Brockway
The American Reformatory (1910)

Mabbott
Punishment (1939)

Andenaes
General Preventive Effects of Punishment (1966)

Packer
The Limits of Criminal Sanction (1968)

Martinson
What Works (1974)

Newman
Defensible Space (1973)

Kretschmer
Physique and Character (1921)

Hooton
American Criminal (1939)

Montagu
Man and Aggression (1968)

Jeffery
Crime Prevention (1971)

E. O. Wilson
Sociobiology (1975)

Goring
The English Convict (1913)

Sheldon
Varieties of Delinquent Youth (1949)

Dalton
The Premenstrual Syndrome (1971)

Tarde
Penal Philosophy (1912)

Freud
General Introduction to Psychoanalysis (1920)

Friedlander
Psychoanalytic Approach to Delinquency (1947)

Eysenck
Crime and Personality (1964)

Bandura
Aggression (1973)

Healy
The Individual Deliquent (1915)

Bonger
Criminality and Economic Conditions (1916)

Rusche & Kircheimer
Punishment and Social Structure (1939)

Vold
Theoretical Criminology (1958)

Chambliss & Seidman
Law, Order & Power (1971)

Goff & Reasons
Corporate Crime in Canada (1978)

Dahrendorf
Class and Class Conflict in Industrial Society (1959)

Taylor, Walton, & Young
The New Criminology (1973)

Park, Burgess, & McKenzie
The City (1925)

Merton
Social Structure and Anomi (1938)

Cloward & Ohlin
Delinquency and Opportunity (1960)

Shaw et al.
Delinquency Areas (1925)

Thrasher
The Gang (1926)

Sellin
Culture, Conflict and Crime (1938)

Lewis
The Culture of Poverty (1966)

Mead
The Psychology of Punitive Justice (1917)

Sutherland
Principles of Criminology (1939)

Lemert
Social Pathology (1951)

Hirschi
Causes of Delinquency (1969)

Schur
Labeling Deviant Behavior (1972)

Sutherland
Criminology (1924)

Sutherland
The Professional Thief (1937)

Becker
Outsiders (1963)

Glueck & Glueck
500 Criminal Careers (1930)

Glueck & Glueck
Unraveling Juvenile Delinquency (1950)

Hathaway & Monachesi
Analyzing and Predicting Juvenile Delinquency with the MMPI (1953)

Eysenck
Crime and Personality (1964)

Wolfgang, Figlio, & Sellin
Delinquency in Birth Cohorts (1972)

1919	1925	1940	1950	1969	1975
World War I	Depression	World War II	Cold War	Vietnam War	Watergate

Time Line of Criminological Theories (continued)

Origin:
Classical Theory

Contemporary Theory:
(Rational) Choice Theory

J.Q. Wilson
Thinking About Crime (1975)

Cohen & Felson
Routine Activities (1979)

Doob & Roberts
*Crime and the Official Response to Crime:
The Views of the Public* (1982)

Brantingham & Brantingham
Environmental Criminology (1981)

Katz
*Seductions of
Crime* (1988)

Origin:
Positivist Theory

Contemporary Theory:
Biosocial Trait Theory

Mednick & Volavka
Biology and Crime (1980)

Ellis
*Evolutionary
Sociobiology* (1989)

Origin:
Positivist Theory

Contemporary Theory:
Psychological Trait Theory

Hirschi & Hindelang
*Intelligence and
Delinquency* (1977)

Leyton
Hunting Humans (1986)

Henggeler
*Delinquency in
Adolescence*
(1989)

Origin:
Marxist Theory

Contemporary Theory:
(Social) Conflict Theory

Reasons, Ross
& Paterson
*Assault on
the Worker:
Occupational Health and
Safety in Canada* (1981)

Lea & Young
Left Realism
(1984)

Fleming
*The New
Criminologies
in Canada: State,
Crime, and
Control* (1985)

MacLean
*The Political
Economy
of Crime* (1986)

Hagan
Structural Criminology
(1989)

Adelberg & Currie
Too Few to Count
(1987)

Daly &
Chesne
*Feminis
Theory*

Origin:
Sociological Theory

Contemporary Theory:
Social Structure Theory

Kornhauser
*Social Sources
of Delinquency* (1978)

Blau & Blau
The Cost of Inequality (1982)

Wilson
The Truly Disadvantaged (1987)

Prus & Irini
*Hookers, Rounders and
Desk Clerks* (1988)

Origin:
Sociological Theory

Contemporary Theory:
Social Process Theory

Akers
Deviant Behavior
(1977)

Smith
*Violence and
Sports* (1983)

Badgley Report
*Committee on Sexual
Offences Against
Children and
Youths* (1984)

Lowman
*Vancouver Field
Study of
Prostitution* (1984)

DeKeseredy & Hin
*Woman Abuse:
Sociological
Perspectives* (1991

Origin:
Multifactor Theory

Contemporary Theory:
Life Course Theory

West & Farrington
Delinquent Way of Life
(1977)

Weis
*Social Development
Theory* (1981)

Thornberry
Interactional Theory
(1987)

Origin:
Multifactor Theory

Contemporary Theory:
Latent Trait Theory

Wilson & Herrnstein
*Crime and Human
Nature* (1985)

Gottfredson & Hirschi
General Theory of Crime (1990)

1980

Reagan Era

1991

Fall of European
Communism

Clarke
Situational Crime Prevention (1992)

Lott
*More Guns,
Less Crime* (2000)

Felson
*Crime and Everyday
Life* (2002)

Kennedy & Sacco
*Crime Counts: A Criminal
Event Analysis* (1996)

Rowe
*The Limits of
Family Influence* (1995)

Harris
The Nurture Assumption (1998)

Rushton
*Race, Evolution, and Behavior:
A Life History Perspective* (1995)

Schoenthaler
*Intelligence, Academic Performance
and Brain Function* (2000)

Moffitt
*Neuropsychology
of Crime* (1992)

Wilson & Daly
Evolutionary Psychology (1997)

Murray & Herrnstein
The Bell Curve (1994)

Bushman & Anderson
Media Violence (2001)

Zehr & Mika
*Fundamental Concepts
of Restorative Justice* (1998)

Sullivan & Tifft
Restorative Justice (2001)

Quinney & Pepinsky
*Criminology as
Peacemaking* (1991)

Barak & Henry
An Integrative-Constitutive Theory of Crime (1999)

Agnew
General Strain Theory (1992)

Courtwright
Violent Land (1996)

Anderson
Code of the Street (1999)

Wolf
*The Rebels:
A Brotherhood of
Outlaw Bikers* (1991)

Messner & Rosenfeld
*Crime and the American
Dream* (1994)

LaFree
Losing Legitimacy
(1998)

Kaplan
*General Theory
of Deviance* (1992)

Akers
*Social Learning
and Social Structure* (1998)

Heimer & Matsueda
Differential Social Control (1994)

Sampson & Laub
Crime in the Making (1993)

Loeber
Pathways to Delinquency (1998)

Moffitt
*Adolescence-Limited and Life-Course
Persistent Antisocial Behavior* (1995)

Tittle
*Control Balance: Toward a General
Theory of Deviance* (1995)

Colvin
Crime and Coercion (2000)

Herrnstein & Murray
The Bell Curve (1996)

1995

1997

2000

2002

Third Edition

Criminology

in Canada

THEORIES, PATTERNS, AND TYPOLOGIES

Third Edition

Criminology
in Canada

THEORIES, PATTERNS, AND TYPOLOGIES

Larry J. Siegel
University of Massachusetts at Lowell

Chris McCormick
St. Thomas University

THOMSON

NELSON

Australia   Canada   Mexico   Singapore   Spain   United Kingdom   United States

THOMSON

NELSON

Criminology in Canada: Theories, Patterns, and Typologies
Third Edition

by Larry J. Siegel and Chris McCormick

Associate Vice President,
Editorial Director:
Evelyn Veitch

Publisher, Social Sciences
& Humanities:
Joanna Cotton

Marketing Managers:
Lenore Taylor
Laura Armstrong

Developmental Editors:
Edward Ikeda
Rebecca Rea

Permissions Coordinator:
Robyn Craig

Production Editor:
Lara Caplan

Copy Editor:
Dawn Hunter

Proofreader:
Wayne Herrington

Indexer:
Belle Wong

Senior Production
Coordinator:
Hedy Sellers

Design Director:
Ken Phipps

Interior Design:
Andrew Adams

Cover Design:
Andrew Adams

Cover Image:
Comstock Images/
Getty Images

Compositor:
Integra

Printer:
Transcontinental

Library and Archives Canada
Cataloguing in Publication Data

Siegel, Larry J.

Criminology in Canada: theories, patterns, and typologies/ Larry J. Siegel, Chris McCormick. — 3rd ed.

Includes bibliographical references and index.
ISBN 0-17-641670-6

1. Criminology—Canada— Textbooks. 2. Crime—Canada— Textbooks.
I. McCormick, Christopher Ray, 1956– II. Title.

HV6025.S53 2005   364.971
C2005-903752-0

*This book is dedicated
to my children, Julie, Andrew,
Eric, and Rachel Siegel, and
to my wife, Theresa G. Libby.*
—Larry J. Siegel

For my students.
—Chris McCormick

Contents

Section 2: Theories of Crime Causation   121

Preface

After launching a massive search at a farm in Port Coquitlam, British Columbia, in early 2002, police were flooded with calls to a special tip line. The farm became the focus of one of the biggest law enforcement investigations in the province's history. A joint task force involving the Vancouver police and the RCMP investigated the disappearance of 50 women since 1983, possibly one of the largest serial homicide cases in the Western world.

The missing women had worked in the sex trade in the lower eastside of Vancouver, and many of them were drug addicts. Many people had speculated for some time that a serial killer was behind the disappearances, and the search at the farm appeared to be a major break in the investigation; several weeks after the investigation began, one of the owners of the farm was charged with the murder of two of the women who had disappeared. The police had been tipped about the farm two years earlier but had failed to act. Some think the indifference came because the victims were prostitutes.

Criminal acts capture public attention in a way that nothing else does. And yet, our ability to determine the validity of those news stories, television documentaries, and magazine articles is compromised by the fact that most of us have little independent knowledge of crime. Unless you hang out with cops (or criminals) or study criminological theory and patterns of crime, it is more than likely that what you know about crime is gleaned from the media.

The media do a good job reporting crime but they also seem to have an inordinate interest in notorious killers, serial murderers, drug lords, and sex criminals. Fraud and counterfeiting do not receive much attention unless the amounts involved are in the millions. It is not surprising, then, that many people are more concerned about violent crime than about almost any other social problem. Most people worry to one degree or another about becoming victims of violent crime, having their houses broken into, or having their cars stolen. People alter their behaviour to limit the risk of victimization and question whether legal punishment alone can control criminal offenders. They are shocked at graphic news accounts of drive-by shootings, police brutality, and prison riots. They are fascinated by books, movies, and TV shows about law firms, clients, fugitives, and hardened killers.

Why do people behave the way they do? What causes one person to become violent and antisocial, while another channels his or her energy into work, school, and family? How do we explain the at-risk kid in a high-crime neighbourhood who successfully resists the temptation of the streets? What accounts for the behaviour of the multimillionaire who cheats on his or her taxes and engages in other fraudulent schemes? The former has nothing yet is able to resist crime; the latter has everything and falls prey to its allure. Is behaviour a function of personal characteristics, or of upbringing and experience? Is it influenced by culture or environment? Or is it a combination of all these influences? This text addresses some of these difficult questions through a typology-based approach.

As a professor of criminology, I have taught more than 1500 students in the last five years, and probably half of those were at the first-year level. To me, what is important is communicating my interest in crime, law, and justice to my classes, and inspiring my students with the same interest in the field that I have. My goal has always been to help students understand a very broad field in a way that is easy to grasp. What could be more important or fascinating than a field of study that deals with such wide-ranging topics as the motivation for mass murder, the association between media violence and interpersonal aggression, the family's influence on drug abuse, and the history of organized crime? Criminology is a dynamic field, changing constantly with the release of major research studies, Supreme

Court rulings, and governmental policy. Its dynamism and diversity make it an important and engrossing area of study. In this book, I have sought to find examples and cases that make the field "come alive."

What makes criminology difficult, but also interesting, is that debate continues over the nature and extent of crime and the causes and prevention of criminality. Some people view criminals as society's victims who are forced to violate the law because of poverty and the lack of opportunity. Others view aggressive, antisocial behaviour as a product of mental and physical abnormalities that persist through the life course. Genetic, neurological, and physiological factors are also felt to influence criminality. Still another view is that crime is a function of the rational choice of greedy, selfish people who can only be deterred through the threat of harsh punishments. For these people there can be no treatment, only punishment. As new research uncovers factors that affect crime, the debate over the nature and cause of crime develops.

Debate also continues over how the criminal justice system should best treat known criminals. Should they be punished by being locked up? Or should they be given a second chance and diverted into alternative justice programs? Should crime control policy focus on punishment or rehabilitation, or even on medical treatment? If the underlying cause is poverty, how could that be remedied? Many of these questions are tied to the current events we learn about through the media. When two British children were accused of abducting and murdering a two-year-old child, the case sparked international outrage, fuelling the call for reforms to juvenile justice. When Melanie Carpenter was abducted from her place of work in Surrey, British Columbia, in broad daylight, there was sufficient public alarm that the dangerous offender legislation was amended. Similarly, when Georgina Leimonis was shot in a Toronto café, there were calls for the deportation of violent criminals.

Because interest in crime and justice is so great and so timely, this text is designed to review these ongoing issues and cover the field of criminology in an organized and comprehensive manner. It is meant as a broad overview of the field, designed to whet the reader's appetite and encourage further and more in-depth exploration. One of my graduating students told me she had kept the first edition of this book throughout university, using it as a reference beyond first year. That type of testimonial inspires me to keep working with Larry Siegel in writing this book to suit student needs, while meeting my interest in communicating my enthusiasm for a rich, growing field of study.

In this third Canadian edition, I have made every effort to make the presentation of material interesting, balanced, objective, and, especially, as distinctly Canadian as possible. No single political or theoretical position dominates the text; instead, the many diverse views that are contained within criminology and that characterize its interdisciplinary nature are presented. The text analyzes the most important scholarly works and scientific research reports, while also presenting topical information on recent cases and events.

ORGANIZATION OF THE TEXT

The text is divided into three main sections or topic areas.

Section 1 provides a framework for studying criminology. Chapter 1 defines the field and discusses its most basic concepts: the definition of crime, the component areas of criminology, the history of criminology, criminological research methods, and the ethical issues that confront the field. Chapter 2 covers the criminal law and its functions, processes, defences, and reform. Much of this information is generic to a justice system anywhere in the Western world, so it was important to add a Canadian face to the material. For example, the topic of wrongful convictions illustrates how mistakes can happen in even the most rationally organized system. There is also material on recent changes to the law, including stalking laws and community notification laws. Chapter 3 deals with the nature, extent, and patterns of crime, covering the various ways we learn about crime in our society: police statistics, victimization surveys, and the media. In the recent past, commissions of inquiry have also become an independent and in-depth source of knowledge about crime. New material is presented on gun control as well as the findings of an important new study that followed chronic juvenile offenders into their adulthood. In addition, new material on international crime rates is included. Chapter 4 is devoted to a relatively rare topic for a criminology text, the concept of victimization. This area includes the nature of victims, theories of victimization, and programs designed to help crime victims. An expanded section on hate crime in Canada has been developed for this edition.

Section 2 contains six chapters that cover criminological theory. Why do people engage in criminal behaviour? These views include theories of criminal choice (Chapter 5); biological and psychological views (Chapter 6); structural, cultural, and ecological theories (Chapter 7); social process theories that focus on socialization and include learning and control (Chapter 8); and theories of social conflict (Chapter 9). Chapter 10 covers attempts by criminologists to integrate various theories into a unified whole. These chapters build on Section 1 and prepare the foundation for the empirical topics discussed in the next section. Of particular interest are the material on closed circuit television in Chapter 5, real cases of sleepwalking used as a defence in Chapter 6, early research done at McGill University in the 1920s in Chapter 7, and research on ethnicity and criminality in Chapter 9.

Section 3 is devoted to the major forms of criminal behaviour. Chapters 11 to 14 cover violent crime, common theft offences, white-collar and organized crimes, and public order crimes, including sex offences and substance abuse. Each of these chapters has been updated from the first Canadian edition, using the latest criminal statistics (2001) and victimization surveys (1999) where possible. Throughout, recent Canadian research is highlighted and current topics keep the text fresh. The latest scandal on Bay Street, as well as the extent of fraud on eBay, can be found here.

The text has been carefully structured to cover relevant material in a comprehensive, balanced, and objective fashion.

KEY FEATURES

Connections boxes are located in appropriate places throughout each chapter. These brief inserts link the material being currently discussed with relevant information located elsewhere in the text. Connections either expand on the subject matter or show how it can be applied to other areas or topics. In a book this comprehensive, they help organize and coordinate the material for quicker learning.

Crime in the News looks at how the media cover crime by reproducing a news story. The media are important resources for our understanding of criminal justice. For example, in Chapter 6, a case from the media is highlighted in which a woman was given leniency after she stabbed her husband. Her defence? She was suffering from premenstrual syndrome, which compromised her ability to make good choices.

Famous Canadian Criminals uses cases from our past to illustrate principles from the text. For example, Chapter 4 highlights the case of Angelique Lyn Lavallee, a battered woman in a violent common-law relationship who killed her partner late one night by shooting him in the back of the head as he left her room. This case ultimately resulted in a decision by the Supreme Court of Canada (1990) that set the legal framework for what has become known as the "battered wife syndrome" defence. Then–Justice Minister Allan Rock also agreed to consider extending that principle to some pre-1990 cases. In this example, we see the origin of an important doctrine of Canadian criminal justice and consider the significance of gender in criminal cases.

Thinking Like a Criminologist asks you to apply reasoning from the chapter to a criminal justice question. For example, in Chapter 12, to deter property

crime, various measures are discussed that could prevent theft from households and cars. Can you think of other preventive measures after reading this chapter?

In addition, each chapter has a section called **Culture, Gender, Ethnicity, and Criminology**, in which broader questions on the relationship between crime and the wider society are addressed. In Chapter 6, for example, some issues concerning the relation between the media and violence are discussed. Are the media implicated in influencing violent behaviour? Do the media simply reflect norms already existing in society? These questions are still open for discussion. In Chapter 4, gay bashing is examined in some detail, and in Chapter 9, issues involving Natives and the criminal justice system are highlighted.

Photos, charts, and figures are important pedagogical features for any text. Each chapter includes a chapter outline, a list of key terms contained in the chapter, and at least one boxed insert. These boxes contain a detailed discussion or reading of an important and intriguing topic, issue, or program. An extensive glossary provides concise definitions of key terms used throughout the text for quick reference.

NEW TO THIS EDITION

The third Canadian edition of *Criminology in Canada* retains many of the same organizational features of the very successful first and second editions, with some notable differences.

Each chapter has a **Famous Canadian Court Case** or a **Famous Canadian Criminals** box, illustrating a theme from the chapter. These are unique features, highlighting important principles of Canadian justice or notable Canadian criminal cases. They help students visualize real-life cases, many of them contemporary, such as the trial of those charged in the Reena Virk case.

A **public opinion poll** on an appropriate topic is included in most chapters. The polls help situate current thinking on criminal issues, such as whether marijuana should be decriminalized.

Each chapter has **Critical Thinking Questions**, designed to get students thinking about key issues in the chapter. These questions follow the popular **Thinking Like a Criminologist** section and are good preparation for essay questions on quizzes.

In addition, **InfoTrac® College Edition** tips are provided to extend reading on relevant research. Students are encouraged to seek out additional, interesting studies on key issues.

New Canadian and international research is included in every chapter, and all statistical tables and exhibits have been updated where possible. Each chapter provides the best from sources that include Canada's General Social Survey, the Uniform Crime Reports, and *Juristat* studies, as well as criminal incident and victimization data from the United States, and information from various international sources, including the International Criminal Victimization Survey.

Chapter-by-Chapter Changes

Changes that are more specific are evident in each chapter. For example, Chapter 1: Crime and Criminology now begins with information about Maurice "Mom" Boucher. There is a greater emphasis on effects of the media, and there are new Famous Canadian Court Case and Crime in the News features. The international crime statistics are updated, and the Famous Canadian Criminals feature has been revised.

In Chapter 2: The Criminal Law and Its Process, there is new material on the history of criminal justice, and the section on the development of criminal justice in Canada has been reorganized. There are new figures on Canada's court system, and new real-life examples of legal defences. Compensation amounts have been added to the Famous Canadian Criminals box for those who were wrongfully convicted, and there is a significant new Crime in the News feature.

In Chapter 3: The Nature and Extent of Crime, there are updated statistics from the UCR, the GSS, and victim surveys. New research studies have been included on factors affecting crime rates, such as youth cases, drug use, offender statistics, and age and crime. In addition, there are new features on international crime statistics, Aboriginal offenders, and the relationship between drugs and crime.

In Chapter 4: Victims and Victimization, there is a new table on international estimates of the costs of crime and new *Juristat* information on victimization and hate crime.

In Chapter 5: Choice Theory, there is new information on drug dealing, bank robbery, capital punishment and deterrence, and closed-circuit television (CCTV) and surveillance. The new Crime in the News feature is written by the author.

Chapter 6: Trait Theories provides new and expanded research notes throughout on a dozen different research topics.

Chapter 7: Social Structure Theories has new updated research on topics such as child poverty, disorganization theory, anomie theory, adolescence, and street youth. There is an important new section on collective efficacy and a new Crime in the News feature.

Chapter 8: Social Process Theories has new theory references on family background, longitudinal surveys, delinquency, the effects of child abuse, bullying, and multisystemic therapy. There are new figures on aggressive behaviour, a significant new Crime in the News feature, and an important new Famous Canadian Criminals feature.

Chapter 9: Social Conflict Theory has new research on policing, Natives, corporate crime, punishment, prostitution, youth, restorative justice, and peacemaking criminology.

Chapter 10: Integrated Theories has two significant exhibits on new directions in integrated theory. There is also new research on integrated theory, antisociality, longitudinal surveys, pathways to delinquency, early-onset delinquency, and criticisms of integrated theories, bringing it more in line with the length of the other theory chapters.

Chapter 11: Violent Crime has new informational and research notes on the *Youth Criminal Justice Act*, firearms, various violent crime statistics, and a significant new Crime in the News feature relating to workplace violence. New material on terrorism and responses to terrorism reflect recent changes in the world that affect us all.

Chapter 12: Property Crimes has updates on most major data sources and features, and new research notes on various topics. There are two new Crime in the News features, one on auto theft and one on identity theft written by the author.

Chapter 13: Crimes of Power: White-Collar, Corporate, and Organized Crime has new research information on corporate crime, white-collar criminals, Internet crime, and computer crime. There is a major new exhibit on computer viruses and new information on Aboriginal organized crime.

Chapter 14: Public Order Crimes: Legislating Morality has updated statistics on offences, such as prostitution, marijuana, substance abuse, drug-related AIDS, and gambling; and new research sections, for example, on Internet pornography.

ANCILLARY MATERIALS

Thomson Nelson provides the following instructional resource supplements to help instructors use this third edition of *Criminology in Canada* in their courses and to aid students in preparing for exams.

Instructor's Manual and Test Bank (0-17-625196-0)

The Instructor's Manual and Test Bank includes lecture outlines, discussion topics, student activities, Internet connections, media resources, and testing suggestions that will help time-pressed instructors more effectively communicate with their students and also strengthen the coverage of course material. Each chapter has multiple-choice and true-or-false test items, as well as sample essay questions.

Computerized Test Bank in Exam View® (0-17-625197-9)

This computerized testing software helps instructors create and customize exams in minutes. It contains all the questions from the printed test bank in the Instructor's Manual. Instructors can easily edit and import their own questions and graphics, change test layouts, and reorganize questions. The Computerized Test Bank is available for both Windows and Macintosh.

Microsoft® PowerPoint® Presentation (0-17-625198-7)

This presentation features important concepts and key points from the textbook and is provided for classroom use to add colour and interest to lectures. The PowerPoint® presentation is available on CD and on the website.

Book-Specific Website: http://www.siegelcriminology3e.nelson.com

This robust and interactive student site is an online study guide that contains chapter-based resources, including quizzes, crossword puzzles, flashcards, and Weblinks. Students will also find a wealth of additional information on topics such as crime and technology, and information on degrees and careers. Students can log on and learn!

Thomson Nelson Criminology Videos

Thomson Nelson offers a compilation of current CBC news clips covering a wide range of topics, including gun control, young offenders, sexual assault, child pornography, crime and punishment, and arson. Clips vary in length from 6 minutes to 20 minutes. The videos include a brief summary of the clips and suggested discussion questions for use in class, making these videos a great enhancement to lectures. Ask your Thomson Nelson sales representative for information on how to order the videos.

CNN Today Videos

Exclusively from Wadsworth/Thomson Learning, the *CNN Today Video Series* offers compelling videos that feature current news footage from the Cable News Network's comprehensive archives. *Criminology* Volumes I through VIII each provide a collection of two- to eight-minute clips on hot topics in criminology, such as children who murder, the insanity defence (in Canada called the not criminally responsible on account of mental disorder defence), hate crimes, cyberterrorism, and much more. Available to qualified adopters, these videotapes are great lecture launchers or classroom discussion pieces. Ask your Thomson Nelson sales representative for information on how to order the videos.

The Wadsworth Criminal Justice Video Library

The Wadsworth Criminal Justice Video Library offers an exciting collection of videos to enrich lectures. Qualified adopters may select from a wide variety of professionally prepared videos covering various aspects of policing, corrections, and other areas of the criminal justice system. The selections include videos from *Rims for the Humanities & Sciences, Court TV* videos that feature provocative one-hour court cases to illustrate seminal and high-profile cases in depth, *A&E American Justice Series* videos, *National Institute of Justice: Crime File* videos, *ABC News* videos, and *MPI Home Videos*. Ask your Thomson Nelson sales representative for information on how to order the videos.

InfoTrac® College Edition

With InfoTrac®, a unique Thomson resource, students receive four months of real-time access to a continually updated online database of full-length articles from hundreds of journals and periodicals. By doing a simple keyword search, users can quickly generate a list of related articles, and then select relevant articles to explore and print out for reference or further study. A free InfoTrac® password and an access instructional card are included with each new copy of *Criminology in Canada,* Third Edition.

Crime Scenes 2.0: Interactive Criminal Justice CD-ROM (0-534-56831-9)

This interactive CD-ROM features six vignettes that allow students to play various roles as they explore all aspects of the criminal justice system. Exciting videos and supporting documents put students in the midst of a juvenile murder trial, a prostitution case that turns into manslaughter, and several other scenarios. This product received the gold medal in higher education and the silver medal for video interface from *NewMedia Magazine's Invision Awards.*

Careers in Criminal Justice 3.0: Interactive CD-ROM (0-534-58571-X)

This self-exploration CD-ROM provides students with extensive career-profiling information and self-assessment testing designed to help them investigate and focus on the criminal justice career choices that are right for them. With links and tools to assist students in finding a professional position, this new version includes 10 new Career Profiles and two new Video Interviews, bringing the total number of careers covered to 58.

Nelson Criminology Dictionary (0-17-640608-5)

Written by Gary Parkinson and Robert Drislane, the *Nelson Criminology Dictionary* is a compact and inexpensive glossary of common criminological terms that students will encounter during their studies in criminology. More than 1400 entries cover the main concepts and events that are used in criminology and criminal justice courses, making this dictionary an invaluable tool.

ACKNOWLEDGMENTS

Many people helped make this book possible. I have attempted to incorporate the suggestions of those who reviewed this edition, including Scot Wortley, University of Toronto; Joanne Simister, Malaspina University-College; Bruce Minore, Lakehead University; Gina Antonacci, Humber College; Michael Young, Camosun College; and Julian Hermida, Dalhousie University.

The list of those who helped with material or advice includes those at Thomson Nelson. Many thanks to Joanna Cotton and Edward Ikeda, in particular, and to Lara Caplan and Laura Armstrong for their assistance. I also thank Larry Siegel (University of Massachusetts at Lowell) for producing such a great text from which to work.

In addition, I also thank copy editor Dawn Hunter and the following research and editorial assistants who helped in many ways to bring this text to its third edition: Andrea Wolf, Vanessa Gallant, and Sarah Gilliss.

Chris McCormick
Department of Criminology
St. Thomas University
Fredericton, New Brunswick
2005

1

Concepts of Crime, Law, and Criminology

How is crime defined? How much crime is there, and what are the trends and patterns in the crime rate? How many people are victims of crime, and who is likely to become a crime victim? How did our system of criminal law develop, and what are the basic elements of crimes? What is the science of criminology all about? These are some of the core issues that will be addressed in the first four chapters of this text, providing a solid foundation for the chapters to come. Chapter 1 introduces the field of criminology: its nature, area of study, methodologies, and historical development. Concern about crime and justice has been an important part of the human condition for more than five thousand years, since the first criminal codes were set down in the Middle East. And although the scientific study of crime—criminology—is considered a contemporary science, it has existed for more than two hundred years.

Chapter 2 introduces one of the key components of criminology: the development of criminal law. It discusses the social history of law and the purpose of law, and how that purpose defines crime. The chapter also briefly examines criminal defences and legal reform using prominent Canadian examples. The final two chapters of this section review the various sources of crime data to create a picture of crime. Chapter 3 focuses on the nature and extent of crime, while Chapter 4 is devoted to victims and victimization. Important and stable patterns in the rates of crime and victimization indicate that these are not random events. The way crime and victimization are organized and patterned profoundly influences how criminologists view the causes of crime.

Crime and Criminology

Maurice "Mom" Boucher was leader of the notorious Nomads chapter of the Hells Angels. Boucher encouraged the murder of rival bikers, members of the Rock Machine, as the Hells Angels sought to expand their territory. He also ordered the murder of two prison guards in an attempt to destabilize the **criminal justice system** and increase fear. For that order, he was convicted of murder and received two life sentences.

In 2003, a high-profile trial was held in a special $16 million courthouse built to accommodate the dozens of bikers swept up in a police raid on 38 locations, called Operation Hurricane. Assets were seized worth $5 million, including houses, luxury cars, and bank accounts. This sweep followed an even larger raid in early 2001 called Operation SPRINGTIME 2001, in which two thousand officers carried out simultaneous raids in 77 municipalities in Quebec. It was the largest one-day police operation of its kind in Canadian history, involving the coordination of police forces at regional, national, and international levels. Twelve million dollars in property, $12 million in cash, narcotics, 28 vehicles, and 70 firearms, including a rocket launcher, were seized.

Nine members of the Angels faced charges of complicity to commit murder, gangsterism, and drug trafficking. After a lengthy trial involving more than two hundred witnesses, the nine Angels members all pleaded guilty.

This case illustrates why crime and criminal behaviour have long fascinated people. Crime touches all segments of society, from the victims of the bikers turf

Maurice "Mom" Boucher was the head of the Nomads, a chapter of the Hells Angels in Montreal. He was arrested in 2002, convicted of murder, and sentenced to 25 years in prison for the deaths of two prison guards in 1997.

war that raged from 1994 to 2001 to those addicted to the drug trade. Crime cuts across racial, class, and gender lines. It involves acts that shock the conscience and others that seem relatively harmless.

In another high-profile case, in 1991 Niagara Region police identified the remains of a woman found dismembered and embedded in concrete in a lake as those of 14-year-old Leslie Mahaffy. Karla Homolka and Paul Bernardo were eventually convicted of her murder and that of 15-year-old Kristen French. In a controversial plea bargain, Homolka cooperated with the prosecution and testified against Bernardo, her husband. She was sentenced to 12 years in jail. Bernardo received a life sentence for the two murders and was declared a dangerous offender for a string of rapes.

Details of the case were subject to a publication ban between the two separate trials of Homolka and Bernardo. However, the ban didn't prevent the public from finding out details of the case. In the United States, *The Washington Post* published a story and Canadians read it in public libraries; *The Buffalo News* also printed an article and Canadians drove across the border to buy the newspaper. Details of the crimes were posted on the Internet faster than news lists and discussion groups could be shut down. Were the media sensationalizing the case, or were they simply responding to the public's need to know? Was a ban necessary to guarantee fair trials for the accused? An Angus Reid survey done in December 1992 reported that despite the media ban, 25 percent of Ontario residents had learned banned details of the trial. However, 35 percent weren't even aware of the case.

Criminal acts can be the work of strangers who prey on people they have never met, or they can involve friends and family members in **intimate violence**.[1] Little consensus exists about the cause of crime or what can be done to prevent it. What might compel a couple like Paul Bernardo and Karla Homolka to commit such crimes? They came from a community with tree-shaded parks, nice homes, and sports fields. They were seen as a young couple with a bright future. Could such outrageous behaviour be better understood if it had been committed by teens who were the product of bad neighbourhoods and dysfunctional homes? Research indicates that habitually aggressive behaviour is often learned in homes in which children are victimized and parents serve as aggressive role models—learned violence then persists into adulthood.[2] Could someone who was really "normal" ever commit such horrible crimes? If this couple were convicted and imprisoned for life, would this extreme punishment deter others? Do the media have any responsibility in reporting such horrific crimes?

Such crime stories as this one take their toll on the public. When Paul Bernardo was on trial for his crimes, about one-third of the Canadian population said that they did not feel safe walking alone in their own neighbourhood at night, and this fear was more likely to be expressed by women than by men. This fear was out of proportion to the actual risk of victimization. Forty-six percent of Canadians aged 15 years and over thought that crime had increased between 1988 and 1993, despite the fact that overall rates of victimization remained the same. The 1993 General Social Survey (GSS) showed that 24 percent of Canadians were victims of crime in 1993, the same percentage as in 1988. Canadians were no more likely to be victims of assault, theft (either of personal or of household property), vandalism, or break and enter in 1993 than they were five years previously.

By 1999, the GSS showed a victimization rate of 25 percent, which is in line with the 2000 International Crime Victimization Survey, which showed an average victimization rate of 22 percent.[3] The percentage of people who believed crime had increased declined to 29 percent, but one-quarter of Canadians said that they didn't walk in their neighbourhoods after dark. Twenty percent worried about being home alone, and 46 percent were fearful waiting for or using public transportation. Although fear may be decreasing, it is still out of proportion to the actual risk of victimization.

The public fear of crime is an important barometer of social health and how people feel about their communities. In a more recent poll conducted in Ottawa, 60 percent of people surveyed thought that the city's crime rate was worse than it was five years ago.

The fact that the public overestimates the likelihood of crime in their own neighbourhoods despite contradictory evidence from their own experience points to the influence of other factors on the public's knowledge of crime. People do not rely on their experience when assessing the likelihood of being a victim of crime; the assessment is derived from such sources as the media. This third-hand fear has long-term effects, creating a negative view of the police and the courts, and an attitude favouring harsher punishments for offenders. The fear of crime also sets the larger social agenda; for example, a poll conducted by the Council for Canadian Unity in 2000 found that more people favoured putting resources into reducing crime than favoured putting resources into reducing poverty.[4]

Connections

Experts have suggested a variety of explanations for bizarre violent episodes, such as serial homicide. Psychologists link violent behaviour to a number of psychological influences, including observational learning from violent TV shows, traumatic childhood experiences, mental illness, impaired cognitive processes, and a psychopathic personality structure. Chapter 6 reviews the most prominent of these explanations of violence.

Concern about crime and the need to develop effective measures to control criminal behaviour has spurred the development of the study of **criminology**. This academic discipline is devoted to the development of valid and reliable information about the causes of crime as well as crime patterns and trends. **Criminologists** use scientific methods to study the nature, extent, cause, and control of criminal behaviour. Unlike media commentators, whose opinions about crime can be coloured by personal experiences, biases, and values, criminologists attempt to bring objectivity and scientific methods to the study of crime and its consequences. Because of the threat of crime and the social problems it represents, the field of criminology has gained prominence as an academic area of study.

This chapter introduces criminology: how it is defined, its goals, and its history. It also addresses such questions as the following: How do criminologists define crime? How do they conduct research? What ethical issues face those wanting to conduct criminological research?

What Is Criminology?

Criminology is the scientific approach to the study of criminal behaviour. In their classic definition, criminologists Edwin Sutherland and Donald Cressey state:

> Criminology is the body of knowledge regarding crime as a social phenomenon. It includes within its scope the processes of making laws, of breaking laws, and of reacting toward the breaking of laws. . . . The objective of criminology is the development of a body of general and verified principles and of other types of knowledge regarding this process of law, crime, and treatment.[5]

Sutherland and Cressey's definition includes the most important areas of interest to criminologists: the development of criminal law and its use to define crime, the cause of law violations, and the methods used to control criminal behaviour. Also important is the use of the scientific method in criminology. Criminologists use objective research methods to pose research questions (hypotheses), gather data, create theories, and test the validity of theories. They use every method of established social science inquiry: analysis of existing records, experimental designs, surveys, historical analysis, and content analysis.

An essential part of criminology is the fact that it is an interdisciplinary science. Relatively few universities in Canada grant graduate degrees in criminology. Many criminologists have been trained in other fields, most commonly sociology but also criminal justice, political science, psychology, history, geography, economics, and the

---

Exhibit 1.1   Criminology, Criminal Justice, and Deviance

Criminology explains the etiology (origin), extent, and nature of crime in society. Criminologists are concerned with identifying the nature, extent, and cause of crime.

Criminal justice refers to the study of agencies of social control that handle criminal offenders. Criminal justice scholars engage in describing, analyzing, and explaining the operations of the agencies of justice, specifically the police departments, courts, and correctional facilities. They seek more effective methods of crime control and offender rehabilitation.

Overlapping areas of concern: Criminal justice experts cannot begin to design effective programs of crime prevention or rehabilitation without understanding the nature and cause of crime. They require accurate criminal statistics and data to test the effectiveness of crime control and prevention programs.

Deviance refers to the study of behaviour that departs from social norms. Included within the broad spectrum of deviant acts are behaviours ranging from violent crimes to joining a nudist colony. Not all crimes are deviant or unusual acts and not all deviant acts are illegal.

Overlapping areas of concern: Under what circumstances do deviant behaviours become crimes? For example, when does sexually oriented material cross the line from merely suggestive to obscene and therefore illegal? If an illegal act becomes a norm, should society reevaluate its criminal status? For example, there is still debate over the legalization and/or decriminalization of abortion, recreational drug use, possession of handguns, and assisted suicide.

---

natural sciences. Today, criminology's orientation is truly interdisciplinary—an integrated approach to the study of criminal behaviour. Criminology combines elements from many other fields in understanding the connections among law, crime, and justice.

Criminology and Criminal Justice

In the late 1960s, research projects were developed to understand the way police, courts, and correctional agencies operated.[6] These academic programs, devoted to studying the criminal justice system, are concentrated in five university departments of criminology in Canada, at Simon Fraser University in Burnaby, the University of Ottawa, the University of Montreal, the University of Toronto, and St. Thomas University in Fredericton.

Although the terms *criminology* and *criminal justice* may seem similar, they have major differences.

Criminologists explain the etiology (origin), extent, and nature of crime in society, while criminal justice scholars describe and analyze the work of the police, courts, and correctional facilities, and how to better design effective methods of crime control.[7]

Because both fields are crime-related, they do overlap. Criminologists must be aware of how the agencies of justice operate; and criminal justice experts design programs of crime prevention or rehabilitation through understanding the nature of crime. Thus, these two fields not only coexist but also help each other grow and develop.

Criminology and Deviance

Criminology is also confused with the study of **deviant behaviour**. However, deviance is more widely defined as behaviour that departs from social norms and that is not always subject to formal sanction.[8] Included within the broad spectrum of deviant acts is sunbathing in the nude, joining a nudist colony, or a woman going topless.

Crime and deviance are often confused, yet not all crimes are deviant or unusual acts, and not all deviant acts are illegal or criminal. For example, using recreational drugs, such as marijuana, may be illegal, but is it deviant? Most Canadians surveyed think that soft drugs should be allowed for individual use.[9] In Vancouver, support for decriminalizing marijuana increased from 47 percent to 57 percent in just three years.[10] When Ross Rebagliati was threatened with losing his gold medal in snowboarding at the 1998 Winter Olympics after testing positive for marijuana, public surveys showed more concern with the high-handedness of officials than with Rebagliati's purported marijuana use. In 2004, a thousand demonstrators rallied at the Ontario legislature as part of the Million Marijuana March, a worldwide event held annually in two hundred cities to demand the full legalization of marijuana.

A 2004 poll by *The Globe and Mail* reported that 50 percent of Canadians said they had used marijuana in the past five years.

Source: Poll conducted by *The Globe and Mail*, November 25, 2004.

Conversely, many deviant acts are not criminal even though they may be shocking. For example, suppose a passerby observes a person drowning and makes no effort to save that victim. Although the general public would probably condemn the passerby's

Figure 1.1	Hagan's Varieties of Deviance

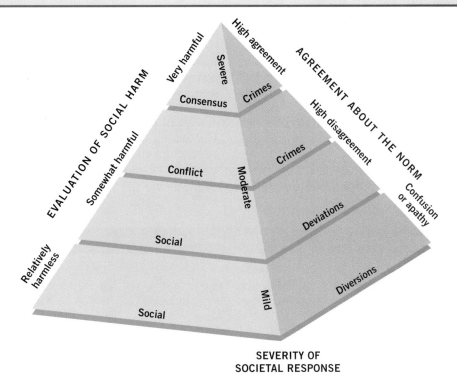

SEVERITY OF
SOCIETAL RESPONSE

Source: © "The Varieties of Deviance" from Hagan, John. *The Disreputable Pleasures: Crime and Deviance in Canada,* 3rd ed. (1991). Toronto: McGraw-Hill Ryerson Ltd., p. 13. Reprinted by permission.

behaviour as callous and immoral, citizens are not required by law to be good samaritans. In sum, many criminal acts, but not all, fall within the concept of deviance. Similarly, some deviant acts, but not all, are considered crimes.

The relationship between crime and deviance is illustrated in Figure 1.1. This model depicts the relationship between crime and deviance along three dimensions: the evaluation of social harm, the level of agreement about the norm, and the severity of societal response. As Figure 1.1 shows, the most serious acts of deviance are also the least likely to occur; however, strong agreement exists over the harmfulness of those acts and the need for a serious societal response.[11]

Two issues that involve deviance are of particular interest to criminologists: (1) How do deviant behaviours become crimes? (2) When should acts considered crimes be legalized? The first issue involves the historical development of law. Many acts that are legally forbidden today were once considered merely unusual or deviant behaviour. Thus, criminologists study the process by which crimes are created from deviance. For example, the sale and possession of marijuana was legal in Canada until 1923, when it was prohibited under federal law by simply being added to the law prohibiting opium.[12] Despite being criminalized,

however, marijuana still enjoys widespread popularity. Health Canada released a survey in 1989 estimating that 60 percent of Canadians between the ages of 20 and 44 had used marijuana.[13] The World Health Organization estimates that more Canadian 15-year-olds have used cannabis in the past year than in any of the other 35 countries studied, more than double the average.

Working with research topics like this, criminologists consider whether outlawed behaviours have evolved into social norms and, if so, whether they should either be legalized or have their penalties reduced (**decriminalization**).

Connections

Some of the drugs considered highly dangerous today were once sold openly and considered medically beneficial. For example, the narcotic drug heroin, now considered extremely addictive, was originally named in the mistaken belief that its painkilling properties would prove "heroic" to medical patients. The history of drug and alcohol use is discussed further in Chapter 14.

The discussion about where to draw the line between behaviour that is merely considered deviant and unusual, and behaviour that is outlawed and criminal can become quite controversial. For example, when does sexually expressive material cross the line from being merely suggestive to being pornographic? Can a line be drawn that separates sexually oriented materials into two groups, one that is legally acceptable and a second that is considered depraved or obscene? And, if such a line can be drawn, who gets to draw it? Many recent efforts have been made to control morally questionable behaviour and restrict the rights of citizens to freedom of their actions. In a very controversial case, a British Columbia man was charged with the possession of violent, pornographic stories involving children. He argued that the law violated his freedom of expression, and he was acquitted. On appeal, the case eventually went to the Supreme Court of Canada. In January 2001 the Court ruled that John Robin Sharpe was deprived of his right to freedom of expression when police seized his pornography, because the stories were for his own personal use.

In sum, criminologists are concerned with the concept of deviance and its relationship to criminality. The shifting definition of deviant behaviour is closely associated with our concepts of crime. The relationship among criminology, criminal justice, and deviance is illustrated in Figure 1.2.

Famous Canadian Court Case

R. v. Sharpe (2001)

It took less than six weeks for Parliament to enact child pornography legislation in 1993, yet section 163.1 of the *Criminal Code of Canada* has been a source of relentless debate ever since. Though not the first of its kind, the Sharpe case is noteworthy because it challenged the federal law against producing, dealing, and possessing child pornography.

John Robin Sharpe was arrested at the Canada–U.S. border in 1995 after customs officers found nude photos of underage boys and explicit written material on several computer disks in his possession. Police later executed a search warrant at the Vancouver home of the retired city planner. Among the materials seized were more than five hundred photos of 91 different boys engaged in sexual activity, as well as a collection of personal stories entitled *Kiddie Kink Classics*. Sharpe was charged with two counts each of possessing and distributing child pornography, but he was acquitted by the British Columbia Supreme Court in 1999.

After the province's Court of Appeal upheld the ruling, Sharpe's case was tried before the Supreme Court of Canada. The country's highest court was forced to decide whether child pornography provisions violated the freedom of expression guarantee in section two of the *Charter*. In 2001, the Court attempted to strike a balance between the need to protect children from sexual exploitation and the need to protect fundamental rights and freedoms. Although section 163.1 of the *Criminal Code* was declared constitutional, exceptions were outlined in certain cases: for materials that have artistic, educational, or scientific merit and for purely personal materials that do not involve children in their production. Sharpe's case was retried the following year as a result and a verdict of not guilty was registered once again in relation to the distribution charges. However, Sharpe was convicted on the possession charges and received a four-month conditional sentence.

Sharpe's legal battle continued when he was arrested in 2003 for indecent assault against a man, now 35, who had come forward after police had issued a public appeal to those pictured in the seized photographs. In July 2004, at the age of 71, Sharpe was handed a prison sentence of two years less a day for the recent charge. Controversy over the Supreme Court ruling prompted the Liberal government to introduce legislation in December 2002 that would tighten the definition of "artistic merit" by introducing a standard of "contribution to the public good." In spite of the government's efforts, the proposed Bill C-12 died on the ledger when the 2004 election was called.

Sources: "Convicted Child Pornographer Sharpe Arrested," CTV News, http://www.ctv.ca (accessed August 27, 2002); "John Sharpe May Defend Himself on New Charges," CTV News, http://www.ctv.ca (accessed May 9, 2002); Robin MacKay and Marilyn Pilon, *Bill C-12: An Act to Amend the Criminal Code (Protection of Children and Other Vulnerable Persons) and the Canada Evidence Act* (Ottawa: Parliament of Canada, Parliamentary Research Branch of the Library of Parliament, February 16, 2004); "Sharpe Avoids Jail Term in B.C. Child Porn Case," CTV News, http://www.ctv.ca (accessed May 3, 2002); "The Supreme Court and Child Porn," CTV News, http://www.ctv.ca (accessed June 22, 2004); Robert Sharpe, Katherine Swinton, and Kent Roach, *The Charter of Rights and Freedoms*, 2nd ed. (Toronto: Irwin Law Inc., 2002).

Prepared by Andrea Wolf.

Figure 1.2	The Relationship among Criminology, Criminal Justice, and Deviance

A Brief History of Criminology

The scientific study of crime and criminality is a relatively recent development. Although written criminal codes have existed for thousands of years, they were, for the most part, restricted to defining crime and setting punishments. What motivated people to violate the law remained a matter of conjecture.

During the Middle Ages, people who violated social norms or religious practices were believed to be witches or possessed by demons. The prescribed method for dealing with the possessed was burning at the stake, a practice that survived into the seventeenth century. For example, between 1575 and 1590, the French Inquisition ordered nine hundred sorcerers and witches burned to death, and the bishop of the German city of Trier ordered the deaths of 6500 people. An estimated 100 000 people were prosecuted throughout Europe for witchcraft during the sixteenth and seventeenth centuries. Even those who questioned demonic possession advocated extremely harsh penalties as a means of punishing criminals and setting an example for others.

Connections

The English common law is the immediate antecedent of the Canadian legal system, except in Quebec, which inherited the Napoleonic Code from France. However, the influence of some of the earliest written codes, such as those of Hebrews and Babylonians, can still be detected. Chapter 2 traces the history of the law in some detail.

During the Middle Ages, the possessed were often burned at the stake, a practice that survived into the seventeenth century. In this painting, *The Trial of George Jacobs, August 5, 1692,* by J.H. Matteson (1855), the ordeal of the Salem patriarch, Jacobs, is depicted. During the witch craze, he had ridiculed the trials, only to find himself being accused, tried, and executed.

Classical Criminology

By the mid-eighteenth century, social philosophers had begun to call for lawmakers to rethink the prevailing concepts of law and justice. They argued for a more rational approach to punishment, stressing that the relationship between crimes and their punishment should be balanced and fair. This view was based on the philosophy called **utilitarianism**, which emphasized that behaviour is purposeful and not motivated by supernatural forces. Rather than cruel public executions designed to frighten people into obedience or to punish those the law failed to deter, reformers called for a more moderate and just approach to penal sanctions. The most famous of these was Cesare Beccaria (1738–1794), an Italian aristocrat whose writings described both a motive for committing crime and methods for its control.

Beccaria believed that people want to achieve pleasure and avoid pain. If crime provides pleasure to the criminal, pain must be used to prevent crime. Beccaria said that "in order for punishment not to be, in every instance, an act of violence of one or many against a private citizen, it must be essentially public, prompt, necessary, the least possible in the given circumstances, proportionate to the crimes, and dictated by the laws."[14]

The ideas are referred to as **classical criminology**, with several basic elements:

1. In every society, people have free will to choose criminal or lawful solutions to meet their needs or settle their problems.
2. Criminal solutions may be more attractive than lawful ones because they usually require less work for a greater payoff.
3. People's choice of criminal solutions may be controlled by their fear of punishment.
4. The more severe, certain, and swift the punishment, the better able it is to control criminal behaviour.

The classical perspective influenced judicial philosophy during much of the late eighteenth and the nineteenth centuries. Prisons began to be used as a form of punishment, and sentences were geared proportionately to the seriousness of the crime. Capital punishment was still widely used but began to be employed for only the most serious crimes. The byword was "Let the punishment fit the crime."

During the nineteenth century, a new vision of the world challenged the validity of classical theory and presented an innovative way of looking at the causes of crime.

Nineteenth-Century Positivism

Although the classical position held sway as a guide to crime, law, and justice for almost one hundred years, during the late nineteenth century a new movement began that would challenge its dominance. **Positivism** developed as the scientific method began to take hold in Europe. This movement was inspired by new discoveries in biology, astronomy, and chemistry. If the scientific method could be applied to the study of nature, why not use it to study human behaviour? Auguste Comte (1798–1857) applied scientific methods to the study of society. He believed societies pass through stages that can be grouped on the basis of how people understand the world. People in primitive societies consider inanimate objects as having life (for example, the sun is a god); in later social stages, people embrace a rational, scientific view of the world.

 InfoTrac®

Positivism can be used as an orientation in shaping the content of the law. To learn about this perspective, use InfoTrac® College Edition to find and read Claire Finkelstein, "Positivism and the Notion of an Offense," *California Law Review* 88, no. 2 (2000): 335.

Positivism has two main elements. The first is the belief that human behaviour is a function of external forces that are beyond individual control. Some of these forces are social, such as the effect of wealth and class, while others are political and historical, such as war and famine. Other forces are more personal and psychological, such as an individual's brain structure and his or her biological makeup or mental ability. All of these forces operate to influence human behaviour.

The second aspect of positivism is its use of the scientific method to solve problems. Positivists would agree that an abstract concept, such as "intelligence," exists because it can be measured by an IQ test. However, they would challenge such a concept as "ghosts" because it cannot be verified by the scientific method. The work of Charles Darwin (1809–1882) encouraged the view that all human activity could be verified by scientific principles.

Positivist Criminology

By the mid-nineteenth century "scientific" methods were being applied to understanding criminality. The earliest of these scientific studies were biological. For example, physiognomists, such as J.K. Lavater (1741–1801), studied the facial features of criminals to determine whether the shape of ears, noses, and eyes and the distance between them were associated with antisocial behaviour. Phrenologists, such as Franz Joseph Gall (1758–1828) and Johann Kaspar Spurzheim (1776–1832), studied the shape of the skull and bumps on the head to determine whether these physical attributes were linked to criminal behaviour. Phrenologists believed that external cranial characteristics dictate which areas of the brain control physical activity. Though their primitive techniques and quasi-scientific methods have been discredited, these efforts were an early attempt to apply a scientific approach to the study of crime (see Figure 1.3).

By the early nineteenth century, abnormality in the human mind was being linked to criminal behaviour patterns. Philippe Pinel (1745–1826), one of the founders of French psychiatry, claimed that some people behave abnormally even without being mentally ill. He coined the phrase *manie sans delire* to denote what eventually was referred to as a psychopathic personality. In 1812 an American, Benjamin Rush (1745–1813), described patients with an "innate preternatural moral depravity."[15] Another early criminological pioneer, English physician Henry Maudsley (1835–1918), believed that insanity and criminal behaviour were strongly linked: "Crime is a sort of outlet in which their unsound tendencies are discharged; they would go mad if they were not criminals, and they do not go mad

because they are criminals."[16] These early research efforts shifted attention to brain functioning and personality as the keys to criminal behaviour.

Cesare Lombroso and the Criminal Man

In Italy, Cesare Lombroso studied the cadavers of executed criminals to scientifically determine whether law violators were physically different from people of conventional values and behaviour. Lombroso (1835–1909) was a physician who served much of his career in the Italian army. That experience gave him ample opportunity to study the physical characteristics of soldiers executed for criminal offences. Later, he studied inmates at institutes for the criminally insane.

Lombrosian theory can be outlined in a few simple statements. First, Lombroso believed that offenders are "born criminals" who engage in repeated assault- or theft-related activities because they have inherited criminal traits that impel them into a life of crime. This view helped spur interest in a **criminal anthropology.**[17] Second, Lombroso held that born criminals suffer from **atavistic anomalies**—physically, they are throwbacks to more primitive times, when people were savages. Thus, criminals supposedly have the enormous jaws and strong canine teeth common to carnivores and savages who devour raw flesh. In addition, Lombroso compared criminals' behaviour with that of people with mental illnesses and those who had certain forms of epilepsy. He concluded that criminogenic traits could be acquired through indirect heredity: from a "degenerate family with frequent cases of insanity, deafness, syphilis, epilepsy, and alcoholism among its members." For Lombroso, this indirect heredity is the primary cause of crime. Direct heredity—being related to a family of criminals—is the second primary cause of crime.

Lombroso's version of criminal anthropology was very popular in North America and Europe, and it was printed in articles and textbooks that adopted his ideas. He attracted a circle of followers who expanded on his vision of biological determinism. By the turn of the twentieth century, authors were already discussing "the science of penology" and "the science of criminology."

Figure 1.3	Early Positivists Believed the Shape of the Skull Was a Key Determinant of Behaviour

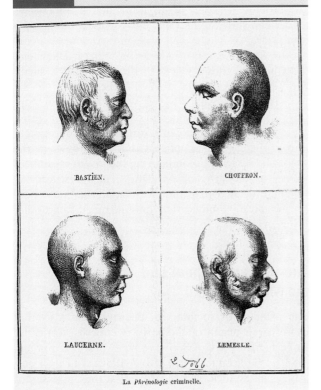

These drawings from the nineteenth century illustrate "typical" criminally shaped heads.

Connections

The theories of criminology that have their roots in Lombroso's biological determinism will be discussed in Chapter 6. Criminologists who today suggest that crime has a biological basis also believe that environmental conditions influence human behaviour. Hence, the term biosocial theory is used to reflect the link among physical and mental traits, the social environment, and behaviour.

The Development of Sociological Criminology

At the same time that biological views were dominating criminology, another group of positivists were developing the field of sociology to scientifically study the major social changes that were taking place in nineteenth-century society.

Sociology was an ideal perspective from which to study society. After thousands of years of stability, the world was undergoing a population explosion: The population, estimated at 600 million in 1700, had risen to 900 million by 1800. People were flocking to cities in ever-increasing numbers. For example, Manchester, England, had 12 000 inhabitants in 1760 and 400 000 in 1850. The development of such machinery as power looms had doomed cottage industries and given rise to a factory system in which large numbers of people toiled for extremely low wages. The spread of agricultural machines increased the food supply while reducing the need for a large rural work force; the excess labourers further swelled the cities' populations.

The foundations of sociological criminology can be traced to the works of L.A.J. (Adolphe) Quetelet (1796–1874) and Emile Durkheim (1858–1917).

L.A.J. Quetelet. Quetelet was a Belgian mathematician who began (along with André-Michel Guerry, from France) what is known as the cartographic school of criminology.[18] Quetelet, made use of social statistics developed in France in the early nineteenth century (called the *Comptes généraux de l'administration de la justice*) and was one of the first social scientists to use objective mathematical techniques to investigate the influence of social factors, such as season, climate, sex, and age, on the propensity to commit crime. Quetelet's most important finding was that social forces were significantly correlated with crime rates. Quetelet showed that the same lawlike mechanical regularity that could be observed in the heavens and in the world of nature also existed in the world of social facts.[19] Quetelet was a pioneer of sociological criminology. He identified many of the relationships between crime and social phenomena that still serve as a basis for criminology today.

Emile Durkheim. (David) Emile Durkheim (1858–1917) was one of the founders of sociology and a significant contributor to criminology.[20] His definition of crime as a normal and necessary social event has been more influential on modern criminology than has any other.

According to Durkheim's vision of social positivism, crime is seen as normal because it has existed in every age, in both poverty and prosperity. Crime is an integral part of all healthy societies because it is virtually impossible to imagine a society in which criminal behaviour is totally absent. Such a society would almost demand that all people be and act exactly alike. The inevitability of crime is linked to the differences within society. Because people are so different from one another and use such a variety of methods and forms of behaviour to meet their needs, some will resort to criminality. Even if "real" crimes were eliminated, human weaknesses and petty vices would be elevated to the status of crimes. As long as human differences exist, crime is inevitable, serving as a symbolic reminder of moral boundaries.

Durkheim argued that crime could be useful, and even healthy, for a society to experience. The existence of crime implies that a way is open for social change and that the social structure is not rigid or inflexible. Put another way, if crime did not exist, it would mean that everyone behaves the same way and agrees totally on what is right and wrong. Such universal conformity would stifle creativity and independent thinking. Durkheim offered the example of the Greek philosopher Socrates, who, simply because he questioned the social order, was considered a criminal and sentenced to death for corrupting the morals of youth. When given the chance to flee to save his life, Socrates refused, saying that doing so would negate his ideal of standing up for what he believed. In addition, Durkheim argued that crime is beneficial because it calls attention to social ills. A rising crime rate can signal the need for social change and promote a variety of programs designed to relieve the human suffering that may have caused crime in the first place.

In *The Division of Labor in Society*, Durkheim described the consequences of the shift from a small, rural society, which he labelled "mechanical," to the more modern "organic" society with a large urban population, division of labour, and personal isolation. From this shift flowed **anomie**, or norm and role confusion, a powerful sociological concept that helps describe the chaos and disarray accompanying the loss of traditional values in modern society. Durkheim's research on suicide indicated that anomic societies maintain high suicide rates; by implication, anomie might cause other forms of deviance to develop.

The Chicago School and the McGill School

The primacy of sociological positivism was secured by research begun in the early twentieth century by Robert Ezra Park (1864–1944), Ernest W. Burgess (1886–1966), Louis Wirth (1897–1952), and their colleagues in the sociology department at the University of Chicago. Known as the **Chicago School**, these sociologists pioneered research on the social ecology of the city and inspired a generation of scholars to conclude that social forces operating in urban areas create criminal interactions; some neighbourhoods become almost natural areas for crime.[21] These urban neighbourhoods maintain such a high level of poverty that critical social institutions, such as the school and the family, break down. The resulting social disorganization reduces the ability of social institutions to control behaviour, and the outcome is a high crime rate.

The Chicago School sociologists and their contemporaries focused on the functions of social institutions and how their breakdown influences behaviour. They pioneered the ecological study of crime—crime as a function of where a person lives. Important works in the Chicago School tradition were *The Gang* (1927) by Frederic Thrasher, *The Ghetto* (1928) by Louis Wirth, *Gold Coast and Slum* (1929) by Harvey Zorbaugh, and *The Hobo* (1923) by Nels Anderson, a professor in the sociology department at the University of New Brunswick.

Less well known is the work of Carl Dawson and his colleagues at McGill University. Dawson, a native of Prince Edward Island and a graduate of Acadia University, studied at the University of Chicago before he went to Montreal to head up McGill's social work and sociology departments. He and his students studied the processes of industrial development, transportation, poverty, ethnicity and immigration, housing, juvenile delinquency, welfare, and physiographic barriers to mobility. This work constituted a significant contribution to early sociology and criminology in Canada.[22]

Connections

The ecological approach of the Chicago School was very influential and was applied to the study of crime in various cities, such as Chicago, New York, and Montreal. In particular, it became known for the concentric zone model of deviance, in which crime is found to be higher in the more socially disorganized areas of a city. For a more in-depth discussion of the work of Carl Dawson and the application of this approach to Montreal, see Chapter 7.

During the 1930s, social psychologists argued that the individual's relationship to education, family life, and peer relations is the key to understanding human behaviour. In any social milieu, children who grow up in a home wracked by conflict, attend an inadequate school, and associate with deviant peers become exposed to pro-crime forces. One position was that people learn criminal attitudes from older, more experienced law violators; another view was that crime occurs when families fail to control adolescent misbehaviour. Each of these views linked criminality to the failure of socialization.

By mid-century, most criminologists had embraced either the ecological or the socialization view of crime. However, these were not the only views of how social institutions influence human behaviour. In Europe, the writings of another social thinker, Karl Marx (1818–1883), had pushed the understanding of social interaction in another direction and sowed the seeds for a new approach in criminology.[23]

InfoTrac®

Use InfoTrac® College Edition to learn more about how socialization affects human development. Narrow the search to find Luoluo Hony's article called "Toward a Transformed Approach to Prevention: Breaking the Link between Masculinity and Violence," published in the *Journal of American College Health* 8, no. 6 (2000): 269.

Conflict Criminology

Oppressive labour conditions prevalent during the rise of industrial capitalism convinced Marx that the character of society is determined by the way people develop and produce material goods. The most important relationship is between the owners of the means of production—the capitalist **bourgeoisie**—and the people who do the actual labour—the **proletariat**. The economic system determines all facets of human life; consequently, people's lives revolve around the means of production. The exploitation of the working class, Marx believed, would eventually lead to class conflict and the end of the capitalist system.

Although Marx did not develop a theory of crime and justice, his writings were applied to legal studies by other social thinkers, including Ralf Dahrendorf, George Vold, and Willem Bonger.[24] Though these writings laid the foundation for a Marxist criminology, decades passed before Marxist theory had an important impact on criminology. The Vietnam War, the development of an anti-establishment counterculture movement in the 1960s, the civil rights movement, and the women's movement were all important events challenging the model of social consensus underlying the functionalism of the Chicago School. Young sociologists who became interested in applying Marxist principles to the study of crime began to analyze the social conditions that were felt to promote class conflict and crime. What emerged from this intellectual ferment was the conflict-oriented radical criminology of the 1970s that indicted the economic system for producing the conditions that support a high crime rate. The radical tradition has played a significant role in criminology ever since.

Criminology Today

The various schools of criminology developed over two hundred years. Although they have undergone great change and innovation, each continues to have an impact on the field. For example, classical theory has evolved into rational choice and deterrence theories. Choice theorists today argue that criminals are rational and use available information to decide whether crime is a worthwhile undertaking; deterrence theory holds that this choice is structured by the fear of punishment.

Criminal anthropology has also evolved considerably. Although criminologists no longer believe that a single trait or inherited characteristic can explain crime, some are convinced that biological and mental traits interact with environmental factors to influence all human behaviour, including criminality. Biological and psychological theorists study the association between criminal behaviour and such traits as diet, hormonal makeup, personality, and intelligence.

Sociological theories, tracing back to Quetelet and Durkheim, maintain that individuals' lifestyles and living conditions directly control their criminal behaviour. Those at the bottom of the social structure cannot achieve success and thus experience anomie, strain, failure, and frustration. This theory today is called the structural perspective.

Some sociologists who have added a social psychological dimension to their views of crime causation find that individuals' learning experiences and socialization directly control their behaviour. In some cases, children learn to commit crime by interacting with and modelling their behaviour after others they admire, while other criminal offenders are people whose life experiences have shattered their social bonds to society. This view is called the social process perspective.

The writings of Marx and his followers continue to be influential. Today conflict criminologists still see social and political conflict as the root cause of crime. In their view, the inherently unfair economic structure of advanced capitalist countries is the engine that drives the high crime rate.

Criminology, then, has had a rich history that still exerts an important influence on the thinking of its current practitioners. These major perspectives are summarized in Figure 1.4.

Figure 1.4   The Major Perspectives of Criminology

CLASSICAL/ CHOICE PERSPECTIVE	**Situational forces** Crime is a function of free will and personal choice. Punishment is a deterrent to crime.
BIOLOGICAL/ PSYCHOLOGICAL PERSPECTIVE	**Internal forces** Crime is a function of chemical, neurological, genetic, personality, intelligence, or mental traits.
STRUCTURAL PERSPECTIVE	**Ecological forces** Crime rates are a function of neighbourhood conditions, cultural forces, and norm conflict.
PROCESS PERSPECTIVE	**Socialization forces** Crime is a function of upbringing, learning, and control. Peers, parents, and teachers influence behaviour.
CONFLICT PERSPECTIVE	**Economic and political forces** Crime is a function of competition for limited resources and power. Class conflict produces crime.
INTEGRATED PERSPECTIVE	**Multiple forces** Biological, social-psychological, economic, and political forces may combine to produce crime.

The focus is on *individual* (biological, psychological, and choice theories), *social* (structural and process theories), *political* and *economic* (conflict), and *multiple* (integrated) factors.

What Criminologists Do: The Criminological Enterprise

Regardless of their background or training, criminologists are primarily interested in studying crime and criminal behaviour. As Marvin Wolfgang and Franco Ferracuti put it,

A criminologist is one whose professional training, occupational role, and pecuniary reward are primarily concentrated on a scientific approach to, and study and analysis of, the phenomenon of crime and criminal behaviour.[25]

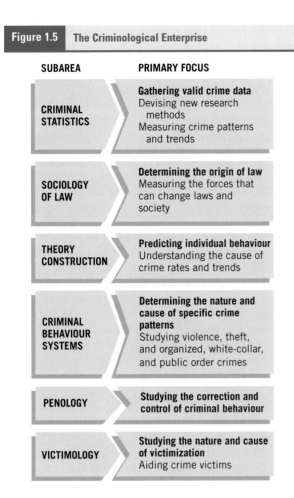

Figure 1.5   The Criminological Enterprise

SUBAREA	PRIMARY FOCUS
CRIMINAL STATISTICS	**Gathering valid crime data** Devising new research methods Measuring crime patterns and trends
SOCIOLOGY OF LAW	**Determining the origin of law** Measuring the forces that can change laws and society
THEORY CONSTRUCTION	**Predicting individual behaviour** Understanding the cause of crime rates and trends
CRIMINAL BEHAVIOUR SYSTEMS	**Determining the nature and cause of specific crime patterns** Studying violence, theft, and organized, white-collar, and public order crimes
PENOLOGY	**Studying the correction and control of criminal behaviour**
VICTIMOLOGY	**Studying the nature and cause of victimization** Aiding crime victims

These subareas constitute the field or discipline of criminology.

Criminal Statistics

The subarea of criminal statistics involves measuring the amount and trends of criminal activity. How much crime occurs annually? Who commits it? When and where does it occur? Which crimes are the most serious? Criminologists interested in criminal statistics try to create valid and reliable measurements of criminal behaviour. For example, they create techniques to use the records of police and court agencies. They develop paper-and-pencil survey instruments and then use them

with large samples of citizens to determine the percentage of people who actually commit crimes and the number of law violators who escape detection by the justice system. They also develop techniques to identify the victims of crime and establish more accurate indicators of the "true" number of criminal acts—how many people are victims of crime and what percentage report crime to police. The study of criminal statistics is one of the most crucial aspects of the criminological enterprise because without valid and reliable data sources, efforts to conduct research on crime and create criminological theories would be futile.

InfoTrac®

To better understand the nature of crime in Eastern European nations that have transitioned from Communism to democracy, and the efforts being made to control crime, use InfoTrac® College Edition to find these articles:

- Christian Caryl, "The Very Long Arm of American Law," *US News & World Report,* July 7, 1997, 49.
- Richard Lotspeich, "Crime in the Transition Economies," *Europe-Asia Studies* 47 (June 1995): 555–590.

Sociology of Law

The sociology of law is a subarea of criminology concerned with the role that social forces play in shaping criminal law and, conversely, the role of criminal law in shaping society. Criminologists study the history of legal thought in an effort to understand how criminal acts, such as theft, rape, and murder, evolved into their present form. Criminologists may also be asked to join in the debate when a new law is proposed to banish or control behaviour. For example, a debate raged over the legality of Napster, an online service that let its 64 million members worldwide share music in apparent violation of copyright law. What role should the law take in curbing the public's access to media and culture? Should society curb actions that some people consider illegal but by which no one is actually harmed? And how is harm defined? Is a child who reads a pornographic magazine "harmed"? Is a company denied profits "harmed"? Is the behaviour Napster allowed any different from videotaping a documentary from the television, or taping a song from the radio or from a cassette owned by a friend?

Most people surveyed think that music file swapping should be legal, even though they know it is theft. It is a crime that is harder to police in Canada than it is

Within the broader arena of criminology are several subareas that, taken together, make up the **criminological enterprise.** Criminologists may specialize in a subarea in the same way that psychologists might specialize in a subfield, such as child development, perception, personality, psychopathology, or sexuality. Some of the more important criminological subareas are described in this section and are summarized in Figure 1.5.

in the United States. Recently, a Canadian court ruled that the music industry can't force Internet service providers to identify online music sharers and that using an online download service for personal use doesn't amount to copyright infringement.

33%   77%
YES   NO

Seventy-seven percent of Canadians surveyed in a 2004 poll by *The Globe and Mail* said "No" to the question of whether music file swapping should be illegal.

Source: Poll conducted by *The Globe and Mail,* May 11, 2004.

InfoTrac®

Use InfoTrac® College Edition to learn more about the sociology of law: Kim Lane Scheppele, "Legal Theory and Social Theory," *Annual Review of Sociology* 20 (1994): 383.

Criminologists also partake in updating the content of criminal law. The law must be flexible and respond to changing times and conditions. Computer fraud, airplane hijacking, theft from automatic teller machines, identity theft, and illegally tapping into TV cable lines are acts that obviously did not exist when criminal law was originally formed. Sometimes, the law must respond to new versions of traditional acts. For example, Sue Rodriguez, who suffered from ALS (amyotrophic lateral sclerosis or Lou Gehrig's disease), committed suicide in February 1994, after losing her bid for legally assisted suicide before the Supreme Court in December 1992.[26] How should the law respond to these controversial issues?

Although some who believe that euthanasia or identity theft are socially harmful, others are not quite so certain. Many Canadians felt great sympathy for Sue Rodriguez's plight, and before international media coverage of the issue, there was no law banning second-party help in suicides. In response to the actions of Jack Kevorkian in the United States, Michigan passed legislation making it a felony to help anyone commit suicide.[27] Is assisted suicide the product of care and concern for human suffering, or is it a callous criminal act? Should

a law be passed that a majority of the general public disapproves of—a condition that makes the law virtually unenforceable? Conversely, should criminal law be restricted to only those acts that are unpopular with the general public?

Theory Construction

A question that has always intrigued criminologists is why do people engage in criminal acts? Why, when they know their actions can bring harsh punishment and social disapproval, do they steal, rape, and murder? Why do people behave the way they do? Does crime have a social or an individual basis? Is it a psychological, a biological, a social, a political, or an economic phenomenon? Some criminologists have a psychological orientation and view crime as a function of personality, development, social learning, or cognition. Others investigate the biology of antisocial behaviour and study the biochemical, genetic, and neurological linkages to crime. Sociologists look at the social forces producing criminal behaviour, including neighbourhood conditions, poverty, socialization, and group interaction.

Understanding the true cause of crime remains a difficult problem. Criminologists are still unsure why, given similar conditions, one person elects criminal solutions to his or her problems while another conforms to accepted social rules of behaviour. Further, understanding crime rates and trends has proved difficult: Why do rates rise and fall? Why are crime rates higher in some areas or regions than in others? Why do some groups seem more crime-prone than others? Is it possible that crime is relative to societal standards and thus a social construction created by the media, politicians, and social alarmists?

Criminal Behaviour Systems

This subarea of criminology involves research on specific criminal types and patterns: violent crime, theft crime, public order crime, and organized crime. Numerous attempts have been made to describe and understand particular crime types. For example, Marvin Wolfgang's famous study *Patterns in Criminal Homicide* is considered a landmark analysis of the nature of homicide and the relationship between victim and offender.[28] Edwin Sutherland's analysis of business-related offences helped coin a new phrase—**white-collar crime**—to describe economic crime activities.[29]

The study of criminal behaviour also involves research on the links between different types of crime and criminals, known as crime typology. Some typologies focus on the criminal, such as professional criminals, psychotic criminals, occasional criminals, and so on. Others focus on the crimes, clustering them into such categories as property crimes, sex crimes, and so on.

Penology

The study of penology involves the correction and control of criminal offenders. Penologists formulate new strategies for crime control and then help implement these policies in "the real world." Some criminologists view penology as involving rehabilitation and treatment, providing behaviour alternatives for those convicted of law violations. This view portrays the criminal as someone whom society has failed; someone under social, psychological, or economic stress; someone who can be helped if society is willing to pay the price.

Others argue that crime can be prevented only through a strict policy of social control. They advocate such strict measures as capital punishment, mandatory prison sentences, and selective incapacitation for repeat offenders.

Connections

In recent years, criminologists have devoted ever-increasing attention to the victim's role in the criminal process, looking at how individuals' lifestyles and behaviour may actually increase the risk that they will become crime victims. Living in a high-crime neighbourhood increases risk, as does associating with dangerous peers and companions. For a discussion of victimization risk, see Chapter 4.

 Culture, Gender, Ethnicity, and Criminology

The Changing Face of International Crime Rates

People in many countries are justifiably concerned about crime, and most people view it as a major social problem. Let's briefly look at some of the recent patterns.

The 2000 International Crime Victimization Survey of 17 industrialized countries found that on average, 21 percent of people aged 16 and older were victims of crime in the previous year. That rate varied from a low of 15 percent for Northern Ireland to 30 percent in Australia. Canada's rate was 24 percent. Most of the countries had no significant changes in crime from 1996. Over the longer term, there were downward trends in Canada, Poland, and the United States.

The crime rate in Canada has declined in recent years. Conversely, the United States has led the world with its murder, rape, and robbery rates. For example, police statistics show that the murder rate was six times higher and the rape rate

was about three times higher in the United States than in England and Wales. The United States also imprisons far more people than other countries. The percentage of the population sent to prison in the United States exceeds those of such notoriously punitive countries as Singapore, Romania, and South Africa.

Explanations for the high American crime rate include urban areas in which the poorest and wealthiest citizens reside in close proximity, racism and discrimination, failure of an underfunded educational system, the troubled American family, easy access to handguns, and a culture that defines success in terms of material wealth.

Many nations are experiencing disturbing upswings in crime. For example, murder rates have sharply increased in England, Germany, and Sweden. Racial assaults and hate crimes have increased dramatically in Germany and England. The most recent data available indicate that robbery, assault, burglary, and motor vehicle theft rates are

actually lower in the United States than they are in England and Wales: Robbery rates rose more than 81 percent in England and Wales between 1981 and 1995, but they fell 28 percent in the United States. Similarly, assault increased by 53 percent in England and Wales but declined by 27 percent in the United States; burglary doubled in England and Wales but fell by half in the United States.

In 2000, the official crime rate in England and Wales showed an average increase of 19 percent and an increase of 38 percent for muggings in London. Officials believed that one-third of all property crime was committed to finance drug abuse. Responding to the crime problem, former Prime Minister Thatcher said in an address,

> [The] permissive society is in fact no society at all. It is little more than a state of nature where the line between right and wrong is first blurred and then obliterated— a place where no one

dares to say no. There can be no order without authority, and authority that is impotent or hesitant in the face of intimidation, crime and violence, cannot endure.

Some feel that the rising crime rate in England is due to a decrease in punitiveness, while the falling crime rate in the United States is due to an increase in punishment. However, it is difficult to know what is causing changes in the crime rates. In England in 1998 it was reported that changes in record keeping, including an end to the practice of counting a string of offences as one crime could create a 20 percent increase in the official rate. And in 2000 it was reported that police tend to downgrade crime by at least 20 percent, artificially decreasing the official rate. However, three thousand fewer police on the beat, the early release of criminals from prison, and the decreased use of police stop and search techniques would mean an increase in crime.

 InfoTrac®

To find out about the factors causing an increase in crime rates in Eastern European countries, check out this article: Richard Lotspeich, "Crime in the Transition Economies," *Europe-Asia Studies* 47, no. 4 (1995): 555–590.

Eastern Europe and Asia

England is not alone in experiencing higher crime rates. Russia and the former Soviet republics have experienced increases in the number of large-scale organized crime gangs, who commonly use violence and intimidation. In 1998 it was reported that economic crimes had increased 20 percent over the previous year, drug trafficking had increased 16 percent, arms trafficking 29 percent, and banditry 52 percent. In other European nations, violence has been fuelled by a dramatic growth in the number of illegal guns smuggled into these countries from the former Soviet republics. Additionally, unrestricted immigration has brought newcomers who face cultural differences, lack of job prospects, and racism. Social and economic pressures, including unemployment and cutbacks in the social welfare system, have also contributed to increased violence. In the formerly communist countries in Eastern Europe especially, weak law enforcement institutions, rapid changes in economic laws, deteriorating economic conditions, incomplete reforms, and destabilized social norms have contributed to rising criminality.

Increased criminal activity in Asia has also been reported. For example, Japan, a nation that prides itself on low crime rates, has experienced an upsurge in juvenile crime. It is estimated that 45 percent of all crimes are committed by people under age 20, about double the percentage in the United States. With so much Japanese crime committed by youths, and with the juvenile crime rate escalating, experts predict an overall increase in future crime rates.

However, Tokyo, the world's safest major city, suffers muggings at the rate of 40 per year per one million inhabitants, compared with New York City's rate of 11 000. Why is the Japanese crime rate so much lower than most developed nations? Japan's homicide rate is two to three times lower than the American rate, and the number of handgun murders in the United States is two hundred times higher than Japan's. Robbery in Japan is about as rare as murder: 1.8 per 100 000 inhabitants, compared with America's rate of 205.4. The American theft rate is 4 times greater than Japan's, the rape rate is nearly 25 times greater, and the robbery rate is 140 times greater. Japan is still considered one of the safest countries in the world, but its crime rate is rising every year. Authorities say that organized crime and juvenile crime are the two biggest contributors to the increase. Criminologists report that violent crime is the highest in 23 years; in 1999 alone, incidents of rape, murder, arson, and assault showed an 11 percent per capita increase.

Juvenile delinquency is also increasing in Singapore; in fact, it more than doubled during the first half of the 1990s. Singapore and Japan are not the only Asian nations experiencing an upsurge in crime. Vietnamese authorities report a troubling increase in street crimes, like burglary and theft. Many crimes are drug-related: Vietnam has an estimated 200 000 opium addicts, and about 20 000 acres of land are now growing the poppies from which heroin is produced.

Although it is difficult to obtain accurate crime data from China, the world's largest nation seems to be cracking down on crime. In recent years, Chinese courts annually have sentenced more than 100 000 street criminals. Death sentences were given to 1000 criminals, and many thousands more were sentenced to life in prison. The current wave of punishment is a response to a significant increase in street crimes, including robberies and drug trafficking.

Violence rates are also increasing in other parts of the world. The homicide rate in Jamaica is 32 per 100 000; in Colombia homicide rates are close to 70 per 100 000, about 10 times the American average! As in Asia and Europe, high regional murder rates are tied to the flourishing drug trade.

International comparisons of crime rates add immeasurably to our understanding of trends.

Sources: John van Kesteren, Pat Mayhew, and Paul Nieuwbeerta, *Criminal Victimisation in Seventeen Industrialised Countries: Key Findings from the 2000 International Crime Victims Survey* (The Hague: Ministry of Justice, WODC, 2000); Jon Hibbs, "Thatcher Hits out at Moral 'Corrosion,'" *London Daily Telegraph,* September 25, 1995.

Victimology

Two classic texts in criminology, one by Hans von Hentig and another by Stephen Schafer, first identified the critical role of the victim in the criminal process. These authors suggested that victim behaviour is often a key determinant of crime, that a victim's actions may precipitate or provide an opportunity for crime, and that the study of crime is not complete unless the victim's role is considered.[30]

The areas of particular interest in victimology include using victim surveys to measure the nature and extent of criminal behaviour, calculating the actual costs of crime to victims, creating probabilities of victimization risk, studying victim culpability or precipitation of crime, and designing services for the victims of crime. Victimology has taken on greater importance as more criminologists focus their attention on the victim's role in the criminal event.

How Do Criminologists View Crime?

Criminology is multidisciplinary, but professional criminologists align themselves with one of several perspectives in their field. Each perspective maintains its own view of what constitutes criminal behaviour and what causes people to engage in criminality. Biologists, psychologists, sociologists, historians, and economists bring conflicting views to research, often disagreeing on the nature and definition of crime itself. Criminologists' theoretical perspectives and conceptualizations of crime affect their research orientations. This section discusses the three most common concepts of crime used by criminologists.

The Consensus View of Crime

This view holds that crimes are repugnant to all elements of society. Thus, criminal law, with its definition of crimes and their punishments, reflects the values, beliefs, and opinions of society's mainstream. The term consensus is used because it implies that general agreement exists among a majority of citizens on what behaviours should be outlawed by the criminal law and viewed as crimes.

Several attempts have been made to create a concise, yet thorough and encompassing, consensus definition of crime. Criminologists Edwin Sutherland and Donald Cressey have taken the popular stance of linking crime with criminal law:

> Criminal behaviour is behaviour in violation of the criminal law. . . . [It] is not a crime unless it is prohibited by the criminal law [which] is defined conventionally as a body of specific rules regarding human conduct which have been promulgated by political authority, which apply uniformly to all members of the classes to which the rules refer, and which are enforced by punishment administered by the state.[31]

This approach implies that the definition of crime is a function of the beliefs, morality, and direction of social authorities, and is applied uniformly to everyone in society. This statement reveals the authors' faith in the concept of an ideal legal system that can deal adequately with all classes and types of people. Although laws banning burglary and robbery are directed at controlling the neediest members of society, laws banning insider trading, embezzlement, and corporate price fixing are aimed at controlling the wealthiest.

The consensus model of crime is probably accepted by a majority of criminologists. Nonetheless, dispute exists over whether the law is applied uniformly.

The Conflict View of Crime

In opposition, the conflict view depicts society as a collection of diverse groups—owners, workers, professionals, students—who are in constant and continuing conflict. Groups able to assert their political power use the law and the criminal justice system to advance their economic and social position. Criminal laws are created to protect the haves from the have-nots. For example, contrast the harsh penalties exacted on the poor for their street crimes (burglary, robbery, and theft) with the minor penalties the wealthy receive for their white-collar crimes (securities violations and other illegal business practices). While the poor go to prison for minor law violations, the wealthy are given lenient sentences for even the most serious breaches of law.

In the conflict view, the definition of crime is controlled by wealth, power, and position and not by moral consensus or the fear of social disruption.[32] Crime is a political concept designed to protect the power and position of the upper classes at the expense of the poor. Even laws prohibiting such violent acts as rape and murder may have political undertones: Banning violent acts ensures domestic tranquillity and guarantees that the anger of the poor will not be directed at the rich. A conflict theorist would see the following as crimes: violations of human rights, unsafe working conditions, inadequate childcare, inadequate opportunities for employment and education, and substandard housing, pollution of the environment, price fixing, police brutality, assassinations, and war making.[33]

The Interactionist View of Crime

The interactionist view of crime has its origins in the symbolic interaction school of sociology, with George Herbert Mead, Charles Horton Cooley, and W.I. Thomas.[34] This position holds that (1) people act according to their own interpretations of reality, according to the meaning things have for them; (2) they learn the meaning of a thing from the way others react to it, either positively or negatively; and (3) they reevaluate and interpret their own behaviour according to the meaning and symbols they have learned from others.

In this perspective, the definition of crime reflects the preferences and opinions of people who impose their definition of right and wrong on the rest of the population. Criminals are individuals whom society chooses to label as outcasts or deviants because they have violated social rules. As sociologist Howard Becker argued: "The deviant is one to whom that label has successfully been applied; deviant behavior is behavior people so label."[35] Crimes are outlawed behaviours because society defines them that way and not because they are inherently evil.

Connections

Interactionists believe that society should intervene as little as possible in the lives of law violators lest they be labelled and stigmatized. Labelling theory, discussed in Chapter 8, is based on interactionist views and holds that the application of negative labels leads first to a damaged identity and then to a criminal career.

The interactionist and conflict perspectives both suggest that behaviour is outlawed when it offends people who maintain the social, economic, and political power necessary to have the law conform to their interests or needs. However, unlike the conflict view, the interactionist perspective does not attribute capitalist economic and political motives to the process of defining crime. Instead, interactionists see criminal law as conforming to the beliefs of "moral crusaders" or **moral entrepreneurs** who use their influence to shape the legal process in the way they see fit. Laws against pornography, prostitution, and drugs are motivated by moral crusades. Interactionists are concerned with shifting moral standards, and crime has no meaning unless people react to it. The one-time criminal, if not caught or labelled, can simply return to a "normal" way of life with little permanent damage—students who try marijuana do not view themselves as criminals or drug addicts. Only when prohibited acts are sanctioned do they become important, life-transforming events.

Defining Crime

The consensus view of crime dominated criminological thought until the late 1960s. Criminologists devoted themselves to learning why lawbreakers violated the rules of society. The criminal was viewed as an outlaw who, for one reason or another, flouted the rules defining acceptable conduct and behaviour. In the 1960s, the interactionist perspective gained prominence. The rapid changes society was experiencing made traditional law and values questionable. Many criminologists were swept along in the social revolution of the 1960s and likewise embraced an ideology that suggested that crimes reflected rules imposed by a conservative majority on nonconforming members of society. During the 1970s, more radical scholars gravitated toward conflict explanations (see Figure 1.6).

Today, each position still has many followers. This fact is important because criminologists' personal definitions of crime dominate their thinking, research, and attitudes toward their profession. Because they view crime differently, criminologists have taken a variety of approaches in explaining its causes and suggesting methods for its control. Considering these differences, it is possible to take elements from each school of thought to formulate an integrated definition of crime: Crime is a violation of societal rules of behaviour as interpreted and expressed by a criminal legal code created by people holding social and political power. Individuals who violate these rules are subject to sanctions by state authority, to social stigma, and to loss of status.

Figure 1.6	The Definition of Crime Affects How Criminologists View the Cause and Control of Illegal Behaviour and Shapes Their Research Orientation

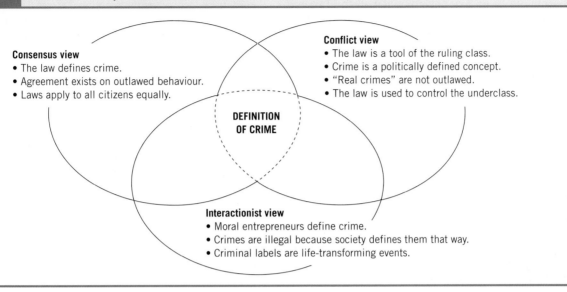

Consensus view
- The law defines crime.
- Agreement exists on outlawed behaviour.
- Laws apply to all citizens equally.

Conflict view
- The law is a tool of the ruling class.
- Crime is a politically defined concept.
- "Real crimes" are not outlawed.
- The law is used to control the underclass.

DEFINITION OF CRIME

Interactionist view
- Moral entrepreneurs define crime.
- Crimes are illegal because society defines them that way.
- Criminal labels are life-transforming events.

This definition combines the consensus view's position that criminal law defines crimes with the conflict perspective's emphasis on political power and control and the interactionist view's concepts of stigma. Thus, crime as defined here is a political, social, and economic function of modern life.

Doing Criminology

Criminologists have used a wide variety of research techniques to measure the nature and extent of criminal behaviour. To understand and evaluate theories and patterns of criminal behaviour, it is important to develop some knowledge of how these data are collected. It is also important to understand the methods used in criminology, as this understanding provides insight into how professional criminologists approach various problems and questions in their field.

Survey Research

Interviewing or questioning subjects is also called **cross-sectional research**, since it involves surveying people who come from a cross-section of the community. Most surveys involve sampling, in which subjects are selected as representative of a larger population. For example, a criminologist might interview a sample of five hundred people drawn from the population of 155 000 offenders who were under the supervision of Canadian correctional agencies in 2001; in this case, the

sample is meant to represent the entire population of inmates. It is assumed that the characteristics of people or events in a carefully selected sample will be quite similar to those of the population at large.

Survey research can be designed to measure the attitudes, beliefs, values, personality traits, and behaviour of participants. Self-report surveys ask participants to describe their criminal activity; victimization surveys seek information from victims of crime; attitude surveys may measure the attitudes, beliefs, and values of various groups, such as prostitutes, students, drug addicts, police officers, judges, or juvenile delinquents.

The cross-sectional survey is a widely used method of criminological study. It is an excellent and cost-effective technique for measuring the characteristics of large numbers of people. Because questions and methods are standardized for all subjects, the statistical analysis of data from the samples enables researchers to generalize their findings from small groups to large populations. Though surveys measure subjects at a single point in their life span, questions can elicit information on subjects' prior behaviour as well as their future goals and aspirations.[36]

Since surveys typically involve a single measurement, they are of limited value in showing how subjects change over time. Also, although efforts are made to ensure the validity of questionnaire items, it is difficult to guard against people misrepresenting information or giving mistaken responses. Surveys of delinquents and criminals are especially suspect, as the surveys rely on the willingness of a group of people not known for their candour about intimate and personal matters. Despite these drawbacks, surveys continue to be an extremely popular method of gathering criminological data.

Longitudinal (Cohort) Research

Longitudinal research involves the observation over time of a group of people who share a characteristic (a **cohort**). For example, researchers might select all girls born in Surrey, British Columbia, in 1970 and follow their behaviour patterns for 30 years. The data might include school experiences, arrests, hospitalizations, and information about their family life (divorces, parental relations). The subjects might be given repeated intelligence tests and physical exams; and their diets could be monitored. Data could be collected directly from the subjects or without their knowledge from schools, police, and other sources. If the research were carefully conducted, it might be possible to determine which life experiences, such as growing up in a broken home or failing at school, typically preceded the onset of crime and delinquency.

It is extremely difficult, expensive, and time-consuming to follow a cohort over time, and most people do not become serious criminals. Another approach is to take a cohort of known offenders and look at their early life experiences by checking their educational, family, police, and hospital records; this format is known as a retrospective cohort study.[37]

Criminologists would use the records of social organizations, such as hospitals, schools, welfare departments, courts, police departments, and prisons. School records contain data on academic performance, attendance, intelligence, disciplinary problems, and teacher ratings. Hospitals record incidents of drug use and suspicious wounds indicative of child abuse. Police files contain reports of criminal activity, arrest data, personal information on suspects, victim reports, and actions taken by police officers. Court records allow researchers to compare the personal characteristics of offenders with conviction rates and types of sentences. Prison records contain information on inmates' personal characteristics, adjustment problems, disciplinary records, rehabilitation efforts, and length of sentence served.

In one retrospective longitudinal survey that used court records to examine the effects of child abuse on a person's adult behaviour, the researcher compared a group of approximately nine hundred people who were reported to have been abused with a group of more than six hundred people with no reported abuse. Interviewing the subjects 15 years after their cases had been heard in court, the research showed that when all possible factors were controlled, a connection existed between child abuse and juvenile delinquency. Being abused or neglected increased the likelihood of arrest as a juvenile by 53 percent and as an adult by 38 percent.[38]

Connections

Some critical criminological research has been based on cohort studies. Some of the most important research has been conducted by University of Pennsylvania criminologist Marvin Wolfgang and his colleagues. Their findings have been instrumental in developing knowledge about the onset and development of a criminal career. Wolfgang's cohort research is discussed in Chapter 3.

Famous Canadian Criminals

Canada's Deadliest Serial Killer

Robert Pickton begins trial in 2006 on 27 cases of first-degree murder. He was charged in connection with the disappearance of more than 60 sex-trade workers. Beginning in 1983, women went missing from Vancouver streets in an area known for drug dealing, addiction, homelessness, and violence. Police wrapped up their $70

million investigation in late 2003 at Pickton's pig farm in Port Coquitlam, B.C. In a scary connection, one of Pickton's victims was Janet Henry, reported missing in 1997; she was also victimized by Clifford Olson in the 1980s.

Canada's First Serial Killer?

Dr. Thomas Neill Cream, born in Glasgow and a graduate of McGill (1876), is estimated to have killed seven women in

Great Britain and North America. Some think that he was Jack the Ripper, responsible for the murder of prostitutes. He worked occasionally as an abortionist, and at one point he was convicted of murder for adding strychnine to a patient's prescription.

Killer in the Making

Michael Wayne McGray, 35, of Nova Scotia, pleaded guilty in 2000 to four counts of murder and implicated himself in 16 others. He testified that he found victims at random, driven by a "boiling urge" to kill. In 1991 he killed two gay men in Montreal, sparking fears of a serial murderer targeting gay men. As a child, McGray was violently beaten by his father, and he became a bully, killing local dogs and cats. He was later assaulted by guards in a reformatory. His criminal career eventually included sexual assault, break and enter, forgery, and dangerous driving. A psychiatrist diagnosed him as suffering from an extreme form of Tourette's syndrome.

A Deal with a Devil

Clifford Robert Olson had a criminal history that included break and enter, burglary, fraud, and theft. As a child he tormented neighbourhood dogs and cats. In 1978, he was charged with indecent assault in Nova Scotia and then imprisoned for fraud in Saskatchewan. In 1981, he killed 11 children in British Columbia. Two weeks after the first murder, he raped a teen prostitute (Janet Henry), but police declined to press charges. In a widely criticized deal with

the RCMP, Olson was paid $100 000 in exchange for information about the murders and the location of six bodies police had been unable to find. In 1996, he applied under Section 745, the faint-hope clause, to have his 25-year parole ineligibility period reviewed, but he was turned down.

The Terror of the Miramichi

Allan Legere, born in 1948, had a long history of crimes, including peeping through windows, theft, and possession of stolen property. In 1989, he escaped from custody, where he was being held for murder, and went on a six-month crime spree. Between May and November 1989, he beat four people to death in New Brunswick. His was the first trial in Canada to use DNA evidence.

The Scarborough Rapist

Paul Bernardo, with the help of his wife, Karla Homolka, was convicted in 1995 of killing teens Leslie Mahaffy and Kristen French. Both girls were held captive before being sexually assaulted and killed.

Bernardo and Homolka were also implicated in the killing of Homolka's sister, Tammy. Bernardo pleaded guilty to more than 50 sexual assaults and was declared a dangerous offender. Police had interviewed him and obtained a forensic sample, but it was months before it was tested. His lawyer was later charged with obstruction of justice for concealing a set of videotapes Bernardo had made of his assaults.

He Did It for Money

Yves "Apache" Trudeau, 58, a former hit man for the Hells Angels, became a police informant after discovering that the Hells Angels put out a contract for his death. In exchange for placement in a witness protection program, Trudeau confessed to 43 murders and helped put 42 former associates behind bars. In 2004, Trudeau faced a number of new charges for sexually assaulting a minor, revoking his parole. Auto-matically facing a life sentence, he returns to prison a marked man as a child molester and informant.

Aggregate Data Research

Criminologists often make use of large databases gathered by government agencies and research foundations, such as Statistics Canada, Correctional Services Canada, and so on. The most important of these sources are crime statistics compiled by the Canadian Centre for Justice Statistics based on the Uniform Crime Reporting system. The UCR is an annual report of the number of crimes reported by citizens to local police departments and the number of arrests made by police agencies in a given year.

Aggregate data can tell us about the effect of overall social trends and patterns on the crime rate. For example, to study the relationship between crime and poverty, criminologists make use of data collected by Statistics Canada on income, the number of people

on welfare, single-parent families in an urban area and then cross-reference this information with official crime statistics from the same locality. The implication that crime is correlated with poverty is not a simple one to explain, but preliminary data would establish whether a pattern exists. We would have to use a different technique, however, if we wanted to study corporate crime because crimes of the powerful are more carefully hidden.

Experimental Research

In experimental research, criminologists manipulate events to see the effect on the subjects. True experiments have three elements: (1) random assignment of subjects,

(2) a control or comparison group, and (3) an experimental condition. For example, a sample of convicted offenders chosen at random would be asked to participate in a community-based treatment program. A follow-up could determine whether those in the community program were less likely to recidivate (repeat their offences) than were those who served time in prison.

In a quasi-experiment, researchers may want to measure the effectiveness of a new law setting a lower blood alcohol threshold for impaired driving. Since this law will be federal, and thus uniform across Canada, the researchers will be more interested in how it is enforced by the police. Since they cannot ask police to randomly arrest drunk drivers, they can compare one province or territory's enforcement patterns to provinces and territories with more lenient impaired-driving enforcement programs. This offence is very sensitive to levels of police enforcement and would show the effectiveness of law enforcement on drunk driving. Enforcement programs can be weak, making it seem as if impaired driving is becoming less of a problem, despite the fact that drunk drivers account for only 1 percent of drivers on the road at night on weekends but nearly half of all the fatal crashes at that time.[39]

Another approach, the time-series design, would record nationwide impaired driving arrest and fatality data for the months and years preceding and following passage of the legislation setting lower limits for impaired driving. The effectiveness of the new limits as a deterrent to impaired driving would be supported if a drop in the arrest and fatality rates coincided with the legislation's adoption.

Criminological experiments are relatively rare because they are difficult and expensive to conduct; they involve the manipulation of subjects' lives, which can cause ethical and legal roadblocks; and they require long follow-up periods to verify results. Those that have been conducted have been an important source of criminological data.

Observational and Interview Research

Sometimes criminologists focus their research on relatively few subjects, interviewing them in depth or observing them as they go about their activities. This research obtains the kind of in-depth data absent in large-scale surveys. For example, interviewing middle-class female drug abusers can provide insight into a group whose behaviour might not be captured in a large-scale

Crime in the News

Olson Once Freed in Assault Case Because of N.S. Prosecutor's Error

Multiple murderer Clifford Olson was allowed to go free several years ago because a Crown prosecutor in Nova Scotia made an error, Attorney-General Harry How said yesterday.

Mr. How said Mr. Olson was charged with indecent assault in an incident involving a young girl in Sydney.

Mr. Olson was sought by Sydney police but avoided arrest. He was later convicted of another offence in Saskatchewan [theft, forgery, and false pretences] and served time in prison there.

Mr. How said that when Mr. Olson applied for parole in

Saskatchewan, he was told that parole would not be granted unless the outstanding charge of indecent assault in Nova Scotia was settled.

Mr. How said the Crown prosecutor assigned to the case did not feel there was sufficient evidence to proceed with a charge of indecent assault against Mr. Olson in the Sydney incident and reduced the charge to one of common assault.

However, Mr. How said that the statute of limitations had expired, making the new charge invalid, so all charges in Nova Scotia were withdrawn.

Earlier yesterday, Premier John Buchanan of Nova Scotia said he was flabbergasted to find out he had signed a letter telling Mr. Olson [Buchanan's] government would try to bring [Olson's]

assault case to a speedy conclusion.

While Mr. Olson was in Nova Scotia in 1978, he tried to pick up a 7-year-old girl in Sydney, and police subsequently issued a warrant for his arrest on a charge of indecent assault. A man fitting his description was found walking hand in hand with the girl after she disappeared from an open-air concert she had been attending with her parents.

The parents called police when they realized the girl was missing.

Although the Sydney police and RCMP suspected Mr. Olson was up to no good, he led them on a chase around industrial Cape Breton before he fled the area. . . .

Source: The Canadian Press, February 12, 1982.

survey.[40] In a different example, a criminologist interviewed youths who lived on the street in Toronto. Using a technique called snowball sampling, in which each person interviewed introduces the researcher to more subjects, he interviewed two hundred youths about their criminal activities. The research found that crime was related to the inability of the subjects to succeed in legitimate jobs.

Another common criminological method is the firsthand observation of criminals to gain insight into their motives and activities. This method may involve going into the field and participating in group activities, such as William Whyte did in his famous study of a Boston gang, *Street Corner Society*.[41] Other observers conduct field studies but remain in the background, observing but not being part of the ongoing activity.[42]

Still another type of observation involves bringing subjects into a structured laboratory setting and observing how they react to a predetermined condition or stimulus. This approach is common in studies testing the effect of observational learning on aggressive behaviour, such as exposing subjects to violent films and observing their subsequent behavioural changes.[43] A set of studies have sought to determine a relationship between explicit sexually violent pornography and attitudes endorsing interpersonal violence against women. These experimental studies have found that exposure to violent sexual material is related to a self-reported tendency to rape, the perception of rape victims as experiencing less trauma, and more callousness toward women in general.[44]

Criminology relies on many of the basic research methods common to other fields, including sociology, psychology, and political science. Multiple methods are needed to ensure that the goals of criminological inquiry can be achieved.

Ethical Issues in Criminology

A critical issue in criminology is recognizing the field's political and social consequences. Criminologists have a social responsibility as experts in the area of crime and justice. Their opinions can influence social policy in debates over gun control, capital punishment, and mandatory sentences. Although some criminologists argue for social service, treatment, and rehabilitation programs to reduce the crime rate, others suggest that only tough prison sentences can bring the crime rate down. Therefore, criminologists must be aware of the ethics of their profession and defend their work in the light of public scrutiny. Major ethical issues include what is to be studied, who is to be studied, and how studies are to be conducted.

When criminologists choose a subject for study, they are guided by their scholarly interests, pressing social needs, the availability of accurate data, and other similar concerns. Nonetheless, in recent years government and institutional funding has influenced the direction of criminological inquiry. In Canada the departments of Health and Welfare, Canadian Heritage, and Justice, and the Office of the Solicitor General historically have been important sources of funding. Private foundations also play an important role in supporting criminological research.

The availability of research money can influence the directions research takes. When governments provide research funds, it dictates areas that can be studied. For example, if funding is given for long-term cohort studies of criminal careers, other areas may be ignored, such as restorative justice. There has been a major decline in academic justice policy research since 1987, research increasingly hired out to consultants designed to satisfy the needs of civil servants, which might not make for informed public debate.[45]

Other limits on research might also arise. For example, governments may be reluctant to fund research on fraud in government. If criminologists are too critical of the government's efforts to reduce or counteract crime, perhaps it will be difficult to receive future funding. This situation is made more difficult because criminologists typically work for universities or public agencies and are under pressure to bring in research funds. Even when criminologists maintain discretion of choice, the direction of their efforts may not be truly objective.

A second major ethical issue in criminology concerns who is to be the subject of inquiries and study. Too often, criminologists have studied the poor and minorities while ignoring white-collar, organized, and government crime, with unfortunate consequences. For example, some research suggests that criminals have lower intelligence quotients than the average citizen and that because minority-group members have lower-than-average IQ scores, their crime rates are high.[46] This was the conclusion reached in *The Bell Curve*, a popular though highly controversial book written by Richard Herrnstein and Charles Murray.[47] Such research is methodologically flawed, and it focuses attention on the criminality of one group while ignoring others. For example, Alan Ryan says in *The Bell Curve Debate* that crime is mainly a male activity, and although IQ can explain male crime, it cannot explain the difference in crime rates between women and men.[48] Perhaps the focus should be on the link between gender and crime, not IQ and crime. This type of research raises ethical issues for criminologists and the research they publish because of the potential social harm the research may cause to minority groups, whose members are more likely to be subject to aggressive policing in general.

Famous Canadian Court Cases

The Russel Ogden Case

Russel Ogden, a former graduate student at Simon Fraser University (SFU), conducted his criminology master's thesis on the topic of assisted suicides and euthanasia among persons infected with HIV/AIDS. In his proposal, which was approved by the SFU Ethics Committee, Ogden stated that he would offer his research participants absolute confidentiality. In 1994, following the completion of his thesis, Ogden received a subpoena to appear at a Coroner's Inquest. Ogden refused to reveal the identities of his research participants and was quickly abandoned by the university. In response to

the situation, SFU made changes to their ethics policy, preventing any researcher from guaranteeing research participants absolute confidentiality.

Facing the threat of charges alone, Ogden appealed to the Wigmore criteria, arguing that the information he obtained was subject to researcher-participant privilege. He won his case and became the first researcher to have researcher-participant privilege recognized in Canadian law.

Ogden incurred approximately $11 500 in legal expenses, but the university provided Ogden with only $2000 on "compassionate grounds." Ogden sued the university for the remaining

amount, but he eventually lost his case in 1998. SFU's president created an independent review board to examine the Ogden case. The board found that SFU acted inappropriately and made the following three recommendations: that the university provide Ogden with a written apology, that Ogden be reimbursed for his lost wages and legal fees, and that the university guarantee to provide graduate students with a legal defence if their ethically approved theses are questioned by a third party. SFU's president accepted and complied with each of the recommendations.

Prepared by Vanessa Gallant.

Subjects can be misled about the purpose of the research. When White and minority youngsters are asked to participate in a survey of their behaviour or take an IQ test, they are rarely told in advance that the data they provide may be used to prove the existence of significant racial differences in their self-reported crime rates. Should subjects be told what the true purpose of a survey is? Would such disclosures make meaningful research impossible? How far should criminologists go when collecting data? Is it ever permissible to deceive subjects when collecting data?

Summary

Criminology is the scientific approach to the study of criminal behaviour and society's reaction to law violations and violators. It has a rich history in the utilitarian philosophy of Beccaria, the biological positivism of Lombroso, the social theory of Durkheim, and the political philosophy of Marx. It is an interdisciplinary field, with many of its practitioners originally trained as sociologists, psychologists, economists, political scientists, historians, and natural scientists. Included among the various subareas that make up the criminological enterprise are criminal statistics, the sociology of law, theory construction, criminal behaviour systems, penology, and victimology. Criminology and criminal justice are mutually dedicated to understanding the nature and control of criminal behaviour. The study of deviant behaviour also overlaps with criminology because many "deviant" acts, but not all, are violations of the criminal law.

In viewing crime, criminologists use one of three perspectives: the consensus view, the conflict view, or the interactionist view. The consensus view is that crime is illegal behaviour defined by the existing criminal law, which reflects the values and morals of a majority of citizens. The conflict view is that crime is behaviour created so that economically powerful individuals can retain their control over society. The interactionist view portrays criminal behaviour as a relativistic, constantly changing concept that reflects society's current moral values. According to the interactionist view, criminal behaviour is behaviour so labelled by those in power; criminals are people society chooses to label as outsiders or deviants.

Criminologists use a variety of research methods. These include cross-sectional surveys, longitudinal cohort studies, experiments, and observations. In doing research, criminologists must be concerned about ethical standards because their findings can have a significant impact on individuals and groups.

Thinking Like a Criminologist

You have been experimenting with various techniques to identify a sure-fire method for predicting violence-prone behaviour in delinquents. Your procedure involves brain scans, DNA testing, and blood analysis. Used with samples of incarcerated adolescents, your procedure has been able to distinguish with 80 percent accuracy between youths with a history of violence and those who are exclusively property offenders.

Your research indicates that your techniques could easily identify for special treatment potentially violence-prone career criminals in any group of youths. For example, children in the local school system could be tested, and those who are identified as violence-prone could be carefully monitored by teachers. Those at risk for future violence could be put into special programs as a precaution.

Some of your colleagues argue that this type of testing is unconstitutional because it violates the subjects' *Charter* guarantee of innocent until proven guilty. There is also the problem of error: some kids may be falsely labelled as violence-prone. How would you answer your critics? Is it fair or ethical to label people as "potentially" criminal and violent even though they have not yet exhibited any antisocial behaviour? Do the risks of such a procedure outweigh its benefits?

Key Terms

anomie

atavistic anomalies

bourgeoisie

Chicago school

classical criminology

cohort

criminal anthropology

criminal justice system

criminological enterprise

criminologists

criminology

cross-sectional research

decriminalization

deviant behaviour

intimate violence

longitudinal research

moral entrepreneurs

positivism

proletariat

utilitarianism

white-collar crime

Critical Thinking Questions

1. Beccaria argued that the threat of punishment controls crime. Are there other forms of social control? Aside from the threat of legal punishments, what else controls your behaviour?

2. What research method would you employ if you wanted to study drug and alcohol abuse at your school?

3. Would it be ethical for a criminologist to observe a teenage gang by "hanging" with them, drinking and watching as they steal cars? Should he or she report that behaviour to the police?

4. Can you identify behaviours that are deviant but not criminal? What about crimes that are not deviant?

5. Do you agree with conflict theorists that some of the most damaging acts in society are not punished as crimes? If so, what are those acts?

 See the book-specific website at http://www.siegelcriminology3e.nelson.com for additional chapter links, discussions, and quizzes.

chapter

2

The Criminal Law and Its Process

The criminal law controls the definition and content of crime. Developed over many generations, it incorporates historical traditions, moral beliefs, and social values, as well as political and economic developments and conditions. The criminal law is a living concept, constantly evolving to keep pace with society. It governs the form and direction of almost all human interaction. Business practices, family life, education, property transfer, inheritance, the availability of certain drugs, and other common forms of social relations must conform to the rules set out by the legal code. Most important for our purposes, the law defines the behaviours that society labels as criminal. Consequently, it is important for students of criminology to have a basic understanding of the law and its relationship to crime and deviance. This chapter will review the nature and purpose of the law, chart its history, and discuss its elements.

The Origins of Law

Crimes were recognized in many early societies.[1] In preliterate societies, common custom and tradition were the equivalents of law. Each group had its own customs created to deal with situations that arose in daily living, often followed long after the reason for their origin was forgotten. Many customs eventually developed into formal or written law.

Early Legal Codes

One of the earliest surviving legal codes was developed in 2000 B.C.E. in Sumer (part of present-day Iraq). It was later adopted by Hammurabi (1792–1750 B.C.E.), king of Babylon, in his written laws, the **Code of Hammurabi**, preserved on basalt rock columns. Punishment was based on physical retaliation, or *lex talionis* ("an eye for an eye"). However, the severity of punishment depended on class standing: For assault, slaves would be put to death; freemen might lose a limb.

Connections

Efforts are now being made to make punishments fit the crimes. See Chapter 5 for more on the view that crime and punishment should be closely aligned.

Babylonian laws were strictly enforced by judges. Burglary and theft was common in ancient Babylon, and local officials were expected to apprehend criminals. If they failed, they had to personally replace lost property; if murderers were not caught, the responsible official paid a fine to the deceased's relatives. Imagine holding police officers to such a standard today!

Another ancient legal code still surviving is the **Mosaic Code** of the Israelites (1200 B.C.E.). According to tradition, God entered into a covenant or contract with the tribes of Israel in which they agreed to obey God's law in return for care and protection. This code is the foundation of Judeo-Christian moral teachings and also a basis for our present-day legal system: Prohibitions against murder, theft, perjury, and adultery precede by several thousand years the same laws found today.

Also surviving is the Roman law contained in the Twelve Tables (451 B.C.E.), formulated by a special commission of 10 men in response to pressure from the lower classes, who believed that an unwritten code gave arbitrary and unlimited power to the wealthy who served as magistrates. The original code was written on bronze plaques that have been lost, but records of sections survive, which were memorized by every Roman male. The laws deal with debt, family relations, property, and other daily matters. Other notable ancient lawgivers through the centuries were Confucius (551–479 B.C.E., China), Mohammed (570–632 C.E., Arabia), Solomon (873–933 C.E., Israel), and Lycurgus (ninth century B.C.E., Greece); a list of important legal documents would certainly have to include the Koran (652 C.E., Arabia).

Early Crime, Punishment, and Law

The early formal legal codes were lost during the Dark Ages, which lasted for hundreds of years after the fall of Rome. During this period, superstition and fear of magic and satanic black arts dominated thinking.

The regulation of crime during the early feudal period involved monetary payments as the main punishments for crimes. For example, the compensation (**wergild**) paid for killing a freewoman of childbearing age was 24 000 denars; if the woman was past childbearing age, the wergild was reduced to 8000 denars.

Guilt was determined by ordeals, such as having the accused place his or her hand in boiling water to see whether God would intervene and heal the wounds. It was also possible to challenge the accuser to a trial by combat. Exhibit 2.1 presents an ordeal called the judgment of the glowing iron, a method of proof used in early Germanic law. Settling trials by ordeal fell out of favour when the Catholic Church decreed that priests could no longer participate. Without the use of the ordeal in disputed criminal cases, courts both in England and in the rest of Europe were not sure how to proceed. Guilt could also be disputed with the aid of **oath-helpers**, who would support the accused's innocence.

Despite reforms, until the eighteenth century, the systems of crime, punishment, law, and justice were chaotic. The law was controlled by the lords of the great

Exhibit 2.1	The Judgment of the Glowing Iron

After the accusation has been lawfully made, and three days have been passed in fasting and prayer, the priest, clad in his sacred vestments with the exception of his outside garment, shall take with a tongs the iron placed before the altar; and, singing the hymn of the three youths, namely, "Bless him all his works," he shall bear it to the fire, and shall say this prayer over the place where the fire is to carry out the judgment: "Bless, O Lord God, this place, that there may be for us in it sanctity, chastity, virtue and victory, and sanctimony, humility, goodness, gentleness and plentitude of law, and obedience to God the Father and the Son and the Holy Ghost." After this, the iron shall be placed in the fire and shall be sprinkled with holy water; and while it is heating, he shall celebrate mass. But when the priest shall have taken the Eucharist, he shall adjure the man who is to be tried . . . and shall cause him to take the communion. Then the priest shall sprinkle holy water above the iron and shall say: "The blessing of God the Father, the Son, and the Holy Ghost descend upon this iron for the discerning of the right judgment of God." And straightway the accused shall carry the iron to a distance of nine feet. Finally his hand shall be covered under seal for three days, and if festering blood be found in the track of the iron, he shall be judged guilty. But if, however, he shall go forth uninjured, praise shall be rendered to God.

Source: Fordham University, Center for Medieval Studies, "The Internet Medieval SourceBook," http://www.fordham.edu/halsall/sbook.html (accessed May 8, 2005).

manors, who tried cases according to local custom and rule. Although people generally agreed that theft, assault, treason, and blasphemy constituted crimes, penalties were often arbitrary and cruel, and included public flogging, branding, beheading, and burning. Peasants who violated the rule of their masters might have their teeth or eyes pulled out, while others were impaled or had their hands cut off; some were burned alive or plunged into boiling lead. Even simple wanderers and vagabonds were viewed as dangerous and subject to these extreme penalties.

Origins of Common Law

Because the ancient legal codes had been lost, law and crime were guided by superstition and local custom during the Middle Ages. Slowly, in England, a common law developed that helped standardize law and justice. This common law became the foundation for Canada's legal system.

Before the Norman Conquest in 1066 C.E., the legal system among the Anglo-Saxons in England was decentralized. Each county (shire) was divided into units of one hundred families, and then further divided into groups of 10 called tithings, which were responsible for maintaining order among themselves and dealing with disturbances, fires, wild animals, and so on.

Petty cases were tried by courts of the hundred group. More serious and important cases could be heard by an assemblage of local landholders or by the local nobleman. If the act concerned spiritual matters, it could be judged in ecclesiastical courts, which were responsible for disciplining the clergy; ensuring church attendance and conformity to church rites; and controlling sexual morality and matrimonial disputes. In early Canadian society, Baptist church courts existed to enforce the moral rules of the faith. Between 1810 and 1880, for example, almost eight thousand people were excluded from Maritime Baptist churches for crimes ranging from fornication to usury.[2]

Crime and Custom. Crimes were viewed as personal wrongs, and compensation was paid to the victims. Even homicide could be settled by payment (wergild) to the deceased's family, unless the crime was carried out by poison or ambush—in which case it was punished by death. If payment was not made, the victims' families would attempt to forcibly collect damages or seek revenge. The result could be a blood feud between two families. Recognized crimes included treason, homicide, rape, property theft, assault, and battery. For treasonous acts, the punishment was death. Theft during the Anglo-Saxon era could result in slavery for the thieves and their families. If caught in the act of fleeing with the stolen goods, the thief could be killed.

A scale of compensation existed for lesser injuries, such as the loss of an arm or an eye. Important persons, churchmen, and nuns received greater restitution than the general population, and they paid more if they were the criminal defendants. This scale became the precursor of the modern-day criminal fine. To a great degree, the criminal law was designed to provide an equitable solution to what was considered a private dispute.

The Norman Conquest. After the Norman Conquest in 1066, Anglo-Saxon justice was administered as it had been in previous centuries. The church courts handled acts that might be considered sin, and the local manorial courts dealt with most secular violations. However, to secure control of the countryside and to ensure military supremacy over his newly won lands, William the Conqueror replaced the local tribunals with royal administrators, who dealt with the most serious breaches of the peace.

Because the royal administrators could not constantly be present in each community, a system was developed in which they travelled in a circuit throughout the land, holding court in each county several times a year. When court was in session, the royal administrator, or judge, would summon a number of citizens who would, on their oath, tell of the crimes and serious breaches of the peace that had occurred since the judge's last visit. The royal judge would then decide what to do in each case, using local custom and rules of conduct as his guide. If, for example, a local freeholder was convicted of theft, he might be executed if those before him had suffered that fate for a similar offence. However, if in previous cases the thief had been forced to make restitution to the victim, then that judgment would be rendered in the current case. This system, known as *stare decisis* ("to stand by decided cases"), meant that courts were bound to follow the law established in previously decided cases (precedent) unless the law was overruled by a higher authority, such as the king or the pope.

The current English system of law came into existence during the reign of Henry II (1154–1189). The Church ban on trial by ordeal meant that a new method of deciding criminal trials needed to be developed. To fill the gap, British justices adapted a method that had long been used to determine real estate taxes. In the time of William the Conqueror, 12 knights in each district had been called before an "inquest" of the king's justices to give local tax information. These "12 free and lawful men of the neighbourhood" would view the land and testify as to who last had peaceful possession and settle "claim jumping" disputes over land. Under King Henry II, these juries (from the Latin *jurati*, to be sworn), were local landholders whom judges called on to decide the facts of cases, investigate crimes, accuse suspected offenders, and even give testimony at trials.

At first, jurors were like witnesses, telling the judge what they knew about the case; these courts were known as *assise* or *assize* (from the Latin *assideo*, to sit together). By the fourteenth century, jurors had become the deciders of fact. Over the centuries, the English jury came to be seen as a check on the government. Gradually, royal prosecutors developed as representatives of the Crown and submitted evidence and brought witnesses to testify before the jury. But not until much later was the accused in a criminal action allowed to use witnesses to rebut charges. Not until the eighteenth century were witnesses required to take oaths. Few formal procedures existed, allowing the judge and the prosecutor to intimidate witnesses and jurors. However, developing routine judicial processes heralded the beginnings of the common law.

The great case that established the principle of jury independence, *Bushell's* case (1670), arose when a London jury acquitted William Penn, a leading Quaker and later the founder of Pennsylvania, of unlawful assembly in connection with his preaching in the street after a Quaker church was padlocked. The jurors were imprisoned by an angry royalist judge and then freed when the same judge said that a jury must reach a verdict based on the evidence, or else the jury would be nothing but a useless rubber stamp.

InfoTrac®

The jury trial continues to be the centrepiece of the legal system. In some ways it is almost like a theatre experience. To learn more about this, read this article: Mark I. Bernstein and Laurence R. Milstein, "Trial as Theater," *Trial* 33, no. 10 (1997): 64–69.

The Common Law

The **common law** is meant to apply to people without regard to social differences. When King Henry's judges began to apply a national law to replace laws in local jurisdictions, they took into account both local custom and Norman feudal law. As new situations arose, judges either invented new solutions or borrowed from European countries. During their gatherings, the circuit judges shared these incidents and discussed their decisions, developing an oral tradition of law. These cases, together with written decisions, filtered through the national court system (see Figure 2.1) and produced a fixed body of legal rule and principles. Thus, common law is judge-made law, or case law derived from previously decided cases. Such crimes as murder, burglary, arson, and rape are common-law crimes—they were initially defined and created by judges.

Common Law and Statutory Law

The common law was and still is the law of the land in England. For example, common law originally defined murder as the unlawful killing of another human being with malice aforethought.[3] For offenders to be found guilty, they must have (1) planned the crime and (2) intentionally killed the victim out of spite or hatred. However, this general definition proved inadequate, so over time English judges added other forms of murder: killing

Connections

Common-law practices still guide modern legal codes. For example, murder statutes still retain different degrees of seriousness based on the intent of the murderer. The degrees of murder and other definitional issues are discussed in Chapter 11.

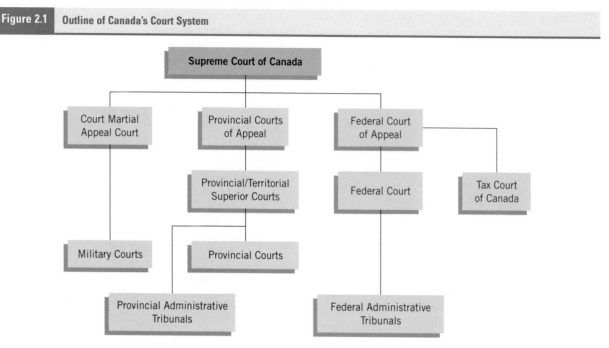

Figure 2.1   Outline of Canada's Court System

Source: Dept. of Justice Outline of Canada's Court System, published in *Canada's System of Justice, 2005,* Dept. of Justice Canada, 2005. Reproduced with the permission of the Minister of Public Works and Government Services, 2005.

someone in the heat of passion, killing someone out of negligence, killing someone in the course of committing another crime, such as during a robbery. Each form of murder was given a different title and a different degree of punishment. Thus, the common law was a constantly evolving legal code, based on legal decisions made from the ground up. Common law is still the basis for understanding statutory law today.

The creation of a new common-law crime can sometimes be traced back to a particular case. For example, an unsuccessful attempt to commit an illegal act was not considered a crime until the 1784 case of *Rex v. Scofield,* who was charged with trying to burn down a house he was renting. Being unsuccessful, Scofield argued that an attempt to commit a misdemeanour was not actually a crime. The court rejected the argument.[4] After *Scofield,* attempt became a common-law crime, and today criminal attempt (called **inchoate crimes**) is defined as a crime in section 24 of the *Criminal Code of Canada* (CCC).

The English Parliament also enacted supplementary legislation, creating statutory crimes. For example, in 1723, the *Waltham Black Act* punished offences against rural property with death, from the poaching of small game to arson, if the criminal was armed or disguised.[5] The Act also allowed execution without a trial if the accused failed to surrender. The underlying purpose was Parliament's desire to control the behaviour of peasants whose poverty forced them to poach on royal lands. In the *Black Act,* then, the British ruling class created a mechanism for protecting its property and power.

Another example also illustrates how the law develops to protect the rights of the privileged. In 1812, the British government proposed a new capital offence, the *Frame Breaking Act,* which enabled people convicted of machine breaking to be sentenced to death (see Figure 2.2). Mill workers were upset by changes occurring in the workplace: wage reductions, the use of unapprenticed workers, and their own replacement by new weaving technology. The Army of Redressers, under the leadership of General Ned Ludd, broke into factories at night to destroy the new power looms. This is the origin of the term "Luddite," which is used today to refer to someone who opposes technical or technological change.

Statutory laws reflect existing social conditions, dealing with issues of morality, such as gambling, sexual activity, and drug-related offences. For example, early in the history of Canada and the United States, it was both legal and relatively easy to obtain narcotics, such as heroin, opium, and cocaine.[6] However, public and governmental concern arose over the use of narcotics by Chinese immigrants who had come to Canada to build railroads and work in mines. By 1910, opium was criminalized in Canada.[7] Conversely, in the case of marijuana, the statutory law has changed in the opposite direction, toward decriminalization. As the use of marijuana became widespread among the middle class in the 1960s, attitudes and enforcement became more relaxed. In 1995, a Health Canada poll discovered that 69 percent of Canadians were against the prohibition of marijuana.

Figure 2.2	The British Parliament Acts against the Luddites

WHEREAS,

Several EVIL-MINDED PERSONS have assembled together in a riotous Manner, and DESTROYED a NUMBER of

FRAMES,

In different Parts of the Country :

THIS IS

TO GIVE NOTICE,

That any Person who will give Information of any Person to Person thus wickedly

BREAKING THE FRAMES,

Shall, upon CONVICTION, receive

50 GUINEAS

REWARD.

And any Person who was actively engaged in RIOTING, who will impeach his Accomplices, shall, upon CONVICTION, receive the same Reward, and every Effort made to procure his Pardon.

☞ Information to be given to Messrs. COLDHAM and ENFIELD.

Nottingham, March 29, 1812.

The Development of Law in Canada

Canada's unique legal system was not achieved overnight or without conflict.[8] The early Canadian criminal justice system was strongly influenced by the common law of England, as well as by geographic, economic, political, and cultural factors. Before Confederation in 1867 Canada did not have a standard criminal justice system. The Hudson's Bay Company was using its employees to enforce its own penal code. And although an infrastructure for justice existed in Eastern Canada, law was being administered by circuit judges in log buildings in Western Canada. The military was the first to maintain law and order, especially in naval ports. Canada's size and the pattern of westward settlement resulted in cases of frontier justice, but by the time the West was opening up, defendants were being taken to the more established parts of Canada for trial. The spread of law enforcement and the development of a legal system gradually became more sophisticated and professional.

Pierre Berton describes the stark difference between the American city of Skagway, which was noted for its lawlessness, and the Canadian city of Dawson, where crime and disorder were kept firmly in check by the North-West Mounted Police (NWMP). In part, the success of the NWMP has been attributed to the unorthodox methods they used, not enforcing some laws and making up others.[9]

The *Police of Canada Act* (1868) created the Dominion Police, and the NWMP began in 1873. Initially given jurisdiction only in the Prairies, the force became the federal Royal Canadian Mounted Police (RCMP) in 1920. The NWMP was sent to protect the Aboriginals from the Americans and to bring the Queen's justice to a dangerous territory. The NWMP was able to use criminal sanctions to repress political dissent, control the Indigenous population, and maintain sovereignty.[10] Maintenance of order helped to encourage settlers, and in the process new markets were created for manufactured goods. The treatment of Aboriginal Canadians by the NWMP is seen by some as benevolent, especially in contrast to the situation in the United States.

Connections

There has been much debate recently about the treatment of Aboriginals in the development of Canada. For more on this topic, see the discussion in Chapter 9.

Before Confederation, British common law was used for criminal prosecutions. With Confederation, however, crime control was centralized in the federal government through the *British North America Act*. The federal government was given the power to create criminal statute law, and the provinces and territories were responsible for its administration. Parliament codified the first CCC in 1892, supplemented by subordinate legislation in municipal bylaws and provincial or territorial department regulations. This centralization was important, because judicial precedent and legislative amendments had created substantial variation across the country. For example, incest was punishable by a severe prison sentence in some provinces and territories but was not even a crime in others.[11]

All existing statute law was eventually consolidated. Some offences prohibited in the 1892 CCC had their origin in seventeenth-century England; for example, offences against public order included inciting to mutiny, unlawful drilling (of soldiers), attending or promoting a prize fight, piracy, possessing a weapon at a public meeting, and pretending to practise witchcraft. Other previously included offences have since been repealed or amended, such as seducing a woman under promise of marriage, carnally knowing idiots, keeping a common bawdy-wigwam, injuring persons by furious driving, leaving holes in the ice unguarded, and abduction of heiresses.

A curious law in the CCC is section 163, offences tending to corrupt morals, where it is an offence to publish, distribute, or possess a crime comic. This section was passed in 1949 out of concern that juveniles were committing murders, robberies, and suicides. Batman and Robin were accused of encouraging

TABLE 2.1   Outdated Canadian Crimes

The *Criminal Code of Canada* includes laws defining the following activities as crimes. Some of them might surprise you.

- Duelling (section 71): It is an indictable offence to challenge or accept a challenge to fight a duel.
- Having a stink bomb (section 178): It is a summary offence for anyone except a peace officer to possess an offensive volatile substance.
- Trespassing at night (section 17): This is a summary, reverse onus offence, which means that the burden of proof lies on defendants to show they have lawful excuse to loiter or prowl.
- Pretending to practise witchcraft (section 365): It is a summary offence to fraudulently pretend to use witchcraft or sorcery; it is legal to be a witch.

homosexuality and Popeye of using marijuana. This law is rarely enforced now, except against marijuana publications. Some other interesting laws still on the books in Canada are displayed in Table 2.1.

Gradually, the reforms taking place in Europe had an impact in Canada, manifested in the construction of prisons designed as places of punishment, the training of professional police, and the declining use of the death penalty.

Classification of Law

Law can be classified in a number of ways that can help us understand its nature and purpose. Three of the most important classifications are (1) crimes and torts, (2) indictable and summary offences, and (3) *mala in se* and *mala prohibitum*. Figure 2.3 shows the relationship among different types of law. These classifications are briefly described here.

Figure 2.3   Types of Law

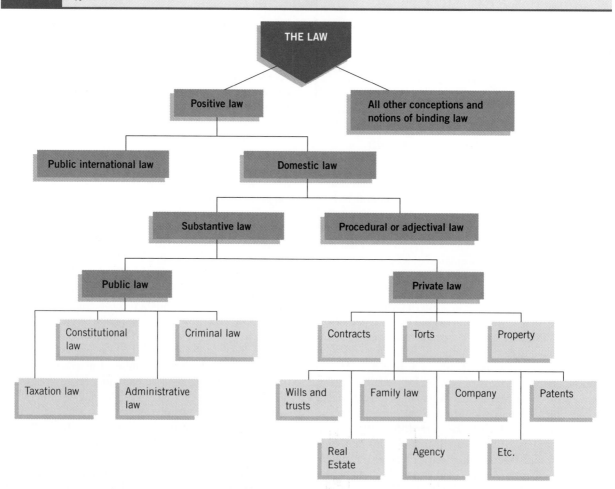

Source: Gerald L. Gall, *The Canadian Legal System*, 5th ed. (Toronto: Carswell, 2005). Reprinted by permission of Carswell, a division of Thomson Canada Limited.

Criminal and Civil Law

Law can be divided into two broad categories: the criminal law and civil law. Civil law is all law other than the criminal law and includes such legal areas as property law (the law governing transfer and ownership of property) and contract law (the law of personal agreements). Of all areas of the civil law, **tort law** (the law of personal wrongs and damage) is most similar in intent and form to the criminal law.

A tort is a civil action in which an individual asks to be compensated for personal harm caused by the actions of another. The harm may be either physical or mental and includes such acts as trespass, assault and battery, invasion of privacy, libel (false and injurious writings), and slander (false and injurious statements). Someone can be sued for damages even if he or she has been acquitted of a criminal act, the reason being that the standards of evidence for a finding are lower in civil cases.

A tort may also occur when a behaviour is an indirect cause of injury, such as when it sets off a chain of events that leads to injury or death. In 1990, for example, the families of two youths who had attempted suicide in 1985 sued the heavy-metal rock group Judas Priest and CBS Records, claiming that the group had put the subliminal message "Do it" in its *Stained Class* album to effect "mind control" over the band's fans. The group was vindicated because the youths were self-destructive before the album was released, engaging in truancy and drug use.[12]

Because some torts are similar to some criminal acts, a person can possibly be held both criminally and civilly liable for one action. For example, if one man punches another, the assailant can be charged with criminal assault, sued by the victim, and required to pay monetary damages.

A difference between the criminal law and civil law is that the state has the power to protect the public from harm by punishing individuals whose actions threaten the social order. In civil law, the harm is considered private, and individuals are compensated for harm done to them by others.

In a criminal action, the state initiates legal proceedings by bringing charges and prosecuting the violator. The victim has a small role. If it is determined that the criminal law has been broken, the state can impose punishment, such as imprisonment, probation (community supervision by the court), or a fine payable to the state. Another major difference is the burden of proof required to establish liability. A criminal defendant's guilt must be proved beyond a reasonable doubt. However, in a civil case, a lower standard of proof is required, based on a balance of probabilities.[13]

Table 2.2 summarizes the differences and similarities between crimes and torts.

TABLE 2.2 Comparison of Criminal and Tort Law

SIMILARITIES

Both criminal and tort law seek to control behaviour and both impose sanctions. Similar areas of legal action exist—for example, personal assault and control of white-collar offences, such as environmental pollution.

DIFFERENCES

Criminal Law	Tort Law
Crime is a public offence.	Tort is a civil or private wrong.
The sanction associated with a criminal law is incarceration or death.	The sanction associated with a tort is monetary damages.
The right of enforcement belongs to the state.	The individual brings the action.
The government ordinarily does not appeal.	Both parties can appeal.
Fines go to the state.	The individual receives compensation for harm done.
The standard of proof is "beyond a reasonable doubt."	Guilt is established by a preponderance of the evidence.

Indictable and Summary Offences

Criminal laws can be further classified as either indictable offences or offences punishable on summary conviction. An **indictable offence** is a serious offence, such as murder (section 231), while a **summary offence**, such as loitering (section 179 on vagrancy), is a minor or petty crime. The main differences involve procedure and penalty. Summary offences have a six-month limitation period on prosecution, they are heard in provincial or territorial court, and the maximum fine is $2000 or a six-month jail term or both.

Indictable offences have no limitation period on prosecution and can result in much more serious penalties if the defendant is found guilty.[14] Indictable offences involve a choice of trial by judge or jury, and section 625.1 of the *Criminal Code* includes the provision for a preliminary inquiry to determine whether enough admissible evidence exists to result in a conviction in a full trial. Most preliminary inquiries are concluded in less than a day.

Figure 2.4   Flow through the Canadian Criminal Justice System

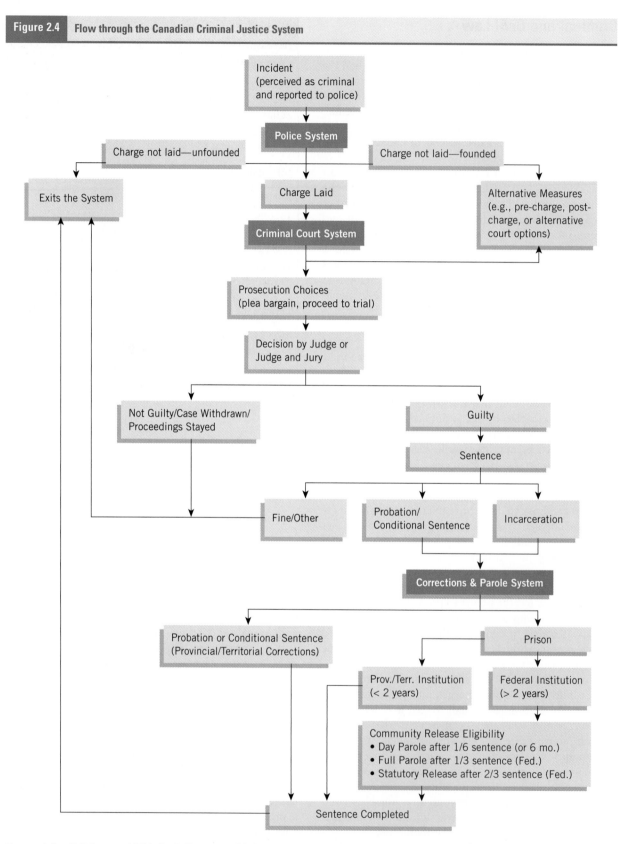

Source: Julian V. Roberts and Michelle G. Grossman, *Criminal Justice in Canada: A Reader*, 2nd ed. (Toronto: Nelson, 2004), 15.

Mala in Se and *Mala Prohibitum*

Criminologists also classify crimes as *mala in se* or *mala prohibitum*. *Mala in se* crimes are rooted in the core values inherent in our culture and are designed to control such behaviours as inflicting physical harm on others (assault, rape, murder), taking possessions that rightfully belong to another (larceny, burglary, robbery), or harming another person's property (malicious damage, trespass).

Mala prohibitum crime involves violations of laws that reflect current public opinion and social values. Actions are periodically designated as crimes to control behaviours that conflict with the functioning of society, such as drug use and possession of unlicensed handguns. Although it is relatively easy to link *mala in se* crimes to an objective concept of morality, it is much more difficult to do so if the acts are *mala prohibitum*. In adjudicating cases of obscenity, for example, the judge must take subjective community standards into account in deciding whether something violates that provision of the code.

See Figure 2.4 for a summary of how incidents move through the Canadian Criminal Justice System.

Functions of the Criminal Law

The substantive criminal law is a written code defining crimes and their punishments. In Canada, it is centralized under the jurisdiction of the federal government, while in the United States, individual states can develop their own criminal codes. This centralization in Canada enables greater social control and perhaps accounts for Canadians' higher respect for authority. Although criminal codes will have their differences, most use comparable terms, and the behaviours they are designed to control are often quite similar, especially in Western countries. Regardless of which culture or jurisdiction created them or when, criminal codes have several distinct functions. The most important of these include (1) providing social control, (2) discouraging revenge, (3) expressing public opinion and morality, (4) deterring criminal behaviour, and (5) maintaining the social order. From the consensus viewpoint (as discussed in Chapter 1), the law reflects the interests of the majority. However, the conflict model sees the law as reflecting the interests of the powerful.[15]

Providing Social Control

The primary purpose of the criminal law is to control people's behaviour. It is a written statement of rules to which people must conform. Societies also have unwritten rules of conduct—ordinary customs and conventions, referred to as **folkways,** and universally followed behaviour called norms and morals, or **mores.** However, the criminal law formally prohibits behaviour believed to threaten societal well-being and that challenges the

Robert Latimer, convicted of killing his daughter, who had severe disabilities, was given a mandatory minimum sentence of 10 years in 2001, despite widespread controversy about his actions. Seventy percent of people polled by *The Globe and Mail* disagreed with the sentence.

political authority. For example, the criminal law incorporates centuries-old prohibitions against the following behaviours harmful to others: taking another's possessions, physically harming another person, and damaging property. Similarly, the law prevents actions that challenge the legitimacy of the government, such as treason and collaborating with enemies. Whereas violations of mores and folkways may be informally enforced by any person, control of the criminal law is given to those in political power and administered and enforced by its agents.

Discouraging Revenge

By delegating enforcement to others, the criminal law controls an individual's need to seek revenge or vengeance against those who have violated their rights. By punishing people who infringe on the rights, property, and freedom of others, the law shifts the burden of retribution from the individual to the state. As Oliver Wendell Holmes stated, this prevents "the greater evil of private retribution."[16]

Although state retaliation may offend the sensibilities of many citizens, it is greatly preferable to a system in which people would have to seek justice for themselves.

Expressing Public Opinion and Morality

The criminal law also reflects constantly changing public opinions and moral values. *Mala in se* crimes, such as murder and forcible rape, are almost universally prohibited, but the prohibition of legislatively created *mala prohibitum* crimes, such as traffic law and gambling violations, changes according to shifting social conditions and attitudes. The criminal law is used to codify these changes. For example, if the government decides to criminalize certain behaviours, such as membership in an organized gang, it will amend the *Criminal Code*. The criminal law then has the power to define the boundaries of moral and immoral behaviour. Nonetheless, it has proved difficult to legally control public morality, because of the problems associated with (1) gauging the will of the majority, (2) respecting the rights of the minority, and (3) enforcing laws that many people consider trivial or self-serving.

The power of the law to express norms and values can be viewed in the development of the crime of **vagrancy** (the moving from place to place by a person who has no visible means of support and who refuses to work). Historically, vagrancy laws were formulated in the fourteenth century after the bubonic plague had killed significant numbers of English peasants, threatening the labour-intensive feudal economy. The law was aimed at preventing workers from leaving their estates to secure higher wages elsewhere. The laws punished migration, thereby mooring peasants to the manors of the nobility and aiding wealthy landowners.[17]

In an opposing view, early English vagrancy laws were less concerned with maintaining capitalism than with controlling beggars and relieving the overburdened public relief and welfare systems.[18] These laws helped town officials deal with the threat to the community posed by vagrants, "Sabbath breakers," paupers, and the wandering poor. The current crime of vagrancy in Canada (section 179) is a summary offence and is restricted to controlling those who support themselves by crime and those who have been convicted of several sexual offences found loitering near playgrounds.

Deterring Criminal Behaviour

The criminal law's social control function is its ability to deter potential law violators. The threat of punishment is designed to prevent crimes before they occur. During the Middle Ages, public executions were held for this reason. Although we don't have public executions today, the impact of criminal law is felt through news accounts of long prison sentences that perform the function of **general deterrence**. That is, people are less likely to commit crimes when they know they will be penalized. Clearly, such an idea is based on the assumption that crime is rational and thought out beforehand; it would not work for crimes of passion committed in the heat of the moment or for impulsive crimes.

The **specific deterrent** power of the criminal law is tied to the power it gives the state to sanction offenders. Whereas violations of folkways and mores are controlled informally through social disapproval, criminal law violators are subject to physical coercion and punishment. Today, the most common punishments are fines, community supervision or probation, and incarceration in prison. Canada last used the death penalty in 1962, and it was finally abolished in 1976.

Exhibit 2.2	The Decriminalization of Homosexuality in Canada

As a result of a case that went to the Supreme Court of Canada (*Klippert v. The Queen,* 1967 S.C.R. 822), Canadian legal history reached a turning point. The case was against Everett Klippert, a homosexual in a small community, well known to the police. Klippert had pleaded guilty in August 1965 to four charges of acts of gross indecency; his criminal record showed 18 similar convictions.

After Klippert's sentencing, the Crown applied to declare him a dangerous sexual offender, and Judge Sissons imposed a sentence of preventive detention. Two psychiatrists had testified that Klippert had never caused injury or pain to any individual, was unlikely to in the future, and would likely recommit the same offence with other consenting male adults; as well, his sexual orientation was viewed by the psychiatrists as incurable. However, the judge declared Klippert a dangerous sexual offender. Klippert appealed to the Northwest Territories Court of Appeal and to the Supreme Court of Canada, both unsuccessfully.

In the Supreme Court decision, Chief Justice J. Cartwright and Mr. Justice Emmett Hall dissented, indicating that they would have allowed the appeal. Their reasons formed part of the government's political decision to decriminalize homosexuality. In response to Klippert's case, Pierre Trudeau made his now-famous comment that "the state has no place in the bedrooms of the nation." Such discrimination and potential for persecution was abolished in Canada when homosexuality was decriminalized in 1969. The *Criminal Law Amendment Act,* 1968–69, amended the *Criminal Code* to exclude homosexuality between consenting adults (persons aged 21 years and older) from the provisions of the code regarding acts of gross indecency.

Source: Based on research by Peggy Scott.

Connections

The social control function of the criminal law assumes that crime is rational and that the threat of punishment will deter crime. This assumption is actually the subject of significant debate: If the criminal law can deter crime, why is there so much crime today? For the answer, see the discussion of general deterrence in Chapter 5.

Maintaining the Social Order

All legal systems are designed to support and maintain the boundaries of the social system. In medieval England, the law protected the feudal system by defining an orderly system of property transfer and ownership. Modern society is also supported and sustained by the criminal law, reflecting generalized needs and protecting the economic and political system. In our society, by meting out punishment to those who damage or steal property, the law promotes the activities needed to sustain an economy based on the accumulation of wealth. It would be impossible to conduct business through the use of contracts, promissory notes, credit, banking, and so on, unless the law protected private capital. Maintaining a legal climate in which capitalism can thrive is an underlying goal of the criminal law.

Historically, if one merchant cheated another, it was considered a private matter. Then in 1473, in the *Carrier's* case, an English court ruled that a merchant who held and transported merchandise for another was guilty of theft if he kept the goods for his own purposes.[19] Before the *Carrier's* case, the law did not consider it a crime for people to keep something that was already in their possession. Breaking with legal precedent, the British court recognized that the new English mercantile trade system could not be sustained if property rights had to be individually enforced. To this day, the substantive criminal law prohibits such business-related acts as fraud, embezzlement, and commercial theft.

The Legal Definition of a Crime

To fulfill the legal definition of a crime, several elements must be proved, including that a law defines the act as criminal.

For the state to prove that a crime occurred and that the defendant committed it, the prosecutor must show that the accused engaged in the guilty act, or *actus reus*, and had the *mens rea*, commonly called the intent to commit the act. The *actus reus* can be taking someone's money or burning a building, or a failure to act when there is a legal duty to do so, such as a parent's neglecting to seek medical attention for a sick child. The *mens rea* is the person's intent to commit the crime at the time of the act. For most crimes, both the *actus reus* and the *mens rea* must be present for the act to be considered a crime. For example, if George decides to kill Bob and then takes a gun and shoots Bob, George can be convicted of the crime of murder because both elements are present. George's shooting of Bob is the *actus reus*; his decision to kill Bob is the *mens rea*. However, if George only thinks about shooting Bob but does nothing about it, the element of *actus reus* is absent, and no crime has been committed. Conversely, if George shoots Bob accidentally, the element of *mens rea* is missing, and it is considered differently. Let us now look more closely at these issues.

Actus Reus

The *actus reus* is the criminal act itself. For an act to be illegal, the action must be voluntary. For example, one person shooting another could certainly be considered a voluntary act. However, if the shooting occurs while the person holding the gun is sleepwalking, he or she will not be held criminally liable, because the act is not voluntary. But if the individual knows he or she has such a condition and does not take precautions to prevent the act from occurring, the person could be held responsible for the criminal act. The central issue concerning voluntariness is whether the individual has control over his or her actions. For instance, in 1992 the Supreme Court of Canada upheld the acquittal of Kenneth Parks, who drove 23 kilometres and stabbed his mother-in-law to death. The trial judge ruled that Parks had been sleepwalking, which is not a mental disorder as defined in law, and was thus acting involuntarily (non-insane automatism). Had he been found guilty, he could have been jailed for life.[20]

Mens Rea

A crime must include the elements of a guilty mind. In the legal sense, "intent" can mean carrying out an act intentionally, knowingly, and willingly. However, the definition also encompasses recklessness or negligence. Some crimes require specific intent, and others require general intent, and criminal liability varies. Most crimes require a general intent or the intent to commit the crime. Thus, when Ann picks Bill's pocket and takes his wallet, her intent is to steal. However, specific intent is the intent to accomplish a specific purpose. For example, burglary is the breaking and entering of a dwelling house with the intent to steal. The break and enter requires a general intent; the theft is a specific intent.

Criminal intent also exists if the results of an action, though unintended, are certain to occur. For example, Kim wants revenge against her former boyfriend John. She poisons the punch bowl at John's party, and several guests die as a result of drinking the punch. Kim killed the guests even though that was not the original purpose of her action. The law would hold that Kim or any other person should be substantially certain that the others at the party would drink the punch and be poisoned along with John.

The concept of *mens rea* also encompasses the situation in which a person intends to commit a crime against one person but injures another party instead. For instance, if Syed, intending to kill Larry, shoots at Larry but misses and kills Jamal, Syed is guilty of murdering Jamal, even though he did not intend to do so. This falls under the doctrine of **transferred intent**.

Mens rea is also found in situations in which harm has resulted because a person has acted negligently or recklessly. Negligence involves a person's acting unreasonably under the circumstances. For example, if a drunk driver hits a pedestrian, criminal negligence exists. In the case of drunk driving, the law maintains that a "reasonable person" would not drive a car when drunk and unable to control the vehicle. This is known as **constructive intent**.

Strict Liability

Both the *actus reus* and the *mens rea* must be present before a person can be convicted of a crime. However, several crimes do not require *mens rea*, because the person is guilty simply by doing what the statute prohibits; mental intent doesn't matter. The Crown needs only to prove the *actus reus* of the offence, unless the accused can show that he or she acted with due diligence or proper care. These offences are known as **strict-liability crimes**, or public welfare offences, and generally apply to statutes other than the *Criminal Code*. Health and safety regulations, traffic laws, and narcotic control laws are strict-liability statutes. For example, a person stopped for speeding is guilty of breaking the traffic laws regardless of whether he or she intended to exceed the speed limit. The underlying purpose of these laws is to protect the public; therefore, intent is not required. Offences of "absolute liability" cannot be defended against by showing that a person acted with due diligence. However, these offences usually violate the *Charter of Rights*.

Connections

Many white-collar crimes, such as pollution of the environment, are considered strict liability. A person who is caught dumping toxic wastes is guilty of a crime; proving intent is usually not required. For an analysis of white-collar law enforcement, see Chapter 13.

Criminal Defences

When people defend themselves against criminal charges, they must refute the elements of the crime of which they have been accused. Several approaches can be taken to criminal defence. First, defendants may deny the *actus reus* by arguing that they were falsely accused and that the real culprit has yet to be identified. Defendants may also claim that although they did engage in the criminal act they are accused of, they lacked the *mens rea* needed to be found guilty of the crime. If a person whose mental state is impaired commits a criminal act, it is possible for the person to claim they lacked the capacity to form sufficient intent to be held criminally responsible for their actions. Ignorance, mental disorder, and intoxication are among the types of excuse defences.

Another type of defence is that of justification. Here, the individual usually admits committing the criminal act but maintains that the act was justified and that he or she should not be held criminally liable. Among the justification defences are necessity, duress, self-defence, and entrapment.

Persons standing trial for criminal offences may defend themselves by claiming either that their actions were justified under the circumstances or that their behaviour can be excused by their lack of *mens rea*. If either the physical or mental elements of a crime cannot be proved, the defendant cannot be convicted. We will now examine some of these defences and justifications in greater detail.

Ignorance or Mistake

As a general rule, ignorance of the law is no excuse (CCC section 19). However, courts have recognized that ignorance can be an excuse if the government fails to make enactment of a new law public or if the offender relied on an official statement of the law that was later deemed incorrect. Ignorance or mistake can be an excuse if it negates an element of a crime. For example, if Andrew purchases stolen merchandise from Eric but is unaware that the material was illegally obtained, he cannot be convicted of receiving stolen merchandise because he had no intent to do so. This is termed a "mistake of fact."

A notable exception is in the law on "consent no defence" (CCC section 150), which says that a belief that a person is of legal age to consent to sex is not a defence unless the accused took all reasonable steps to ascertain the person's age.

In a classic example, the English case of *Tolson* (1889), a woman thought she had been widowed, but her husband was alive and he resurfaced after she remarried. Although she was convicted of bigamy, Tolson was acquitted on appeal because of honest mistake of fact.

This same defence was rejected by the Yukon Court of Appeal in the 1965 *Ladue* case. This accused was charged with "indecently interfering with a dead human body" after initiating sexual activity with a deceased female. Ladue claimed that, in his intoxicated state, he believed the woman was merely unconscious.

Not Criminally Responsible on Account of Mental Disorder

In 2002 the Standing Committee on Justice and Human Rights examined section 16 of the *Criminal Code* and changed the former "insanity" defence to one of mental disorder. Before 1992, a person could be found "not guilty by reason of insanity" (NGRI) and held indefinitely at the pleasure of the lieutenant governor. However, in *R. v. Swain* (1991), the Supreme Court of Canada ruled that indefinite sentences were a violation of the accused's constitutional rights. Although section 16 exempts an accused from criminal responsibility, he or she is not acquitted. A verdict of not criminally responsible on account of mental disorder (NCRMD) will result in a disposition ranging from community living under supervision to detention in a psychiatric facility until fit for release.

A **mental disorder** is defined in section 2 of the *Criminal Code* as a "disease of the mind" as determined by a trial judge. It includes an illness, disorder, or abnormal condition that impairs the functioning of the mind, excluding self-induced states caused by alcohol or drugs and transitory mental states, such as hysteria and concussion.

Everyone is presumed to be sane, and thus the burden of proving mental disorder rests on the accused. Sometimes, a person who was sane when he or she committed a crime becomes insane soon afterward. In that instance, the person receives psychiatric care until capable of standing trial and is then tried on the criminal charge, since the person actually had *mens rea* at the time the crime was committed. This defence traces its origins to the eighteenth century, the English common law, and the M'Naghten rule.

Fitness to Stand Trial. To be exempt from criminal responsibility, the accused must have had a mental disorder at the time of the offence that made it impossible to appreciate the nature of the act or to know that it was wrong. Under 615 of the *Code*, the accused must also be "fit to stand trial," which includes being able to understand the proceedings against them and to instruct a lawyer. The percentage of individuals found unfit for trial represented less than 1 percent of those charged with a criminal offence in 2000 for both indictable and summary offences.

A basic legal principle is that responsibility requires an operating mind, and the law exempts from criminal responsibility those who are incapable of making a rational choice because of mental disorder or immaturity. Experts agree that the law works well to balance the rights of people with mental disorders and the protection of society.

 InfoTrac®

To research the impact of the former insanity plea on criminal defences, check out the following article: Richard J. Bonnie, Norman G. Poythress, Steven K. Hoge, John Monahan, and Marlene Eisenberg, "Decision-Making in Criminal Defense: An Empirical Study of Insanity Pleas and the Impact of Doubted Client Competence," *Journal of Criminal Law and Criminology* 87, no. 1 (1996): 48–62.

The M'Naghten Rule. In 1843 Daniel M'Naghten, believing Edward Drummond to be Sir Robert Peel, the prime minister of Great Britain, shot and killed Drummond (Peel's secretary). At his trial for murder, M'Naghten claimed that he could not be held responsible because his delusions had caused him to act. The jury agreed and found him not guilty by reason of insanity.

Because of the importance of the people involved in the case, the verdict was not well received. The British House of Lords reviewed the decision and requested the court to clarify the law with respect to insane delusions. The court's response became known as the **M'Naghten rule:**

> To establish a defence on the ground of insanity, it must be proved that at the time of the committing of the act the party accused was labouring under such a defect of reason from disease of the mind, as not to know the nature and quality of the act he was doing; or, if he did know, that he did not know he was doing what was wrong.[21]

The M'Naghten rule maintains that an individual has a mental disorder if he or she is unable to tell the difference between right and wrong because of some mental disability. The M'Naghten rule is a widely used test for legal mental disorder; however, over the years it has attracted much criticism. First, "disease of the mind" has never been properly clarified. Second, the rule does not cover situations in which people know right from wrong but cannot control their actions. Third, a defendant's psychological makeup is an issue best raised at the sentencing stage after guilt has been determined. Fourth, criminal responsibility is separate from mental illness. Criminal responsibility is not a trait or quality that can be detected by a psychiatric evaluation. Moreover, some offenders are erroneously judged by psychiatrists as having a mental illness. Conversely, some people who are found NCRMD because they had a mild personality disturbance in the past have been incarcerated in mental institutions far longer than they would have been imprisoned if they had been convicted of a criminal offence.

Connections

One reason that mental disorder pleas are seldom successful is that there may be relatively few criminals with mental disorders. The association between mental illness and crimes seems to be tenuous at best. For a discussion of this issue, see the sections in Chapter 6 on mental illness and crime.

Intoxication

Self-induced intoxication, which includes the taking of alcohol or drugs, is not a defence to a general intent crime of violence, such as sexual assault and assault. Bill C-72, *An Act to Amend the Criminal Code (Self-induced intoxication)*, was passed in 1995 and made people accountable for violent acts they committed while intoxicated. This change in the law creates a standard of care, and breach of this standard is criminal fault. However, there are two exceptions to this rule. First, an individual who becomes intoxicated by mistake, through force, or under duress can use involuntary intoxication as a defence. Second, voluntary intoxication is a defence when specific intent is needed and the person could not have formed the intent because of his or her intoxicated condition. For example, if a person breaks into and enters another's house but is so drunk that he or she cannot form the intent to commit a robbery, the intoxication is a defence against theft but not against the break and enter.

In a classic intoxication defence case, *Otis* (1978), two men consumed a considerable amount of alcohol together. Otis, the accused, struck his friend about the face and head with a lamp and wine bottle. The victim experienced a massive brain hemorrhage and died. Although Otis was convicted of second-degree murder, the Ontario Court of Appeal ordered a retrial. This charge requires specific intent, and the Court ruled that the trial judge had not directed the jury to consider whether the accused had actually formed the intent to kill.

Duress

When a defendant commits an illegal act because the defendant or a third person has been threatened by another with death or serious bodily harm, this is called **duress**. This defence, however, does not cover the situation in which defendants commit a serious crime, such as murder or sexual assault, to save themselves or others.

The threat has to be immediate, and the accused cannot be a member of the group planning to commit the offence.

The defence of duress was successfully applied in the 1993 *Langlois* case, in which the accused was caught smuggling drugs into a penitentiary where he worked. After receiving several anonymous phone calls threatening him and his family, Langlois had followed an inmate's orders to pick up drugs and deliver them to motorcycle gang members inside the institution. Langlois claimed he did not alert authorities out of fear for his family's safety and doubt that police could offer adequate protection.

Necessity

The defence of necessity is applied in situations in which a person must break the law to avoid a greater evil caused by natural physical forces (storms, earthquakes, illness). This defence is available only when committing the crime is the lesser of two evils. For example, in the 1981 *Morris* case, the defendant was charged with assault and later acquitted by an Alberta Court. Morris admitted to grabbing his wife's neck during an altercation but successfully argued that he immobilized his wife to prevent her from jumping from their moving vehicle.

However, as the famous English case *Regina v. Dudley and Stephens* indicates, necessity does not justify the intentional killing of another.[22] In that case, three sailors and a cabin boy had been shipwrecked and were floating in the open seas in a lifeboat. After nine days without food and seven without water, two of the sailors, Dudley and Stephens, killed and ate the cabin boy. Four days later, the sailors were rescued. The court acknowledged that the cabin boy most likely would have died naturally because he was in the weakest condition, but nevertheless judged the killing as unjustified.

In Canada, a similar situation involved Martin Hartwell, who piloted a plane that crashed in the Northwest Territories on November 8, 1972. Severely injured, he survived for 31 days in mid-winter until he was rescued. One passenger, a nurse, died on impact, and another, a pregnant woman needing surgery for a premature baby, was injured in the crash and died a few days later. A young boy suffering from acute appendicitis survived for three weeks, during which time he and the pilot ate corned beef, sugar cubes, snow, soap, and candles. During an inquest into events surrounding the crash, it was revealed that the pilot had survived by eventually resorting to cannibalism. Criminal charges were never brought against the pilot, but his actions would certainly have fallen under the defence of necessity.[23]

Self-Defence

Self-defence involves a claim that the defendant's actions were a justified response to the provocative behaviour of the victim to protect the defendant's person or property.

In August 2000, tension erupted at the Burnt Church Native reserve. In a standoff between the Department of Fisheries and Oceans and Native fishers, the Natives pressed for their demand to have their fishing rights recognized, rights that had been affirmed by the Supreme Court of Canada. Sometimes the defence is that no illegality is involved, as in this case, and the conflict becomes whether a law has been broken.

An individual is justified in using force against another to protect himself or herself against unprovoked assault (CCC section 34) and is not guilty of the harm done. This defence can excuse such crimes as murder, manslaughter, and assault. However, there are limits. First, defendants must have a reasonable belief that they are in danger of death or great harm and that it is necessary for them to use force to prevent harm to themselves.

In 1990 the Supreme Court of Canada ruled that in the case of a battered woman, the threat need not be imminent if it is part of a pattern of domestic violence (*R. v. Lavallee*, S.C.C. 852). Angelique Lyn Lavallee was a battered woman in a volatile relationship; she killed her partner late one night by shooting him in the back of the head as he left her room. The shooting occurred after an argument in which the appellant had been physically abused and was fearful for her life after being taunted with the threat that either she kill him or he would get her. This case created what has become known as the "battered woman syndrome," an area of law in which Canada is the world leader.

 Culture, Gender, Ethnicity, and Criminology

What Happens When People Go outside the Law to Uphold the Law

On November 11, 1986, Stephen Kesler, his wife, and two daughters were working in their small drugstore in Calgary when two men entered. One demanded that Mrs. Kesler fill a pillowcase with drugs. The other man removed $150 from the cash register. Kesler attacked him and chased him from the store with a shotgun. Kesler shouted at the fleeing robber to stop, but when he continued to run, Kesler shot him fatally in the back.

Kesler returned to the store to confront the other man who was armed with a .22. Five shots were fired and Kesler was hit in the shoulder. When the man fled, Kesler chased him and beat him with the butt of his shotgun. When police arrived, Kesler was charged

with second-degree murder. He was eventually found not guilty, even though the prosecution argued Kesler was not preventing an assault on himself (Grayson 1992). In a poll undertaken by Gallup in January 1985 just after the Kesler incident, 70 percent specified that such actions were "sometimes" justified.

The idea of going outside the law to enforce social order is not new. Instead of asking why people deviate, perhaps it would be better to ask why people conform.

On the American frontier, vigilantism was common in the absence of organized law enforcement. However, Canada had a different tradition, with the North-West Mounted Police an important force in maintaining order. In some areas, before the arrival of the NWMP, the law was administered in a different way. In Yukon, for example, in the mid-1890s, law was administered

in a process called the miners' meeting, an example of frontier justice. Anyone could air a grievance, criminal or civil, and the assembled parties reached a verdict and decided on the disposition in the case.

Palmer (1978) notes that in the nineteenth century, people who violated certain standards of behaviour might be subject to various forms of "misrule." The offender might be seized, put on a donkey or wooden beam, and ridden about town or along a country road to the derision of the crowd. Physical beatings, tar and featherings, and even killings occurred. However, an escalating pattern of violence in the early 1800s led to a series of local bylaws outlawing these practices. Hundreds of such ritualized confrontations took place over the course of the nineteenth century and were common until the beginning of the twentieth century.

It might be surprising to realize that Canadians and Americans are equally supportive of spontaneous vigilantism, even though Canada has a lower crime rate and high confidence in its police. When individuals identify with the established order but resort to means that break the law to uphold the established order, they are called vigilantes. Given that spontaneous vigilantes may be victims of crimes and that juries frequently acquit them, vigilantism might be seen as extra-legal, meant to repair a break in social custom. The police and juries are sometimes prepared to accept what some might feel to be excessive actions.

Ritualized confrontations were means of maintaining social control, but this is not desirable in the twenty-first century. For example, Dobash and Dobash (1981) describe how misrules and charivaris were sometimes carried out against men who beat their wives. The intent was to set limits on the husband's right to discipline his wife. In France in the eighteenth century, rituals for men who beat their wives were restricted to May. In England in the nineteenth century, wife beaters were subject to a parade of men, women, and children beating bells, kettles, and frying pans who proceeded to the house of the offending man, where they would chant rhymes and songs.

In the cuckold's court, men were ridiculed publicly if it was thought they were doing women's work, if they were henpecked, or if they were cuckolded. Their crime was permitting an inversion of the proper roles men and women should occupy in a marriage.

In Britain in 1500, and for at least two hundred years, a woman could be subject to public ridicule if she was domineering or quarrelsome. Forced to wear a "scold's bridle" she would be paraded through the village. By the twentieth century, such ritual shaming and confrontations had pretty much disappeared. Conflict resolutions have been appropriated by the state, which reserves to itself the right to try an accused and subject him or her to punishment if found guilty. Regulation and surveillance have become part of the monopoly of the state.

Existing law does not recognize the legitimacy of retribution carried out by individual citizens. However, a large proportion of Canadians report qualified support for vigilantism. Given the objective differences in crime rates between Canada and the United States, it is not surprising that more Americans than Canadians feel threatened by the circumstances in which they live. However, the Canadian support is surprising.

Sources: Russell P. Dobash and R. Emerson Dobash, "Community Response to Violence Against Wives: Charivari, Abstract Justice and Patriarchy," *Social Problems* 28 (1981): 563–78; J. Paul Grayson, "Vigilantism in Canada and the United States," *Legal Studies Forum* 16 (1992): 21–39; W.R. Morrison, *Showing the Flag: The Mounted Police and Canadian Sovereignty in the North, 1894–1925* (Vancouver: University of British Columbia Press, 1985); Bryan D. Palmer, "Discordant Music: Charivaris and Whitecapping in Nineteenth Century North America," *Labour* 3 (1978): 5–62; Thomas Stone, "The Mounties as Vigilantes: Perceptions of Community and the Transformation of Law in the Yukon," *Law and Society Review* 14, Fall (1979): 83–114.

The second limit is that the amount of force used must be no greater than that necessary to prevent personal harm. For example, the accused in the 1998 *Berrigan* case stabbed and killed an unarmed man in the mistaken belief that the victim was drawing a gun from his pocket. Although Berrigan's violent response was not proportionate to the degree of force threatened by the victim, who was actually reaching for a cell phone, the British Columbia Court of Appeal allowed the accused to raise this defence.

The rules concerning self-defence also apply to situations involving the defence of a third person. Thus, if a person reasonably believes that another is in danger of unlawful bodily harm from an assailant, the person may use the force necessary to prevent the danger. Using force to defend property from trespass or theft is allowable if the force is reasonable. This means that the use of force should be a last resort after requests to stop interfering with the property or legal action have failed. This limit is based on the social policy that human life is more important than property.

Entrapment

The defence of **entrapment** allows the defendant to argue that law enforcement officers encouraged the commission of a crime, which would not have been committed had it not been for trickery, persuasion, or fraud on the officers' part. If law enforcement officers plan a crime, implant the idea in a person's mind, and pressure that person into committing the act, the person may plead entrapment. The police cannot induce a person to break the law. This situation is different from that in which an officer simply provides an opportunity for the crime to be committed and the defendant is willing and ready to act. For example, if a plainclothes police officer poses as a potential customer and is approached by a prostitute, no entrapment has occurred. However, if the same officer approaches a woman and persuades her to commit an act of prostitution, the defence of entrapment is appropriate. Several Supreme Court cases have ruled that the police cannot randomly test a citizen's virtue.

The *Canadian Charter of Rights and Freedoms*

The *Charter of Rights and Freedoms* is the ultimate arbiter of law and legal rights in Canada. The *Charter* is included in the *Constitution Act*, which was repatriated

from Britain in 1982 (see Table 2.3 for a sample of the legal rights that the *Charter* contains). All laws must uphold the rights guaranteed under the *Charter*. The impact of the *Charter* has been great.

Because the *Charter* guarantees rights to the individual that cannot be abridged except in unusual circumstances, these rights are said to be "inalienable." For example, a person has a right to a lawyer, and appeals of convictions have been launched based on an accused person being denied access to legal advice. The prosecution must also give all the evidence gathered by the police to the defendant so that he or she can make a complete defence to the charges. This is known as **disclosure**, and it has become a fundamental principle of Canadian justice. The principle of disclosure figured largely in the discussion of the wrongful conviction of Donald Marshall, in which it was found that the prosecution had evidence that could have been the basis for his release had it been known to the defence.

In the case of Donald Marshall, a special provision in the *Criminal Code* was invoked and was instrumental in

---

TABLE 2.3 *Constitution Act 1982—Canadian Charter of Rights and Freedoms—*Legal Rights

Whereas Canada is founded upon principles that recognize the supremacy of God and the rule of law . . .

LIFE, LIBERTY AND SECURITY OF THE PERSON

7. Everyone has the right to life, liberty and security of the person and the right not to be deprived thereof except in accordance with the principles of fundamental justice.

SEARCH OR SEIZURE

8. Everyone has the right to be secure against unreasonable search or seizure.

DETENTION OR IMPRISONMENT

9. Everyone has the right not to be arbitrarily detained or imprisoned.

ARREST OR DETENTION

10. Everyone has the right on arrest or detention
    (a) to be informed promptly of the reasons therefor;
    (b) to retain and instruct counsel without delay and to be informed of that right; and
    (c) to have the validity of the detention determined by way of habeas corpus and to be released if the detention is not lawful.

PROCEEDINGS IN CRIMINAL AND PENAL MATTERS

11. Any person charged with an offence has the right
    (a) to be informed without unreasonable delay of the specific offence;
    (b) to be tried within a reasonable time;
    (c) not to be compelled to be a witness in proceedings against that person in respect of that offence;
    (d) to be presumed innocent until proven guilty according to law in a fair and public hearing by an independent and impartial tribunal;
    (e) not to be denied reasonable bail without just cause;
    (f) except in the case of an offence under military law tried before a military tribunal, to the benefit of trial by jury where the maximum punishment for the offence is imprisonment for five years or a more severe punishment;
    (g) not to be found guilty on account of any act or omission unless, at the time of the act or omission, it constituted an offence under Canadian or international law or was criminal according to the general principles of law recognized by the community of nations;

(h) if finally acquitted of the offence, not to be tried for it again and, if finally found guilty and punished for the offence, not to be tried or punished for it again; and

(i) if found guilty for the offence and if the punishment for the offence has been varied between the time of commission and the time of sentencing, to the benefit of the lesser punishment.

TREATMENT OR PUNISHMENT

12. Everyone has the right not to be subjected to any cruel or unusual treatment or punishment.

SELF-INCRIMINATION

13. A witness who testified in any proceedings has the right not to have any incriminating evidence so given used to incriminate that witness in any other proceedings except in a prosecution for perjury or for the giving of contradictory evidence.

INTERPRETER

14. A party or witness in any proceedings who does not understand or speak the language in which the proceedings are conducted or who is deaf has the right to the assistance of an interpreter.

 Famous Canadian Criminals

Wrongfully Convicted

David Milgaard was sentenced in 1970 to life imprisonment for the murder of Gail Miller; a second section 690 application was granted in 1991. A new trial was ordered by the Supreme Court in 1992 and the charges were stayed. Milgaard was subsequently exonerated by DNA testing arranged by AIDWYC in 1997. Milgaard was awarded $10 million.

Donald Marshall Jr. was sentenced in 1971 to life imprisonment for the murder of Sandy Seale; a section 690 application was granted in 1982. He was acquitted by the Nova Scotia Court of Appeal in 1983. In 1984 Marshall was awarded $270 000, less legal fees of $100 000, for 11 years in jail, subsequently amended in 1990. The whole package is worth more than $10 million.

Wilson Nepoose was sentenced in 1987 to life imprisonment for murder; a section 690 application in 1991 resulted in the Alberta

Court of Appeal ordering a new trial in 1992. A retrial was not proceeded with. Nepoose continually suffered from depression, and he was found dead in 1998.

Wilfred Beaulieu was sentenced in 1992 to three-and-a-half years' imprisonment for two sexual assaults. A section 690 was allowed in 1996. His appeal was allowed by the Alberta Court of Appeal and an acquittal was subsequently entered in 1997.

Richard McArthur was sentenced in 1986 to life imprisonment for murder; a section 690 reference was granted in 1998 and was heard by the Alberta Court of Appeal in April 1999. The AIDWYC was advised that an acquittal would be entered at the Crown's request.

Clayton Johnson was sentenced in 1993 to life imprisonment for murder; a section 690 application was filed by AIDWYC in March 1998. His case was referred to the Nova Scotia Court of Appeal in September 1998. Johnson was free on bail in 2002 when he

heard that the Crown was dropping all charges. In 2004 he received $2.5 million for legal fees and compensation.

Rejean Hinse was sentenced in 1964 to 15 years' imprisonment for armed robbery; he was acquitted by the Supreme Court of Canada in 1997 after being granted an extension of time to appeal.

Richard Norris was sentenced in 1980 to 23 months' imprisonment for sexual assault; he was acquitted in 1991 by the Ontario Court of Appeal and awarded compensation of $507 000 in 1993. A former friend confessed that he had committed the crime.

Norman Fox was sentenced to 10 years for sexual assault; he was granted a pardon in 1984 after evidence indicated that he had been mistakenly identified. Fox was given $275 000 in compensation.

Michael McTaggart (Subway Elvis) was sentenced in 1988 to five years' imprisonment for bank robbery; a new trial was ordered by the Ontario Court of Appeal in 1990. Police evidence not disclosed to the defence was crucial to his wrongful conviction; in 2001, he received $380 000.

Thomas Sophonow was convicted in 1983 and 1985 to life imprisonment for the 1981 murder of Barbara Stoppel after three trials; both convictions were overturned and an acquittal was entered in December 1985 by the Manitoba Court of Appeal. DNA tests cleared him in 2000, and the next year it was recommended he be awarded $2.6 million.

Gregory Parsons was sentenced in 1994 to life imprisonment for murder; the Newfoundland Court of Appeal ordered a new trial in 1996. A stay of proceedings was entered in 1998 based on DNA testing. AIDWYC intervened before the Newfoundland Supreme Court on a *Charter* application to set aside the stay and have an acquittal entered. An acquittal was entered with the consent of the Crown in November 1998. Parsons received $650 000 in compensation.

Ronald Dalton, wrongfully convicted of murdering his wife in 1989, spent more than eight years in prison before being

acquitted on retrial in 2000. His case was one subject of an inquiry into Newfoundland's justice system in 2003, along with Gregory Parsons and Randy Druken.

Guy Paul Morin was sentenced in 1992 to life imprisonment for murdering Christine Jessop. The Ontario Court of Appeal acquitted him in 1995 as a result of DNA testing. Morin and his parents received $1.25 million as a settlement.

Herman Kaglik, convicted in 1992 of sexual assault, spent almost five years in jail before being exonerated by DNA evidence. The Northwest Territories Court of Appeal entered an acquittal in 1998. The federal government paid him $1.1 million, the largest compensation package for wrongful conviction for something other than murder.

Benoit Proulx was awarded $1.6 million for being wrongfully jailed in the 1982 murder of his ex-girlfriend.

Steven Truscott was sentenced to death in 1959 for capital murder; his sentence was commuted to life imprisonment in 1960. His conviction was upheld in 1967 after a Reference to the Supreme Court of Canada. In 2004 the Minister of

Justice sent the case to appeal court for review.

Donzel Young was sentenced in 1991 to life imprisonment for murder; a section 690 application was filed in 1995, but Young was murdered in prison. Mr. Justice Kaufman was appointed by the minister of justice to review the case; however, due to witnesses disappearing, his case is now in limbo.

Section 690 of the CCC, amended in 2000, allows the minister of justice to use his or her discretion in assisting people believed to have been wrongfully convicted.

The AIDWYC, founded in 1993, is dedicated to preventing wrongful convictions and reversing those that have already occurred. The AIDWYC believes that these cases represent a small percentage of those people wrongly convicted in Canada. Three largest reasons for wrongful convictions are lack of disclosure, faulty eyewitness evidence, and false confessions.

Sources: injusticebusters, http://www.injusticebusters.com (accessed May 11, 2005), ForJustice, http://www.forejustice.org (accessed May 11, 2005), and Innocence Project, http://www.innocenceproject.org (accessed May 11, 2005).

his eventual release. The statute is section 690, by which the minister of justice can direct a new trial or appeal if it seems warranted. A group called the Association in Defence of the Wrongfully Convicted (AIDWYC) has played a very important role in securing reviews of wrongful convictions, as seen in the Famous Canadian Criminals box.

The *Charter* has been criticized for doing too much to protect the rights of individuals and not enough to protect society.

Although there are occasional debates in our society as to whether certain procedural rights have been extended too far, a comparison with other countries can

serve as an eye-opener. In the Crime in the News feature, we see the result of an Iranian court case against a man accused of killing a Montreal woman who had been in custody for taking photographs outside a prison. Canadian officials had been barred from the trial and the media ordered not to report on the case. The court acquitted the defendant and ordered compensation. The average compensation paid to relatives of a Muslim man is $25 000, half that if the victim is Christian, Jewish, or a woman. Rights that we would take for granted around imprisonment and prosecution were apparently not observed.

Crime in the News

UN Rights Experts Concerned about Iran

Geneva—Key UN human-rights experts expressed their "profound" concern Tuesday about Iranian legal proceedings in the death of Iranian-Canadian photojournalist Zahra Kazemi.

"Many reports indicate that the proceedings did not meet international standards of fair trial because key evidence that might have incriminated judiciary officials, the prosecutor's office as well as the intelligence ministry were ignored by the court," a UN statement said.

Ms. Kazemi was arrested in June, 2003, while working outside Evin prison in Tehran. She died of a fractured skull and brain hemorrhage while in detention last July.

A Tehran court cleared secret agent Mohammad Reza Aghdam Ahmadi, the sole defendant, on Saturday of killing Ms. Kazemi.

An Iranian judiciary statement released Monday said Mr. Ahmadi was acquitted for "lack of sufficient evidence," the official Islamic Republic News Agency reported.

The UN experts—specialists in free speech, torture and independent judges—said Iranian authorities failed to ensure an open trial and the independent functioning of the judiciary.

The statement noted that journalists and other foreign observers were barred from full access to the courtroom from the third day of the trial.

The experts said they feared Iranian authorities "are favouring a climate of impunity for law-enforcement officials and setting the ground for the recurrence of

similar human-rights violations in the future."

The statement was made by Ambeyi Ligabo, who specializes in freedom of opinion; Leandro Despouy, expert on the independence of judges and lawyers; and Theo van Boven, who reports on torture.

It said they "express their profound concern regarding the unanswered questions which have resulted from the acquittal."

On Monday, Foreign Affairs Minister Pierre Pettigrew phoned Ms. Kazemi's son, Stephan Hachemi, to express sympathy. Hachemi has been harshly critical of Ottawa's handling of the affair and is pushing for the case to be taken to the International Court of Justice at The Hague.

Source: Associated Press and Canadian Press, July 27, 2004.

Famous Canadian Court Cases

Legal Rights and the *Charter*

Numerous high-profile cases have branded Canadian criminal justice history, serving as glaring reminders of the disadvantaged position that individuals occupy when accused by the state. Procedural protections have been introduced at all stages of the criminal process to alleviate power and resource imbalances, and to safeguard individuals from the abuse and oppression that can plague crime control efforts. As the following cases testify, enshrining legal rights in the *Charter* has substantially affected the criminal law.

R. v. Oakes

David Oakes was found guilty of unlawful possession of a narcotic in 1982, a time when section 8 of the *Narcotic Control Act* contained a "reverse onus" clause. Essentially, any person found by the Court to be in possession of illegal drugs was presumed to have the intent of trafficking and was to be convicted accordingly unless the defence could prove otherwise. In 1986, the Supreme Court of Canada upheld the Ontario Court of Appeal's judgment in this case. The narcotics provision was rendered invalid because it unreasonably interfered with the section 11 *Charter* right to be presumed

innocent until proven guilty. However, this case is best known for its impact on section 1 of the *Charter*. Oakes established the proportionality test, the basic framework of analysis that judges use to determine whether or not limitations on rights and freedoms are justifiable.

R. v. Swain

This *Charter* challenge involved sections 7 (right to life, liberty and security of the person), 9 (right against arbitrary detention/ imprisonment), and 15 (equality rights). Owen Swain was found not guilty of common and aggravated assault by reason of insanity. As such, he was subject to automatic and indefinite detention pursuant to section 542(2) of the *Criminal Code*. Both the trial judge and the Ontario Court of Appeal disagreed with the defence submission that such a sentence infringed on Swain's constitutional rights. However, the Supreme Court of Canada overturned the lower court judgments in 1991. Detaining an insanity acquittee "at the pleasure of the lieutenant governor" was deemed an unjustifiable *Charter* violation. Since 1991, section 672.54 of the *Criminal Code* has instructed courts to impose the least restrictive disposition possible after taking into account public safety concerns, the mental condition of the accused, and the goal of reintegrating offenders into society.

R. v. Stinchcombe

Suspected of wrongfully appropriating a client's property, lawyer William Stinchcombe was charged with numerous counts of criminal breach of trust, theft, and fraud. He was convicted after both the Crown and trial judge denied disclosure of witness statements that may have operated in his favour. In response to this case, the Supreme Court of Canada established general disclosure principles respecting the section 11 *Charter* right to make a full answer and defence. Prosecutors are now obligated to provide the defence with all case information that might be relevant to the accused, even if it will not be presented in court. Despite the landmark 1991 ruling, disclosure issues jeopardized Stinchcombe's retrial and prompted the Crown in his third trial to call no evidence. Consequently, the 51-year-old Calgary man was found not guilty after a decade-long legal battle and two trips to Canada's highest court.

R. v. Askov

At stake in Askov was the section 11 *Charter* right to be tried within a reasonable time. The four accused in this case were charged with conspiracy to commit extortion and several other offences in November 1983, but they were not tried until September 1986. Attributed mainly to an overburdened system, this lengthy delay prompted an Ontario judge to stay the proceedings. In October 1990, the Supreme Court of Canada affirmed that the postponement was unreasonably excessive. The Court recommended that delays not exceed six to eight months, which spurred the withdrawal or dismissal of 51 000 cases in Ontario alone within months. The Askov verdict created powerful incentives for officials to better allocate judicial resources and for prosecutors to resolve cases in a more timely fashion.

Sources: Bob Beaty, "Lawyer Acquitted at Start of Third Trial," *Calgary Herald*, March 24, 1996; "Case Summary *R. v. Stinchcombe*," Mapleleafweb, http://www .mapleleafweb.com (accessed October 23, 2002); Connie Utrecht, "Lower BAC Will Increase Court Backlogs," *Canada Safety Council: Canada's Voice and Resource for Safety*, February 11, 2003; David Pomerant and Glenn Gilmour, "The Impact of *R. v. Stinchcombe* and the New Disclosure Policies of the Attorneys-General," *A Survey of the Preliminary Inquiry in Canada*, April 1993; Jake Rupert, "Delays Sink Case against Former 67," *The Ottawa Citizen*, http://www.edelsonandassociates .com/news/Galbraith/Galbraith%20trial%20 08-15-02-3.htm (accessed August 15, 2002); Robert Sharpe, Katherine Swinton, and Kent Roach, *The Charter of Rights and Freedoms*, 2nd ed. (Toronto: Irwin Law, 2002); *R. v. Askov*, [1990] 2 S.C.R. 1199; *R. v. Oakes*, [1986] 1 S.C.R. 103, http://www .canlii.org/ca/cas/scc/1986/1986scc7.html (accessed May 10, 2005); *R. v. Swain*, [1991] 1 S.C.R. 933, http://www.canlii .org/ca/cas/scc/1991/1991scc41.html (accessed May 10, 2005).

Prepared by Andrea Wolf.

Changing the Criminal Law

Governments routinely examine the substantive criminal law. Since the law reflects public opinion regarding various forms of behaviour, what was a crime 40 years ago may not be considered so today. Gambling, for example, has been almost totally legalized and all criminal penalties have been removed. With respect to some other laws, however, new criminal laws have been created and penalties have been toughened to conform to emerging social issues. Let's look at some examples.

Marijuana. The crime of possessing marijuana has been virtually decriminalized with penalties reduced to a fine instead of a prison sentence. In May 1999, Health Minister Allan Rock allowed people to apply to use marijuana for medicinal purposes. However, because initially there was no legal way to obtain the drug, it was inevitable that someone would be charged for growing it. In 2000, an Alberta judge stayed a charge against Grant Krieger for cultivating marijuana, and in 2001, it was announced that Canada would become the only country in the world with a government-regulated system for using marijuana as medicine. The health minister denied that this was the thin edge of the wedge for legalizing marijuana.

In 2003, the Supreme Court heard the case of *R. v. Clay*, who was convicted of drug possession and trafficking. It decided that Parliament has the constitutional right to prohibit possession despite evidence that it doesn't harm and is essentially unenforceable. In 2004 the government reintroduced Bill C-10, *An Act to amend the Contraventions Act and the Controlled Drugs and Substances Act.* This Bill died on the order paper.

The Canadian Centre for Justice Statistics (CCJS) reports that following nearly a decade of increases, the rate of drug crimes fell by 8 percent in 2003. This decline was due to an 18 percent drop in cannabis possession incidents, which compose about half of all drug crimes reported by police. The overall rate of persons charged with cannabis possession fell dramatically by 30 percent in 2003. This drop is probably due to uncertainty within law enforcement because of legislation introduced to decriminalize possession of small amounts of cannabis, as well as recent court rulings questioning the constitutionality of laws on cannabis possession. The police have also wisely reallocated resources toward more serious drug offences.

Youth Justice. In 2002, Parliament passed the *Youth Criminal Justice Act* (YCJA) to replace the *Young Offenders Act.* The YCJA addresses various problems in the youth justice system: the lack of a coherent youth justice philosophy; the highest youth incarceration rate in the Western world; the over-use of courts for minor cases that can be dealt with better outside the courts; sentencing disparities and unfairness in youth sentencing; the lack of reintegration after being released from custody; unfairness in transfers to the adult system; the blurring of serious and less serious offences; and insufficient recognition to the concerns and interests of victims.

Assisted Suicide. Assisted suicide has become the subject of legal debate in both Canada and the United States. In Michigan, a ban was passed to stop Dr. Jack Kevorkian from practising obitiatry, helping people take their lives.[24] A similar law in Canada was challenged in 1998, when a respirologist at Victoria General Hospital in Halifax, Nova Scotia, was charged with ending the life of a terminally ill cancer patient after he had been taken off life support.[25] A SCC decision denied Sue Rodriguez the right to assisted suicide, which prompted the call for change in the criminal law.

Connections

Euthanasia and assisted suicide are discussed in more detail in Chapter 14, where issues surrounding the rightful connection between the law and morality are debated.

Stalking. Another evolving concern has come to be known as **stalking.** The Canadian federal government enacted a provision against criminal harassment in 1993, which prohibits and punishes acts described typically as "the willful, malicious and repeated following and harassing of another person."[26] Stalking is not

an insignificant event. A 2003 Ipsos poll showed that 10 percent of Canadians admit to having stalked an ex-partner after a break-up, while 7 percent say they have sought revenge on a former partner. The pattern varies inversely by age and by social class, with the young and lower income more likely to stalk and seek revenge.

The CCJS reports that in 2003 the rate of criminal harassment incidents has increased over the past five years and is now 26 percent higher than in 1998. Three-quarters of all criminal harassment victims in 2003 were female, and 86 percent of all accused were male. One-third of female victims were harassed by ex-spouses, 22 percent by close friends (which includes ex-boyfriends), 22 percent by casual acquaintances, 12 percent by strangers, and 3 percent by current spouses. In 8 percent of cases, the relationship could not be determined. Male victims were most commonly harassed by casual acquaintances (35 percent), followed by close friends (18 percent), strangers (15 percent), ex-spouses (14 percent), and current spouses (1 percent). In 17 percent of cases, the relationship could not be determined.

Exhibit 2.3 | **Quick Code: Criminal Harassment, Section 264, CCC**

264(1) Criminal harassment

(1) No person shall, without lawful authority and knowing that another person is harassed or recklessly as to whether the other person is harassed, engage in conduct referred to in subsection (2) that causes that other person reasonably, in all the circumstances, to fear for their safety or the safety of anyone known to them.

264(2) Prohibited conduct

(2) The conduct mentioned in subsection (1) consists of

   (a) repeatedly following from place to place the other person or anyone known to them;

   (b) repeatedly communicating with, either directly or indirectly, the other person or anyone known to them;

   (c) besetting or watching the dwelling-house, or place where the other person, or anyone known to them, resides, works, carries on business or happens to be; or

   (d) engaging in threatening conduct directed at the other person or any member of their family.

Source: R.S., 1985, c. C-46, s. 264; R.S., 1985, c. 27 (1st Supp.), s. 37; 1993, c. 45, s. 2.

David Milgaard, wrongfully convicted of murder in 1970 and subsequently exonerated by DNA testing in 1997.

Although stalking laws were originally formulated to protect women terrorized by former husbands and boyfriends, the laws have often been applied to people stalked by strangers or casual acquaintances. There has been criticism that the reaction to the perceived threat of stalking has been exaggerated and that stalking covers other behaviours that are already against the law, such as trespassing. However, others have argued that the gendered character of the crime has finally been recognized.

Sex offender registration is a response to public concern about sexual predators moving into neighbourhoods. In 1996, the United States passed legislation requiring that the public be informed of the existence of convicted pedophiles in their midst.[27] New laws, such as California's "sexual predator" law, were passed to keep sexually dangerous individuals in custody even after their sentences are served. In 2001, Ontario became the first province to enact legislation (called Christopher's Law) to develop a sex offender registry, but there was no general policy on **community notification**. In 2004, the minister of public safety announced the *Sex Offender Information Registration Act*, which requires released offenders to report to the police.

The Crown can already apply on conviction, before sentencing, to have an offender classified as a "dangerous offender" (CCC section 753). Such offenders can be held in jail indefinitely. Although fewer than three hundred dangerous offenders live in Canada, public concern is that they pose a very serious threat to public safety. The Crown can also classify these offenders as long-term offenders (LTO), which places them under 10 years, 25 years, or life-long parole.

Related to societal concerns about dangerous sexual predators, in 2000 a National DNA Databank was launched in Canada, which enables judges to authorize the collection of DNA samples from convicted offenders. In 2004, the databank was reinforced with legislation to include criminal harassment and those found NCRMD, and expanded to include retroactive offences. DNA was first used in an RCMP investigation in 1989, and the trial of Alan Legere was the first to use DNA evidence. Following the 2004 murder of Holly Jones, police sought saliva samples from all men over age 16 in the area, a very controversial tactic. The Toronto police chief is now asking that DNA be obtained on arrest, in the same way that fingerprints are.

A majority of people in an April 2004 poll believed that the rights of society should take precedence over the rights of the individual. When it came to a specific issue, such as the right of the community to be informed when an offender is released from prison, the number agreeing jumped dramatically.

Source: Poll conducted by *The Globe and Mail,* April 29, 2004.

Cybercrime. Millions of people worldwide are on the Internet. Criminal entrepreneurs are now developing a whole new breed of high-tech crimes that contain elements of fraud, theft, swindles, and false claims. These crimes are difficult to categorize because they can be committed by corporations and individuals, can be singular or ongoing, and can involve the theft of information, identity, resources, or funds. High-tech crimes cost consumers billions of dollars each year and will increase dramatically in the years to come. They are also difficult to detect and police. There have been a number of highly publicized cases in which adults have solicited teenagers in Internet chat rooms. Others have used the Internet to sell and distribute obscene material, prompting some service providers to censor or control sexually explicit material.

In March 2001, legislation was introduced to create tough penalties to rid the Internet of child pornography. The new crime of "Internet luring," with a maximum penalty of five years in prison, is the response to reports that pedophiles use Internet chat rooms and false identities to entice children away from their homes. The legislation makes it a crime to transmit child pornography on the Internet, make child pornography available in cyberspace, or possess it for the purposes of transmitting it, making it available, or exporting it. The offences all carry a maximum penalty of 10 years in prison.

Bogus get-rich-quick schemes, weight-loss scams, and investment swindles have also been pitched on the Internet. In some cases, these fraudulent acts can be dangerous to clients. For example, in a 1995 case a Minnesota woman advertised the health benefits of "germanium" on the Internet, claiming that it could cure AIDS, cancer, and other diseases. Germanium products, however, have been banned because they cause irreversible kidney damage.[28] The Canadian Medical Association warns of a case in which potential customers were told that a device that used an electric current could kill parasites that cause cancer and Alzheimer's.

Corporate Crime. In 2004, the minister of justice announced the passage of Bill C-45 regarding the criminal liability of corporations. It is commonly referred to as the Westray bill and makes organizations criminally liable when senior officers commit or do not stop criminal actions within the organization or act in such a way as to constitute criminal negligence. The maximum penalty is $100 000. Canada now follows Australia, Britain, and the United States in developing legislation on "workplace homicide."

Other future directions of the criminal law remain unclear. Crimes by corporations will certainly be given more attention. Other offences, such as recreational drug use, may be reduced in importance or removed entirely from the criminal law system. In addition, changing technology will require modification in the criminal law. For example, such technologies as automated teller machines and cellular phones have already spawned a new generation of criminal acts involving "theft" of access numbers and cards and software piracy. As the information highway grows, as the nation's computer network advances, and as biotechnology produces new substances, the criminal law will be forced to address threats to the public safety that today are unknown. However, developments in technology, such as DNA testing and electronic monitoring, will change the way in which criminal investigation and punishment are carried out.

Connections

The criminal law must be constantly modified to include areas that only a few years earlier were unknown. Chapter 13 contains sections on technological crimes, including the emerging areas of computer crime.

Summary

The substantive criminal law is a set of rules that specifies the behaviour society has outlawed. The criminal law can be distinguished from the civil law on the basis that the former involves powers given to the state to enforce social rules, while the latter controls interactions between private citizens. The criminal law serves several important purposes: It represents public opinion and moral values, it enforces social controls, it deters criminal behaviour and wrongdoing, it punishes transgressors, and it banishes private retribution. It can also entrench the interests of the powerful and be used to resist social change. The criminal law used in Canada traces its origin to the English common law, which was formulated during the Middle Ages when King Henry II's judges began to use precedents set in one case to guide their decisions.

In Canada's legal system, common-law crimes have been codified into the federal *Criminal Code*. Today, most crimes fall into the category of indictable offences—serious crimes usually punished by a prison term—or summary offences—minor crimes that carry a fine or a light jail sentence. The former include murder, rape, assault with a deadly weapon, and robbery; the latter include simple assault and the possession of small amounts of drugs.

Every crime has specific elements. In most instances, these elements include the *actus reus* (guilty act), which is the actual physical part of the crime (for example, taking money or burning a building), and the *mens rea* (guilty mind), which refers to the state of mind of the individual who commits a crime—more specifically, the person's intent to do the act.

At trial, accused individuals can defend themselves by claiming to have lacked *mens rea* and, therefore, not being responsible for the criminal actions. One type of defence is excuse for mental reasons, such as mental disorder, intoxication, necessity, or duress. Another defence is justification by reason of self-defence or entrapment. Of all defences, mental disorder is perhaps the most controversial. In most cases, defendants using a mental disorder defence claim that they did not know what they were doing when they committed a crime or that their mental state did not allow them to tell the difference between right and wrong (the M'Naghten rule). Mental disorder defences can also include the claims that the offender lacked the substantial capacity to conform his or her conduct to the criminal law. Regardless of the mental disorder defence used, critics charge that mental illness is separate from legal responsibility and that the two should not be equated. Supporters counter that the mental disorder defence allows people who have mental illness to avoid penal sanctions.

The criminal law is undergoing constant reform. Some acts are being decriminalized—their penalties are being reduced—while laws are being revised to make penalties for some acts more severe. The law must confront social and technological change.

Thinking Like a Criminologist

The Canadian Parliament is considering Bill C-210, An Act to prevent the use of the Internet to distribute material that advocates, promotes or incites racial hatred, violence against woman or child pornography. The parliamentarians have asked you, a criminologist, to appear before the Justice Committee on Criminal Code reform in order to identify whether legal controls are needed to control the use of the Internet. The fear is that unscrupulous entrepreneurs may use the Internet to sell undesirable material, such as pornography. Would you advise Parliament to control the Internet closely? What dangers might be presented by such an attempt at regulation? Is there a tradeoff between individual rights and social security?

Key Terms

actus reus	inchoate crimes	sex offender registration
assisted suicide	indictable offence	specific deterrence
Code of Hammurabi	*lex talionis*	stalking
common law	M'Naghten rule	*stare decisis*
community notification	*mala in se*	strict-liability crimes
constructive intent	*mala prohibitum*	summary offence
disclosure	*mens rea*	tort law
duress	mental disorder	transferred intent
entrapment	mores	vagrancy
folkways	Mosaic Code	wergild
general deterrence	oath-helpers	

Critical Thinking Questions

1. What are the specific aims and purposes of the criminal law? To what extent is the criminal law aimed at controlling social harm?

2. What kinds of activities should be labelled criminal in contemporary society? Do you believe some acts that are now legal should be criminalized and some that are now criminal should be legalized?

3. Under common law, a person must have *mens rea* to be guilty of a crime. Would society be better off if criminal intent were not considered? After all, aren't we merely guessing about a person's actual motivation for committing crime?

4. When is it permissible to use force in self-defence? Considering that the law seeks to prevent crime, not promote it, should the permissible use of self-defence be tightened?

5. Should a person's past history of abuse be considered in judging criminal responsibility? Should the fact that a person was sexually abused as a child be used to defend his or her actions as an adult?

 See the book-specific website at http://www.siegelcriminology3e.nelson.com for additional chapter links, discussions, and quizzes.

chapter

3

The Nature and Extent of Crime

How much crime is there? What are the patterns and trends in crime? Who commits crime? What is the nature of criminality? These are some of the most important questions in the study of criminology. Without such information, it would not be possible to formulate theories that explain the onset of crime or to devise social policies that facilitate its control or elimination. With knowledge, we have prediction and then control.

In this chapter, data collected on criminal offences are reviewed to provide a summary of crime patterns and trends. These topics are also discussed elsewhere in the book, particularly Chapters 11 to 14. This chapter addresses a number of questions: Are crime rates increasing? What factors influence crime rate trends? Where and when does crime take place? What are the social and individual patterns that affect the crime rate? What effect do social class, age, gender, and race have on the crime rate? Finally, the chapter reviews the concept of criminal careers and what available crime data can tell us about the onset, continuation, and termination of criminality.

The above questions address the issue of how to explain crime. However, the factors that *cause* criminal behaviour are different from those forces that affect what we *know* about crime. The causes of crime are discussed in more detail elsewhere, particularly Chapters 5 to 10. In terms of what we know about crime, it is important to state that a "crime rate" does more than reflect the simple increase or decrease of crime. Crime rates change for five reasons: (1) some crimes are **report-sensitive**, which means that the willingness of the public to report the crime determines whether we know about it; (2) **policing-sensitive** crimes reflect the level of police enforcement; (3) crimes are **definition-sensitive**, so a change in the law changes the rate; (4) **media-sensitive** crimes cause a "feedback loop" when they are publicized, changing the perceptions of the public and their willingness to report; and (5) of course, sometimes a real change occurs in the number of crimes in society, which leads us to ask what factors are responsible.

In this first section of the chapter, we will look at the official statistics on crime and consider what they do and do not tell us about crime. In the second section, we will look at such factors as age and class and briefly consider how they might be causes of crime.

The Uniform Crime Report

The Canadian Centre for Justice Statistics (CCJS) has collected information on crime reported by the police every year since 1962 through the **Uniform Crime Report (UCR)** survey. This aggregate count is based on reports from 420 different police forces across Canada and represents crimes substantiated through police investigation. It is an invaluable base from which to study crime in society. In 1984, the UCR was revised so that it could collect more detailed information, such as accused and victim characteristics (e.g., age, sex, alcohol and drug consumption, victim–offender relationship, and level of injury) and incident characteristics (e.g., location, time, secondary violations, and weapons). The revised version, the UCR2, gives the police and the public a more specific sense of how and why offences occur. The first police departments to collect and report **incident-based data** were the Niagara Regional and Fredericton police departments. In 2003, 122 police agencies supplied data to the UCR2 survey, representing 61 percent of the national volume of crime. As well as the two UCR surveys, the CCJS has collected detailed information on murder in the Homicide Survey since 1961.

Collecting the UCR

The methods used to compile the UCR are quite complex. Each month, police agencies report to the CCJS the **incidence** or number of crimes known to them. This official crime count is taken from all complaints of crime received from victims or from officers who discovered the infractions. This crime database represents only what the police know about crime, since some crimes are never detected and others are not reported to the police. Various checks are performed on the validity of the crime statistics before the results are made public.

Whenever complaints of crime are determined, through investigation, to be unfounded or false, they are eliminated from the count. The standard way to display the incidence of crime is to show all the crimes reported to the police that are felt to be **founded**—excluding false reports. This happens even if no one is arrested for the crime, or if stolen property is recovered, or if a prosecution is undertaken.

The UCR uses several terms to express crime data. First, the number of crimes reported to the police and arrests made are expressed as raw figures (for example, 548 murders occurred in 2003). Second, the **percentage change** in the amount of crime between years is computed (for example, reported crime increased 6 percent in 2003). The percentage change is important, because it is a soft indicator of whether society is becoming more dangerous. In 2003, the property crime rate increased 4 percent, the first substantial increase since 1991. The violent crime rate dropped 1 percent, with all violent crime categories recording declines except robbery (+5 percent) and attempted murder (+4 percent).

The third, and perhaps most important, way of expressing crime data is the crime rate per 100 000 people. Calculating the **crime rate** involves dividing the total crimes by the population, which enables changes in the population to be ignored when looking at changes

TABLE 3.1	Incidence, Rate, and Clearance Status of Selected Crimes, Canada, 2003			
	Actual	**Rate**	**% change**	**Clearance (%)**
CRIMES OF VIOLENCE	**304 515**	**963**	**−0.7**	**70**
Homicide	548	2	−6.6	74
Sexual assault	23 425	74	−5.2	61
Nonsexual assault	236 103	746	−0.7	75
Abduction	560	2	−8.2	50
Robbery	28 332	90	5.4	35
PROPERTY CRIME	**1 303 569**	**4 121**	**3.7**	**20**
Break and enter	284 496	899	2.4	15
Motor vehicle theft	171 017	541	4.7	11
Theft over $5000	20 124	64	0.7	17
Theft $5000 and under	702 317	2 220	4.4	18
Fraud	92 838	294	0.3	44
OTHER CRIMES	**964 159**	**3 048**	**10.3**	**38**
Prostitution	5 658	18	−2.8	79
Arson	13 851	44	4.6	16
Offensive weapons	16 940	54	5.4	71
TOTAL *CRIMINAL CODE* (excluding traffick)	**2 572 243**	**8 132**	**5.5**	**33**
DRUGS	**85 953**	**272**	**−8.1**	**76**
TOTAL INCIDENTS	**2 810 236**	**8 885**	**4.4**	**36**

Canada's population in 2003 was 31 629 677.

Source: Adapted from the Statistics Canada publication "Crime Statistics in Canada," 2003, *Juristat*, Catalogue 85-002, vol. 24, no. 6, July 28, 2004.

in crime. For example, when the UCR indicates that the murder rate was 1.7 in 2003, it means that about 2 people in every 100 000 were murdered between January 1 and December 31 in 2003. Out of a population of 31.6 million people, 548 murders occurred. Therefore, the likelihood of a person being murdered is very low in Canada. The formula would look like this:

$$\text{crimes/population} \times 100\,000 = \text{rate}$$

548 homicides/31.6 million population $\times$ 100 000 = 1.7

The result is a measure not weighted by the relative population. For example, Ontario had 178 murders in 2003, while Prince Edward Island had 1. However, Ontario also had a far greater population base than did Prince Edward Island, skewing the absolute number of crimes. When the population is factored in, Prince Edward Island's murder rate is 0.7, and Ontario's is 1.5.

Table 3.1 shows information about selected crimes in Canada. It's apparent that the incidence of violent crime is low compared with the amount of property crime committed in Canada. In 2003 there were 2 572 243 total *Criminal Code* offences in Canada (including traffic), 304 515 of which were violent crimes (12 percent). Property crime, however, accounted for 1 303 569 offences or 51 percent of all offences. "Other" *Criminal Code* offences, such as prostitution and gaming, accounted for almost one million more offences (37 percent).

Historically, crime rates have increased moving from east to west across Canada. However, in recent years, the pattern has begun to change. Crimes rates in the Atlantic provinces are now surpassing those in Ontario and Quebec (see Figure 3.1). Little attempt has been made to measure this phenomenon. Hartnagel suggests that provinces and territories with a high rate of

---

| Figure 3.1 | Crime Rates by Province and Territory, 2003 |

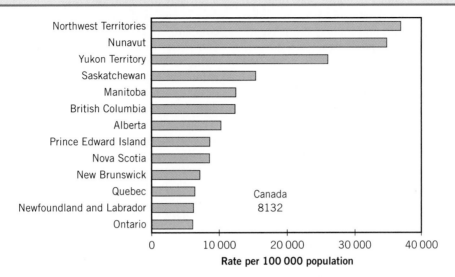

Source: Adapted from Statistics Canada, "Crime Statistics," *The Daily*, Catalogue 11-001, Wednesday, July 28, 2004, http://www.statcan.ca/Daily/English/040728/d040728a.htm (accessed May 10, 2005).

---

in-migration have higher rates of property and violent crime because geographic mobility produces weakened informal social control.[1] Large-scale changes in the economy combined with a rapid change in population are destabilizing.

In addition, police agencies report the total number of crimes that were **cleared**, which does not mean that a person was cleared of suspicion. Crimes are cleared in two ways: (1) when at least one person is arrested, charged, and turned over to the court for prosecution, or (2) when some element beyond police control precludes the physical arrest of an offender (exceptional means), such as when a suspect dies or leaves the country. A case can be "cleared otherwise" even if no charge is laid, as in the case of a young offender diverted to an alternative measures program.

The clearance rate for homicide was 74 percent in 2003, while theft under $5000 was cleared 18 percent of the time. The lowest clearance rates were theft from cars at 4 percent and bike theft at 5 percent. If 70 percent of violent offences and 20 percent of property violations were cleared, that means 30 percent of violent crime and 80 percent of property violations go uncleared.

As we proceed through the system, the number of cases being dealt with gradually drops. This process is called **attrition**, or a **crime funnel**, illustrating how the number of crimes punished by the criminal justice system is lower than that committed or reported. Of all crimes committed, only 37 percent were reported in 1999 (the last time the victimization survey was conducted). The clearance rate was 73 percent for violent crimes, 27 percent for property crimes, and 47 percent

for "other," giving a 37 percent clearance rate overall. In other words, out of a hundred crimes, 37 were reported, and 14 were solved. Fifteen percent of all cases reported to the police result in a conviction, and 4 percent receive a custodial sentence. Violent crimes are more likely to be solved than are property crimes, because police devote more resources to these more serious acts and because witnesses and the victim are available to identify offenders since usually the victim and offender are previously acquainted.

The Accuracy of the UCR

Despite the importance and wide use by criminologists of the UCR, its accuracy has limitations. We'll address the five main areas of concern: reporting practices, law enforcement practices, legal definitions, media practices, and methodological problems.

Reporting Practices. Many serious crimes are not reported to police by victims and do not become part of the UCR, which means that many crimes are report-sensitive. The reasons for not reporting vary. Some people do not have property insurance and therefore believe it is useless to report theft-related crimes. In other cases, the victim may fear reprisals from the offender's friends or family. In some cases people simply want to deal with it their way, whether that means forgetting it or getting revenge. The increase in levels of violence reported by women in recent years is probably due to an increase in the reporting of sexual assault and domestic violence. The likelihood of victims reporting crime to the police also varies by crime. Between 1982 and 1991, the sexual assault rate more than doubled, compared with the rate for assault (63 percent), other violent offences (32 percent), and robbery (10 percent).

Because of the difficulties posed by underreporting, victimization surveys are used to measure the number of crimes not reported to the police. The 1993 General Social Survey showed that crime reports ranged from a low of 10 percent for sexual assault to a high of 68 percent for attempted break and enter. The average report rate for all household offences was 42 percent. The 1999 GSS (the most recent one available) estimated that 78 percent of sexual assaults and 67 percent of household thefts were not reported. The report rate overall declined to 37 percent.[2] The reasons given for not reporting crime included the victim believing the incident was "a private matter," that "nothing could be done," that the "victimization was not important enough," or that the offender would seek revenge.[3] Thus, UCR data significantly underrepresent the total number of annual criminal events.

Victimization surveys, also discussed later in this chapter, are now used in many countries to complement UCR data. The 2000 British Crime Survey (BCS) showed that four and a half as many crimes were reported by victims in the survey as were reported to police.[4] The 2000 Scottish Crime Survey showed a survey report rate three times the official police crime rate. The United States uses the National Crime Victimization Survey to supplement its UCR data.

Connections

Victimization surveys are covered in more detail in Chapter 4. They have become a vitally important way of measuring the "dark figure" of crime—crime not reported to police and thus not included in statistics.

Law Enforcement Practices. The way in which police departments enforce and record criminal and delinquent activity also affects the validity of UCR statistics. This means that some crimes are police-sensitive. This effect was recognized more than 40 years ago, when researchers found that the number of burglaries in New York City rose from 2726 in 1948 to 42 491 in 1952. The increase was related to the change to a centralized crime reporting system.[5] Now, to correct possible mistakes in UCR reporting, the CCJS does extensive checks on the data it receives.

It might be appealing to try to improve a police department's public image by lowering the crime rate. Research published in 1983 found there were provincial and territorial differences in charge rates because of discretion on the part of the police.[6] However, this was probably more of a problem in the past than today.

Ironically, boosting police efficiency and professionalism may also increase crime rates. Higher crime rates may occur as departments adopt more sophisticated computer-aided technology and hire better-educated and better-trained employees. One study found that crime rates are significantly affected by the way law enforcement agencies process UCR data. As the number of unsworn (civilian) police employees assigned to dispatching, record keeping, and criminal incident reporting increased, so too did national crime rates. What appears to be a rising crime rate may be an artifact of improved police record-keeping ability.[7] How law enforcement agencies interpret the definitions of crimes also affects crime rates. Some departments may define crimes loosely—for example, not reporting a trespass as a burglary, while others pay strict attention to guidelines. These reporting practices may help explain interjurisdictional differences in crime.[8]

In the past, arson has been seriously underreported in the United States because many fire departments didn't report to the Federal Bureau of Investigation, and those that did defined as accidental or spontaneous many fires that were probably set by arsonists.[9] In a more contemporary example, the introduction of the National Crime Recording Standard (NCRS) created changes in police recording practices and inflated the numbers of crimes in the British Crime Survey. In 2003, the CCJS noted that when the Toronto police implemented a new records management system, the transition had an effect on data quality. In addition, a discrepancy in methodology applied by forces using the Ontario Municipal and Provincial Police Automation Cooperative (OMPPAC) data system was detected in 2002, and 2001 data had to be revised.

In addition, the way in which police enforce the law affects the crime rate. Such crimes as prostitution, drug crime, traffic offences, and crime on the Internet are sensitive to the resources police devote to detecting the crime. Clearly, if the police go undercover, they will be able to arrest far more prostitutes, johns, and pimps than if they wait for someone to report the crime to them. Similarly, there were only 25 convictions for cannabis possession in Canada between 1930 and 1946. In 1962, there were 20 cases; in 1968, there were 2300 cases; and in 1972, there were 12 000 cases. Part of this explosion of cannabis possession charges was an increased interest in its use, but police enforcement was relevant as well.

It is difficult to know for certain how important variations in police charging practices are.[10] Although the police have a lot of discretion in deciding whether to lay charges, the Crown, screening agencies, and alternative measures programs also affect the laying of charges in different jurisdictions. The development of zero-tolerance school violence policies has influenced the number of youths charged with nonsexual assault. This crime accounted for 73 percent of all youth violent offences in 2000 and 80 percent in 2003.

Figure 3.2	Arson Incidents 1978 to 1993

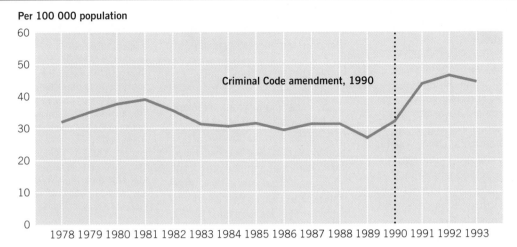

Per 100 000 population

Criminal Code amendment, 1990

1978 1979 1980 1981 1982 1983 1984 1985 1986 1987 1988 1989 1990 1991 1992 1993

Source: Adapted from Statistics Canada, *Canadian Crime Statistics, 1993* (Catalogue No. 85-205), p. 50.

Legal Definitions. Changes to the law also affect crime rates. For example, amendments to the *Criminal Code* in 1990 broadened the definition of arson to include mischief fires. Given that the cause was "unknown" in almost half of fires with losses of more than $500 000, what counts as a suspicious fire has some latitude. The result was an increase in arson statistics.[11] As Figure 3.2 shows, arson varied from approximately 30 to 40 incidents per 100 000 population from 1978 to 1990, except for a slight dip in 1989. Then it suddenly increased by 17 percent between 1989 and 1990 because of a change in the definition of arson.

An arsonist is not always a lone pyromaniac who likes to watch fires; some fires are set to collect insurance money, while others are set for revenge. Sometimes in the case of insurance fraud, arson is difficult to investigate because of a high public tolerance for the crime.

An even more dramatic example of a definition-sensitive crime is sexual assault. Before 1983, a man could not be charged for sexually assaulting his wife; however, changes made to increase reporting also increased the number of men charged with the crime. Canada's sexual assault legislation was amended in 1988 to better deal with child sexual abuse and in 1991 to include the concept of consent.

Other legislative changes that have affected criminal justice statistics are the *Young Offenders Act* (1984); *Dangerous and Impaired Operation* (1985), which allowed the police to take breath and blood samples; *Property Value Limits* (1985, 1995); and Bill C-68 (1997), which requires firearm owners to be licensed and to register their guns. We could also look at new terrorism and organized crime laws, hate crime laws, and juvenile crime legislation.

InfoTrac®

One method of reducing gun violence may be to make guns safer. Read more about this plan in Krista D. Robinson, Stephen P. Teret, Susan DeFrancesco, and Stephen W. Hargarten, "Making Guns Safer," *Issues in Science and Technology* 14, no. 4 (1998): 37–41.

Media Practices. An additional factor to consider when looking at crime is the effect of the media. We often hear of random crimes, committed in public by strangers against innocent victims, which encourages the perception that crime is random. A good example is shown in the Crime in the News feature. Distorted media coverage sensitizes the public to fear crime, which then is transformed into police enforcement or legislative changes.

For example, the concern over youth crime shows that the public is being overexposed to a relatively infrequent type of crime. Between 1996 and 2002, 7 percent of those charged with violent offences in Canada were youths and this rate was consistent. However, there is a feeling that youth crime is out of control and that "something must be done about it." In 2003, the rate of youths charged by the police dropped 15 percent, but there was an overall increase of 5 percent in the youth crime rate. The 30 percent increase in the rate of youths cleared otherwise is attributable in part to increased reporting by police of youths not formally charged, because of the new provisions of the *Youth Criminal Justice Act* (YCJA).

Crime in the News

Man Gets 10 Years for Attack

A man has been sentenced to 10 years in prison for attacking a bank machine user with a sledgehammer. Trevor Stang, 32, was found guilty of aggravated assault after Jaafar Omar was hit over the head three times with a two-kilogram sledgehammer while trying to pay a gas bill at an automated teller. Stang then fled with $30 and Mr. Omar's car.

"Mr. Omar could've been anyone," said Justice Denis Hart. "Random violence . . . strikes at the heart of a civilized society. Everyone is a potential victim, no one is immune."

Later that night, Stang attacked Tara McDonald while she was working alone in a Subway sandwich shop. She too was hit with a hammer, and she died from her injuries. Stang ran off with the cash register, which contained less than $50. He was later caught, tried, and convicted of first-degree murder. He is serving a life sentence.

Sources: *The National Post,* May 12, 2001; Kevin Martin, "Employees Placed at Risk," *Calgary Sun,* February 10, 2005, http://www.canoe .ca/NewsStand/Columnists/Calgary/Kevi n_Martin/2005/02/10/925826.html (accessed May 11, 2005); Peter Smith, "Mom's Breathing Easier," *Calgary Sun,* March 9, 2000, http://www.canoe .ca/CNEWSLaw0003/09_safe.html (accessed May 11, 2005).

Youth courts in Canada have heard fewer cases in recent years. Total cases processed in youth court dropped 20 percent between 1991 and 2003. The most common crimes heard in youth court were theft of goods under $5000 and assault. Murder accounted for less than 1 percent of the cases heard in youth court.[12]

One way to explain the discrepancy between the reality of dropping rates of youth crime and the perception that youth crime is out of control is media coverage. The media may distort the frequency of youth crime, causing unease on the part of the public.

For example, as shown in Table 3.2, violent youth crime is overrepresented in the media, while youth property crime is underrepresented. The public gets the message that violent youth crime is a large problem. This message distorts perception, which in turn affects the reported rates of youth crime and the public's willingness to press charges, eventually resulting in pressure on politicians to change the law. Figure 3.3 begins to map out this relationship.

The CCJS *Juristat* series is an important source of data for the media, and the series presents complex information in a way that makes it appealing for the media to report without misrepresenting the facts.[13] The creation of UCR statistics in the United States in the 1920s was as much about providing journalists with information about crime as it was about measuring police workload.[14] Today, the media influence the timing and wording of press releases, the type of statistics used, and the types of information presented. The CCJS, the police, and the government employ "information officers" who will provide the media with stories, as it is often beyond the scope of a reporter's ability to question the production of statistical knowledge.[15]

TABLE 3.2   Comparing Young Offenders in the Courts and the News, 1993–1994

	Ontario Youth Court		Toronto News	
Violent crime	11 004	(22%)	106	(94%)
Property crime	25 008	(50%)	6	(5%)
Other	8 942	(18%)	1	(1%)
YOA*	3 622	(7%)	—	
Total	50 008	(100%)	113	(100%)

Source: Jane B. Sprott, "Understanding Public Views of Crime and the Youth Justice System," *Canadian Journal of Criminology* (July 1996): 271–90. Reproduced by permission of the *Canadian Journal of Criminology and Criminal Justice.* Copyright by the Canadian Criminal Justice Association.

Note: Numbers may not add up to 100 percent because of missing categories.

*Statutory breaches of the *Young Offenders Act*

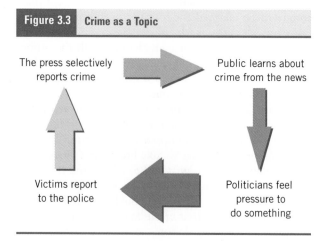

Figure 3.3   Crime as a Topic

The press selectively reports crime → Public learns about crime from the news → Politicians feel pressure to do something → Victims report to the police → The press selectively reports crime

Methodological Problems. Methodological issues also raise questions about the accuracy of the UCR. Among the most often cited are the following:

- The definition of a crime can change.
- Nonviolent crimes are underreported.
- Cases are screened as unfounded and founded.
- The notation "cleared by charge" may not be made in the month the offence was committed.
- Reports can sometimes vary in accuracy and completeness.
- If an offender commits multiple crimes, only the most serious is recorded.
- Each act is listed as a single offence for some crimes but not for others.[16]

What does the future hold for the UCR? The changes made in the form of the Revised UCR will enable better analysis of incidents and the characteristics of accused persons and their relationships to victims.

Self-Report Surveys

The limits of official statistics have led criminologists to seek alternative sources of information to measure crime patterns. As well, since official statistics don't record the personality, attitudes, and behaviour of individual criminals, and underreport such victimless crimes as substance abuse, criminologists have used **self-report surveys** to supplement and expand official data.

Self-report studies ask participants to reveal information about their law violations. For example, the criminologist can interview people who have been arrested or imprisoned. Subjects can also be telephoned at home or mailed a survey form. Most often, anonymous self-report surveys are administered to large groups through questionnaires. Self-reports are viewed as another mechanism to get at the "dark figures of crime," the figures missed by official statistics.

The Focus of Self-Reports

Most self-report studies have focused on juvenile delinquency and youth crime.[17] First, the school setting makes it convenient to test thousands of subjects simultaneously, all of them with the means (pens, desks, time) to respond to a research questionnaire. Second, since school attendance is universal, a school-based self-report survey is an estimate of the activities of a cross-section of the community. Self-reports, though, are not restricted to youth crime and have been used to examine the offence histories of prison inmates, drug users, and other groups.

Self-reports can assess the number and frequency of people who have committed illegal acts. They are particularly useful for assessing substance abuse, as most drug use goes undetected by police. Because most surveys also contain items measuring subjects' attitudes, values, personal characteristics, and behaviours, the data obtained from them can be used to test theories, measure attitudes toward crime, and measure the association between crime and family relations, educational attainment, and income.

Self-reports provide a broader picture of the distribution of criminality than do official data, because self-reports can estimate the number of criminal offenders unknown to police, some of whom may even be serious or chronic offenders.[18] Self-reports also allow for evaluation of the distribution of criminal behaviour across racial, class, and gender lines, to determine whether official arrest data are truly representative of the offender population or whether they reflect bias, discrimination, and selective enforcement. For example, racial bias may be present if surveys indicate that Black and White people report equal amounts of crime, but the official data indicate that minorities are arrested more often than Whites.

In sum, self-reports can provide a significant amount of information about offenders that cannot be found in the official statistics. However, self-reports are not used very often.[19] A few important self-reports have recently released their results. A 1999 study surveyed 2001 students aged 12 to 18 from 67 Alberta public and Catholic junior and senior high schools. Participants completed a questionnaire about their perceptions of youth crime, violence, and personal safety; victimization at school and away from school; the extent to which they had engaged in delinquent behaviour; weapons possession at school; and their perceptions of and contact with the police and the criminal justice system. Another study, released in 2002, by Tanner and Wortley, surveyed 3400 high-school students and 400 street youth in Toronto on issues ranging from experiences of victimization and perception of the city's youth crime problem to participation in gangs.

The Centre for Addiction and Mental Health and the University of Montreal released the first national survey of alcohol and other drug use on university campuses, the Canadian Campus Survey (CCS), in 2000. The survey collected responses from 7800 undergraduate students in 16 Canadian universities. Heavy drinking was extensive, and 47 percent of students reported using cannabis at some point in their lives. Ten percent of students had used other illicit drugs during the previous year. This type of study demonstrates the value of self-report studies, where the behaviour in question is unlikely to be reported to the police and for which there is no victim in the traditional sense. Various other drug use surveys done in Canada include those done by the Addiction Research Foundation and the Canadian Centre on Substance Abuse.

The 2002 Canadian Community Health Survey reported that three million people used marijuana or hashish at least once in the previous year. Seven percent reported using cannabis in 1989 and 12 percent in 2002. Although half said they used it only once a month, 10 percent reported they used it on a weekly basis, and 10 percent said they used it daily. The survey also collected data on the use of cocaine or crack, ecstasy, lysergic acid diethylamide (LSD), other hallucinogens, amphetamines (speed), and heroin. About 2 percent of people aged 15 or older reported using at least one of these drugs in the past year, up from 1 percent in 1994.

The Accuracy of Self-Reports

Though self-report data are useful, there are some methodological issues about their accuracy. People will not candidly admit illegal acts. They have nothing to gain, and the ones taking the greatest risk are the respondents with official records who may be engaging in the most criminality. Conversely, some people may exaggerate their criminal acts, may forget the acts, or be confused about what is being asked. Most surveys contain questions on trivial offences—skipping school, running away, using a fake ID—lumped together with serious crimes, making it difficult to compare the groups. We cannot be certain how valid self-report studies are because we have nothing reliable to measure them against. Correlation with official reports is low, because the inadequacies of those reports were largely responsible for the development of self-reports in the first place. Official statistics can show a declining youth crime rate, while self-report and survey data show the opposite.[20]

Various techniques have been used to verify self-report data.[21] The "known group" method compares incarcerated youths with "normal" groups to see whether the former report more delinquency. Another approach uses peer informants to verify a subject's answers. Another approach is to ask youths whether they have ever been arrested or convicted of a delinquent act and then check the official record against their responses. Studies using this method have found a remarkable uniformity between self-reported answers and the official record. The conclusions are that (1) the problems of accuracy in self-reports are surmountable, (2) self-reports are more accurate than most criminologists believe, and (3) self-reports and official statistics are quite compatible.[22]

Connections

Criminologists suspect that a few repeat juvenile offenders are responsible for a disproportionate share of serious adult crime. Results would be skewed if even a few of these chronic offenders were absent or refused to participate in a schoolwide self-report survey. For more on chronic offenders, see the discussion in this chapter.

The "Missing Cases" Issue

Although these findings are encouraging, questions remain about the validity of self-reports. Even if 90 percent of a school population voluntarily participate in a self-report study, researchers don't know whether the few who refuse to participate or who are absent that day make up a significant portion of the school's population of persistent high-rate offenders. School surveys also fail to count incarcerated youth and dropouts, whose numbers may include some of the most serious offenders. Some research suggests that the "missing cases" in self-reports may be more crime-prone than the general population.[23]

Self-reports are weakest in measuring substance abuse.[24] Drug users may significantly underreport the frequency of their substance abuse. Gray and Wish surveyed a group of juvenile detainees and also tested them with urinalysis. They found that less than one-third of the kids who tested positive for marijuana also reported using it, while only 15 percent of those testing positive for cocaine admitted to having used it during the previous month. Although this research involves a sample of incarcerated youth who might be expected to underreport drug use, the findings illustrate another problem of self-report surveys.[25]

Self-reports are a widely used measure of criminal behaviour, but their accuracy is limited in determining the behaviour of chronic offenders and persistent drug abusers.

Connections

Self-report data are used as the standard measure of the nation's youth drug population. When reading the results of national drug use surveys in Chapter 14, keep in mind this research on the validity of self-report surveys. Are heavy crack cocaine users likely to respond accurately to a self-report survey?

Victim Surveys

After the UCR and self-report surveys, a third source of crime data is surveys that ask people whether they have been victims of crime. Because many victims do not report their experiences to the police, such surveys are another method of getting at the dark figures of crime.

In Canada, telephone surveys are conducted to ask residents questions about whether they have experienced crimes such as sexual assault, robbery, assault, break and enter, motor vehicle theft, household property theft, personal theft, and vandalism. They also examine the victim's experience of crime, the reasons victims decide not to report crimes to the police, and victims' perception of crime overall. It is through such surveys that we find that many crimes are not reported to the police.

The first national survey in the United States was conducted in 1966. It indicated that the number of criminal victimizations was far higher than previously believed and that many victims failed to report crime to the police, fearing retaliation or official indifference. These results prompted the National Crime Victimization Survey (NCVS) in 1973. In Canada, the first national study of violence against women was conducted in 1993. Now, international comparisons can be made with the International Criminal Victimization Survey and the World Crime Surveys, both under the auspices of the United Nations.

Surveys on criminal victimization were conducted as part of the GSS in 1988, 1993, and 1999. The most recent survey involved telephone interviews with approximately 26 000 people. All respondents were asked about their experiences with criminal victimization and their opinions on a variety of justice-related topics. These topics included their fear of crime and their perceptions about the performance of the police, criminal courts, and prison and parole systems.

Like the UCR and self-report surveys, victimization surveys may suffer from some methodological problems, so their findings must be interpreted with caution. Among the potential problems are the following:

- Overreporting owing to victims' misinterpretation of events. For example, a lost wallet is reported as stolen, or an open door is viewed as a burglary attempt.
- "Telescoping" events from the past, in which victims think that events happened more recently than they really did.
- Underreporting owing to embarrassment of reporting crime to interviewers, fear of getting in trouble, or simply forgetting an incident.
- Inability to record the personal criminal activity of those interviewed, such as drug use or gambling; murder is also not included, for obvious reasons.
- Sampling errors that produce a group of respondents who are not representative of the population.
- Inadequate question format that invalidates responses. Some groups such as adolescents may be particularly susceptible to error because of question format.[26]

In 1993 the GSS was much improved from that of 1988. For example, in 1993 the word "rape" was left off the list of examples of an attack, and questions were asked instead about forced sexual activity. The change in wording resulted in far more sexual assaults being reported in the 1993 survey.

Connections

Not only do victim surveys provide indications of criminal incidents, but they can also describe the individuals who are most at risk for being hurt by crime and where and when they are most likely to become victimized. Data from crime surveys are used in Chapter 4 to draw a portrait of the nature and extent of victimization in Canada.

Are Crime Statistics Sources Compatible?

Are the various sources of criminal statistics compatible? Each has its own strengths and weaknesses, and although they are difficult to compare, they are complementary.

The UCR is carefully tallied and contains data on an extensive list of crimes, yet it omits the many crimes that victims choose not to report to the police. The GSS does contain unreported crime and important information on the personal characteristics of victims, but it relies on personal recollections that may be inaccurate. Self-report surveys can provide information on the personal characteristics of offenders—their attitudes, values, beliefs, and psychological profile—that is unavailable from any other source. Yet, at their core, self-reports rely on the honesty of criminal offenders and drug users, a population not generally known for accuracy and integrity.

Some criminologists believe that the data sources are more compatible than was first believed possible. Although their tallies of crimes are different, the crime patterns and trends they record are often quite similar.[27] For example, all three sources are in general agreement about the personal characteristics of serious criminals (such as age and gender) and where and when crime occurs (such as urban areas, night time, and summer months).

Other criminologists say that the data sources measure separate concepts (for example, reported crimes, actual crimes, and victimization rates). This debate underlines the fact that gathering information about crime and interpreting it is often problematic. Because each source of data uses a different method to obtain results, differences will inevitably occur among them. These differences must be carefully considered when interpreting the data on the nature of and trends in crime.[28]

The following section considers different ways of displaying information about crime, to expand the idea that there are alternative sources of information than official crime statistics.

Alternative Sources of Information

Commissions of Inquiry. So far, three major sources of crime data have been discussed: police reports, self-reports, and victim surveys. Other sources of information exist, which are often overlooked in criminological inquiry but are very useful.

The commission of inquiry is unparalleled in its richness as a resource. Some notable examples are the Commission on Systemic Racism in the Ontario Criminal Justice System,[29] the Royal Commission on the Wrongful Incarceration of Donald Marshall Jr. in Nova Scotia,[30] the Report of the Task Force on the Criminal Justice System and Its Impact on the Indian and Métis People of Alberta,[31] the Report of the Aboriginal Justice Inquiry (1991), the Report of the Saskatchewan Indian Justice Review Committee,[32] and the Report of the Commission of Inquiry into the Shooting Death of Leo Lachance.[33] Others include the Cohen Commission on hate crime, the Arbour Commission on the closing of the Kingston Prison for Women, the inquiry into the federal sponsorship program, the Miller Inquiry into Kingsclear, and the announced RCMP inquiry on the same.

Commissions of inquiry are appointed by provincial, territorial, or federal governments. They are quasi-judicial, which means they have broad-ranging powers of investigation similar to a court's. They cannot establish individual criminal liability, but they have a broader mandate than a court trial. The information revealed in a commission of inquiry might have been undiscovered or not investigated by the police. Similarly, it might not have been disclosed to victims or publicized in the media.

The commissions of inquiry mentioned above add significantly to our knowledge of the treatment of Natives and ethnic minorities in the criminal justice system. Inquiries have contributed to our knowledge of institutional child abuse, for example, in the Mount Cashel Orphanage Inquiry.[34] The children in the orphanage, run by the Irish Christian Brothers, were wards of the welfare system and were subject to extreme physical and sexual abuse. Even though the police investigated in 1975, charges were not laid, under the direction of the minister of justice.

In Nova Scotia, Chief Justice Stratton of New Brunswick was appointed by the minister of justice to hold an investigation into sexual and physical abuse at various provincial schools and training centres. The inquiry found "a conspiracy of silence and inaction," as those in positions of trust "turned a blind eye and deaf ears and . . . chose not to implicate themselves or their co-workers."[35]

Many other commissions of inquiry could be mentioned, from the inquiry into tainted blood to the Dubin inquiry on drug doping in professional sports. They are a fertile source of information on crime that might not be brought to light in any other way.

Crisis Index for Justice. Another interesting attempt to measure the rate and impact of crime was the report released by the Mennonite Central Committee in Winnipeg, Manitoba, in 1997.[36] The report is critical of a system that "responds to crime primarily by punishing offenders, yet virtually ignores the victims and communities hurt by crime," and it argues that simply

increasing the amount of money spent on corrections has had little effect on the crime rate. The crime index is based on four measurable areas of criminal justice: the crime rate, the incarceration rate, spending on prisons, and spending allocated to community corrections. Community corrections includes electronic monitoring, probation, services for victims and offenders, and alternative justice approaches. Research has found that such approaches improve rehabilitation and reintegration, and cost less in the bargain.

By ranking the provinces and territories in relation to one another, the report maps the relative degree of crisis. Saskatchewan, with a crime rate similar to Nova Scotia's, spends 147 percent more on corrections and has a 94 percent higher rate of imprisonment. With the second-highest incarceration rate among developed Western nations, Canada annually spends four times more per prisoner than it does per university student! Prison accounts for 85 percent of the corrections budget in Ontario, 15 percent higher than in Nova Scotia. Conversely, Nova Scotia spends 24 percent of its corrections budget on community corrections, while Ontario spends half that, at 12 percent.

Official Crime Trends in Canada

Criminologists use official statistics to determine changes in the crime rate. Figure 3.4 shows the trend going back to 1962. Since 1991, the crime rate decreased from 1 percent to 5 percent per year until 2003, which saw an

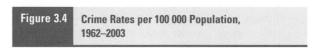

| Figure 3.4 | Crime Rates per 100 000 Population, 1962–2003 |

Rate per 100 000 population

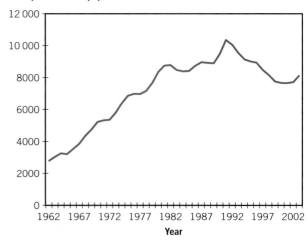

Source: Statistics Canada, "Crime Statistics," *The Daily,* July 28, 2004, http://www.statcan.ca/Daily/English/040728/d040728a.htm (accessed May 10, 2005).

Famous Canadian Criminals

A Man Who Abused Boys

FOR IMMEDIATE RELEASE
Edmonton Police Department
August 2, 2001
PUBLIC INFORMATION AND
WARNING

In the interest of public safety, the Edmonton Police Service is issuing the following warning:

Karl Richard TOFT will be released from the Bowden Institution on Friday, August 3, 2001, after serving a sentence for numerous convictions for sexual assault, buggery and indecent assault. TOFT has received some Sex Offender treatment, however, he is still considered to be a risk of significant harm and a high-risk Sex Offender.

His criminal convictions date back to 1992 for numerous sexual offences perpetrated against male children aged 12 to 17 years of age, over an 18–20 year period. The Edmonton Police Service acknowledges that while Karl TOFT has received some Sex Offender Programming, and indications are that he has a desire to seek further treatment, at this time the EPS still has serious concerns about his

Karl Toft was employed as a guard at the New Brunswick Kingsclear Youth Training School. By his own admission he abused more than 200 boys under his care. He was convicted of 34 charges of sexual assault against 18 boys at his trial in 1992. He certainly ranks as one of the most notorious pedophiles in Canadian history.

Karl Toft's crimes became known to the authorities in 1984, but he was not investigated by the police until 1990. The RCMP then concluded that they would not pursue charges. In 1991 he was finally arrested and charged by the Fredericton city police. A commission of inquiry (the Miller Inquiry, 1995) heard testimony from 157 witnesses. During the three decades that Toft served as a guard, he had access to children, whom he exploited. A provincial compensation report says there could be as many as 1400 offences in total. It is alleged by some, and recorded in the inquiry's report, that some provincial officials who knew of the abuse did nothing about it.

Toft was released from Bowden Institution in August 2001. He had served two-thirds of a 13-year sentence and was due for statutory release. When it was announced he was to be released to a halfway house, Edmonton police issued a public alert that listed his convictions, his participation in a sex offender program, a physical description, and a photo. Public protests ensued and Toft was sent to a psychiatric hospital instead. There were also concerns for his safety, as his life was threatened by a former inmate. However, in a poll on August 28, 2001, 61 percent of those surveyed felt that Toft's personal safety should not be a reason to keep him in prison.

In 2004, the RCMP public complaints commission announced that it would conduct an inquiry into complaints concerning the RCMP investigation, following renewed allegations of criminal conduct by Kingsclear staff and RCMP Staff Sergeant Clifford McCann. The inquiry will also investigate whether the RCMP tried to cover up the alleged criminal conduct.

continued high risk to the community.

The Edmonton Police Service is issuing this information and warning after careful deliberation

and consideration of all related issues, including privacy concerns, in the belief that it is clearly in the public interest to inform the members of the community about Karl Richard TOFT.

The Edmonton Police Service believes that his presence on the street poses a risk of significant harm to the health or safety of the public.

Members of the public are advised that the intent of this process is to enable citizens to take suitable precautionary measures. Releasing this information is NOT intended to encourage people to

engage in any form of vigilante action.

Note: This information is released under the authority of the *Freedom of Information and Protection of Privacy Act*, S.A. 1994 c. F–18.5

increase of 6 percent, the first substantial increase in more than a decade.[37] Some have argued that the drop in crime is a result of an increase in private security and new crime prevention measures, such as proactive community policing.[38] However, there are probably other reasons as well.

Explaining Crime Trends

What factors produce increases or decreases in the crime rate? How can the recent decline in the violence rate be explained? A number of critical factors have been used to explain crime rate trends. Given the shift in crime rates happening in many countries, as Table 3.3 indicates, a few of the most important are discussed here.

Age. The age distribution of the population has a great influence on violent crime trends. As a general rule, the crime rate follows the proportion of young males in the population. The postwar baby-boom generation reached their teenage years in the 1960s, when the crime rate began a sharp increase. Since both the victims and the perpetrators of crime tend to fall into the 18- to 25-year age category, the rise in crime reflected the age structure of society. With the "greying" of society in the 1980s and a decline in the birth rate, it was not surprising that the overall crime rate stabilized between 1990 and 1995. Because the number of juveniles is likely to increase over the

next decade (baby-boom-echo babies), criminologists fear this will signal a return to escalating crime rates.[39]

Increases in youth crime are also influenced by bureaucratic processes. In some provinces and territories, a youth can be recommended for alternative measures only at the post-charge stage. Thus, trying to divert more youths from formal court processes might result in more charges being laid initially. In addition, the total number of cases is quite low, and any change calculated as a percentage will thus seem higher. In 2003, 17 551 youths were charged with break and enter, a shocking increase of 6.6 percent.[40] The overall rate of increase for break and enter was only 2.4 percent. However, 284 496 break and enters took place in Canada in 2003. The general impression is that youth crime, and especially that committed by young women, is increasing in seriousness.[41]

Race. There is also no simple relationship between race and crime (see the Culture, Gender, Ethnicity, and Criminology box). Any relationship that does exist is most likely a product of various factors, including lack of social opportunity, discrimination, and selective reporting and surveillance by the police. The Commission on Systemic Racism in the Ontario Criminal Justice System was established (1992) after Black youths rioted, angered by the killing of a young Black man by the police. The commission examined whether criminal justice practices, procedures, and policies reflected systemic racism. The inquiry found

TABLE 3.3   Crime Rates in Canada, the United States, and England and Wales

	1992	1993	1994	1995	1996	1997	1998	1999	2000	2001	2002	2003
	(year-to-year percentage change in rate)											
Canada	−3	−5	−4	−2	−2	−5	−4	−5	−1	+1	−0.6	+6
United States	−3	−2	−1	−1	−3	−4	−5	−3	−0.3	+2	−0.2	—
England/Wales	+5	−2	−5	−3	−2	−9	−8	−1	−0.2	−3	+2	−2

Sources: Canadian Crime Statistics collected by the Canadian Centre for Justice Statistics; Crime in England and Wales 2002/03, in *Home Office Statistical Bulletin*, July 2003.

that Blacks have a disproportionate chance of being charged and imprisoned in Ontario compared with Whites. When charged with drug trafficking, Blacks are 27 times more likely than are Whites to be held in pretrial detention and 20 times as likely to be imprisoned when found guilty. Blacks make up 3 percent of Ontario's population but 15 percent of the prison population. Defence counsel who represent racial minorities believe there were problems in the bail system and that police laid multiple charges on street-level addicts and drug dealers if they were from a minority.

Federal prison system statistics show that the percentage of the prison population that is Black is up to three times higher than the percentage of Blacks in the population. For instance, nationally, Blacks make up 7 percent of inmates, but in Ontario they are 14 percent of the inmate population.

When we compare American criminal justice statistics that include race with victimization surveys, the overrepresentation of Blacks diminishes. Although

 Culture, Gender, Ethnicity, and Criminology

The Politics of Statistics

In 1989, an inspector with the Metro Toronto Police Department said that Black people committed a disproportionate amount of the street crime in the Jane-Finch area. Although this area does have a high rate of crime, the fact that he linked it to an ethnic group provoked controversy. Similarly, in 1991, when a Metro Toronto police sergeant said that Vietnamese and Mainland Chinese immigrants committed a high percentage of the crime in the Asian community, he was publicly reprimanded. This was despite the fact that he himself was Chinese, and many people in the Chinese community supported him. In 1990 the CCJS had proposed including statistics on the race of suspects and victims in its crime reports. The idea was quickly abandoned in the face of political pressure. Is this a matter of political correctness?

The criminal justice system already collects statistics on identifiers, such as age and sex, that are beyond an individual's control. Furthermore, Correctional Services notes the race of an inmate on its admission forms. Such information is integral to an informed analysis of crime patterns and a criminal's treatment. Statistics on the proportion of Natives in the criminal justice system, for example, show the extreme overrepresentation of Natives in prison. In 1998–99, Aboriginals represented 3 percent of the general population in Canada but 15 percent of the offenders in federal custody. Such disparities can alert us to socioeconomic conditions on reserves and possible bias on the part of the justice system. The collection of these data shouldn't be abandoned just because it might be politically incorrect (Gabor 1994).

Statistics on race-related crime are routinely collected in the United States, where race is felt to be a strong predictor of criminal activity. The FBI reports that in 1999, 69 percent of those arrested were White and 29 percent were Black. As of 2000, the U.S. Census Bureau estimated that 93 percent of the American population was White, and 13 percent was Black. These statistics mean that Blacks are overrepresented in arrest statistics, while Whites are underrepresented relative to their proportion of the population. Blacks are more likely to be arrested for murder (52 percent), robbery (54 percent), and being in possession of stolen property (43 percent). However, they are less likely to be arrested for arson (24 percent), vandalism (22 percent), and driving under the influence (10 percent).

There are several reasons why the relationship between race and crime is underdeveloped in Canada (Hatt 1994; Johnston 1994; Wortley 1999). The first is found in the innate problem of crime statistics. Again, going back to the United States, 1986 FBI data indicate that 47 percent of violent crimes reported to the police were committed by Blacks. However, when we go to alternative sources of information, such as victim surveys, the ratio of crimes committed by Blacks goes down. The NCVS found that Blacks were responsible for 24 percent of violent crimes, about half the official rate. Moreover, self-report surveys found no relationship between ethnicity and crime (Roberts and Gabor 1990; Roberts 1994). One conclusion that can be drawn from these data is that people are more likely to report to the police those crimes committed by ethnic minorities.

The second reason is the inherent difficulty of measuring race. Ethnicity is not homogeneous. More than 10 million people identified themselves as being from multiple ethnic origins in the 1996 census, a full 35 percent of Canada's population. As Haggerty (2001) points out, there are real problems in categorizing ethnicity. Is ethnicity a matter of skin colour, country of origin, or self-identification?

The third reason that the relationship between race and crime is not studied more is the possibility that racial information will be used to justify racism. Wortley and Brownfield (1996) found that Blacks report a higher rate of stops and searches by police. In a survey of Black, Chinese, and White residents of Toronto, Blacks were most likely to describe experiences of discrimination (Wortley 1996).

Forty-three percent of Black males reported being stopped by the police, compared with 25 percent of Whites, and 19 percent of Chinese. Four out of 10 Black respondents reported that they were treated unfairly, compared with 15 percent of Chinese and 10 percent of Whites. Between 1986 and 1993, the number of Whites incarcerated for drug trafficking increased 151 percent, while the number of Blacks committed to detention increased 1164 percent (Wortley 1999). Research also shows that Blacks are less likely to be granted bail (Ontario 1995). The "racialization" of crime occurs when an ethnic group becomes identified with criminal activity. A Toronto survey (1995) found that 45 percent of people believed there was a relationship between ethnicity and crime. Furthermore, two-thirds of those people thought that Blacks committed more crime (Henry, Hastings, and Freer 1996).

In the early 1990s, after University of Western Ontario professor Phillippe Rushton published work relating race and crime (1987, 1988), a debate ensued in the *Canadian Journal of Criminology* (Roberts and Gabor 1990; Cernovsky and Litman 1993; Hatt 1994; Rushton 1994; Johnston 1994). Julian Roberts and Thomas Gabor of the University of Ottawa wrote that the overrepresentation of certain ethnic minorities in crime statistics was misleading and should not be construed as support for a genetic theory of crime (Roberts and Gabor 1990). Rushton had proposed a theory that Blacks were less intelligent and less law-abiding than Whites or Asians. Roberts and Gabor argued that there was a link between ethnicity and crime, but it was easily exaggerated and more

often misunderstood. Blacks are underrepresented in tax fraud and securities violations, and arrests for white-collar crimes are much higher for Whites.

This debate over race is not new. The practice of assigning a racial category to offenders has a long history. Cesare Beccaria, for example, used a racial typology of criminals as part of his explanation for criminality.

When plans were underway to develop the incident-based UCR2 crime survey in the late 1980s, it was recognized that there was the potential to significantly increase the amount of data available on crimes (Haggerty 2001). Specifically, it would be possible to trace links between crime and numerous contextual factors associated with the accused, including ethnicity. The Canadian police community was a strong advocate for introducing racial variables. Such data would make it possible to better control the criminality of certain ethnic groups, as well as reveal systemic racism within the criminal justice system. The common-sense demarcation of race chosen was European origin (White); South Asian; Black; East/Southeast Asian; Central and South American; and Aboriginal. By 1991, police forces were providing the centre with data on racial origin, but after objections were raised by the prime minister's office, the privacy commissioner of Canada, the media, and academics, the project was abandoned. One fear was that the police would assign criminals to ethnic groupings already perceived as being "criminogenic" and reinforce dominant stereotypes.

In fact, two commissions at the time advocated increasing the variety of statistics on the status of Aboriginals in the criminal justice system (Alberta 1991; Saskatchewan 1993). And other reports, including one on racism in the criminal justice system in Manitoba (Manitoba 1991), were damning in their conclusion that racism was systemic. The Commission of Inquiry that looked at the shooting of Leo Lachance (Saskatchewan 1993) concluded that a major obstacle in the investigation in the case was that racism was not seen to be an issue. The 1989 Royal Commission into the Wrongful Conviction of Donald Marshall Jr. was unequivocal in its finding that racism played a part in his miscarriage of justice (Nova Scotia 1989). So perhaps there are solid grounds for wanting to conduct research on the relationship among race, crime, and victimization.

Sources: Thomas Gabor, "The Suppression of Crime Statistics on Race and Ethnicity: The Price of Political Correctness," *Canadian Journal of Criminology* 36 (1994): 153–63; Ken Hatt, "Reservations about Race and Crime Statistics," *Canadian Journal of Criminology* 36 (1994): 164–66; J. Phillip Johnston, "Academic Approaches to Race–Crime Statistics Do Not Justify Their Collection," *Canadian Journal of Criminology* 36 (1994): 166–74; Scot Wortley, "A Northern Taboo: Research on Race, Crime, and Criminal Justice in Canada," *Canadian Journal of Criminology* 41 (1999): 261–75; Scot Wortley, "Justice for All? Race and Perceptions of Bias in the Ontario Criminal Justice System—A Toronto Survey," *Canadian Journal of Criminology* (October 1996): 439–67; Scot Wortley and David Brownfield, "The Usual Suspects: Race, Age, and Gender Differences in Involuntary Police Contact," 48th Annual Conference of the American Society of Criminology, Chicago, 1996; Julian V. Roberts, "Crime and Race Statistics: Toward a Canadian Solution," *Canadian Journal of Criminology* 36 (1994): 175–85; Julian V. Roberts and Thomas Gabor, "Lombrosian Wine in a New Bottle: Research on Crime and Race," *Canadian Journal of Criminology* 32 (1990): 291–313; J. Phillippe Rushton, "Population Differences in Rule-Following Behaviour: Race, Evolution and Crime," presented to the 39th Annual Meeting of the American Society of Criminology, 1987; J. Phillippe Rushton, "Race Differences in Behaviour: A Review and Evolutionary Analysis," *Personality and Individual Differences* 9 (1988): 1009–24; J. Phillippe Rushton, "Race and Crime: A Reply to Roberts and Gabor," *Canadian Journal of Criminology* 32 (1990): 315–34; J. Phillippe Rushton, "Race and Crime: A Reply to Cernovsky and Litman," *Canadian Journal of Criminology* 36 (1994): 79–83; Nathalie L. Quann and Shelley Trevethan, *Police Reported Aboriginal Crime in Saskatchewan* (Ottawa: Statistics Canada, 2000); Zack Z. Cernovsky and Larry C. Litman, "Re-analyses of J.P. Rushton's Crime Data," *Canadian Journal of Criminology* 35 (1993): 31–7; Thomas Gabor and Julian V. Roberts, "Rushton on Race and Crime: The Evidence Remains Unconvincing," *Canadian Journal of Criminology* 32 (1990): 335; Frances Henry, Patricia Hastings, and Brian Freer, "Perceptions of Race and Crime in Ontario: Empirical Evidence from the Toronto and Durham Region," *Canadian Journal of Criminology* (October 1996): 46–476; Kevin Haggerty, *Making Crime Count* (Toronto: University of Toronto Press, 2001); Julian V. Roberts, "Racism and the Collection of Statistics Relating to Race and Ethnicity," in *Crimes of Colour: Racialization and CJS in Canada*, eds. Wendy Chan and Kilran Mirchandani, 101–12 (Peterborough, ON: Broadview Press, 2002); R.A. Cawsey, Mr. Justice, *Justice on Trial. Report of the Task Force on the Criminal Justice System and its Impact on the Indian and Métis People of Alberta* (Edmonton: Attorney General and Solicitor General of Alberta, 1996); A.C. Hamilton and C.M. Sinclair (Commissioners), *Report of the Aboriginal Justice Inquiry of Manitoba: The Justice System and Aboriginal People*, Chapter 13: Women (Winnipeg: Public Inquiry into the Administration of Justice and Aboriginal People, 1991); Nova Scotia, *Royal Commission on the Donald Marshall, Jr., Prosecution*, Vol. 1, *Findings and Recommendations* (Halifax: The Commission, 1989); M. Gittens and D. Cole, *Report of the Commission on Systemic Racism in the Ontario Criminal Justice System* (Toronto: Queen's Printer for Ontario, 1995); E.N. Hughes (Chair), *Report of Commission of Inquiry into the Shooting Death of Leo Lachance* (Saskatchewan: Queen's Printer, Government of Saskatchewan, 1993).

46 percent of arrests for violent crime involved Blacks, victimization surveys reveal that the percentage of offenders identified by the victim as Black was less than 25 percent.

Aboriginal offenders represent less than 3 percent of the adult population but compose 18 percent of the people incarcerated. In addition, on conviction Aboriginal offenders are more likely to be incarcerated, and as Figure 3.5 shows, the number of incarcerated Aboriginal offenders is increasing. In 2002–03, 70 percent of Aboriginal offenders were in prison, compared with 58 percent for non-Aboriginals. Aboriginal women represent 29 percent of incarcerated women, while Aboriginal men represent 18 percent of incarcerated men. In Manitoba, Aboriginal women compose 14 percent of the provincial population but 80 percent of the female jail population.

The statistical overrepresentation of certain ethnic groups isn't a surprise, but the causes are not clear.[42] Thus, racism in the criminal justice system has become an important issue.

Natives and Crime. The CCJS Profile Series notes that in the 1996 census, about 800 000 people, or 3 percent of the total population of Canada, identified themselves as Aboriginal.[43] In the 1999 GSS, 35 percent of the Aboriginal population had been victims of a crime in the previous year, much higher than the rate

Figure 3.5	The Proportion of Aboriginal Offenders Incarcerated Is Higher Than for Non-Aboriginal

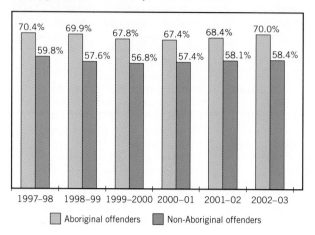

Percentage of Federal Offender Population Incarcerated

	1997–98	1998–99	1999–2000	2000–01	2001–02	2002–03
Aboriginal offenders	70.4%	69.9%	67.8%	67.4%	68.4%	70.0%
Non-Aboriginal offenders	59.8%	57.6%	56.8%	57.4%	58.1%	58.4%

Source: *Corrections and Conditional Release Statistical Overview 2003* (Ottawa: Solicitor General Canada, Correctional Services Canada, 2004).

Exhibit 3.1	Quick Facts: General Profile of the Native Offender

- The Aboriginal population, at 800 000, represents about 3 percent of the Canadian population.
- In provincial and territorial jurisdictions, about 15 000 (15 percent) of offenders sentenced in 1998 were Native.
- In federal jurisdiction, about 17 percent of inmates are Native.
- About 12 percent of inmates are Native males, and 17 percent are Native females.
- Those in the 18- to 37-year-old age group make up 76 percent of Inuit offenders, 85 percent of Métis offenders, and 83 percent of First Nations offenders.
- Sixty-five percent of Aboriginal offenders had prior convictions.
- Natives are five times as likely to be convicted of serious assault as non-Natives are.
- Natives are four times as likely to be victimized by crime as non-Natives are.
- The on-reserve rate of violence is five times higher than off reserve.
- Almost 90 percent of Aboriginals report being victims of childhood or adult violence.
- One-third of those under age 15 live in single-parent families.
- In Manitoba, Natives represent 16 percent of 12- to 17-year-olds but make up 71 percent of youths sentenced to custody.

Sources: National Crime Prevention Centre, *Aboriginal Canadians: Violence, Victimization and Prevention* (Ottawa: Department of Justice, 2001); Nathalie L. Quann and Shelley Trevethan, *Police Reported Aboriginal Crime in Saskatchewan* (Ottawa: Statistics Canada, 2000).

for non-Aboriginals (26 percent). Nineteen percent of the Natives reported being victimized two or more times, compared with 10 percent of the non-Native population. Aboriginal people were nearly three times more likely to be victims of violent crime (307 versus 110 incidents per 1000 population) and more likely to be victims of spousal violence. Approximately 20 percent of Aboriginal people reported being assaulted by their spouse, compared with 7 percent of non-Aboriginal people. Eighty percent of Native women are victims of violence; death from violence occurs at a rate three times higher than that of non-Native communities. Suicide among males is four times higher than the non-Native rate.[44]

Natives are more likely to have contact with police and for more serious reasons. For example, they were more likely to come into contact with the police as victims of a crime (17 percent to 13 percent), as witnesses to a crime (11 percent to 6 percent), and by being arrested (4 percent to 1 percent). Natives are also less satisfied with the police and less likely to rate the police as being approachable (58 percent to 67 percent), as ensuring the safety of citizens (55 percent to 63 percent), as enforcing the laws (48 percent to 61 percent), as supplying information on ways to reduce crime (46 percent to 55 percent), and as responding promptly to calls (43 percent to 50 percent).

The Economy. Debate remains over the effects the economy has on crime rates. Some criminologists believe that a poor economy actually helps lower crime rates. Unemployed parents are at home to supervise children and guard their homes. And because there is less money to spend, a poor economy means that there are fewer valuables around worth stealing. It also seems unlikely that law-abiding, middle-aged workers will suddenly turn to a life of crime if they are laid off during an economic downturn.

However, long-term periods of sustained economic weakness and unemployment eventually affect the crime rate. The recession that occurred in the late 1980s may have produced a climate of hopelessness in North America's largest cities, which saw increased violence rates between 1985 and 1990. Research shows that those people born in the 1960s had higher levels of criminal involvement due to more serious difficulties integrating into the job market in the early 1980s.[45] Inmates are more likely to have been unemployed at the time they committed their offence. Teenage unemployment rates are especially high in urban areas that contain large at-risk populations. Property crimes, such as arson and insurance fraud, also go up in times of economic recession.[46]

Social Malaise. Other social problems also affect the crime rate. Increases in the number of single-parent families, in divorce and dropout rates, in drug abuse, and in teen pregnancies are significant. Cross-national research indicates that child homicide rates are greatest in those nations that have the highest rates of illegitimacy and teenage mothers.[47] This conclusion is very controversial, because it neglects the social reasons for child poverty and contributes to the invisibility of teenage dads. As illegitimacy rates rise and social spending is cut, the rate of violent crime might trend upward. Social malaise may explain why some cities and regions have higher crime rates than others do. Conversely, some research shows that legalized abortion in the early 1970s contributed to a lowering of the crime rate in the 1990s. The point is that improved policing and better prisons, plus a strong economy, can account for only half of the 30 percent crime rate decline.[48]

Culture and Crime Rates. Culture makes a difference as well. For example, Japan is a large industrialized country whose population is jammed into overcrowded urban areas, but its crime rate is extremely low compared with many Western countries. The fear of crime is relatively low, even though the Japanese news media focus a lot of attention on violent crime. How can this difference be explained?

Cultural differences play an important role in controlling crime in Japan. In North America, individualism and self-gratification are emphasized, and success is defined by material goods and possessions. People are more willing to engage in confrontations, increasing the likelihood of violence. In Japan, honour is an important personal trait, and people are deeply loyal to historical traditions, which provide a sense of moral order. Networks of social groups create a strong commitment to social norms. An important cultural norm is patience when seeking change, a cooperative approach to decision making, respect for seniority and age, and concern for society at the expense of the individual. Japanese customs that subordinate personal feelings for the good of the group produce fewer violent confrontations. Research by Gartner and Parker shows that murder rates in Japan and Scotland have been unaffected by population trends because in these nations violence is considered shameful.[49]

Nowhere are obedience and respect more important in Japan than in relationships with family members and friends. Children owe parents total respect; younger siblings must obey older brothers and sisters; younger friends show reverence toward older acquaintances; and all show respect to the emperor. Bowing symbolizes this respect. The Japanese, then, are deterred from criminal behaviour not only by moral principles of right and wrong but also by the need to avoid embarrassment to self, family, and acquaintances. This fear of shame is the key to the crime rate.[50] In Japan shameful acts are confronted in an effort to reintegrate offenders into society.

Although Japanese crime rates are low, what crime there is tends to involve organized criminal gangs. Youth in the *bosozoku* (hot-rodder) and "Yankee" gangs flout the conventional dress and speech codes so important in Japan. Members embrace an overtly macho behavioural code, featuring violence, reckless driving, and drug use. They may "graduate" into *yakuza* gangs, huge organized crime groups that are responsible for drug trafficking, extortion, gambling, and other criminal conspiracies. They are often hired by legitimate enterprises to "settle" labour disputes, close business deals, and collect debts. Although membership in traditional organized crime families is on the wane in North America, the number of Japanese *yakuza* members has increased sharply.[51]

Connections

The link among the economy, social malaise, and the crime rate is important for criminological theory. If crime rates are higher in poor or distressed regions, an association may exist between poverty and crime. This is the assumption made by the social structure theorists, who are discussed in Chapter 7.

Guns. A lot of controversy exists over whether the availability of firearms may influence the crime rate. More guns than ever before are finding their way into the hands of young people. In 2002, 21 percent of those charged with robbery with a firearm were youths. Numbers in the United States are even higher,[52] which suggests that in at least some areas, juvenile gun possession is all too prevalent and may in part be responsible for increasing violence rates.

Connections

Bill C-68 was introduced to the legislature in 1995 as an attempt to control this problem. Gun control is discussed in more depth in Chapter 11.

According to the CCJS, firearms were used in 26 percent of homicides, 28 percent of attempted murders, and 13 percent of robberies. Of all violations against the person, only 2 percent involve firearms.[53]

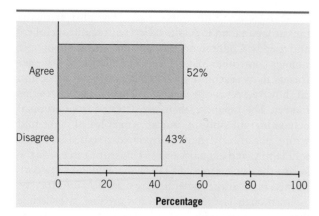

Canadians are divided on whether the gun registry should be abolished.

Source: Poll conducted by Ipsos Reid/CTV/*The Globe and Mail*, February 1, 2004.

There is some debate about the extent to which Canadians use firearms for self-protection. Some research shows that Canadians are three times more likely to use guns in self-defence than to commit violent crimes. However, other research shows that self-defence killings were outnumbered by the death of residents in the homes by 40 to 1. If a gun is available, it also increases the likelihood it will be used in a suicide.[54]

Drugs. Increasing drug use may affect crime rates. Groups and gangs involved in the urban drug trade recruit juveniles because they work cheaply, are immune from heavy criminal penalties, and are willing to take risks.[55] Arming themselves for protection, these drug-dealing kids present a menace that persuades neighbourhood adolescents to arm themselves for protection. The result is an increasing spiral of violence. The criminalization of drugs creates an illegal drug trade that in turns makes for more gun-related violence.

The violent crime rate between 1980 and 1990 was due in part to the crack cocaine epidemic that swept North America's largest cities and the drug-trafficking gangs that fought over turf. These well-armed gangs did not hesitate to use violence to control territories, intimidate rivals, and increase their market share. In Washington, D.C., 21 percent of homicides were drug-related in 1985; by 1988, this figure had increased to 80 percent.[56] In Canada, the CCJS says that 1 in 13 homicides is gang-related; and in 2002, 1 in 3 gang-related homicides was drug-related. In addition, 48 drug-related homicides were not related to gang activity. Table 3.4 summarizes the relationship between drugs and crime.

Connections

The drug–crime connection is a critical one for lawmakers. If drug use causes crime rates to increase, then the outright ban on drugs is warranted. If there is no drug–crime connection, efforts to legalize drug use might be justified. For sections on the drug–crime connection see Chapter 14.

TABLE 3.4 Summary of the Relationship between Drugs and Crime

Drugs/Crime Relationship	Definition	Examples
Drug-defined offences	Violation of laws that prohibit or regulate the possession, use, distribution, or manufacture of illegal drugs	growing marijuana; making methamphetamine; selling cocaine, heroin, or marijuana
Drug-related offences	Offences to which a drug's pharmacological effects contribute; offences motivated by the user's need for money to support continued use	violence; stealing; prostitution
Drug-using lifestyle	The likelihood and frequency of involvement in crime is increased because drug users don't participate in the legitimate economy and are exposed to situations that encourage crime	emphasis on short-term goals; learning criminal skills from other offenders

Source: Adapted from the White House, "Drug Policy Information Clearinghouse Fact Sheet, 2000," http://www.whitehousedrugpolicy.gov (accessed May 10, 2005).

Justice Policy. Law enforcement experts suggest that reduction in crime rates may be attributed to aggressive police practices that target "quality of life" crimes such as panhandling, graffiti, petty drug dealing, and loitering. By showing that even the smallest infractions will be dealt with seriously, aggressive police departments may be able to discourage potential criminals from committing more serious crimes. This has been called the "broken windows" approach, discussed elsewhere in this book, which attempts to reduce the incivilities experienced by neighbourhood residents. The issue is open to debate, but reducing fear among residents might enlist their help in fighting crime.[57]

Tough laws targeting drug dealing and repeat offenders with lengthy prison terms can have an effect on crime rates. The fear of punishment may inhibit some would-be criminals. Lengthy sentences also help boost the nation's prison population. It is possible that placing a significant number of potentially high-rate offenders behind bars helps stabilize crime rates. This is called selective incapacitation.

Connections

Although there is still a great deal of debate over the impact that incarcerating criminals has on the crime rate, most scholars dispute the idea that locking them up by itself can bring crime rates down. New criminals are continually coming along to replace those behind bars. For more on this topic, see the sections in Chapter 5 on incapacitation.

InfoTrac®

- To read about the effect of age on crime, look at "Researchers Link Youth Marijuana Epidemic and Crime," *Alcoholism and Drug Abuse Weekly* 13, no. 26 (July 2, 2001): 4.
- Gang activity may have an impact on crime; see Terry O'Neil, "Biker Gangs—Stronger Than Ever: Police Admit That Their Campaign Has Failed to Stop Hells Angels from Spreading," *Alberta Report* 29, no. 4 (2002): 18–22.

What the Future Holds

Current conditions can change to affect crime trends; however, prediction of future patterns is possible. Steffensmeier and Harer accurately predicted that violent crime would drop during the 1990s as baby boomers passed into middle age. They also predicted property crime rates would at first decline, then level off and begin rising toward the end of the decade as the baby-boom-echo kids born in the early 1980s began to hit their "peak" crime years. After the year 2000, both property and violent crimes were predicted to increase.[58] The age structure of society is considered to be a very powerful influence on the crime rate, and a significant increase in teen violence is expected if current trends persist.[59]

In 2002, the Canadian Police Survey on Youth Gangs said that the youth gang problem is growing. The United States has seen the youth gang population increase exponentially, and Canadian trends in crime usually follow a decade behind the United States'.

Of course, such predictions are based on population trends and can be thrown off by changes in the economy, justice policy, drug use, gun availability, gang membership, and other sociocultural forces. For example, in 2000 it was predicted that the number of adults charged with drug offences would increase between 1998 and 2003. However the CCJS reported that after nearly a decade of increases, the rate of drug crimes fell by 8 percent in 2003. It is also possible that outrage over violent crime will help encourage local residents to take actions to reduce crime, including assisting police, enforcing curfews, participating in Neighbourhood Watch, developing recreational facilities for youths, addressing poverty, and so on.

A particularly ambitious attempt to predict crime trends is seen Table 3.5. The level of recorded crime is forecast to fall to 85 percent of its 1999 level by 2026 and to 81 percent by 2041.

Crime Patterns

What do the various sources of criminological statistics tell us about crime? What is known about the nature of crime and criminals? What trends or patterns exist in the crime rate that can help us understand the causes of crime?

Criminologists look for patterns in crime to gain insight into the nature of crime. If crime rates are consistently higher at certain times, in certain areas, and among certain groups, this knowledge helps explain the cause of crime. For example, if criminal statistics show that crime rates are consistently highest in poor neighbourhoods in large urban areas, then crime may be a function of poverty and neighbourhood decline. If, in contrast, crime rates are spread evenly across the social structure, there would be little evidence that crime has an economic basis; crime might then be linked to socialization, personality, intelligence, or some other trait

TABLE 3.5 Actual and Forecast Rates of Specific Offences, 1999, 2026, 2041

	Incidents per 100 000			Ratio	
	1999 (actual)	2026	2041	2026/1999	2041/1999
Homicide, attempt	4	3	3	0.86	0.83
Assault and sexual assault, Levels 2 and 3	129	111	107	0.86	0.82
Robbery	92	75	72	0.82	0.78
Sexual assault, Level 1	74	67	64	0.91	0.87
Assault, Level 1	578	499	477	0.86	0.82
Other person	79	69	66	0.88	0.84
Total person	**955**	**825**	**789**	**0.86**	**0.83**
Break and enter	1 044	860	828	0.82	0.79
Other indictable property	645	531	515	0.82	0.80
Theft under	2 227	1 908	1 338	0.83	0.83
Other summary and hybrid property	1 416	1 187	1 138	0.84	0.80
Total property	**5 332**	**4 487**	**4 318**	**0.84**	**0.81**
Administration of justice	287	237	228	0.83	0.79
Public order, morals, weapons	331	278	267	0.87	0.83
Drugs	265	216	209	0.81	0.79
Criminal Code traffic	455	404	388	0.89	0.85
Miscellaneous	953	813	780	0.85	0.82
Total other	**2 283**	**1 949**	**1 872**	**0.85**	**0.82**
Total	**8 570**	**7 261**	**6978**	**0.85**	**0.81**

Source: Peter Carrington, "Population Aging and Crime in Canada, 2000–2041," *Canadian Journal of Criminology* 43, no. 3 (July 2001): 331–357. Reproduced by permission of the *Canadian Journal of Criminology and Criminal Justice.* Copyright by the Canadian Criminal Justice Association.

unrelated to class position or income. What, then, are the main traits and patterns in crime statistics?

The Ecology of Crime

A curious pattern is the link to temporal and ecological factors. Some of the most important of these factors are the day, season, and climate; temperature; the density of the population; and geographical region.

Day, Season, and Climate. Most reported crimes occur during warm summer months. During the summer, teenagers, who usually have the highest crime levels as a group, are out of school and have greater opportunity to commit crime. People spend more time outdoors, making themselves easier targets, and homes are left vacant, which makes them more vulnerable to property crimes.

Crime rates may also be higher on the day government welfare and social security cheques arrive, increasing such activities as breaking into mailboxes and accosting recipients on the streets. Also, people may have more disposable income at this time, and the availability of extra money may relate to behaviours associated with crime, such as drinking, partying, gambling, and so on.[60]

Temperature. Some crimes increase with a rise in temperature and then begin to decline when it becomes too hot for physical exertion. However, field studies indicate that the rates of some crimes (such as domestic assault) but not all (such as rape) continue to increase as temperatures rise. Research has shown that a long stretch of highly hot and uncomfortable weather is related to an increase in the number of homicides. The relationship between temperature and assault is strong during the morning and evening hours: A person is four times as likely to be assaulted at midnight when the temperature exceeds 30°C than when the temperature is –20°C![61]

Population Density. Areas with low per capita crime rates tend to be rural—large urban areas have by far the highest violence rates. These findings are also supported by victim data.

Region. Definite differences are apparent in regional crime rates. Historically, Canada has had a pattern of crime rising from east to west, although this is beginning to change. Earlier in the chapter it was suggested that internal migration has resulted in weaker social control in Western provinces. For many years, southern American states also had significantly higher rates in almost all crime categories than were found in other regions of the country, indicating a southern subculture of violence.

Social Class and Crime

Traditionally, crime has been thought of as a lower-class phenomenon. People at the lowest rungs of the social structure would appear to have the greatest incentive to commit crimes. Those unable to obtain desired goods and services through conventional means may resort to theft and selling narcotics to obtain them; these activities are referred to as **instrumental crimes**. Those living in areas of poverty are also believed to engage in disproportionate amounts of **expressive crimes**, such as rape and assault, as a means of expressing their rage, frustration, and anger against society. Alcohol and other drug abuse helps fuel violent episodes.[62]

In the United States, crime rates in inner-city, high-poverty areas are generally higher than those in suburban or wealthier areas; for example, the highest homicide victimization levels are in deteriorated inner-city areas.[63] Studies using arrest records have consistently shown that crime rates in lower-class areas are higher than in wealthier neighbourhoods. Surveys of prison inmates show that most prisoners were members of the lower class and unemployed or underemployed in the years before their incarceration.

An alternative explanation is that official crime rates are a function of law enforcement practices and not of actual criminal behaviour. Police may devote more resources to poverty areas, and, consequently, apprehension rates may be higher there. Similarly, police may be more likely to formally arrest and prosecute lower-class citizens than those in the middle and upper classes, which may account for the lower class's overrepresentation in the official statistics and the prison population. The third explanation is that crimes are class-related; that is, the rich are more likely to commit tax fraud, while the poor are more likely to commit welfare fraud.

Connections

Crimes of power cause more harm to society than does street crime, discussed in Chapter 13.

Evidence for a Class–Crime Relationship. Using self-report data to test the class–crime relationship, early studies conducted in the 1950s did not find a direct relationship between social class and youth crime. They found that socioeconomic class was related to official processing by police, court, and correctional agencies but not to the actual commission of crimes. In addition, factors generally associated with lower-class membership, such as broken homes, were found to be related to institutionalization but not to admissions of delinquency.[64]

For more than 20 years, self-report studies could not prove a class–crime relationship: If the poor possessed more extensive criminal records than the wealthy, it was because of differential law enforcement and not because of behaviour. The definitive work on this subject, a meta-review of 35 studies on the relationship between class and crime, concluded that there was little support for a lower-class crime connection.[65] In 1990, an update again found little evidence to support it.[66] Consequently, official statistics probably reflect class bias in the processing of lower-class offenders.

If a study includes trivial offences, such as using a false ID or drinking alcohol, this inflates the overall statistics. Youth often engage in such offences as petty larceny, drug use, and simple assault.[67] Those studies showing middle- and lower-class youths to be equally delinquent rely on measures weighted toward minor crimes (for example, using a false ID or skipping school); when serious crimes, such as burglary and assault, are used in the comparison, lower-class youths are more delinquent.[68]

A 2001 *Juristat* study on youth delinquency concluded that there was not a strong link between property crime and income. Furthermore, between 39 percent and 44 percent of children from all income groups reported being involved in some or a lot of aggressiveness.[69]

The Class–Crime Controversy. The relationship between class and crime is an important one for criminological theory. If crime is related to social class, then such socioeconomic factors as poverty and neighbourhood disorganization are a cause of criminal behaviour.

One difficulty is in how we measure "class." So many different indicators are used that findings are ambiguous. For example, father's occupation and education are only weakly related to self-reported crime, while unemployment or being a welfare recipient is a much stronger correlate of criminality.[70]

The class–crime relationship may also be more complex than "the poorer a person is, the more crime he or she commits." Age, race, and gender may all influence the connection between class and crime.[71] Unemployment, racism, sexism, and unrealistic expectations can all create resentment.[72] It is not surprising that the true relationship between class and crime is difficult to determine.

Connections

If class and crime are unrelated, the causes of crime must be found in factors experienced by members of all social classes—psychological impairment, family conflict, peer pressure, and school failure. Theories that view crime as a function of problems experienced by members of all social classes are reviewed in Chapter 8.

Recent evidence suggests that serious street and official crime is more prevalent among the lower classes, while less serious and self-reported crime is spread more evenly throughout the social structure.[73] Income inequality, poverty, and resource deprivation are all associated with the most serious violent crimes, including homicide and assault.[74] Nonetheless, although crime rates may be higher in lower-class areas, poverty alone cannot explain why a particular individual becomes a chronic violent criminal; if it could, the crime problem would be much worse than it is now.[75]

Age and Crime

Age is inversely related to criminality.[76] Regardless of economic status, marital status, race, sex, and so on, younger people are more likely (in terms of their proportion of the population) to commit crime than are their older peers. This pattern has remained stable from 1935 to the present.[77] Official statistics tell us that young people are arrested at a disproportionate rate to their numbers in the population; and victim surveys generate similar findings for crimes in which the age of the assailant can be determined.

Youth crime has caused a lot of concern, especially since youth commit some crimes at a much higher rate than their share of the population would warrant. Sensational cases in the media also exacerbate the problem. One such case is the trial of the killers of Reena Virk, described in the Famous Canadian Court Case.

Cases like the savage beating and murder of Reena Virk, and the media spectacles that ensue, help explain people's exaggerated fears about youth violence. The circumstances surrounding this particular young woman's death thrust the issues of bullying and female violence into the public spotlight—not just in the small British Columbia suburb where this crime occurred, but also on national and international levels. Meanwhile, a number of other pertinent issues, like racism, may have been overlooked. The FREDA Centre for Research on Violence against Women and Children maintains that Reena was targeted because of her East Indian

The Winnipeg Police Gang Unit arrests a member of the youth gang called Indian Posse in a big sweep in August 1995. It is estimated that the gang and the Manitoba Warriors have 1500 members in Winnipeg and have been connected to crimes such as murder, robbery, and drug dealing.

heritage. The majority of perpetrators were White, including the two killers, and the attack was initiated by butting out a cigarette on Virk's forehead.

The Age–Crime Controversy. The inverse relationship between age and crime, called **aging out** or the **desistance phenomenon**, has been the subject of considerable academic debate. Hirschi and Gottfredson say that the relationship between age and crime is constant and that the age variable is actually irrelevant. Because all people, regardless of race, gender, class, family structure, domicile, work status, and so on, commit fewer crimes as they age, it is not important to consider age as a factor in explaining crime. Even hard-core chronic offenders commit fewer crimes as they age. Differences in offending rates for groups (males and females or rich and poor) that exist at any point in their respective life cycles will be maintained throughout their lives.[78]

In a replication of Hirschi's research, Laub and Sampson studied with a delinquent group of five hundred men. From age 7 to 70, they committed 9500 crime events and confirmed the classic age–crime pattern, even within a population characterized by serious, persistent criminal activity.[79]

Famous Canadian Court Case

The Murder of Reena Virk

Reena Virk was a troubled 14-year-old whose struggle to be free from the confines of family and to gain the acceptance of peers ended in tragedy. The long history of harassment Reena endured began at an early age with insults regarding her appearance and ended in 1997 with allegations of spreading rumours. On a November evening that year, Virk was lured by a group of fellow teenagers to a muddy bank under the Craigflower Bridge in Saanich, Victoria, where she was brutally attacked twice by her accusers and then drowned in a nearby waterway. Reena sustained injuries so severe, a pathologist later testified, that it was as though she had been run over by a car.

A week after the incident, a day before police divers found Reena's body, charges were laid against seven girls and one boy aged 14 to 17. Six of the girls were accused of aggravated assault in relation to the initial beating. Although half pleaded guilty and the other three were tried, convictions were registered for all of them in February 1998.

These girls faced consequences ranging from a two-month conditional sentence to a yearlong prison term. The only boy among the accused, Warren Glowatski, and the remaining girl, Kelly Ellard, were charged with second-degree murder for committing the second attack and the drowning. Glowatski admitted to participating in both assaults but insisted that Ellard was solely responsible for killing Virk. Nevertheless, he was convicted in June 1999 and sentenced to life in prison with no chance of parole for seven years.

Kelly Ellard's case has attracted widespread media coverage and is probably the most notorious in connection with Virk's death. In April 2000, Ellard received a life sentence after being convicted in adult court of second-degree murder. However, this verdict was overturned in 2003 when the British Columbia Court of Appeal ruled that Ellard was improperly cross-examined by the Crown and thus denied a fair trial. The Court released the now 21-year-old pending a retrial but revoked her bail after she was arrested for assaulting a 58-year-old woman in Vancouver. Ellard's second trial, which commenced in June 2004, resulted in a mistrial because of a deadlocked jury. On April 12, 2005, Ellard was found guilty of second-degree murder in her third trial.

Sources: "Ellard Admits Punching Virk," *CBC News*, July 7, 2004, http://www.cbc.ca/stories/2004/07/06/canada/ellard_testify040706 (accessed May 10, 2005); "Second Trial Begins for Virk Murder Suspect," *CBC News*, June 14, 2004, http://www.cbc.ca/stories/2004/06/14/canada/ellard040614 (accessed May 10, 2005); Sid Tafler, "The Lonely Death of Reena Virk," PWAC Victoria, April, 1998, http://www.islandnet.com/pwacvic/tafler04.html (accessed May 10, 2005); "The Murder of Reena Virk: A Timeline," *CBC News*, July 20, 2004, http://www.cbc.ca/news/background/virk/ (accessed May 10, 2005); Yasmin Jiwani, "The Denial of Race in the Murder of Reena Virk," The FREDA Centre for Research on Violence against Women and Children, April 2000, http://www.rajweb.com/cassa/eMag/Articles/Articles2.htm (accessed May 10, 2005); Yasmin Jiwani and Annabel Webb, "Violence, Racism, and Power—The Ellard Trial," The FREDA Centre for Research on Violence against Women and Children, April 2000, http://www.rajweb.com/cassa/eMag/Articles/Articles4.htm (accessed May 10, 2005).

Prepared by Andrea Wolf.

Connections

Hirschi and Gottfredson have used their views on the age–crime relationship as a basis for their general theory of crime. This important theory holds that the factors that produce crime change little after birth and that the association between crime and age is a constant. For more on their views, see Chapter 10.

Those who do not support the view of an inverse relationship between age and crime suggest that personal factors (gender and race) and social factors (lifestyle, economic situation, and peer relations) have a significant impact. Evolving patterns or cycles of criminal behaviour may be keyed to personal characteristics and lifestyle, including gender, race, and class. For example, the male-to-female crime ratio difference declines with age. The female homicide rate peaks between ages 25 and 29, doesn't fluctuate much, and is at a low rate throughout adulthood; in contrast, the male homicide rate is much higher, peaks between ages 8 and 25, and drops thereafter.[80]

The likelihood of a long-term criminal career is also determined by the age at which offending commences. People who get involved in criminality at a very early age (**early onset**) and who gain official records will be the ones most likely to become chronic offenders. Research shows that preschoolers (under age five) who are labelled "troublesome" or "difficult" by parents are most likely to become persistent offenders through adolescence and resistant to the aging-out process.[81]

Desistance is also influenced by criminal specialization. Crimes that provide significant economic gain, such as gambling, embezzlement, and fraud, are less likely to decline with maturity than are high-risk, low-profit offences, such as assault. People who are frequent cocaine and heroin users continue to commit criminal acts 10 years or more past the age when nonusers have terminated their criminal activity.[82]

Two Classes of Criminals? The population thus may contain different sets of criminal offenders: one or more groups whose criminality declines with age and another group whose criminal behaviour remains constant through their maturity.[83] The age–crime pattern may also undergo change, as a greater proportion of violent behaviour is concentrated among youthful offenders than it was 40 years ago.

In sum, some criminologists view the relationship between crime and age as constant, while others believe that it varies according to offence and offender. This difference has important implications for criminological research and theory. If age is a constant, then the criminality of any group can be accurately measured at any single point in time. If, however, the relationship between age and crime varies, then it would be necessary to conduct longitudinal studies that follow criminals over their life cycle to fully understand how their age influences their offending patterns.[84] Crime is also a type of social event that takes on different meanings at different times in a person's life.[85]

Various experiments have tried to deal with the problem of young offenders, such as boot camps and early intervention programs. In Scotland, the Freagarrach Project for persistent offenders (those who committed more than five offences) was able to achieve a 20 percent to 50 percent reduction in repeat offences. These youths had an average of 18 offences against them. Close counselling, education, and exercise, and a system of rewards achieved more significant results than a simple prison sentence would achieve.

In London, multisystemic therapy (MT) is a low-cost alternative to traditional mental health services, aimed at reducing recidivism. The program appears to be successful in treating antisocial behaviour in young offenders. The program targets chronic, violent, and substance-abusing high-risk juveniles. Randomized, clinical trials found few rearrests, fewer self-reported offences, and reduced time spent in corrections facilities. The four-year recidivism rate was 22 percent for MT participants, compared with 87 percent for those with no treatment. Those who received treatment and were rearrested had committed less serious offences than those in a control group.[86]

Debates over the relationship between age and crime, and what to do about it, has sponsored new research in Canada, the United States, Sweden, and Britain.[87] Clearly, more research is required on this important topic.

Why Does Aging out Occur? Despite the debate over the age–crime relationship, the overall crime rate does decline with age. Why does this phenomenon take place? One view is that a direct relationship exists between aging and desistance. As they mature, troubled youths are able to develop a long-term life view and resist the need for immediate gratification.[88] Teenage crime is "fun," a social activity that provides adventure in an otherwise boring life. As people grow older, life patterns become inconsistent with criminality, so delinquents literally grow out of crime.[89]

Wilson and Herrnstein argue that the aging-out process is a function of the natural history of the human life cycle. Deviance in adolescence is fuelled by the need for conventionally unobtainable money and sex and reinforced by close relationships with peers who defy conventional morality. At the same time, teenagers are becoming independent from parents and other adults who enforce conventional standards. Teens have a new sense of energy and strength and are involved with peers who are similarly vigorous and frustrated. Adulthood brings increasingly powerful ties to conventional society, such as a family. Adults also develop the ability to delay gratification and forgo the immediate gains that law violations bring.

> When you're a teenager, you're rowdy. Nowadays, you aren't rowdy. You know, you want to settle down because you can go to jail now. [When] you are a boy, you can be put into a detention home. But you can go to jail now. Jail ain't no place to go.[90]

Aging out of crime is also influenced by the success or failure of interpersonal relationships. Children who are labelled antisocial by teachers, police, parents, and neighbours find they have little choice but to remain committed to their criminal careers.[91] However, if youths believe they have little chance of achieving success, money, and happiness through crime, they are more likely to desist.[92] Individuals are also influenced by their adult relationships. For example, people who maintain successful marriages are more likely to desist from antisocial behaviours than those whose marriages fail.[93]

Even those who persist in a criminal career will eventually slow down as they age. Crime is too dangerous, physically taxing, and unrewarding, and punishments are too harsh and long lasting, to become a long-term way of

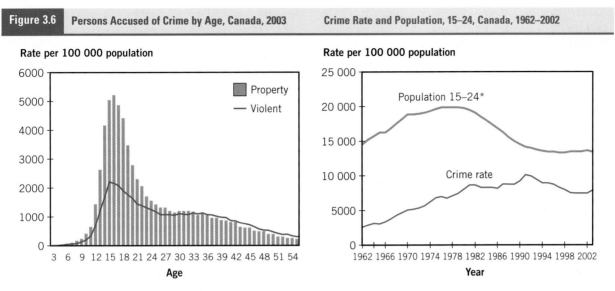

Figure 3.6 | Persons Accused of Crime by Age, Canada, 2003   Crime Rate and Population, 15–24, Canada, 1962–2002

*This line represents the number of 15 to 24 years olds expressed as a rate of 100 000 population and not the crime rate of this age group.

Source: Adapted from the Statistics Canada publication "Crime Statistics in Canada," 2003, *Juristat,* Catalogue 85-002, vol. 24, no. 6, July 28, 2004.

life for most people. The uniformity of maturational changes in the crime rate suggests to some that it must be part of a biological "evolutionary process."[94]

Connections

The belief that life events influence behaviour choices is at the core of life-course theories. These theories hold that as people and their social environment change, so do their criminal behaviour patterns. Theories of the criminal life course are discussed in Chapter 10.

Changing Demographics. The general decline in crime rates during the 1990s coincided with the decreasing proportion of persons aged 15 to 24. This age group has the highest rate for committing crimes and being a victim of crime. In 2003, the CCJS reported that people aged 15 to 24 years were 14 percent of the population and accounted for 45 percent of property crimes and 31 percent of violent crimes. Figure 3.6 shows the relationship between age and crime in 2003 and from 1962 to 2002. The changing age structure can explain only some of the change in crime rates. However, it is expected that all types of crimes will continue to decrease because of the aging of the population. Although an increase in the number of youths is forecast within a decade, there will also be an increase in older adults as well, driving the trend downward.[95]

Gender and Crime

The three major forms of criminal statistics generally agree on the finding that male crime rates are probably much higher than those for females. However, women are more at risk of committing, and being victimized by, certain crimes, as shown in Exhibit 3.2.

Explaining Gender Differences: Biosocial Differences. How can the gender differences in the crime rate be explained? Early criminologists pointed to the emotional, physical, and psychological differences between males and females. They maintained that because females were weaker and more passive, they were less likely to commit crimes. The most widely cited evidence was contained in Cesare Lombroso's 1895 book *The Female Offender.*[96] Lombroso argued that a small group of female criminals lacked "typical" female traits of "piety, maternity, undeveloped intelligence, and weakness." In physical appearance as well as in emotionality, delinquent females appeared more similar to men than to other women. Lombroso's theory became known as the **masculinity hypothesis**; in essence, a few "masculine" females were responsible for the handful of crimes committed by women.

Another early view of female crime focused on the dynamics of sexual relationships. Female criminals were viewed as either sexually controlling or sexually naive, either manipulating men for profit or being manipulated by them. The female's criminality was often masked,

Exhibit 3.2	Quick Facts: Profile of Women and the Criminal Justice System

- Twenty-five percent of women and 27 percent of men report being victimized in the past year.

- Women are more likely to be victims of sexual assault (33/1000) than are men (8/1000).

- Men represented 97 percent of the persons accused of sexual offences, compared with 82 percent of persons accused of all remaining types of violent offences.

- Men are more likely to victims of robbery (12/1000) than are women (7/1000).

- Men are more likely to be victims of assault (92/1000) than are women (70/1000).

- More than 60 percent of victimizations against men and women are not reported to the police.

- Women report more difficulty (33 percent) than do men (17 percent) in daily activities after victimization.

- Women know their perpetrator (78 percent of the time): they are related to them (40 percent) or are friends (38 percent).

- Women are victimized by strangers 17 percent and men are 37 percent of the time.

- Women are more likely to be murdered by a spouse (38 percent) than are men (2 percent).

- Sixty-five percent of women who were assaulted by a partner were victimized more than once.

- Women are a minority of offenders (17 percent of all adults).

- Women commit 22 percent of property crimes and 16 percent of violent crimes.

- The most common charge against women is theft (25 percent adult women; 32 percent young women).

- Women are less likely to be found guilty (53 percent of the time) than are men (63 percent).

- Females represent 21 percent of the youth court caseload.

- Female inmates are most likely to be young, of Aboriginal descent, single, and unemployed, and have little education.

- Drug-related offences account for 27 percent of federal and 13 percent of admissions to provincial or territorial facilities.

Sources: Based on the 1999 General Social Survey; CCJS, *Canadian Crime Statistics*, Catalogue 85205XIE, 2002; CCJS, "Sexual Offences in Canada," *Juristat* 23, no. 6 (July 2003), Catalogue 85002XIE; CCJS, "Women in Canada," *Profile Series* (June 2001), Catalogue 85F0033MIE.

because criminal justice authorities were reluctant to take action against a woman.[97] Referred to as the **chivalry hypothesis**, Pollack's view was that much of the criminality of females is hidden because of the generally protective and benevolent attitudes toward them in our culture.[98] In other words, police are less likely to arrest, juries less likely to convict, and judges less likely to incarcerate female offenders.

Although these early writings are now seen as sexist and androcentric (male-centred), trait differences are a determinant of crime rate differences. For example, some criminologists link antisocial behaviour to hormones, arguing that male sex hormones (**androgens**) account for aggressive behaviour and that gender-related hormonal differences explain the gender gap in the crime rate.[99]

Explaining Gender Differences: Socialization.
By the mid-twentieth century, it was common for criminologists to describe gender differences in the crime rate as a function of socialization. Textbooks explained the relatively low female crime rate by citing the fact that in contrast to boys, girls were supervised more closely and protected from competition.[100] The few female criminals were seen as troubled individuals, alienated at home, who pursued crime as a means of compensating for their disrupted personal lives.[101] The streets became a "second home" to girls whose physical and emotional adjustment was hampered by a strained home life, such as absent fathers and overly competitive mothers.

InfoTrac®

Use "sex differences" as a subject guide on InfoTrac® College Edition to learn more about male–female differences in socialization. Here's a sample: Darrell Steffensmeier and Emelie Allan, "Gender and Crime: Toward a Gendered Theory of Female Offending," *Annual Review of Sociology* 22 (1996): 459–488.

Connections

Gender differences in the crime rate may be a function of androgen levels because these hormones cause areas of the brain to become less sensitive to environmental stimuli, making males more likely to seek high levels of stimulation and to tolerate more pain in the process. Chapter 6's discussion of the biosocial causes of crime reviews this issue in greater detail.

Gender-based crime is also influenced by socialization. Traditionally, girls are socialized to be less aggressive than boys are, and girls are supervised more closely by their parents. Girls are more likely to learn to respond to provocation by feeling anxious and depressed, whereas boys are encouraged to retaliate with aggression. Although females get angry as often as males, they are taught to blame themselves for harbouring negative feelings and are therefore much more likely than males to respond to anger with feelings of depression, anxiety, fear, and shame. Although females are socialized to fear that their anger will harm valued relationships, males react with "moral outrage," looking to blame others for their discomfort.[102] Overall, women are much more likely to feel distressed than are men, experiencing sadness, anxiety, and uneasiness. The relatively few females who commit violent crimes report having home and family relationships that are more troubled than those experienced by male delinquents.[103]

Explaining Gender Differences: Feminist Views. In the 1970s, feminist writing revolutionized thinking on gender differences in the crime rate.[104] This writing, known as **liberal feminist theory**, focused attention on the social and economic roles of women in society and their relationship to female crime rates. The traditionally lower crime rate for women was explained by their "second-class" economic and social position, and it was predicted that as women's social roles changed and their lifestyles became more like those of men, the crime rates would converge.[105]

Criminologists began to refer to the "new female criminal." The rapid increase in the female crime rate during the 1960s and 1970s, especially in traditional male-oriented crimes (burglary, larceny), lent support to the convergence model. Support for convergence model is also found in gangs, where police have seen increased recruitment of female gang members in the predominantly male world of street gangs. In addition, self-report studies indicate that (1) the pattern of female criminality, if not its frequency, is quite similar to that of male criminality, and (2) the factors that predispose male criminals to crime have an equal impact on female criminals.[106]

Will gender differences in the crime rate eventually dissolve? Are gender differences permanent and unchanging? Some criminologists find that gender-based crime rate differences remain significant and argue that the emancipation of women has had relatively little influence on female crime rates.[107] They dispute the idea that increases in the female arrest rate reflect economic or social changes brought about by the women's movement. Many female criminals come from the socioeconomic class least affected by the women's movement, and their crimes are more a function of economic inequality than of women's rights. Also, the offence patterns of women are quite different from those of men, who are still committing a disproportionate share of serious crimes, such as robbery, burglary, murder, and assault.[108] In 2003, women committed 16 percent of violent crimes in Canada, 18 percent of assaults, 10 percent of homicides, and 2 percent of the sexual assaults. In contrast, young women committed 26 percent of violent crimes, 29 percent of assaults, 21 percent of homicides, and 3 percent of sexual assaults. Although this could be taken as gender convergence, much international research has failed to find an association between economic development and female crime rates.[109] There is little evidence that nations undergoing economic development also experience increases in the female violence rate.

Perhaps it is too soon for criminologists to write off "the new female criminal." After all, though male arrest rates are still considerably higher than female rates are, the female rates seem to be increasing at a faster pace. It is possible that convergence has been delayed by a slower-than-expected change in gender roles; the women's movement has not yet achieved its full impact on social life.[110] One reason is that while expanding their economic role, women have not abandoned their conventional role of taking care of family and home; women today are being forced to cope with added financial and social burdens. If gender roles are truly equivalent, crime rates may eventually converge; these changes appear to be taking place now.

Connections

Critical criminologists view gender inequality as stemming from the unequal power of men and women in a capitalist society and the exploitation of females by fathers and husbands. Female crime patterns can be explained by these unequal power relationships. These views, referred to as Marxist or radical feminism, are considered more fully in Chapter 9.

Connections

The concept of relative deprivation refers to the fact that people compare their success with that of the people they are in immediate contact with. Even if conditions improve, people may still feel as if they are falling behind. A sense of relative deprivation, discussed in Chapter 7, may lead to criminal activity.

InfoTrac®

Many explanations exist for the gender differences in the crime rate. To research this topic on InfoTrac® College Edition, use "gender" and "crime" as key words. Here's one result: Daniel P. Mears, Matthew Ploeger, and Mark Warr, "Explaining the Gender Gap in Delinquency: Peer Influence and Moral Evaluations of Behaviour," *Journal of Research in Crime and Delinquency* 35, no. 3 (1998): 251–257.

Criminal Careers

Most offenders commit a single criminal act and on arrest discontinue their antisocial activity. Others commit a few crimes of a less serious nature. However, a small group of individuals accounts for a majority of all crimes committed. These persistent offenders are referred to as **career criminals** or **chronic offenders**. The significance of this research is that it addresses elements within a criminal's life that are related to crime, rather than factors that differentiate offenders from nonoffenders.

Recent research shows that in 1999 in Canada, 60 percent of convicted offenders had at least one previous conviction. Among those recidivists, 28 percent had one prior conviction, and 72 percent had multiple prior convictions. The majority (62 percent) had been previously convicted at least once in youth court.[111] In 2002, almost two-thirds of people accused of homicide had a Canadian criminal record; among those, 73 percent had been previously convicted of a violent offence. These life-course persisters, as they are called, do a lot of damage to society because they are responsible for such a large share of adult misconduct.

Connections

More than 70 years ago, the Gluecks found that almost all of the reformatory inmates in their study of criminal careers had backgrounds in serious antisocial conduct. Read about their research in Chapter 6.

Delinquency in a Birth Cohort

The concept of the chronic or career offender is most closely associated with the research of Wolfgang, Figlio, and Sellin.[112] In their landmark study, *Delinquency in a Birth Cohort*, official records were used to follow the criminal careers of a cohort of 9945 boys born in Philadelphia in 1945. The cohort members were followed from the time of their birth until they reached 18 years of age. Official police records were used to identify delinquents. About one-third of the boys (3475) had some police contact. The remaining two-thirds (6470) had none.[113] Their delinquent acts were weighted to allow the researchers to differentiate, for example, between a simple assault requiring no medical attention for the victim and a serious assault in which the victim needed hospitalization.

The best-known discovery was of the chronic offender. Fully 54 percent of the delinquent youths were repeat offenders, while the remaining 46 percent were one-time offenders. However, the repeaters could be further categorized as nonchronic recidivists and chronic recidivists. The former consisted of 1235 youths who had been arrested more than once but fewer than five times and who made up 36 percent of all delinquents. The latter were a group of 627 boys arrested five times or more, who accounted for 18 percent of the delinquents and 6 percent of the total sample.

It was the chronic offenders (known today as "the chronic 6 percent") who were involved in the most dramatic amounts of delinquent behaviour; they were responsible for 5305 offences, or 59 percent of all offences. Even more striking was the involvement of chronic offenders in serious criminal acts. Of the entire sample, they committed 71 percent of the homicides, 73 percent of the rapes, 82 percent of the robberies, and 69 percent of the aggravated assaults.

Wolfgang and his associates found that arrest and court experience did little to deter the chronic offender. In fact, punishment was inversely related to chronic offending: The more stringent the sanctions chronic offenders received, the more likely they were to engage in repeated criminal behaviour.

Birth Cohort II

The subjects who made up Wolfgang's original birth cohort were born in 1945. How have behaviour patterns changed in subsequent years? To answer this question, a new, larger birth cohort of 27 000 subjects (13 000 males and 14 000 females), born in Philadelphia in 1958, were followed until their maturity.[114] Although the proportion of delinquent youths was about the same as that in the 1945 cohort, those in the larger sample were involved in 20 089 delinquent arrests. Chronic offenders (five or more arrests as juveniles) made up 7.5 percent of the 1958 sample (compared with 6.3 percent in 1945) and 23 percent of all delinquent offenders (compared with 18 percent in 1945). Chronic female delinquency was relatively rare—only 1 percent of the females in the survey were chronic offenders.

Chronic male delinquents continued to commit more than their share of criminal behaviour. They accounted for 61 percent of the total offences and a disproportionate amount of the most serious crimes: 61 percent of the homicides, 76 percent of the rapes, 73 percent of the robberies, and 65 percent of the aggravated assaults. The chronic female offender was less likely to be involved in serious crimes.

As a group, the 1958 cohort was involved in significantly more serious crimes than was the 1945 group. For example, the violent offence rate (149 per 1000 in the sample) was three times higher than the rate for the 1945 cohort (47 per 1000 subjects).

In the 1945 cohort, chronic offenders dominated the total crime rate and continued their law-violating careers as adults. The newer cohort study showed that the chronic offender syndrome was maintained in the group of subjects born 13 years later than the original cohort and, if anything, the newer group was more violent than that first group. Finally, the efforts of the justice system seem to have little preventive effect on the behaviour of chronic offenders: The more often a person was arrested, the more likely he or she was to be arrested again. For males, 26 percent of the entire group had one violent-offence arrest; of that 26 percent, 34 percent went on to commit a second violent offence, while 43 percent of the three-time losers went on to a fourth arrest, and so on.

Chronic Offender Research

This effort to identify the chronic career offender has been replicated by a number of other important research studies. Shannon also used the cohort approach to investigate career delinquency patterns.[115] West and Farrington's ongoing study of London youths has shown that a small number of recidivists continue their behaviour as adults and that arrest and conviction have little influence on their behaviour other than to amplify the problem that youths with multiple convictions as juveniles tend to have multiple convictions as adults. The most important childhood risk factors associated with chronic offending include a history of troublesomeness, a personality that reveres daring behaviour, a delinquent sibling, and a convicted parent. Farrington finds that the most chronic offenders could be identified by age 10 on the basis of personality and background features.[116]

In another study, a sample was followed through adulthood to age 30.[117] Seventy percent of the "persistent" adult offenders had been chronic juvenile offenders, who had an 80 percent chance of becoming adult offenders and a 50 percent chance of being arrested four or more times as adults. In comparison, subjects with no juvenile arrests had only an 18 percent chance of being arrested as an adult. The chronic offenders also continued to engage in the most serious crimes. Although they accounted for only 15 percent of the follow-up sample, the former chronic delinquents were involved in 74 percent of all arrests and 82 percent of all serious crimes, such as homicide, rape, and robbery.

The cohort follow-ups clearly show that chronic juvenile offenders continue their law-violating careers as adults, a concept referred to as the **continuity of crime**. Kids who are disruptive and antisocial as early as age five are the most likely to exhibit stable, long-term patterns of disruptive behaviour through adolescence. They have measurable behavioural problems in such areas as learning and motor skills, cognitive abilities, family relations, and other areas of social, psychological, and physical functioning. Youthful offenders who persist are more likely to abuse alcohol, get into trouble while in military service, become economically dependent on their families or on society, have lower aspirations, get divorced or separated, and have a weak employment record.[118] Canadian research shows that aggressive children are more likely to feel unhappy and rejected.[119] Criminalizing their behaviour by lowering the age of criminal responsibility would do nothing to deal with the problems that might cause the behaviour in the first place.

Additional studies conducted in Europe, such as the Stockholm cohort project (Project Metropolitan, which contains 15 117 male and female subjects), indicate that criminal career development in Sweden follows many of the same patterns found in American cohorts. Similarly, data from a sample of 411 males born in London found that the frequency of offending was predicted by early onset of antisocial behaviour, associating with deviant peers, certain personality traits (such as a low level of anxiety), poor school achievement, and dysfunctional family relations. Those delinquents who persisted into adulthood (ages 21 to 32) exhibited low IQs, substance abuse, chronic unemployment, and a low degree of commitment to school.[120] Further analysis shows that the persistent offender group may be further subdivided into high- and low-rate offenders, with the former committing two or three times as many offences as the latter.[121] Punishment does little to deter their behaviour and, if anything, prompts escalation of their criminal activities.

Correctional Services Canada reports that of 14 091 male offenders incarcerated in 1997, 54 percent had no term of previous federal incarceration, 17 percent had one term, 11 percent had two, 7 percent had three, and 10 percent had more than three. Women were far more likely to have had no previous term of federal incarceration (75 percent) and less likely to have more than three (4 percent). Of provincial and territorial inmates, 83 percent had at least one prior conviction. In a "snapshot" of inmates done in 1996, it was found that 96 percent of those classified as high risk had previous convictions.[122]

In sum, research shows that a small group of offenders are responsible for a great deal of all crime. These youths begin their offending career at an extremely young age and persist into their adulthood.

Implications of the Chronic Offender Concept

The findings of the cohort studies and the discovery of the chronic offender is a puzzle for criminological theory. If relatively few offenders become chronic, persistent criminals, it is possible that they possess some individual trait that is responsible for their criminality. Most people exposed to troublesome social conditions, such as poverty, do not become chronic offenders; thus, it is unlikely that social conditions alone can cause chronic offending. So, what does?

Traditional theories of criminal behaviour have failed to distinguish between chronic and occasional offenders. They have concentrated more on explaining why people begin to commit crime and paid scant attention to the reasons that people stop offending. The "discovery" of the chronic offender has forced criminologists to consider the role of persistence and desistence in the onset of criminality and also in its termination. Why do most offenders "age out" of crime? Why do some persist into adulthood? Ongoing research efforts are now aimed at answering these critical questions.

The chronic offender concept has also raised questions about the treatment of known offenders: If we can identify chronic offenders, what should we do about them? How can chronic offenders be controlled if punishment actually escalates the frequency of their criminal activity? The chronic offender has thus become

Studies in Europe show that persistent chronic offenders account for a significant portion of all criminal acts. Frequency of offences has been associated with early onset of antisocial behaviour, association with deviant peers, personality disorders, poor school achievement, dysfunctional family relations, low IQ, substance abuse, chronic unemployment, and a low degree of commitment to school. Could these youths be influenced by the personal characteristics that promote and sustain chronic criminal offending?

a central focus of crime control policy. Concern about repeat offenders has been translated into programs at various stages of the justice process.

Even more important has been the effect of the chronic offender on sentencing policy. Sentencing policies are increasingly designed to incapacitate serious offenders for long periods without hope of probation or parole. In the United States, a mandatory sentence for violent or drug-related crimes in most states is commonly known as a "three strikes and you're out" policy. Whether such policies can be effective in reducing crime rates or are merely "get tough" measures designed to placate conservative voters remains to be seen.

Summary

There are three primary sources of crime statistics: the UCR based on police data accumulated by the CCJS, self-reports of criminal behaviour, and victim surveys. All three sources, pieced together, overlap to tell us about crime in Canada. Each data source has its strengths and weaknesses, and though quite different from one another, they agree on the nature of criminal behaviour. Commissions of inquiry are also a quasi-judicial source of information about crime that can provide detailed investigation of criminal issues.

The data sources show some stable patterns in the crime rate. Until the early 1990s, the amount of violent crime was increasing, only to go into a decade of decline. Ecological patterns show that some areas of the country are more crime-prone than others, that there are seasons and times for crime, and these patterns are quite stable. There is also evidence of a gender and age gap in the crime rate. Men usually commit more crimes than do women, and young people commit more crimes than the elderly do. The crime data show that people commit fewer crimes as they age, but the significance and cause of this pattern is still not completely understood. A class pattern also exists in the crime rate. However, it is still unclear whether these are true differences or a function of discriminatory law enforcement.

One of the most important findings of cohort research is the existence of the chronic offender, a repeat criminal responsible for a significant number of all law violations. Chronic offenders begin their career early in life and, rather than aging out of crime, persist in their criminal behaviour into adulthood. The discovery of the chronic offender has led to the study of developmental criminology—why people persist, desist, escalate, or terminate their deviant behaviour.

This chapter shows that with the right tools, we can better understand the patterns of crime and the reasons that it occurs. However, we also need to be aware that crime statistics seldom portray at face value the reality they purport to describe. Crime statistics can be an artifact of reporting practices, police enforcement, changing legal definitions of crime, and media representations.

Thinking Like a Criminologist

An assistant deputy minister in the federal Department of Justice has asked for your professional advice on how to reduce the threat of young offenders becoming chronic offenders. Some of the more conservative members of the government believe that juvenile delinquents who are punished harshly are less likely to recidivate than are youths who receive lesser punishments, such as community corrections or probation.

The bureaucrat is unsure whether such an approach can reduce the threat of chronic offending. Can tough punishment produce deviant identities that lock kids in a criminal way of life? This would be counterproductive. Conversely, will a strategy stressing punishment have relatively little impact if these are serious chronic offenders? You find it difficult to offer advice, because you remember a lecture given by the Minister of Corrections, John Edwards, at St. Thomas University in 1996, in which he described the profile of the federal offender.

Ninety-seven percent are male, most are single, and 75 percent have committed serious violent offences. Two-thirds of the admissions have done provincial or territorial time, and most have records going back into juvenile years. The average educational level of offenders is grade 7, and 68 percent test below grade 8 in language and mathematics. More than half claim to have been abused as children, and three-quarters have unstable job histories. Does punishment begin to get at these underlying issues?

Key Terms

aging out	crime rate	liberal feminist theory
androgens	definition-sensitive crimes	masculinity hypothesis
attrition	desistance phenomenon	media-sensitive crimes
career criminals	early onset	percentage change
chivalry hypothesis	expressive crimes	policing-sensitive crimes
chronic offenders	founded	report-sensitive crimes
cleared	incidence	self-report surveys
continuity of crime	incident-based data	Uniform Crime Report (UCR)
crime funnel	instrumental crimes	

Critical Thinking Questions

1. Would you answer honestly if a national crime survey asked you about your criminal behaviour, including drinking and drug use? If not, why not? If you said "no," do you question the accuracy of self-report surveys?

2. How would you explain gender differences in the crime rate? Why do you think males are more violent than females?

3. Assuming that males are more violent than females, does that mean crime has a biological rather than a social basis (because males and females share a similar environment)?

4. The UCR reports that crime rates are higher in large cities than they are in small towns. What does that tell us about the effects of TV, films, and music on teenage behaviour?

5. What social and environmental factors do you believe influence the crime rate? For example, do you think a national emergency would increase or decrease crime rates?

See the book-specific website at http://www.siegelcriminology3e.nelson.com for additional chapter links, discussions, and quizzes.

Victims and Victimization

For many years, crime victims were not considered an important topic for criminological study. Victims were viewed as the passive receptors of a criminal's anger, greed, or frustration; they were people considered to be in the "wrong place at the wrong time." In the late 1960s, a number of pioneering studies found that, contrary to popular belief, the victim's function is an important one in the crime process. Victims can influence criminal behaviour by playing an active role in the criminal incident—for example, if an assault victim insults and provokes his or her eventual attacker. Research efforts have found that victims also play an indirect role in the criminal incident—for example, when people adopt work or lifestyles that brings them into high-crime areas.

"Gutless politicians are only concerned for the rights of criminals" reads a protest sign outside the Just Desserts café in Toronto. The criticism became especially vehement after it was revealed that the suspect in the shooting at the café was an illegal immigrant convicted previously of violent offences. There was an outcry demanding that "aliens" who commit crimes be deported.

The discovery that the victim plays an important role in the crime process has prompted the scientific study of the victim, or **victimology**. Victim studies have also taken on great importance because of concern for those who are injured in violent crimes or who suffer loss owing to economic crimes. The 1999 General Social Survey (GSS) in Canada indicates that 25 percent of Canadians were the victims of at least one crime in the previous year. Of 8.3 million victimization incidents reported to the GSS in 1999, one-third involved a household crime (break and enter, motor vehicle/parts theft, theft of household property, or vandalism). The advantage of using the GSS to measure victimization is that it enables us to count crimes not reported to the police.

In this chapter, the focus is on victims and their relationship to the criminal process. First, using available victim data, we analyze the nature and extent of victimization. We then turn to a discussion of the relationship between victims and criminal offenders, and we summarize the various theories of victimization. Finally, we look at how society has responded to the needs of victims and at the special problems they still face.

Problems of Crime Victims: Loss and Suffering

Being the target or a victim of rape, robbery, or assault can have considerable long-term consequences.[1] The Insurance Board of Canada estimates that more than $1 billion a year is paid in claims due to property crime, and theft is the cause of one-third of all homeowner claims paid, with a recovery rate of only 23 percent in the 1990s.

However, property losses are only a small part of the toll that crime takes on victims.[2] Productivity losses due to injury, medical costs, psychological pain, and emotional trauma also take their toll. Then factor in insurance premiums, security, and surveillance costs. This figure does not include the cost of white-collar crime, tax evasion, or stock market manipulation. There are also the costs that cannot be easily measured. Crime makes people feel unsafe and decreases their quality of life. The ripple effects are felt in a broad range of sectors, including health, social services, education, labour, and employment. Table 4.1 provides some international estimates of these costs.

Victims are likely to suffer serious physical injury, often requiring medical treatment. And victims' suffering does not end when the attacker leaves the scene of the crime. They may suffer more "victimization" at the hands of the justice system. While the crime is still fresh in their minds, victims may be subjected to insensitive questioning by police, including innuendos or suspicion

TABLE 4.1 Some International Estimates of the Costs of Crime

Cost of crime in Canada (2004) ($1500/person)	
police, courts, corrections	$10 billion
with pain, suffering, lost wages, health, insurance costs	$46 billion
Cost of crime in the United States (1999) ($4100/person)	$1 trillion
Cost of crime in Australia (2003) ($1600/person)	$32 billion
Cost of crime in England and Wales (2000)	
cost of property	£19 billion
emotional and physical impact on victims	£18 billion
criminal justice system costs	£12 billion
costs in anticipation of crime	£5 billion
Total	£60 billion

Sources: Australian Institute of Criminology; (British) Home Office Research Studies; Department of Justice (Canada).

Connections

Some crimes are called "victimless" crimes, not because no one is hurt, but because an agreement exists between two parties. See Chapter 14 for more on this type of crime.

that the victims were somehow at fault. Victims may have difficulty learning what is going on in the case. In addition, their property is often kept for a long time as evidence and may never be returned. They lose wages because of time spent testifying in court.

Time may be wasted when victims appear in court only to have their case postponed or dismissed. Furthermore, they may find that authorities are indifferent to their fear of retaliation if they cooperate in the offender's prosecution, and they may be fearful of testifying in court and being embarrassed by defence attorneys. Only a few courthouses have services on site to assist victims who are appearing in court as witnesses.[3]

After the incident is over, the victim may suffer stress and anxiety, even when the physical traumas, financial losses, and justice process have been forgotten. For example, women who were sexually and physically

abused as children are more suicidal as adults than are nonabused females.[4] Those who suffered the pains of abuse also have significantly higher levels of homelessness; a history of physical and sexual abuse is especially common among homeless women, who may also display symptoms of mental illness.[5] The long-term emotional trauma suffered by women in the aftermath of spousal assault is also well documented.[6] Spousal abuse victims suffer an extremely high prevalence of depression, posttraumatic stress disorder, anxiety disorder, and obsessive-compulsive disorder. Symptoms include nightmares, hyperarousal, and repression of the abuse.

Many Canadians are victimized every year by robbery, and if the crime is marked by violence and loss of property, the psychological consequences can be as serious as posttraumatic stress disorder. Women generally suffer more than men do, and the elderly experience more distress than the young do. Virtually every victim experiences an emotional reaction, and up to a third of robbery victims suffer severe short-term trauma. After six months, the effects diminish, but 5 percent to 10 percent of victims continue to suffer significant psychopathology. The effects last even longer for victims of domestic violence. Child abuse is also more pervasive than official statistics indicate, and children who are victims of physical assault will have problems, such as noncompliance, tantrums and aggression, serious intellectual deficits, language delays, and interpersonal problems.[7]

Male victims of violent attacks also suffer postcrime stress disorders. Viewing themselves from a male frame of reference, these victims express feelings of being weak and helpless. Whereas female victims internalize and blame themselves, males are more likely to externalize blame and express anger toward their attackers.[8] Often, men who have been incarcerated for violent crimes have themselves been subjected to multiple forms of abuse.[9]

Victims are more likely than nonvictims to think that crime rates have increased, to worry about neighbourhood safety, and to experience a lower quality of life.[10] In short, the pain and suffering experienced by crime victims does not stop after the criminal incident is over. Many go through a fundamental life change, viewing the world more suspiciously and less as a safe, controllable, and meaningful place, becoming more likely to suffer psychological stress for extended periods.[11]

Some victims may find that the physical wounds received during a criminal incident haunt them for the rest of their lives, especially if they become physically disabled because of wounds sustained during episodes of violence. Many victims have no insurance, and specialized treatment costs add to the overload on an overburdened health care system.[12]

Hate crime adds a new dimension to victimization. Hate crimes are more likely to involve excessive violence and greater psychological trauma. They are seven times more likely to be directed against a person than against property than are crimes in which hate isn't the motivating factor. They are twice as likely to involve physical injury and four times as likely to require hospitalization. The ensuing depression can cause intense feelings of vulnerability, and lead to physical ailments, learning problems, and interpersonal conflicts.[13]

The Perception of the Risk of Being a Victim

Consistently in national surveys, people's fears of victimization outstrip their actual likelihood of experiencing a crime. Such results raise questions about the public's perception of risk.[14] The fact that the public overestimates the likelihood of crime, despite contradictory evidence from their own experience, points to the influence of extraneous factors in the public's knowledge of crime. People do not rely on their own experience in assessing the likelihood of being a victim of crime. A 2003 poll in Toronto found that 43 percent of people are very concerned about child abductions, 42 percent about drugs and dealers, 36 percent about sexual assault, 24 percent about police chases.[15] As Figure 4.1 shows, in a separate poll, a full 60 percent of people surveyed worried about being a victim of a home break-in.

The media help create a distorted expectation of victimization. In 1996, Canada's murder rate declined for the fourth year in a row. However, television news had increased its coverage of murder stories (Figure 4.2).[16] According to the National Media Archive's annual study of murder stories, coverage tended to focus on sensational murders—the Bernardo and Simpson trials each made up 18 percent of the CBC's murder stories in 1995. Furthermore, 16 percent of the murders in 1995 were committed by someone unknown to the victim, but on television the murders most likely to be reported are random ones. Although 83 percent of murders are committed by a spouse or acquaintance, 54 percent of CBC and 66 percent of CTV coverage focused on random murders. Only 18 percent of CBC and 11 percent of CTV murder stories focused on murders committed by someone known to the victim.[17]

It is reassuring that the fear of crime seems to be decreasing,[18] yet we have to be conscious of how crime can be distorted in the media, because it has an effect on demands for police services, the public's perception of the courts, and how politicians develop programs to prevent and fight crime.[19]

> In a poll of 11 countries worldwide, a majority of citizens said that the world has become a more dangerous place.

Source: Poll conducted by Ipsos Reid, May 16, 2002, "Global Poll Shows World Perceived As More Dangerous Place."

Figure 4.1	British Columbians' Worries about Being a Victim of Crime

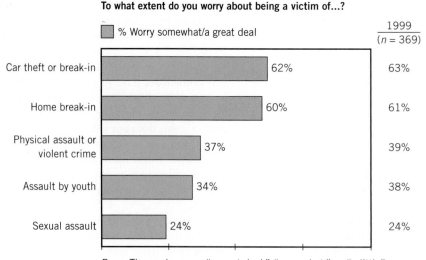

To what extent do you worry about being a victim of...?

☐ % Worry somewhat/a great deal

		1999 (n = 369)
Car theft or break-in	62%	63%
Home break-in	60%	61%
Physical assault or violent crime	37%	39%
Assault by youth	34%	38%
Sexual assault	24%	24%

Base: Those who worry "a great deal," "somewhat," or "a little" about being the victim of a specific crime.

Source: Poll conducted by Ipsos Reid, *British Columbians on Crime*, March 26, 2004.

| Figure 4.2 | Murder Rate Compared with Television Attention, 1989–2000 |

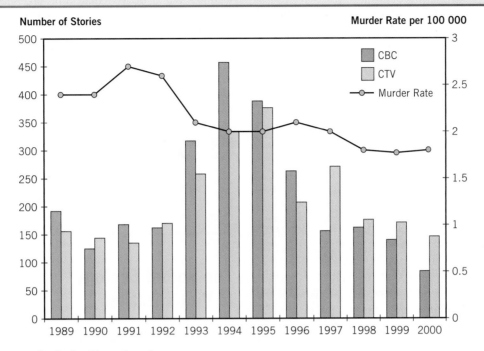

Note: *2000 figures are for the first 11 months only.

Source: National Media Archive 2004.

Problems of Crime Victims: Antisocial Behaviour

In the 1996 film *Never Talk to Strangers*, a psychiatrist played by Rebecca DeMornay suspects that her new boyfriend (Antonio Banderas) is a killer. As the bodies begin to pile up, the audience begins to share her suspicions. In the film's surprise ending, we learn that DeMornay is the real killer. It seems her personality was irrevocably damaged when her father sexually abused her as a child and murdered her mother while she watched.

The association between early victimization and later criminality is not merely the subject of Hollywood films; victims of certain crimes are more likely to commit crime themselves. For example, in an analysis of juvenile court records, Cathy Spatz Widom found that child maltreatment was a significant predictor of future criminality. Having been abused or neglected increased the odds of being arrested as a juvenile and also of having at least one alcohol- or drug-related arrest in adulthood. The odds of adult arrest were 39 percent greater for maltreated adolescents than for nonabused ones. This was further confirmed by later research.[20] The phenomenon of child victims later becoming adult criminals is called the **cycle of violence**.[21]

The cycle of violence hypothesis is supported by research showing that young males are more likely to engage in violent behaviour if they were (1) the target of physical abuse and (2) exposed to interadult violence.[22] The association between victimization and future behavioural difficulties is not limited to males; research efforts have found that females exposed to family violence may be even more likely to manifest behavioural and adjustment problems as they mature.[23]

A 2001 *Juristat* study also found that children who experience high levels of punitive parenting and lower parental nurturance exhibit more aggressive behaviour and are more likely to be involved in property offences.[24] A 2003 report on the correctional services system found that an extremely high percentage of Aboriginal offenders report early drug and alcohol use (80 percent), physical abuse (45 percent), parental absence or neglect (41 percent), and poverty (35 percent) in their family backgrounds.[25] A study of family violence cites the 1998 National Longitudinal Survey of Children finding that 8 percent of children between the ages of four and seven witness some type of physical violence in the home. Seeing physical violence was found to be related to long-term behaviour problems, such as aggression, and emotional problems, such as anxiety.[26]

Connections

It has become common for Hollywood to depict women as psychopathic serial killers (*Friday the 14th, Black Widow, The Crush*). Are female serial killers common? No, women are rarely involved in multiple murders. Chapter 11 reviews serial murder in some detail.

The Nature of Victimization

Although criminologists depend largely on official statistics, victimization surveys are an important source of information about the nature and extent of victimization. The surveys were originally conceived as a way to estimate the distribution of unreported crime and can be used to make estimates of overall victimization patterns.

Victimization Surveys. In 1982 the Ministry of the Solicitor General conducted the Canadian Urban Victimization Survey (CUVS), whose purpose was to acquire information on the extent of crime, the impact of victimization, public perception of crime and the criminal justice system, and public knowledge of crime prevention and compensation programs.[27] The survey showed that many offences were not reported to the police. Robberies, for example, were estimated to occur at a rate of 993 per 100 000 population, compared with the official police rate of 108 per 100 000![28]

The next victimization survey was conducted in 1988 as part of the General Social Survey (GSS). A sample of people 15 years of age and older were asked about their knowledge of victim services, perceived risk of victimization, and the number and kind of accidents and crimes respondents had been involved in during 1987. It was estimated that there were 143 personal victimizations per 1000 people and 216 household incidents of victimization per 1000 people.[29] Two other victimization surveys have been conducted as part of the GSS in 1993 and 1999.

International patterns of victimization show that Canadians are relatively free from contact with crime compared with people in some other countries, as shown in Table 4.2. Canada ranked sixth in car theft, seventh in burglary, and eighth in violent crime. In overall victimization, Canada's rate was lower than Australia's, England and Wales's, the Netherlands', and Sweden's.

The patterns in victimization surveys are stable and repetitive, indicating that victimization is not random but rather is a function of personal and ecological factors. Studying these patterns informs us about the nature of victimization, and policies can be created that

might eventually reduce the victimization rate. Who are victims? Where does victimization take place? What is the relationship between victims and criminals? Is there a difference in the report rate between crime that is **acquaintance-related** and crime that is **stranger-related**? Answers to these questions can come from crime victimization surveys. In the following sections, some of the most important patterns and trends in victimization are discussed.

Connections

The importance of victimization is more apparent in the context of other sources of information about crime. Chapter 3 presents an overview of major issues related to the measurement of crime.

The Social Ecology of Victimization

The GSS survey data can tell us a lot about the social and demographic patterns of victimization: where, when, and how it occurs, and whether a victim's involvement in crime is random.

In general terms, the risk of personal injury increases moving from east to west across Canada, is higher for males than for females, and is lower for the elderly than the young. Those living in urban areas have higher rates of theft, sexual assault, and robbery than do people living in rural areas. Some violent victimizations, such as robbery, are more likely to be committed by strangers and in public, while sexual assaults are more likely to be committed by acquaintances. Eighty percent of robberies were committed by a stranger in 2004, compared with 24 percent of non-sexual assaults.

 InfoTrac®

Did you know that a great deal of victimization occurs in school buildings? Although school violence may be declining, about one-third of all students are injured in a physical altercation each year. To learn more about this phenomenon, using InfoTrac® College Edition, read "Violence Decreasing in U.S. High Schools," *The Brown University Child and Adolescent Behavior Letter* 15, no. 12 (1999): 3.

TABLE 4.2 The Profile of Crime in Different Countries[1]

(PERCENTAGE OF ALL OFFENCES: TOTAL = 100%): 2000 ICVS

	Thefts from and of cars	Car vandalism	Motorcycle & bicycle theft	Burglary with entry and attempts	All contact crime[2]	Theft of personal property
Australia	18	20	4	15	29	14
Belgium	14	23	15	17	19	13
Canada	20	15	10	13	27	15
Catalonia (Spain)	25	38	4	7	14	12
Denmark	14	13	26	13	21	12
England & Wales	19	23	6	12	30	10
Finland	11	16	19	6	36	13
France	23	31	6	8	24	9
Japan	8	26	40	13	11	2
Netherlands	12	26	21	10	19	12
Northern Ireland	20	25	10	11	22	11
Poland	21	23	10	10	20	16
Portugal	29	33	4	13	14	8
Scotland	16	30	6	9	28	12
Sweden	19	14	21	7	24	16
USA	20	22	7	15	20	16
Average	18	24	13	11	22	12

1 Based on incidence rates. Percentages add to 100%.
2 Based on robbery, sexual incidents, and assaults and threats.

Source: John von Kesteren, Pat Mayhew, Paul Nieuwbeerta, "Criminal Victimisation in Seven Industrialized Countries. Key Findings from the 2000 International Crime Victims Survey." *Research Policy*, no. 187. © NI Syndication.

Victim Characteristics

A number of social and demographic characteristics distinguish victims from nonvictims. The most important of these factors are gender, age, social status, and relationship.

Gender. The GSS provides information on the background characteristics of the victims of crime, including gender. Gender is related to risk, fear, and sense of control.

Men are more likely to be victims of robbery (12 per 1000 men versus 7 per 1000 for women) and assault (92 per 1000 for men, 70 per 1000 for women). Women are more likely to be victims of sexual assault (33 per 1000 for women, compared with 8 per 1000 for men) and theft (80 per 1000 for women, 71 per 1000 for men). Women's overall personal victimization was 189 per 1000, compared with 183 for men.

When men are victims of violent crime, the perpetrator is usually a stranger. Women are much more likely to be attacked by a relative than men are; about two-thirds of all attacks against women are committed by a husband, a boyfriend, a family member, or an acquaintance.[30] In two-thirds of sexual assaults, the victim is acquainted with her attacker.

Gender is a significant factor in such crimes as stalking, in which women account for 78 percent of victims in criminal harassment cases.[31] The way in which authorities deal with such crimes can be crucial. In the infamous Jane Doe case, the Metropolitan Toronto police failed to warn women that a serial rapist was committing crimes in their neighbourhood because they didn't want to alert the suspect. In 2000 a woman sued the Toronto police for $4.5 million in damages for failing to warn women in the city's north end that a sexual predator was attacking women in underground parking garages.

Risk is gendered and affects how women think of how to go about their everyday activities. Because they are more likely to think that crime has increased, and to worry about being victimized, women engage in defensive behaviours, managing their fear of crime by making decisions on where to walk, where to park, and whom to see.[32]

Age. Young people commit a greater proportion of certain crimes than do other age groups. In 2003, youths 16 to 24 years represented 14 percent of the total population but were responsible for 45 percent of property crimes and 32 percent of violent crimes.[33] *Juristat* statistics show that 37 percent of all personal crimes were committed against those between the ages of 15 and 24 (17 percent of the population). Moreover, 49 percent of sexual assaults and 57 percent of robberies occurred in that age group.

In the case of homicide, these youths are especially likely to kill parents and other family members.[34] Moreover, because much crime is intra-age (within the same age group), youths themselves face a much greater victimization risk than do older persons. Victim risk is highest in the 15 to 24 age group (405 per 1000), dropping abruptly to 262 incidents per 1000 between the ages of 25 and 34 years.

The elderly, who are thought of as being the helpless targets of predatory criminals, are actually much safer than are young people, with a victimization rate of 12 per 1000. Those over 65 years of age (15 percent of the population) experience 2 percent of total violations against the person. As people age, they are more likely to be a homeowner, more likely to think that crime has increased, and more likely to have higher levels of satisfaction with the criminal justice system.

The association between age and victimization may be bound up in the lifestyle shared by young people. Adolescents often stay out late at night, go to public places, and hang out with kids who have a high risk of criminal involvement. Most adolescents aged 12 to 19 are attacked by offenders in the same age category, while a great majority of adults are victimized by adult criminals. Approximately 50 percent of victimizations occur in or around a private residence, about 30 percent at a public institution (such as a school), and about 20 percent in public places, such as a parking lot.

In their now benchmark research, sociologists Gelles and Straus found extensive physical abuse of children by their parents. In addition, they found that 16 percent of the couples in their sample reported a violent act toward a spouse, 50 percent of multichild families reported attacks between siblings, and 20 percent had incidents in which children attacked parents.[35] The U.S. National Committee to Prevent Child Abuse indicates that in 1995, there was a 50 percent increase in cases of child abuse reported to police and social service agencies compared with 1985.[36] It is uncertain whether this increase in reported abuse is a result of an increase in incidents or a greater public awareness of the problem.

As discussed below, age of victimization is also linked to relationship as a factor. Nearly three-quarters of murdered children are killed by a parent, children are most likely to be sexually victimized by family members, and rates of family-related assault have gone up since 1998. Table 4.3 shows that sexual and physical assaults against children are more likely to occur against the young.

InfoTrac®

Australia, the United States, and other developed countries offer elementary school programs that heighten children's awareness about the possibility of abduction. To read about these and other programs on InfoTrac® College Edition, use "crime victims" as a subject guide and look for the subcategory "youth–crimes against."

Social Status. The poorest Canadians are more likely to be victims of crime, since they are more likely to live in areas that are crime-prone: inner-city, urban neighbourhoods. Households with incomes of less than $15 000 had a victimization rate of 254 per 1000, compared with the national average of 186 for personal crimes. The rate for violent crimes in this income category was 192 per 1000, compared with a national average of 111. The $60 000-and-over income group had the next highest victimization rate. Street youths also report higher rates of physical assaults than do high-school students, 69 percent versus 39 percent, and higher rates of sexual assault as well (29 percent versus 6 percent).

One fact that is particularly disturbing is that poverty increases the risk of child abuse. A 1998 report, *The Canadian Incidence Study of Reported Child Abuse and Neglect*, documents that 40 percent of child abuse cases stem from neglect, 19 percent from emotional maltreatment, 31 percent from physical abuse, and 10 percent from sexual abuse. Many of the children also suffered from depression and anxiety, and in three-quarters of the cases, at least one parent suffered from drug abuse or domestic violence. Nearly half the families were led by a single parent, and 36 percent were collecting social assistance.[37]

Although the poor are more likely to be the victims of assault, the wealthy are more likely to be the targets of theft. Perhaps the affluent, who sport more expensive attire and drive better cars, earn the attention of thieves

TABLE 4.3 Age and Type of Assault against Children and Youth by Family Member, 2002[1,2,3]

Relationship of victim to accused		Sexual assault[4] Age of victim							Physical assault[5] Age of victim						
		Total No.	<3	3–5	6–8	9–11	12–14	15–17	Total No.	<3	3–5	6–8	9–11	12–14	15–17
Parent[6]	%	1 219	61	44	37	37	46	48	3 852	89	86	84	75	70	53
Sibling[7]	%	832	21	30	34	31	27	23	1 025	7	6	11	17	21	24
Extended family[8]	%	779	18	26	29	32	25	24	419	4	7	6	8	7	9
Spouse[9]	%	33	...	...	...	...	2	6	301	...	...	...	...	1	14
Family total	%		100	100	100	100	100	100		100	100	100	100	100	100
Total victims	no.	**2 663**	92	550	575	599	667	380	**5 597**	322	432	682	842	1 361	1 838

Source: Statistics Canada, Canadian Centre for Justice Statistics, *Incident-Based Uniform Crime Reporting (UCR2) Survey*, 2003.

Note: Percentages may not add up to 100% due to rounding.

... not applicable

1 Excludes incidents where the sex and/or the age of the victim was unknown.

2 Data are not nationally representative. Based on data from 94 police departments representing 56% of the national volume of crime in 2002.

3 Children and youth include all those under the age of 18.

4 Sexual assault includes assault, sexual assault with a weapon, aggravated sexual assault and the "other sexual crimes" category, which includes sexual interference, sexual touching, sexual exploitation, incest, etc.

5 Physical assault includes common assault (level 1), major assault (levels 2 and 3), unlawfully causing bodily harm, discharge firearm with intent, criminal negligence causing bodily harm and other assaults.

6 Includes a small number of cases where age or the relationship between the accused and the victim have been miscoded.

7 Sibling includes natural, step, half, foster or adopted siblings.

8 Extended family includes others related by blood, marriage, adoption or foster care.

9 Spouses include legally married, separated, divorced, and common-law partners.

TABLE 4.4 Violations against the Person, by Relationship of Accused to Victim[1] and Sex*, 2002

	Total	Family				Friend[5]	Acquaintance			Stranger	Unknown[6]
		Spouse/ Ex-spouse	Parent	Other Family[4]	Total Family		Business	Acquaintance	Total		
					percentage						
TOTAL VICTIMS											
Homicide[2]	356	4.0	5.1	7.3	26.4	6.2	3.4	15.7	25.3	15.7	32.6
Criminal Negligence/ Other Violations Causing Death	68	5.9	8.8	4.4	18.1	13.2	2.9	16.2	32.4	29.4	19.1
Attempt/Conspire Murder	571	5.1	2.5	5.1	22.6	6.3	4.6	24.3	35.2	28.5	13.7
Sexual Assault— Total	13 967	4.1	6.7	13.1	26.0	10.5	6.2	29.8	48.5	18.8	6.7
Aggravated Sexual Assault	84	0.7	6.0	7.1	23.8	6.0	7.1	26.2	38.3	25.0	11.9
Sexual Assault with Weapon	256	1.7	2.0	3.0	17.6	11.7	6.1	18.8	38.8	40.0	6.0
Sexual Assault	13 627	3.9	8.9	13.3	26.1	10.5	8.2	30.1	46.6	18.4	6.7
Nonsexual Assault	140 135	3.9	3.9	6.7	30.5	9.9	7.2	21.9	39.0	24.2	6.3
Aggravated Assault	1 791	9.2	2.3	5.5	17.0	9.0	3.6	25.2	37.9	32.3	12.8
Assault with weapon/CBH[3]	28 564	9.8	3.7	6.7	26.9	8.7	5.6	23.2	37.5	28.9	7.3
Assault	101 016	2.8	4.3	7.2	34.3	11.0	7.3	22.8	41.0	18.9	5.8
Discharge Firearm with Intent	64	7.1	0.0	2.4	9.5	2.4	1.2	31.0	34.5	41.7	14.3
Assault Peace Officer	6 825	0.1	0.0	0.1	0.2	0.1	14.5	3.3	17.9	73.8	8.1
Other Assaults	2 855	4.6	2.0	2.8	9.4	4.7	10.5	13.3	28.5	56.6	5.5
Assault—Total	184 102	8.5	4.4	7.3	30.1	10.0	7.3	22.6	39.9	23.7	6.3

Other Sexual Offences	1 805	0.7	12.7	17.3	30.7	5.2	8.0	30.0	49.2	19.4	6.7
Kidnapping/Hostage Taking	2 473	4.7	2.8	3.1	30.8	16.5	3.0	15.2	34.8	28.6	6.0
Abduction	318	0.0	58.8	9.7	68.6	1.3	0.0	5.3	6.6	16.0	6.8
Robbery	19 509	0.5	0.0	0.2	0.7	0.8	1.4	8.3	10.5	80.4	8.4
Extortion	726	3.7	0.7	4.4	8.8	5.8	14.5	38.4	58.7	25.9	5.6
Criminal Harassment	9 706	6.9	0.9	3.4	31.2	20.2	8.2	28.4	52.8	9.5	6.5
Other	35 524	2.4	2.7	7.5	22.6	6.9	10.7	33.0	50.6	18.9	7.8
Total Violations Against the Person	**225 157**	**6.1**	**3.7**	**6.6**	**26.4**	**9.1**	**7.2**	**23.2**	**39.5**	**27.3**	**6.6**

Source: Incident-based UCR2. Policing Service Program, Canadian Centre for Justice Statistics.

Note: Data are provided from a non-representative subset of 123 police departments accounting for approximately 59% of the national volume of crime.
*Box breakdown may not add to the total because in some situations the sex of the person is not identified.

1 Relationship establishes the identity of the accused (spouse, friend) relative to a victim at the time the incident occurred. Spouse or ex-spouse denote marriage or common-law.
2 Homicide characteristics reported to UCR2 may not match them on the homicide data batch. For detailed analysis on homicide refer to the most recent release from the Homicide Survey. Homicide in Canada, 2002 *Juristat* vol. 23. no. 8, released October, 2003.
3 CBH is an abbreviation for causing bodily harm.
4 Other family includes child, sibling, grandparents, aunts, uncles, cousins, and all other relatives to the victim either by blood or marriage.
5 Friend relationship includes long-term and/or close relationship with the victim (include intimates, ex-friends, ex-intimates).
6 Unknown is included when the identity of the accused is not known or the relationship cannot be established.

looking for attractive targets. Victim data suggest that thieves choose their targets carefully. In contrast, the targets of violence, an expressive crime, are the nation's poorest people.

Relationship. As well as varying by age and gender, crimes vary by the relationship between the victim and the offender. Although an increasing number of violent crimes are committed by strangers, a surprising number of violent crime victims are either related to or acquainted with their attackers. However, one problem with crime statistics is that they provide little information on crime victims, especially with regard to relationships. Victimization surveys and some changes in the UCR are trying to rectify this.

The 1999 GSS shows that the overall violent victimization rate was highest for those who are single (21 percent), with married people and common-law partners lower (5 percent and 16 percent, respectively). For those who engaged in 30 or more evening activities per month, the accused was a family member in 27 percent of the cases, a friend or acquaintance in 36 percent, and a stranger in 26 percent. However, UCR data from 2002 show a different relationship pattern for certain types of crimes. Homicide is more likely to be committed by a family member (26 percent) or acquaintance (25 percent) than by a stranger (16 percent). This same pattern exists for sexual assault, nonsexual assault, criminal harassment, and abduction, as shown in Table 4.4.

The GSS of 1988 and 1993 were designed to gather information on attacks by family members, but its estimated incidence of wife assault (15 per 1000 women) is conservative. Statistics Canada's national survey of violence against women, conversely, found that 30 percent of women currently or previously married had experienced at least one incident of abuse. The rate of assault among young women was four times the national average and twice the national average in the lowest income group. With statistics like these, it is obvious that we are only starting to understand the extent of violence against women in relationships.[38]

Women in relationships are more likely to experience violence than are men: They are four times more likely to be killed, three times more likely to suffer injury, five times more likely to need medical attention, and five times more likely to fear for their lives as a result of the violence. Since 1974, nearly 2600 spousal homicides have been recorded in Canada, with more than three-quarters of them against women. Young separated women are at the highest risk. In 2002, females accounted for 85 percent of all victims of spousal violence. Women aged 25 to 34 had the highest rates, and the rates were five times lower for

men than for women.[39] Recently, spousal homicide rates have dropped. Several societal changes explain this decline, including more equality in relationships, changes in the law, and better training for the police and judges.

In 1996, British Columbia announced an updated policy on violence against women in relationships, including a central registry of protection orders to ensure that police have access to information on peace bonds and restraining orders; to improve rights and services for victims; to fund transition houses, treatment, and violence prevention and public education programs. British Columbia's actions reflect those taken in many provinces and territories and represent an effort to deal with an entrenched problem.[40]

When a spouse is killed, it is usually the woman; and when women kill, it is usually in self-defence. After Jane Stafford shot her sleeping common-law husband, the trial evidence indicated that he was domineering and abusive. He had threatened to kill all the members of her family, one by one, if she tried to leave him. On the night in question, he had threatened to kill her son.[41] It is only within the last 15 or so years that the Canadian courts have come to realize that standards for assessing the violence of women compared with that of men must be different in some situations, as discussed in the Famous Canadian Criminals feature.

The home can be a dangerous place for children as well. Official statistics for 1994 show that 37 percent of all offenders in solved violent incidents against children under 12 were family members, and 25 percent were parents. Incidents in the home involving nonfamily members as offenders accounted for 63 percent of all offences, of which 16 percent were committed by strangers.[42] One survey estimated that more than 46 000 children in Ontario were suspected victims of abuse, which would be a rate of 21 per 1000 people or 2.1 percent.[43]

Repeat Victimization

Does prior victimization enhance or reduce the chances of future victimization? Certain patterns of behaviour encourage victimization, and people who maintain them become "chronic victims" who are constantly the target of predatory crimes.

Research shows that prior victimization is a strong predictor of future victimization.[44] Research also shows that households that have experienced victimization in the past are the ones most likely to experience it again.[45] Fully one-half of incidents reported by the GSS in 1988 were repeat victimizations. Offences that are more likely to be stranger-related, such as robbery, are not as likely to be repeat offences. This pattern is seen internationally.[46]

Famous Canadian Criminals

A Woman Who Killed

"In 1991 a charge of second degree murder was stayed against a Nelson, B.C., woman who blew away her husband with a shotgun while he was talking on the telephone."

So starts the article "New Hope for Husband Murderers" from a 1995 issue of *Alberta Report*. The article discusses then–Justice Minister Allan Rock's decision to appoint a judge to review the cases of more than a dozen women convicted before 1990 of killing their abusive partners. The federal government had the authority to release the women, shorten their sentences, or order new trials. This decision followed a 1990 Supreme Court of Canada ruling that set the legal framework for what has become known as the "battered wife syndrome" defence.

The Supreme Court said in its decision, "It is difficult for the layperson to comprehend the battered wife syndrome. It is commonly thought that battered women are not really beaten as badly as they claim, otherwise they would have left the relationship. Alternatively, some believe that women enjoy being beaten, that they have a masochistic strain in them." Luckily we have left such views behind, and it is clear that the Supreme Court did not agree with these views.

Angelique Lyn Lavallee was a battered woman in a violent common-law relationship. She killed her partner late one night by shooting him in the back of the head as he left her room. They had had an argument and she was fearful for her life. He had frequently abused her and she concocted excuses to explain her injuries. A psychiatrist with experience in treating battered wives prepared a psychiatric

assessment of the appellant that was used to support her claim of self-defence. The psychiatrist explained Lavallee's ongoing terror and her inability to escape the relationship, despite the violence that put her life in danger. He testified that when Lavallee shot her partner, it was the desperate act of a woman who believed that she would be killed.

Lavallee was acquitted on the grounds that she was psychologically trapped in an abusive relationship and that to protect herself, she had the right to take steps that would not otherwise be tolerated. This conclusion differs from the traditional right of self-defence in that a woman can excusably kill her husband in self-defence even if no threat is imminent. Although the jury acquitted the appellant, its verdict was overturned by the Manitoba Court of Appeal.

Lavallee did not testify, but the statement she made to police on the night of the shooting was put into evidence. In it she described a party with friends:

"Me and Wendy argued as usual and I ran in the house after Kevin pushed me. I was scared, I was really scared. I locked the door. Herb was downstairs with Joanne and I called for Herb but I was crying when I called him. I said, 'Herb come up here please.' Herb came up to the top of the stairs and I told him that Kevin was going to hit me, actually beat on me again. Herb said he knew and that if I was his old lady things would be different; he gave me a hug. . . . He went outside to talk to Kevin leaving the door unlocked. I went upstairs and hid in my closet from Kevin. I was so scared. . . . My window was open and I could hear Kevin asking questions about what I was doing

and what I was saying. Next thing I know he was coming up the stairs for me. He came into my bedroom and said, 'Wench, where are you?' And he turned on my light and he said, 'Your purse is on the floor' and he kicked it. Okay, then he turned and he saw me in the closet. He wanted me to come out but I didn't want to come out because I was scared. I was so scared. He grabbed me by the arm right there. There's a bruise on my face also where he slapped me. He didn't slap me right then, first he yelled at me then he pushed me and I pushed him back and he hit me twice on the right hand side of my head. I was scared. All I thought about was all the other times he used to beat me, I was scared, I was shaking as usual. The rest is a blank, all I remember is he gave me the gun and a shot was fired through my screen. This is all so fast. And then the guns were in another room and he loaded it the second shot and gave it to me. And I was going to shoot myself. I pointed it to myself, I was so upset. Okay, and then he went and I was sitting on the bed and he started going like this with his finger [the appellant made a shaking motion with an index finger] and said something like 'You're my old lady and you do as you're told' or something like that. He said, 'Wait till everybody leaves, you'll get it then' and he said something to the effect of 'either you kill me or I'll get you'— that was what it was. He kind of smiled and then he turned around. I shot him but I aimed out. I thought I aimed above him and a piece of his head went that way."

Sources: Les Sillars, "New Hope for Husband Murderers," *Alberta Report* 22 (1995): 18; *R. v. Lavallee,* [1990] 1 S.C.R.: 852; "Ministers Respond to Self-Defence Review," Department of Justice News Release, Ottawa, September 26, 1997.

David Finkelhor and Nancy Asdigian identified three specific types of characteristics that increase the potential for victimization:

1. *Target vulnerability.* The victims' physical weakness or psychological distress renders them incapable of deterring crime and makes them easy targets (e.g., drinking).
2. *Target gratifiability.* The victims' characteristics increase their risk because they have some quality or possession that an offender wants to obtain (e.g., leather coat).
3. *Target antagonism.* Some characteristics increase risk because they arouse anger, jealousy, or destructive impulses in the offender (e.g., dressing differently).[47]

What factors predict chronic victimization? It is a combination of personal and social factors. For example, repeat victimizations are most likely to occur in areas with high crime rates. Some personal characteristics are also important.[48] Kids who are shy, physically weak, or socially isolated may be prone to being bullied in the schoolyard. This bullying then enhances chronic victimization. For example, boys who are bullied at school may become even more introverted after being victimized, increasing their chances for future victimization.[49]

Repeat victimization is also a function of rational choice and offender decision making: Offenders "learn" the weaknesses of victims. For example, the abusive husband learns that his battered wife will not call the police; thus, domestic violence is particularly susceptible to repeat offences. When the police do not respond to reported hate crimes, perpetrators learn they have little to fear from the law.[50]

A study in British Columbia found that 18 percent of respondents were victims of multiple offences. Furthermore, 18 percent of the sample accounted for 69 percent of the offences. The 6 percent of the respondents who were victimized three times or more accounted for 30 percent of all incidents.[51]

Connections

Efforts to understand the causes of the problems in Native communities today focus on their wider relations with the dominant White society. Chapter 9 discusses issues of inequality and ethnicity in more detail.

Theories of Victimization

For most of its history, criminological theory has focused on the actions of the criminal offender, and the role of the victim was virtually ignored. The resultant focus has sometimes been called "offenderology."[52] Then a number of scholars noted that the victim is not a passive target in crime but someone whose behaviour can influence his or

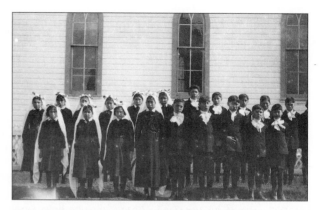

Abuse committed at residential and mission schools for Natives run by religious orders gained national prominence during the 1980s. Children were physically, emotionally, and sexually abused by priests and nuns after the children had been forcibly taken from their families and transported hundreds of kilometres to schools in which they were not allowed to speak their own languages.

her own fate. Crime is seldom random or gratuitous, but it is an outcome of an organizational process that involves both victim and offender. One of the first criminologists to comment on the role that victims play was Hans Von Hentig in the 1940s. He portrayed the crime victim as someone who "shapes and molds the criminal."[53] The criminal might be a predator, but the victim may have helped the offender by providing an opportunity for the crime to happen. Another pioneering **victimologist**, Stephen Schafer, focused on the victim's responsibility in the "genesis of crime" for provoking or encouraging the criminal.[54] These early works helped focus attention on the role of the victim in the crime problem. Today, a number of theories attempt to explain the causes of victimization, including victim precipitation, lifestyles, and routine activities.

Victim Precipitation Theory

Is it possible that people cause their own victimization? According to the **victim precipitation** view, some people may "initiate" the confrontation that eventually leads to their injury or death. Victim precipitation can be either active or passive. This theory is not meant to blame the victim but to explain why some people become victims; it does not try to excuse the actions of the offender.

Active precipitation occurs when victims act provocatively, use threats or "fighting words," or even attack first. This model of victim-precipitated crime was first popularized by Marvin Wolfgang in his 1958 study of criminal homicide. He defined the term victim precipitation as follows:

> "Victim-precipitated" is applied to those criminal homicides in which the victim is a direct, positive precipitator in the crime.

The role of the victim is characterized by his having been the first in the homicide drama to use physical force against his subsequent slayer. The victim-precipitated cases are those in which the victim was the first to show and use a deadly weapon, to strike a blow in an altercation—in short, the first to commence the interplay or resort to physical violence.[55]

Examples of a victim-precipitated homicide include the death of an aggressor in a barroom brawl or a wife who kills her husband after he attacks and threatens to kill her. Wolfgang found that 150, or 26 percent, of the 588 homicides in his sample could be classified as victim-precipitated. Clearly this theory applies more readily to violent crime than to property crime. In most cases where victims precipitate a violent confrontation, they are more likely to suffer harm as a result than is the person targeted.

InfoTrac®

Study sexual and nonsexual victimization when drinking in a sample of college students in "College Women Have Much Higher Risk of Victimization on Days They Drink," *Women's Health Weekly,* May 6, 2004, 124.

Active Precipitation and Rape. Nowhere is the concept of victim precipitation more controversial than in the crime of rape. In 1971, Menachim Amir suggested that female victims often contribute to their attacks through a relationship with the rapist.[56] This statement is controversial, because it diverts our attention (and blame) from the man to the woman. However, it focuses our attention on court cases in which the defendant is acquitted because the victim's actions are construed as consenting to sexual intimacy. Date rapes are rarely treated with the same degree of punitiveness as stranger rapes.[57]

However, sometimes defendants are found not guilty because judges believe that a sexual assault was victim-precipitated. In a Northwest Territories case in 1989, the judge said, "The majority of rapes occur when the woman is drunk and passed out. A man comes along and sees a pair of hips and helps himself." In Alberta, a judge explained his acquittal of a man who sexually assaulted a young woman who was being interviewed for a job in this way: "The complainant did not present herself in a bonnet and crinolines, she was the mother of a six-month-old baby, and along with her boyfriend shared an apartment with another friend."[58] In another case, a mathematics professor said that "a girl who had sexual intercourse with a large number of boys would not suffer as a result of an unwanted sexual encounter. . . . When a boy invites a girl to his bedroom . . . she should consider it an invitation for sexual intercourse."[59]

Such cases involve blaming the victim. Ezzat Fattah, one of the early pioneers in the discipline of victimology, says we have to clearly identify that the interactions of victim and perpetrator involve unequal relations of power, which are exploited by the aggressor.[60]

Connections

Efforts to separate the causes of rape from the concept of victim precipitation have resulted in modification of rape laws in Canada, including the banning of testimony in court about the sexual history and reputation of the victim, the banning of publishing the identity of the victim in the news media, and a clearer definition of consent. Rape and the law are discussed further in Chapter 11.

Passive Precipitation. **Passive precipitation** occurs when the victim exhibits some personal characteristic that unknowingly threatens or encourages the attacker. The threat can occur because of personal conflict, such as when two people are in competition over a job, promotion, love interest, or some other scarce and coveted commodity. Although the victim may never have met his or her attacker or even known of the attacker's existence, the attacker feels menaced and acts accordingly.[61]

For example, Sandy Welsh at the University of Toronto researches the causes and consequences of sexual harassment in the workplace. This is typically a gendered crime against women, where their gender is used against them. Sexual harassment is a relatively new area of study, since official complaints to the Canadian Human Rights Commission have only been possible since 1978. The more serious a complaint is, the more likely it is to be resolved, because women must demonstrate they have either suffered physically or psychologically. This is a double victimization.

In another scenario, the victim may belong to a group whose mere presence threatens the attacker's reputation, status, or economic well-being. For example, hate crime violence may be precipitated when immigrant group members move into a community to compete for jobs and housing; women in the work force may be seen as threatening by insecure and emotionally unstable men.

It is estimated that 40 organized hate groups are operating in Canada. The Media Awareness Network and Hatewatch.org say that there were five hundred hardcore hate sites on the Internet in 2000. The advantage of the Internet is that it can be used to reach and recruit more people than ever before.

In 1996, sentencing provisions in the Canadian *Criminal Code* were amended so that if a judge determined hatred was the motivation in an attack, it would be considered an **aggravating** rather than a **mitigating** factor, thus requiring a more severe sentence. When this Bill was proposed in 1995, the justice minister was accused of promoting the special interests of homosexuals and had to defend the proposal by saying that he was not promoting a gay lifestyle.[62] In 2004, a new hate-crime bill passed the Senate, again, under vigorous opposition.

The first case to use the enhanced sentence provision was the racially motivated murder of a Sikh cleric, Nirmal Singh Gill, in 1998. RCMP infiltrated a skinhead gang and collected evidence crucial to the prosecution, and the five defendants were sentenced to 12 to 15 years incarceration.

Research indicates that passive precipitation is related to power; if the target group can establish themselves economically or gain political power in the community, their vulnerability will diminish. They become too formidable a target to attack and are no longer passive precipitators. For example, employed women in Canada are less likely to be homicide victims, whereas unemployed women suffer higher homicide victimization rates.[63] By implication, gaining economic power reduces the victimization risk for women.

Exhibit 4.1   Quick Code: Hate Crime

Section 718.2 A court that imposes a sentence shall also take into consideration the following principles:

(a) a sentence should be increased or reduced to account for any relevant aggravating or mitigating circumstances relating to the offence or the offender, and, without limiting the generality of the foregoing,

   (i) evidence that the offence was motivated by bias, prejudice or hate based on race, national or ethnic origin, language, colour, religion, sex, age, mental or physical disability, sexual orientation, or any other similar factor,

   (ii) evidence that the offender, in committing the offence, abused the offender's spouse or common-law partner or child,

   (iii) evidence that the offender, in committing the offence, abused a position of trust or authority in relation to the victim, or

   (iv) evidence that the offence was committed for the benefit of, at the direction of or in association with a criminal organization

shall be deemed to be aggravating circumstances. . . .

Source: *Criminal Code of Canada,* 1995, c. 22, s. 6; 1997, c. 23, s. 17; 2000, c. 12, s. 95.

In 2004, the federal government finalized a nationwide plan to combat racism, including asking law enforcement agencies to establish hate crime units. Initiatives also include an educational campaign to promote antiracism and new money for crime prevention programs. It is the first national antiracism program undertaken by the government, and it is considered necessary in light of recent incidents across the country. B'nai Brith Canada reports there were more incidents of harassment and vandalism against Jews in 2003 than any year in the past two decades.

Whether active or passive, the concept of victim precipitation implies that in some crimes, the offender's crime begins as a reaction to a victim's actions. The crime, as reaction, could not take place without action on the part of the victim. The victim's actions might consciously put him or her in harm's way, but the actions might be inadvertent as well. Routine activities theory, discussed later in this chapter, will explore this further. One important point, however, is that modern crime prevention programs involve making targets harder to victimize, which requires that the programs be victim centred.

The Extent of Hate Crime. Until now there has been no systematic collection of hate crime statistics in Canada. However, preliminary research (see Crime in the News) shows that hate crime occurs primarily on the basis of race, religion, and sexual orientation. One estimate is that 60 000 hate crimes are committed annually in Canada.[64] The Ottawa Police have an established specialized hate/bias crime unit. In the United States, the FBI collects data on hate crimes under the *Hate Crime Statistics Act* of 1990 from more than 12 000 law enforcement agencies.[65] Some organizations, such as the League for Human Rights of B'nai Brith, have produced an annual report on the number of anti-Semitic incidents in Canada since 1982.

In 1999 the GSS measured self-reported hate crime victimization incidents at the national level for the first time, finding 272 732 incidents considered by the victim to be motivated by hate.[66] Whereas almost half (49 percent) of all hate crime incidents are assaults, fewer than one in five (18 percent) nonhate crime incidents are assaults. And whereas police-reported statistics indicate that in 30 percent of nonhate crimes, the perpetrator is a stranger, in almost half (46 percent) of all violent hate crime incidents the offender is a stranger to the victim. See Exhibit 4.2 for the most recent statistics.

Hate/bias crime is slowly being recognized as a widespread and serious problem and as a new category of violent personal crime.[67] This crime is displayed in violent acts directed toward a particular person or members of a group merely because the targets share

Hate Crimes Not So Uncommon

In June [2004], the Canadian Centre for Justice Statistics published the results of a four-year pilot survey on hate crime. The survey was done in collaboration with 12 major police forces across the country. It used the definition that "hate crimes are offences motivated by bias, prejudice or hate based on race, national or ethnic origin, language, colour, religion, sex, age, mental or physical disability, sexual orientation, or any other similar factor."

These police services represent 43 percent of the total volume of crime in Canada, and thus [the survey] represents a significant advance in our understanding of hate crime. The police departments reported 1,119 total hate incidents, of which 928 were criminal hate offences.

Behind the statistics are stories.

An elderly Pakistani commissionaire is set upon by neo-Nazi thugs in a random attack. They don't know anything about him or his experiences. He is beaten and killed.

Two men leaving a gay bar are attacked by a group of men they do not know. They are beaten severely enough they have to go to the hospital. The attackers are charged with assault. In another incident, a young gay man is enticed from a bar, tied with wire to a fence and killed. His attackers face the death penalty.

A young black man is picked up hitchhiking by two white guys, tied with a chain to the back of their truck and dragged to his death.

A teen is charged with distributing hate literature at a high school. A schoolteacher is barred from the classroom after teaching that the Holocaust was a hoax. The police are called to investigate the distribution of alleged hate literature found in the downtown area on Canada Day.

Vandals spray paint swastikas on vehicles, fences, bus shelters and sidewalks in Toronto. In Montreal, an 18-year-old man has been charged with firebombing a Jewish school. A children's library is destroyed by arson.

How often do such crimes happen? Well, it all depends on whether the question is asked.

Hate crime in Canada was measured nationally for the first time in 1999. The General Social Survey was a victimization survey, unlike the police study reported above. It interviewed 26,000 people aged fifteen years of age and older. The Survey found a quarter of a million incidents, or 4 percent of total criminal offenses reported, to be motivated by hate. The victim's ethnicity was the motive in 43 percent of hate offences, and religion and sexual orientation in [a total of] 37 percent. This is a crime against minorities, and it amounts to an assault against their identity. They did nothing to bring the violence upon themselves. The victims of hate crime incidents lived in urban areas, where there is a larger, and more diverse, population.

What is surprising is that this survey was done only five years ago. Even in the United States, data has been collected by the FBI only since the early 1990s.

What have we learned about the larger pattern of hate crime?

We know that hate crimes are more likely to be personal offences than most crimes. Three-quarters of hate crimes are assault, robbery, theft, and sexual assault. These are offenses against the person, not against property. In comparison one half of all offenses not motivated by hate are directed against the person.

Being assaulted because of who you represent is a crime of hate. It is a crime against a person's identity, against who they are and what they represent. These are crimes of intolerance. These crimes are usually between strangers, but they are not random because there is a pattern.

According to the 2004 police pilot study, the most common types of hate crime included mischief, followed by assault, uttering threats, and hate propaganda. While ethnicity was the most common reason for hate crime, individuals targeted because of their sexual orientation were more likely than other groups to suffer violent crimes including assault. The offenders are usually male.

In fact, those accused of hate crime are men in 84 percent of all cases. The average age of the accused was 30 years. In 86 percent of the cases, there was a single offender. Less than 10 percent of the offenders had been involved in previous criminal activity.

Almost all hate crime incidents involved a single victim. The average age of the victim was 37 years. Sixty-seven percent were male. Physical force was used in 34 percent of incidents, and weapons in 17 percent.

Unfortunately, most victims of hate crime will not report the crime to the police. The 1999 victimization survey showed that only 45 percent of hate-motivated [crimes] were reported. However, hate crimes actually have a higher report rate than non-hate crimes. Only

37 percent of all crimes are reported to the police. The higher report rate for hate crimes is due to the fact that they are more likely to be committed by strangers. People are less likely to report offenses committed by someone they know.

In a multicultural society like Canada, such crimes are unconscionable, and should not be tolerated.

Source: © Chris McCormick, "Hate Crimes Not So Uncommon," *Daily Gleaner,* July 22, 2004.

Exhibit 4.2 | **Quick Facts: Hate Crime in Canada**

The following figures are drawn from the 2001/2002 Canadian Hate Crime Pilot Survey. Twelve major police forces participated, representing approximately 43 percent of the national crime volume.

- Of 928 recorded hate crime incidents, 57 percent were motivated by race/ethnicity, 43 percent by religion, 10 percent by sexual orientation, and 3 percent by language, sex, age, or disability.
- One-quarter of incidents were anti-Semitic in nature, involving Jewish people or institutions. The second most common group targeted was Blacks (17 percent) followed by Muslims (11 percent), South Asians (10 percent), and gays and lesbians (9 percent).
- Most hate crimes involved offences against the person (52 percent), followed by property offences (31 percent) and other offences (17 percent), such as hate propaganda.
- About 1 in 5 victims of violent hate crime had a weapon used against them; one-quarter suffered an injury, 45 percent of which were minor.
- Incidents motivated by sexual orientation were most likely to be violent (65 percent). Gays and lesbians were almost twice as likely as hate crime victims in general to suffer an injury (46 percent versus 25 percent).
- When the victim–accused relationship was identified, 83 percent of victims did not know their perpetrator; 15 percent stated that the accused was a casual acquaintance or business associate (in 2 percent of cases, the relationship was not identified).
- A chargeable accused was identified 48 percent of the time. Most were male (84 percent) and the average age was 29.5 years; fewer than 1 in 10 were involved in previous criminal activity.
- A victim was identified 86 percent of the time. Most were male (67 percent) and the average age was 36.6 years.

Prepared by Andrea Wolf.

a discernible racial, ethnic, religious, gender or physical characteristic or sexual orientation. Hate crimes can include the desecration of a house of worship or cemetery, harassment of a minority-group family that has moved into a previously all-White neighbourhood, or a racially motivated murder of an individual.[68]

A number of conditions may influence hate crime offending:

- economic recessions, increased crime, and unemployment being blamed on minorities
- the movement of minorities into an area seen as a threat to a traditional way of life
- the desire to alleviate boredom
- feelings of resentment for the economic or social success of minorities
- historical animosities that have been transmitted from one generation to another
- belief that actions of the offenders are condoned by the larger society or community

Hate crimes usually involve convenient and vulnerable targets who are incapable of fighting back, for example, teenagers attacking vagrants and the homeless.[69]

 InfoTrac®

For an article on the relationship between gang enlistment based on race and hate crime, see Eric Tischler, "Can Tolerance Be Taught?" *Corrections Today* 61, no. 15 (1999): 76–80.

The Roots of Hate. Why do people commit bias crimes? Hate crimes are generally spontaneous incidents motivated by the victims' walking, driving, shopping, or socializing in an area in which their attacker believes they do not belong.[70] Other reasons found for bias attacks are that the victim had moved into an ethnically distinct neighbourhood or had dated a member of a different racial or ethnic group. Although hate crimes are often unplanned, a majority of these crimes were serious incidents involving assaults and robberies.[71]

Although hate crimes are often mindless attacks directed toward "traditional" minority victims, political and economic trends may cause violent attacks to be redirected. For example, after September 11, 2001, there was a short-term but significant increase in hate crimes against East Asian Americans. The CCJS reports that there were three times more hate crimes in the following two months than at any other time. Hate crimes associated with terrorism are more likely to be violent.[72]

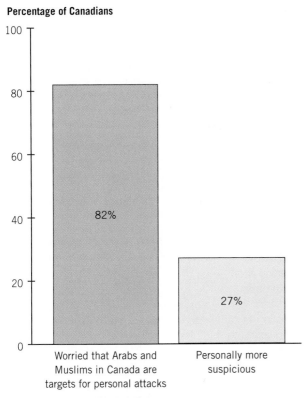

Percentage of Canadians

A poll released September 2001 indicates that 82 percent are worried that Arabs and Muslims in Canada may be the target of racism and personal attacks; 27 percent indicate they are personally more suspicious.

Source: Poll conducted by Ipsos-Reid/CTV/*The Globe and Mail,* September 2001.

Lifestyle Theories

Some criminologists believe that people may become crime victims because they have a **lifestyle** that increases their exposure to criminal offenders. Both GSS and UCR data sources show that victimization risk is increased by such characteristics as being single, associating with young men, going out in public places late at night, and living in an urban area. Conversely, a person's chances of victimization can be reduced by staying home at night, moving to a rural area, staying out of public places, earning more money, associating

with young women, or getting married. The important point is that crime is not a random occurrence but rather is, in part, a function of the behaviour and actions of its targets.

Criminality and victimization thus seem bound in an association in which the probability of crime depends on the activities of the potential victim.[73] Crime occurs because victims have a lifestyle that places them in jeopardy: A person's chances of being robbed by a stranger are much greater in downtown Montreal at 2 a.m. than they are if the person is in a locked farmhouse in rural Manitoba.

The likelihood of victimization is greatest among groups with high-risk lifestyles. For example, teens may have the greatest risk of victimization because their lifestyle places them in an at-risk location—the neighbourhood high school. That's where the most criminal element of the population, teenage males, congregate. In half of nonsexual assaults against children, the accused was an acquaintance, especially in the case of male victims. Physical force was the most common weapon (81 percent of cases), and 60 percent took place in a public or open area.[74]

In 1997, the Centre for Research on Youth at Risk estimated that 56 percent of all victims of youth violence were other youths; 12 to 17 year olds were identified as victims in common assault cases involving young accused as often as adults (55 percent in both cases). Children under the age of twelve were more likely to be the victims of youths in common assault (43 percent) or sexual assault (34 percent).

An adolescent's lifestyle continues to place him or her at risk after leaving the school grounds. Kids who hang out with their friends and get involved in the "recreational pursuit of fun" face an elevated risk for victimization. For example, their friends may give them a false ID so that they can go drinking; hanging out in bars places them at risk because many fights and assaults occur in places that serve liquor.[75]

Adolescents are not the only ones with high-risk lifestyles. A number of studies have found that the homeless population is extremely vulnerable to physical harm because its members are constantly exposed to the criminal population in large urban areas. The homeless have a high victimization risk compared to the general population, and homeless victims are more likely to have a history of mental hospitalization, depression, and physical problems.[76]

Women who work for escort services don't turn up as murder victims at the same rate as street-involved women. Similarly, women who work in body-rub and massage parlours don't encounter the same kind of victimization from clients as do street prostitutes. Women working on the street are particularly vulnerable to predatory violence, especially since they face criminal prosecution themselves. When a conflict with a client occurs, he may use violence

Famous Canadian Court Case

R. v. Keegstra

Responding to a spread of hate propaganda in Canada in the 1960s, then–Justice Minister Guy Favreau appointed the Cohen Commission, which concluded that hate propaganda poses a serious threat to society. Their 1966 report was largely responsible for a number of 1970 *Criminal Code* amendments, such as section 319(2), which prohibits the communication of statements that willfully promote hatred against an identifiable group. Section 319(3) affords certain defences to this charge, such as when an accused can prove that the objectionable statements he or she communicated are in fact true.

This law was disputed in a notorious case involving Alberta high-school teacher James Keegstra, who lectured and tested his class on anti-Semitic material. Keegstra was known to penalize students for challenging his inflammatory depiction of Jews as a "treacherous" and "sadistic" people who "created the Holocaust to gain sympathy." He was fired in 1982 and

decertified after being confronted by parents, inspected by the school superintendent, and suspended for disregarding the curriculum. Two years later, his clash with education officials had transformed into a full-fledged battle with the criminal justice system when police charged him for violating Canada's anti-hate statutes.

Defence counsel unsuccessfully argued that section 319 of the *Criminal Code* is unconstitutional because it infringes on the rights to free speech and presumption of innocence. Although Keegstra was tried and convicted, the country's highest court was forced to resolve his case in 1990 after a contradictory judgment was handed down on appeal. The Supreme Court justices all agreed that hate propaganda is protected under section 2 of the *Charter* because it conveys meaning and, therefore, constitutes expression. They also ruled that the "truth" defence contravenes section 11 of the *Charter* by permitting courts to register a conviction in spite of reasonable doubt. However, the justices were divided as to whether the anti-hate statute can

be considered a reasonable limitation of rights and freedoms. By a margin of four votes to three, the Supreme Court ultimately answered this question in the affirmative and upheld section 319.

Sources: "Freedom of Speech: James Keegstra," *Spirit of Democracy*, March 29, 2004, http://www.Spiritofdemocracy .com (accessed May 10, 2005); Ian Mulgrew, "Hate Crime Laws Don't Work—Witness the World after 9/11: Incidents of Intolerance Occur against the Old, the Different, the Disliked and the Disabled," *Vancouver Sun*, May19, 2003, http://www.canada .com (accessed May 10, 2005); Karen Mock, "Recognizing and Reacting to Hate Crime in Canada Today," Canadian Race Relations Foundation et al., http://www.crr.ca/ EN/Publications/EducationalTools/ RecognizingandReacting.htm (accessed May 10, 2005); *R. v. Keegstra*, [1990] 3 S.C.R. 697, http://www.canlii .org/ca/cas/scc/1990/1990scc128.html (accessed May 10, 2005); Robert Sharpe, Katherine Swinton, and Kent Roach, *The Charter of Rights and Freedoms*, 2nd ed. (Toronto: Irwin Law Inc., 2002); "Testing the Limits of Freedom of Expression: The Keegstra Case," *Human Rights in Canada: A Historical Perspective*, December 13, 1990.

Prepared by Andrea Wolf.

because he knows she is unlikely to report it to the police. Statistics on violence against street prostitutes suggest that it is probably the most dangerous form of work in Canada. Other high-risk professions include police, taxi drivers, security guards, bouncers, and retail business managers.[77]

The Equivalent Group Hypothesis. The lifestyle view suggests that victims and criminals share similar characteristics because they are not actually separate groups and that a criminal lifestyle exposes people to increased levels of victimization risk. The **equivalent group hypothesis** is supported by research showing that crime victims self-report significant amounts of criminal behaviour. In 2002, the CCJS reported that

half of all homicide victims 12 years and older had a criminal record; 47 percent of this group had been previously convicted of a violent crime.[78] A number of studies have shown that adolescents who engage in delinquent behaviour or join gangs also face the greatest risk of victimization. For example, young victims of school crime were likely to strike back at other students in order to regain lost possessions or recover their self-respect.[79] In another study, it was found that the victims of violent assault were those most likely to become offenders themselves.[80] Similarly, an association has been found between participation in self-reported delinquent behaviour and personal victimization in such crimes as robbery and assault.[81] The conclusion is that for personal victimizations,

Culture, Gender, Ethnicity, and Criminology

Heterosexual Panic or Homo-cide: The Extent of Hate Crime

Hate crime is slowly being recognized as a widespread and serious problem, and in recent years criminologists have begun studying the issue. One group targeted for hate crimes is gay men and lesbian women.

A community survey conducted by Ellen Faulkner of Brock University at the 519 Church Street Community Centre in Toronto showed that 78 percent of respondents had experienced verbal assaults and 50 percent had been threatened with physical violence. Toronto's Wellesley Hospital created a program to help its emergency staff to be more sensitive and effective when caring for victims of gay bashing.

A New Brunswick study on discrimination and violence against lesbians, gays, and bisexuals found that 82 percent had been verbally abused; 34 percent had been chased or followed; 10 percent had been spat on; 19 percent had had their property damaged; 17 percent had had objects thrown at them; 18 percent had been punched, kicked, hit or beaten; and 23 percent had been harassed or assaulted by the police.

A Nova Scotia study on homophobic abuse and discrimination found that 72 percent of gays and lesbians had been verbally abused because of their sexual orientation; 42 percent had been threatened with violence; 33 percent had been chased or followed; 9 percent had been spat on; 12 percent had had their property damaged; 25 percent had had objects thrown at them; 18 percent had been assaulted

with a weapon, punched, kicked, or beaten; 16.5 percent had been harassed; and another 2 percent had been beaten by the police.

In a survey of homophobic violence reported in the *Gay Times* (1996), one in three gay men and one in four lesbians said they had been bashed in the previous five years. For those under age 18, the figures were even higher. Avoidance techniques were adopted, such as not holding hands or kissing in public (88 percent), avoiding telling people they are gay (65 percent), and avoiding looking "obviously gay" (59 percent).

- In 1985 Kenn Zeller was murdered in a Toronto park by five teenagers who had gone to the park to "beat up a fag."
- In 1989 a gay AIDS activist, Joe Rose, was murdered on a crowded Montreal bus by a gang of 15 youths who taunted him with shouts of "faggot" and stabbed him to death.
- In 1992 Daniel Lacombe was killed in Montreal by a group of young adults who had gone out to beat up gays.
- At least 14 gay men were murdered in Montreal between 1989 and 1994 as a result of homophobic violence.

The FBI reports that of the 17 murders reported among hate-motivated incidents, racial bias motivated 9 of the murders; sexual-orientation bias and ethnicity or national origin bias motivated 3 each; and religious bias motivated 2. In the Matthew Shepard case, which galvanized public attention in 1998, two men were tried and found guilty for luring a gay man from a bar, pistol-whipping him, and leaving him to die tied to a fence. The defendants

tried to argue that his sexual advances provoked them into a homosexual panic and that they were just defending themselves.

In 1995 Scott Amedure was killed by Jonathan Schmitz after appearing on the *Jenny Jones* television talk show. Scott admitted a crush on Jonathan, who turned out to be homophobic. The show made a $25 million settlement with the victim's family.

Victor Janoff, in *Pink Blood: Queer-bashing in Canada,* provides a comprehensive overview of queer-bashing. The M.A. thesis analyzes the impact of violence on gays and lesbians and assembles evidence on the prevalence of homophobic violence in Canada. In an extensive series of interviews with police officers, community activists, victims, and prosecutors, Janoff details more than 300 incidents, including 85 homicides. In particular he highlights the problem of the "homosexual panic defence."

This so-called defence is based on the idea that a homosexual proposition can cause a reaction akin to temporary insanity in a person with latent homosexual tendencies or in someone who has been abused. Usually, a homosexual advance is used as evidence of provocation in order to reduce the attacker's sentence, for example, from murder to manslaughter. The *Gay Times* reports that the defence of homosexual panic has been used in the United States at least 15 times in the past 10 years to reduce charges from murder to manslaughter.

In a recent case in British Columbia, the Crown accepted a plea bargain of manslaughter in a murder case, on the grounds that the defendant had been provoked by an aggressive homosexual assault. The court accepted the argument that a heterosexual man should react to an alleged advance with extreme violence. In another case, the Manitoba Court of Appeal said there can be no doubt that a homosexual advance may be provocation. However in Alberta, in a case where the defendant alleged that the victim had reached toward the accused as if to grab him, the Court of Appeal decided it would be impossible for a jury to conclude that an ordinary man's sensitivity to a homosexual approach should lead to anything more than annoyance.

Violence against homosexuals is on the rise in Australia, and since 1993 this defence has been used in 13 cases that resulted in death. Since 1990, the police have systematically recorded gay hate-related killings in New South Wales. Using data from the National Homicide Monitoring Program, the Australian Institute of Criminology has compared the victims and offenders in such homicides with other male homicides in New South Wales and found that the victims are generally older than other male homicide victims and are more likely to have

been beaten to death. The offenders are much more likely to be younger than other homicide offenders and more likely to be unemployed (82 percent) and unmarried (77 percent). In a 1998 report on the "homosexual advance defence," the Criminal Law Division recommended that this defence be excluded through legislation because of its prejudicial basis.

InfoTrac®

- For research on gay and lesbian domestic violence, see Sarah Wellard, "Victim on the Margins," *Community Care,* March 6, 2003, 32.
- For information on harassment and bullying of gay and lesbian students, look at David Kurby, "What Makes a Bully?" *The Advocate,* July 3, 2001, 30.

Sources: L. Still, "Homophobe Who Killed Gay Handed Five-Year Sentence," *The Vancouver Sun,* June 29, 1995; D. Dahl, "Bias in the Criminal Justice System—The 'Homosexual Panic Defence,'" *The Vancouver Sun,* December 28, 1995; *R. v. Ryznar,* [1986] 6 WWR 210 (Man CA); *R. v. Hansford* (1987), 55 CR (3d) 347 (Alta CA) at 363; "Anti-Gay Crimes Are Reported on Rise in 5 Cities," *New York Times,* March 20, 1992; "Gay Discrimination Focus of Probe," *The Globe and Mail,* November 15, 1993; Jenny Mouzos and Sue Thompson, "Gay-Hate Related Homicides: An Overview of Major Findings in New South Wales," Australian Institute of Criminology, *Trends and Issues in Crime and Criminal Justice* 155 (June 2000); C. Petersen, "A Queer Response to Bashing: Legislating Against Hate," *Queen's Law Journal* 16 (1991), 237 at 246; S. Samis, "An Injury to One Is an Injury to All: Heterosexism, Homophobia and Anti-Gay/Lesbian Violence in Greater Vancouver," M.A. (Sociology) thesis, Simon Fraser University, 1994; Quebec Human Rights Commission; "Discrimination and Violence Encountered by Lesbian, Gay and Bisexual New Brunswickers," *New Brunswick Coalition for Human Rights Reform,* 1990; "Proud but Cautious: Homophobic Abuse and Discrimination in Nova Scotia," Nova Scotia Public Interest Research Group, 1994; Ellen Faulkner, *Anti-Gay/Lesbian Violence in Toronto: The Impact on Individuals and Communities, Department of Justice Canada: Research and Statistics Division/Policy Sector.* TR1997-5e. (A Project of the 519 Church Street Community Centre Victim Assistance program, 519 Church Street, Toronto, Ontario: p. 40.)

those most likely to be the victims of crime are those who have been most involved in crime.[82]

The criminal–victim connection may exist because the conditions that create criminality also predispose people to victimization. Both share similar lifestyle and residence characteristics. Some former criminals may later become targets because they are perceived as vulnerable: Criminal offenders are unlikely to call the police, and if they do, who will believe them? Some victims may commit crime out of frustration; others may use violence as a means of revenge, self-defence, or social control. Some may have learned antisocial behaviour as a consequence of their own victimization experiences, as in the case of abused children.[83] Research cited in one study showed that more than 85 percent of

female offenders had experienced physical and sexual violence both inside and outside the home, at the hands of parents, intimate partners, and strangers.[84]

The Proximity Hypothesis. Lifestyle theory implies that some people willingly put themselves in jeopardy by choosing high-risk lifestyles or that some people become victims because they are forced to live in close physical proximity to criminals and are selected because they share similar backgrounds and circumstances.[85] Early research by Hindelang, Gottfredson, and Garofalo, advanced the idea that association with and exposure to high-risk people in high-risk locations at high-risk periods increases the incidence of the risk of crime.[86] For example, people who reside in socially disorganized "high-crime areas" have the greatest risk of coming into contact with criminal offenders, irrespective of their own behaviour or lifestyle. Thus, according to the **proximity hypothesis**, victims do not encourage crime; they are simply in the "wrong place at the wrong time."[87] Thus, there may be little reason for residents in lower-class areas to alter their lifestyle or take safety precautions, since personal behaviour choices do not, in fact, influence the likelihood of victimization.[88]

Thus, victimization is more dependent on where people live than how people live. People who live in close proximity to criminals are at greater risk of victimization than are people who reside in less risky areas but have attractive, unguarded homes.[89] Neighbourhood crime levels are more important for determining the chances of victimization than are individual characteristics. People who exhibit high-risk traits, such as unmarried males, will further increase their chances of victimization if they reside in a high-crime area.[90]

The Deviant Place Hypothesis. The **deviant place hypothesis** theory suggests that there are natural areas for crime, places in which crime flourishes regardless of precautions taken by residents. These areas are poor, densely populated, highly transient neighbourhoods in which commercial and residential property exist side by side. The commercial property provides criminals with easy access to targets for theft crimes, such as shoplifting and larceny. Successful people stay out of these stigmatized areas; they are homes for "demoralized kinds of people" who are easy targets for crime: the homeless, people with addictions, people with mental disabilities, and the elderly poor.[91]

People who can afford to leave dangerous areas do so.[92] More affluent people realize that criminal victimization can be avoided by moving to an area with greater law enforcement and lower crime rates. As residents leave inner-city high-crime areas, those left behind suffer higher victimization rates.

Both victim lifestyle and place of domicile interact to produce crime and victimization rates. People who live in more affluent areas and take safety precautions significantly lower their chances of becoming crime victims. Residents of poor areas have a much greater risk of becoming victims because they live in areas with many motivated offenders; to protect themselves, they have to try harder to be safe than do the more affluent. People who take chances, who live in high-risk neighbourhoods, and who are law violators themselves share the greatest risk of victimization. Although victim behaviour cannot explain the onset of criminality, it can influence the occasion of crime. Although criminal motivation may be acquired early in life, the decision to commit a particular crime may depend on the actions and reactions of potential victims.

Routine Activities Theory

An important attempt to formally describe the conditions that produce victim risk is Cohen and Felson's **routine activities theory**.[93] They assume that the motivation to commit crime is constant. In every society, there will always be people willing to break the law for gain, revenge, greed, or some other motive. Consequently, the volume and distribution of **predatory crime** (violent crimes against the person and crimes in which an offender attempts to steal an object directly) are closely related to the interaction of three variables that reflect the routine activities of the typical Canadian lifestyle: the availability of **suitable targets** (such as homes containing easily saleable goods); the absence of **capable guardians** (such as police, homeowners, neighbours, friends, and relatives); and the presence of **motivated offenders** (such as a large number of unemployed teenagers). The presence of these components increases the likelihood that a predatory crime will take place: Targets are more likely to be victimized if they are poorly guarded and are exposed to a large group of motivated offenders (see Figure 4.3).

The routine activities approach can explain the rise in crime between 1960 and 1980. The number of adult caretakers at home during the day (guardians) decreased because of increased female participation in the work force; while mothers are at work and children are in daycare, homes are left unguarded. Similarly, with the growth of suburbia and the decline of the traditional neighbourhood, the number of such familiar "guardians" as family, neighbours, and friends diminished. At the same time, the volume of easily transportable wealth increased, creating a greater number of available targets. In one study, burglary rates are linked to the proliferation of a commodity easily stolen and disposed of: television sets.[94] Finally, with the baby-boom generation coming of age from 1960 to 1980, there were an excess of motivated offenders, and the crime rate increased in predictable fashion. The implication of this theory is that crime is not a product of social disorder but of both prosperity and the changing economy.

 InfoTrac®

To see how the routine activities approach is used to explain violent victimizations, see Thoroddur Bjarnason, Thordis J. Sigurdardottir, and Thorolfur Thorlindsson, "Human Agency, Capable Guardians, and Structural Constraints: A Lifestyle Approach to the Study of Violent Victimization," *Journal of Youth and Adolescence* 28, no. 1 (1999): 105.

| Figure 4.3 | Routine Activity Theory Posits the Interaction of Three Factors |

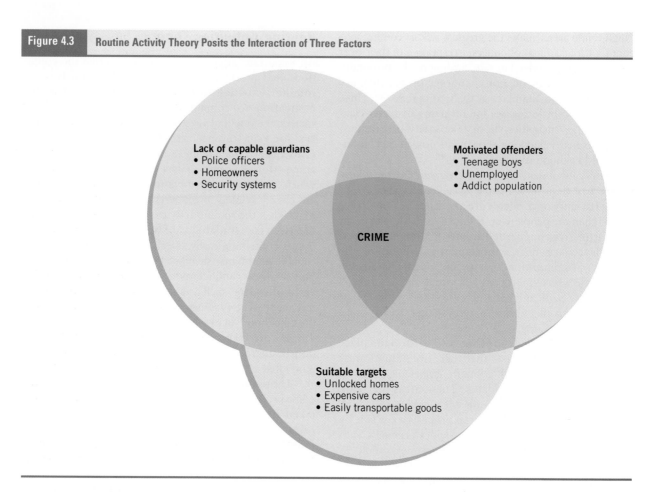

Lack of capable guardians
• Police officers
• Homeowners
• Security systems

Motivated offenders
• Teenage boys
• Unemployed
• Addict population

CRIME

Suitable targets
• Unlocked homes
• Expensive cars
• Easily transportable goods

Crime and Everyday Life. A core premise of routine activities theory is that the greater the opportunity to commit crime, the higher the crime and victimization rate. Accordingly, crime has grown as society changed from a nation of small villages and towns to one of large urban environments. In a village, not only could thieves be easily recognized, but the commodities they stole could also be identified long after the crime occurred. Cities provided a population mass that allowed predatory criminals to hide and evade apprehension. After the crime, criminals could blend into the crowd and disperse their loot; in the modern city, the public transportation system provides a quick escape.

As suburbs grew in importance, labour and family life moved away from the household, decreasing guardianship. The microwave, freezer, and automatic dishwasher freed adolescents from common household chores. Rather than help prepare the family dinner and wash dishes afterward, adolescents had the freedom to meet with their peers and avoid parental controls. As car ownership increased, teens had greater access to transportation and independence. Greater mobility makes it impossible for neighbours to know whether a teen belongs in an area or is an intruder planning to commit a crime. Schools have become larger and more complex,

providing an ideal site for crime. Teachers might not know who belongs where, and spacious school grounds reduce teacher supervision. In the shopping mall, strangers converge in large numbers and youths hang out. The interior is filled with people, so drug deals can be concealed in the pedestrian flow. Stores have attractively displayed goods, encouraging shoplifting and employee pilferage. Substantial numbers of cars are parked in areas that make larceny and car theft virtually undetectable. Who notices people taking items from a car in a parking lot? In addition, shoppers can be attacked in parking lots as they walk in isolation to and from their cars.

These changes in the structure of society helped increase and sustain crime rates into the early 1990s. The upshot is that rather than change people, crime prevention strategies must reduce the opportunity to commit crime.

Moral Guardianship. Some criminologists believe moral beliefs and socialization may influence the routine activities that produce crime. Even in the presence of criminal opportunities, people may refrain from crime if they are bonded with or attached to conventional peers and have been socialized to hold conventional attitudes.

The strength of social bonds may serve as a buffer, a form of moral guardianship, sufficient to counteract the lure of criminal opportunities.[95]

When Martin Schwartz and his associates studied date rape on college campuses, they found that men whose peer group supported emotional and physical violence against women were the ones most likely to engage in date rape (especially if they drank on a weekly basis). Those who believed their peers would reject and disapprove of their behaviour were deterred from victimizing women. Peer rejection and disapproval may be forms of moral guardianship that can deter even motivated offenders from engaging in law-violating behavior.[96]

Routine Activities and Lifestyle. Routine activities theory is similar to the lifestyle approach because it shows how routine living arrangements can affect victim risk: People who live in unguarded areas are going to be at the mercy of motivated offenders. Miethe and Meier argue that there is a congruence between the two theories, each relying on four basic concepts: (1) proximity to criminals, (2) time of exposure to criminals, (3) target attractiveness, and (4) guardianship.[97] For example, both routine activities theory and lifestyle theory would predict that (1) people who live in high-crime areas (2) who go out late at night (3) carrying valuables, such as an expensive watch, (4) without friends or family to watch or help them increase their victimization risk.

Exhibit 4.3 is from a test that lets you rate your risk of being assaulted. The test was developed by the Metro Nashville Police Department and includes questions on factors that affect assault rates. The key elements reflect

the ideas discussed here, that the lifestyle and routine activities people engage in can put them at relative danger from crime.

Testing Routine Activities Theory. Numerous attempts have been made to substantiate the principles of routine activities theory.[98] Personal characteristics increase the likelihood that people's routine activities will place them at a greater risk for victimization. These characteristics include being a young minority-group member, having a low socioeconomic status, living in an urban area, and being a single parent. Maxfield found that victimization was most common in homes comprising a single parent and several children. Single parents may be less able to protect their families and themselves from the most common predatory criminals: other family members and former loved ones.[99] Note that this implies that going out of the home may not be the best predictor of risk, given the characteristics of violence in the family, especially for women and children.

Homes that are well guarded are the least likely to be burglarized.[100] Rape rates are high in areas where socioeconomic distress results in divorce, unemployment, and overcrowded living conditions—factors that reduce the number of guardians and increase the number of potential offenders.[101] However, some empirical research has failed to find a relationship between property victimization and guardianship, seeming to provide weak support for routine activities theory.[102]

The routine activities view also suggests that lifestyle plays an important role in victimization risk. Those who maintain a high-risk lifestyle by staying out late at night and having frequent activity outside the home also run

Exhibit 4.3	**Rate Your Risk of Being Assaulted on the Street**

The following test lets you rate your risk of being assaulted on the street. This test uses known risk factors taken from executive security courses, police detectives, and security consultants. Some of the questions may seem unusual but they are all factors that affect aggravated assault statistics.

1. How much do you travel outside of the city where you live in one year?
   - You travel under 1,000 miles total.
   - You travel about 1,000 to 5,000 miles in the U.S.
   - You travel in the U.S. more than 5,000 miles.
   - You travel worldwide.

2. When you fly
   - You fly by commercial carrier.
   - You regularly fly using small, foreign-owned carriers.

- You travel (fly, drive, etc.) with more than one suitcase and one carry-on type bag.

3. Security Techniques
   - You go to conventions or seminars in other cities even occasionally.
   - You wear a convention badge while out of the meeting room itself on such a trip.
   - You regularly wear your last name visible when you work.
   - You (or other family members) open the door of your home for visitors without positive identification.
   - You never open your door to strangers when you are unarmed.
   - You only open a door when armed.
   - Your mailbox doesn't lock.

- You have a solid door without a "peephole" or way to view who is outside.
- You have a lock on your bedroom door.

4. How much cash do you carry?
   - You rarely carry any cash.
   - You carry $20 to $50.
   - You carry $50 to $400.
   - You carry over $400.
   - You separate the money you need from other large denomination bills.

5. Credit and Bank Cards
   - How many credit cards do you carry?
   - How many major oil credit cards [gas cards] do you carry?
   - How many major credit cards do you carry (MasterCard, Visa, American Express, Carte Blanche, Discover, etc.)?
   - You carry one or more ATM cards.
   - You carry secret code numbers to cards written down (even though you might hide them).
   - You never use outside ATM (anytime teller machines) after dark. (Leave this blank if the ATM is at a police sub-station.)

6. Sundry Habits
   - How many acts of adultery have you committed (in the last two years)? Count each meeting during this marriage.
   - You are unmarried and you have dated a married person in the last year. How many dates have you had with this married person?
   - You are unmarried and you steadily cohabit with one person but you have dated on the sly in the last year.
   - Indicate your total number of partners.
   - You go to nightclubs and take home partners or go somewhere with them.
   - If so, are you male or female?
   - Do you ever use prostitutes?
   - Do you ever hitchhike or pick up hitchhikers?
   - Do you walk in public more than five times per month?
   - Do you generally walk at night with one or more companions?
   - Do you ever use cocaine, crack, uppers, downers or narcotics away from home on any occasion?
   - Do you ever get drunk in public to the point where your speech is even slightly slurred or your balance is affected?

7. On the Street
   - You visibly wear lots of gold chains when in public.
   - You wear rings, bracelets, or other jewelry worth over $2,000 while in public.
   - You wear an overcoat or full-length rain suit over a suit jacket in public.
   - You wear a natural fur in public.
   - Do you carry an umbrella or cane without necessity?
   - Do you walk with young children (age eight or under) or a dog?

8. Outings
   - Do you drive with any car door unlocked?
   - You have a remote starting device on your car.
   - You regularly commute by bus or subway.
   - You cannot change a car tire yourself and you drive.
   - You drive (more than once a month) with an eighth of a tank of gas or less.
   - You carry a tire inflator/puncture sealant screw-on canister in your car.
   - You frequent the same gas station.
   - You work at a gas station, bar, fast food restaurant, or drive-in market.
   - You are going camping or partying in a boat in the next year.
   - There is no controlled access in and out of your work.

9. Other Factors
   - You are a black male between the ages of 14 and 26.
   - You are over 60 years old.
   - You can run over 300 m without stopping to walk.
   - You are a first-degree black belt or higher in any martial art (Karate, Judo, Tae Kwon Do, Kung Fu, etc.).
   - You speak quietly when you talk.
   - You are considered calm but assertive when you talk.
   - You are afraid of guns and can't stand to touch one.
   - You are commissioned to or otherwise legally carry a handgun.
   - You always carry a handgun and you aren't commissioned or registered.
   - You know others illegally carry firearms where you drink or gamble.

Source: © Ken Pence, "Rate Your Risk," http://rateyourrisk.org/ (accessed May 10, 2002).

increased chances of victimization.[103] This idea was corroborated in the Greater Vancouver Victimization Survey conducted by Statistics Canada.[104] When Messner and Tardiff studied patterns of urban homicide, they found that lifestyles significantly influenced victimization: People who tended to stay at home were the ones most likely to be killed by family or friends.[105] Lasley found that youths in Britain who stayed out late at night and used excessive amounts of alcohol stood the greatest risk of becoming crime victims.[106] A connection has also been found between the developmental level of a society and the amount of theft that occurs, but there does not appear to be a relationship with homicide, which is a more conflict-linked expressive crime.[107]

Because of the uniformity of this supporting research, routine activities theory has become a very popular theory of victimization.

Is the Routine Activity Approach Valid? Not all criminologists support this model.[108] According to routine activities theory, the affluent should have a lower victimization risk than the poor because they have the means to purchase security. Yet affluence allows people to increase activity outside the home, and wealth makes for a tempting target and for greater risk. Routine activities theory may explain why some people become victims, but it fails to explain whether others were first considered potential targets and then discarded, and if so, why that decision was made. Furthermore, the model does not explain why some people are not victimized despite the presence of risk factors.[109]

It has also been suggested that routine activities theory overemphasizes the victim and overlooks offender differences. Why do offenders choose to commit crime? Offender motivation is assumed to be rational and offenders assumed to act from similar motives. However, it is unlikely that all offenders perceive criminal opportunity or the risk of apprehension in a similar fashion. Other researchers have suggested that peer group pressure and cultural norms exert pressure on potential offenders, guide their motivation, and influence their choices; routine activities theory, they conclude, neglects to account for the factors that shape criminal choice.[110] And finally, the model is especially inadequate for measuring violence in the home committed by acquaintances. We cannot assume that women are less vulnerable because they spend more time with family members, given the high rates of assault and sexual abuse that occurs in families.[111]

Caring for the Victim

The 1994 GSS indicated that 24 percent of Canadians were victims of at least one crime in 1993, which represented no change since 1988. According to the 1999 GSS, 25 percent of Canadians aged 15 and older were victims of at least one crime in the previous year. In Britain it is estimated that the average person can expect to be the victim of a car theft once in his or her life; however, the risk of robbery is lower than that of being admitted to hospital as a psychiatric patient.[112] In the aftermath of a crime, a victim will suffer financial problems, mental stress, and physical hardship.[113] In one study of 391 adult females 75 percent had been victimized by crime at least once in their lives; 25 percent had developed posttraumatic stress syndrome, the symptoms of which lasted for more than a decade after the crime occurred.[114] The long-term effect of sexual victimization can include years of problem avoidance, social withdrawal, and self-criticism.[115]

Helping victims cope is the responsibility of all members of society. Law enforcement agencies, courts, and correctional and human service systems have come to realize that due process and human rights exist both for the defendant and for the victim of criminal behaviour.

InfoTrac®

To learn more about victims and how they see the justice system, see Catherine Kaukinen and Sandra Colavecchia, "Public Perceptions of the Courts: An Examination of Attitudes Toward the Treatment of Victims and Accused," *Canadian Journal of Criminology* 41, no. 3 (1999): 365–384.

The Government's Response

In 1998, Anne McLellan, minister of justice and attorney general of Canada, and Andy Scott, solicitor general of Canada, announced a $32-million-a-year National Crime Prevention Strategy (NCPS) aimed at developing community-based responses to crime, with an emphasis on children and youth, women, and Native people. It was designed to increase public safety for individuals and the community by providing them with resources to enhance crime prevention in their communities by developing sustainable approaches to crime prevention that deal with the root causes of crime. The emphasis has recently been broadened to address other at-risk groups including seniors, ethnic groups, gays and lesbians, and those with disabilities. The NCPS has funded more than 2400 projects in more than 60 communities and will provide more support for community projects and reduce the burden on the traditional justice system.

In the United States, the Task Force on Victims of Crime undertook an extensive study of crime victimization.[116] Its most significant recommendation was that victims be present and heard at all critical stages of the judicial proceedings. Other recommendations included protecting witnesses and victims from intimidation, requiring restitution in criminal cases, setting up programs of victim compensation, expanding victim–witness programs, requiring the use of victim impact statements at sentencing in federal criminal cases, and providing federal funding for state victim compensation and assistance projects.[117]

In Canada, the government's response to a 1998 Committee on Justice and Human Rights report was a federal strategy to include code amendments, develop new policy to assist victims, and conduct research on the effectiveness of existing programs.[118]

The following is a discussion of the most prominent forms of victim services in operation in Canada.

Victim Impact Statements

In 1986 the Canadian Department of Justice funded projects to test and evaluate victim impact statements. The evaluations included measuring the effect of the statements on the criminal justice system, how satisfied the victim was with the program, and the success of project implementation. In 1988 section 735 of the *Criminal Code* allowed victims to record a statement describing physical injury, financial loss, and personal reactions to criminal victimization, which would be introduced after conviction and before sentencing. Victim impact statements are most often used in cases involving interpersonal victimization, but they can be used in conjunction with any offence; however, most victims choose not to participate. In 1992, the Department of Justice found a lot of variation across jurisdictions, but statements were completed in less than 6 percent of cases and filed in less than 2 percent.

Chapter 22 of the *Statutes of Canada on Sentencing Reform* proclaimed in 1996 included the provision that victim impact statements (VIS) be considered in sentencing.[119] In 1999, section 722 of the *Criminal Code of Canada* was amended to permit victims to deliver the VIS openly in court orally if so desired and to require the judge to inquire whether the victim had been advised of his or her right to make this statement. The *Corrections and Conditional Release Act* was also amended to permit the introduction of these statements at parole hearings.

Notable differences exist in how each province and territory organizes and implements the use of the VIS; however, it is generally agreed that the VIS allow prosecutors and judges to experience the impact of crime more fully and that they help victims recover from crime and reduce their feeling of powerlessness as participants in the criminal justice system.

Victim Compensation

One agenda of victim advocates has been to lobby for legislation creating crime **victim compensation** programs.[120] The first program was launched in Alberta in 1969; and in 1989, the victim surcharge was created to collect revenue for provincial assistance programs. A 1994 Department of Justice study showed that collected revenues across Canada were lower than expected, with only 15 percent of potential surcharges actually imposed and only 3 percent collected. However, Parliament amended legislation in 1999 to strengthen the surcharge, to increase the rate, and for it to be imposed automatically.

As a result of such legislation, the offender pays the surcharge, and the victim can apply for compensation from the state to pay for damages associated with the crime. Each provincial and territorial compensation scheme is unique, however, and the amount of awards varies. Although victims typically seek compensation in property crimes, the most common way victims receive compensation is through private insurance. Compensation may be made for medical and dental bills, loss of present and future wages, counselling, and in some cases for pain and suffering. In the case of death, the victim's survivors can receive aid for loss of support.

In 2004, the Ontario government announced new funding for organizations that provide assistance to victims. The money comes from surcharges and provides counselling, peer support networks, educational campaigns, and coordinate programs.

An important service of most victim programs is to familiarize clients with compensation options and help them apply for aid. The usual time limit for applying for compensation is one year, although this can be waived, as in cases of childhood victimization. Victims can be disqualified if they are found to have contributed to their injuries, to have provoked the offender, or to have been in the process of committing a criminal offence.

Court Services

A common victim program service involves helping victims and witnesses deal with the criminal justice system. This aid might involve explaining court procedures: how to be a witness, how bail works, or what to do if the defendant makes a threat. Lack of such knowledge can cause confusion, making some victims reluctant to testify in court proceedings. Transportation to court might be provided, along with counsellors who remain in the courtroom during hearings to explain procedures and provide support. Although some courthouses have on-site services to aid witnesses, most do not. Court escorts are particularly important for elderly victims, people with disabilities, victims of child abuse and assault, and those who have been intimidated by friends or relatives of the defendant.

In this context, pretrial safety for victims and their families needs to be ensured in court as well. This safety is achieved through peace bonds, restraining orders, and provisions against communication with witnesses. Legislation also aids victims who are testifying, such as publication bans to protect the victim's identity, "rape-shield" provisions to prohibit evidence about a victim's sexual history, and public exclusion orders in the case of child witnesses.[121] Victim services are funded in part by a victim fine surcharge of 15 percent of a fine; if no fine is specified, the judge can set the amount up to $10 000.

Public Education

Some victim programs engage in public education that helps familiarize the general public with agencies that help crime victims. These include education programs that teach methods of dealing with conflict without resorting to violence, school-based programs that present information on spousal and dating abuse, and discussions of how to reduce violent incidents.[122] Some victim assistance projects seek to help victims learn about victim compensation services and related programs. For example, CAVEAT (Canadians Against Violence Everywhere Advocating Its Termination) developed its educational programs based on information from victims of violence and current research. Their crime prevention workshops and forums examine both prevention and response strategies, such as increasing awareness of issues, learning prevention skills, and developing early identification and intervention strategies.

Other programs help employers understand the plight of employees who have been victims of crime. Because victims may miss work or suffer postcrime emotional trauma, they may need to be absent from work for extended periods. If employers are unwilling to give them leave, victims may refuse to participate in the criminal justice process.

Crisis Intervention

Victim programs also make referrals to social services agencies to help victims recover from their ordeal by providing emergency and long-term assistance with transportation, medical care, shelter, food, and clothing. In addition, some programs provide **crisis intervention** to victims who feel isolated, vulnerable, and in need of immediate services. Some programs offer counselling at the service's office, while others do outreach in victims' homes, at the crime scene, or in a hospital. For example, after years of rape being ignored by the justice system, increased sensitivity to sexual assault victims has spurred the opening of crisis centres around the country. These centres typically feature 24-hour-a-day emergency phone lines and information on police, medical, and court procedures. Some provide volunteers to assist the victim as her case is processed through the justice system. The growth of these services has been so explosive that services are now available in many major cities and college communities.[123] Some services maintain websites on the Internet as well. Most rape crisis centres provide emergency assistance, information, referral, crisis intervention, and counselling in a variety of settings.[124]

Victim–Offender Reconciliation Programs

In reconciliation programs, mediators facilitate face-to-face encounters between victims and their attackers in an attempt to create restitution agreements and possibly reconciliation between the two parties.[125] Included in this are alternative measures or diversion programs that exist for young offenders in all provinces and territories, and for adults since 1996 in most provinces and territories. In most cases, charges are either stayed or not laid, providing that community service work is carried out. Although they were at first designed to handle routine misdemeanours, such as petty theft and vandalism, these programs now commonly facilitate restitution agreements in more serious incidents.

One of the first contemporary victim–offender mediation programs in the world was established in Kitchener, Ontario, in 1974. Today, Winnipeg has the largest victim–offender mediation program in North America and Europe. The continued growth of mediation programs is certain because restorative principles of sentencing have been incorporated into the *Criminal Code* (sections 717, 718). Unlike studies of victim participation in sentencing, evaluations of mediation programs indicate that they are successful and lead to victim and offender satisfaction.

Connections

Reconciliation programs are based on the concept of restorative justice, which rejects punitive correctional measures and suggests that crime should be viewed as an interpersonal conflict that needs to be settled in the community through noncoercive means. The theoretical roots of the restorative justice concept can be found in Chapter 9's discussion of peacemaking criminology.

Victims' Rights

In 1985, the UN Declaration on *Basic Principles of Justice for Victims of Crime and Abuse of Power* set the framework for a victim's bill of rights. In 1986 Manitoba made world history by being the first jurisdiction to adopt that framework.

Just as the law guarantees that offenders have the right to counsel and a fair trial, society also has the obligation to ensure basic rights for law-abiding citizens.[126] These rights range from adequate protection under the law from violent crimes, to victim compensation and assistance from the criminal justice system.

In 1988 the provincial, territorial, and federal governments agreed on principles for the treatment of victims. Some of these principles are the following:

- Victims should be treated with courtesy and receive redress for the crime committed against them.
- Victims should receive information about their role in criminal justice proceedings and be asked what assistance they need.
- The victim and his or her family's safety should be ensured, and there should be an opportunity for the victim and his or her family's views about the impact of the crime to be heard.
- Criminal justice system personnel should be made sensitive to the needs of victims.[127]

Ontario's *Victim's Bill of Rights* was made law in 1996.[128] It includes principles supporting victims through the criminal justice process; improving information services; allowing victims of sexual assault to be interviewed by officials of the same gender; making it easier for victims to sue assailants in civil actions; recognizing emotional distress; making amendments to support child witnesses; and expanding the Victims' Justice Fund.

Victim advocacy today is offered by an eclectic group of organizations, some independent, some government-sponsored, and some self-help. Advocates can be especially helpful when victims need, for example, to lobby police departments to keep investigations open and request the return of recovered stolen property. They can ask prosecutors and judges to help protect them from harassment and reprisals, such as making "no contact" a condition of bail. They can help victims make statements during sentencing hearings and probation and parole revocation procedures. Victim advocates can also interact with the news media, making sure that reporting is accurate and that victim privacy is not violated. Legal counsel is not usually provided to victims, but that would be useful too.

Self-Protection

Although the public is generally satisfied with the police, fear of crime and concern about community safety have prompted many people to become their own "police force" and take an active role in community protection and citizen crime control groups. The more crime in an area, the greater the amount of fear and the more likely residents will engage in self-protective measures.[129] Leslie Kennedy writes that a significant number of crimes may not be reported to police simply because victims prefer to take matters into their own hands.[130] Gartner and Doob report that 70 percent of robbery victims and 64 percent of assault victims said they didn't report their victimization to the police because they "dealt with it another way."[131] However, attitudes supporting taking the law into your own hands are probably more conservative in Canada than in the United States. For example, one author of this text saw a bumper sticker on a car from Texas and marvelled at its message: "Fight Crime. Shoot Back!" That would be unusual to see in Canada.

One self-protection trend is **target hardening**, or making a home and business crime-proof through locks, bars, alarms, and other devices.[132] This approach is based on routine activities theory and places the onus on the victim to prevent crime. Many people take specific steps to secure their homes or place of employment, such as installing burglar alarms, participating in Neighbourhood Watch programs, or engraving valuables with an identification number. Other crime prevention techniques include building a fence at the entrance of a home or business; installing an intercom or phone to gain access to the building; installing surveillance cameras, window bars, or warning signs; hiring a doorkeeper, guard, or receptionist in an apartment building; and obtaining dogs known for their ability to guard premises. The use of these measures is inversely proportional to perception of neighbourhood safety: People who fear crime are more likely to use crime prevention techniques, if they can afford it.

Connections

Target hardening is based on the idea of rational deterrence, that making a crime difficult to complete will make it unattractive to the instrumentalist criminal. For more on rational choice and deterrence theory, see Chapter 5.

People who engage in household protection are less likely to become victims of property crimes;[133] for example, people who install burglar alarms are less likely to become burglary victims.[134] When such measures are effective in deterring crime, what sometimes occurs is crime **displacement**, in which crime moves to weaker targets.[135]

Fighting Back

Some people take self-protection to its ultimate end and are prepared to fight back when they are attacked by criminals. How successful is this? Research indicates that victims who fight back often frustrate their attackers, but they also face increased odds of being physically harmed during the attack. For example, fighting back does decrease the odds of a sexual assault being completed, but it increases the victim's chances of receiving other physical injuries.[136] Robbery victims who fight back are less likely to experience completed crimes than are passive victims, but they are also more likely to be injured during the robbery. In 2003, robberies were one of the few crimes to increase (5 percent), and those committed by using a firearm increased 10 percent. The victims who escape both serious injury and property loss were the ones who used the most violent responses to crime, such as a weapon, or the least violent, such as reasoning with their attackers. Those who fought back with their fists or who tried to get help were the most likely to experience both injury and theft.[137]

Armed victims are often ready and willing to use their guns against offenders—2.5 million times a year in the United States, where about one-third of households contain guns.[138] It is estimated that armed victims kill 1500 to 2800 potential felons each year in the United States, more than the estimated 250 to 1000 killed annually by police.[139] One researcher has found that the risk of collateral injury is relatively rare and that potential victims should be encouraged to fight back; empirical research studies unanimously show that defensive gun use is associated with both lower rates of crime completion and lower rates of injury to the victim.[140]

In Canada, some support an "armed citizenry," and some research done by Gary Mauser supports the view that Canadians do use guns for self-defence. The estimate is that Canadians use firearms to protect themselves between 60 000 and 80 000 times per year and that 19 000 to 37 500 of these incidents involve defence against human threats.[141] Other criminologists, such as Gary Green, speculate that firearm ownership brings with it a number of problems, including accidental deaths, suicides, and the use of stolen guns in other crimes.[142] The issue of gun control will be discussed in depth in later chapters.

Community Organization

Not everyone is capable of buying a handgun or semiautomatic weapon and doing battle with predatory criminals. A better approach is for communities to organize on the neighbourhood level against crime. Citizens usually work in cooperation with local police agencies in neighbourhood patrol and block watch programs. These programs organize local citizens in urban areas to patrol neighbourhoods, watch for suspicious people, lobby for improvements, such as better lighting, report crime to police, put out community newsletters, conduct home security surveys, and serve as a source for crime information or tips, as in Crime Stoppers.[143]

Although such programs are welcome additions to police services, little evidence exists that they have an appreciable effect on the crime rate. There is also concern that their effectiveness is spottier in low-income, high-crime areas, which are in the most need of crime prevention assistance.[144] Block watches and neighbourhood patrols seem more successful when they are part of general-purpose or multi-issue community groups, rather than when they focus directly on crime problems.

Another community-based program is National Night Out, an event involving citizens and law-enforcement agencies. The program was created by the National Association of Town Watch, a nonprofit organization dedicated to developing crime- and drug-prevention programs, generating support and participation in local anticrime programs, and strengthening police and community relations. Between the hours of 7 and 10 p.m., residents are urged to keep their porch lights on to warn criminals that neighbourhoods are fighting back against crime.

In Manitoba, civilians and the law are working on a partnership with ChildFind to establish an anonymous tip line to combat the sexual exploitation of children. Since it is illegal to intentionally view child pornography, staffers at ChildFind run the risk of prosecution. In British Columbia, Active Youth Network, comprising various youth-serving agencies is working to facilitate improved communication and information sharing among those who work with high-risk youth. In Ottawa, programs are in place to identify and work with high-risk youth.

In sum, community crime prevention programs, target hardening, and self-defence measures are flourishing across North America. They are a response to the fear of crime and the perceived shortcomings of police

WHY ARE GUYS LIKE THIS OUT ON THE STREETS?

BECAUSE GUYS LIKE *THESE* ARE CLOGGING UP THE JAILS:

RELEASED AFTER SLITTING A MAN'S THROAT; NOW SUSPECTED OF MURDERING FIVE PEOPLE

SERVING MINIMUM MANDATORY SENTENCE FOR GROWING A POT PLANT IN HIS CLOSET

agencies in ensuring community safety. Along with private security, they represent attempts to supplement municipal police agencies and expand the "war on crime" to become a personal, neighbourhood, and community concern.

Summary

Criminologists now consider victims and victimization a major focus of study. More than 24 percent of Canadian citizens are victims of crime each year, and the social and economic costs of crime are in the billions of dollars. Like crime, victimization has stable patterns and trends. In general, victims of violent crime tend to be young, poor, single males living in large cities. Crime takes place more often at night in public places. However, many victimizations also occur in the home, and women and female children are often the target of intrafamilial violence. Many women who are killed are the victims of their husbands.

A number of theories of victimization exist. One view, called victim precipitation, contends that victims provoke criminals. Lifestyle theories suggest that victims put themselves in danger by engaging in high-risk activities. The routine activities theory maintains that a pool of motivated offenders exists and that they will take advantage of unguarded, suitable targets. The major theories of victimization are summarized in Table 4.5.

Numerous programs help victims by providing court services, economic compensation, public education, and crisis intervention. However, victims still complain about feeling victimized by the criminal justice system, whether that means being interviewed by unsympathetic police officers, being forced to wait for their court hearing in the same area of the courthouse as the defendant, not qualifying for legal aid, or not receiving compensation.

Rather than depend on the justice system, some victims have attempted to help themselves. In some instances, this self-help means community organization for self-protection. In other instances, victims have armed themselves and fought back against their attackers. There is evidence that fighting back reduces the number of completed crimes but is also related to victim injury. The development of victimology certainly adds to the complexity of studying the crime problem.

TABLE 4.5 Victim Theories

Theory	Major Premise	Strengths
Victim precipitation	Victims trigger criminal acts by their provocative behaviour. Active precipitation involves fighting words or gestures. Passive precipitation occurs when victims unknowingly threaten their attacker.	Explains multiple victimizations. If people precipitate crime, it follows that they will become repeat victims if their behaviour persists over time.
Lifestyle theories	Victimization risk is increased when people have a high-risk lifestyle. Placing themselves at risk by going to dangerous places results in increased victimization.	Explains victimization patterns in the social structure. Males, young people, and the poor have high victim rates because they have a higher-risk lifestyle than females, the elderly, and the affluent.
Equivalent group hypothesis	Criminals and victims are one and the same. Both crime and victimization are part of a high-risk lifestyle.	Shows that the conditions that create criminality also produce high victimization risk. Victims may commit crime out of a need for revenge or frustration.
Routine activities theory	Crime rates can be explained by the availability of suitable targets, the absence of capable guardians, and the presence of motivated offenders.	Can explain crime rates and trends. Shows how victim behaviour can influence criminal opportunity. Suggests that victim risk can be reduced by increasing guardianship and reducing target vulnerability.
Proximity hypothesis	People who live in deviant places are at high risk for crime. Victim behaviour has little influence over the criminal act.	Places the focus of crime on deviant places. Shows why people with conventional lifestyles become crime victims.

Thinking Like a Criminologist

The solicitor general of Canada has asked you to prepare a report on the relationship between physical abuse and criminal acts among adolescents ages 10 to 18. As a result of the self-report survey you conduct, you are able to provide the following information.

Adolescents experiencing abuse or violence are at high risk of immediate and lasting negative effects on health and well-being. Of the high-school students surveyed, an alarming one in five (21 percent) said they had been physically abused. Of the older students, ages 15 to 18, 29 percent said they had been physically abused. Younger students also reported significant rates of abuse: 17 percent responded "yes" when questioned whether they had been physically abused. Although girls were far less likely to report abuse than were boys, 12 percent said they had been physically abused. Most abuse occurs at home; it occurs more than once; and the abuser is usually a family member. More than half of those physically abused had tried alcohol and drugs, and 60 percent had admitted to a violent act. Nonabused children were significantly less likely to abuse substances, and only 30 percent indicated they had committed a violent act.

What is your interpretation of the association between abuse and delinquency? What recommendations would you make about current discussions to reform the *Youth Criminal Justice Act* to make it more responsive to underlying factors that affect youth crime?

Key Terms

acquaintance-related crime

active precipitation

aggravating factor

capable guardians

crisis intervention

cycle of violence

deviant place hypothesis

displacement

equivalent group hypothesis

lifestyle

mitigating factor

motivated offenders

passive precipitation

predatory crime

proximity hypothesis

routine activities theory

stranger-related crime

suitable targets

target hardening

victim compensation

victim precipitation

victimologist

victimology

Critical Thinking Questions

1. Considering what we learned in this chapter about crime victimization, what measures can you take to better protect yourself from crime?

2. Do you agree with the assessment that a school is one of the most dangerous locations in the community? Did you find your high school to be a dangerous environment?

3. Does a person bear some of the responsibility for his or her victimization if the person maintains a lifestyle that contributes to the chances of becoming a crime victim? That is, should we "blame the victim"?

4. Have you ever experienced someone precipitating crime? If so, did you do anything to help resolve the situation?

 See the book-specific website at http://www.siegelcriminology3e.nelson.com for additional chapter links, discussions, and quizzes.

Theories of Crime Causation

An important goal of the criminological enterprise is to create valid and accurate theories of crime causation. Social scientists have defined theory as sets of statements that explain why and how several concepts are related. For a set of statements to qualify as a theory, we must be able to deduce some conclusions from it that are subject to empirical verification; that is, theories must predict or prohibit certain observable events or conditions.*

Criminologists have sought to collect vital facts about crime and interpret them in a scientifically meaningful fashion. By developing empirically verifiable statements, or hypotheses, and organizing them into theories of crime causation, criminologists hope to identify the causes of crime.

Since the late nineteenth century, criminological theory has pointed to various underlying causes of crime. The earliest theories generally attributed crime to a single underlying cause: atypical body build, genetic abnormality, insanity, physical anomalies, and poverty. Later theories attributed crime causation to multiple factors: poverty, peer influence, school problems, and family dysfunction.

In this section, theories of crime causation are grouped into six chapters. Chapters 5 and 6 focus on theories based on individual traits. These theories hold that crime is either a free-will choice made by an individual, a function of personal psychological or biological abnormality, or both. Chapters 7 through 9 investigate theories based in sociology and political economy. These theories portray crime as a function of the structure, process, and conflicts of social living. Chapter 10 is devoted to theories that combine or integrate these various concepts into a cohesive, complex view of crime.

*Rodney Stark, *Sociology,* 2nd ed. (Belmont, Calif.: Wadsworth, 1987), 618.

Choice Theory

chapter 5

Crime data tell us that criminality is a young man's game: Most offenders are young males who desist from crime as they mature; the bulk of adult offending is committed by relatively few persistent offenders. Why do these youths commit criminal acts? Furthermore, given that most young offenders age out or desist from crime, why do some continue to violate the law and risk apprehension, trial, and punishment well into adulthood?

To some criminologists, persistence is a function of personal choice. The decision to violate the law—commit a robbery, sell drugs, attack a rival, fill out a false tax return—is made for a variety of personal reasons, including greed, revenge, need, anger, lust, jealousy, thrill seeking, and vanity. The central issue is that the illegal act is a matter of individual decision making, a rational choice made after weighing the potential benefits and consequences of crime. The jealous suitor concludes that the risk of punishment is worth the satisfaction of punching a rival; the greedy shopper considers the chance of apprehension by store detectives so small that she takes a new sweater; the drug dealer concludes that the huge profits possible from a single shipment of cocaine outweigh the cost of apprehension. In the final analysis, people choose crime simply because it is rewarding, satisfying, easy, or fun.

This chapter will review the philosophical underpinnings of **choice theory**, which first appeared as **classical criminology**, and the recent theoretical models that have developed. Because the central premise is that criminals are rational, their behaviour can be controlled or deterred by the fear of punishment. Desistence is thus explained by a growing and intense fear of punishment. These models include situational crime prevention, general deterrence theory, specific deterrence theory, and incapacitation. Finally, the chapter briefly reviews how choice theory has influenced policymaking in the area of criminal justice.

The Development of Classical Theory

Theories of crime based on the rational decision making of motivated criminals can trace their roots to the classical school of criminology. In Chapter 1, we saw that classical criminology was based on the works of Beccaria, Bentham, and other utilitarian philosophers. At its core are the following concepts:

- People choose all behaviour, including crime.
- A violation of another person is a violation of the social contract.
- Society must provide the greatest good for the greatest number.

- The law shouldn't try to legislate morality.
- People should be presumed innocent until proven guilty, with no torture.
- Laws should be written out with punishments prescribed in advance.
- Individuals give up some of their liberty in exchange for social protection.
- People are motivated by pain and pleasure.
- Punishment should be limited to what is necessary to deter people from crime.
- Punishment should be severe, certain, and swift.
- The law must be rational, transparent, and just, or is itself a crime.
- People's choices can be controlled by the fear of punishment.
- Severity, certainty, and swiftness of punishment are the most effective in controlling criminal behaviour.[1]

Beccaria saw people as egotistical and self-centred, needing to be goaded by the fear of punishment. However, he also called for fair and certain punishment to deter crime.

 InfoTrac®

To read about Beccaria's life history and the formulation of his ideas, go to http://www.criminology.fsu.edu/crimtheory/beccaria.htm. For an up-to-date list of weblinks on Beccaria, go to http://info.wadsworth.com/siegel.

Beccaria felt that punishments must be proportional to the crimes, otherwise people would not be deterred from committing more serious offences. For example, if both rape and murder were punished by death, a rapist would have little reason to refrain from killing the victim to eliminate the potential threat of the victim contacting the police and giving evidence in court.

Beccaria was one of those rare reformers to have an enduring influence on justice policy,[2] inspiring criminologists who believe that criminals choose to commit crime and that crime can be controlled by the judicious application of criminal punishments. The result was a foundation for criminal justice that is still with us today.

Beccaria's vision has had a powerful influence on events in the criminal justice system.[3] The belief that punishment should fit the crime and that people should be punished proportionately for what they did was widely adopted throughout Europe and North America. In Britain, philosopher Jeremy Bentham (1748–1833) helped popularize Beccaria's views in his writings on **utilitarianism**. According to this theory, actions are evaluated by their tendency to produce advantage, pleasure, and happiness, and to avoid or prevent mischief, pain, evil, or unhappiness.[4] Bentham believed that the purpose of all law is to produce and support the total happiness of the community it serves. Since punishment is in itself harmful, its existence is justified only if it promises to prevent greater evil than it creates. Punishment, therefore, has four main objectives:

1. To prevent all criminal offences
2. To convince the offender to commit a less serious crime when it cannot prevent a crime
3. To ensure that a criminal uses no more force than is necessary
4. To prevent crime as cheaply as possible

The most stunning example of how the classical philosophy of Beccaria and Bentham was embraced in Europe occurred in 1789, when France's postrevolutionary Constituent Assembly adopted these ideas in the *Declaration of the Rights of Man*:

> The law has the right to prohibit only actions harmful to society. . . . The law shall inflict only such punishments as are strictly and clearly necessary. . . . No person shall be punished except by virtue of a law enacted and promulgated previous to the crime and applicable to its terms.

Similarly, a prohibition against "cruel and unusual punishments" was incorporated into Canada's *Charter of Rights and Freedoms*, as section 12: "Everyone has the right not to be subjected to any cruel and unusual treatment or punishment."

The use of torture was largely abandoned in the nineteenth century, with the increased use of incarcerating criminals and structuring prison sentences to fit the severity of the crime. Although the proportionality demanded by Beccaria was often ignored by the legal system, the general theme of gearing punishment to deter crime was widely accepted.

By the end of the nineteenth century, the popularity of the classical approach began to decline, after one hundred years of dominance, and by the mid-twentieth century this perspective was neglected by mainstream criminologists. During this period, positivist criminologists focused on the internal and external factors—poverty, low IQ, poor education, inadequate home life—believed to be the true cause of criminality. Since these conditions could not be easily curbed, the concept of punishing people for behaviours beyond their control seemed both foolish and cruel. Although classical principles still controlled the way police, courts, and correctional agencies operated, most criminologists rejected classical criminology as an explanation of criminal behaviour.

 InfoTrac®

For a contrasting take on whether prisons work, see the following:

- Daniel P. Mears, Sarah Lawrence, Amy L. Solomon, and Michelle Waul, "Prison Based Programming: What It Can Do and Why It Is Needed," *Corrections Today* 64, no. 2 (2002): 66.
- Ralph A. Rossum, "Rehabilitating Rehabilitation: One Reason Why Prisons Are Failing to Rehabilitate Inmates Is That Rehabilitation Seeks to Improve the Character of Offenders While Most Prisons Degrade Prisoners," *World and I* 18, no. 12 (2003): 24.

Choice Theory Emerges

The classical approach began to enjoy a resurgence of popularity in the mid-1970s. According to positivist criminology, if crime were caused by some social or psychological problem, such as poverty, crime rates could be reduced by providing good jobs and economic opportunities. However, national surveys (such as Martinson's "What Works?") failed to uncover examples of rehabilitation programs that prevented future criminal activity.[5] Some went as far as suggesting that punishment-oriented programs could suppress future criminality much more effectively than could those that relied on rehabilitation and treatment efforts.[6] Reviving classical concepts of social control and punishment seemed to make more sense than did futilely trying to improve entrenched social conditions or rehabilitate criminals using ineffectual methods.[7]

Beginning in the late 1970s, a number of criminologists began producing books and monographs expounding the theme that criminals are rational actors who plan their crimes, fear punishment, and deserve to be penalized for their misdeeds. In a 1975 classic, *Thinking About Crime*, political scientist James Q. Wilson debunked the positivist view that crime is a function of such forces as poverty that can be altered by government programs. Instead, he argued, efforts should be made to reduce criminal opportunity by deterring would-be offenders and incarcerating known criminals.

People likely to commit crime were said to lack inhibition against misconduct, to value the excitement and thrills of breaking the law, to have a low stake in conformity, and to be willing to take greater chances than was the average person. If they can be convinced that their actions will bring severe punishment, only the totally irrational will be willing to engage in crime. Although incapacitating criminals should not be the sole goal of the justice system, such a policy does have the advantage of restraining offenders and preventing their future criminality without having to figure out how to change their attitudes or nature—a goal that has proved difficult to accomplish. Wilson made this famous, albeit cynical, observation:

> Wicked people exist. Nothing avails except to set them apart from innocent people. And many people, neither wicked nor innocent, but watchful, dissembling, and calculating of their chances, ponder our reaction to wickedness as a clue to what they might profitably do.[8]

Wilson seems to be saying that unless we react forcefully to crime, those "sitting on the fence" will get a clear message: Crime pays.

Coinciding with the publication of Wilson's book was a conservative shift in public policy in many Western countries. Political decision makers embraced these ideas as a means of bringing the crime rate down because they focused blame on the individual. These views have helped shape criminal justice policy for the past two decades.

Does Crime Pay? Rational offenders are induced to commit crime if they perceive that crime pays more than they could earn from a legitimate job. Crime pays if the benefits of employment are lower than the expected benefits of theft. Does crime, in fact, pay?

To answer this question, Wilson and Abrahams (1992) used a sample of incarcerated inmates to determine their perceived and actual "take" from crime. Wilson and Abrahams divided the group into mid- and high-rate offenders in one of six crime categories: burglary, theft, swindling, auto theft, robbery, and mixed offences predominantly involving drug sales.

Using crime loss estimates derived from the National Crime Victimization Survey (NCVS), Wilson and Abrahams found that mid-rate burglars on average earn about 32 percent of what they could have earned in a legitimate job. High-rate burglars, who commit an average of 193 crimes per year, earn roughly what they would have earned from a job (but they spend more time behind bars). Even if free for the entire year, high-rate burglars would earn about the same as if they had held a job for the same period. Research shows that criminals may be motivated to commit crime when they know people who have made "big scores" and are quite successful at crime. Though the prevailing wisdom is that "crime does not pay," a small but significant subset of criminals actually enjoy earnings of close to $50 000 per year from crime, and their success may help motivate other would-be offenders.[9]

Crime profits are reduced by the costs of a criminal career: legal fees, bail bonds, the loss of family income, and the psychic cost of a prison sentence. Given these costs, most criminals actually earn little from crime. Would you be willing to become a high-rate robber if you knew that you would be spending half your life in prison for an annual salary of less than $15 000? In 1986, the average take for a gas station robbery was $300. Bank robberies netted on average $2500 in 1993, but the clearance rate was as high as 80 percent, with an even higher conviction rate.[10]

If crime pays so little, why are there so many criminals? There are a number of reasons criminals choose crime despite its relatively low payoff. One reason is that criminals tend to overestimate the money they can earn. In some cases, criminals' estimates were more than 12 times higher than a realistic assessment of their earning potential. For example, burglars estimated they could earn $2674 per month from crime, while a more realistic figure is only $230! In 1992, when three young man robbed a McDonald's restaurant in Sydney River, Nova Scotia, they had convinced themselves they could get $200 000 from the robbery. For a take that was only a fraction of what they had estimated, they killed three people and received long prison sentences.[11]

Some criminals believe they have no choice but to commit crime because legitimate work is unavailable. However, about two-thirds of the inmates reported having been employed before they were imprisoned. Rather than being excluded from the job market, criminals are more likely to be underemployed than to be unemployed.

Criminals are realistic, believing that eventually everyone is caught and punished. However, they are overly optimistic about getting away with each individual crime, and being impulsive, they take the short-term view that each particular crime is worth the risk.

From these roots, a more contemporary version of classical theory evolved that is based on decision making, referred to as the rational choice approach to crime causation.[12]

The Concepts of Rational Choice

According to the rational choice approach, law-violating behaviour occurs when an offender decides to commit crime after considering both personal factors (need for money, revenge, thrills, and entertainment) and situational factors (how well a target is protected, the efficiency of the local police force). Before choosing to commit a crime, the reasoning criminal evaluates the risk of apprehension, the seriousness of expected punishment, the potential value of the criminal enterprise, and the need for criminal gain.

Famous Canadian Criminals

The Curious Career Choice of Edwin Alonzo Boyd

Edwin Alonzo Boyd, the son of a Toronto policeman, embarked on his career as a bank robber in1949. He undertook this first robbery on his own, taking in just over $2000. Sometimes he had a partner, Howard Gault, a former jail guard. Boyd's efforts were not always successful. In one robbery, the bank manager grabbed a gun and shot at Boyd, who had no choice but to run without the loot. Another time, Boyd was chased in his stolen car by a bank employee and just barely escaped.

Boyd was finally captured in 1951 and sent to Toronto's Don Jail, where he met "Tough Lennie" Jackson, another bank robber, and Willie "The Clown" Jackson, a small-time criminal. Lennie had a hacksaw blade hidden in his wooden leg, which they used to saw through the bars. Together with another bank robber, Steve Suchan, they slid through the window, landing in an exercise yard. They used bed sheets to make a rope that they threw to the top of a wall, clambering up to make their way to freedom. They went on a 10-month bank-robbing spree that included the biggest cash haul in Toronto's history. It made exciting newspaper coverage. Willie Jackson was soon caught and sent back to the Don Jail.

It all came to an end in 1952, when two police detectives, Edmund Tong and Roy Perry, pulled over a car. Tong had been on the trail of the Boyd gang but didn't know the black Mercury contained Suchan and Lennie Jackson. As Tong approached the suspect vehicle, he was gunned down, and Perry was wounded in the arm.

In response to the public outrage, a manhunt was quickly mounted. Suchan and Lennie Jackson were captured in Montreal, but Boyd, who had had nothing to do with the murder, eluded capture for a while. He was arrested peacefully at his brother's house. The four were reunited in the Don Jail. Once again, they took advantage of Lennie's artificial foot by using it to hide a piece of metal, a file, and hacksaw blades. They made a key to their cell door with the metal and file and used the hacksaw blades to cut through the bars. Rewards totalling $26 000 were posted for their capture. After a huge manhunt, police captured the gang in an abandoned barn near Yonge Street and Sheppard Avenue. All four were convicted on charges of armed robbery and auto theft. Leonard Jackson and Steve Suchan were executed by hanging for the murder of Edmund Tong.

Edwin Alonzo Boyd was sentenced to life in prison but was eventually paroled in 1966 and retired to a private life under a different name in British Columbia. He died in 2002. William Jackson also served a lengthy jail term in the Kingston Penitentiary, before being released.

Source: Brian Vallee, *Edwin Alonzo Boyd* (Toronto: Doubleday, 1998); torontopolice.on.c/d32/history; tv.cbc.ca/lifeandtimes/bio1998/boyd.

The decision to commit a crime, then, is a matter of personal decision making based on weighing the available information. The decision to forgo crime may also be based on the perception that the economic benefits are no longer there or that the risk of apprehension is too great. For example, studies of residential burglary indicate that criminals will forgo activity if they believe a neighbourhood is well patrolled by police.[13] In fact, evidence exists that when police begin to concentrate patrols in a particular area of the city, crime rates tend to increase in adjacent areas that may be perceived by criminals as "safer" (**crime displacement**).[14]

Offence and Offender Specifications

Crime is both offence- and offender-specific.[15] **Offence-specific crime** refers to how offenders react selectively to the characteristics of particular offences. The decision of whether to commit a burglary, for example, might involve evaluating the target's likely cash yield; the availability of a getaway car; and the probability of capture by police.

Offender-specific crime refers to how criminals do not usually engage in random acts of antisocial behaviour. They analyze whether they have the prerequisites for committing a criminal act, including their skills, motives, needs, and fears. Criminal acts might be ruled out if the potential offenders perceive that they can reach a desired personal goal through legitimate means or if they are too afraid of getting caught.[16]

Note the distinction made here between crime and criminality.[17] Crime is an event; criminality is a personal trait. Criminals do not commit crime all the time, and even the most honest citizens may on occasion violate the law. Some high-risk people lacking opportunity may never commit crime, whereas given enough provocation or opportunity, a low-risk, law-abiding person may commit crime. What, then, are the conditions that promote crime and criminality?

Structuring Criminality. A number of personal factors condition people to choose criminality, such as the perception of economic opportunity: Offenders are more likely to desist from crime if they believe that (1) their future criminal earnings will be relatively low and (2) attractive and legal income-generating opportunities are available.[18]

Fluctuations in the perceptions of risk over a person's lifetime also influence choices. Experienced criminals may desist when they believe that the risks are greater than the profit.[19] The veteran criminal discovers personal limitations and knows when to take a chance and when to be cautious. Learning and experience are important elements in the choice of crime.[20]

Personality and lifestyle also help structure criminal choices. According to Agnew, people who choose crime over conformity share similar personal traits: (1) They feel as if they can do what they want to and perceive a lack of social constraints, (2) they have less self-control than other people and seem unaffected by fear of punishment, and (3) they are typically under stress or facing some serious personal problem or condition that forces them to choose risky behaviour.[21]

Structuring Crime

The decision to commit crime is structured by the choice of (1) location, (2) target characteristics, and (3) the techniques available for its completion.

Choosing the Place of Crime. In choosing the place of crime, interviews with crack cocaine street dealers showed that they evaluated the desirability of their "sales area" before setting up shop.[22] The middle of a long block was considered the best choice because they could see everything coming toward them from both directions; police raids could then be spotted ahead of time. Another tactic was to entice buyers of whom they were suspicious either into spaces between apartment buildings or into back lots to do drug deals. The dealer gained a measure of protection because confederates could watch over the operation and come to the rescue if the buyer tried to "pull something."

Choosing Targets. Rational choice is also used in locating targets. Studies of professional and occasional criminals show that choosing targets is a rational event. Burglars check to make sure that no one is home before they enter a residence. Some call ahead, while others ring the doorbell, preparing to claim they had the wrong address if someone answers. Some check to find out which families have star high-school athletes, since those that do are sure to be at the game, leaving their houses unguarded.[23] In Waterloo recently, "obituary bandits" robbed homes when people were at funerals and viewings, after looking at newspapers for death notices. Others seek the unlocked door and avoid the one with a deadbolt; houses with dogs are usually considered off-limits.

Some burglars avoid freestanding buildings, which are more easily surrounded by police; others select targets that are known to do a primarily cash business, such as bars, supermarkets, and restaurants.[24] Homemakers develop predictable patterns, which helps burglars plan their crimes.[25] Burglars prefer working between 9 a.m. and 11 a.m. and in mid-afternoon, when parents are either working or dropping off or picking up kids at school. Burglars avoid Saturdays because families are at home, but Sunday during church hours is a prime time for weekend burglaries. Bank robbers choose city banks over country banks, because subway routes and areas with heavy pedestrian traffic make escape easier.

Learning Criminal Techniques. Criminals learn techniques that help them avoid detection; for example, crack dealers learn how to "stash" crack cocaine in undisclosed locations so they will not have to carry drugs on them. Females drawn into drug dealing tell how they have learned the "trade" in a businesslike manner:

> He taught me how to "recon" [reconstitute] cocaine, cutting and repacking a brick from 91 proof to 50 proof, just like a business. He treats me like an equal partner, and many of the friends are business associates. I am a catalyst. . . . I even get guys turned on to drugs.[26]

In sum, rational choice involves shaping criminality and structuring crime. Personality, age, status, risk, and opportunity influence the decision to become a criminal; place, target, and techniques help to structure crime.

 InfoTrac®

Security measures can quickly become outdated; for example, see "Wireless Internet Users Can Be Inviting Targets for Crime," *Knight Ridder/Tribune Business News*, February 18, 2004.

Rational Choice and Routine Activities

Rational choice theory dovetails with **routine activities theory**, which maintains that a supply of motivated offenders, the absence of capable guardians, and the presence of suitable targets determine crime trends.[27] Routine activities theory provides a **macro perspective** on crime, predicting how change in social and economic conditions influences the overall crime and victimization rates. In contrast, **rational choice theory** provides a **micro perspective** on why individual offenders decide to commit specific crimes. These approaches overlap in saying that crime rates are a product of criminal opportunity: Increase the number of guardians, decrease the suitability of targets, or reduce the offender population, and crime rates should likewise decline; increase opportunity and reduce guardianship and crime rates should increase.

What are the connections between rational choice and routine activities?

Connections

In Chapter 4, routine activities theory discussed how victimization is patterned, not random or accidental. This theory gives a macro perspective on some of the causes of crime.

Suitable Targets. Criminal choice is influenced by the perception of target vulnerability. As they go about their daily activities, potential criminals may encounter targets of illegal opportunity: an empty carport, an open door, an unlocked car, a bike left on the street. Corner homes, usually near traffic lights or stop signs, are more likely to be burglarized. Secluded homes, such as those at the end of a cul-de-sac, surrounded by wooded areas, also make suitable targets.[28] Thieves also choose sites that are convenient, familiar, and located in easily accessible and open areas.[29]

Criminals are unlikely to travel long distances to commit crimes and are more likely to drift toward the centre of a city.[30] White found that "permeable neighbourhoods," those with a greater than usual number of access streets from traffic arteries into the neighbourhood, are the ones most likely to have high crime rates.[31] This fact might lend credence to the idea of having "gated communities," where access is strictly controlled. It is possible that thieves choose open neighbourhoods because they are familiar, well travelled, open and vulnerable, and offer more potential escape routes. Familiarity with the area gives thieves ready knowledge of escape routes; this is

referred to as their "awareness space."[32] Robbers may be wary of people who are watching the community for signs of trouble: Research by Paul Bellair shows that robbery levels are relatively low in neighbourhoods where residents keep a watchful eye on their neighbours' property.[33] Here, we can see the influence of a routine activity on criminal choice: The more suitable and accessible the target, the more likely that crime will occur.[34]

Capable Guardians. The presence of **capable guardians** deters crime, because criminals tend to shy away from victims who are perceived to be armed and potentially dangerous.[35] In interviews conducted with career property offenders, Tunnell found that burglars will avoid targets if they feel police are in the area or if "nosy neighbours" might be suspicious.[36] Predatory criminals are aware of law enforcement capability: Communities that enjoy the reputation of employing aggressive "crime-fighting" cops are less likely to attract offenders than areas perceived as having passive law enforcers.[37]

Guardianship can also involve passive or mechanical devices, such as security fences or burglar alarms. Physical security measures can improve guardianship and limit offender access to targets.[38]

Research has also shown that living in a cohesive community reduces the likelihood of victimization. Tightly knit communities have higher levels of informal guardianship, with members more active in intervening in public deviant or criminal activities. In a study of 19 000 respondents to national victimization surveys in 15 countries, and 10 000 respondents to city-level surveys in another 12 countries, community cohesion was found to reduce robbery and assault near the home by strangers.[39] Arguably, for the same reasons, Block Parent and Neighbourhood Watch programs also work to create cohesion and reduce crime.

Motivated Criminals. Crime rates also correspond to the number of **motivated criminals** in the population (that is, teenage males, drug users, unemployed adults). Rational offenders are less likely to commit crimes if they can achieve personal goals through legitimate means, so job availability reduces crime. In contrast, criminal motivation increases when the cost of living rises.[40] Criminal motivation can be reduced if offenders perceive alternatives to crime; in contrast, the perception of blocked legitimate opportunities increases criminal motivation.

Tunnell's career criminals said they committed crimes because they considered legitimate opportunities unavailable to people with their limited education and background. One offender told him:

I tried to stay away from crime. . . . Nobody would hire me. I was an ex-con and I tried, I really tried to get gainful employment. There was nobody looking to hire me with my record. I went in as a juvenile and came out as an adult and didn't have any legitimate employment résumé to submit. Employment was impossible. So, I started robbing.[41]

Note how crime became the choice when legitimate alternatives were absent. In contrast, potential offenders who perceive legitimate alternatives, such as high-paying jobs, are less likely to choose crime.[42]

Connections

Lack of conventional opportunity is a persistent theme in sociological theories of crime. The frustration caused by a lack of opportunity explains high crime rates in lower-class areas. Chapter 7 sections on strain theories provide an alternative explanation of how lack of opportunity is associated with crime.

Interactive Effects. Motivation, opportunity, and targets are interactive. Motivated criminals will not commit crime unless they have suitable targets and the opportunity to attack them. The presence of guardians will deter most offenders, rendering even attractive targets off-limits. These principles apply to crimes from shoplifting to bank robbery.[43] Exhibit 5.1 shows three basic approaches to crime prevention, depending on the level of intervention required.

Figure 5.1 illustrates the interrelationship among opportunity, routine activities, and environmental factors. Criminal opportunities, suitable victims, and targets abound in urban environments where facilitators (guns, drugs) are readily found. Environmental factors, such as physical layout and cultural style, may facilitate or restrict criminal opportunity. Motivated offenders living in these urban "hot spots" continually learn about criminal opportunities from peers, the media, and their own perceptions. This information may either escalate their criminal motivation or warn them of its danger.[44]

Warr found that kids who are attached to their parents and spend their weekends at home report little in the way of criminal motivation; lack of opportunity may reduce motivation.[45] Similarly, Hagan indicates that kids whose family relationships are strained, distant, and unrewarding are more likely to become attached to deviant peers, which in turn helps increase criminal motivation.[46]

In a national study of 1700 youths aged 18 to 26, researchers found that adolescents who spend a great deal of time socializing with peers in the absence of authority figures (riding around in cars, going to parties, going out at night for fun) are also most likely to engage in deviance.[47] The presence of motivated peers, with the lack of guardianship, leaves more opportunity for substance abuse, crime, and dangerous driving. Participation in unstructured activities helps explain the association among crime rates and gender, age, and status: Teenage boys have the highest crime rates because they are the group most likely to engage in unsupervised socialization.

Opportunity combined with lack of guardianship increases criminal motivation.

Mapping. Since crime is a rational choice and involves guardianship, opportunity, and motivation, it can be mapped. For years, statisticians have been measuring things to discover patterns in the social and natural worlds. Figure 5.2 shows the distribution of homicide in Division 51, Toronto, from 1990 to 1999. Producing such maps based on either police reports or calls for service enables the police to understand where the "hot spots" are and where enforcement would be most effective. A former Vancouver police officer, Kim Rossmo, has developed a mathematical geographic profiling system that shows the probability of where an offender might live, based on the distance-delay concept: Offenders don't travel far from home, and the frequency of offending is in inverse proportion to the distance from home.[48]

Is Crime Rational?

It is obvious that some crimes are the product of rational and objective thought, especially when they involve an ongoing criminal conspiracy centred on

Exhibit 5.1	Basic Approaches to Crime Prevention
Primary prevention	Actions taken to reduce the occurrence of criminal acts (e.g., Neighbourhood Watch, Block Parents)
Secondary prevention	Detecting early signs of high-risk individuals or situations before a crime takes place (e.g., Mothers Against Drunk Driving)
Tertiary prevention	Intervention programs for youth or adult offenders to prevent further offences (e.g., community notification programs)

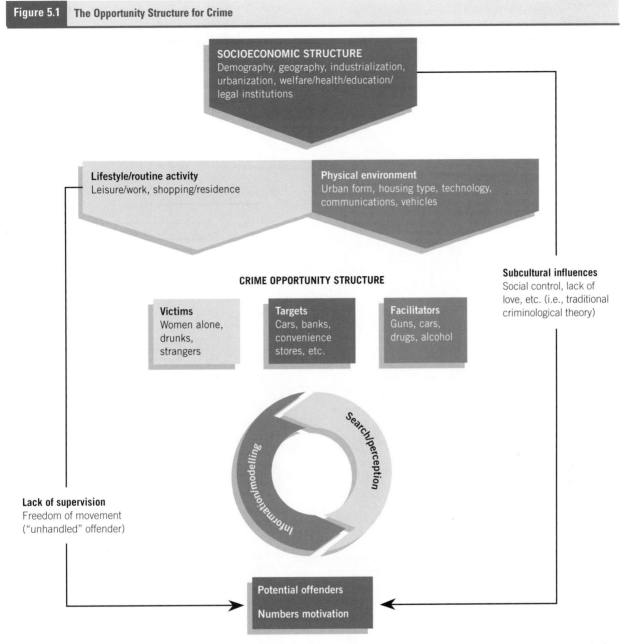

Figure 5.1   The Opportunity Structure for Crime

Source: Ronald Clarke, "Situational Crime Prevention," in *Building a Safer Society: Strategic Approaches to Crime Prevention,* volume 19 of *Crime and Justice, A Review of Research,* ed. Michael Tonry and David Farrington, 103 (Chicago University of Chicago Press, 1995). Reprinted by permission.

economic gain. When prominent bankers in the United States savings and loan industry were indicted for criminal fraud, their elaborate financial schemes not only showed signs of rationality but also exhibited brilliant financial expertise.[49] The stock market manipulations of Wall Street insiders, such as Boesky, Milken, and Martha Stewart, and the problems of Enron demonstrate an analysis of market conditions, interests, and risks.

Connections

In Chapter 13, various criminal enterprises run by white-collar professionals and involving corporate interests are discussed. Learn how workers are exposed to risks, how consumers are sold faulty products, and how environmental pollution is a cost of doing business.

Figure 5.2   Homicides in Police Division 51, Toronto, 1990–1999

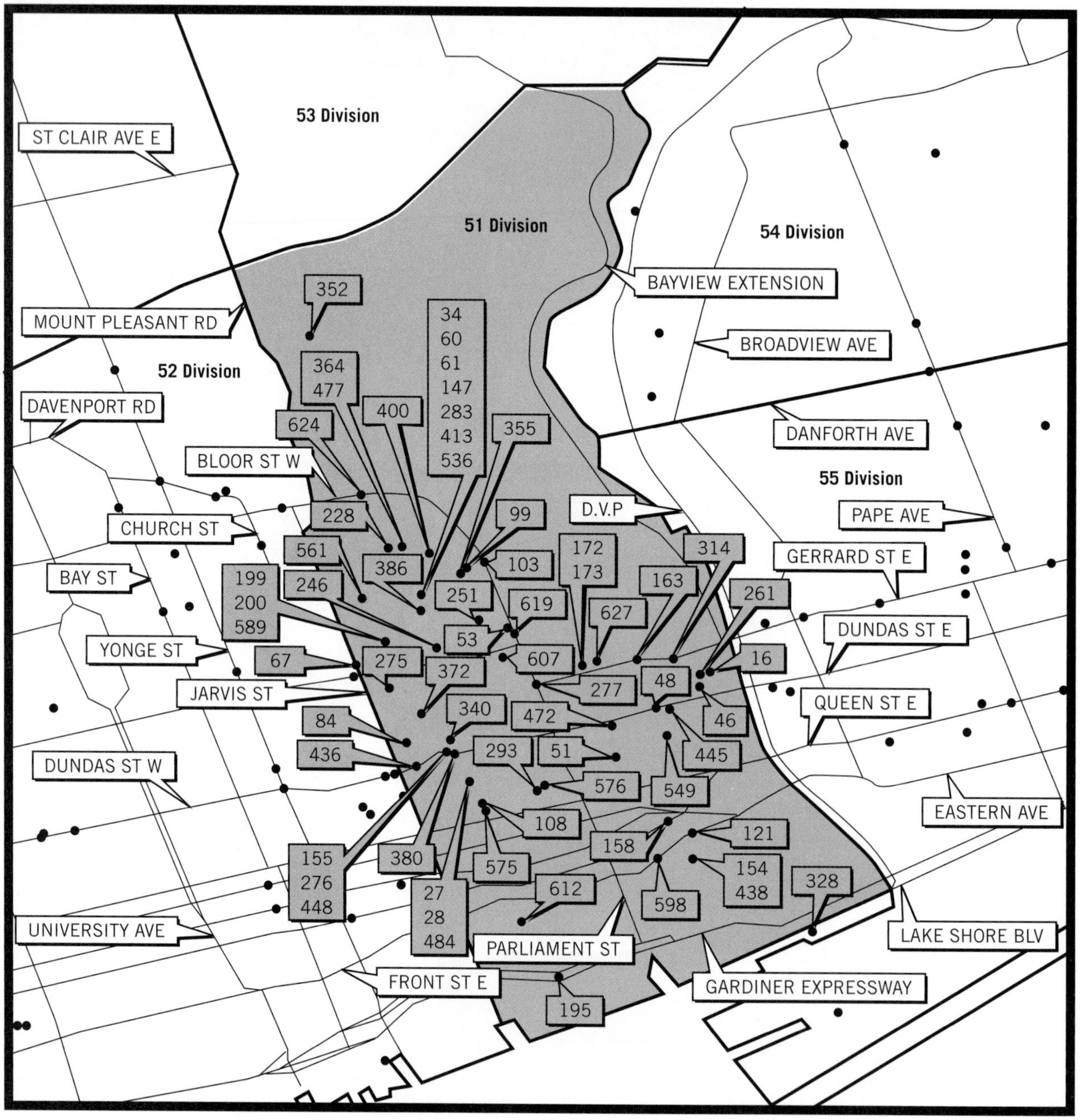

Source: Reprinted with permission of the Toronto Star Syndicate.

Are Street Crimes Rational?

Do common street crimes, such as prostitution and petty theft, exhibit rationality? They are not random acts but are the product of careful risk assessment, including environmental, social, and structural factors. Serial killer John Martin Crawford, the topic of *Just Another Indian* by Warren Goulding, reputedly picked up Native prostitutes because they were less likely to be missed.

Criminologists Clarke and Harris found that auto thieves are highly selective in their choice of targets. If they want to strip cars for their parts, thieves are most likely to choose Volkswagens; if they want to sell the cars or keep them permanently, they choose Mercedes; for temporary use, Buicks are top-ranked.[50] Vehicle selection is based on the cars' attractiveness and suitability for a particular purpose: German automobiles are selected for stripping because they usually have high-quality audio equipment that has good value on the secondhand market; thus, target selection is highly rational.

Studies of prostitutes suggest that these women make clear choices in their daily activities. For example, Maher's interviews with street-level sex workers in Brooklyn showed that prices were declining and competition was increasing because increased drug use produced an influx of new women willing to charge little to support their habits. Despite fierce competition, more-experienced street workers still resist sex practices that compromise their chances of survival, such as sex without condoms, they refuse to trade sex for drugs, and they refuse to service clients they consider too dangerous or distasteful.[51] These activities show clear signs of rational choice.

Similarly, there has been an attempt to influence johns in their choice of soliciting. Some jurisdictions confiscate johns' cars, and others require men to go to "john school" after conviction, where they learn more about the exploitation hidden in prostitution.

Is Drug Use Rational?

Research shows that drug use is controlled by rational decision making. Users report that they begin taking drugs when they believe that the benefits of substance use outweigh its costs, that drugs will provide an enjoyable, exciting, thrilling experience. Their entry into substance abuse is facilitated if friends and family members encourage drug use and abuse substances themselves.[52]

In adulthood, heavy drug users and dealers show signs of rationality and cunning in their daily activity. Jacobs found that users and dealers used specific techniques to avoid apprehension by police. They scope out the territory to make sure nothing is out of place that may be a potential threat, such as police officers or rival gang members.[53] One crack dealer told Jacobs:

> There was this red Pontiac sittin' on the corner one day with two white guys inside. They was just sittin' there for an hour, not doin' nothin'. Another day, diff'rent people be walkin' up and down the street you don't really recognize. You think they might be kin of someone but then you be askin' around and they [neighbours] ain't never seen them before neither. When ya' see strange things like that, you think somethin' be goin' on [and you don't deal].

Drug dealers are also careful about whether they should deal alone or in groups: Large groups draw more attention from the police but can offer more protection. Drug-dealing gangs can also help divert the attention of police: If their drug dealing is noticed by detectives, a dealer can walk away or dispose of evidence while confederates distract the cops.

Morgan and Joe's three-city (San Francisco, San Diego, Honolulu) study of female drug abusers also found a great deal of rationality and careful decision making. One dealer who earns $50 000 per year told them:

> I stayed within my goals, basically. . . . I don't go around doing stupid things. I don't walk around telling people I have drugs for sale, I don't have people sitting out in front of my house. I don't have traffic in and out of my house. . . . I control the people I sell to.[54]

These dealers viewed drug distribution positively, because it provides them with economic independence, self-esteem, and the ability to maintain control over their lives.

Some research shows that dealing drugs is more of a complement to a regular income than a replacement. Dealers that sell on a daily basis sold on average only four hours a day. Surprisingly, instead of being highly lucrative, earnings are generally lower than the public perceives. For the occasional dealer, such as a university student, it is a way to make extra income, not unlike waiting tables.[55]

Can Violence Be Rational?

Although there is evidence that **instrumental crimes**, such as drug dealing and burglaries, are rational, is it possible that violent acts through which the offender gains little material benefit are the product of a reasoned decision-making process?

Hollywood likes to portray deranged people killing innocent victims at random, but people who carry guns and are ready to use them typically do so for more rational reasons. They may perceive that they live in a dangerous environment and carry a weapon for self-protection.[56] Some are involved in dangerous illegal activities, such as drug dealing, and carry weapons as part of the job.[57]

Even violent criminals are selective in their choice of suitable targets, picking people who are vulnerable. For example, robbers choose victims who are vulnerable and do not pose any threat.[58] Wright and Rossi found that violent offenders avoid victims who may be armed and dangerous. About three-fifths of all felons surveyed were more afraid of armed victims than of police, about 40 percent had avoided a victim because they believed the victim was armed, and almost one-third reported that they had been scared off, wounded, or captured by armed victims.[59] Even serial murderers, outwardly the most irrational of all offenders, choose victims who are defenceless or cannot count on police protection: prostitutes, gay men, hitchhikers, children, hospital patients, the elderly, the homeless. Rarely do serial killers target weightlifters, martial arts experts, or any other potentially powerful person.[60]

Recent studies have found that even the most violent interactions are motivated by rational thought and not unthinking rage. Decker found that people most often killed acquaintances in disputes involving drug deals gone awry. Even in apparently senseless killings among strangers, the "real" motive was revenge for a prior dispute or disagreement among the parties involved (or their families).[61] Similarly, Felson and Messner found that many homicides were motivated by the offenders' desire to avoid retaliation from a victim they had assaulted or to avoid future prosecutions by getting rid of witnesses.[62] Although some killings are the result of angry aggression, others seem to show signs of rational planning. So, although violent acts appear to be irrational, they do involve calculation of risk and reward.

What Are the Seductions of Crime?

The focus of rational choice theory is on the opportunity to commit crime and on how criminal choices are structured by the social environment. Some people will always be willing and able to bypass the law, given the proper conditions and opportunity. Some irrational people or those with mental disturbances may commit crimes without thought to potential hazard, but situational variables guide most criminal behaviour: People commit crimes when they view the outcome as beneficial.[63] For many, crime is attractive; it brings rewards, excitement, prestige, and other desirable outcomes without lengthy work or effort.

Katz talks about the benefits to criminality, which he labels the **seductions of crime**,[64] that precede the commission of a crime and draw offenders into law violations. Someone challenges the "bad-ass" with a bump or a stare, and the tough person beats up the challenger. Youths want to do something exciting, so they break into and vandalize a school building.[65] Choosing crime can satisfy personal needs; for example, shoplifting and vandalism are attractive because getting away with it is a thrilling demonstration of personal competence. Even murder can have an emotional payoff. Killers have life-or-death control over their victims.

Situational inducements created from emotional upheaval can also structure the decision to commit crime. When an individual is faced with humiliation, righteousness, arrogance, or ridicule, violent reactions seem a natural response. When someone is rebuked at a party because he or she is disturbing people, the person responds, "So, I'm acting like a fool, am I?" and attacks because of the public embarrassment.

People are most likely to be "seduced" if they fear neither the risk of apprehension nor its social consequences. People who fear either losing the respect of their peers or suffering legal punishments are the ones most likely to forgo the seductions of crime.[66]

We have been speaking of crime in its usual sense, as predatory, unwanted behaviour. What do we do about violations that are nonetheless accepted by everyone involved? In 1994, the government of Ontario implemented the *Ontario Tobacco Control Act*. This Act fined merchants who sold tobacco to minors up to $25 000; however, 60 percent of retailers remained willing to sell to minors. This crime would clearly be an instrumental one, where the threat of punishment would hold most weight. One study concluded that four factors influenced the retailer's decision to sell: time of day, his or her gender, his or her age, and his or her compliance with other regulations.

In Alberta, fines have been increased for retailers selling tobacco to minors: $3000 for a first offence, $50 000 for a second. Under the *Prevention of Youth Tobacco Use Act*, those 17 years and under face a $100 fine if caught smoking in public, and their tobacco products can be confiscated.

Such research clearly demonstrates the principles of rational choice theory.[67] However, how can illegal acts be prevented? That is the challenge and the focus of the next section.

Eliminating Crime

If crime is rational, then it can be controlled by convincing potential offenders that the choice of crime is a poor one and that it will not bring rewards but instead pain, hardship, and deprivation.

For example, jurisdictions with low incarceration rates also experience the highest crime rates.[68] Perhaps "street smart" offenders know which areas offer the least threat and plan their crimes accordingly. A number of potential strategies flow from this premise:

1. Situational crime prevention is aimed at convincing would-be criminals to avoid specific targets. When people install security systems in their homes or hire security guards, they are broadcasting the message: Guardianship is great here; stay away—the potential reward is not worth the risk of apprehension.

2. General deterrence strategies are aimed at making potential criminals fear the consequences of crime. The threat of punishment is aimed at convincing rational criminals that crime does not pay.

3. Specific deterrence refers to punishing known criminals severely so that they will never be tempted to repeat their offences.

4. Incapacitation strategies attempt to reduce crime rates by denying motivated offenders the opportunity to commit crime. If, despite the threat of law and punishment, some people still find crime attractive, the only way to control their behaviour is to take them out of society.

In the following sections, each of these crime reduction or control strategies based on the rationality of criminal behaviour is discussed in detail.

Situational Crime Prevention

Because criminal activity is offence-specific, crime prevention and crime reduction should be achieved through policies that convince potential criminals to desist from criminal activities, delay their actions, or avoid a particular target. Table 5.1 presents 16 techniques for preventing crime, from target-hardening to facilitating compliance.

Criminal acts will be avoided if (1) potential targets are carefully guarded, (2) the means to commit crime are controlled, and (3) potential offenders are carefully monitored. Desperate people may contemplate crime, but only the truly irrational will attack a well-defended, inaccessible target and risk strict punishments. Crime prevention can be achieved by reducing the opportunities people have to commit particular crimes, a practice known as **situational crime prevention.**

Situational crime prevention was popularized in the early 1970s by Oscar Newman, who coined the term **defensible space** to signify that crime can be prevented or displaced through the use of residential architectural designs that reduce criminal opportunity, such as well-lit housing projects that maximize surveillance.[69] In 1971 C. Ray Jeffery wrote *Crime Prevention through Environmental Design*, in which he extended Newman's concepts and applied them to nonresidential areas, such as schools and factories.[70] According to this view, such mechanisms as security systems, deadbolt locks, high-intensity street lighting, and Neighbourhood Watch patrols should be able to reduce criminal opportunity.[71] In 1992 Ronald Clarke published *Situational Crime Prevention*, which compiled the best-known strategies and tactics to reduce criminal incidents.[72]

In Canada, Patricia and Paul Brantingham of Simon Fraser University are leaders in research on situational crime prevention. They say that despite the claims of many programs, most crime prevention efforts have mixed success. Generic programs cannot address the diversity of criminal behaviour and need to be targeted toward specific social-order problems. The motive for stealing a car for a joyride is different from that for stealing a car for parts. Therefore, the prevention strategy should also be different. Assuming a rational basis for committing a crime might overestimate the extent to which people consider the legal consequences of their actions and underestimate the demand for such crimes as prostitution. Despite tough new laws making it easier for the police to deal with the buying and selling of sex, the overall volume of prostitution has remained relatively unchanged.

Neighbourhood Watch programs are also very popular, but their main effect is probably to improve people's attitudes about their neighbourhoods. Situational variables, such as traffic flow, pedestrian walkways, and public lighting, become part of an environment that can enable or discourage crime.[73]

Crime Prevention Strategies

A number of situational crime prevention efforts might reduce crime rates. One approach is to create an overall community strategy to reduce crime in general. For example, Felson suggests that such a strategy might include some or all of the following elements:

- Uniform school release schedules so that there is no doubt when kids belong in school and when they are truant; combined with effective truancy control efforts
- After-school and weekend activities to keep kids under adult supervision
- School lunch programs designed to keep kids in school and away from shopping areas
- No-cash policies in schools to reduce kids' opportunity to either be targets or to buy drugs or alcohol
- Shopping areas and schools kept separate
- Construction of housing to maximize guardianship and minimize illegal behaviour
- Encouragement of neighbourhood stability so residents will be acquainted with one another
- Privatization of parks and recreation facilities so people will be responsible for their area's security[74]

Felson's suggestions are designed to reduce crime by limiting the access that members of a highly motivated offender group (high-school kids) have to tempting targets. Crime maps show that robberies and vandalism occur close to urban high schools. Some features of the "total community strategy" are designed to eliminate specific crimes (for example, by youths) but mainly to reduce the overall crime rate.

 InfoTrac®

For an interesting discussion of crime prevention applied to teens, see Jacquelynne S. Eales, Bonnie L. Barber, Margaret Stone, and James Hunt, "Extracurricular Activities and Adolescent Development," *Journal of Social Issues* 59, no. 4 (2003): 965.

TABLE 5.1 Sixteen Techniques of Situational Crime Prevention

Increasing Perceived Effort	Increasing Perceived Risks	Reducing Anticipated Rewards	Inducing Guilt or Shame
1. Target hardening Slug rejector devices Steering locks Bandit screens	5. Entry/exit screening Automatic ticket gates Baggage screening Merchandise tags	9. Target removal Removable car radio Women's refuges Phone card	13. Rule setting Harassment codes Customs declaration Hotel registrations
2. Access control Parking lot barriers Fenced yard Entry phones	6. Formal surveillance Burglar alarms Speed cameras Security guards	10. Identifying property Property marking Vehicle licensing Cattle branding	14. Moral condemnation "Shoplifting is stealing" Roadside speedometers "Bloody idiots drink and thrive"
3. Deflecting offenders Bus stop placement Tavern location Street closures	7. Surveillance by employees Pay phone location Park attendants CCTV [closed-circuit television] systems	11. Reducing temptation Gender-neutral phone lists Off-street parking	15. Controlling disinhibitors Drinking age laws Ignition interlock Server intervention
4. Controlling facilitators Credit card photo Caller ID Gun controls	8. Natural surveillance Defensible space Street lighting Cab driver ID	12. Denying benefits Ink merchandise tags PIN for car radios Graffiti cleaning	16. Facilitating compliance Improved library checkout Public lavatories Trash bins

Source: Ronald Clarke and Ross Homel, "A Revised Classification of Situational Crime Prevention Techniques," in *Crime Prevention at a Crossroads*, ed. Steven Lab, 17–33 (Cincinnati: Anderson Publishing Company, 1997).

Connections

Chapter 12 discusses many types of property crime, the total cost to society, and some tips on how to discourage it. For crimes of opportunity, especially, prevention measures are usually fairly inexpensive and uncomplicated.

Targeting Specific Crimes

Situational crime prevention involves developing tactics to reduce or eliminate a specific crime problem, such as shoplifting in an urban mall or street-level drug dealing. It is useful to target specific subsets of the criminal population. Boston's Operation Ceasefire, for example, is a successful problem-oriented policing intervention aimed at reducing youth homicides.[75] Crime prevention tactics in use today generally fall into one of four categories: (1) increasing the effort needed to commit the crime, (2) increasing the risks of committing the crime, (3) reducing the rewards for committing the crime, and (4) inducing guilt or shame for committing the crime.

Some basic techniques and some specific methods that can be used to prevent auto crime are listed in Exhibit 5.2.

Some tactics designed to increase the offender's effort include target-hardening techniques, such as putting unbreakable glass on storefronts, locking gates, and

Exhibit 5.2	Neighbourhood Watch Tips on Vehicle Security

In Canada, vehicle thefts occur every eight minutes.

- Always lock the doors and roll up the windows tightly
- Leave your valuables out of view and securely locked away
- Park in well lit areas with pedestrian traffic
- Do not leave personal identification such as ownership, credit card slips in your vehicle
- Do not hide spare keys—they can be found
- Never put your name/address on your house or car keys; keep vehicle and house keys on a separate key ring
- If you have a garage use it. Lock both the vehicle and garage doors
- Consider installing anti-theft devices

Source: Kanata Neighbourhood Watch Security Tips, "Safety and Security Tips," http://www.atkanata.com/KNW/tips.htm (accessed May 10, 2005).

fencing yards. Technological advances can be used to make it more difficult to commit crimes, such as having an owner's photo on credit cards to reduce the use of stolen cards. The development of new products also makes it more difficult to commit crimes. For example, the use of steering locks has helped reduce car theft in the United States, Britain, and Germany.[76] Installing a locking device on cars that prevents inebriated drivers from starting the vehicle significantly reduces drunk-driving rates.[77]

An excellent example of comprehensive crime prevention is one developed at a Canadian bank. The bank has more than 400 branches, and one in four had been robbed the previous year, some more than once. Fourteen percent of the branches were considered at high risk. Based on interviews with convicted bank robbers, a robbery prevention program was instituted that centred on a target-hardening floor plan, robbery prevention procedures, and enhanced training for personnel. Robberies of the branches decreased 65 percent over a two-year period.[78]

It is also important to increase the chances of apprehension. Improving surveillance lighting, creating Neighbourhood Watch programs, controlling building entrances and exits, installing burglar alarms and security systems, increasing the number of private security officers, and modifying police patrols all help reduce crime rates.[79] Research on gasoline "drive-offs" from convenience stores found that removing signs from store windows, installing brighter lights, and instituting a pay-first policy reduces the number of incidents of people driving off without paying.[80]

Target reduction strategies include such simple steps as making car radios removable, marking property so that it is more difficult to sell when stolen, and having gender-neutral phone listings. Caller ID has resulted in significant reductions in the number of obscene phone calls with the consequent threat of exposure.[81] Tracking systems similar to global positioning systems help police locate and return stolen vehicles.

Inducing guilt or shame might include such techniques as setting strict rules that embarrass offenders, such as publishing "john lists" in the newspaper to shame those arrested for soliciting prostitutes. In 2000, a Canadian police officer recommended that drunk drivers be forced to have a large sign with the letter "D" placed on their car. This penalty for drunkenness hearkens back to the seventeenth century, when in Boston, for example, Robert Coles was "fyned ten shillings and enjoyned to stand with a white sheet of paper on his back whereon Drunkard shalbe written in great lres & to stand therewith soe longe as the Courte finde meete, fo abuseing himself shamefully with drinke."[82]

Research on the use of shaming against financial criminals is less encouraging. It suggests that potential damage to business prospects is more effective than shame. Eighty-eight percent of British executives in the *Times* 1000 largest companies survey said they would refuse to do business with people convicted of fraud. Thus, the inducement for corporate misbehaviour is not as easily corrected by shaming individuals.[83]

Crime Discouragers

The success of situational crime prevention may also rest on the behaviour of people whose actions directly influence the prevention of crime. Crime discouragers can be grouped into three categories: guardians, who monitor targets (such as store security guards); handlers, who monitor potential offenders (such as parole officers and parents); and managers, who monitor places (such as homeowners and doorkeepers). Crime discouragers have different levels of responsibility, ranging from highly personal involvement, such as homeowners protecting their house and parents controlling their children, to the most impersonal involvement, such as a stranger who stops someone from shoplifting in the mall (see Table 5.2).[84]

The concept of crime discouragement can be useful to plan situational crime prevention tactics. More effective crime reduction may occur if (1) managers are given tools to better monitor places, (2) guardians are better equipped to protect targets, and (3) handlers are allowed to exert greater control over offenders. For example, store clerks can enhance their discouragement role with a mirror to watch merchandise and a button to summon supervisory

help. A handler will become more effective if supplied with hidden cameras and eavesdropping devices. Managers given greater supervisory powers will help reduce crime by exerting better control over their charges.

Ramifications of Situational Prevention

Situational crime prevention can also produce unforeseen and unwanted consequences. Preventing crime from occurring in one locale might do little to deter criminal motivation, so crime is not prevented but displaced to alternative targets.[85] For example, a 2003 drug crackdown by Vancouver police spread drug activity from a concentrated area to a much wider area through the downtown eastside. Because enforcement does not address deeper issues, like health, unemployment, and harm reduction, it cannot reduce crime overall.[86]

There are six kinds of crime displacement:

1. *Temporal.* Offenders perpetrate crimes at times seen as less risky.
2. *Target.* Difficult targets are given up in favour of those easier to hit.
3. *Spatial.* Offenders move from high-target areas to less-protected areas.
4. *Tactical.* Tactics are changed to get around security measures.
5. *Perpetrator.* New offenders take the place of those who are apprehended.
6. *Type of crime.* Offenders take up another type of crime if one type is too difficult.[87]

TABLE 5.2 Crime Discouragers

TYPES OF SUPERVISORS AND OBJECTS OF SUPERVISION

Level of Responsibility	A. Guardians (monitoring suitable targets)	B. Handlers (monitoring likely offenders)	C. Managers (monitoring amenable places)
1. Personal (owners, family, friends)	Student keeps eye on own bookbag	Parent makes sure child gets home	Homeowner monitors area near home
2. Assigned (employees with general assignment)	Store clerk monitors jewellery	Principal sends kids back to school	Doorman protects building
3. Diffuse (employees with general assignment)	Accountant notes shoplifting	School clerk discourages truancy	Hotel maid impairs trespasser
4. General (strangers, other citizens)	Bystander inhibits shoplifting	Stranger questions boys at mall	Customer observes parking structure

Source: Marcus Felson, "Those Who Discourage Crime," in *Crime and Place*, eds. John Eck and David Weisburd, 59 (Monsey, N.Y.: Criminal Justice Press, 1995). Reprinted by permission.

Displacement assumes an equilibrium that crime might "spill over" from one area to the next. However, this might not be the result of displacement but the result of offenders casually drifting in and out of crime. The offender's willingness to commit crime has to be accompanied by an opportunity. Therefore, there might be a net preventive effect.[88]

There is also the problem of **extinction**: Crime reduction programs may produce a short-term positive effect but dissipate as criminals adjust to new conditions. Criminals learn to dismantle alarms or avoid patrols, or become motivated to try new offences they had previously avoided. For example, if every residence is provided with a burglar alarm system, motivated offenders might then turn to armed robbery, a riskier and more violent crime. However, some offenders are unlikely to turn to crimes they find morally repugnant, for example, from shoplifting to armed robbery.

Although displacement and extinction may be a problem, a hidden benefit of situational crime prevention has been noted: **diffusion of benefits**.[89] Diffusion occurs when (1) efforts to prevent one crime cause the unintended prevention of another and (2) crime control efforts in one locale reduce crime in other, nontarget areas.

Crime control may deter criminals by causing them to fear apprehension. For example, video cameras set up in a mall to reduce shoplifting can also reduce property damage, because would-be vandals or prostitutes fear being caught on camera.[90]

Another type of diffusion effect is called **discouragement**. By limiting one type of target, would-be lawbreakers may forgo other criminal activity because crime no longer pays. Drug enforcement programs that use municipal codes and nuisance abatement laws not only decrease drug dealing in targeted areas but also reduce it in surrounding areas as well.[91]

General Deterrence

According to the rational choice view, motivated people will violate the law if left free and unrestricted. Rational offenders want the goods and services crime provides without having to work for them, committing crime if there is no fear of apprehension or punishment. The concept of **general deterrence** holds that crime rates are influenced and controlled by the threat of criminal punishment. If people fear apprehension and punishment, they will not risk breaking the law. An inverse relationship should thus exist between crime rates and the certainty, severity, and celerity (speed) of legal sanctions. If, for example, the punishment for a crime is increased and if the effectiveness and efficiency of the criminal justice system in enforcing the law prohibiting

that act are improved, then the number of people engaging in that act should decline.

The factors of certainty, severity, and celerity also influence one another. For example, if a crime, such as robbery, is punished severely but few robbers are ever caught or punished, it is likely that the severity of punishment for robbery will not deter people from robbing. However, if the certainty of apprehension is increased by modern technology, or more efficient police work, even minor punishments might deter the potential robber.

In Western society, support has increased in favour of more punitive measures. This change reflects the fact that the middle class no longer sees crime as just affecting the poor but as a problem affecting society as a whole. Harsher punishments, three-strikes-and-you're-out legislation, and mandatory minimum sentences are still, and increasingly, in favour.[92]

Certainty of Punishment

According to deterrence theory, if the probability of arrest, conviction, and sanctioning increases, crime rates should decline. Rational offenders will realize that the increased likelihood of being punished outweighs any benefit they perceive from committing crimes.

Research does show an inverse relationship between crime rates and the certainty of punishment.[93] Evidence shows that people who believe that they will be punished for future crimes also say that they will not commit those crimes.[94] In a study of arrest probability, Tittle and Rowe concluded that if police could make an arrest in at least 30 percent of all reported crimes, the crime rate would significantly decline.[95] However, other research has found little relationship between the likelihood of being arrested or imprisoned and corresponding crime rates.[96]

One reason for this ambivalent finding is that the punishment–crime association may be both crime- and group-specific. For example, the arrest probability for Black people influences Black offence rates alone, while the arrest probabilities for White people affect White offending patterns. In large cities, the threat of arrest is communicated within neighbourhoods and has an independent effect on residents of each racial grouping.[97]

Some research shows a crime-specific deterrent effect. For example, the increased certainty of arrest helps lower the burglary rate, while theft rates remain unaffected by law enforcement efforts.[98] In Varma and Doob's analysis of the deterrence of tax evasion, they found that the certainty of being caught was a stronger deterrent than was the size of the penalty. This lends more weight to the certainty of than to the severity of the punishment.[99]

In corporate crime, punishment is far from certain. In July 1998, the Toronto Stock Exchange assessed a $4-million penalty against the brokerage firm First Marathon Securities Ltd. for failing to supervise its business operations and employees. Some of those employees were involved in a conflict of interest in the promotion of Cartaway Resources, one of the most spectacular stock flops in Canadian mining history. Because the employees were not properly supervised, they were able to act as promoters, underwriters, and investors in the stock. The fine, while embarrassing to the company, did not have a big impact on its estimated profit of $50 million per year. The Ontario Securities Commission, which oversees the 80 percent of the country's capital market located in Ontario, had a budget of $20 million in 1997, and the "compliance" department had a staff of only six to oversee hundreds of companies.[100]

Connections

In cases we will look at in Chapter 13, the rewards for engaging in corporate criminality are too great, and the oversight too minimal, for crimes not to occur.

General deterrence is difficult in cases of corporate crime because quite often the penalties are administrative, not criminal. The Ontario Securities Commission is not a department of the criminal justice system, and it does not have the authority to lay criminal charges. However, that may be about to change. Australia, the United States, Britain, and now Canada have adopted changes to their *Criminal Codes* to make corporations more accountable for their actions. In the 1997 report into the Westray mine disaster, Mr. Justice Peter Richard said:

> The Government of Canada . . . should introduce in the Parliament of Canada such amendments to legislation as are necessary to ensure that corporate executives and directors are held properly accountable for workplace safety.[101]

A bill named after Westray, which criminalizes corporate inaction in cases of homicide, was passed in 2003.

The Effect of Police Actions. If the increased certainty of apprehension and punishment deters criminal behaviour, increasing the number of police officers should be able to bring the crime rate down. Moreover, if these police officers are active and aggressive crime fighters, would-be criminals should be convinced that the risk of apprehension outweighs the benefits they can gain from crime. However, research does not show a simple increase in police presence to be a crime deterrent.[102]

Although this result is discouraging, it might simply be difficult to measure the association between police presence and crime rates. When crime rates increase, communities add police officers. More officers will process more crime, making it appear that adding police actually increases community crime rates! However, recent research using sophisticated methodological tools has found evidence that increasing levels of crime only cause small increases in the number of police officers, whereas increased police levels cause substantial reductions in crime over time.[103] When crime rates go down, it may be due to other factors, such as a decrease in the number of young males in the population.

Conversely, another study estimated that for every officer added, there would be 24 fewer crimes per year.[104] This result indicates that adding police officers may, in the long run, provide a general deterrent effect.

Police Experiments. Some police departments have conducted experiments to determine whether increasing police activities or allocation of services can influence crime rates. In 1988, for example, Edmonton implemented a Neighbourhood Foot Patrol, with constables assigned to 21 neighbourhoods. This initiative in "community policing" identified city areas by repeat calls for service and occurrence data. The result was that community and police satisfaction increased, and calls for service went down.[105] Similar studies have found bike patrols to be effective, as police are more in contact with their surroundings and better able to patrol ball fields and parks to crack down on public drinking and vandalism.

In such initiatives, police and crime prevention organizations need evaluation to be implemented from the very beginning alongside the initiative.[106]

In another well-known experiment to evaluate the effectiveness of police patrols and the general deterrent effect of police activity, the Kansas City police department's 15 independent police beats or districts were divided into three groups.[107] The first retained a normal police patrol; the second (proactive) was supplied with two to three times the normal number of patrol forces; and the third (reactive) eliminated its preventive patrol entirely, and police officers responded only when summoned by citizens to a crime. Surprisingly, data indicated that variations in patrol techniques had little effect on the crime patterns. The presence or absence of patrol forces did not seem to affect residential or business burglaries, auto thefts, larcenies involving auto accessories, robberies, vandalism, or other criminal behaviour.

Other police departments have instituted **crackdowns**, sudden changes in police activity designed to increase the communicated threat or actual certainty of punishment, to lower crime rates. Crackdowns can target specific neighbourhoods or specific offences and even efforts to decrease the signs of public disorder that create fear. Initial and residual deterrent effects vary, sometimes based on factors outside the scope of the crackdowns themselves. For example, a police task force that targets street-level narcotics dealers by using undercover agents and surveillance cameras in known drug-dealing locales may have an initial deterrent effect on controlling crime but suffer diffusion over time. However, a recent analysis of a crackdown and clean-up initiative in seven city neighbourhoods in Richmond, Virginia, found that crime rates declined by 92 percent during the month-long crackdown period, the effects persisted up to six months after the crackdown ended, and no displacement was observed. Clearly more research is needed in this important area of deterrence.[108]

These crackdowns illustrate what has become known as the "broken-windows approach," first developed by George Kelling, in which the police deal with what the public sees as symptoms of crime, such as people urinating and sleeping in public, littering and loitering, creating graffiti, and being drunk in public.[109] Efforts to crack down on crime can target specific neighbourhoods or specific offences. In an example from Toronto, police took a zero-tolerance approach to crime, targeting such minor offences as panhandling and urinating in public. This is similar to a crackdown on illegal parking and disorder in Washington, D.C., and a similarly huge effort to reduce crime in New York City's subways.[110]

Severity of Punishment

The threat of severe punishments should also bring the crime rate down. Some studies have found that increasing sanction levels can, in fact, control common criminal behaviours, for example, using an illegal, unauthorized descrambler to obtain pay cable television programs.[111] In one study, threatening letters were sent to violators who were using a descrambler and avoiding payments to the local cable company, which conveyed the general message that illegal theft of cable signals would be criminally prosecuted. The letter did not indicate that the subject's personal violation had been discovered, but it was found that about two-thirds of the violators reacted to the threat by desisting and trying to hide their crime by removing the illegal device; a six-month follow-up showed that the intervention had a long-lasting effect.

Although research shows that the threat of strict punishment can sometimes deter crime, it is not clear that severe sanctions alone can reduce criminal activities. The analysis of the deterrent effects of anti-drunk-driving laws on motor vehicular violations is an example of the limited utility of sanctioning severity. Research found that when laws are toughened, a short-term deterrent effect is produced; however, because the likelihood of getting caught is low, the deterrent effect is small over the long term.[112] In a later study that evaluated the effect of a new law in mandating jail sentences for drunk-driving convictions, time series analysis indicated little deterrent effect.[113]

Research has also looked at what effect firearm sentencing laws have on violent crime rates. Some research efforts claim that these laws can lower crime rates, while others question their deterrent effect;[114] there is little evidence that they can reduce crime in general.[115]

In sum, despite the hope of those espousing a law and order agenda, little evidence exists that increasing the punishments for specific crimes can alone deter their occurrence.

Connections

The last execution in Canada happened in 1962. Read about this famous Canadian case of Arthur Lucas and Ronald Turpin, in Chapter 11.

The Special Case of Capital Punishment

If punishment severity can have a deterrent effect on crime, fear of the death penalty, the ultimate legal deterrent, should significantly reduce murder rates. Because no one denies its emotional impact, failure of the death penalty to deter violent crime jeopardizes the validity of the entire deterrence concept. Various studies have tested the assumption that capital punishment deters violent crime. The research can be divided into three types: immediate impact studies, comparative research, and time series analysis.

Capital punishment was abolished in Canada in 1976, and the last executions took place in 1962. However, half of Canadians would like to see capital punishment reinstated. Because there is a perception that perpetrators of heinous crimes should face the death penalty, we will briefly look at the research to evaluate its effectiveness.

Immediate Impact Studies. If capital punishment is a deterrent, it should have the greatest impact after a well-publicized execution has taken place. Dann began testing this assumption in 1935, when he chose five highly publicized executions of convicted murderers in different years and determined the number of homicides in the 60 days before and after each execution.[116] The research showed that an average of 4.4 more homicides occurred during the 60 days following an execution than during those preceding it, suggesting that the overall impact of executions might actually increase the incidence of homicide. That executions may increase the likelihood of murder has been labelled the **brutalization effect.**[117]

Some research indicates that in the short run, executing criminals can bring the murder rate down.

Phillips studied the immediate effect of executions in Britain from 1858 to 1914 and found a temporary deterrent effect based on the publicity following the execution.[118] A more contemporary (1950 to 1980) evaluation of executions by Stack concluded that capital punishment does indeed have an immediate impact and that 16 well-publicized executions may have saved 480 lives.[119] However, this finding is controversial and not well-accepted in the field.

Comparative Research. Another type of research compares the murder rates in jurisdictions that have abolished the death penalty with the rates of those that have the death penalty. Using this approach, research shows that homicide rates and execution risks move independently of each other and that the death penalty has no deterrent effect on violent crime rates.[120] However, criminologist James Yunker, using an American national data set, has found evidence that a deterrent effect of capital punishment exists but that it may be hidden when state-by-state comparisons are made.[121] The most significant effect has been achieved in recent years when the pace of executions has accelerated.

The failure to show a deterrent effect of the death penalty is not limited to cross-state comparisons. Research on 14 nations around the world found little evidence that countries with a death penalty have lower violence rates, but research has found evidence that homicide rates decline after capital punishment is abolished.[122] These findings help explain the contradictory findings of immediate impact studies.

Time Series Analysis. The development of statistical analysis helps in gauging whether the murder rate changes when death penalty statutes are created or eliminated. Based on the idea that the perception of execution is a determinant of whether one individual will murder another,[123] it has been suggested that each execution could save seven or eight people from being victims of murder. This research is widely cited by advocates of the death penalty as empirical proof of the deterrent effect of capital punishment. However, other research shows that punishment doesn't need to be that extreme, as life imprisonment is just as effective.[124]

A recent amendment to the law in Louisiana that now allows juries to consider imposing the death penalty found that there seemed to be no deterrent effect. The only significant change was the reduction of trials, with defendants more willing to pursue plea bargains.[125]

In sum, studies trying to show the deterrent effect of capital punishment on the murder rate indicate that execution has relatively little influence on behaviour.[126] Although it is still uncertain why the threat of capital punishment has failed as a deterrent, the cause may lie in the nature of homicide itself: Murder is often an expressive "crime of passion" involving people who know each other and who may be under the influence of drugs or suffering from the burdens of poverty.[127] These factors may either prevent or inhibit rational evaluation of the long-term consequences of an immediate violent act. Overall, it is probably safe to say that much murder is a **conflict-linked crime** not committed during the course of another crime.

Perception and Deterrence

A core element of general deterrence theory is that people who believe that they are likely to be caught and severely punished will abstain from crime; thus, deterrence theory would be discredited if perceptions of future punishment have little or no effect on behaviour.[128]

Some research has found that the greater the perceived risk of apprehension, the less likely criminals will be to risk committing a crime.[129] However, others have found little association between fear of future punishments and criminal activity.[130] This would be especially true for "conflict-linked" crime, as mentioned above.

Where deterrence has been found, it is the certainty and not the severity of punishment that seems to influence people.[131] A cross-sectional survey found that people who believe they will be caught and subjected to criminal prosecution are less likely to engage in tax evasion.[132] Other research found that the perceived risk of getting caught influenced active burglars, while the threat of severe punishments had relatively little effect.[133] This suggests that perceived risk of apprehension rather than punishment severity can deter active criminal offenders.

One criticism of this **perceptual deterrence** research is that it usually involves samples of noncriminals, such as college students, and crimes of minor seriousness, such as smoking marijuana. Experienced offenders, who are more criminally motivated and less committed to moral values, are less likely to be deterred by the perception that they will be punished in the future[134] and are the ones least threatened by the idea of future punishment.[135] Other research has found that prior sanctions actually lower the perception that crime is a risky undertaking; criminals with the greatest number of prior convictions have the lowest fear of legal sanctions. Perhaps punishments were less fearsome than they had anticipated; only the most severe punishments seem to have any influence on experienced criminals.[136]

A recent study conducted as part of the Dunedin (New Zealand) Study, a longitudinal study of individuals from birth to age 26, found that deterrence had its greatest effect in criminally prone study members. This result shows the difficulty in extrapolating from studies of the general population.[137]

In sum, research measuring the perceptions of punishment shows that the certainty of punishment has a greater influence on the choice of crime than does the severity of punishment, and people who believe they are certain to be arrested and punished for a crime are less likely to break the law regardless of the severity of the punishment.[138]

Informal Sanctions

The fear of **informal sanctions** may have a greater crime-reducing impact does than the fear of formal legal punishments. Informal sanctions occur when significant others, such as parents, peers, neighbours, and teachers, direct their disapproval, anger, and indignation toward an offender. If this happens, law violators run the risk of feeling shame, being embarrassed, and suffering a loss of respect.[139] Can the fear of public humiliation deter crime?

Research efforts have in fact established the influence of informal sanctions. In a national survey of almost two thousand subjects, Tittle found that perception of informal sanctions was a more effective determinant of deterrence than was perception of formal sanctions.[140] Social control is rooted in how people perceive negative reactions from interpersonal acquaintances (family, friends). Legal sanctions supplement informal control processes by influencing a small segment of "criminally inclined" persons.[141] If this conclusion is accurate, it also means that family and friends who don't react negatively to crime are facilitating it.

Other studies have also found that people who are committed to conventional moral values and believe crime to be sinful are unlikely to violate the law. Evidence from Britain shows that efforts to control drunk driving by shaming offenders produced a moral climate that helped reduce the incidence.[142] Perhaps the same moral effect can help reduce drug use in Canada.

Those fearful of being rejected by family and peers are also reluctant to engage in deviant behaviour.[143] Two factors seem to stand out: personal shame over violating the law and the fear of public humiliation if the deviant behaviour becomes public knowledge. A series of studies found that people who say that involvement in crime will cause them to feel ashamed are less likely to commit theft, fraud, and motor vehicular offences than are those who report not feeling ashamed about crime.[144] People have been found to be more likely to respond to anti-littering drives and anti-drunk-driving campaigns if the thought of being accused of littering or driving drunk makes them feel ashamed or embarrassed.[145] Women are much more likely to fear shame and embarrassment than are men, a finding that may help explain gender differences in the crime rate.[146]

Fear of shame and embarrassment can be a powerful deterrent to crime.[147] One study found that spouse abusers were more afraid of social costs (for example, loss of friends and family disapproval) than they were of legal punishments (such as going to jail). The researchers found that in cases of wife assault, the potential for self-stigma and personal humiliation was the greatest deterrent to crime.[148]

The effect of informal sanctions may vary according to the cohesiveness of community structure and type of crime. Informal sanctions may be most effective in highly unified areas where everyone knows one another and the crime cannot be hidden from public view. The threat of informal sanctions may also have the greatest influence on instrumental crimes, which involve planning, and not on impulsive or expressive criminal behaviours or those associated with substance abuse.[149]

This research seems to indicate that public education on the social cost of crime that stresses the risk of shame and humiliation may be a more effective crime-prevention tool than are the creation and distribution of legal punishments; potential offenders may be deterred if they can be convinced that crime is sinful or immoral.[150]

Closed-Circuit Television and Public Surveillance

Debate exists over whether to mount closed-circuit television (CCTV) cameras in public places to deter crime. CCTV has been around for quite some time and can be actively monitored (by a person watching in real time) or passively monitored (recorded). The Scottish government's Central Research Unit analyzed CCTV surveillance in two cities, Ardrie and Glasgow. It concluded that 21 percent fewer offences took place in the two years after introduction of the cameras. Housebreaking, shoplifting, and theft from vehicles fell by 48 percent. Significantly, the unit concluded that no displacement effect to nonmonitored areas occurred.[151]

England's use of video surveillance goes back to 1986. However, Canada, France, Italy, Monaco, Russia, Spain, Ireland, and others are all increasing their use of CCTV. In the United States, about 75 percent of businesses use some form of CCTV to protect their premises.[152] The International Center for the Prevention of Crime estimates that delinquency in public areas can be reduced by up to 68 percent with the use of CCTV, but it has to be used in conjunction with a quick response by the police and video hard-copies have to be stored for future prosecution.[153] The type of surveillance (active or passive) also makes an important difference. Several Canadian studies show that unmonitored cameras are one of the least effective deterrents to robberies in banks and convenience stores. For example, the Peel Regional Police have concluded that closed-circuit television is expensive to implement and is not a major deterrence.

Some legal and social issues surround the use of CCTV surveillance techniques. First, is the notion that such techniques will damage the image of the police by creating a "big brother" mentality. Second, there is fear that the recordings will be sold for their commercial value, violating the rights of those recorded on these tapes. In the United States, legal challenges have dealt with issues of privacy and the distinction between public and private places. The trend has been to allow surveillance so long as it does not occur in truly private areas and as long as its use has helped save money or lives.[154]

Video surveillance has been in use in Canada since 1992 by law enforcement agencies, banks, libraries, restaurants, and convenience stores, and at industrial sites, offices, apartment buildings, and public transit stations. In 1995, 70 percent of all bank robberies in Canada were videorecorded, and CCTV surveillance tapes captured 75 percent of all crimes investigated by law enforcement or private security. CCTV video cameras in commercial areas have also been instrumental in helping to find missing persons.[155]

In British Columbia, the use of CCTV systems is controlled by the *Freedom of Information and Protection of Privacy Act, 1996*. Some fear that acceptance of video surveillance may be the first step in a series of more intrusive surveillance techniques. In 2001, the RCMP violated privacy laws when they set up a surveillance camera on a Kelowna, B.C., street. The federal privacy commissioner said the $22 000 crime camera in downtown Kelowna contravened federal law. Vancouver police have proposed setting up 23 cameras in the city's crime-ridden downtown eastside. London, Toronto, and Winnipeg are also considering them.

There is a concern that once installed, CCTV systems will be used to serve a wide range of social-control functions. Another concern is inadvertent "function creep" whereby a camera system installed to watch for criminal behaviour may end up being used as a tool to monitor performance.[156] Another criticism is that since the state is indirectly behind most public-space CCTV systems, the systems permit the state to maintain a high degree of control over its population.[157]

In conclusion, there is a difference of opinion as to the effectiveness of CCTV surveillance. Such systems reinforce the traditional view that violence takes place in the public sphere. However, CCTV can be used as a tool to ensure the success of local economies by providing a safe place for businesses to set up and for consumers to gather.

New Developments in Surveillance. The average person is caught on videotape up to a dozen times a day. However, many other forms of surveillance are being developed that are potentially more invasive.

The average person is caught on videotape up to a dozen times a day.

A growing number of police departments use handheld wireless devices that contain records culled from motor vehicle registries, credit bureaus, and telephone directories. One private sector company in particular can provide information on 98 percent of the American population. Broad searching through records and commercial files, called data mining, is very poorly regulated. However, although there is a push to acquire more information about people who might not even be suspected of committing crime, the public is becomingly less compliant. In 2004, Canadian police chiefs proposed a surcharge on phone bills to pay for police wiretaps, but 88 percent of those replying to a poll by *The Globe and Mail* said no.

The 2004 Olympics saw a significant increase in the use of surveillance, all in the effort to detect and deter crime. Street-level cameras and speech recognition software, combined with helicopters, patrol boats, and mobile command centres, all created an extensive network of surveillance. Another development is radio frequency identification (RFID) chips implanted in commercial products, which can track their purchase and customer preferences. RFIDs can also be embedded subcutaneously for tracking purposes, for example, in the case of offenders under house arrest or pedophiles ordered to stay away from areas with children.

The future can only be imagined.

General Deterrence in Review

Some experts believe that the purpose of the law and the justice system is to create a "threat system,"[158] that the threat of legal punishment should deter lawbreakers through fear. Who among us can claim that they never had an urge to commit crime but were deterred by fear of discovery and its consequences? Nonetheless, the relationship between crime rates and deterrent measures is far less than choice theorists might expect. Despite

Crime in the News

Curfews Are for Adults

Opinion. Some people think that keeping kids in at night would take care of most crime. Youths hang out at night with nothing to do, committing acts of vandalism and property damage.

Fact. Contrary to what people might think, the peak time for the commission of crimes by young people is not at night, but between 2 and 6 in the afternoon. This is borne out by research from the US Department of Justice, and it makes sense. Youths get out of school, they're waiting for their parents to get home, and many places have no community programs or places for kids to hang out. So what do you do if the problem is kids with nothing to do?

Opinion. Kids are responsible for most crime in our society. Despite the decrease in crime in the 1990s, it is juveniles that keep the crime rate up.

Fact. Youths between the ages of 12 and 17 committed twenty-nine percent of property crime, and seventeen percent of violent crime in 2002. This means that adults over the age of eighteen are responsible for eighty-two percent of violent crimes and sixty-nine percent of property crimes. In total adults commit seventy-seven percent of all Criminal Code offences. So what do you do if the problem is adults?

Opinion. Kids are more likely to commit crime than other age groups.

Well, that might be true, although it depends on how you interpret the numbers. The Canadian Centre for Justice Statistics says that in 2003 persons aged 15 to 24 had higher rates of offending and victimization than other age groups. This age group represents fourteen percent of the total population while accounting for forty-five percent of those accused of property crimes and thirty-two percent of persons accused of violent offences. This age group is at a higher risk of offending. But what crimes are they committing?

In the majority of youth court cases heard in Canada in 1998–99, fifteen percent of cases were for shoplifting, and 5 percent for stolen property, 5 percent for mischief, eleven percent for break and enter, and 10 percent for minor assault. It is unlikely that much of this will be corrected by a curfew, since it occurs after school. It is also unlikely that a curfew will even withstand a constitutional challenge. But we're exasperated, isn't there anything we can do?

Well, let's start with the premise that curfews are a good idea. They have become very popular, adopted as a panacea, a cure-all, in many US municipalities where it is feared that parents do not know where their children are. Many towns and cities in Canada also have bylaws, but they are enforced with discretion, used to deal with minor incidents.

Huntingdon, Quebec, has been in the news recently for imposing a curfew between 10:30 p.m. and 6 a.m. for those under sixteen. The mayor says he just wants parents to supervise their children at night and that citizens are fed up with vandalism and loitering. Well, is this a crime issue or a parenting issue? You can't force parents to be more responsible by imposing a $100 fine. Why not solve such crimes as vandalism with the existing criminal law? Well, the municipality says it can't afford the extra policing costs. But if that's the case, why create a bylaw, which itself has to be enforced, to solve a problem the criminal law hasn't been able to solve?

What does the experience with curfews in other jurisdictions show? The Justice Policy Institute compared curfew-arrest rates and youth-crime rates from 1978 to 1996. The results were clear: curfews don't reduce youth crime. Furthermore, they have been challenged as unconstitutional, too vague, and denying parents' discretion in raising their children.

The JPI says that in one jurisdiction youth crime rates actually increased during the school year when the curfew was in force and fell in the summer when it was suspended. Rates go up as enforcement goes up, that's easy, but the reason for the decrease? It's simple. There were free youth recreation programs, what I would call positive intervention.

A curfew law with clearly defined exceptions, combined with anti-loitering provisions in the daytime, might decrease crime if it's enforced. But it's yet another layer of law to deal with issues that are already illegal. If there is a problem with such crimes as vandalism and break and enter, then deal with it that way. If there is a lack of recreational programs, then provide them. Harden the targets, turn the outside lights on at night, get involved in Neighbourhood Watch, and volunteer to spend time with kids. But don't think that a curfew will solve the problem. That's an anodyne to sooth disturbed feelings, to make us think that something is

being done. However, it's a political solution to a social problem.

Huntingdon's mayor says that leaders shouldn't be wimps. Well,

I think that a soft touch is exactly what we need.

Source: © Chris McCormick, *Daily Gleaner,* August 11, 2004.

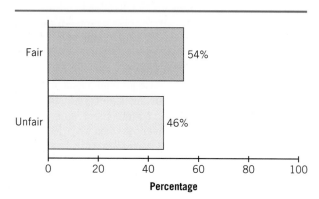

In a recent poll, 54 percent of Canadians said that it was fair to impose curfews on teenagers.

Source: Poll conducted by *The Globe and Mail,* July 27, 2004.

efforts to punish criminals and make them fear crime, there is little evidence that the fear of apprehension and punishment can reduce crime rates. How can this discrepancy be explained?

First, deterrence theory assumes an offender is rational and weighs the costs and benefits of a criminal act before deciding on a course of action. However, some criminals are desperate people acting under the influence of drugs and alcohol or suffering from personality disorders. Surveys show that a significant portion of all offenders, perhaps up to 80 percent, are substance abusers.[159] Chronic offender research indicates that a relatively small group of offenders commit a significant percentage of all serious crimes. Some psychologists believe that members of this select group suffer from an innate or inherited emotional state that renders them both (1) incapable of fearing punishment and (2) less likely to appreciate the consequences of crime.[160] It is likely that the threat of future punishment has little deterrent effect on these people.

Second, many offenders are members of what is referred to as the underclass—people cut off from society, lacking the education and skills they need to be in demand in the modern economy.[161] It may be unlikely that such desperate people will be deterred from crime by fear of punishment because, in reality, they perceive few other options for success.

Third, as Beccaria's famous equation tells us, the threat of punishment involves not only its severity but also its certainty and speed. Our legal system is not very effective. Only 10 percent of all serious offences result in apprehension (since half go unreported and police make arrests in about 20 percent of reported crimes). Police routinely do not arrest suspects in personal disputes, even when they lead to violence, as in the case of wife assault.[162] As apprehended offenders are processed through all the stages of the criminal justice system, the odds of their receiving serious punishment diminish. Thus, some offenders may believe that they will not be severely punished for their acts and consequently have little regard for the law's deterrent power.

Only offenders who suffer the most severe sanctions are likely to fear future legal punishments. Adolescents as a group are responsible for a disproportionate amount of crime, but may be well aware that the juvenile court "is generally lenient in the imposition of meaningful sanctions on even the most serious offenders."[163] Research shows that even those accused of murder, the most serious of crimes, are often convicted of lesser offences and spend relatively short amounts of time behind bars.[164] In 1995 the maximum penalty for murder for juveniles was extended to 10 years, far below that for adults. In making their "rational choice," offenders may be aware that the deterrent effect of the law is minimal.

Fourth, in such cases as white-collar crime, it would seem that the rational deterrence of sanctions would be most likely to have an effect, since the crime is rationally calculated and planned; however, it is also likely that offenders perceive their actions as "normatively" acceptable within their subculture. In such an environment, it is the sanctions that would seem unfair and deviant to the offender, not the criminal actions.

Specific Deterrence

The general deterrence model focuses on future or potential criminals. In contrast, the theory of **specific deterrence** (also called special or particular deterrence) holds that criminal sanctions should be so powerful that known criminals will never repeat their criminal acts. For example, we hope the drunk driver whose sentence is a large fine and a week in the county jail will be convinced that the price to be paid for drinking and driving is too great to consider future violations; burglars who spend five years in a tough, maximum-security prison should find their enthusiasm for theft dampened.[165] In principle, punishment works to prevent or reduce crime if a connection can be established between the planned action and its consequence.[166]

Does Specific Deterrence Deter Crime?

At first glance, specific deterrence does not seem to work, as a majority of known criminals are not deterred by their punishment. However, these are people who are already in a criminal career pattern. Chronic offender research indicates that a stay in a juvenile justice facility has little deterrent effect on whether a persistent delinquent will become an adult criminal.[167] It is no surprise, then, that most prison inmates have prior records of arrest and conviction before their current offence. In 1997, Correctional Services Canada reported that 46 percent of incarcerated male offenders (6510), and 25 percent of female offenders (90), had served a previous term of federal incarceration.[168] Research in the United States shows that two-thirds of all convicted felons are rearrested within three years of their release from prison, and those who have been punished in the past are the most likely to recidivate.[169]

A pilot analysis of recidivism among convicted youth in Canada showed that 60 percent of the 57 000 convicted offenders between the ages of 18 and 25 had at least one previous conviction. Among recidivists, 72 percent had multiple prior convictions. The earlier the offender was convicted, the more likely he or she was to recidivate. The average number of prior convictions for offenders first convicted at age 19 was four, compared with eight for those convicted at age 12.[170]

However, research also shows that offenders sentenced to prison have no lower rates of recidivism than do those receiving community sentences for similar crimes. For example, white-collar offenders who received a prison sentence were as likely to recidivate as was a matched group of offenders who received an alternative sanction.[171]

Some research has shown that rather than reducing the frequency of crime, punishment increases reoffending.[172] It is possible that (1) punishment brings defiance rather than deterrence or (2) the stigma of apprehension helps lock offenders into a criminal career instead of convincing them to avoid one. Recent changes in drunk-driving legislation in Ontario impose stiff sanctions, an automatic year-long suspension, a mandatory program, and a quadrupling of insurance premiums. The result has been an increase of people driving with suspended licences and no insurance. Research in Alberta on 514 incarcerated drunk drivers, however, did find that if the sentencing threshold were properly applied, there was a consistent deterrent effect even on chronic offenders. Shorter sentences were less effective, but sentences longer than six months did not produce additional benefits.[173]

Some empirical research does exist indicating that in a few instances, offenders who receive harsher punishments than do their peers will be less likely to recidivate, or if they do commit crimes again, they will do so less frequently.[174] However, the consensus is that the association between crime and specific deterrent measures is complex.

Connections

Theoretically, experiencing punishment should deter future crime. However, punishment stigmatizes people and "spoils" their identity, a turn of events that may encourage antisocial behaviour. The two factors may cancel each other out, helping to explain why punishment does not substantially reduce future criminality. The effects of stigma and negative labels are discussed further in Chapter 8.

InfoTrac®

For information on domestic violence screening by physicians, see "Screening for Domestic Violence: Who, What, When, Why, and How?" *OB/GYN Clinical Alert* 17, no. 8 (2002): 62.

Culture, Gender, Ethnicity, and Criminology

Deterrence and Domestic Violence

Is it possible to reduce the incidence of spouse abuse and domestic violence through

mandatory arrest policies? Groundbreaking research that illustrates the specific deterrent effect of legal punishment was conducted in Minneapolis, Minnesota, by Sherman and Berk.

They had police officers randomly assign treatments to the domestic assault cases they encountered on their beat. The first approach was to give advice and mediation, the second was to send the assailant from the home for eight hours, and the third was to arrest the assailant. They found that when police took formal action (arrest), the chance of recidivism was substantially less than when they took less punitive measures, such as warning the offenders or ordering them out of the house for a cooling-off period. A six-month follow-up found that only 10 percent of the arrested group had repeated their violent behaviour, compared with 19 percent of the advised group and 24 percent of the sent-away group.

Sherman and Berk concluded that a formal arrest, the most punitive alternative, was the most effective means of controlling domestic violence, regardless of what happened to the offender in court. This research finding was considered highly significant, because it was one of the few instances in which a specific deterrent effect could be identified, and because it promised a solution to one of society's most intractable problems—wife abuse.

Although the findings of the Minneapolis experiment seemed to affirm the effectiveness of specific deterrence, efforts to replicate the experimental design found it difficult to duplicate the original findings. In other locales, formal arrest was not a greater deterrent to spouse abuse than was warning or advising the assailant; in fact, in some cases, the frequency of domestic assaults increased after arrest. Although there was an initial cooling-off period, in the long term, resentment seemed to build in the offender. There are also indications that police officers in the original experiment failed to assign cases in a random fashion, which altered the experimental findings.

Despite these setbacks, it is still unclear whether the findings of the original Minneapolis experiment were invalid. An in-depth review of the replication studies concludes that the available information is still incomplete and inadequate for knowing the true effect of arrest on spousal abuse.

It is premature to dismiss the specific deterrent effect of arrest on spouse abuse. There are indications that specific deterrence policies can, under some circumstances, deter domestic abuse. One study showed that a period of short-term custody lasting about three hours may reduce recidivism; unfortunately, deterrent effects decayed over time. Evidence also exists that one subset of offenders—those with a greater stake in conformity—are more deterrable than those with little social commitment; deterrence seems to work with those who have more to lose, such as a high-paying job.

It is difficult to explain why the specific deterrent effect of arrest can be absent, decay over time, or only affect a subset of offenders (those married and employed). It is possible that offenders who suffer arrest are initially fearful of punishment but eventually replace fear with anger and violent intent toward their mate when their case does not result in severe punishment.

Sources: Lawrence Sherman and Richard Berk, "The Specific Deterrent Effects of Arrest for Domestic Assault," *American Sociological Review* 49 (1984): 261–72; Richard Berk and Phyllis J. Newman, "Does Arrest Really Deter Wife Battery? An Effort to Replicate the Findings of the Minneapolis Spouse Abuse Experiment," *American Sociological Review* 50 (1985): 253–62; Franklyn Dunford, "The Measurement of Recidivism in Cases of Spouse Assault," *Journal of Criminal Law and Criminology* 83 (1992): 120–36; J. David Hirschel, Ira Hutchinson, and Charles Dean, "The Failure of Arrest to Deter Spouse Abuse," *Journal of Research in Crime and Delinquency* 29 (1992): 7–33; J. David Hirschel and Ira Hutchinson, "Female Spouse Abuse and the Police Response: The Charlotte, North Carolina Experiment," *Journal of Criminal Law and Criminology* 83 (1992): 73–119; David Huizinga and Delbert Elliott, "The Role of Arrest in Domestic Assault: The Omaha Experiment," *Criminology* 28 (1990): 183–206; David Hirschel, Ira Hutchinson, Charles Dean, Joseph Kelley, and Carolyn Pesackis, *Charlotte Spouse Abuse Replication Project: Final Report* (Washington, D.C.: National Institute of Justice, 1990); Richard Berk, Gordon Smyth, and Lawrence Sherman, "When Random Assignment Fails: Some Lessons from the Minneapolis Spouse Abuse Experiment," *Journal of Quantitative Criminology* 4 (1989): 209–23; Joel Garner, Jeffrey Fagan, and Christopher Maxwell, "Published Findings from the Spouse Assault Replication Program: A Critical Review," *Journal of Quantitative Criminology* 11 (1995): 2–28; Lawrence Sherman, Janell Schmidt, Dennis Rogan, Patrick Gartin, Ellen Cohn, Dean Collins, and Anthony Bacich, "From Initial Deterrence to Long-Term Escalation: Short-Custody Arrest for Poverty Ghetto Domestic Violence," *Criminology* 29 (1991): 821–50; Anthony Pate and Edwin Hamilton, "Formal and Informal Deterrents to Domestic Violence: The Dade County Spouse Assault Experiment," *American Sociological Review* 57 (1992): 691–97; Richard Berk, Alec Campbell, Ruth Klap, and Bruce Western, "The Deterrent Effect of Arrest in Incidents of Domestic Violence: A Bayesian Analysis of Four Field Experiments," *American Sociological Review* 57 (1992): 698–708; Jeffrey Fagan, "Cessation of Family Violence: Deterrence and Dissuasion," in *Family Violence,* eds. Lloyd Ohlin and Michael Tonry, 377–426 (Chicago: University of Chicago Press, 1989).

Pain versus Shame

If current efforts at specific deterrence are less than successful, should new approaches be attempted? In their two widely discussed works on specific deterrence, criminologists Newman and Braithwaite take opposing approaches to reforming criminals.

Newman embraces traditional concepts of specific deterrence.[175] However, he adds a new wrinkle in his provocative suggestion that society should return to the use of corporal punishment. He advocates the use of electric shocks to punish offenders because the shocks are over with quickly, have no lasting effect, and can easily be adjusted to fit the severity of a crime.

According to Newman, corporal punishment could be used as an alternative sanction to fill the gap between the severe punishment of prison and the nonpunishment of probation. Electric shocks can be controlled and calibrated to fit the crime. For violent crimes in which the victim was terrified and humiliated and for which a local community does not want to incarcerate, a violent corporal punishment should be considered, such as whipping. In these cases, humiliation of the offender is seen as justifiably deserved. In sum, Newman embraces specific deterrence strategies if they can be relatively inexpensive, immediate, and individualized and leave no lasting disabilities.

In 1994, when a young American boy was flogged in Singapore after he pleaded guilty to vandalizing property, an international debate was provoked over the value of corporal punishment. In Canada, we have generally moved away from corporal punishment as undesirable in a civilized society.

Braithwaite takes a radically different approach.[176] Braithwaite notes that countries, such as Japan, in which conviction for crimes brings an inordinate amount of shame have extremely low crime rates. In Japan, prosecution of the criminal proceeds only when the normal process of public apology, compensation, and forgiveness by the victim breaks down. In Japan reintegrative shaming is used extensively as an alternative to humiliating offenders. Japan is the only nation with a sustained decline in the crime rate over the past 50 years (37 per 100 000 population compared with 699 per 100 000 population in the United States).[177]

Shame is a powerful tool of informal social control. Citizens in cultures in which crime is not shameful do not internalize an abhorrence for crime because when they are punished, they view themselves as merely "victims" of the justice system; their punishment comes at the hands of neutral strangers being paid to act. In contrast, shaming relies on the participation of victims. Imagine the deterrent effect of the "brank," shown in the picture.

Braithwaite divides the concept of shame into two distinct types. The most common form of shaming typically involves **stigmatization**. This form of shaming is an ongoing process of **degradation** in which the offender is branded as an evil person and cast out of society. Shaming can occur at a school disciplinary hearing or a criminal court trial. Harold Garfinkel called trials "degradation ceremonies."[178]

The brank or scold's bridle was used in the sixteenth and seventeenth centuries. Also called a witch's bridle, it had a metal cage for the head and spikes to pierce the tongue. Some also had a bell, which would humiliate the "scold" as she was paraded through the streets in a cart. A scold was a troublesome woman who nagged her husband and wrangled with her neighbours. It was usually a husband who brought his wife to court, where a judge would decide if she were a public nuisance. Source: Karen Farrington, *Dark Justice: A History of Punishment and Torture* (Toronto: Reed Consumer Books Limited, 1996).

Bestowing stigma and degradation may have a general deterrent effect: It makes people afraid of social rejection and public humiliation. However, as a specific deterrent, stigma can sometimes fail, since people who suffer humiliation at the hands of the justice system "reject their rejectors" by joining a deviant subculture of like-minded people who, collectively, resist social control, such as outlaw motorcycle gangs.

Braithwaite argues that crime control can be better achieved through a policy of **reintegrative shaming**. Here, disapproval is applied to the offenders' deeds, while they are cast as people who can be reaccepted by society. A critical element of reintegrative shaming occurs when the offenders begin to understand and recognize their wrongdoing and internalize shame. To be reintegrative, shaming must be brief and controlled and then followed by "ceremonies" of forgiveness, apology, and repentance.

Ahmed and Braithwaite developed a shame-management measurement tool to assess how individuals manage their shame after wrongdoing. The study involved 1401 students in grades 4 to 7 and 978 of their primary caregivers. The results indicated the importance of shaming in managing school bullying, shaped in part by signals about what is acceptable. Children who are impulsive, who perceive their school as unable to control bullying, and whose families are enmeshed in conflict are at a greater risk of becoming bullies. An adaptive strategy for handling shame, rather than a displacement strategy, reduced the risk of bullying in part because it required greater empathy with victims.[179]

To prevent crime, Braithwaite charges, society must encourage reintegrative shaming. For example, people interested in reducing domestic violence may mount a crusade to shame spouse abusers.[180] Early rough

---

Famous Canadian Court Cases

Effects of the *Charter* on Deterrence

The state is a mighty adversary. By further defining and guaranteeing individual rights and freedoms, the *Charter* attempts to balance power differentials between the government and the citizenry. But have the scales tipped too far in the opposite direction? Many people argue that rights afforded to accused and convicted people interfere with the administration of justice. How can we expect to curb crime if police have limited means to enforce the law and offenders deserving of punishment can get off on technicalities?

Consider the section 8 *Charter* prohibition of unreasonable searches and seizures. The Supreme Court has ruled that this provision protects not only property but also an individual's reasonable expectation of privacy. Such an interpretation can seriously compromise the principles of certainty, swiftness, and severity that are central to deterrence theory. Repercussions may include a significant reduction in

the odds of offenders being captured and held accountable. Even if the state is successful in these respects, a defendant's opportunity to challenge the legality of searches and seizures may create lengthy court delays.

Numerous precedent-setting cases involving section 8 have been heard since the implementation of the *Charter*. Deemed triumphs by some and setbacks by others, these cases include the following:

- *R. v. Kokesch* (1990): Police confirmed suspicions that Kokesch was cultivating marijuana when officers conducted a perimeter search of his residence. Based on their observations, police obtained a search warrant and seized a number of plants from the defendant's home. Kokesch was acquitted because officers did not secure a warrant before initially trespassing on his property.
- *R. v. Wong* (1990): In the course of an illegal gambling investigation, police installed video cameras in a hotel room registered to Wong without

prior judicial authorization. Officers eventually raided the room and seized profit lists, gambling paraphernalia, and a large sum of money. This evidence was admitted, but the Supreme Court ruled that this type of surveillance necessitates a warrant.

- *R. v. Dersch* (1993): Doctors withdrew some of the defendant's blood for medical purposes as he lay unconscious in hospital after a motor vehicle accident. When Dersch later refused a blood alcohol test, police requested a hospital report detailing the results of his blood work. Based on this information, a warrant was issued permitting officers to seize the initial blood sample. This evidence facilitated charges of impaired driving and criminal negligence causing death and bodily harm, but it was subsequently deemed inadmissible in court.

Source: Robert Sharpe, Katherine Swinton, and Kent Roach, *The Charter of Rights and Freedoms*, 2nd ed. (Toronto: Irwin Law Inc., 2002). *Prepared by Andrea Wolf.*

justice in Canada was often used to control the excesses of spousal abuse, a process that involved the whole community in shaming the individual involved. In addition, an effort must be made to create pride in solving problems nonviolently, in caring for others, and in respecting the rights of women.

Reintegrative shaming can have a general deterrent effect and produce specific deterrence in individuals. Parents who use reintegrative shaming techniques in their child-rearing practices may improve parent–child relationships and ultimately reduce the delinquent involvement of their children.[181] Braithwaite and Mugford's research in Australia shows how offenders are brought together with victims (so that they can experience shame) and with close family members and peers (who help with reintegration).[182] Efforts like these can humanize a system of justice that today relies on repression and not forgiveness as the basis of specific deterrence.

In the next section, we look at efforts to rethink the nature and value of deterrence. The Famous Canadian Court Cases are particularly appropriate to consider, because there is some concern that deterrence as we have envisioned it is not tough enough on offenders.

Rethinking Deterrence

So far, both specific and general deterrence strategies have not yielded the results predicted by choice theorists. Although a few studies have shown expected effects, there is still little conclusive evidence that formal sanctions can convince would-be criminals to forgo their intended behaviour or convince experienced offenders that "crime does not pay."

Some criminologists argue that the concepts of specific and general deterrence should be considered interactive.[183] Most people have had experience with the direct effect of punishment (specific deterrence) and the indirect effect of the fear of punishment (general deterrence). In addition, they may have experienced punishment avoidance, either getting away with crime themselves or knowing about others who have escaped detection or have been punished (vicarious deterrence). The total deterrent effect includes a combination of personal and vicarious experiences with punishment and its aftermath.[184]

However, the two effects may cancel each other out. An experienced criminal may fear apprehension but know that the law's "bark is worse than its bite." For example, in a study of male offenders, only half said that their sentence would prevent them from reoffending.[185] A person with criminal friends will find the fear of punishment diminished when the friends describe how easy it is to get away with crime.

Incapacitation Strategies

If more criminals are sent to prison, the crime rate should go down. Because most people age out of crime, the duration of a criminal career is limited. Placing offenders behind bars during their "prime crime" years should lessen their lifetime opportunity to commit crime. The shorter the span of opportunity, the fewer the number of offences they can commit over their life course; hence, crime is reduced.

This idea seems logical, but does it work? For the past 20 years, there has been significant growth in the number and percentage of the population held in prisons, with 24 000 people incarcerated in 2001–02. Between 1988 and 1998, Canada's prison population rose 24 percent. Canada has the fourth-highest incarceration rate (118 per 100 000 population) in the world, after the United States (699 per 100 000 population), New Zealand (149 per 100 000 population), and the United Kingdom (124 per 100 000 population). Advocates of incapacitation suggest that this effort was responsible for the overall stabilization and actual decline in crime rates in the 1990s. Others suggest that this association is illusory and that a stable crime rate is actually controlled by such factors as the size of the teenage population, the threat of tough new mandatory sentences, a healthy economy, the initiation of tougher gun laws, the end of the "crack epidemic," and the implementation of tough and aggressive policing strategies in large cities, such as Montreal and Toronto.[186] If, for example, the crime rate drops as more and more people are sent to prison, it would appear that incapacitation works. However, crime rates may really be dropping because potential criminals now fear punishment and are being deterred from crime. What appears to be an incapacitation effect may actually be an effect of general deterrence.[187]

Can Incapacitation Reduce Crime?

Research on the direct benefits of incapacitation has not shown that increasing the number of people behind bars or the length of their stay can effectively reduce crime. A number of studies have set out to measure this, and the results have not supported a strict incarceration policy. In a study using FBI index crime data, it was found that if the prison population were cut in half, the crime rate would most likely go up only 4 percent; if prisons were entirely eliminated, crime might increase 8 percent. Looking at this relationship from another perspective, if the average prison sentence were increased 50 percent, the crime rate might be reduced only 4 percent. One researcher concluded that prisons may be terribly unpleasant, psychologically destructive, and at times dangerous to life and limb, but there is no compelling evidence that imprisonment substantially decreases the likelihood of criminal involvement.[188]

A similar study of prison rates and incapacitation estimated that a 50 percent reduction in average time served would result in a 4.6 percent increase in property crime and a 2.5 percent increase in violent crime, while another found that an increase in incarceration rates may actually lead to an increase in crime rates.[189] Other research suggested that a policy of mandatory prison sentences of five years for violent crime and three for property offences could reduce the reported crime rate by a factor of four or five.[190] Further, other estimates are that a mandatory prison sentence of five years for repeat offences, such as murder, rape, robbery, and serious assault, would reduce the rate of these crimes by 6 percent to 17 percent.[191]

With these few exceptions, existing research indicates that the crime control effects of a strict incapacitation policy are modest at best.[192] The solicitor general of Canada's position is that incarceration is limited as a deterrence and that the best solution is to use alternative measures, such as conditional sentencing, and to try to return the offender to the community.

The Logic of Incarceration

Why hasn't an incarceration strategy worked? There is little evidence that incapacitating criminals will deter them from future criminality and even more reason to believe that they may be more inclined to commit crimes on release. The more prior incarceration experiences inmates had, the more likely they were to recidivate (and return to prison) within 12 months of their release.[193] Whatever reason they had to commit crime before their incarceration, there is little to suggest that a prison sentence will reduce those criminogenic forces. The criminal label precludes their entry into many legitimate occupations and solidifies their attachment to criminal careers.

The economics of crime suggest that if money can be made from criminal activity, there will always be someone to take the place of the incarcerated offender. New criminals will be recruited and trained, offsetting any benefit accrued by incarceration. Putting established offenders in prison may open new opportunities for competitors who were suppressed by the more experienced criminals. For example, the incarceration of organized crime members helped open drug markets to new gangs; the flow of narcotics into the country increased after organized crime leaders were imprisoned.

Incarceration may not work because the majority of criminal offences are committed by teens and very young adult offenders who are unlikely to be sent to prison for a single felony conviction. Incarcerated criminals, aging behind bars, are already past the age at which they are "at risk" to commit crime. A strict incarceration policy may result in people being kept in prison beyond the time that they are a threat to society, while a new cohort of high-rate adolescent offenders is on the street.

It is also expensive to maintain an incapacitation strategy. Correctional services cost $2.6 billion in 2001–02. However, the combined cost of all justice spending was $11 billion in 2000–01, spent on policing (61 percent), adult corrections (22 percent), courts (9 percent), legal aid (5 percent), and criminal prosecutions (3 percent).[194] The average annual cost of keeping an adult offender in maximum security is $72 834! Even if incarceration could reduce the crime rate, the costs would be enormous. At a time of cutbacks, should we be spending billions on this type of crime control strategy?

Selective Incapacitation: Three Strikes and You're Out

A more efficient incapacitation model is suggested by the "discovery" of the chronic career criminal. If small numbers of people account for a relatively large percentage of the nation's crime rates, then an effort to incapacitate these few troublemakers might have a significant payoff. Some have suggested that a policy of **selective incapacitation** could be an effective crime-reduction strategy.[195] In a widely cited study of more than two thousand inmates serving time for theft offences in California, Michigan, and Texas, Greenwood found that the selective incapacitation of chronic offenders could reduce the rate of robbery offences by 15 percent and the inmate population by 5 percent.

Chronic offenders can be distinguished on the basis of their offending patterns and lifestyle (for example, their employment record and history of substance abuse). Once identified, high-risk offenders would be eligible for sentencing enhancements that would substantially increase the time they serve in prison.

Another concept receiving widespread international attention is the three-strikes-and-you're-out policy now used in many American states; it gives people convicted of three violent offences a mandatory life term without parole. This policy seems to offer an attractive solution to the problem of chronic offending and is being considered in Britain. Many states already have habitual offender laws that provide long (or life) sentences for repeat offenders. Some criminologists argue that such strategies, though attractive to the public, will not work, because (1) most "three-time losers" are at the verge of aging out of crime anyway, (2) current sentences for violent crimes are already severe, (3) an expanding prison population will drive up already high prison costs, (4) there would be racial disparity in sentencing, and (5) the police would be in danger because two-time offenders would violently resist a third arrest, knowing they face a life sentence.

In a meta-analysis of 50 studies dating from 1958 and involving 336 052 offenders, it was found that a prison sentence increased the likelihood of a repeat offence, compared with a community-based sanction. Also, there was some tendency for lower-risk offenders to be more negatively affected by the prison experience. The conclusion was that prisons should not be used with the expectation of reducing criminal behaviour and that the use of incarceration has enormous cost implications. However, the researchers also feel that the primary justification of prison should be to incapacitate offenders (particularly, those of a chronic, higher-risk nature) for reasonable periods and to exact retribution.[196]

Policy Implications of Choice Theory

From the origins of classical theory to the development of modern rational choice views, the belief that criminals choose to commit crime has had an important influence on the relationship among law, punishment, and crime. When police patrol in well-marked cars, it is assumed that their presence will deter would-be criminals. When the harsh realities of prison life are portrayed in movies and TV shows, the lesson is not lost on potential criminals. Nowhere is the idea that the threat of punishment can control crime more evident than in the implementation of tough, mandatory criminal sentences to control violent crime and drug trafficking.

Despite its questionable deterrent effect, severe penalties, such as life imprisonment or capital punishment, are also viewed as effective means of restricting criminal choice. Many observers are dismayed because people who are convicted of murder sometimes kill again when released on parole. One study of 52 000 incarcerated murderers found that 810 had been previously convicted of murder and had killed 821 people following their previous release from prison.[197] About 9 percent of all inmates on death row in the United States have prior convictions for homicide; if they had been executed for their first offence, hundreds of people would be alive today.[198]

So although research on the core principles of choice theory and deterrence theories produces mixed results, there is little doubt that these models have had an important impact on crime prevention strategies.

The concept of criminal choice has also prompted the creation of justice policies referred to as **just desert**.[199] The just desert position can be summarized in these three statements:

1. Those who violate others' rights deserve to be punished.
2. We should not deliberately add to human suffering; punishment makes those punished suffer.
3. However, punishment may prevent more misery than it inflicts; this conclusion reestablishes the need for desert-based punishment.

This utilitarian view is the key to the desert approach: Punishment is needed to preserve the social equity disturbed by crime; nonetheless, the severity of the punishment should be commensurate with the seriousness of the crime. These principles were laid out by Cesare Beccaria more than two hundred years ago and still form a foundation of our criminal justice system.

Desert theory is also concerned with the rights of the accused. It alleges that the rights of the person being punished should not be unduly sacrificed for the good of others (as with deterrence). The offender should not be treated as more (or less) **blameworthy** than is warranted by the character of his or her offence. For example, if two crimes, A and B, are equally serious, but if severe penalties are shown to have a deterrent effect only with respect to A, would it be fair to punish the person who has committed crime A more harshly simply to deter others from committing the crime? Conversely, imposing a light sentence for a serious crime would be unfair, because it would treat offenders as being less blameworthy.

In sum, the just desert model suggests that retribution justifies punishment because people deserve what they get for past deeds. Punishment based on deterrence or incapacitation is wrong because it involves an

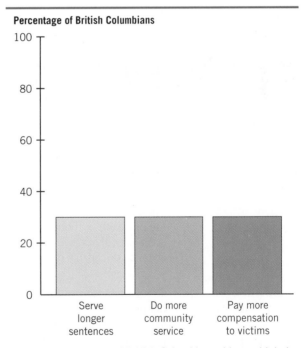

Percentage of British Columbians

Seventy-one percent of British Columbia residents think the courts are too soft in dealing with offenders. One-third favours having offenders serve longer sentences; one-third favours more community service; and one-third wants offenders to pay more compensation to victims.

Source: Poll conducted by Ipsos Reid, December 31, 2002, "Crime in British Columbia."

offender's future actions, which cannot accurately be predicted. Punishment should be the same for all people who commit the same crime. Criminal sentences based on individual needs or characteristics are inherently unfair, as all people are equally blameworthy for their misdeeds.

The influence of these views can be seen in sentencing models that give the same punishments to all people who commit the same type of crime.

Summary

Choice theory assumes that criminals carefully choose whether to commit criminal acts. These theories are summarized in Table 5.3. However, people are influenced by their fear of the criminal penalties associated with being caught and convicted for law violations. The more severe, certain, and swift the punishment, the more likely it is to control crime. The choice approach is rooted in the classical criminology of eighteenth-century social philosophers Cesare Beccaria and Jeremy Bentham.

The growth of positivist criminology, which stressed external causes of crime and rehabilitation of known offenders, reduced the popularity of the classical approach in the twentieth century. However, in the late 1970s the concept of criminal choice once again became an important perspective of criminologists. Today, choice theorists view crime as offence- and offender-specific. Research shows that offenders consider their targets carefully before choosing a course of action. By implication, crime can be prevented or displaced by convincing potential criminals that the risks of violating the law exceed the benefits.

Deterrence theory holds that if criminals are indeed rational, an inverse relationship should exist between punishment and crime. However, a number of factors confound the relationship. For example, if people do not believe they will be caught, even harsh punishment may not deter crime. Deterrence theory has been criticized on the grounds that it wrongfully assumes that criminals make a rational choice before committing crimes, it ignores the intricacies of the criminal justice system, and it does not take into account the social and psychological factors that may influence criminality. Research designed to test the validity of the deterrence concept has not indicated that deterrent measures actually reduce the crime rate.

Specific deterrence theory holds that the crime rate can be reduced if known offenders are punished so severely that they never commit crimes again. However, there is little evidence that harsh punishments actually reduce the crime rate. Incapacitation theory maintains that if deterrence does not work, the best course of

TABLE 5.3   Choice Theories

Theory	Major Premise	Strengths
Rational choice	Law-violating behaviour is an event that occurs after offenders weigh information on their personal needs and the situational factors involved in the difficulty and risk of committing a crime.	Explains why high-risk youths do not constantly engage in delinquent acts. Relates theory to delinquency control policy. It is not limited by class or other social variables.
Routine activities	Crime and delinquency are a function of the presence of motivated offenders, the availability of suitable targets, and the absence of capable guardians.	Can explain fluctuations in crime and delinquency rates. Shows how victim behaviour influences criminal choice.
General deterrence	People will commit crime and delinquency if they perceive that the benefits outweigh the risks. Crime is a function of the severity, certainty, and speed of punishment.	Shows the relationship between crime and punishment. Suggests a real solution to crime.
Specific deterrence	If punishment is severe enough, criminals will not repeat their illegal acts.	Provides a strategy to reduce crime.
Incapacitation	Keeping known criminals out of circulation will reduce crime rates.	Recognizes the role opportunity plays in criminal behaviour. Provides a solution to chronic offending.

action is to incarcerate known offenders for long periods so that they lack criminal opportunity. Research efforts have not provided clear-cut proof that increasing the number of people in prison, and increasing prison sentences, will reduce crime rates.

Choice theory has been influential in shaping public policy. The criminal law is designed to deter potential criminals and fairly punish those who have been caught in illegal acts. Some courts have changed sentencing policies to adapt to classical principles, and the correctional system seems geared toward incapacitation and special deterrence. The renewed interest in the use of the death penalty is testimony to the importance of classical theory.

Thinking Like a Criminologist

The solicitor general has issued a request for proposals for a national survey of sentencing practices. The government is interested in recommendations about criminal punishment. Specifically, do the length of criminal sentences and the way they are served have an impact on crime rates? What could be gained by either increasing punishment or requiring inmates to spend more time behind bars before their release? Are we being too lenient or too punitive as a society?

As someone who has studied choice theory, you have some ideas on how crime rates might be affected if the way we punished offenders was radically changed. Initially, you favour selective incapacitation. However, you have come across research called "Deterrence and Homeless Male Street Youth" in the *Canadian Journal of Criminology* (1998) that causes you to question yourself. The research has found that although street youths fear legal sanctions, more serious offenders do not. Instead, their fear of punishment is reduced by their poverty. Drug use and association with criminal peers cause a lack of normative constraints. The more serious street youth offenders are immersed in a lifestyle in which crime, drugs, and criminal peers feed off one another, isolating them from conventional society. What would you propose with regard to sentencing for this group of offenders?

Key Terms

blameworthy

brutalization effect

capable guardians

choice theory

classical criminology

conflict-linked crime

crackdowns

crime displacement

defensible space

degradation

diffusion of benefits

discouragement

extinction

general deterrence

informal sanctions

instrumental crimes

just desert

macro perspective

micro perspective

motivated criminals

offence-specific crime

offender-specific crime

perceptual deterrence

rational choice theory

reintegrative shaming

routine activities theory

seductions of crime

selective incapacitation

situational crime prevention

specific deterrence

stigmatization

target reduction strategies

utilitarianism

Critical Thinking Questions

1. If drug dealing is similar to any type of commercial sales, can it be controlled or eliminated in the same way a competitor is put out of business—for example, by driving down the price of goods and offering a much cheaper alternative? If so, what sort of legal alternative could you suggest?

2. If crime is rational, rather than motivated by uncontrollable psychological drives, would you want to live in a society in which crime rates are low because criminals are subjected to extremely harsh punishments, such as flogging for committing vandalism?

3. Why do arrests seem to have little effect on future domestic violence? Could it be that getting arrested increases feelings of strain and hostility and does little to reduce the problems that led to domestic conflict in the first place? Explain how you think this works.

4. Is it possible to create a method of capital punishment that would actually deter murder, for example, by televising executions? What might be some of the negative consequences of such a policy?

 See the book-specific website at http://www.siegelcriminology3e.nelson.com for additional chapter links, discussions, and quizzes.

Trait Theories

TV shows and movies that portray violent criminals as mentally deranged and physically abnormal play an important part in our culture. The classic film is Alfred Hitchcock's *Psycho*, and since then, producers have made millions depicting the ghoulish acts of people who at first seem normal but turn out to be demented and dangerous. There are crazed babysitters (*The Hand That Rocks the Cradle*), frenzied airline passengers (*Turbulence*), disturbed roommates (*Single, White Female*), psychotic tenants (*Pacific Heights*), demented secretaries (*The Temp*), unhinged police officers (*Maniac Cop*), irrational fans (*The Fan, Misery*), abnormal girlfriends (*Fatal Attraction*) and boyfriends (*Fear*), unstable husbands (*Sleeping with the Enemy*) and wives (*Black Widow*), loony fathers (*The Stepfather*) and mothers (*Friday the 13th, Part 1*), maniacal children (*The Good Son*), and psychotic teenaged admirers (*The Crush*). No one is safe, when even the psychologists and psychiatrists who should be treating these people turn out to be demonic murderers themselves (*Silence of the Lambs, Dressed to Kill, Never Talk to Strangers*). Is it any wonder that we respond to a particularly horrible crime by saying of the perpetrator, "That guy must be crazy," or "She's a monster!"

Real life can sometimes seem just as crazy. In 2004, a man whom police described as "mentally ill" loaded his car with weapons and headed to Toronto. He was unemployed and depressed, and he had diabetes and a hereditary heart condition. His plan was to shoot as many people as possible so that he would spend the rest of his life in jail. On arrest, he was charged with weapons-related offences and remanded for psychiatric examination. The only reason that he didn't go on his rampage was that a dog befriended him when he stopped for a rest in a park. He figured that if there was a nice dog in the area, there must be nice people, too.[1]

Connections

Some critics have called for the strict regulation of all media, believing them harmful to their mostly adolescent audience. Does watching all these aggressive, crazed people cause viewers to act violently themselves? For more on this issue, see the Culture, Gender, Ethnicity, and Criminology box on media violence later in this chapter.

The view that criminals have physical or mental traits that make them "different" and "abnormal" is not new. Since the nineteenth century, criminologists have suggested that biological and psychological traits may influence behaviour. For example, low-birth-weight babies have been found to perform poorly in educational achievement later in life. Academic deficiency has been linked to delinquency and drug abuse, so it is possible that

a condition present at birth will influence antisocial behaviour during later adolescence.[2] These personal differences explain why, when faced with the same life situations, one person commits crime and becomes a chronic offender, while another attends school, church, and neighbourhood functions and obeys the laws of society. One person reacts to being cut off in traffic with "road rage," while another barely notices. All people are aware of the law, but some are unable to control their urges and passions. The variations on this view of crime causation are referred to as **trait theories** or constitutional theories.

Trait theorists do not suggest that a single biological or psychological attribute is adequate to explain all criminality. Rather, for each offender there is a unique explanation for his or her behaviour. Some have inherited criminal tendencies; others have nervous system (neurological) problems; some have a blood chemistry disorder that heightens their antisocial activity. What we want is to understand the basic influences on behaviour.

Trait theorists are not concerned with legal definitions of crime or explaining why people violate particular statutory laws, such as car theft or burglary. Instead, trait theorists focus on basic human drives—aggression, violence, and impulsivity—that are linked to antisocial behaviour. They recognize that crime involves both personal traits (intelligence, personality, chemical and genetic makeup) and environmental factors (family life, educational attainment, and neighbourhood conditions). Although some people have a predisposition toward aggression, environmental stimuli can either suppress or trigger antisocial acts. Physical or mental traits are but one part of a large pool of factors that account for criminality.

Trait theories have gained prominence because of what is known about chronic recidivism and the development of criminal careers. If only a small percentage of all offenders go on to become persistent repeaters, it is possible that what sets them apart from the criminal population is an abnormal biochemistry, brain structure, or genetic makeup.[3] Even if criminals do "choose crime," the fact that some repeatedly make that choice could well be linked to their physical and mental makeup.

This chapter reviews the two major divisions of trait theory: the biological and the psychological.

Biological Trait Theory

Development of Biological Theories

Cesare Lombroso's work on the "born criminal" and identification of primitive atavistic anomalies was based on what he believed to be sound empirical research using established scientific methods.

A contemporary, Raffaele Garofalo (1852–1934), also believed that certain physical characteristics indicate a criminal nature. For example, among criminals, "a lower degree of sensibility to physical pain seems to be demonstrated by the readiness with which prisoners submit to the operation of tattooing."[4] A student, Enrico Ferri (1856–1929), believed that biological and organic factors cause delinquency and crime.[5] However, he also added a social dimension and held the view that criminals should not be held personally or morally responsible for their actions, because forces outside their control cause criminality.

Connections

Biological explanations of criminal behaviour first became popular during the middle part of the nineteenth century with the introduction of positivism—the use of the scientific method and empirical analysis to study behaviour, discussed in Chapter 1.

Advocates of the inheritance school traced the activities of several generations of families believed to have an especially large number of criminal members. The most famous study of a "degenerate family" was Richard Dugdale's *The Jukes: A Study in Crime, Pauperism, Disease, and Heredity* (1875), which traced a family's history over 150 years. Dugdale claimed to have proved the existence of hereditary criminality, saying: "Fornication is the backbone of their habits, flanked on one side by pauperism, on the other by crime. The secondary features are prostitution, with its complement of bastardy, and its resultant neglected and miseducated childhood; exhaustion, with its complement intemperance and its resultant unbalanced minds; and disease with its complement extinction."[6]

A later attempt at criminal anthropology was the **somatype** school developed by William Sheldon, which held that criminals manifest distinct physiques susceptible to particular types of delinquent behaviour. Mesomorphs have well-developed muscles and are active, aggressive, and the most likely to become criminals. Endomorphs have heavy builds and are known for lethargic behaviour. Ectomorphs are tall, thin, less social, and more intellectual than the other types.[7]

The work of Lombroso and his contemporaries is regarded today as faulty because they did not use control groups from the general population to compare the results. Many of the traits they assumed to be inherited are not genetically determined. Many of the biological features they identified could have been caused by deprivation in surroundings and diet. Even if most criminals shared certain biological traits, these might have resulted from environmental conditions, such as poor nutrition or health care. Because of these deficiencies in the research design, the validity of individual-oriented explanations of criminality became questionable.

InfoTrac®

Use "morphology" as a keyword on InfoTrac® College Edition to learn more about this topic.

Sociobiology. During the early twentieth century, criminologists became concerned about the sociological influences on crime. The work of biocriminologists had been viewed as methodologically unsound,[8] but this situation changed:

> What seems no longer tenable at this juncture is any theory of human behaviour which ignores biology and relies exclusively on sociocultural learning. . . . Most social scientists have been wrong in their dogmatic rejection and blissful ignorance of the biological parameters of our behaviour.[9]

In the 1970s, Edmund O. Wilson published *Sociobiology*, and the biological basis for crime again emerged into the limelight.[10] **Sociobiology** differs from earlier theories of behaviour in stressing how biological and genetic conditions affect the perception and learning of social behaviours. Sociobiologists view the gene as the ultimate unit of life that controls all human destiny, with environment and experience having an impact on behaviour. Most important, sociobiology holds that people are controlled by the innate need to have their genetic material survive. Consequently, they want to ensure their own survival and that of others who share their gene pool (relatives, fellow citizens). Even when they are altruistic and come to the aid of others, people are motivated by the belief that their actions will be reciprocated.

Sociobiologists view biology, environment, and learning as mutually interdependent factors. Problems in one area can be altered by efforts in another. In this view, people are biosocial organisms whose behaviours are influenced by physical as well as environmental conditions.

Sociobiology has been criticized, but it has revived interest in finding a biological basis for crime and delinquency.

| Exhibit 6.1 | Sheldon's Somatypes |

In the 1940s, psychologist William Sheldon proposed the idea that body types were associated with personality characteristics. After studying four thousand photographs of college-age men, and connecting body type and temperament, he said there were three categories of human bodies: the endomorph, characterized by a preponderance of body fat; the mesomorph, characterized by a well-developed musculature; and the ectomorph, who had neither much muscle tissue nor body fat. Ectomorphic people tend to be quiet, mesomorphs are energetic, and endomorphic people love to eat. In Sheldon's words, "the somatype is intended as a kind of identification tag . . . a rather crude tool fashioned to reflect a basic structural orderliness which can be perceived in human life." For example, consider the following:

"Somatype 117—Walking Sticks—Fragile stretched-out creatures with the utmost surface exposure in proportion to mass. . . . This extremely rare somatype (incidence 2 per ten thousand), with his extreme predominance of surface over mass, seems caught in a predicament of biological overexposure, and for such an organism the ordinary circumstances of social life may amount to chronic overstimulation. Hebephrenic psychopathy may be one natural response to such a situation. The 117 is more common in the mental hospitals than in the general population, and his diagnosis is usually hebephrenic schizophrenia. But also he is encountered more frequently on college campuses than in the general population, and there the diagnosis is sometimes Phi Beta Kappa."

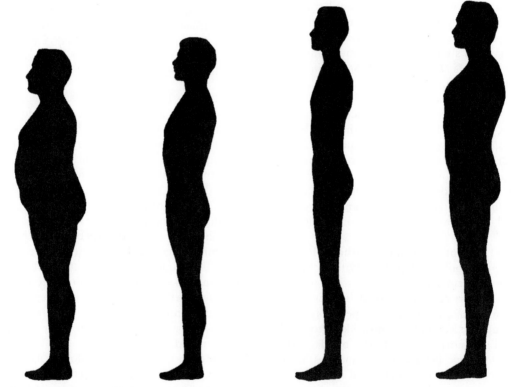

From left to right: endomorph, mesomorph, ectomorph, normal

Source: William Sheldon, *Atlas of Men. A Guide for Somatyping the Adult Male at All Ages* (New York: Harper and Brothers, 1954).

InfoTrac®

Can sociobiology explain behaviour patterns across all animal species and show how it is linked to mating behaviour? To find out, read about the mechanism of natural selection in this InfoTrac® College Edition article: Gerald Holton, "The New Synthesis?" *Society* 35, no. 2 (1998): 203–213.

Modern Biological Theories. Sociobiology has helped revive interest in the biological basis of crime. Rather than view the criminal as a person whose behaviour is controlled by biological conditions determined at birth, modern biological trait theorists believe that physical, environmental, and social conditions work together to produce human behaviour. Environmental forces can "trigger" antisocial behaviour in people biologically predisposed to deviance, or if conditions are right, mediate or offset the effects of biological predisposition. For example, perhaps chronic offenders suffer some biological/psychological condition or trait that renders them incapable of resisting social pressures and problems.[11]

Biological trait theory has several principles.[12] First, genetic makeup means not all humans are born with equal potential to learn and achieve (**equipotentiality**). Whereas sociological criminologists say that everyone is born equal and their behaviour is controlled by social forces (parents, schools, neighbourhoods, friends), biosocial theorists argue that no two people are alike (with rare exceptions, such as identical twins) and that the combination of human genetic traits and the environment produces individual behaviour patterns.

Another focus is the importance of brain functioning, mental processes, and learning. Although physical and social environments affect learning, people also learn through a process involving the brain and central nervous system, via biochemistry, cellular interaction, and physical changes that occur in the brain.[13]

Some biosocial theorists believe that learning is influenced by instinctual drives developed over history. **Instincts** are inherited and non-learned dispositions that activate behaviour patterns. For example, a drive to "possess and control" other people and things means theft is motivated by the instinctual need to possess goods. Rape and other sex crimes may be linked to an instinctual drive males have to "possess and control" females.[14] However, such a theory shouldn't be taken as legitimating rape as natural.

The following subsections examine some of the more important subbranches within biological criminology (see Figure 6.1 for an overview).[15] First, we will

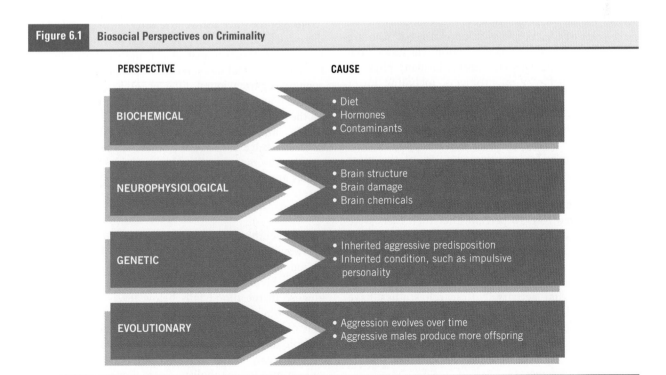

| Figure 6.1 | Biosocial Perspectives on Criminality |

PERSPECTIVE

CAUSE

BIOCHEMICAL
- Diet
- Hormones
- Contaminants

NEUROPHYSIOLOGICAL
- Brain structure
- Brain damage
- Brain chemicals

GENETIC
- Inherited aggressive predisposition
- Inherited condition, such as impulsive personality

EVOLUTIONARY
- Aggression evolves over time
- Aggressive males produce more offspring

review the biochemical factors believed to affect the learning of proper behaviour patterns. Then, we'll consider the relationship of brain function and crime, and current ideas about the association between genetic factors and crime. Finally, we will evaluate evolutionary views of crime causation.

Biochemical Conditions and Crime

Some trait theorists believe that biochemical conditions, both those that are genetically predetermined and those acquired through diet and environment, control and influence antisocial behaviour. This view of crime received national attention in 1979 when Dan White, the killer of San Francisco Mayor George Moscone and City Councillor Harvey Milk, claimed his behaviour was precipitated by an addiction to sugar-laden junk foods.[16] However, Milk was the first openly gay councillor of San Francisco and responsible for the city's first gay rights ordinance. White, a former police officer also on city council, opposed Milk's political reforms. When White's "Twinkie defence" was supported by psychiatric evidence of hypoglycemia, the jury found him guilty of the lesser offence of diminished capacity manslaughter rather than first-degree murder. (White committed suicide after serving his prison sentence.)

Some of the more important biochemical factors that have been linked to criminality range from nutrition to hormones.

Nutritional Deficiencies. Biocriminologists maintain that minimum levels of vitamins and minerals are needed for normal brain functioning, especially in the early years of life. People with normal needs who are not receiving the appropriate nutrition will suffer from vitamin deficiency. This lack results in many physical, mental, and behavioural problems, including lower intelligence.[17] Alcoholics often suffer from thiamine deficiency because of their poor diets and consequently are susceptible to the serious, often fatal, Korsakoff's syndrome.[18]

Schoenthaler has conducted some of the most important research on diet and crime. In one study of 803 New York City public schools, Schoenthaler found that the academic performance of 1.1 million school children rose 16 percent after their diets were modified.[19] Other research shows that the dietary inadequacy of sodium, potassium, calcium, amino acids, monoamines, and peptides can lead to depression, mania, cognitive problems, memory loss, and abnormal sexual activity.[20] Research studies have found a link between antisocial behaviour and insufficient quantities of vitamins B3, B6, and C. In addition, a major proportion of all schizophrenics and children with learning and behaviour disorders require vitamin B3 and B6 supplements.

 InfoTrac®

For relevant information on nutritional deficiencies, see Willow Lawson, "Fighting Crime One Bite at a Time: Diet Supplements Cut Violence in Prison," *Psychology Today* 36, no. 2 (2003): 22.

Sugar and Crime. Another suspected nutritional influence on behaviour is a diet especially high in carbohydrates and sugar.[21] For example, how the brain processes glucose was related to scores on tests measuring reasoning power.[22] High sugar intake levels have been associated with attention-span deficiencies.

Diets high in sugar and carbohydrates are linked to violence and aggression. An experiment with 276 incarcerated youths was conducted to determine whether a change in the amount of sugar in their diet would have a corresponding influence on their behaviour.[23] In the experiment, several dietary changes were made: Sweet drinks were replaced with fruit juices, table sugar was replaced with honey, and breakfast cereals high in sugar were eliminated. These changes produced a decline of 45 percent in the number of assaults, thefts, fights, and incidents of disobedience within the institution.

Although research linking sugar intake to emotional, cognitive, and behavioural performance is impressive, some researchers have failed to find a link between sugar consumption and violence.[24] For example, one group of researchers had 25 preschool children and 23 school-aged children described as sensitive to sugar follow a different diet for three consecutive three-week periods. One diet was high in sucrose, the second substituted aspartame (Nutrasweet) as a sweetener, and the third relied on saccharin. Careful measurement found little evidence of cognitive or behavioural differences that could be linked to diet. If anything, sugar seemed to have a calming effect on the children.[25]

In sum, although some research efforts allege a sugar–violence association, others suggest that many people who maintain diets high in sugar and carbohydrates are not violent or crime-prone, and that in some cases, sugar intake may actually reduce or curtail violent tendencies.[26]

Hypoglycemia. Research shows that abnormalities in the way the brain metabolizes glucose (sugar) can be linked to antisocial behaviours, such as substance abuse.[27] **Hypoglycemia** is a condition that occurs when glucose in the blood falls below levels necessary for normal brain functioning. The brain is the only organ that obtains its energy solely from the combustion of carbohydrates. Thus, when the brain is deprived of blood sugar, it has no alternative food supply to call on and its metabolism slows down. Symptoms of hypoglycemia include irritability, anxiety, depression, crying spells, fatigue, insomnia, nervousness, mood swings, phobias, temper outbursts, headaches, and confusion.

Hypoglycemia has been linked to outbursts of antisocial behaviour and violence. As early as 1943, murder was linked to hypoglycemia, while other studies have related assaults and fatal sexual offences to hypoglycemic reactions.[28] Hypoglycemia has also been connected with a syndrome characterized by aggressive and assaultive behaviour, and brain dysfunction. Studies of jail and prison inmate populations have found a higher than normal level of hypoglycemia, as well as in groups of habitually violent and impulsive offenders.[29]

Hormonal Influences. Criminologist James Q. Wilson, in *The Moral Sense*, concludes that hormones, enzymes, and neurotransmitters are the keys to understanding human behaviour and that they explain gender differences in the crime rate. Males are biologically and naturally more aggressive than females, while women are more nurturing of the young and more important for survival of the species.[30] Hormone levels also explain the aging-out process: Levels of the principal male steroid hormone decline during the life cycle, reducing violence rates.[31]

Biosocial theorists are now evaluating the association between violent behaviour episodes and hormone levels, and the findings suggest that abnormal levels of male sex hormones (**androgens**) do, in fact, produce aggressive behaviour.[32] This link among hormonal changes, mood, and behaviour may explain why adolescents experience more intense mood swings, anxiety, and restlessness than do their elders.[33] Both hormonal activity and antisocial behaviour peak in adolescence.[34] In the case of adolescents, researchers believe that prepubertal development is a significant factor in peer-to-peer sexual harassment.[35]

Testosterone is the most abundant androgen, controlling secondary sex characteristics, such as facial hair and voice timbre. Research on both humans and animals has found that prenatal exposure to unnaturally high levels of androgens permanently alters behaviour. Girls who were unintentionally exposed to elevated androgen levels during fetal development display a high long-term tendency toward aggression; boys prenatally exposed to steroids that decrease androgens displayed decreased aggressiveness.[36] In contrast, inmate studies indicate that testosterone levels are higher in men who committed violent crimes.[37] In 2001, the science journal *Nature* reported on a study showing that fish that watched two other males attack each other had higher levels of testosterone than fish that didn't watch the fighting. This shows that the body's biology reacts to social behaviour and influences individual behaviour.

In animals, the relationship between testosterone and aggression is well established, but it is more controversial in humans and is influenced by culture and experience.[38] In an extensive meta-analysis, psychologists at Queen's University found a weak but positive relationship. Results in human studies vary widely in part because testosterone levels change from moment to moment.[39]

Hormone levels influence violent behaviour because areas of the brain become less sensitive to environmental stimuli. Males who possess high androgen levels are more likely than females to need excess stimulation and to be willing to tolerate pain in their quest for thrills. Androgens are linked to brain seizures that, under stressful conditions, can result in emotional volatility. Androgens affect brain structure, influencing the left hemisphere of the neocortex, the part of the brain that controls sympathetic feelings toward others. Some other physical reactions produced by hormones linked to violence include the need to seek unusually high levels of environmental stimulation, impulsive emotional responses to stressful environmental encounters, and a rightward shift in neocortical functioning, which is less prone to reason or to respond to linguistic commands.[40]

Drugs that decrease testosterone are used to treat male sex offenders.[41] The female hormones estrogen and progesterone have been administered to sex offenders to decrease their sexual potency.[42] Chemical castration is used in some American states for repeat sex offences, especially those against children. Surgical castration is used in some countries, however, not in Canada. A problem with sex offenders is that most will have substance-abuse disorders, antisocial personality disorders, mood disorders, or psychological problems. The identification of the problem is not a simple one.

Premenstrual Syndrome (PMS). The suspicion has long existed that the onset of the menstrual cycle triggers excessive amounts of the female sex hormones, affecting antisocial, aggressive behaviour. During the nineteenth century, "disordered menstruation" was often introduced as a factor in defending women on serious charges, such as arson or homicide. Today, this condition is commonly referred to as **premenstrual syndrome (PMS)**.[43] The link between PMS and delinquency was first popularized by Katharina Dalton, whose studies of English women indicated that females are more likely to commit suicide and be aggressive just before or during menstruation.[44] The syndrome includes about 150 symptoms.

Debate continues over any link between PMS and aggression. For example, perhaps psychological and physical stress brings on menstruation and not vice versa.[45] Diana Fishbein, an expert on biosocial theory, says an association exists between elevated levels of female aggression and menstruation. She says that a significant number of incarcerated females committed their crimes during the premenstrual phase.[46]

Only a few criminal trials in Canada, Britain, and the United States have successfully used PMS as a mitigating factor in a woman's defence. The usual result has been the defendant being required to receive hormone injections as a condition of the sentence.[47]

However, the overwhelming majority of females who suffer anxiety and hostility before and during menstruation do not actually engage in violent criminal behaviour.[48]

Another mental disorder believed to be typically female is Munchausen's syndrome by proxy (MSBP), in which the mother either induces or fabricates illness in a child in order to achieve repeat contact with the health care system. The syndrome was identified in the late 1970s; however, there is little consensus as to what type of disorder it is.

Allergies. Allergies are excessive reactions of the body to foreign substances.[49] For example, hay fever is an allergic reaction caused when pollen cells enter the body and are fought or neutralized by the body's natural defences. The result is itching, red eyes, and active sinuses.

Cerebral allergies cause a reaction in the brain, whereas neuroallergies affect the nervous system, believed to cause enzymes that cause swelling of the brain and sensitivity in the central nervous system linked to mental, emotional, and behavioural problems. Research indicates a connection between these allergies and hyperemotionality, depression, aggressiveness, and violent behaviour.[50]

Neuroallergy and cerebral allergy problems have been linked to hyperactivity in children. The foods most commonly involved in producing such allergies are cow's milk, wheat, corn, chocolate, citrus, and eggs; however, about three hundred other foods have been identified as allergens. Corn is a suspected cerebral allergen, which has been linked to cross-national homicide rates.[51]

Environmental Contaminants. Dangerous quantities of copper, cadmium, mercury, and inorganic gases, such as chlorine and nitrogen dioxide, in the ecosystem influence behaviour and are linked to emotional and behavioural disorders, severe illness, or death.[52] The ingestion of food dyes and artificial colours and flavours has been linked to hostile, impulsive, and antisocial behaviour in youths.[53] Radiation from artificial lighting, such as fluorescent tubes and television sets, may be another important environmental influence on antisocial behaviour.[54]

A number of recent research studies have suggested that lead ingestion is linked to aggressive behaviours on

Crime in the News

Woman's Syndrome Brings Leniency

A woman who stabbed her husband in the back last year while suffering from premenstrual syndrome was placed on probation Monday because she couldn't get proper treatment in a correctional institution.

District Court Judge Joseph Winter suspended sentencing Marsali Edwards, 29, for three years.

"For what I am about to do, I am of course going to be severely criticized," Judge Winter said before passing sentence.

But he warned that his decision should not be viewed as a license for other women to repeat Edwards's actions.

Winter also ordered her to report regularly to a probation officer and to undergo treatment by a "competent, appropriate, knowledgeable medical practitioner other than a psychiatrist."

The case establishes a precedent in Canadian law for the use of premenstrual syndrome as a mitigating factor in sentencing people charged with violent crimes.

The disorder, which experts say affects 20 to 40 percent of women, has been blamed for a wide range of symptoms, [from] hostility, anxiety and depression to food cravings, acne and changes in hair texture.

It has been used in a few cases in the United States to win acquittals.

Winter stressed his sentence was also based on Edwards's background, which he described as "very unfortunate."

During a four-day trial last December, court was told Edwards was adopted at the age of three after being abused by her natural parents. During her adolescence, she ran away to marry a high school teacher who was three times her age.

The marriage lasted six months, after which she began living with Brian Edwards, 41.

Edwards, who later married her, was described as a "wife-beating drunk" by Winter, who said the man's alcohol problem was so severe that it caused him to be discharged from the Canadian Forces. That marriage also broke down, court was told.

Source: Canadian Press, *Vancouver Sun*, February 10, 1987.

both a macro and micro level. For example, areas with the highest concentrations of lead in the air also reported the highest levels of homicide.[55] Studies have linked lead to conduct problems and antisocial behaviour in hyperactive children.[56] A study of 900 Black youth found that lead poisoning was one of the most significant predictors of male delinquency and persistent adult criminality. Needleman tracked three hundred boys from ages 7 to 11 and found that those who had high lead concentrations in their bones were much more likely to report attention problems, delinquency, aggressiveness, and poor language skills.[57] High lead ingestion is also related to lower IQ scores, a factor linked to aggressive behaviour.[58] Lead has also been linked to attention deficit disorder. A study of 216 youths convicted in a juvenile court showed higher levels of lead in their bones than in the control group, with elevated lead levels leading to antisocial activities like bullying, vandalism, truancy, and shoplifting.

Neurophysiological Conditions and Crime

Some criminologists, looking at brain activity (**neurophysiology**), believe that neurological and physical abnormalities acquired as early as the fetal stage control behaviour throughout the life span.[59]

The relationship between neurological dysfunction and crime received a great deal of attention in 1968, when Charles Whitman killed his wife and his mother, barricaded himself in a tower at the University of Texas with a high-powered rifle, and killed 14 people and wounded 24 others before he was killed by police. An autopsy revealed that Whitman suffered from a malignant brain tumour; he had experienced urges to kill and had gone to a psychiatrist.[60]

Since then, attention has focused on the association between neurological impairment in brain functions (abstract reasoning, problem-solving skills, motor behaviour skills) and aggressive behaviour.[61]

Neurological Impairments and Crime. There are numerous ways to measure neurological functioning, including visual awareness tests, short-term auditory memory tests, and verbal IQ tests. These can distinguish criminal offenders from noncriminal control groups.[62]

Probably the most important measure of neurophysiological functioning is the **electroencephalograph.** An EEG records the electrical impulses given off brain waves, which can be recorded by electrodes placed on the scalp.[63] Studies find that violent criminals have far higher levels of abnormal EEG recordings than do nonviolent or one-time offenders.[64] In what is considered the most significant investigation of EEG abnormality and crime, a randomly selected group of 335 violent delinquents was divided into those who were habitually violent and those who had committed only a single violent act. Sixty-five percent of the habitually aggressive had abnormal EEG recordings, while only 24 percent of the one-time offenders had recordings that deviated from the norm. When those with brain damage, mental retardation, or epilepsy were removed from the sample, the percentage of abnormality among boys who had committed a solitary violent crime was the same as that of the general population, about 12 percent. However, the habitually aggressive subjects showed a 57 percent abnormality.

Although 5 percent to 15 percent of the population have abnormal EEG readings, 50 percent to 60 percent of adolescents with known behaviour disorders display abnormal recordings.[65] These disorders include poor impulse control, inadequate social adaptation, hostility, temper tantrums, and destructiveness.[66]

Studies of adults have associated slow and bilateral brain waves with hostile, hypercritical, irritable, nonconforming, and impulsive behaviour.[67] Psychiatric patients with EEG abnormalities are highly combative and suffer episodes of rage. Studies of murderers have shown a disproportionate number manifest abnormal EEG recordings.[68] EEG analysis, then, shows that measures of brain activity are significantly associated with antisocial behaviour.

Fetal Alcohol Syndrome. Fetal alcohol syndrome (FAS), or fetal alcohol spectrum disorder (FASD), occurs when children are exposed to alcohol in the womb and later experience developmental delays and often display crime-related behaviour. Half of all children with FASD are diagnosed with AD/HD and they are more likely to have secondary disabilities, such as disruptive school experiences. Common cognitive and behavioural problems are learning difficulties, poor impulse control, speech problems, and inability to foresee consequences. Overall, it is estimated that FASD affects 1 percent of all babies, but between 40 percent and 80 percent of children in foster care. Half of young offenders appearing in provincial or territorial court are there because their mothers drank during pregnancy.[69]

Minimal Brain Dysfunction. Minimal brain dysfunction (MBD) is related to an abnormality in cerebral structure. It is sometimes simply maladaptive behaviour that interrupts the lifestyle of an individual. However, in its most serious form, MBD has been linked to serious antisocial acts, an imbalance in the urge-control mechanisms of the brain, and chemical abnormality. The category of minimal brain dysfunction includes behaviour patterns, such as dyslexia, visual perception problems, hyperactivity, poor attention span, temper tantrums, and aggressiveness. One type of minimal brain dysfunction is manifested through episodic periods of explosive rage and is considered an important cause of such behaviour as spouse beating, child abuse, suicide, aggressiveness, and motiveless homicide.

Some studies measuring the presence of minimal brain dysfunction in offender populations have found that up to 60 percent of offenders exhibit brain dysfunction on psychological tests.[70] Criminals have been characterized as having dysfunction of the dominant hemisphere of the brain.[71] Researchers using brain-wave data have predicted with 95 percent accuracy the recidivism of violent criminals.[72]

Attention Deficit/Hyperactivity Disorder. Many parents have noticed that their children do not pay attention to them—they run around and do things in their own way. Sometimes this inattention is a function of age; in other instances, it is a symptom of **attention deficit/hyperactivity disorder (AD/HD)**, in which a child shows impulsivity, hyperactivity, and a developmentally inappropriate lack of attention. The various symptoms of AD/HD are described in Table 6.1.

Between 3 percent and 5 percent of children, most often boys, are believed to have AD/HD, and it is the most common reason children are referred to mental health clinics. AD/HD is associated with poor school performance, grade retention, placement in special needs classes, bullying, stubbornness, and lack of response to discipline.[73] Suspected causes include neurological

---

Table 6.1   Symptoms of Attention Deficit/Hyperactivity Disorder

Lack of Attention
Frequently fails to finish projects
Does not seem to pay attention
Does not sustain interest in play activities
Cannot sustain concentration on schoolwork
   or related tasks
Is easily distracted

Impulsivity
Frequently acts without thinking
Often "calls out" in class
Does not want to wait his or her turn in lines
   or games
Shifts from activity to activity
Cannot organize tasks or work
Requires constant supervision

Hyperactivity
Constantly runs around and climbs on things
Shows excessive motor activity while asleep
Cannot sit still; is constantly fidgeting
Does not remain in his or her seat in class
Is constantly on the go like a "motor"

Source: Adapted from American Psychiatric Association, *Diagnostic and Statistical Manual of Mental Disorders,* 4th ed. (Washington, D.C.: American Psychiatric Press, 1994); also online at http://web.cs.mun.ca/~jamie/dsm4.html.

---

damage, prenatal stress, food additive and chemical allergies, and perhaps a genetic link.

Research now links AD/HD, minimal brain dysfunctions (such as poor motor function), hyperactivity, and below-average written and verbal cognitive ability to the onset and sustenance of a delinquent career. Youths who have both AD/HD and MBD and grow up in a dysfunctional family are the ones most vulnerable to chronic and persistent delinquency.[74] The relationship between chronic delinquency and attention disorders may be mediated by school failure: Kids who are poor readers are the most prone to antisocial behaviour; many poor readers also have attention problems.[75]

Although AD/HD has historically been characterized as a childhood disease, it is a lifelong disorder affecting 2 percent to 6 percent of adults, and symptoms of AD/HD seem to remain stable through adolescence into adulthood.[76] AD/HD has a high likelihood of inheritance and is associated with various impairments, such as high levels of substance abuse.[77]

Early diagnosis and treatment of children with AD/HD may enhance their life chances. Today, the most typical treatment is doses of stimulants, such as Ritalin and Dexedrine, which help control emotional and behavioural outbursts.

Other Brain Dysfunctions. Persistent criminality has been linked to dysfunction in the frontal and temporal regions of the brain, which regulate and inhibit human behaviour, and the formation of plans and intentions.[78] Brain lesions that occur in the neurological system can have permanent effects on behaviour, and clinical evaluation of depressed and aggressive psychopathic subjects showed a significant number (75 percent) had dysfunction of the temporal and frontal regions of the brain.[79]

In an analysis of uxoricide (wife homicide), Dutton found that most offenders had experienced traumatic childhoods and had personality disorders. In addition, he speculates that attachment dysfunction in childhood coupled with low levels of serotonin and high levels of norepinephrine are implicated in aggression.[80]

Tumours, Injury, and Disease. The presence of brain tumours has been linked to psychological problems, including personality changes, hallucinations, and psychotic episodes. People with tumours are more prone to depression, irritability, temper outbursts, and even homicidal attacks. Previously docile people may undergo behaviour changes so great that they attempt to harm their families and friends; when the tumour is removed, their behaviour returns to normal.[81] In addition, head injuries caused by accidents have been linked to personality reversals marked by outbursts of antisocial and violent behaviour.[82] Brain scans can show the presence of underlying trauma.

A variety of central nervous system diseases, including cerebral arteriosclerosis, epilepsy, senile dementia, Korsakoff's syndrome, and Huntington's chorea, have also been associated with memory deficiency, orientation loss, and affective (emotional) disturbances dominated by rage, anger, and increased irritability.[83]

In a study of interaction between obstetrical complications and early family adversity, researchers looked at 849 boys from low-socioeconomic areas of Montreal. They found that such complications as preeclampsia and umbilical cord prolapse, coupled with the psychosocial factors of an adverse family environment, increased the risk of violence in the boys when they reached 16 to 17 years of age. It seems that neuropsychological deficits leading to behavioural problems are engendered by fetal brain damage, essentially rewiring the brain.[84]

Brain Chemistry and Crime. Neurotransmitters are chemical compounds that influence or activate brain functions. Abnormal levels of some neurotransmitters, including androgens, dopamine, norepinephrine, serotonin, monoamine oxidase, and GABA, have been linked with aggression. For example, people with histories of impulsive violence usually have a reduction in the function of the serotonin system. Studies of habitually violent Finnish criminals show that low serotonin levels are associated with poor impulse control and hyperactivity. Prozac, which is commonly prescribed for depression, is a serotonin enhancer. Low levels of certain chemicals in the brain are also linked with increased irritability, sensation seeking, and depression.[85]

Since the 1990s, doctors have prescribed selective serotonin reuptake inhibitors (SSRIs) to children with major depressive disorders. But in 2003, an advisory was issued that possible side effects included an increased risk of suicide, aggression, conduct problems, and hostility.[86]

Prenatal exposure of the brain to high levels of androgens can result in a brain structure that is less sensitive to environmental inputs. Affected individuals seek more intense and varied stimulation and are willing to tolerate more adverse consequences.[87] Such exposure results in a rightward shift in brain functioning and a lessening of cognitive and emotional tendencies. Interestingly, left-handers are disproportionately represented in the criminal population, since the movement of each hand tends to be controlled by the hemisphere of the brain on the opposite side of the body.

Individuals with a low supply of the enzyme monoamine oxidase (MAO) engage in behaviours linked with violence and property crime, including defiance of punishment, impulsivity, hyperactivity, poor academic performance, sensation seeking and risk taking, and recreational drug use. Females have higher levels of MAO than males, which might explain gender differences in the crime rate.[88]

A deficiency of MAOA (a subtype of MAO) in abused children, especially boys, is a good predictor of future violence and criminality. In a study of 442 males in New Zealand, 37 percent had low levels of MAOA. Abused children with low MAOA activity (12 percent of the study) accounted for 44 percent of the violent crime connections. The researchers concluded that genetic characteristics moderate children's sensitivity to environmental insults, such as abuse, and help explain why not all victims of abuse grow up to victimize others.[89]

Because this linkage has been found, violence-prone people are treated with antipsychotic drugs that help control levels of neurotransmitters, sometimes referred to as "chemical straitjackets." The brain can also produce natural opiates, chemically similar to the narcotics opium and morphine. Perhaps the risk and thrills involved in crime cause the brain to produce increased amounts of these natural narcotics. The result is an elevated mood state, perceived as an exciting and rewarding experience, that acts as a positive reinforcer to crime.[90]

The brain then produces its own natural "high" as a reward for risk-taking behaviour. While some people achieve this high by rock climbing and skydiving, others engage in crimes of violence.

Arousal Theory. If obtaining thrills is a motivator of crime, adolescents may engage in shoplifting and vandalism simply because these acts offer the attraction of "getting away with it."[91] Is it possible that thrill seekers are people who have some form of abnormal brain functioning that directs their behaviour?

According to **arousal theory**, people's brains function differently in response to environmental stimuli. People seek to maintain a preferred or optimal level of arousal. Too much stimulation leaves them anxious; too little makes them feel bored. There is, however, variation in the way people's brains process sensory input. Some nearly always feel comfortable with little stimulation, while others require a high degree of environmental input to feel comfortable. The "sensation seekers" seek out stimulating activities, which may include aggressive, violent behaviour patterns.[92]

The factors that determine a person's optimal level of arousal are not fully determined. Suspected sources include brain chemistry (serotonin levels) and brain structure. For instance, some people's brains have many more nerve cells with receptor sites for neurotransmitters than do other people's.

Connections

Jack Katz has written on the seductions of crime and how some people may be drawn into crime because it produces the natural high they crave. The seduction of crime is discussed in Chapter 5.

Genetics and Crime

Early biological theorists believed that criminality ran in families, conducting research on deviant families, such as the Jukes and Kallikaks. Modern biosocial theorists are still interested in genetics and how heredity influences antisocial tendencies. Animals bred to have aggressive traits include pit bull dogs, fighting bulls, and fighting cocks. Genetic factors associated with human behaviour include extraversion, openness, agreeableness, and conscientiousness.[93] Human personality traits associated with criminality, such as aggression (psychopathy, impulsivity, and neuroticism), and psychopathology (such as schizophrenia), may be heritable.[94]

Richard Speck, the convicted killer of eight nurses in Chicago, was said to have inherited an abnormal XYY chromosomal structure (XY is the normal sex chromosome pattern in males), raising concern that all XYYs were potential killers and should be closely controlled.[95] However, neither Speck nor most violent offenders actually had an extra Y chromosome, so interest in the XYY theory dissipated.

Is it possible that the tendency for crime and aggression is inherited? Since the Speck case, numerous researchers have carefully explored the heritability of criminal tendencies using a variety of techniques, the most common being twin studies and adoption studies.

Twin Studies. If inherited traits cause criminal behaviours, twins should be quite similar in their antisocial activities. However, since twins are usually brought up in the same household and are exposed to the same set of social conditions, determining whether their behaviour is a result of biological, sociological, or psychological conditions is difficult. Trait theorists have tried to overcome this dilemma by comparing identical monozygotic (MZ) twins with fraternal dizygotic (DZ) twins of the same sex. MZ twins are genetically identical, while DZ twins have only half their genes in common. If heredity does determine criminal behaviour, the MZ twins should be much more similar in their antisocial activities than are the DZ twins.

Early studies on the behaviour of twins detected a significant relationship between the criminal activities of MZ twins and a much lower association between those of DZ twins. Sixty percent of MZ twins shared criminal behaviour patterns (if one twin was criminal, so was the other), while only 30 percent of DZ twins were similarly related. This was viewed as evidence of a genetic basis to criminality. More recently Christiansen studied 3586 male twin pairs and found a 52 percent similarity for MZ pairs and only 22 percent for DZ pairs, suggesting that MZ twins share a genetic characteristic that increases the risk of their engaging in criminality.[96] Genetic effects have been found to be a significant predictor of problem behaviours in children as young as three years old.[97] Although the behaviour of some twin pairs seems to be influenced by their environment, others displayed behaviour disturbances that could only be explained by their genetic similarity.[98]

The controversy over the heritability of crime persists. On the one hand, evidence provides little conclusive proof that crime is genetically predetermined. Not all research efforts have found that MZ twin pairs are more closely related in their criminal behaviour than are DZ or ordinary sibling pairs.[99] On the other hand, some experts have concluded that individuals who share genes are alike in personality regardless of how they are reared, with the environment inducing little or no personality resemblance in twin pairs.[100]

Adoption Studies. If the behaviour of adopted children is more similar to their biological parents than to their adoptive parents, the idea of a genetic basis for criminality would be supported. If, however, adoptees are more similar to their adoptive parents than to their biological parents, an environmental basis for crime would seem more valid.

Several studies indicate a relationship between biological parents' behaviour and the behaviour of their children, even with infrequent contact.[101] In the most significant study in this area, 1145 male adoptees born in Copenhagen, Denmark, between 1927 and 1941 were examined; of these, 185 had criminal records.[102] After following up on 143 of the criminal adoptees and matching them with a control group of 143 noncriminal adoptees, Hutchings and Mednick found that the criminality of the biological father was a strong predictor of the child's criminal behaviour. When both the biological and the adoptive fathers were criminal, the probability that the youth would engage in criminal behaviour greatly expanded: 25 percent of the boys whose adoptive and biological fathers were criminals had been convicted of a criminal law violation; only 14 percent of those whose biological and adoptive fathers were not criminals had similar conviction records.[103]

A more recent analysis of Swedish adoptees found that genetic factors were highly significant. Boys who had criminal parents were significantly more likely to violate the law, while environmental influences were significantly less important. Nonetheless, having a positive environment, such as being adopted into a more affluent home, helped inhibit genetic predisposition.[104]

Evaluating Genetic Research. The findings of the twin and adoption studies give some support to a genetic basis for criminality. However, inadequate research designs and weak methodologies undermine the research. Newer, better-designed research studies provide less support than did earlier studies.[105]

It is possible that the apparent genetic effect is actually the effect of sibling influence on criminality, referred to as the contagion effect: Genetic predispositions and early experiences make some people, including twins, susceptible to the deviant behaviour displayed by antisocial siblings in the household.[106] Sibling pairs with warm relationships are most likely to behave similarly; those who maintain a close relationship also have similar rates of drug abuse and delinquency.[107]

These findings can be interpreted in a number of ways:

- Siblings in the same environment are influenced by similar social and economic factors.
- Deviant siblings may grow closer because of shared interests.
- Younger siblings who admire their older siblings may imitate the elder's behaviour.

What seems to be a genetic effect may actually be the result of warm and close sibling interaction.

Contagion may explain the higher concordance of deviant behaviours found in identical twins as compared with fraternal twins or mere siblings. The relationship between identical twins may be more enduring than between other sibling pairs so that contagion and not genetics explains their behavioural similarities. Accordingly, the contagion effect may also explain why the behaviour of twins is more similar in adulthood than adolescence. Youthful misbehaviour is influenced by friends and peer group relationships. As adults, the influence of peers may wane as people marry and find employment. In contrast, twin influence is everlasting; if one twin is antisocial, it legitimizes and supports the criminal behaviour in the co-twin. This effect may grow even stronger in adulthood because twin relations are more enduring than any other. What seems to be a genetic effect may actually be the result of sibling interaction with a brother or sister who engages in antisocial activity.

The genes–crime relationship is controversial since it implies that the propensity to commit crime is present at birth and cannot be altered. It thus raises moral dilemmas. For example, if genetic testing could detect a gene for violence, should a fetus be aborted?

Evolutionary Views of Crime

Recent biosocial research has focused on evolutionary factors in criminality.[108] As human beings have evolved, certain traits have become ingrained and responsible for some crime patterns. Jealousy, for example, is theorized to have developed in ancient times as a way to keep families intact. Women benefit from jealousy because they can keep a provider attached to them, while for men it increases the likelihood that they will reproduce. Aggression is also favoured in evolution, especially for men who benefit from being pro-risk, while women

benefit from being risk-averse. Similar behaviour has been observed in both humans and chimpanzees.[109]

Gender differences in the violence rate have been explained by the evolution of mammalian mating patterns. Hypothetically, to ensure the survival of the gene pool, it is beneficial for a male to mate with as many suitable females as possible. In contrast, because of the long period of gestation, females require a secure home and stable nurturing partner to ensure their survival. Because of these differences in mating patterns, the most aggressive males mate most often and have the greatest number of offspring. However, it is not clear how the offspring survive despite the lack of a stable, nurturing father. Nonetheless, it is felt that the descendants of these aggressive males now account for the disproportionate amount of male aggression and violence.[110]

Two general evolutionary theories of crime are "r/k theory" and the "cheater theory."[111]

InfoTrac®

For a broad overview of evolutionary psychology, read this article on InfoTrac® College Edition: Linnda R. Caporael, "Evolutionary Psychology: Toward a Unifying Theory and a Hybrid Science," *Annual Review of Psychology* 52 (2001): 607–628.

R/K Selection Theory. **R/k theory** holds that all organisms can be located along a continuum based on their reproductive drives in relation to their environment. Those along one end (r-selection individuals) reproduce whenever they can and invest little in their offspring, while those along the other end (k-selection individuals) reproduce slowly and take care in raising their offspring. K-oriented people are more cooperative and sensitive to others, while r-oriented people are more cunning and deceptive. People who commit violent crimes seem to exhibit r-selection traits, such as a premature birth, early and frequent sexual activity, neglect as a child, and a short life expectancy.

This theory is based on the idea that natural selection favours different sets of adaptations. In environments with excess resources, rapid growth and early reproduction are favoured at the expense of competitive ability. In an environment with limited resources, competitive ability is important, even if the tradeoff is slower growth and delayed reproduction. Populations subjected to the first set of forces of boom and bust are called opportunistic populations, in contrast with the more stable equilibrium populations that occur in more constant environments.

"Cheater Theory." Cheater theory suggests that a subpopulation of men has evolved with genes that incline them toward extremely low parental involvement.

Sexually aggressive, they use cunning to secure sexual conquests with as many females as possible. Because females would not willingly choose them as mates, these men use stealth to gain sexual access, such as mimicking the behaviour of more stable males. They use devious means for sexual domination, and their deceptive tactics spill over into areas where their talent for irresponsible, opportunistic behaviour supports their antisocial activities. Deception in reproductive strategies is thus linked to a deceitful lifestyle.

Connections

Researchers have just begun studying the relationship between evolutionary factors and crime, with criminologists exploring how social organizations and institutions interact with biological traits to influence criminal strategies. See the sections on latent trait theories in Chapter 10 for more on the integration of biological and environmental factors.

Cheater males may be especially attractive to younger, less intelligent women, who begin having children at an early age. State-sponsored welfare removes the need for potential mates to have the resources needed to be stable providers. The fleeting courtships that ensue produce children with low IQs, aggressive personalities, and little chance of proper socialization in father-absent families. Because the criminal justice system treats them leniently, sexually irresponsible men are free to prey on young girls. Over time, their offspring will supply an ever-expanding supply of cheaters who are both antisocial and sexually aggressive.

InfoTrac®

For a review of similar takes on evolution and deviant behaviour, go to InfoTrac® College Edition and read "Shotgun Solutions for the Family Crisis: A Survey of Recent Articles," *The Wilson Quarterly* 21, no. 1 (1997): 113–115.

Evaluation of the Biological Branch of Trait Theory

Biosocial perspectives on crime raise some challenging questions for criminology. If biology can explain the cause of street crimes and if poor and minority-group members commit a disproportionate number of such acts, then by implication members of these groups are biologically different, flawed, or inferior.

Connections

Biosocial theory focuses on the violent crimes of the lower classes while ignoring the white-collar crimes of the upper and middle classes. That is, although it seems logical to believe that there is a biological basis to aggression and violence, it is more difficult to explain how insider trading and fraud are biologically related. For the causes of white-collar crime, see Chapter 13.

Biological explanations for the geographic, social, and temporal patterns in the crime rate are also problematic. Is it possible that more people are genetically predisposed to crime in different areas of the country?

Biosocial theorists counter that their views are not deterministic. Rather than suggest that there are born criminals, these researchers believe that some people carry the potential to be violent or antisocial and that environmental conditions can trigger antisocial responses.[112] This would explain why some otherwise law-abiding citizens engage in a single antisocial act and why some people with long criminal careers often engage in conventional behaviour. It also explains why geographic and temporal patterns occur in the crime rate: People who are predisposed to crime may simply have more opportunities to commit illegal acts in the summer in Vancouver and Toronto than in the winter in Gander, Newfoundland.

The biosocial view is that behaviour is a product of interacting biological and environmental events.[113] For example, girls who reach physical maturity at an early age are the ones most likely to engage in delinquent acts, suggesting a relationship between biological traits (hormonal activity) and crime. However, the association may also have an environmental basis. Physically mature girls are the ones most likely to have prolonged contact with a crime-prone group: older adolescent boys.[114] Here, the combination of biological change, social relationships, and routine opportunities predicts crime rates.

The most significant criticism of biosocial theory has been the lack of adequate empirical testing, with small, nonrepresentative samples, such as adjudicated offenders in clinical treatment settings. Methodological problems make it impossible to determine whether findings apply only to offenders who have been convicted of crimes and placed in treatment or to the population of criminals as a whole.[115]

Psychological Trait Theories

The second branch of trait theory focuses on the mental aspects of crime, including the association among intelligence, personality, learning, and criminal behaviour.

In *The English Convict*, Charles Goring (1870–1919) used his "biometric method" to study the characteristics of three thousand English convicts. He found little difference in the physical characteristics of criminals and noncriminals but uncovered a relationship between crime and a condition he called "defective intelligence." Goring believed that criminal behaviour was inherited and could be controlled by regulating the reproduction of families exhibiting such traits as "feeblemindedness, epilepsy, insanity, and defective social instinct."[116]

Gabriel Tarde (1843–1904) used a different psychological approach as the forerunner of modern-day learning theorists.[117] Unlike Goring, who viewed criminals as having a mental impairment, Tarde believed people learn from one another through a process of imitation. Tarde proposed three laws of imitation to describe why people engaged in crime. First, individuals in close and intimate contact imitate one another's behaviour. Second, imitation spreads from the top down; consequently, youngsters imitate older individuals. Crime among young, poor, or low-status people is really their effort to imitate wealthy, older, high-status people (for example, through gambling, drunkenness, accumulation of wealth). Third, new acts and behaviours are superimposed on old ones and either reinforce or discourage previous customs (the law of insertion). For example, drug taking may be a popular fad among university students who previously used alcohol. However, students may find that a combination of both substances provides even greater stimulation, causing the use of both drugs and alcohol to increase. Tarde's ideas are similar to those of modern **social learning** theorists, who believe that both interpersonal and observed behaviour, such as watching a movie or television, can influence criminality.

This section is organized along the lines of the predominant psychological views most closely associated with the cause of criminal behaviour; these perspectives are outlined in Figure 6.2. Some psychologists view antisocial behaviour from a psychoanalytic perspective. Their focus is on early childhood experience and its effect on personality. In contrast, behaviourists stress social learning and behaviour modelling as the keys to criminality. Cognitive theorists analyze human thought and perception and how they affect behaviour. Other psychologists are concerned about the influence of personality or intelligence on behaviour.

Connections

Chapter 1 discussed how some of the early founders of psychiatry tried to develop an understanding of the "criminal mind." Later theories suggested that mental illness and insanity were inherited and that deviants were inherently mentally damaged by reason of their inferior genetic makeup.

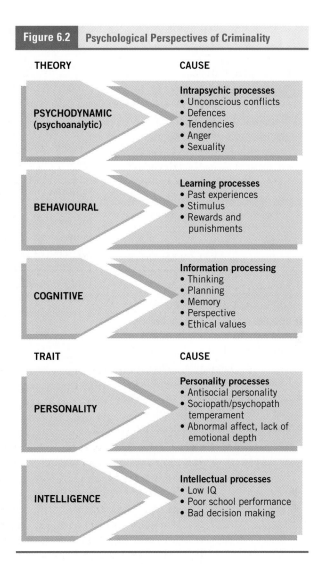

Figure 6.2 **Psychological Perspectives of Criminality**

THEORY — CAUSE

PSYCHODYNAMIC (psychoanalytic) — **Intrapsychic processes**
- Unconscious conflicts
- Defences
- Tendencies
- Anger
- Sexuality

BEHAVIOURAL — **Learning processes**
- Past experiences
- Stimulus
- Rewards and punishments

COGNITIVE — **Information processing**
- Thinking
- Planning
- Memory
- Perspective
- Ethical values

TRAIT — CAUSE

PERSONALITY — **Personality processes**
- Antisocial personality
- Sociopath/psychopath temperament
- Abnormal affect, lack of emotional depth

INTELLIGENCE — **Intellectual processes**
- Low IQ
- Poor school performance
- Bad decision making

Psychodynamic Perspective

Psychodynamic or psychoanalytic psychology was originated by Sigmund Freud (1856–1939) and is still an important psychological theory.[118]

According to **psychodynamic theory**, the human mind performs three separate functions. The conscious mind is the aspect of the mind that people are most aware of—everyday thoughts. The preconscious mind contains elements of experiences that are out of awareness but can be brought back to consciousness at any time—memories, experiences. The unconscious part of the mind contains biological desires and urges that cannot readily be experienced as thoughts. Part of the unconscious contains feelings about sex and hostility, which people keep below the surface of consciousness by a process called **repression**.

Psychodynamic theory also holds that the human personality contains a three-part structure. The id, the primitive part of people's mental makeup, represents

Famous Canadian Criminals

Kenneth Parks, Sleepwalker

In the early morning hours of May 24, 1987, 23-year-old Kenneth Parks drove 23 km and attacked his parents-in-law with a kitchen knife as they lay sleeping. His mother-in-law was killed and his father-in-law seriously injured. Immediately after the incident, Parks went to the police station and told the police, "I just killed someone with my bare hands. Oh, my God, I just killed someone; I've just killed two people; my God, I've just killed two people with my hands; my God, I've just killed two people. My hands; I just killed two people. I killed them; I just killed two people; I've just killed my mother- and father-in-law. I stabbed and beat them to death. It's all my fault."

He claimed to have been sleepwalking during the crime. He had always been a deep sleeper and had a great deal of trouble waking up. Several members of his family also suffered from sleep problems, such as sleepwalking, adult enuresis, nightmares, and sleeptalking. The year before the incident was particularly stressful. He worked 10 hours a day as a project coordinator for Revere Electric. In addition, he had lost money betting on horse racing. When he stole $30 000 from his employer, he was dismissed and charged. His personal life suffered. His parents-in-law, with whom he got on well, were aware of the situation and supported him.

Kenneth Parks was charged with the first-degree murder of Barbara Ann Woods and the attempted murder of Denis Woods. At the trial, he presented a defence of automatism. The testimony of five expert witnesses called by the defence was not contradicted by the Crown. This evidence was that Parks was sleepwalking and that sleepwalking is not a neurological, psychiatric, or other illness. At issue was whether sleepwalking should be classified as non-insane automatism, which would result in an acquittal, or as a "disease of the mind" (insane automatism), leading to a special verdict of not guilty by reason of insanity. The trial judge presented only the defence of automatism to the jury, who acquitted Parks of first-degree murder and then of second-degree murder. The judge then acquitted Parks of attempted murder. Two subsequent appeals upheld his acquittals.

unconscious biological drives for sex, food, and other life-sustaining necessities. The id follows the pleasure principle, requiring instant gratification without concern for the rights of others. The ego develops early in life, when a child learns that wants cannot be instantly gratified. The ego compensates for the demands of the id by helping the individual guide his or her actions to remain within the boundaries of social convention. The superego develops as a result of incorporating within the personality the moral standards and values of parents, community, and significant others. This moral aspect of personality passes judgments on their behaviour.

Human Development. The most basic human drive present at birth is eros, the instinct to preserve and create life, which is expressed sexually. Consequently, early in their development humans experience the seeking of pleasure through the body. During the first year of life, a child attains pleasure by sucking and biting: the oral stage. During the second and third years of life, the focus of sexual attention is on the elimination of bodily wastes: the anal stage. The phallic stage occurs during ages four and five, as children focus their attention on their genitals. Males begin to have sexual feelings for their mother (the Oedipus complex) and girls for their father (the Electra complex). The latency stage begins at age six, and during this period, feelings of sexuality are repressed until the genital stage begins at puberty, which marks the beginning of adult sexuality.

If conflicts are encountered during any of these psychosexual stages of development, a person can become fixated. For example, an infant who does not receive enough oral gratification during the first year of life is likely as an adult to engage in smoking, drinking, or drug abuse, or to be clinging and dependent in personal relationships. Thus, the root of adult behaviour problems can be traced to problems developed in the earliest years of life.

Psychodynamics of Abnormal Behaviour. According to the psychodynamic perspective, people who experience feelings of mental anguish and are afraid they are losing control of their personalities have a **neurosis**. Those people who have lost total control and who are dominated by their primitive id suffer from **psychosis**, with behaviour marked by bizarre episodes, hallucinations, and inappropriate responses. According to the psychodynamic view, the most serious types of antisocial behaviour, such as murder, might be motivated by psychosis, while neurotic feelings would be responsible for less serious delinquent acts and status offences, such as petty theft and truancy.

Psychosis takes many forms. The most common is **schizophrenia**, in which persons exhibit illogical and incoherent thought processes and a lack of insight into their behaviour. They may experience delusions and hallucinate, for example, seeing themselves as agents of the devil, avenging angels, or the recipients of messages from animals and plants. David Berkowitz, the "Son of Sam," exhibited these traits when he claimed that his killing spree began when he received messages from a neighbour's dog. Paranoid schizophrenics also suffer complex delusions involving wrongdoing or persecution, and they think everyone is out to get them. In a study of 50 stalkers, psychotic illness was associated with the stalking of strangers (see Table 6.2). Almost three-quarters of those who stalked strangers and acquaintances had a psychotic illness, while only 20 percent of those who were former sexual intimates were psychotic. Although there was no relationship between serious violence and psychosis, there was a strong relationship between violence and former sexual intimacy, as shown in Table 6.2.[119]

In 1994, Ralph Tortorici, brandishing a high-calibre rifle, walked into a classroom at the State University of New York and held the class hostage. In a dramatic example of the link between schizophrenia and crime, he was clearly delusional and psychotic. This sort of offender should be treated in a hospital, but he was committed to jail, where he eventually committed suicide.

Medical research shows that schizophrenia is also related to urban living, with birth cohort studies showing that the incidence of schizophrenia is twice as high in cities than anywhere else and that the incidence increases with city size. Where a person is born and brought up is a larger contributing factor to risk than is genetic predisposition: 35 percent of schizophrenia cases would be prevented if people were not brought up in cities, compared with 5 percent of cases that would

be prevented if people did not have parents or siblings who had the illness.[120]

Connections

See the Famous Canadian Court Case later in the chapter for an interesting case of criminality and paranoid schizophrenia.

Psychosis and Crime. Freud did not theorize much about crime, but he linked criminality to the unconscious sense of guilt a person retains because of an Oedipus complex or Electra complex. He believed that in criminals, especially youthful ones, guilt that existed before the crime is not the result of crime but its motive. It is as if the person is relieved to be able to fasten the unconscious sense of guilt onto something real and immediate.[121]

Psychologists have used psychoanalytic concepts to link criminality to abnormal mental states produced by early childhood trauma. Alfred Adler (1870–1937), the founder of individual psychology, used "**inferiority complex**" to describe people who compensate for feelings of inferiority by controlling others. Erik Erikson (1902–1984) identified the **identity crisis**—a period of serious personal questioning that young people undertake in an effort to determine their own values and sense of direction. Adolescents undergoing an identity crisis might exhibit out-of-control behaviour and experiment with drugs and other forms of deviance.

The psychoanalyst most closely associated with criminality is August Aichorn.[122] After examining many delinquent youths, he concluded that societal stress could not result in a life of crime unless a predisposition existed that prepared youths psychologically for antisocial acts. This mental state, called **latent delinquency**, is found in youngsters whose personality requires them (1) to seek immediate gratification (to act impulsively), (2) to consider satisfaction of their personal needs more important than relating to others, and (3) to satisfy instinctive urges without consideration of right and wrong (that is, they lack guilt).

Table 6.2   Violence, Psychosis, and Relationship to Victim of Stalkers

	Strangers	Acquaintances	Former sexual intimates
Serious violence	25%	28%	78%
Psychotic illness	75%	72%	12%
Total = 50	subtotal = 12	subtotal = 18	subtotal = 18

Source: Frank R. Farnham, David V. James, and Paul Cantrell, "Association between Violence, Psychosis, and Relationship to Victim in Stalkers," *The Lancet*, January 15, 2000: 199. Reprinted by permission of Elsevier Science.

InfoTrac®

The following article discusses the relationship between mental disorder (specifically schizophrenia) and violent criminal behaviour: "A Ten-Year Follow-up of Criminality in Stockholm Mental Patients: New Evidence for a Relationship Between Mental Disorder and Crime," *British Journal of Criminology* 38, no. 1 (1998): 145–156.

Psychodynamics of Criminal Behaviour. Since this early work, psychoanalysts have viewed the criminal as an id-dominated person who suffers from the inability to control impulsive, pleasure-seeking drives.[123] Perhaps because they suffered unhappy experiences in childhood or had families that could not provide proper love and care, criminals suffer from weak or damaged egos that make them unable to cope with conventional society. Weak egos are associated with immaturity, poor social skills, excessive dependence on others, and being easily led by antisocial peers into crime and drug abuse. Some offenders have undeveloped superegos and consequently commit crimes because they have difficulty understanding the wrongfulness of their actions.[124]

Personality conflict or underdevelopment may result in neurotic or psychotic behaviour patterns.[125] Offenders classified as neurotics have an unconscious desire to be punished for prior sins and violate the law to gain attention or punishment from their parents. In its most extreme form, criminality is viewed as a form of psychosis that prevents offenders from appreciating the feelings of victims or controlling their own impulsive needs for gratification.

Crime is a manifestation of feelings of oppression and the inability of people to develop the proper defence mechanisms to keep these feelings under control. Criminality actually allows troubled people to survive by producing positive psychic results: It helps them feel free and independent, gives them excitement and the chance to use their skills and imagination, provides them with positive gain, allows them to blame others for their predicament, and allows them to rationalize their sense of failure ("If I hadn't gotten into trouble, I could have been a success").

The psychodynamic model of the criminal offender depicts an aggressive, frustrated person dominated by events that occurred early in childhood.

Behavioural Theories

Behaviour theory maintains that human actions are developed through learning experiences. Rather than focus on unconscious personality traits or biological predispositions, behaviour theorists are concerned with what people do during their daily lives. The major premise is that people alter their behaviour according to the reactions they receive from others—rewards and punishments. Behaviour is constantly being shaped by life experiences, and crimes are learned responses to life situations that do not necessarily represent abnormal or morally immature responses.

Social learning theorists, such as Albert Bandura, argue that people are not actually born with the ability to act violently but learn to be aggressive.[126] These experiences include personally observing others acting aggressively to achieve some goal or watching people being rewarded for violent acts in the media. People learn to act aggressively when, as children, they model their behaviour after the violent acts of adults. Later in life, these patterns persist in social relationships. The boy who sees his father repeatedly strike his mother is more likely to grow up to become a battering parent and husband.

Although mental or physical traits may predispose a person to violence, the activation of a person's violent tendencies is achieved by environmental factors. The specific forms that aggressive behaviour takes, its frequency, the situations in which it is displayed, and the specific targets selected for attack are largely determined by social learning. An adolescent who spends a weekend in jail for drunk driving may find it a lesson about not drinking and driving; another may find it an exciting experience to brag about to his friends.

This process of learning is called **behaviour modelling**. Studies of family life show that children who use aggressive tactics have parents who use similar behaviours when dealing with others. A second influence on the social learning of violence is provided by environmental experiences. People who live in areas where violence is a daily occurrence are more likely to act violently than those who dwell in low-crime areas that stress conventional behaviour. A third source of behaviour modelling is the mass media, which commonly depicts violence graphically, and as acceptable behaviour, especially for heroes who never have to face legal consequences for their actions. For example, David Phillips found that the homicide rate increases significantly immediately after a heavyweight championship prizefight, which models the acceptability of violent behaviour.[127]

What triggers violent acts? One idea is that a direct, pain-producing physical assault will usually trigger a violent response. Yet the relationship between painful attacks and aggressive responses is inconsistent. Whether people counterattack in the face of physical attack depends in part on their fighting skill and their perception of their attacker's strength. Verbal taunts and insults are also linked to aggressive responses. People who are predisposed to aggression by their learning experiences are likely to view insults from others as a challenge to their social status and to react with violence. Still another violence-triggering mechanism is a perceived reduction in life conditions. Prime examples of this phenomenon are riots and demonstrations in poverty-stricken areas. Discontent produces aggression in members of lower-class groups who have been led to believe they can succeed but who cannot now succeed. This relationship is complex. No matter how deprived some individuals are, they will not resort to violence. People's perceptions of their position have differing effects on their aggressive responses.

In summary, social learning theorists have said that the following four factors help produce violence and aggression:

1. An event that heightens arousal, such as being provoked through physical assault or verbal abuse
2. Aggressive skills learned from observing others, either personally or through the media
3. Expected outcomes, or the belief that aggression will be rewarded, either in money, reduced tension or anger, enhanced self-esteem, or the praise of others
4. Consistency of behaviour with values, or the belief that aggression is justified and appropriate, given the circumstances of the current situation

Percentage of Canadians

Two-thirds of Canadians say they rely mostly on television for accurate news and information, while approximately one in ten opts for radio or daily newspapers.

Source: Poll conducted by Ipsos Reid, May 13, 2003.

Cognitive Theory

One area of psychology that has received increasing recognition in recent years has been the **cognitive school**. Cognitive psychologists focus on how people perceive the world and solve problems. Pioneers of this school were Wilhelm Wundt (1832–1920), Edward Titchener (1867–1927), and William James (1842–1920). Today, there are several subareas within the cognitive area. For example, the moral development branch is concerned about the way people morally reason about the world, while the information-processing branch focuses on the way people process, store, encode, retrieve, and manipulate information to make decisions and solve problems.

Moral and Intellectual Development Theory. The moral and intellectual development branch of cognitive psychology is identified with Jean Piaget (1896–1980), who hypothesized that people's reasoning processes develop in an orderly fashion, beginning from birth.[128] At first, during the sensorimotor stage, children respond to the environment in a simple manner, seeking interesting objects and developing their reflexes. By the fourth and final stage, the formal operations stage, they have developed into mature adults who can use logic and abstract thought.

Lawrence Kohlberg applied the concept of moral development to criminology.[129] He found that people travel through stages of moral development, during which decisions on issues of right and wrong are based on different reasoning, with serious offenders having a moral orientation that differs from that of law-abiding citizens. Kohlberg's stages of development are:

Stage 1:   Right is obedience to power and avoidance of punishment.

Stage 2:   Right is taking responsibility for yourself, meeting your own needs and leaving to others the responsibility for themselves.

Stage 3:   Right is being good in the sense of having good motives, having concern for others, and putting yourself in the other person's shoes.

Stage 4:   Right is maintaining the rules of society and serving the welfare of the group or society.

Stage 5:   Right is based on recognized individual rights within a society with agreed-on rules—a social contract.

Stage 6:   Right is an assumed obligation to principles applying to all humankind—principles of justice, equality, and respect for human life.

As we can see, a person is classified at different levels of increasing abstraction, extending personal rights to others, and then to all society. In studies conducted by

Culture, Gender, Ethnicity, and Criminology

The Media and Violence

In 1995, thieves ignited flammable liquid in a New York City subway token booth, seriously injuring the clerk. The crime was virtually identical to a robbery scene in the film *Money Train*, which had been released a few days before.

Whether broadcast violence causes aggressive behaviour in viewers is a hot topic. Critics have called for drastic measures, from banning TV violence to putting warning labels on heavy metal albums out of the fear that listening to hard-rock lyrics produces delinquency.

If a TV–violence link exists, then the problem is an alarming one, given the amount of television that young people watch. Viewing of TV begins at age two and a half and continues at a high level during the preschool and early school years. It is estimated that children aged 2 to 5 watch TV for 28 hours per week; children aged 6 to 11, watch 24 hours per week; and teens watch 23 hours per week. Marketing research says adolescents aged 11 to 14 rent violent horror movies at a higher rate than any other age group, even gaining access to R-rated films. Most households have cable TV, which airs violent films and shows. Even children's programming is saturated with violence. The average child views eight thousand TV murders before finishing elementary school.

The fact that kids watch so much violent TV is not surprising. A study in 1995 said that of 161 television movies monitored (every one that aired that season), 23 raised concerns about the use of violence, a violent theme, a violent title, or the inappropriate graphic nature of a scene. Of the 118 theatrical films monitored (all that aired that season), 50 raised concerns about their use of violence.

Even some children's television shows feature "sinister combat" as the theme. The characters are happy to fight and do so with little provocation. One study found children's programming contained an average of 32 violent acts per hour, 56 percent had violent characters, and 74 percent had characters who became the victims of violence.

In 1977 Ronald Zamora killed an elderly woman and then pleaded not guilty by reason of insanity. His attorney claimed that Zamora was addicted to TV violence and could no longer differentiate between reality and fantasy, but Zamora was found guilty. At least 43 deaths have been linked to the movie *The Deer Hunter*, which featured a scene in which a main character kills himself while playing Russian roulette for money.

John Hinckley Jr. shot then–U.S. President Ronald Reagan as a result of his obsession with actress Jodie Foster, after he watched her in the movie *Taxi Driver*. Hinckley had viewed the film at least 15 times. In October 1993, a five-year-old Ohio boy set a fire that caused the death of his two-year-old sister. The boy's mother charged that the youth had been influenced by the MTV show *Beavis and Butt-Head*, whose cartoon heroes started fires and chanted, "Fire is good." MTV responded to the public outcry by moving the show's broadcast time to 10:30 p.m. A national survey conducted in the wake of the controversy found that almost 80 percent of the public believes that violence on TV can cause violence in real life.

Psychologists believe that media violence does not in itself cause violent behaviour, because if it did, there would be millions of incidents in which viewers imitated aggression seen in the media. The concern is that media violence contributes to aggression. There are several explanations for the effects of television and film violence on behaviour:

- Media violence can provide aggressive "scripts" that children store in memory. Repeated exposure can lead to changes in attitudes and to aggressive behaviour.
- Observational learning occurs when violence seen on television is copied by children, who learn to be violent in the same way as they learn behaviours from parents and friends.
- Television violence increases the arousal levels of viewers, making them more prone to act aggressively. The galvanic skin response of subjects, based on electricity conducted across skin, shows that viewing violent shows led to increased arousal levels.
- Television violence promotes attitudinal and behavioural changes by promoting positive attitudes toward aggression when violence is socially acceptable.
- Television violence helps already aggressive youths justify their behaviour as a socially acceptable and common activity.
- Television violence disinhibits aggressive behaviour, normally controlled by other learning processes, when adults are rewarded for violence that is socially acceptable.

In experiments, subjects are exposed to media and compared with control groups, or observations are made in playgrounds, athletic fields, and residences. Other experiments require subjects to answer attitude surveys after watching violent TV shows. In some cases, longitudinal surveys are employed.

A follow-up study of 557 children originally interviewed in 1977 found that childhood exposure to television violence was more likely to result in physical aggression in adulthood. Other factors, such as childhood neglect, family income, neighbourhood violence, parental education and psychiatric disorders, are significant as well and may well undermine the media–violence link.

Most evaluations of experimental data indicate that watching violence on TV is correlated with aggressive behaviours or at least has a short-term impact on behaviour. Subjects who view violent TV shows are likely to begin aggressive behaviour almost immediately.

Although this evidence is persuasive, some critics argue that the evidence does not support the claim that watching TV or movies and listening to heavy metal music is related to antisocial behaviour.

Millions of children watch violence every night yet fail to become violent criminals. If violent TV shows cause interpersonal violence, there should be few ecological and regional patterns in the crime rate. How can regional differences in the violence rate be explained when people all across the nation watch the same TV shows and films?

Critics also assert that experimental results are short-lived. People may have an immediate reaction to viewing violence on TV, but aggression quickly ends. Experiments that show a correlation between aggression and TV fail to link the association with actual criminal behaviours, such as rape or assault. Experimental results indicate that violent media have an immediate impact on people with a preexisting tendency toward crime and violence. But do kids who act more aggressively after watching violent TV later grow up to become rapists and killers?

Violent TV shows can be controlled with government regulations that limit the content of programs or restrict times that violent shows are aired. The TV and film industries now place advisory warnings on shows that have objectionable content, and parents can purchase a "V-Chip" to screen out violent or objectionable programming on television. Although such practices help guide parents, they do little to restrict TV watching when children are home alone.

When the local football team wins, violent assaults on women increase; sports dominance may trigger feelings of power and control, which results in sexual aggression in males. This research received nationwide attention and prompted antibattering public service announcements during the 1997 Super Bowl. If such findings are valid, it is unlikely that those concerned with media violence can engineer a ban of pro football games on television.

A new crime–media concern is video games and whether violent games are linked to aggressive behaviours. In one study of 607 students in grades 8 and 9, adolescents who played violent video games were generally more hostile, got into fights and arguments more, and performed more poorly in school. A study of 150 students in grades 4 and 5 found that exposure to video game violence was associated with lower empathy and stronger proviolence attitudes, higher than the measure for any media, except movies. The intense engagement involved in playing violent video games leads to the automatic learning of aggressive self-views, acceptance of norms condoning physical aggression, cardiovascular arousal, and decreases in helping behaviour.

 InfoTrac®

The first article looks at the media's positive influence rather than the negative: Jane Rosenzweig, "Can TV Improve Us?" *The American Prospect* (July 1999): 58.

The other two debate whether media violence is actually desired by the public:

- James T. Hamilton, "The Market for Television Violence," *National Forum* 80, no. 4 (2000): 15.
- Cheri W. Sparks and Glenn G. Sparks, "Why Do Hollywood and TV Keep Showing Us Violence?" *USA Today*, January 2001, 56.

Sources: UCLA Center for Communication Policy, *Television Violence Monitoring Project* (Los Angeles, CA, 1995); Associated Press, "Hollywood Is Blamed in Token Booth Attack," *Boston Globe,*

November 28, 1995; Garland White, Janet Katz, and Kathryn Scarborough, "The Impact of Professional Football Games upon Violent Assaults on Women," *Violence and Victims* 7 (1992): 157–71; Simon Singer, "Rethinking Subcultural Theories of Delinquency and the Cultural Resources of Youth," paper presented at the annual meeting of the American Society of Criminology, Phoenix, Arizona, November 1993; Albert Reiss and Jeffrey Roth, eds., *Understanding and Preventing Violence* (Washington, D.C.: National Academy Press, 1993); Reuters, "Seventy-Nine Percent in Survey Link Violence on TV and Crime," *Boston Globe,* December 19, 1993; Scott Snyder, "Movies and Juvenile Delinquency: An Overview," *Adolescence* 26 (1991): 121–31; Steven Messner, "Television Violence and Violent

Crime: An Aggregate Analysis," *Social Problems* 33 (1986): 218–35; Candace Kruttschnitt, Linda Heath, and David Ward, "Family Violence, Television Viewing Habits, and Other Adolescent Experiences Related to Violent Criminal Behaviour," *Criminology* 243 (1986): 235–67; Jonathan Freedman, "Television Violence and Aggression: A Rejoinder," *Psychological Bulletin* 100 (1986): 372–78; Wendy Wood, Frank Wong, and J. Gregory Chachere, "Effects of Media Violence on Viewers' Aggression in Unconstrained Social Interaction," *Psychological Bulletin* 109 (1991): 371–83; Craig A. Anderson, "An Update on the Effects of Playing Violent Video Games," *Journal of Adolescence* 27 (2004): 113–22; Barbara Krahe and Ingrid Moller, "Playing Violent Electronic Games, Hostile

Attributional Style, and Aggression-Related Norms in German Adolescents," *Journal of Adolescence* 27 (2004): 53–69; Erica Uhlmann and Jane Swanson, "Exposure to Violent Video Games Increases Automatic Aggressiveness," *Journal of Adolescence* 27 (2004): 41–52; Jeanne B. Funk, Heidi Bechtoldt Baldacci, Tracie Pasold, and Jennifer Baumgardner, "Violent Exposure in Real-Life, Video Games, Television, Movies, and the Internet: Is There Desensitization?" *Journal of Adolescence* 27 (2004): 23–39; Douglas A. Gentile, Paul J. Lynch, Jennifer Ruh Linder, and David A. Walsh, "The Effects of Violent Video Game Habits on Adolescent Hostility, Aggressive Behaviors, and School Performance," *Journal of Adolescence* 27 (2004): 5–22.

Kohlberg, criminals were found to be significantly lower in their moral judgment development than were noncriminals of the same social background.[130] Since Kohlberg's pioneering efforts, researchers have continued to show that criminal offenders are more likely to be classified in the lowest levels of moral reasoning (stages 1 and 2), while noncriminals have reached a higher stage of moral development.

Research indicates that the decision not to commit crimes may be influenced by a person's stage of moral development. People at the lowest levels report that they are deterred from crime because of their fear of sanctions; those in the middle consider the reactions of family and friends; those at the highest stages believe in a duty to others and universal rights.[131]

Moral development theory suggests that people who obey the law simply to avoid punishment or who have outlooks mainly characterized by self-interest are more likely to commit crimes than are those who view the law as something that benefits all of society and who sympathize with the rights of others. Higher stages of moral reasoning are associated with conventional behaviours, such as honesty, generosity, and nonviolence.

Information Processing. When cognitive theorists who study information processing try to explain antisocial behaviour, they do so in terms of perception and analysis of data. When people make decisions, they engage in a sequence of thought processes. They first encode information so that it can be interpreted, search for a proper response and decide on the most appropriate action, and, finally, they act on their decision.[132]

Connections

The deterrent effect of informal sanctions and feelings of shame discussed in Chapter 5 may hinge on the level of a person's moral development. The lower the person's state of moral development, the less impact informal sanctions may have. If moral development increases, informal sanctions may be better able to control crime.

According to this approach, violence-prone people may be using information incorrectly when they make decisions. They may be relying on mental "scripts" learned in childhood that tell them how to interpret events, what to expect, how they should react, and what the outcome of the interaction should be.[133] Hostile children may have learned improper scripts by observing how others react to events and acting out their own parents' aggressive and inappropriate behaviour. Violence becomes a stable behaviour because the scripts that emphasize aggressive responses are repeatedly rehearsed as the child matures.

Violence-prone kids see people as more aggressive than they actually are and as intending them ill when there is no reason for alarm. As these children mature, they use fewer cues than do most people to process information. Some use violence in a calculating fashion as a means of getting what they want; others react in an overly volatile fashion to the slightest provocation. Aggressors are more likely to be vigilant, on edge, or suspicious. When they attack victims, they may believe they are defending themselves, even though they are misreading the situation.[134]

Does playing video games cause kids to act aggressively? Although laboratory observations suggest a media–violence link, there is less evidence that such an association occurs in the real world. Millions of kids play video games every day, yet few become violent criminals. It is possible, however, that playing violent video games can reinforce a predisposition to aggressive behaviour.

Recent research on cognitive processes in sexual assault has found that rapists lack empathy toward their victims but not toward the women who are sexually abused by other offenders. This works as a refusal to recognize the harm they are inflicting.[135]

Information-processing theory has been used to explain date rape. Sexually violent males believe that when their dates say no to sexual advances, the women are really "playing games" and actually want to be taken forcefully.[136] This type of attitude is self-justifying, of course.

Treatment based on information processing acknowledges that people are more likely to respond aggressively to a provocation when thoughts intensify the insult or otherwise stir feelings of anger. Cognitive therapists teach explosive people to control aggressive impulses by viewing social provocations as problems demanding a solution rather than as insults requiring retaliation. Problem-solving skills may include listening, following instructions, joining in, and using self-control. Treatment interventions based on learning social skills are relatively new, but this approach can have long-term benefits for reducing criminal behaviour.

Mental Illness and Crime

Each school of psychology has a unique approach to the concept of mental abnormality. Psychoanalysts view mental illness as a retreat from unbearable stress and conflict; cognitive psychologists link it to thought disorders and overstimulation; behavioural theorists might look to environmental influences, such as early family experiences and social rejection. Regardless of the cause of mental illness, is there a link between it and crime?

A recent survey of more than six thousand adults in 14 countries found that mental ailments affect more than 10 percent of people queried in more than half the countries surveyed. Treatment rates ranged from 64 percent in developed countries to only 15 percent in developing countries. In Canada, it's estimated that 20 percent of children are experiencing emotional problems requiring treatment. The most common ailments were anxiety disorders and posttraumatic stress disorders. Unfortunately, if left untreated, the criminal justice system becomes the avenue into the health system.[137]

A great deal of early research efforts found that many offenders who engage in serious, violent crimes suffer from some sort of mental disturbance. Sorrells's study of juvenile murderers found that many homicidal youths were hostile, explosive, anxious, and depressed.[138] Likewise, in a study of 45 males accused of murder, Rosner found 75 percent could be classified as having some form of mental illness, including schizophrenia.[139] Abusive mothers have been found to have mood and personality disorders and a history of psychiatric diagnoses.[140]

There is some indication that those who are diagnosed as having a mental illness are more likely to violate the law than are those who do not have a mental illness. Substance abuse among people with mental illnesses is significantly higher than among the general population.[141] Furthermore, people with diagnosed mental illnesses appear in arrest and court statistics at a rate disproportionate to their presence in the population.[142]

However, the question remains whether people with mental illnesses are any more criminal than those without mental illnesses. They may be more likely to withdraw or harm themselves than to act aggressively toward others.[143] Prisoners who had prior histories of hospitalization for mental disorders were less likely to be rearrested than were those who had never been hospitalized.[144] The great majority of known criminals do not have a mental illness.

This research gives only tentative support to the proposition that mental disturbance or illness can be an underlying cause of violent crime. However, certain symptoms of mental illness are connected to violence, including the feelings that others are wishing the person harm, that his or her mind is dominated by forces beyond that person's control, and that thoughts are being put into his or her head by others.[145] People who have other psychological disorders, such as substance abuse, psychopathy, and neuroticism, are the ones most at risk for chronic criminal behaviour.[146]

It is also possible that the link between mental illness and crime is spurious and an artifact of structural factors: people with mental illnesses often lack the financial resources to live in affluent areas and are therefore more likely to reside in deteriorated, high-crime neighbourhoods, which are linked to violence (see Chapter 7).[147] Living in a stress-filled, urban environment may produce both symptoms of mental illness and crime.[148] It is also possible that a lack of resources may inhibit the mentally ill from obtaining the proper treatment, which would result in reduced criminality. For example, in a recent comparison of patients with mental illness who received outpatient treatment and an untreated comparison group, treatment significantly reduced the probability of arrest (12 percent versus 45 percent).[149] Interest in this topic continues to influence research.

Personality and Crime

Personality can be defined as the reasonably stable patterns of behaviour, thoughts, and emotions that distinguish one person from another. Personality reflects a characteristic way of adapting to life's demands and problems. The way people behave is a function of how their personality enables them to interpret life events and make appropriate behavioural choices. The issue of whether crime can be linked to personality has always caused significant debate.[150] In their early work, the Gluecks identified a number of personality traits that they believed characterized antisocial youth:[151]

self-assertiveness	sadism
defiance	lack of concern for others
extroversion	feelings of being unappreciated
ambivalence	distrust of authority
impulsiveness	poor personal skills
narcissism	mental instability
suspicion	hostility
destructiveness	resentment

Several other research efforts have attempted to identify criminal personality traits.[152] Suspected traits include impulsivity, hostility, and aggressiveness.[153] Hans Eysenck identified two personality traits associated with antisocial behaviour: extroversion-introversion and stability-instability. Extreme introverts are overaroused and avoid sources of stimulation, while extreme extroverts are unaroused and seek sensation. Introverts are slow to learn and be conditioned; extroverts are impulsive individuals who lack the ability to examine their own motives and behaviours. Those with neuroticism are anxious, tense, and emotionally unstable.[154] People who are both neurotic and extroverted lack self-insight, are impulsive and emotionally unstable, and are unlikely to have reasoned judgments of life events. While extrovert neurotics may act self-destructively—for example, by abusing drugs—more-stable people will be able to reason that such behaviour is ultimately harmful and life threatening. Eysenck believes that the direction of the personality is controlled by genetic factors and is heritable.

In a recent study evaluating the most widely used measures of personality, agreeableness and conscientiousness seem to be most closely related to antisocial behaviours. *Agreeableness* involves the ability to use appropriate interpersonal strategies when dealing with others; *conscientiousness* involves a person's ability to control impulses, carry out plans and tasks, maintain organizational skills, and follow an internal moral code. Personality researchers now link antisocial behaviours to such traits as hostility, self-centredness, spitefulness, jealousy, and indifference to others. Law violators tend to lack ambition, motivation, and perseverance; have difficulty controlling their impulses; and hold unconventional values and beliefs. These personality traits are linked to crime, but there is still some question about the direction of the linkage. On the one hand, it is possible that people who share these personality traits are programmed to commit crimes. On the other hand, it is possible that personality traits interact with environmental factors to alter behaviour. For example, kids who are low in conscientiousness will most likely have poor educational and occupational histories, which limit their opportunity for advancement; this blocked opportunity renders them crime-prone.[155]

Other personality deficits in criminals include hyperactivity, impulsiveness, short attention spans, conduct disorders, anxiety disorders, and depression. These traits make criminals prone to problems ranging from psychopathology and drug abuse to sexual promiscuity and violence.[156] As a group, people who share these traits are believed to have a character defect referred to as the antisocial, sociopathic, or psychopathic personality. Although these terms are often used interchangeably, some psychologists do distinguish between sociopaths and psychopaths by suggesting that the former are a product of a destructive home environment, while the latter are a product of a defect or aberration within themselves.[157]

 InfoTrac®

To learn more about personality traits as predictors of delinquency, look for Jan ter Caak, Nartijn de Goede, Liesbeth Aleva, and Gerald Bauman, "Incarcerated Girls: Personality, Social Competence and Delinquency," *Adolescence* 38, no. 150 (2003): 251–265.

The Antisocial Personality. Some, but not all, serious violent offenders may have a disturbed character structure commonly called **psychopathy, sociopathy,** or **antisocial personality.** Psychopaths have a low level of guilt and anxiety and persistently violate the rights of others. Although they may exhibit superficial charm and above-average intelligence, this surface often masks a disturbed personality that makes them incapable of forming enduring relationships with others and continually involves them in such deviant behaviours as violence, risk taking, substance abuse, and impulsivity.

Connections

The Glueck research is representative of the view that antisocial people maintain a distinct set of personal traits that makes them particularly sensitive to environmental stimuli. Once dismissed by mainstream criminologists, the Gluecks' views, reviewed in Chapter 10's section of life-course theories, still influence contemporary criminological theory.

From an early age, the psychopath's home life is filled with frustrations, bitterness, and quarrelling. Consequently, throughout life, he or she is unreliable, unstable, demanding, and egocentric. Psychopaths are risk-taking sensation seekers who are constantly involved in a variety of antisocial behaviours. They have been described as grandiose, egocentric, manipulative, forceful, and cold-hearted, with shallow emotions and the inability to feel empathy with others, remorse, or anxiety over their misdeeds. They are also able to rationalize their behaviour so that it appears warranted, reasonable, and justified.

Psychopaths are cold-blooded, planning their murders out carefully. The acts are seldom spontaneous, and the killer is more likely to use excessive force. The psychopath is at a higher risk of reoffending than the nonpsychopath and will benefit the least from anger management. If they are not classified as dangerous offenders, then there is serious risk to the public when they are released.

Considering these personality traits, it is not surprising that studies show that psychopaths are significantly more criminal prone and that psychopaths continue their criminal careers long after other offenders burn out or age out of crime. Psychopaths are continually in trouble with the law and therefore are likely to wind up in penal institutions. It has been estimated that up to 30 percent of all inmates can be classified as psychopaths or sociopaths, but a more realistic figure is probably 10 percent; not all psychopaths become criminals, and, conversely, most criminals are not psychopaths.

 InfoTrac®

- Multisystemic therapy is being used to provide effective treatment for a growing number of antisocial youth in New Zealand: Nicola Curtis et al., "Antisocial Behaviours in New Zealand Youth: Prevalence, Interventions and Promising New Directions," *New Zealand Journal of Psychology* 31, no. 2 (2002): 53–58.
- Drug dependent adults in the following study report a history of antisocial dependency: "Antisocial Tendency Among Drug-Addicted Adults: Potential Long-Term Effects of Parental Absence, Support, and Conflict During Childhood," *American Journal of Drug and Alcohol Abuse* 24, no. 3 (1998): 361–375.

What Causes Psychopathy? Psychologists think a number of factors contribute to the development of a psychopathic or sociopathic personality: an unstable parent, parental rejection, lack of love during childhood, and inconsistent discipline. Early childhood experiences seem quite important. Children who lack the opportunity to form an attachment to a mother figure in the first three years of life, who suffer sudden separation from the mother figure, or who see changes in the mother figure are the most likely to develop sociopathic personalities. Psychopathy may also be related to personal traits. Children with AD/HD are more likely to experience conduct problems in childhood.

Psychopaths may also suffer from lower than normal levels of arousal. If psychopathy is caused by damage to the frontal and temporal lobes, psychopaths may need greater-than-average stimulation to bring them up to comfortable levels (similar to arousal theory). Antisocial individuals are often sensation seekers who desire pleasure, an extroverted lifestyle, drinking, and a variety of sexual partners. The desire for this stimulation may originate in their physical differences.

Psychopaths have a "low fear quotient" that inhibits their fear of punishment. All people have a natural or innate fear of certain stimuli—spiders, snakes, fires, strangers. Psychopaths fall on the low end of the fearfulness continuum. Since the normal socialization process depends on the current punishment of antisocial behaviour, someone who does not fear punishment is harder to socialize.

Psychopaths also have ineffective coping mechanisms for dealing with negative stimuli and are less capable of regulating their activities. Although nonpsychopaths may become anxious and afraid when facing the prospect of

Famous Canadian Court Case

Andre Dallaire

The tale of Andre Dallaire's dramatic encounter with former prime minister Jean Chrétien and his wife is a strange one. Early one November morning in 1995, Aline Chrétien found a knife-wielding intruder in an upstairs hallway at 24 Sussex Drive. After quickly retreating to the bedroom she shared with her husband, Aline locked the doors and alerted the prime minister. Chrétien armed himself with a soapstone carving until RCMP officers arrested the trespasser.

This unprecedented security breach was not only shocking but also incredibly embarrassing for the Mounties. Remaining undetected by the officers responsible for Chrétien's safety, Dallaire roamed the government property and its perimeter for more than three hours before his confrontation with Aline. Although he likened himself to James Bond, this 34-year-old Montreal convenience store clerk's not-so-stealthy tactics included tripping alarms, waving at surveillance cameras, and hurling rocks at windows. He even paused to tour the prime minister's home before deciding to resume his mission to slit Chrétien's throat. Dallaire relented when Aline locked him out of the couple's bedroom; he laid his knife on the floor and sat down to wait for the RCMP.

Dallaire was charged with four criminal charges: break and enter, being unlawfully in a dwelling, possession of a weapon, and attempted murder. The motives of this would-be assassin were initially thought to be political. A sovereignty referendum had been held in Quebec just a week before the incident, and Dallaire had vanished from his home and job two days after the narrow separatist loss. In his statements to police, Dallaire described Chrétien as a traitor to Quebeckers and remarked that he would have acquired hero status for slaying the prime minister. Following a preliminary psychiatric evaluation, Dallaire was deemed fit to stand trial. However, acknowledging the defendant's history of mental health issues, a judge released Dallaire into the care of the Royal Ottawa Hospital while awaiting trial. He was transferred to a group home when his condition stabilized.

At Dallaire's trial, a psychiatrist testified that the accused had committed his crimes in a paranoid schizophrenic state and that his obsession with the referendum outcome was a delusional one. Furthermore, the judge was assured that medication had absolved any threat Dallaire posed. The defendant expressed remorse in court and apologized to the Chrétien family. Although the Crown did not contest Dallaire's diagnosis, the prosecution did argue that a conviction for attempted murder was warranted, because the accused had purchased a knife and explored the crime scene in advance. Yet the defence lawyer emphasized that his client had merely put himself in a position to kill the prime minister. The judge ultimately sided with the Crown by staying the charge of being unlawfully in a dwelling house and finding Dallaire guilty but not criminally responsible for his actions on the remaining three counts.

Prepared by Andrea Wolf.

committing a criminal act, psychopaths in the same circumstances feel no such fear. These reduced anxiety levels result in impulsive and inappropriate behaviour, apprehension, and incarceration. Psychologists have attempted to treat patients diagnosed as psychopaths by giving them adrenaline, which increases their arousal levels.

Antisocial Personality and Chronic Offending. The antisocial personality concept jibes with what is known about chronic offending. Chronic offending is a continuum of behaviour at whose apex lies the most extremely dangerous and predatory criminals. As many as 80 percent of chronic offenders exhibit sociopathic behaviour. Though making up about 4 percent of the male population and less than 1 percent of the female population, sociopathic chronic offenders are responsible for half of all the serious felony offences committed annually. Not all high-rate chronic offenders are sociopaths, but enough are to support a strong link between personality dysfunction and long-term criminal careers.

Should people diagnosed as psychopaths be separated and treated even if they have not yet committed a crime? Should psychopathic murderers be spared the death penalty because they lack the capacity to control their behaviour? These are difficult questions, and ones that will probably not go away.[158]

Research on Personality. Since maintaining a deviant personality has been related to crime and delinquency, numerous attempts have been made to devise accurate measures of personality and determine whether they can predict antisocial behaviour. Two types of standardized personality tests have been constructed. The first are projective techniques, such as the Rorschach inkblot test and the Thematic Apperception Test, which require a subject to react to an ambiguous picture or shape by describing what it represents or by telling a story about it. Clinicians interpret the responses and categorize them according to established behavioural patterns. Although these tests were not used extensively, some early research found that delinquents and nondelinquents could be separated on the basis of their personality profiles.[159]

The second frequently used method of psychological testing is the personality inventory, such as the Minnesota Multiphasic Personality Inventory (MMPI).[160] This test requires subjects to agree or disagree with groups of questions in a self-administered survey. In one study, the MMPI was given to a sample of boys and girls in grade 9 in Minneapolis; the scores had a significant relationship to later delinquent involvement.[161]

The MMPI and other scales used to predict crime and delinquency have proved inconclusive.[162] The Hare Psychopathy Checklist has also been used for diagnosing psychopathy. Although some law violators may suffer from an abnormal personality structure, there are also many more whose personalities are indistinguishable from the norm. Efforts to improve the MMPI have resulted in a new scale with, it is hoped, improved validity.[163] Interestingly, one problem with attempting to treat psychopaths is that it makes them better manipulators.

Are Some People Crime-Prone? Interest in the personality characteristics of criminals has been increasing. Because the most commonly used scales have not been very successful in predicting criminality, psychologists have turned to other measures, including the Multidimensional Personality Questionnaire (MPQ), to assess such personality traits as control, aggression, alienation, and well-being. Such scales can show how personality is linked to delinquency, and these measures are valid across genders, races, and cultures.[164] Adolescent offenders who are crime-prone respond to frustrating events with strong negative emotions. They feel stressed and harassed, and are adversarial, experiencing anger, anxiety, and irritability. They also have weak personal constraints and have difficulty controlling impulsive urges. Because they are both impulsive and aggressive, crime-prone people are quick to take action against perceived threats.

In research on the link between stalking and domestic violence, researchers found that both stalkers and abusers possessed traits, such as emotional volatility, attachment dysfunction, substance abuse, and early childhood trauma. Other research has found a high correspondence with risk-taking, low self-control, and offending behaviour.[165]

Evidence that personality traits predict crime and violence is important because it suggests that the root cause of crime is found in the forces that influence human development at an early stage of life. If this is valid, rather than focus on job creation and neighbourhood improvement, crime control efforts might be better focused on helping families raise children who are reasoned and reflective and enjoy a safe environment.

Intelligence and Crime

Early criminologists maintained that delinquents and criminals have below-average intelligence and that this is a cause of their criminality. They believed criminals to be inherently substandard in intelligence and naturally inclined to commit more crimes than were more intelligent people. It was thought that if authorities could determine which individuals had low IQs, they might identify potential criminals before they could commit socially harmful acts.

Because social scientists had a captive group of subjects in juvenile training schools and penal institutions, they measured the correlation between IQ and crime by testing offenders. These inmates were used as a test group on which numerous theories about intelligence were built, leading ultimately to the nature versus nurture controversy that is still going on today.

Canada's Experiment with Eugenics. In the 1920s, acting on the idea that IQ is related to delinquency, several provincial governments passed laws in an attempt to weed out undesirable characteristics, a practice known as "negative eugenics." Alberta passed its *Sexual Sterilization Act* and created a Provincial Eugenics Board in 1928. This law was in force until 1972. British Columbia's law existed from 1933 to 1973. Ontario and Quebec only narrowly missed passing such laws under opposition by the Roman Catholic Church.

In 1965, Leilana Muir sued the Alberta government for her involuntary sterilization in 1959 and for falsely categorizing her as a moron under this law. She had been physically abused by her mother and abandoned at the Provincial Training School for Mental Defectives at the age of 11. The government in British Columbia sterilized at least two hundred people, and Alberta's government sterilized almost three thousand people whom they believed had "mental defects." In total, almost five thousand people with disabilities were approved for sterilization. Female youths underwent tubal ligations or hysterectomies for "menstrual management," while males had vasectomies or were castrated.

The Eugenics Board acted arbitrarily and falsely—who can imagine approving such procedures for children? In 1997, when Ms. Muir sued again, she was awarded $750 000 in compensation, but the Alberta government refused to compensate the other victims. Finally, in 1999, it agreed to an $82-million settlement to 247 victims. The belief that mental illness, mental disability, and criminality were inherited was one born from poorly constructed evolutionist thinking and has since been discounted.

Nature Theory. Nature theory argues that intelligence is largely determined genetically and that low intelligence in a low IQ score is linked to behaviour, including criminal behaviour. When IQ tests were administered to inmates of prisons and juvenile training schools in the first decades of the twentieth century, the nature position gained support because a large proportion of the inmates scored low on the tests. Henry Goddard concluded during his studies in 1920 that many institutionalized persons were "feebleminded" and that at least half of all juvenile delinquents were "mental defectives."[166] In 1926, Healy and Bronner tested groups of delinquent boys in Chicago and Boston and found 37 percent were below normal, concluding delinquents were five to ten times more likely to have mental deficiencies than were nondelinquent boys.[167] Low IQ scores were seen to indicate potentially delinquent children and to prove a correlation between innate low intelligence and deviant behaviour. Criminologists accepted the idea that individuals with substandard IQs were predisposed toward delinquency and adult criminality, because IQ tests were believed to measure the inborn genetic makeup of individuals.

Nurture Theory. The rise of cultural explanations of human behaviour in the 1930s led to the nurture school of intelligence. Here intelligence is viewed as partly biological but primarily sociological. Nurture theorists discredited the notion that persons commit crimes because they have low IQs. Because intelligence is not inherited, parents with low IQs do not necessarily produce children who have low IQs.[168] Instead, environmental stimulation from parents, relatives, social contacts, schools, and peer groups can improve a child's IQ level; low IQs can result from an environment that also encourages delinquent and criminal behaviour. Thus, if low IQ scores are recorded among criminals, these scores may reflect the criminals' cultural backgrounds, not their mental ability.

Studies challenging the IQ–crime assumption began to appear as early as the 1920s. In 1926, Slawson studied 1543 delinquent boys in New York institutions and compared them with a control group.[169] Although 80 percent of the delinquents achieved lower scores in abstract verbal intelligence, they were normal in mechanical aptitude and nonverbal intelligence. These results indicated the possibility of cultural bias in portions of the IQ tests. Slawson found no relationship among the number of arrests, the types of offences, and IQ.

In 1931, Edwin Sutherland evaluated IQ studies of criminals and delinquents and noted discrepancies in testing methods rather than differences in mental ability.[170] Sutherland's research all but put an end to the belief that crime is caused by low intelligence, and the IQ–crime link was all but forgotten in the criminological literature.

Rediscovering IQ and Criminality. Although the IQ–crime link had been dismissed by mainstream criminologists, it became an important area of study once again when Hirschi and Hindelang reexamined existing data and concluded that "the weight of evidence is that IQ is more important than race and social class" for predicting criminal and delinquent involvement.[171] Rejecting the notion that IQ tests are race- and class-biased, they concluded that major differences exist between criminals and noncriminals within similar racial and socioeconomic class categories. Low IQ increases the likelihood of criminal behaviour through its effect on school performance because youths with low IQs do poorly in school, and school failure is highly related to delinquency and later to adult criminality.

Hirschi and Hindelang's inferences have been supported by research conducted by international scholars.[172] Some studies have found a direct IQ–delinquency link among samples of adolescent boys.[173] When Alex Piquero examined violent behaviour among groups of children in Philadelphia, he found that scores on intelligence tests were the best predictors of violent behaviour and could be used to distinguish between groups of violent and nonviolent offenders.[174]

Other research supports these conclusions.[175] In *Crime and Human Nature*, James Q. Wilson and Richard Herrnstein feel that the IQ–crime link is an indirect one: Low intelligence leads to poor school performance, which enhances the chances of criminality.[176] They concluded, "A child who chronically loses standing in the competition of the classroom may feel justified in settling the score outside, by violence, theft, and other forms of defiant illegality."

The IQ–crime relationship has also been found in some cross-national studies.[177] However, the IQ–crime relationship might be small.[178] A recent evaluation of existing knowledge on intelligence conducted by the American Psychological Association concluded that the strength of an IQ–crime link is "very low."[179] In contrast, *The Bell Curve* comes down firmly on the side of an IQ–crime link, with an extensive summary showing that people with low IQs are more likely to commit crime, get caught, and be sent to prison. Conversely, at-risk kids with higher IQs seem to be protected from becoming criminals. The authors conclude that criminal offenders have an average IQ of 92, about 8 points below the mean; chronic offenders score even lower than the "average" criminal. And it is not only low-IQ criminals who get caught; data show little difference in IQ scores between self-reported and official criminals.[180]

This debate will not be settled soon. Measurement is beset by many methodological problems. The criticism that IQ tests are race- and class-biased would certainly influence the testing of the criminal population, who are inundated with a multitude of socioeconomic problems. Even if known offenders have lower IQs than does the general population, it is difficult to explain many patterns in the crime rate: Why are males more criminal than females? Why do crime rates vary by region, time of year, and even weather patterns? Why does aging out occur? IQ does not increase with age— why should crime rates fall with age? Such an approach has critical theoretical problems as well: Various issues that are ignored include the role of the police in enforcing the law, their use of discretion, and the ability of the law to reinforce social inequality. These issues are discussed in Chapter 9, "Social Conflict Theory."

Social Policy Implications

For most of the twentieth century, biological and psychological views of criminality have had an important influence on crime control and prevention policy. These views can be seen in primary prevention programs that treat personal problems before they manifest themselves as crime: family therapy organizations, substance abuse clinics, and mental health associations. Referrals to these resources are made by teachers, employers, courts, and welfare agencies. If a person's problems can be treated before they become overwhelming, then future crimes might be prevented. Secondary prevention programs provide psychological counselling to youths and adults after they have violated the law. Attendance in such programs may be a mandatory requirement of a probation order, part of a diversionary sentence, or aftercare at the end of a prison sentence.

Comparative research shows that therapeutic and preventive treatment works. However, health care differences between Canada and the United States have not resulted in fewer people with mental disorders in correctional institutions here. Yet neither are they being used to warehouse offenders with mental disorders. The long-term trend in Canada has been to deinstitutionalize people who have mental illnesses, to increase the use of medication, and to treat them in community clinics. The Supreme Court itself has reviewed how the better use of conditional sentencing can make health care a better solution than incarceration.[181]

Connections

The law recognizes the psychological aspects of crime when it permits a plea of not criminally responsible on account of mental disorder (NCRMD) as an excuse for criminal liability or when it allows trial delay because of mental incompetence. See Chapter 2 for more on the NCRMD defence.

Biologically oriented therapy is also being used in the criminal justice system. Programs have altered diet, changed lighting, compensated for learning disabilities,

Is it nature or nurture? Even if some aspects of intelligence are inherited, if children are raised in an environment that lacks economic resources and parental support, they will fail to maximize their intellectual potential. The mother here is going to college while on welfare to better support herself and her child. Is it the responsibility of society to provide resources sufficient to enable all youth to achieve their rightful share of intellectual development?

treated allergies, and so on.[182] What is more controversial has been the use of mood-altering chemicals, such as lithium and benzodiazepines, or the use of brain surgery, to control the behaviour of antisocial individuals.[183]

Some criminologists view biologically oriented treatments as a key to solving the problem of the chronic offender. They argue that a number of inherited physical traits that cause disease have been successfully treated with medication after their genetic code has been broken; why not, then, a genetic solution to crime?[184]

Whereas such biological treatment is a relatively new phenomenon, it has become commonplace since the 1920s to offer psychological treatment to offenders before, during, and after a criminal conviction. For example, since the 1970s, pretrial programs have sought to divert offenders into nonpunitive rehabilitative programs designed to treat rather than to punish them. Based on some type of counselling regime, diversion programs are commonly used with first offenders, nonviolent offenders, and so on. At the trial stage, judges often order psychological profiles of convicted offenders so that a treatment program can be planned. Should offenders be kept in the community? Do they need a more secure confinement to deal with their problems? If correctional confinement is called for, inmates are commonly evaluated at a correctional centre to measure their personality traits or disorders. Correctional facilities almost universally require inmates to participate in some form of psychological therapy: group therapy, individual analysis, transactional analysis, and so on. Parole decisions may be influenced by the prison psychologist's evaluation of the offender's adjustment.

Summary

The earliest positivist criminologists were biologists. Led by Cesare Lombroso, these early researchers believed that some people manifested primitive traits that made them born criminals. Biological views fell out of favour in the early twentieth century, but in the 1970s, criminologists again turned to the study of the biological basis of criminality. For the most part, the effort has focused on the causes of violent crime. Interest has been revived in several areas: (1) biochemical factors, such as diet, allergies, hormonal imbalances, and environmental contaminants (such as lead); (2) neurophysiological factors, such as brain disorders, EEG abnormalities, tumours, and head injuries; and (3) genetic factors, such as XYY syndrome and inherited traits. There is also an evolutionary

branch, which holds that changes in the human condition that have taken thousands of years to evolve may help explain crime rate differences.

Table 6.3 reviews the biological and psychological theories of criminal behaviour.

Psychological attempts to explain criminal behaviour no longer suggest that all criminals are insane or have mental damage. Today, there are three main psychological perspectives. The psychodynamic theorists say that aggressive behaviour is linked to personality conflicts developed in childhood. However, behavioural and social learning theorists believe criminality is a learned behaviour: Children who are exposed to violence and see it rewarded may become violent as adults. In contrast, cognitive psychologists are concerned with human development and how people perceive the world. They see criminality as a function of improper information processing or moral development.

Psychological traits, such as personality and intelligence, have been linked to criminality, for example, to the psychopath, a person who lacks emotion and concern for others. The controversial issue of the relationship of IQ to criminality has been resurrected once again with the publication of studies purporting to show that criminals have lower IQs than do noncriminals. Psychologists have developed standardized tests with which to measure personality traits. One avenue of research has been to determine whether criminals and noncriminals manifest any differences in their responses to test items.

TABLE 6.3 Biological and Psychological Theories

Theory	Major Premise	Strengths
Biological		
Biochemical	Crime, especially violence, is a function of diet, vitamin intake, hormonal imbalance, or food allergies.	Explains irrational violence. Shows how the environment interacts with personal traits to influence behaviour.
Neurological	Criminals and delinquents often suffer brain impairment, as measured by the EEG. Attention deficit/hyperactivity disorder and minimum brain dysfunction are related to antisocial behaviour.	Explains irrational violence. Shows how the environment interacts with personal traits to influence behaviour.
Genetic	Criminal traits and predispositions are inherited. The criminality of parents can predict the delinquency of children.	Explains why only a small percentage of youth in a high-crime area become chronic offenders.
Evolutionary	As the human race evolved, traits and characteristics became ingrained. Some of these traits make people aggressive and predisposed to commit crime.	Explains high violence rates and aggregate gender differences in the crime rate.

Psychological

Psychodynamic	The development of the unconscious personality early in childhood influences behaviour for the rest of a person's life. Criminals have weak egos and damaged personalities.	Explains the onset of crime and why crime and drug abuse cut across class lines.
Behavioural	People commit crime when they model their behaviour after others they see being rewarded for the same acts. Behaviour is reinforced by rewards and extinguished by punishment.	Explains the role of significant others in the crime process. Shows how family life and media can influence crime and violence.
Cognitive	Individual reasoning processes influence behaviour. Reasoning is influenced by the way people perceive their environment and by their moral and intellectual development.	Shows why criminal behaviour patterns change over time as people mature and develop their moral reasoning. May explain the aging-out process.

Thinking Like a Criminologist

In our culture, we believe that people should not be blamed for actions that are beyond their control. We think that a person cannot be legally responsible if he or she cannot meet certain tests. An obvious test of competence is cognitive, that there is a criminal intent. Thus, the M'Naghten rule (1843) says that every person is to be presumed to be sane and that to establish a not criminally responsible on account of mental disorder defence, it must be proved that, at the time of committing the act, the accused was suffering from a disease of the mind that meant he or she did not know the nature of the act being committed; or if he or she did know it, there was no knowledge that it was wrong. Used in this way, the definition seems overly restrictive and psychiatric. As a criminologist with expertise of trait theories of crime, do you think this goes far enough in explaining aberrant behaviour?

Key Terms

androgens

antisocial personality

arousal theory

attention deficit/hyperactivity disorder (AD/HD)

behaviour modelling

behaviour theory

cognitive school

electroencephalograph (EEG)

equipotentiality

hypoglycemia

identity crisis

inferiority complex

instincts

latent delinquency

minimal brain dysfunction (MBD)

neurophysiology

neurosis

personality

premenstrual syndrome (PMS)

psychodynamic theory

psychopathy

psychosis

r/k theory

repression

schizophrenia

social learning

sociobiology

sociopathy

somatype

testosterone

trait theories

Critical Thinking Questions

1. What should be done with the young children of violence-prone criminals if, in fact, research could show that the tendency to commit crime is inherited?

2. After considering the existing research on the subject, would you recommend that young children be forbidden from eating foods with a heavy sugar content?

3. Knowing what you do about trends and patterns in crime, how would you counteract the assertion that people who commit crime have a physical or mental abnormality? For example, how would you explain the fact that crime is more likely to occur in Western and urban areas than in Eastern or rural areas?

4. Aside from becoming a criminal, what other career paths are open to psychopaths?

5. Research shows that kids who watch a lot of TV in adolescence are more likely to behave aggressively in adulthood. This result has led some to conclude that TV watching is responsible for adult violence. Can this relationship be explained in another way?

 See the book-specific website at http://www.siegelcriminology3e.nelson.com for additional chapter links, discussions, and quizzes.

Social Structure Theories

chapter 7

Motivations for crime do not result simply from the flaws, failures, or free choices of individuals. A complete explanation of crime ultimately must consider the sociocultural environments in which people are located.[1]

Sociology has been the primary focus used in criminology since early in the twentieth century, with Robert Ezra Park, Ernest W. Burgess, and their colleagues at the University of Chicago pioneering research on the social ecology of the city.

Connections

As discussed in Chapter 1, sociological positivism can be traced to the works of Quetelet and Comte; the work of Durkheim will be reviewed here in the section on anomie theory.

Park applied anthropological methods of description and observation to urban life.[2] He was concerned about how neighbourhood structure develops, how isolated pockets of poverty form, and what social policies could be used to alleviate urban problems. Later, with Burgess, they studied the social ecology of the city and found that some neighbourhoods form **natural areas** of wealth and affluence, while others suffer poverty and disintegration.[3] Regardless of their race, religion, or ethnicity, the everyday behaviour of people living in these areas is controlled by the social and ecological climate.

Over the next 20 years, **Chicago School** sociologists carried out research that produced Harvey Zorbaugh's *The Gold Coast and the Slum,* Frederic Thrasher's *The Gang,* and Louis Wirth's *The Ghetto.*[4]

Sociological Criminology

Sociologists look at how patterns of behaviour exist within the social structure. Criminologists attempt to discover why criminal patterns exist and how they can be eliminated. Explanations of crime as an individual-level phenomenon fail to account for these consistent patterns in the crime rate. If violence, for example, is related to chemical or chromosome abnormality, how can ecological differences and similarities in the crime rate be explained? There is a lot of debate over the effects of violent TV shows on adolescent aggression, yet adolescents in cities and towns with widely disparate crime rates, from St. John's, Newfoundland, to Vancouver, British Columbia, all watch the same shows and movies. How can crime rate differences in these areas be explained? If violence has a biological or psychological origin, should it not be distributed more evenly throughout the social structure?

Sociology is concerned with social change and the dynamic aspects of human behaviour. It follows transformations in cultural norms and institutions and the subsequent effect they have on individual and group behaviour.[5] In modern society, a reduction in the influence of the family has been accompanied by an increased emphasis on individuality, independence, and isolation, with weakened family ties linked to crime and delinquency.[6]

Rapid advances in technology have also influenced society. People who lack the requisite social and educational training have found that the road to success through upward occupational mobility has become almost impossible. Even today, in one of the most industrialized countries in the world, most children grow up to occupy the same social class position as their parents. Lack of upward mobility may make drug dealing and other crimes an attractive solution to socially deprived but economically enterprising people, especially if they are only marginally employed.[7]

Connections

The association between crime and social class is confusing. Crime rates sometimes go up during periods of full employment and drop during periods of relatively high unemployment. Chapter 13 discusses a type of crime linked to employment: elite or white-collar crime.

Criminologists believe that understanding the dynamics of interactions between individuals and their families, peers, schools, work, and the like, is important for understanding the cause of crime.[8] Sociology is concerned with the benefits of positive human interactions and the costs of negative ones. Crime is itself an interaction and therefore should not be studied without considering the interactions of all participants in a criminal act: the law violator, the victim, the law enforcers, the lawmakers, and the social institutions.

To summarize, concern about the ecological distribution of crime, the effect of social change, and the interactive nature of crime itself has made sociology the foundation of modern criminology. This chapter reviews sociological theories that emphasize the relationship between social status and criminal behaviour. In Chapter 8, the focus will shift to theories that emphasize socialization and its influence on crime and deviance; Chapter 9 covers theories based on the concept of social conflict.

Economic Structure and Crime

All societies are characterized by social stratification. Social classes are created by the unequal distribution of wealth, power, and prestige; their members have similar possessions and share attitudes, values, norms, and lifestyle. In our society, it is common to identify people as upper-, middle-, and lower-class citizens. The upper-upper class is reserved for a small number of exceptionally well-to-do families who maintain enormous financial and social resources. The lower class consists of those people who live in poverty and includes the working poor. The middle class are the managers, professionals, and white-collar workers.

A new shift is occurring in the distribution of poverty. For the first time, the elderly are better off than working-class people are, with universal medical care, social security, and private pensions improving the lifestyle of most retirees. At the same time, a large proportion of Canada's children now live in poverty, a frightening reality once being designated by the United Nations as one of the best countries in which to live.

The National Council of Welfare says that many Canadians with full-time jobs were living below the poverty line in 2000. Furthermore, although the proportion of children living in poverty dropped between 1990 and 2000, half of all food bank recipients were children. In 2004, the child poverty rate increased for the first time since 1996, with 16 percent of children living below the poverty line, 15 years after Parliament made a unanimous declaration to end child poverty.

When these children become adolescents, legitimate opportunities are more likely to be limited. As Baron and Hartnagel point out in their extensive survey of street youth, the resulting occupational strain is more likely to be solved through crime. Similarly, Bolland found in a survey of 2468 inner-city adolescents that that feelings of hopelessness increased violent behaviour, substance use, sexual behaviour, and accidental injury.[9]

InfoTrac®

You can use "poverty" as a keyword to search for articles like these:

- Suzanne Lewis-Johnson, "Left in the Cracks," *Christianity Today,* March 5, 2001, 26, 45.
- "Government Defines Ambition of a Society Free of Child Poverty by 2020," *Ma Pressuire,* December 18, 2003.

Inequality

Lower-class slum areas are scenes of inadequate housing and health care, disrupted family lives, underemployment, depression, and despair. Some people are driven to desperate measures to cope with their economic plight.

Members of the lower class are constantly bombarded with a flood of advertisements linking material possessions to self-worth, but they are often unable to attain desired goods and services through conventional means. Although

they are members of a society that extols material success above any other, they are unable to satisfactorily compete for such success with members of the upper classes.

The social problems found in lower-class slum areas have been described as an "epidemic."[10] As neighbourhood quality decreases, the probability that residents will develop problems sharply increases. Adolescents in the worst neighbourhoods have the greatest risk of dropping out of school and becoming teenage parents, further limiting their mobility.

The disadvantages of lower-class citizens are particularly acute for racial minorities. Blacks and Native people in Canada have a mean income level significantly lower than that of Whites, and an unemployment rate that is markedly higher. Although many of the urban poor are White, minorities are overrepresented within the poverty classes. Statistics Canada says that immigrants who arrived in Canada in the late 1990s have experienced a decline in income of 24 percent versus those who arrived 30 years earlier.

Economic problems are not the only ones faced by racial minorities. Native Canadians, for example, have a much shorter life span than do Whites. It has now been established that a link exists between entrenched poverty and HIV infection. In Vancouver, Aboriginal injection drug users are becoming HIV positive at twice the rate of non-Natives.[11] It has also been suggested that the concentration of poor, single-parent, and poorly educated Aboriginal people in large cities disadvantages them in ways that might account for their overrepresentation in the justice system.[12]

Racial segregation and isolation of poor African Americans and Hispanics in American urban areas has been increasing.[13] A recent survey found that low-income Native-American women are at least twice as likely to suffer physical or sexual assault by a partner as the national average. More than half the women had been assaulted by a partner during their lifetime, and one in eight had been raped by a partner. Policy implications of such findings are echoed in a report from Ontario that low incomes of people receiving welfare contribute to women staying in abusive relationships, giving weight to the relationship between poverty and victimization.[14]

InfoTrac®

For more on poverty, unemployment, and crime, check out:

- Gunnar Almgren, Avery Guest, George Immerwahr, and Michael Spittel, "Joblessness, Family Disruption, and Violent Death in Chicago, 1970–90," *Social Forces* 76, no. 4 (1998): 1465.
- William Julius Wilson, "Inner-City Dislocations," *Society* 35, no. 2 (1998): 270.

In this picture of a downtown Canadian city, we see the conditions in which some people live. Does this provide an enriched environment in which to grow up and escape poverty and crime, or a deprived one in which crime prospers?

In 1966, Oscar Lewis argued that the crushing lifestyle of slum areas produces a "culture of poverty" passed from one generation to the next.[15] The **culture of poverty** is marked by apathy, cynicism, helplessness, and mistrust of social institutions, such as schools, government agencies, and the police. This mistrust prevents slum dwellers from taking advantage of the meagre opportunities available to them. In 1970, Gunnar Myrdal described a worldwide **underclass** cut off from society, its members lacking the education and skills in demand in modern society.[16]

Are the Poor Undeserving?

Despite all our technological success, the fact that a significant percentage of citizens are either homeless or living in areas of concentrated poverty is an important social problem. Yet some view impoverished people as somehow responsible for their own fate, believing that if they tried, they could "improve themselves."[17]

This conclusion is baseless. People living in poverty in physically deteriorated, inner-city neighbourhoods experience high crime, poor schools, and excessive mortality.[18] They have higher rates of unemployment, are more dependent on welfare, and are more likely to live in single-parent households. The burden of living in these high-poverty areas goes beyond merely being poor. Under these conditions, self-help and upward mobility are highly difficult. The barriers to getting ahead are not personal but systemic.

Adolescents residing in areas of concentrated poverty are more likely to suffer in their cognitive development, sexual and family formation practices, school attendance habits, and transition to employment.

The poor confront obstacles far greater than the mere lack of financial resources in that they are ill-prepared to take advantage of employment opportunities even in favourable labour markets. The fact that many of the underclass are children who can expect to spend all their life in poverty is probably the single most important problem facing the nation today.

Unemployment and Crime

The social structure approach links crime to economic deprivation. If people do not hold jobs, they are more likely to turn to crime as a means of support. If jobs are available, crime rates should go down. People who hold jobs should be less criminal than are people who are unemployed. What is the relationship between crime and unemployment?

The crime rate has risen dramatically since the 1960s; however, this occurs even during prosperous times. There is little indication that changing market conditions cause offenders to renounce crime and choose legitimate earning opportunities. Crime rates are slightly linked to labour market conditions, but the relationship between them is one of many.

A routine activities theorist (Chapter 5) might suggest that although joblessness increases the motivation to commit crime, it simultaneously decreases the opportunity to gain from criminal enterprise. During periods of economic hardship, potential victims have fewer valuable items in their possession and guard those valuables more closely. Parents who are unemployed can be at home to supervise their children, reducing the opportunity for the kids to commit crime. However, teenagers have higher crime rates than any other age group because they are not yet part of the work force and are unlikely to be directly affected by employment rates.

When individual offenders are the unit of analysis, we see that unemployed individuals are more likely to commit crime. Surveys of adult inmates show that many were unemployed and underemployed before their incarceration, with a median income below the poverty level. It is possible that unemployment increases crime because it reduces people's stake in conformity. By severing attachments to coworkers and reducing parents' ability to be breadwinners, unemployment reduces the attachment people have to conventional institutions and their ability to exert authority over their children.

A number of possible explanations exist for the rather weak crime–unemployment association. It may be that only extremely high unemployment rates are associated with crime. Crime rates peaked in the 1930s during the Great Depression, and it is possible that only such a sustained period of economic chaos can affect crime rates. Recent short-term fluctuations in the economy may be of too short a duration to have a measurable effect.

The unemployment–crime relationship may also be offence specific, having the greatest influence on opportunistic property crimes, such as burglary, and the least on violent assaultive crimes, which are more likely to be motivated by such factors as rage, jealousy, or substance abuse.

It is also possible to formulate the direction of the crime–unemployment relationship in a different way. Rather than joblessness motivating people to commit crime, criminal behaviour can exclude offenders from work. An early experience with delinquent behaviour and drug abuse may later result in unemployment as an adult. Hagan explains this relationship as social embeddedness: early behaviour patterns become stable, lifelong habits and tendencies. Kids with early criminal experiences, whose friends are delinquent and whose parents are criminals, become embedded in behaviours that result in later unemployment. The chain of events runs from having criminal friends and parents, engaging in delinquency, and gaining police and court contacts to losing the opportunity for meaningful employment as adults. Embeddedness in a deviant lifestyle is contrasted with the establishment of roots in a conventional one: Youths who get early work experience, who make contacts, and who learn the ropes of the job market establish the groundwork for a successful career.

So, is there an association between crime and unemployment? The data suggest that these two variables are interrelated in a variety of ways.

Branches of Social Structure Theory

The disadvantages of economic inequality have been viewed by many criminologists as a primary cause of crime, referred to here as **social structure theory**. These theories suggest that forces operating in deteriorated lower-class areas push many of their residents into criminal behaviour patterns. Unsupervised teenage gangs, high crime rates, and social disorder in slum areas are seen as major social problems.

Lower-class crime is often the violent, destructive product of youth gangs and marginally employed young adults, which suggests that the social forces that cause crime begin to affect people while they are relatively young and continue to influence them throughout their life. Although not all youthful offenders become adult criminals, many begin their training and learn criminal values as members of youth gangs and groups.

Social structure theorists don't believe that crime is caused by psychological imbalance, biological traits, insensitivity to social controls, personal choice, or any other individual-level factor. People living in equivalent social environments behave in similar ways, and if the environment did not influence human behaviour, crime rates would be distributed equally across the social structure. Because crime rates are higher in lower-class urban centres than in middle-class suburbs, social forces must be operating in urban areas that influence or control behaviour.[19]

There are three independent yet overlapping branches within the social structure perspective: social disorganization theory, strain theory, and cultural deviance theory, as outlined in Figure 7.1.

| Figure 7.1 | The Three Branches of Social Structure Theory |

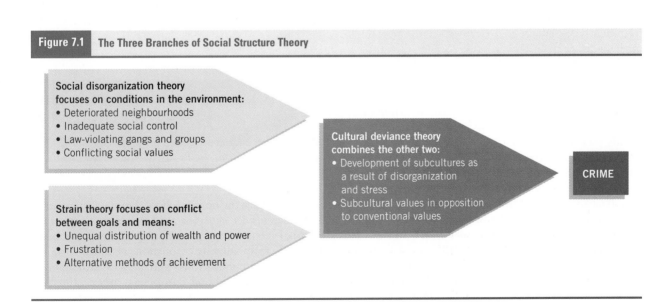

Social disorganization theory, the first branch, focuses on conditions within the urban environment that affect crime rates. A disorganized area is one in which institutions of social control, such as the family, commercial establishments, and schools can no longer carry out their functions. Indicators include high unemployment and school dropout rates, deteriorated housing, low income levels, and large numbers of single-parent households. Residents in these areas experience conflict and despair, and antisocial behaviour flourishes.

Strain theory, the second branch of social structure theory, holds that crime is a product of conflict between goals and means. Although social and economic goals are common, the ability to obtain these goals is class-dependent. Most people desire wealth, material possessions, power, and prestige; however, the lower class is less able to achieve these symbols of success through conventional means. Consequently, they feel anger, frustration, and resentment: "strain." Either they can accept their condition as socially responsible citizens, or they can choose an alternative means of achieving success, such as theft, violence, or drug trafficking.

Cultural deviance theory, the third variation of structural theory, combines elements of both strain and social disorganization. According to this view, unique lower-class cultures develop in disorganized neighbourhoods, creating a unique set of values in conflict with conventional social norms. Criminal behaviour is an expression of conformity to lower-class subcultural values and traditions and not a rebellion against conventional society.

Each of these separate theories supports the view that socially isolated people, living in disorganized neighbourhoods, are the ones most likely to experience crime-producing social forces. We will now examine each branch of social structure theory in some detail.

Social Disorganization Theory

Social disorganization theory links crime rates to neighbourhood ecological characteristics. Crime rates are elevated in highly transient, mixed-use neighbourhoods (residential and commercial properties exist side by side) or changing neighbourhoods, in which the fabric of social life has become frayed. These localities are unable to provide essential services, such as education, health care, and proper housing, and experience significant levels of unemployment, single-parent families, and families on welfare and aid to dependent children (see Figure 7.2).

Social disorganization theory views crime-ridden neighbourhoods as ones in which residents are trying to leave at the earliest opportunity. Common sources of

Figure 7.2   Social Disorganization Theory

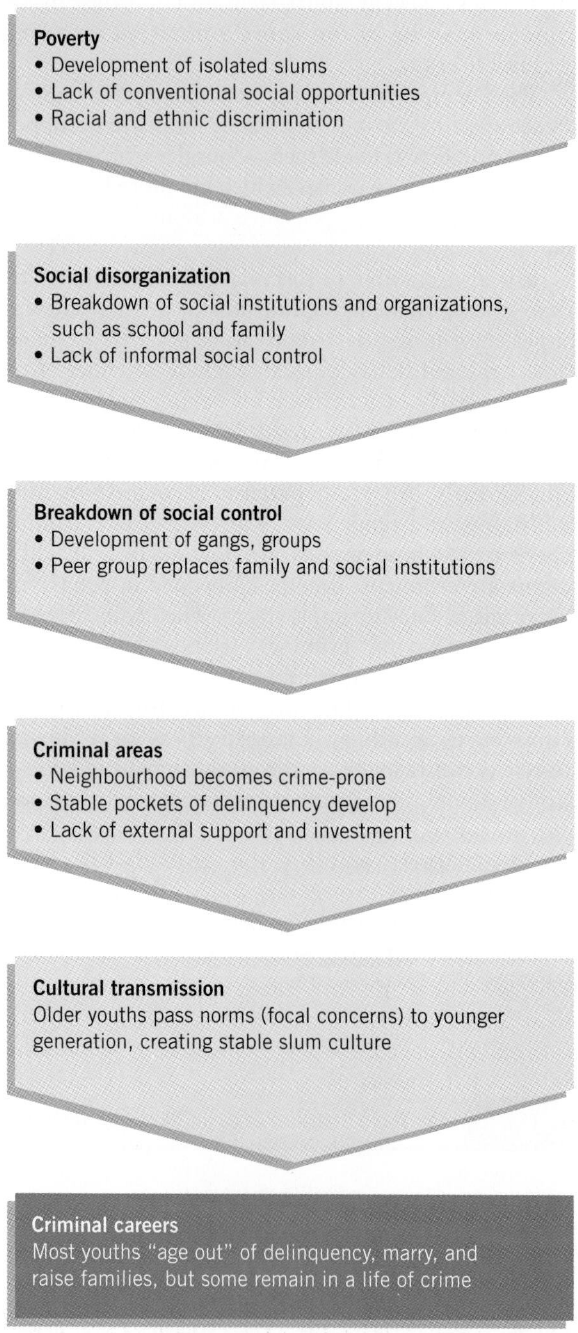

Poverty
- Development of isolated slums
- Lack of conventional social opportunities
- Racial and ethnic discrimination

Social disorganization
- Breakdown of social institutions and organizations, such as school and family
- Lack of informal social control

Breakdown of social control
- Development of gangs, groups
- Peer group replaces family and social institutions

Criminal areas
- Neighbourhood becomes crime-prone
- Stable pockets of delinquency develop
- Lack of external support and investment

Cultural transmission
Older youths pass norms (focal concerns) to younger generation, creating stable slum culture

Criminal careers
Most youths "age out" of delinquency, marry, and raise families, but some remain in a life of crime

control, such as the family, school, business community, and social service agencies, are weak and disorganized. Personal relationships are strained because neighbours are constantly moving. Constant resident turnover weakens communications and blocks attempts at solving neighbourhood problems or establishing common goals.[20]

Concentric Zone Theory

Social disorganization theory was popularized by the work of two Chicago sociologists, Shaw and McKay, who linked life in transitional slum areas to crime. They began their research during the 1920s while working for a state-supported social service agency.[21]

During this time, Chicago was experiencing a transition that was also taking place in many other urban areas: a mid-nineteenth-century population expansion, fuelled by a dramatic influx of foreign-born immigrants. Congregating in the central city, the newcomers occupied the oldest housing.

As the city core began to deteriorate, the city's wealthy, established citizens became concerned about the moral fabric of society. The belief was widespread that immigrants from Europe were crime-prone and morally dissolute, and local groups were created for the purpose of "saving" the children of poor families from moral decadence.[22] It was popular to view crime as the province of inferior racial and ethnic groups, but this belief was rooted in the anxiety over social changes altering the face of twentieth-century society: industrialization, urbanization, immigration, and increased geographic and social mobility.

Transitional Neighbourhoods. Shaw and McKay explained crime and delinquency within the context of the changing urban environment and ecological development of the city. They said Chicago had developed into distinct "natural areas," some affluent and others wracked by extreme poverty. So-called transitional areas had high rates of population turnover and were incapable of inducing residents to remain and defend the neighbourhood against criminal groups.

Low rents in these areas attracted newly arrived immigrants from Europe who congregated in these **transitional neighbourhoods**. Their children were torn between being assimilated into a new culture and abiding by the traditional values of their parents. Informal social control mechanisms that had restrained behaviour in the "old country" or in rural areas were disrupted in the city.

In transitional slum areas, successive changes in the composition of the population, the disintegration of traditional cultures, the divergent cultural standards, and the gradual industrialization of the area resulted in dissolution of neighbourhood culture and organization. The effectiveness of the neighbourhood as a unit of control and as a medium for the transmission of the moral standards of society was greatly diminished. High population turnover impeded the establishment of common values, and children had little access to the cultural heritages of conventional society, leaving them more susceptible to the organized gangs that developed in these areas. Subcultural values developed, which were then passed down through succeeding generations

through **cultural transmission**. Frederic Thrasher documents this well in his 1927 classic *The Gang*.

Concentric Zones. Shaw and McKay noted that distinct ecological areas had developed in the city, composing a series of five concentric circles, or zones, that had significant differences in interzone crime rates (see Figure 7.3). The heaviest concentration of crime appeared to be in the transitional inner-city zones, where large numbers of foreign-born citizens had recently settled. The zones farthest from the city's centre had correspondingly lower crime rates. Analysis of these data indicated a surprisingly stable pattern of criminal activity in the five ecological zones over a 65-year period.

Shaw and McKay concluded that in transitional neighbourhoods, multiple cultures and diverse values, both conventional and deviant, coexist. Kids growing up in the street culture often find that adults who have adopted a deviant lifestyle, such as the gambler, the pimp, or the drug dealer, are the most financially successful people in the neighbourhood. They join with like-minded youths and form law-violating gangs and cliques, but because of their deviant values, slum youths come into conflict with middle-class norms, which are more in line with the legal code. Consequently, a **value conflict** occurs, and the result is a fuller acceptance of deviant goals and behaviour. Shut out of conventional society, neighbourhood street gangs become fixed institutions, recruiting new members and passing on delinquent traditions from one generation to the next.

Shaw and McKay's statistical analysis confirmed their suspicions. They found that even though crime rates changed, the highest rates were always in zones I and II (central city and transitional areas). The areas with the highest crime rates retained high rates even when, over time, families moved out to the suburbs and the ethnic composition changed (in this case, from German and Irish to Italian and Polish).[23]

The Legacy of Shaw and McKay. Social disorganization concepts originally articulated by Shaw and McKay have remained prominent within criminology for more than 75 years. The most important is that crime is a result of the destructive ecological conditions in urban slums. Criminals are not, as some criminologists of the time believed, biologically inferior, intellectually impaired, or psychologically damaged. Crime is a constant fixture in a slum area regardless of the racial or ethnic identity of its residents.

Since the basis of their theory was that neighbourhood disintegration and slum conditions are the primary causes of criminal behaviour, Shaw and McKay paved the way for the many community action and treatment programs developed in the past half-century. Shaw was the founder of one very influential community-based treatment program, the Chicago Area Project.

Figure 7.3   Thrasher's Concentric Zone Map of Chicago Gangland

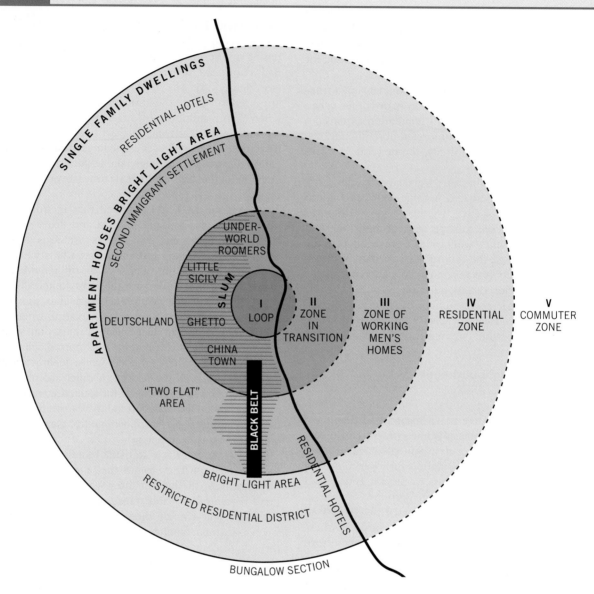

Source: Frederic M. Thrasher, *The Gang: A Study of 1,313 Gangs in Chicago* (Chicago: University of Chicago Press, 1927), p. 24.

Another important feature of this theory is that it depicted criminality as a normal response to adverse social conditions.

Despite these noteworthy achievements, some have faulted Shaw and McKay's assumption that neighbourhoods are essentially stable, while others have found their definition of social disorganization confusing.[24] The most important criticism is that the researchers used police records to calculate neighbourhood crime rates. Research indicates that police use extensive discretion when arresting people and that social status is one factor that influences their decisions. Middle-class people might commit criminal acts that never show up in official statistics, while people in lower-class areas face a far greater chance of arrest and court adjudication.[25] Thus, the relationship between environment and crime rates may reflect police enforcement.

These criticisms aside, the theory provides a valuable contribution to our understanding of the causes of criminal behaviour. By introducing a new variable—the ecology of the city—into the study of crime, the authors paved the way for succeeding generations of criminologists to focus on the social influences on criminal and delinquent behaviour.

Connections

If social disorganization causes crime, why are the majority of low-income people law abiding? To explain this anomaly, some sociologists have devised theoretical models suggesting that individual socialization experiences mediate the effect of environmental influences. These theories will be discussed in Chapter 9.

The Social Ecology School

During the 1970s, theories with a more social psychological orientation developed critiques of social disorganization theory. However, the social disorganization tradition was kept alive by area studies showing that ecological conditions, such as substandard housing, low income, and unrelated people living together, predicted a high incidence of delinquency.[26]

In the 1980s, criminologists revived concern about the effects of social disorganization,[27] and **social ecologists** developed an approach that stressed the relation of community deterioration and economic decline to criminality while placing less emphasis on value conflict. Sampson and Groves produced a study using data from the 1982 British Crime Survey, and the social disorganization theory seemed to be vindicated.[28]

In the following sections, some of the more recent social ecological research is discussed in some detail.

Community Deterioration. Crime rates are associated with community-level indicators of social disorganization, including disorder, poverty, alienation, disassociation, and fear of crime.[29] Neighbourhoods with deserted houses and apartments experience high crime rates, as abandoned buildings serve as a "magnet for crime."[30] Areas in which houses are in poor repair, boarded up, and burned out and whose owners are best described as "slumlords" are also sites of the highest violence rates and gun crime.[31] The percentage of people living in poverty and the percentage of single-parent homes are strongly related to neighbourhood crime rates.[32] Gangs flourish in deteriorated neighbourhoods, adding to the crime rate. Curry and Spergel found that gang homicide rates were associated with the percentage of the neighbourhood living below the poverty line, the lack of mortgage investment in a neighbourhood, the unemployment rate, and the influx of new immigrant groups, factors usually found in disorganized areas.[33]

In a study of police charging practices in 447 Canadian communities, Schulenberg found that, of four different ecological theories, social disorganization theory was the strongest predictor of crime rates.[34]

Research conducted in Scandinavia and Great Britain also found that socially disorganized neighbourhoods experienced the highest amounts of crime and victimization.[35] Communities characterized by sparse friendship networks, unsupervised teenage peer groups, and low organizational participation had the greatest amounts of criminality. This model, then, has the power to explain crime rates in countries with similar socioeconomic conditions.[36]

Employment Opportunities. The relationship between unemployment and crime is unsettled: crime rates sometimes rise during periods of economic prosperity and fall during periods of economic decline.[37] Yet high unemployment rates may have crime-producing effects in particular neighbourhoods or in areas wracked by poverty and social disorganization.[38] Even though short-term economic trends may have little effect on crime, it is possible that long-term unemployment rates will eventually produce higher levels of antisocial behaviours.[39]

Neighbourhoods with few employment opportunities are the most vulnerable to predatory crime. Unemployment helps destabilize households, and unstable families are the ones most likely to contain children who put a premium on violence and aggression as a means of dealing with limited opportunity. Crime rates increase when large groups or cohorts of people of the same age compete for relatively scant resources.[40]

Limited employment opportunities also reduce the stabilizing influence of parents and other adults, who once counteracted the allure of youth gangs.[41] Even the most deteriorated neighbourhoods have a surprising degree of familial and kinship strength. Yet the consistent pattern of crime and neighbourhood disorganization that follows periods of high unemployment can neutralize their social control capability.

 InfoTrac®

For an article on the relationship between unemployment rates and crime in New Zealand, look at Kerry Papps and Rainer Winkelmann, "Unemployment and Crime: New Evidence for an Old Question," *New Zealand Economic Papers* 34, no. 1 (2000): 53.

Community Fear. Disorganized neighbourhoods suffer social and physical incivilities—rowdy youth, trash and litter, graffiti, abandoned storefronts, burned-out buildings, littered lots, strangers, drunks, vagabonds, loiterers, prostitutes, noise, congestion, angry words, dirt, and stench. The presence of such incivilities helps

Culture, Gender, Ethnicity, and Criminology

Carl Dawson and the McGill School

Carl Addington Dawson was born in 1887 in Augustine Cove, Prince Edward Island. He studied sociology at Acadia University in the 1890s and then served as pastor of a Baptist church in Lockeport, Nova Scotia. Acadia was one of the first universities to offer courses in sociology, which was seen by urban reformers, settlement-house workers, and social-gospel ministers as a way to deal with the problems of urbanization and industrialization.

Dawson did not think that social reform was the best way to improve social conditions, but he believed that research and investigation of urban communities and their institutions would provide the insight to create a better society. Many churches were convinced that sin was not so much a product of an individual's shortcomings as it was a condition forced on that person by his or her position in society. The Baptists, for example, talked about improving the social environment as a way of preventing the production of criminals; they advocated prison reform, prohibition, and justice for Native Canadians. They argued for inner-city missions, protection for children, and women's rights. Prohibitionists in Nova Scotia were motivated by a desire to eliminate the roots of human unhappiness and to create a society in which crime, disease, and **social injustice** would not exist.

Dawson had studied at Chicago and was brought to McGill University to research the problems of postwar Montreal. He was hired as the director of the School of Social Work and then became head of the first

Canadian department of sociology in 1924. The new science of sociology gave the observer the opportunity to understand the forces that led to social fragmentation and social cohesion. Human ecology combined ideas borrowed from plant and animal ecology, physiology, and cultural anthropology. This became the framework within which all McGill sociology courses were taught and the frame of reference for all research projects undertaken by Dawson and his students throughout the 1920s and 1930s.

Sociologists turned to biology for guidelines because they found suggestions for explaining the flux that characterized human society. Existence was a struggle for survival, yet all beings were bound up in a web of relations with other beings and not because they were bound to the physical environment alone. Higher life forms succeeded the lower ones by "invading" an area and forcing the inhabitants to settle in a zone on the rim of their original habitat, which created instability.

Dawson saw society as an order that transcended its individual members, and the ultimate end of the evolutionary process was to establish an equilibrium and a harmonious social order. In keeping with his training, he chose not to focus on social pathology but rather to investigate the broader structure of the city and the way in which it moulded the behaviour and institutions of its inhabitants. His research was in ordinary areas to ascertain through careful observation the social changes that were caused by advances in communication and transportation.

The city, he said, was an organism, with a centre of dominance—the business sector—around which were arranged a

number of zones in concentric circles, their use and occupants varying with the value of the land and the distance from the centre. Each zone was divided into "natural areas," marked off from each other by natural or artificial boundaries and distinguished by their own characteristic institutions and populations. Inhabitants were "sifted" to these areas by a selective process, and their attitudes and behaviour were shaped by the areas. Dawson and his students looked at industrial development, transportation innovations, immigration, housing, labour organization, crime, juvenile delinquency, family disorganization, welfare work, and child labour. They plotted railroad property, industrial and commercial frontage, parks, boulevards, and physiographic barriers on maps of the city.

At the turn of the twentieth century, only about one-third of the province's population were urban dwellers, but by 1928, Montreal had become the fifth-largest city in North America. Its port, industries, and services drew immigrants by the thousands every year. Electric streetcars, first introduced in 1892, contributed to the expansion of the city and enabled thousands of workers to move out of the city's inner core into the numerous residential neighbourhoods and suburbs that were springing up all around the city. Although the main tendencies of expansion radially from the centre held true for Montreal, its topographic features distorted the concentric circles in a kidney shape around Mont Royal, as shown in Figure 7.4.

As the city grew, business institutions that had been located near the river encroached on the residential district, where the old walled town of Ville Marie had once

Figure 7.4   **A Kidney-Zone Map of Social Differentiation in Montreal**

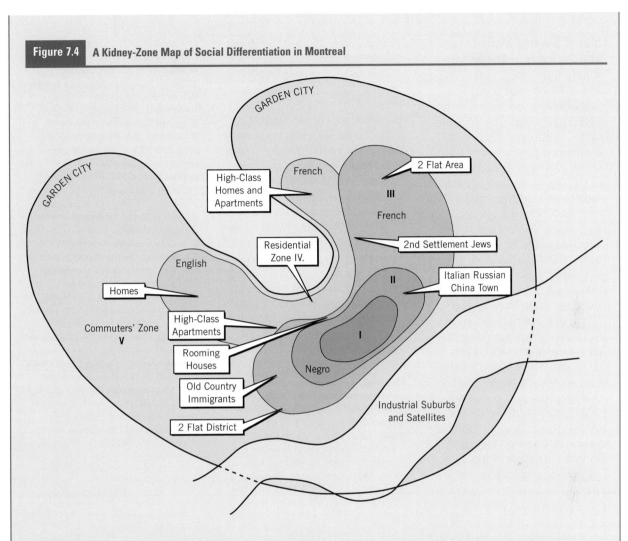

Source: Adapted from C.A. Dawson and W.E. Gettys, *An Introduction to Sociology* (New York: Romald Press, 1929, 1935), p. 130.

stood. The St. Antoine district, on the verge of becoming a slum in the 1920s, had been created by the expansion of the business section. The area's more successful residents had already moved above the hill and to the west. The part of Montreal that experienced the most disruption as the business centre expanded was Dufferin district, a neighbourhood that lay in the city's transitional zone.

Robert Percy, an M.A. student who studied the area, found that the Dufferin district became a slum at the turn of the twentieth century, when the commercial sector of Montreal expanded and a flood of Asian and European immigrants poured into the city. Its boundaries were invaded by machine shops, warehouses, and light manufacturing. The more successful among the English, Irish, Scottish, and French families who lived in the district departed, and their vacated homes were remodelled into flats and occupied by the less prosperous.

Although stable residential neighbourhoods were well equipped with churches and schools, Dufferin district did not have many such institutions, and rescue missions first made their appearance in Dufferin district in the 1890s. Constant noise, dirt, stimulation, vice, and despair characterized this disorganized physical environment.

Although the work of Carl Dawson and his students has been largely overlooked, it represents an important period in Canadian criminology: an attempt to apply scientific principles to the study of the natural organization of crime.

Muriel Bernice McCall and the Study of Social Disorganization

Muriel McCall was one of the first people to graduate with an M.A. in Sociology from McGill. In her 1928 thesis, McCall says that the population of any great city is heterogeneous. In the area of transition, "they are crowded together for the most part in cheap boarding houses under most unsatisfactory conditions. They are casual by nature and by choice preferring work as lackeys and porters or even bootblacks to employment of a more permanent nature. Their sense of moral right and wrong is practically lacking. When they do enter into any legal marriage relationship they regard it very lightly. They are ready to air their troubles on the slightest provocation and therefore contribute a great deal of disintegration. . . . [However,] the fourth zone is the habitat of the upper middle and professional classes.

Private ownership of a home and restrictions upon how and where it shall be built appear here for the first time. The homes in Westmount and in Notre Dame de Grace are homes of this kind. Small lawns appear in front of the house and some attempt is made to have the exterior of the home as attractive as the interior. There are children but the families tend to be small and the care of them is often left to nurse maids hired for the purpose. Husband and wife are on an equality of footing. Father has his club and mother has hers. If they find it impossible to get any enjoyment out of being together there are always a multiplicity of other activities ready to claim them."

Sources: I am indebted to Marlene Shore for her excellent overview to this neglected period in Canadian criminological history, in *The Science of Social Redemption: McGill, the Chicago School, and the Origins of Social Research in Canada* (Toronto: University of Toronto Press, 1987). Carl Dawson, "Research

and Social Action," *Social Welfare* 5 (1923): 93–5; S.D. Clark, "Sociology in Canada: An Historical Overview," *Canadian Journal of Sociology* 1, 1975; V.A. Tomovic, "Sociology in Canada: An Analysis of Its Growth in English Language Universities, 1908–1972," Ph.D. thesis, University of Waterloo, 1975; E.R. Forbes, "Prohibition and the Social Gospel in Nova Scotia," *Acadiensis* 1 (1971); John S. Moir, "The Canadian Baptist and the Social Gospel Movement, 1879–1914," in *Baptists in Canada: A Search for Identity Amidst Diversity,* ed. Jarold K. Zeman (Burlington: G.R. Welsh, 1980); C.A. Dawson, "Human Ecology," in *The Fields and Methods of Sociology,* ed. L.L. Bernard (New York: Ray Lang and Richard Smith, 1934); C.A. Dawson, "The City as an Organism. With Special Reference to Montreal," in *McGill University Publications* 13 (1926); Muriel Bernice McCall, "A Study of Family Disorganization in Canada," M.A. thesis, McGill, 1928; Wilfrid Emmerson Israel, "The Montreal Negro Community," M.A. thesis, McGill, 1928; Margaret Millicent Wade, "A Sociological Study of the Dependent Child," M.A. thesis, McGill, 1931.

---

convince residents of disorganized areas that their neighbourhood is dangerous and that they face a considerable chance of becoming crime victims. Not surprisingly, when crime rates are actually high in these disorganized areas, fear levels undergo a dramatic increase.[42] Perceptions of crime and victimization produce neighbourhood fear.[43] People who report living in neighbourhoods that have high levels of crime and civil disorder become suspicious and mistrusting.[44]

Fear becomes most pronounced in areas undergoing rapid and unexpected racial and age-composition changes.[45] Fear can become contagious, as people talk of their personal involvement with victimization, spreading the word that the neighbourhood is getting dangerous and that the chance of future victimization is high.[46] People dread leaving their homes at night and withdraw from community life. Not surprisingly, people who have already been victimized are more fearful of the future than those who have escaped crime.[47]

When fear grips a neighbourhood, business conditions begin to deteriorate, population mobility increases,

and a criminal element begins to drift into the area. Fear helps produce more crime, as people decrease their level of "ownership" and stay off the street, increasing the chances of victimization, producing even more fear, in a never-ending loop.

Connections

Chapter 5's discussion of choice theory mentioned that communities characterized by broken windows had higher crime rates.

Siege Mentality. One unique aspect of community fear is the development of a **siege mentality**.[48] This mindset results in mistrust of critical social institutions, including business, government, and schools. When police ignore crime in poor areas, or when police are violent and corrupt, anger flares and people take to the streets and react in violent ways.

In 1992, after the Rodney King verdict acquitting four police officers in Los Angeles, California, people rioted as far away as Toronto, a city with certainly less minority and police conflict. There has long been tension between the police and ethnic minorities in large Canadian cities, where immigration has swelled the numbers of the non-White population.

Population Turnover. In our industrial society, urban areas undergoing rapid structural changes in racial and economic composition also seem to experience the greatest change in crime rates. Change, not stability, is the hallmark of inner-city areas. A neighbourhood's residents, wealth, and density are constantly changing. Some neighbourhoods may become multiracial, while others become racially homogeneous; some areas become stable and family-oriented, while in others, mobile, never-married people predominate.

As areas decline, residents flee to safer, more stable localities. Those who can't leave face an even greater risk of victimization. Because of racial differences, those "left behind" are all too often members of minority groups, who find themselves surrounded by an influx of new residents. High population turnover affects community culture because it interrupts communication and information flow.[49] A culture may develop that dictates standards of dress, language, and behaviour to neighbourhood youth that are in opposition to those of conventional society. All these factors are likely to produce increasing crime rates.

Community Change. Social ecologists have charted the life cycles of urban areas, which begin with the building of residential dwellings, followed by a period of decline with marked decreases in socioeconomic status and increases in population density. Later stages in this life cycle include changing racial or ethnic makeup, population thinning, and, finally, a renewal stage in which obsolete housing is replaced or upgraded (gentrification). Areas undergoing such change experience increases in their crime rates.[50] Communities go through cycles in which neighbourhood deterioration precedes increasing rates of crime and delinquency.[51] Those communities most likely to experience a rapid increase in antisocial behaviour contain large numbers of single-parent families and unrelated people living together. These areas have gone from having owner-occupied units to having renter-occupied units and have an economic base that has lost semiskilled and unskilled jobs. These ecological disruptions strain existing social control mechanisms and inhibit their ability to control crime and delinquency.

Research shows that changing lifestyles in urban neighbourhoods, including declining economic status, increasing population, and racial shifts, are associated with increased neighbourhood crime rates, and even areas adjoining neighbourhoods undergoing racial change will experience corresponding increases in their own crime rates.[52] This phenomenon may reflect community reaction to perceived racial and class conflict. In changing neighbourhoods, adults support the law-violating behaviour of youths and encourage them to protect their property and way of life by violently resisting newcomers.

Poverty Concentration. One aspect of community change is the concentration of poverty in deteriorated neighbourhoods. Although poverty rates or unemployment may not be direct causes of crime, the most deteriorated areas have much higher crime rates than more stable lower-class environments. Working and middle-class families flee inner-city poverty areas, resulting in a **concentration effect** in which elements of the most disadvantaged population are consolidated in urban ghettos. As the working and middle classes move out, they take with them their financial and institutional resources and support. Businesses are disinclined to locate in poverty areas; banks become reluctant to lend money for new housing or businesses.[53] Minorities living in these areas suffer race-based inequality, such as **income inequality** and institutional racism.[54]

Areas marked by concentrated poverty become isolated from the social mainstream and more prone to the criminal activity of gangs.[55] The concentration effect contradicts Shaw and McKay's assumption that crime rates increase in transitional neighbourhoods. Today, the most crime-prone areas may be stable, homogeneous areas whose residents are "trapped" in public housing and urban ghettos.[56]

Weak Social Controls. Most neighbourhood residents share the common goal of living in a crime-free area. Some communities can regulate the behaviour of residents through the influence of community institutions, such as family and school. Other neighbourhoods, experiencing social disorganization, find that efforts at social control are weak. When community social control efforts are blunted, crime rates increase, further weakening neighbourhood cohesiveness in a never-ending cycle.

Neighbourhood agencies of social control operate on the primary level, with peers, families, and relatives exerting informal control through awarding approval and respect. Informal control mechanisms include criticism and ridicule.[57] Businesses, schools, churches, and organizations are part of the internal networks that communities can use control crime.

Stable neighbourhoods are able to arrange for external sources of social control, such as additional law enforcement. The presence of police sends a message that the area will not tolerate deviant behaviour. Criminals and drug dealers avoid such areas and relocate to easier and more appealing targets.[58]

As neighbourhood disadvantage increases, its level of informal social control decreases.[59] Since the population is transient in disorganized areas, interpersonal relationships remain superficial; social institutions, such as schools and churches, cannot work effectively in a climate of alienation and mistrust. In these areas, the absence of local political power limits access to external funding and police protection. Neighbourhoods need an injection of funds from the outside to rebuild properly.[60]

Social control is also weakened because unsupervised peer groups and gangs, which flourish in disorganized areas, disrupt the influence of neighbourhood control agents.[61] Children who live in these neighbourhoods may want to attend school and other programs, but they may instead find themselves drafted into those gangs.[62]

InfoTrac®

To learn more about making better, safer communities, look at Julian E. Barnes, "Reclaiming Our Cities, Block by Block: How a Little Rock Program Offers Hope for Countering Urban Decay," *Washington Monthly* 28, no. 4 (1996): 42–45.

Collective Efficacy. Communities that are cohesive and maintain high levels of social control develop collective efficacy—mutual trust and a willingness to intervene in the supervision of children and the maintenance of public order.[63] Cohesion among neighbourhood residents combined with shared expectations for informal social control of public space promotes collective efficacy.[64] Communities with high collective efficacy experience low violence rates and low levels of physical and social disorder (for example, drinking in the street, spray-painting graffiti, and breaking windows). In contrast, neighbourhoods with low collective efficacy suffer high rates of violence and significant physical and social disorder. Local organizations designed to control crime, such as neighbourhood associations, may only be effective if they promote a sense of collective efficacy.[65] Moreover, spillover effects can extend beyond the geographic boundaries of a single neighbourhood. There are three forms of collective efficacy:

1. *Informal social control:* This form of social control works on the primary level and involves peers, families, and relatives exerting informal control through positive and negative reinforcement.[66] For example, families may exert control by awarding privileges or ridiculing lazy or disrespectful children.

    In some neighbourhoods, neighbours practise informal social control through surveillance practices: for example, by keeping an eye out for intruders when their neighbours go out of town. This vigilance initially reduces the levels of such crimes as street robberies; however, if robbery rates remain high, people become fearful for their safety and reduce surveillance.[67]

2. *Institutional social control:* Social institutions, such as schools and churches, cannot work effectively in a climate of alienation and mistrust. As noted, the positive impact that neighbourhood control agents can have is easily disturbed by the gangs that are often found in disorganized areas. Children who reside in these neighbourhoods find that involvement with conventional social institutions, such as schools and afternoon programs, is blocked; they are instead at risk for recruitment into gangs and law-violating groups.[68] As crime flourishes, neighbourhood fear increases, which in turn decreases a community's cohesion and thwarts the ability of its institutions to exert social control over its residents.[69]

    Communities that have collective efficacy attempt to use their local institutions to control crime. Sources of institutional social control include businesses, stores, schools, churches, and social service and volunteer organizations.[70] Some institutions, such as recreation centres for teens, have been found to lower crime rates because they exert a positive effect; others, such as taverns and bars, can destabilize neighbourhoods and increase the rate of violent crimes, such as rape and robbery.[71]

3. *Public social control:* Stable neighbourhoods are also able to secure external resources and are better able to reduce the effects of disorganization and maintain lower levels of crime and victimization.[72] The police presence is typically greatest when community organizations and local leaders have sufficient political clout to get funding for additional law enforcement personnel,[73] and offenders relocate to other areas.[74]

    In more disorganized areas, the absence of political power brokers limits access to external funding and protection. Without money from the outside, the neighbourhood lacks the ability to "get back on its feet."[75] In these areas, fewer police are on patrol and those who do patrol the area are less motivated and their resources are stretched more tightly. These communities cannot mount an effective social control effort because, as neighbourhood disadvantage increases, the level of informal social control decreases.[76]

In areas where collective efficacy is sufficient, children are less likely to become involved with deviant peers and engage in problem behaviours. When social control is weak, there may be an overreliance on formal punishment, such as arrest and prosecution, to control offenders, a situation that helps destabilize neighbourhoods by putting many of its residents behind bars.

Social Altruism. The inverse of communities that provide weak social controls are those that provide strong social supports for their members. Residents teach one another that they have moral and social obligations to their fellow citizens; children learn to be sensitive to the rights of others and respect differences.

People living in disorganized areas may also be able to draw on resources from their neighbours in more affluent surrounding communities, helping to keep crime rates down.[77] This phenomenon may explain, in part, why violence rates are high in poor neighbourhoods that are cut off from outside areas for support.[78]

Areas that place a greater stress on caring for fellow citizens seem, not surprisingly, less crime-prone. In an important survey, Chamlin and Cochran found that social altruism (which they define as the ratio of contributions given to the United Way charity by area income levels) is inversely related to crime rates.[79] Their findings can be interpreted in two ways: (1) crime rates are lower in altruistic areas; (2) well-funded charities help lower crime rates by providing a secure safety net for "**at-risk**" families.

Taken in sum, the writings of the social ecology school show that (1) social disorganization produces criminality and (2) the quality of community life, including levels of change, fear, incivility, poverty, and deterioration, has a direct influence on an area's crime rate. It is not some individual property or trait that causes some people to commit crime but the quality and ambiance of the community in which they reside.

InfoTrac®

This article looks at Canada (an individualistic society) and Nigeria (a collectivist society) and compares their procedural preferences for conflict resolution: James T. Gire and D.W. Carment, "Dealing with Disputes: The Influence of Individualism-Collectivism," *Journal of Social Psychology* 133, no. 1 (1993): 81–96.

Strain Theory

Inhabitants of a disorganized inner-city area feel isolated, frustrated, and left out of the economic mainstream. What effect do these feelings have on criminal activities?

Criminologists who view crime as a result of lower-class frustration and anger are called strain theorists. They believe that although most people share similar values and goals, the ability to achieve personal goals is stratified by socioeconomic class. Those in affluent areas feel less strain because educational and vocational opportunities are available. In socially disorganized

areas, however, strain occurs because legitimate avenues for success are less open. To relieve strain, indigent people may be forced to either use deviant methods to achieve their goals, such as theft or drug trafficking, or reject socially accepted goals outright and substitute other, more deviant goals, such as being tough and aggressive (see Figure 7.5).

Figure 7.5	The Basic Components of Strain Theory

Poverty
- Development of isolated slum culture
- Lack of conventional social opportunities
- Racial and ethnic discrimination

Maintenance of conventional rules and norms
Lower-class slum-dwellers remain loyal to conventional values and rules of dominant middle-class culture

Strain
Lack of opportunity coupled with desire for conventional success produces strain and frustration

Formation of gangs and groups
Youths form law-violating groups to seek alternative means of achieving success

Crime and delinquency
Methods of groups—theft, violence, substance abuse—are defined as illegal by dominant culture

Criminal careers
Most youthful gang members "age out" of crime, but some continue as adult criminals

Anomie Theory

The roots of strain theories can be traced to Emile Durkheim's notion of anomie (from the Greek *a nomos*, "without norms"). Anomie occurs when norms of behaviour are broken down during periods of rapid social change. Anomie is most likely to occur in societies that are moving from a preindustrial model held together by traditions, shared values, and unquestioned beliefs. In industrial societies, which are highly developed and dependent on the division of labour, people are connected by their interdependent needs for one another's services and production. This shift in traditions and values creates social turmoil. Established norms begin to erode and lose meaning, a theme we saw in disorganization theory. If a division occurs between what the population expects and what society can realistically deliver, frustration and normlessness occurs.

Society works to limit people's goals and desires. If a society becomes anomic, it can no longer maintain control over its population's wants and desires. Since people find it difficult to control their appetites, their demands become unlimited. Under these circumstances, obedience to legal codes may be strained, making alternative behaviour choices, such as crimes, inevitable.

Durkheim's ideas were applied to criminology by sociologist Robert Merton in his theory of anomie.[80] Merton found that two elements of culture interact to produce potentially anomic conditions: culturally defined goals and socially approved means for obtaining them. For example, modern societies stress the goals of acquiring wealth, success, and power, and the socially permissible means of achieving those goals, which include hard work, education, and thrift.

Merton argued that the legitimate means to acquire wealth are not available to all. Those with little formal education, for example, find that they are

 Famous Canadian Criminals

Women Who Kill Their Children

Before the twentieth century, killing an infant was classed as murder and the current conception of postpartum depression did not exist. In the eighteenth century, the main offence under which women were charged was concealment of birth. And if a "bastard" child was born dead, it was assumed that the mother had killed the baby. Given the circumstances, juries were often unwilling to convict. In 1867, infanticide was formally added to the *Criminal Code* as a form of murder, and in 1948, the mental component (postpartum depression) was added to the *Criminal Code.* However, even before those changes, it was commonly understood that some women lived lives of desperation that might result in them killing their babies. Contraception had been criminalized, abortion was not legally available, and single

mothers were seen as deviant. Homes in which unwed mothers could have their babies and give them up for adoption were common.

Consider the case of Marie McCabe, who in 1880 came to Canada with the help of a charitable organization. When she was six, her mother died and her father suffered an industrial accident. The nine children were placed in an orphanage, but only Marie and her sister survived. Working as a chambermaid in a Quebec City hotel, she became pregnant by a local businessman, who promptly abandoned her. The local city welfare officials and private charity sources refused to help her, even after her child was born. In desperation she struck a deal with a family who agreed to keep her and the baby and then adopt the child at the age of one.

However, the deal was not a happy one, and when the baby was four months old, McCabe abandoned it in a cistern, where

it drowned. The corpse was discovered six months later, and McCabe was charged by the police. She pleaded guilty at the coroner's inquest and then at the trial. She was sentenced to death in 1883; however, her case was trumpeted in the local newspaper. Calls for clemency resulted in the commutation of her death penalty, and she was eventually released in 1889.

Today, it is recognized that emotional imbalance, as well as social situations, have an effect on mothers. Very few cases of infanticide come forward in any year, and they are treated very differently now from the way they were in the past. Mothers are more likely to be seen as needing medical treatment rather than criminal punishment.

Sources: I am indebted to Frank Anderson's *A Dance with Death: Canadian Women on the Gallows, 1754–1954* (Saskatoon: Fifth House, 1996). Also Helen Boritch, *Fallen Women: Female Crime and Criminal Justice in Canada* (Toronto: ITP Nelson, 1997).

Crime in the News

Concealment of Birth

In another example reported in *The Globe and Mail* in 1881, the state tried to charge the mother as an accessory to murder; however, in return for a guilty plea, the prosecution withdrew the charge:

"Mr. Fenton stated that he did not wish to press the charge against Mrs. Phair, and he did not think that anything could be proved against her.

"Mrs. Phair was then discharged.

"Mr. Murphy, on behalf of Emma Phair, said that he would withdraw the plea of not guilty, and put in one of guilty. He would also ask to be allowed to call witnesses to testify to the character borne by the defendants.

"A number of witnesses were called, and all gave the unfortunate girl an excellent character, stating that she was a hard-working, quiet girl, and the sole support of her mother.

"The Magistrate reserved judgment to the 21st.

"This finished the business, and the Court rose."

Source: "Concealment of Birth," *The Globe and Mail,* 1881.

---

denied the ability to legally acquire wealth, the preeminent success symbol.

When socially desirable goals are uniform throughout society but access to legitimate means is bound by class and status, a strain occurs among those who are locked out of the legitimate opportunity structure. Consequently, they may develop criminal or delinquent solutions to the problem of attaining goals.

Social Adaptations. Merton argued that some people have inadequate means of attaining success, and others who do have the means reject societal goals as being unsuited to them. His typology included five social goals and the means for getting them.

Conformity occurs when individuals both embrace conventional social goals and have the means at their disposal to attain them. In a balanced, stable society, this is the most common social adaptation. If a majority of its people did not practise conformity, the society would cease to exist.

Innovation occurs when an individual accepts the goals of society but is incapable of attaining them through conventional means. Many people desire material goods and luxuries but lack the financial ability to attain them. The resulting conflict forces them to adopt innovative solutions to their dilemma: They steal, sell drugs, or extort money. Of the five adaptations, innovation is most closely associated with criminal behaviour.

If successful, innovation can have serious, long-term social consequences. Criminal success helps convince otherwise law-abiding people that crime pays. "The process thus enlarges the extent of anomie within the system," claims Merton, "so that others, who did not respond in the form of deviant behaviour to the relatively slight anomie which they first obtained, come to do so as anomie is spread and is intensified."[81] This explains why crime is created and sustained in certain low-income ecological areas.

Ritualism occurs when social goals are lowered in importance. Ritualists gain pleasure from the practice of traditional ceremonies that have neither a real purpose nor a goal. The strict set of manners and customs in religious orders, feudal societies, clubs, and fraternities and sororities encourage and appeal to ritualists, who have the lowest level of criminal behaviour because they have abandoned the success goal that is at the root of criminal activity.

Retreatists reject both the goals and the means of society. Merton suggested that people who adjust in this fashion are "in the society but not of it," such as psychotics, outcasts, vagrants, vagabonds, tramps, chronic drunkards, and drug addicts. Such people attempt to escape their lack of success by withdrawing, either mentally or physically, which is itself deviant.

Rebellion involves substituting an alternative set of goals and means for conventional ones. Revolutionaries who want to promote radical change in the existing social structure and who call for alternative lifestyles, goals, and beliefs are engaging in rebellion. Rebellion may be a reaction against a corrupt and hated government or an effort to create alternative opportunities and lifestyles within the existing system.

Evaluation of Anomie Theory. To resolve the goals–means conflict or relieve their sense of strain, some people innovate by stealing or extorting money; others retreat into drugs and alcohol, rebel by joining revolutionary groups, or get involved in ritualistic behaviour by joining a religious cult.

Merton's theory is influential because by linking deviance to the success goals that control social behaviour, it pinpoints the conflict that produces personal frustration and consequent criminality. Society unfairly distributes the means to achieving success, which explains the existence of high-crime areas and the predominance of delinquent and criminal behaviour among the lower class. By suggesting that social conditions, not individual personalities, produce crime, Merton greatly influenced the directions taken to reduce and control criminality during the last half of the twentieth century.

Several questions are left unanswered by anomie theory.[82] Merton did not explain why people differ in their choice of criminal behaviour. Why does one anomic person become a mugger while another deals drugs? Anomie may be used to explain differences in crime rates, but it cannot explain why most young criminals desist from crime as adults. Does this mean that perceptions of anomie dwindle with age? Is anomie short-lived?

Critics have also suggested that people pursue a number of different goals, including educational, athletic, and social success. Juveniles may be more interested in immediate goals, such as being a good athlete, than in long-term achievements, such as monetary success. Other factors, including athletic ability, intelligence, personality, and family life, can also either hinder or assist goal attainment.[83] Any assumption that all people share the same goals and values is false.[84] Ethnic minorities, for example, tend to subscribe to different goals from those of the majority.[85] Because of these and other criticisms, the theory of anomie, along with other structural theories, fell into disuse for almost 20 years.

Anomie Reconsidered. Strain theories fell out of favour when criminologists turned their attention to social-psychological views of criminality. However, in the 1990s there was a resurgence of interest in strain and anomie because of the economic displacement brought on by a shifting economy. The "truly disadvantaged" are at risk for both normlessness and high crime rates. For example, recent research on five historical periods shows that gangs respond to social changes, confirming that poverty is a significant precondition generating gang formation.[86] In addition, some researchers are now reexamining concepts more precisely, which is important because some of the criticism of Merton was based on inadequate research.[87] Cross-cultural research also confirms the concepts of anomie.[88]

Criminologists are now producing newer versions of anomie. On the macro level, some say that North America's materialistic culture influences the nature and extent of the aggregate crime rate. Micro-level versions suggest that individuals who experience anomie are more likely to commit crime than are those who are immune to feelings of strain or goal conflict. Examples of both of these views are discussed next.

Institutional Anomie Theory

At the macro level, antisocial behaviour is seen as a function of cultural and institutional influences in society. As a goal, the North American dream involves

There is growing concern about squeegee kids who walk up to cars stopped in traffic and clean their windows. People are threatened by the tattoos, clothing, and hairstyle of these kids, who are often homeless. Some cities, such as Vancouver, Winnipeg, and Toronto, have either passed or are considering bylaws limiting public panhandling in an effort to control the "squeegees."

Moncton, New Brunswick, passed a bylaw this week cracking down on panhandling in the city. How would you like to see your community deal with street beggars? Forty-three percent said build more shelters and make welfare easily available to the indigent.

Source: Poll conducted by *The Globe and Mail,* April 9, 2004.

the accumulation of material goods and wealth. As a process, it involves both socialization to the pursuit of material success and the belief that prosperity is an achievable goal. Anomic conditions occur because the desire to succeed at any cost drives people apart, weakens the collective sense of community, fosters ambition, and restricts the desirability of other kinds of achievement, such as a good name and respected reputation.

That we are conditioned to succeed at all costs should come as no surprise. Businesspeople hold esteemed positions in society. What is distinct about modern North American society, according to Messner and Rosenfeld, and what most likely determines high national crime rates, is that anomic conditions have been allowed to "develop to such an extraordinary degree."[89]

Why does anomie pervade our culture? Perhaps institutions that might otherwise control the exaggerated emphasis on financial success have been rendered powerless or obsolete. There are three reasons that social institutions have been undermined:

1. Performance in noneconomic institutional settings—the family, school, or community—is assigned a lower priority than the goal of financial success.
2. When conflicts emerge, the schedules, routines, and demands of the workplace take priority over those of the home, the school, the community.
3. Economic terms become part of the common language: People want to get to the "bottom line"; spouses are "partners" who "manage" the household. Corporate leaders run for public office promising to "run the country like a business."

High crime rates in Western society can be explained at the cultural level because the desire for material goods cannot always be achieved by legitimate means. Anomie becomes a norm, and extralegal means (crime) become a strategy for attaining material wealth. At the institutional level, the dominance of economic concerns weakens informal social control exerted by the family, church, and school. These institutions have lost their ability to regulate behaviour and have instead become a conduit for promoting material success. For example, schools are not evaluated for conveying knowledge but for their ability to train students to get high-paying jobs.

Thus, crime rates may rise in a healthy economy because national prosperity heightens the attractiveness of monetary rewards, encouraging people to gain financial success by any means possible, including illegal ones, while reducing the importance of social institutions and lessening their abilities to exert social control.

InfoTrac®

For some further research on institutional anomie theory, see Steven F. Messner and Richard Rosenfeld, "Political Restraint of the Market and Levels of Criminal Homicide: A Cross-National Application of Institutional Anomie Theory," *Social Forces* 75, no. 4 (1997): 139–163.

Supporting Research. However, areas with high levels of church membership, lower levels of divorce, and high voter turnouts also enjoy lower crime rates. Strong institutional controls (family, church, and polity), researchers have found, may counteract the influence of economic deprivation, a finding in sync with institutional anomie theory.[90] In an analysis of survey data, people who valued the North American dream but failed to achieve economic success were found to be crime-prone. The effect was more substantial for Whites than for non-Whites, who may have greater expectations of material success. When Whites experience strain, they are more apt to react with anger and antisocial behaviour.[91]

The Messner-Rosenfeld version of anomie strain may be a blueprint for crime-reduction strategies: If citizens are provided with an economic safety net, they may be able to resist the influence of economic deprivation and commit less crime. Nations that provide such resources—welfare, pension benefits, health care—have significantly lower crime rates, even though some of their citizens are beset by income inequality.[92]

This version of anomie builds on Merton's macro-level views by trying to explain why the success goal has reached such a place of prominence in Western culture. The message "succeed by any means necessary" has become a national maxim.

Relative Deprivation Theory

Ample evidence shows that neighbourhood-level income inequality is a significant predictor of neighbourhood crime rates.[93] Income inequality increases both perceptions of strain and crime rates because divisions between the rich and poor create an atmosphere of envy and mistrust. Braithwaite says those societies in which income inequality flourishes are especially demeaning to the poor. Criminal motivation is fuelled by both perceived humiliation and the right to humiliate a victim in return.[94]

Areas in which the affluent and indigent live in close proximity create **relative deprivation**, a concept developed by the Blaus.[95] Lower-class people who feel deprived because of their race or class and who reside in urban areas that also house the affluent eventually develop a sense of injustice and discontent. They feel blocked and the constant frustration produces aggression, hostility, and, eventually, violence and crime.[96] The relatively enriched also feel threatened, but they retreat to gated communities.

Adolescents raised in inner-city poverty areas will experience this crime-producing relative deprivation, since their neighbourhoods are usually located close to the most affluent neighbourhoods.[97] Wage inequality may motivate young males to enter the drug trade, an endeavour that increases the likelihood that they will become involved in violent crimes.[98]

Testing Relative Deprivation. Crime rates increase under conditions of relative deprivation when contiguous neighbourhoods become polarized along class lines.[99] Income inequality predicts violent and general area crime rates, even during times of improvement in income level and educational attainment.[100] Crime can increase during times of relative affluence and declining unemployment: The standard of living may improve, but people may find that they are still losing ground in comparison with other groups. It is the perception of relative deprivation and not absolute poverty levels that ushers in higher crime rates.

Famous Canadian Court Cases

Svend Robinson

During a nationally televised news conference in April 2004, member of Parliament Svend Robinson announced that he had committed theft and was embarking on a much-needed stress leave. The New Democrat, who had occupied the same Vancouver riding for 25 years, was highly respected by colleagues and quite popular among constituents. Robinson may not personify the disadvantaged individual who is turned into an offender by the tension of socioeconomic constraints, but he is certainly not precluded from experiencing strain.

Because he pleaded guilty to the crime, Robinson's true motives for stealing a diamond ring, appraised at almost $65 000, might never be uncovered. However, anyone trying to understand the 52-year-old's actions should take into account his demanding public position as Canada's first openly gay member of Parliament, his recent near-fatal

hiking accident, and his sister's struggle with multiple sclerosis. Undoubtedly, another important piece of the puzzle is the suspicion that Robinson could not afford to buy a $10 000 ring that he had been eyeing for his partner just two days before the shoplifting incident.

The scene of the crime was an auction house that Robinson attended. Not only were patrons required to sign a form and surrender a piece of identification on arrival, but they were also monitored by electronic surveillance for the duration of their stay. The combined force of these security measures and Robinson's status as a well-known public figure was still not powerful enough to deter him from pocketing the ring. Over the next few days, spent at his cottage, Robinson wrestled with a desire to return the merchandise and the fear of being caught. He finally approached police when his efforts to contact the auction service company were unsuccessful. Meanwhile, RCMP officers had

already visited the government official's home and office on two occasions.

The injured party in this case declined to pursue the matter after receiving an apology from Robinson, but a specially appointed prosecutor elected to press charges in June. Two months later, a judge ruled that the scales of justice were tipped in the defendant's favour after considering Robinson's contributions to society, the remorseful guilty plea, his support network, and the shame he had experienced. Robinson was spared the burden of a criminal record as long as he fulfilled the provisions of a one-year conditional sentence that required him to attend counselling and perform one hundred hours of community service. In September 2004, Robinson applied for readmission to the Law Society of British Columbia in hopes of pursuing the legal career he set aside on entering politics.

Prepared by Andrea Wolf.

38%   62%
YES   NO

Svend Robinson has applied to the Law Society of British Columbia for reinstatement. Should he be allowed to practise law? Sixty-two percent of respondents said "no."

Source: Poll conducted by *The Globe and Mail,* September 9, 2004.

Recent research comparing income inequality and homicide rates in Canada and the United States confirms inequality as a strong determinant of levels of lethal violence.[101]

The weight of the evidence supports relative deprivation, and it remains an important concept for understanding area crime rates.

Is Relative Deprivation "Relative"? Relative deprivation theory holds that people who live in deteriorated urban areas; who lack proper health care, decent clothing, and adequate shelter; and who reside in close proximity to those who enjoy the benefits of higher social position, will inevitably resort to such crimes as homicide, robbery, and aggravated assault.[102] Is this view restricted to the lower classes, or can it also be responsible for crimes of the affluent? In other words, is relative deprivation "relative"?

Even the most affluent North Americans will feel strain when they fail to achieve "unlimited goals."[103] No matter what their level of affluence, people may perceive strain because the goals they set for themselves can never be achieved or when their expected standard of living or economic security declines. Research indicates that residing in an economically integrated neighbourhood harms the children of the more affluent families, producing greater dropout rates and more out-of-wedlock births among the prosperous than among the indigent.[104]

Some affluent people may feel relatively deprived when they compare their accomplishments with those of their even more socially successful peers. The relatively affluent may then use illegal means to satisfy their own "unrealistic" success goals:

> Upper-class individuals . . . are by no means shielded against frustrations, relative deprivation and anomie created by a discrepancy between cultural ends and available means, especially in the context of industrial societies, where the ends are renewed as soon as they are reached.[105]

Perhaps some of the individuals involved in Bay Street securities scandals or Wall Street insider-trading cases feel "relatively deprived" and socially frustrated when they compare the paltry few millions they have already accumulated with the hundreds of millions held by the "truly wealthy," whom they envy.

As economic inequality decreases between ethnic groups, White crime rates increase. Although Whites maintain a distinct advantage in power and resources, some perceive the economic progress made by ethnic minorities as a step backward for themselves. Feelings of relative deprivation result in the rise of White power groups when lower-class Whites begin to feel threatened. Many countries have experienced waves of anti-immigrant violence, for example, which supports the model and indicates relative deprivation is quite complex.

General Strain Theory

Robert Agnew's **general strain theory (GST)** differs from the previously discussed models because of its focus on the micro-level, or individual, effects of strain and not the macro-level (social) effects. Although Merton tried to explain social class differences in the crime rate, Agnew tries to explain why individuals who feel stress and strain are more likely to commit crimes. Agnew also attempts to offer a more general explanation of criminal activity among all elements of society rather than restrict his views to lower-class crime.[106]

Multiple Sources of Stress. Criminality is the direct result of **negative affective states**, such as anger, frustration, and adverse emotions that come in the wake of negative and destructive social relationships. Negative affective states are produced by a variety of sources of strain:

1. *Strain caused by the failure to achieve positively valued goals.* This type of strain is a result of the disjunction between aspirations and expectations. It occurs when, for example, a youth aspires to wealth and fame but, lacking financial and educational resources, assumes that such goals are impossible to achieve.

2. *Strain caused by the disjunction of expectations and achievements.* Strain can also be produced when a disjunction exists between expectations and achievements. When people compare themselves with peers who are doing better financially or socially (or making more money or getting better grades), even those doing relatively well feel strain. For example, they may get into university but not into a prestigious school. Perceptions of inequity may result in many adverse reactions, including lowering the benefits others have through physical attacks or vandalism of their property.

3. *Strain as the removal of positively valued stimuli from the individual.* The loss of a positively valued stimulus from the individual, for example, of a girlfriend or boyfriend, can produce strain, as can the death of a loved one, moving to a new neighbourhood or school, and the divorce or separation of parents. The person tries to prevent the loss, retrieve what has been lost, obtain substitutes, or seek revenge against those responsible for the loss.

4. *Strain as the presentation of negative stimuli.* Strain may also be caused by the presence of negative stimuli, such as child abuse and neglect, crime victimization, physical punishment, family and peer conflict, school failure, and stressful life events ranging from verbal threats to air pollution.

Although these sources of strain are independent of one another, they may overlap and be cumulative in practice. For example, insults from a teacher may be viewed as an unfair application of negative stimuli, which interferes with academic aspirations. The greater the intensity and frequency of strain experiences, the greater their impact and the more likely they are to cause delinquency.

Each type of strain will increase the likelihood of experiencing such negative emotions as disappointment, depression, fear, and, most important, anger. Anger increases perceptions of being wronged and produces a desire for revenge and lowers inhibitions.

Because it produces these emotions, strain can be considered a predisposing factor for crime when it is chronic and repetitive and creates a hostile, suspicious, and aggressive attitude. Individual strain episodes may serve as a situational event or trigger that produces criminality, such as when a particularly stressful event ignites a violent reaction (see Figure 7.6).

Coping with Strain. Not all people who experience strain become criminals. Some marshal their emotional, mental, and behavioural resources to cope with anger and frustration. Some defences are cognitive, as when individuals rationalize frustrating circumstances, such

Figure 7.6	Elements of General Strain Theory (GST)

SOURCES OF STRAIN

Failure to achieve goals

Disjunction of expectations and achievements

Removal of positive stimuli

Presentation of negative stimuli

Negative affective states
- Anger
- Frustration
- Disappointment
- Depression
- Fear

ANTISOCIAL BEHAVIOUR
- Drug abuse
- Delinquency
- Violence
- Dropping out

Crime in the News

Once Upon a Crime

Svend Robinson's bid for reinstatement as a legal beagle reminds us how thin the line is between them dastardly criminals and us good, law-abiding folk. The former politician pleaded guilty . . . to stealing a diamond ring but managed to escape a criminal record. Instead he was sentenced to a year's probation and 100 hours of community work. The judge decided Robinson was no sinner, just a victim of stress. So he also sentenced him to psychological counselling.

Robinson's punishment got up the nose of Burnaby's Bill Cooper who penned a letter to the Vancouver *Province*. "In the case of politicians breaking the law, it appears it is forgivable to steal a $64,000 ring if you're NDP MP Svend Robinson, but not OK to pass a joint if you're BC Marijuana party leader Marc Emery," Cooper

huffed. "Robinson got a slap on the wrist for stealing. Emery got three months in jail. I think the whole judicial system needs an overhaul."

Cooper's letter referred to Marc Emery's drug trafficking conviction in a Saskatoon court. . . . Emery admitted to passing a joint in a crowd of supporters after a pro-pot rally at the University of Saskatchewan last March. Passing a joint constitutes trafficking under Canada's enlightened drug laws. Since pot smokers often pass joints, maybe the cops should charge all three million people who inhale the herb every year. Mind you, the cops are already pretty busy. Last year, they laid more than 41,000 charges for pot possession and 10,000 more for trafficking weed. Emery's drug conviction was his 11th. According to the Saskatoon *StarPhoenix*, his lawyer told the judge Emery was making a political statement and

that public attitudes toward marijuana have changed. The judge cut her off. "No democratic society can have any freedoms unless the underlying value is respect for the law," the paper quotes him as snapping. Oh yes, freedom and respect for the law! See how thin the line is between them criminals and us law-abiders?

Which brings me to Conrad Black, newspaper mogul extraordinaire, former owner of the Halifax *Daily News*, affectionately known as Tubby to his colleagues in the journalism game. Lord Tubs stands accused of stealing $400 million from other shareholders in Hollinger Inc. A Hollinger committee investigating allegations of theft, fraud and racketeering sent a detailed, 500-page report to US financial regulators last week. It accuses Tubby of operating a "corporate kleptocracy" in which he, his cronies and second-in-command David Radler (affectionately known as Rattlesnake Radler) grabbed 95 percent of Hollinger's income over the past seven years. "Black and Radler made it their business to line their pockets at the expense of Hollinger almost every day, in almost every way," the report says poetically.

It accuses Tubby and wife Babs of milking Hollinger to finance a lifestyle that Pharaoh Ramses II would envy. Aside from a private jet ($3 to $4 million per year) and subsidies for a New York apartment, Tubs and Babs dinged Hollinger for a shitload of living expenses.

Black's corporate expense reports charge the company for items such as "handbags for Mrs. BB" ($2,463), "jogging attire for Mrs. BB" ($140), exercise equipment ($2,083), "T. Anthony Ltd. Leather Briefcase" ($2,057), opera tickets for "C&BB" ($2,785), stereo equipment for the New York apartment ($828), "silverware for Blacks' corporate jet" ($3,530), "Summer Drinks" ($24,950), a "Happy Birthday, Barbara" dinner party at New York's La Grenouille Restaurant ($42,870), and $90,000 to refurbish a Rolls Royce. The report also alleges that Black evaded income taxes and that he made lavish charitable donations in his own name but charged them to Hollinger.

Please, don't get me wrong. I ain't saying Conrad Black is any more a criminal than Svend Robinson or Marc Emery. Nothing's been proven in court. But if it does turn out that old Tubby hijacked a few hundred million, I think we need a new definition of crime. The bandit who knocks over a bank is obviously a vicious thug. The tycoon who steals millions is an entrepreneur. There but for the grace of god, go the rest of us.

Source: Reproduced courtesy of Bruce Wark. Originally published in *The Coast*, September 9–16, 2004, 12, 15.

as saying that not getting the career they desire is "just not that important." Others seek behavioural solutions by running away or seeking revenge. Some will try to regain emotional equilibrium with techniques ranging from physical exercise to drug abuse.

The GST acknowledges that the ability to cope with strain varies with personal experiences over the life course. Kids who lack economic means are less likely to cope than those who have sufficient financial resources at their command. Personal temperament, prior learning of criminal attitudes and behaviours, and association with criminal peers who reinforce anger are also important. When individuals can identify a target to blame for their problems, they are more likely to respond with retaliatory action ("Joe stole my girl by lying about me, so I beat him up!"). When individuals internalize blame, they are less likely to engage in criminal behaviour ("I lost my girlfriend because I was unfaithful; it's all my fault"). Sometimes the source of strain is difficult to pinpoint ("I feel depressed because my parents got divorced"). This last type of strain is ambiguous and unlikely to produce an aggressive response.[107]

Strain and Criminal Careers. How does GST explain both chronic offending and the stability of crime over the life course? GST recognizes that certain people have traits that may make them particularly sensitive to strain. These include having a difficult temperament, being overly sensitive or emotional, having a low tolerance for adversity, and having poor problem-solving skills. Kids who suffer from this form of "negative emotionality" are much more likely to engage in antisocial behaviours, especially if they also lack self-control.[108] These traits, linked to aggressive and antisocial behaviour, seem to be stable over a person's life cycle.[109]

Connections

Cohort studies show that criminal behaviour begins early in life, then remains stable over the life course. Considering that strain-producing interactions are not constant, explaining the stability of chronic offending is an important task, as discussed in Chapter 3.

Aggressive people who have these traits are likely to have poor interpersonal skills and are more likely to be treated negatively by others; their combative personalities make them feared and disliked. They are likely to live in families whose caretakers share similar personality traits. They are also more likely to reject conventional peers and join deviant groups. Such individuals are more likely to be subjected to a high degree of strain over the course of their lives.

Crime peaks during late adolescence because this is a period of social stress caused by the weakening of parental supervision and the development of relationships with a diverse peer group. Many kids going through the trauma of family break-up and frequent changes in family structure find themselves under stress and react with involvement in precocious sexuality and substance abuse. Young girls of any social class are more likely to bear out-of-wedlock children if they themselves experienced an unstable family life.[110] In adolescence, hormone levels peak and the behaviour-moderating aspects of the brain are not fully developed, which make adolescent males susceptible to environmental sources of strain.[111]

As teens mature, their expectations increase, and some are unable to meet academic and social demands. Adolescents are concerned about their standing with peers, and some become social outcasts. Feelings of strain and being overwhelmed become magnified as individuals attempt to comply with peer group demands. Kids may, for example, get involved in a shoplifting spree to pay for drugs.[112] In adulthood, these sources of strain are reduced, and as new sources of self-esteem emerge, adults are able to bring their goals in line with reality.

Evaluating GST. Agnew's work is important because it both clarifies the concept of strain and directs future research into how social and life history events influence offending patterns. Because sources of strain vary over the life course, crime rates vary too.

Connections

Explaining continuity and change in offending rates over the life course is looked at in the analysis of latent trait and life-course theories in Chapter 10.

Recent research on GST using longitudinal survey data found that adolescents who score high on scales measuring perceptions of strain labelled "life hassles" (for example, "My classmates do not like me," adults and friends "don't respect my opinions") and "negative life events" (being a victim of crime, the death of a close friend, serious illness) are the ones most likely to engage in crime.[113]

Other research efforts shows that indicators of strain—family break-up, unemployment, moving, feelings of dissatisfaction with friends and school—are positively related to criminality.[114] Middle-class youth who drop out of school are more likely to engage in criminal behaviour, because removing this "positive stimulus" has a greater strain on those who are expected to succeed.[115]

Adolescents who report feelings of stress and anger are more likely to interact with delinquent peers and to engage in criminal behaviours.[116] Persistent drug abusers report feeling a great deal of "life stress" and associate with peers who are themselves substance users.[117] This criminal interaction may serve as an effective "coping" mechanism that helps relieve feelings of anger and resentment.[118]

In interviews with two hundred male street youth, Baron explored how their perceptions of unemployment are linked to criminal behaviour. He found that those who remained bonded to conventional society and believed in the dominant idea of getting ahead responded with depression and guilt, which lead to being withdrawn and inhibited criminal behaviour. In contrast, those youth who dismissed the idea of getting ahead felt that criminal activities were superior to available employment.[119]

GST and Gender. GST doesn't explain gender differences in the crime rate. Compared with males, females experience as much or more strain, frustration, and anger, yet their crime rate is much lower. Is it possible that gender differences exist either in the relationship between strain and criminality or in the ability to cope with the effects of strain? For example, some research shows that males may be more deeply affected by interpersonal stress,[120] while other studies show that stressful life events have a similar impact on delinquency and drug abuse for both males and females.[121]

If stress is experienced equally by males and females and produces criminal behaviour in both, how can the much greater male crime rate be explained? It is possible that females use different coping mechanisms to deal with strain. Psychologist Lisa Broidy suggests that even when presented with similar types of strain, males and females respond with a different constellation of negative emotions.[122] Females may be socialized to internalize stress, blaming themselves for their problems; males can relieve strain by deflecting criticism with aggression. Only those females who face overwhelming stress may succumb to criminality.[123]

Cultural Deviance Theory

The third branch of social structure theory combines the effects of social disorganization and strain to explain how people living in deteriorated neighbourhoods react to social isolation and economic deprivation. Although middle-class culture stresses hard work, delayed gratification, formal education, and caution, the lower-class subculture stresses excitement, toughness, risk taking, fearlessness, immediate gratification, and "street smarts." The lower-class subculture is an attractive alternative because the urban poor find it impossible to meet the behavioural demands of middle-class society. Unfortunately, subcultural norms often clash with conventional values (see Figure 7.7).

Figure 7.7   Elements of Cultural Deviance Theory

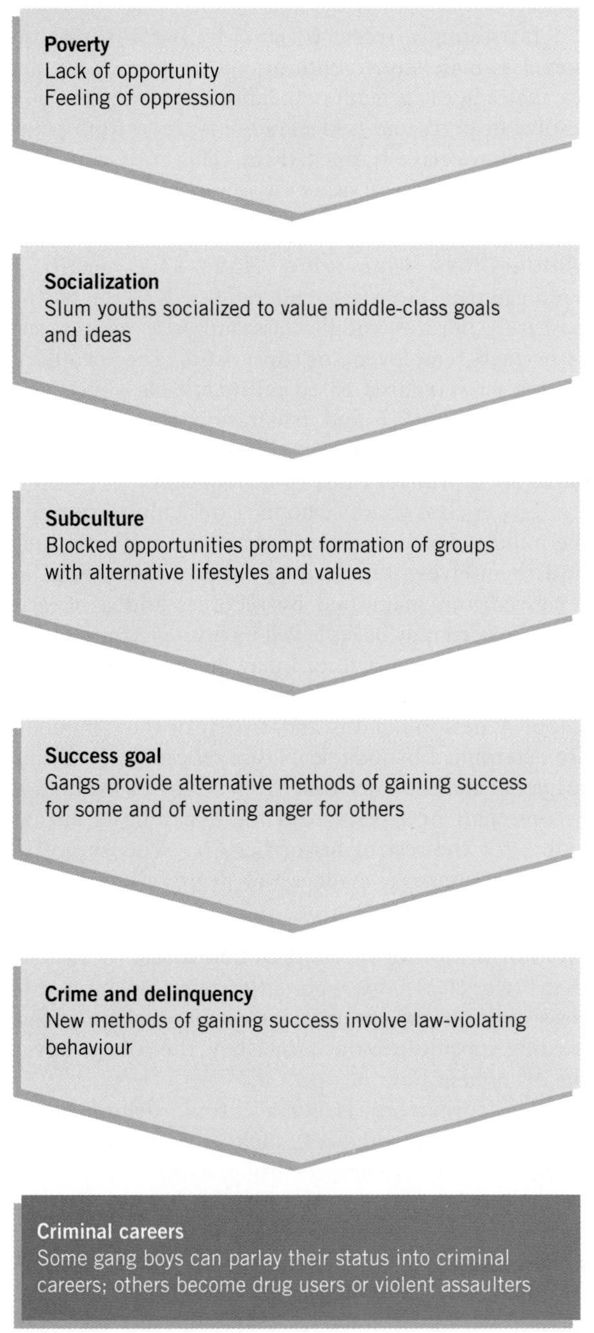

Poverty
Lack of opportunity
Feeling of oppression

Socialization
Slum youths socialized to value middle-class goals
and ideas

Subculture
Blocked opportunities prompt formation of groups
with alternative lifestyles and values

Success goal
Gangs provide alternative methods of gaining success
for some and of venting anger for others

Crime and delinquency
New methods of gaining success involve law-violating
behaviour

Criminal careers
Some gang boys can parlay their status into criminal
careers; others become drug users or violent assaulters

Conduct Norms

The concept that the lower class develops a unique culture in response to strain can be traced to Thorsten Sellin's classic 1938 work, *Culture Conflict and Crime*.[124] The criminal law was seen as an expression of the dominant culture, creating a clash between conventional, middle-class rules and those excluded from the social mainstream. A conflict of norms exists when divergent rules of conduct govern the specific life situation in which a person may find himself or herself. For example, **culture conflict** occurs when the rules expressed in the criminal law clash with the demands of group **conduct norms**. To make his point, Sellin cited the case of a Sicilian father in New Jersey who killed the 16-year-old seducer of his daughter and then expressed surprise at being arrested; he had merely defended his family honour in a traditional way. Conduct norms are universal; they are not the product of one group, culture, or political structure.

Focal Concerns

In his classic 1958 paper, "Lower-Class Culture as a Generating Milieu of Gang Delinquency," Walter Miller identified the unique value system that defines lower-class culture.[125] Obedience is maintained to certain values that have evolved specifically to fit conditions in poor areas, including the following:

1. *Trouble.* This includes fighting, drinking, and sexual misconduct, in which people are evaluated by their involvement in troublemaking activity. Dealing with trouble can confer prestige, as when a man gets a reputation for being able to handle himself well in a fight. Not being able to handle trouble can make a person look foolish and incompetent.

2. *Toughness.* Lower-class males want local recognition of their physical toughness. They refuse to be soft and instead value strength, fighting ability, and athletic skill. Those who cannot measure up risk getting a reputation for being weak, inept, and effeminate.

3. *Smartness.* Members of the lower-class culture want to maintain an image of being "street-wise" and savvy, and of having the ability to "out-con" the opponent. Although formal education is not admired, knowing essential survival techniques, such as gambling, conning, and outsmarting the law, is a requirement.

4. *Excitement.* Another important feature of the lower-class lifestyle is the search for fun and excitement. This pursuit may lead to gambling, fighting, getting drunk, and having sexual adventures. In between, the lower-class citizen may simply "hang out" and "be cool."

5. *Fate.* Lower-class citizens believe their lives are in the hands of strong spiritual forces that guide their destinies, whether it's getting lucky, finding good fortune, or hitting the jackpot.

6. *Autonomy.* A general concern exists in lower-class cultures about personal freedom and autonomy. Being independent of authority figures, such as the police, teachers, and parents, is required; losing control is a weakness, incompatible with toughness.

According to Miller, clinging to lower-class **focal concerns** promotes behaviour that often runs afoul of the law. Toughness may mean displaying fighting prowess; street smarts lead to drug deals; excitement may result in drinking, gambling, or drug abuse. It is this obedience to the prevailing cultural demands of lower-class society, and not alienation from conventional society, that causes urban crime. Sociologist Elijah Anderson says lower-class areas maintain competing value systems.[126] One that he labels "decent" is committed to family and middle-class values; the other is an oppositional culture of "the streets," whose norms are often diametrically opposed to those of mainstream society. At the heart of the code is respect, which is the need to be treated with deference. Respect is hard won but easily lost and so must constantly be guarded. Lower-class focal concerns seem as relevant today as when first identified by Miller more than forty years ago.

These views of a lower-class subculture formed by strain inspired a number of formal theories that predicted the onset of gang delinquency in lower-class areas. The two best known are the theory of delinquent **subcultures** and the theory of **differential opportunity**.

Theory of Delinquent Subcultures

In his classic 1955 book *Delinquent Boys*,[127] Albert Cohen said the delinquent behaviour of lower-class youths is a protest against the norms and values of the middle-class culture. Because legitimate success is difficult, lower-class youths experience **status frustration**. As a result, many of them join gangs and engage in behaviour that is nonutilitarian, malicious, and negativistic.

Cohen viewed the gang as a subculture, possessing an oppositional value system that takes its norms from the larger culture but turns them upside down. The delinquent's conduct is normal in the context of the subculture because it is deviant according to the norms of the larger cultures. For example, recent research based on interviews with inmates shows that transactions involving illegal firearms take place through informal, personal networks, despite the weight of gun control legislation.[128]

Accordingly, the development of the delinquent subculture is a consequence of socialization practices found in a poor environment. Deficient socialization renders lower-class kids unable to achieve conventional success. Cohen suggests that lower-class parents are incapable of teaching children the necessary techniques for entering the dominant middle-class culture. Developmental handicaps suffered by lower-class kids include lack of education, poor speech and communication skills, and an inability to delay gratification. These children lack the basic skills necessary to achieve social and economic success in a demanding "credentialist" society.

Interestingly, recent research by Baron shows that homeless male street youth are much more likely than are males in the general population to use aggression to resolve disputes and to demand reparation from people they believe have harmed them. This trait would not serve them well in an office environment perhaps, but it is highly adaptable and functional on the street.[129]

Middle-Class Measuring Rods. One significant handicap that lower-class children face is the inability to positively impress middle-class authority figures, such as teachers, employers, or supervisors. These authority figures set standards based on middle-class measuring rods. The conflict and frustration that lower-class youths experience when they fail to meet these standards are a primary cause of delinquency.

Lower-class youths who have difficulty adjusting to the middle-class measuring rods of one institution may find themselves prejudged by others. The ratings are reviewed and magnified by records, and a negative school record may be reviewed by juvenile court authorities; a juvenile court record may be opened by the military; and a military record can influence the securing of a job. A person's status and esteem in the community are determined by judgments that reflect the traditional values of mainstream society.[130] Negative evaluations become part of a permanent file that follows an individual for the rest of his or her life. When he or she wants to improve, evidence of prior failures is used to discourage advancement.

The Formation of Deviant Subcultures. Cohen said that lower-class boys who suffer rejection by middle-class decision makers usually elect to join one of three existing subcultures: the corner boy, the college boy, or the delinquent boy.

The corner boy is not a chronic delinquent but engages in petty offences, such as recreational drug abuse. He is loyal to his peer group, which he depends on for support, motivation, and interest. His values, therefore, are those of the group with which he is in close personal contact. He is well aware of his failure to achieve the standards of the "dream," retreats into the comforting world of lower-class peers, and eventually becomes a stable member of the neighbourhood, holding a menial job, marrying, and remaining in the community.

The college boy embraces the cultural and social values of the middle class. Rather than scorning middle-class measuring rods, he strives to be successful by those standards. Cohen views this type of youth as one who is embarking on an almost hopeless path, since he is ill-equipped academically, socially, and linguistically to achieve the rewards of middle-class life.

The delinquent boy adopts a set of norms in opposition to middle-class values, living for today and letting "tomorrow take care of itself." Delinquent boys resist efforts by family, school, and authority to control their behaviour and join a gang because it is autonomous and independent. Frustrated by their inability to succeed, these boys exhibit **reaction formation**, an exaggerated response disproportionate to the stimulus. This reaction takes the form of irrational and unaccountable hostility, causing these youth to overreact to any perceived threat or slight, making them more willing to take risks and violate the law.

Cohen's work helps explain how social factors, such as status frustration and middle-class measuring rods, promote a delinquent subculture. The corner boy–college boy–delinquent boy triad explains why many lower-class youths fail to become chronic offenders: There is more than one social path open to poor youth.[131] His work is a skillful integration of strain and social disorganization theories.

Strain and Street Youths. In their application of strain theory, Baron and Kennedy look at the growing problem of youths under the age of 24 who have left school and hang out on the street. This population is usually underemployed or unemployed and homeless, with lives characterized by poverty and hunger.

For many of these youths, criminal activity is the primary way to gain material wealth. The culturally produced feelings of failure and rejection lead to a sense of relative deprivation and thwarted ambition in a culture where the idea is that hard work is the way to get ahead. Youths in this situation gravitate together and develop a new frame of reference in which status is attained and alternative routes to financial success organized. Together they attempt to develop new norms, new standards, and new criteria for success that are more readily achieved.

Baron and Kennedy's study of two hundred homeless male youths took place in the downtown business core of a city bordered by the local skid row. The area contained a mix of commercial and financial establishments surrounded by bars, pawnshops, hotels, shelters, detoxification centres, rooming houses, rundown residential units, and abandoned buildings.

Respondents reported an average legal income of $335 a month in the previous year. The average respondent reported more than 1600 offences in the prior 12 months, mostly for selling illegal drugs. They also reported an average of 348 property offences and 48 robberies throughout the year (thefts from cars, shoplifting, and break and enters).

The youths reported that their failure to find employment destroyed their motivation and made them less likely to think that lawbreaking is wrong: "Because I could make more money selling drugs than working for five bucks an hour"; "'Cause I don't feel guilty about it 'cause I hate flipping burgers. If you're going to have a job you might as well be doing something you like, like robbing people." Crime not only gave them money but also provided a structure to their day and a sense of doing something.[132]

Theory of Differential Opportunity

In *Delinquency and Opportunity*, Cloward and Ohlin portray the gang-sustaining criminal subculture by combining strain and social disorganization principles to describe how delinquent activity is a requirement for "fitting in." [133]

Youth gangs are an important part of the delinquent subculture. Delinquent gangs spring up in disorganized areas where youths lack the opportunity to gain success through conventional means. True to strain theory principles, slum kids are individuals who want to conform to middle-class values but lack the means to do so; reaching out for socially approved goals under conditions that made it impossible to achieve them may become a prelude to deviance.

Differential Opportunities. The centrepiece of the theory is the concept of **differential opportunity**, in which people share the same success goals; however, those in the lower class have limited means of achieving those goals. People who perceive themselves as failures within conventional society will seek alternative or innovative ways to gain success, joining with like-minded peers to form a gang. Gang members provide the emotional support to handle the shame, fear, or guilt they may develop while engaging in illegal acts. The youth who is considered a failure at school and is only qualified for a menial job at a minimum wage can earn thousands of dollars plus the respect of his or her peers by joining a gang and engaging in drug deals or armed robberies.

The opportunity for success in either conventional or criminal careers is limited. In stable areas, adolescents may be recruited by professional criminals, drug traffickers, or organized crime groups. Unstable areas cannot support flourishing criminal opportunities, so adult role models are absent and young criminals have few opportunities to join established gangs or learn the fine points of professional crime. Cloward and Ohlin's most important finding, then, is that all opportunities for success, both illegal and conventional, are closed for the most "truly disadvantaged" youth.

Because of differential opportunity, kids are likely to join one of three types of gangs:

1. *Criminal gangs.* Criminal gangs exist in stable but poor areas in which close connections among adolescent and adult offenders create an environment

for successful crime. Youths are recruited into established criminal gangs that provide training in criminal knowledge and skills. During this "apprenticeship stage," older, more experienced members of the criminal subculture hold youthful "trainees" on tight reins, limiting activities that might jeopardize the gang's profits (for example, engaging in nonfunctional, irrational violence). The new recruits learn the techniques and attitudes of the criminal world. To become fully accepted, novices must prove themselves reliable and dependable. They are introduced to the intermediaries—drug importers, fences, pawnshop operators—and to legal connections—crooked police officers and shady lawyers.

2. *Conflict gangs.* Conflict gangs develop in communities unable to provide either legitimate or illegitimate opportunities. These highly disorganized areas are marked by transient residents and physical deterioration. Crime in these areas is individualistic, unorganized, petty, poorly paid, and unprotected because successful adult criminal role models are missing. With such severe limitations on criminal opportunity, violence is a means of gaining status. The swaggering toughs fight with weapons to win respect from rivals and engage in unpredictable and destructive assaults on people and property to protect their own and their gang's honour. By doing so, they gain admiration from their peers and develop their own self-image. Conflict gangs help get the scarce

According to Cloward and Ohlin's theory of differential opportunity, those who perceive themselves as failures within conventional society or who conclude that there is little hope for advancement by legitimate means may join with like-minded peers to form a gang.

resources for adolescent pleasure and opportunity in underprivileged areas.

3. *Retreatist gangs.* Retreatists are double failures, unable to gain success through legitimate means and unwilling to do so through illegal ones. Some retreatists have tried crime or violence but are too clumsy, too weak, or too scared to be accepted in criminal or violent gangs. They then "retreat" into a role on the fringe of society. Members of the retreatist subculture constantly search for ways of getting high with alcohol, pot, heroin, unusual sexual experiences, or music. To feed their habits, retreatists develop a "hustle"—pimping, conning, selling drugs, and committing petty crimes. Personal status in the retreatist subculture is derived from peer approval.

Analysis of Differential Opportunity Theory. Cloward and Ohlin's theory is important because of its integration of cultural deviance and social disorganization variables and its recognition of different modes of criminal adaptation. The fact that criminal cultures can be supportive, rational, and profitable seems to be a more realistic reflection of the actual world of the criminal gang than was Cohen's original view of purely negativistic, destructive criminal youths who oppose all social values. The tripartite model of urban delinquency also relates directly to the treatment and rehabilitation of delinquents. Although other social structure theorists portray delinquent youths as having values and attitudes in opposition to middle-class culture, Cloward and Ohlin suggest that many delinquents share the goals and values of the general society but lack the means to obtain success. This position suggests that delinquency prevention can be achieved by providing youths with the means for obtaining the success they truly desire without the need to change their basic attitudes and beliefs.[134]

In the United States, the nation with perhaps the most gangs, a 1992 survey of police departments found that 91 percent (72 cities) reported the presence of youth gangs involved in criminal activity. Data from these cities, along with data collected from 29 smaller cities and 11 county jurisdictions, showed a total of 4881 gangs with 249 324 members. A 1994 survey indicated 8625 to 16 643 gangs containing between 378 807 and 555 181 members. It was estimated that gang members commit between 437 066 and 580 331 crimes each year, that gang activity is higher than ever before, and that gang membership accelerated in the 1990s.[135]

Another survey of "gang cities" found that 94 percent of cities with populations of one hundred thousand or more and eight hundred to nine hundred smaller cities have gang problems. Combining these would create a total of more than one thousand gang locations. Although smaller cities have relatively few gang members, half of the larger cities report having five hundred or more members, including 14 cities with more than four thousand gang members. Los Angeles alone has more than a thousand gangs.[136]

Connections

Chapter 13 looks at gangs in Canada and their relationship to ethnic minorities.

Gang activity has increased because of the involvement of youth gangs in the distribution and sale of illegal drugs, replacing traditional organized crime families as the dominant supplier of illegal substances. The introduction of crack cocaine, which provides a cheap and powerful albeit short-term high, helped open new markets in the drug trade.[137]

A report on female gang association in Manitoba supports social structure theories and differential opportunity theory in particular. Female gang members typically come from poor socioeconomic backgrounds, survive dysfunctional childhoods, and are predominantly Aboriginal. Gang life provides a sense of family and acceptance, supplies them with money and drugs, and gives them a sense of power.[138]

Gang formation may be the natural consequence of the evolution of Western society from a manufacturing economy to a low-wage service economy.[139] The modern city, which traditionally required a large population base for its manufacturing plants, now faces economic stress as these plants shut down. In this uneasy economic climate, gangs form and flourish in areas where the moderating influence of successful adult role models and stable families declines and where adolescents face constrained choices and weak social controls.[140] Gang activity provides members with a stable income, so from this perspective, youth gangs are a response to the economy.

The rise of gang memberships in a declining industrial market and the development of drug profits as an alternative or innovative method of financial success are social conditions predicted by opportunity theory. The prevalence of gang activity in urban North American society provides staunch support for the social structure approach.

Evaluation of Social Structure Theories

The social structure approach has influenced both criminological theory and crime-prevention strategies. Its core concepts seem valid in view of the high crime and delinquency rates and the gang activity occurring in the deteriorated inner-city areas of large cities. The public's image includes roaming bands of violent teenage gangs, drug users, prostitutes, muggers, and similar frightening examples of criminality. All of these are present today in urban areas.

Each branch of the general structural model supports and amplifies others. Some theorists, such as Sampson and Wilson, suggest that these concepts are actually interdependent.[141] Factors that cause strain, such as lack of access to legitimate economic opportunities and economic inequality, also produce social disorganization. Stress leads to alcohol abuse and unprotected sex, causing an increase in dysfunctional families, urban hostility, and the deterioration of informal social controls.

Critics say that lower-class culture and residence in urban areas are not sufficient to cause people to violate the law.[142] They say that lower-class crime rates are due to bias in the criminal justice system. Lower-class areas seem to have higher crime rates because residents are arrested and prosecuted by the police.[143] Class bias is coupled with discrimination against minority-group members, who have long suffered at the hands of the justice system.

Even if the higher crime rates recorded in lower-class areas are valid, it is still true that most members of the lower class are not criminals. The discovery of the chronic offender indicates that a significant majority of people living in lower-class environments are not criminals and that a relatively small proportion of the population commits most crimes. If social forces alone could be used to explain crime, how could we account for the vast number of urban poor who remain honest and law-abiding? Given these circumstances, it is tempting to say that law violators must be motivated by some individual mental, physical, or social process or trait.[144]

It is also questionable whether a distinct lower-class culture actually exists. Several researchers have found that gang members and other delinquent youths value such concepts as sharing, earning money, having an education, and respecting the law as highly as do middle-class youths.[145] Opinion polls show that most lower-class citizens maintain middle-class values, such as tougher drug laws, more police protection, and greater control over criminal offenders. These opinions seem similar to conventional middle-class values rather than representative of an independent, deviant subculture. Thus, income does not seem to be a good predictor of youth delinquency.

Although this evidence contradicts some of the central ideas of social structure theory, the discovery of stable patterns of lower-class crime, the high crime rates found in disorganized inner-city areas, and the rise of teenage gangs and groups support a close association between crime rates and social class position.

Social Structure Theory and Social Policy

Social structure theory has had a significant influence on social policy. If the cause of criminality is viewed as a separation between lower-class individuals and conventional goals, norms, and rules, it seems logical that alternatives to criminal behaviour can be provided by giving those who are deprived opportunities a chance to share in the rewards of conventional society.

One approach is to give indigent people direct financial aid through welfare and to give aid to dependent children. Crime rates are reduced when families receive supplemental income through public assistance payments.[146]

Efforts have been made to reduce crime rates by directly applying concepts suggested by social structure theories to social policy, such as Shaw's Chicago Area Project, which attempted to organize existing community structures to develop social stability in otherwise disorganized slums. The project sponsored recreation programs for children in the neighbourhoods, including summer camps. It campaigned for community improvements in education, sanitation, traffic safety, physical conservation, and law enforcement. Project members also worked with police and court agencies to supervise and treat gang youth and adult offenders. In a 25-year assessment of the project, it was successful in demonstrating the feasibility of creating youth welfare organizations in high-delinquency areas.[147]

Social structure concepts have been a critical ingredient in social reform projects, particularly those that sought to attack the crime-producing structures of poor areas. The crime-prevention effort called Mobilization for Youth was designed to provide teacher training to help educators deal with problem youth, create work opportunities through a youth job centre, organize neighbourhood councils and associations, provide street workers to deal with teen gangs, and set up counselling services and assistance to neighbourhood families. Subsequent programs included the Job Corps, Head Start, and Upward Bound (educational enrichment programs) and Neighbourhood Legal Services. Such programs sought to reduce crime by developing community pride in poverty areas and providing educational and job opportunities for crime-prone youths.

Since then, the tendency has been to adopt more selective crime-prevention policies.

Connections

Across Canada, more than one hundred Head Start projects have been instituted. Designed as an early intervention strategy for Natives and non-Natives alike, funded by more than $20 million annually from the federal government, these projects are designed to increase self-esteem and develop a positive sense of self. This initiative is described in more detail in Chapter 8.

Summary

Sociology has been the main orientation of criminologists because crime rates vary among social classes, society goes through changes that affect crime, and social interaction relates to criminality. Social structure theories suggest that people's places in the socioeconomic structure of society influence their chances of becoming a criminal. Poor people are more likely to commit certain crimes because they are unable to achieve monetary or social success in any other way. Social structure theory has three schools of thought: social disorganization, strain, and cultural deviance theory (summarized in Table 7.1).

Social disorganization theory suggests that poor urban dwellers violate the law because they live in areas in which social control has broken down. The origin of social disorganization theory can be traced originally to Shaw and McKay, who concluded that disorganized areas marked by divergent values and transitional populations produce criminality. This research was also conducted at McGill University in Canada, as part of a larger process of social reform. Modern social ecology theory looks at such neighbourhood issues as community fear, unemployment, siege mentality, and deterioration.

Strain theories compose the second branch of the social structure approach. They view crime as a result of the anger people experience over their inability to achieve legitimate social and economic success. Strain theories hold that most people share common values and beliefs, but the ability to achieve them is differentiated throughout the social structure. The best-known is Merton's theory of anomie, which describes what happens when the means people have at their disposal are not adequate to satisfy their goals. This theory was subsequently developed by others to show that strain has multiple sources.

Cultural deviance theories hold that a unique value system develops in lower-class areas. Lower-class values approve of such behaviours as being tough, never showing fear, and defying authority. People

TABLE 7.1 Social Structure Theories

Theory	Major Premise	Strengths
Social Disorganization Theory		
Shaw and McKay's concentric zone theory	Crime is a product of transitional neighbourhoods that manifest social disorganization and value conflict.	Identifies why crime rates are highest in slum areas. Points out the factors that produce crime. Suggests programs to help reduce crime.
Social economy theory	The conflicts and problems of urban social life and communities, including fear, unemployment, deterioration, and siege mentality, influence crime rates.	Accounts for urban crime rates and trends.
Strain Theory		
Anomie theory	People who adopt the goals of society but lack the means to attain them seek alternatives, such as crime.	Points out how competition for success creates conflict and crime. Suggests that social conditions and not personality can account for crime. Can explain middle- and upper-class crime.
General strain theory	Strain has a variety of sources. Strain causes crime in the absence of adequate coping mechanisms.	Identifies the complexities of strain in modern society. Expands on anomie theory. Shows the influences of social events on behaviour over the life course.
Institutional anomie theory	Material goals pervade all aspects of Canadian life.	Explains why crime rates are so high in North American culture.
Relative deprivation theory	Crime occurs when the wealthy and poor live in close proximity to each other.	Explains high crime rates in deteriorated inner-city areas located near more affluent neighbourhoods.
Cultural Deviance Theory		
Sellin's culture conflict theory	Obedience to the norms of their lower-class culture puts people in conflict with the norms of the dominant culture.	Identifies the aspects of lower-class life that produce street crime. Adds to Shaw and McKay's analysis. Creates the concept of culture conflict.
Miller's focal concern theory	Citizens who obey the street rules of lower-class life (local concerns) find themselves in conflict with the dominant culture.	Identifies the core values of lower-class culture and shows their association to crime.
Cohen's theory of delinquent gangs	Status frustration of lower-class boys, created by their failure to achieve middle-class success, causes them to join gangs.	Shows how conditions of lower-class life produce crime. Explains violence and destructive acts. Identifies conflict of lower class with middle class.
Cloward and Ohlin's theory of opportunity	Blockage of conventional opportunities causes lower-class youths to join criminal, conflict, or retreatist gangs.	Shows that even illegal opportunities are structured in society. Indicates why people become involved in a particular type of criminal activity. Presents a way of preventing crime.

perceiving strain will bond together in their own groups or subcultures for support and recognition. Cohen links the formation of subcultures to the failure of lower-class citizens to achieve recognition from middle-class decision makers, such as teachers, employers, and police officers. Cloward and Ohlin have argued that crime results from lower-class people's perception that their opportunity for success is limited. Consequently, youths in low-income areas may join criminal, conflict, or retreatist gangs.

Thinking Like a Criminologist

You are a criminologist at a university and are serving as an adviser to the mayor of Central City, a capital city with a population of 150 000. The mayor wants to initiate a project to show that government can reduce vandalism, petty crime, and disturbances in an area suffering from a disorganized community structure. Efforts by the police to reduce public disorder and crime rates are not working.

Delinquent youths run free at night, vandalizing property and committing minor thefts. The school system is unable to do anything, and public education campaigns seem fruitless. Residents feel little can be done to bring the neighbourhood back to life.

A recently published research report suggests that the key to reducing neighbourhood crime is to create a sense of "collective efficacy" in city neighbourhoods. The report defined collective efficacy as "cohesion among neighbourhood residents combined with shared expectations for informal social control of public space."

The basic premise is that when people mistrust one another, they are unlikely to take action against disorder and crime. However, when there is cohesion and mutual trust among neighbours, the likelihood is greater that they will share a willingness to intervene for the common good. The report found that in neighbourhoods where this sense of collective efficacy was strong, rates of violence were low, regardless of neighbourhood composition or socioeconomic conditions. Collective efficacy also appeared to deter disorder: Where it was strong, observed levels of physical and social disorder were low.

The mayor wants to apply these concepts to Central City. She asks you to come up with a plan for increasing the collective efficacy of local neighbourhoods and to determine whether such measures can actually reduce crime. You can bring any public or private element to bear on this overwhelming problem.

Your problem is twofold: (1) How can collective efficacy be improved? (2) What test will show whether improvements in collective efficacy levels are responsible for lower violent crime rates?

Key Terms

at-risk	focal concerns	social ecologists
Chicago School	general strain theory (GST)	social injustice
concentration effect	income inequality	social structure theory
conduct norms	natural areas	status frustration
cultural deviance theory	negative affective states	strain theory
cultural transmission	reaction formation	subcultures
culture conflict	relative deprivation	transitional neighbourhoods
culture of poverty	siege mentality	underclass
differential opportunity	social disorganization theory	value conflict

Critical Thinking Questions

1. Is there a "transition" area in your town or city? Does the crime rate remain constant in this neighbourhood, regardless of the racial, ethnic, or cultural composition of its residents?

2. Do you believe a distinct lower-class culture exists? Do you know anyone who has the focal concerns Miller talks about? Did you experience elements of these focal concerns while you were in high school? Will emerging forms of communication, such as the Internet, reduce cultural differences and create a more homogeneous society, or are subcultures resistant to such influences?

3. Do you agree with Agnew that there is more than one cause of strain? If so, are there other sources of strain that he did not consider?

4. How would a structural theorist explain the presence of middle-class crime?

5. How would biosocial theories explain the high levels of violent crime in lower-class areas?

 See the book-specific website at http://www.siegelcriminology3e.nelson.com for additional chapter links, discussions, and quizzes.

chapter

8

Social Process Theories

Many criminologists question whether a person's place in the social structure can alone control the onset of criminality. After all, the majority of people residing in the nation's most deteriorated urban areas are law-abiding citizens who hold conventional values and compensate for their lack of social standing and financial problems by working hard, living frugally, and looking to the future. Conversely, self-report studies tell us that many members of the privileged classes engage in theft, drug use, and other crimes.

Even if it is assumed that all criminals come from the lower classes (which they don't), it is evident that the great majority of even the poorest Canadians do not commit criminal acts.[1] In the United States, the National Crime Victimization Survey has estimated that although 26 million serious crimes occur annually, about two million people could account for most of those offences.[2]

Therefore, neighbourhood deterioration and disorganization alone cannot explain why one person commits crime while another person living in the same environment obeys the law, gets an education, and has a legitimate job.[3] Relatively few delinquent offenders living in the most deteriorated areas remain persistent, chronic offenders, despite the continuing pressure of social decay. Some other social forces must be at work to explain why the majority of at-risk individuals do not become persistent criminal offenders.

To explain these contradictory findings, attention has focused on social-psychological processes and interactions common to all people. **Social process theories** hold that criminality is a function of **socialization** and draw attention to the interactions people have with others. As they pass through life, people are influenced by familial relationships, peer group associations, educational experiences, and interactions with authorities, such as teachers and employers. If these relationships are positive and supportive, people will be able to succeed within the rules of society; if these relationships are dysfunctional and destructive, conventional success is more difficult.

Social process theories share one basic concept: All people, regardless of race, class, or gender, have the potential to become delinquent or law-abiding citizens. Although some have the burden of poverty, racism, poor schools, and disrupted family lives, these social forces may be counteracted by positive peer relations, a supportive family, and educational success. Even the most affluent may turn to antisocial behaviour if their life experiences are intolerable or destructive.

Social process theorists focus attention on the socialization of youths and attempt to identify supportive developmental factors—family relationships, peer influences, educational attainment, self-image development—that can lead to a successful life. If these developmental factors are dysfunctional, they can result in antisocial behaviours.

The influence of social process theories has endured. Most residents of inner-city areas refrain from

criminal activity, and few of those who do commit crimes remain persistent, chronic offenders in their adulthood. If poverty were the sole cause of crime, poor adults would be as criminal as would be poor teenagers; class position alone cannot explain crime rates.[4]

Research shows that even in the most deteriorated areas, it is the quality of interpersonal interactions with parents, peers, and schools that controls criminality; income and environment alone cannot determine behaviour.[5] Socialization is as important as social structure to understanding crime.

Connections

Chapter 3's analysis of the class–crime relationship showed why that relationship is still a hotly debated topic. Although serious criminals may be disproportionately found in lower-class areas, self-report studies show that criminality cuts across class lines. The discussion of drug use in Chapter 14 also shows that many members of the middle class engage in recreational substance abuse, an indication that many law violators are not economically motivated.

Social Processes and Crime

Criminologists study the critical elements of socialization, such as family, peer group, and school, to determine how those elements contribute to the development of a criminal career.

InfoTrac®

For information on how a disordered attachment-related behavioural pattern has been linked to severe caregiving neglect and maltreatment, see Adrian D. Sandler, "Attachment Disorder Behavior Following Early Severe Deprivation: Extension and Longitudinal Follow-Up," *Journal of Developmental and Behavioral Pediatrics* 22, no. 1 (2001): 80.

Family Relations

Evidence that parenting factors play a critical role in determining whether individuals misbehave as children and as adults is well established, with research going back decades.[6] Youths who grow up in a household characterized by tension, where familial love and support are lacking, will be susceptible to the crime-promoting forces in the environment, placing them at "higher risk."[7]

Children possessing disruptive characteristics at an early age are more likely to engage in later risky behaviour, adolescent delinquency, and adult crime. However, there is a window of opportunity between the ages of four and nine when quality of parental intervention is significant.[8]

Even those children living in high-crime areas will be better able to resist the temptations of the streets if they receive fair discipline, care, and support from parents who provide them with strong, positive role models.[9]

Nonetheless, living in a disadvantaged neighbourhood places a strain on family functioning, especially in single-parent families experiencing social isolation from relatives, friends, and neighbours. Kids who are raised within such distressed families are at risk for delinquency.[10] The relationship between family structure and crime is critical when the high rates of divorce and single parenthood are considered.

The United States Census Bureau predicts that the percentage of children living in homes headed by married couples will decline from 35 percent today to about 29 percent in 2010. In Canada, the rate of "other" family household types, including lone-parent family households, increased 5 percent between 1996 and 2001.[11] Such trends are important when we consider the fact that since 1960, the number of single-parent households in the population has been significantly related to arrest rates.[12]

At one time, growing up in a broken home was considered a primary cause of criminal behaviour. However, many criminologists today discount any easy association between family structure and the onset of criminality, claiming that family conflict and discord are more important determinants of behaviour than is family structure.[13] However, Wilson and Herrnstein claim that it is difficult for single mothers or fathers to make up for the loss of a second parent, and the chances of failure increase.[14] Single parents may find it difficult to provide adequate supervision, and children with single parents receive less encouragement and less help with schoolwork. They may be more prone to rebellious acts, such as running away and truancy.[15] Children in two-parent households are more likely to want to go on to postsecondary education than are kids in single-parent homes; poor school achievement and limited educational aspirations have been associated with delinquent behaviour.[16]

InfoTrac®

Does remarriage help the educational achievement of kids who live in single-parent households? To find out, read this article in InfoTrac® College Edition: William Jeynes, "Effects of Remarriage Following Divorce on the Academic Achievement of Children," *Journal of Youth and Adolescence* 28, no. 3 (1999): 385(9).

Because their incomes are often reduced in the aftermath of marital break-up, many divorced mothers are forced to move to residences in deteriorated neighbourhoods, which places children at risk for crime and drug abuse.[17]

However, new research complicates the picture somewhat. It has been found that a mother's delinquency before marriage not only predicts her future divorce but also accounts for the behaviour problems of her children after divorce.

In a review of data on 1204 mothers and their children from the United States National Longitudinal Survey of Youth, researchers concluded that an adolescent mother's delinquent behaviour in 1980 (abusing drugs and being delinquent at school) predicted her divorced status in 1994 and whether her child was antisocial, anxious, or depressed. Parents' personal behaviour and personality characteristics have a greater impact on their children's behaviour than does their married, never-married, or divorced status.[18]

It has also been thought that remarriage does not mitigate the effects of divorce on youths: Children living with a stepparent exhibit as many problems as youths in divorce situations and considerably more problems than those living with both biological parents.[19]

However, again, new research complicates the picture. Although crime rates for adolescents from two-parent families are lower than for teens from single-parent families, evidence collected in the American National Youth Survey suggests that divorce will have an effect on delinquency only when a two-parent family structure is not reestablished.

Data on 1169 boys and girls between the ages of 13 and 19 showed that having two adult caretakers in a household allows less opportunity for delinquency. Although children from single-parent families face a higher risk of delinquency than do those from two-parent families, it is having an intact family structure that's important.

The study found the family structure–delinquency relationship was also gender based. The difference in delinquent behaviour between girls from one-parent families and girls from two-parent families was greater than was the difference in delinquency for boys.[20]

Other family factors that have predictive value for criminal behaviour include inconsistent discipline, poor supervision, and the lack of a warm, loving, supportive parent–child relationship.[21] Parents who are supportive and control their children in a noncoercive fashion (parental efficacy) are more successful.[22] Delinquency is reduced if parents provide a structure that integrates children into families while giving them the ability to assert their individuality and regulate their own behaviour.[23] Children who have warm and affectionate ties to their parents report greater levels of self-esteem beginning in adolescence and extending into their adulthood; high self-esteem is inversely related to criminal behaviour.[24]

Parental deviance has also been linked to a child's criminal behaviour. Children growing up in homes in which parents have a mental impairment are at risk for delinquency.[25] Even at age two, the children of drug abusers exhibit personality defects, such as excessive anger and negativity.[26] Kids whose parents abuse drugs are more likely to become persistent substance abusers than are the children of nonabusers.[27] The children of parents who engage in criminality and substance abuse are more likely to engage in law-violating behaviour than are the children of conventional parents.[28]

There is also a link between child abuse, neglect, sexual abuse, and crime.[29] Studies show an association between child maltreatment and serious self-reported and official delinquency.[30] Victims of child abuse are more likely to mature into abusing and violent adults than are nonvictims.[31] This cycle of violence means that children who are physically victimized and who witness interparental violence have an increased risk of adulthood child and partner abuse. The results also point to same-gender modelling for perpetration of violence against women and children: Men's risk was increased by exposure to father to mother violence, and women's risk for being in an abusive relationship was increased by childhood victimization.[32]

Childhood sexual abuse victims also report twice as many sexual assaults, four times more self-inflicted harm, higher rates of domestic violence, and more significant lifetime traumas.[33] Child abuse is most prevalent among families living in socially disorganized neighbourhoods, explaining in part the association between poverty and violence.[34]

Results from interviews with parents in the 1998–99 National Longitudinal Survey of Children and Youth indicate that 8 percent of children between the ages of four and seven had witnessed some type of physical violence in the home, with one-third witnessing it sometime and 5 percent often. Witnessing violence in the home is related to short-term and long-term behavioural problems, such as aggression and anxiety. Furthermore, rates of violence in the home are on the rise.[35]

The cycle of violence is not automatic, and the most typical outcome for individuals exposed to violence in their families is to be nonviolent in their adult lives.

Connections

The cycle of violence is also discussed in Chapter 4.

The effect of the family on delinquency has also been observed in other cultures. For example, research on Chinese families shows that those who provide firm support inhibit delinquency, whereas families who experience parental deviance are more likely to contain youths involved in antisocial behaviours.[36]

Connections

The age-graded theory of Sampson and Laub is discussed in Chapter 10. Although deviant parents may encourage offending, Sampson and Laub believe that life experiences can either encourage crime-prone people to offend or aid them in their return to a conventional lifestyle.

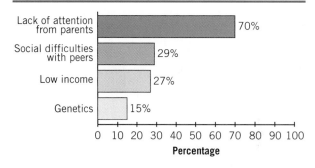

Percentage

Seven in 10 parents (70 percent) point to "lack of attention from parents" as a severe negative risk factor, while 3 in 10 (29 percent) consider "social difficulties with peers" a severe negative risk factor. Three in 10 (27 percent) think that "low income is a severe negative risk factor," while 1 in 7 (15 percent) say that "genetics" are a severe negative risk factor.

Source: Poll conducted by Ipsos Reid, "Parents Spending More Time With Their Children" *Part III: Parents On Parenting: How Are Canada's Children Being Raised?* April 3, 2004, Ipsos News Centre, http://www.ipsos-na.com/news/pressrelease.cfm?id=2112 (accessed May 15, 2005).

Educational Experience

Adolescent achievement in school has also been linked to criminality. Studies show that children who do poorly in school, lack motivation, and feel alienated are the most likely to engage in criminal acts.[37] An analysis of 118 studies of educational achievement found academic performance to be a significant predictor of crime and delinquency. Although White children and males seem more deeply influenced by school failure, all children who fail in school offend more frequently, commit more serious and violent offences, and persist in their offending into adulthood.[38]

The Canadian Centre for Justice Statistics found that children's social relationships at school are related to aggression. Figure 8.1 demonstrates that when children feel unsafe and bullied at school, they feel like outsiders and are more likely to be involved in aggressive behaviours.

Furthermore, a relationship exists between property offences and school risk factors (Figure 8.2). Of children who reported liking school a lot, 5 percent were involved in high numbers of property offences, compared with 16 percent of those who did not like

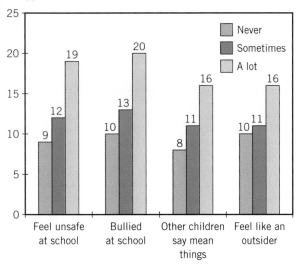

Figure 8.1 Percentage of Children Aged 12 to 13 Reporting High Levels of Aggressive Behaviour as a Function of School Relationships

Percentage of Children Reporting High Levels of Aggressive Behaviours

Source: Adapted from the Statistics Canada publication "Children Witnessing Family Violence," 2001, *Juristat,* Catalogue 85-002, vol. 21, no. 4, June 12, 2001.

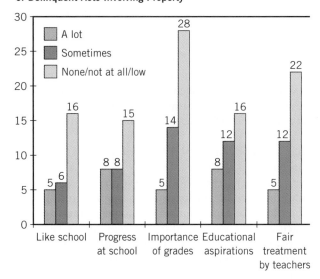

Figure 8.2 Percentage of Children Aged 12 to 13 Reporting High Levels of Delinquent Acts Involving Property as a Function of Relative Academic Ability and Aspirations

Percentage of Children Reporting High Levels of Delinquent Acts Involving Property

Source: Adapted from the Statistics Canada publication "Children Witnessing Family Violence," 2001, *Juristat,* Catalogue 85-002, vol. 21, no. 4, June 12, 2001.

school. Children who do not like school, whose school progress is poor, and who think grades are unimportant are also more likely to be involved in property offences. In addition, children who have lower educational aspirations and who skip classes are more likely to report being involved in high levels of property offences. Finally, those children who scored higher on reading achievement tests were less likely to be involved in delinquent acts.[39]

Schools help contribute to criminality when they label "problem" youths, setting them apart from conventional society. A system that identifies some students as university-bound and others as academic under-achievers **stigmatizes** youths.[40] Research indicates that many school dropouts, especially those who have been expelled, face a significant chance of entering a criminal career.[41] In contrast, doing well in school and developing feelings of attachment to teachers have been linked to resistance to crime.[42]

It is not surprising that the school system has been the subject of criticism concerning its methods, goals, and objectives. Often educational systems are under-funded and understaffed. Reading and math ability levels are in question. These trends do not bode well for the crime rate. Most important, surveys indicate that a lot of youth crime occurs within the schools themselves.

 InfoTrac®

Does delinquency cause educational failure? Or does educational failure cause delinquency? To find out, read Julian Tanner, Scott Davies, and Bill O'Grady, "Whatever Happened to Yesterday's Rebels? Longitudinal Effects of Youth Delinquency on Education and Employment," *Social Problems* 46, no. 2 (1999): 250(1).

Peer Relations

The peer group has a powerful psychological effect on human conduct, influencing decision making and behaviour choices, and this effect has been observed in many cultures.[43]

Early in children's lives, parents are the primary source of influence. Between the ages of 8 and 14, children seek out a stable peer group, and the number and variety of friendships increase as children go through adolescence. Soon, friends begin to have a greater influence over decision making than do parents.[44] By their early teens, children report that their friends give them emotional support when they are feeling bad and that they can confide intimate feelings to peers without worrying about their confidences being betrayed. As they go through adolescence, children form small groups of friends who share activities, confidences, and interests. They share intimate knowledge, as well as activities, such as sports, religion, or hobbies. Although bonds in this wider circle of friends may not be intimate, kids learn a lot about themselves and their world while navigating through these relationships, some of it good, some of it negative.[45]

For example, research by the Department of Community Health and Epidemiology at Queen's University with a sample of 5749 boys and girls aged 11 to 16 found that obese children and teenagers are more likely to be bullied. Part of a 35-country World Health Organization survey, the research found that one in seven overweight children was bullied and that the behaviour grew intensely more violent as the kids aged. Boys were most likely to be the victims of physical bullying, while girls were victims of relational bullying (being ostracized).[46]

In this example, we see how peer approval has a major impact on socialization. Popular youths do well in school and are socially astute. In contrast, children rejected by their peers are more likely to display aggressive behaviour and disrupt group activities through bickering or other antisocial behaviour.[47]

Peer relations are a significant aspect of maturation. In a self-report study of 526 students in grades 8 and 9, researchers found that interparental violence and peer dating violence predicted adolescent dating violence, with the latter being the consistent predictor.[48]

Peers pressure youths to conform to group values. Peers guide children and help them learn to share and cooperate, cope with aggressive impulses, and discuss feelings they would not dare bring up at home. With peers, youths can compare their own experiences, learn that others have similar concerns and problems, and realize that they are not alone. It should come as no surprise, then, that much adolescent criminal activity begins as a group process.[49]

Delinquent peers exert influence on behaviour and beliefs.[50] In every level of the social structure, youths who fall in with a "bad crowd" become more susceptible to criminal behaviour patterns.[51] Deviant peers provide friendship networks that support delinquency and drug use.[52] Riding around, staying out late, and partying with deviant peers provide youths with the opportunity to commit deviant acts.[53] And because delinquent friends are not easily lost, peer influence may continue through the life span.[54] Even though many groups are short-lived and transitory, being exposed to deviant influences in multiple groups helps explain why deviant group membership is highly correlated with personal rates of offending.[55]

 InfoTrac®

In searching for articles on peers and delinquency we found these:

- Stu Kwong Wong, "Peer Relations and Chinese-Canadian Delinquency," *Journal of Youth and Adolescence* 27, no. 5 (1988): 641.
- Rutger Engles and Tom ter Bogt, "Influence of Risk Behaviors on the Quality of Peer Relations in Adolescence," *Journal of Youth and Adolescence* 30, no. 6 (2001): 675.

Institutional Involvement and Belief

People with strong moral values and beliefs, who have learned to distinguish right from wrong, and who regularly attend religious services should also eschew crime and other antisocial behaviours. Religion binds people together and forces them to confront the effect their behaviour has on others; committing crimes would violate the principles of all organized religions. Therefore, it's no surprise that in studying bullying behaviour, researchers have found that children who engage in such positive social activities as going to church are generally less likely to be violent.[56]

In 1969, the association between religious attendance and delinquent behaviour was thought to be negligible.[57] However, recent research has reached an opposing conclusion: Attendance at religious services has a significant impact on crime.[58] For example, kids living in disorganized high-crime areas who attend religious services are better able to resist illegal drug use.[59] Obviously, ongoing participation is a more significant inhibitor of crime than is the mere holding of religious beliefs and values.[60] Cross-national research shows that countries with high rates of church membership and attendance have the lowest crime rates.[61]

 InfoTrac®

What can institutions do? See Clyde A. Winters, "Learning Disabilities, Crime, Delinquency, and Special Education Placement," *Adolescence* 32 (1997): 451–458.

Connections

Arousal theory would also predict that church attendance is inversely correlated with crime rates, because criminals are people who need large amounts of stimulation and they would not be able to sit through religious services. See Chapter 6 for more on arousal theory.

Branches of Social Process Theory

To criminologists, the elements of socialization just described are chief determinants of criminal behaviour. People living in even deteriorated urban areas can successfully resist crime if they have a good self-image, have learned moral values, and have the support of parents, peers, teachers, and neighbours. The girl with a positive self-image who is chosen for a university scholarship, has the warm, loving support of her parents, and is viewed as someone "going places" by friends and neighbours is less likely to adopt a criminal way of life than is another adolescent who is abused at home, who lives with criminal parents, and whose bond to the school and peer group is shattered because she is labelled as a "troublemaker."[62]

Like social structure theory, the social process approach has several independent branches (see Figure 8.3). The first, **social learning theory**, suggests that people learn the techniques and attitudes of crime from close relationships with criminal peers: Crime is a learned behaviour. The second branch, **control theory**, maintains that most people are controlled by their bond to society: Crime occurs when the forces that bind people are weakened or broken. The third branch, **labelling theory**, says that people become criminals when significant members of society label them as such and they accept those labels as a personal identity.

Put another way, social learning theory assumes that people are born "good" and learn to be "bad"; control theory assumes that people are born "bad" and must be controlled in order to be "good"; labelling theory assumes that whether "good" or "bad," people are controlled by the reactions of others.

Social Learning Theory

Social learning theorists say crime is a product of learning norms, values, and behaviours associated with criminal activity. Social learning can involve the actual techniques of crime—how to hot-wire a car or roll a joint—as well as the psychological aspects of criminality—how to deal with the guilt or shame associated with illegal activities.

Figure 8.3   **The Complex Web of Social Processes That Control Human Behaviour**

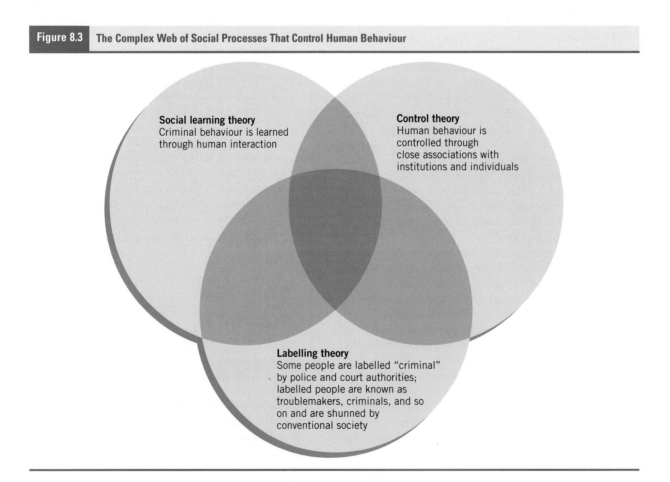

Social learning theory
Criminal behaviour is learned through human interaction

Control theory
Human behaviour is controlled through close associations with institutions and individuals

Labelling theory
Some people are labelled "criminal" by police and court authorities; labelled people are known as troublemakers, criminals, and so on and are shunned by conventional society

This section briefly reviews the three most prominent forms of social learning theory: differential association theory, differential reinforcement theory, and neutralization theory.

Connections

In the late nineteenth century, Gabriel Tarde's theory of imitation held that criminals imitate "superiors" they admire and respect. Tarde's work, discussed in Chapter 6, is thus a precursor to modern learning theories.

Differential Association Theory

Edwin H. Sutherland (1883–1950) first put forth the **differential association (DA) theory** in 1939 in *Principles of Criminology*.[63] It remains one of the most enduring explanations of criminal behaviour.

Sutherland's research on white-collar crime and professional theft led him to dispute the notion that crime is a function of the inadequacy of people in the lower classes.[64] Criminality stemmed from neither individual traits nor socioeconomic position; instead, he believed it to be a function of a learning process that could affect anyone.

A few ideas are basic to the theory of differential association.[65] For example, crime is politically defined by government authorities but may be rejected by some groups of people because of their relative acceptance of criminal definitions. The acquisition of behaviour is a social learning process, and criminal skills and motives are learned as a result of contacts with pro-crime values.

Principles of Differential Association. The basic principles of differential association are as follows:[66]

1. Criminal behaviour is learned in the same manner as any other learned behaviour, such as writing, painting, or reading. It is not inherent or a matter of mere imitation.
2. Criminal behaviour is learned actively in symbolic interaction with other persons and not simply by living in a criminogenic environment or by having personal characteristics, such as low IQ or family problems.
3. Learning deviance occurs within intimate personal groups, such as family, friends, and peers. For example, children who grow up in homes where parents abuse alcohol are more likely to view drinking as being socially and physically beneficial.[67] Social support overrides dominant social controls.
4. Learning deviance includes learning the techniques for committing crime and learning motives, rationalizations, and attitudes. The actual techniques of criminality must be acquired. Young delinquents learn from their associates the proper way to pick a lock, shoplift, and obtain and use narcotics. For example, using marijuana requires learning how to smoke a joint and how to rationalize it.
5. The specific direction of motives and drives is learned from perceptions of various aspects of the legal code as being favourable or unfavourable. Since the reaction to social rules and laws is not uniform across society, people constantly come into contact with others who maintain different views on whether to obey the legal code. When definitions of right and wrong are extremely varied, this creates culture conflict. The conflict of social attitudes is the basis for the concept of differential association.
6. A person becomes a criminal when he or she perceives more benefits than unfavourable consequences to violating the law (see Figure 8.4). Individuals become law violators when they are in contact with persons, groups, or events that have more definitions that are favourable toward criminality and are isolated from counteracting forces. For example, friends sneaking into a theatre to avoid paying for a ticket creates a favourable definition. An unfavourable definition occurs when parents demonstrate disapproval of such actions.
7. Differential associations vary in frequency, duration, priority, and intensity. Whether a person learns to obey the law or to disregard it is influenced by the quality of social interactions. Interactions that are frequent and long have greater influence than those that are brief or haphazard. Furthermore, contacts made early in life probably have a greater and more far-reaching influence than do those developed later on. Finally, the prestige of others is important. For example, the influence of a father, mother, or trusted friend outweighs the effect of more socially distant figures.
8. Although criminal behaviour is an expression of general needs and values, the motives for criminal behaviour are not the same as for conventional behaviour. The motive to accumulate money or social status, such as personal frustration or low self-concept, is an unlikely cause of crime, since it is just as likely to produce noncriminal behaviour, such as getting a better education or working harder on a job. Learning definitions favourable to criminality produces illegal behaviour.

In sum, DA theory holds that people learn criminal attitudes and behaviour while in their adolescence from close and trusted relatives and companions. A criminal career develops if learned antisocial values and behaviours are not exceeded by conventional attitudes and

Figure 8.4 | Differential Association Theory Assumes That Criminal Behaviour Will Occur When the Definitions for Crime Outweigh the Definitions Against Crime

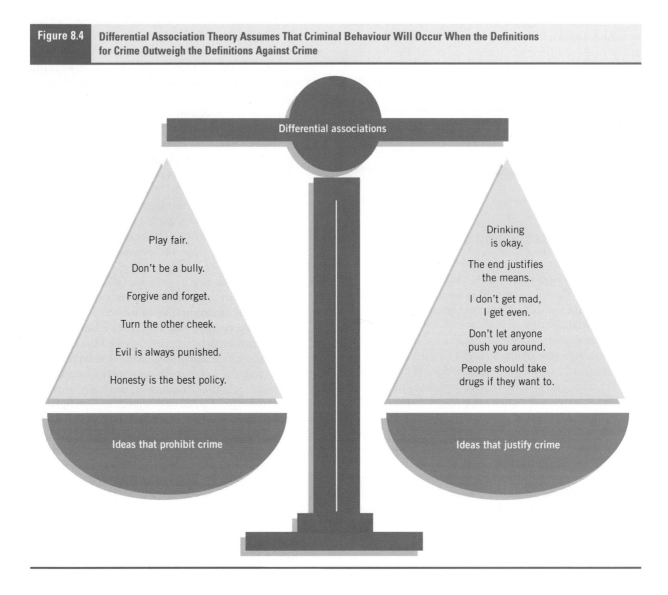

Differential associations

Play fair.

Don't be a bully.

Forgive and forget.

Turn the other cheek.

Evil is always punished.

Honesty is the best policy.

Ideas that prohibit crime

Drinking is okay.

The end justifies the means.

I don't get mad, I get even.

Don't let anyone push you around.

People should take drugs if they want to.

Ideas that justify crime

behaviours. Criminal behaviour is learned in a process similar to learning any other human behaviour.

Testing Differential Association. Despite its importance, research devoted to testing DA theory's assumptions has proven difficult to conduct. For example, social scientists find it difficult to evaluate such vague concepts as "definition toward criminality." It is also difficult to follow people over time, establish precisely when definitions toward criminality begin to outweigh pro-social definitions, and determine whether this imbalance produces criminal behaviour.

However, one important area of research is the friendship patterns of delinquent youths. DA theory implies that criminals maintain close and intimate relations with deviant peers.[68] For example, Short surveyed institutionalized youths and found that they had

maintained close associations with delinquent youths before their law-violating acts.[69] Similarly, Reiss and Rhodes found an association between delinquent friendship patterns and youth crime.[70]

Law violators maintain close relationships with deviant peers.[71] For example, Warr found that antisocial kids who maintain delinquent friends over a long duration are more likely to persist in delinquent behaviour. However, recently cultivated friendships had a greater influence on criminality than friends acquired earlier in life, a finding that contradicts DA theory's emphasis on the "priority" of criminal influences.

DA theory's principles are relevant in explaining the onset of substance abuse and a career in the drug trade.[72] In his interview study of low-level drug dealers, Tunnell found that many novices were tutored by a more experienced dealer who helped them make connections with buyers and sellers. One told him:

> I had a friend of mine who was an older guy and he introduced me to selling marijuana to make a few dollars. I started selling a little and made a few dollars. For a young guy to be making a hundred dollars or so, it was a lot of money. So I got kind of tied up in that aspect of selling drugs.[73]

Making connections is an important part of the dealer's world. Adolescent drug users are likely to have intimate relationships with a peer friendship network that supports their substance abuse.[74]

Another approach to assessing DA theory tests the assumption that people who have assimilated pro-crime attitudes are also the ones most likely to engage in criminal activity.[75] In one cross-cultural study conducted in Hong Kong, Cheung and Ng found that DA items were the most significant predictor of delinquent behaviour in a sample of 1139 secondary-school students. They conclude that deviant youths may be imitating friends' behaviour.[76]

Self-report research must be interpreted cautiously. Since subjects are usually asked about their peer relations, learning experiences, perceptions of differential associations, and criminal behaviours simultaneously, it is impossible to determine whether differential associations were the cause or the result of criminal behaviour. Youths may learn about crime and then commit criminal acts, but it is also possible that experienced delinquents and criminals seek out like-minded peers after they engage in antisocial acts. The internalization of deviant attitudes may follow, rather than precede, criminality.[77]

Researchers must develop more valid measures of differential associations.[78] One possibility is that longitudinal analysis might be used to measure subjects repeatedly over time to determine the effect of exposure to excess definitions toward deviance. Even then, it is difficult to show whether people who continually break the law develop a group of like-minded peers who support their behaviour, rather than a process in which "innocent" people are "seduced" into crime.

Another approach may be to follow a cohort over time to assess the impact of criminal associations: Does repeated exposure escalate deviance? Recent research found that adolescents who acquire criminal friends are also the ones most likely to eventually engage in criminal behaviour—a finding that supports DA theory. Criminal friends are hard to shake, locking people into antisocial behaviour patterns through the life course. People who maintain deviant friendships are the ones most likely to persist in their offending careers, counteracting the crime-reducing effects of the aging-out process.[79]

Analysis of Differential Association Theory. Misconceptions about DA theory have produced some unwarranted criticisms.[80] For example, some criminologists claim that the theory is concerned solely with the number of personal contacts and associations a delinquent has with other criminal or delinquent offenders.[81] If this were true, and we pushed the idea to the extreme, those most likely to become criminals would be police, judges, and correctional authorities, since they are constantly associating with criminals. Sutherland stressed "excess definitions toward criminality," not mere association with criminals. Personnel of the juvenile justice system do have extensive associations with criminals, but these are more than counterbalanced by their associations with law-abiding citizens.

Another misconception is that definitions toward delinquency are acquired only from learning the values of a deviant subculture.[82] However, some people become criminals because they have been socialized into a deviant culture or improperly socialized into the normative culture.[83]

Although DA theory stresses an excess of definitions toward delinquency, these definitions need not come solely from the lower class. Law-abiding middle-class parents can encourage delinquent behaviour by their own drinking, drug use, or family violence. And all youths are exposed to media images that express open admiration for violent heroes, such as those played by Tom Cruise and Vin Diesel, who take the law into their own hands. The influence of differential association is not affected by social class, supporting Sutherland's belief that deviant learning can affect middle-class as well as lower-class youths.[84]

Sutherland's work is criticized for not explaining why one youth who is exposed to delinquent definitions succumbs to them, while another living under similar conditions doesn't.[85] Another criticism of DA theory is that it assumes criminal and delinquent acts are rational and systematic, ignoring spontaneous acts of violence, such as isolated psychopathic killings, which are virtually unsolvable because of the killer's anonymity and lack of criminal associations.

The most serious criticism is the vagueness of terms, such as an "excess of definition toward criminality." How can we determine whether an individual actually has a pro-criminal imbalance of these definitions or a majority of definitions toward criminality?

Despite these criticisms, DA theory maintains an important place in the study of criminal behaviour, providing a consistent explanation of all types of delinquent and criminal behaviour. Unlike social structure theories, DA theory is not limited to lower-class gang activity. The theory also accounts for criminal behaviour in middle- and upper-class areas, where youths are exposed to pro-criminal definitions from such sources as overly opportunistic parents and friends. And the research that suggests that criminal friends are "sticky" indicates that differential associations might be one of the keys to explaining deviance through the life course.

Crime in the News

Children's Aid Probing Khadrs

Agency examines treatment of son in Afghanistan: "Counselling one's child to become suicidal or homicidal constitutes emotional abuse"

Don Martin

National Post, April 20, 2004

The Children's Aid Society has launched an investigation into whether the parents of 14-year-old Karim Khadr are guilty of child abuse for counseling him to become a terrorist.

Maha Elsamnah Khadr arrived in Toronto from Pakistan with her paralyzed son two weeks ago, demanding health care and triggering a debate on the boy's right to medicare. Ms. Elsamnah wants treatment for the spinal injury the boy received in a gunfight with Pakistani troops that killed his father, Ahmed Said Khadr, an al-Qaeda fundraiser and Osama bin Laden operative.

An official says the Children's Aid Society of Toronto "has already begun" looking into Karim's treatment from his parents while the family lived in Afghan terrorism circles.

Authorities will start by investigating a report received yesterday from psychologist Marty McKay, an expert witness in more than 200 child welfare cases.

"We're treating it seriously," said agency spokeswoman Melanie Persaud. "If we're going to get good quality information and that's what our next steps will be."

Since Canada has legislated aggressive spankings as child abuse, the 14-year-old's involvement with terrorists and

his brush with violent death could cause his mother serious legal complications.

Ms. Elsamnah, who left Canada many years ago, denouncing it as a place unworthy of raising children lest they be exposed to drugs and homosexuality, has promised the glories of heaven to her offspring should they become martyrs for extremist Islamic causes. She has also declared her pride in another teenage son being held in Guantanamo Bay, Cuba, for killing a U.S. medic.

That brand of parental guidance prompted Dr. McKay to raise the alarm with Children's Aid authorities, arguing it is part of her professional mandate as a clinical psychologist with 28 years in the field.

"I am sure that you would agree that counseling one's child to become suicidal or homicidal constitutes emotional child abuse, leading to physical abuse when the child acts upon these teachings," she said in her report.

A U.S. security chief says the coming months are "rich with symbolic opportunities for the terrorists to try to shake our will."

Having worked with thousands of abused children, Dr. McKay predicts authorities will find Karim is suffering multiple mental problems stemming from his upbringing.

"I'd be surprised if the child wasn't suffering from two or three disorders, be it anxiety or depression suffered by the loss of family members and the fact he's paralyzed," Dr. McKay said in an interview yesterday. "Psychologically, I'm sure he's quite a mess."

For the Khadrs, the child abuse investigation could become a reminder that claiming the

benefits of Canadian citizenship also comes with legal consequences for their actions taken beyond our borders.

Children's Aid officials waited barely two hours after receiving Dr. McKay's report before launching the Khadr probe. And they confirmed Dr. McKay's view that child abuse on foreign soil is not immune from Canadian investigation, child apprehension and parental prosecution.

"Whether or not the child has experienced the hardship in another country or in this country is a red herring," Ms. Persaud said.

"We're concerned with the type of parenting the child is receiving here. If it happened in another country, it very well could happen again here. The parent is the constant, not the country."

Police could be involved if evidence of abuse is found, she added.

During a CBC television interview in March, Karim's 23-year-old sister, Zaynab, expressed her support for suicide bombing.

"We believe in dying by the hand of your enemy," she said. "My father had always wished that he would be killed . . . he would be killed for the sake of Allah. I remember when we were very young he would say, if you guys love me, pray for me that I get jihaded, which is killed."

Karim's mother said she would be happy if her children died the same way.

"You know we are promised that we go to Heaven," Ms. Elsamnah said.

Abdurahman Khadr, 21, Karim's older brother, who was released from a U.S. jail and returned to Toronto last year, told the CBC he was "raised to become an al-Qaeda, was raised to become a suicide bomber, was raised to become a bad person. . . . I decided on my own that I do not want to be that."

Dr. McKay has personally been involved in two incidents where parents were arrested in Canada after their children complained of being sexually assaulted in Thailand. She sees parallels here.

"While Ms. Khadr may have the right to her religious and political views, it is also imperative to note that all children ... have equal rights of protection under the law and exceptions cannot be made based on cultural difference," she said. "Child abuse is still a crime."

For the Khadrs, the Children's Aid investigation adds to a difficult homecoming, where the family's views and actions have triggered political reaction federally and provincially.

While Prime Minister Paul Martin washed his hands of any retaliation against the Khadrs, Ontario Premier Dalton McGuinty has demanded they apologize for their views before receiving provincial benefits and federal Immigration Minister Judy Sgro called on the widow to apologize and show more respect for her citizenship.

Source: Don Martin, *National Post,* April 20, 2004. Material reprinted with the express permission of "National Post Company," a CanWest Partnership.

Differential Reinforcement Theory

Differential reinforcement (DR) theory (social learning theory) also explains crime as a type of learned behaviour. First proposed by Akers and Burgess, it is a version of the social learning view that combines differential association concepts with elements of psychological learning theory.[86]

The same process is involved in learning both deviant and conventional behaviour. People neither learn to be "all deviant" or "all conforming" but rather strike a balance between the two.[87]

Various learning processes shape behaviour. Direct conditioning occurs when behaviour is either rewarded or punished during interaction with others. Differential association involves learning from direct or indirect interaction with others. Imitation occurs from observational learning experiences, such as from watching TV and films. People also learn cognitive definitions, which are attitudes that are favourable or unfavourable toward a behaviour and can either stimulate or extinguish that behaviour.

Behaviour is reinforced when positive rewards are gained or when punishment is avoided (negative reinforcement). It is weakened by negative stimuli (punishment) and loss of reward. Whether deviant or criminal behaviour is begun or persists depends on the degree to which it has been rewarded or punished and the rewards or punishments attached to its alternatives.

In a shocking study of reinforcement, researchers in Toronto found that correctional staff in juvenile institutions allowed and encouraged peer violence. Of one hundred juvenile offenders interviewed, half reported that staff ignored violence by other inmates and a third saw guards offering incentives to young offenders to intimidate or assault other inmates.[88]

People evaluate their behaviour through interaction with significant others and groups who control sources of reinforcement, define behaviour as right or wrong, and model behaviours. The more individuals learn to justify their behaviour, the more likely they are to engage in it. For example, kids in a peer group whose members value drugs and alcohol, encourage their use, and provide opportunities to observe drug use, will be encouraged through this social learning experience to use drugs themselves.

The principal influence on behaviour comes from groups that control individuals' reinforcement and punishment.[89] The important groups are the ones with which a person is in differential association—peer and friendship groups, schools, churches, and similar institutions. Within the context of these groups, deviance is expected to the extent that it has been differentially reinforced over alternative behaviour and is defined as desirable or justified. Once people are initiated into crime, their actions are reinforced by exposure to deviant models, association with deviant peers, and lack of negative sanctions from parents or peers. The deviant behaviour, originated by imitation, is sustained by social support, establishing criminal careers and explaining persistent criminality.

Akers surveyed 3065 male and female adolescents on drug- and alcohol-related activities and their perception of variables related to social learning and DR theory. Included were respondents' perception of peers' attitudes toward drug and alcohol abuse, people they admired who used controlled substances, and whether people they admired would reward or punish them for substance abuse. A strong association between drug and alcohol abuse and social learning variables was found: Kids who believed they would be rewarded for deviance by those they respect were the ones most likely to engage in deviant behaviour.[90]

Learning experience continues within a deviant group as behaviour is both influenced by and exerts influence over group processes. For example, kids may learn to smoke because of social reinforcement by peers;

over time, smoking influences friendships and peer group memberships.[91]

DR theory is an important view of the cause of criminal activity, looking at how socialization conditions crime. Because not all socialization is positive, it accounts for how negative reinforcements can produce criminal results. Research shows that parental deviance is related to adolescent antisocial behaviour.[92] This fits well with rational choice theory because they both suggest that people learn the techniques and attitudes necessary to commit crime through experience. After considering the outcome of their past experiences, potential offenders decide which criminal acts will be profitable and which are dangerous and should be avoided.[93] Why do people make rational choices about crime? Because they have learned to balance risks against the potential for criminal gain.

Neutralization Theory

Neutralization theory is identified with Matza and Sykes, who also viewed the process of becoming a criminal as a learning experience.[94] While such theorists as Sutherland and Akers look at the learning of techniques, values, and attitudes necessary for performing criminal acts, Sykes and Matza maintain that most delinquents and criminals hold conventional values and attitudes but master techniques that enable them to neutralize these values and drift back and forth between illegitimate and conventional behaviour. One reason is that what Matza called **"subterranean values"** exist alongside conventional values, which, although condemned in public, may be practised in private, such as viewing pornographic videos. In contemporary culture, it is common to hold both subterranean and conventional values; few people are "all good" or "all bad."

Even the most committed criminals and delinquents are not involved in criminality all the time; they also attend schools, family functions, and religious services. Their behaviour falls along a continuum between total freedom and total restraint. This process of **drift** refers to the movement between deviance and constraint. Learning **techniques of neutralization** allows a person to temporarily drift from conventional behaviour and get involved in more subterranean values and behaviours, including crime and drug abuse.[95]

Techniques of Neutralization. Sykes and Matza suggest that offenders develop a distinct set of justifications for law-violating behaviour.

First, criminals sometimes voice a sense of guilt over their illegal acts. Second, offenders frequently respect and admire honest, law-abiding persons, such as sports figures, priests, parents, teachers, and neighbours. Third,

criminals draw a line between those whom they can victimize and those whom they cannot. Members of similar ethnic groups, churches, or neighbourhoods are often off-limits. This practice implies that criminals are aware of the wrongfulness of their acts. Why else limit them? Finally, criminals are not immune to the demands of conformity. Most criminals frequently participate in many of the same social functions as law-abiding people, such as school, church, and family activities.

Because of these factors, criminality is seen as the result of the neutralization of accepted social values through the learning of a standard set of techniques that allow people to counteract the moral dilemmas posed by illegal behaviour. Sykes and Matza identify the following techniques of neutralization:

1. *Denial of responsibility.* Offenders claim that their unlawful acts were not their fault but resulted from forces beyond their control.
2. *Denial of injury.* In denying the wrongfulness of an act, harm can be neutralized. For example, stealing is viewed as borrowing; vandalism is considered mischief that has gotten out of hand.
3. *Denial of victim.* Criminals can maintain that the victim of crime "had it coming," such as vandalism directed against a disliked teacher or neighbour, or assaults against homosexuals. Denying the victim makes the crime morally acceptable because the victims cannot be sympathized with or respected.
4. *Condemnation of the condemners.* An offender views the world as a corrupt place with a dog-eat-dog code. Since police and judges are on the take, teachers show favouritism, and parents take out their frustrations on their kids, it is ironic and unfair for these authorities to condemn misconduct. This shifts the blame to others.
5. *Appeal to higher loyalties.* Novice criminals often argue that they are caught in the dilemma of being loyal to their own peer group while at the same time attempting to abide by the rules of the larger society.

In sum, the theory of neutralization presupposes a condition in which such slogans as "I didn't mean to do it," "I didn't really hurt anybody," "They had it coming to them," "Everybody's picking on me," and "I didn't do it for myself" are used by people to neutralize unconventional norms and values so they can drift into criminal modes of behaviour (see Figure 8.5).

Testing Neutralization Theory. A test of neutralization theory would have to show that a person neutralized his or her moral beliefs and then drifted into criminality. Otherwise, people who commit crime could later attempt to rationalize their behaviour. It is also possible that criminals and noncriminals have different moral values and that neutralizing them is therefore

| Figure 8.5 | Techniques of Neutralization |

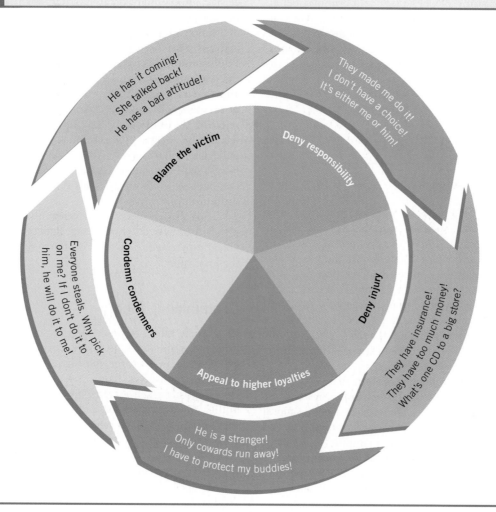

He has it coming!
She talked back!
He has a bad attitude!

They made me do it!
I don't have a choice!
It's either me or him!

Blame the victim

Deny responsibility

Everyone steals. Why pick on me? If I don't do it to him, he will do it to me!

They have insurance!
They have too much money!
What's one CD to a big store?

Condemn condemners

Deny injury

Appeal to higher loyalties

He is a stranger!
Only cowards run away!
I have to protect my buddies!

unnecessary.[96] The validity of the model depends on showing that all people share similar moral values and must neutralize them first to engage in criminal behaviour. Research tries to empirically verify those assumptions.[97]

Agnew indicates that delinquents do not value or condone violent behaviour and that they use neutralizations, such as "It is all right to physically beat up people who call you names," to justify their aggressive activities.[98] Research also shows that institutionalized youths excuse deviant behaviours to a significantly greater degree than the general population does.[99] People who commit criminal acts also have learned to rationalize their guilt. One study found that psychotherapists accused of sexually exploiting their clients express neutralizations for their behaviour, blaming the victim for "seducing them" or claiming there was little injury caused by the sexual encounter.[100]

Are Social Learning Theories Valid?

Social learning theories make a significant contribution to our understanding of the onset of criminal behaviour. Nonetheless, the general learning model has been subject to some criticism.

Learning theories imply that people learn techniques that allow them to be active and successful criminals, but these theories don't explain spontaneous acts of violence and other expressive crimes that have little utility or purpose. Is it possible that a random shooting is caused by an excess of deviant definitions? It is estimated that about 70 percent of all people arrested were under the influence of drugs and alcohol when they committed their crime. Do addicts pause to neutralize their moral inhibitions before mugging a victim? Do drug-involved kids stop to consider what they have "learned" about moral values?[101]

However, learning theories have an important place in the study of delinquent and criminal behaviour, because they can explain criminality across class structures. Even corporate executives are exposed to a variety of pro-criminal definitions and learn to neutralize moral constraints. Social learning theories can be applied to a wide assortment of criminal activity.

Social Control Theories

Social control theories maintain that all people have the potential to violate the law and that modern society presents many opportunities for illegal activity. Criminal activities, such as drug abuse or shoplifting, are often exciting and hold the promise of immediate reward and gratification. Considering the attractions of crime, the question control theorists pose is, "Why do people obey the rules of society?" To a choice theorist, the answer is fear of punishment; to a structural theorist, obedience is due to access to legitimate opportunities; to a learning theorist, obedience is acquired through contact with law-abiding parents and peers.

In contrast, control theorists argue that people obey the law because behaviour and passions are controlled by internal and external forces. Some have a strong moral sense that renders them incapable of hurting others and violating social norms. Some maintain self-control because they have a **commitment to conformity**—a reason to obey the rules of society.[102] Perhaps they believe that being caught in a criminal activity will hurt a dearly loved parent or jeopardize their chance at a university scholarship or perhaps their job will be forfeited if they get in trouble with the law. In other words, a person's behaviour is controlled by attachment and commitment to conventional institutions, individuals, and processes. If that commitment is absent, people are free to violate the law and engage in deviant behaviour; the "uncommitted" are not deterred by the threat of legal punishments.[103]

Self-Concept and Crime

Early control theory speculated that low self-control was a product of weak self-esteem. Youths who felt good about themselves could maintain a positive attitude and were able to resist the temptations of delinquency. Reiss described how delinquents had weak "ego ideals" and lacked the "personal controls" to produce conforming behaviour.[104] Others noted that youths who believe criminal activity would damage their self-image and their relationships with others will be most likely to conform to social rules; they have a commitment to conformity. In contrast, those less concerned about their social standing are free to violate the law.

Empirical research indicates that an important association exists between self-image and delinquency.[105] Kaplan found that youths with poor self-concepts are the ones most likely to engage in delinquent behaviour and that successful participation in criminality helped raise their self-esteem.[106] Youths who perceive **self-rejection** ("I feel I do not have much to be proud of"; "I feel useless at times") are the ones most likely to engage in deviant behaviours.[107] Youths who maintain both the lowest self-image and the greatest need for approval are the ones most likely to seek self-enhancement from delinquency.[108]

Kids who are having problems in school feel better if they drop out and join a gang. However, this is a self-defeating strategy that usually hurts the individual in the long run.

Containment Theory

In an early effort to describe how self-image controls criminal tendencies, Reckless argued that youths growing up in even the most criminogenic areas can insulate themselves from crime if they have sufficiently positive self-esteem. He called the individual's ability to resist criminal inducements **containments**, the most important of which are a positive self-image and "ego strength."[109] Kids with these traits can resist crime-producing "pushes and pulls." Here are some of the crime-producing forces that a strong self-image counteracts:

- *Internal pushes.* Internal pushes include such personal factors as restlessness, discontent, hostility, rebellion, mental conflict, anxieties, and need for immediate gratification.
- *External pressures.* External pressures are adverse living conditions that influence deviant behaviour, such as poverty, unemployment, minority status, and limited opportunities.
- *External pulls.* External pulls are represented by deviant companions, membership in criminal subcultures or other deviant groups, and such influences as mass media and pornography.

To test containment theory in a school setting, Reckless concluded that the ability of youths to resist crime depends on their maintaining a positive self-image in the face of environmental pressures toward delinquency. This version of control theory set the stage for subsequent theoretical developments, following the idea that people are "controlled" by their feelings about themselves and others with whom they are in contact. In general, control theory maintains that although all people perceive inducements to crime, some are better able to resist them than are others.

InfoTrac®

Not only can learning theories be applied to a wide assortment of criminal activity, but they are also used to explain noncriminal activities. To find out more, go to InfoTrac® College Edition and look for Brian Cambourne, "Turning Learning Theory into Classroom Instruction: A Minicase Study," *The Reading Teacher* 54, no. 4 (2000): 414.

Social Control Theory

Social control theory, originally articulated by Travis Hirschi in his influential 1969 book *Causes of Delinquency*, replaced containment theory as the dominant version of control theory.[110]

Hirschi linked the onset of criminality to the weakening of ties that bind people to society. Hirschi assumed that all individuals are potential law violators but are kept under control because they fear that illegal behaviour will damage their relationships with friends, parents, neighbours, teachers, and employers. Without these social ties or bonds, and in the absence of sensitivity to others, a person is free to commit criminal acts. Society is not seen as containing competing subcultures with unique value systems. Most people are aware of the prevailing moral and legal code. Hirschi suggested, however, that in all elements of society, people vary in their responses to conventional social rules and values. Among all ethnic, religious, racial, and social groups, people whose bond to society is weak may fall prey to crime.

InfoTrac®

How does self-concept influence delinquent and criminal behaviour? To find out, read this article on InfoTrac® College Edition: Kenneth St. C. Levy, "The Contribution of Self-Concept in the Etiology of Adolescent Delinquents," *Adolescence* 32, no. 127 (1997): 671(16).

Elements of the Social Bond. The social bond a person maintains with society is divided into four main elements: attachment, commitment, involvement, and belief (see Figure 8.6).

Attachment refers to a person's sensitivity to and interest in others. Psychologists believe that without a sense of attachment, a person loses the ability to relate coherently to others. The development of a social conscience depends on caring for other human beings. Parents, peers, and schools are the important social institutions with which a person should maintain ties. Attachment to parents and family is primary, leading later to feelings of respect for secondary others and for those in authority.

Commitment involves the time, energy, and effort expended in conventional lines of action, such as getting an education and saving money for the future. If people build a strong involvement in life, property, and reputation, they will be less likely to engage in acts that will jeopardize their positions. Conversely, lack of commitment to conventional values may lead to seeing risk-taking behaviour as reasonable.

Heavy involvement in conventional activities leaves little time for illegal behaviour. Involvement in school, recreation, and family insulates a person from the potential lure of criminal behaviour, while idleness enhances it.

People who live in the same social setting often share common moral beliefs, such as sharing, sensitivity to the rights of others, and respect for the law. If these beliefs are absent or weakened, individuals are more likely to participate in antisocial acts.

It is the interrelationship of elements of the social bond that controls behaviour. For example, people who feel kinship and sensitivity to parents and friends are more likely to adopt and work toward legitimate goals. Conversely, a person who rejects social relationships lacks commitment to conventional goals. Similarly, people who are highly committed to conventional acts and beliefs are more likely to be involved in conventional activities.

Testing Social Control Theory. Hirschi tested social control theory by giving a self-report survey to more than four thousand high-school students in grades 11 and 12, finding evidence to support the control theory model:

- Youths who were strongly attached to their parents were less likely to commit criminal acts.
- Commitment to conventional values, such as striving to get a good education and refusing to drink and "cruise around," was related to conventional behaviour.
- Youths involved in conventional activity, such as homework, were less likely to engage in criminal behaviour.
- Youths involved in unconventional behaviour, such as smoking and drinking, were more delinquency-prone.
- Delinquent youths maintained weak and distant relationships with people, while nondelinquent youths were attached to their peers.
- Delinquent and nondelinquent youths shared similar beliefs about society.

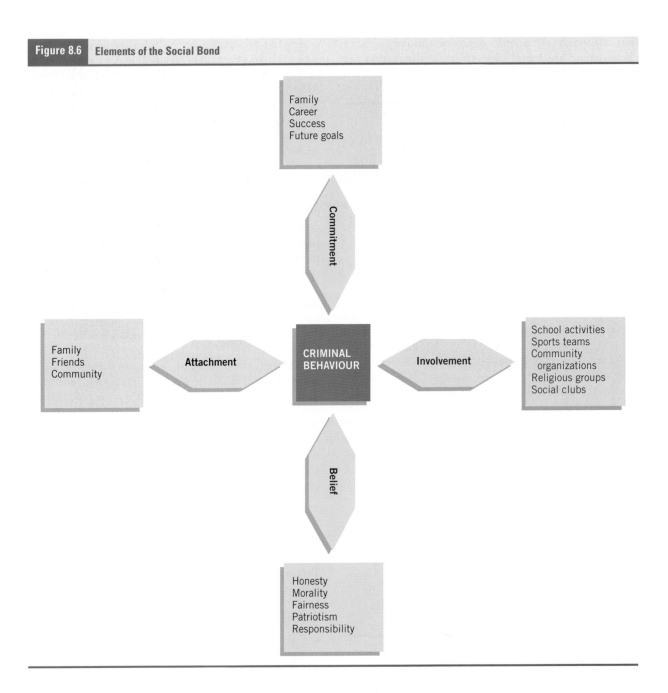

Figure 8.6   Elements of the Social Bond

Supporting Research. Because of its importance, social control theory has been the focus of numerous research efforts. Associations among indicators of attachment, belief, commitment, and involvement with measures of delinquency have tended to be positive and significant.[111] Research indicates that family detachment, including intrafamily conflict, abuse of children, and lack of affection, supervision, and family pride, are predictive of delinquent conduct.[112] Youths who are detached from the educational experience are at risk of criminality.[113] Lack of attachment to family, peers, and school has been found to predict delinquency in cross-cultural samples of youths.[114]

High peer tolerance of deviance and low parental empathy are also linked to offending, as are low academic achievement and low parental monitoring.[115] Conversely, high levels of parental attachment and individual self-reliance are associated with higher social and coping competencies, lower levels of marijuana use, and fewer problems associated with substance use.[116] This points to the importance of social control in predicting youth delinquency.[117]

Other research efforts have shown that positive beliefs are inversely related to criminality. That is, children who are involved in religious activities and hold conventional religious beliefs are less likely to become

According to Hirschi, potential law violators are normally kept under control because they fear that illegal behaviour will damage their social relationships. Without such social ties, a person may feel free to commit criminal acts. Kids who commit crimes with their friends may appear attached, but they actually have few emotional commitments to their deviant peers.

involved in substance abuse.[118] Similarly, youths who are involved in conventional leisure activities, such as supervised social activities and noncompetitive sports, are less likely to engage in delinquency.[119]

In a study of youths in Edmonton, Alberta, parental attachment was the strongest predictor of delinquent or law-abiding behaviour.[120] Teens who are attached to their parents may develop the social skills that equip them both to maintain harmonious social ties and to escape life stresses, such as school failure.[121]

Opposing Views. Many attempts have been made to corroborate social control theory by replicating Hirschi's original survey techniques.[122] Although significant empirical support exists for the model, some question part or all of its elements.

One criticism concerns the contention that delinquents are detached loners whose bond to their family and friends has been broken. Do delinquents have strained relations with family and peers, or are they actually influenced by close relationships with deviant peers and family members? A number of research efforts show that delinquents maintain relationships with deviant peers and are influenced by members of their deviant peer group.[123] Delinquents may not be "lone

wolves" whose only personal relationships are exploitive; their friendship patterns seem quite close to those of conventional youths.[124] For example, young male drug abusers maintained even more intimate relations with their peers than nonabusers did; illicit drug abuse can be used to predict strong social ties and high levels of intimacy.[125]

Hirschi made little distinction in the importance of the elements of the social bond. For example, research shows that high levels of involvement, which Hirschi suggested should reduce delinquency, may actually increase delinquent behaviour. The more kids are involved in unsupervised, and possibly illegal, behaviours outside the home, the less contact they have with parental supervision and the greater the opportunity they have to commit crime.[126] Research with younger children found that the concepts of "involvement" and "belief" had relatively little influence over behaviour patterns.[127]

Hirschi's conclusion that any form of social attachment is beneficial, even to deviant peers and parents, has also been disputed. For example, Hindelang found that attachment to delinquent peers escalated rather than restricted criminality.[128] Furthermore, youths attached to drug-abusing parents are more likely to become drug

Famous Canadian Criminals

Fateful Turns in the Difficult Life of Tyrone Conn

The life of Tyrone William Conn was not an easy one. Given up for adoption at the age of three, he spent eight years with abusive adoptive parents before being returned to the state in 1978. After that, he went from one group home to another, experiencing abandonment and deprivation.

He went from breaking into houses to eventually holding up a bank at the age of 16. In his criminal career, he was charged with almost 30 criminal offences. At the age of 25, he was ordered to serve 47 years in jail and would not be eligible for release until 2032. In prison, he completed his high-school education and took university-level sociology and psychology courses.

In 1989 at the age of 22, Conn escaped while on medical leave from Millhaven Penitentiary in Kingston, Ontario, and remained at large for 68 days. In 1991, he broke out of the Collins Bay Penitentiary and remained free for 46 days. Police found him in an apartment building in Ottawa, where he evaded escape for 90 minutes by climbing between fourth-floor balconies. By this time, Conn was suffering from anxiety caused by being confined in prisons.

In 1999, at the age of 32, Conn became the first inmate to break out of Kingston Penitentiary in 40 years, causing a media frenzy. He visited his mother in Belleville and then later robbed a bank in Colborne, the same bank he had robbed before. To his credit, Conn never caused physical harm to anyone during his career as an armed robber.

Conn spent his last hours in a dingy basement apartment in Toronto, listening to a police scanner. On May 20, 1999, at 10:30 p.m., after a standoff with police that began around 9 p.m., Conn called a CBC producer who had interviewed him years before. Conn had met the producer and broadcaster Linden MacIntyre while the latter was working on a story about the effects of child abuse. At Conn's request, the producer phoned high-profile defence attorney Clayton Ruby. She then tried to get Conn to surrender, but the police set off a flash grenade to incapacitate him. When they entered the apartment Conn was dead, apparently from a self-inflicted shotgun blast. His hard life finally ended.

---

users themselves.[129] And in another important study in Edmonton, this one of dropouts, Samuelson, Hartnagel, and Krahn found that attachment to deviant peers helped motivate dropouts to commit crime and helped facilitate their delinquent acts.[130] Finally, attachment to delinquent friends is a powerful predictor of delinquency, strong enough to overcome the controlling effect of positive family relationships.[131]

Can social control theory explain all modes of criminality, or is it restricted to particular groups or forms of criminality? A survey of 3065 high-school students in grades 11 and 12 found that control variables were better able to explain female delinquency than male delinquency and minor delinquency, such as alcohol and marijuana abuse, than more serious criminal acts.[132] Other school-based research also found gender differences in that social control variables were more predictive of female than of male behaviour.[133] Perhaps girls are more deeply influenced by the quality of their bond to society than are boys.

Social bonds also seem to change over time. For example, in a sample of 12-, 15-, and 18-year-old boys, researchers found age differences in the perceptions of the social bond: Mid-teens are surprisingly likely to be influenced by their parents and teachers; boys in the other two age groups are more deeply influenced by their deviant peers.[134] This finding can be attributed to the problems of mid-adolescence, in which there is a great need to develop "psychological anchors" to conformity. It is possible, then, that at one age level, weak bonds (to parents) lead to delinquency, while at another, strong bonds (to peers) lead to delinquency.

Sociologist Robert Agnew claims that Hirschi miscalculated the direction of the relationship between criminality and a weakened social bond.[135] Although Hirschi says that a weakened bond leads to delinquency, Agnew suggests that the chain of events may flow in the opposite direction: Kids who break the law find that their bond to parents, schools, and society eventually becomes weak and attenuated. Other studies have also found that weakened social bonds are a consequence of criminality, not the reverse.[136]

However, the overall weight of evidence supports control theory, and it has emerged as one of the preeminent theories in criminology.[137] For many criminologists, it is perhaps the most important way of understanding the onset of criminal misbehaviour.

Connections

Hirschi and Gottfredson have restructured the concept of control by integrating biosocial, psychological, and rational choice theory ideas into a general theory of crime. This theory is discussed in Chapter 10.

Labelling Theory

Labelling theory explains criminal career formation in terms of destructive social interactions and encounters. Its roots are in the **symbolic interaction theory** of sociologists Charles Horton Cooley, George Herbert Mead, and Herbert Blumer.[138] Symbolic interaction theory holds that people communicate via representational symbols, such as gestures, signs, words, or images. People interpret symbolic gestures from others and incorporate them into their self-image. Symbols are used by others to let people know how well they are doing and whether they are liked and appreciated. How people view reality depends on the content of the messages and the situations they encounter, the subjective interpretation of these interactions, and the way they shape future behaviour. In this view, no simple objective reality exists. People interpret the actions of others, and this interpretation defines meaning.

Throughout their lives, people are given a variety of symbolic labels in their interactions with others, such as "mental disorder."[139] These labels imply a variety of behaviours and attitudes, and define not just one trait but also the whole person. For example, people labelled "insane" are also assumed to be dangerous, dishonest, unstable, violent, strange, and otherwise unsound. Labels including "smart," "honest," and "hard worker" suggest overall competence, which improves self-image and social standing. People given a positive trait, such as "attractive," are assumed to have others, such as intelligence and competence.[140] In contrast, negative labels, including "troublemaker," "mentally ill," and "stupid," stigmatize their targets and reduce their self-image.

Both positive and negative labels entail subjective interpretations. Being called a "troublemaker" need not be based on any objective proof that the person is actually a troublemaker. However, although a label may be a function of rumour, innuendo, or unfounded suspicion, its adverse impact can be immense.

A devalued status conferred by a significant other, such as a teacher, police officer, elder, parent, or valued peer, can cause permanent harm. Being perceived as a **social deviant** may affect treatment at home, at work, at school, and in other social situations. School officials may limit these people to classes for students with behaviour problems. Adults labelled "criminal," "ex-con," or "drug addict" may find their employment severely restricted. And, of course, if the label is the result of conviction for a crime, the labelled person may be subject to official sanctions ranging from a mild reprimand to incarceration. Research on 16 636 Canadian youth court cases found that prior dispositions were a significant factor in both stabilizing and escalating dispositions, showing support for societal-reaction theory.[141]

InfoTrac®

For an interesting discussion, see the following:

- Mike S. Adams, Craig T. Robertson, Phyllis Gray-Kay, and Melvin C. Ray, "Labeling and Delinquency," *Adolescence* 38, no. 149 (2003): 171(16).
- Bruce G. Link and Jo C. Phelan, "Conceptualizing Stigma," *Annual Review of Sociology* (2001): 363.

Connections

Fear of stigma has prompted efforts to reduce the impact of criminal labels through such programs as pretrial diversion and community treatment programs. In addition, some criminologists have called for noncoercive "peacemaking" solutions to interpersonal conflict. This peacemaking or restorative justice movement is reviewed in Chapter 9.

Labelling also means that a person will have an increasing commitment to a deviant career and turn to others similarly stigmatized for support and companionship. Isolated from conventional society, they may identify themselves as members of an outcast group and become locked into deviant careers.

Because stigmatization is an interactive process, control institutions, such as the police, courts, and correctional agencies, produce the stigmas that are so harmful to the very people they are trying to help, treat, or correct. Rather than reduce deviant behaviour, for which they were designed, they actually help maintain and amplify criminal behaviour (see Figure 8.7).

| Figure 8.7 | The Labelling Process |

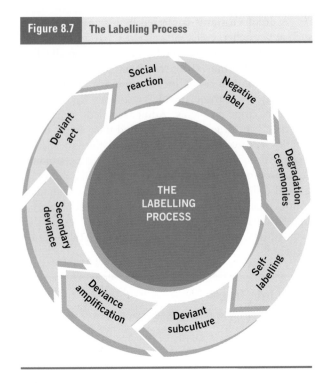

Crime and Labelling Theory

As sociologist Kai Erickson said, "Deviance is not a property inherent in certain forms of behaviour, it is a property conferred upon those forms by the audience which directly or indirectly witnesses them."[142] This definition was amplified by Edwin Schur, who stated:

> Human behavior is deviant to the extent that it comes to be viewed as involving a personally discreditable departure from a group's normative expectation, and it elicits interpersonal and collective reactions that serve to "isolate," "treat," "correct" or "punish" individuals engaged in such behavior.[143]

Crime and deviance are defined by the social audience's reaction to a person's behaviour and the subsequent effects of that reaction; they are not defined by the moral content of the illegal act itself. As difficult as it sounds, a crime, such as murder, is bad because it is labelled as such. After all, the difference between an excusable act and a criminal one is a matter of legal definition. A killing can be a murder, an execution, an accident, self-defence, or a legitimate act in war. Such acts as abortion, marijuana use, possession of a handgun, and gambling have all been legal at some points and places in history and illegal at others. What's important is who does the labelling.

Howard Becker refers to people who create rules as **moral entrepreneurs**. In a famous statement in his book *The Outsiders*, he summed up their effect as follows:

> Social groups create deviance by making rules whose infractions constitute deviance, and by applying those rules to particular people and labeling them as outsiders. From this point of view, deviance is not a quality of the act a person commits, but rather a consequence of the application by others of rules and sanctions to an "offender." The deviant is one to whom the label has successfully been applied; deviant behavior is behavior that people so label.[144]

Differential Enforcement

An important principle of labelling theory is that the law is differentially applied, benefiting those who hold economic and social power and penalizing the powerless. The probability of being brought before legal authority is a function of a person's race, wealth, gender, and social standing. Police officers are more likely to arrest males, minority-group members, and those in the lower class and to use their discretionary powers to give beneficial treatment to more favoured groups.[145] Similarly, minorities and the poor are more likely to be prosecuted for criminal offences and receive harsher punishments when convicted.[146] This evidence shows that personal characteristics and social interactions are actually more important variables in the criminal career formation process than is the mere violation of the criminal law.

Labelling theorists also argue that the content of the law reflects power relationships in society. White-collar crimes are most often punished by a relatively small fine and rarely result in prison sentences, but long prison sentences are given to those convicted of "street crimes," such as burglary or car theft.[147] In sum, a major premise of labelling theory is that the law is differentially constructed and applied. It favours the powerful members of society who direct its content and penalizes people whose actions represent a threat to those in control.[148]

Becoming Labelled

Labelling theorists are not especially concerned with explaining why people originally engage in acts that result in their being labelled.[149] Crime may be a result of greed, personality, social structure, learning, or control, but labelling's concern is with criminal career formation and not the origin of criminal acts.

Labelling suggests that the less personal power and fewer resources a person has, the greater the chance of becoming labelled. In this view, a person is labelled deviant primarily as a consequence of the **social distance** between the labeller and the person labelled. Race, class, and ethnic differences influence the likelihood of labelling. For example, a poor or minority-group teenager may run a greater chance of being officially processed for criminal acts by police, courts, and correctional agencies than a wealthy White youth does.

Of course, not all labelled people have chosen to engage in crime. Some labels are bestowed on people for behaviours over which they have little control, such as "mentally unbalanced" and "mentally deficient." The probability of being labelled may depend on the visibility of the person in the community, the tolerance of the community for diversity, and the person's own power to combat labels.

Consequences of Labelling

Criminologists are most concerned with two effects of labelling: the creation of stigma and the effect on self-image. The social outcast may be prevented from enjoying higher education, well-paying jobs, and other social benefits. Public condemnation is an important part of the label-producing process and is accomplished in "degradation ceremonies," such as a hearing in which a person is found to have a mental illness or a trial in which an individual is convicted of crime.[150] A public record of the deviant acts causes the denounced person to be ritually separated from citizens of good standing.

The label redefines the whole person, for example, "ex-con" connotes tough, mean, dangerous, aggressive, dishonest, sneaky, even though a person who has been in prison may not possess those traits. People react to the "master status" of the label and what the label signifies and not necessarily to actual behaviour. In addition, in a retrospective reading, the past of the labelled person is often reviewed and reevaluated to fit his or her current outcast status. For example, boyhood friends of an assassin or killer are interviewed by the media and report that the suspect was withdrawn, suspicious, and negativistic as a youth. This information appears to explain his current behaviour, confirming the label as accurate.[151]

Labels become the basis of personal identity, as negative feedback from law enforcement agencies, parents, friends, and teachers amplifies the force of the original label and stigmatized offenders reevaluate their own identities. Frank Tannenbaum referred to this process as the **dramatization of evil:**

> The process of making the criminal, therefore, is a process of tagging, defining, identifying, making conscious and self-conscious; it becomes a way of stimulating, suggesting and evoking the very traits that are complained of. If the theory of relation of response to stimulus has any meaning, the entire process of dealing with the young delinquent is mischievous insofar as it identifies him to himself or to the environment as a delinquent person. The person becomes the thing he is described as being.[152]

Primary and Secondary Deviance

One well-known views of the labelling process is Edwin Lemert's concept of primary and secondary deviance.[153]

Primary deviance involves norm violations that have little influence on the actor and can be quickly forgotten. For example, a university student takes a "five-finger discount" at the campus bookstore. He successfully steals a textbook, uses it to get an A in a course, goes on to graduate, is admitted into law school, and later becomes a famous judge. Because his shoplifting goes unnoticed, it is a relatively unimportant event that has little bearing on his life.

In contrast, **secondary deviance** occurs when a deviant event comes to the attention of those who apply a negative label. The newly labelled offender then reorganizes his or her behaviour and personality around the consequences of the deviant act. The shoplifting student is caught by a security guard and expelled from university. With his law school dreams dashed and future cloudy, his options are limited; people who know him say he "lacks character," and he begins to share their opinion. He eventually becomes a drug dealer and winds up in prison, where he commits suicide. One little act begins a slippery slide.

If successful, secondary deviance involves resocialization into a deviant role. There is a deviance amplification effect in which offenders feel isolated from the mainstream of society. They become firmly locked into their deviant role and seek out others similarly labelled to form deviant subcultures or groups. They become locked into an escalating cycle of deviance, apprehension, more powerful labels, and identity transformation. This is the core of labelling theory, that deviance is a process in which a person's identity is transformed. Efforts to control the offenders, whether by treatment or punishment, simply help solidify them in their deviant role.

A number of attempts have been made to formulate theories of deviant career formation using a labelling perspective. What follows is a discussion of two such efforts.

General Theory of Deviance

Howard Kaplan's general theory of deviance begins with the assumption that people who cannot conform to social group standards face negative sanctions. They are considered failures either because they lack desirable physical, social, or psychological traits or because they fail to behave according to group expectations.

Those exposed to negative social sanctions experience self-rejection and a lower self-image. The experience of self-rejecting attitudes ("At times, I think I am no good at all") results in both a weakened commitment to conventional values and behaviours and the acquisition of motives to deviate from social norms. Facilitating this attitude and value transformation is the bond social outcasts form with similarly labelled peers.[154] Membership in a deviant subculture involves conforming to group norms that conflict with those of conventional society. Deviant group membership then encourages criminality and drug abuse.

Deviant behaviours that defy conventional values can serve a number of purposes. Some acts are defiant, showing contempt for the source of the negative labels, while others are planned to distance the target from further contact with the source of criticism (for example, an adolescent runs away from critical parents).[155]

Kaplan has found in adolescents that social sanctions lead to self-rejection, deviant peer associations, and eventual deviance amplification.[156] This model is important because it accounts for the creation of labels, their impact on self-image, and the long-term effect they have on criminal careers. Negative sanctions also have a labelling effect if they help undermine conventional relationships and encourage deviant peer group memberships.

According to Lemert's theory, if these kids are caught and labelled as "druggies," they may become secondary deviants, taking on an identity associated with their negative label, and enter a life of crime. If their actions go undetected, their behaviour remains primary and their drug use remains nothing more than an easily forgotten youthful indiscretion.

Differential Social Control

Heimer and Matsueda's theory of differential social control says that self-evaluations reflect actual or perceived appraisals made by others.[157] Kids who view themselves as delinquents are giving an inner voice to their perceptions of how parents, teachers, peers, and neighbours feel about them. Kids who believe that others view them as troublemakers, for example, expect to be rejected. Labelled youths may then join with similarly outcast delinquent peers who facilitate their behaviour. Eventually, antisocial behaviour becomes habitual and automatic. This is a self-fulfilling prophecy, and the process has been linked to delinquent behaviour and other social problems, including depression.[158]

This **reflective role-taking** is affected by families, schools, and peers, who can either help control kids and dissuade them from crime or encourage and sustain their deviance. When these groups are dysfunctional, such as when parents use drugs, they encourage, rather than control, antisocial behaviour.

Empirical research supports the core of the model. **Reflected appraisal** as a rule violator has a significant effect on delinquency: Kids who believe that their parents and friends consider them troublemakers are the ones most likely to engage in delinquency and to engage in risk-taking behaviours.[159]

This work is important because it is an alternative to "traditional" labelling theory and focuses on social control and symbolic interaction.

Research on Labelling Theory

Research on labelling theory can be classified into two distinct categories. The first says that offenders who are chosen for negative labels are likely to be powerless people unable to defend themselves. The second type of research attempts to discover the effects of being labelled.

Who Gets Labelled? It is widely believed that poor and powerless people are victimized by the law and justice system and that labels are not equally distributed across class and racial lines. Although substantive and procedural laws govern almost every aspect of the criminal justice system, discretionary decision making also comes into play. From the police officer's decision on whom to arrest, to the prosecutor's decisions on whom to charge, to the court's decision on whom to release or for whom to permit bail, to the judge's decision on the length of the sentence, discretion works against minorities.[160] A meta-review of 30 years of research on minorities in the juvenile justice system found that race bias adversely influences decision making.[161]

Connections

In Chapter 9, we look at some of the ways in which the powerless are discriminated against by the criminal justice system and how it is necessary to develop a critical perspective to analyze that process. In a multicultural society, ethnic discrimination is a very important topic.

Those in power try to streamline the labelling process by discounting or ignoring the "protestations of innocence" made by suspects accused of socially undesirable acts, such as child abuse. For example, people accused of child abuse are routinely defined as "noncredible" when they deny accusations of abuse and are only believed when they confess their guilt. In contrast, victims are believed when they make accusations but are considered "noncredible" when they claim the suspect is innocent.[162]

This doesn't mean the justice system is inherently unfair and biased. Such procedures as arrest, prosecution, and sentencing are usually based on legal factors, such as prior record and crime seriousness, rather than on personal characteristics, such as class and race.[163]

The Effects of Labelling. However, empirical evidence exists that negative labels actually have a dramatic influence on the self-image of offenders, leading to self-labelling and deviance amplification.[164]

Parents negatively label their children, who suffer a variety of problems, including antisocial behaviour and school failure.[165] Once labelled as troublemakers, adolescents begin to reassess their self-image in a process of deviance amplification, causing parents to become alienated from their child, further reducing the child's self-image and increasing delinquency.[166]

Connections

Chapter 5 looked at Braithwaite's research on how parental attributions that are negative are linked to bullying.

Intensive official labelling can produce self-labelling and damaged identities.[167] Kids labelled as troublemakers in school are the ones most likely to drop out, which has been linked to delinquent behaviour.[168] Male drug users labelled as addicts by social control agencies eventually became self-labelled and increase their drug use.[169] People arrested in domestic violence cases with a low "stake in conformity"—that is, who were jobless and unmarried—increased offending after being given official labels.[170] This outcome could be seen as a mischievous or perverse effect.

Labelling and Criminal Careers. Until recently, scant attention has been paid to the fact that stigmatization and negative labels may sustain chronic offending and criminal careers.[171] In fact, the very definition of a chronic offender is a person who has been arrested and therefore labelled multiple times in his or her offending career.

Although labels may not cause adolescents to initiate criminal behaviours, experienced delinquents are significantly more likely to continue offending if they believe their parents and peers view them in a negative light.[172] Labelling thus sustains criminality over time.

In sum, considerable evidence exists that people who are labelled by parents, schools, and the criminal justice system stand a good chance of getting involved in deviance. The labelling effect and other personal and social factors that cause the labelling to occur are interwoven.

Is Labelling Theory Valid?

Those who criticize labelling theory point to its inability to specify the conditions that must exist before an act or individual is labelled deviant—that is, why some people are labelled while others remain "secret deviants."[173] Critics also say labelling theory fails to explain differences in crime rates; if crime is a function of stigma and labels, why are crime rates higher in some parts of the country at particular times of the year? Labelling theory also ignores the onset of deviant behaviour and does not deal with the decision to forgo a deviant career.[174]

In addition, others question whether deviance is relative. They argue that some crimes, such as rape and homicide, are universally sanctioned.[175] Furthermore, crime is situationally motivated and depends more on ecological and personal conditions than on labels and stigma. Some charge that it all too often focuses on "nuts, sluts, and perverts" and ignores the root causes of crime.[176]

With the "discovery" of the chronic offender, it was believed that labelling theory would receive renewed interest, because the chronic offender is defined as someone who has been repeatedly labelled by the justice system. This idea has met with criticism.[177] In an indepth analysis of research on the crime-producing effects of labels, Tittle found little evidence that stigma produces crime.[178] He claims that many criminal careers occur without labelling, often coming after rather than before chronic offending, and that criminal careers may not follow even when labelling takes place. If criminal careers begin early in life, those who go on to a "life of crime" are burdened with so many social, physical, and psychological problems that negative labelling may be a relatively insignificant event.[179]

Sometimes people are able to successfully organize to resist deviant labels. One technique is to appropriate the label and use it proudly, like the word "gay." Another is to proclaim that there is, in fact, nothing deviant about the behaviour. Here, Delwin Vriend (right) gets a congratulatory kiss from his partner at a rally in Edmonton after the Supreme Court of Canada ruled in Vriend's favour, forcing the Alberta government to amend its Human Rights Code to include sexual orientation.

Although criticisms of labelling theory exist, its utility as an explanation of crime and deviance should not be dismissed. Here are some other features of the labelling perspective that are important contributions to the study of criminality:[180]

1. The labelling perspective identifies the role played by social control agents in the process of crime causation.
2. Labelling theory recognizes that criminality is not a disease or pathological behaviour. It focuses attention on the social interactions and reactions that shape individuals.
3. Labelling theory distinguishes between criminal acts (primary deviance) and criminal careers (secondary deviance), showing that these concepts require different views.

Labelling theory is also important because of its focus on interaction and the situation of crime. Rather than view the criminal as a robotlike creature whose actions are predetermined, it recognizes that crime is often the result of complex interactions and processes. The decision to commit crime involves the actions of a variety of people, including peers, the victim, the police, and other key characters. Labels may expedite crime because they guide the actions of all parties in criminal interactions. Actions deemed innocent when performed by one person are considered provocative when engaged in by another labelled as a deviant. Similarly, labelled people may be quick to judge, take offence, or misinterpret behaviour because of past experience. They experienced conflict in the past, so why not now?

An Evaluation of Social Process Theory

The branches of social process theory—social learning, social control, and labelling—are compatible because they suggest that criminal behaviour is part of the socialization process. Criminals are people whose interactions with critically important social institutions and processes—the family, schools, the justice system, peer groups, employers, and neighbours—are troubled and disturbed. Although there is disagreement about the relative importance of those influences, there is little question that social interactions shape the behaviour, beliefs, values, and self-image of the offender. People who have learned deviant social values, who find themselves detached from conventional social relationships, or who are the subject of stigma and labels from significant others will be the most likely to fall prey to the attractions of criminal behaviour. These negative influences can affect anyone, beginning in youth and continuing into adulthood. The major strength of the social process view is the vast body of empirical data showing that delinquents and criminals are indeed people who grew up in dysfunctional families, who had troubled childhoods, and who failed at school, at work, and in marriage. Prison data show that these characteristics are typical of inmates.

Although persuasive, these theories have trouble accounting for some of the patterns and fluctuations in the crime rate. For example, people in the Western provinces must be socialized differently from those in the Eastern provinces, since these latter regions have much lower crime rates. Or how can the fact that crime rates are lower in October than in July be explained if crime is a function of learning or control? How can social processes explain why criminals escalate their activity or why they desist from crime? Once a social bond is broken, how can it be "reattached"? Once crime is "learned," how can it be "unlearned"?

Social Process Theory and Social Policy

Social process theories have had a major influence on social policy since the 1950s. Learning theories have influenced concepts of treatment of the offender, especially young offenders, who are viewed as being more salvageable than are "hardened" criminals. Advocates argue that if people become criminal by learning definitions and attitudes toward criminality, they can "unlearn" them by being exposed to definitions toward conventional behaviour. This philosophy has been used in numerous treatment facilities, which use group interaction sessions to attack the criminal behaviour orientations held by residents (being tough, using alcohol and drugs, believing that school is for "sissies") while promoting conventional lines of behaviour (going straight, saving money, giving

up drugs). It is common today for residential and nonresidential programs to offer such treatment programs. They teach kids to say no to drugs, to forgo delinquent behaviour, or to stay in school. It is even common for celebrities to return to their old neighbourhood to tell kids to stay in school or off drugs. After Ben Johnson was banned from international competition for using steroids, for example, he gave talks to school kids on the value of being drug-free. If learning did not affect behaviour, such exercises would be futile.

Making changes in how the system reacts can be an important part of the solution. Youth diversion programs are springing up all over the country that force offenders to be more accountable to the community. For minor crimes, offenders make restitution, apologize, and do volunteer work. Research shows that intervening early, in a nonjudicial way, does work for delinquents. However, catching problems before they develop is important too. In 2004, Ontario announced new spending to help students in danger of dropping out of school. In British Columbia, early intervention initiatives have begun in high schools to encourage Aboriginals to go to university, which is key to them finding better jobs.[181]

Control theories have also influenced criminal justice and other social policymaking. Programs have been developed to improve people's commitments to conventional lines of action and to create and strengthen bonds early in life before the onset of criminality. The educational system has been the scene of numerous programs designed to improve basic skills and create an atmosphere in which youths will develop a bond to their schools. The Head Start program is one of the largest and best-known attempts to solidify social bonds.

Given the emphasis of the new *Youth Criminal Justice Act*, restorative justice options are being explored. Extra-legal, community-oriented approaches, such as family group conferencing and sentencing circles, are being developed as a way to strengthen the relationships among offender, family, and community. Changes in funding priorities, with more emphasis on noncustodial programs and services, are helping to shift the balance in youth justice toward a community-based model, providing and relying on support from parents, for example.[182]

An approach that has proved effective in other countries is multisystemic therapy (MST). This is a home-based treatment for juvenile delinquents that addresses the relationships among family, peers, school, and community. MST targets chronic, violent, and substance-abusing juveniles who are at high risk. The aim is to empower parents with the skills and resources needed to help them cope. Families reported increased cohesion, and decreased

Culture, Gender, Ethnicity, and Criminology

The Head Start Program

Head Start is probably the best-known effort to help lower-class youths achieve proper socialization and, in so doing, reduce their potential for future criminality.

Head Start programs were first instituted in the United States in the 1960s as part of the War on Poverty. In the beginning, Head Start was a two-month summer program, providing comprehensive programming and promoting physical health and enhanced mental processes. It worked to improve social and emotional development, self-image, and interpersonal relationships. Preschoolers were provided with an enriched educational environment to develop their learning and cognitive skills. They were given the opportunity to use materials that middle-class children take for granted— pegs and pegboards, puzzles, toy animals, and so forth.

Today, services have been expanded beyond the two-month summer program. More than 1300 centres with 36 000 classrooms in the United States service 740 000 children and their families. Learning experiences appropriate to the child's age and development focus on reading books, understanding cultural diversity, and the expression of feelings and play with their peers. Students are guided in developing gross and fine motor skills and self-confidence. Health care is also an issue, and most children enrolled in the program receive comprehensive health screening, physical and dental examinations, and appropriate follow-up. Many programs provide meals and in so doing help children receive proper nourishment.

Head Start programs now serve parents in addition to their preschoolers. Some programs allow parents to enroll in classes that cover parenting, literacy, nutrition, domestic violence prevention, and other social issues. Social services, health, and education services are also available.

Some controversy has surrounded the success of the Head Start program. In 1970, an evaluation of the Head Start effort found no evidence of lasting cognitive gains on the part of the participating children. Initial gains seemed to evaporate during the elementary school years, and by grade 3, the performance of the Head Start children was no different from that of their peers.

Although disappointing, this evaluation focused on IQ levels and not whether social competence improved. More recent research has produced dramatically different results. One report found that by age five, children who experienced the enriched daycare offered by Head Start averaged more than 10 points higher on their IQ scores than did their peers who did not participate in the program. Other research that carefully compared Head Start children with similar youths who did not attend the program found that the former made significant intellectual gains. Head Start children were less likely to have been retained in a grade or placed in classes for slow learners; they outperformed peers on achievement tests; and they were more likely to graduate from high school. Head Start kids also make strides in nonacademic areas: They had better health, immunization rates, and nutrition, and they had enhanced emotional characteristics after leaving the program.

Research also shows that the Head Start program can have important psychological benefits for the mothers of participants, decreasing depression and anxiety and increasing feelings of life satisfaction. Although findings in some areas may be tentative, Head Start enhances school readiness and has enduring effects on social competence.

If, as many experts believe, there is a close link between school performance, family life, and crime, such programs as Head Start can help some potentially criminal youths avoid problems with the law. By implication, their success indicates that programs that help socialize youngsters can be used to combat urban criminality.

In Canada, the federal Aboriginal Head Start program is aimed at children two to five years of age and focuses on school readiness, healthy living, language, and cultural identity. This program is oriented to high-risk children: those in single-parent families, those with special needs, those with low incomes, or those whose caregivers have low education levels.

More than 70 percent of the children came from families in which the parents had grade 12 or less education. Children identified as high risk were less likely to have both parents in the same household and were more likely to have a history of family violence. Other relevant factors were parents who had histories of drug or alcohol abuse or who were survivors of residential school. In a 1998 evaluation report, success was reported at identifying those with risk factors, in retention through the whole program, and in addressing their needs.

conflict. The overall rate of recidivism in one study was 22 percent, compared with 71 percent in a control group. It was estimated that the program paid for itself more than eight times over in terms of savings in criminal justice. Results in family court in London, Ontario, are not optimistic, but the program has the promise of avoiding some of the deleterious effects of incarceration.[183]

Control theory's focus on the family has been put into operation in programs designed to strengthen the bond between parent and child. Other programs attempt to "repair" bonds that have been broken and frayed. Examples of this approach are the career, work furlough, and educational opportunity programs being developed in the nation's prisons. These programs are designed to help inmates maintain a stake in society so they will be less willing to resort to criminal activity on their release. An important change was the establishment of federal guidelines on the use of conditional sentencing, which came into force in 1996. This is a good example of social process theory informing social policy. Offenders serve their time in the community, reducing incarceration costs and making it is easier to reintegrate the offender into the community.

Labelling theorists caution against too much intervention. Rather than ask social agencies to attempt to rehabilitate people who are having problems with the law, theorists argue that "less is better." Put another way, the more institutions try to "help" people, the more these people will be stigmatized and labelled. For example, a special education program designed to help problem readers may cause them to be labelled by themselves and others as slow or stupid; a mental health rehabilitation program created with the best intentions may cause clients to be labelled as crazy or dangerous.

The influence of labelling theory can be viewed in the development of diversion and restitution programs. Diversion programs are designed to remove both juvenile and adult offenders from the normal channels of the criminal justice process by placing them in programs designed for rehabilitation. For example, a university student whose drunk driving causes injury to a pedestrian may, before a trial occurs, be placed for six months in an alcohol treatment program. If he or she successfully completes the program, the charges will be dismissed. Often, diversion programs offer counselling; vocational, educational, and family services; and medical advice. Another label-avoiding innovation that has gained popularity is restitution. Rather than face the stigma of a formal trial, an offender is asked either to pay back the victim of the crime for any loss incurred or to do some useful work in the community in lieu of receiving a court-ordered sentence.

Despite their good intentions, stigma-reducing programs have not met with great success. Critics charge that they substitute one kind of stigma for another—for instance, attending a mental health program in lieu of a criminal trial. In addition, diversion and restitution programs usually screen out violent offenders and repeat offenders. Finally, there is little hard evidence that the recidivism rate of people who have attended alternative programs represents an improvement over the rate of people who have been involved in the traditional criminal justice process.

Summary

Social process theories view criminality as a function of people's interaction with various organizations, institutions, and processes in society. Everyone has the potential to become a criminal if he or she maintains destructive social relationships. Social process theory has three main branches: Social learning theory stresses that people learn how to commit crimes; control theory analyzes the failure of society to control criminal tendencies; and labelling theory maintains that negative labels produce criminal careers. These theories are summarized in Table 8.1.

The social learning branch of social process theory suggests that people learn criminal behaviours much as they learn conventional behaviour. Differential association theory, formulated by Edwin Sutherland, holds that criminality is a result of a person's perceiving an excess of pro-crime definitions over definitions that uphold conventional values. Ronald Akers has reformulated Sutherland's work using psychological learning theory. He calls his approach differential reinforcement theory. Sykes and Matza's theory of neutralization stresses youths' learning of behaviour rationalizations that enable them to overcome societal values and norms and engage in illegal behaviour.

Control theories maintain that all people have the potential to become criminals but that their bonds to conventional society prevent them from violating the law. Walter Reckless's containment theory suggests that a person's self-concept aids his or her commitment to conventional action. Travis Hirschi describes the social bond as containing elements of belief, commitment, attachment, and involvement. Weakened bonds allow youths to become active in antisocial behaviour.

Labelling theory holds that criminality is promoted by becoming negatively labelled by significant others. Such labels as "criminal," "ex-con," and "junkie" serve to isolate people from society and lock

TABLE 8.1 Social Process Theories

Theory	Major Premise	Strengths
Differential association theory	People learn to commit crime from exposure to antisocial definitions.	Explains onset of criminality. Explains the presence of crime in all elements of social structure. Explains why some people in high-crime areas refrain from criminality. Can apply to adults and juveniles.
Differential reinforcement theory	Criminal behaviour depends on the person's experiences with rewards for conventional behaviours and punishment for deviant ones. Being rewarded for deviance leads to crime.	Adds learning theory principles to differential association. Links sociological and psychological principles.
Neutralization theory	Youths learn ways of neutralizing moral restraints and periodically drift in and out of criminal behaviour patterns.	Explains why many delinquents do not become adult criminals. Explains why youthful law violators can participate in conventional behaviour.
Control theories		
Containment theory	Society produces pushes and pulls toward crime. In some people, they are counteracted by internal and external containments, such as a good self-concept and group cohesiveness.	Brings together psychological and sociological principles. Can explain why some people are able to resist the strongest social pressure to commit crime.
Control theory	A person's bond to society prevents him or her from violating social rules. If the bond weakens, the person is free to commit crime.	Explains the onset of crime; can apply to both middle- and lower-class crime. Explains its theoretical constructs adequately so they can be measured. Has been empirically tested.
Labelling theories		
Labelling theory	People enter into law-violating careers when they are labelled for their acts and organize their personalities around the labels.	Explains the role of society in creating deviance. Explains why some juvenile offenders do not become adult criminals. Develops concept of criminal careers.
General theory of deviance	People exposed to negative labels experience self-rejection, which causes them to bond with social outcasts.	Considers the relationship among negative labels, self-image, and personal relations.
Differential social control	Social rejection leads to self-fulfilling prophecy. Weak social controls encourage deviance.	Considers the role of social control in the labelling process.

them into lives of crime. Labels create expectations that the labelled person will act in a certain way; so-labelled people are always watched and suspected. Eventually, these people begin to accept their labels as personal identities, locking them further into lives of

crime and deviance. Edwin Lemert has said that people who accept labels are involved in secondary deviance.

Social process theories have had a great influence on social policy. They have controlled treatment orientations as well as community action policies.

Thinking Like a Criminologist

The federal government is considering a bill that requires the names of people convicted of certain offences, such as vandalism, soliciting a prostitute, or nonpayment of child support, to be posted in local newspapers under the heading "For Shame." Those who favour the bill cite the fact that in Boston, men arrested for soliciting prostitutes are forced to clean streets. In Dallas shoplifters are made to stand outside stores with signs stating their misdeeds. In some states, convicted sex offenders have been required to put signs on their lawn stating their offence.

The Canadian Civil Liberties Union opposes the idea, stating, "It's simply needless humiliation

of the individual." They argue that public shaming is inhumane and further alienates criminals who already have little stake in society, further ostracizing them from the mainstream. For the one-time offender, shaming damages their reputation and puts them at risk of further offending.

This "liberal" position is challenged by those who believe that convicted lawbreakers have no right to conceal their crimes from the public. Shaming penalties seem attractive as cost-effective alternatives to imprisonment. These critics ask what could be wrong with requiring a teenage vandal to personally apologize at the school and wear a shirt with

a big "V" on it while cleaning up the mess. Similarly, drunk drivers should have a big "D" placed on their car. If you do something wrong, they argue, you should have to pay the consequences.

As a social process theorist, you believe criminal attitudes and behaviours are learned. Weak ties to parents and families, poor school performance, and so on, effect the actions of the individual. Considering this, do you believe a "get tough" program could actually work, or does it miss the underlying causes of the behaviour? You have been asked to address the Justice Committee on the issue of whether shaming could deter crime. What would you say?

Key Terms

commitment to conformity

containments

control theory

differential association (DA) theory

differential reinforcement (DR) theory

dramatization of evil

drift

labelling theory

moral entrepreneurs

neutralization theory

primary deviance

reflected appraisal

reflective role-taking

secondary deviance

self-rejection

social control theory

social deviant

social distance

social learning theory

social process theories

socialization

stigmatize

subterranean values

symbolic interaction theory

techniques of neutralization

Critical Thinking Questions

1. Do negative labels cause crime? Or do people who commit crime become negatively labelled? That is, are labels a cause of crime or a result?

2. Once weakened, can a person's bonds to society become reattached? What social processes might help reattachment?

3. Can you devise a test of Sutherland's differential association theory? How would you go about measuring an excess of definitions toward criminality?

4. Can you think of ways you may have supported your peers' or siblings' antisocial behaviour by helping them learn criminal techniques or attitudes?

5. Do you recall neutralizing any guilt you might have felt for committing a criminal or illegal act? Did your neutralizations come before or after you committed the act in question?

 See the book-specific website at http://www.siegelcriminology3e.nelson.com for additional chapter links, discussions, and quizzes.

Social Conflict Theory

It would be unusual to pick up the morning paper and not see headlines loudly proclaiming renewed strife between countries, between union negotiators and company attorneys, or between citizens and police authorities. The world is filled with conflict. Conflict is destructive when it leads to war, violence, and death; but conflict can also result in positive social change. Those who view crime as a function of social and economic conflict are referred to as the conflict, critical, Marxist, or radical criminologists (see Figure 9.1).

The goal of social conflict theorists is to explain crime within economic and social contexts and to express the connections among social class, crime, and social control.[1] Social conflict theorists are concerned with such issues as the role government plays in creating a criminogenic environment, the relationship of personal or group power in controlling and shaping the criminal law, the role of bias in the operations of the justice system, and the relationship between a capitalist free-enterprise economy and crime rates.

Figure 9.1 **The Branches of Social Conflict Theory**

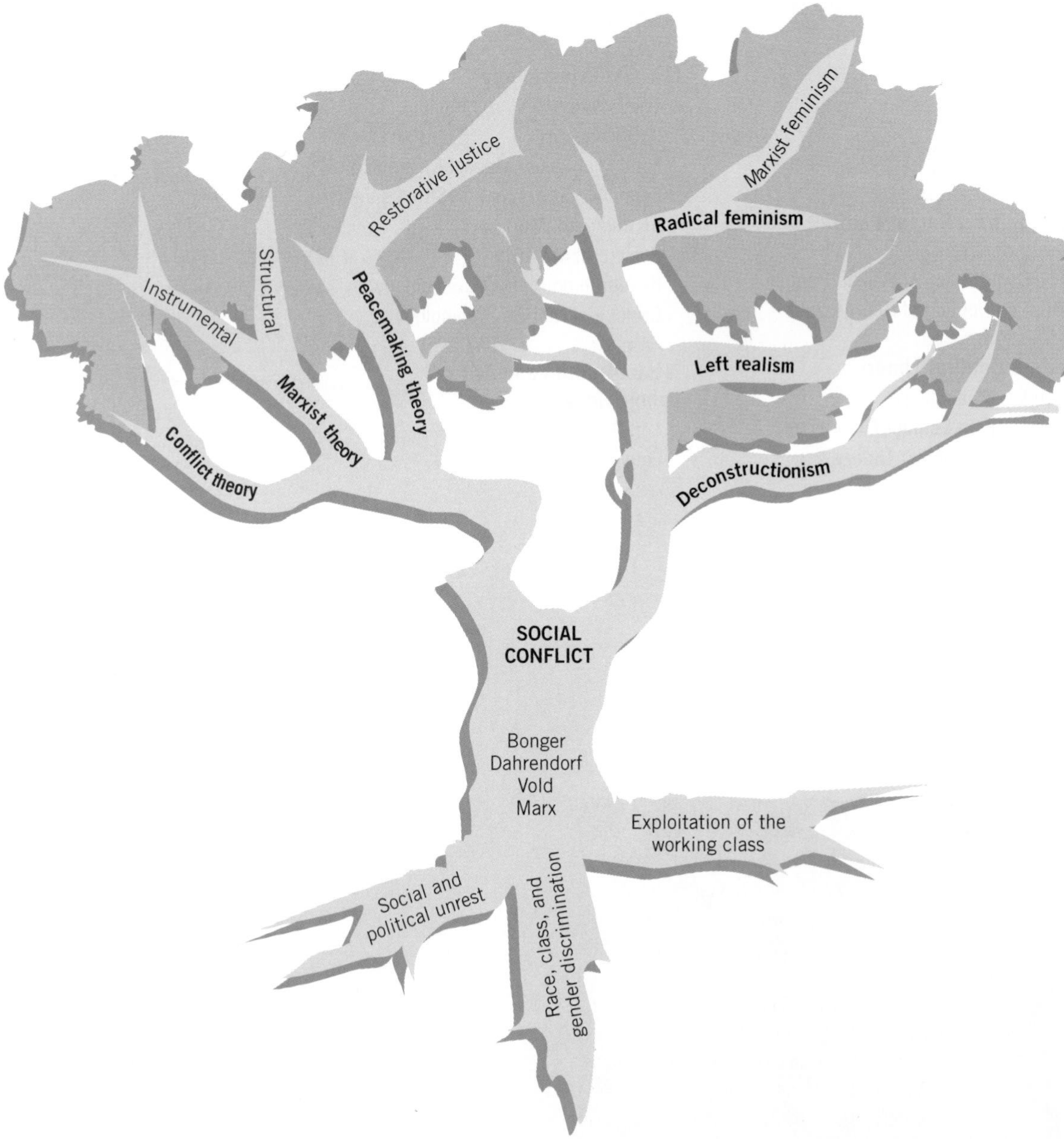

Conflict theorists view crime as the outcome of class struggle. Conflict works to promote crime by creating a social atmosphere in which the law is a mechanism for controlling dissatisfied members of society while maintaining the position of the powerful. That is why crimes that are the province of the wealthy, such as illegal corporate activities, are sanctioned much more leniently than are those, such as burglary, that are considered lower-class activities.

Conflict theorists reject the notion that law is designed to maintain a tranquil and fair society, and that criminals are simply violent and predatory people. Rather, racism, sexism, imperialism, unsafe working conditions, inadequate childcare, substandard housing, pollution of the environment, and war are the "true crimes." However, the crimes of the powerless, such as burglary, robbery, and assault, are more likely to be prosecuted.[2]

This chapter reviews criminological theories that allege that criminal behaviour is a function of conflict, a reaction to the unfair distribution of wealth and power in society. The social conflict perspective has several independent branches. One, generally referred to as **conflict theory**, assumes that crime is caused by the intergroup rivalry that exists in every society. A second branch focuses more directly on the crime-producing traits of capitalist society; the various schools of thought in this area of scholarship include critical, radical, and Marxist criminology. Other sections are devoted to feminist, new realist, and peacemaking criminology.

Connections

As discussed in Chapter 1, the philosophical and economic analysis of Karl Marx forms the historical roots of the conflict perspective of criminology.

Marxist Thought

Karl Marx lived in an era of unrestrained capitalist expansion.[3] By 1850, the tools of the Industrial Revolution, mechanized factories, the use of coal to drive steam engines, and modern transportation had become regular features of society. Production had shifted from cottage industries to large factories. Conditions in industrial factories were atrocious, and trade unions were ruthlessly suppressed by owners and government agents.

Marx had found his early career as a journalist interrupted by government suppression of the newspaper where he worked because of its liberal editorial policy. He then moved to Paris, where he met Friedrich Engels (1820–95), who became his friend and economic patron. By 1847, Marx and Engels had joined with a group of primarily German socialist revolutionaries known as the Communist League.

Productive Forces and Productive Relations

Marx believed the economic conditions of capitalism had put workers at the mercy of their capitalist employers. For example, young children worked in mines and factories from dawn to dusk with no protection under the labour law. Analysis of such conditions as this led Marx to conclude that this method of developing and producing material goods was oppressive.

Production has two components: (1) productive forces, which include technology, energy sources, and material resources, and (2) productive relations, which exist among the people producing goods and services. The most important relationship in industrial culture is between the owners of the means of production and the people who do the actual labour. Throughout history, society has been organized this way—master–slave, lord–serf, and now capitalist–proletarian. Capitalism is subject to the development of a rigid class structure: the capitalist bourgeoisie at the top and the working proletariat, who actually produce goods and services, at the bottom.

The term *class* denotes position in relation to others. Thus, it is not necessary to have a particular amount of wealth or prestige; it is more important to have the power to exploit others economically, legally, and socially. The political and economic philosophy of the dominant class influences all aspects of life, as people's lives revolve around the means of production.[4]

Marx believed that societies change through slow evolution or sudden violence because of contradictions or conflicts present in a society. If these social conflicts are not resolved, they tend to destabilize society, leading to social change.

Marx on Crime

Marx viewed crime as the product of law enforcement policies akin to a labelling process theory. He also saw a connection between criminality and inequality, stating: "There must be something rotten in the very core of a social system which increases in wealth without diminishing its misery, and increases in crime even more rapidly than in numbers."[5]

 InfoTrac®

To read an excerpt in Marx's own words on the nature of crime look up this article: Karl Marx, "Criminals on the Development of Productive Power," *Journal of Contemporary Asia* 31, no. 3 (2001): 288.

In *The Condition of the Working Class in England in 1844*, Engels portrayed crime as a function of social demoralization: workers, demoralized by capitalist society, are caught up in a process that leads to crime and violence.[6] Working people commit crime because their choice is a slow death of starvation or a speedy one at the hands of the law.

Developing a Social Conflict Theory of Crime

Conflict theory was first applied to criminology by Willem Bonger and George Vold.

The Contribution of Willem Bonger

Bonger was born in 1876 in Holland and committed suicide in 1940 rather than submit to Nazi rule. His Marxist/socialist concepts of crime causation were first published in 1916.[7]

Bonger believed that crime is social, lying within the boundaries of normal human behaviour. The response to crime is punishment—the application of penalties considered more severe than spontaneous moral condemnation administered by the state. No act is naturally immoral; what is considered antisocial reflects current morality. Since society changes continually, ideas of what is immoral also change.

Bonger believed that society is divided unequally because of the system of production. In societies divided into a ruling class and an inferior class, penal law serves the will of the former. Even though criminal laws may appear to protect members of both classes, crimes are acts considered harmful to those who have the power to control society at their command.

The capitalist system is competitive, held together by force rather than by consensus. Bonger argued that all people desire wealth and happiness; however, few people can achieve it. People are encouraged by capitalist society to be egoistic, caring only for their own pleasures and ignoring the disadvantaged. As a consequence of this environment, people have become more capable of crime than they would be if the system had developed under a socialist philosophy.

Although capitalism makes both the proletariat and the bourgeoisie crime-prone, only the former are likely to become officially recognized as criminals. The key to this problem is that the legal system discriminates against the poor by legalizing the egoistic actions of the wealthy. Upper-class individuals will commit crime if (1) they have an opportunity to gain an illegal advantage and (2) their lack of moral sense enables them to violate social rules. It is success at any price that pushes wealthier individuals toward criminality.

If wealth is distributed unequally through the social structure and people are taught to equate economic advantage with superiority, those who are poor and therefore inferior will be crime-prone. The economic system will intensify any personal disadvantage people have and increase their propensity to commit crime.

Bonger concluded that almost all crime would disappear if society could progress to a form in which property was distributed based on "each according to his [or her] needs." The remaining crimes will be the irrational psychopathic type caused by individual mental problems.

In formulating their views, today's conflict theorists also rely heavily on the writings of pioneering social thinker Ralf Dahrendorf,[8] who believed that every society is based on the coercion of some of its members by others.

The Contribution of George Vold

Social conflict theory was actually adapted to criminology by George Vold.[9] Laws are created by politically oriented groups who seek the assistance of the government to help them defend their interests and curb the interests of others. Lawmaking and enforcement reflect conflicts between interest groups and their struggle to control the power of the state. Every stage of the process—from the passage of the law, through the prosecution of the case, to the relationships between inmate and guard or parole agent and parolee—is marked by conflict.

Criminal acts are a consequence of direct contact between forces struggling to control society, and examination of even basic violent acts often reveals political undertones. Vold's model is limited to situations in which rival group loyalties collide. It cannot explain impulsive, irrational acts unrelated to any group's interest.

 InfoTrac®

To learn more about the effect of conflict on everyday life, look at a study that urges educators to allow students to respond to conflict and promote resolution through peace and nonviolence rather than avoiding conflict: Irene McHenry, "Conflict in Schools—Fertile Ground for Moral Growth," *Phi Delta Kappan* 82, no. 3 (2000): 223.

Modern Conflict Theory

In the 1960s, self-report studies suggested that crime and delinquency were much more evenly distributed through the social structure than shown by the official statistics.[10] If this were true, then middle-class participation in crime was going unrecorded, while the lower class was the subject of discriminatory law enforcement practices.

Criminologists began to view the justice system as a mechanism to control the lower class and maintain the status quo, rather than as the means of dispensing fair and evenhanded justice.[11] The publication of important labelling perspective works, such as Lemert's *Social Pathology* and Becker's *Outsiders*, also contributed to the development of the conflict model.[12] Labelling theorists rejected the notion that crime is morally wrong and studied the interaction among crime, criminal, victim, and social control agencies.[13]

A group of criminologists began to produce scholarship and research directed at (1) identifying "real" crimes in society, such as profiteering, sexism, and racism; (2) evaluating how the criminal law is used as a mechanism of social control; and (3) turning the attention of citizens to the inequities in society.[14] David Greenberg comments on the scholarship that was produced:

> The theme that dominated much of the work in this area was the contention that criminal legislation was determined not by moral consensus or the common interests of the entire society, but by relative power of groups determined to use the criminal law to advance their own special interests or to impose their moral preferences on others.[15]

This movement was aided by the general and widespread social and political upheaval of the late 1960s and early 1970s. This included demonstrations against the Vietnam War, counterculture movements, and political protest. Conflict theory flourished within this framework, since it provided a systematic basis for challenging the legitimacy of the government. The crackdown on political dissidents by agents of the federal government, and the prosecution of draft resisters, seemed designed to maintain control in the hands of political powerbrokers.

Conflict Criminology

In the early 1970s, conflict theory began to have a significant influence on criminology. Chambliss and Seidman wrote *Law, Order and Power*, which documented how the justice system operates to protect the rich and powerful:

> To maintain the existing legal system requires a choice . . . between maintaining a legal system that . . . supports the existing economic system with its power structure and developing an equitable legal system accompanied by the loss of "personal freedom." But the old question comes back to plague us: Freedom for whom? Is the black man who provides such a ready source of cases for the welfare workers, the

mental hospitals, and the prisons "free"? Are the slum dwellers who are arrested night after night for "loitering," "drunkenness," or being "suspicious" free?[16]

The objectives of conflict criminology are to describe how the control of the political and economic system affects the administration of criminal justice, to show how the definitions of crime favour those who control the justice system, and to show how justice in society is skewed so that those who deserve to be punished the most (wealthy white-collar criminals whose crimes cost society millions of dollars) are actually punished the least, while those whose crimes are relatively minor and committed out of economic necessity (petty, lower-class thieves) receive the stricter sanctions.[17]

Power Relations. The unequal distribution of power produces conflict. People use power to shape public opinion to meet their personal interests, and crime is defined by those in power. This is criminogenic, because laws are culturally relative, and no absolute standard of right and wrong exists.[18]

The power to control people is exemplified by the relationship between the justice system and minorities. For example, in policing, only 13 percent of public police officers and 20 percent of security guards are women. Visible minorities constitute 10 percent of the paid labour force but only 3 percent of the public police force in Canada. Only in Aboriginal policing has Native representation exceeded the national average, because of self-administered police services in Aboriginal communities. These types of underrepresentation affect the ability of the police to address the needs of these groups.[19]

The subtle ways that the justice system victimizes ethnic minorities have been well documented.[20] Socioeconomic conditions that favour Whites create an environment in which minority people commit crimes that get them processed by the system. Discretionary decisions by law enforcement officers have them charged with more serious offences; they are less likely to be advised to speak to a lawyer; they are shunted into the criminal courts and not diversion programs. Busy public defenders too often give their clients short shrift and force them into plea bargains that ensure early criminal records; and ethnic minorities are more likely to be encouraged to plead guilty. Health care workers and teachers report suspected violent acts to the police, resulting in frequent and early arrests of minority adults and youths. Police departments routinely use policies of searching, questioning, and detaining ethnic males in an area if a violent criminal has been described as non-White. And media accounts create the image of pervasive minority-group criminality by mentioning race when it concerns a Black or Native suspect, but not when it concerns a White suspect. When this

A Mohawk calling himself Kadahfi leads demonstrators onto the Oka golf course. Plans to expand the golf course triggered the Oka crisis in 1990.

InfoTrac®

Does race discrimination still exist in modern society? See Francis T. Cullen et al., "Stop or I'll Shoot: Racial Differences in Support for Police Use of Deadly Force," *American Behavioral Scientist* 39, no. 4 (1996): 449(12).

stereotyping is coupled with unfair treatment, those in power further alienate minorities from the mainstream, perpetuating a class- and race-divided society in which minority-group members are more likely to perceive "criminal injustice."[21]

The Social Reality of Crime. Richard Quinney integrated his beliefs about power, society, and criminality into a theory called the **social reality of crime.** The theory's six propositions are contained in Table 9.1.[22] Criminal definitions (law) represent the interests of those who hold power in society. Where conflict exists between social groups—for example, the wealthy and the poor—those who hold power will create laws to benefit themselves. So harsh punishments for property crime are designed to help those who already have

TABLE 9.1 Propositions of the Social Reality of Crime

1. Crime is a definition of human conduct that is created by authorized agents in a politically organized society.
2. Criminal definitions describe behaviours that conflict with the interests of the segments of society that have the power to shape public policy.
3. Criminal definitions are applied by the segments of society that have the power to shape the enforcement and administration of the criminal law.
4. Behaviour patterns are structured in segmentally organized society in relation to criminal definitions, and within this context, persons engage in actions that have relative probabilities of being defined as criminal.
5. Conceptions of crime are constructed and diffused in the segments of society by various means of communication.
6. The social reality of crime is constructed by the formulation and applications of criminal definitions, the development of behaviour patterns to criminal definitions, and the construction of criminal conceptions.

Source: Adapted from Richard Quinney, *The Social Reality of Crime* (Boston: Little, Brown, 1970), 15–23.

wealth keep it in their possession; in contrast, the lenient sanctions attached to corporate crimes are designed to give the already powerful a free hand at economic exploitation.

Quinney wrote that criminal definitions are based on such factors as (1) changing social conditions; (2) emerging interests; (3) increasing demands that political, economic, and religious interests be protected; and (4) changing conceptions of public interest. Quinney pulled together these ideas to say that concepts of crime are controlled by the powerful and that the criminal justice system works to secure the needs of the powerful. Criminal definitions are a constantly changing set of concepts that mirror the political organization of society. Criminals are people who have come up short in the struggle for success and are seeking alternative means of achieving wealth, status, or even survival.[23] Consequently, law violations can be viewed as political or even quasi-revolutionary acts.[24]

For example, in 2004, arson, vandalism, and other disturbances occurred in Kanesatake, a Native community outside Montreal, bringing back memories of violence in 1990 when police and Natives were locked in a deadly land claims standoff. Part of the underlying conflict relates to **norm resistance**, because for years the official policy toward Natives was assimilation. Today, Aboriginal communities react more in protest to threats of outside interference.[25]

Connections

Quinney has changed his theoretical outlook over his long and distinguished career. He is now a leader of the Zen-inspired peacemaking movement, which seeks to remove violence and coercion from the criminal justice system and promotes healing or "restorative justice." See the section on peacemaking later in this chapter.

Norm Resistance. Other writers, such as Austin Turk, write that social conflict is inevitable when authorities in society are in conflict with those who are controlled by, but have little ability to control, the law. Conflict is inherent because both groups have their own sets of cultural norms (those that express ideals and values) and social norms (actual group behaviours). Interaction between authorities and subjects eventually produces norm resistance, or open conflict, which is highest under certain conditions:

- Authorities and subjects are both committed to opposing cultural norms.
- People with group support will be resistant to authority or change.
- People who are sophisticated at assessing the strengths and weaknesses of their opponents will be better able to avoid conflict with authorities.[26]

Research on Conflict Theory

Testing conflict theory is different from evaluating consensus models. Similar methodologies are often used,

Culture, Gender, Ethnicity, and Criminology

Native People in Canada

- In the 1930s, Native workers were used at Port Radium to bag and haul uranium ore; they were not allowed to use the White showers to clean themselves of the poison.
- A Native woman taken to a Vancouver Island residential school in the 1950s when she was six years old suffered 12 years of degradation, abuse, and rape.
- In 1989, Ontario's task force on policing and race relations heard testimony from Native people about beatings, racial slurs, and neglect by police on northern reserves.
- In 1993, six Innu children were found in an unheated shack in Davis Inlet, sniffing gasoline and saying that they wanted to die.
- Militant loggers from the Listuguj reserve in Quebec blockaded a road for three weeks in the summer of 1998

in a protest to improve Aboriginal logging rights.
- In 2001, two Saskatchewan police officers were convicted of abandoning Native men outside of Saskatoon in the middle of the winter without proper clothing.

Stories like these are just the tip of the iceberg in the study of relations between Native people and the Canadian criminal justice system. Research into the issue could take many directions. We could look at the socioeconomic conditions of Native people in Canada: the poverty rates they experience, the higher than normal rate of suicide, the violence and despair that are felt by those living in isolated reserves and in large cities. We could also question why Native people are overrepresented in prisons in Western Canada, why they are more likely to experience discrimination by the police, and why they are more likely to be advised to plead guilty and be sent to prison than are Whites.

We need only look at the case of Donald Marshall, Jr. for a prominent and clear example of how Native people are treated by the justice system. On May 28, 1971, Marshall, a 17-year-old Micmac, and Sandy Seale, a 17-year-old Black teenager, were walking through Wentworth Park in Sydney, Nova Scotia. There they met Roy Ebsary and Jimmy MacNeil. When they asked Ebsary for money, he responded by fatally stabbing Seale and wounding Marshall. The police officers who responded to the incident did not cordon off the crime scene, search the area, or question witnesses. The sergeant of detectives subsequently accused Marshall of stabbing Seale during an argument and pressured two youths to claim that they had witnessed the attack. Information from MacNeil was discounted by the police, as was that provided by Ebsary's daughter. Marshall was charged with murder and spent 11 years in jail for a murder he didn't commit. The RCMP reopened the case in 1982. Then Justice Minister Jean Chrétien referred the case to the Nova Scotia Court of Appeal, which acquitted Marshall in 1983 but concluded that he was partly to blame for his misfortune. In 1989, a Royal Commission investigating the wrongful conviction and incarceration of Donald Marshall, Jr. concluded that the criminal justice system had failed him at every turn.

The commission's seven-volume report did not whitewash problems in the criminal justice system; it commissioned research to show that Native and Black minorities were discriminated against by the system. In this larger context, what happened to Donald Marshall was certainly not an isolated case.

In 1999, Donald Marshall was in the news again in another case that put Native people in conflict with the law on different grounds, when the Supreme Court of

Canada heard a case on appeal from Nova Scotia. In 1993 in a case called *R. v. Marshall* [1999, 3 S.C.R.] Marshall had been charged and convicted of three offences set out in the federal fishery regulations: the selling of eels without a licence, fishing without a licence, and fishing during the closed season with illegal nets. Marshall admitted he had caught and sold 463 pounds (210 kilograms) of eels worth $787.10, without a licence and with a prohibited net within closed times, but he argued that he possessed a treaty right to catch and sell fish under the treaties of 1760–61. In its decision, the Supreme Court overturned the two lower court decisions. It specifically concluded that prohibitions on catching, retaining, and selling fish without a licence, and on fishing during the closed time, as set out in Maritime Provinces Fishery Regulations were inconsistent with the treaty rights of Native people.

The federal government, through its Department of Fisheries and Oceans (DFO), subsequently set out to negotiate interim agreements with Native bands throughout the Maritime region, but the Burnt Church reserve decided to develop its own management scheme and fish for lobster independently. The DFO declared that the Native people were acting "in defiance of the law" and moved in. With the RCMP looking on, the DFO, with their boats and helicopters, conducted surveillance and seized traps and gear. Native people are now more likely to challenge discrimination in the criminal justice system and to press for their rights under historic treaties. However, change will be slow.

Sources: Royal Commission on the Donald Marshall, Jr., Prosecution, Digest of Findings and Recommendations (Province of Nova Scotia: King's Printer, 1989); R. v. Marshall, Supreme Court of Canada 1999.

but conflict-centred research places attempts to show that conflict principles hold up under empirical scrutiny. Areas of interest include comparing the crime rates of members of powerless groups with those of members of the elite classes, examining the operation of the justice system to uncover bias and discrimination, charting the historical development of the criminal law, and identifying laws created to preserve the power of the elite classes at the expense of the poor.

Conflict theorists say that such crimes as burglary and larceny are a means of social and economic survival, and others, such as assault, homicide, and drug use, are a means of expressing rage, frustration, and anger. Crime rates also vary according to indicators of poverty and need. For example, a comparison of homicide rates with infant mortality rates over a 50-year period (since the latter variable is an efficient measure of poverty) found that the two rates were significantly interrelated.[27] Other data collected by ecologists show that crime is strongly related to income level, deteriorated living conditions, and relative economic deprivation.[28]

Another area of research focuses on the criminal justice system. For example, American states with significant poverty levels were also the most likely to have the largest number of fatal shootings by police, suggesting that police act more forcefully in areas of class conflict.[29] Similarly, an examination of criminal cases processed by the Chicago criminal courts found that members of powerless groups are the most likely to receive prejudicial sentences in criminal courts.[30] Other research shows that both White and Black offenders are more likely to receive stricter sentences in criminal courts if their personal characteristics (single, young, urban, male) give them the appearance of being a member of the **dangerous classes**.[31]

Studies of bail hearings show moral assessments by police have a strong influence on decisions to remand those suspected of crimes. Pretrial detention is important, because it can be used to encourage (or coerce) guilty pleas from accused persons. Those accused who are not held in pretrial custody are more likely to have their charges withdrawn by the prosecution. The overpolicing of stigmatized groups is related

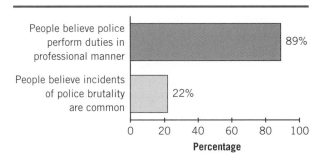

Do you trust your local law enforcement group? Forty-eight percent of Canadians say "no."

Source: Poll conducted by *The Globe and Mail*, May 4, 2004.

People believe police perform duties in professional manner — 89%

People believe incidents of police brutality are common — 22%

Percentage

Eight-nine percent of the public overwhelmingly thinks that the police perform their duties in a professional and respectful manner; however, 22 percent say that incidents of police brutality are common.

Source: Poll conducted by Ipsos-Reid, October 30, 2003, "BC Public Provides Backup to Police on Issue of Police Brutality."

to views held by the police that create a conservative and authoritarian culture. The Royal Commission on Aboriginal People found that Natives are more likely to be denied bail, to be subjected to pretrial detention, and to plead guilty without knowing the consequences of doing so.

The Commission on Systemic Racism in the Ontario Criminal Justice System found that Blacks were more likely than were Whites to be stopped by the police, but Whites were more likely to be granted bail.[32] When the Toronto police were accused in 2002 of racial profiling, a lot of controversy ensued over whether the facts supported that conclusion.[33] The police launched a $2.7 billion lawsuit in their own defence.

Conflict theorists show that the criminal justice system is quick to take action when the victim of crime is wealthy, White, and male but is uninterested when the victim is poor, non-White, and female, indicating how power positions affect justice.[34] It is not surprising that an analysis of national population trends and imprisonment rates shows that as the percentage of minority-group members increases, the imprisonment rate does likewise.[35] This outcome may be a function of society becoming "less tolerant of nonwhite populations and/or feeling more threatened by them."[36] Data showing racial and class discrimination by the justice system support conflict theory.

One reason for discrimination may be the attitudes of decision makers. For example, justice professionals

who express racist values are also more punitive, believe that courts should be stricter, and believe that the death penalty is an effective deterrent.[37] Race has varying and subtle effects on decision making in the juvenile justice system.[38] Critical thinkers say the powerless need a greater voice to express their needs and concerns, if these inequities are to be addressed.[39] There is also a need for more research, for example, on police–citizen encounters in domestic disputes.[40]

Social policy stems directly from such research. For example, a pilot project developed in New Brunswick to serve the Native population found that providing legal aid services in an Aboriginal's first language reduced adjournments and resulted in a higher rate of not guilty pleas.[41] The significance of being sensitive to the plight of minority groups when they come in conflict with the criminal justice system is illustrated in the Famous Canadian Court Case, *R. v. Gladue.*

Analysis of Conflict Theory

Conflict theorists identify power relations in society and their role in promoting criminal behaviour. They reject the view that the law represents the values of the majority or that legal codes create a just society and criminals are simple predators. Some criminologists disagree, suggesting instead that crime is a matter of rational choice made by offenders motivated more by greed and selfishness than by poverty and hopelessness.[42] Critics also say that crime is less likely to be a function of poverty and class conflict than a product of personal needs, socialization, or some other related factor.[43]

Similarly, studies of police discretion, criminal court sentencing, and correctional policy have not always found indicators of class or race bias, an outcome predicted by conflict theory.[44] An examination of the prison sentences of 10 488 inmates in three southeastern American states concluded that socioeconomic status was unrelated to the length of prison terms assigned by the courts.[45] Sentencing decisions in California also found little evidence of race bias; African Americans were neither more likely to be sent to prison than were White offenders nor more likely to receive longer prison terms.[46]

Cross-cultural research indicates that crime rates are not reduced when a free-market system is replaced by a less competitive economic model. Analysis of crime in Tanzania found that when the free enterprise system was replaced by a socialist system, the crime rate actually increased. New crimes, such as theft by public servants and corruption, also appear to increase.[47]

More radical versions of the general conflict model have developed, and attention has now turned to these more critical versions of social conflict theory.

Famous Canadian Court Case

R. v. Gladue

Jamie Gladue's 19th birthday was an exceptional one, but for very different reasons from the average person her age. On the same night she celebrated this special occasion, she took her partner's life and changed her own forever. In the process, this young Cree woman from Alberta set the stage for a legal drama that has significantly affected the lives of Aboriginals right across the country.

In June 1996, Gladue was charged with second-degree murder for stabbing her common-law husband to death during a domestic dispute. She pleaded guilty to a reduced count of manslaughter about eight months later. Had the federal government not recently modified Canada's sentencing laws, this might have been an open and shut case.

On entering the disposition phase of the proceedings, a newly enacted *Criminal Code* provision was automatically invoked.

Section 718.2(e) compels adjudicators to consider all available and reasonable sanctions other than imprisonment, paying particular attention to the circumstances of Aboriginal offenders. The presiding judge questioned the relevance of this provision to the matter at hand, noting that the couple lived in an urban area off-reserve. Gladue was handed a three-year prison term.

Gladue challenged her disposition before the British Columbia Court of Appeal, targeting the lower court's reading of section 718.2(e). Although the judge's reasoning was opposed, his decision was defended. Ultimately, the higher court agreed that there was no basis for a special focus on the appellant's heritage in this particular situation.

The battle reached a climax in April 1999, when the Supreme Court of Canada evaluated both the Gladue case and the *Criminal Code* provision. The concern that due consideration had not been given

to Gladue's Aboriginal background was legitimated, but her sentence was upheld yet again. Although the defendant was defeated in one sense, the judgment was successful in other respects. First and foremost, the Supreme Court validated section 718.2(e). Principles were also established to guide the proper interpretation and application of this provision.

The legal effects of the Gladue decision have proven to be far-reaching. For example, three provinces have established Aboriginal-only courts. Not everyone is receptive to the Supreme Court decision, however. Some complain that Aboriginal offenders are treated too leniently. Others criticize the government for concentrating on sentencing practices when the overrepresentation of Aboriginals in prison stems from socioeconomic inequalities.

Prepared by Andrea Wolf.

Marxist Criminology

Above all, Marxism is a critique of capitalism. Capitalism produces haves and have-nots, each engaging in a particular branch of criminality.[48] Those in political power also control the definition of crime.[49] Consequently, the only crimes available to the poor are the severely sanctioned "street crimes": rape, murder, theft, and mugging. Members of the middle class cheat on their taxes and engage in petty corporate crime, acts that generate social disapproval but are rarely punished severely. The wealthy are involved in acts that should be described as crimes but are not, such as corporate crime. Though regulatory laws control business activities, these are rarely enforced, and violations are lightly punished. Laws regulating corporate crime are window dressing designed to create the impression that the justice system is fair.[50]

The Development of a Radical Criminology

Radical theory can be traced to the National Deviancy Conference (NDC) of 1968 in Britain. Members were critical of the positivist criminology being taught in British and American universities. They rejected the conservative stance of criminologists and their close financial relationship with government funding agencies. They investigated the concept of deviance from a labelling perspective, looking at how social control might be a cause of, rather than a response to, antisocial behaviour.

Radical theory was given a powerful boost when Taylor, Walton, and Young published *The New Criminology*, followed by *Critical Criminology*, criticizing existing concepts in criminology.[51] Those books became important resources for scholars critical of both the field of criminology and the existing legal process.

Meanwhile, American scholars began to follow a new radical approach to criminology, focused on the criminology program at the University of California. These scholars, and others, such as Richard Quinney and William Chambliss, were influenced by social criticism of the Vietnam War, prison struggles, and the civil rights and feminist movements. Mainstream criminology was criticized as conservative, pro-government, and antihuman. Critical criminologists scoffed when their fellow scholars used statistical analysis of computerized data to describe criminal and delinquent behaviour:

> Many of our scientific heroes of the past, upon rereading, turned out to be racists or, more generally, apologists for social injustice. In response to the widespread protests on campuses and throughout society, many of the contemporary giants of social science emerged as defenders of the status quo and vocally dismissed the claims of the oppressed for social justice.[52]

Marxists did not meet with widespread approval. The criminology school at Berkeley was eventually closed for what many believe were political reasons. Even today, conflict exists between critical thinkers and mainstream academics. The prestigious Harvard Law School and other law centres have been the scenes of conflict and charges of purges and tenure denials because some professors held critical views of law and society, victimized by "academic McCarthyism."[53]

In the ensuing years, new branches of a radical criminology were developing elsewhere. In the early 1980s, the **left realism** school was started by scholars affiliated with the Middlesex Polytechnic and the University of Edinburgh in Great Britain. In the United States, scholars influenced in part by the pioneering work of Dennis Sullivan and Larry Tifft created the peacemaking movement.[54] At the same time, feminist scholars began to apply critical analysis to the relationship among gender, power, and criminality. These movements have coalesced into a rich and complex criminological tradition.

Fundamentals of Marxist Criminology

Marxist criminologists ignore formal theory construction, with its heavy emphasis on empirical value-free testing, arguing that criminological scholarship should have a political and ideological basis.[55] Crime and criminal justice must be viewed in a historical, social, and economic context. Leftist criminologists see the definition of crime designed to protect the power and position of the upper classes at the expense of the poor. Part of the radical agenda, then, is to make the public aware that crimes of power are crimes just as much as burglary and robbery are.[56]

Criminals are not social misfits but rather a product of the society and its economic system in which they reside. Capitalism has always produced a relatively high level of crime and violence. Three implications follow from this view:

1. Each society will produce its own types and amounts of crime.
2. Each society will have its own distinctive ways of dealing with criminal behaviour.
3. Each society gets the amount and type of crime that it deserves.

Criminals are not outsiders who can be controlled by an increase in law enforcement. Criminality is a function of the social and economic organization of society. To control crime and reduce criminality is to end the social conditions that promote crime.

Economic Structure and Surplus Value

Marxist criminology's general theme is the relationship between crime and the ownership and control of private property in a capitalist society.[57] That ownership and control, according to sociologist Gregg Barak, is the principal basis of power in capitalist society.[58] Social conflict is fundamentally related to the historical and social distribution of productive private property and **surplus value** (profit).

One important aspect of capitalism is the effect of surplus value, which refers to the value resulting from production when the cost of labour is less than the cost of the goods it produces. The profit can be reinvested or used to enrich the owners. To increase the rate of surplus value, workers can be made to work harder for less pay, be made more efficient, or be replaced by "labour-saving" technology.

As surplus value increases, more people are displaced from productive relationships, and the size of the "marginal" population swells. As corporations downsize to increase profits, high-paying labour and managerial jobs are lost to computer-driven machinery. Displaced workers are forced into service jobs at minimum wage or become temporary employees without benefits or a secure position.

As more people are thrust outside the economic mainstream (**marginalization**), a larger portion of the population is forced to live in areas conducive to crime. Once people are marginalized, commitment to the system declines, producing another criminogenic force: a weakened bond to society.[59]

This effect has also been observed in former socialist republics that have converted to free-market economies. Both China and the former Soviet Union have experienced an upsurge in gang activity as they embrace market economies; Russia may now have a murder rate higher than that of the United States.

There are a number of schools of thought within the radical literature. Some of these different approaches are discussed in further detail in the following sections.

Instrumental Marxism

These Marxists view the criminal law and criminal justice system solely as an instrument for controlling the poor; the state is the "tool" of the capitalists. Accordingly, capitalist justice serves the powerful and enables them to impose their morality on the entire society.[60]

The poor may or may not commit more crimes than the rich do, but they certainly are arrested and punished more often. The poor are driven to crime because a natural frustration exists in a society in which affluence is well publicized but unattainable. When class conflict becomes unbearable, frustration can spill out in riots, such as the one that occurred in Los Angeles on April 29, 1992, described as a "class rebellion of the underprivileged against the privileged."[61] Extensive work to rebuild police–community relationships ensued after the U.S. Federal Justice Department identified a pattern of civil rights violations by the Los Angeles police department.

Because of class conflict, hostility is generated among members of the lower class toward the social order. The focus of conventional criminology on social conditions that cause crime, such as family structure, intelligence, peer relations, and school performance, serves to keep the lower classes servile by showing why its members are more criminal, less intelligent, and more prone to school failure and family problems than are members of the middle class. Rather, the goal of criminology should be to show how law in capitalist society works to preserve ruling-class power, summarized in the following statements:

- Society is based on an advanced capitalist economy.
- The state is organized to serve the interests of the dominant economic class.
- The criminal law is a state instrument used to maintain the existing social and economic order.
- Crime control occurs through institutions established and administered by an elite.
- Contradictions in advanced capitalism require that the subordinate classes remain oppressed through the coercion and violence of the legal system.
- Only with the collapse of capitalist society and the creation of a new society, based on socialist principles, will there be a solution to the crime problem.[62]

Concepts of Instrumental Marxism. Legal relations underpin the infrastructure required by capitalism. Legal relations maintain the family and school structure so as to secure the labour force. The system may at times secure the interests of the working class, for example, to protect collective bargaining. Yet legal relations maintain patterns of individualism and selfishness and perpetuate a class system characterized by anarchy, oppression, and crime.[63]

At its core, instrumental Marxism defines the state, the law, and the ruling class as a single entity. The law is shaped by the economic, social, and political interests of the ruling class and used by the ruling class to its own advantage; the definition of crime deflects attention from social injustice.[64]

Privilege. Barry Krisberg has linked crime to the differentials in **privilege**, which include such rights as life, liberty, and happiness; such traits as intelligence, sensitivity,

and humanity; and such material goods as monetary wealth, luxuries, land, and the like. The effective use of violence and coercion is the major factor in determining which social group ascends to the position of defining and holding privilege.

Class discrimination based on privilege can be quite subtle. When the Ontario government announced that it was going to require mandatory drug testing and treatment for welfare recipients suspected of having a substance abuse problem, the policy was condemned by the Centre for Addiction and Mental Health as being discriminatory and ineffective. Another legislative move criticized for being an attack on the poor is the *Safe Streets Act* introduced in British Columbia in 2004. Modelled on Ontario legislation, it makes it illegal to solicit money in a threatening manner, to panhandle within five metres of an automated bank machine, and to solicit money from vehicles that are stopped or parked, eliminating the market for window-washing squeegee kids.

Conversely, criminologists, such as Laureen Snider, argue that corporate crime has disappeared through decriminalization, deregulation, and downsizing of enforcement capability. As she says:

> While punishment for corporate criminals was being eliminated, incarceration rates for traditional, blue-collar criminals were doubling and tripling. Increasing penality—through criminalizing behaviours previously tolerated, through the "war on drugs," by abolishing parole and statutory remission, lengthening minimum sentences, instituting compulsory urinalysis for "at risk" populations—became a growth business in the 1980s and 1990s.[65]

Some say criminology itself helps support state repression:

> Criminology has serviced domestic repression. . . . This system has been used to repress and maintain the powerlessness of poor people, people of colour, and young people. In the past, we have been constrained by a legal definition of crime which restricts us to studying and ultimately helping to control only legally defined "criminals." We need a more humanistic definition of crime, one which reflects the reality of a legal system based on power. . . . A human rights definition of crime frees us to examine imperialism, racism, sexism, capitalism, exploitation, and other political or economic systems which contribute to human misery.[66]

Michael Lynch observes that instrumental Marxist theory may be limited because it is based on assumptions that are incorrect: that law and justice always operate in the interests of the ruling class, that members of the ruling class "conspire" to control society, and that what benefits one member of the ruling class benefits them all. In reality, some laws benefit the lower classes, and capitalists compete with one another rather than conspire. Because of these deficiencies, some radicals have turned from instrumental theory and embraced structural Marxism.

Structural Marxism

Structural Marxists disagree with the view that the relationship between law and capitalism always works for the rich and against the poor.[67] Law is not the exclusive domain of the rich but is used to maintain the long-term interests of the capitalist system and control members of any class who pose a threat to its existence. This is perhaps why the sponsorship scandal in Canada became such a boondoggle; favouring Liberal-friendly companies threatened the legitimacy of the whole system. If law and justice were purely instruments of the capitalist class, why would laws controlling corporate crimes, such as price fixing, false advertising, and illegal restraint of trade, have been created and enforced? To a structuralist, the law is designed to keep the capitalist system operating in an efficient manner, and anyone who "rocks the boat" will be sanctioned. For example, antitrust legislation is designed to prevent any single capitalist from dominating the system and preventing others from "playing the game."

In Stephen Spitzer's Marxian theory of deviance, he says that law defines as deviant any person who disturbs, hinders, or calls into question any of the following: [68]

- Capitalist modes of appropriating the product of human labour
- The social conditions under which capitalist production takes place (for example, when some people refuse or are unable to perform wage labour)
- Patterns of distribution and consumption in capitalist society (for example, when people use drugs for escape rather than for adjustment)
- The process of socialization for productive and nonproductive roles (for example, when youths refuse to be schooled or they deny the validity of family life)
- The ideology that supports the functioning of capitalist society

Capitalism has special ways of dealing with those who oppose its operation. One is to normalize formerly illegal acts—for example, through legalizing abortions. Another is conversion, co-opting deviants by making them part of the system—for example, a gang leader may be recruited to work with younger delinquents.

Protests are one way the public has to communicate their disapproval in a democratic society. However, sometimes these protests are not seen as legitimate. In 2001, protestors massed in Quebec City to demonstrate against the Free Trade Summit. One of their weapons of choice: a teddy-bear launching catapult. The police responded with tear gas and rubber bullets.

 InfoTrac®

For an interesting take on American economic booms and busts (e.g., NASDAQ), throughout history, look at Richard D. Wolff, "The US Economic Crisis and Marxism Analysis," *Theoria* (June 2001): 82(18).

Containment involves segregating deviants into isolated geographic areas so that they can easily be controlled—for example, by creating a ghetto. Finally, capitalist society actively supports some criminal enterprises, such as organized crime.

Research on Marxist Criminology

Marxist criminologists rarely use standard social science methodologies.[69] Marxists believe that the research conducted by mainstream liberal/positivist criminologists is designed to unmask powerless members of society so they can be better dealt with by the legal system—a process called correctionalism. They are particularly offended by purely empirical studies, such as those showing that minority-group members have lower IQs than the White majority, or that the inner city is the site of the most serious crime while middle-class areas are relatively crime-free.

However, empirical research is not totally incompatible with Marxist criminology, and some important efforts have been made to test its assumptions.[70] For example, Alan Lizotte has shown that the property crime rate reflects a change in the level of surplus value; the capitalist system's emphasis on excessive profits accounts for the need of the working class to commit property crime.[71]

Marxist research tends to be historical and analytical. Social trends are interpreted to understand how capitalism has affected human interaction: how the accumulation of wealth affects crime rates and the effect of criminal interactions on individuals. Of particular importance is the analysis of the historical development of capitalist social control institutions, such as the criminal law, police agencies, courts, and prison systems.

Famous Canadian Criminals

Louis Riel (1844–1885), Métis Leader

In 1869, the newly confederated Dominion of Canada was in the process of purchasing Rupert's Land from the Hudson's Bay Company, causing the Métis of Manitoba to worry about their land rights and the preservation of their culture. As a result, they proclaimed a provisional government and appointed as its secretary Louis Riel, a young Métis lawyer. During the Red River Rebellion of 1869, an armed group representing the committee seized Upper Fort Garry and ordered the lieutenant governor of the North-Western Territory not to enter the territory. In addition, Riel issued the "Declaration of the People of Rupert's Land and the North-West" and became head of the provisional government of Red River.

In an attempt to overthrow Riel, a group of men travelled from Portage la Prairie to Fort Garry, but they were captured and imprisoned. The Métis tried and sentenced one of the men, Thomas Scott, to death for insubordination in captivity. They executed him by firing squad. Responding to appeals from a bishop, they then released the remaining prisoners. After land negotiations between the federal government and the Métis were completed, the government sent a military force on a "mission of peace" to Red River. Riel, fearing its true purpose, fled to the United States.

Although the federal government preferred that Riel stay in the United States—the province of Ontario considered him a murderer—his supporters in Manitoba and Quebec persuaded him to run for election in Canada. He was as elected a member of Parliament three times, but when he attempted to take his seat in 1874, he was expelled from the House of Commons. In 1875, he was exiled for five years. In the winter of 1878–79, Riel tried to assemble a coalition of Métis and Indians to invade Western Canada, but Poundmaker and Sitting Bull refused. He even wrote to Ulysses S. Grant, asking for his help in an invasion of Western Canada. In 1884, he was asked to become political leader of a Métis movement in Saskatchewan, and the North-West Rebellion ensued. Riel seized a church at Batoche in 1885, but after less than two months of fighting he surrendered.

He was taken to Regina rather than stand trial before a 12-member mixed race jury in Winnipeg. His six-member jury was English, White, and Protestant, presided over by a part-time magistrate. The *Criminal Code of Canada* did not yet exist, so the charge was laid under the British *Statute of Treasons*. Riel pleaded not guilty to the charge of treason, although his lawyer wanted him to plead insanity. On August 1, 1885, he was found guilty with a recommendation for mercy. After appeals to the Manitoba Court of Appeal and to the Privy Council in London failed, Riel was hanged on November 16, 1885. The Métis dream was over.

Relations between the North-West Mounted Police and the Native residents eroded after the establishment of the federal Department of Indian Affairs in the early 1880s and the official policy of total assimilation and segregation on reserves.

One hundred and twenty years later, the federal government announced it would review Riel's case and look into pardoning him.

Sources: The Northwest Resistance 1885, "Louis Riel," University of Saskatchewan Library, http://library.usask .ca/northwest/background/riel.htm (accessed May 15, 2005); *Canadian Encyclopedia* (Toronto: McClelland and Stewart, 1988).

Crime, the Individual, and the State. Marxists study the relationships among crime, victims, the criminal, and the state. Two common themes emerge: (1) Crime and its control are a function of capitalism, and (2) the justice system is biased against the working class and favours upper-class interests. Marxian analysis of the criminal justice system is designed to identify the processes that exert control over people's lives.[72] It might show how sentencing in a juvenile court is a function of social class,[73] how power relationships help undermine any benefit the lower class gets from sentencing reforms,[74] how the justice system is class biased,[75] or the relationship between capitalism and rape.[76] It is not surprising to conflict theorists that police brutality complaints are highest in minority neighbourhoods. Critical research of this sort is designed to reinterpret commonly held beliefs about society within the framework of Marxist social and economic ideas.[77] The goal is to show that capitalism creates an environment in which crime is inevitable.

In addition to conducting studies showing the relationship between crime and the state, some critical researchers have attempted to show how capitalism influences the distribution of punishment. For example, between 1971 and 1991 the rate of imprisonment grew substantially in those American states with (1) the highest revenues, (2) the highest unemployment rates, and (3) the largest African American populations.[78] In wealthier states, where income is concentrated in the hands of a few affluent people, those in power will be willing to spend enormous sums to keep the poor and minority-group members under state control.

An increasing prison population masks unemployment rates. Many inmates were chronically unemployed before their imprisonment. When the large numbers of people who are on probation and parole and who must maintain jobs are added to the mix, the correctional system is now playing an ever-more important role in suppressing wages and maintaining the profitability of capitalism.[79]

Historical Analysis. A second type of Marxist research focuses on the historical background of commonly held institutional beliefs and practices, to show how changes in the criminal law corresponded to the development of capitalist economy.

For example, the Highland Clearances involved burning townships and dispossessing feudal peasants, all for the sake of clearing land for sheep. In Canada, capitalism had already been imported from Europe, but resistance from Natives, Métis, and then later trade unions had to be suppressed in the interests of economic reform.[80]

Analysis of historical records shows that law reform in nineteenth-century England was largely a response to pressure from the business community to make the punishment for property law violations more acceptable.[81]

Another topic of importance is the development of modern police agencies. Police often play an active role in putting down labour disputes and controlling the activities of political dissidents. Prominent examples include research on the history of private police and historical analysis of police excesses in the repression of an early union, the International Workers of the World.[82] Analysis of the development of modern policing shows how police developed as an antilabour force that provided muscle for industrialists at the turn of the century.[83]

Critique of Marxist Criminology

Marxist criminology has met with criticism.[84] Some mainstream criminologists argue that Marxist theory is the old tradition of helping the underdog, such as Robin Hood stealing from the rich to help feed the poor. In reality, they claim, most theft is for luxury, not survival. Moreover, they dispute the idea that the crimes of the rich are more reprehensible and less understandable than those who live in poverty. Criminality and immoral behaviour occurs at every social level, but the relatively disadvantaged contribute disproportionately to crime and delinquency rates.

Other critics charge that Marxists ignore the varied interest groups that exist in a pluralistic society and focus unilaterally on class differentials.[85] For example, if social reforms are disguised attempts to control the underclass, is it logical to believe that giving people more rights is a trick to allow greater control to be exerted over them? Consider the right to a jury, the rights of free speech, free press, free association, public trial, habeas corpus, and so on.

The problems of Marxist theory are summarized in the following statements:

- Marxist criminologists refuse to confront the problems of socialist countries, such as the gulags and purges of the Soviet Union under Stalin.
- Capitalism is blamed for every human vice and predatory and personal crime.
- Marxist criminology doesn't explain criminality existing in states that have abolished private ownership of the means of production, such as Cuba.
- Marxists overlook distinctions that exist between people in different classes.
- Marxists attempt to explain issues that are obvious, such as politicians are corrupt and businesspeople are greedy.
- Marxists suspect even those practices and freedoms that most people cherish as the cornerstones of democracy (right to trial, free press, religious freedom, and so on).

In response, Marxist scholars charge that critics rely on "traditional" variables, such as "class" and "poverty," in their analysis of radical thought. Although important, these concepts do not reflect the key issues in the structural and economic process. In fact, like crime, they, too, may be the outcome of the capitalist system.[86]

Although radical criminologists dispute criticisms, they have also responded by creating new theoretical models that incorporate Marxist ideas in an innovative manner. In the following section, we discuss some recent forms of radical theory in some detail.

New Directions in Critical Criminology

Mainstream criminology has been criticized for focusing too much on crimes committed by working-class, poor, or unemployed people. They are the most easy to subject to surveillance, and they are the least likely to know their rights. However, critical criminology looks at crimes of the powerful and how crime is a consequence of unequal power relations in society. In particular, left realism explains and measures street crime and proposes short-term solutions.

Left Realism

Some radical scholars are troubled by the emergence of a strict "law and order" philosophy that places crime control above due process. As shown in the Crime in the News box, there is a tendency to think that anything is justified in the war against crime, even if it violates a person's rights. At the same time, the focus of most left-wing scholarship, the abuse of power by the ruling elite, is sometimes seen as too narrow. Is it wrong to ignore the problem of inner-city gang crime and violence, which all too often targets indigent people?[87] Those who share these concerns are referred to as left realists.[88]

Left realism is connected to British scholars Lea and Young, especially their 1984 work *What Is to Be Done about Law and Order?* They rejected utopian views of "idealistic" Marxists who portrayed street criminals as revolutionaries and took the "realistic" approach that street criminals prey on the poor and disenfranchised, thus making them doubly abused, first by the capitalist system and then by members of their own class.[89]

Lea and Young's view of crime causation closely resembles the relative deprivation approach. As they put it,

---

Crime in the News

Police Should Find Real Crimes to Solve in Halifax

by Parker Barss Donham

A police review board that fails to condemn police violations of civil liberties emboldens police to intrude even further upon the rights of citizens.

Last week, the Nova Scotia Police Review Board endorsed a Halifax Regional Police strip search of thirty-four citizens working at a dance. The police had a warrant, based on a dubious informant, to search the dance hall for a bottle of ecstasy pills supposedly hidden in the ceiling. When they found nothing, the cops proceeded to strip search everyone present.

The board justified this humiliating excess on the grounds

that "the only logical" possibility was that someone present had hidden the drugs on their person—patently false, given that the strip search turned up no ecstasy. The board declined to consider whether the charter protection against arbitrary search and seizure applied.

A stupid ruling begets stupider police thinking.

Sunday's *Daily News* canvassed legal opinion as to what people should do if police with a warrant to search a public building demand to strip everyone inside.

Most of the lawyers said citizens needn't comply with a search demand unless they are arrested, and they can't be arrested without reasonable and probable grounds they have committed an offence. The lawyers suggested citizens ask politely whether they are under

arrest, and if not, decline to submit.

"Then you'd probably get placed under arrest," said police spokeswoman Sgt. Brenda Zima. "Certainly, that's not something we would encourage. It's not advisable, put it that way."

In other words, the mere assertion of one's constitutional rights may provoke arrest.

"That's an outrageous statement by a spokesperson for a police department in a democratic society," said Dalhousie law professor Archie Kaiser. "If you stand by your right to be left alone, you are somehow doing something suspicious."

Source: Parker Barss Donham, "Police Should Find Real Crimes to Solve in Halifax," Sunday *Daily News*, http://www.rabble.ca. (acessed May 15, 2001). Copyright © 2001 by Parker Donham.

Exhibit 9.1	Basic Principles of Left Realism

- Crime is a symbol of the antisocial nature of capitalism.
- The relationship between the police and the public determines the efficacy of policing.
- The relationship between the victim and the offender determines the impact of crime.
- The relationship between the state and the offender is a major factor in recidivism.
- Relative deprivation leads to discontent; discontent plus lack of political solutions leads to crime.
- Local crime surveys provide the best measure of crime because national surveys may be irrelevant in any one area.
- Anticrime strategies should be short term and avoid easy "crime control" solutions, such as more police.

"The equation is simple: relative deprivation equals discontent; discontent plus lack of political solution equals crime."

Left realists argue that crime victims in all classes need protection, and crime control reflects community needs. The police and courts are not inherently evil tools of capitalism whose tough tactics alienate the lower classes. These institutions would, in fact, offer life-saving public services if their use of force could be reduced and their sensitivity to the public increased.[90] Another approach is **preemptive deterrence,** in which community organization efforts eliminate or reduce crime before it becomes necessary to use police forces. This tactic aims at reducing the number of marginalized youth, those who feel they are not part of society and have nothing to lose by committing crime.[91]

Street crime is real, and the fear of violence among the lower classes has allowed the right wing to seize law and order as a political issue. Most gang kids prey on members of their own race and class and are happy to keep the proceeds for themselves. Gang kids are capitalists, hustling their way to obtain coveted symbols of success.

Left realists want crime control policy to build on the work of strain theorists, social ecologists, and other "mainstream" views. Community-based efforts seem to hold the most promise as crime control techniques.

Left realism has been critiqued as legitimizing the existing power structure: By supporting existing definitions of law and justice, it suggests that the "deviant" and not the capitalist system is the cause of society's problems. However, left realists say it is unrealistic to speak of a socialist state as lacking a police force or system of laws and justice; the *Criminal Code* does in fact represent public opinion.

Feminist Theory

Like so many theories in criminology, most of the efforts of radical theorists have been devoted to explaining male criminality.[92] To remedy this, feminist writers explain the cause of crime, gender differences in the crime rate, and the exploitation of female victims from a gendered perspective. Scholars usually hold one of two related philosophical orientations: Marxist feminism or radical feminism.

Marxist Feminism. The first group views gender inequality as stemming from the unequal power of men and women in a capitalist society. Gender inequality is a function of the exploitation of females by fathers and husbands; women are considered a "commodity" worth possessing, like land or money.[93] The origin of gender differences can be traced to the development of private property and male domination over the laws of inheritance.

Bernard Schissel, for example, says that violence by male youth against female youth originates largely within the confines of patriarchal, profit-driven culture, and feelings of powerlessness and depression increase the likelihood of violence against women, all of which are related closely to our moneymaking culture.[94]

Marxist feminists link criminal behaviour patterns to the gender conflict created by the economic and social struggles common in postindustrial societies. In *Capitalism, Patriarchy, and Crime,* Messerschmidt argues that capitalist society is marked by both patriarchy and class conflict. Capitalists control the labour of workers, while men control women both economically and biologically.[95] This "double marginality" explains why females in a capitalist society commit fewer crimes than males do: they are isolated in the family, with fewer opportunities to engage in elite deviance, and denied access to male-dominated street crimes.[96] Since capitalism renders women powerless, they are forced to commit less serious, nonviolent, self-destructive crimes, such as drug abuse.

Powerlessness also increases the likelihood that women will become the target of violent acts.[97] Lower-class males are shut out of the economic opportunity structure. One way to improve their self-image is through acts that may involve violence or abuse of women. A significant percentage of female victims are attacked by a spouse or an intimate partner.

In *Masculinities and Crime,* Messerschmidt suggests that in every culture, males try to emulate what are considered ideal masculine behaviours.[98] In Western culture this means being authoritative, in charge, combative, and controlling. Failure to adapt to these roles leaves men feeling effeminate and unmanly. Crime is a good way for men to "do gender" because abusers believe it separates them from the weak and allows them to demonstrate physical bravery.

Radical Feminism. In contrast, **radical feminists** view the cause of female crime as originating with the onset of male supremacy (patriarchy), the subsequent subordination of women, male aggression, and the efforts of men to control females sexually.[99] Radical feminists focus on social forces that shape women's lives and experiences to explain female criminality.[100] For example, the sexual victimization of girls is a function of male socialization because so many young males learn to be aggressive and exploitive of women in same-sex peer groups. On university campuses, peers encourage sexual violence against women whom they define as "teasers," "pickups," or "sluts"; a code of secrecy then protects the aggressors from retribution.[101] Sexual and physical exploitation of young girls may cause the girls to run away or abuse substances, itself labelled deviant behaviour.[102]

A survey conducted by the Centre for Research on Women at Wellesley College found that 90 percent of adolescent girls are sexually harassed in school, almost 30 percent report having been pressured to "do something sexual," and 10 percent said they were forced to do something sexual.[103]

In a sense, the female criminal is a victim herself. Feminists have struggled to have youth prostitution looked at as a form of child abuse. And in one notorious case, former judge David Ramsay was sentenced in 2004 for taking advantage of and molesting young Native girls. He knew his victim: The typical female inmate is Native, without skills, and a single mother who has a history of illegal drug dependency and childhood sexual abuse.[104]

Accordingly, exploitation acts as a trigger for the onset of delinquent and deviant behaviour. When female victims run away and abuse substances, reacting to abuse at home and school, their attempts at survival are labelled deviant, and victim-blaming occurs. Research shows that a significant number (86 percent) of girls who had been sent to the hospital emergency room to be treated for sexual abuse later reported engaging in physical fighting as a teen or as an adult; many of these abused girls later formed a romantic attachment with an abusive partner. Many girls involved in delinquency, crime, and violence have themselves been the victims of violence in their youth and later as adults.[105]

The Wellesley survey of sexual harassment found that teachers and school officials ignore about 45 percent of complaints made by female students; school officials responded to reports of sexual harassment by asking the young victim, "Do you like it?" and saying, "They must be doing it for a reason." Because agents of social control often choose to ignore reports of abuse and harassment, young girls may feel trapped and desperate.

One criticism is that radical feminism focuses on the problems and viewpoints of White, middle-class, heterosexual women, without taking into account the special interests of lesbians and women of colour.[106]

InfoTrac®

Here is an interesting article: H. Gottfried, "Beyond Patriarchy? Theorising Gender and Class," *Sociology* 32, no. 3 (1998): 451–468.

How the Justice System Penalizes Women. Radical feminists have said that the justice system contributes to the onset of female delinquency. From its inception, the juvenile justice system has viewed female delinquents as sexually precocious girls who have to be brought under control. Writing on the "girl problem," Ruth Alexander has described how working-class young women desiring autonomy and freedom in the 1920s were considered delinquents and placed in reformatories. These young girls were considered outlaws in a male-dominated society because they flouted the rules of appropriate behaviour applied to females in Victorian society. Girls who rebelled against parental authority or who engaged in inappropriate sexual behaviour were incarcerated to protect them from a career in prostitution.[107] In fact, young women were much more likely to be prosecuted for sexual promiscuity under the *Juvenile Delinquents Act* than were young men, even though these girls had to be promiscuous with someone.

Current attempts to redefine how youth prostitution is dealt with under "secure care" legislation in various provinces can also be criticized for not dealing with the unequal power relations that give rise to the youth sex trade.[108] The pull of addiction, pimps/boyfriends, and peers, coupled with the lack of noncustodial alternatives, results in higher incarceration rates for these young women.[109]

In a similar vein, a study of the early Los Angeles Juvenile Court found that in 1920, so-called delinquency experts identified young female "sex delinquents" as a major social problem. Civic leaders who were concerned about immorality mounted a eugenics and social hygiene campaign that identified the "sex delinquent" as a moral and sexual threat to society. These experts advocated a policy of eugenics or sterilization to prevent these inferior individuals from having children. Female police officers were hired to deal with girls under arrest and female judges to hear girls' cases in juvenile court; they also established a female detention centre and a girls' reformatory.

The majority of these delinquent girls were petitioned for either suspected sexual activity or behaviour that placed them at risk of sexual relations. Despite the limited seriousness of these charges, the majority of girls were detained before their trials and given a compulsory pelvic exam. Girls adjudged sexually delinquent on the basis of the exam were segregated from the merely incorrigible girls to prevent moral corruption. Those testing positive for venereal disease were confined in the Juvenile Hall hospital for usually from one to three months. More than 29 percent of these female adolescents were eventually committed to custodial institutions.[110]

Looking at the judicial victimization of female delinquents, Meda Chesney-Lind has written extensively on how police in Honolulu were more likely to arrest female adolescents for sexual activity and to ignore the same behaviour among male delinquents.[111] Although 74 percent of the females in her sample were charged with sexual activity or incorrigibility, only 27 percent of the boys faced the same charges. The court ordered physical examinations in more than 70 percent of the female cases, but only 15 percent of the males were forced to undergo this embarrassing procedure. Girls were also more likely to be sent to a detention facility before trial, and the length of their detention averaged three times that of the boys. Because female adolescents have a much narrower range of acceptable behaviour than do males, any sign of misbehaviour in girls is seen as a substantial challenge to authority and the double standard of sexual inequality. Female delinquency is viewed as relatively more serious than male delinquency and therefore is more likely to be severely sanctioned.

Power-Control Theory. John Hagan has created a radical feminist model that uses gender differences to explain the onset of criminality. The most significant statements are expanded in Hagan's 1989 book, *Structural Criminology*. Crime and delinquency rates are a function of two factors: (1) class position (power) and (2) family functions (control).[112] Within the family, parents reproduce the power relationships they hold in the workplace. The class position and work experiences of parents influence the criminality of children.[113] A position of dominance at work is equated with control in the household.

In **paternalistic** families, fathers assume the traditional role of breadwinners, while mothers have menial jobs or remain at home to supervise domestic matters. Within the home, mothers are expected to control the behaviour of their daughters while granting greater freedom to sons. In such a home, the parent–daughter relationship can be viewed as a preparation for the "cult of domesticity," while boys are freer to deviate because they are not subject to maternal control. Consequently, male siblings exhibit a higher degree of delinquent behaviour than do their sisters.

Conversely, in **egalitarian** families—those in which the husband and the wife share similar positions of power at home and in the workplace—daughters gain a kind of freedom that reflects reduced parental control. These families produce daughters whose law-violating behaviour mirrors their brothers'. Ironically, these kinds of relationships also occur in female-headed households with absent fathers. Similarly, when both fathers and mothers hold equally valued managerial positions, the similarity between the rates of their daughters' and sons' delinquency is greatest.

By implication, middle-class girls are the most likely to violate the law because they are less closely controlled than their lower-class counterparts are. And in homes in which both parents hold positions of power, girls are more likely to have the same expectations of career success as their brothers. Consequently, siblings of both sexes will be socialized to take risks and engage in other behaviour related to delinquency. Power-control theory, then, implies that middle-class youth of both sexes will have higher overall crime rates than their lower-class peers (although lower-class males may commit the more serious crimes).

Power-control theory has received a great deal of attention in criminology because it encourages studying gender differences, class position, and the structure of the family. There is evidence that parental power and control in the workplace increases male antisocial behaviour and that in more egalitarian families, female crime rates are higher. For example, some research found support for a key element of power-control theory: Females in paternalistic households have been socialized to fear legal sanctions more than their brothers have.[114]

Not all research is as supportive.[115] Although its basic premises have not yet been thoroughly tested, some critics have questioned the assumption that power and control variables can explain crime.[116] More specifically, critics fail to replicate the finding that upper-class kids are more likely to deviate than are their lower-class peers or that class and power interact to produce delinquency.[117] However, empirical testing may produce further refinement of the theory. For example, Kevin Thompson found few gender-based supervision and behaviour differences in worker-, manager-, or owner-dominated households.[118] However, parental supervision practices were quite different in families headed by the chronically unemployed, and these findings conformed to the power-control model. The research indicates that the concept of class used by Hagan may have to be reconsidered: Power-control theory may actually explain criminality among the truly disadvantaged and not among the working class.

Deconstructionism

Radical criminologists often use **deconstructionism**, which focuses on the critical analysis of communication and language in legal codes. Rules and regulations are analyzed to determine whether they contain language and content that institutionalizes relations of power: gender, ethnicity, and social class.

Deconstructionists rely on various types of discourse analysis, such as **semiotics**, to conduct their research efforts. This means seeing language as signs that indicate more than the mere meaning of words. There are many signs or language groupings in operation today. For example, sports rely very heavily on the use of signs, and to become a sports "expert" means becoming familiar with terminology, such as "blitzing the quarterback" and a "hat trick." These terms convey meaning that is far greater than the words themselves and provide images to sports fans familiar with the signs that would be lost on others.

Deconstructionists believe that language is value-laden and contains the same sorts of inequities present in the rest of the social structure. Capitalism puts a price tag on all merchandise. Law, legal skill, and justice are "commodities" that can be bought and sold like any other.[119]

We can apply an analysis of discourse to various social issues in order to dissect power relations. Certain groups are defined as dangerous, as in racial profiles that result in discriminatory enforcement. The police are able to use discourse to create constructions of street gangs, for example, which are often based on race and gender stereotypes.[120] Discourse on critical social issues is also a way in which the state legitimates social policy. For example, since the mid-1980s, successive federal governments attempted to mediate debate concerning amendments to the *Young Offenders Act* through a series of parliamentary hearings. Through an analysis of these hearings, we can see how the problem of youth crime is constructed.[121]

Restorative Justice

As an outgrowth of critical criminology, **restorative justice** is based on a social rather than a legal view of crime. Restorative justice views crime as an injury to personal and community relations rather than as an abstract legal violation against society. Accordingly, restorative justice theorists and practitioners emphasize the need for a holistic or inclusive response to crime.

In his pioneering work on how the retributive and restorative justice models can be distinguished from each other, Howard Zehr stated that crime is a violation of relationships that creates certain obligations: "Justice involves the victim, the offender, and the community in a search for solutions which promote repair, reconciliation, and reassurance."[122]

Zehr's emphasis on viewing criminal behaviour as a violation of people and relationships continues to serve as the basis of restorative justice programming throughout Canada. Distinct from the legal definition of crime, in which criminal activity is addressed in an impersonal and potentially dehumanizing way, restorative justice rests on understanding the cause or causes of conflict and then exercising compassion when responding to criminal justice and social justice issues. Restorative justice is what the peacemaking churches define as an expression of Agape or loving our brothers and sister.[123]

According to the legal view, "society" consists of (1) formal institutions and (2) individuals. Society is defined as an aggregation of people over which the state has jurisdiction. Legally, this aggregation possesses group qualities: common meanings and values, sustained interaction, and symbolic bonds. In the restorative view, the bureaucratic nature of society is not capable of manifesting such social qualities. It is only in smaller, less formal, and more cohesive social groups, such as families, congregations, and residential communities, that such qualities are found. Therefore, the potential for restoring social relations damaged by crime is to be found not in the state but in social groups, in the community.

Restorative justice theorists, such Sullivan and Tifft, and practitioners, such as Mark Umbreit, are critical of the traditional role that the state has played in the criminal justice system.[124]

The needs of victims, offenders, and communities are not met except in smaller, less formal, and more cohesive social groups. Only in groups where strong interpersonal communication is facilitated and encouraged to take place can social justice–related issues be successfully addressed. The potential for restoring social relationships damaged by crime is to be found not in the state but in communities.[125]

In small northern Aboriginal communities where most inhabitants know each other, sentencing circles are usually held in a band hall or a church. The setting is informal, with participants (including the judge) in casual attire. The space is free from the ritualistic legal language and furniture of the regular courtroom. Participants usually include the offender; the victim; their families, friends, and support systems; others from the community (e.g., alcohol/drug treatment specialists); and the judge, prosecutor, and defence attorney.[126]

In this way, collective life draws its strength not from threat, coercion, and fear, but from motivation, based on trust, participation, and support.[127]

In the restorative view, the state and formal legal institutions inhibit qualities that encourage healing and harmony. In addition, proponents say that individuals who are typically marginalized by the state and the formal legal institutions, individuals who hold little or no power or economic clout, will be included in the criminal justice process.

Restorative justice is in opposition to the adversary system. Without the capacity to restore damaged social relations, society's response to crime has been almost exclusively punitive. In attempting to ensure equal protection under the law, the procedural design of the adversarial system limits consideration of the unique personal and social qualities of particular crimes. As a result of its preoccupation with the protection of individual rights, the adversarial system encourages the accused to deny, justify, or excuse his or her actions, thereby precluding the acceptance of responsibility. In addition, the central role of trained professionals in the adversarial process (prosecution and defence attorneys) severely limits the possibility of direct exchanges between the victim and the offender. Because the adversaries are narrowly defined as the "accused" and the "state," little consideration can be given to community concerns and participation. Restorative justice is a direct response to the inadequacies of the adversarial process.

Restorative justice is guided by three principles: (1) community ownership of conflict (including crime), (2) material and symbolic reparation for victims and the community, and (3) social reintegration of the offender. The restorative process begins by redefining crime in terms of a conflict among the offender, the victim, and the affected constituencies (families, schools, workplaces, and so on). Therefore, the resolution takes place within the context in which the conflict originally occurred rather than being transferred to a specialized institution that has no social connection to the community. By maintaining ownership over the conflict, the community is able to express its shared outrage about the offence, which can be communicated to the offender. The victim is given a chance to voice his or her story, and the offender can directly communicate the need for social reintegration and treatment.

The restoration process depends on encouraging people to discuss problems and developing an informal communicative exchange among victim, offender, and community. Although restorative processes differ in structure and style, they include a recognition of the injury to personal and social relations, a determination and acceptance of responsibility (ideally accompanied by a statement of remorse), a commitment to both material and symbolic (e.g., an apology) reparation, and a determination of community support and assistance for both victim and offender. The intended result of the restorative process is to repair injuries suffered by the victim and the community while ensuring reintegration of the offender.

One of the first contemporary victim–offender mediation programs in the world was established in Kitchener, Ontario, in 1974, and since then, there has been an explosion of restorative justice programs around the world.[128]

The continued growth of mediation programs in Canada is due to restorative principles of sentencing incorporated into the *Criminal Code* as part of the fundamental purpose of sentencing (section 718), as well as alternative measures also incorporated into the *Code* (section 717).

However, although widespread agreement exists among proponents of restorative justice as to what constitutes restoration, not all believe that restorative justice can be achieved within the context of the existing social structure.

Canadian legal theorist Robert C. Depew states that in some non-Aboriginal community settings, traditional Aboriginal restorative justice practices may not be suitable.[129] Additionally, in Aboriginal communities where traditional cultural practices have been lost, it may be impossible to follow an Aboriginal restorative model. In her criticism of restorative justice, Ruth Morris states that for restorative practices to be truly successful, individuals must first address social structural issues that promote racism and classism. Following what Morris terms as a transformative justice model, significant social structural changes must occur for the true potential of restorative justice to be realized.[130]

Some argue that the social qualities of the group can be re-created within such processes as family group conferencing, victim–offender reconciliation, and sentencing circles. The latter suggest that such social qualities cannot be effectively re-created; rather, they must exist before the restorative process begins.

The effectiveness of restorative justice ultimately depends on the stake a person has in the community (or a particular social group). Persons who do not value group membership will be unlikely to accept responsibility, show remorse, or repair the injuries caused by their actions. Existing restorative justice programs, such as mediation programs, will be unable to effectively reach those persons who are disengaged from all community institutions. Therefore, the relative effectiveness of existing restorative justice programs provides us with a measurement of the need for structural change.[131]

Peacemaking Criminology[132]

Suffering can be ended only with the return of all sentient beings to a condition of wholeness.[133]

One of the newer movements in radical theory is **peacemaking criminology**, based on principles that promote increased understanding among individuals, institutions, and nations. The transformation of human beings and the transformation of the Canadian criminal justice system are actively promoted. Rather than attempting to create a good society first and then trying to make ourselves better human beings, peacemaking theorists and practitioners state that we have to work on bettering society and ourselves simultaneously.

The inner being and the outer world are interconnected.[134] This is one of the newer branches in radical criminological theory, and theorists believe that the main purpose of criminology is to promote a peaceful and just society.

Moving from cultures of conflict and war-making to cultures of cooperation and peacemaking shifts the focus from violence and repression to nonviolence and emancipation.[135] Rather than standing on empirical analysis of data sets, peacemaking draws its inspiration from religious and philosophical teachings ranging from Quakerism to Zen.

Peacemakers view the efforts of the state to punish and control as crime-encouraging rather than crime-discouraging, views first articulated in a series of books written by Larry Tifft and Dennis Sullivan:[136]

> The violent punishing acts of the state and its controlling professions are of the same genre as the violent acts of individuals. In each instance these acts reflect an attempt to monopolize human interaction.

Sullivan recognizes the futility of correcting and punishing criminals in the context of our conflict-ridden society:

> The reality we must grasp is that we live in a culture of severed relationships, where every available institution provides a form of banishment but no place or means for people to become connected, to be responsible to and for each other.

Sullivan suggests that mutual aid rather than coercive punishment is the key to a harmonious society. In *Restorative Justice*, Sullivan and Tifft reaffirm their belief that society must seek humanitarian forms of justice without resorting to brutal punishments:

> By allowing feelings of vengeance or retribution to narrow our focus on the harmful event and the person responsible for it—as others might focus solely on a sin committed and the "sinner"—we tell ourselves we are taking steps to free ourselves from the effects of the harm or the sin in question. But, in fact, we are putting ourselves in a servile position with respect to life, human growth, and the further enjoyment of relationships with others.[137]

Mutual aid rather than coercive punishment is the key to a harmonious society. Today, advocates of the peacemaking movement, such as Pepinsky and Quinney, try to find humanist solutions to crime and other social problems.[138] Rather than punishment and prison, they advocate such policies as mediation and conflict resolution, closely related to the principles of restorative justice.

In *The Mystic Heart of Justice*, Breton and Lehman state that true justice will only be attained when individuals who are harmed by crime are understood in a holistic way that promotes connectedness and positive growth.[139] This requires that individuals develop and utilize strong communication skills, promote inclusiveness so that marginalization is no longer a problem, and challenge existing social structures that promote violence through power. Peacemaking criminologists believe that the administration of justice can become more compassionate.

Today, advocates of the peacemaking movement try to find and apply humanist solutions to violence or conflict situations, encouraging active communication and positive conflict resolution. Peacebuilding is responsive to the experiential and subjective realities shaping people's perspectives and needs.[140]

The Canadian criminal justice system must therefore respond to conflict situations in ways that promote greater understanding among those who have been harmed by crime. Sustainable peace can be established. Violent conflict situations cannot be avoided; however, what can change are the ways that individuals and communities respond to unjust and harmful occurrences.

Much literature has been developed in this area, and it constitutes a significant new direction in criminology.[141]

 InfoTrac®

Using InfoTrac® we found the following article, which gives a good description of restorative justice and its background; it also discusses studies examining its effectiveness: Gary Hill, "Restorative Justice: A Canadian Approach," *Corrections Compendium* 27, no. 8 (2002): 6(2).

Other articles worth reading are the following:

- Gordon Bazemore, "Restorative Justice and Earned Redemption: Communities, Victims, and Offender Reintegration," *American Behavioral Scientist* 41 (1998): 768.
- Carol LaPrairie, "The Impact of Aboriginal Justice Research on Policy: A Marginal Past and an Even More Uncertain Future," *Canadian Journal of Criminology* 41 (1999): 249.

Summary

Social conflict theorists view crime as a function of the conflict that exists in society. Social conflict has its theoretical basis in the works of Karl Marx, as interpreted by Willem Bonger and George Vold. Conflict theorists suggest that crime in any society is caused by class conflict. Laws are created by those in power to protect their rights and interests. All criminal acts have political undertones. Richard Quinney has called this concept the social reality of crime. One of conflict theory's most important premises is that the justice system is biased and designed to protect the wealthy. Research has not been unanimous in supporting this point.

Marxist criminology views the competitive nature of the capitalist system as a major cause of crime. The poor commit crimes because of their frustration, anger, and need. The wealthy engage in illegal acts because they are used to competition and because they must do so to keep their positions in society. Marxist scholars have attempted to show that the law is designed to protect the wealthy and powerful and to control the poor, have-not members of society. Branches of radical theory include instrumental Marxism and structural Marxism (see Table 9.2 for a summary of these theories).

Research on Marxist theory focuses on how the system of justice was designed and how it operates to further class interests. Quite often, this research uses historical analysis to show how the capitalist classes have exerted their control over the police, courts, and correctional agencies. Both Marxist and conflict criminology have been heavily criticized by consensus criminologists.

During the 1990s, new forms of conflict theory emerged. Feminist writers drew attention to the influence of patriarchal society on crime; left realism took a centrist position on crime by showing crime's rational and destructive nature; peacemaking criminology brought a call for humanism to criminology; and deconstructionism looked at the symbolic meaning of law and culture.

TABLE 9.2 Social Conflict Theories

Theory	Major Premise	Strengths
Conflict theory	Crime is a function of class conflict. The definition of the law is controlled by people who hold social and political power.	Accounts for class differentials in the crime rate. Shows how class conflict influences behaviour.
Marxist theory	The capitalist means of production creates class conflict. Crime is a rebellion of the lower class. The criminal justice system is an agent of class warfare.	Accounts for the associations between economic structure and crime rates.
Instrumental Marxist theory	Criminals are revolutionaries. The real crimes are sexism, racism, and profiteering.	Broadens the definition of crime and demystifies or explains the historical development of law.
Structural Marxist theory	The law is designed to sustain the capitalist economic system.	Explains the existence of white-collar crime and business control laws.
Radical feminist theory	The capitalist system creates patriarchy, which oppresses women.	Explains gender bias, violence against women, and repression.
Left realism	Crime is a function of relative deprivation; criminals prey on the poor.	Represents a compromise between conflict and traditional criminology.
Deconstructionism	Language controls the meaning and use of the law.	Provides a critical analysis of meaning.
Peacemaking	Peace and humanism can reduce crime; conflict resolution strategies can work.	Offers a new approach to crime control through mediation.

Thinking Like a Criminologist

A local school board has just announced a plan to have police officers patrol schools daily with drug-sniffing dogs. Despite the lack of evidence that there is a drug problem, the dogs will be sniffing lockers, gym bags, and people. If any drugs are found, criminal charges may be filed against students who get caught.

You are a lawyer and a member of the British Columbia Civil Liberties Association. Concerned students come to you for advice. They want you to answer the following questions:

1. Are civil liberties being violated? If so, which ones? Provide some details.

2. What type of legal or other action would you advise your clients to take? Estimate their chances of success.

Source: Adapted from Rights Talk: Students and Civil Liberties at School, "Legal Rights: Search and Seizure," B.C. Civil Liberties Association, http://www.bccla.org/rightstalk/legal .html (accessed May 15, 2005).

Key Terms

conflict theory
dangerous classes
deconstructionism
egalitarian
left realism
marginalization

Marxist feminists
norm resistance
paternalistic
peacemaking criminology
preemptive deterrence
privilege

radical feminists
restorative justice
semiotics
social reality of crime
structural Marxists
surplus value

Critical Thinking Questions

1. How would a conservative reply to a call for more restorative justice? How would a restorative justice advocate respond to a conservative call for more prisons?

2. How would a power-control theorist explain recent drops in the crime rate?

3. If Marx were alive today, what would he think about the prosperity enjoyed by the working class in industrial societies? Might he alter his vision of the capitalist system?

4. How can restorative justice be sold as an alternative sanction when the public supports more punitive sanctions? For example, would it be feasible for people to believe that using restorative justice with nonviolent offenders frees up resources for the relatively few dangerous people in the criminal population? Explain.

 See the book-specific website at http://www.siegelcriminology3e.nelson.com for additional chapter links, discussions, and quizzes.

chapter 10

Integrated Theories

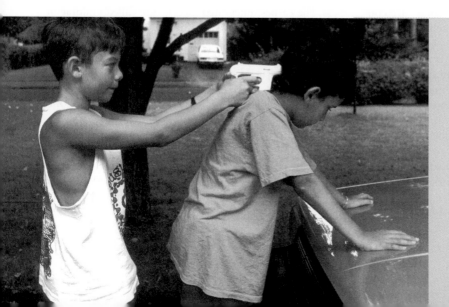

Whereas early criminologists readily embraced the theoretical work of their colleagues, modern criminologists have tended to specialize; they classify themselves as choice, conflict, labelling, control, or some other kind of theorist.[1] As a result, criminological theory ranges from the most radical (Marxist, conflict, and deconstructionist theory) to the most conservative (rational choice and trait theory) views. The ideological differences among these positions create a gulf that sometimes seems impossible to bridge, especially when advocates are dismissive of competing viewpoints. Recently, however, to derive a more powerful explanation of crime, some criminologists have begun integrating these individual factors into multifactor theories that attempt to blend seemingly independent concepts into complex explanations of criminality.

A number of reasons account for the current popularity of integrated theory. One is practical: The development of large, computerized databases and software that facilitate statistical analysis now makes theory integration practical. Criminologists of an earlier era simply did not have the tools to conduct the sophisticated computations necessary for theory integration.

The other reason is substantive. Single-factor theories focus on the onset of crime; they tend to divide the world simply into criminals and noncriminals, those who have a crime-producing condition and those who do not. For example, people who feel anomie become deviant, while those who do not remain law-abiding; people with high testosterone levels are violent, while people with low levels are not.

Connections

The issue of age and crime and the "desistance" phenomenon was discussed in Chapter 3. Crime rates peak in the teenage years and then decline over the life course. Explaining this decline has become an important focus of criminology.

The view that criminality is stable over the lifetime is now being challenged. Criminologists today are concerned not only with the onset of criminality but also with its termination: Why do people age out of or desist from crime? If, for example, criminality is a function of intelligence, as some criminologists claim, why do most delinquents fail to become adult criminals? It seems unlikely that intelligence level increases as young offenders mature. If the onset of criminality can be explained by intelligence level, then some other factor must explain its termination.

In charting a criminal career, why do some offenders escalate their criminal activities, while others decrease? Why do some specialize in a particular crime, while others become generalists? Why do some criminals

reduce criminal activity and then resume it once again? Research now shows that some offenders begin their criminal career at a very early age while others begin at a later point in their lives. How can early- and late-onset criminality be explained?[2] This approach is sometimes referred to as **developmental criminology**.

Connections

As you may recall from Chapter 3, the Philadelphia cohort studies conducted by Wolfgang and his associates identified the existence of a relatively small group of chronic offenders who committed a significant amount of all serious crimes and persisted in criminal careers into their adulthood.

Single-factor theories have trouble explaining why only relatively few of the many individuals exposed to criminogenic influences in the environment actually become chronic offenders.

For example, structural theories make a convincing case for a link between crime and social variables, such as neighbourhood disorganization and cultural deviance. Why do so many underprivileged youths resist crime despite their exposure to social disorganization and cultural deviance? There may be more than a single reason that one person engages in criminal behaviour and another person, living under similar circumstances, can avoid a criminal career.

By integrating a variety of ecological, socialization, psychological, biological, and economic factors into a coherent structure, criminologists are attempting to answer complex questions like these. This chapter summarizes these integrated theories.

Overview of Integrated Theories

Integrated theories can be divided into three groups on the basis of their view of human development and change: multifactor theories, latent trait theories, and life-course theories.

The earliest integrated theories are called **multifactor theories,** which combine the influences of variables that have been used in structural, socialization, conflict, choice, and trait theories.

The multifactor approach explains both criminal career formation and desistence from crime: Although many youths are at risk, relatively few face the complete set of hazards that result in a criminal career, including an impulsive personality, a dysfunctional family, a disorganized neighbourhood, deviant friends, and school failure. For example, a model based on the concept of latent traits could explain the flow of crime over the life cycle, by looking at personal attributes or characteristics that control the inclination to commit crimes.[3] **Latent traits** may be present at birth and remain stable over time, such as defective intelligence, impulsive personality, and genetic abnormalities. Those who carry these latent traits are in danger of becoming career criminals. Latent traits affect the behaviour choices of all people equally, regardless of their gender or personal characteristics.[4]

The positive association between past and future criminality detected in the cohort studies of career criminals may reflect the presence of underlying criminogenic traits. That is, if low IQ causes delinquency in childhood, it should also cause the same people to offend as adults, since intelligence is usually stable over the life span. Similarly, people who are antisocial during their adolescence are the ones most likely to be persistent criminals throughout their life span.

Because latent traits are stable, fluctuations in offending over time reflect criminal opportunities and not the propensity to commit crime. For example, assume that a stable latent trait, such as low IQ, causes some people to commit crime. Teenagers have more opportunity to commit crime than do adults of equal intelligence; therefore, adolescent crime rates are higher. As they mature, low-IQ teens will commit fewer crimes because they have fewer criminal opportunities. Although the propensity to commit crime is stable, the opportunity to commit crime fluctuates. Latent trait theories thus integrate concepts usually associated with trait theories (personality and temperament) with rational choice theories (criminal opportunity and suitable targets).

Another approach that has emerged is **life-course theory**. In contrast to the latent trait view, life-course theories hold that the propensity to commit crimes is not stable and does change over time; it is a developmental process.

Accordingly, some career criminals may desist from crime for a while, only to resume later. Some commit offences at a steady pace, while others escalate their rate of criminal involvement. Offenders may specialize in one type of crime or become generalists who commit a variety of illegal acts. Criminals may be influenced by family matters, financial needs, and changes in lifestyle and interests. Although latent traits may be important, they alone neither control the direction of criminal careers nor ensure that criminal acts are predetermined at birth or soon afterward.

Life-course theories also recognize that as people mature, the factors that influence their behaviour change.[5] At first, family relations may be most influential; in later adolescence, school and peer relations predominate; in adulthood, vocational achievement and marital relations may be the most critical. For example, antisocial kids who are in trouble as adolescents may manage to find stable work and maintain intact marriages as adults; these life events help them desist from crime. In contrast, the less fortunate who have arrest records can find only menial jobs and are at risk for criminal careers. Social forces that are critical at one stage of life may have little meaning or influence at another.

Connections

Social process theories lay the foundation for assuming that peer, family, educational, and other interactions that vary over the life course influence behaviours. See the first few sections of Chapter 8 for a review of these issues.

Multifactor theories, latent trait theories, and life-course theories share some common ground.[6] The criminal career is a passage along which people travel, with events and circumstances that influence the journey, such as the following:

- Structural factors: income and status
- Socialization factors: family and peer relations
- Biological factors: size and strength
- Psychological factors: intelligence and personality
- Opportunity factors: free time, inadequate protection, easily stolen merchandise

Life-course and multifactor theories stress the influence of changing interpersonal and structural factors; latent trait theories assume that it is not people but criminal opportunities that change.

These perspectives differ in their view of human development: Do people change, as life-course theories suggest, or are they stable, constant, and changeless, as the latent trait view indicates? Is there a dominant key that controls human destiny, or are there multiple influences on human behaviour? Are the social and personal factors that influence people stable, or do they change as a person matures?

In the remainder of the chapter, we discuss in some detail some of the most important integrated theories that address the development and sustenance of a criminal career.

Multifactor Theories

Multifactor theories integrate a range of variables into a cohesive explanation of criminality. These theories recognize that factors that appear later in life, such as peer relations, exert an important influence on people.

Efforts to create multifactor theories are not new. For example, Daniel Glazer's differential anticipation theory says, "A person's crime or restraint from crime is determined by the consequences he anticipates from it."[7] According to Glazer, people commit crimes when the expectations of gain exceed the expectations of losses (rational choice). This decision is tempered by the quality of social bonds (control theory), as well as prior learning experiences (learning theory).

A few prominent examples of integrated theory are discussed next, including two important new developments.

Exhibit 10.1	New Directions in Integrated Theory: The Dependency, Availability, and Deterrence (DAD) Model of Woman Abuse

Family violence researchers fail to examine cohabiting relationships separately from marital relationships when examining the causes of violence against women. The risk is in assuming that violence against women is the same for both groups. However, studies have consistently found that women in cohabiting relationships experience higher rates of violence than those in marital unions.

In an attempt to fill this gap in research, a number of theories (including feminist theory, routine activities theory, and subculture of violence theory) have been used to explain why women in cohabiting relationships experience this higher rate of violence. Criminologists Ellis and DeKeseredy have created an integrated theory of woman abuse comprised of three components: dependency, availability, and deterrence (DAD). Variations in each of these three components contribute to the rates of woman abuse in cohabiting unions.

Dependency. Women in cohabiting relationships have higher rates of employment and are less likely to be economically dependent on their partners than are married women. Men in cohabiting relationships tend to be less educated, earn less than their partners, and live in unemployment. These men struggle to retain dominance and sometimes resort to violence in order to maintain the patriarchal structure. Alcohol and drug dependency may also contribute to the higher rates of woman abuse.

Availability. The time that cohabiters spend together may be more "risky." The male may feel insecure due to his economic dependency. He may also fear that his partner may be cheating. Thus, cohabiting men may resort to violence to force their partners into loyalty and fidelity.

Deterrence. Cohabiting men, who live in social isolation and with low income have less to lose in being abusive than do married men.

Source: Reprinted from D.A. Brownridge and S.H. Shiva, "'Living in Sin' and Sinful Living: Toward Filling the Gap in the Explanation of Violence Against Women," *Aggression and Violent Behavior* 5, no. 6 (2000): 565–583. Copyright 2000, with permission from Elsevier. *Prepared by Vanessa Gallant.*

The Social Development Model (SDM)

The **social development model (SDM)** attempts to integrate social control, social learning, and structural models (see Figure 10.1).[8]

Accordingly, a number of community-level "risk factors" make some people susceptible to the development of antisocial behaviours. For example, in a low-income, disorganized community, families are under great stress, educational facilities are inadequate, fewer material goods are available, and respect for the law is weak. Because crime rates are high, there are greater opportunities for law violation, putting even more strain on the agencies of social control.

As a child matures, elements of socialization control the developmental process. Preexisting risk factors are either reinforced or neutralized through socialization. Children are socialized and develop bonds to their family through four processes:

1. Perceived opportunities for involvement in activities and interactions with others
2. The degree of involvement and interaction
3. The skills to participate in these interactions
4. The reinforcement (feedback) they perceive for their participation

A child must maintain **pro-social bonds**, developed within the context of family life, which provide pro-social opportunities and reinforce them by offering consistent positive feedback. Parental attachment affects a child's behaviour throughout the life course, determining both school experiences and personal beliefs and values. For those with strong family relationships, school will be a meaningful experience marked by academic success and commitment to education. Youths are more likely to develop conventional beliefs and values, become committed to conventional activities, and form attachments to conventional others.

Children's antisocial behaviour also depends on the quality of their attachments to others. Unlike Hirschi's control theory, which assumes that all attachments are beneficial, SDM suggests that interaction with antisocial peers and adults promotes participation in delinquency and substance abuse over the life course.[9] Whereas Hirschi maintains that early family attachments are the key determinants of future behaviour, SDM suggests that later involvement in pro-social or antisocial behaviour determines the quality of attachments. Adolescents who perceive opportunities and rewards for deviance will form deep attachments to deviant peers, will become committed to delinquency, and will develop antisocial values and behaviour. In contrast, those who perceive opportunities and rewards for normalcy will get involved in conventional activities, form attachments to pro-social others, and develop moral beliefs.

Figure 10.1   **The Social Development Model of Antisocial Behaviour**

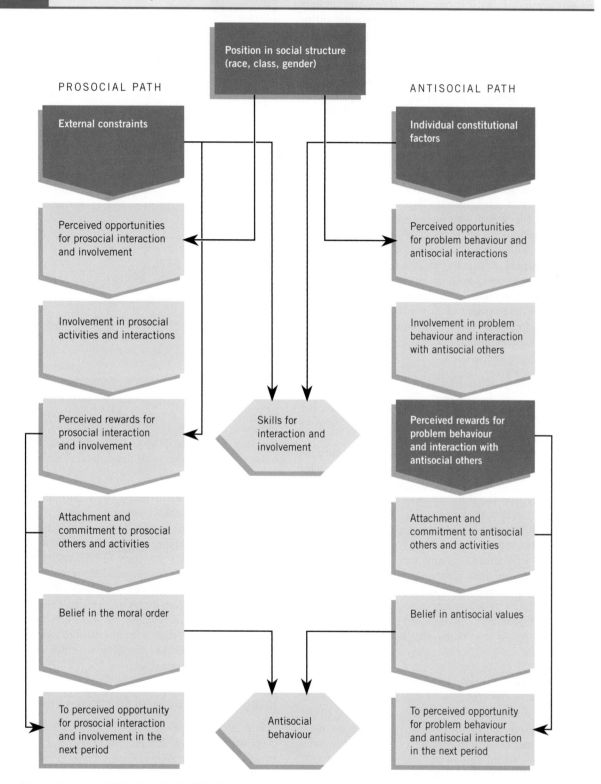

Source: Adapted from J. David Hawkins, Karl G. Hill, Richard F. Catalano, Rick Kosterman, and Robert Abbot, *Seattle Social Development Project* (University of Washington).

SDM thus holds that commitment and attachment to conventional institutions, activities, and beliefs work to insulate youths from the criminogenic influences of their environment; the pro-social path inhibits deviance by strengthening bonds to pro-social others and activities.

Many of these assumptions have been tested empirically.[10] SDM seems to provide an accurate picture of the onset and continuation of violent and antisocial behaviour both for early-onset offenders who engage in antisocial acts in childhood and later-onset offenders who begin offending in their teens.[11] It also predicts the onset and continuation of delinquency and drug abuse, with research showing that both social learning and control bonding predict gang membership.[12] Kids who learn deviant attitudes and who have weak ties to conventional institutions are more likely to engage in criminal behaviours. Kids who maintain antisocial opportunities and involvement, and who perceive that it is easy and rewarding to get away with deviance, are the ones most likely to engage in crime.[13] Treatment interventions, then, promote the development of strong bonds to family and school to help youth resist the motivation to take drugs and engage in delinquency.[14]

Elliott's Integrated Theory

Another attempt at theory integration combines the features of strain, social learning, and control theories into a single theoretical model.[15]

According to this view (see Figure 10.2), adolescents who live in socially disorganized areas (A), who are improperly socialized (B), face a significant risk of perceiving strain (C); perceptions of strain then lead to weakened bonds with conventional groups, activities, and norms (D). Weak conventional bonds and high levels of perceived strain lead some youths to reject conventional social values (E) and seek out deviant peer groups (F). From these delinquent associations come positive reinforcements and role models for deviance (G). Attachment to delinquent groups, when combined with weak bonding to conventional groups and norms, leads to a high level of delinquent behaviour and drug abuse (H).

Social Factors. Elliott's integrated theory is similar to SDM, with the addition of the concept of strain. Living in a disorganized neighbourhood, feeling hopeless and unable to get ahead, and becoming involved in petty crimes eventually lead to a condition in which conventional social values and respect for the social order are weakened. A deviant peer group becomes an acceptable substitute; consequently, attitudes that support delinquency are amplified. The result is early

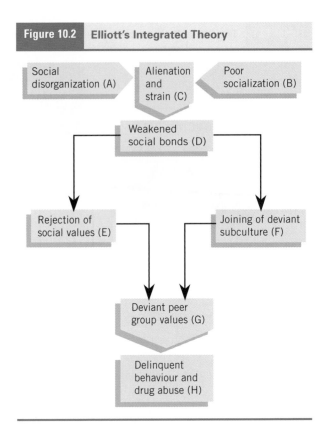

Figure 10.2   Elliott's Integrated Theory

experimentation with drugs, and delinquency becomes a way of life. Both SDM and Elliott's integrated theory assume involvement with delinquent friends increases risk of crime.

Testing Integrated Theory. In a national survey of 1800 youths interviewed over three years, the results supported integrated theory. However, some subjects reported developing strong bonds to delinquent peers even if they did not reject conventional values, suggesting that youths living in disorganized areas may have to join law-violating youth groups since conventional groups don't exist. Moreover, initial experimentation with drugs predicted joining a teenage law-violating peer group. Another national survey of more than one thousand youths also found that bonding to a delinquent peer group escalates criminal activity.[16]

Integrated Structural Marxist Theory

A multifactor theory developed to integrate conflict concepts with structural and process factors is the **integrated structural Marxist theory,** illustrated in Figure 10.3.[17]

Crime is a result of family relationships marked by conflict and despair, and it is influenced by the quality of a person's work experience. Wage earners who occupy

Figure 10.3	Integrated Structural Marxist Theory

Capitalist economic system
- Workplace environment
- Competition

Family relations
- Strain
- Alienation

Adolescent conflict
- Poor schools
- Social maladjustment
- Strain

Deviant peers
- Violence
- Theft

Exhibit 10.2	New Directions in Integrated Theory: The Gendered Social Bond/Male Peer Support Model

In an attempt to determine why offenders are motivated to harm females in a university setting, criminologists have examined Hirschi's social bond theory from a critical and feminist perspective. The gendered social bond/male peer support model incorporates gender where Hirschi ignored it and uses Hirschi's idea of the criminal bond to explain why individuals are motivated to harm women. This model is based on the premise that abusive behaviour is learned, whereas Hirschi maintains that criminality is naturally predisposed.

Hirschi argues that delinquent acts are the result of weak or broken bonds to conventional society. The gendered social bond/male peer support model suggests that the acts that have been defined as deviant may actually be the result of conformity to conventional norms. When a university legitimates gender inequalities, it helps to create a social bond that could support violence against women. This theory may explain why sexual assault rates are high compared with other forms of serious or violent crime in the university environment:

- Men who have an *attachment* to groups that idealize a heterosexual hypermasculine subculture (such as athletic teams and social fraternities) display their masculinity through sexual and aggressive behaviours.

- Members may prove their *commitment* and loyalty to the group through the use of force and even date rape drugs.

- *Involvement* in activities, such as clubs, sports, and fraternities, may promote rather than deter men from engaging in deviant activities.

- The *belief* in the common patriarchal value system among male students supports the use of abuse against challenging females and excuses sexual abuse against women by claiming that the women deserved it.

Through attachment, commitment, involvement, and belief in the patriarchal order, abuse of women is learned and viewed as a normal way of interacting with females in the North American society.

Source: A. Godenzi, M.D. Schwartz, and W.S. DeKeseredy, "Toward a Gendered Social Bond/Male Peer Support Theory of University Woman Abuse," *Critical Criminology* 10 (2001): 1–16. *Prepared by Vanessa Gallant.*

an inferior position will experience negative relationships with supervisors and employers. This creates strain and alienation within the family, especially if there is inconsistent and overly punitive discipline. Juveniles in such families become alienated from their parents and experience adjustment problems in school. They are more likely to go to underfunded schools, do poorly on standardized tests, and be placed in slow-learner tracks, all of which are correlated with delinquent behaviour.

Negative social relations at home and school result in strain, which is reinforced by alienated peers and results in patterns of violent behaviour or economic crime.

According to integrated structural theory, a crime control policy has to address root causes. Coercive punishments cannot be effective unless those who produce goods are given greater opportunity and power to shape their lives.[18]

The Latent Trait Approach

The second main approach considered here, latent trait theory, assumes that some latent trait or condition can account for criminal onset. The propensity for crime remains stable throughout the person's life, when social forces and opportunity can influence the likelihood of crime. People age out of crime because as they mature there are simply fewer opportunities to commit crime and greater inducements to remain law-abiding.

Some of the suspected traits linked to crime include biosocial factors, such as attention deficit/hyperactivity disorder, and psychological traits, such as impulsivity. Yet almost all biosocial and psychological advocates recognize the multidimensionality of crime. For example, as biosocial theorist Lee Ellis maintains, (1) the physical–chemical functioning of the brain is responsible for all human behaviour, (2) brain function is controlled by genetic and environmental factors, and (3) environmental influences on brain function encompass both physical (drugs, chemicals, and injuries) and experiential (social) factors. All three components of modern biocriminology (biochemistry, genetics, and neurology) work in concert with social and experiential factors to control crime.[19]

Here we discuss in some detail two integrated theories that assume that crime is a function of a latent trait.

Connections

Individual-level factors seem ideally suited for a role in theory integration because, as noted in Chapter 6, it is evident that alone they cannot explain crime rate patterns and changes.

Crime and Human Nature

In *Crime and Human Nature*, Wilson and Herrnstein make the argument that personal traits, such as genetic makeup, intelligence, and body build, may outweigh the importance of social variables as predictors of criminal behaviour.[20] Their integrated theory of criminality includes elements of biosocial makeup, personality, rational choice, and structure and social process.

Accordingly, all behaviour, including criminality, is determined by its perceived consequences. A criminal incident occurs when an individual chooses criminal over conventional behaviour (referred to as "noncrime") after weighing the potential gains and losses of each. Rationally, the larger the ratio of net rewards of crime to the net rewards of noncrime, the greater the tendency to commit the crime.

Rewards include material gain, sexual gratification, revenge, and peer approval. The consequences can include pangs of conscience, victim reprisals, social disapproval, and the threat of legal punishment. Although negative consequences may deter some, the impact may be neutralized by the fact that these consequences are typically distant, whereas rewards are immediate and current. The rewards for choosing noncrime are also gained in the future: If you "stay clean," someday people will learn to respect you, your self-image and reputation will improve, and you may achieve happiness and freedom.

The process is unpredictable. The burglar hoping for the "big score" may instead experience arrest, conviction, and incarceration; people who "play it straight" may find that their sacrifice does not get them to the place in society they desire.

Choosing Crime or Noncrime. The choice between crime and noncrime is often difficult. Criminal choices are reinforced by the desire to obtain basic rewards (food, clothing, shelter, sex) or learned goals (wealth, power, status) without having to work and save for them. Even if an individual has been socialized to choose noncrime, crime can be an attractive alternative, especially if any potential negative consequences are uncertain. By analogy, cigarette smoking is common because its consequences are distant and uncertain, while taking cyanide is rare because the effects are immediate and certain.

Integrating Social and Individual Traits. The model of crime and human nature assumes that both biological and psychological traits influence choice. There is a close link between a person's decision to choose crime and such biosocial factors as low intelligence, body type, genetic influences, and the possession of an autonomic nervous system that responds too quickly to stimuli. Psychological traits, including an impulsive personality and low intelligence, also determine the potential to commit crime. Having these traits will not by itself guarantee a person will become a criminal; however, those who have them will be more likely to choose crime over noncrime.

In addition, social factors, such as a turbulent family life, school failure, and membership in a deviant teenage subculture, also have a powerful influence. Thus, biosocial, psychological, and social conditions, working in concert, can influence thought and behaviour patterns. For example, intelligence is mediated by school performance: A child who performs poorly may feel justified in settling the score outside by violence, theft, and other forms of defiant illegality. School failure enhances the rewards for crime by engendering feelings of unfairness. In addition, failure in school predicts failure in the marketplace. For someone who stands to gain little from legitimate work, the rewards of noncrime are relatively weak.

In this viewpoint, harsh punishment is not the answer to the crime problem. Strengthening the family and helping orient children toward noncrime solutions to their problems is better. The family can help a child cultivate character and respect for the moral order, and schools can teach the benefits of accepting personal responsibility.

This work represents a dramatic attempt to integrate two of the most prominent theoretical movements in the study of criminality.

General Theory of Crime

In *A General Theory of Crime*, Gottfredson and Hirschi have modified the principles in Hirschi's social control theory by integrating the concepts of control with those of biosocial, psychological, routine activities, and rational choice theories.[21]

The Act and the Offender. In their **general theory of crime (GTC)**, Gottfredson and Hirschi consider the offender and the criminal act as separate concepts (see Figure 10.4). On the one hand, criminal acts, such as robberies or burglaries, are illegal events that people perceive to be advantageous. For example, burglaries are typically committed by young males looking for cash, liquor, and entertainment. Even if the number of offenders remains constant, crime rates may fluctuate because of the presence or absence of criminal opportunities, familiar in rational choice and routine activities theories: People commit crime when it promises rewards with minimum threat of pain or punishment. If targets are well protected by effective guardians, crime rates will diminish.

On the other hand, criminal offenders are people predisposed to commit crimes. They are not robots who commit crime without restraint; their days are also filled with conventional behaviours, such as going to school, parties, concerts, and church. But given the same set of criminal opportunities, criminogenic people have a much higher probability of violating the law.

Connections

In the discussion of control theory in Chapter 8, Hirschi focused on social controls that attach people to conventional society; in this new work, he concentrates on self-control as a stabilizing force. The two views are connected, however, because both social control (or social bonds) and self-control are acquired through early experiences with effective parenting.

By recognizing stable differences in people's propensity to commit crime, the general theory adds a biosocial element to the concept of social control. Individual differences are stable over the life course and so is the propensity to commit crime; it is only opportunity that changes.

Figure 10.4 The General Theory of Crime

Impulsive personality
- Physical
- Insensitive
- Risk taking
- Short-sighted
- Nonverbal

Low self-control
- Poor parenting
- Deviant parents
- Lack of supervision
- Active
- Self-centred

Weakening of social bonds
- Attachment
- Involvement
- Commitment
- Belief

Criminal opportunity
- Gangs
- Free time
- Drugs
- Suitable targets

Crime and deviance
- Delinquency
- Smoking
- Drinking
- Sex
- Crime

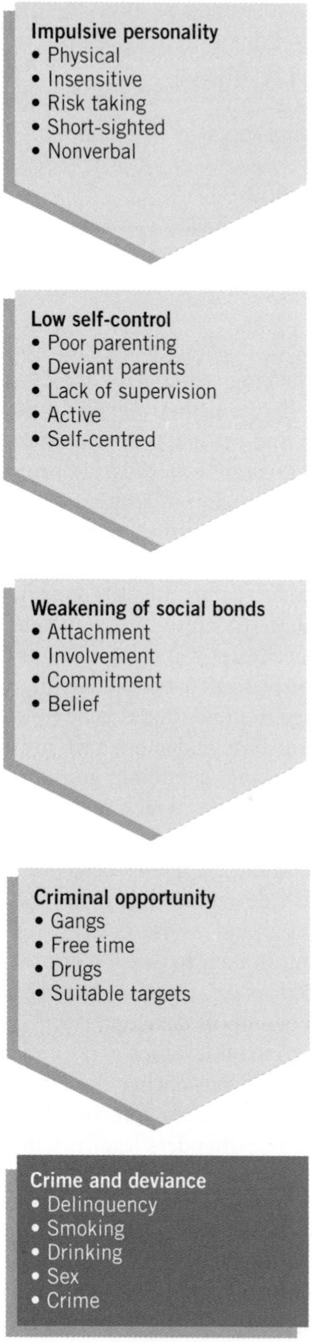

What Makes People Crime-Prone? What, then, causes people to become excessively crime-prone? Those with limited self-control are impulsive, making them less sensitive, physical (rather than mental), risk-takers, shortsighted, and nonverbal. They have a "here and now" orientation; they lack diligence in a course of action. They are adventuresome, active, physical, and

InfoTrac®

To read a critique of the GTC, use InfoTrac® College Edition to access this article: Charles R. Tittle and Harold G. Grasmick, "Criminal Behavior and Age: A Test of Three Provocative Hypotheses," *Journal of Criminal Law and Criminology* 88, no. 1 (1997): 309–342.

self-centred, with unstable marriages, jobs, and friendships. People lacking self-control are less likely than are others to feel shame if they engage in deviant acts and more likely to find these acts pleasurable.[22]

Crime is attractive because it provides easy and immediate gratification: "money without work, sex without courtship, revenge without court delays." People with limited self-control are more likely to enjoy criminal acts that require stealth, danger, agility, speed, and power than to enjoy conventional acts, which demand long-term study and cognitive and verbal skills.

It is no surprise that people lacking in self-control will also engage in noncriminal behaviours that provide them with immediate and short-term gratification, such as smoking, drinking, gambling, and illicit sexuality.

What causes people to lack self-control? The origins of poor self-control are felt to be linked to parents who are unable to monitor a child's behaviour and to recognize and punish deviance when it occurs. Kids who are poorly supervised and whose parents are deviant themselves are the most likely to develop poor self-control. It is a "natural occurrence" that will happen in the absence of steps taken to stop its development.[23]

Low self-control develops early and remains stable into adulthood.[24] Considering the continuity of criminal motivation, we might question why we separate youthful and adult offenders legally, when the source of their criminality is essentially the same.[25]

Self-Control and Crime. The principles of self-control theory apply to all varieties of criminal behaviour, such as burglary, robbery, embezzlement, drug dealing, murder, rape, and insider trading. Likewise, gender, racial, and ecological differences in the crime rate can be explained by discrepancies in self-control. The male crime rate is higher than the female crime rate, and the discrepancy can be explained by the fact that males have lower levels of self-control.

Rates of white-collar crime are quite low because people lacking in self-control rarely attain the position necessary to commit those crimes. As well, people become less crime-prone as they age. Although the criminal activity of low-self-control individuals also declines, they maintain an offence rate that remains consistently higher than those with strong self-control do.

Supporting Evidence for the GTC. Research to support this viewpoint would identify indicators of impulsiveness and self-control and measure whether they correlate with criminal activity.[26] For example, both male and female drunk drivers were found to be impulsive individuals who manifest low self-control.[27] Research on violent recidivists indicates that they can be distinguished from other offenders on the basis of their impulsive personality structure.[28] Studies of incarcerated youths show that they enjoy risk-taking behaviour.[29] Kids who take drugs and commit crime are impulsive.[30] Low self-control predicts deviant behaviour (cutting class and drinking) among college students.[31] The quality of parental supervision influences both self-control and subsequent deviant behaviour.[32] One study of Canadian youth found that kids with an "egocentric personality" develop weak social ties and are more likely to engage in delinquency and unconventional behaviours.[33]

Vazsonyi analyzed self-control and deviant behaviour with samples drawn from four different countries (Hungary, Switzerland, the Netherlands, and the United States).[34] The findings indicate that, as predicted by Gottfredson and Hirschi, low self-control is significantly related to antisocial behaviour and that the association can be seen regardless of culture or national settings.

Low self-control interacts with criminal opportunity in the decision to commit crimes.[35] The causal chain flows from (1) an impulsive personality to (2) lack of self-control to (3) the withering of social bonds to (4) the opportunity to commit crime and delinquency to (5) deviant behaviour.[36]

Analyzing the General Theory of Crime. Gottfredson and Hirschi's general theory provides answers to many of the questions left unresolved by Hirschi's original single-factor control model. Integrating the concepts of criminality and crime helps explain that even people who lack self-control can escape criminality, if they lack criminal opportunity. People who are at risk because they have an impulsive personality may forgo criminal careers because they have noncriminal opportunities that satisfy their impulsive needs: They enroll in tennis lessons, they go to church, they join the Boy Scouts, they enter the military, or they have great athletic ability and make the team.

Integrating criminal propensity and criminal opportunity can explain why the so-called good kid, who has a strong school record and positive parental relationships, gets involved in drugs or vandalism or why the corporate executive with a spotless record gets caught up in business fraud. Even a successful executive may find his or her self-control inadequate if the potential for illegal gain is high. The fear of failure, and not the mere desire for excessive profits, overwhelms an affluent businessperson's self-control. The impulsive manager who fears dismissal may be tempted to circumvent the law to improve the bottom line.[37]

Although the general theory of crime seems persuasive, several questions and criticisms remain unanswered, including the following.[38]

1. *Tautological.* The theory involves circular reasoning: How do we know when people are impulsive? When they commit crimes. Are all criminals impulsive? Of course, or else they would not have broken the law.[39] However, impulsivity is not in itself a propensity to commit crime but a condition that inhibits people from appreciating the long-term consequences of their behaviour. If given the opportunity, they are more likely to indulge in criminal acts than are the nonimpulsive, if they can't channel their reckless energies into noncrime activity.

2. *Personality disorder.* Saying someone lacks self-control implies a personality defect. Psychologists have sought evidence of a "criminal personality,"[40] yet there is no conclusive proof that criminals can be distinguished on the basis of personality alone.

3. *Ecological differences.* GTC also fails to address ecological patterns in the crime rate. For example, if crime rates are higher in Vancouver than in London, Ontario, are Vancouverites more impulsive than Londoners? Can these differences be explained solely by variation in criminal opportunity? Crime rate differences may simply reflect criminal opportunity, as some areas have different levels of effective law enforcement, stricter laws, and higher levels of guardianship.

4. *Individual differences.* Although distinct gender differences in the crime rate exist, there is little evidence that males are more impulsive than females. Similarly, can racial differences in crime be explained as a failure of childrearing practices in minority families? Institutional racism, poverty, and relative deprivation have a significant impact on crime rate differentials.

5. *Moral beliefs.* The general theory also ignores the moral concept of right and wrong, or "belief."[41] Does this mean that learning and assimilation of moral values have little effect on criminality? Belief is a central concept of social bond theory but not of control theory.

6. *Do people change?* The general theory assumes that people do not change; it is opportunity that changes. However, research indicates that factors that help control criminal behaviour, such as peer relations and school performance, vary over time. Factors that have a controlling effect in early adolescence may fade and be replaced by others.[42] For example, having delinquent peers encourages future criminality, and the propensity to commit crimes is influenced by peer relations that develop in adolescence.[43] As children mature, peer influence over delinquent behaviour choices continues to grow.[44] Changing life circumstances all have an influence on the frequency of offending.[45] People are more likely to commit crimes when using illegal drugs and less likely when they are living with a spouse. These findings contradict self-control theory, which assumes that criminality is independent of personal relationships.

7. *Cross-cultural differences.* There is evidence that criminals in other countries do not lack self-control, indicating that GTC may be culturally limited.[46] Behaviour that may be considered imprudent and risky in one culture may be socially acceptable in another and therefore cannot be explained by a "lack of self-control."[47]

8. *Different classes of criminals.* There are two classes of criminals—adolescent-limited and life-course persistent,[48] with different criminal paths or trajectories. People offend at a different pace, commit different kinds of crimes, and are influenced by different external forces.[49] This contradicts the idea of a single factor causing crime and the idea that there is a single class of offender.

9. *Peer influence.* The quality of peer relations either enhances or controls criminal behaviour and this influence varies over time.[50] As children mature, peer influence continues to grow.[51] Kids who lack self-control also have trouble maintaining relationships with law-abiding peers. Establishing friendships with low-self-control individuals increases the likelihood of involvement in criminal behaviours.[52] This finding contradicts the GTC, which suggests that the influence of friends should be stable and unchanging and that a relationship established later in life (for example, making new friends) should not influence criminal propensity. However, impulsive kids lacking in self-control seek out peers with similar personality characteristics, and membership in a group of impulsive peers increases both the opportunity and the support to commit crime.

10. *Modest relationship.* The proposition is that self-control is a causal factor in criminal and other forms of deviant behaviour, but the association is fairly weak.[53] This indicates that other forces influence criminal behaviour, and low self-control alone cannot predict the onset of a deviant career. Perhaps antisocial behaviour is best explained by a condition that either develops subsequent to the development of self-control or is independent of a person's level of impulsivity.[54] This alternative quality, which may be the real stable latent trait, is still unknown.

Although these questions remain, the strength of the general theory lies in its scope and breadth, explaining all forms of crime and deviance, from lower-class gang delinquency to sexual harassment in the business community.[55] By integrating concepts of criminal choice, criminal opportunity, socialization, and personality, deviant behaviour may originate at the same source.

Life-Course Theories

What causes the onset of criminality and sustains a criminal career over the life course? One theme is that the seeds of a criminal career are planted early in life. Kids who later become delinquents begin their deviant careers at a very early (preschool) age.[56] For narcotics addicts, the earlier the onset of substance abuse, the more frequent, varied, and sustained the addict's criminal career.[57]

Another theme is the **continuity of crime:** The best predictor of future criminality is past criminality. Kids who are repeatedly in trouble during adolescence are the ones who will still be antisocial as adults. Criminal activity beginning early in life is likely to be sustained, because these offenders lack the "social survival skills" necessary to find work or develop the interpersonal relationships needed to allow them to "drop out" of crime.[58]

The third of the integrated approaches considered here, life-course theory, sees criminality as multidimensional or having multiple roots: maladaptive personality traits, educational failure, and dysfunctional family relations. It comes as no shock to life-course theorists when research shows that criminality runs in families and that having criminal relatives is a significant predictor of future misbehaviours.[59] Criminality cannot be attributed to a single cause, and it does not represent a single underlying tendency.[60]

Life-course theorists conclude that multiple social, personal, and economic factors can influence criminality and that as these factors change over time, so too does criminal involvement.[61] As people make important transitions in their life—from child to adolescent, from adolescent to adult, from unwed to married—the nature of their social interactions changes and so too does their behaviour. Children whose socialization is ineffective because of improper, maladaptive parenting later build on this improper interactional style and engage in behaviour that leads them to be rejected by their peers and to experience academic failure.[62] They then turn to deviant peers from whom they learn new forms of antisocial behaviour. Early childhood family conflicts and lack of a strong bond with parents open the door for social conflict in later adolescence.[63]

| Connections |

As you may recall from Chapter 3, a great deal of research has been conducted on the relationship of age and crime and the activities of chronic offenders. This body of scholarship has prompted interest in the life cycle of crime. It is also buttressed by social process theories, as discussed in Chapter 8.

The Glueck Research

While at Harvard University in the 1930s, Sheldon and Eleanor Glueck researched the life cycle of delinquent careers, in longitudinal research studies following the careers of known delinquents to determine the factors that predicted persistent offending.[64] They made extensive use of interviews and records.[65]

This "life-course" research focused on **early onset** of delinquency as a harbinger of a criminal career: The deeper the roots of childhood maladjustment, the smaller the chance of adult adjustment. Offending careers were also stable: Children who are antisocial early in life are the ones most likely to continue their offending careers into adulthood.

Of personal and social factors related to persistent offending, the most important are family relations, such as the quality of discipline and emotional ties with parents.

As well, biological and psychological traits, such as body type, intelligence, and personality, were found to play a role. Children with low intelligence, with a background of mental illness, and with a powerful physique (mesomorphs) were the ones most likely to become persistent offenders.

This research was ignored for nearly 30 years as the study of crime and delinquency shifted almost exclusively to the social and social-psychological factors (poverty, neighbourhood deterioration, socialization) that formed the nucleus of structural and process theories.

Life Course Emerges

The rediscovery of the Gluecks' research has renewed interest in criminal careers.[66] It has revived interest in asking basic questions about how a criminal career unfolds over a person's life:[67]

1. Why do people begin committing antisocial acts?
2. Why do some stop or desist while others continue or persist?
3. Why do some escalate the severity of their criminality while others deescalate?
4. If some terminate their criminal activity, what, if anything, causes them to begin again?
5. Why do some specialize in certain types of crime while others are generalists?

Criminogenic influences change and develop over time. In studies on delinquency prevention, it has been found that poor discipline and monitoring by parents are key to the onset of criminality in early childhood. Then, in middle childhood, social rejection by conventional peers and academic failure sustain antisocial behaviour. In later adolescence, commitment to a deviant peer group creates a "training ground" for crime. Kids who are improperly socialized by unskilled parents are the ones most likely to rebel by wandering the streets with their deviant peers.[68] Although the onset of a criminal career is a function of poor parenting skills, its maintenance and support are connected to social relations that emerge later in life.[69] Similar results have been obtained from longitudinal analyses of elementary-school-aged boys that indicate that early onset is correlated with social withdrawal, depression, deviant peers, and family problems, while later onset (at ages 13 or 14) is related to low educational motivation.[70]

From this has emerged a view of crime that incorporates personal change and growth. The factors that produce crime and delinquency at one point in the life cycle may not be relevant at another; as people mature, the social, physical, and environmental influences on their behaviour are transformed.

In the following sections, we review some of the more important concepts associated with the life-course perspective and discuss three prominent life-course theories.

Is There a Problem Behaviour Syndrome?

Most criminological theories portray crime as the result of social problems rather than as their cause. For example, learning theorists view a troubled home life and deviant friends as precursors of criminality; structural theorists maintain that acquiring deviant cultural values is causal. In contrast, the life-course view is that criminality is one of many social problems faced by at-risk youth. Criminality may be part of a **problem behaviour syndrome (PBS)**, a cluster of antisocial behaviours, typically involving family dysfunction, substance abuse, smoking, precocious sexuality and early pregnancy, educational underachievement, suicide attempts, sensation seeking, and unemployment.[71] People with one condition typically exhibit symptoms of the rest.[72] These conditions are usually interconnected.[73] All varieties of criminal behaviour, including violence, theft, and public order crimes, may be part of a generalized PBS.[74]

Those who suffer PBS have a range of social problems, from abusing drugs to being accident-prone.[75] They also require more health care and hospitalization, and have more mental health problems. PBS has been linked to personality (rebelliousness and low ego), family problems (interfamily conflict, parental mental disorder), and educational failure (school rejection).[76] Youth with PBS are also more likely to become teenage parents.[77] Kids who suffer PBS, including drug use, delinquency, and precocious sexuality, display symptoms at a very early age.[78]

Using longitudinal data from the Pittsburgh Youth Study, White examined the relationship between substance abuse and aggression among adolescents and found that kids who committed offences while "under the influence" were also more likely to be heavy alcohol and drug users, commit serious delinquent acts, have impulsive personalities, and associate with deviant peers.[79] A survey of students in grades 6, 9, and 12 showed that children who experienced physical and sexual abuse at the hands of parents or other adults were also likely to have eating disorders (binge eating, purging, anorexia) and increased levels of cigarette smoking, alcohol consumption, stress, anxiety, hard-drug use, and suicidal thoughts.[80] Other research links family violence to a variety of family and environmental problems that seem to cluster together: low income, single-parent household, residence in an isolated poor area, lack of family support or resources, racism, and prolonged exposure to poverty.[81] Studies of inmates show that many had mental health problems and were also undereducated and unemployed. Many also have histories of alcohol, marijuana, cocaine, and heroin abuse.[82]

In a study of four hundred youths over six years, behaviours that clustered together included delinquency, substance abuse, school misconduct and underachievement, precocious sexual behaviour, violence, suicide, and mental health problems.[83] Problem behaviours were also stable: Those who had multiple problems at age 15 continued to experience them at age 21. In adolescent misbehaviour, PBS might involve one of several clusters of behaviour, including drug "specialists," crime specialists, and "generalists" who engage in both delinquency and drug abuse. Generalists are the most likely to suffer PBS, displaying higher levels of psychological problems, a lack of control, and lower emotional stability.[84]

So problem behaviours—including violence, drug abuse, and theft—may cluster in a number of ways, affecting people as they mature from adolescence into adulthood.[85] The interconnection of problem behaviours increases the risk of teenage pregnancy, AIDS, and other sources of social distress.

The Course of Criminal Careers

More than a single road may be travelled by career criminals: Some specialize in violence and extortion; some are involved in theft and fraud; others engage in a variety of criminal acts. Some offenders may begin their career early in life, while others are "late bloomers" who begin committing crime at the age when most people desist.

InfoTrac®

What are the problems that plague troubled youth, and how are they linked? Use InfoTrac® College Edition to access this article for answers to these questions: Gabriel Kuperminca and Joseph Allen, "Social Orientation: Problem Behavior and Motivations toward Interpersonal Problem Solving among High-Risk Adolescents," *Journal of Youth and Adolescence* 30, no. 5 (2001): 597.

| Figure 10.5 | Pathways to Crime |

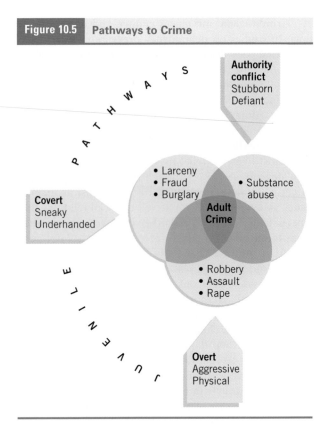

Pathways to Crime. Are there different pathways to crime? In a study of a longitudinal cohort,[86] three distinct paths to a criminal career were identified (see Figure 10.5):

1. The **authority conflict pathway** begins at an early age with stubborn behaviour and defiance of parents (doing things one's own way, refusing to do things, disobedience) and then moves to authority avoidance (staying out late, truancy, running away).

2. The **covert pathway** begins with minor underhanded behaviour (lying, shoplifting) that leads to property damage (setting fires, vandalism) and escalates to more serious crimes (joyriding, pocket-picking, larceny, and fencing to passing bad cheques, using bad credit cards, stealing cars, dealing drugs, and breaking and entering).

3. The **overt pathway** consists of an escalation of aggressive acts beginning with aggression (annoying others, bullying) leading to physical (and gang) fighting and on to violence (attacking someone, strong-arming, forced theft).

Each path may lead to a sustained deviant career. Some youths enter two and even three paths simultaneously: They are stubborn, lie to teachers and parents, are bullies, and commit petty thefts. These are the adolescents most likely to become persistent offenders as they mature. Although some specialize in one type of behaviour, others engage in a variety. For example, they may start out cheating on tests and bullying kids in the schoolyard, then move on to shoplifting from a store, and end by taking drugs, committing a burglary, and stealing a car.

Maxwell and Maxwell, in their study of the career paths of young female offenders, found one distinct group of women who used drugs and engaged in a variety of illegal activities, including theft and prostitution, to generate capital for further drug purchases. The second group specialized in drug selling and avoided prostitution and other illegal activities.[87] This suggests the existence of a multitude of criminal career subgroupings (for

InfoTrac®

To read an article in which the pathways model is explained, use InfoTrac® College Edition to access this article: Rolf Loeber and Dale Hay, "Key Issues in the Development of Aggression and Violence from Childhood to Early Adulthood," *Annual Review of Psychology* 48 (1997): 371(40).

example, prostitutes and drug dealers) that each have their own distinctive career paths.

Adolescent-Limited Offenders and Life-Course Persisters. In addition to taking different paths to criminality, people may begin at different times. Some are precocious, beginning their criminal careers at an early age; others are late bloomers who stay out of trouble until their teenage years. These kids may be considered "typical teenagers" who get into minor scrapes and engage in rebellious behaviour with their friends.[88] Some offenders peak at an early age, while others persist into their adulthood, reflecting changes in the life course.[89]

Whereas antisocial behaviour peaks in adolescence and then diminishes for most offenders (these offenders are **adolescent-limited**), a small group of life-course persistent deviants offend well into adulthood.[90] Life-course persistents combine family dysfunction with severe neurological problems, the result of maternal drug abuse, poor perinatal nutrition, or exposure to toxic agents, such as lead. Lower verbal ability inhibits reasoning skills, learning ability, and school achievement. Adolescent-limited delinquents mimic the behaviour of more troubled teens but reduce the frequency of offending as they mature at around age 18.[91]

Kids who mature faster (**pseudomaturity**) have a greater chance of becoming life-course persisters. The earlier an adolescent engages in substance abuse and sexuality or suffers emotional distress, the more likely it is that he or she will be involved in adult deviance.[92]

InfoTrac®

To learn more about the relationship between crime and age, use these terms as subject guides on InfoTrac® College Edition to find specific articles on the early stages of police contact and the onset and development of criminal careers, such as Bruce L. Arnold and Fiona M. Kerry, "Early Transition Stages and Heterogeneity in Criminal Careers among Young Offenders," *Canadian Review of Sociology and Anthropology* 36, no. 2 (1999): 157(2).

Culture, Gender, Ethnicity, and Criminology

Violent Female Criminals

Are paths taken by males and females similar? Although considerable research is now being devoted to gender differences in the crime rate, little has been done to chart the life course of violent female street criminals.

Baskin, Sommers, and Brownstein, in interviews with violent female criminals, found that 60 percent of violent female offenders begin their criminal career at a very early age; half reported regular fighting as early as 10 years, and 40 percent reported that they regularly left home carrying a weapon. In contrast, the other 50 percent reported that they did not engage in fighting until they had left school. Because of the clear time differential in when these females began their criminal careers, Baskin and Sommers conducted an independent analysis of the early- and late-onset offenders.

Women in both groups suffered from severe social and emotional problems. All were likely to have been raised in single-parent families and to have received little

parental supervision. Both groups experienced physical and sexual abuse at the hand of a parent or guardian and were likely to have witnessed abuse. Almost half were raised in households that relied on public welfare assistance. More than half had a parent who was either a substance abuser or who had been incarcerated sometime during childhood.

Women in the early-onset group were the ones most likely to reside in areas with high concentrations of poverty and to have family histories of psychiatric problems requiring hospitalization. They were more likely to be truant, leave school early, and associate with delinquent peers while in school, and more likely to be placed in a juvenile detention centre.

The major distinction, however, was in the scale and direction of their offending careers. Although both groups were drug users, early-onset women began abusing substances two years ahead of the late-onset group. The early-onset group were involved in a variety of crimes, including serious robberies, assaults, and burglaries, even before they became involved with

drug use. In contrast, the later-onset group were involved mostly in nonviolent crimes, such as shoplifting and prostitution, until they began taking drugs. The violent offending of the latter group was thus clearly part of a drug–crime connection. In contrast, the violent behaviour of the early-onset women was part of a generalized PBS.

Other research supports these findings. White and Hansell found that girls who begin using alcohol early in life are the ones most likely to be aggressive and violent in their later years. Brownstein conducted interviews with 215 women convicted of murder. Most of these women told a familiar story: The most violent had histories of juvenile violence, drug abuse, and personal victimization. Researchers found that 65 percent had participated in some violent activity and 64 percent claimed to have seriously harmed someone when they were growing up; 58 percent had been the victim of serious physical harm, and 49 percent had been sexually abused.

These women had a long-term commitment to crime, beginning in early childhood and continuing through their use of deadly violence in their adulthood. Of 19 women who had killed in the context of drug dealing, some were motivated by money, while others killed on behalf of a man or out of fear of a man.

This research contradicts the latent trait theory and supports the life-course view: Events in these women's adult lives shaped the direction of their offending careers. The researchers found that there are, in fact, different pathways to a crime and that both environmental and serendipitous life circumstances (such as meeting the wrong man) influence offending.

 InfoTrac®

There is a growing body of literature on the violent behaviour of female offenders. To read more about this phenomenon, access these articles:

- Denise Hien and Nina Hien, "Women, Violence with Intimates, and Substance Abuse: Relevant Theory, Empirical Findings, and Recommendations for Future Research," *American Journal of Drug and Alcohol*

Abuse 24, no. 3 (1998): 419.
- Karen Joe Laidler and Geoffrey Hunt, "Violence and Social Organization in Female Gangs," *Social Justice* 24, no. 4 (1997): 148.

Sources: Deborah Baskin and Ira Sommers, "Females' Initiation into Violent Street Crime," *Justice Quarterly* 10 (1993): 559–81; Helene Raskin White and Stephen Hansell, "The Moderating Effects of Gender and Hostility on the Alcohol–Aggression Relationship," *Journal of Research in Crime and Delinquency* 33 (1996): 450–70; Henry Brownstein, Barry Spunt, Susan Crimmins, and Sandra Langley, "Women Who Kill in Drug Market Situations," *Justice Quarterly* 12 (1995): 473–98.

Early versus Late Onset. Although most life-course persisters are "early starters," some begin their offending career in late adolescence, after age 14. These "late starters" are also at high risk for adult criminality regardless of what age they began their offending careers.[93] Early-onset delinquents are both more prevalent and more generalized in their delinquent activity, for both male and female delinquents.[94]

Most life-course theories assume that criminal careers begin early in life and that early onset of deviance strongly predicts later and more serious criminality.[95] Research supports this idea by showing that as early as preschool, children begin to show deviance and that the earlier this happens, the longer their criminal careers will be. A thorough review of the literature found that early-onset criminals typically have a history of disruptive behaviour beginning in early childhood, with truancy, cruelty to animals, lying, and theft.

Kids who later become delinquents begin their deviant careers at a very early (preschool) age.[56] For narcotics addicts, the earlier the onset of substance abuse, the more frequent, varied, and sustained the addict's criminal career.[57]

Why do some people enter a path to crime later rather than sooner? Research shows that early-starter adolescents experience (1) poor parenting, which leads them into (2) deviant behaviours and then (3) involvement with delinquent groups. In contrast,

late starters follow a somewhat different path: (1) poor parenting leads to (2) identification with a delinquent group, and then into (3) deviant involvement. By implication, adolescents who suffer poor parenting and are at risk for deviant careers can avoid criminality if they can bypass involvement with delinquent peers.[97]

Early- and late-onset offenders take different paths into crime and are influenced by different life factors. Criminal peers exert a greater influence on the late bloomers than on their more precocious peers.[98] In a study of incarcerated criminals, early starters were more likely to be the victims of child abuse than later starters were. In addition, criminal punishments seemed to have a greater deterrent effect on early starters. It is possible that early starters learn from their experiences and become more cunning criminals, increasing their offending rates while avoiding detection.[99]

Not all persistent offenders begin at an early age. Some are precocious, beginning their criminal careers early and persisting into adulthood.[100] Others stay out of trouble in adolescence and do not violate the law until their teenage years. Some offenders may peak at an early age, whereas others persist into adulthood. Some youth maximize their offending rates at a relatively early age and then reduce their criminal activity; others persist into their twenties. Some are high-rate offenders, whereas others offend at relatively low rates.[101]

If all criminals have a singular latent trait that makes them crime-prone, it would be unlikely that these variations in criminal careers would be observed. It is difficult to explain such concepts as "late onset" and "adolescent-limited behaviour" from the perspective of latent trait theory.

Tracking persistent offenders over their life course supports what is known about delinquent–criminal career patterns.[102] Early onset predicts later offending, there is continuity in crime (juvenile offenders are the ones most likely to become adult criminals), and chronic offenders commit a significant portion of all crimes.[103]

Based on these findings, a number of systematic theories that account for the onset, continuance, and desistance from crime have been formulated. In the following sections, we discuss three life-course theories in some detail.

Farrington's Theory of Delinquent Development

One of the most important of the cohort longitudinal studies tracking persistent offenders is the Cambridge Study in Delinquent Development, which followed the

---

Famous Canadian Criminals

The Socialite Who Bought a Gun

On January 21, 1995, Earl Joudrie, a Calgary business tycoon, was leaving his condo after an emotional meeting with his wife in which he said he was seeking a divorce. Suddenly, he was stunned by a "whack across his back which felt like a . . . two by four." Joudrie fell to the ground, where Dorothy Joudrie pumped five more shots into him. She was "cold and controlled," he testified, "like a person I had never known." At her trial for attempted murder, Mrs. Joudrie relied on the controversial defence of automatism, a robot-like state in which she was unaware of her actions. Her lawyer based his argument on a ruling by Canadian Supreme Court Justice Bertha Wilson: "The mental state of an accused at the critical moment she pulls the trigger cannot be understood except in terms of the cumulative effect of months or years of brutality." Abuse in her marriage had resulted in hospitalization on three previous occasions, leaving her nose broken, her eyes blackened, and her ribs bruised.

Mrs. Joudrie was found not criminally responsible by reason

of mental disorder and was required to attend the Alberta Hospital Edmonton (AHE) for assessment by the Provincial Board of Review to determine whether she was a significant threat to public safety. Initially, this was to be a mere formality, but the hospital board decided to keep her in hospital for further testing. While Mrs. Joudrie was there, she was assaulted by a patient who broke her nose. She was confined to the mental hospital for five months, before being set free in 1996 by Alberta's Provincial Board of Review. The ruling meant that she was no longer considered a threat.

Mrs. Joudrie also spent a month at the Betty Ford Center for alcohol treatment in California, followed by a stay in Calgary's Foothills Hospital, where she was diagnosed with Graves' disease (a thyroid condition) as well as lymphatic cancer. Restrictions were placed on her travel and she was not allowed to drink alcohol.

Mrs. Joudrie later said of her five months in the mental hospital that it "was punishment, there was no therapy, there was no treatment, and no compassion." She also said, "What got me out

of the mental hospital was the fact that I had the money to fight the system. I want to speak up for the people who aren't so fortunate." Mrs. Joudrie and her lawyer credit her release to the fact that her money purchased the best legal and psychiatric specialists available.

Having recovered from surgery for her cancer, Mrs. Joudrie was looking forward to resuming her extensive charity work, her golf, and her bridge, and "trying to make a difference with others less fortunate" than she was. However, after a difficult life, she died in 2002.

Sources: Canadian Press, October 20, 1998; Kevin Udahl, "The 'Scariest Place in the World': How Dorothy Joudrie's Money Rescued Her from Hell," *Alberta Report,* November 16, 1998; Mary Nemeth, "A Turbulent and Troubled Life Laid Bare," *Maclean's,* May 13, 1996; Randy Olson, "Courts Confront the Question of Free Will," *Alberta Report/Western Report,* April 24, 1995; Les Sillars, "Unequal Before the Law?" *Alberta Report/Western Report,* March 6, 1995; Mary Nemeth, "Dorothy Joudrie's 'Nightmare' Ends," *Maclean's,* May 20, 1996; Les Sillars, "Until Fists, Alcoholism and Betrayal Do Us Part," *Alberta Report/Western Report,* May 20, 1996; Joe Woodward "Behind Robo-wife Stands Tyranny," *Alberta Report/Western Report,* May 27, 1996.

offending careers of 411 London boys born in 1953.[104] Farrington's study is one of the most serious attempts to isolate the factors that predict the continuity of criminal behaviour throughout the life course. Using self-report data, in-depth interviews, and psychological testing, the boys were interviewed eight times over a period of 24 years, beginning at age 8 and continuing to age 32.[105]

The Cambridge study is important because it shows the same patterns found in other research: the existence of chronic offenders, the continuity of offending, and the presence of early onset leading to persistent criminality. The traits of persistent offenders can be observed as early as age eight. The chronic criminal, typically a male, has been born into a low-income, large family headed by parents who have criminal records, and has delinquent older siblings. The future criminal receives poor parental supervision, including the use of harsh or erratic punishment and childrearing techniques; his parents are likely to divorce or separate.

The chronic offender associates with friends who are also future criminals. By age eight, he is already exhibiting antisocial behaviour, including dishonesty and aggressiveness. At school, he has low educational achievement and is restless, troublesome, hyperactive, impulsive, and often truant.

After leaving school at age 18, the persistent criminal tends to maintain a relatively well-paid but low-status job and is likely to have an erratic work history and periods of unemployment. Deviant behaviour is specialized, as the typical offender commits property offences, such as theft and burglary, and engages in violence, vandalism, drug use, excessive drinking, drunk driving, smoking, reckless driving, and sexual promiscuity. This is evidence of generalized problem behaviour syndrome. Chronic offenders are more likely to live away from home and have conflict with their parents. They wear tattoos, go out most evenings, and enjoy hanging out with groups of their friends. They are much more likely than are nonoffenders to get involved in fights, to carry weapons, and to use weapons in violent encounters. The frequency of offending reaches a peak in the teenage years (about 17 or 18) and then declines in the 20s, when the offender "settles down."

By the time he reaches his 30s, the former delinquent is likely to be separated or divorced from his wife and to be an absent parent. His employment record remains spotty, and he moves often to rental units rather than owner-occupied housing. His life is still characterized by evenings out, heavy drinking and substance abuse, and violent behaviour. Because the typical offender provides the same kind of deprived and disrupted family life for his own children that he experienced, the social experiences and conditions that produce delinquency are carried on from one generation to the next.

Nonoffenders and Desisters. Farrington has also identified factors that predict the discontinuity of criminal offences: These offenders have a background that puts them at risk to crime, but they are able to remain nonoffenders or begin a criminal career and later desist. The factors that "protect" high-risk youth from even beginning a criminal career include having a shy personality, having few friends (at age eight), having a nondeviant family, and being highly regarded by their mother. Shy kids with few friends avoid the damaging relationships with other adolescent boys and are therefore able to avoid criminality.

What causes offenders to desist? Holding a relatively good job helps reduce criminal activity. Unemployment is related to the escalation of theft offences, but violence and substance abuse are unaffected by unemployment. Being married also helps diminish criminal activity. However, finding a spouse who is also involved in criminal activity and has a criminal record increases criminal involvement.

Physical relocation, such as going to a more rural or suburban area, was linked to reductions in criminal activity. Relocation forces offenders to sever ties with co-offenders.

Although employment, marriage, and relocation helped offenders desist, not all found the key to success. At-risk youth who managed to avoid criminal convictions were unlikely to avoid other social problems. Rather than becoming prosperous homeowners with flourishing careers, they tended to live in unkempt homes and have large debts and low-paying jobs. Desisters were more likely to remain single and live alone: Youths who experience social isolation at age 8 also experience it at age 32.

Theoretical Modelling. Farrington's theoretical model of criminality can be summarized in seven points:

1. Childhood factors predict a continuity of teenage antisocial behaviour and adult dysfunction.
2. The personal and social factors associated with criminal propensity are economic deprivation, poor parenting, and an antisocial family, and personalities marked by impulsivity, hyperactivity, and attention deficit/hyperactivity disorder.
3. Adolescents who have criminogenic tendencies are motivated to offend by the desire for material goods, excitement, and status with peers. Boys from less affluent families are unable to achieve these goals through legitimate means so they tend to commit offences.
4. Life events influence behaviour, and family life is critical to a deviant career. Adolescents exposed to effective childrearing, including consistent discipline and close supervision, build internal inhibitions against offending in a social learning process.

5. The chance of offending in any particular situation depends on the perception of the costs and benefits of crime and noncrime alternatives. Boys who are more impulsive are more likely to offend because they are less likely to consider possible future consequences.

6. Factors that encourage criminality at one period during the life course may inhibit it in another. Being nervous and withdrawn and having few friends is negatively related to adolescent and teenage offending but positively related to adult social dysfunction.

7. Adult criminal behaviour is predicted by external behaviour (engaging in violence and getting arrested and convicted for crimes) and internal behaviour (psychiatric disorders, substance abuse, nervousness, and social isolation).

Experiences over the life course shape the direction and flow of behaviour choices. People are not controlled by a single, unalterable latent trait. Although there may be continuity in offending, the factors that predict criminality at one point in the life course may not be the ones that predict criminality at another. Although most adult criminals began their career in childhood, life events may help some children forgo criminality as they mature.

Interactional Theory

Terence Thornberry has also proposed an age-graded view of crime that he calls **interactional theory** (see Figure 10.6).[106] The onset of crime can be traced to a deterioration of the social bond during adolescence, a weakened attachment to parents, low commitment to school, and lack of belief in conventional values. This view recognizes structural variables, for example, that growing up in a socially disorganized area will also create the greatest risk of a weakened social bond and subsequent delinquency. The onset of a criminal career is supported by residence in a social setting in which deviant values and attitudes can be learned and reinforced by delinquent peers.

Serious delinquent youths form belief systems that are consistent with their deviant lifestyle, seeking out kids who share their interests, who reinforce their beliefs about the world, and who support their delinquent behaviour. Accordingly, delinquents seek out a criminal peer group, but deviant peers do not turn an otherwise "innocent" boy into a delinquent. They support and amplify the behaviour of kids who have already accepted a delinquent way of life; they support and amplify offending patterns.

The key idea is that causal influences are bidirectional. Weak bonds lead kids to develop relationships with deviant peers and get involved in high-rate

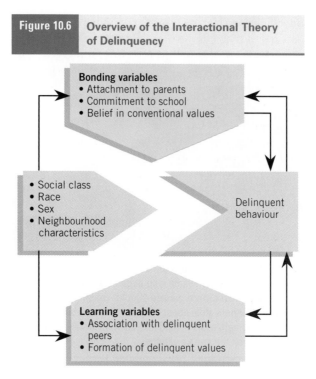

Figure 10.6   Overview of the Interactional Theory of Delinquency

Bonding variables
• Attachment to parents
• Commitment to school
• Belief in conventional values

• Social class
• Race
• Sex
• Neighbourhood characteristics

Delinquent behaviour

Learning variables
• Association with delinquent peers
• Formation of delinquent values

Source: Terence Thornberry, Margaret Farnsworth, Alan Lizotte, and Susan Stern, "A Longitudinal Examination of the Causes and Correlates of Delinquency," working paper No. 1, Rochester Youth Development Study (Albany, NY: Hindelang Criminal Justice Research Center, 1987), p. 11.

delinquency. Frequent delinquency involvement further weakens bonds and makes it difficult to reestablish conventional ones. Delinquency-promoting factors tend to reinforce one another and sustain a chronic criminal career.

Interactional theory is considered age-graded because it incorporates an element of the **cognitive perspective** in psychology: As people mature, they pass through different stages of reasoning and sophistication.[107] Criminality is a dynamic, developmental process that takes on different meaning and form as a person matures. During early adolescence, attachment to the family is the single most important determinant of whether a youth will adjust to conventional society and be shielded from delinquency. By mid-adolescence, the influence of the family is replaced by the world of friends, school, and youth culture. In adulthood, a person's behavioural choices are shaped by his or her place in conventional society and his or her own nuclear family.

One test of this model is to look at youths who will be followed through their offending careers.[108] Preliminary results support interactional theory hypotheses, including the deviance-amplifying powers

David Farrington's longitudinal research found the persistent offender was typically a male who began his criminal career as a property offender. Here we see a looter robbing a dépanneur in Montreal. Others stole about 15 cases of beer while a stunned cashier stood helplessly behind the counter. Looters threw beer bottles to break the store's window.

of associating with a delinquent peer group.[109] Associating with delinquent peers increases delinquent involvement because the peer group reinforces deviance.[110] As delinquent behaviour escalates, kids seek out deviant friends who reinforce delinquent beliefs (thinking it is okay to commit crimes). In contrast, conventional youths seek out friends equally conforming, who then reinforce their pro-social lifestyle. Antisocial kids will become part of a deviant peer network that will reinforce their behaviour; conventional youths will, in turn, be reinforced by their conventional friends.[111]

Similar patterns have been found for family and school relations: Delinquency is related to weakened attachments to family and the educational process; delinquent behaviour further weakens the strength of the bonds to family and school.[112] There is an interactional relationship between criminal behaviour and moral values (antisocial behaviour weakens moral beliefs and weakened beliefs encourage criminality).[113]

Life events can make even high-risk youths resilient to delinquency. Kids who grow up in indigent households with unemployment, high mobility, and parental criminality and who are placed in the care of social service agencies can resist delinquent involvements if they have pro-social life experiences. Among those encounters are forming a commitment to school, developing an attachment to teachers, establishing the goal of a postsecondary education, and scoring high on reading and math tests.[114]

In sum, interactional theory suggests that criminality is part of a dynamic social process and not simply an outcome of that process. Although crime is influenced by social forces, it also influences these processes and associations to create behavioural trajectories toward increasing law violations for some people. In so doing, the interactional theory integrates elements of social disorganization, social control, social learning, and cognitive theory into a powerful model of the development of a criminal career.

Sampson and Laub's Age-Graded Theory

If there are various pathways to crime and delinquency, are there trails back to conformity? In *Crime in the Making*, Sampson and Laub identify the turning points in a criminal career.[115] They say that the stability of delinquent behaviour is affected by events that occur later in life, even after a chronic delinquent career has been undertaken. They agree with Gottfredson and Hirschi that formal and informal social controls restrict criminality and that the onset of crime begins early in life and continues over the life course. They disagree that once this course is set, nothing can impede its progress.

Laub and Sampson reanalyzed the data originally collected by the Gluecks. Using modern computerized statistical analysis, they found evidence supportive of the life-course view. They have found that children who enter delinquent careers are those who have trouble at home and at school and who maintain deviant friends—findings not dissimilar from earlier research on delinquent careers.

Turning Points in Crime. Laub and Sampson's most important contribution has been identifying the life events that enable adult offenders to desist from crime (see Figure 10.7). Two critical **turning points** are marriage and career. For example, adolescents who are at risk for crime are able to live "normal" or conventional lives if they can find good jobs or achieve successful careers. Their success may hinge on a "lucky break": employers who are willing to give them a chance despite their record.

InfoTrac®

The following article found through InfoTrac® discusses the importance of marital attachment and job stability associated with distance from crime: Peggy C. Giordano, Stephen A. Cernkovich, and Jennifer L. Rudolph, "Gender, Crime and Distance: Toward a Theory of Cognitive Transformation," *American Journal of Sociology* 101, no. 4 (2002): 990(76).

Famous Canadian Court Case

John Martin Crawford

Clifford Olson, Paul Bernardo, Robert Pickton—these individuals top the ranks of Canadian serial killers. So does John Crawford, but chances are his name does not come to mind. He was convicted of slaying four women and is the prime suspect in at least three other brutal murders and disappearances. Nevertheless, very few people know about Crawford, his crimes, or his victims.

Born to a young, unwed mother in 1962, this Manitoba native was scarred in a childhood accident, both literally and figuratively. Crawford was severely burned and other children teased him about his scars. Despite the many authority figures in his life, Crawford had few positive role models. He instead had an alcoholic stepfather and sexually abusive babysitters.

Growing up, behavioural problems and failing grades warned of Crawford's impending transgressions. This glue-sniffing runaway who was picked on by his peers transformed into a drug-abusing car thief who bullied other kids. Crawford's deviant

sexual tendencies first emerged at the age of 13, when he paid a younger girl for sex. He soon began to hear voices and display other psychotic symptoms.

By the age of 19, Crawford had become a sadistic predator and claimed his first victim. Crawford viciously attacked and murdered Mary Jane Serloin in Lethbridge, Alberta. After pleading guilty to manslaughter in 1982, he served seven years of a decade-long sentence. Crawford's coping difficulties followed him to prison, where they manifested as anxiety and self-mutilation.

Crawford's appetite for sex, drugs, and violence escalated on his release from prison in 1989. While living with his then-divorced mother in Saskatoon, the parolee was fined for soliciting a prostitute and charged with sexual assault. In 1992, Crawford savagely raped, tortured, and killed Calinda Waterhen, Shelly Napope, and Eva Taysup.

These women's remains were not discovered until 1994 and it took two more years for Crawford's trial to commence. With the aid of an informant paid $15 000 by the police,

one first-degree and two second-degree murder convictions were eventually secured. The judge imposed three concurrent life sentences with no chance of parole. Professing her son's innocence, Crawford's mother hired lawyers to push the case forward. A higher Saskatchewan court rejected their appeal in 1999, as did the Supreme Court of Canada in 2000. Now in his early forties, Crawford is housed in a Prince Albert penitentiary.

To date, his conviction record is surpassed only by that of Clifford Olson. Despite this fact, the reporters who flocked to Paul Bernardo's 1995 trial were nowhere to be found when Crawford was brought to justice a year later. This indifference has been attributed to the same systematic racism and sexism that allowed Robert Pickton to evade authorities for more than a decade: Crawford and Pickton preyed on Aboriginal women with high-risk lifestyles. As the sister of Crawford's first victim lamented, "It seems any time a Native is murdered, it isn't a major case. It's just another dead Indian."

Prepared by Andrea Wolf.

When they achieve adulthood, even adolescents with significant problems with the law are able to desist if they become attached to a spouse who supports and sustains them even though they were in trouble when they were younger. Happy marriages are life-sustaining, and marital quality improves over time (as people work less and have fewer parental responsibilities); people who are married even tend to live longer.[116] Children who grow up in two-parent families are more likely to have happier marriages themselves than are children who are the product of divorced or never-married parents.[117] The marriage–crime association may be intergenerational: If people who have marital problems are more crime-prone, their children will also suffer a greater long-term risk of marital failure and antisocial

activity. People who cannot sustain secure marital relations or who are unemployed are less likely to desist from crime.

Social Capital. People build **social capital**—positive relations with individuals and institutions that are life-sustaining. Building social capital supports conventional behaviour and inhibits deviant behaviour. For example, a successful marriage creates social capital when it improves a person's stature, creates feelings of self-worth, and encourages people to take a chance on the individual. A successful career inhibits crime by creating a stake in conformity; why commit crime when you are doing well at your job? The relationship is reciprocal: If a person is chosen as an employee, he or she will return the favour

Figure 10.7	Sampson and Laub's Age-Graded Theory

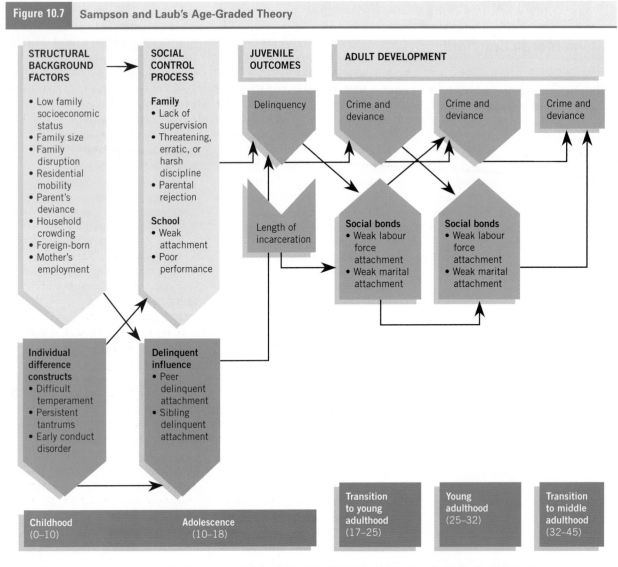

Source: Robert Sampson and John Laub, *Crime in the Making* (Cambridge, MA: Harvard University Press, 1993), pp. 244–45.

by doing the best job possible; if the person is chosen as a spouse, he or she can become a devoted partner. In contrast, moving to a new city reduces social capital by closing people off from long-term relationships.[118]

 InfoTrac®

To learn more about the concept of social capital, use it as a keyword term on InfoTrac® College Edition and find articles like Daniel Lederman, Norman Locynza, and Ana Maria Menendey, "Violent Crime: Does Social Capital Matter?" *Economic Development and Cultural Change* 50, no. 3 (2002): 509(31).

Building social capital and strong social bonds reduces the likelihood of long-term deviance, suggesting that, in contrast to latent trait theories, events that occur in later adolescence and adulthood do, in fact, influence the direction of delinquent and criminal careers. Life events can either help terminate or help sustain deviant careers. For example, getting arrested and punished may have little direct effect on future criminality, but it can help sustain a criminal career because it reduces the chances of employment and job stability, two factors directly related to crime.

Testing Age-Graded Theory. At-risk youth with a history of delinquent behaviours have been found to desist if they later improve their peer relations, do better in school, and make effective use of their leisure time. Once begun,

According to Sampson and Laub, building social capital helps inhibit the onset of criminality. Some treatment programs put these views into action, for example, by helping addicted homeless mothers become drug-free and develop marketable skills.

Laub and Sampson's life-course model while contradicting one of the key assumptions of the latent trait approach of Gottfredson and Hirschi.[123] Although change is possible, some important questions need answering:

1. Why do some kids change while others resist?
2. Why do some people enter strong marriages while others fail?
3. What is it about a military career that helps reduce future criminality?
4. Does the connection between military service and desistance suggest universal military service as a crime-prevention alternative?
5. Why are some troubled youths able to conform to the requirements of a job or career while others cannot?

Perversely, an in-depth case study of a female crack dealer showed that social capital, family, friends, education, marriage, and employment can also aid in a "successful" career as a crack dealer. The addict's own crack consumption was kept under control, and she remained competent as a "manager," keeping her family life and drug dealing separate.[124]

The Marriage Factor. Marriage stabilizes people and helps them build social capital; it also may discourage crime by reducing contact with criminal peers. As Mark Warr states:

> For many individuals, it seems, marriage marks a transition from heavy peer involvement to a preoccupation with one's spouse. That transition is likely to reduce interaction with former friends and accomplices and thereby reduce the opportunities as well as the motivation to engage in crime.[125]

Even people who have histories of criminal activity and have been convicted of serious offences reduce the frequency of their offending if they live with spouses and maintain employment when they are in the community.[126]

Confirming the benefits of marriage as a crime-reducing social event, Piquero, Parker, and MacDonald tracked 524 men in their late teens and early 20s for seven years after they were paroled from the California Youth Authority during the 1970s and 1980s. The men had been incarcerated for lengthy periods, and 49 percent were White, 33 percent were Black, 17 percent were Hispanic, and 2 percent were other races.[127] Former offenders were far less likely to return to crime if they settled down into the routines of a solid marriage. Common-law marriages or living with a partner did not have the same crime-reducing effect as did traditional marriages in which the knot is tied, the union is registered at the courthouse, and there is a general expectation to lead a steady life. Among non-Caucasians, parolees cohabiting without the benefit of marriage actually increased their recidivism rates.

These findings suggest that married people have schedules where they work nine-to-five jobs, come home

a delinquent career can be reversed if life conditions improve.[119] Men who are unemployed or underemployed report higher criminal participation rates than do employed men; men released from prison on parole who obtain jobs are less likely to recidivate.[120] There is evidence that substance abusers who maintain a successful marriage in their 20s and become parents are the ones most likely to mature out of crime.[121] Employment and marriage are two cornerstones of age-graded theory. Delinquents who enter the military and serve overseas also enhance their occupational status and economic well-being—clearly a turning point in the life course.[122]

Paternoster found that people who are self-centred and present-oriented are less likely to accumulate social capital and more prone to commit criminal acts. In contrast, people who have accumulated social capital are unwilling to risk damage to that investment and therefore are less likely to commit crime. Because behaviour is influenced by considerations of future punishment, as social capital increases, the risk of crime decreases. This supports

for dinner, take care of children, watch television, go to bed, and repeat that cycle over and over again; people who are not married have a lot of free rein to do much of what they want, especially if they are not employed. There's something about crossing the line of getting married that helps these men stay away from crime.

However, some important questions still need to be answered: Why do some people enter strong marriages while others fail? Does the influence of marriage have an equal effect on men and women? Although marriage improves a woman's life chances, it has less impact on men.[128] However, for both males and females, having an antisocial romantic partner as a young adult increased the likelihood of later criminal behaviour, a finding that supports Laub and Sampson's theory.

Summary

Recently, criminologists have been combining elements from a number of different theoretical models into integrated theories of crime, as outlined in Table 10.1. One approach is to use multiple factors derived from a

TABLE 10.1 Integrated Theories		
Theory	**Major Premise**	**Strengths**
Multifactor Theories		
Social development model (SDM)	Weak social controls produce crime. A person's place in the structure influences his or her bond to society.	Combines elements of social structural and social process theories. Accounts for variations in the crime rate.
Elliott's integrated theory	Strained and weak social bonds lead youths to associate with and learn from deviant peers.	Combines elements of learning, strain, and control theories.
Integrated structural theory	Delinquency is a function of family life, which is in turn controlled by the family's place in the economic system.	Explains the relationship between family problems and delinquency in terms of social and economic conditions.
Latent Trait Theories		
General theory	Crime and criminality are separate concepts. People choose to commit crime when they lack self-control. People lacking self-control will seize criminal opportunities.	Integrates choice and social control concepts. Identifies the difference between crime and criminality.
Human nature theory	People choose to commit crime when they have biological and psychological impairments.	Shows how physical traits interact with social conditions to produce crime. Can account for noncriminal behaviour in high-crime areas. Integrates choice and developmental theories.
Life-Course Theories		
Farrington's theory of delinquent development	Personal and social factors control the onset and stability of criminal careers.	Makes use of data collected over a 20-year period to substantiate hypothesis.
Interactional theory	Criminals go through lifestyle changes during their offending career.	Combines sociological and psychological theories.
Age-graded theory	As people mature, the factors that influence their propensity to commit crime change. In childhood, family factors are critical; in adulthood, marital and job factors are key.	Shows how crime is a developmental process that shifts in direction over the life course.

number of structural and process theories. Examples of this approach include the social development model and Elliott's integrated theory, both of which hold that social position controls life events. The social development model suggests that living in a disorganized area helps weaken social bonds; Elliott's theory holds that strain leads to weakened bonds. Both theories find that weakened bonds lead to the development of deviant peer group associations. In another variation, integrated structural theory, Colvin and Pauly add conflict variables to structural and process factors.

Latent trait theories hold that some underlying condition present at birth or soon after controls behaviour. Suspect traits include low IQ, impulsivity, and personality structure. This underlying trait explains the continuity of offending because once present, it remains with a person throughout his or her life. The latent trait theories developed by Gottfredson and Hirschi and by Wilson and Herrnstein both integrate choice theory concepts: People with latent traits choose crime over noncrime. The opportunity for crime mediates their choice.

Life-course theories argue that events that take place over the life course influence criminal choices. The cause of crime is constantly changing as people mature. At first, the nuclear family influences behaviour; during adolescence, the peer group dominates; in adulthood, marriage and career are critical. There are a variety of pathways to crime: Some kids are sneaky; others are hostile; and still others, defiant. Crime may be part of a garden variety of social problems, including health, physical, and interpersonal troubles. Important life-course theories have been formulated by Terence Thornberry, David Farrington, and John Laub and Robert Sampson.

Thinking Like a Criminologist

Luis Francisco is the leader of a Hispanic gang in Montreal. He was convicted of murder in 1998 and sentenced to life imprisonment.

Luis Francisco's life has been filled with displacement, poverty, and chronic predatory crime. The son of a prostitute in Haiti, he was sent to prison for robbery at the age of nine. He had trouble in school, and teachers described him as having attention problems; he dropped out in grade 7. On his 19th birthday in 1980, he immigrated to Canada and soon

after became a member of the Montreal criminal gang the Latin Kings. He shot and killed his girlfriend in 1981 and was not apprehended until 1984. Sentenced to nine years for second-degree manslaughter, Luis Francisco ended up in a maximum-security prison in Manitoba, where he started a prison chapter of his gang. As King Blood, Francisco ruled his gang in and out of prison. Disciplinary troubles erupted when some Kings were stealing from the organization. Infuriated,

King Blood phoned his street lieutenants and ordered their termination. The RCMP, who had been monitoring his communications, arrested 35 gang members. Thirty-four pleaded guilty; only Francisco insisted on a trial, where he was found guilty of conspiracy to commit murder.

Explain Luis's behaviour patterns from a developmental view. How would a latent trait theorist explain his escalating criminal activities?

Key Terms

adolescent-limited

authority conflict pathway

cognitive perspective

continuity of crime

covert pathway

developmental criminology

early onset

general theory of crime (GTC)

integrated structural Marxist theory

interactional theory

latent traits

life-course theory

multifactor theories

overt pathway

problem behaviour syndrome (PBS)

pro-social bonds

pseudomaturity

social capital

social development model (SDM)

turning points

Critical Thinking Questions

1. Crime data tell us that women are significantly less violent than are men. Are the pathways to chronic offending different among violent females than among violent males?

2. What conditions present at birth can control future criminal behaviour?

3. A person is accepted at three universities. Without knowing this person, what personal, family, and social characteristics do you think this person has? Another person becomes a serial killer. Without knowing this person, what personal, family, and social characteristics do you think this person has? If "bad behaviour" is explained by multiple problems, is "good behaviour" explained by multiple strengths?

4. Do you believe it is a latent trait that makes a person crime-prone, or is crime a function of environment and socialization?

5. What factors (for example, a military career) that influenced the men in the original Glueck sample are still relevant for change today? Would it be possible for such men as these to join the military today?

 See the book-specific website at http://www.siegelcriminology3e.nelson.com for additional chapter links, discussions, and quizzes.

section 3

Crime Typologies

Regardless of the reasons that people commit crime in the first place, their actions are defined by law as falling into particular crime categories. Criminologists often seek to group individual criminal offenders or behaviours so they may be more easily studied and understood. These are referred to as offender typologies.

In this section, crime patterns are clustered into four groups: violent crime (Chapter 11); economic crimes involving common theft offences (Chapter 12); economic crimes involving white-collar criminals or criminal organizations (Chapter 13); and public order crimes, such as prostitution and drug abuse (Chapter 14). These groupings focus our attention on bringing physical harm to others; misappropriating other people's property; and violating laws designed to protect public morals.

Typologies can be useful in classifying large numbers of criminal offences or offenders into easily understood categories. This text has grouped offences and offenders on the basis of (1) their legal definitions, (2) their collective goals, objectives, and consequences, and (3) societal reaction.

Violent Crime

In our society, people are afraid of becoming crime victims. TV news stories and newspaper articles feature grisly accounts of mass murder, child abuse, and serial rape. Moreover, despite recent declines, rates of violent crime have risen in the past 30 years. The rate of violence in the United States exceeds that of any other industrialized nation, but even Canada is not the "peaceable kingdom" everyone would like to think it is.[1]

Many people have personally experienced violence or have a friend who has been victimized; almost everyone has heard about someone being robbed, beaten, or killed; riots and violent protests have recently made the headlines; "hate crime" has become a common phrase; assassination has claimed the lives of political, religious, and social leaders all over the world; and "terrorism" has become a household word.

Because of such events, the public believes that the government should take a "get-tough" approach to violent crime, especially when the perpetrators are young offenders. However, there is a perception that youth criminal legislation, reflected in the *Youth Criminal Justice Act,* might not go far enough. In the United States, the Supreme Court has made teenage criminals over the age of 16 eligible for the death penalty.[2] In Canada, public opinion polls indicate that almost half of Canadians favour the return of the death penalty, three decades after it was abolished. Many people believe that society is becoming more violent and that things are not as they were in the "good old days." And maybe they are right—since the mid-1970s, the homicide rate was declining, but in 2002, it rose 4 percent.[3] But is longing for the serenity of earlier days appropriate when we consider that violence has been a long-standing feature of social life? Perhaps we are just hearing more highly publicized accounts of violent crime.

Some experts suggest that violence originates in a relatively small number of inherently violence-prone individuals who themselves may have been the victims of physical violence or who may have psychological abnormalities. Other social scientists consider violence and aggression inherently human traits, while others believe that there are violence-prone subcultures within society whose members value force and routinely carry weapons.[4]

Connections

As discussed in Chapter 6, biosocial theorists link violence to a number of biological irregularities, including genetic influences and inheritance, hormones, neurotransmitters, brain structure, and diet. Psychologists link violent behaviour to observational learning from violent TV shows, traumatic childhood experiences, low intelligence, mental illness, impaired cognitive processes, and abnormal (psychopathic) personality structure.

This chapter surveys the nature and extent of violent crime. First, we briefly review some hypothetical causes of violence. Then, we turn our attention to specific types of interpersonal violence: rape, homicide, assault, and robbery. Finally, we look at political violence, state-sponsored violence, and terrorism.

The Roots of Violence

What causes people to behave violently? There are a number of competing explanations for behaviour as violent as the following:

- In 1984, Denis Lortie opened fire in Quebec's National Assembly with a machine gun, killing three and wounding 13 others; he pleaded guilty by reason of insanity.
- In 1989, a male gunman killed 14 women and wounded 12 others at the École Polytechnique in Montreal. After his suicide, a statement found on his body blamed feminists for spoiling his life.[5]
- In 1992, Valery Fabrikant walked into Concordia University's engineering department and killed three professors; the university had previously asked the police not to approve Fabrikant's gun permit.
- In 1995, an ex-Boy Scout leader named Thomas Hamilton took four high-powered rifles into the primary school of the Scottish town of Dunblane and slaughtered 16 children and their teacher. This horrific crime shocked the British Isles into passing strict controls on all guns.
- In 2004, Chechen rebels claimed responsibility for the school hostage-taking in southern Russia. More than 320 hostages were killed, half of them children. There was speculation that al-Qaeda was involved in the attack.

Bizarre outbursts, such as these acts of mass violence, exacerbate our worst fears that we could be victimized by brutal, random crime committed by strangers in public places. Fear distorts the experience of living in modern society. And the fear is not totally groundless.

Canada has a homicide rate higher than most Western societies (2.1 homicides per 100 000 people in 1999 compared with England's 0.8 homicides). In Aboriginal communities, the suicide rate is three times higher than the average, and violent crime is more than three times the average. Our society can't prevent the victimization of women and children, and we have many instances of police and prison violence.

Figure 11.1 shows some of the known sources of violence.

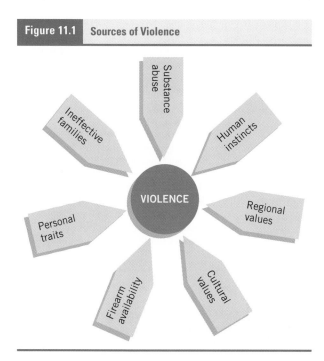

Figure 11.1   Sources of Violence

Personal Traits

Some see a link between violence and personal traits. More than 35 years ago, Laura Bender examined convicted juveniles who had killed their victims and concluded that they suffered from abnormal electroencephalogram (EEG) readings, learning disabilities, and psychosis.[6]

More recent research has found that murderous youths suffer signs of major neurological impairment (abnormal EEGs, multiple psychomotor impairment, and severe seizures), low intelligence, and psychotic symptoms, such as paranoia, illogical thinking, and hallucinations.[7] Similarly, studies of male batterers indicate that abnormal personality structure, including depression, borderline personality syndrome, and psychopathology, is associated with various forms of spousal and family abuse.[8] However, there are other theories as well.

Ineffective Families

In 1990, residents of Gainesville, Florida, were shocked when five young students were brutally murdered.

Famous Canadian Criminals

The Killer

Few people would have otherwise recognized his name: Marc Lepine. He was considered a loser, unable to keep a girlfriend and ineligible for the military because of his mental instability and antisocial personality. Then on December 6, 1989, Marc Lepine dressed in military fatigues, hid his guns under his coat, and went to the École Polytechnique. He went into an engineering classroom and ordered all the men out, after which he shot the women, cursing them for being feminists. He walked through the school systematically shooting women until he turned the gun on himself. Was he a lunatic or part of the wider continuum of violence against women? Was this act an isolated one or the extreme end of everyday misogyny?

A letter found on his body said that he had decided to kill women because they had ruined

The Women Victims

Genevieve Bergeron, 21, civil engineering

Helene Colgan, 23, mechanical engineering

Nathalie Croteau, 23, mechanical engineering

Barbara Daigneault, 22, mechanical engineering

Anne-Marie Edward, 21, chemical engineering

Maud Haviernick, 29, environmental design

Barbara Maria Klucznik, 31, materials

Maryse Laganiere, 25, Polytechnique budget department

Maryse Leclair, 23, engineering materials

Anne-Marie Lemay, 27, mechanical engineering

Sonia Pelletier, 28, mechanical engineering

Michele Richard, 21, engineering materials

Annie St-Arneault, 23, mechanical engineering

Annie Turcotte, 21, engineering materials

his life. He had tried to enter the Polytechnique as a student but was turned down. He admired Denis Lortie for going into the legislature and shooting politicians and wanted to emulate him.

The initial reaction to the Montreal Massacre was incredulity and anger. How could a person be in possession of such weapons? Why did the police take so long to respond? Why did Lepine single out women?

For many, this event has come to symbolize wider patterns of violence against women in society.

When Suzanne Lapointe-Edward speaks about what happened to her daughter, she calls Lepine "the killer." She believes that the media made Lepine an anti-hero while the women became nameless victims. Lapointe-Edward lectures across the country to promote action and healing with respect to violence against women, advocating stricter gun control legislation.

Women are usually killed by men they know, after withstanding repeated assaults. That night in Montreal, the women were selected because of their sex. They had done nothing to Lepine and nothing to deserve what happened to them.

Not all men are violent, but most violence is committed by men—a fact that is hard to overlook. However, men and women have joined together in

trying to overcome a legacy of gendered violence and to work for change.

Sources: *After the Montreal Massacre,* 1990, National Film Board documentary; Elizabeth Stanko, *Everyday Violence* (London: Pandora, 1990); "Media Literacy: Ten Years Later, Media Still Don't Get the Montreal Massacre," Judy Rebick, *CBC Straight From the Hip,* December 12, 1999; *Canadian Crime Statistics 2000* (Ottawa: Canadian Centre for Justice Statistics, 2001).

Newspaper accounts told how the victims had been stabbed dozens of times and raped, and how their mutilated bodies were posed in sexually suggestive positions.[9] Danny Harold Rolling was convicted for committing these horrible crimes, and the jury recommended the death penalty. During sentencing, Rolling pleaded for mercy and claimed his behaviour was a result of emotional and physical abuse by his father. His mother backed up his claim of abuse, saying that she had failed him somewhere.

Research linking violence to ineffective, abusive, or inadequate parenting shows that parents reinforce a child's coercive behaviour by failing to set adequate limits or use proper and consistent discipline. Such factors are all linked to persistent violent offending.[10]

The Canadian Centre for Justice Statistics (CCJS) confirms this pattern. As part of the National Longitudinal Survey of Children and Youth, more than 20 000 children or their caregivers are interviewed every two years until they are 25 years of age. In 1994, the ages of the first group of children were newborn to age 11. A key finding is that children who are exposed to fighting in the home are more likely to be physically aggressive themselves. Figure 11.2 shows that almost three times as many children who witness violence are likely to be violent compared with those who don't witness violence. There is also a direct relationship among seeing violence; being hyperactive, anxious, or depressed; and committing property crimes.

InfoTrac®

To read an interview with Dorothy Otnow Lewis in which she discusses how the problems in an aggressive boy's life should be evaluated and how appropriate treatment should be provided, see Rena Large, "New Path for Aggressive Boys," *NEA Today* 17, no. 2 (1998): 29(1).

| Figure 11.2 | Child Behavioural Outcomes in Homes Where Children Witnessed Violence |

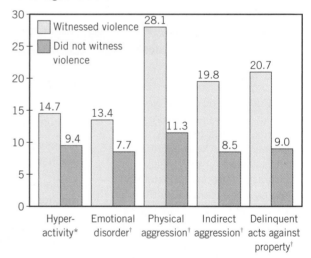

Percentage of Children

* Chi-square = < .05; *df* = 1
† Chi-square = < .001; *df* = 1
Those who fell within the bottom 10% of the scale were considered to have behavioural problems.
Source: Statistics Canada, *National Longitudinal Survey of Children and Youth, 1998–1999.*

Source: Adapted from the Statistics Canada publication "Children Witnessing Family Violence," *Juristat,* Catalogue 85-002, vol. 21, no. 6, June 28, 2001.

Abused Kids. Victims of childhood abuse later engage in violent delinquent behaviour at a rate greater than do unabused children.[11] Samples of convicted murderers contain a high percentage of seriously abused youths.[12] Abuse is a factor in many cases when parents have been killed by their children.[13]

Children who are physically punished are the ones most likely to physically abuse a sibling and later engage in spouse abuse.[14]

The Brutalization Process. Case studies of violent criminals show that antisocial careers are created in stages, beginning with brutal episodes during early adolescence. The first stage is the **brutalization process**, during which abusive parents or caretakers cause the young victim to develop a belligerent, angry demeanour. When confronted at home, at school, or on the street, these youths respond with hostility. The success of their confrontations provides them with a sense of power. In the virulency stage, they develop a violent identity that makes them feared; they enjoy intimidating others. This process takes now-violent youths full circle, from being the victim of aggression to being its initiator; they are now the same person they grew up despising, ready to begin the process with their own children.[15]

Although evidence shows the association between abuse and violent crime, many offenders have not suffered abuse, and many abused youths do not grow up to become persistent adult offenders.[16]

Evolutionary Factors/Human Instinct

It is possible that violent responses are inherent in all humans, needing only the right trigger. Freud believed human aggression and violence were produced by instinctual drives.[17] Freud said that humans have two opposing instinctual drives that control behaviour: **Eros**, the life instinct, drives people to self-fulfillment and enjoyment; **thanatos**, the death instinct, produces self-destruction. Thanatos can be expressed externally (as violence and sadism) or internally (as suicide, alcoholism, or other self-destructive habits).

Biologists and anthropologists speculate that instinctual violence-promoting traits may be common to the human species. Aggression and violence are the results of instincts inborn in all animals. Konrad Lorenz developed this theory in *On Aggression*,[18] arguing that aggressive energy is produced by inbred instincts independent of environmental forces. In the animal kingdom, aggression serves a productive purpose—for example, leading members of grazing species to spread out over available territory to ensure an ample food supply and the survival of the fittest.

Lorenz felt that humans have some of the same aggressive instincts as animals but without some important inhibitions. Among lower species, aggression is rarely fatal; when a conflict occurs, the winner is determined through a test of skill or endurance. This inhibition against killing members of their own species protects animals from self-extinction.

Evolutionary theories suggest that violence may have become instinctual because of the long-term influences of reproductive behaviour: Males who are sexually aggressive are the ones most likely to produce children. Over time, male aggression has become predominant.[19]

Cultural Values

Explanations of the cause of violent behaviour that focus on the individual fail to account for larger patterns of societal violence. Is interpersonal violence more common in large, urban, inner-city areas? Are violent crime rates linked to socially disorganized areas?[20]

Subculture of Violence. To explain the existence of areas and groups with disproportionately high violence rates, Marvin Wolfgang suggests the existence of a subculture of violence.[21] The subculture's norms are separate from society's central, dominant value system, and violence becomes a way to solve conflicts.[22]

Ganging. Empirical evidence shows that violence is highest in urban areas in which subcultural values support teenage gangs whose members embrace the use of violence.[23] Gang members are more likely to own guns and other weapons.[24] Gang violence may be used to retaliate against rivals and to protect turf from incursions by outsiders.[25] The number of gang-related killings has increased significantly in recent years.[26] In Canada, increasing attention is being paid to Chinese and Vietnamese gangs as well as to outlaw motorcycle gangs.[27]

Regional Values

Do regional values promote violence.[28] Research in the southern United States attributed high homicide rates to a culture that stresses a frontier mentality, mob violence, personal vengeance, and easily available firearms.[29] Not all criminologists agree with these conclusions.[30]

Police data and victimization surveys in Canada show that Western provinces have a higher overall rate of violent crime. This pattern is consistent for property and violent crime, with provincial and territorial variations due to age, sex, urban concentration, and social disorganization.[31] However, Kennedy and Silverman suggest that crime rates increase, moving from low rates in the East and gradually increasing in a westward direction, because of relative disadvantage. That is, crime is likely to be higher in the West because there is a broader range of social inequality. In areas of absolute disadvantage, as in much of Eastern Canada, there is little animosity because there is little difference among individuals.[32]

InfoTrac®

To find out more about violence around the world, use "violence Europe," "violence Asia," and "violence Africa" as keywords on InfoTrac® College Edition.

Substance Abuse

Violence can also be linked to substance abuse, which influences violence in three ways: through the actual effects of drugs, out of the need to obtain drugs, and in relation to drug trafficking.[33]

The relationship is **psychopharmacological** when it is the direct consequence of ingesting mood-altering substances. Drugs, such as PCP and amphetamines, produce violence and aggression. Alcohol abuse is also associated with violence, especially since drinking reduces cognition.[34]

Drug ingestion may result in economic compulsive behaviour when drug users resort to violence to gain funds to support their habit. In a Corrections Canada survey of six thousand offenders entering federal institutions between 1994 and 1996, 48 percent admitted having used a drug on the day of their offence, and 30 percent said they had used cocaine in the six months before arrest. The U.S. Drug Use Forecasting (DUF) survey shows that 80 percent of people arrested for violent crimes test positively for drugs.[35] Surveys of American prison inmates show a majority report being under the influence of drugs and alcohol at the time of their offence.[36]

A bond between violent crime and substance abuse is also forged by the activities of drug-trafficking gangs whose members sell and use drugs. Drug-related deaths are motivated by drug trafficking and interpersonal conflict brought on by drug abuse; relatively few people are killed by drug users trying to get drug money.[37]

Firearm Availability

Although firearm availability is not in itself a cause of violence, it is certainly a facilitating factor: An argument can escalate into a fatality if one party has a handgun. In Canada, 26 percent of all homicides involved shootings in 2002, down from 42 percent in 1961. Handguns are used in three-quarters of all firearm homicides.[38]

Shootings are a major cause of death for police officers who are killed, and the presence of firearms in the home significantly increases suicide, regardless of how carefully the guns are secured or stored.[39] As Exhibit 11.1 shows, 81 percent of all firearm deaths in Canada are suicides. In the United States, assaults and violence among family members are 12 times more likely to result in death if a handgun is used than if the attacks do not involve firearms.[40]

Between 1970 and 1995, probably as a result of more stringent firearms regulations, the use of firearms for suicide and homicide decreased. Unintentional firearms deaths have also decreased.[41]

Exhibit 11.1	Quick Facts about Weapons and Violent Crime, 1995

- Homicide is the violent crime that most frequently involves the use of weapons. This includes first-degree murder, second-degree murder, manslaughter, and infanticide.

- Firearm use in spousal homicides declined from 36 percent to 28 percent between 1985 and 1995. This includes registered marriages, common-law unions, separations, and divorces.

- Only 2 percent of all violent-crime victims encountered firearms.

- Thirty-one percent of assault victims encountering knives sustained major injury, compared with 16 percent facing guns.

- From 1991 to 1995 the proportion of firearm deaths involving handguns increased from 29 percent to 50 percent.

- From 1991 to 1995, rates declined for homicide (26 percent) and for firearm homicide (39 percent).

- Canadians have 3.1 million rifles, 2.3 million shotguns, and 1 million handguns (estimated, 1990).

- In 1997, almost all Canadian households with a firearm possessed a long gun (95.1 percent). These households represented 19.2 percent of all Canadian households. In contrast, 12 percent of Canadian gun-owning households possessed a handgun and this represented 2.3 percent of all Canadian households. Only about 2.2 percent of Canadian households owned both a handgun and a long gun.

- Suicides accounted for 81 percent of all firearm deaths.

- Types of weapons used in violent incidents were similar for adults or youths.

- Handguns are more common in homicides in large urban areas.

Sources: Adapted from the Statistics Canada publication "Weapons and Violent Crime," *Juristat* 17 (1997); Richard Block, Firearms in Canada and Eight Other Western Countries: Selected Findings of the 1996 International Crime (Victim) Survey, Working Document, January, 1998, http://canada.justice.gc.ca/en/ps/rs/rep/wd97-3a-e.html (accessed May 19, 2005).

Connections

Some criminologists have focused on "violent" business or corporate crimes, such as the release of toxic pollutants into the environment. Because these acts are linked to business organizations, they will be covered in the sections on corporate crime in Chapter 13.

Although gun control is a hotly debated topic in Canada, we have had a gun registry since the 1930s for handguns and from the early 1940s for long guns, both occurring during wartime. Changes to the law in the form of Bill C-51 in 1979, Bill C-17 in 1991, and Bill C-68 in 1995 occurred during peacetime.[42] There are many obstacles to acquiring a gun: firearm acquisition certificate screening, penalties for gun-related offences, strengthened prohibition orders, and provisions for safe handling and storage. Following the Montreal Massacre, carbines and high-capacity magazines became restricted.

Other legislative changes have involved mandatory reporting of gunshot wounds and firearm mandatory registration.[43] The gun registry was again revamped in 2004 to focus more on the criminal use of guns and to decriminalize registry offences. Public opinion is widely divided on the necessity of gun registration, with a majority favouring stricter laws for gun ownership in 2001, and then thinking that the gun registry should be scrapped in 2002.[44] Those who see crime as motivated by internal factors are less likely to support gun registration than are those who believe that it is access to guns that facilitates crime.[45]

So far, we have reviewed a few of the factors suspected to be causes of violent crime. In the remainder of the chapter, we turn our attention to the individual acts that make up violent crime in our society. When violence is directed toward strangers, it is said to be **instrumental**—designed to improve the financial or social position of the criminal, such as armed robbery. This is also **crime-related violence**. In contrast, **expressive violence** is designed to vent rage, anger, or frustration, as when a romantic triangle results in a murder. This is called **conflict-related violence**.

Among the common-law violent crimes are rape, murder, assault, and robbery. Newly recognized forms of violence are directed at specific targets. Included within this category are workplace crimes. In addition, violent, politically motivated crimes are commonly referred to as acts of terrorism.

Sexual Assault

Rape is defined under common law as "carnal knowledge of a female forcibly and against her will."[46] Under traditional common law, rape involved nonconsensual

Exhibit 11.2	Quick Code: Sexual Assault Law in Canada before 1983

143. A male person commits rape when he has sexual intercourse with a female person who is not his wife,

   a. Without her consent, or

   b. With her consent if the consent

       i. Is extorted by threats or fear of bodily harm,

       ii. Is obtained by personating her husband, or

       iii. Is obtained by false and fraudulent representations as to the nature and quality of the act

Source: C. Boyle, "Sexual Assault: A Case Study of Legal Policy Options," in *Canadian Criminology: Perspectives on Crime and Criminality*, ed. M. Jackson and C. Griffiths (Toronto: Harcourt Brace, 1991), p. 101.

sexual intercourse performed by a male against a female he is neither married to nor cohabiting with.[47] Until 1983, Canadian law provided an exemption for husbands accused of raping their wives (see Exhibit 11.2). This definition was removed in 1983 under a series of sweeping changes to sexual assault laws. The situation is different in some countries, however. In 1993, for example, Italy's Supreme Court accepted a husband's argument that he raped his wife in order to save their marriage.[48]

Traditionally, rape was viewed as a sexual offence. Even today, some men view rape as a sexual act, including one Tennessee judge who in 1994 released an accused rapist after stating that all the man needed was a girlfriend and telling the public defender's office to arrange for a dating service.[49]

Criminologists now consider rape to be a violent, coercive act of aggression, and the term has been changed to "sexual assault." The campaign to alert the public to the seriousness of rape, to initiate help for victims, and to change legal definitions to facilitate the prosecution of rape offenders has increased the reported rate of sexual assault because victims feel less reluctant to come forward and report the crime to police.

History of Rape

In early civilization, rape was common. Men staked a claim of ownership on women by forcibly abducting and raping them. This was part of male domination of women. In *Against Our Will*, Susan Brownmiller says the criminalization of rape occurred after the development of a monetary economy.[50] Thereafter, the violation of a virgin caused an economic hardship on her family, who expected a significant dowry for her hand in marriage. In Babylonian and Hebraic law, the rape of a virgin was a crime punishable by death. However, if the victim was a married woman, both she and her attacker were equally to blame. Unless her husband chose to intervene, the victim and her attacker were put to death.

During the Middle Ages, it was common for ambitious men to abduct and rape wealthy women to force them into marriage. "Heiress stealing" illustrates how feudal law gave little protection to women and equated them with property. Only in the fifteenth century was forcible sex outlawed and then only if the victim was of the nobility; raped peasant women and married women were not considered rape victims until well into sixteenth century. A woman who was raped was suspected of contributing to her attack.

InfoTrac®

If you are interested in reading more about the early history of violence in the West, look up Margaret Walsh, "New Horizons for the American West," *History Today* 44, no. 3 (1994): 44–51.

Sexual Assault and the Military

In 1998, allegations began to surface of sexual assault in the Canadian military. Although such stories are not new, what was shocking were accounts of women going to their superiors only to have their complaints discounted, to be told nothing could be done, or to hear it suggested *they* were to blame for the incidents.

Rape is associated with warfare, as conquering armies have long considered rape of their enemies' women one of the spoils of war. Among the ancient Greeks, rape was socially acceptable and well within the rules of warfare. During the Crusades, even knights and pilgrims, bound by vows of chivalry and Christian piety, raped as they marched toward Constantinople.

The practice has continued, from the Crusades through the war in Vietnam, to more recent conflicts. The systematic rape of Bosnian women by Serbian army officers during the civil war in Yugoslavia, part of an official policy of genocide, horrified the world. In Haiti, the rape of politically involved women became a norm in the wake of the 1991 military coup that ousted President Jean-Bertrand Aristide.[51] In Shabunda, an area of the Congo, it is estimated that more than three thousand women were raped between late 1999 and mid-2001. In Darfur, in the Sudan, thousands of women and girls have been raped since 2003, when an armed conflict began.

Incidence of Sexual Assault

How many sexual assaults occur each year, and what is known about rape patterns? In 2003, a total of 23 425 sexual assaults occurred in Canada, a rate of 74 per 100 000. Sexual assault has a lower clearance rate than do crimes of violence in general, partially due to the fact that the rate of sexual assault reported to the police has continued to increase over the years.[52]

Population density influences the rape rate: Metropolitan areas have a rape rate significantly higher than do rural areas. Nonetheless, urban areas have experienced a much higher drop in rape reports than have rural areas. Rape is also a warm-weather crime, usually occurring during July and August, with the lowest rates occurring during December, January, and February.

Data must be interpreted cautiously, because sexual assault is frequently underreported by victims. In Canada less than 10 percent of victims report the crime to the police.[53] Many are embarrassed, they believe nothing can be done, or they blame themselves. In a major American study on date rape, researchers found that only 27 percent of the women whose sexual assault met the legal definition of rape thought of themselves as rape victims.[54]

Males are victims of sexual assault too, although not nearly to the extent that women are. However, what we find are similar effects: depression, self-blame, low self-esteem, anger, anxiety, and sexuality problems.[55] Although most sexual assault perpetrators are male, females are responsible for between 1 percent and 4 percent of offences against youths.[56]

Official data often reflect reporting practices. Chapter 3 refers to this phenomenon as report-sensitive crime. At least 20 percent of adult women, 15 percent of university-aged women, and 12 percent of adolescent girls have experienced sexual abuse or assault sometime during their lifetime, so it is evident that both the official and the victimization statistics significantly undercount rape.[57] In Canada, 39 percent of women over 18 years of age report having experienced sexual assault in their adult lifetime, 5 percent in the previous year.[58] An independent study of sexual contact between physicians and patients conducted by the Ontario College of Physicians and Surgeons estimated that the rate of sexual abuse by doctors was nearly 10 percent.[59]

As Exhibit 11.3 shows, a large continuum of violence against women exists in our society, ranging from date rape and sexual assault to wife abuse and domestic violence. The fact that such crimes are examples of **gendered violence** should be obvious from the proportion of female victims and male offenders.

Types of Rapists

Some rapes are planned, others are spontaneous; some focus on a particular victim, while others occur during

Exhibit 11.3   Quick Facts about Sexual Assault

- The 2002 rate was 47 percent higher than the rate in 1983, the date reform legislation passed.

- The most common offence was unwanted touching (77 percent) rather than sexual attack (23 percent).

- Among spousal victims, 20 percent of women and 3 percent of men report incidents of sexual attack.

- More than 80 percent of victims are female, and more than half are between 15 and 25 years of age.

- In 2003, 60 percent of sexual assaults took place in residences, 8 percent on the street, and 4 percent in public institutions.

- Twenty-nine percent of child victims are male, as are 8 percent of adult victims and 12 percent of youth victims.

- Rates of victimization are highest among female teenagers.

- Rates of offending are highest among male teenagers.

- In 2002, rates varied from 160 per 100 000 in Saskatchewan to a low of 71 in Quebec.

- The rate of offending in the cities with the highest rates is more than three times the rate in cities with lowest rates.

- Sexual offences are the offences least likely to be reported to the police.

- The reasons for not reporting include the belief that it is a personal matter (50 percent), the person not wanting the police involved (47 percent), and the victim fearing revenge (19 percent).

- Sexual offences are the least likely violent crime to be founded and to result in charges.

Sources: Rebecca Kong, Holly Johnson, Sara Beattie, and Andrea Cardillo, "Sexual Offences in Canada," *Juristat* 23, no. 6 (2003); Statistics Canada, *Canadian Crime Statistics 2003* (Ottawa: Canadian Centre for Justice Statistics, 2004).

the commission of other crimes, such as burglary.[60] Some rapists are one-time offenders, while others engage in multiple or serial rapes. Some attack their victims without warning ("blitz rapes"); others try to "capture" their victims by striking up a conversation or by offering them a ride; others use a personal relationship to gain access to their target.[61]

One of the best-known attempts to classify the personality of rapists was made by Groth, a psychological expert on classification of sex offenders. He said every rape encounter contains three elements: anger, power, and sexuality:[62]

- *Anger rapes* are a discharge of pent-up anger and rage. The rapist uses brutality to hurt the victim as much as possible; the sexual aspect may be an afterthought. Often the anger rapist acts spontaneously after an upsetting incident has caused him conflict or aggravation. The woman is usually physically beaten; more likely to receive sympathy from her peers, relatives, and the justice system; and less likely to be accused of precipitating the attack.

- *Power rapes* involve an attacker whose goal is sexual conquest using only the amount of force necessary. He wants to be in control and to have women at his mercy. It is not sexual gratification that drives the power rapist, but personal insecurities about heterosexuality and manhood. The victim is usually younger, and the lack of evidence of physical violence may reduce the support given to the victim.

- *Sadistic rapes* involve aggression, and the victim might be abused, degraded, or tortured. Victims are usually related to a personal characteristic he wants to harm or destroy. This victim needs psychiatric care long after physical wounds have healed.

About 55 percent of rapists are of the power type; 40 percent, the anger type; and 5 percent, the sadistic type. The key issue is that rape is a crime of violence and not a sexual act. Rape might be committed during the course of another crime or be caused by intense anger toward women, but it is almost always a gendered crime committed by men against women.[63]

Types of Rape

Criminologists divide rapes into two categories: stranger rapes and acquaintance rapes. The former involve people who have never met, the latter involve someone known to the victim, even family members and friends. So-called date rape involves a sexual attack during a courting relationship.

It is difficult to estimate the ratio of rapes involving strangers to those in which victim and assailant were in some way acquainted, as women are more reluctant to report acts involving acquaintances. It used to be thought that 90 percent of sexual assaults involved strangers. However, in 2002 the CCJS reported the percentage of stranger sexual assaults at 20 percent, ranging from a low of 9 percent for children under age 12, to a high of 31 percent for adults over 18 years.[64]

Date Rape. In 1999, 26 percent of rapes involved family members, 14 percent were committed by strangers, 5 percent were unknown, and fully 55 percent involved acquaintances.[65] Since women are less likely to report crimes involving acquaintances, it is possible that acquaintance rape, referred to as **date rape**, constitutes the bulk of sexual assaults.

Some date rapes occur on first dates, others after a relationship has been developing, and still others after the couple have been involved. The male may feel he has invested so much time and money in his partner that he is owed sexual relations or that sexual intimacy is an expression that the involvement is progressing.[66]

A survey of Canadian college women found that about one-third had experienced an episode of physical, verbal, or psychological sexual coercion; 25 percent said they had had unwanted sexual relations during the previous year.[67]

The incidence of date rape may be even higher than surveys indicate because many victims blame themselves and do not recognize the incident as a rape, saying, for example, "I should have fought back harder," "I should not have gotten drunk." Some victims do not report because they do not view their experiences as a "real rape," which they believe involves a strange man "jumping out of the bushes"; others are too embarrassed or frightened to report the crime.[68]

To fight back, some campus women's groups have taken to writing on bathroom walls the names of men accused of date rape and sexual assault, as a way to alert potential victims to the danger they face from men whom they might have considered trustworthy friends.[69]

Another disturbing phenomenon is campus gang rape, in which a group of men attack a defenceless or inebriated victim; another trend is the growing number of women reporting that they have been raped while sedated by the "date rape drug," Rohypnol.[70]

 InfoTrac®

Does watching films that degrade women influence the commission of a date rape? To find out, read Michael Milburn, Roxanne Mather, and Sheree D. Conrad, "The Effects of Viewing R-Rated Movie Scenes That Objectify Women on Perceptions of Date Rape," *Sex Roles* 43 (2000): 645.

Marital Rape. Some women are raped by their husbands as part of an overall pattern of spousal abuse, often accompanied by brutal and sadistic beatings.[71]

Until recently, a legally married husband could not be charged with raping his wife, referred to as the **marital exemption**. This legal doctrine can be traced to the sixteenth-century pronouncement of Matthew Hale, England's chief justice, who wrote, "The husband cannot be guilty of rape committed by himself upon his lawful wife, for by their mutual matrimonial consent and contract the wife hath given up herself in this kind unto the husband which she cannot retract."[72] The exemption was abolished in Canada in 1983.[73] In 1980 only three American states had laws against marital rape; today almost every state recognizes marital rape as a crime.

The Cause of Rape

What factors cause rape? The answers formulated by criminologists are varied; however, most explanations can be grouped into a few categories.

Evolutionary/Biological Factors. One explanation focuses on evolutionary/biological aspects of the male sexual drive that may have once served the purpose of maximizing offspring. Some believe that males still have a natural sexual drive that encourages them to have intimate relations with as many women as possible.[74] Men who are sexually aggressive will have the reproductive edge over their more passive peers. In contrast, women are more cautious and want to choose stable partners who are willing to make a long-term commitment to childrearing. This difference produces sexual tension that causes men to use forceful copulatory tactics, especially when the chances of punishment are quite low.[75]

Male Socialization. In contrast, some researchers argue that rape is a function of male socialization.[76] Boys are taught to be aggressive and led to believe that females want to be dominated. If males learn to separate sexual feelings from love and affection and are socialized to be the aggressors, then sexual inexperience is a mark of shame. Similarly, sexually aggressive women frighten men and cause them to doubt their own masculinity. Sexual insecurity may lead some men to commit rape to bolster their self-image and masculine identity.

If rape is an expression of male anger and the devaluation of women, men socialized into traditional sex-role stereotypes are more likely to be sexually aggressive.

Connections

In Chapter 9 Messerschmidt described how the need to prove their masculinity helps men to justify their abuse of women. Men who are sexually violent need to prove that they are not effeminate.

Psychological Views. Another view is that rapists have some type of personality disorder or mental illness. Incarcerated rapists often exhibit psychotic tendencies, while others have hostile and sadistic feelings toward women.[77]

Social Learning. Men often learn to commit rapes and are influenced by watching violent or pornographic films featuring women who are beaten, raped, or tortured.[78] In one case, a 12-year-old boy in Providence, Rhode Island, sexually assaulted a 10-year-old girl on a pool table after watching TV coverage of a case in which a woman was similarly raped.[79] (The case was made into a film, *The Accused*, starring Jodie Foster.)

Connections

The social learning view is explored further in Chapter 14, where the issue of pornography and violence is analyzed in greater detail. Most research does not link watching "porno films" to sexual violence, but there may be a link between sexual aggression and viewing movies with sexual violence as their theme.

Sexual Motivation. Most current views of rape hold that it is a violent act. Yet there might still be a sexual motive from some rapes:[80] Although older criminals may be raping for motives of power and control, younger offenders are seeking sexual gratification.

In sum, rape is the product of a number of social, cultural, and psychological forces.[81] Although some experts view rape as a normal response to an abnormal environment, others view it as the product of a disturbed mind and deviant life experiences.

Rape and the Law

Women are reluctant to report this crime because of how rape victims are often treated by police, prosecutors, and court personnel. In the past, police were reluctant to make arrests, and courts reluctant to convict, in cases where the woman was not beaten seriously or in which she had previously known her attacker. Laws made rape so difficult to prove that women believed the chances of their attacker being convicted were insufficient to warrant their participation in the prosecutorial process.

However, police and courts have become more sensitive and are now just as likely to investigate "acquaintance" rapes as they are "aggravated" rapes involving multiple offenders, weapons, and victim injuries. The justice system is more willing to take rape cases seriously and not ignore those in which the victim and attacker had a prior relationship or those that did not involve serious injury.[82]

Proving Rape. Proving guilt in a rape case is challenging because some psychiatrists still maintain that women create false accusations.[83]

Sexism has created a cultural suspicion of women. Consequently, there is an attempt to shift the burden to the woman and prove that she provoked the rape.

Jurors are sometimes swayed by the insinuation that the rape was victim-precipitated, thus shifting blame from rapist to victim. To get a conviction, prosecutors must establish that the act was forced and that voluntary compliance doesn't exist.

Rape represents a major legal challenge.[84] One issue is **consent.** Proving victim dissent is not a requirement in any other violent crime (robbery victims do not have to prove they did not entice their attacker by flaunting expensive jewellery), yet in rape cases defence counsel can try to create a reasonable doubt about the woman's credibility under sections 265.4 and 276.1 of the *Criminal Code.* A defence attorney might try to introduce suspicion in the minds of the jury that the woman may have consented to the sexual act and later regretted her decision.[85]

Law Reform. Because of the difficulty victims have had in receiving justice in rape cases, legislation in Canada has undergone significant change since 1983. Efforts for reform have included changing the language of statutes, dropping the conditions of recent complaint and corroboration, and developing **shield laws** protecting women from being questioned about their sexual history unless it is judged to have a direct bearing on the case. These changes are quickly becoming an international standard.[86]

In addition to requiring evidence that consent was not given, the common law of rape required **corroboration** that the crime of rape actually took place. This involved the need for independent or third-party evidence from police officers, physicians, and witnesses that the accused was actually the person who committed the crime, that sexual penetration took place, and that force was present and consent absent.[87] Current law does not require corroboration, intercourse, or a complaint to be filed immediately.

In the early 1990s, consent became legally required, and it is considered impossible for consent to be given when the victim is too drunk to know what was happening. Section 273.1 of Canada's *Criminal Code* requires that sexual activity be voluntary. No consent is obtained, where

- the agreement is expressed by someone else
- the complainant is incapable of consenting to the activity
- the accused induces the complainant to engage in the activity by abusing a position of trust, power, or authority
- the complainant expresses, by words or conduct, a lack of agreement to engage in the activity
- the complainant, having consented to engage in sexual activity, expresses, by words or conduct, a lack of agreement to continue to engage in the activity

Therefore, sexual assault laws make illegal any type of forcible or nonconsensual sex. However, the credibility of sexual assault victims is still more likely to be challenged than is testimony of victims of nonsexual assault.[88]

For example, a psychologist found that judges tend to characterize sexual assault as erotic rather than as violent, that the consent laws are not applied uniformly, and that only when the victim resists an unwanted advance will the court recognize lack of consent.[89]

Clearly, more efforts are needed to improve the prosecution rate in sexual assault cases.

Murder

To prove murder has been committed with malice, prosecutors must prove that the accused intentionally desired the death of the victim. Malice is assumed to exist when someone kills another in the absence of apparent provocation. Implied malice exists when death results from negligent behaviour; even though the perpetrator did not want to kill the victim, the killing was the result of a dangerous act and is considered murder.

Degrees of Murder

Murder is defined in the common law as "the unlawful killing of a human being with malice aforethought." Exhibit 11.4 details some facts about homicide in Canada.

There are different levels or degrees of homicide.[90] This categorization came about with the abolition of capital punishment in 1976. Murder in the first degree occurs when a person kills after deliberation. **Premeditation** means that the killing was considered beforehand and that it was more than an act of impulse.

Second-degree murder requires the actor to have malice but not premeditation, and it occurs when disregard for the victim or the desire to inflict serious bodily harm results in the loss of life.

An unlawful homicide without malice is called manslaughter. Voluntary manslaughter refers to a killing committed in the heat of passion or during a sudden quarrel with sufficient provocation to produce violence; although intent may be present, malice is not. Involuntary or negligent manslaughter refers to a killing that occurs when a person's acts are negligent and without regard for the harm that they may cause others. Most involuntary manslaughter cases involve motor vehicle deaths, as when a drunk driver causes the death of a pedestrian. However, people can be held criminally liable for the death of another in any instance in which the actor's disregard of safety causes the death.

Exhibit 11.4	**Quick Facts about Homicide in Canada**

- Police departments reported 548 homicides in Canada in 2003, down from the number in 2002.
- Stabbing (31 percent) accounted for most deaths in 2002, followed by shooting (26 percent), beating (21 percent), and strangulation (11 percent).
- Homicide rates increase from East to West, with Newfoundland and Labrador having the lowest rate (0.4 per 100 000 population), compared with Manitoba (3.1 per 100 000 population), in 2002.
- Canada's largest urban areas have homicide rates consistent with nonurban areas.
- Homicide between gang members dropped substantially in 2002, after tripling between 1992 and 2000.
- In 2003, acquaintances were the perpetrators in 29 percent of solved homicides, family members in 18 percent, and strangers in 21 percent. In 32 percent of cases, the relationship was unknown.
- In 75 percent of the murder cases of a child under 12 years, the killer is a parent.
- The father is more than twice as likely to be the killer of a child than is the mother.
- Two-thirds of those accused of homicide had a prior criminal history, 73 percent of which were for a violent offence in 2002.
- Spousal-related homicides account for one out of every five solved homicides in 2002.
- The greatest risk of being a homicide victim occurs during the first two years of life.
- Natives account for 3 percent of the population but 21 percent of those accused of homicide and 14 percent of homicide victims.
- Youths represent 8 percent of those accused of homicide, and most of them are males.
- Almost one-third of all homicides occur during the commission of another offence.
- Police reported that 52 percent of homicide victims and 68 percent of accused had consumed alcohol and/or drugs.

Source: Adapted from the Statistics Canada publication "Homicide in Canada," 2002, *Juristat*, Catalogue 85-002, vol. 23, no. 8, October 1, 2003.

The Nature and Extent of Murder

The Homicide Survey details information on all homicide offences in Canada since 1961. Homicide is relatively rare, with only 548 offences in 2003. The rate of homicide in the United States was 5.5 per 100 000 in 2003, compared with 1.8 in Canada.[91]

What else do the official crime statistics tell us about murder today? Murder victims tend to be males over 18 years of age. Murder, like many crimes, tends to be an intraracial crime, committed by people against members of their own ethnic group. Most homicides involve a single victim, and most (75 percent to 85 percent) are solved by the police. Few people are killed by a stranger, and most are killed during a conflict (57 percent), not during the course of another crime. Youths (12 to 17) accounted for 8 percent of all accused persons in 2002, which was lower than the 1992–2001 average. Males represented 65 percent of homicide victims in 2002, and 52 percent were between 18 and 39 years of age.

The next section explores the relationship between social and ecological factors and murder.

Murderous Relations

One factor that has received a great deal of attention from criminologists is the relationship between the murderer and the victim. Criminologists separate murders into those involving strangers—typically stemming from a crime, such as a robbery or drug deal—and acquaintance homicides involving disputes between family, friends, and acquaintances. The quality of relationships and interpersonal interactions may thus influence murder.

Connections

Chapter 4's discussion of victim precipitation theory mentioned the argument made by some criminologists that murder victims help create the "transaction" that leads to their death.

Spousal Relations. Women are more likely to be killed by their mates than are men. In Canada since 1974, three-quarters of victims who were killed by someone they had an intimate relationship with were women. Although the number of unmarried men killed by their partners declined in the late 1990s, the rate of women killed by the men they lived with increased dramatically. Men kill their spouses because they fear losing control and power. Because people who live together without marriage have a legally and socially more "open" relationship, cohabiting males are more likely to feel loss of control and exert their power by using violence. In contrast, research indicates that females who kill their mates do so after suffering repeated violent attacks.[92] Between 1991 and 2000, separated women aged 15 to 24 were killed at a rate of 113 per million, compared with fewer than 10 women

per million among separated women aged 55 years and older. Women have a heightened risk of homicide after separation, and the motive is most often male jealousy.[93]

Women Who Kill. Statistics Canada data show that although the killing of children represents a small proportion of the total number of homicides in Canada, it represents the largest proportion of killing done by women (24 percent). Infanticide is usually committed by very young women (69 percent are under 21 years old), and the vast majority of accused (70 percent) are single. Finally, 67 percent of these women have a mental illness.[94]

Children Who Kill. There are five categories of homicide for youths: parents, siblings, other family, friends, and no relationship. The rate of homicide committed by youths rises as youth approach 18 years of age, and most of the homicides involve only one offender and one victim. The most common method of homicide for youths is guns, followed by knives. The most common targets are friends and acquaintances. Seventy percent of all homicides committed by youths in Canada are theft-related. Contrary to predictions, young children are more likely to use guns than are older children. Also, younger children's victims are more likely to be family members, whereas older children are more likely to kill in the commission of other crimes and are more likely to kill strangers.[95]

Stranger Relations. Although people fear stranger homicide, the actual number is fairly low. Most stranger homicides occur during the commission of other offences, such as assault, robbery, and sexual assault. Very few murders are random or motiveless, such as would occur if a homeowner told a motorist to move his car because it is blocking the driveway and in the ensuing argument got a pistol and killed the motorist.[96]

How do murderous relations develop between two people who have never met? Luckenbill's study of murder transactions found common sequential patterns of behaviour in the transaction between killer and victim: The victim makes what the perpetrator considers an offensive move; the perpetrator typically retaliates in a verbal or physical manner; and in the ensuing fight, the victim is slain or injured.[97]

Conversely, Kennedy and Silverman found that the elderly are likely to be the victims of theft-based homicide, by strangers, in their homes. Even though routine activities theory would suggest that the elderly are least likely to be victimized by homicide, in cases of household theft, they stand a high risk. This is because it is usually the house that is the intended victim of the crime, and the elderly are victimized during the course of the crime.[98]

Youths living on the street, however, experience violence certainly as a result of the activities they engage in and almost as a part of their culture.[99]

InfoTrac®

In some school shooting incidents, the perpetrators claim to have been picked on and bullied by the school's star athletes. Did you know that in sports, a team often reflects the personality of the coach? If the coach is very aggressive, players may follow this example. To research the effects of coaching on team violence, use "sports violence" as keywords. You may want to read this article as well: Edgar Shields, "Intimidation and Violence by Males in High School Athletics," *Adolescence* 34, no. 135 (1999): 503.

Homicide Networks

Although some murders may be the result of wanton violence by a stranger, others involve a social interaction between people who know each other and whose destructive social interaction leads to death.[100] These seemingly senseless deaths often mask an underlying cause: revenge, dispute resolution, jealousy, bad drug deals, racial bias, or threats to identity or status.[101] Perpetrators and victims are joined in a "homicide network" that links victims, suspects, and witnesses together.

Often a prior act of violence, motivated by profit or greed, generates revenge killings. The instigator of one criminal act becomes the victim in another. Those individuals who are most isolated from conventional society are those most likely to seek "street justice." Witness the battle between the Hells Angels and the Rock Machine motorcycle gangs in Quebec. The combatants take the victimization of family and friends seriously, setting up a murderous exchange with the people they feel are responsible.[102]

Types of Murderers

Other forms of stranger homicides take a toll on society. **Thrill killings** involve impulsive violence motivated by the killer's decision to kill a stranger as an act of daring or recklessness.

Gang killings involve members of gangs who make violence part of their group activity. Some of these gangs engage in warfare over territory or control of the drug trade; in drive-by shootings, enemies are killed and strangers are sometimes caught in the crossfire.

Cult killings occur when members of religious cults are ordered to kill by their leaders. On some occasions, the cult members kill peers who deviate from the leader's teachings. Other crimes involve random violence against strangers, either as a show of loyalty or because of the misguided belief that the strangers are a threat to the cult's existence. In Matamoros, Mexico, police uncovered the grave of a 21-year-old American college student who had served as a human sacrifice for members of a Mexican drug ring that practised *palo mayombe*, a form of black magic; killing the youth was believed to bring immunity from bullets and criminal prosecution.[103]

In 1994, bodies were recovered in homes belonging to the Order of the Solar Temple cult in Switzerland and Montreal. Some members of the apocalyptic cult were murdered, while others committed suicide. The cult combined teachings from medieval orders, such as the Knights Templar, and the leaders appropriated their followers' wealth for their own personal gain. Police speculated the cult's leaders were involved in an international money-laundering and arms-smuggling operation as well.

Some murders blamed on Satanism are not carried out by members of an organized group but are perpetrated by individuals who have visions of the Devil. In 1993, a 15-year-old Houston boy killed his mother after hearing the Devil tell him to "kill all the Christians"; law enforcement officials linked the boy's passion for heavy metal music to the crime.[104]

InfoTrac®

Serial killers are not a new phenomenon. To read about the history of such gruesome acts, read Bernard Capp, "Serial Killers in Seventeenth-Century England," *History Today* 46, no. 3 (1996): 21.

Serial Murder

Donald Harvey was described as pleasant and normal by those who knew him best. However, his coworkers in a Cincinnati-area hospital where he worked as a nurse's aide referred to Harvey as the "angel of death" because so many patients died in his ward. An investigation led to Harvey being convicted of killing at least 21 patients. He said he was a mercy killer who "gained relief for the patients."[105]

Some serial murderers, such as Theodore (Ted) Bundy, roam the country killing at random. Others terrorize a city, such as the Los Angeles–based Night Stalker; the Green River Killer, who is believed to have slain more than four dozen young women in Seattle;

and the Hillside Stranglers, Kenneth Bianchi and Angelo Buono, who tortured and killed 10 women in the Los Angeles area. Others, such as Donald Harvey and Milwaukee cannibal Jeffrey Dahmer, kill so cunningly that many victims are dispatched before the authorities even realize the deaths can be attributed to a single perpetrator.[106]

Robert Pickton, a Canadian pig farmer, has been charged with murdering at least 23 of Vancouver's missing women. It is alleged that he lured women to his farm, where he assaulted and killed them. If he is convicted on all counts, he will be Canada's worst serial killer.

Serial killers operate over a long period and can be distinguished from the **mass murderer**, who kills many victims in a single, violent outburst, such as Thomas Hamilton's outburst in Dunblane, Scotland, or James Huberty's murder of 21 people in a McDonald's restaurant in San Ysidro, California.

Types of Serial Murderers. Research shows that serial killers have long histories of violence, beginning in childhood with the targeting of other children, siblings, and small animals.[107] They maintain superficial relationships with others, have trouble relating to the opposite sex, and have guilt feelings about sex. Despite these commonalities, there is no single distinct type of serial killer.

Mental illness, sexual frustration, neurological damage, child abuse and neglect, smothering relationships

Culture, Gender, Ethnicity, and Criminology

The Death of James Bulger

On February 12, 1993, the security cameras at a shopping centre near Liverpool, England, recorded two-year-old James Bulger being abducted by two strangers. He was taken on a long walk, cruelly tortured, sexually abused, beaten to death, and abandoned on the railroad tracks. Jon Venables and Robert Thompson, his murderers, were 10 years old. When arrested and questioned, they each denied their role in the murder and blamed the other.

Jon's psychological profile showed that he was generally well behaved but sometimes hyperactive. His mother thought that Jon was the victim of bullies

Preacher Spells out Britain's Moral Decline

By Victoria Combe, Churches Correspondent

The American evangelist Morris Cerullo yesterday took two full-page adverts in broadsheet newspapers, costing more than £40,000, to outline Britain's "rapid moral and spiritual decline". . . .

Mr Cerullo claimed Britain's laws, formerly a model of Christian principles for other governments, had been "eroded" since the 1960s by "atheists, rationalists and confused spiritual leaders". . . .

Listing disasters such as Hillsborough, Lockerbie and the Jamie Bulger killing, he said Britain was in a state of "rapid decline morally, spiritually and materially". [The] British people want political leaders who tell them the truth. Men and women who live honestly. They want unconfused Church leaders. "The nation wants men of integrity who lead by what God of the Bible has to say, not what they think may be politically acceptable."

Source: *Electronic Telegraph*, Monday, July 29, 1996.

at school. Jon's parents had repeatedly split up and reunited, undermining the family as a source of stability. Jon seemed to have low self-esteem and was defensive about his family. He had a history of self-inflicted violence: banging his head against the wall and cutting himself with scissors. He was also destructive at school. Both his siblings had

developmental problems, and his parents had histories of clinical depression. His mother had, on occasion, physically and verbally assaulted Jon.

Robert's psychological profile showed that he was intelligent and had no sign of mental illness or depression. However, he was often assaulted by his older brothers and alcoholic mother.

His father beat his wife and eventually abandoned the family. Both his mother and father came from abusive families. One of his brothers had been placed in protective services after he had been abused. Another was a thief, and another was an arsonist and suspected of sexually abusing young children.

An important issue in the trial was whether the boys knew the difference between right and wrong. The concept of *doli incapax* was established to protect innocent children from punishment and dates back to Roman law. If a child cannot grasp the consequences of his or her actions, he or she is legally incapable of wrongdoing. Jon and Robert's teachers and psychiatrists testified that they believed the defendants knew the severity of their crime. The interviews recorded by the police also revealed that the boys understood the charges against them.

The judge addressed the boys: "The killing of James Bulger was an act of unparalleled evil and barbarity. This child of two was taken from his mother on a journey of over two miles and then, on the railway line, was battered to death without mercy. Then his body was placed across the railway line so it would be run over by a train in an attempt to conceal his murder. In my judgment your conduct was both cunning and very wicked."

With their conviction for the murder of James Bulger, Jon Venables and Robert Thompson became the youngest convicted murderers in Britain in 250 years. Their original sentence of 15 years was overturned when the European Court of Human Rights decreed in 1999 that the boys had not received a fair trial and mandated their release after eight years in jail. In a newspaper phone poll, 96 percent of the British public protested that the boys had been released. Because of the public outcry over the killing, Jon and Robert have been given false identities for their own safety.

Sources: Blake Morrison, "Children of Circumstance," *The New Yorker,* February 14, 1994, 48–60; Shirley Lynn Scott, "The Death of James Bulger," Court TV's Crime Library, http://www .crimelibrary.com/classics3/bulger/ (accessed May 14, 2005).

---

with mothers, and childhood anxiety are possible reasons that people become serial killers. However, most experts view serial killers as sociopaths who, from early childhood, demonstrate bizarre behaviour, such as torturing animals, who are immune to their victims' suffering, and who bask in the media limelight. However, Philip Jenkins's study of serial murder in England identified one group of offenders who had no apparent personality problems until late in their lives, were married and respectable, and even had careers in the armed services and police.[108]

Holmes and DeBurger have studied serial killers and found that they can be divided into at least four types:

1. *Visionary killers*: commit psychotic murders in response to an inner voice or vision that demands that some person be killed
2. *Mission-oriented killers*: are motivated to rid the world of a particular type of person that they consider undesirable, such as prostitutes
3. *Hedonistic killers*: are thrill-seeking murderers who get excitement and sexual pleasure from their acts
4. *Power/control-oriented killers*: enjoy having complete control over their victims[109]

Other types of serial killers include the sadistic child killer, who gains sexual satisfaction from torturing and killing children; the psychopathic killer, who is motivated by a character disorder that results in their being unable to experience feelings of shame, guilt, or other normal human emotions; and professional hit killers, who assassinate complete strangers for economic, political, or ideological reasons (terrorists and organized crime figures fall within this category).

When the Serial Killer Is a Woman. An estimated 10 percent to 15 percent of serial killers are women.[110] Female killers are older than males and usually abuse both alcohol and drugs. These women are often diagnosed as having histrionic, bipolar, borderline, dissociative, and antisocial personality disorders.

The female serial killer is a person who smothers or poisons someone she knows. During childhood, she suffered from an abusive relationship in a disrupted family. Female killers' education levels are below average, and if they work, it is in a low-status position.

Controlling Serial Killers. Serial killers come from diverse backgrounds. Police are often at a loss to control random killers who leave few clues, constantly move, and have little connection with victims. In the 1980s, because of a series of high-profile serial homicides that encompassed multiple jurisdictions, a better way for police to share information was proposed. The "automated case linkage system," called ViCLAS (Violent Crime Linkage Analysis System), helps police profile cases and identify potential suspects. It was modelled on the computerized information service developed by the FBI, called the Violent Criminal Apprehension Program (VICAP), which

gathers information and matches offence characteristics on violent crimes around the country.[111]

Philip Jenkins has studied serial killing over the past 50 years and reports an upsurge since the 1960s. In addition, the number of victims per criminal and the ferocity and savagery of the killings also seem to be increasing. Jenkins attributes this increase to a variety of influences, ranging from a permissive, drug-abusing culture to a mental health system so overcrowded that potentially dangerous people are released without supervision.[112]

 Famous Canadian Court Cases

Arthur Lucas and Ronald Turpin

The exact number of Canadian executions for capital offences is unknown because the government began systematically recording the names, dates, and places involved only after Confederation in 1867. Although the identities of many Canadians condemned to death will never be uncovered, Ronald Turpin and Arthur Lucas will likely always be remembered. Shortly after midnight on December 11, 1962, theirs were the final two of more than seven hundred names to be entered in Department of Justice ledgers. Lucas and Turpin are thus associated with a defining moment in Canadian criminal justice history: the abolition of capital punishment.

Surprisingly, these doomed men were actually quite advantaged compared to individuals executed in earlier years. Lucas and Turpin lived during a time when the only crimes warranting the death penalty were certain types of murders: those that were planned and deliberate, those occurring during the commission of violent crimes, and those involving on-duty

police and corrections officers. The days were long over when people could be executed for almost any offence, like one unfortunate man hanged in Halifax in 1795 for stealing a few potatoes. Lucas and Turpin had the right to secure legal counsel, give evidence on their own behalf, and appeal their death sentence, unlike many of their predecessors. Nevertheless, both of these men received the ultimate sanction for the ultimate crime.

Lucas had murder on his mind when he drove to Toronto to confront Therland Carter, a pimp and material witness in a pending American narcotics trial. The Detroit native stabbed Carter to death on November 17, 1961. He chose not to spare Carol Newman, a prostitute who was with Carter at the time of the altercation. On February 12, 1962, Turpin shot and killed Metropolitan Toronto police constable Frederick Nash. Not only was Turpin wanted for questioning in relation to a shooting that transpired the year before, but he had also just robbed the Red Rooster Restaurant of $632.84 when he was pulled over for a broken

taillight. Turpin shot Nash in the chest with a .32 calibre handgun before attempting to flee in the slain officer's cruiser.

Lucas and Turpin came from different walks of life, but they shared the same fate. Both were arrested, tried, convicted, and executed within 14 months. They were represented by the same defence counsel and ate the same last meal. At the ages of 54 and 29, Lucas and Turpin were hanged at Toronto's Don Jail while an angry crowd protested outside the prison gates. They were buried side by side in unmarked graves. Although Lucas and Turpin were shown no mercy by the governor general, all remaining death sentences in Canada were thereafter commuted to life imprisonment. In July 1976, capital punishment officially met its end when Parliament passed a bill to abolish the practice by a meagre six votes. The government rejected a motion to reinstate the death penalty 11 years later by 148 votes to 127, but the debate over capital punishment continues.

Prepared by Andrea Wolf.

43%   57%
YES NO

When asked whether the death penalty should be restored as a sentencing option for particularly heinous murders, 43 percent of respondents said yes, while 57 percent said no.

Source: Poll conducted by *The Globe and Mail*, June 18, 2004.

Assault

In 2003, the Canadian Centre for Justice Statistics reported 248 402 nonsexual assaults had occurred, a rate of 785 per 100 000 inhabitants. Assaults have a clearance rate of 75 percent. The majority of the perpetrators are male (81 percent), and only 13 percent are youths.

Assault in the Home

One of the most frightening aspects of assault is the incidence of violent attacks in the home. Exhibit 11.5 displays some facts about violence against children. Intrafamily violence is a serious social problem in our society, and one area that has received a great deal of media attention is **child abuse**. This term describes any physical or emotional trauma to a child for which no reasonable explanation, such as an accident, can be found.[113]

Some people believe that ordinary disciplinary practices, such as spanking, are abuse, but spanking is protected under Section 43 of the *Criminal Code*. It allows parents and teachers to use reasonable force when correcting a child.

Child abuse can result from actual physical beatings administered to a child by hands, feet, weapons, belts, sticks, burning, and so on. An estimated three to five babies per million are affected by shaken baby syndrome in North America every year. Another form of abuse results from neglect—not providing a child with the care and shelter to which he or she is entitled. It is difficult to estimate the actual number of child abuse cases, since so many incidents are never reported to the police.

According to the 1998 *Canadian Incidence Study of Reported Child Abuse and Neglect*, the main reasons for child maltreatment investigations are neglect (40 percent), physical abuse (31 percent), emotional maltreatment (19 percent), and sexual abuse (10 percent).[114]

Exhibit 11.5	Quick Facts about Violence Against Children and Youths in Families, 2002

- Children under 18 make up 23 percent of the population, but account for 61 percent of sexual offence victims.
- Physical assault victims are usually male (62 percent); sexual assault victims are usually female (80 percent).
- Between 1974 and 2000, 63 percent of youth and child homicides were perpetrated by family members.
- Offenders are usually male in physical assault cases (78 percent) and sexual assault cases (98 percent).
- The estimated rate of abuse and neglect is 21 cases per 100 children.
- In assaults against children and youths, 52 percent were assaulted by acquaintances, 23 percent by family members, and 19 percent by strangers. In 6 percent of cases, the relationship was unknown.
- In sexual assaults against children and youths, 49 percent were assaulted by acquaintances, 30 percent by family members, and 15 percent by strangers. In 6 percent of cases, the relationship was unknown.
- For victims sexually assaulted by a family member, parents were the main perpetrator (39 percent), followed by siblings (32 percent), and extended family members (29 percent).
- For victims of physical assault by a family member, parents were the main perpetrator (67 percent), followed by siblings (18 percent), and extended family members (8 percent). In 7 percent of cases, the relationship was unknown.
- In 1994, in cases of the kidnapping/abduction of boys, parents were the perpetrators in 43 percent and friends in 19 percent. In cases of the kidnapping/abduction of girls, parents were the perpetrators in 25 percent and friends in 35 percent.
- Overall, in cases of kidnapping/abduction, the parents were the perpetrators in 33 percent, acquaintances in 28 percent, and strangers in 25 percent in 1994.
- In 1994, 11 percent of violent incidents involving children and youths occurred on school property.

Sources: Catherine Trainor, ed., *Family Violence in Canada: A Statistical Profile 2002* (Ottawa: Canadian Centre for Justice Statistics, 2002); CCJS, "Children and Youths as Victims of Violent Crimes," *Juristat* 15, no. 15 (1995).

In Canada, 6 percent of the victims of violent crime are children under 12, while 20 percent are aged 12 to 19. In general, boys and girls are equally likely to be the victims of violent crimes. However, boys are more likely to be the victims of homicide, while girls are more likely to be sexually abused.[115] More than one million children a year in the United States are subject to physical abuse from their parents.[116] Physical abuse is rarely a one-time event, and children of all ages suffer abuse.

Another aspect of the abuse syndrome is **sexual abuse**—the exploitation of children through rape, incest, and molestation by parents or other adults. It is difficult to estimate the incidence of sexual abuse. Many allegations of sexual impropriety have been made against religious figures, such as priests, and Boy Scout leaders.[117] Many Canadian organizations that use the services of volunteers now have their applicants screened by the police for a criminal record.

One survey found that 38 percent of women had experienced intrafamilial or extrafamilial sexual abuse by the time they reached age 18.[118] A survey of students in grades 6, 9, and 12 found about 2 percent of males and 7 percent of females had experienced incest, while 4 percent of males and 13 percent of females had suffered extrafamilial sexual abuse. Other research indicates one in five girls suffers sexual abuse.[119]

These results likely underestimate the incidence of sexual abuse. It is difficult to get people to answer questions about youthful sexual abuse, and young victims might not understand their abuse or have repressed their memories of the incidents. Children, the most common target, may be inhibited because parents are reluctant to admit abuse occurred. One study found that 57 percent of children referred to a clinic because they had sexually transmitted diseases claimed not to have been molested despite this irrefutable physical evidence. Parental response significantly influences reporting abuse: Kids whose caretakers admitted the possibility of abuse were 3.5 times more likely to report abuse than those whose parents denied any possibility that their children were victims.[120]

The growing incidence of sexual abuse is of particular concern when its long-term impacts are considered. Abused kids experience fear, posttraumatic stress disorder, behaviour problems, sexualized behaviour, and poor self-esteem. The amount of force used, its duration, and its frequency are all related to the extent of the long-term effects and the length of time needed for recovery.[121]

Causes of Child Abuse

Why do parents physically assault their children? This is a highly complex problem, cutting across ethnic, religious, and socioeconomic lines. Abusive parents come from all walks of life.

However, one factor associated with systematic child abuse is familial stress. Abusive parents are unable to cope with life crises—divorce, financial problems, alcohol and other drug abuse, poor housing conditions. This inability leads them to maltreat their children. A higher rate of assault on children occurs among lower economic classes; however, this doesn't mean that lower-class parents are more abusive than those in the upper classes. First, low-income people are often subject to greater levels of environmental stress and have fewer resources to deal with it. Second, abuse among poor families is more likely to be dealt with by public agencies and therefore is more frequently counted in official statistics.[122]

Other characteristics that are related are the presence of a stepparent in the household, young parents, poor parenting skills, marital violence, alcohol or other drug abuse, large family size, poverty, unemployment, and disability in the child.[123]

Two other factors have a direct correlation with abuse and neglect. First, parents who themselves suffered abuse as children tend to abuse their own children; second, isolated and alienated families tend to become abusive. A cyclical pattern of family violence is perpetuated from one generation to another. A large number of abused and neglected children grow into adolescence and adulthood with a tendency to engage in violent behaviour. The behaviour of abusive parents can be traced to negative experiences in their own childhood—physical abuse, lack of love, emotional neglect, and incest. These parents become unable to separate their own childhood traumas from their relationships with their children. They have unrealistic perceptions of the appropriate stages of childhood development. Thus, when their children are unable to act "appropriately"—when they cry, throw food, or strike their parents—the parents may react in an abusive manner: "A fussy baby can be the lighted match."[124]

Parents can also become abusive if they are isolated. Potentially or actually abusing parents live in states of alienation, cut off from contact with other people in the neighbourhood and lacking close relationships with people who could provide help and support.

Public concern about child abuse has led to the development of programs designed to prevent and deter it. The reporting of child abuse by doctors, social workers, and other such persons is mandated by law. As well, Human Resources Development Canada (HRDC) implemented the National Longitudinal Survey of Children and Youth in 1994, which follows 25 000 children as they grow to adulthood, in order to collect data about child welfare in Canada.

Spouse Abuse

On the evening of June 23, 1993, John Wayne Bobbitt came home and, according to his wife, Lorena, committed a marital rape. Afterward, while he slept, Lorena used a 30-centimetre (12-inch) kitchen knife to slice off two-thirds of his penis, which she then threw into a field. Police officers recovered the penis, and it was surgically reattached.

Bobbitt was acquitted on charges of sexual assault and Lorena was found not guilty by reason of insanity on a charge of malicious wounding. No longer considered a threat (at least to anyone other than her former husband), she was released.[125]

Although highly publicized, this case is misleading: Spouse abuse overwhelmingly involves a physical assault in which a wife is injured by a husband.[126] There are indeed some cases of husband battering, but they typically involve a defensive measure taken by a previously abused spouse, according to Schwartz and DeKeseredy.[127]

Connections

In Chapter 4, the case of Angelique Lyn Lavallee is considered in relation to victimization theory.

Spouse abuse has occurred throughout recorded history. During the Roman era, men had the legal right to beat their wives for attending public games without permission, drinking wine, or walking outdoors with their faces uncovered, while adultery was punishable by death. However, by the fourth century, excessive violence on the part of husband or wife could be used as sufficient grounds for divorce. During the Middle Ages, the wife was guarded jealously and could be punished severely for violations of duty. A husband was expected to beat his wife for "misbehaviours" and might himself be punished by neighbours in the cuckold's court if he failed to do so.

By the mid-nineteenth century, severe wife beating had fallen into disfavour, and accused wife beaters were subject to public ridicule. By the twentieth century, England had outlawed wife beating, yet the tradition of husbands' domination over wives made physical coercion difficult to control. Even after World War II, some English courts found domestic assault to be a reasonable punishment for a disobedient wife.[128]

Brinkerhoff and Lupri, in their study of family violence, found that both women and men are the agitators of violence, and that much abuse goes unreported. Furthermore, if there was one violent episode, it was likely to occur again. Violent couples came from all socioeconomic classes, and occupational/educational attainment had an insignificant role in predicting interspousal violence.[129]

Tragically, family members convicted of violent crimes against spouses are less likely than other violent offenders to get prison terms.

The Nature and Extent of Spouse Abuse. Statistics Canada's National Survey on Violence Against Women estimated that 29 percent of women who have ever been married have been assaulted. The rate was highest in British Columbia (36 percent) and lowest in Newfoundland and Labrador (17 percent). In cases of previous marriages, 48 percent of the women had been assaulted, while 15 percent of currently married women reported being assaulted.[130] In a national survey of college students, more than 20 percent of the females had experienced violence during their dating and courtship relationships.[131]

Characteristic traits of the wife assaulter include excessive alcohol abuse, hostility and dependency based on resentment, and brooding over a wife's behaviour. Being under economic stress, serving in the military, being given to a sudden burst of anger after a verbal dispute, and having been battered as a child are also factors.[132]

Is Spouse Abuse Intergenerational? Although it is generally agreed that child abuse is intergenerational, do the same patterns apply to spouse abuse? Although

---

Exhibit 11.6	Public Attitudes toward Family Violence

- Those who agree that someone who insults other family members will eventually move to slapping and punching them: 59 percent
- Those who agree that people who are violent with family members are not responsible for their actions: 23 percent
- Those who agree that spousal violence involving hitting is a crime: 86 percent
- Those who say that stress due to money problems and unemployment is a cause of violence in families: 54 percent
- Those who believe that the greatest impact on individuals is negative psychological effects: 44 percent
- Those who believe that children in violent homes are more likely to be bullies: 79 percent
- Those who believe that living with family violence affects people's health: 81 percent
- Those who believe that the media has overstated the problem: 17 percent
- Those who say that the problem is more serious than is was 10 years ago: 62 percent
- Those who say that family violence does not occur in their own community "very often": 39 percent

Source: EKOS Research Associates Inc., *Public Attitudes Towards Family Violence: A Syndicated Study, Final Report* (Ottawa: Author, 2002).

there is little conclusive evidence that spouse abusers grew up in homes where spouses were abused, some research indicates that abused children later act abusively toward their own children and their spouses.[133]

One view on why this occurs is that children learn the role of parent/spouse through observation, and those who grow up in abusive households believe that harsh parenting and violent behaviour are "normal" in the typical family. A second view is that harsh parenting teaches kids that it is necessary to hit those you love. A third view is that harsh and incompetent parenting produces children who have behavioural problems. People who have experienced abusive and incompetent parenting are more likely to use drugs and commit crimes. The relationship between deviant behaviour and physical punishment is constant across race, ethnic origin, and socioeconomic status.

Support given to battered women includes transition houses and shelters. Police departments have made enforcement of domestic abuse laws a top priority with presumptive arrest policies, where charges are laid where there are reasonable grounds to believe an offence has been committed.

Robbery

The common-law definition of **robbery** is taking anything of value from the custody or control of a person by force or threat or by putting the victim in fear. A robbery is different from a theft because robbery involves the use of force. Robbery is punished severely because the victim's life is put in jeopardy; the amount of force used and not the value of the items taken determines the level of punishment.

In Canada in 1996, there were 3877 robberies with firearms, 10 660 with other offensive weapons, and 13 795 other kinds of robberies, for a total of 28 332 incidents. The combined rate for robbery in Canada in 2003 was 90 per 100 000 population, down from 104 in 1996. The clearance rate is only 35 percent, and about 70 percent of robberies are committed by adults.[134]

The Ecology of Robbery

The ecological pattern for robbery is similar to that of other violent crimes. Robbery is most often a public crime—that is, fewer robberies occur in the home (8 percent) than in public places (42 percent), such as parking lots (6 percent), streets (32 percent), and open areas (4 percent). Commercial areas, including bars, restaurants, hallways, and office buildings, accounted for 41 percent of all robberies in 2003. The public nature of robbery has greatly influenced people's behaviour. Most people believe that the most serious instances of violent crimes occur in large cities, and they move to suburban communities for this reason.

Robber Typologies

Attempts have been made to classify and explain the nature and dynamics of robbery, and several types of robberies have been identified:[135]

- Robbery of persons who work in places where money changes hands, such as banks, or valuable goods are sold, such as jewellery stores
- Robbery in an open area, such as muggings or purse snatchings, in the street and parking lots, on public transit, and in open areas
- Robbery on private premises, such as breaking into homes
- Robbery in the aftermath of a chance meeting, such as at a bar or a party
- Robbery after previous association of some duration between the victim and offender

Robbers can also be categorized into the following specialties:[136]

- Professional robbers have a commitment to crime as a livelihood because it is fast and very profitable (as opposed to the nonprofessional criminals discussed earlier). With planning and skill and by operating in groups, professionals usually steal large amounts from commercial establishments.
- Opportunist robbers steal small amounts of money from accessible and vulnerable targets: cab drivers, drunks, and the elderly. They are usually youths who do not plan their crimes, who operate within juvenile gangs, and who spend little time discussing weapon use, getaway plans, or other strategies.
- Addict robbers steal to support drug habits. They have a low commitment to robbery because of its danger but commit theft because it supplies needed funds. The addict is less likely to plan crime or use weapons than is the professional robber but is more cautious than the opportunist. Targets are chosen on the basis of risk.
- Alcoholic robbers steal to get money to buy liquor and have no commitment to robbery as a way of life. Their crimes are random, with little thought to victim, circumstance, or escape. They are the most likely to be caught.

As these typologies indicate, the typical armed robber is unlikely to be a professional who carefully studies targets while planning a crime. Convenience stores, gas stations, and people walking along the street are much more likely to be the target of robberies than are banks or other highly secure environments.

Robbers, therefore, seem to be diverted by modest defensive measures, such as having more than one clerk in a store or locating stores in strip malls rather than in stand-alone isolation.[137]

InfoTrac®

To learn more about robbery, see the following articles:

- Peter J. van Koppen and Robert W.J. Jansen, "The Road to the Robbery: Travel Patterns in Commercial Robberies," *British Journal of Criminology* 38, no. 2 (1998): 230.
- D.J. Pyle and D.F. Deadman, "Crime and the Business Cycle in Post-War Britain," *British Journal of Criminology* 34, no. 3 (1994): 339–357.

Evolving Forms of Violence

Assault, rape, robbery, and murder are traditional forms of interpersonal violence. However, criminologists have recognized new categories within these crime types, such as serial murder, date rape, and hate crime. In this section, we briefly discuss a new crime concern: workplace violence.

Connections

Hate crimes are another "newly discovered" form of violence, discussed in the context of passive precipitation theory in Chapter 4 on victimization.

Workplace Violence

In August 1992, after a long history of disciplinary problems and increasingly erratic behaviour, Dr. Valery Fabrikant walked into the engineering department at Concordia University and opened fire, killing three people and wounding two others because he had been denied a tenured position.[138]

In 1999, a former employee at the Ottawa bus terminal took a high-powered rifle to work and shot six employees (see the Crime in the News feature). Although it is alleged that he had a history of mental illness, he selected parts department employees only.

As of April 2005, Canada was ranked as the fourth-worst country in the world for violence in

---

Crime in the News

Pierre Lebrun

One of the most tragic examples of workplace violence in Canada unfolded at Ottawa's largest bus depot in April 1999. Former city transit worker Pierre Lebrun fatally shot four of his coworkers with a high-powered rifle and wounded two others before turning the gun on himself. Exactly what triggered Lebrun's murderous rampage and subsequent suicide may never be known, but it is clear that any social ties he had at the time of the incident were little more than dangling threads.

Lebrun's rocky career with the Ottawa Carleton Transpo began in 1986. He took on a garage attendant position after a five-year stretch of bus driving, which rates as one of the most stressful occupations, according to Statistics Canada. Not only did Lebrun have to deal with the routine hassles of this job, but he was also relentlessly ridiculed by colleagues. His status as an unmarried, middle-aged man with a speech impediment made him a vulnerable target.

The harsh treatment Lebrun received at work and his history of depression proved to be a volatile combination. Several complaints and transfers later, he finally retaliated by assaulting another employee. Lebrun was promptly fired, then reinstated and shuffled yet again into an isolating, nonunion position as an audit clerk. He decided to resign in January 1999, citing personal reasons, and virtually disappeared for three months before ambushing the station.

The case of this 40-year-old with no criminal record turned mass murderer warranted a coroner's inquest. Witnesses depicted Lebrun as "a quiet, withdrawn loner who often slept during his breaks or buried his head in newspapers." In a letter introduced as evidence, Lebrun described himself as "tired, exhausted and completely backed against the wall." City transit employees either denied or downplayed the harassment Lebrun suffered, but his anguish and thirst for revenge resounded in a suicide note left to his parents. The product of this six-week hearing was a list of 77 recommendations to various agencies, the majority of which addressed workplace violence and harassment issues.

Prepared by Andrea Wolf.

the workplace, just behind Argentina, Romania, and France, according to the International Labour Organization (ILO). In the United States, the Bureau of Labour Statistics notes that workplace homicide is the third-most frequent cause of employee deaths after highway accidents and falls.[139]

It has become commonplace to read of irate employees or former employees attacking coworkers or sabotaging machinery and production lines. Workplace violence is now considered the third-leading cause of occupational injury or death in the United States.[140] A majority of respondents in a Canadian survey felt that workplace violence was increasing, and significant sources are psychological violence and aggression. Canada ranks fourth in the world when it comes to workplace aggression.

The typical offender is a middle-aged White male who faces losing his job. In businesses, long-term employees fear job loss because of automation and reorganization. The common name for this type of mass violence is "going postal," due to some high-profile shootings by postal employees in 1986.

Another cause may be leadership styles. Some companies have authoritarian management styles that demand performance above all else from employees. Managers who are unsympathetic and unsupportive may help trigger workplace violence.

Not all workplace violence is caused by an injustice by management. There have been incidents in which coworkers have been killed because they refused a romantic relationship with the assailant or had reported him for sexual harassment; others have been killed because they got a job the assailant coveted. In a few cases, irate clients and customers have killed because of poor service or perceived slights.[141]

There are also a variety of responses to workplace "provocations." Some former employees attack supervisors to punish the company that dismissed them. Disgruntled employees may attack family members or friends, ignoring the actual cause of their rage and frustration. Others sabotage company equipment. Over time, if there is an unresolved conflict, some other events may eventually cause an eruption.

In his study of workplace violence in British Columbia's health care industry, Neil Boyd found more than 70 percent of nurses in British Columbia reported some form of violence at work, and 20 percent of these involved physical injury from an attack. Female workers were far more likely to experience violence at work than were males, probably due to the fact that 80 percent of workers in health care are female. Cutbacks have increased workload and tensions and have decreased the standard of medical care expected by many patients.[142]

Can workplace violence be controlled? Dispute resolution may help, and some researchers argue for aggressive job retraining, continued medical coverage in case of layoffs, and due process guarantees to thwart unfair terminations.

Political Violence and Terrorism

Violent behaviour also involves acts that have a political motivation, such as terrorism. Political crime has been with us throughout history.[143]

It is often difficult to separate political from interpersonal crimes of violence. For example, in the 1960s the FLQ (Front de Libération du Québec or the Quebec Liberation Front) robbed banks and credit unions to finance its revolutionary activity in Quebec. Was this terrorism or bank robbery?

To be a political crime, an act must carry with it the intent to disrupt and change the government and not simply a common-law crime committed for reasons of greed. Perpetrators believe their actions will benefit society and are necessary to create social changes.

Terrorism is a complex phenomenon that generally involves the illegal use of force against innocent people to achieve a coercive political objective.[144]

Terrorism is a political crime that uses violence to promote change. Whereas other political criminals may engage in demonstrating, counterfeiting, selling secrets, spying, and the like, terrorists make systematic use of murder and destruction to terrorize governments into conceding to political demands.[145] Terrorist actions are aimed at political change or economic or social reform. Terrorism is distinguished from conventional warfare because it requires secrecy and clandestine operations.[146]

The term *terrorist* is sometimes used interchangeably with *guerrilla*. The latter term, meaning "little war," developed out of the Spanish rebellion against French troops after Napoleon's invasion in 1808. Guerrillas are often located in rural areas, and the objects of their attacks include the military, the police, and government officials.[147] Guerrillas can often become effective military organizations, as the Russians found out when occupying Afghanistan in the 1980s.

Historical Perspective on Terrorism

Terrorism is known throughout history, becoming widespread in the Middle Ages, when political leaders were assassinated by their enemies. The word *assassin* is derived from an Arabic term meaning "hashish eater" and refers to members of a drug-using Muslim terrorist organization that carried out plots against prominent Christians and other religious enemies.[148]

European states have encouraged terrorism against enemies. For example, Queen Elizabeth I empowered Francis Drake to carry out attacks against the Spanish fleet. These privateers would have been considered pirates, but they operated with government approval. American privateers operated against the British during the Revolutionary War and the War of 1812. History can turn terrorists into heroes, depending on which side wins.

The term *terrorist* became popular during the French Revolution. From the fall of the Bastille in 1789 until 1794, thousands suspected of counterrevolutionary activity went to their deaths on the guillotine. The end of the terror was signalled by the death of its

Culture, Gender, Ethnicity, and Criminology

Transnational Terrorism

In 1998, terrorism expert Harvey Kushner wrote: "Today, international terrorists likely to target the United States are individuals. . . . The greatest threat to the security of the US in the next millennium will come from the hands of the freelancer."

The traditional image of the armed professional terrorist group with a clear-cut goal, such as nationalism or independence, is giving way to a new breed of terrorist with diverse motives. They do not have a unified central command, they are not located in any particular area, and they are capable of attacking anyone at any time with great destructive force. They may employ any number of weapons.

The new terrorist is more lethal, with fatalities steadily increasing in recent years. Terrorism expert Bruce Hoffman believes this is due to the rise of religiously motivated terrorist groups, such as al-Qaeda. Religiously inspired terrorist attacks are more likely to result in higher casualties because they are motivated not by efforts to obtain political freedom but by conflicting cultural values. Maintaining a differing value system allows the perpetrators to justify the deaths of large numbers of people: "For the religious terrorist, violence is a divine duty . . . executed in direct response to some theological

demand . . . and justified by scripture."

The al-Qaeda network is the paradigm of the new value-oriented terrorist organization. The September 11, 2001, attack was not designed to restore a homeland or bring about a new political state but to have a value structure adopted by Muslim nations. Osama bin Laden's attack may have been designed to create a military invasion of Afghanistan, which he hoped to exploit for revolution. According to Michael Scott Doran, bin Laden believed his acts would reach the audience that concerned him the most: the *umma* or universal Islamic community. The media would show Americans killing innocent civilians in Afghanistan, and the *umma* would find it shocking. The ensuing outrage would open a chasm between the Muslim population of the Middle East and the ruling governments in such states as Saudi Arabia, which were allied with the West. On October 7, 2001, bin Laden made a broadcast in which he said that the Americans and the British "have divided the entire world into two regions—one of faith, where there is no hypocrisy, and another of infidelity, from which we hope God will protect us."

Accordingly, his aim was to cause an Islamic revolution within the Muslim world. His attack was designed to force those governments to choose: You are either with the idol-

worshipping enemies of God, or you are with the true believers. The attack on the United States was designed to help his brand of extremist Islam survive and flourish among the believers who could bring down these corrupt governments.

This new generation of terrorists is especially frightening because its members are willing to engage in suicide missions to achieve their goals and willing to martyr themselves because they consider themselves true believers surrounded by blasphemers.

 InfoTrac®

What can be done to prevent terrorism? Can technology hold the key? Find out by reading Richard K. Betts, "Fixing Intelligence," *Foreign Affairs* 81, no. 1 (2002): 43.

Sources: Michael Scott Doran, "Somebody Else's Civil War," *Foreign Affairs* 81 (2002): 22–25; Bruce Hoffman, "Change and Continuity in Terrorism," *Studies in Conflict and Terrorism* 24 (2001); Harvey Kushner, *Terrorism in America, A Structured Approach to Understanding the Terrorist Threat* (Springfield: Charles C. Thomas, 1998); Ian Lesser, Bruce Hoffman, John Arquilla, David Ronfeldt, and Michele Zanini, *Countering the New Terrorism* (Washington, D.C.: Rand, 1999); Jessica Stern, *The Ultimate Terrorists* (Cambridge, Mass.: Harvard University Press, 1999).

prime mover, Maximilien Robespierre, in 1794, who was executed on the same guillotine to which he had sent almost 20 000 people to their deaths.

In the hundred years after, the world saw the Hur Brotherhood in India, the Internal Macedonian Revolutionary Organization in Turkey, and the Black Hand in Serbia. The Irish Republican Army battled British forces from 1919 to 1923, culminating in the southern part of Ireland's gaining independence.

Between the world wars, right-wing terrorism existed in Germany, Spain, and Italy. Russian left-wing revolutionary activity led to the death of the czar in 1917 and the rise of the Marxist state. During World War II, resistance to Germans was common throughout Europe; these terrorists are now considered heroes. In Palestine, Jewish terrorist groups—the Haganah, Irgun, and Stern Gang, whose leaders included Menachim Begin, who later became prime minister—waged war against the British to force them to allow Jewish survivors of the Holocaust to settle in their traditional homeland. Today, Palestinian and Islamic terrorist groups carry out violent political action against the Israeli state.

Forms of Terrorism

Today, the term *terrorism* is used to describe many behaviours and goals. We will briefly describe some of the more common forms.[149]

Revolutionary Terrorism. Revolutionary terrorists use violence as a tool to invoke fear in those in power and their supporters. The ultimate goal is to replace the existing government with a regime that holds acceptable political views. Such actions as kidnapping and assassination, such as the beheadings carried out in Iraq, are designed to draw repressive responses from governments trying to defend themselves. These responses help revolutionaries expose, through the skilled use of media coverage, the government's inhumane nature.

In Europe, a Marxist group called the Baader-Meinhof group in Germany conducted a series of robberies, bombings, and kidnappings in the 1980s. With the reunification of Germany, terrorist actions were believed over. Yet in 1991, the Baader-Meinhof group's successor, the Red Army Faction, claimed credit for assassinating the head of the government agency charged with rebuilding the East German economy.[150] In Italy, the Red Brigade kidnapped and executed a former Italian president and abducted an American general, who was later rescued by security forces.[151]

In the Middle East, the Palestine Liberation Organization (PLO) has directed terrorist activities against Israel. More radical splinter groups have broken from the PLO, including the Abu Nidal group, the Popular Front for the Liberation of Palestine, Hamas, and the Iranian-backed Hezbollah group, continuing the conflict. When the World Trade Center in New York City was bombed in 1993, the group responsible was demonstrating its hatred of American policies in the Middle East. And again, on September 11, 2001, when the World Trade Center towers were brought down by hijacked airliners, it was a Middle Eastern group, al-Qaeda, headed by Islamic extremist and millionaire Osama bin Laden, that was held responsible.

There have been numerous tragic incidents, but several stand out because of the large loss of life: Agents of the pro-Iranian Islamic Jihad used a truck bomb to blow up the U.S. Marine compound in Beirut, Lebanon, on April 18, 1983, killing 241; Libyan agents are the main suspects in the Christmas Day 1988 bombing of PanAm Flight 103 over Lockerbie, Scotland, which killed 270 people; and the August 7, 1998, bombings of American embassies in Kenya and Sudan by agents of Osama bin Laden killed at least 250 and injured more than four thousand.[152] The attacks on September 11 killed approximately five thousand people.

Political Terrorism. In 1996, after an 11-month federal investigation had resulted in their indictment on fraud charges, members of the U.S. Freemen movement held federal officers at bay in a month-long standoff before surrendering in Jordan, Montana. Heavily armed, the Freemen are one of many right-wing groups who have conducted or plan to conduct antigovernment activities. Their peaceful surrender prevented another in a long line of bloody engagements between federal agents and right-wing militants, such as the 1992 siege at Ruby Ridge, Idaho, or the infamous standoff in Waco, Texas, that resulted in the fiery deaths of followers of Branch Davidian leader David Koresh.[153]

Political terrorism is directed at those who oppose the terrorists' political ideology or against those whom terrorists define as "outsiders." Political terrorists in the United States tend to be heavily armed groups organized around such themes as White supremacy, Nazism, militant tax resistance, and religious revisionism. Identified groups include the Aryan Republican Army, Aryan Nation, and Posse Comitatus, as well as the traditional Ku Klux Klan organizations. Some of these groups have formed their own churches; for example, the Church of Jesus Christ Christian claims that Jesus was born an Aryan rather than a Jew and that White Anglo-Saxons are the true "chosen" people. Some groups have committed common-law crimes, such as bank robberies, to fund their activities, including bombings and other terror tactics.[154] The Oklahoma City bombing may have been the most tragic example of such activities.

Nationalistic Terrorism. Nationalistic terrorism promotes the interests of minority ethnic or religious groups that feel they have been persecuted under majority rule. In India, Sikh radicals assassinated Indian prime minister Indira Gandhi in 1984 in retaliation for the government's storming of their Golden Temple religious shrine.[155] In Egypt, fundamentalist Muslims have attacked foreign tourists in an effort to wreck the tourist industry, topple the secular government, and turn Egypt into an Islamic state.[156] In Algeria, fundamentalist Muslim groups have waged a decade-long battle against the government. In 1997, 50 militants armed with axes decapitated 31 people in the city of Medea.[157] The best-known nationalistic terrorist group operating today is the Provisional Irish Republican Army (IRA), which is dedicated to unifying Northern Ireland with the Republic of Ireland under home rule.

A Canadian nationalist terrorist group, the Front de Libération du Québec (FLQ) or Quebec Liberation Front, planted bombs, robbed banks, and raided military armouries for weapons in the 1960s. Their actions are thought to have signalled the modern age of terrorism. They had suspected links with the Black Panthers, Cuba's revolutionary government, and radical groups in Algeria. On October 5, 1970, James Cross, a British trade official, was kidnapped by the FLQ. The group demanded $500 000, the release of political prisoners, and safe passage to Cuba. The Quebec premier refused to negotiate and asked the federal government to send in troops. On October 10, Quebec cabinet minister Pierre Laporte was also abducted and murdered a week later. The imposition of the *War Measures Act* resulted in the arrest without warrant of 450 people, of which few were ever charged with a crime. When asked to justify his use of such extreme legal measures to fight terrorism, then–Prime Minister Pierre Trudeau said: "There's a lot of bleeding hearts who don't like to see people with helmets and guns . . . but it is more important to keep law and order in society."[158]

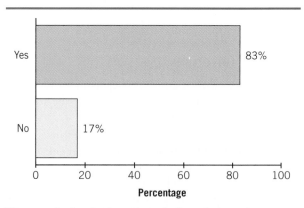

When asked whether they believed that the recent American terror alert was more about politics than about security, 83 percent voted yes and 17 percent voted no.

Source: Poll conducted by *The Globe and Mail,* August 7, 2004.

The World Trade Center towers collapse after a terrorist attack on September 11, 2001.

Nonpolitical Terrorism. Terrorist activity also involves groups that espouse a particular social or religious cause and use violence to address their grievances. For example, anti-abortion groups have sponsored demonstrations at abortion clinics, and some members have gone so far as to attack clients, bomb offices, and kill doctors who perform abortions.

Animal rights organization members have harassed and thrown blood at people wearing fur coats. It has also become common for environmental groups to resort to terror tactics to sabotage their enemies' ability to harm the environment. One of the biggest targets is the livestock and research animal–producing industry.

A soldier stands guard at Parliament Hill. Security was stepped up because of terrorist kidnappings in Montreal during the FLQ crisis.

Members of such groups as the Animal Liberation Front (ALF) and Earth First! acknowledge making attacks against ranches and packing plants. ALF members free animals, such as by raiding turkey farms before Thanksgiving and rabbit farms before Easter.[159]

State-Sponsored Terrorism. State-sponsored terrorism occurs when a repressive government forces its citizens into obedience, oppresses minorities, and stifles political dissent. Death squads and the use of government troops to destroy political opposition parties are often associated with Latin American political terrorism.[160]

Some governments have been accused of using terrorist-type actions to control political dissidents. For example, in the first 18 months of its deployment, members of the Haitian National Police allegedly executed 15 political opponents of the regime.[161]

Much of what we know about state-sponsored terrorism comes from the efforts of human rights groups. London-based Amnesty International maintains that tens of thousands of people continue to become victims of security operations that result in disappearances and extrajudicial executions.[162] Political prisoners are tortured in about one hundred countries, people have disappeared or are being held in secret detention in 20 countries, and government-sponsored death squads operate in more than 35. Countries known for encouraging violent control of dissidents include Brazil, Colombia, Guatemala, Honduras, Peru, Iraq, and the Sudan. When Tupac Amaru rebels seized and held hostages at the Japanese ambassador's villa in Peru in 1996, Amnesty International charged that the action came in response to a decade-long campaign of human rights violations by national security forces and extensive abuses against opposition groups. Between January 1983 and December 1992, Amnesty International documented at least 4200 cases of people who had "disappeared" in Peru following detention by the security forces. Thousands more were killed by government forces in extrajudicial executions, including some 500 people in 19 separate massacres.[163]

Human Rights Watch, reporting on state-sponsored terrorism around the world, has charged that serious human rights violations, including disappearances, torture, and extrajudicial executions, persist at alarming levels in Guatemala.[164]

Another form of state-sponsored terrorism is **structural violence**, which involves the physical harm caused by the unequal distribution of wealth. Structural violence involves a set of social conditions from which flows poverty, disease, hunger, malnutrition, poor sanitation, premature death, and high infant mortality.[165]

It is also possible for state-sponsored terrorism to be directed at people and governments outside the state's borders. Particularly disturbing is the possibility that some "outlaw" state, such as Libya or North Korea, will carry out a nuclear-based attack against a nation viewed as the enemy.[166] Although special expertise is needed to build such a bomb, there are so many existing nuclear bombs in the hands of unstable Eastern European states that nuclear terrorists might be able to purchase what they need to build a bomb, as is allegedly the case with Osama bin Laden. If the World Trade Center in New York had been attacked with a low-yield nuclear device rather than chemical explosives, both towers would have collapsed and as many as 50 000 people would have been killed. Instead, it was airliners flown by hijackers armed with box-cutters that brought down the towers.

Crime in the News

Police in Montreal Defuse 150-Pound Bomb in Car

by Clair Balfour

Montreal—A Volkswagen, converted into a mobile bomb, was discovered and defused behind the head office of the Bank of Montreal in the St. James Street financial district of Montreal early yesterday.

With its cargo of 150 pounds of dynamite, it was the biggest of four bombs investigated by city and district police in 48 hours. One went off and killed a man on Saturday as he drove on Metropolitan Boulevard, which carries the Trans-Canada Highway across the north side of Montreal.

Montreal police received a call at 12:55 a.m. yesterday about the car behind the bank. Police said the car contained a bomb composed of two sticks of dynamite wired to a clock set for 4:15 a.m. The 150 pounds of explosives were in a case in the car and police said the small bomb would have triggered the case.

Sgt. Bob Cote of the Montreal police department's technical squad, said his men had a difficult time in disengaging the timing device.

The bomb, one of the largest dismantled by the city's bomb squad, would have leveled the building and caused considerable damage to the surroundings.

Source: Clair Balfour, "Police in Montreal Defuse 150-Pound Bomb in Car," ©*The Globe and Mail*, July 13, 1970, A1. Reprinted with permission of The Globe & Mail.

The extreme form of state-sponsored terrorism occurs when a government seeks to wipe out a minority group within the jurisdiction it controls, referred to as **genocide**. The Holocaust during World War II is the most notorious example of genocide, but more recent atrocities have taken place in Cambodia, Rwanda, and Bosnia.

Criminal Terrorism. In 2001, six men were arrested by Russian security forces as they were making a deal to sell weapons-grade uranium. Some of the men were members of the Balashikha criminal gang, who were in possession of almost one kilogram of top-grade radioactive material, which can be used to build weapons. They were asking $30 000 for the deadly merchandise.[167] Since 1990, there have been half a dozen cases involving theft and transportation of nuclear material and other cases involving people who offered to sell agents material that was not yet in their possession. These are the known cases.

In some instances, there has been close cooperation between organized criminal groups and guerrillas. In other instances the relationship is more superficial. For example, the Revolutionary Armed Forces of Colombia (FARC) impose a tax on Colombian drug producers, but evidence indicates that the group cooperates with Colombia's top drug barons in running the trade. In some cases, the line between being a terrorist organization with political support and vast resources and an organized criminal group engaging in illicit activities for profit becomes blurred. This similarity can be confusing for counterterrorism authorities: Are they dealing with convictional criminals or criminals for profit? For example, financially motivated terrorists are more likely to follow through on their end of a kidnapping negotiation than is a traditionally motivated political terrorist.[168]

What Motivates Terrorists?

In the aftermath of the September 11, 2001, destruction of the World Trade Center in New York City, people asked what could motivate someone like Osama bin Laden to order the deaths of thousands of innocent people?

Some experts believe that the attacks had a political basis, an outgrowth of America's Middle East policies. Others saw a religious motivation: The terrorists were radical Muslims at war with the liberal religions of the West. Another view was that bin Laden's rage was fuelled by deep-rooted psychological problems.

On the surface, Osama bin Laden, the favoured son of a wealthy Saudi Arabian family, financed his terrorist activities from an inheritance of more than $300 million.[169] Although it is possible that he had some mental disorder, his actions may have stemmed from his efforts to gain his father's approval. He once told an interviewer that his father wanted his sons to fight against the enemies of Islam. Perhaps this need for acceptance explained bin Laden's religious zeal, which was in excess of anyone else's in his large extended family.

After his father's death, bin Laden was mentored by a Jordanian named Abdullah Azzam, whose credo was not to negotiate. When Azzam was killed in 1989 by a car bomb in Pakistan, bin Laden vowed to carry on Azzam's "holy war" against the West. He threw himself into the Afghan conflict against the Soviet Union, and when the Russians withdrew, he was convinced that the West was vulnerable.

Bin Laden's motivations will probably never be fully understood, but is it possible that his violent urges stemmed from the same web of emotions that fuel the thousands of predatory criminals who prowl society looking for unwary victims? If so, his actions, although extreme, are certainly not unique. Many people have personally experienced violence or have a friend who has been victimized. Almost everyone has heard about someone being robbed, beaten, or killed. Riots and mass disturbances have ravaged urban areas; racial attacks plague schools and university campuses; assassination has claimed the lives of political, religious, and social leaders all over the world.

What motivates these individuals to risk their lives and those of innocent people? One view is that terrorists are emotionally disturbed, acting out their psychosis within violent groups. According to this view, "terrorist" violence is not so much a political instrument as it is the result of compulsion or psychopathology. Terrorists act out of emotional problems, including but not limited to self-destructive urges, disturbed emotions, problems with authority, and inconsistent and troubled parenting.[170] As terrorism expert Jerrold M. Post puts it, "political terrorists are driven to commit acts of violence as a consequence of psychological forces, and . . . their special psychology is constructed to rationalize acts they are psychologically compelled to commit."[171]

Terrorists hold extreme ideological beliefs that prompt their behaviour. They have heightened perceptions of oppressive conditions, believing that they are being victimized by some group or government, and conclude they must resort to violence to encourage change. "Successful" terrorists believe that their "self-sacrifice" outweighs the guilt created by harming innocent people.

Ironically, Osama bin Laden was a multimillionaire and at least some of his followers were highly educated and trained. The acts of the modern terrorist—using the Internet, planning logistically complex and expensive assaults, and writing and disseminating formal critiques, manifestos, and theories—require the training and education of the social elite, not the poor and oppressed.

In some instances, terrorists may be motivated by feelings of alienation and failure to comprehend technological society. Japanese novelist Haruki Murakami interviewed members of the Aum Shinrikyo, a radical religious group that released poison gas into a Tokyo subway in 1995, killing 12 and injuring five thousand.[172] Murakami found that the terrorists thought modern society was too complex, with few clear-cut goals and values. Surprisingly, the cult members that Murakami interviewed were relatively ordinary people; some were dropouts with few prospects, but others were highly educated professionals. All seemed alienated from modern society; some felt that a suicide mission would cleanse them from the corruption of the modern world. One told him that since he had been a child, he had realized that everything in life was heading straight for destruction and there was no turning back. Once he joined the terrorist group, he was on a path to salvation and once again life had meaning.

 InfoTrac®

To find out more about terrorism, use "terrorism" as a keyword in InfoTrac® College Edition.

The Extent of Terrorism

The number of international terrorist incidents has decreased in recent years (296 in 1996). However, Iran, Iraq, Libya, North Korea, and Cuba continue their policy of giving material, logistic, and financial support to the groups that are committing terrorism.

Who Is the Terrorist?

Terrorists engage in criminal activities, such as bombings, shootings, and kidnappings. One view of their motivation is that they have heightened perceptions of oppressive conditions—they feel relative deprivation.[173] The terrorists conclude that they must resort to violence to encourage change.

The violence need not be aimed at a specific goal. Rather, terror tactics must contribute to setting in motion a series of events that enlist others in the cause and lead to long-term change. It also requires violence without guilt. The cause justifies the need for violence.[174]

According to Austin Turk, terrorists tend to come from upper- rather than lower-class backgrounds.[175] This was clearly the case in the September 11, 2001, airplane hijackings. It may be because the upper classes can produce people who are more politically sensitive, articulate, and focused in their resentments. Since their position in the class structure gives them the feeling that they can influence society, upper-class citizens are more likely to seek confrontations with authorities. Class differences are also manifested in different approaches to political violence. The violence of the lower class is more often associated with spontaneous expressions of dissatisfaction, collective riots, and politically inconsequential acts. Higher-class violence tends to be more calculated and organized and uses elaborate strategies of resistance. Revolutionary cells, campaigns of terror and assassination, logistically complex and expensive assaults, and writing and disseminating formal critiques, manifestos, and theories are typically acts of the socially elite.

Upper-class political terrorism has been manifested in the death squads operating in Latin America and

Asia, which use violence to intimidate those opposing the ruling party. One graphic example occurred in Sri Lanka in 1989, when a death squad made up of members of the ruling party's security forces beheaded 18 suspected members of the antigovernment People's Liberation Front and placed the heads around a pond at a university campus.[176]

Responses to Terrorism

Governments have tried various responses to terrorism. Law enforcement agencies have infiltrated terrorist groups and turned members over to police. Rewards have been given for information leading to the arrest of terrorists, as was the case with the FLQ. Democratic elections have been held to discredit terrorists' complaints that the state is oppressive. The United States, probably the biggest target of terrorist attacks, has antiterrorist legislation for terrorist acts committed abroad against American citizens and for the killing of foreign officials and politically protected persons. In 1996 the American *Antiterrorism and Effective Death Penalty Act* was signed into law, banning fundraising to

support terrorist organizations. It also allowed American officials to deport terrorists from American soil and to bar terrorists from entering the United States in the first place. Its other provisions include:

- Requiring plastic explosives to contain chemical markers so that criminals who use them can be tracked down and prosecuted
- Increasing controls over biological and chemical weapons
- Toughening penalties over a range of terrorist crimes
- Banning the sale of defence goods and services to countries that are not "cooperating fully" with American antiterrorism efforts

In Canada, as a result of the events of September 11, 2001, various measures were taken, including the passage of Bill C-36 and Bill C-42 through Parliament.[177] Among other powers, Bill C-36 gave the police broad new powers of arrest without warrant, increased the period for which a person could be detained, and enabled the government to place a ban on the release of information related to terrorist investigations. As an

---

Culture, Gender, Ethnicity, and Criminology

Genocide

The most extreme form of political violence is genocide—the attempt to eliminate a whole group of people defined by their race, religion, ethnicity, or political beliefs. Genocidal episodes have included the attempted destruction of European Jews by the Nazis during the Holocaust, the killing of the Armenians in Turkey at the beginning of the twentieth century, the annihilation of native tribes during the Spanish conquest of Latin America, the "ethnic cleansing" that occurred during the recent wars in the former Yugoslavia, and the horrifying military attacks against civilians throughout Darfur since 2003.

A framework for understanding how these unimaginable outbreaks of political mass murder can occur in a civilized society

must include conditions that have preceded the onset of genocide in Western society, such as the following:

- *Difficult life conditions*: Basic physical and material needs are not being met, and social groups lack a sense of positive identity, effectiveness, and control.
- *Scapegoating*: A group is identified as the cause of life's problems, which affirms the group identity by diminishing individual responsibility for problems.
- *New ideology*: Ideologies emerge that offer the hope of a better life. The scapegoated group is seen as a roadblock to its fulfillment.
- *Devaluation*: Members of a scapegoated group who are devalued can be harmed at will. The perpetrators become

increasingly prone to act aggressively.

- *"Just world" thinking*: As members of the scapegoated group are harmed, both perpetrators and bystanders believe the people who suffer deserve their fate.
- *Commitment*: As harm increases, so does commitment to group process and ideology. The more harm they cause, the less likely perpetrators are to be willing to change.
- *Passive bystanders*: Bystanders within and outside the society remain passive, affirming the perpetrators' belief that they are right to victimize the outcast group.
- *Authority orientation*: Groups with unquestioning respect for authority are more prone to group violence and less likely to oppose leaders.

- *Monolithic culture*: A limited set of cultural values inhibits intergroup relations; nonmembers are kept from important cultural and professional offices and from the legal process they could use to speak out against or halt destructive practices.
- *Group self-concept*: Shared belief that a group is either superior or inferior; life's difficulties become more frustrating when they conflict with a group's feelings of superiority. Frustrated feelings of superiority combined with feelings of weakness and vulnerability lead to the embrace of destructive ideologies and scapegoating.
- *History of aggression*: Some cultures have a long history of violence and aggression. Using aggressive tactics to solve problems thus may seem normal, appropriate, and even desirable.

How does this model fit twentieth-century genocides, such as the Holocaust, and those that have occurred since? The Germans had a long history of violence and aggression. Their culture was monolithic and featured such values as loyalty, obedience, and order. Life conditions in Germany were difficult after World War I, and the Jews were scapegoated as responsible for the economic catastrophe that followed. The Nazi ideology promised a better tomorrow that would elevate the Germans as the "purest" race and that conditions could be improved by eliminating lesser races. The Nazi ideology was appealing, with its emphasis on the superiority of the German people, nationalism, and unquestioning obedience to a leader.

Because the Jews were relatively successful, it was easy to portray them as dishonest and manipulative, enhancing their devalued status. Although there was a progression of anti-Semitic actions after Hitler came to power, nonaligned Germans distanced themselves from Jews, and the rest of the world stood idly by, attending the Berlin Olympics in 1936. American corporations conducted business in Germany throughout the 1930s. These conditions provoked an escalating round of violence that eventually led to genocide and mass destruction.

By setting out the factors that support genocide, we can get some insight into how the risk of political mass murder can be avoided. For example, societies must stress inclusion rather than exclusion, including education about other cultures in school curriculums, in order to lay the groundwork for understanding and acceptance.

Sources: Ervin Staub, "Cultural-Societal Roots of Violence," *American Psychologist* 51 (1996): 117–32; *The Roots of Evil: The Origins of Genocide and Other Group Violence* (New York: Cambridge University Press, 1989); Eric Reeves, "Unnoticed Genocide," Genocide Watch, http://www.genocidewatch.org/UnnoticedGenocide.htm (accessed May 15, 2005).

---

omnibus bill, it included acts to amend the *Criminal Code*, the *Official Secrets Act*, the *Canada Evidence Act*, the *Proceeds of Crime (Money Laundering) Act*, and other acts. Bill C-42 gave the federal government the power to designate an area as vital to national security, after which the military could compel everyone to leave and seal it off. These two bills came under heavy fire for violating civil rights. The American antiterrorism bill is called the *Patriot Act*. Given the ability of the FBI to monitor Internet traffic, civil libertarians fear that there will be increasing violations of civil rights.[178]

Despite the development of antiterrorism statutes in North America and Europe, most politically motivated acts are prosecuted as common-law crimes. In Canada it is probably easier to deport a person under immigration law than it is to detain that person under the new antiterrorism legislation.

Some countries have specially trained antiterrorist squads. The American military, for example, has created the renowned Delta Force, made up of members from the four service areas. Delta Force activities are generally secret, but it is known that the force saw action in Iran (1980), Honduras (1982), Sudan (1983), and during the Grenada invasion (1983), and it was prepared to take action against the hijacking of the ship *Achille Lauro* in 1985. The American government's counterrevolutionary study, Project Camelot, had a branch studying the secession movement in Quebec.

Any attempts to meet force with force are fraught with danger. If the government's response is retaliation in kind, it could provoke increased terrorist activity. Of course, a weak response may be interpreted as a licence for terrorists to operate with impunity. The American government bombed Libya in 1986, in an attempt to convince its leader, Colonel Muammar Qaddafi, to desist from sponsoring terrorist organizations. Although the raid made a dramatic statement, preventing terrorism is a task that so far has stymied the governments of most nations.

Efforts Made since September 11, 2001

The World Trade Center attack forever changed American policy on terrorism. What have been some of the major efforts to combat terrorist groups?

Legal Efforts. In the wake of the September 11 attacks, the United States moved to freeze the financial assets of groups thought to engage in, or support, terrorist activities. For example, the assets of the Holy Land Foundation for Relief and Development, Beit Al-Mal Holdings, and Al-Aqsa Islamic Bank were frozen because they were suspected of funding Hamas, a Middle Eastern terrorist group. The United States blocked more than $27 million in assets of the Taliban and al-Qaeda, and other nations have blocked at least $33 million. To help monitor terrorist assets, the Foreign Terrorist Asset Tracking Center was founded.

Soon after the attack, Congress moved quickly to pass legislation giving the law enforcement agencies a freer hand to investigate and apprehend suspected terrorists. The American *Patriot Act* made changes to existing statutes to give new powers to domestic law enforcement and international intelligence agencies in an effort to fight terrorism, to expand the definition of terrorist activities, and to alter sanctions for violent terrorism.[179]

Traditional tools of surveillance have been expanded, such as wiretaps, search warrants, and subpoenas. Greater power was given to the FBI to check and monitor phone, Internet, and computer records without first needing to demonstrate that these systems were being used by a suspect or target of a court order. The government does not need to show a court that the information or communication is relevant to a criminal investigation, nor do enforcement agencies have to report where they served the order or what information they received.

Although law enforcement agencies may applaud these new laws, civil libertarians are troubled because they view the laws as eroding civil rights. The new and sweeping authority might not be limited to true terrorism investigations but actually cover a much broader range of activity involving reasonable political activities.[180]

Canada, of course, has also experienced its problems because of increased security around terrorism. Congested border crossings cost us more than $8 billion a year, and those travelling to the United States face new restrictions. Canada's own *Anti-terrorism Act* was tested in the Supreme Court in 2004. In a set of dual hearings, the SCC ruled that someone could be compelled to testify in investigative hearings and that these court hearings could not be held in private. The fight against terrorism makes it easy to seek to tighten up the law and restrict important rights. Ontario's "terror czar" wanted the power to ban travel, destroy property, and search and seize property without a warrant, actions that would have been impossible without the threat of terrorism. Transport Canada decided to check into the backgrounds of 130 000 airport workers. Under the new *Public Safety Act*, the Canadian Security Intelligence Service would create a no-fly list of passengers banned from domestic flights.[181]

We will be living with this new reality for some time.

Summary

It seems that we live in an extremely violent time, with new forms of violence being identified and publicized more than ever before. Among the various explanations for violent crimes are personal traits, ineffective families, the presence of a subculture of violence that stresses violent solutions to interpersonal problems, substance abuse, and the availability of firearms.

There are many types of interpersonal violent crime. Sexual assault has been known throughout history, and at one time it was believed that a woman was as guilty as her attacker was for her rape. At present, it is estimated that less than 10 percent of all sexual assaults are reported to police each year; the true number is probably much higher. Rape is an extremely difficult charge to prove in court.

Murder is the unlawful killing of a human being with malice. There are different degrees of murder, and punishments vary accordingly. One important characteristic of murder is that the victim and criminal often know each other. This fact has caused some criminologists to believe that murder is a victim-precipitated crime. Murder victims and offenders both tend to be young and male.

Assault is another serious interpersonal violent crime. One important type of assault occurs in the home, including child abuse and spouse abuse. It has been estimated that many children are abused by their parents each year, and a significant proportion of families report husband–wife violence. There is also a trend toward violence between dating couples on university and college campuses.

Robbery involves theft by force, usually in a public place. Types of offenders include professional, opportunist, addict, and alcoholic robbers.

Political violence is another serious problem. Many terrorist groups exist, at both the national and the international levels. Hundreds of terrorist acts are reported each year in the United States alone. There are political terrorists, nationalists, and state-sponsored terrorists.

Violence is an important topic facing society today, and the tasks of criminology are to identify and explain it and to work toward solutions. It is also our task to show that because we live in an information age, we are also more sensitive to reports of violent crime as well.

Thinking Like a Criminologist

The provincial government has hired you to prepare a report on what used to be called "statutory rape," that is, sex with an underage youth. The government is concerned because of the growing number of underage girls who have been impregnated by adult men. Studies reveal that many teenage pregnancies result from affairs that underage girls have with older men, with age gaps ranging up to 10 years. The girl typically drops out of school and goes on welfare. Some outraged parents want the provincial government to more strictly enforce the law.

However, some critics suggest that implementing statutory rape laws to punish males who have relationships with minor girls does not solve the problems of teenage pregnancies and out-of-wedlock births. Liberals dislike the idea of using the criminal law to solve social problems because it does not provide for the girls and their young children and focuses only on punishing offenders.

In contrast, conservatives fear that such laws give the state power to prosecute people for victimless crimes, thereby adding to the government's ability to control people's private lives. Not all cases involve much older men, and critics ask whether we should criminalize the behaviour of 17-year-old boys and their 15-year-old girlfriends.

As a criminologist with expertise on rape and its effects, what would you recommend regarding implementation of the law?

Key Terms

brutalization process

child abuse

conflict-related violence

consent

corroboration

crime-related violence

cult killings

date rape

eros

expressive violence

gang killings

gendered violence

genocide

instrumental violence

marital exemption

mass murderer

murder

premeditation

psychopharmacological

robbery

sexual abuse

shield laws

structural violence

terrorism

thanatos

thrill killings

Critical Thinking Questions

1. Should different types of rape receive different legal sanctions? For example, should someone who rapes a stranger be punished more severely than someone who is convicted of marital rape or date rape?

2. There have been significant changes in rape laws regarding issues, such as corroboration and shield laws. What other measures would you take to protect the victims of rape when they are forced to testify in court?

3. Should hate crimes be punished more severely than crimes motivated by greed, anger, or revenge? Why should crimes be distinguished by the motivations of the perpetrator? Is hate a more heinous motivation than revenge?

4. Should acts of terrorism be treated differently from other common-law violent crimes? For example, should terrorists be executed for their acts even if no one is killed during their attack?

5. Crime rates were exceedingly high in the nineteenth century before TV, movies, and rap videos had been created. What, if anything, does this say about the effect of media on crime? What were some of the other factors that provoked violence in the nineteenth century? Do you think that these factors still cause violence today?

6. It is unlikely that the threat of punishment can deter robbery, but eliminating cash and relying on debit and credit cards may be the most productive method to reduce robbery. Although this seems far-fetched, our society is becoming progressively more cashless; it is now possible to buy both gas and groceries with credit cards and debit cards. Would a cashless society end the threat of robbery, or would innovative robbers find new targets?

7. Based on what you know about how robbers target victims, how can you better protect yourself from robbery?

 See the book-specific website at http://www.siegelcriminology3e.nelson.com for additional chapter links, discussions, and quizzes.

Property Crimes

Economic crimes are acts in violation of the criminal law designed to bring financial reward to an offender. In our society, the range and scope of criminal activity motivated by financial gain are tremendous. Official statistics indicate that of the 2.6 million offences in Canada in 2003, 51 percent were property crimes. Self-report studies show that property crime among the young of every social class is widespread, and youths make up 28 percent of those charged in property offences. Although the violent crime rate decreased in 2003, the property crime rate increased almost 4 percent, the first increase since 1991. We also know that corporate and other white-collar crimes are commonplace; political scandals indicate that even high-ranking government officials can be suspected of criminal acts.

Whereas average citizens may be puzzled and enraged by violent crimes, they often view economic crimes ambivalently. Although it is true that society generally disapproves of crimes involving theft and corruption, the public seems quite tolerant of "gentlemen bandits," even to the point of admiring such figures. They pop up as characters in popular myths and legends—Robin Hood, Jesse James, Bonnie and Clyde, Edwin Alonzo Boyd. They are the semiheroic subjects of books and films, such as *48 Hours*, *Pulp Fiction*, and *Heat*.

How can ambivalence toward criminality be explained? For one thing, tolerance toward economic criminals may be prompted by the fact that almost everybody has been involved in economic crime. Even law-abiding people may have at one time engaged in petty theft, cheated on their income taxes, stolen a textbook from a university bookstore, or pilfered from their place of employment.

People may also be more tolerant of economic crimes because these crimes never seem to seriously hurt anyone—banks are insured, large businesses pass along losses to consumers, stolen cars can be replaced. Convicted offenders, especially businesspeople who commit white-collar crimes involving millions of dollars, are often punished lightly. We fail to realize how great the cost of economic crime is. In Nova Scotia, for example, a GPI Atlantic study found that crime costs $550 million a year in economic losses to victims, including public spending on police, courts, and prisons, and private spending on burglar alarms, security guards, electronic surveillance, and theft insurance. This amounted to $600 per person in 1997. When unreported crimes, such as insurance fraud, are added, the cost is $1.2 billion a year, or $1250 per person. And this is lower than the national average!

This chapter is the first of two that review the nature and extent of economic crime in our society.

Property crimes are not new to this century. This painting illustrates fourteenth-century thieves plundering a home in Paris.

It is divided into two principal sections. The first deals with the concept of professional crime and focuses on different types of professional criminals, including the **fence**, a buyer and seller of stolen merchandise. Then the chapter turns to a discussion of common theft-related offences, or **street crimes**. This includes the major forms of common theft: shoplifting, auto theft, theft by false pretences, bad cheques, credit card fraud, and embezzlement. Then the chapter discusses a more serious form of theft—burglary, or break and enter—that involves forcible entry into a person's home or place of work for the purpose of theft. Finally, arson is discussed briefly. In Chapter 13, attention will be given to white-collar crimes and economic crimes that involve organizations devoted to criminal enterprise.

A Brief History of Theft

Theft is known throughout recorded history. The Crusades of the eleventh century inspired peasants and downtrodden noblemen to leave their estates to prey on passing pilgrims.[1] Not surprisingly, Crusaders felt it within their rights to appropriate the possessions of any infidels, Greeks, Jews, or Muslims, they encountered during their travels. By the thirteenth century, returning pilgrims, not content to live as serfs on feudal estates, gathered in the forests of England and the Continent to poach on game that was the rightful property of their lord or king and to steal from passing strangers. By the fourteenth century, many highwaymen and poachers were full-time livestock thieves, stealing cattle and sheep. Interestingly enough, the origin of the vagrancy statutes are rooted in the need to control people who wandered about, with no lawful occupation, and preyed on travellers.

Culture, Gender, Ethnicity, and Criminology

Catching Thieves in Eighteenth-Century England

By the eighteenth century, the Industrial Revolution had lured thousands from the English countryside to work in the factory towns. The swelling population of urban poor, whose minuscule wages could hardly sustain them, increased the crime rates. In the London area, law enforcement was provided by thief-takers—organized groups of private police who earned a living by catching thieves and collecting rewards for their capture. Between 30 and 40 thief-takers were active in London by the mid-eighteenth century.

Most thief-takers started as prison turnkeys, constables, court bailiffs, or other minor court officers. They were called "monied police" because they made a living not only from catching and informing on criminals but also from receiving stolen property, stealing, perjury, and blackmail. Typically corrupt, they took hush money and stolen goods from prisoners, gave perjured evidence, swore false oaths, and operated extortion rackets. Petty debtors were easy targets for those who combined thief-taking with the keeping of taverns. The health and safety of incarcerated prisoners was entirely at the whim of the keepers/thief-takers, who were free to charge what their prisoners could pay for board and other necessities.

Thief-takers' use of violence was notorious. Among the most infamous violent thief-takers was Jack Wild. He pursued armed thieves and was prepared to maim or kill. Before he was hanged in 1725, Wild had two fractures in his skull, and his bald head was covered with silver plates. He had 17 wounds in various parts of his body from swords, daggers, and gunshots, and his throat had been cut in the course of his duties.

Henry Fielding sought to clean up the thief-taking system. As a city magistrate in 1748, Fielding operated his own group of monied police from Bow Street in London, deploying them throughout the city, deciding which cases to investigate and what streets to protect. Fielding's "Bow Street Runners" were an improvement over earlier monied police because their administrative structure improved record-keeping and investigative procedures, and they were instructed on legitimate duties. However, by the nineteenth century state police officers were needed.

InfoTrac®

The Crusades actually lasted for centuries. Read about them and why they ended in this article on InfoTrac® College Edition: Nigel Saul, "The Vanishing Vision: Late Medieval Crusading," *History Today* 47, no. 6 (1997): 23–29.

The fifteenth century brought hostilities between England and France in the Hundred Years' War. Foreign mercenary troops roamed the countryside, and looting and pillaging were viewed as part of their pay. Theft became more professional with the rise of the city and the establishment of a class of urban poor.[2] By the eighteenth century, three separate groups of property criminals were active. In larger cities, such as London and Paris, groups of skilled thieves, pickpockets, forgers, and counterfeiters operated freely. As noted in the Culture, Gender, Ethnicity, and Criminology feature above, some of the earliest organized police operated in London.

Thieves congregated in **flash houses**, public meeting places, such as taverns, that were headquarters for gangs. Deals were made, crimes plotted, and the sale of stolen goods negotiated. There were also smugglers, who moved freely in sparsely populated areas and transported goods without paying tax or duty. The third group were poachers, who lived in the country and supplemented their diet and income with game that belonged to a landlord. By the eighteenth century, professional thieves in larger cities had banded into gangs to protect themselves, increase their activities, and dispose of stolen goods.

Sometimes the difference between cop and criminal was difficult to see. Jack Wild, London's most famous thief and thief-taker perfected the process of buying and selling stolen goods and gave himself the title of "Thief-Taker General of Great Britain and Ireland." Before he was hanged, Wild controlled numerous gangs and dealt harshly with any thief who violated his strict code of conduct.[3] During this period, individual theft-related crimes began to be defined by the common law. The most important of these categories are still used today.

InfoTrac®

Is poaching still a crime? To find out, use "poaching" as a subject guide; you might also find the following articles interesting. The first discusses the fight by forensic criminologists to stop the illegal trade in wildlife:

- Kathleen F. Doyle, "Dead Reckoning: Wildlife Super Sleuths Use Sophisticated Forensics to Track Poachers," *Earth Action* 6, no. 2 (1995): 20–23.

- Ed Ricciuti, "Subtle Poaching: The Rules That Govern Hunting and Fishing Cannot Bend without Breaking," *Field and Stream* 103, no. 1 (1998): 12.

Modern Thieves

Hundreds of thousands of property-related crimes occur each year. In 2003, 702 317 thefts under $5000 and 284 496 break and enters were committed in Canada. Most are committed by occasional criminals who act opportunistically and are not committed career criminals; other theft-offenders are skilled, professional criminals. The following sections review these two orientations toward property crime.

Occasional Criminals

The majority of economic crimes are the work of amateur criminals whose decision to steal is spontaneous and whose acts are unskilled, unplanned, and haphazard. These do not involve the threat of violence, and many occur at domestic residences. Twenty-two percent of those accused in thefts under $5000 are youths.

It is likely that millions of theft-related crimes occur each year, and most are not reported to police agencies. In 1999 the General Social Survey or GSS (Canada's national victimization study) found that only 35 percent of thefts of personal property, 32 percent of household thefts, and 60 percent of motor vehicle thefts were reported to the police.[4] This represents a 5 percent decline in reporting since 1993. Of those crimes not reported, 59 percent were felt to be not important enough, and in 50 percent of cases, victims felt that the police couldn't do anything.

Most school-aged youths who commit thefts won't enter a criminal career and their behaviour drifts between conventional and criminal behaviour. Added to the pool of amateur thieves are millions of adults whose behaviour may occasionally violate the criminal law, such as shoplifters, pilferers, and tax cheats, but whose main source of income comes from conventional means and whose self-identity is noncriminal. Added together, their behaviours form the bulk of theft crimes.

According to routine activity theory, occasional property crime occurs when there is a **situational inducement** to commit crime.[5] Opportunities are available to members of all classes, but the upper class can engage in more crimes of price fixing, bribery, and embezzlement, which are closed to the lower classes, and lower-class individuals are overrepresented in street crime. Situational inducements are short-run influences on a person's behaviour that increase risk taking. These include psychological factors, such as financial problems, and social factors, such as peer pressure. Seasonality contributes to the opportunity to commit crime, with almost 10 percent more crime occurring in the summer than in the winter. Opportunity and situational inducements are not the cause of crime; rather, they are the occasion for crime—hence, the term **occasional criminal**.[6]

Opportunity and inducements are not randomly situated, and vary by age, class, and gender. Young persons, single women, high-income earners, urbanites, and homeowners are at greatest risk.[7]

Occasional offenders are not professionals. They do not rely on special skills to commit their crimes, and they are not committed to crime as a way of life. Unlike professionals, occasional criminals do not receive peer group support for their crimes. They will deny any connection to a criminal lifestyle and view their transgressions as being "out of character." They see their crimes as being motivated by necessity, but because of the lack of commitment may be the most likely to respond to general deterrence.

Professional Criminals

In contrast, **professional criminals** make a significant portion of their income from crime. They don't believe their acts are impulsive, nor do they use rationalizations to excuse the harmfulness of their action. Consequently, professionals pursue their craft with vigour, learning from experienced criminals the techniques that will earn them the most money with the least risk. Although few in number, professional criminals produce the greater losses to society and cause significant social harm.

Professional theft is nonviolent criminal behaviour undertaken with a high degree of skill for monetary gain that maximizes financial opportunities and minimizes the possibilities of apprehension. The most typical forms include pocket-picking, burglary, shoplifting, forgery and counterfeiting, extortion, sneak theft, and confidence swindling.

Three patterns emerge in the career patterns of professional criminals: (1) Youths come under the influence of older, experienced criminals who teach them the trade; (2) juvenile gang members continue their illegal activities at a time when most of their peers have "dropped out" to marry, raise families, and take conventional jobs; and (3) youths sent to prison for minor offences learn the techniques of crime from more experienced thieves. For example, this professional thief relates this story of his entry into crime:

> It was while I was at this parental school that I learned that some of the kids had been committed there by the court for stealing bikes. They taught me how to steal and where to steal them and where to sell them. Incidentally, some of the "nicer people" were the ones who bought bikes from the kids. They would dismantle the bike and use the parts: the wheels, chains, handlebars, and so forth.[8]

Edwin Sutherland used the term "professional criminal" to refer to thieves who do not use force or physical violence in their crimes and live solely by their wits and skill.[9] However, some criminologists use the term to refer to any criminal who identifies with a criminal subculture, makes their main living from crime, and possesses skill in their chosen trade.[10] Thus, one can become a professional safecracker, burglar, car thief, or fence.

Figure 12.1   Sutherland's Typology of Professional Thieves

Pickpocket ("cannon")

Sneak thief from stores, banks, and offices ("heel")

Shoplifter ("booster")

Jewel thief who substitutes fake gems for real ones ("pennyweighter")

Thief who steals from hotel rooms ("hotel prowl")

Confidence game artist

Thief in rackets related to confidence games

Forger

Extortionist from those engaging in illegal acts ("shakedown artist")

Source: Edwin Sutherland and Chic Conwell, *The Professional Thief* (Chicago: University of Chicago Press, 1937).

InfoTrac®

To read about the lives of three professional criminals, use InfoTrac® College Edition to access this article: Dick Hobbs, "Professional Crime: Change, Continuity and the Enduring Myth of the Underworld," *Sociology* 31, no. 1 (1997): 57–73.

InfoTrac®

To read about the life of an actual train robber, check out this article: Stephen Fox, "Chris Evans Could Always Be Relied on to Pull a Fast One," *Smithsonian* 26, no. 2 (1995): 84–92.

Sutherland's Professional Criminal. What we know about the lives of professional criminals has come to us through journals, diaries, autobiographies, and first-person accounts given to criminologists. The best-known account is Edwin Sutherland's in *The Professional Thief*.[11] This concept of professional theft has two dimensions. First, professional thieves engage in limited types of crime, which are described in Figure 12.1.

Second, professional thieves exclusively use their wits, a believable demeanour, and talking ability. Manual dexterity and physical force are of little importance. Professional areas of activity include bank robbery, car theft, burglary, and safecracking.

Professional thieves acquire status in their profession based on technical skill, financial standing, and connections. Sutherland and Conwell say that professional thieves share feelings, sentiments, and behaviours, none more important than the code of honour of the underworld; even under threat of the most severe punishment, a professional thief must never inform on his fellows.

Professional Criminals: The Fence. This view of the professional thief may be outdated because modern thieves often work alone and are not part of a criminal subculture.[12] However, Sutherland's principles certainly apply to the professional fence, a person who earns a living solely by buying and reselling stolen merchandise. In 2003, there were 32 777 cases of people having stolen goods in Canada, and certainly some would involve professional fences.

The fence's critical role in criminal transactions has been recognized since the eighteenth century. Fences act as intermediaries who purchase stolen merchandise, ranging from diamonds to outboard motors, and then resell it to merchants who market the goods to legitimate customers. Much of what is known about fencing comes from three in-depth studies.[13]

Klockars study of the fence Vincent Swaggi found that this highly professional criminal had developed techniques that made him almost immune to prosecution. During the course of a long and profitable career, Vincent spent only four months in prison because of his sophisticated knowledge of the law of stolen property.

To convict someone of receiving stolen goods, the prosecution must prove that the accused was in possession of the goods and knew that the goods had been stolen. Vincent had the skills to make sure that this could never be proved. He maintained close ties with influential members of the justice system, helping them purchase items at below-cost, bargain prices. He also helped authorities recover stolen goods, suggesting that fences customarily cheat their thief-clients and at the same time cooperate with the law.

In another study, the fence Sam Goodman also purchased stolen goods from a wide variety of thieves and suppliers, including burglars, drug addicts, shoplifters, dockworkers, and truck drivers. According to Sam, a successful fence must meet the following conditions:

1. *Upfront cash.* All deals are cash transactions, so a fence must have ready cash on hand.
2. *Knowledge of dealing: learning the ropes.* The fence must know the trade, develop a "larceny sense," learn to buy at acceptable prices, be able to not get caught, make the right contacts, and know how to wheel and deal and create opportunities for profit.
3. *Connections with suppliers of stolen goods.* The successful fence engages in long-term relationships with suppliers of high-value stolen goods. The warehouse worker who pilfers is a better supplier than is the narcotics addict, who is more likely to be apprehended and talk to police.
4. *Connections with buyers.* The successful fence must have continuing access to buyers of stolen merchandise who are inaccessible to the common thief.

5. *Complicity with law enforcers.* The fence must work out a relationship with law enforcement officials, who invariably find out about the fence's operations. The fence must either bribe officials with good deals on merchandise and cash or act as an informer to help police recover particularly important merchandise and arrest thieves.

Fences handle products from televisions to cigarettes, stereo equipment, watches, autos, and cameras. They operate through many legitimate fronts, including art dealers, antique stores, furniture and appliance retailers, remodelling companies, salvage companies, trucking companies, and jewellery stores. When deciding what to pay for goods, the fence uses a pricing policy. Professional thieves who steal high-priced items are given the highest amounts, 30 percent to 50 percent of wholesale price. For example, furs valued at $5000 may be bought for $1200. However, the amateur thief or drug addict who is not in a good bargaining position may receive only ten cents on the dollar.

Fencing contains many elements of professional theft as described by Sutherland: Fences live by their wits, never engage in violence, depend on their skill in negotiating, and maintain community standing based on connections and power. The only divergence between Sutherland's thief and the fence is the code of honour; the fence is more willing to cooperate with authorities than are professional criminals.

In a striking twist on an old trade, fencing stolen merchandise has now hit the World Wide Web. According to the National Fraud Information Center, online auction frauds account for 78 percent of all frauds and cost more than $300 each (see the Crime in the News feature).

The Nonprofessional Fence

Professional fences are the ones who have attracted the attention of criminologists. Yet fencing is also performed by amateur or occasional criminals. The guy who steals an outboard motor and sells it out of the back of a truck in the parking lot of a coffee shop is unlikely to be making that his steady occupation (and is most likely to get caught).

In interviews with convicted thieves, fences, and people who bought stolen property, criminologists discovered that novice burglars, such as juveniles and drug addicts, often find it so difficult to establish relationships with professional fences they turn instead to nonprofessionals to unload their stolen goods.[14]

One type of occasional fence is the part-timer who, unlike professional fences, has other sources of income. Part-timers are often "legitimate" businesspeople who integrate the stolen merchandise into their regular stock.

Crime in the News

eBay: Den of Thieves?

by Laura Lorek

Crooks looking to unload stolen goods are increasingly turning to eBay to find buyers and reap some quick cash.

In the past few years, police have busted at least three major fencing rings on eBay in which burglars and thieves from Boston, Chicago and Jackson, Mich., used the online auction marketplace to sell thousands of dollars worth of jewelry, electronics, coin collections, baseball cards, designer clothes and household goods.

In late February, Chicago investigators nabbed two Marshall Field's window dressers who allegedly stole more than $2 million in highend merchandise and then posted the stolen items for sale on eBay. The thieves stole a slew of pricey items, including $5,000 purses, $3,000 men's suits, $1,500 sweaters, computers, jewelry and even a $450 cashmere baby blanket and then posted the merchandise on eBay's auction site for sale to the highest bidder.

In June 2000, two men in the Boston area were arrested for burglarizing more than 100 homes and selling the stolen goods— baseball cards, collectors' edition coins, jewelry and silverware—on the popular auction site.

And in August 1999, two men from Jackson, Mich., were charged with selling stolen goods on eBay. They sold at least $19,000 worth of shoplifted merchandise, including digital cameras, fishing lures and radios, to buyers around the globe.

Kevin Pursglove, spokesman at eBay, said the San Jose company and its shoppers would have little reason to suspect that a particular item up for bid was stolen. Pursglove said eBay has 22 million items up for bid each day, which generate more than $22 million in daily sales. With that amount of traffic, there is no way to completely police all commerce, he said.

"With the overall level of ecommerce activity on eBay, problems like this are minuscule," Pursglove said. eBay limits its liability by calling itself a "venue."

Caveat Emptor

"We are not involved in the actual transaction between buyers and sellers," according to eBay's user agreement. "As a result, we have no control over the quality, safety or legality of the items advertised."

eBay does insure goods up to $200 with a $25 deductible, and it offers an escrow service by which a seller is not paid until the bidder has inspected his or her purchase.

Of course, fencing stolen goods is not a new crime. But

before the rise in popularity of online auctions, thieves had few options to dispose of stolen goods quickly. They often dumped them at pawnshops for much less than they were worth.

Police said criminals usually collect only 25 cents on the dollar when they pass off fenced material. But on an auction site like eBay, a bidding war can result in much higher profits.

However, selling stolen goods on eBay and other Internet auction sites is a very risky proposition. Instead of anonymously fencing stolen goods in a pawn shop for a handful of cash, the criminals are creating a paper trail that is easy to trace, said Angela Bell, spokeswoman at the FBI.

However, selling stolen goods online is a cybercrime some experts believe could become more common and more sophisticated.

In 1997, the Federal Trade Commission received about 100 complaints about fraud through online auction sites. Last year, the FTC recorded 10,700 online auction fraud complaints making Internet auctions the biggest source of online consumer complaints.

Source: Laura Lorek, "eBay: Den of Thieves?" *Interactive Week*, ZDNet News, May 14, 2001.

For example, the manager of a local video store buys stolen VCRs and tapes and rents them along with his legitimate merchandise (and does not report the income for tax purposes).

Some merchants become actively involved in theft either by specifying the merchandise they want the burglars to steal or by "fingering" victims. Some businesspeople sell merchandise to people and then

describe the customers' homes and vacation plans to known burglars so they can steal it back!

Some amateur fences barter stolen goods for services rendered. These "associational fences" typically have legitimate professional dealings with known criminals and include bail bonds agents, police officers, and attorneys. One lawyer bragged of getting a $12 000 Rolex watch from one client in exchange for

The Toronto and Regional CrimeStoppers is one of dozens of similar programs across the country responsible for recovering millions in stolen property every year. Recently, they redesigned their website to incorporate their new logo.

legal services. Bartering for stolen merchandise avoids taxes and becomes a transaction in the "underground economy."

"Neighbourhood hustlers" buy and sell stolen property as one of many ways they make a living; they keep some of the booty for themselves and sell the rest in the neighbourhood.

"Amateur receivers" can be complete strangers approached in a public place by someone offering a great deal on valuable commodities. Anyone buying a diamond ring for $50 cash should suspect it has been stolen. Some amateur receivers make a habit of buying merchandise at reasonable prices from a "trusted friend" and may account for a great deal of criminal receiving.

Common theft falls into several categories linked together because they involve the intentional misappropriation of property for personal gain. In such cases as fencing, the property is bought from another who is in illegal possession of the goods. In the case of embezzlement or burglary, the property is taken through stealth, while in such cases as bad cheques, fraud, and false pretenses, it is obtained through deception. Some of the major categories of common theft offences are discussed in the rest of this chapter in detail.

Theft

Theft was one of the earliest common-law crimes created by English judges to define acts in which one person took for their own use the property of another.[15] In common law, **larceny** was defined as "the trespassory taking and carrying away of the personal property of another with intent to steal." Today, definitions of theft include such acts as shoplifting and other theft offences that do not involve using force or threats on the victim or forcibly breaking into a person's home or place of work. (The former is robbery; the latter, break and enter.)

Originally, larceny involved only taking property that was in the possession of the rightful owners. For example, it would have been considered larceny for someone to go secretly into a farmer's field and steal a cow. Thus, the original common-law definition required a "trespass in the taking"; this meant that goods must have been taken from the physical possession of the owner.

In creating this definition, English judges were more concerned with disturbance of the peace than they were with thefts because if someone stole property from another's possession, the act could eventually lead to a confrontation. Consequently, the original definition did not include crimes in which the thief had come into the possession of the stolen property by trickery or deceit. For example, if someone entrusted with another person's property decided to keep it, it was not considered larceny.

The growth of manufacturing and the development of the free enterprise system required greater protection for private property. Commercial enterprise often required that property be entrusted to another for legitimate means.

To get around the element of "trespass in the taking," English judges created the concept of **constructive possession**, which applied to situations in which persons voluntarily and temporarily gave up custody of their property but still believed that the property was legally theirs. For example, if a person gave a jeweller a watch for repair, that person would believe that he or she owned the watch, although it was handed over to the jeweller. Similarly, when a person misplaces his or her wallet and someone else finds it and keeps it, although identification of the owner can be plainly seen, the concept of constructive possession makes the person who has kept the wallet guilty of larceny.

Theft Today

The criminal justice system separates theft into two classes according to the value of the goods involved: theft over and under $5000. The former involves small amounts of money or property and accounts for the majority of thefts in Canada. The latter is more likely to be punished by a sentence in prison. In Canada in 2003, there were 20 124 cases of theft over $5000, and 702 317 thefts under $5000. Of the latter, 9 percent were bicycles, 12 percent were a result of shoplifting, and 38 percent were from motor vehicles.

Theft is the most common criminal offence, accounting for about 69 percent of all property crime in Canada. It was estimated to have cost $3 billion in 1993, the costliest year for property crime in our society.[16] Satellite signal theft alone is estimated to cost more than $400 million annually in lost revenues to broadcasters, artists, and actors. Theft has increased by 1 percent a year since 1979. As society becomes more affluent and mobile and people spend less time at home, guardianship decreases and opportunities for theft continue to increase.[17]

Connections

Chapter 5 looks at routine activities theory and how situational variables affect crime rates.

Connections

Although Chapter 11 looks at rape as a violent crime, this chapter considers its relationship to capitalism as a property crime.

Shoplifting

Shoplifting is a common form of theft that involves taking goods from stores. The Retail Council of Canada estimates that "inventory shrinkage" cost

---

Culture, Gender, Ethnicity, and Criminology

How Capitalism Influences Rape

Herman and Julia Schwendinger's classic study of rape provides an excellent example of Marxian critical analysis. In looking at why women who are raped often feel guilty, the researchers came to believe that a rape victim has internalized discriminatory norms because she has been raised in a sexist society. Women have traditionally been viewed as the weaker sex, dependent on parents or husbands, so rape was seen as a property crime against those men.

During the early stages of capitalism, families underwent strain when industry demanded a labour force of men, only infrequently supplemented by single women. The role of father was strained as men were separated from their households. The woman's role became more narrowly defined as childbearer and childraiser. The limited economic role of women helped define them as dependants. Married women were viewed as

nonproductive, since they did not participate in commodity markets and earn money.

In reality, women's household productivity must be viewed as an essential contribution to the family and the economy. A woman is dependent on her husband's wage to buy things for the family, and her sense of self-worth reflects her dependency. Negative evaluations, such as those created by a rape experience, are likely to be turned inward by the woman, creating unwarranted self-recrimination and remorse.

In addition, schools and the media traditionally reinforce dependency in the curriculum. Textbooks used to stereotype the woman's role: Girls were depicted as helpless and frightened. Vocational tests provide fewer opportunities for girls. In media presentations, women are usually depicted as housewives and mothers. When women are portrayed on television commercials, they seem "concerned mainly with clean floors and clean hair—housework and their personal appearance."

Although women have made great advances, their labour is often in low-paid, low-mobility occupations and does little to improve their economic dependency. For these reasons women often blame themselves for being raped. The Schwendingers imply that women feel they have "let down" the people they depend on when they are trapped in a rape encounter. This self-blame for the attack prevents a woman from focusing on the true culprits: the rapist and the capitalist system whose economic structure results in a rape-producing climate in which women are undervalued. The Schwendingers' research approach illustrates the effect of material economic conditions.

It is not accidental that rape was traditionally seen as a crime of property.

Sources: Herman Schwendinger and Julia Schwendinger, *Rape and Inequality* (Newbury Park, Calif.: Sage, 1983); Herman Schwendinger and Julia Schwendinger, "Rape Victims and the False Sense of Guilt," *Crime and Social Justice* 13 (1980): 4–17.

businesses more than $3 billion in 2000. Usually, shoplifters try to snatch goods—jewellery, clothes, records, appliances—when store personnel are otherwise occupied. The "five-finger discount" is an extremely common form of crime.[18] Retail security measures add to the already high cost of this crime, which is passed on to the consumer. Shoplifting incidents have increased dramatically in the past 20 years, and retailers now expect an annual increase of 10 percent to 15 percent. Some studies estimate that about one in every nine shoppers steals from department stores. Discount stores have a minimum of sales help and depend on highly visible merchandise displays to attract purchasers, which make the merchandise vulnerable to shoplifters.

The Shoplifter. Only 10 percent of all shoplifters are professionals who derive the majority of their income from shoplifting.[19] Sometimes called **boosters** or **heels**, professional shoplifters resell stolen merchandise to pawnshops or fences, usually at half the original price.

The majority of shoplifters are amateurs. These **snitches** are usually respectable persons who do not conceive of themselves as thieves but are systematic shoplifters who steal merchandise for their own use. They are not simply seized by an uncontrollable urge to take something that attracts them; they come equipped to steal. Usually, they have never been apprehended before, lack criminal experience, and lack association with a criminal subculture.

Shoplifters are likely to reform if apprehended because they are not part of a criminal subculture. Getting arrested has a traumatic effect, and they will not risk a second offence.[20] Apprehension sometimes has a labelling effect that can result in repeated offending, but youths who are apprehended for shoplifting are usually deterred by official processing.[21]

Exhibit 12.2 | Quick Facts about Theft in Canada

- In 2003 theft was the largest property crime category, at 69 percent of the total.

- Of thefts with a value under $5000 in 2003, 38 percent were from motor vehicles.

- In 2003 theft was lowest in Newfoundland and Labrador (65 percent of the national average under $5000).

- British Columbia was 185 percent of the national average under $5000 in 2003.

- The 15 to 24 age group is nine times as likely to be victimized as the 65-plus age group.

- In 1993–94 "theft under" accounted for 78 percent of youth court theft cases; 64 percent were found guilty.

- Those earning $60 000 are twice as likely to be victimized as those in the $15 000 to $30 000 income group.

- The highest theft rate occurs in June to August, the lowest in December to February.

- For adults charged (over $5000), 75 percent were males; for theft under $5000, 71 percent were males.

- The clearance rate for having stolen goods was 86 percent in 2003; for property crime overall, it was 20 percent.

- In 2003, the most likely single item to be stolen was a motor vehicle (20 percent); firearms were the least likely (0.2 percent).

- A motor vehicle was most likely to be stolen from a parking lot (40 percent), rather than from a residence (22 percent) in 2003.

- Thefts were highest from commercial establishments (26 percent over $5000, 31 percent under $5000).

- Victimization surveys show that personal theft in 1999 was 17 percent higher than in 1993.

Sources: Statistics Canada, *Canadian Crime Statistics 2003* (Ottawa: Canadian Centre for Justice Statistics, 2004); Sandra Besserer and Catherine Trainor, "Criminal Victimization in Canada, 1999," *Juristat* 20 (2000); Dianne Hendrick, "Theft," in *Crime Counts: A Criminal Event Analysis,* ed. Leslie W. Kennedy and Vincent F. Sacco (Toronto: ITP Nelson, 1996).

Exhibit 12.3 | Quick Code: Theft

Section 322. (1) Every one commits theft who fraudulently and without colour of right takes, or fraudulently and without colour of right converts to his use or to the use of another person, anything, whether animate or inanimate, with intent,

  (a) to deprive, temporarily, or absolutely, the owner of it, . . .

Section 334. Except where otherwise provided by law, every one who commits theft

  (a) is guilty of an indictable offence and liable to imprisonment for a term not exceeding ten years, . . .

[Other relevant sections: sections 323, 324, 326, 327, 328, 329, 330, 331, 332, 338, 356]

Source: Rodrigues, Gary P., ed. *Pocket Criminal Code 1996* (Scarborough, Ont.: Carswell, 1995).

InfoTrac®

- Who shoplifts? Are they professionals or amateurs? To find out, read the following article: Read Hayes, "When Shoplifters Attack," *Security Management* 42, no. 6 (1998): 14.

- Can something be done to prevent shoplifting? To find out, read Katherine Hobson, "Hey, Security Tag Makers: You're It," *U.S. News & World Report* 130, no. 19 (2001): 34.

Controlling Shoplifting. One major problem associated with combating shoplifting is that many customers who observe pilferage are reluctant to report it to security agents. Store employees themselves often hesitate to get involved in apprehending a shoplifter. For example, in a controlled experiment, customers observed only 28 percent of staged shoplifting incidents that had been designed to get their attention. Furthermore, less than one-third of people who said they had observed an incident reported it to store employees.

In another controlled experiment using staged shoplifting incidents, less than 10 percent of shoplifting was detected by store employees, and customers appeared unwilling to report even serious cases.[22] Even in stores with an announced policy of full reporting and prosecution, only 70 percent of the shoplifting detected by employees was actually reported to managers, and only 5 percent was prosecuted. Foreigners, adults, and blue-collar workers were disproportionately represented among those officially punished. The store owner's decision to prosecute shoplifters is based on the value of the goods stolen, the nature of the goods stolen, and the manner in which the theft was realized. For example, shoplifters who planned their crime by using a concealed apparatus, such as a bag pinned to the inside of their clothing, were more apt to be prosecuted than were those who had impulsively put merchandise into their pockets.[23]

To aid in the arrest of shoplifters, some American jurisdictions have passed merchant privilege laws that are designed to protect retailers and their employers from litigation stemming from improper or false arrests of suspected shoplifters.[24] These laws protect but do not immunize merchants from lawsuits. The laws require that arrests be made on reasonable grounds or probable cause, detention be of short duration, and store employees or security guards conduct themselves in a reasonable fashion.

Prevention Strategies. Retail stores are now initiating a number of strategies designed to reduce or eliminate shoplifting. Security devices are just one way to combat shoplifting.

Target removal strategies involve using dummy goods on display while having the "real" merchandise kept under lock and key. Some stores sell from a catalogue while keeping merchandise in stockrooms. In one incident at the Bay, a shopper stole a box that he believed to contain a VCR from a display, but unfortunately, the box was full of bricks. He was caught when he returned it for a refund.

Target hardening strategies involve locking goods into place or having them monitored by electronic systems. Clothing stores may use racks designed to prevent large quantities of garments from being slipped off easily.

Situational measures place the most valuable goods in the least vulnerable places, use warning signs to deter potential thieves, and have closed-circuit cameras. Goods may be tagged with devices that give off an alarm or spray a dye if they are taken out of the shop.

Exhibit 12.4 describes some of the steps retail insurers recommend to reduce the incidence of shoplifting.

Exhibit 12.4 How to Stop Shoplifting: Some Useful Tips

- Train employees to watch for suspicious behaviour, such as a shopper loitering over a trivial item. Have them keep an eye out for shoppers wearing baggy clothes, carrying their own bag, or using some other method to conceal products.

- Develop a call code. When employees suspect that a customer is shoplifting, they can use the call to bring store management or security to the area.

- Products on lower floors face the greatest risk. Relocate the most tempting targets to upper floors.

- Use smaller exits and avoid placing the most expensive merchandise near these exits.

- Design routes within stores to make theft less tempting and funnel customers toward cashiers.

- Place service departments (credit and packaging) near areas where shoplifters are likely to stash goods. Extra supervision reduces the problem.

- Avoid creating corners in which there are no supervision sight lines. Restrict and supervise areas where electronic tags can be removed.

Sources: Marcus Felson, "Preventing Retail Theft: An Application of Environmental Criminology," *Security Journal* 7 (1996): 71–75; Marc Brandeberry, "$15 Billion Lost to Shoplifting," *Today's Coverage, A Newsletter of the Grocers Insurance Group,* Portland, OR, 1997.

InfoTrac®

To learn more about shoplifting control, use InfoTrac® College Edition, and read Ann Longmore-Etheridge, "Bagging Profits Instead of Thieves," *Security Management* 45, no. 10 (2001): 70.

Private Justice. Efforts to control the spread of shoplifting have prompted some retail chains to establish loss prevention units, private justice systems that work parallel to but independent of the public justice system. Private security officers have many of the law enforcement powers granted to municipal police officers, including arrest of suspects and search and seizure.[25]

Shoplifters may be required to compensate store owners for the value of the goods they attempted to steal, costs incurred because of their illegal acts, and punitive damages. Some major Canadian retailers practise this form of "cost recovery" but with some controversy, especially when the parents of a youth who steals are sued. The availability of civil damages affects decision making, if store owners go after affluent shoplifters for civil recovery and ship the poor to the public criminal justice system for prosecution.

Auto Theft

The rate of motor vehicle theft was 514 per 100 000 people in 2003. In 2001, the Canadian Coalition Against Insurance Fraud estimated that more than 450 cars were stolen in Canada every day. Thirty-four percent of all *Criminal Code* property offences in 2003 involved the theft of a car or of property from a car, not including trucks or motorcycles. One in a hundred vehicles was reported stolen, and losses from motor vehicle thefts, thefts from motor vehicles, and vandalism against motor vehicles amounted to $1.6 billion in 1993.[26] In contrast, credit card fraud cost $55 million, and bank robberies $3.5 million! The 2000 International Crime Victimization Survey estimated that car vandalism was the most prevalent crime measured, with 7 percent of the population having been a victim of this crime.

The cost of auto theft is estimated to be $1 billion per year. Thirty years ago, 95 percent of the cars were recovered, but this has dropped to 72 percent today. The clearance rate in auto theft is 11 percent. This means that in the past, the typical car thief was out for a joyride; today, however, the car is stolen for resale or to be chopped into parts.[27]

One typology uncovered five categories of auto theft transactions:[28]

1. *Joyriding:* Motivated by teenagers' desire to acquire power and prestige, joyriders do not steal cars for profit but to experience the benefits of having an automobile.
2. *Short-term transportation:* Auto theft for short-term transportation involves the theft of a car to drive to another place, and then perhaps another theft to continue the journey.
3. *Long-term transportation:* Stealing cars for long-term transportation means keeping the car; usually older and lower class, these thieves may paint and disguise cars to avoid detection.
4. *Profit:* Auto theft is motivated by monetary gain; organized professionals resell expensive cars after altering identification numbers; amateur auto strippers steal batteries, tires, and wheel covers to sell them or equip their own cars.
5. *Commission of another crime:* A small portion of auto thieves steal cars to use in other crimes, such as robberies and thefts.

At one time, joyriding was the predominant motive for auto theft, and most cars were taken by relatively affluent, White, middle-class teenagers looking for excitement.[29] Youths represented 58 percent of those charged with motor vehicle theft in 2003, up from 40 percent in 1999. However, there appears to be a change in this pattern: Fewer cars are being taken today while, concomitantly, fewer stolen cars are being recovered. Part of the reason is the increase in the number of professional car thieves who are linked to "chop shops" or export rings. Export of stolen vehicles has become a global problem, and the emergence of capitalism in Eastern Europe has increased the demand for Western-made cars.[30]

In 2001, Interpol reported that more than three million cars are stolen in the world annually. The value of vehicles stolen from 45 countries in Europe, North America, Africa, and Asia is estimated at U.S.$21 billion per year. Interpol's Automated Search Facility database for stolen motor vehicles contains records for more than 2.5 million stolen cars from 59 countries and is used by police forces worldwide to track stolen vehicles. Interpol alleges that profits from smuggling stolen cars are used to fund terrorist organizations.[31]

Apparently, high-ranking members of the Hezbollah, an Iranian-backed terrorist group, favour the $70 000 Lincoln Navigator, quite often stolen in Ontario!

Which Cars Are Taken Most? Car thieves show signs of rational choice when they make their target selections, as the Crime in the News feature shows. Luxury cars and utility vehicles are popular, and older Japanese models are more valuable because of the interchangeability of their parts.

Crime in the News

Surrey, B.C., Is Auto Theft Capital of Canada

When you're a cop in charge of dealing with auto thefts and the vehicles disappear at a rate of about 90 a day, it helps to have a sense of humour. RCMP Sgt. Enzo Nadalin does.

The head of the RCMP Auto Theft Task Force has the dubious task of trying to deal with what has been described as an epidemic—about 33,000 vehicles stolen in British Columbia in 2001.

He appears to be losing the battle and is appealing to courts, lawmakers and the honest citizenry.

Recently, in an effort to draw the media's attention to the startling statistic, Nadalin issued a news release this summer entitled Driving Miss Daisy, after the popular movie starring Morgan Freeman and Jessica Tandy in which Freeman played Tandy's chauffeur in the Deep South.

But the duo in Nadalin's story was a mother and son auto theft team.

"Mom was driving around in a stolen car driven by the son," Nadalin says in a recent interview. "Mom was in her 60s."

The Crown laid several charges against the son but felt it didn't have a substantial likelihood of conviction regarding Mom, said Nadalin, even though the son had been caught before with Mom nearby.

"We did them once before and she was there," says Nadalin, his voice resonating with frustration. "All of a sudden we're doing it again and there's stolen vehicles in the yard, in the garage and stolen motorcycles in the basement." Nadalin was successful in getting the media's attention.

Last week he did it again by releasing new, non-humorous auto theft statistics that focused on the much-maligned Vancouver suburb of Surrey.

The sprawling community was dubbed the auto theft capital of North America based on the number of vehicles stolen per 100,000 population.

RCMP figures show that the city had about 6,100 vehicles stolen in 2001—a rate of 1,743 automobiles stolen per 100,000 residents.

In Los Angeles and New York, the rate is about 400 autos per 100,000 residents. A recent study by the U.S. National Insurance Crime Bureau says the U.S.'s highest auto-theft rate is in Phoenix, where 1,081 cars are stolen per 100,000 population.

Surrey is tops for auto theft in Canada, followed by Winnipeg and Regina—a close second and third. London, Ont., is fourth.

Why Surrey?

"I've got to be careful how I answer this one," says Nadalin, who doesn't want to offend the vast majority of law-abiding citizens but is aware of Surrey's reputation for crime and transients.

"These people get out of jail and double up (for accommodation) and SkyTrain brings a lot of people out here. They can do their crime and go back to wherever they live."

Last week, as newspapers and TV milked the auto theft story, Nadalin issued another news release aimed at getting more publicity.

This one he headlined, "I'll be out in the morning," and described a 17-year-old who was caught trying to steal a car. He assaulted an arresting officer, fled and was picked up later.

"He bragged that 'I'll be out (of custody) in the morning,'" said Nadalin.

Since 1999, the youth has been arrested 19 times by Surrey RCMP and has nine prior Criminal Code convictions.

Police feel handcuffed by the seemingly endless parade of repeat offenders and their treatment in the justice system.

"We've arrested about 400 people since we've been in operation, and out of that 400 there's only a half dozen that don't have a prior criminal record," says Nadalin.

Many have between six and 15 prior convictions "and one guy has 52 prior convictions, including car theft and break and enter."

"We're not asking that all car thieves be put in jail. What we're saying is a small percentage of car thieves be put in jail. These are the career criminals."

There is some progress, however.

Most vehicle models since 2000 have built-in anti-theft devices in the form of a key that has a built-in computer chip that makes the car almost impossible to steal even through the tried-and-true hot wiring.

The auto task force also has compiled the most popular cars to steal.

The top 10 in B.C. include Honda Civic and Accord, the Acura, the Dodge Caravan and Plymouth Voyager vans, and Toyota Camry.

They're popular because "with a butter knife and a screwdriver, you can enter that vehicle and start it in less than 60 seconds."

The "typical" car thief is also no candidate for the junior achievement award.

He is a white male, 16 to 25 years old, unemployed, with trouble holding a steady job.

He is usually on welfare and has a prior, extensive criminal record. The thief has low self-esteem, comes from a dysfunctional family, has no people skills, is a poor student, smokes and uses drugs and has poor grooming habits.

Most car thefts in B.C., says Nadalin, are done alone or with another person and are not part of organized crime rings to the extent they are in other parts of Canada.

While more than 90 per cent of stolen vehicles are recovered, others are never seen again or are taken to chop shops.

The auto theft task force has broken up about 35 chop shops since it started, but has no handle on the number out there.

"That's almost like saying, 'How many (marijuana) grow-ops are in an area?'" says Nadalin.

While Surrey is the latest public relations victim in terms of car thefts, Vancouver held the distinction for many years. The latest statistics place it second in British Columbia while Burnaby, New Westminster and Langley are next.

Doug McClelland of the Insurance Corp. of B.C. cites another array of astounding theft or vandalism statistics.

ICBC in 2001 paid out $167 million in claims for vehicles that were stolen, damaged or vandalized.

That included $40 million in claims for 56,000 vehicle break-ins in which the car was not stolen and another $30 million for the 53,000 claims of vehicle vandalism.

"It truly is an epidemic and it's growing out of control," says McClelland.

Surrey Mayor Doug McCallum called for more jail time and a five-year driving ban for convicted car thieves.

Solicitor General Rich Coleman supported McCallum's plan,

> **The 10 most-stolen vehicles in Canada:**
>
> 1. Hyundai Tiburon FX
> 2. Volkswagen Golf
> 3. Accura Integra
> 4. Jeep TJ
> 5. Hyundai Accent
> 6. Chevy Cavalier Z-24
> 7. Dodge Durango
> 8. Dodge Dakota
> 9. Toyota 4-Runner
> 10. Dodge Ram pickup
>
> Source: RCMP auto theft task force.

saying the Superintendent of Motor Vehicles may issue a driving prohibition "if it is in the public interest."

Source: Canadian Press, "Surrey, B.C., Is Auto Theft Capital of Canada," September 15, 2002.

Car models that have been in production for a few years without many design changes stand the greatest risk of theft. Camrys made between 1988 and 1991 are attractive because they have parts that are most valued in the secondary market. Luxury cars typically experience a sharp decline in their theft rate soon after a design change. Older cars are more likely to be uninsured, and demand for stolen used parts is higher for these vehicles.

The economics of auto theft are interesting. The Insurance Board of Canada estimates that an organized theft ring will pay between $150 and $500 for a stolen Jeep Grand Cherokee. The VIN from a wrecked model purchased for $2000 will be placed on the stolen SUV for a cost between $500 and $1500. It can then be sold "legitimately" in another jurisdiction to an unsuspecting buyer for about $45 000, creating a profit of about $40 000. If it is sold in Eastern Europe, the profit could be as high as $95 000!

InfoTrac®

Look for the link between the movie *The Fast and the Furious* and car theft rates in Texas; read "Street-Racing Culture Has Impact on Auto-Theft Rates, Say Texas Investigators," *Knight Ridder/Tribune Business News,* February 18, 2004.

Connections

Chapter 5 discusses the rational choice view of car theft. As you may recall, cars with expensive radios and parts are more often the target of rational thieves.

Carjacking. You may have read about gunmen approaching a car and forcing the owner to give up the

| Exhibit 12.5 | **Quick Facts about Auto Theft in Canada** |

- The auto theft rate increased 5 percent in 2001, for the first time in five years, and is now 10 percent higher than it was a decade ago.

- Since 1991, motor vehicle theft rates have doubled in London and Hamilton, tripled in Regina, and more than quadrupled in Winnipeg.

- Canada ranked fifth highest of 17 countries for risk of car theft in the 1999 International Crime Victimization Survey.

- Cars are the most commonly stolen vehicle, but truck and sport utility vehicles theft has increased 59 percent in 10 years.

- Parking lots, streets, garages, and driveways account for 87 percent of all motor vehicle thefts.

- One-quarter of all stolen vehicles were never recovered, were sold for resale, were exported, or were chopped for parts.

- Motor vehicle thefts are characterized by very low clearance rates: 13 percent in 2001.

- Although the rate of youths 12 to 17 years of age charged with motor vehicle theft is 35 percent lower than a decade ago, youths account for 42 percent of all persons charged.

- Thefts from motor vehicles increased (+1.3 percent) in 2001 for the first time in 10 years, with audio equipment the item most likely to be stolen.

Source: CCJS, "Motor Vehicle Theft in Canada, 2001," *Juristat* 23, no. 1 (2003).

keys; in some cases, people have been killed when they reacted too slowly. This type of auto theft has become common enough that it has its own name, **carjacking**.[32] This is considered a type of robbery because it involves the use of force.

Carjacking is a new form of crime that some have dubbed "urban terrorism." Such high-profile crime attracts widespread media coverage. In Florida, for example, the killing of tourists in out-of-state rental cars received international attention several years ago. In a form of carjacking, called the "bump and grab," cars are stolen when they are hit from behind and the driver pulls off to the side of the road.

In another form of urban terrorism, called a "home invasion," armed robbers force their way into a home while the residents are there and extort money by force.[33] Such crimes strike at the heart of our safest places, our homes, and cause a lot of concern. In two-thirds of home invasions, all the accused are strangers to

the homeowners; half of the home invasions involve a weapon; the elderly are most frequently the victims; and the rates of home invasions have remained stable at about 23 per 100 000 population.[34]

Figure 12.2 shows the risk of carjacking compared with other life events.

Combating Auto Theft. Because of its commonality and high loss potential, auto theft has been a target of situational crime prevention efforts.[35] One approach has been to increase the risk of apprehension. Information hotlines offer rewards for information leading to the arrest of car thieves. Another approach has been to place fluorescent decals on windows that indicate that the car is never used between 1 a.m. and 5 a.m.; if police spot a car with the decal being operated during this period, they know it is stolen. Cars have also been equipped with radio transmitters. The LoJack system involves a tracking device installed in the car that gives off a signal, enabling the police to pinpoint the car's location.

Other prevention measures make it more difficult to steal cars. The most common method of stealing a car is by using the keys (43 percent), with most cars in Canada stolen using the keys left in them.[36] Parking lots have been equipped with theft-deterring closed-circuit TV cameras and barriers. Manufacturers have installed more sophisticated steering-column locking devices and other security systems that make theft harder. Improved security measures, such as lighting and patrols, probably deter auto crime but displace it to other areas.[37]

A study by the Highway Loss Data Institute (HLDI) in the United States, however, found that most car theft prevention methods, especially alarms, have little effect on theft rates. The most effective methods appear to be devices that immobilize a vehicle by cutting off the electrical power needed to start the engine.

Or alternatively, a person could drive a car that nobody would want to steal.

False Pretences or Fraud

False pretences, or **fraud,** involves misrepresenting a fact to cause a victim to willingly give his or her property to the wrongdoer, who keeps it.[38] The definition of false pretences was created by the English Parliament in 1757 to cover an area of law left untouched by larceny statutes. The first false pretences law punished people who "knowingly and designedly by false pretense or pretenses, [obtained] from any person or persons, money, goods, wares or merchandise with intent to cheat or defraud any person or persons of the same."[39] False pretences differs from traditional larceny because the victims willingly give their possessions to the offender.

| Figure 12.2 | Carjacking Compared with Risks of Other Life Events |

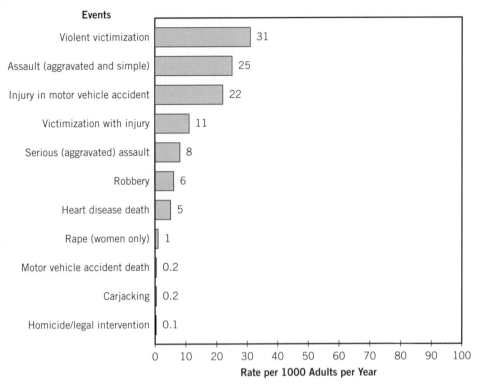

Source: *Highlights from 20 Years of Surveying Crime Victims*, October 1993, NCJ-144525. Online: http:www/ojp.usdoj.gov/bjs/pub/ascii/c.txt (U.S. Department of Justice).

An example of false pretences would be an unscrupulous merchant selling someone a chair by claiming it was an antique but knowing all the while that it was a cheap copy. Another example would be a phony healer selling a victim a bottle of coloured sugar water as an elixir that would cure a disease. A report issued in 2004 estimated that hazardous fake products now commonly found include cosmetics laced with toxins, toys made with contaminated material, and faulty electrical switches. The total cost of lost revenue from the sale of counterfeit products was estimated to be in the billions of dollars.[40]

Exhibit 12.6 illustrates some facts and trends about fraud in Canada in recent years.

Confidence games are run by swindlers and usually involve getting a "mark" interested in some get-rich-quick scheme, which may have illegal overtones. The criminal's hope is that when victims lose their money, they will be too embarrassed and afraid to call the police. There are hundreds of varieties of con games. The most common is called the pigeon drop.[41] A package or wallet containing money is "found" by a con man or woman. A passing victim is asked for

advice about what to do since the wallet contains no identification. Another "stranger," who is part of the con, approaches and enters the discussion. The three decide to split the money. But first, one of the swindlers goes off to consult a lawyer; and on returning says that the money can be split up, but each must have the means to reimburse the original owner. The victim is asked to give some good-faith money for the lawyer to hold. When the victim goes to the lawyer's office to pick up a share of the loot, the address is bogus and the money is gone.

In the 1990s con games were appropriated by corrupt telemarketers, who contacted people, typically elderly people, over the phone to defraud them. The FBI estimates that illicit telephone pitches cost $3 billion to $40 billion a year in the United States and $80 million to $100 million in Canada.[42] In one scam, a salesman tried to get $500 from a 78-year-old woman by telling her the money was needed as a deposit to make sure she would get $50 000 cash she had supposedly won in a contest. A Las Vegas-based telephone con game defrauded people out of more than $1.3 million by soliciting donations for families of

Exhibit 12.6	Quick Facts about Fraud in Canada

- In 2003, 92 838 cases of fraud were reported to the police, with a clearance rate of 44 percent.

- Cheque fraud outnumbered credit card fraud three to one in 1995; it was reversed to two to three in 2003.

- The cost of credit card fraud in 2001 was almost $2 million.

- Eight percent of those charged with break and enter were women in 2003, compared with 41 percent of those charged with fraud.

- The national fraud rate is 294 per 100 000, with the lowest rate in Prince Edward Island at 123 and the highest rate in Alberta at 439.

- Youths compose only 7 percent of those charged with fraud offences.

- Primary targets for fraud are businesses (53 percent), banks (28 percent), and individuals (6 percent).

- The elderly are most often victimized by telephone fraud, making up 61 percent of victims in 2003.

- Credit card counterfeiting is the fastest-growing fraudulent crime.

- The cost of fraud is more than $3 billion annually.

- Insurance fraud costs about $1.3 billion per year, representing 10 percent to 15 percent of auto, household, and commercial claims.

- Telemarketing prize and lottery fraud cost more than $2 million in 2003.

Sources: Statistics Canada, *Canadian Crime Statistics 2003* (Ottawa: Canadian Centre for Justice Statistics, 2004); Statistics Canada, *Canadian Crime Statistics 1999* (Ottawa: Canadian Centre for Justice Statistics, 2000); Derek E. Janhevich, "The Changing Nature of Fraud in Canada," *Juristat* 18 (1998); "Counterfeiting and Credit Card Fraud," Royal Canadian Mounted Police, http://www.rcmp-grc.gc.ca/scams/ccandpc_e.htm (accessed May 17, 2005); "Statistics on Phone Fraud, 2003," PhoneBusters, http://www.phonebusters.com (accessed May 20, 2001); Derek Paul McPhie, "Fraud," in *Crime Counts: A Criminal Event Analysis,* ed. Leslie W. Kennedy and Vincent F. Sacco (Toronto: ITP Nelson, 1996).

 Famous Canadian Criminals

Albert Johnson Walker

When Albert Walker (left) fled Canada, he took his daughter Sheena (right) with him. Walker was sought by Interpol for defrauding clients of more than $3 million in pension and investment funds.

After his company defrauded 30 clients of more than $3 million from pension and investment funds, Albert Walker, a financial adviser, fled to England in 1990 with his daughter Sheena, 15. With an arrest warrant issued for him in Woodstock, Ontario, he was soon on Interpol's most wanted list. If he had stayed in Canada, he would have faced more than three dozen fraud-related charges, including money-laundering.

When Walker was arrested in 1996 in a tiny village northwest of London, he was living with his daughter and her two children. However, he was living under the name of David Davis. His daughter posed as his wife, Noel Davis. The paternity of the children was described as "unknown."

Through his personal secretary, Walker had met a man named Ronald Platt and arranged to use his identity in exchange for money. However, in 1996, Walker killed Platt and dumped his body in the ocean, assuming his identity completely. Police were able to trace Walker's whereabouts on the day Platt was killed from information retrieved from his global posi-tioning satellite (GPS) device. In 1998, Walker was found guilty of murder. In 2000, he asked for a transfer to a Canadian prison, but was flatly turned down.

Albert Walker still faced a number of charges in Canada. This was a fraud of magnificent proportions, made possible because of his privileged position. Walker came back to Canada in late February. He'll be serving the rest of his sentence here, and police still plan to prosecute him for the 37 fraud charges here.

Exhibit 12.7	Telemarketing Scams

1. *The prize scam*: The caller says you have won a valuable prize, but you must first submit a payment for taxes, transportation, customs, insurance, or legal fees. Response: When you're a winner, you don't have to pay for your prize. Don't send money in advance.

2. *The lottery scam*: The caller wants you to be part of a syndicate, or group, to buy a large number of lottery tickets in foreign lotteries. Response: No matter what the caller says, the odds per ticket remain millions to one. Don't buy lottery tickets from a telephone solicitation.

3. *The advanced fee loan scam*: This usually starts with an advertisement for an easy loan. If victims have a bad credit history, they can call a number to be approved for a loan. However, they're told an advance fee is required, usually about 10 percent of the amount. Response: It is illegal to require an advance fee for a loan. Don't deal with any lender who charges an advance fee for a loan.

4. *Vacation scams*: The caller offers savings to popular destinations, and certificates are issued

in the victim's name for a reservation. Response: When travelling, deal with a reputable agent.

5. *Charity scams*: The caller solicits for a worthy cause. Response: You should carefully select causes you wish to support; call and arrange to have your contribution sent directly. Don't send money to a charity with which you are not completely familiar.

6. *Police/firefighter magazines*: The caller wants you to advertise in the magazine, to support a police or fire department. Response: Police or fire departments don't support such magazines.

With the growth of direct-mail marketing and 1-900 telephone numbers that charge callers more than $2.50 per minute for conversations with beautiful and willing sex partners, new confidence games will increase. However, 64 percent of fraud offences were cleared in 1995—most likely a small percentage of all swindlers, scam artists, and frauds.

Source: © 1997 Toronto Police Service, www.TorontoPolice.on.ca.

those killed in the Oklahoma City bombing. The Phone Busters unit of the Ontario Provincial Police estimates that one Canadian per week loses more than $5000 in such schemes. Some common telemarketing scams are detailed in Exhibit 12.7.

In a study conducted for the Insurance Board of Canada's investigative division by a team at St. Francis Xavier University, it was determined that 26 percent of four thousand closed personal injury claims were fraudulent. Opportunistic fraud, such as inflating medical expenses, was the most common type. The rate is highest in Ontario and lowest in Alberta. It also tends to be higher in major cities and metropolitan areas.

In 2001, an organized ring of 25 people were sued for staging car accidents, allegedly defrauding the Insurance Corporation of British Columbia of $400 000. They would stage the accidents between 9:30 p.m. and midnight, in an area where there would be no witnesses, and then submit claims for about $30 000.

In 2004, several sellers on eBay were fined and ordered to pay restitution for fraudulently bidding up prices to unsuspecting buyers of motor vehicles.

Identity Theft. A new form of fraud or false pretences is identity theft. The Canadian Council of Better Business Bureaus estimates that identity theft takes $2.5 billion out of the Canadian economy annually.

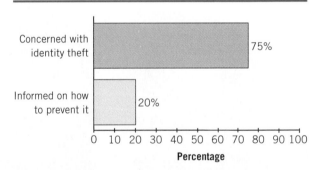

Seventy-five percent of Canadian adults are concerned about identity theft, but only 20 percent said that they were very well informed about how to prevent it.

Source: Poll conducted by Ipsos Reid, June 30, 2004, "Canadians Concerned About Identity Theft."

With fake driver's licences available on the Internet, illegitimate identities are much easier to build. A jump in counterfeiting was a significant factor in the increase in the crime rate in 2003. In the same year, it was reported that hundreds of social insurance numbers were stolen at Canada Customs. SINs allow access to databases that include employment records, and allow a person to apply for employment insurance, credit cards, and welfare.

Bad Cheques

Another form of fraud is cashing a bank cheque drawn on a nonexistent or underfunded bank account. Cheque fraud accounted for 68 percent of all reported frauds in 1979. By 1993 this had declined to 50 percent, in 1999 to 33 percent, and in 2003 to 21 percent. This form of fraud has a high clearance rate: 55 percent in 2003, higher than for fraud (44 percent) and for property crime (20 percent).

Edwin Lemert found that the majority of "naive" cheque forgers are amateurs who do not believe their actions will hurt anyone.[43] They come from middle-class backgrounds and have little identification with a criminal subculture. They cash bad cheques because of a financial crisis—perhaps they have lost money gambling and have some pressing bills to pay. Often socially isolated, they are unsuccessful in their relationships and are risk-prone when faced with a situation that is unusually stressful. The willingness of stores and other commercial establishments to cash cheques with a minimum of fuss to promote business encourages the cheque forger to risk committing a criminal act.

Lemert found that a few professionals, **systematic forgers**, make a substantial living by passing bad cheques. However, professionals constitute a relatively small segment of the total population of cheque forgers. It is estimated that the 15 000 known incidents in 1993 resulted in a loss of $100 million. Stores and banks may choose not to press charges, since the effort to collect the money due them is often not worth their while. It is also difficult to separate the true cheque forger from the neglectful shopper.

Crime in the News

Identity Theft a Nightmare

I stole a car today. And I used your credit card.

I walked into the car rental shop, and in five minutes drove out with a new minivan. I went shopping, bought a DVD player, a digital camera, some sports equipment and a computer, which I promptly hawked. On the way to Montreal I stayed in motels, bought meals, and received cash advances, all with your credit card. I sold the car for $5000, which went into a cargo container destined for a foreign country. All told, you're on the hook for ten thousand dollars. Your credit rating will be ruined.

This is called identity theft.

The RCMP says that with your name, address, date of birth, and social insurance number, a thief can take over your financial accounts, open new bank accounts, transfer money between accounts, apply for loans or credit cards, all the things that you can do yourself. Except you are no longer yourself.

In fact, the basic information needed to apply for credit, to receive cell phone service, to rent an apartment, to purchase goods online, could be used to steal your identity.

Maybe it started with stealing your purse in the grocery store, or the gym, or out of your car. I found your driver's licence, credit cards, social insurance card, and your employee identification card. Have you checked your wallet lately to see how much personal information is there? We carry a lot of plastic, and credit card fraud is the most common type of identity theft complaint. Or maybe I simply found your credit card invoice in the garbage, or your blue box, and took that information. Or perhaps I found a letter soliciting reapproval of your credit card in the mailbox after you moved.

Identity theft is simple.

I could redirect all your mail to a new address, or fill out a preapproved credit card application in your name. There is no guarantee that even a legitimate company's database is invulnerable to infiltration. Maybe

you ordered something online through an unsecured website, or over the phone using a credit card number. Today's business practices involve collecting a lot of personal information to ensure more effective marketing. However, creating intensive consumer profiles also leaves consumers susceptible to identify theft.

It is unfortunate, but you will spend hundreds of hours, and thousands of dollars trying to clear your name, and it will probably never come to trial. The Ontario government is introducing new legislation to deal with what it calls the fastest growing and most serious consumer crime in North America. We are not yet sure how good that legislation will be. The PhoneBusters organization estimates that the number of identity theft victims grew 8 percent in 2003 over the previous year, and that the losses increased 60 percent. This is definitely the tip of the iceberg. Most victims probably don't realize they've been taken, or report the crime if they are. The three major credit bureaus estimate the problem to be very large, not the 8000 cases reported by PhoneBusters, but at least 20 000 cases a year. This shows a shocking non-report rate of staggering dimensions. All told, identity-theft costs consumers, banks, credit card firms, and business at least $2.5 billion per year.

The cost to society will include money spent by the business community, costs to you for legal assistance from lawyers, costs to the government for judicial and law enforcement, investigation and prosecution. And we are at an infancy in terms of estimating the costs. The FBI estimates the average cost for this type of crime investigation is $20 000; and for prosecution, a minimum of $10 000. There is the cost of the theft itself, the cost of time to deal with the problem personally, the cost of policing and professional

assistance, and most importantly, the cost of the loss of public trust.

The Privacy Rights Clearing House estimates the average victim spends 175 hours to restore their identity, if they know of the theft. You might eventually be cleared of fault, but in the intervening period the debts appear on your credit record.

What can you do? Well, it's quite simple. Most people are worried about the misuse of personal information, even at the same time as they are increasingly unable to control that information. So, first, only carry as much plastic as you need. Second, keep your eye on your mail if it's delivered to an unsecured place; and make sure the change of address works. Third, never give personal information over the phone, over the Internet, or to someone who has no need to know. Fourth, if someone calls

wanting to know personal banking information, you should call the police. Fifth, know your payment cycles on your credit card, and call if the bill is late. If a change of address is requested for your credit card billing, it might be a while before you notice not receiving a bill. And then it's too late.

The U.S. National Centre for Victims of Crime estimates that 12 months pass between the first misuse of the victim's identity and its discovery. There are other estimates that are even higher. If research shows that it may be over a year before you even realize that your identity and financial security have been compromised—you may never do so.

To report an incident of identity theft, contact your local RCMP.

Source: © Chris McCormick, *Daily Gleaner*, June 24, 2004.

Credit Card Theft

The use of stolen credit cards has become a major problem. Credit card companies sustained an $84 million loss due to credit card fraud in 1996. Almost 78 000 credit card files were open, with more than 18 000 of those stolen credit cards. Fully 24 percent of credit cards used fraudulently were lost or stolen. Counterfeit or forged cards accounted for more than 30 percent of fraud cases in 1995–96, as reported by the Canadian Bankers' Association.[44]

Most credit card abuse is the work of amateurs who acquire stolen cards through theft and then use them for two days. However, members of professional credit card rings get jobs as clerks in stores, where they collect names and credit card numbers of customers. Gang members buy plain plastic cards and have the names and numbers embossed on them. The gang then creates a fictitious wholesale jewellery company, receives authorization to accept credit cards from the customers, and uses the phony cards to charge nonexistent jewellery purchases on the accounts of the people whose names and card numbers they had collected. The thieves withdraw the money from their business account and leave town.

Embezzlement

The crime of **embezzlement** was observed in early Greek culture when Aristotle alluded to theft by road commissioners and other government officials.[45] It was first codified into law by the English Parliament during the sixteenth century to fill a gap in the larceny law.[46] Until then, to be guilty of theft a person had to take goods from the physical possession of another. However, as explained earlier, this definition did not cover instances in which one person willingly gave another temporary custody of his or her property. For example, in everyday commerce, store clerks, bank tellers, brokers, and merchants gain lawful possession but not legal ownership of other people's money.

Embezzlement occurs when someone trusted with property fraudulently keeps it for his or her own use, distinguished from fraud on the basis of when the criminal intent was formed. The mere act of moving property without the owner's consent, or damaging it or using it, is not considered embezzlement. However, using it up, selling it, pledging it, giving it away, or holding it against the owner's will is held to be embezzlement.

Although it is impossible to know how many embezzlement incidents occur annually, the FBI found that only

GST Fraud Ring

In 1991, the Canadian government introduced a Goods and Services Tax. This move generated another category of national revenue as well as a new opportunity for criminal gain. Although some individuals pointed fingers at federal officials for cheating the public out of hard-earned money, others were busy detecting ways to exploit the system. Loopholes in GST rebate procedures quickly registered on their radar.

The path to crime can be paved with good intentions. To promote business, the government reimburses Canadian companies for certain GST payments. However, weaknesses in the administration of these tax breaks have managed to boost illicit activity. Authorities rely on self-reports of GST payment amounts and they tend to issue refunds before verifying any submitted paperwork. Both real and phony companies have defrauded the government by

fabricating business transactions and forwarding bogus tax claims.

In the most complex and lucrative GST rebate scam to date, automobiles were the merchandise of choice. Between April 1995 and December 1998, a ring of swindlers staged thousands of sales involving vehicles that were sometimes nonexistent. This "Cadillac of GST frauds" was exposed in the late 1990s through Project Phantom, a police probe that lasted 10 months. Investigators from the Halton Regional Police Service, the Royal Canadian Mounted Police, the Ontario Provincial Police, the Ontario Motor Vehicle Industry Council, and Revenue Canada (now the Canada Customs and Revenue Agency) joined forces in the operation.

Although an estimated $50 million in rebates were illegally obtained, the legal value of this scheme was capped at $20 million. Auditors were able to track this amount through flagged bank accounts. Most of the

money disappeared before it could be seized, so Revenue Canada only recovered a few thousand dollars. Regardless, 219 fraud-related charges were laid against 18 suspects and one car dealership in 1999.

Although many counts were processed separately, seven accused stood tried together in November 2002. Their fate was decided after a court in Milton, Ontario, considered seven months of testimony and more than 100 000 exhibits. Five years after the crackdown, 11 convictions had been registered. The penalties imposed varied between an 18-month conditional sentence and a five-year prison term, accompanied by restitution orders ranging from $15 000 to $1 million.

It has been said that death and taxes are the only two certainties in life. Judging by the tremendous risks that some people take to get rich quick, greed may very well qualify as a third.

Prepared by Andrea Wolf.

---

15 200 people were arrested for embezzlement in 1995—probably an extremely small percentage of all embezzlers. In the United States, the number of people arrested for embezzlement has increased 22 percent since 1986, indicating that (1) more employees are willing to steal from their employers, (2) more employers are willing to report instances of embezzlement, or (3) law enforcement officials are more willing to prosecute embezzlers.

Break and Enter

Under common law, the crime of **break and enter**, sometimes called **burglary**, is defined as "the breaking and entering of a dwelling house of another in the nighttime with the intent to commit a felony within." Burglary is more serious than theft, since it involves entering another's home, which increases the threat of harm even though the premises may be unoccupied.

The legal definition of burglary has undergone considerable change since its common-law origins. When first created by English judges during the late Middle Ages, laws against burglary were designed to protect people whose home might be set upon by wandering criminals. Including the phrase "breaking and entering" in the definition protected people from unwarranted intrusions; if an invited guest stole something, it would not be considered a burglary. Similarly, the requirement that the crime be committed at nighttime was added because evening was considered the time when honest people might fall prey to criminals.[47]

The Extent of Break and Enter

The definition of burglary includes any unlawful entry into a structure to commit an indictable offence. Break and enter is categorized into those against businesses, residences, and other. According to the Uniform Crime

| Exhibit 12.8 | Quick Facts about Break and Enter in Canada |

- Break and enters (B&Es) were the second most frequent kind of property crime in 2002 at 22 percent.

- This crime accounts for 11 percent of *Criminal Code* incidents reported to the police.

- There were 275 000 reported cases in 2002, a 25-year low.

- The majority of adult suspects (92 percent) charged with B&E in 2002 were male.

- Youths as a percentage of those charged overall increased to 56 percent.

- Sixty percent of victims in 1993 knew the perpetrator: acquaintance/friend (38 percent), ex/spouse (17 percent), family (5 percent).

- Main locations included private residences (67 percent) and businesses (27 percent).

- Audiovideo equipment is the single item most often stolen (22 percent).

- One in 16 residences had a B&E in 1996, an increase from 1991; overall property crime decreased.

- Break and enters cost the insurance industry $299 million in 1999.

- In 2002, of 865 residential robberies with violence, almost two-thirds involved a weapon being present (firearm, 33 percent; knife, 30 percent).

- Persons aged 60 or over were victimized in 15 percent of such incidents, compared with 4 percent for all violent crimes.

- The clearance rate for break and enters in 2003 was 15 percent; for property crimes in general, it was 20 percent.

Sources: Statistics Canada, *Canadian Crime Statistics 2003* (Ottawa: Canadian Centre for Justice Statistics, 2004); Statistics Canada, *Canadian Crime Statistics 1999* (Ottawa: Canadian Centre for Justice Statistics, 2000); "Canadian Crime Statistics, 1996," *Juristat* 17 (1997); Rosemary Gartner and Anthony N. Doob, "Trends in Criminal Victimization: 1988–1993," *Juristat* 14 (1994); Peter Greenberg, "Break and Enter," in *Crime Counts: A Criminal Event Analysis,* ed. Leslie W. Kennedy and Vincent F. Sacco (Toronto: ITP Nelson, 1996); "Breaking and Entering in Canada, 2002," *Juristat* 24, no. 5 (2004).

Reports (UCR), 284 496 break and enters occurred in 2003. Break and enter represented 26 percent of property crimes in 1993, 25 percent in 1999, and 21 percent in 2003. Most burglaries (62 percent) were of residences; 26 percent were business-related. Break and enter victims suffered losses of about $3 billion in 1993, with an average loss of about $3000. In 2001,

the insurance industry paid out $243 million in claims for residential and commercial B&Es.

The General Social Survey (GSS) reported that 232 per thousand of Canadian households were victimized by break and enter in 1999 in urban areas and 164 per thousand in rural areas. The difference between the UCR and GSS statistics is explained by the fact that some types of offences are reported more often than others are. In 1999, sexual assault had the highest percentage of incidents that were not reported to police (78 percent), while break and enter had the lowest percentage that was not reported (35 percent). Overall, household crimes were reported more frequently than were personal crimes. Part of the reason people report household crimes to the police is to be able to make insurance claims.

Those most likely to be burglarized are living in renting dwellings in urban areas and have the lowest incomes.

Careers in Burglary

Within the ranks of burglars are crude thieves who will smash a window and enter a vacant home or structure. However, because it involves planning, risk, and skill, burglary has been a crime long associated with professional thieves. The burglar must learn the craft. For example, this experienced professional burglar describes how another educated him in the craft of burglary when the two were serving time in prison:

> Never wear deodorant or shaving lotion;
> the strange scent might wake someone up.
> The more people there are in a house, the safer
> you are. If someone hears you moving around,
> they will think it's someone else. . . . If they
> call, answer in a muffled sleepy voice. . . .
> Never be afraid of dogs, they can sense fear.
> Most dogs are friendly; snap your finger, they
> come right to you.[48]

Despite his elaborate preparations, Hoheimer spent many years in confinement, so perhaps his advice is not the best.

Burglars on the Job

Burglars must master the skills of their trade, learning to spot environmental cues that nonprofessionals fail to notice.[49] In *Burglars on the Job*, Richard Wright and Scott Decker describe the working conditions of active burglars.[50] Most are motivated by the need for cash in order to get high; they want to enjoy the good life without the need for working. Although, as Exhibit 12.9 shows, they approach their "job" in a rational fashion, their lives are controlled by their

Exhibit 12.9	How Burglars Approach Their "Job"

- Targets are often acquaintances.
- Drug dealers are a favoured target because they have lots of cash and drugs, and victims aren't going to call police.
- Tipsters help the burglars select attractive targets.
- Some stake out residences to learn the occupants' routine.
- Many burglars approach a target masquerading as workers, such as carpenters or housepainters.
- Most avoid occupied residences, considering them high-risk targets.
- Alarms and elaborate locks do not deter burglars but do tell them there is something inside worth stealing.
- After entering a residence, their anxiety turns to calm as they turn first to the master bedroom for money and drugs.
- Most work in groups, one serving as a lookout while the other(s) ransack the place.
- Some dispose of goods through a professional fence; others try to pawn the goods, exchange the goods for drugs, or sell them to friends and relatives. A few keep the stolen items for themselves, especially guns and jewellery.

Source: Richard Wright and Scott Decker, *Burglars on the Job: Streetlife and Residential Break-Ins* (Boston, Mass.: Northeastern University Press, 1994).

Exhibit 12.10	Quick Code: Break and Enter

Section 348. (1) Every one who
(a) breaks and enters a place with intent to commit an indictable offence therein,
(b) breaks and enters a place and commits an indictable offence therein, or
(c) breaks out of a place after

 (i) committing an indictable offence therein, or
 (ii) entering the place with intent to commit an indictable offence therein, is guilty of an indictable offence and liable

(d) to imprisonment for life, if the offence is committed in relation to a dwelling-house, or
(e) to imprisonment for a term not exceeding fourteen years, if the offence is committed in relation to a place other than a dwelling-house . . .

[Other relevant sections: 321, 349, 350, 351, 352]

Source: From *Martin's Annual Code 2005*. Reproduced with the permission of Canada Law Book Inc. (1-800-263-3269, www.canadalawbook.ca).

culture and environment. Unskilled and uneducated, urban burglars make the choices they do because they have had few conventional opportunities for success.

The Good Burglar. This characterization is applied by professional burglars to colleagues who have distinguished themselves by their (1) technical competence, (2) maintenance of personal integrity, (3) specialization in burglary, (4) financial success at crime, and (5) ability to avoid prison sentences.[51]

To receive recognition as good burglars, novices must learn the skills needed to commit lucrative burglaries, such as how to gain entry into homes and apartment houses; select targets with high potential payoffs; choose items with a high resale value; properly open safes without damaging their contents; and use the proper equipment, including cutting torches, electric saws, explosives, and metal bars. Second, the good burglar must be able to team up to form a criminal gang. Choosing trustworthy companions is essential if the obstacles to completing a successful job—police, alarms, secure safes—are to be overcome.

Third, the good burglar must have inside information. Without knowledge of what awaits them inside, burglars can spend a tremendous amount of time and effort on empty safes and jewellery boxes. Finally, the good burglar must cultivate fences or buyers for stolen wares. Once the burglar gains access to people who buy and sell stolen goods, he or she must also learn how to successfully sell these goods for a profit.

The process of becoming a professional burglar is similar to the process Sutherland described in his theory of differential association. A person becomes a good burglar through learning the techniques of the trade from older, more experienced burglars. The older burglar teaches the novice how to deal with defence attorneys, bail bond agents, and other agents of the justice system. Consequently, the opportunity to become a good burglar is not open to everyone. Apprentices must have the appropriate character before they are taken under the wing of the "old pro." Usually, the opportunity to learn burglary comes as a reward for being a highly respected juvenile gang member, from knowing someone in the neighbourhood who has made a living at burglary, or, more often, from having built a reputation for being solid while serving time in prison.

The Burglary "Career Ladder." Burglars go through stages of career development.[52] They begin as young novices who learn the trade from older, more experienced burglars, often relatives. They continue to get this tutoring as long as they can develop their own markets (fences) for stolen goods. After their education is over, novices enter the journeyperson stage, characterized by forays in search of lucrative targets and by careful planning; they develop reputations as experienced, reliable criminals. Finally, they become professional burglars when they have developed advanced skills and organizational abilities that give them the highest esteem among their peers; they plan and execute their crimes after careful deliberation.

These burglars display rational decision making, carefully evaluating potential costs and benefits. They follow this pattern in their choice of burglary sites, preferring corner houses because they are easily observed (surveilability) and offer the maximum number of escape routes. Other issues are occupancy and accessibility. They look for houses that show evidence of long-term care and wealth. Although people may erect fences and other barriers to deter burglars, these devices may actually attract crime because they protect something worth stealing: If there were nothing valuable inside, why go to so much trouble to secure the premises?[53]

Connections

According to the rational choice approach discussed in Chapter 5, burglars make rational and calculated decisions before committing crimes. If circumstances and culture dictate their activities, can their decisions be considered a matter of choice?

The researchers also found that many burglars had serious drug habits and that their criminal activity was in part aimed at supporting their substance abuse.

Repeat Burglary. Research suggests that burglars may return to the "scene of the crime" in order to repeat their offences. One reason is that many burgled items are deemed indispensable (such as televisions and VCRs), so it is safe to assume they will be quickly replaced.[54] Other reasons include the following:

- It takes less effort to burgle a home or apartment known to be a suitable target than it does to burgle an unknown or unsuitable one.
- The burglar is already aware of the target's layout.
- The ease of entry of the target has probably not changed, and escape routes are known.
- The lack of protective measures and the absence of nosy and intrusive neighbours, which made the first burglary a success, have probably not changed.
- Goods were observed that could not be taken out the first time.[55]

Connections

Chapter 4 discussed repeat victimization. As you may recall, it is common for particular people and places to be the target of numerous predatory crimes.

The Female Burglar

Relatively little is known about female burglars, even though 8 percent of adults charged are female.

Researchers interviewed 18 females, ranging in age from 15 to 51, who were actively engaged in residential burglary. They found that female burglars had offending patterns similar to those of males and engaged in other thefts, such as shoplifting and assault. The major difference between male and female burglars is that females tend to avoid auto theft.[56]

Another difference is that females almost always work with a partner, but only 40 percent of males do. Females begin their offending careers earlier than males do, and they commit fewer offences. Considering that they start earlier and commit more crimes, it is not surprising that males had a much greater chance of doing time (26 percent) than did females (6 percent).

Most male and female burglars report substance abuse problems, including cocaine, heroin, and marijuana use. Males report less addiction, drug use, and alcohol abuse than do females.

Female burglars who work as accomplices commit burglaries because they feel compelled to commit crimes because of a relationship. Accomplices got into crime because they lacked legitimate employment, were drug dependent, or had alcohol problems. Accomplices exercised little control over their crimes and commonly acted as a lookout or driver.

In contrast, partners are involved in planning and carrying out crimes because they enjoy both the reward and the excitement of burglary. In planning their crimes, partners displayed many of the characteristics of the rational criminal: They helped spot targets and planned entries. As one female burglar stated:

> That's one reason why we got so many
> youngsters in jail today. I see this, so
> let's go make a hit. No, no, no. If they
> see this and it looks good, then it's going
> to be there for a while. So the point is,
> you have to case it and make sure you
> know everything. I want to know what
> time you go to work, the time the children
> go to school. I know there's no one coming
> home for lunch. So plan it with somebody
> else. We'll take the new dishwasher, washing
> machine, and this other stuff. We just put it

in the truck. Do you know when people rent a truck, nobody ever pays that any attention? They think you're moving [but] only if you rent a truck.

In conclusion, most female burglars maintain roles and identities quite similar to those of their male colleagues. Although some gender-based differences are evident (males more often work alone; women almost always work with others), both male and female burglars plan crimes for many of the same reasons. This research shows that for the majority of both male and female burglars, criminal careers may be a function of economic need and role equality, a finding that supports a feminist view of crime. It also illustrates that repeat criminals use rational choice in planning their activities.

Arson

Arson is the willful and malicious burning of a home, public building, vehicle, or commercial building. UCR statistics for 2003 show there were 13 851 arsons known to the police, an increase of 9 percent since 1999. This is a very difficult crime to solve, with a clearance rate of 16 percent. Of those charged, 42 percent were youths and 85 percent were males.

There are several motives for arson. Juvenile firesetters fall into three general groups.[57] The first is made up of children under seven years of age who start fires as the result of accidents or curiosity. In the second group are children ranging in age from 8 to 12, with a greater proportion representing underlying psychosocial conflicts. The third group includes adolescents between the ages of 13 and 18 with a long history of undetected fire play and firestarting behaviour. Their current firesetting episodes are usually the result of either psychosocial conflict and turmoil or intentional criminal behaviour.

Studies show that juvenile arsonists can be classified in one of four categories:

1. *The "playing with matches" firesetter.* This is the youngest, usually between the ages of four and nine, who sets fires because parents are careless with matches and lighters. Proper instruction on fire safety can help prevent fires set by these young children.
2. *The "crying for help" firesetter.* This type is a 7- to 13-year-old who turns to fire to reduce stress caused by family conflict, divorce, death, or abuse. These youngsters have difficulty expressing their feelings of sorrow, rage, or anger and turn to fire as a means of relieving stress or getting back at their antagonists.
3. *The "delinquent" firesetter.* Some youths set fire to school property or surrounding areas to retaliate for some slight experienced at school. These kids may break into the school to vandalize property with friends and later set a fire to cover up their activities.
4. *The "severely disturbed" firesetter.* This youngster is obsessed with fires and often dreams about them in "vibrant colours." This is the most disturbed and the one most likely to set numerous fires with the potential for death and damage.[58]

Adult arson may also be a function of severe emotional turmoil. Some psychologists view firestarting as a function of a disturbed personality and thus as a mental health problem and not a criminal act.[59]

Arsonists often experience sexual pleasure from starting fires and then observing their destructive effects.[60] It is equally likely that fires are started by angry people looking for revenge against property owners or by teenagers out to vandalize property.

Other arsons are set by "professional" arsonists who engage in arson for profit. This is often related to arson fraud, in which a business owner burns his or her property, or hires someone to do it, to escape financial problems.[61] Over the years, investigators have found that businesspeople are willing to become involved in arson to collect fire insurance or for various other reasons:

- Obtaining money during a period of financial crisis
- Getting rid of outdated or slow-moving inventory
- Destroying outmoded machines and technology
- Paying off legal and illegal debt
- Relocating or remodelling a business

Throughout the 1990s hundreds of mysterious burnings of churches occurred. It is as yet undetermined whether the fires were part of a coordinated plot or were individual acts of arson. In 1998 in Toronto, Christ Church St. James, one of the oldest Black churches in Canada, was gutted by fire set by an arsonist.

- Taking advantage of government funds available for redevelopment
- Applying for government building money, pocketing it without making repairs, and then claiming that fire destroyed the "rehabilitated" building
- Planning bankruptcies to eliminate debts, after the merchandise supposedly destroyed was secretly sold before the fire
- Eliminating business competition by burning out rivals
- Using extortion schemes to demand that victims pay or the rest of their property will be burned
- Showing displeasure during labour-management problems
- Concealing another crime, such as embezzlement

 ### InfoTrac®

The following article discusses the prevalence of childhood firesetting and what is considered "normal": Ian Lambie, Shane McCandle, and Ray Coleman, "Where There's Smoke There's Fire: Firesetting Behaviour in Children and Adolescents," *New Zealand Journal of Psychology* 31, no. 2, (2000): 73–79.

Some recent technological advances may help prove that many alleged arsons were actually accidental fires. For example, a flashover occurs during the course of an ordinary fire, and heat and gas at the ceiling of a room can reach 1093°C. This causes clothes and furniture to burst into flame, duplicating the effects of an arsonist's gasoline or explosives. It is possible that many suspected arsons are actually the result of flashover.[62] Arson is a difficult crime to investigate and prosecute because of the tendency on the part of the public to see arson as a "victimless" crime or to feel compassion for the defendant.

Summary

Economic crimes are designed to bring financial reward to the offender. The majority of economic crimes are committed by opportunistic amateurs. However, economic crime has also attracted professional criminals who earn the bulk of their income from crime, view themselves as criminals, and have skills that aid them in their lawbreaking. Edwin Sutherland's *The Professional Thief* is perhaps the most famous portrayal of professional crime, showing how professionals live by their wits and never resort to violence. A good example of the professional criminal

Exhibit 12.11	Quick Facts about Arson in Canada

- In 1990, 57 people were killed and 551 injured in fires costing $244 million.
- Arson is an underreported crime, but 13 851 incidents were reported in 2003.
- The percentage of arson cases in which an accused was identified has dropped from 30 percent in 1974 to 21 percent in 1991, to 19 percent in 1999, to 16 percent in 2003.
- Fifty percent of all fires with losses of more than $500 000 in 1989 had an unknown cause.
- The peak for arson in the 1980s coincided with an economic recession.
- Adults accounted for 58 percent of all arson charges in 2003, 85 percent of whom were male.
- The most favoured locations are homes (31 percent) and commercial locations (20 percent).
- Arson was redefined in 1990, with the maximum penalty increased to life in prison.
- Arson is a difficult crime to investigate.

Sources: Statistics Canada, *Canadian Crime Statistics 2003* (Ottawa: Canadian Centre for Justice Statistics, 2004); Statistics Canada, *Canadian Crime Statistics 1999* (Ottawa: Canadian Centre for Justice Statistics, 2000); Statistics Canada, *Canadian Crime Statistics 1995* (Ottawa: Canadian Centre for Justice Statistics, 1996); Lee Wolff, "Arson in Canada," *Juristat* 12 (1992); John L. McMullan and Peter D. Swan, "Social Economy and Arson in Nova Scotia," *Canadian Journal of Criminology* 31 (1989): 281–308.

Exhibit 12.12	Quick Code: Arson

Section 433. Every person who intentionally or recklessly causes damage by fire or explosion to property, whether or not that person owns the property, is guilty of an indictable offence and liable to imprisonment for life where

(a) the person knows that or is reckless with respect to whether the property is inhabited or occupied

(b) the fire or explosion causes bodily harm to another person.

[Other relevant sections: 434, 435, 436, 437]

Source: Rodrigues, Gary P., *Pocket Criminal Code 1996* (Scarborough, Ont.: Carswell, 1995).

is the fence who buys and sells stolen merchandise. There are also occasional thieves whose skill level and commitment fall below the professional level.

Common theft offences include larceny, fraud, embezzlement, and burglary. These are common-law crimes, created by English judges to meet social needs. Theft involves taking the legal possessions of another, divided into theft over and under $5000. The crime of false pretences, or fraud, is similar to larceny because it involves the theft of goods or money, but it differs because the criminal tricks victims into voluntarily giving up their possessions. Embezzlement is another larceny crime. It involves people taking something that was temporarily entrusted to them, such as bank tellers taking money out of the cash drawer and keeping it for themselves.

Newer larceny crimes have also been defined to keep abreast of changing social conditions: passing bad cheques, stealing or illegally using credit cards, shoplifting, stealing autos to sell on the international underground market, and Internet fraud. The top Internet fraud in 2001 was online auctions. Overall losses topped $6 million.[63]

Burglary, a more serious theft offence, was defined in the common law as the "breaking and entering of a dwelling house of another in the nighttime with the intent to commit a felony within." Today, the definition of burglary includes theft from any structure at any time of day. Because burglary involves planning and risk, it attracts professional thieves. The most competent have technical competence and personal integrity, specialize in burglary, are financially successful, and avoid prison sentences.

Arson is another serious property crime. Although many arsonists are teenage vandals, professional arsonists specialize in burning commercial buildings for profit.

Thinking Like a Criminologist

To reduce the risk of loss during the Christmas holidays, the Association of Household Insurers (AHI) suggests that you don't display presents where they can be seen from a window or doorway and that you put gifts in a safe place before leaving the house or taking a trip. Moreover, closing drapes or blinds during even short trips away from home is a good habit.

It is important to trick burglars into believing someone is home. If you are away, the AHI suggests having lights on timers, stopping mail and newspaper delivery, and arranging, if possible, to have the walkways shovelled and have a car parked in the driveway as additional security measures. Other suggestions include installing a good dead-bolt lock with at least a 2.5-centimetre (one-inch) throat into a solid wood or a steel door that fits securely into a sturdy frame, keeping doors locked, putting a chain-link fence around a yard, getting a dog, and having police inspect the house for security. Putting a mannequin in a chair by the window might be a good idea too. Also, buy a weighted safe deposit box to secure items that can't be replaced, and engrave your driver's licence number and province or territory of residence on your property to give police a way to contact you if your home is burglarized and the stolen items are later found.

Con artists may take advantage of people's generosity during the holidays by making appeals for nonexistent charities. Always ask for identification from solicitors.

As a criminologist, can you come up with any new ideas that the Association of Household Insurers failed to cover?

Key Terms

arson	economic crimes	larceny
boosters	embezzlement	occasional criminals
break and enter	false pretences	professional criminals
burglary	fence	situational inducement
carjacking	flash houses	snitches
confidence games	fraud	street crimes
constructive possession	heels	systematic forgers

Critical Thinking Questions

1. Differentiate between an occasional and a professional criminal. Which one would be more likely to resort to violence? Which one would be more easily deterred?

2. What crime occurs when a person who owns an antique store sells a client an "original" Tiffany lamp that the seller knows is a fake? Would it still be a crime if the seller were not aware that the lamp was a fake? As an antique dealer, should the seller have a duty to determine the authenticity of the products he or she sells?

3. You have been the victim of repeat burglaries. What could you do to reduce the chances of future victimization? (Hint: buying a gun is not an option!)

4. Technology changes the nature and extent of theft crimes. Although train robbing and safecracking may be rare today, using bogus credit cards and stealing from ATMs have increased in both number of crimes and value. What are some other crime patterns that have been created by technological innovation?

5. If you knew of someone who frequently tampered with matches to the point of causing you concern, how would you handle this situation? What other danger signs would you look for?

 See the book-specific website at http://www.siegelcriminology3e.nelson.com for additional chapter links, discussions, and quizzes.

Crimes of Power: White-Collar, Corporate, and Organized Crime

chapter 13

Dr. Samuel Waksal, founder of a biotech company called ImClone Systems, pleaded guilty in 2002 to charges of securities fraud, perjury, and obstruction of justice. The charges were the result of an investigation into the dumping of stock by Waksal, his friends and family shortly before the company announced that the U.S. Food and Drug Administration had rejected its application for approval of a cancer drug. The announcement would have depressed the value of company shares.

As part of his guilty plea, Dr. Waksal read a detailed description of how he had phoned his daughter, urging her to sell her stock ahead of the critical announcement about the cancer drug, and how he directed her to cover up those conversations when she was questioned by government investigators. Waksal's friend Martha Stewart also dumped her shares just before the negative announcement, and quickly became the target of a government probe.[1]

The ending is now well known, with Stewart going to jail for obstructing justice.

In 2003, Ken Lay quit as CEO of Enron, the seventh largest corporation in the United States. The bankruptcy of Enron cost thousands their jobs and became the largest collapse in corporate history. Accused of hiding billions in debts, the accounting firm that audited Enron was complicit in masking the problem and shredding important documents. The two biggest banks in the United States were required to pay $236 million to compensate victims of the fraud.

It has become easy in our global economy to use illegal tactics to make profit. We refer here to these crimes of the marketplace as **enterprise crimes**, and divide these crimes into three categories. **White-collar crime** involves the illegal activities of people and institutions whose acknowledged purpose is profit through legitimate business transactions. **Cybercrime** involves people using the instruments of modern technology for criminal purposes. **Organized crime** involves the illegal activities of people and organizations whose acknowledged purpose is profit through illegitimate business enterprise.

These organizational crimes involve all phases of illegal commercial activity. Organized crime involves individuals or groups whose marketing techniques (threat, extortion, and smuggling) and product lines (drugs, sex, gambling, and loan sharking) have been outlawed. White-collar crimes include the use of illegal business practices (embezzlement, price-fixing, bribery, and so on) to market what are ordinarily legitimate commercial products; cybercriminals use their technical expertise for criminal misappropriations.

In contrast to the previous chapter on street crimes, statistics on white-collar crime, cybercrime, and organized crime are not readily available, so much of the evidence will be presented through cases. What is similar to the property crimes is enterprise, just on a much grander scale:

> White-collar crime is not simply a dysfunctional aberration. Organized crime is not something ominously alien to the . . . economic system. Both are made criminal by laws declaring that certain ways of doing business, or certain products of business, are illegal. In other words, criminality is not an inherent characteristic either of certain persons or of certain business activities but rather, an externally imposed evaluation of alternative modes of behaviour and action.[2]

Business enterprise is a spectrum of acts ranging from the most "saintly" to the most "sinful."[3] White-collar and organized crime share a similarity, for example, the sale of illegal goods and services to customers who know these goods and services are illegal.[4]

Although organizational practices may be desirable to many consumers (for example, the sale of narcotics) or an efficient way of doing business (such as the dumping of hazardous wastes), society tries to regulate or outlaw these behaviours. Unfortunately, this means that **corporate crime** is not prosecuted criminally in the same way that street crime is. For example, in 2003, California voted to defeat a bill that would put any company convicted of three felonies in a 10-year period out of business.

The *Corporate Crime Reporter* compiled a list of the top one hundred corporate criminals of the 1990s using only corporations that pleaded guilty to crimes and had been criminally fined. They found that corporate criminals fell into 14 categories: environmental (38), antitrust (20), fraud (13), campaign finance (7), food and drug (6), financial crimes (4), false statements (3), illegal exports (3), illegal boycott (1), worker death (1), bribery (1), obstruction of justice (1), public corruption (1), and tax evasion (1).

The use of force and coercion by organized crime members has been popularized in the media; however, the fact that white-collar and corporate crimes may result in the infliction of pain and suffering seems more astonishing. Yet experts claim that 200 000 or more occupational deaths occur each year and that corporate violence annually kills and injures more people than all street crimes combined.[5]

Some criminal enterprises involve both organized and white-collar crime. Organized criminals may seek out legitimate enterprises to launder money, diversify their sources of income, increase their power and influence, and gain and enhance respectability.[6] Legitimate businesspeople may turn to organized criminals to help them with problems of an economic nature (such as breaking up a strike or dumping hazardous waste products), stifle or threaten competition, and increase the businesspeople's influence. The distinction between

Exhibit 13.1	Quick Facts about the Cost of Corporate Crime in Canada

- Between 1972 and 1981, more than 10 000 Canadians died from work-related injuries.

- In Canada there are about five hundred homicide victims per year, but about 15 000 die from corporate inaction.

- Failure to remit payroll deductions costs society more than bank robbery, extortion, and kidnapping combined.

- Occupational deaths are the third leading cause of death, after heart disease and cancer.

- Hundreds of thousands of workers are exposed to radioactive and chemical pollutants every year.

- In 1993, the Canadian Union of Public Employees estimated that 61 percent of workers were victimized by violence; 43 percent said no action was taken after a violent incident.

- The Canadian Labour Congress (1993) reports that deaths from workplace disease are largely uncompensated.

- Of those killed in fatal workplace accidents, 97 percent are men.

- Women are at risk of reproductive health hazards due to exposure to toxic substances.

Sources: John L. McMullan, *Beyond the Limits of the Law: Corporate Crime and Law and Order* (Halifax: Fernwood, 1992); Desmond Ellis and Walter DeKeseredy, *The Wrong Stuff: An Introduction to the Sociological Study of Deviance*, 2nd ed. (Scarborough, Ont.: Allyn and Bacon, 1996); Brian MacLean, ed., *The Political Economy of Crime* (Scarborough, Ont.: Prentice Hall, 1986).

organized crime and white-collar and corporate criminals often overlap, as we see in Figure 13.1.

Some forms of white-collar crime may be more like organized crime than others.[7] Although some corporate executives cheat to improve their company's position in the business world, others are motivated purely by personal gain. It is this latter group, people who engage in ongoing criminal conspiracies for their own profit, that most resembles organized crime.[8]

White-Collar Crime

Edwin Sutherland first used the term *white-collar crime* to describe criminal activities of the rich and powerful.[9]

Sutherland said that white-collar crime involved conspiracies by members of the wealthy classes to use their position for personal gain without regard to the law. All too often, these actions were handled by civil courts, since injured parties were more concerned with

recovering their losses than with seeing the offenders punished criminally. Consequently, the great majority of white-collar criminals are not studied by criminology. Yet the financial cost of white-collar crime is many times greater than what is customarily regarded as the "crime problem." Moreover, damage to social relations occurs. White-collar crimes violate trust between consumers and corporations, clients and professionals, citizens and their government. This lowers social morale, in contrast to other crimes, which produce relatively little effect on social institutions or social organization.[10]

Redefining White-Collar Crime

Modern criminologists have developed Sutherland's work and broadened their definition of white-collar crime. Edelhertz described it as "an illegal act committed by nonphysical means to obtain money or property or to obtain business or personal advantage."[11] This definition encompasses crimes even with little connection to business enterprise,[12] so a symposium of experts on white-collar crime formulated the following definition:

> White-collar crime consists of the illegal or unethical acts that violate fiduciary responsibility or public trust, committed by an individual or organization, usually during the course of legitimate occupational activity by persons of high or respectable social status for personal or organizational gain.[13]

Today's definition of white-collar crime includes all individuals who use the marketplace for their criminal activity, from middle-income Canadians to corporate titans.[14]

Included in this definition are "middle-class" acts such as income tax evasion, credit card fraud, and bankruptcy fraud. White-collar individuals use their positions of trust in business or government to commit crimes, such as pilfering, soliciting bribes or kickbacks, and embezzlement. Some white-collar criminals victimize the public, for example in land swindles, securities thefts, medical or health frauds, and so on. Some white-collar criminals become involved in criminal conspiracies designed to improve the market share or profitability of their corporations, such as antitrust violations, price-fixing, and false advertising.

State–corporate crimes are illegal or socially injurious actions resulting from cooperation between governmental and corporate institutions.[15] Some say the explosion of the *Challenger* space shuttle in 1986 was the result of a state–corporate crime involving the cooperative and criminally negligent actions of the National Aeronautics and Space Administration (NASA) and Morton Thiokol, Inc., the shuttle builder.

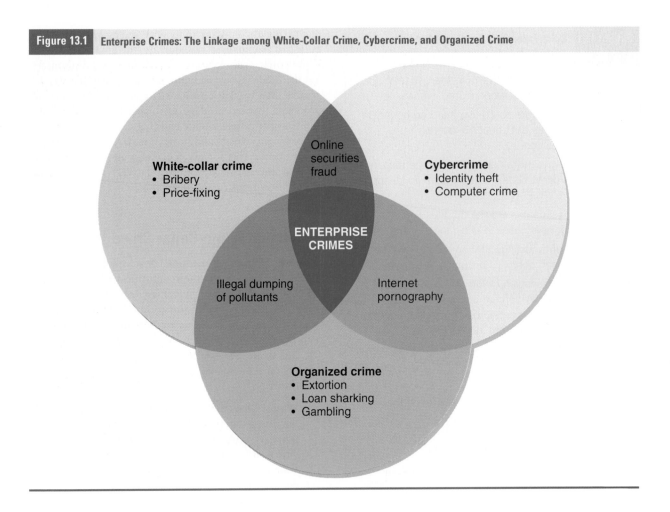

Figure 13.1   Enterprise Crimes: The Linkage among White-Collar Crime, Cybercrime, and Organized Crime

The White-Collar Crime Problem

Despite being difficult to estimate,[16] experts place the cost of white-collar crime at hundreds of billions of dollars, far outstripping any other crime. For example, **occupational crime** alone, such as loss due to employee theft from businesses, amounts to billions of dollars per year.[17] KPMG's investigation and security unit does an annual survey of Canada's one thousand largest companies. In 1997, 57 percent of respondents said they had been defrauded in the last year by their own employees. Inflated expense accounts, false invoices, and personal use of company supplies were estimated to cost an average of $1.3 million. A 1998 KPMG survey of five thousand American businesses, agencies, and nonprofit organizations showed an average loss of $624 000 from cheque fraud by employees, twice as much as reported in 1994.

White-collar crimes also involve property damage and loss of human life, violations of safety standards, environmental pollution, and industrial accidents due to negligence. In the United States, corporate crime annually results in 20 million serious injuries, including 110 000 people who become permanently disabled, and 30 000

deaths. The potential impact ranges from acute environmental catastrophes, such as the collapse of a dam, to the chronic effects of diseases resulting from industrial pollution.[18]

Gilbert Geis says white-collar crime is much more serious than is street crime:

> It destroys confidence, saps the integrity of commercial life and has the potential for devastating destruction. Think of the possible results if nuclear regulatory rules are flouted or if toxic wastes are dumped into a community's drinking water supply.[19]

The public has begun to recognize the seriousness of white-collar crimes and demand that they be controlled—such as a judge taking a bribe to give a light sentence, a doctor cheating on medical insurance claims, and a factory owner knowingly disposing of waste in a way that pollutes the water supply.[20] However, white-collar criminals generally face monetary fines and relatively short sentences; judges and prosecutors are sometimes reluctant to incarcerate offenders who do not fit the image of "common criminals."

Mining's dam problem. A bulldozer plugs a gap in the tailings dam at Boliden's minesite in the south of Spain, where five million cubic metres of sludge poured onto nearby farms.

InfoTrac®

Look up this research study, which uses a personality-based integrity test to discriminate white-collar criminals from other white-collar employees: Judith M. Collins and Frank L. Schmidt, "Personality, Integrity, and White Collar Crime: A Construct Validity Study," *Personnel Psychology* 46, no. 2 (1993): 295–312.

International White-Collar Crime

White-collar crime occurs in other countries as well. In China, cases of corruption account for a high percentage of all cases of economic crime and have been the subject of extreme crackdowns. Despite the fact that the penalty for corruption in China is death, most of the people involved in corruption and bribery are state personnel. In the late 1980s there were no more than 10 000 corruption cases each year; by 1996 there were six times as many.[21]

In Thailand, crime and corruption are skyrocketing; top executives of the Bangkok Bank of Commerce are believed to have absconded with billions in depositors' money.[22] It is suspected that North American companies are also the targets of white-collar criminals overseas. Agents have been inserted into companies abroad to steal trade secrets, confidential procedures, and intellectual property, such as computer programs and technology. The cost is somewhere between a conservative $50 billion and an astounding $240 billion a year.[23]

Offences perpetrated against the European Community (EC) can be grouped into four categories:[24]

1. *Corporate crime*, in which legitimate companies or organizations, in the course of their usual business, cheat the EC, a crime fostered by a strongly competitive environment
2. *Government crime*, which includes illegal acts committed by government officials or with their knowledge and support, as well as cover-ups of other persons' crimes

3. *Occupational crime*, which involves people making extra money by bending or breaking the rules, perhaps because of financial straits or other business-related problems

4. *Organized/professional crime*, which involves people or groups of people whose primary source of income is illegal

Crimes within these categories amount to billions in losses each year. For example, fraud in the agricultural sector, which ranges from evasion of taxes and deceitful claims to phantom operations and false or forged documentation, may amount to $8 billion per year.[25]

Components of White-Collar Crime

White-collar crimes involve individuals acting alone or within a business structure. The victims can be the public, the organization that employs the offender, or a competing organization. Clinard and Quinney divide white-collar crime into an occupational category, (offences committed by individuals in the course of their occupation and by employees against their employers) and into corporate crime, which is "the offenses committed by corporate officials for the corporation and the offenses of the corporation itself."[26]

Edelhertz divides white-collar criminality into four categories:

1. *Ad-hoc violations*. Committed episodically for personal profit, such as welfare fraud or tax cheating

2. *Abuses of trust*. Committed by a person in a place of trust in an organization against the organization; for example, embezzlement, bribery, or kickbacks

3. *Collateral business crimes*. Committed by organizations to further their business interests; for example, antitrust violations, or the concealment of environmental crimes

4. *Con games*. Committed for the sole purpose of cheating clients; for example, fraudulent land sales, sales of bogus securities, or sales of questionable tax shelters

Edelhertz's typology captures the diverse nature of white-collar criminality and illustrates how both individuals and institutions can be the victims of and the offenders in a white-collar crime.

The Famous Canadian Criminals feature details some of the activity of Christopher Horne, who committed an outrageous fraud while at RBC Securities. In a case on a grander scale, German financier Wolfgang Stolzenberg of Montreal-based Castor Holdings is alleged to have been involved in a 15-year Ponzi scheme, a pyramid scam in which money raised from new investors is used to pay off earlier investors. He faced 41 counts of fraud and conspiracy and is alleged to have defrauded investors of $200 million in the $1.5 billion bankruptcy of Castor Holdings

Exhibit 13.2	A Typology of Corporate Crime
Victim	**Crime**
Consumer	False advertising, harmful products, price gouging, abuse of credit information
Environment	Pollution, resource mismanagement, destruction of way of life
Worker	Unsafe work conditions, pension fund abuse, failure to pay legal wages
Competitors	Price-fixing, illegal takeovers, industrial espionage, corruption, and influence peddling
State	Fraudulent billing, tax evasion, bribing politicians, illegal exporting of products

Sources: Adapted from John L. McMullan, *Beyond the Limits of the Law: Corporate Crime and Law and Order* (Halifax: Fernwood, 1992); C. Goff and C. Reasons, "Organizational Crimes against Employees, Consumers, and the Public," in *The Political Economy of Crime: Readings for a Critical Criminology*, ed. B. Maclean (Scarborough, Ont.: Prentice Hall, 1986); Desmond Ellis and Walter DeKeseredy, *The Wrong Stuff: An Introduction to the Sociological Study of Deviance*, 2nd ed. (Scarborough, Ont.: Allyn and Bacon, 1996).

Ltd. It is the second largest fraud investigation ever conducted by the Royal Canadian Mounted Police, after the inquiry into the failure of mining company Bre-X Minerals Ltd.

Types of White-Collar Crime

Mark Moore's typology of white-collar crime ranges from an individual using a business enterprise to commit theft-related crimes, through individuals using their place within a business for illegal gain, to business enterprises collectively engaging in crime.[27] This typology tries to encompass the complex array of acts possible in white-collar crime: (1) stings and swindles, (2) chiselling, (3) individual exploitation of institutional position, (4) influence peddling and bribery, (5) embezzlement and employee fraud, (6) client frauds, and (7) corporate crime.

Stings and Swindles

Swindling is stealing through deception by individuals who have no continuing institutional or business position and whose entire purpose is to bilk people out of their money. Offences range from door-to-door sale of faulty merchandise to the passing of millions of dollars in

Famous Canadian Criminals

The High Life of Christopher Horne

In 1996, RBC Dominion Securities Inc. was fined $250 000 for failing to properly supervise former vice-president and stockbroker Christopher Horne. Horne was a Toronto-based broker who defrauded elderly clients of millions of dollars over a 10-year period. Horne had quit his job with RBC Dominion Securities in 1994 but in 1996 was charged with fraud and theft. The Royal Bank, which owned RBC Dominion,

reimbursed more than $5 million to his victims.

Horne had misappropriated millions of dollars from client accounts, channelling the money into the Toronto and Grand Cayman bank accounts of a shell company, International Haven Services, which he had founded in Panama City in 1980. Horne had sat on the board of the Art Gallery of Ontario and had used his ill-gotten gains to finance his own art collection, worth more than $4 million. Horne was sentenced to five years in prison in August 1996. Horne's collection

of paintings, photographs, and sculptures was seized to pay back creditors.

The Cayman Islands is a tax haven where individuals and corporations pay no taxes and benefit from absolute secrecy. The Bahamas is another tax haven with no personal or corporate taxes. It is well established, with more than four hundred banks and U.S.$320 billion on deposit. More than 44 000 offshore companies are registered there. Because of its unique financial position, money laundering is a problem there.

---

counterfeit stock certificates to established brokerage firms. If caught, white-collar swindlers are usually charged with common-law crimes, such as embezzlement or fraud.

Connections

In Chapter 12, the crime of fraud was discussed in the context of individual-level crimes that involve con games. Although similar, swindles here involve organizations that are devoted to fleecing the public.

Financial Swindles. Although swindlers are often considered petty thieves, swindles can run into millions of dollars.[28]

The collapse of the Bank of Credit and Commerce International (BCCI) is a swindle that cost depositors billions of dollars. BCCI was the world's seventh-largest private bank, with assets of about $23 billion. Investigators allege that bank officials made billions in loans to confederates without intent to repay. BCCI officers also used false accounting methods to defraud depositors. Its officers helped clients, such as Colombian drug cartel leaders and dictators Saddam Hussein and Ferdinand Marcos, finance terrorist organizations, smuggle illegal arms, and launder money for narcotics traffickers.[29] After the bank was shut down, auditors liquidated the bank's holdings; English liquidators alone were paid $360 million in fees between 1991 and 1994.[30]

Canadians had $107 million invested, only a quarter of which was insured by the Canada Deposit Insurance Corporation (CDIC). Assets were seized by Canada's top

financial regulator in 1991, after concerns were raised over its mounting loan losses and its poor internal financial controls.

Despite the notoriety of such cases, investors continue to bite at bogus investment schemes that promise quick riches, as you will see in other examples in this chapter. In 1997, the economy of Albania was virtually wiped out in a gigantic Ponzi scheme.

Religious Swindles. One of the most cold-blooded swindles is an investment scam that uses religious affiliations to steal from trusting investors. For example, TV evangelist Jim Bakker was convicted of defrauding followers of $3.7 million when he oversold "lifetime partnerships" at his Heritage USA religious retreat. Bakker had diverted ministry funds for personal use while knowing that his PTL ministry was in financial trouble. He bought vacation homes in California and Florida, a houseboat, expensive cars, and an air-conditioned dog house. Bakker had sold hotel rooms to 153 000 people yet built only 258 rooms to accommodate them.[31] Bakker was sentenced to 45 years in prison, reduced on appeal, and released from prison in 1996.

The Bakker case is not unique. The North American Securities Administrators Association estimates that swindlers using fake religious identities bilk thousands of people out of $100 million per year.[32] Swindlers take in worshippers of all persuasions: Jews, Baptists, Lutherans, Catholics, Mormons, and Greek Orthodox have all fallen prey to religious swindles. Religious swindlers join close-knit churches and establish a position of trust that enables them to operate without the normal investor

In the best-known case involving a religious swindle, TV evangelist Jim Bakker was convicted of defrauding followers of $3.7 million when he oversold "lifetime partnerships" at his Heritage USA religious retreat.

skepticism. Some use religious television and radio shows to sell their product. Others place verses from the scriptures on their promotional literature to comfort hesitant investors. Religious swindles are tough to guard against because they are promoted in the same manner as legitimate religious fundraising.

Chiselling

Chiselling, the second category of white-collar crime, refers to cheating an organization or its consumers. Chisellers are looking to make quick profits, or are employees who decide to cheat on obligations to customers by doing something contrary to company policy. Chiselling may involve charging for bogus auto repairs, cheating customers on home repairs, short-weighting (tampering with scales used to weigh products) in supermarkets or dairies, or fraudulently selling securities at inflated prices. It may even involve illegal use of information about company

policies that have not been disclosed to the public. The secret information can be sold to speculators or used to make money in the stock market.

Corporations can engage in large-scale chiselling when they misrepresent products or alter their content. The Beech-Nut Nutrition Corporation paid a $2 million fine for illegally selling a product labelled "apple juice" that was nothing more than sweetened water. Despite enforcement efforts, it is estimated that 10 percent of all fruit juices use illegal additives.[33]

Professional Chiselling. Professionals can use their positions to chisel clients. Pharmacists can alter prescriptions or substitute low-cost generic drugs for more expensive name brands. Pharmacists who are business-oriented are the ones most inclined to chisel customers.[34]

The 1970s American Watergate hearings revealed the unethical behaviour of high-ranking government attorneys. The American Bar Association subsequently required that law students take a course in legal ethics. This action is needed, since lawyers chisel clients out of millions of dollars each year in such schemes as forging signatures on clients' compensation cheques and tapping escrow accounts and other funds for personal investments.[35] Special funds are often set up by bar associations to reimburse chiselled clients.

Securities Fraud. Chiselling can also take place in the commodity and stock markets. The **churning** of a client's account by an unscrupulous stockbroker involves repeated, excessive, and unnecessary buying and selling of stock with either the intent to defraud the client or the disregard of the client's investment interest.[36]

The organization that deals with stock market regulation in Canada is the Toronto Stock Exchange. This is a nonprofit organization governed by a 15-member board. The TSX is overseen by the Ontario Securities Commission. The Exchange investigates rules regarding insider trading or market manipulation, among others. The Vancouver Stock Exchange especially has been plagued with allegations of professional improprieties involving stock trading, and a former premier of British Columbia was once investigated for insider trading.

In 1989 the American federal government indicted prominent brokers on the Chicago Board of Trade on racketeering and other statutes.[37] The brokers had engaged in prearranged trading in which two or more brokers agree to buy and sell commodity futures among themselves without offering the orders to other brokers for competitive bidding; "front running," in which brokers place personal orders ahead of a customer's large order to profit from the market effects of the trade; and "bucketing," or skimming customer trading profits.[38]

Another form of securities fraud involves using a position of trust to profit from inside business information.

The information can then be used to buy and sell securities, giving the trader an unfair advantage over the public.

It is illegal for corporate employees with direct knowledge of market-sensitive information to use it for their own benefit—for example, by buying stock in a company that they have learned will be taken over by the larger concern. In recent years, the definition of **insider trading** has been expanded to include employees of financial institutions, such as law or banking firms, who use confidential information to purchase stock or give the information to a third party so that party can buy shares in the company. Such actions are deceptive and in violation of security trading codes.[39]

Interpretations of what constitutes insider trading vary widely. To many, the "hot tip" is the bread and butter of stock market speculators, and the point at which a tip becomes a criminal act is often fuzzy. In the most celebrated insider trading cases, billionaires Ivan Boesky and Michael Milken, two of Wall Street's most prominent **arbitrage** experts, were convicted and sentenced to prison. Arbitragers speculate on the stock of companies that are rumoured to be takeover targets and make a profit on the difference between current stock prices and the price the acquiring company is willing to pay. Boesky used inside information on such deals as the merger negotiations between International Telephone and Telegraph and Sperry Corporation, and Coastal Corporation's takeover of American Natural Resources. Possession of this information allowed Boesky to profit in the millions; he received a three-year prison sentence, was barred from dealing in securities, and was ordered to pay $100 million in penalties. Milken was indicted on 98 counts of security fraud, pleaded guilty to six relatively minor counts, and received a billion-dollar fine; his 10-year sentence was later reduced because of his cooperation with authorities in other cases.[40]

Individual Exploitation of Institutional Position

Individuals can exploit their power or position to take advantage of others; for example, a fire inspector can demand that a restaurant owner pay him to be granted an operating licence. This type of offence occurs when the victim has a clear right to expect a service and the offender threatens to withhold the service unless an additional payment or bribe is paid.

Exploitation in Government. Throughout history, political and government figures have been accused of using their positions to profit from bribes and kickbacks.[41] Political leaders have used their position to control and profit from the city's police force. Politicians have used their offices to buy and sell political favours.

The use of political office for economic gain is tempting. On the local level, scandals can involve liquor licence board members, food inspectors, and fire inspectors wanting "consideration."[42] Even powerful politicians have been implicated in corrupt practices. In 1998, Conservative senator Michel Cogger was sentenced to pay a $3000 fine and do 120 hours of community work for peddling his influence to a Montreal businessman. In 1996, U.S. representative Dan Rostenkowski pleaded guilty to two federal corruption charges in return for a 17-month prison sentence and a $100 000 fine.[43]

Exploitation in Industry. Purchasing agents in large companies can demand a kickback for awarding contracts to suppliers and distributors. In one case, a J.C. Penney employee received $1.4 million from a contractor who eventually did $23 million of business with the company.[44] In another case, a purchasing agent

Crime in the News

How Corporate Criminals Hide Their Money

Nauru Gets Tough on Illicit Banking
by Adrian Humphreys

The government of the world's smallest republic, branded a gangster's paradise because of its lax banking laws, says international pressure can be eased now that it has strengthened anti-money laundering regulations.

The Republic of Nauru amended legislation on banking and corporate secrecy in a bid to avoid sanctions by the Financial Action Task Force (FATF), an agency supported by about 30 countries, Mathew Batsiua, the island's Chief Secretary, said yesterday.

Nauru is a desolate South Pacific island of 24 square kilometres and with a population of 12,088. Money laundering specialists say the island is home to more shell corporations and banks than people. For years, its use by the Russian mafia, tax dodgers and other gangsters to hide money has enraged banks, police and tax collectors around the world. However, attempts to shame the tiny country into tightening regulations have failed.

Source: Adrian Humphreys, "Nauru Gets Tough on Illicit Banking," *National Post*, December 8, 2001: A16.

for the American Chiclets division of Warner-Lambert (maker of Dentyne, Chiclets, Trident, and Dynamints) received a $300 000 kickback from the makers of the wire racks on which gum products are displayed in supermarkets.[45]

In some foreign countries, soliciting bribes to do business is a common practice. In European countries, such as Italy and France, giving bribes to secure contracts is perfectly legal, and in Germany, corporate bribes are actually tax-deductible. Some government officials will solicit bribes to allow firms to do business in their countries. The medical supply firm Baxter International allegedly bribed officials to do business in Arab nations after it had been placed on a blacklist for owning a plant in Israel.

In China, corruption has been targeted in its Strike Hard campaign, with more than 800 000 people given the death penalty or long sentences. Corruption, bribery, and embezzlement are among the highest charges.

Influence Peddling and Bribery

Individuals in important institutional positions can sell power, influence, and information to outsiders, such as government employees taking kickbacks from contractors in return for awarding them contracts, or outsiders bribing government officials who might sell information about future government activities. Political leaders have been convicted of securing bribes to obtain funds to rig elections and allow their party to control state politics.[46]

In an investigation into the sale of B.C.'s publicly owned railway to CN Rail, the RCMP raided the legislature to collect documents and alleged that at least two officials were offered personal benefits for their cooperation.[47] In a scandal in Toronto in 2004, police officers were charged with breach of trust, fraud, and obstructing justice after demanding cash for receiving tips about liquor inspectors. Six members of the now-disbanded drug squad were charged after a corruption probe by the RCMP.[48]

Also in 2004, the RCMP laid charges against a retired bureaucrat and the president of an advertising firm for their involvement in the sponsorship scandal, a deal that saw lucrative government contracts go to firms friendly to the Liberal government. The RCMP alleged that contracts worth about $100 million were awarded noncompetitively and that work was not done before payments were made.[49]

One major difference distinguishes influence peddling from exploitation of an institutional position: Exploitation involves forcing victims to pay for services to which they have a clear right, while influence peddlers and bribe-takers use their institutional positions to grant favours and sell information to which their co-conspirators are not entitled.

> Ninety percent of those polled say that former Prime Minister Chrétien should come clean and testify on the sponsorship program.

Source: Poll conducted by Ipsos Reid, February 16, 2004.

Influence Peddling in Government. In 1995, a scandal erupted in Canada over alleged kickbacks in the airline industry. It was alleged that former prime minister Brian Mulroney, along with former premier of Newfoundland and Labrador Frank Moores, had accepted payments from a private company in return for procuring a lucrative contract with the federal government to buy passenger airplanes. A Bavarian intermediary, Franz Schreiber, had set up a shell company, International Airlines, to influence Air Canada to purchase the Airbus 330. In a *Fifth Estate* documentary on the CBC, it was alleged that $20 million was paid in kickbacks. The allegations were never proved, and the federal government was forced to pay out a settlement of $1 million to Mulroney when he sued.

In 1981, FBI agents posed as wealthy Arabs looking for favourable treatment from high-ranking American politicians. The agents said they wanted to obtain American citizenship and receive favourable treatment in business ventures. As a result of this "sting," several officeholders were indicted, including a U.S. senator, who was convicted of accepting an interest in an Arab-backed mining venture in return for promising to use his influence to obtain government contracts.[50]

In a case at the Pentagon, senior officials received hundreds of thousands of dollars in bribes for granting contracts for military clothing. The corruption was so pervasive that the military found it difficult to locate sufficient replacement manufacturers who were not involved in the scandal. More than $1 billion worth of contracts were suspended. The scandal touched some of the largest defence contractors in the United States, including Raytheon, Litton Industries, and Lockheed.[51]

In the mid-1980s, officials at the U.S. Department of Housing and Urban Development (HUD) used their power to dispense huge grants to political figures, a number of whom were later convicted of taking bribes and defrauding the government. In Louisiana, the state insurance commissioner was convicted in 1991 on money laundering, conspiracy, fraud, and for taking $2 million in bribes in return for regulatory favours.[52]

Corruption in the Criminal Justice System. Agents of the criminal justice system have also gotten caught up in official corruption, which is disturbing because society expects a higher standard of moral integrity from people empowered to uphold the law. The credibility of the justice process is weakened when officials who hold power over other people engage in criminal behaviour.

In 2001, the RCMP was called in to investigate the drug squad of Toronto's police. Officers were suspected of corruption and the theft of money from the squad's "fink fund." The way the fraud worked was that the officers would send out users to buy drugs from traffickers. They would attribute the source as a police informant, requisition money to pay them, and pocket the cash instead. More than one hundred court cases were compromised as a result.

This example shows how the police are particularly vulnerable to charges of corruption. In New York, the Knapp Commission found that police corruption was widespread, ranging from patrol officers accepting small gratuities from local businesspeople to senior officers receiving payoffs in the thousands of dollars from gamblers and narcotics violators.[53] Construction firms made payoffs to have police ignore violations of city ordinances, such as double parking, obstruction of sidewalks, and noise pollution. Bar owners paid police to allow them to operate after hours or to give free rein to the prostitutes, drug pushers, and gamblers operating on their premises. Drug dealers allowed police to keep money and narcotics confiscated during raids in return for their freedom.

In 1993 New York City's Mollen Commission investigated corruption among city police who were immersed in violence, coercion, theft, and drug dealing. Testifying before the commission to gain a reduced sentence on a narcotics charge, one officer told of "shaking down" drug dealers, brutalizing innocent citizens, and intimidating fellow officers to force their silence. Protected by the police officer code of secrecy, these cops were able to purchase luxury homes and cars with the profits from their illegal thefts, extortion, and drug sales.[54]

Such cases show the difficulty of eradicating police corruption without changing the social context of policing. Police operations must be visible, with more oversight, and better public complaints procedures.

Influence Peddling in Business. In the 1970s, revelations were made that multinational corporations regularly made payoffs to foreign officials and businesspeople to secure business contracts. Gulf Oil executives admitted paying $4 million to the South Korean ruling party; Burroughs Corporation admitted paying $1.5 million to foreign officials. McDonnell-Douglas Aircraft Corporation was indicted for paying $1 million in bribes to officials of Pakistani International Airlines to secure orders.[55]

Despite legal changes, corporations that deal in foreign trade have continued to give bribes to secure favourable trade agreements.[56] In 1995, for example, several former executives of the Lockheed Aircraft Corporation pleaded guilty to bribery in the sale of transport aircraft to the Egyptian government.[57]

Embezzlement and Employee Fraud

The fifth type of white-collar crime involves individuals' use of their positions to embezzle company funds or appropriate company property for themselves. Here, the company or organization that employs the criminal is the victim of the white-collar crime.

Twenty percent of Canadians say that they are personally aware of people stealing from their employers.

Source: A poll conducted by Ernst & Young, August 8, 2002, "One in Five Canadians Say Fraud Occurs in Their Workplace."

Blue-Collar Fraud. Employee theft can reach all levels of the organizational structure. Blue-collar employees have been involved in systematic theft of company property, commonly called **pilferage**. The techniques of employee theft are quite varied:

- Piece workers zip completed garments into their clothing and take them home.
- Cashiers ring up lower prices on single-item purchases and pocket the difference.
- Clerks sell untagged sale merchandise at its original cost, pocketing the difference.
- Receiving clerks obtain duplicate keys to storage facilities, returning later to steal.
- Truck drivers make fictitious purchases of fuel, splitting the gains with the truck stop.
- Employees hide items in garbage pails or under trash heaps for retrieval later.[58]

In one study, 35 percent of employees surveyed reported involvement in pilferage.[59] Employee theft can be explained by factors related to the work setting, such as job dissatisfaction and the belief they are being exploited by employers or supervisors. It has been estimated that pilferage accounts for 30 percent to 75 percent of all shrinkage and amounts to losses of billions of dollars annually.[60]

Management Fraud. Management-level fraud includes (1) converting company assets for personal benefit, (2) fraudulently receiving increases in compensation (such as raises or bonuses), (3) fraudulently increasing personal holdings of company stock, (4) retaining a position within the company by manipulating accounts, and (5) concealing unacceptable performance from stockholders.[61] An example of management fraud is overstating company profits, which pays off if bonuses are tied to company profits.[62]

In a survey of three hundred American companies by KPMG Peat Marwick, 75 percent reported having experienced employee fraud during the previous 12 months; the estimated total loss was $250 million. In the 2003 KPMG Fraud Survey, 75 percent of companies had experienced fraud in the previous year. This ranged from employee fraud ($464 000) to financial reporting fraud $258 million).[63]

A serious violation of the public trust occurred in the Bre-X scandal in 1996, involving insider trading, stock manipulation, and management fraud on a scale hardly ever accomplished in Canada, as shown in Exhibit 13.3.

A Case in Point: The Savings and Loan Scandal. In 1985–86 the Canadian Commercial Bank of Canada (CCB) and the Northland Bank collapsed because of unacceptable financial practices. The Canada Deposit Insurance Corporation estimated the loss from the collapse of the CCB to be almost $250 million.

Exhibit 13.3	The Bre-X Scandal

In March 1997, Mike de Guzman, the top geologist of the Bre-X mine in Busang, Indonesia, leapt to his death from a helicopter. De Guzman had been credited with helping Calgary-based Bre-X discover what was believed to be the world's biggest gold deposit at the Busang mine.

The site was alleged to contain 200 million ounces of gold. However, suspicions surfaced that Bre-X's core samples had been "salted" with alluvial gold to increase the gold content. Tests conducted by Barrick Gold, a Toronto-based gold mining corporation, in 1996 showed no gold in 148 out of 150 samples. When news leaked out that the massive gold discovery was a fraud, Bre-X shares dropped substantially from a high of $286.50. Shortly after, trading in the company was halted by regulators at the Toronto Stock Exchange until an independent audit of drilling tests was completed.

The executive chief geologist of the company, Jon Felderhof, was sued for $3 billion by Bre-X's receiver-manager, Deloitte and Touche. Felderhof is believed to have made at least $70 million trading in Bre-X stock. The total amount acquired by company insiders was estimated to be on the order of $150 million. It is estimated that 40 000 Canadian investors lost more than $3 billion investing in Bre-X, looking for that lucky strike.

Sources: Glen Whelon, "Felderhof Hit by Suit," *Calgary Sun*, December 31, 1997; Sandra Roubin, "Bre-X Board Told in Late 1996 Tests Showed No Busang Gold," *Financial Post*, April 13, 1998.

The most significant case of management fraud in American history occurred in the savings and loan (S&L) industry. For more than a decade, the owners and managers of some of America's largest savings and loan banks swindled investors, depositors, and the public. The fraud cost $500 billion, 1700 banks collapsed, and criminal activity was a central factor in 70 percent to 80 percent of these cases.

How could crimes of this magnitude have been committed? In 1980, the American federal government allowed the S&Ls to expand their business operations beyond residential housing loans so that they could get involved in high-risk commercial real estate lending. The S&Ls were allowed to compete for deposits with commercial banks by offering high interest rates. The S&Ls also made deals with brokerage firms to sell high-interest certificates of deposit, encouraging investors to pour billions of dollars into banks they had never seen.

Surprisingly, the government insured all deposits. Even if crooked owners offered outlandish interest rates to attract deposits and then lent them to shady businesspeople, the federal government guaranteed that depositors could not lose money. The S&Ls made irresponsible and fraudulent loans, and losses began to mushroom. The first type of violation involved risky loans to commercial real estate developers, sometimes involving kickbacks.

A second criminal activity was collective embezzlement, siphoning funds for personal gain. For example, Erwin Hansen took over Centennial Savings and Loan of California in 1980 and threw a Christmas party for five hundred friends and their guests that cost $148 000 and included a 10-course, sit-down dinner, roving minstrels, court jesters, and pantomimes. Hansen travelled around the world in the bank's private airplanes, purchased antique furniture, and refurbished his home at a cost of more than $1 million. Before it went bankrupt, the bank bought a fleet of luxury cars and an extensive art collection. The commissioner of the California Department of Savings and Loans said in 1987, "The best way to rob a bank is to own one."

Other practices involved outright fraud. Land was sold or "flipped" between conspirators, driving up the assessed evaluation. The overpriced land could then be sold to or mortgaged by a friendly bank owned by a co-conspirator for far more than it was worth. One loan broker bought a piece of property in 1979 for $874 000, flipped it, and sold it two years later for $55 million to an S&L he had bought. Another method was reciprocal lending in which bank insiders would lend each other money that was never paid back and then trade the bad loans back and forth to delay discovery of the fraud.

In the aftermath of these white-collar crimes, owners tried to cover up their crimes by using shady accounting practices or fabricated income statements, some of them respected businesspeople with political connections. For example, the collapse of Denver-based Silverado Banking Savings and Loan cost taxpayers $1 billion, and President George Bush Sr.'s son Neil was on Silverado's board of directors. Neil Bush was called to testify before the House Banking Committee on his relationships with two developers who owed the bank considerable sums. One had given Bush $100 000 to invest with the condition that they share in the profits but not the losses. Even Neil Bush admitted, "I know it sounds a little fishy."

The crimes were difficult to detect because they involved acts of business out of the public view and revolved around seemingly innocent loans and mortgages made to associates for investment purposes. Of course, the investments later turned out to be worthless, and the bank and its stockholders were left accountable. Because the government guarantees deposits, it was forced to take over the banks and reorganize their assets.

The S&L crisis was a result of the unregulated finance capitalism that dominated the American economy in the 1980s. Because nothing is produced or sold, financial institutions are ripe for fraud. Their business is the manipulation of money, and the line between smart business practices and white-collar crime is often thin. However, between 1988 and 1992, more than 3200 defendants had been charged, 2600 convicted, and 1700 sent to prison.[64]

Client Frauds

A sixth component of white-collar crime is theft by a client from an organization that advances credit to its clients. Included in this category are insurance fraud, credit card fraud, welfare and medical insurance fraud, and tax evasion. For example, about 2 percent of welfare recipients cheat the federal government. In 2001, it was made public that Canada Customs routinely makes available its lists of people crossing the border to Employment Canada, so that the latter can check to see who is not "available for work."

These offences are grouped together because they involve theft from organizations that have many individual clients who may take advantage of their positions of trust to steal from the organizations.

InfoTrac®

Search for this article, which looks at employee theft and prevention strategies: R.A. Wilson, "The Enemy Within," *Risk and Insurance* 15, no. 8 (2004), 18–22.

Health Care Fraud. Client frauds may be common even among upper-income people.[65] Some physicians have been caught cheating the federal government out of Medicare or Medicaid payments, such as the Toronto chiropractor caught billing the government in 1996 for $65 000 in services he never delivered. In Ontario a study by the Canadian Medical Association found that in one in three thousand cases, prescription drug benefits were claimed by someone after an individual was dead. Other abusive practices include such techniques as "ping-ponging" (referring patients to other physicians in the same office), "gang visits" (billing for multiple services), and "steering" (directing patients to particular pharmacies).[66]

Of a more serious nature are fraudulent acts designed to cheat both the government and the consumer, such as billing for services not rendered, billing excessive amounts, setting up kickback schemes, and providing false identification on reimbursement forms. For example, a 1997 undercover operation in New York State netted 20 professionals who were fraudulently overbilling insurance companies. One doctor saw a patient 11 times and billed for 150 office visits; another treated a patient once and sent in 90 claims. One of the chiropractors was secretly videotaped coaching a patient on how to fake injuries when examined by physicians evaluating his insurance claim.[67] Doctors involved in these schemes are liable to criminal prosecution under the law, and the dollar losses are astronomical.[68]

Bank Fraud. Bank fraud can encompass such diverse schemes as cheque kiting (see Exhibit 13.4), cheque forgery, false statements on loan applications, money laundering, sale of stolen cheques, bank credit card

Exhibit 13.4	Cheque Kiting

Cheque kiting is a scheme in which a client with accounts in two or more banks takes advantage of the time required for cheques to clear to obtain unauthorized use of bank funds. For example, a person has $5000 on account in a bank and cashes a cheque for $3000 from an account in another bank in which he or she has no funds. The bank cashes the cheque because this person is already a customer. He then closes his original account before the bad cheque is discovered or writes cheques on his account that total $5000, which clear because he has funds in his account. In some instances, the kiter expects the bank to cover a withdrawal before a cheque is presented to another bank for collection: He simply wants a short-term interest-free loan. Others have no intention of ever covering the transaction but instead want to take cash out of the system after building accounts to artificially high amounts. Kiting can be a multimillion-dollar offence involving cheques written and deposited in banks in two or more provinces or territories and sometimes among banks in multiple countries.

fraud, unauthorized use of automatic teller machines (ATMs), auto title frauds, and illegal transactions with offshore banks. For example, a car dealership could commit bank fraud by securing loans on titles to cars it no longer owns. Or a real estate owner would be guilty of bank fraud if he or she obtained a false appraisal on a piece of property with the intention of obtaining a bank loan in excess of the property's real worth.

Tax Evasion. Another important aspect of client fraud is tax evasion. This is a particularly challenging area for criminological study, since (1) so many citizens regularly underreport their income, and (2) it is often difficult to separate honest error from deliberate tax evasion.

To prove tax fraud, the government must find that the taxpayer either underreported income or did not report taxable income. A second element of tax fraud is "willfulness" on the part of the tax evader. Finally, the government must show that the taxpayer has purposely attempted to evade or defeat a tax payment.

Tax evasion is a difficult crime to prosecute. It is hard to prove the difference between a careless mistake and willful fraud. However, the temptation is there, such as construction workers who provide services under the table and off the books.[69]

In Canada the value of the underground economy is estimated to be as high as 16 percent of the gross national product (GNP), or $130 billion, based on a study by the Canadian Tax Foundation. In the United States the IRS estimates that more than $120 billion in taxes go uncollected each year because individuals fail to report all their income; nearly one-third of that amount is from self-employed workers, including professionals, labourers, and door-to-door salespeople.[70]

If the temptation is high, the likelihood of getting caught is low. In the United States, for example, the number of tax audits declined from 8 percent in 1980 to about 2 percent currently.[71] Computer models are used to target anomalies. Despite some well-publicized cases involving the wealthy, such as a $16-million judgment against singer Willie Nelson and the prosecution and conviction of multimillionaire Leona Helmsley, the IRS has been accused of targeting middle-income taxpayers and ignoring the upper classes and large corporations.

Corporate Crime

The final component of white-collar crime is corporate representatives violating laws that restrain these institutions from doing social harm. This is also known as corporate or organizational crime.

Interest in corporate crime first emerged in the 1900s, when writers targeted the unscrupulous business practices of John D. Rockefeller, Andrew Carnegie, J.P. Morgan, and other corporate business leaders.[72] In 1907, sociologist E.A. Ross described the "criminaloid," a business leader who victimized an unsuspecting public. However, it was Edwin Sutherland who focused theoretical attention on the subject in the 1940s.[73]

Corporate crimes are socially injurious acts committed by companies to further their business interests, as can be seen from some of the examples in Exhibit 13.5 and in Exhibit 13.2. The target of their crimes can be the general public, the environment, or even their company's workers. They can range from the thousands of women with immune system disorders from breast implants, to the 26 miners who died in the Westray coal mine. In a recent case, Firestone Tire was sued after one hundred people were killed when the tread separated from their tires, causing their vehicles to crash, a problem that could have been fixed for as little as 90 cents a tire (see the Crime in the News feature).

What makes corporate crimes unique is that the corporation is a legal fiction, not an individual. In reality, it is company employees or owners who commit corporate

---

Exhibit 13.5   Quick Facts on Cases of Corporate Crime

- In 1987 the ferry *Herald of Free Enterprise* sank in the English Channel, killing two hundred people; the bow doors were improperly secured because proper safety measures had been rejected as too costly.

- In the early 1970s Reed Paper, a processing plant in Dryden, Ontario, dumped nine thousand kilograms of mercury into a nearby river, causing extensive brain damage among members of the Grassy Narrows Ojibwa band.

- Between 1958 and 1978, it is estimated that the cost of overcharging by the major oil companies cost Canadians $12 billion due to lack of competition and price-fixing.

- The Sydney Steel Corporation in Cape Breton is estimated to have released emissions 6000 percent above allowable standards; 700 000 tons of toxic materials in the tar ponds resist all attempts at clean-up or cover-up.

- In 1982 the oil platform *Ocean Ranger* sank off the coast of Newfoundland, killing all 84 people on board; among other problems, safety standards were inadequate.

- In 1992 the Westray coal mine in Plymouth, Nova Scotia, exploded, killing 26 miners; safety standards were lax and unenforced by government inspectors.

Sources: M. Clarke, *Business Crime* (Cambridge: Polity Press, 1990); Russell Mokhiber, *Corporate Crime and Violence: Big Business, Power and the Abuse of the Public Trust* (San Francisco: Sierra Club, 1988); Laureen Snider, *Bad Business: Corporate Crime in Canada* (Scarborough, Ont.: Nelson, 1993).

Crime in the News

Corporate Disregard for Human Life

Lessons of the Ford/Firestone Scandal: Profit Motive Turns Consumers into Road Kill
by Anthony D. Prince

The year was 1981, the case was encaptioned *Grimshaw v. Ford Motor Company* and at issue was the auto giant's liability for permanently disfiguring burns and other severe injuries sustained by a 13-year-old boy named Richard Grimshaw who barely escaped a flaming Ford Pinto with his life. The driver, Mrs. Lilly Gray, was dead within days of the fiery rear-end collision. A California jury subsequently returned a $126 million civil judgment for young Richard; the Pinto was seared into the national consciousness as a symbol of corporate greed in America.

Rejecting safety designs costing between only $1.80 and $15.30 per Pinto, Ford had calculated the damages it would likely pay in wrongful death and injury cases and pocketed the difference. In a cold and calculating "costs/benefits" analysis, Ford projected that the Pinto would probably cause 180 burn deaths, 180 serious burn injuries, 2,100 burned vehicles each year. Also, Ford estimated civil suits of $200,000 per death, $67,000 per injury, $700 per vehicle for a grand total of $49.5 million. The costs for installing safety features would cost approximately $137 million per year. As a result, the Pinto became a moving target, its unguarded fuel tank subject to rupture by exposed differential bolts shoved into it by rear-end collisions at speeds of as little as 21 miles per hour. Spewing gasoline into the passenger compartment, the car and its passengers became engulfed in a raging inferno.

Only months before, an Elkhart, Indiana County, prosecutor had, for the first time in history, filed homicide charges against Ford Motor Company for the deaths of three Indiana girls in another Pinto rear-end collision. Ultimately, however, District Attorney Michael Cosentino, whose entire budget for the prosecution was $20,000, was no match for millions of dollars worth of corporate legal talent brought in by Ford. Cosentino could not even prevent the trial-court judge from systematically excluding Ford crash-test films and other inculpatory evidence. Yet, while an acquittal was a foregone conclusion, a precedent was established for criminally charging a product manufacturer in the death of a consumer.

As the Ford SUV/Firestone-Bridgestone tire scandal continues to dominate the headlines 20 years after Grimshaw and the *People of Indiana v. Ford Motor Company*, the only law to which these corporate giants seem beholden is the "law of maximum profits." At last count, more than 100 deaths worldwide have been directly attributed to Firestone tire failures and dozens more to fatal rollover accidents involving the top-heavy Ford Explorer, one of the best-selling vehicles in history. . . .

Far from being the exception, Firestone and Ford are only the most recent examples of the rule. The list is long and not pretty. In the 1970s, the Dalkon Shield, A.H. Robbins' toxic intrauterine device, cut a swath of death and injury to the reproductive systems of tens of thousands of women. In the 1980s, the carcinogenic poisoning of Woburn, Massachusetts, was still a buried secret until Jonathan Harr's book *A Civil Action* and the subsequently released movie starring John Travolta told the sordid story of W.R. Grace Corporation's thirst for profits at the expense of children's lives. Add to the list of victims the millions of asbestos insulators, coal miners, textile workers and addicted cigarette smokers whose life-breath is choked off every minute of every day all in pursuit of the almighty dollar.

Anthony Prince is an Oakland, Calif., product liability attorney and former union safety committeeman.

Source: Excerpted from an article in the People's Tribune (Online Edition), Vol. 26 No. 11/November, 2000; P.O. Box 3524, Chicago, IL 60654, http://www.lrna.org. For free electronic subscription, email pt-dist@noc.org with "Subscribe" in the subject line. For the full version of the article, visit http://www.lrna.org/league/PT/PT.2000.11/PT.2000.11.7.html (accessed May 18, 2005).

crimes and who ultimately benefit through career advancement or greater profits. Some of the acts included in corporate crime are price-fixing and illegal restraint of trade, false advertising, and company practices that violate environmental protection statutes. The variety of crimes contained within this category is great, and the damage they cause is vast. The following subsections will examine some of the most important offences.

Illegal Restraint of Trade and Price-Fixing. Restraint of trade involves a contract or conspiracy designed to stifle competition, create a monopoly, artificially maintain prices, or otherwise interfere with competition.

A good example of restraint of trade is **price-fixing**. This act usually takes one of four forms.[74] The first is *predation*, in which large firms agree among themselves to sell their products below market prices to drive out weaker firms. A second scheme is *identical bidding*, in which competitors agree to submit identical bids for each contract, above what would have been expected if collusion had not occurred. Purchasing agents use their discretion to choose among bidders; however, identical bidding usually ensures all vendors get a share of the market. In the third scheme, the market might be *divided into territories* within which only one member of the conspiring group is permitted a low bid. The remaining conspirators either refrain from bidding or give artificially high bids. The fourth scheme, *rotational bidding*, involves a conspiracy in which the opportunity to submit a winning bid for a government or business contract is rotated among the institutional bidders. The conspirators meet in advance and determine who will give the low bid. The winning bid is higher than it should be, since the losers have all submitted abnormally high bids. Close coordination among the bidders is essential.

False Claims and Advertising. Executives in even the largest corporations are sometimes caught in the position in which the expectation of profits demands that sales be increased. At times, executives respond to this challenge by making claims about their product that cannot be justified by its actual performance. The line between clever, aggressive sales techniques and fraudulent claims is a fine one in business but a large one morally. It is not fraudulent to show a delivery service vehicle taking off into outer space. However, it is illegal to knowingly and purposely advertise a product as possessing qualities that the manufacturer realizes it does not have.

In 1991 the U.S. Food and Drug Administration seized all the Citrus Hill orange juice stored in a Minneapolis warehouse. The third-largest-selling breakfast drink in the United States, Citrus Hill had billed itself as "pure squeezed," "100 percent pure," and "fresh," despite the fact that it was made from concentrate.[75]

Orange juice might seem like a minor example. However, what if a car manufacturer claims that its car gets higher gas mileage than it really does, or a mouthwash maker claims its product can cure colds? The list is endless.

In the pharmaceutical industry, it has been common for medicines to be advertised as cures for previously incurable diseases.[76] Such medicines include alleged cures for cancer and arthritis and drugs advertised to give energy and sexual potency. The problem arises because competing companies market similar products and the key to successful sales is convincing the public that one product is superior to the rest. This drive for profits leads to the falsification of data and unethical sales promotions.[77]

It is difficult for authorities to police such violations of the public trust. The most serious consequence is usually an order that the company refrain from using the advertising or that it withdraw the advertising claims. Criminal penalties for false claims are rarely given.

Environmental Crimes. There are many types of environmental crimes, from endangering the lives of workers by maintaining unsafe conditions in plants and mines, to exposing workers to hazardous materials while on the job. For example, the asbestos industry was inundated with lawsuits after environmental scientists found a close association between exposure to asbestos and the development of cancer.

A second type of environmental crime committed by large corporations is illegal pollution of the environment. Two cases stand out. The first was the leaking of methyl isocyanate from a Union Carbide plant in Bhopal, India, in 1984. Estimates of the death toll range from 5000 to 20 000 people; another 60 000 were injured. Union Carbide later reported that the plant had not been operating safely and blamed the negligence on local officials.[78] The second case occurred when the tanker *Exxon Valdez* ran aground on a reef off the coast of Alaska on March 24, 1989, dumping just over five hundred million litres (11 million gallons) of crude oil and fouling 1100 kilometres (700 miles) of shoreline. In 1991, Exxon agreed to pay $1 billion in criminal and civil fines rather than face trial, the largest amount paid as a result of environmental pollution to date.[79] However, initially, the American government announced that it would not pursue charges; Exxon was then the largest multinational in the world, with an annual budget exceeding that of most countries.

Some recent environmental disasters in the news illustrate the fine line between an accident and a crime. At the Canadian-owned Los Frailes mine in Spain, five million cubic metres of toxic mine waste spilled through a break in a mine tailings pond in 1998. Boliden said that the waste had contaminated thousands of hectares of farming land. Environmentalists accused the company of failing to properly maintain the reservoir and of firing an engineer who had predicted the disaster. In 1996 the Canadian-owned Omai gold mine in Georgetown, Guyana, was the site of a massive cyanide spill from a tailings pond. The mine was developed by Canadian Robert Friedland, who had been sued by the American government for a huge environmental spill of cyanide at the Summitville gold mine in Colorado. He also developed the Voisey's Bay nickel mine in Labrador, and the assets from the sale to Inco were briefly seized by an American court to pay for Summitville. Could these disasters have been prevented with adequate environmental safeguards; are they more likely to happen in poor countries that are heavily dependent on resource extraction?

Considering the uncertainties of federal budget allocations, there is some question whether environmental legislation can be enforced well enough to deter environmental crime. Lack of effective regulation was certainly an issue at the Westray mine. But in Parliament in 2004, Bill C-45, or the Westray bill, came into effect, which makes organizations and senior officers liable for criminal acts related to workplace safety. See Exhibit 13.6 for more on the Westray Mine disaster.

Exhibit 13.6	The Tragedy of Westray

In 1987 the Nova Scotia government was looking for someone to take over the stalled Westray mine in Plymouth, Pictou County. Clifford Frame of Curragh Mining agreed to develop the mine, despite studies pointing out dangers such as the high concentrations of methane gas.

A deal brokered between provincial and federal politicians and Frame was announced three days before the provincial election in 1988. Westray was to receive $85 million in the form of a federal loan guarantee, plus a $12 million provincial loan. A lucrative 15-year contract was signed with Nova Scotia Power, despite the fact that there was cleaner, cheaper coal to be found elsewhere.

Between February 1991 and April 1992, Labour Department inspection reports show that the mine's owners were cautioned about methane gas levels, improper storage of flammable materials, and the use of unauthorized equipment. No charges were laid. Despite cave-ins and a roof collapse, mining began in 1991. In November of that year changes were made to the mine's design without the knowledge or approval of the Department of Natural Resources.

On May 9, 1992, at 5:18 a.m., a methane explosion ignited a build-up of coal dust in the mine, and 26 miners were killed. As Figure 13.2 shows, the explosion happened deep underground, where it would have been impossible for workers to escape.

Figure 13.2	Westray Mine Disaster Map

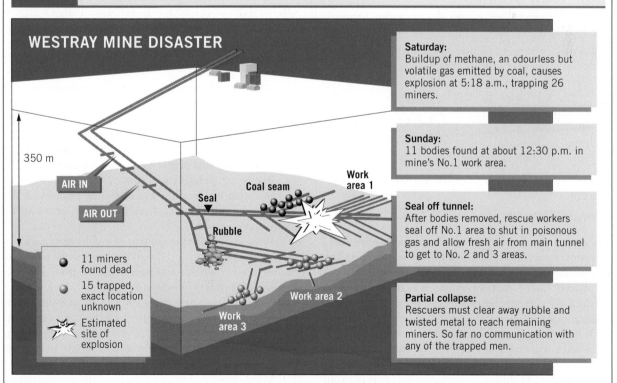

Source: *The Toronto Star,* May 11, 1992, p. A1. Reproduced with permission of Torstar Syndication Services.

The RCMP launched a criminal investigation, and a provincial inquiry was commissioned to determine whether neglect had contributed to the disaster. In October, the Nova Scotia Department of Labour charged Curragh and four mine managers with 52 violations of the *Occupational Health and Safety Act*; the maximum penalty was $10 000. In November 1992, the Supreme Court of Nova Scotia quashed the inquiry, and in December the safety charges were dropped so as to not interfere with the RCMP investigation. In April 1993, Curragh and two underground managers were charged with manslaughter and criminal negligence, but charges were thrown out three months later for being too vague. The charges were relaid, but Curragh went into receivership, reducing the number of defendants to two.

In 1995 the criminal trial began, but four months later the proceedings were stayed by the judge, who ruled that the prosecution did not properly disclose evidence. In December the Nova Scotia Court of Appeal subsequently quashed the appeal, and the likelihood that anyone would face criminal charges looked increasingly grim. In March 1997 the Supreme Court of Canada upheld the new trial order.

By 1998, six years had elapsed since the explosion. The Government of Nova Scotia announced that it would not pursue criminal charges, Curragh was bankrupt, and Frame wouldn't testify before the provincial inquiry. The inquiry's report, based on 17 000 pages of oral testimony, was released, citing extensive problems with government regulation. The John T. Ryan Trophy Committee of the Canadian Institute of Mining, Metallurgy and Petroleum, which declared the Westray mine the safest colliery in Canada a month before it exploded, announced that it would adopt measures to ensure that companies do not fudge accident statistics. The miners' families decided that they must move on, and the province announced that it would dismantle the Westray minehead.

Sources: Shaun Comish, *The Westray Tragedy: A Miner's Story* (Halifax: Fernwood, 1993); Dean Jobb, *Calculated Risk: Greed, Politics, and the Westray Tragedy* (Halifax: Nimbus, 1994); *The Westray Story: A Predictable Path to Disaster, Report of the Westray Mine Public Inquiry* (Halifax, 1997).

High-Tech Crime

The Moore typology of white-collar crime organized traditional entrepreneurial crime. However, high-tech crimes are emerging that contain elements of fraud, theft, swindles, and false claims. The crimes are difficult to categorize because they can be committed by corporations and individuals, can be singular or ongoing, and can involve the theft of information, resources, or funds. High-tech crimes cost consumers billions of dollars each year and will increase dramatically. They are also difficult to detect and police.

Internet Crimes

Millions of people worldwide are on the Internet, and the number entering cyberspace is growing rapidly. This vast pool is a target for high-tech crimes.

There have been cases in which adults have solicited teenagers in Internet chat rooms, distributed obscene material, or allowed right-wing hate groups to publish Web pages on the Internet.

Until it was raided by federal authorities on August 8, 2001, Landslide Productions Inc. of Fort Worth, Texas, was a highly profitable Internet-based pornography ring, taking in as much as $1.4 million in one month.[80] It was the largest-known commercial child pornography enterprise, having at least 250 000 subscribers worldwide.

The crackdown led to convictions of the owners, who had offered subscribers access to websites that advertised themselves with such phrases as "Child Rape" or "Cyber Lolita." The sites were off-limits to control by American authorities because the sites were located in Russia and Indonesia.

Selling child pornography on the Internet isn't the only illegal use. The Computer Security Institute found that 78 percent of employers had detected employee abuse of Internet access privileges, such as employees downloading pirated software. Thirty-eight percent report unauthorized access or misuse of their websites.[81]

Bogus get-rich-quick schemes, weight-loss scams, and investment swindles have also been pitched on the Internet. In some cases, these fraudulent acts can be dangerous to clients.

With the continuing growth of e-commerce, a study by Meridien Research predicted that payment-card fraud on the Internet would increase worldwide from $1.6 billion in 2000 to $15.5 billion by 2005.[82] The European Commission reported that in 2000, payment-card fraud in the European Union rose by 50 percent to $553 million in fraudulent transactions; the International Chamber of Commerce reported that nearly two-thirds of all cases it handled in 2000 involved online fraud.[83]

Some other recent cases include the conclusion in 2004 of an investigation targeting various Internet crimes, including the use of spam e-mail to steal credit card numbers. It was estimated that the crimes had

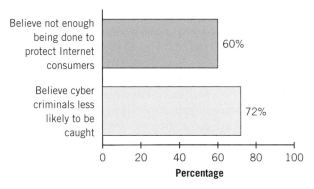

Sixty percent of Canadians don't believe that enough is being done to protect Internet consumers from cybercrime; 72 percent say that cybercriminals have less chance of being caught than do criminals in the real world.

Source: Poll conducted by Ipsos Reid, March 26, 2001, "Canadians Worried About Cybercrime."

InfoTrac®

Internet information theft and access violations threaten companies worldwide. To read how business leaders are fighting back, go to InfoTrac® College Edition and read this article: Luis Ramiro Hernandez, "Integrated Risk Management in the Internet Age," *Risk Management* 47, no. 6 (2000): 29.

| Exhibit 13.7 | Common Internet Fraud Schemes |

- **Online Auction/Retail:** misrepresentation of product advertised for sale, or nondelivery of merchandise or goods purchased through Internet auction site

- **Investment Fraud:** fraudulent claims to solicit investments or loans, or that provides for the purchase, use, or trade of forged or counterfeit securities

- **Business Opportunity/Work at Home:** offering phony job opportunities, often with associated charges such as "processing" or "application" fees

- **Financial Institution Fraud:** misrepresentation of truth by a person to induce a business or organization that manages money or credit to perform a fraudulent activity

- **Credit Card Theft/Fraud:** unauthorized use of a credit/debit card or credit/debit card number to fraudulently obtain money or property; stolen from unsecured Web sites

- **Ponzi/Pyramid Schemes:** investment scheme in which investors are promised abnormally high profits on their investments. Early investors are paid returns with the investment money received from the late-comers. The system usually collapses, and the later investors do not receive dividends and lose their initial investment.

Source: FBI, *Common Internet Fraud Schemes* (Washington, D.C.: Author, 2001).

victimized 150 000 people and caused $215 million in losses. In 2004 the Royal Bank warned its customers that fake e-mail messages were being sent out to clients asking them to verify their account numbers and PIN information. The scam was probably accomplished through a "phishing" software package that enables the user to create legitimate looking e-mail. It's estimated that 16 percent of attacks on businesses are in the e-commerce area.[84]

What is obvious is that the Internet magnifies the proportion of the crime. For example, in one of the first cased of its kind, an Ontario judge awarded an archaeologist $125 000 in damages after a Native man used e-mails to smear her as a "grave robber."

The ruling is precedent-setting in the emerging field of Internet libel, or "cyberlibel." Posting slanderous remarks on a popular website, where millions of users might pick them up and circulate them, or e-mailing libellous remarks in an attempt to smear someone's reputation is illegal.

Connections

In Chapter 12 we looked at ordinary forms of fraud. With the amount of power corporations have in the information age, they can commit larger frauds than ever before.

Computer Crimes

Computer-related thefts are a new trend in employee theft and embezzlement. The widespread use of computers for business transactions has encouraged people to use them for illegal purposes, usually in five categories:[85]

1. Theft of services or using the computer for unauthorized purposes
2. Use of data in a computer system for personal gain

3. Unauthorized use of computers employed for financial processing to obtain assets
4. Theft of property by computer for personal use or conversion to profit
5. Use of a computer as the object of a crime, such as spreading a computer virus

Although most of these crimes involve using computers for personal gain, the last category typically encompasses activities that are motivated more by malice than by profit. Computer criminals are typically motivated by (1) revenge for some perceived wrong, (2) a need to exhibit their technical prowess and superiority, (3) a desire to highlight the vulnerability of computer security systems (so that they will be hired as consultants), (4) a need to spy on other people's private financial and personal information (computer voyeurism), and (5) the desire to assert a philosophy of open access to all systems and programs.[86]

Types of Computer Crime. Several common techniques are used by computer criminals. In fact, theft via computers has become so common that experts have created their own jargon to describe theft styles and methods:

1. *The Trojan horse.* One computer is used to reprogram another for illicit purposes.
2. *The salami slice.* An employee sets up a dummy account, and a small amount is subtracted from all other customers' accounts and added to the thief's account.
3. *Super-zapping.* An employees use a maintenance program to order the system to issue cheques to his or her private account.
4. *The logic bomb.* A virus program is secretly attached to the company's computer system.
5. *Impersonation.* An unauthorized person uses the identity of an authorized computer user to access the computer system.
6. *Data leakage.* A person illegally obtains data from a computer system by leaking them out in small amounts.

A different type of computer crime involves the installation of a virus in a computer system that disrupts existing programs and networks. This high-tech vandalism is the work of hackers, who consider their efforts to be pranks. In one case, a 25-year-old computer whiz named Robert Morris unleashed a program that wrecked a nationwide electronic mail network. His efforts netted him three years' probation, a $10 000 fine, and four hundred hours of community service.[87]

Shift magazine estimates that the number of computer viruses that exist in the world today is in excess of 56 000. The number doubled between 1999 and 2000.

In 1998, the first major Internet virus, the Morris worm, infected more than six thousand computers. In 2000, the Love Bug worm infected more than 15 million computers, costing $14 billion; 40 people were involved in writing it. With the growth of the Internet, the ability to spread these viruses has grown. In 1999 it took about three days for the Melissa macro virus to spread to more than 10 million computers worldwide.

An accurate accounting of computer crime is not possible since many offences go unreported. Sometimes company managers refuse to report the crime to police lest they display their incompetence to stockholders, or because it involves such "low-visibility" acts as copying computer software in violation of copyright laws.[88]

The Extent of Computer Crime. How much computer crime is there? The Computer Crime and Security Survey, based on a survey of more than five hundred computer security practitioners in corporations, government agencies, financial institutions, medical institutions, and universities, indicates that the threat from computer crime and other information security breaches is rapidly expanding. Among the survey's most important findings are the following:

- Eighty percent of respondents detected computer security breaches.
- Eighty percent acknowledged financial losses due to computer breaches.
- Forty-four percent reported $455 million in financial losses, up from $378 million in 2001.
- Theft of proprietary information cost $170 million, and financial fraud cost $115 million.
- Seventy-four percent cited their Internet connection as a frequent point of attack.
- Thirty-four percent reported the intrusions to law enforcement.[89]

The Business Software Alliance estimated that $11 billion or more is lost each year to the unauthorized use of software. Software piracy was highest in Asia ($4.7 billion) and amounted to about $2 billion in North America.[90]

 InfoTrac®

Look for the following articles:

- Peter Plazza, "Low Security Means Crime Pays," *Securities Management* 45, no. 3 (2001): 38.
- John Sullivan and Daniel Tsai, "The Developing Law of Internet Jurisdiction," *The Advocate* 61, no. 4 (2003): 521–538.

Exhibit 13.8   A Short History of Computer Viruses and Attacks

1945: Rear Admiral Grace Murray Hopper calls a moth trapped between relays in a Navy computer a "bug," a term used since the late nineteenth century to refer to problems with electrical devices.

1964: AT&T begins monitoring telephone calls to try to discover the identities of "phone phreaks" who use tone generators to make free phone calls. The company monitors 33 million toll calls and scores two hundred convictions by the time the investigation ends in 1970.

1972: John Draper discovers that the plastic whistle in a box of breakfast cereal reproduces a 2600-hertz tone that can be used to unlock AT&T's phone network, allowing free calls. Among other phreakers of the 1970s is famous future hacker Kevin Mitnick.

1979: Engineers at Xerox Palo Alto Research Center discover the computer "worm," a short program that scours a network for idle processors. Designed to provide more efficient computer use, the worm is the ancestor of modern worms—destructive computer viruses that alter or erase data on computers, often leaving files irretrievably corrupted.

1983: The FBI busts the "414s," a group of young hackers who break into several U.S. government networks using only an Apple II+ computer and a modem.

1983: University of Southern California doctoral candidate Fred Cohen coins the term "computer virus" to describe a computer program that can "affect other computer programs by modifying them in such a way as to include a (possibly evolved) copy of itself."

1986: One of the first PC viruses ever created, "The Brain," is released in Pakistan.

1988: Twenty-three-year-old programmer Robert Morris unleashes a worm that invades ARPANET computers (the forerunner of the Internet). The small program disables roughly six thousand computers on the network by flooding their memory banks with copies of itself. Confessing to creating the worm out of boredom, he is fined $10 000.

1991: Symantec releases its Norton Anti-Virus software.

1994: Inexperienced e-mail users dutifully forward an e-mail hoax warning people not to open any message with the phrase "Good Times" in the subject line.

1998: Intruders infiltrate and take control of more than five hundred military, government, and private sector computer systems. The incidents, first thought to have originated in Iraq, were committed by two California teenagers.

1999: The "Melissa" virus infects thousands of computers, causing an estimated $80 million in damage. The virus starts a program that sends copies of itself to the first 50 names listed in the recipient's Outlook e-mail address book. In 2002, Melissa virus author David L. Smith, 33, is sentenced to 20 months in federal prison.

2000: The "I Love You" virus infects millions of computers virtually overnight, sending passwords and usernames stored on infected computers back to the virus's author. Authorities trace the virus to a young Filipino computer student, but he goes free because the Philippines has no laws against hacking and spreading computer viruses. This spurs the creation of the European Union's global Cybercrime Treaty.

2000: Yahoo, eBay, Amazon, and Datek are knocked offline following a series of "distributed denial-of-service attacks." Investigators discover that the attacks—in which a target system is disabled by a flood of traffic from hundreds of computers simultaneously—were orchestrated when the hackers co-opted powerful computers at the University of California–Santa Barbara.

2001: The "Anna Kournikova" virus mails itself to every person listed in the victim's Microsoft Outlook address book. This relatively benign virus frightens computer security analysts, who believe it was written using a software toolkit that allows even the most inexperienced programmer to create a computer virus.

2001: The Code Red worm infects tens of thousands of systems, causing $2 billion in damages. The worm is programmed to use the power of all infected machines against the White House website. In a partnership with virus hunters and technology companies, the White House deciphers the virus's code and blocks traffic as the worm begins its attack.

2001: Just days after September 11, the "Nimda" virus infects hundreds of thousands of computers around the world. The virus is considered one of the most sophisticated, with up to five methods of infecting systems and replicating itself.

2002: The "Klez" worm sends copies of itself to all of the e-mail addresses in the victim's Microsoft Outlook directory.

2002: A denial-of-service attack hits the 13 servers for almost all Internet communications.

2003: The "Slammer" worm infects hundreds of thousands of computers in less than three hours. The fastest-spreading worm ever wreaks havoc on businesses worldwide, knocking cash machines offline and delaying airline flights.

Source: Adapted from Brian Krebs, "A Short History of Computer Viruses and Attacks," *Washington Post,* February 14, 2003, www.washingtonpost.com.

The Cause of White-Collar Crime

When Ivan Boesky pleaded guilty to security fraud, he paid a fine of $100 million, the largest at that time in U.S. Securities Exchange Commission (SEC) history. Boesky's fine was later superseded by Michael Milken's fine of more than $1 billion. How, people asked, can people with so much disposable wealth get involved in a risky scheme to produce even more?

Offenders can engage in business crime because they can rationalize its effects and convince themselves that their actions are not really crimes because the acts involved do not resemble street crimes. For example, a banker who uses a position of trust to lend an institution's assets to a company he secretly controls may see himself as doing shrewd business. A pharmacist who chisels customers on prescription drugs may rationalize that it does not really hurt anyone. Businesspeople feel justified in committing white-collar crimes because they believe that government regulators do not understand the problems of competing in the free enterprise system. Some white-collar criminals believe that everyone violates business laws, so it is not so bad if they do so themselves. Rationalizing or "neutralizing" greed is a common trait of white-collar criminals not unlike those other criminals use. It is just a matter of scale.

Greedy or Needy?

Greed and need motivate white-collar crime. Executives tamper with company books because they feel the need to keep or improve their jobs, satisfy their egos, or support their children. Blue-collar workers may pilfer because they need to keep pace with inflation or buy a new car. Many white-collar crimes involve relatively trivial amounts: Women convicted of white-collar crime typically work in lower-echelon positions, and their acts are motivated more by economic survival than by greed and power.[91] Sometimes, perhaps, even people in the upper echelons of the financial world, such as Ivan Boesky, may be working from a more basic emotional insecurity.[92]

Embezzlement is caused by a "nonshareable financial problem."[93] This condition may be the result of offenders' living beyond their means and piling up gambling debts, for example. Solving personal financial problems through criminal means is opened by the rationalizations that society has developed for white-collar crime, as in these typical phrases: "Many people get their start in life by using other people's money"; "in real estate, there is nothing wrong with using deposits before the deal is closed"; "anybody will steal if they get in a tight spot." Rationalizations allow offenders' financial needs to be met without compromising their values.

There are a number of more formal theories of white-collar crime. In the following sections, we examine two of the more prominent ones in detail.

Corporate Culture Theory

Some business organizations promote white-collar criminality in the same way that lower-class culture encourages the development of juvenile gangs and street crime. Business enterprises cause crime by placing excessive demands on employees while maintaining a business climate tolerant of employee deviance. New employees learn attitudes and techniques needed to commit white-collar crime from business peers in a learning process similar to how gang boys learn the techniques of drug dealing and burglary from older youths through differential association.

Criminologists use corporate culture and structure to explain white-collar crime. For example, business organizations will encourage employee criminality if they encounter difficulties in attaining goals, especially making profits. Some organizations will create cost-reduction policies that inspire lawbreaking and corner-cutting to become norms passed on to employees. When new employees balk at violating business laws, they are told: "This is the way things are done here, don't worry about it." A business's organizational environment influences white-collar crime. If market conditions are weak, competition intense, law enforcement lax, and managers willing to stress success at any cost, conditions for corporate crime are maximized.[94]

Corporate culture theory is analogous to the cultural deviance approach, suggesting that crime occurs when obedience to subculture norms and values causes people to break the rules of conventional society. However,

WorldCom controller David Myers, one example of high-profile executives facing charges for white-collar crime.

cultural deviance theory was originally directed at lower-class slum boys, not business executives. However, the same crime-producing forces may be operating in both socioeconomic groups.

Corporate Climate. John Braithwaite, in his writings on white-collar crime, has said that businesspeople in any society may find themselves in a situation where their organization's stated goals cannot be achieved through conventional business practices.[95] In a capitalist society, young executives may find that their profit ratios are below par and that illegitimate opportunities are the only solution to their problem. So when a government official is willing to take a bribe to overlook costly safety violations, the bribe is gratefully offered. Or when insider trading can increase profits, the investment banker leaps at the chance to engage in it. But how can traditionally law-abiding people overcome the ties of conventional law and morality?

If corporations contain an employee subculture that resists government regulation and socializes new workers in the skills and attitudes necessary to violate the law, junior executives may learn from seniors how to meet with competitors to fix prices. When governmental agencies are viewed as uncooperative, untrustworthy, and resistant to change, corporations will be more likely to develop clandestine, law-violating subcultures. A positive working relationship with governmental overseers will reduce the need for a secret, law-violating infrastructure to develop. Illegal corporate behaviour can exist only in secrecy; public scrutiny brings the "shame" of a criminal label to people whose social life and community standing rests on their good name and character.

Shame of Discovery. The shame of discovery has an important moderating influence on corporate crime. Its source may be external: the community, professional or industry peers, or government regulatory agencies. The source of shame and disapproval can also be internal: corporate policies that admonish employees to obey the rule of law. For example, some corporations encourage whistle-blowing by coworkers to sanction workers who violate the law and cause embarrassment. In a sense, corporations that maintain an excess of definitions unfavourable to violating the law will be less likely than those that don't to contain deviant subcultures and business violations. In contrast, corporate crime thrives in organizations that isolate people within spheres of responsibility, where lines of communication are blocked, where deviant subcultures can develop.

Those holding the corporate culture theory would view the savings and loan scandal as a prime example of what happens when people work in organizations whose cultural values stress profit over fair play, in which government scrutiny is limited and regulators are viewed as the enemy, and in which senior members encourage newcomers to believe that greed is good.

The Self-Control View

Hirschi and Gottfredson take exception to the idea that white-collar crime is a product of the corporate culture.[96] If that were true, there would be much more white-collar crime, and white-collar criminals would not be embarrassed. Instead, the motives that produce white-collar crimes are those that produce any other crime: the desire for quick, certain benefit, with minimal effort. Their general theory holds that criminals lack self-control. White-collar criminals are people with low self-control who follow momentary impulses without consideration of long-term costs. White-collar crime is rare because executives hire people with self-control, limiting the number of potential white-collar criminals. Data show that the demographic distribution of white-collar crime is similar to that for other crimes. For example, gender, race, and age ratios are the same for such crimes as embezzlement and fraud as they are for street crimes, such as burglary and robbery.

Business executives and corporate executives seem to be people who would have above-average self-control.[97] However, there is some evidence that white-collar criminals are often repeat offenders, sharing characteristics with street criminals (such as being impulsive and egocentric), although they begin their careers later in life and offend at a slower pace.[98]

Even if this view is accurate, white-collar offenders may manifest a wide range of self-control, which determines the path they take to crime. People with low self-control of their impulsivity commit fraud and other crimes in self-interest, as do common criminals. Others with high self-control pursue ego gratification in an aggressive and calculating fashion. In the middle are offenders who take advantage of criminal opportunities to satisfy an immediate personal need; in them, self-control becomes overwhelmed by special problems. Self-control is a variable that interacts with need and opportunity to produce white-collar crimes.[99]

 InfoTrac®

Look for Abeb David Lowell and Kathryn C. Arnold, "Corporate Crime after 2000: A New Law Enforcement Challenge or Déjà Vu?" *American Law Review* 41, no. 2 (2003): 219–241.

Controlling White-Collar Crime

Conflict theorists argue that, unlike lower-class street criminals, white-collar criminals are rarely prosecuted and, when convicted, receive relatively light sentences.[100] Physicians who engage in medical insurance fraud are rarely prosecuted, and when they are, judges are reluctant to severely punish them. As one official told them, "When we convicted a guy, I wanted to see him do hard time. But what the hell, seeing what's going on in prisons these days and things like that, I think to put one of these guys in prison for hard time doesn't make any sense."[101] An analysis of 477 corporations found that only one in 10 serious and one in 20 moderate violations resulted in sanctions. When white-collar statutes are enforced, the tendency is to investigate, prosecute, and penalize small, powerless businesses while treating the market leaders more leniently.[102]

There are a number of reasons for the leniency afforded white-collar criminals. Although white-collar criminals may produce millions of dollars of losses and endanger human life, some judges believe they are not "real criminals" but businesspeople just trying to make a living. Businesspeople seek legal advice, are well aware of the loopholes in the law, and can claim that they had sought legal advice and believed they were in compliance with the law. White-collar criminals are often considered nondangerous offenders because they are respectable, older citizens who have families to support. These "pillars of the community" are not seen in the same light as a teenager who breaks into a drugstore to steal a few dollars. Their public humiliation at being caught is usually deemed punishment enough; a prison sentence seems unnecessarily cruel.

Judges and prosecutors may identify with the white-collar criminal based on shared background and worldviews.[103] Another factor complicating white-collar crime enforcement is that many legal business and governmental acts seem as morally tinged as those made illegal by government regulation. For example, the U.S. Air Force required a general to step down for mismanaging the manufacture of a C-17 cargo plane, which accrued $1.5 billion in cost overruns, including $450 million in illegal payments to the contractor, McDonnell Douglas.[104] These acts were not treated as crimes, but compared with other business practices made illegal by government regulation, such as price-fixing, the distinctions are hard to see. It may seem unfair to prosecutors and judges to penalize some government and business officials for actions not too dissimilar from those applauded on Bay Street or in the *Financial Post*.[105]

Finally, some corporate practices that result in death or disfigurement are treated as civil actions in which victims receive monetary damages. The A.H. Robins Company's Dalkon Shield intrauterine device caused massive trauma to hundreds of thousands of women, including pelvic disease, infertility, septic abortions, and a suspected 20 deaths. The company went bankrupt and set up a multibillion-dollar trust for the survivors.[106] Other drug companies, including Bristol

Myers Squibb, set up a similar trust fund to compensate victims who suffered because their products used in breast implant surgery were deemed defective and dangerous. In 1997 the leading American tobacco companies agreed to set up a multibillion-dollar trust to compensate smokers and their families for illness and death related to smoking. Although these cases involve much more serious injury than, say, insider trading, they are not considered criminal matters.

White-Collar Law Enforcement Systems

The detection of white-collar crime is primarily in the hands of government administrative departments, inspectorates, commissions, and agencies.[107] Usually, the decision to pursue criminal rather than civil violations is based on the seriousness of the case and the perpetrator's intent, actions to conceal the violation, and prior record.

Any evidence of criminal activity is then sent to agencies for investigation. Provincial and territorial departments of labour have their own investigators, and enforcement is reactive (generated by complaints) rather than proactive (involving ongoing investigations or the monitoring of activities). In Canada, the RCMP has made enforcement of white-collar laws one of its top three priorities (along with combating foreign counter-intelligence and organized crime).

Prosecutors will pursue white-collar criminals more vigorously if they are part of a team effort that includes a network of law enforcement agencies.[108] However, local prosecutors might not consider white-collar crimes particularly serious. They are more willing to prosecute cases if the offence caused substantial harm and other agencies failed to take action. Relatively few prosecutors participate in interagency task forces designed to investigate white-collar criminal activity.

The number of prosecutors who believe that upper-class criminals are not above the law is growing. However, funds and staff needed for local white-collar prosecutions are often scarce. Crimes considered more serious, such as drug trafficking, usually take precedence over corporate violations. Coordination is uncommon, and there is relatively little resource sharing. It is likely that concern over the environment may encourage local prosecutors to take action against those who violate state pollution and antidumping laws.

Corporate Policing

White-collar crime law enforcement is often left to business organizations themselves. However, corporate structures can be crime facilitative or crime inhibiting.

Culture, Gender, Ethnicity, and Criminology

Why the Mounties Can't Get Their Man

Canada has been the setting for some spectacular frauds: John C. Doyle and Canadian Javelin; Lenny Rosenberg, Bill Player, and Ontario's $500-million Cadillac Fairview apartment flip; the collapse of the Principal Group of companies in Alberta; and, most recently, the Bre-X gold stock scam. Some of the swindles have been stunningly well-planned and daringly executed. Toronto stockbroker Christopher Horne, for example, built a world-class art collection with money he embezzled from clients. Montreal-based Castor Holdings sucked as much as $1.8 billion from victims around the world in a 15-year Ponzi scheme, a pyramid scam where money raised from new investors was used to pay off earlier investors.

Toronto has achieved the distinction of many experts as the North American capital of organized criminal fraud, surpassing even such hotbeds of white-collar crime as south Florida, Houston, Orange County in California, and the suburbs of New York City. Extradition laws that make it difficult to expel white-collar crooks are part of the problem. Cutbacks in the justice system have forced compromises in both law enforcement and prosecution. Crown attorneys across the country have been given extraordinary powers to choose cases to prosecute, and police forces deploy resources to address the concerns of interest groups. These factors, combined with Canada's lax banking and securities laws, tough privacy legislation, increasing constitutional restrictions on the police, and a disinclination by

politicians to declare all-out war on white-collar crime, have created fertile ground for fraudulent business practices to flourish.

Some experts say that the conditions are close to ideal. "If a fraud is committed against a bank or a Fortune 500 company, the police aren't interested," says Toronto forensic accountant Tedd Avey. "The big companies are on their own. All the police want to deal with are investment scams, widows and orphans and, perhaps, government as victims." Twenty years ago the RCMP was internationally renowned for its success in putting fraud artists behind bars. "Today," he says, "criminals know it's pretty well open season in Canada. They know they're not going to go to jail."

Others agree. "There's so much fraud that the police can't keep up," says Pat McKernan, a commercial crime officer who left the Mounties in 1995 and now heads security for Western Canada at Imperial Oil Ltd. in Calgary. A veteran RCMP officer says that if a crook wants to commit fraud, "Canada is the place to come and do it." Added the Mountie: "Over the years, we have lost the ability and will to investigate fraud. As a result, the criminals have no fear of the police. It's a terrible situation."

So what are the authorities doing to combat white-collar crime? The answer, according to police and civilian experts, is that financially strapped police forces across the country— following the lead of the RCMP— are getting out of commercial crime investigation. Metropolitan Toronto police have a two-year backlog of fraud investigations— and will not even look at scams involving less than $1 million. . . .

Over the years, the RCMP has attempted to adjust to the changing demands of its political masters. It has made itself less militaristic, promoted bilingualism, opened its ranks to women, recruited members of visible minorities, hired civilians for non-policing jobs, decentralized administration and operations, and embraced advanced technology. It has even learned to act more like a business, generating revenue for the government by, among other things, confiscating the assets of drug dealers and other criminals.

Despite its efforts to modernize, however, the RCMP keeps running up against one immutable fact—there are not enough resources available for the force to carry out its panoply of federal, provincial and municipal policing tasks, let alone keep pace with today's sophisticated criminals. Since 1992, the number of RCMP officers has declined 4.2 per cent, to 14,997 from 15,661, while the population has grown 6.3 per cent. And over the same period, far from seeing an increase in their annual budget— $1.8 billion this year—the Mounties have had to absorb cutbacks of $173 million. Wages have been frozen for five years, with the result that RCMP officers now earn barely half as much as their counterparts in US federal police agencies do. Because the force will not pay housing allowances, even Mounties with 20 years' experience find they cannot afford to live in high-cost centres like Vancouver and Toronto. Restrictions on overtime are so tight that in some places policing has become essentially a 9 to 5 operation. Police sources say that in Hamilton, shift changes and a ban on overtime caused the RCMP to refuse to respond in two cases—one involving the sale of guns, the other a cocaine shipment. . . .

The part of the RCMP's operations that has been most affected by budget cuts and policy changes is the investigation of white-collar crime. In the mid-1960s, partly in response to a series of gruesome murders in Quebec linked to a phoney bankruptcy scheme—a case known as the "limepit murders"—the Mounties pioneered a new approach to commercial crime investigation. Until then, fraud had generally been treated as a civil matter. But when it was evident that organized crime was making inroads into the business world, the RCMP felt it had to establish a powerful presence.

As a result, the Mounties created the specialized Commercial Crime Branch, which quickly attracted some of the force's best and brightest investigators. Widely copied in other countries, the elite branch had some high-profile successes

in the late 1960s and 1970s. As a result of its investigations, the criminal-infested Canadian Stock Exchange in Montreal was shut down, and charges were brought against leading businessmen and companies in the patronage and fraud scandals related to the dredging of the Hamilton harbour and the licensing of airport kiosks called Sky Shops.

In 1997, however, the branch was downgraded and incorporated into a much larger operation called Federal Services, which has borne the brunt of the budget cutbacks. Commercial crime investigators, especially, are starved for resources and manpower. This year, the Mounties will spend just $36.7 million investigating commercial crime of all types in all parts of the country. That is barely 2 per cent of the RCMP's overall budget and less than half of the amount—$83 million—that Canadian businesses lost last year to just one form of commercial crime: credit-card fraud.

The Mounties have largely taken themselves out of the business of investigating white-collar crime—except where the

government itself is the victim or there is money to be recovered for the treasury. Today, if a corporation is targeted by criminals, it has little choice but to hire forensic accountants and other private investigators—at rates that can run as high as $600 per hour—to root out the crooks. Sonny Saunders, director of corporate security at the Royal Bank of Canada, says that budget cutbacks have caused most police forces in Canada to give low priority to fraud investigations. "Violent crime takes priority," Saunders said. "I don't think anybody would argue against that. But it means increasingly that most corporations are going to do their own fraud investigations. Every day there seems to be more and more withdrawal of police services."

For better or worse, Canada now has a two-tier system of law enforcement: the Mounties look after the interests of the state, and businesses look after themselves.

Source: Paul Palango, "Mountie Misery," *Maclean's,* July 28, 1997, pp. 10–15.

Corporations spend hundreds of millions of dollars each year on internal audits that help unearth white-collar offences:

- *Security strategies* involve employing contract security personnel and private police officers who guard merchandise and conduct surveillance. Passive security measures include use of badges, passes, key cards, and checkpoints to restrict access to merchandise. Closed-circuit TV and other monitoring devices are used for surveillance.
- *Screening and education strategies* involve using preemployment screening and background checks to weed out problems. Personality and integrity tests screen applicants. Stores teach employees how to spot theft and how to report problems.

- *Whistle-blowing strategies* involve creating hotlines so employees can report theft anonymously. Third-party firms may be called in to maintain hotlines because employees may be reluctant to report fellow workers to their own employer.[109]

Many jurisdictions have passed laws protecting workers from being fired if they testify about violations.[110] Without such help, the hands of justice are tied.

White-Collar Control Strategies: Compliance

The prevailing wisdom is that white-collar criminals avoid prosecution and that those who are prosecuted receive lenient punishments. What efforts have been made to bring violators of the public trust to justice? White-collar enforcement typically involves two strategies designed to control organizational deviance: compliance and deterrence.[111]

Compliance strategies aim for law conformity without the necessity of detecting, processing, or penalizing individual violators. They seek cooperation and self-policing within the business community and attempt to create conformity by providing economic incentives to companies to obey the law. Compliance systems depend on the threat of economic sanctions or civil penalties (referred to as economism) to control corporate violators, such as prosecuting securities violations.

One method is to set up administrative agencies to oversee business activity, with legislation spelling out penalties for violating regulatory standards. This approach has been used to control environmental crimes, by levying heavy fines based on the quantity and the quality of pollution released into the environment.[112] One case involved a lawsuit brought against the Sherwin-Williams paint company for a longtime pattern of dumping dangerous chemicals into sewers.[113]

In another form of economism, people and businesses are sometimes barred from receiving government contracts if they are found to have engaged in fraudulent practices, such as bribing public officials.[114]

Although it is difficult to gauge the effectiveness of compliance, strict enforcement of penalties under the *Occupational Health and Safety Act* can significantly reduce workplace injuries.[115]

In sum, compliance strategies attempt to create a marketplace incentive to obey the law; for example, the more a company pollutes, the more costly and unprofitable that pollution becomes. Compliance strategies limit individual blame and avoid stigmatizing and "shaming" businesspeople by focusing on the act rather than on the actor.[116]

Economic sanctions have limited value in controlling white-collar crime because penalties are imposed after crimes have occurred, require careful governmental regulation, and often amount to only a slap on the wrist.[117] Compliance is particularly difficult to achieve if the federal government adopts a pro-business, antiregulation policy that encourages economic growth by removing controls over business. It is also difficult to achieve when multinational corporations have sufficient resources to not only resist prosecution but also to use the courts to their own advantage.

It is also possible for corporations that are hit with fines and regulatory fees to pass the costs on to consumers in the form of higher prices or reduced services. Shareholders who had little to do with the crime may see their stock dividends cut or share prices fall.

Fines and penalties involved in compliance strategies may be insignificant for a company doing billions of dollars in annual business. For a large brokerage

Canadian company, like First Marathon, a fine of millions of dollars represents a small fraction of its total revenue. Similarly, when Baxter International was banned from bidding on new federal contracts for one year because it had deceived American government purchasing agents, the punishment was a blow to its corporate reputation, but its total annual revenue still amounted to $8.5 billion.[118]

Because of this, the punishment of white-collar crimes should contain a retributive component similar to that used in common-law crimes. White-collar crimes, after all, are immoral activities that have harmed social values and deserve commensurate punishment.[119] Furthermore, corporations can get around economic sanctions by moving their rule-violating activities overseas, where legal controls over injurious corporate activities are lax or nonexistent.[120]

White-Collar Control Strategies: Deterrence

Deterrence strategies involve detecting criminal violations, determining who is responsible, and penalizing them to deter future violations. Punishment serves as a warning to potential violators who might break the rules. Deterrence systems are oriented toward apprehending violators and punishing them rather than creating conditions that induce conformity to the law.

Deterrence strategies should work since white-collar crime is a rational act whose perpetrators are extremely sensitive to the threat of criminal sanctions. There are numerous instances in which prison sentences for corporate crimes have produced a significant decline in white-collar activity; and the perceptions of detection and punishment for white-collar crimes appear to be a powerful deterrent to future law violations.[121]

 InfoTrac®

Some federal courts are quite likely to send convicted white-collar criminals to prison, whereas others seem reluctant to use incarceration. For a news report on this phenomenon, go to InfoTrac® College Edition and read this article: "Wide Disparity in White-Collar Sentences," *USA Today* (Magazine) 128, no. 2659 (2000): 11.

Punishing White-Collar Criminals. There have been dramatic examples of deterrence strategies used by federal and provincial or territorial justice systems to prevent white-collar crime. It is not extraordinary to hear of corporate officers receiving long prison sentences in conjunction with corporate crimes.[122] Corporate executives have even been charged with murder because of the actions of their companies.[123] However, in other cases prosecution fails, as in the Westray mine explosion.

Are such stiff penalties the norm, or infrequent instances of government resolve? A survey conducted by the U.S. Bureau of Justice Statistics reviewed enforcement practices in nine states and found that (1) white-collar crimes account for about 6 percent of all arrest dispositions, (2) 88 percent of all those arrested for white-collar crimes were prosecuted, and (3) 74 percent were subsequently convicted in criminal court. The survey also showed that although 60 percent of white-collar criminals convicted in state courts were incarcerated (a number comparable to the punishment given most other kinds of offenders), relatively few white-collar offenders (18 percent) received a prison term of more than a year.[124]

Is the Tide Turning? This new "get tough" deterrence approach appears to be affecting all classes of white-collar criminals. Although the prevailing wisdom is that the affluent corporate executive usually avoids serious punishment, high-status offenders are more likely to be punished than was previously believed.[125] Research indicates that public displeasure with highly publicized white-collar crimes may produce a backlash resulting in more frequent use of prison sentences. Governments may be going overboard in their efforts to punish white-collar criminals, especially for crimes that are the result of negligent business practices rather than intentional criminal conspiracy.[126] Nonetheless, relatively few white-collar offenders are prosecuted, and when they are convicted, many escape serious punishment.

Organized Crime

The second branch of organizational criminality is organized crime, ongoing criminal groups whose purpose is gain through crime. A structured enterprise system is set up to supply consumers with merchandise and services banned by criminal law but for which a ready market exists: prostitution, some kinds of pornography, some gambling, and narcotics—the classic victimless crimes. The system may even resemble a legitimate business, with assistants, staff attorneys, and accountants.[127]

Because of secrecy, power, and wealth, a mystique has grown up about organized crime. Legendary leaders, such as Al Capone, have been the subjects of books and films. The famous *Godfather* films

popularized organized crime figures, and the media all too often glamorize them.[128] Most citizens believe that organized criminals are capable of taking over legitimate business enterprises if given the opportunity. Almost everyone is familiar with such synonyms as the mob, underworld, Mafia, syndicate, or La Cosa Nostra. This section briefly defines organized crime, reviews its history, and discusses its economic effect and control.

80% but 60%

of Canadians think that
organized crime is a
serious problem

think that the police do
not have the resources
necessary to fight it

Source: Canadian Press/Leger Marketing, *How Canadians Perceive Organized Crime in Canada: Executive Report* (Montreal: Leger Marketing, 2001).

Characteristics of Organized Crime

A description of organized crime has some of these general traits:

- *Organized crime is a conspiratorial activity* involving the coordination of numerous people in the planning and execution of illegal acts. Organized crime requires a commitment by primary members, with assistance by individuals with specialized skills.
- *Organized crime has economic gain as its primary goal*, although power and status may also be motivating factors. Economic gain is achieved through maintaining a monopoly on illegal goods and services, including drugs, gambling, some types of pornography, and prostitution.
- *Organized crime activities also encompass seemingly legitimate activities*, such as laundering illegal money through legitimate businesses.
- *Organized crime employs predatory tactics*, such as intimidation, violence, and corruption. It appeals to greed to accomplish its objectives and preserve its gains.
- *Organized crime's conspiratorial groups are quick and effective in controlling and disciplining their members, associates, and victims.* Any deviation from organizational rules will evoke a prompt response from reduction in rank to a death sentence.

- *Organized crime is not synonymous with the Mafia*, which is actually a stereotype. Although several families in the organization called the Mafia are important components of organized crime activities, they do not hold a monopoly on underworld activities.
- *Organized crime does not include terrorists* dedicated to political change, although violent acts are a major tactic of organized crime.

Activities of Organized Crime

Traditionally, income comes from providing illicit materials, narcotics distribution, loan-sharking, and prostitution.[129] The annual gross income in the United States from criminal activity is between $50 billion and $90 billion, outranking most major industries, with more from gambling, theft rings, and some types of pornography.[130] In 2004, the RCMP estimated that the drug trade and organized crime have made money laundering the second-largest global industry with the circulation of "dirty" money estimated at $3 trillion worldwide.

In some cases, organized criminals have infiltrated labour unions, taking control of their pension funds and dues.[131] Hijacking of shipments and cargo theft are other sources of income, as is the fencing of high-value items. In recent years, organized criminals have branched into computer crime and other white-collar activities.

Organized Crime and Legitimate Enterprise

Outside of criminal enterprises, billions are earned by organized crime figures who force or buy their way into legitimate businesses for profit. Businesses most likely to be affected are low technology (garbage collection), have uniform products, and operate in markets where increases in price will not result in reduced demand. Industries most affected by labour pressure are susceptible to takeovers because a mob-controlled work stoppage would interfere with meeting deadlines. Organized criminals today become involved in legitimate enterprise in five ways: (1) business activity that supports illegal enterprise by providing a front, (2) predatory exploitation in which protection money is demanded, (3) organization of monopolies or cartels to limit competition, (4) unfair advantages gained by such practices as manipulation of labour unions and corruption of public officials, and (5) illegal manipulation of legal vehicles, particularly stocks and bonds.[132]

These traits show how organized crime is more like a business enterprise than like a confederation of criminals seeking to merely enhance their power.[133] Thus, controlling organized crime today involves a cooperative relationship among big business, politicians, and racketeers.

The Concept of Organized Crime

The term *organized crime* conjures up images of strong men in dark suits, machine-gun-toting bodyguards, and professional gangland killings. Criminologists refer to this as the **alien conspiracy theory** concept of organized crime, the belief that organized crime is a direct offshoot of the Mafia that first originated in Italy and Sicily. A major premise is that the Mafia is centrally coordinated by a national committee that settles disputes, dictates policy, and assigns territory.[134] Not all criminologists believe in this narrow concept of organized crime.[135] Instead, they characterize organized crime as a group of ethnically diverse gangs or groups who independently compete for profit in the sale of illegal goods and services or who use force and violence to extort money from legitimate enterprises.

The Development of a Syndicate

According to the alien conspiracy theory, organized crime really consists of a national syndicate of Italian-dominated crime families, La Cosa Nostra.[136]

The first "organized" gangs consisted of Irish immigrants who made their home in the slum districts of New York City.[137] The first New York gang members with a definite, acknowledged leadership were muggers, thieves, and pickpockets on the Lower East Side of Manhattan from the 1820s to just before the Civil War. Around 1890, Italian immigrants began forming gangs modelled after the Mafia called the Black Hand. Prohibition created a multimillion-dollar bootlegging industry overnight, and bloody wars for control of rackets and profits became common. However, the problems of supplying liquor to thousands of illegal drinking establishments (speakeasies) required organization and an end to open warfare.

The end of Prohibition required a new source of profits, so narcotics and selling information on horse racing created a national network of gang-dominated bookmakers. After World War II, organized crime families began using their profits from liquor, gambling, and narcotics to buy into legitimate businesses, such as entertainment, legal gambling in Cuba and Las Vegas, hotel chains, jukebox concerns, restaurants, and taverns. By paying off politicians, police, and judges and by using blackmail and coercion, organized criminals became almost immune to prosecution. The machine-gun-toting gangster had given way to the businessman-racketeer. Gang activity expanded into legitimate businesses, challenging traditional stereotypes.

The Cosa Nostra version of organized crime is fanciful, heavily influenced by media accounts.[138] In an alternative view, Philip Jenkins studied organized crime in Philadelphia and found little evidence that it was controlled by an Italian-dominated crime family.[139]

Famous Canadian Court Cases

Tobacco Smuggling

Tobacco companies are notorious for generating two things: smoke and controversy. They have been condemned for manufacturing lethal products, misleading the public about the dangers of smoking, and aggressively marketing cigarettes to youth. At the root of all this criticism, the burning question seems to be one of legality rather than of morality. Are industry executives criminal conspirators? Canadian courts may soon provide an answer. Currently, cigarette makers are at the centre of the largest corporate fraud case ever filed in this country.

Ottawa tried to encourage smokers to kick the habit by doubling tobacco taxes in 1991. However, these barriers to smoking soon buckled under a flood of contraband. Federal and provincial or territorial governments lost more than $10 billion in total revenue after nearly $1 billion of cigarettes were smuggled into Canada. Struggling to curb the black market tobacco trade, politicians were forced to backpedal. Taxes were slashed in 1994 but began to surge again five years later,

when one of America's top cigarette manufacturers came under investigation.

As the allegations stand, R.J. Reynolds Tobacco spearheaded an elaborate smuggling ring. Plants in Montreal and Puerto Rico shipped loads of Export A cigarettes to the United States. Much of the merchandise was funnelled through Northern Brand International (NBI), a shell company created by RJR to avert suspicion. In turn, the goods were leaked into Canada through Mohawk reserves along the New York–Ontario border and sold at discount prices.

Ironically, while the corporation evaded cigarette taxes, RJR officials lobbied the government for tax relief to help combat the smuggling problem. RJR managed to hide behind this smokescreen for some time after the scandal was exposed. A New York court indicted more than 20 people in 1997, none of them employed in the tobacco business. All were eventually convicted, along with NBI and the sham company's sales director, while the industry giant remained untouched.

RJR finally came under fire in December 1999. Following an RCMP investigation that lasted

more than four years, the Canadian government decided to recoup some of its losses. Ottawa refused a $100 million settlement, filing a $1 billion civil racketeering case in New York instead. Authorities accused RJR, its Canadian subsidiary RJR-Macdonald, several other affiliated companies and the Canadian Tobacco Manufacturers' Council of plotting to stock the black market on this side of the border.

Hopes for legal redress almost went up in smoke after the United States Supreme Court rejected Ottawa's claim in November 2002. Fortunately, the case was dismissed on technical grounds alone. An American rule of law regarding jurisdiction presented the problem, so authorities brought the matter home. In February 2003, fraud and conspiracy charges were laid against RJR, a number of its affiliates, and eight senior executives. A trial is not expected until at least the fall of 2005. Meanwhile, the federal government is suing the tobacco companies for $1.5 billion in an Ontario Court.

Prepared by Andrea Wolf.

Organized crime is a loosely constructed social system, comprising relationships that bind professional criminals, politicians, law enforcers, and various entrepreneurs. In contrast, the social world of organized crime is often chaotic because of the constant power struggle between competing groups.

Some criminologists view the world of professional criminals as one shaped by the political economy. Madams, drug distributors, and bookmakers are workers in the world of illegal enterprise. This view of organized crime is revisionist since it portrays mob activity as an enterprise system and not a tightly knit cartel dominated by ethnic minorities carrying out European traditions.

This world of organized crime is dominated by business leaders, politicians, and union leaders who work hand in hand with criminals. Moreover, the violent, chaotic social world of power struggles does not lend itself to a tightly controlled syndicate.

Organized Crime Groups

Organized crime is a loose confederation of ethnic and regional crime groups, bound together by a commonality of economic and political objectives. There are four or five main organized crime groups in Canada.[140] They commit a variety of offences, as shown in Figure 13.3.

| Figure 13.3 | Crimes Committed by Organized Crime Groups in Canada |

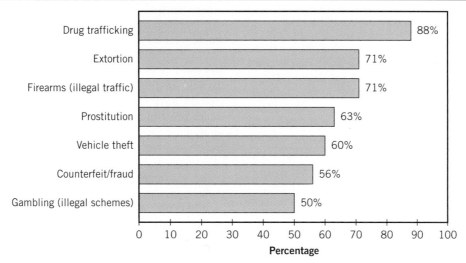

Source: Adapted from the Statistics Canada publication "Organized Crime Activity in Canada: A Pilot Survey of 16 Police Services," 1998, Catalogue 85-548, no. 01, May 20, 1999.

Asian-Based Organized Crime. These groups are extensively involved in trafficking cocaine and ecstasy; the production, trafficking, and exporting of marijuana; and the importation and distribution of Southeast Asian heroin. They are also involved in large-scale illegal migrant smuggling operations, to Canada and into the United States. Based primarily in Vancouver, Calgary, Edmonton, Toronto, and Montreal, these groups include criminal youths and members of street gangs. They are involved in home invasions, kidnapping, theft, shoplifting, prostitution, assaults, illegal gambling, loan-sharking, and the production and distribution of counterfeit currency, software, manufactured goods, and credit and debit cards. They are also involved in the laundering of criminal proceeds and the investment of laundered money into legitimate businesses. An investigation by the RCMP in 2004 concluded that more than $200 million was laundered in one cross-border operation.

East European–Based Organized Crime. Groups from Eastern Europe continue to expand their activities in Canada, particularly in larger urban centres. They are well-connected to established criminal organizations around the world and exploit technology to commit sophisticated financial and Internet-based frauds. For a decade, Canada has experienced the growth of organized crime groups from the former Soviet Union. These groups engage in crimes ranging from petty theft to sophisticated fraud. Using legitimate business ventures as fronts for their illegal activities, the most frequently reported criminal activities include financial frauds, prostitution, theft, contraband smuggling, illicit drug

importation, vehicle theft and illegal export (remember those stolen vehicles in Chapter 12?), and money laundering. Credit card "skimming," e-commerce site hacking, and fraudulent credit card purchases are examples of activity they engage in, all of which are made easier by the Internet.

Traditional (Italian-Based) Organized Crime. The traditional organized crime associated with Italy remains a threat and includes the Sicilian Mafia, which has ties to other Sicilian clans in Venezuela, the United States, and Italy. They participate in joint criminal ventures, such as importing illegal narcotics, laundering drug proceeds, drug trafficking, illegal gaming, extortion, and loan-sharking. Illegal gaming activities include backroom gambling, sports betting, and illegal video lottery gaming terminals. Profits from these criminal activities are invested in both legitimate commercial enterprises as well as their ongoing criminal operations.

Aboriginal-Based Organized Crime. Various Aboriginal gangs have emerged, including the Manitoba Warriors, Indian Posse, Redd Alert, and Native Syndicate. Aboriginal-based street gangs are generally involved in street crime, such as trafficking marijuana, cocaine and crack cocaine, and, to a lesser extent, methamphetamine. The gangs are also involved in prostitution, break and enters, robberies, assaults, intimidation, vehicle theft, and illicit drug debt collection. The gangs' capability to plan and commit sophisticated or large-scale criminal activities is low, but they are very violent. Gangs frequently use handguns that have been domestically stolen or smuggled from the United States.[141] Some experts argue that minority gangs will have a tough time developing the network of organized corruption, which involves working with government officials and unions, that traditional crime families enjoyed.[142]

Organized Crime at Marine Ports. Marine ports are used by organized crime groups to move illegal commodities into Canada for sale and for export. Drugs seized at marine ports include cocaine, heroin, hashish, and ecstasy. In addition, tobacco, alcohol, and firearms have been seized. Criminal associates are placed within the port, giving them access to port information and the movement of commercial cargo from the vessels and through the port environment. In some instances, conspirators take contraband from marine containers before inspection, while in other instances, containers may simply disappear.

Outlaw Motorcycle Gangs. Motorcycle gangs use violence to accomplish their goals and are involved in money laundering, intimidation, assaults, attempted murder, murder, fraud, theft, counterfeiting, loansharking, extortion, prostitution, escort agencies, strip clubs, illegal booze cans, and the possession and trafficking of illegal weapons, stolen goods, contraband, alcohol, and cigarettes. Members of the Hells Angels are involved in the importation and trafficking of cocaine, the cultivation and exportation of high-grade marijuana and, to a lesser extent, the production and trafficking of methamphetamine, the trafficking of ecstasy and other synthetic illicit drugs. The Hells Angels are the largest and most criminally active outlaw motorcycle gang (OMG) in the country. The RCMP says that OMGs make up the largest proportion of people on the annual Strategic Threat Assessment list and constitute a significant threat because of their criminal activity.[143]

One important recent change in organized crime is the interweaving of ethnic groups. Asian racketeers and Native gangs now collaborate or compete with more traditional groups, such as the Hells Angels, overseeing the distribution of drugs, prostitution, and gambling in a symbiotic relationship with old-line racketeers. Since 1970, Russia and other Eastern European countries have cooperated with Mafia families in narcotics trafficking, fencing of stolen property, money laundering, and other "traditional" organized crime schemes.[144]

Part of the evolution of organized crime is created by patterns of law enforcement. Pressure on traditional organized crime encouraged the Hells Angels to become the leading distributor of narcotics in Canada. A recent series of bombings erupted in Montreal as part of a turf war between the Hells Angels and the Rock Machine, another motorcycle gang. Chinese criminal gangs have taken over the dominant role in New York City's heroin market from the traditional Italian-run syndicates.[145] In Canada, Chinese Triad gangs traditionally relied on extortion as a source of illegal wealth, extending activity to include the sale of drugs. One reason for their persistence is their cell structure; unlike the hierarchical structure of the traditional Mafia, using cells ensures that no one member of the criminal organization knows the whole picture.

Overall, it is estimated that organized crime generates more than $20 billion a year in Canada, half from the sale of drugs alone, and the rest from crimes that include auto thefts, money laundering, smuggling, fraud, prostitution, and violent crime. Selling restricted weapons, providing access to illicit toxic waste dumps, and selling high-technology secrets are also profitable. Most experts agree it is simplistic to view organized crime as a national syndicate that controls illegitimate rackets, ignoring the variety of gangs and groups, their membership, and their relationship to the outside world.[146] Mafia-type groups are not the only organized criminals.[147]

 InfoTrac®

To read more about Russian organized crime, go to InfoTrac® College Edition and access this article: Scott O'Neal, "Russian Organized Crime," *FBI Law Enforcement Bulletin* 69, no. 5 (2000): 1.

Organized Crime Abroad

Many countries confront the problem of organized criminal gangs. The Cali and Medellin drug cartels in Colombia are world famous for both their vast drug trafficking profits and their use of violence to achieve their objectives. When Pablo Escobar, the head of the Medellin cartel, was captured and killed by police and soldiers in 1993, experts predicted that drug smuggling would increase with the shift of the cocaine trade to the control of the smoother and more businesslike Cali cartel.[148]

Japan also has a long history of organized criminal activity by Yakuza gangs. In 1993 officials of the Kirin Brewery, Japan's largest beer maker, resigned after allegations were made that they had paid more than 33 million yen in *sokaiya* (extortion money) to racketeers who threatened their business.[149] In China, organized gangs use violence to enforce contracts between companies, serving as an alternative to the legal system. They also help smuggle many of the 100 000 people from mainland China who enter the United States each year.[150]

Russia has been beset by organized crime activity since the break-up of the Soviet Union, with an estimated three thousand active criminal gangs. Bloody shootouts have become common as gangs stake out territory and extort businesses.[151]

Computer and communications technology has fostered international cooperation among crime cartels. East European and Russian gangs sell arms seized from the former Soviet Army to members of the Sicilian Mafia; Japanese and Italian mob members have met in Paris; drug money from South America is laundered in Canada and England.

Controlling Organized Crime

George Vold argued that the development of organized crime parallels early capitalist enterprises. Organized crime uses ruthless and monopolistic tactics to maximize profits; it is also secretive and protective of its operations and defensive against any outside intrusion.[152] Consequently, controlling its activities is extremely difficult, and little has been done to combat organized crime until fairly recently.

One measure aimed directly at organized crime in the United States was the (1970) *Organized Crime Control Act* and the *Racketeer Influenced and Corrupt Organization Act.* RICO did not create new categories of crimes but rather new categories of offences in racketeering activity, such as murder, kidnapping, gambling, arson, robbery, bribery, extortion, and narcotics violations and such federally defined crimes as bribery, counterfeiting, transmission of gambling information, prostitution, and mail fraud.

In Canada attempts to control organized crime include Bill C-69, which gives the police more power to

---

Exhibit 13.9	The Fight against Organized Crime

The Organized Crime Impact Study, commissioned by the Department of the Solicitor General in 1988, indicated the following:

- The Canadian illicit drug market is between $7 billion and $10 billion each year.

- Securities fraud and telemarketing scams cost Canadians at least $5 billion each year.

- Between $5 billion and $17 billion is laundered in Canada each year.

- As many as 16 000 people may be smuggled into Canada every year.

- The production and sale of counterfeit products—clothing, software, and pharmaceuticals—may cost Canadians more than $1 billion each year.

- The illegal smuggling of tobacco, alcohol, and jewellery may cost up to $1.5 billion in government tax revenues.

In recent years, the federal government, the provinces and territories, and the police have taken steps against organized crime:

- The *Anti-Smuggling Initiative* (1994), to provide resources for the RCMP, Justice Agency, and the Canada Customs and Revenue Agency to target smuggling and distribution networks at the border; it has led to 17 000 smuggling-related charges resulting in fines in excess of $113 million, and $118 million in evaded taxes and duties has been identified.

- The *Witness Protection Program Act* (1996), a national program to protect those who risk their lives to assist police investigations.

- The Solicitor General Canada and Justice Canada organizing a National Forum on Organized Crime (1996), to bring the police, federal and provincial governments, the private sector, the legal community, and academics together.

- Five Regional Coordinating Committees and a National Coordinating Committee on Organized Crime (1997), providing a foundation for further cooperation to combat organized crime.

- Integrated Proceeds of Crime units (1997), which combine the resources of RCMP, local and provincial police officers, Canada Customs and Revenue Agency officers, Crown counsel, and forensic accountants to target organized crime groups and seize their assets, over $110 million so far.

- Legislative amendments to the *Criminal Code* (1997), to make participation in a criminal organization an indictable offence, punishable by up to 14 years in prison.

- The Solicitor General providing $115 million to the RCMP (1999) to modernize the Canadian Police Information Centre (CPIC), the computerized information system for Canadian law enforcement, to improve information-sharing with other law enforcement, provincial, and federal databases.

Source: Solicitor General of Canada, "Organized Crime Impact Study Highlights," Public Safety and Emergency Prepardness Canada, http://www.sgc.gc.ca/Publications/Policing/1998orgcrim_e.asp (accessed May 17, 2005).

seize goods suspected of being purchased with the proceeds of crime. Section 312 of the Canadian *Criminal Code* makes it an offence to possess anything derived indirectly or directly from an indictable offence. During the confrontation between rival bike gangs in Montreal, a joint police task force (the RCMP and the Montreal Urban Community Police) made significant arrests and seized explosive devices, including one thousand sticks of dynamite. In addition, the Canadian Security Intelligence Service (CSIS) has asked that the $1000 bill be eliminated and that the movement of large sums of money be reported by financial institutions. Bill C-24, created after September 2001, freed up $200 million over five years to give police new measures to fight organized crime.

New developments in the enforcement of laws designed to control organized crime include police anti-drug-profiteering units. A joint Canada–United States agreement on sharing the proceeds of crime was signed in 1995. In 1994 a money-laundering operation was broken in Montreal with cooperation from American authorities, and police seized almost $1 million. Some provincial police organizations have their own antibiker squads, and the *Witness Protection Act* was designed to encourage witnesses to come forward with reports on crime. The National Action Plan to Combat Smuggling was launched in 1994, and $2 billion of smuggled goods were confiscated.

Human smuggling and trafficking in humans continues to be a problem linked to organized crime. The former involves assisting those wanting to illegally immigrate to Canada, while the latter involves the transportation of people by means of coercion or violence. Most of these victims are women and children forced into illegal activities, such as labour, slavery, and prostitution. Legislation to combat these crimes includes the *UN Convention Against Transnational Organized Crime*, the *Immigration and Refugee Protection Act*, and the *Anti-Smuggling Initiative*.

The Future of Organized Crime

Indications are that the traditional organized crime syndicates are in decline.[153] Active government enforcement policies have reduced the membership in organized crime from 20 years ago, and high-ranking leaders have been imprisoned. Additional pressure comes from newly emerging ethnic gangs that want to "muscle in" on traditional syndicate activities. For example, Chinese Triad gangs have been active in the drug trade, loan-sharking, and labour racketeering. Other ethnic crime groups include Black and Colombian drug cartels and the Sicilian Mafia.

White, ethnic, inner-city neighbourhoods, once the locus of Mafia power, have been reduced in size as families have moved to the suburbs. Organized crime groups have consequently lost their political and social base of operations. In addition, the "code of silence," which served to protect Mafia leaders, is now being broken by younger members who turn informer rather than face prison. For example, the reign of John Gotti, the most powerful mob boss in New York, was ended by testimony given at his murder trial by his one-time ally Sammy "The Bull" Gravano.

Jay Albanese, a leading expert on organized crime, predicts that pressure by government will encourage organized crime figures to engage in "safer" activities, such as credit card and airline ticket counterfeiting and illicit toxic waste disposal. Instead of running illegal enterprises, established families may be content with financing younger entrepreneurs and channelling or laundering profits through their legitimate business enterprises. There may be greater effort among organized criminals in the future to infiltrate legitimate business enterprises to obtain access to money for financing and the means to launder illicitly obtained cash. Labour unions and the construction industry have been favourite targets in the past.[154]

Although these actions are considered a major blow to Italian-dominated organized crime cartels, they are unlikely to stifle criminal entrepreneurship. As long as vast profits can be made from selling narcotics, producing pornography for the Internet, or taking illegal bets, many groups stand ready to fill the gaps and reap the profits of providing illegal goods and services.

Summary

White-collar and organized criminals are similar because they both use ongoing illegal business enterprises to make personal profits. There are several types of white-collar crime. Stings and swindles involve the use of deception to bilk people out of their money. Chiselling customers, businesses, or the government on a regular basis is a second common type of white-collar crime. Surprisingly, many professionals engage in chiselling offences. Other white-collar criminals use their positions in business and the marketplace to commit economic crimes, involving illegal payments, embezzlement, employee pilferage, fraud, client fraud, influence peddling, and bribery. Further, corporate officers sometimes violate the law to improve the position and profitability of their businesses, which might include price-fixing, false advertising, and environmental offences. More recently, computers have been used to commit high-tech crimes, such as counterfeiting, or variations on old crimes, such as libel.

So far, little has been done to combat white-collar crimes. Most offenders do not view themselves as criminals and therefore do not seem to be deterred by criminal statutes. Although thousands of white-collar criminals are prosecuted each year, their numbers are insignificant compared with the magnitude of the problem. Law enforcement strategies to combat white-collar crime involve deterrence, which uses punishment to frighten potential abusers, and compliance, which creates economic incentives to obey the law.

The demand for illegal goods and services has produced a symbiotic relationship between the public and an organized criminal network. Organized crime supplies alcohol, smuggled tobacco, gambling, drugs, prostitutes, and some types of pornography to the public. It is immune from prosecution because of public apathy and because of its own strong political connections. Organized criminals used to be White ethnics—Jews, Italians, and Irish—but today Blacks, Hispanics, Asians, and other groups have become involved in organized crime activities. The old-line "families" are more likely to use their criminal wealth and power to buy into legitimate businesses.

There is debate over the control of organized crime. Some experts believe there is a national crime cartel that controls all activities. Others view organized crime as a group of disorganized, competing gangs dedicated to extortion or to providing illegal goods and services. Efforts to control organized crime have been stepped up. But as long as there are vast profits to be made, illegal enterprises will continue to flourish.

Thinking Like a Criminologist

People who commit computer crime are found in every segment of society. They range in age from 10 to 60, and their skill level runs from novice to professional. They are otherwise average people, not super-criminals possessing unique abilities and talents. Any person of any age with even a little skill is a potential computer criminal. Most studies indicate that employees represent the greatest threat to computers. Almost 90 percent of computer crimes against businesses are inside jobs. Ironically, as advances continue in remote data processing, the threat from external sources will probably increase. With the networking of systems and the adoption of more user-friendly software, the sociological profile of the computer offender may change. For example, computer criminals may soon be members of organized crime syndicates. They will use computer systems to monitor law enforcement activities. In the twenty-first-century organized crime family, the recruit will have to develop knowledge of the equipment used for audio surveillance of law enforcement communications: computers with sound cards or microphones, modems, and software programs for the remote operation of the systems.

Which theories of criminal behaviour best explain the actions of computer criminals, and which ones fail to account for computer crime?

Key Terms

alien conspiracy theory	cybercrime	organized crime
arbitrage	deterrence	pilferage
churning	enterprise crimes	price-fixing
compliance	insider trading	swindling
corporate crime	occupational crime	white-collar crime

Critical Thinking Questions

1. How would you punish a corporate executive whose product killed people if the executive had no knowledge that the product was potentially lethal? What if the executive did know?

2. Is organized crime inevitable as long as immigrant groups seek to become part of the "North American Dream"?

3. Does the media glamorize organized crime? Does it paint an inaccurate picture of noble crime lords fighting to protect their families?

4. Apply traditional theories of criminal behaviour to white-collar and organized crime. Which one seems to best predict why someone would engage in these behaviours?

 See the book-specific website at http://www.siegelcriminology3e.nelson.com for additional chapter links, discussions, and quizzes.

chapter 14

Public Order Crimes: Legislating Morality

Gillian Guess was a member of the jury in the murder trial of Peter Gill in 1995. Three years later, she was on trial herself for her conduct on that jury: The Crown attorney said she had openly flirted with Gill, sat in the jury box in a manner that allowed Gill to look up her skirt, had a sexual relationship with him, and then swayed the jury, resulting in Gill's acquittal. During the controversial trial, Ms. Guess maintained a website on which she compared her prosecution with a witch hunt. She denounced the RCMP for recording her sexual encounters with Gill and regularly briefed the media despite warnings by the judge.[1]

Gillian Guess became the first person in North America to be convicted for obstructing a jury by having a relationship with an accused. Was it possible for her to act impartially while having an affair? Would it have helped to have juror counselling, a common practice elsewhere? Would it have prevented such a problem? Or is it

---

Culture, Gender, Ethnicity, and Criminology

Results of the Great Canadian Moral Scruples Challenge

The Scruples Challenge is based on a telephone survey conducted in 1996, commissioned by the Canadian Coalition Against Insurance Fraud, an organisation of consumer advocates, police and fire services, and insurers.

The survey measured Canadians' attitudes toward insurance fraud in fourteen different ethical dilemmas. Participants were asked what they would do, and what they thought other people would do, in the same situations.

The survey showed that younger people are less likely to behave ethically than older people. In some instances people in Atlantic Canada were more likely to behave ethically than people in other parts of the country. However, in general, class, education, and religion did not make a difference.

One of the most interesting results of the survey was the gap between what people said they would do and their perception of what others would do. For example, if a friendly bank teller accidentally gives you an extra $100, what would you do? Eighty-three percent said they would give the money back.

In another scenario, a bank machine gives a customer $20 more than it records on the bank receipt. A lower number, 53 percent, said they would return the extra $20 to the bank, but in the phone poll, 28 percent thought that 70 percent of other Canadians would keep the money.

Two friends are discussing their home businesses. One asks the other to make a copy of an expensive piece of computer software. The self-report survey says that 37 percent would refuse to copy the software. However, 24 percent would copy the software with no question asked, 12 percent would copy the software, but tell him it's wrong, and 23 percent would let him use their computer. In the phone poll, 52 percent of Canadians would give away a copy of the software, and they felt that 68 percent would do the same.

Let's take a couple more examples. For instance, a car mechanic does extra work on a car after an accident and includes the cost on the insurance bill. An honest 47 percent said they would pay for the repairs and report the body shop, while 27 percent would take the car "as is." Nine percent would pay extra for the repairs, but not tell the insurance company, while 13 percent would refuse to sign the form releasing the car from the body shop.

In the phone poll, 25 percent said they would go along with the mechanic and take the car "as is," but they felt that 72 percent would simply take the car. So they felt others would not be as moral as themselves.

Finally, a man is on leave from work because of an injury requiring a neck brace. When a colleague drops in on him, he finds the man is not wearing the brace and is doing heavy yard work. Fifty percent said they would tell him he's wrong, while 20 percent would do nothing, and think less of him. Nineteen percent would report the co-worker, and 6 percent would call Crime Stoppers.

In the phone poll, 40 percent said they would confront their colleague, but felt that only 14 percent of other Canadians would do the same.

What happens when you compare these results to your ethical standards? What do they tell you about the standards of Canadians?

Source: The Great Canadian Moral Scruples Challenge, conducted by Insight Canada Research (POLLARA), 1996. Reproduced courtesy of the Canadian Coalition Against Insurance Fraud, copyright 1997.

possible that her behaviour was irrelevant, that the jury acquitted Gill on the basis of the evidence, regardless of Guess's actions? Was this even a simple legal issue, or was it a matter of moral impropriety?

Societies have always limited behaviours *believed* to run contrary to social norms, customs, and values. These acts are referred to as **public order crimes** or **victimless crimes**.[2] Public order crimes usually include acts that offend our moral sense of how people should act. Put another way, although such common-law crimes as rape or robbery are considered *mala in se*, inherently evil and wrong, there are also *mala prohibitum* crimes, which are behaviours outlawed because they conflict with social policy, moral sensibilities, and current public opinion.

Laws to uphold public order usually prohibit the distribution of morally questionable things, such as erotic material and mood-altering drugs. They may also ban acts that some people holding political power consider immoral, such as abortion, prostitution, marijuana use, or assisted suicide. These acts are controversial because sometimes law-abiding citizens engage in them. However, as the Culture, Gender, Ethnicity, and Criminology box shows, the line between good and bad behaviour is often a thin one.

This chapter is divided into four main sections: (1) the relationship between law and morality, (2) public order crimes of a sexual nature, (3) drug and alcohol abuse, and (4) emerging issues, such as the decriminalization of gambling and euthanasia.

Law and Morality

The legislation of moral issues is a continual source of frustration. There is little debate that the purpose of the criminal law is to protect society and reduce social harm. When a store is robbed or a child assaulted, it is relatively easy to condemn the social harm done to the victim. It is more difficult to identify the victim of immoral acts, such as prostitution, in which the parties may be willing participants. If there is no victim, can there be a crime? Should acts be made illegal merely because they violate prevailing moral standards? If so, who defines morality? The absolute letter of the law might be unrealistically strict.

Should a person be punished for providing a service other people are willing to pay for? If people willingly pay to purchase sexual services, are they crime victims? Many, but not all, prostitutes willingly engage in sexual activity for money, and their income is far higher than they would have earned in "legitimate jobs." Although "immoral," should a prostitute and his or her clients be considered criminals for engaging in this "victimless crime"?

We might first consider whether there is actually a victim in victimless crimes. Some participants may have been forced into their acts, for example, some women involved in adult films.[3] Young runaways can be coerced into a life on the streets, where they are cruelly treated and held as virtual captives.[4] Asian girls are trafficked into Canada and sold into debt bondage to brothels. Although less than 20 percent of prostitutes are juveniles, a majority of street prostitutes interviewed had become sex trade workers before the age of 18.[5]

Society as a whole should consider the victim of these crimes.

Conversely, when consenting behaviour between adults is criminalized, it sends out a message that repression is an acceptable way to enforce conformity. People quite often feel that the state has no business regulating the private sexual relationships of consenting adults.[6]

InfoTrac®

For an interesting essay on the association between law and morality, use InfoTrac® College Edition and read this article: M. Cathleen Kaveny, "Law, Morality and Common Ground: Law Can Still Function as a Powerful Moral Teacher," *America* 183, no. 19 (2000): 7.

Debating Morality

Some argue that pornography, prostitution, and drug use erode the moral fabric of society and should be punished by law, because of a collective feeling of revulsion toward certain acts, even when they are not dangerous.[7] In his classic statement on the function of morality in the law, Sir Patrick Devlin stated:

> Without shared ideas on politics, morals, and ethics no society can exist. . . . If men and women try to create a society in which there is no fundamental agreement about good and evil, they will fail; if having based it on common agreement, the society will disintegrate. For society is not something that is kept together physically; it is held by the invisible bonds of common thought. If the bonds were too far relaxed, the members would drift apart. A common morality is part of the bondage . . . which is part of the price of society; and mankind, which needs society, must pay its price.[8]

Accordingly, criminal law must express public morality and prohibit victimless crimes.[9]

Gusfield says that outlawing acts shows the moral superiority of those who condemn the acts over those who commit them. The legislation of morality "enhances the social status of groups carrying the affirmed culture and degrades groups carrying that which is condemned as deviant."[13] Legislating morality thus creates insiders who are normal and outsiders who are deviant.

InfoTrac®

Although almost universally condemned in the West, female circumcision is still quite common in parts of Africa and the Middle East. To find out why, read this article on InfoTrac® College Edition: Richard A. Shweder, "What about 'Female Genital Mutilation'? And Why Understanding Culture Matters in the First Place," *Daedalus* 129, no. 4 (2000): 209.

Criminal or Immoral?

Acts that we might feel are immoral are not necessarily criminal. There is no law against pride, sloth, lust, gluttony, wrath, avarice, or envy, although they are considered the "seven deadly sins."

Violations of conventional morality may be tolerated because they serve a useful social function. Watching sexually explicit films can release tension; immoral behaviour may provide benefits to legitimate enterprises.[14]

Some acts also seem well intentioned, but are still criminal in Canada, such as killing a loved one who is suffering from an incurable disease (euthanasia), stealing to feed a poor family (theft), or marrying many women (polygamy) in conforming to religious beliefs.[15]

It might be possible to settle this argument by saying that immoral acts become crimes if they are harmful to the public. Yet some acts that cause social harm are legal, such as the use of tobacco and alcohol, and driving vehicles that can accelerate to more than 160 km/h. More people die each year from alcohol-, tobacco-, and auto-related deaths than from all drug-related deaths combined. Should drugs be legalized and fast cars outlawed?

Even if an act were outlawed, the law might prove difficult to enforce if the public was divided. For example, assisted suicide may be against the law because it causes social harm, but prosecutors have failed to gain convictions in assisted suicide cases because so many people view it as a humanitarian act and refuse to convict. Although Sue Rodriguez failed in her request to the Supreme Court of Canada for legal assisted suicide, many people were sympathetic to her cause (see the Famous Canadian Court Case later in the chapter).

A "game" unfolds nightly on the streets and alleys of downtown Canadian cities—a picture of prostitution that masks the hidden world of pimps and johns.

Some argue that basing criminal definitions on moral beliefs is an impossible task: Who defines morality? Are we not punishing differences rather than social harm? If morals are really the expression of the majority, does that mean they should be the basis for regulating the conduct of all? Are photographs by Robert Mapplethorpe art or obscenity? As U.S. Supreme Court Justice William O. Douglas put it, "What may be trash to me may be prized by others."[10]

In the Puritan society of Salem, Massachusetts, women were burned at the stake as witches because their behaviour seemed strange. In parts of Africa today, female circumcision is performed to ensure virginity and make girls suitable for marriage. Critics of this practice consider it an act of mutilation and torture, while others argue that this ancient custom should be left to the discretion of people who consider it part of their culture. Can an outsider define the morality of another culture?[11] Or, in a democracy, should a majority dictate how all should live?[12]

When asked whether they favour or oppose legalized euthanasia, 49 percent of people surveyed said they were in favour, while 37 percent were opposed and 14 percent were undecided.[16]

Vigilante Justice

Canada doesn't have the "wild west" history of the United States, where "vigilance committees" were set up in boomtowns to pursue cattle rustlers and stagecoach robbers. However, there is a largely unknown history of "popular justice" in early Canada. These vigilantes held to a strict standard of morality, punishing moral transgressions such as sexual deviance, drunkenness, severe wife beating, and adultery. The popularity of such vigilante movements diminished with the growth of state institutions and the development of the police.[17]

The avenging vigilante is an important part of North American popular culture, enforcing the law and social customs. From Superman to Captain Canada, the righteous **vigilante** goes on **moral crusades** without authorization from legal authorities. Popular targets of moral crusaders are abortion clinics, pornographers, gun dealers, and logging companies. What else but moral issues could explain the thousands of acts of violence against abortion clinics over the last 30 years?

Howard Becker has labelled such people **moral entrepreneurs**, who operate with an absolute certainty that their way is right and that any means are justified to get their way; "the crusader is fervent and righteous, often self-righteous."[18]

Moral crusades are directed against people defined as evil by a segment of the population. For example, anti-smut campaigns attempt to ban books by an author from the library or prevent a "controversial" figure from speaking at a university. One way to accomplish their goal is to prove that their target is evil, polarizing people into "bad guys" and "good guys," creating a climate where the good are deified while the bad are demonized.[19]

Categorizing people as all good or all bad creates crime control policies that may be overly punitive. For example, the death penalty is justified if murderers are bad guys—unrepentant monsters who commit serial murders and mutilate their victims. If, instead, murderers were seen as disturbed victims of child abuse and neglect, it would be out of the question to consider the death penalty.

Enforcement of morally tinged statutes has become a significant problem for law enforcement agencies. In Vancouver, several stores selling marijuana paraphernalia have been raided, and pipes and seeds were seized under section 462.2 of the *Criminal Code of Canada* (CCC).[20] If laws governing marijuana use are enforced too vigorously, local authorities are branded as reactionaries who waste time on petty issues. But if the authorities confiscate marijuana destined for alleviating pain, they risk being seen as insensitive. However, if police agencies ignore public order crimes, they are accused of being soft on immorality. "Society would be a lot better off," the argument goes, "if the cops cracked down on 'those people.'" Who "those people" are and what should be done about them is a matter of great public debate.

Let us now turn to specific examples of public order crimes.

Illegal Sexuality

One type of public order crime relates to what conventional society considers deviant sexual practices, such as paraphilia, prostitution, and pornography.

Paraphilia

In 1996, 250 000 Belgians took to the streets to protest the government's inept handling of a case involving the deaths of four children at the hands of a pedophile ring led by convicted rapist, Marc Dutroux. Two of the victims (eight-year-old girls) had been imprisoned and molested for months in Dutroux's home. They starved to death when he was arrested and sent to jail on an unrelated charge. Other children had been kidnapped, raped, tortured, and sold into sexual slavery by the ring.[21]

This is an extreme example of **paraphilia**, abnormal sexual practices involving recurrent sexual urges focused on (1) nonhuman objects (underwear, shoes, leather), (2) humiliation or the experience of receiving or giving pain (sadomasochism, bondage), or (3) children or others who cannot grant consent.[22] Some paraphilias, such as wearing clothes normally worn by the opposite sex (transvestitism), can be engaged in by adults in the privacy of their homes and do not involve a third party. Others, however, present a risk of social harm and are subject to criminal penalties, such as exposure of genitals in public (indecent exposure, section 173 CCC) and sexual interference with a person under the age of 14 (section 153 CCC). Voyeurism is handled under trespassing (section 177 CCC) or stalking (section 264 CCC).

Paraphilias that involve unwilling or underage victims show that quite often the victim and offender have a prior relationship as family members, intimates, or acquaintances. Based on data for 2003, family members were involved in 26 percent of sexual assaults and 31 percent of other sexual offences; acquaintances committed 48 percent and 44 percent, respectively. Twenty percent of all sexual assaults and 43 percent of "other sexual offences" involved a child under 12 years of age. These statistics point to a sex offender who is older than other violent offenders, heterosexual, and more likely to

Famous Canadian Criminals

The Case of Everett Klippert

In 1965, during a police investigation, a man named Everett Klippert said he was homosexual. At the time, a man having sex with men was categorized as gross indecency under the criminal law. Sentenced to three years in prison, he was interviewed by two psychiatrists who concluded that Klippert fitted under Canada's law respecting dangerous sexual offenders, simply because he was likely to repeat his behaviour. Klippert was incarcerated for life, a sentence confirmed by the Supreme Court of Canada in 1967.

Reaction to the judgment was swift. An editorial in the *Toronto Star* called the decision "a return to the Middle Ages," and Pierre Elliott Trudeau, then justice minister, said that "the state has no place in the bedrooms of the nation."

Two years later, in 1969, Bill C-150, an omnibus bill dealing with offences from gross indecency through abortion to gambling, decriminalized homosexuality by suggesting that sexual acts between consenting adults in private were legal. The bill caused heated debate in the House of Commons. John Diefenbaker, recorded in the *Hansard Debates* of January 27, 1969, said, "I am opposed to these homosexuality amendments. I think they are wrong. . . . I know there is no individual more subject to intimidation and threat by the USSR as it endeavours to obtain information detrimental to the security of Canada than those who are believed to be homosexuals."

Trudeau said, "It's certainly the most extensive revision of the *Criminal Code* since the 1950s and . . . I feel that it has knocked down a lot of totems and over-ridden a lot of taboos. . . . It's bringing the laws of the land up to contemporary society. . . . The view we take here is that there's no place for the state in the bedrooms of the nation. . . . What's done in private between adults doesn't concern the *Criminal Code*. When it becomes public, this is a different matter, or when it relates to minors, this is a different matter."

On July 20, 1971, Everett Klippert was released from prison.

Sources: Anne Vassal, John Fisher, Ralf Jürgens, and Robert Hughes, "Gay and Lesbian Issues and HIV/AIDS, A Discussion Paper," Canadian HIV/AIDS Legal Network and Canadian AIDS Society, July 1997, http://www.aidslaw.ca/Maincontent/issues/gaylesbian/07p2bE.html (accessed May 19, 2005); Owen Wood, "The Fight for Gay Rights: Canada Timeline," Pride News, http://www.caw2002tca.ca/e/pride.htm (accessed May 19, 2005).

be related to or known by the victim and exploiting a position of authority.[23]

This picture of the sex offender is very different from an earlier image of sexual danger.

In the 1950s and 1960s in Canada, hundreds of suspected gay men and lesbians lost their jobs, were demoted from high-security positions in the Canadian civil service, or were purged from the military (see the Famous Canadian Criminals feature). By the late 1960s, the RCMP had collected the names of nine thousand suspected lesbians and gay men.[24] There was also government-funded research into a means to detect homosexuals, known as the "fruit machine" (see the Crime in the News feature). However, homosexuality was dropped from the list of deviant sexualities by the Canadian Psychological Association in the late 1970s.

Prostitution

The earliest record of prostitution appears in ancient Mesopotamia, where priests engaged in sex to promote fertility in the community. All women were required to do temple duty, and passing strangers were expected to make donations to the temple after enjoying its services.

Modern commercial sex has its roots in ancient Greece, where Solon established licensed brothels in 500 B.C.E. The earnings of Greek prostitutes helped pay for the temple of Aphrodite, where famous men went to enjoy intellectual, aesthetic, and sexual stimulation.

Although some early Christian religious leaders, such as St. Augustine and St. Thomas Aquinas, were tolerant of prostitution, this attitude disappeared after the Reformation. Lutheran doctrine depicted prostitutes as emissaries of the devil who were sent to destroy the faith.[25]

In more recent times, prostitution was tied to the rise of English brewery companies during the early nineteenth century. The breweries employed prostitutes in saloons to attract patrons and encourage them to drink.

Today, **prostitution** is defined as the consensual exchange of sex for money, and money for sex. This exchange itself is not illegal, although it is virtually impossible not to break some part of the law. For example, section 213 of the *Criminal Code of Canada* (CCC) makes it illegal to either ask for or offer a money–sex exchange in public. This law has been challenged on constitutional grounds as violating the constitutionally

Crime in the News

The "Fruit Machine"

by Dean Bibby, Canadian Press

The federal government's "fruit machine," intended to root out homosexuals in the civil service, was one of the most bizarre medical devices ever developed with taxpayers' money.

An individual peered into the narrow opening of a large box in which sometimes lewd pictures from magazines were shown. A camera recorded pupil size as each new image was flashed.

In one hand, the subject clutched a small mesh bag of anhydrous silica gel and anhydrous cobalt chloride. Around one finger was an aluminum ring that used a cadmium selemide photocrystal to record blood flow electronically.

The contraption drew on a grab-bag of poorly tested medical theories that nevertheless got support from the National Research Council, the Health and Welfare Department, and Privy Council.

The brains behind the machine was Robert Wake, a psychologist at Carleton University in Ottawa who used a 1962 sabbatical to launch the project. . . .

To identify gays, Wake proposed reading a list of "homosexual words" to an individual who was holding a mesh bag of crystals. Only a gay person would be stimulated to sweat, he reasoned. The so-called homosexual word list that Wake compiled included circus, bagpipe, blind, camp, fish, sew, house, and restaurant.

Source: Dean Bibby, "Privy Council, NRC Backed 'Fruit Machine,'" Canadian Press, April 24, 1992.

---

protected right to communication; however, the Supreme Court ruled that the law is a "reasonable infringement" on civil liberties, because of the nuisance caused by the public solicitation of sex for money.[26]

The definition of the offence of prostitution is gender neutral, since prostitutes can, of course, be male or female, straight or gay. Other sections of the code include "Keeping a common bawdy-house" (section 210 CCC), "Transporting person to bawdy-house" (section 211 CCC), and "Procuring," otherwise known as pimping (section 212 CCC). The most usual offence for which a person is charged under prostitution law is section 213, "Communicating for the purposes of prostitution."

In 1990, Metropolitan Toronto Police charged *NOW* magazine with "Communicating for the purposes of prostitution," because some of its classified advertising offered sexual services for sale. The charges were laid by morality bureau officers despite the lack of official approval by the attorney general's office and were subsequently dropped.[27]

The commercial sexual transaction usually involves activity with sexual significance for the customer: intercourse, exhibitionism, sadomasochism, oral sex; an economic transaction: money or drugs are exchanged for the activity; and emotional indifference: the interaction has nothing to do with affection.[28]

Incidence of Prostitution. The Uniform Crime Reports (UCR) for 2003 indicate that there were 5658 prostitution-related offences (PROs), an increase of 12 percent since 1990. More than 90 percent of PROs are for communication. Of adults charged, 47 percent are male, down from 49 percent in 1990. This gender imbalance in charging is surprising, given that one

Exhibit 14.1	**Quick Code on Prostitution**

213. (1) Every person who in a public place or in any place open to public view

(a) stops or attempts to stop any motor vehicle,

(b) impedes the free flow of pedestrian or vehicular traffic or ingress to or egress from premises adjacent to that place, or

(c) stops or attempts to stop any person or in any manner communicates or attempts to communicate with any person for the purpose of engaging in prostitution or of obtaining the sexual services of a prostitute is guilty of an offence punishable on summary conviction.

(2) Definition of "public place"

(a) In this section, "public place" includes any place to which the public have access as of right or by invitation, express or implied, and any motor vehicle located in a public place or in any place open to public view.

prostitute will service hundreds of different clients each year. The clearance rate has decreased from 87 percent to 79 percent, which is also surprising. Prostitution is a policing-sensitive crime, and the crime rate reflects the level of police enforcement. As Figure 14.1 shows, probation and fines account for 69 percent of the sanctions given to males, and 54 percent of those given to women. Males, however, are much less likely to receive a jail sentence (3 percent) than are women (39 percent).

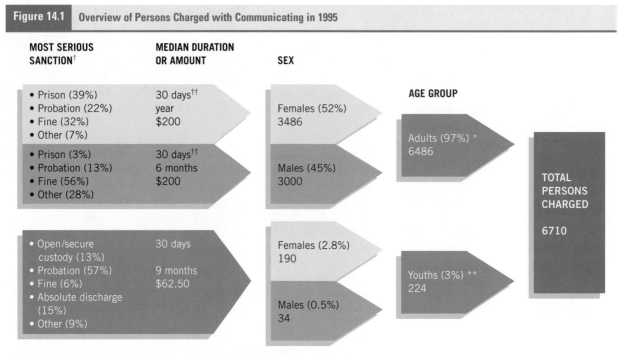

Figure 14.1   Overview of Persons Charged with Communicating in 1995

*Persons aged 18 and over.

**Persons aged 12 to 17. Many youths are diverted to social service agencies in lieu of being charged.

† Adult court cases: Adults convicted of this offence in 1993 and 1994 (1993–94 and 1994–95 fiscal years in Ontario). Excludes New Brunswick, Manitoba, and British Columbia; coverage is incomplete for Newfoundland and Labrador, Nova Soctia, and Quebec. Youth court cases: Youths convicted in Canada in 1993–94 and 1994–95 fiscal years.

†† Based on cases where the sentence duration was known.

Source: Adapted from the Statistics Canada publication "Street Prostitution in Canada," *Juristat*, Catalogue 85-002, vol. 17, no. 2, February 13, 1997.

Types of Prostitution. Prostitutes who work the streets are called hustlers, hookers, or streetwalkers. Although glamorized by the Julia Roberts character in the film *Pretty Woman* (who winds up with multimillionaire Richard Gere), streetwalkers are considered the least attractive, lowest-paid, most vulnerable men and women in the profession. Streetwalkers wear bright clothing and makeup, and take their customers to hotels or cars.[29] Streetwalkers are most likely to be members of ethnic or racial minorities who live in poverty. Many are young runaways who gravitate to major cities to find an exciting life and escape from sexual and physical abuse at home.[30] Of all prostitutes, streetwalkers have the highest incidence of drug abuse and larceny arrests.

Bar girls (B-girls) spend their time in bars, drinking and waiting to be picked up by customers. B-girls work out an arrangement with the bartender so they are served diluted drinks or water coloured with dye or tea, for which the customer is charged an exorbitant price. It is common to find B-girls in towns with military bases and large transient populations.

 InfoTrac®

Read about prostitution in other countries, such as prostitution and sex trafficking in southeast Asia, in Michelle Kuo, "Asia's Dirty Secret," *Harvard International Review* 22, no. 2 (2000): 42; or the sex trade in China, in Sarah Schafer, "Not Just Another Pretty Face," *Newsweek International*, October 3, 2003, p. 36.

Brothels flourished in the nineteenth and early twentieth centuries. Some operate legally in Nevada today. They are establishments run by **madams** that house several prostitutes. The madam employs and supervises the prostitutes and takes a cut of the prostitutes' earnings. The madam's role may include recruiting women into prostitution and socializing them in the "trade."[31] The madam attracts prostitutes and customers, works out understandings with police authorities, and pacifies neighbours.

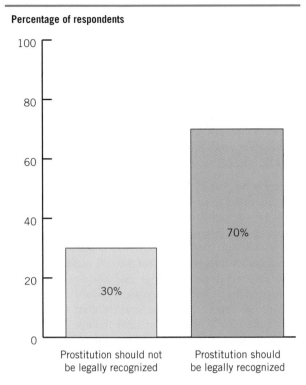

Percentage of respondents

In a recent poll, 4714 people were asked, "Do you believe prostitution should be legally recognized as a business?"

Source: Poll conducted by *The Globe and Mail,* November 18, 2004.

The aristocrats of prostitution are **call girls**. They charge customers up to $1500 per night and may net more than $100 000 per year. Some gain clients through employment in escort services, while others develop independent customer lists. Many call girls come from middle-class backgrounds and service upper-class customers. Working exclusively via telephone "dates," call girls get their clients by word of mouth or by making arrangements with bellhops, cab drivers, and so on. They either entertain clients in their own apartments or make "outcalls" to clients' hotels and apartments. Call girls are at risk by being alone with strangers, so they might request the business cards of their clients to make sure they are dealing with "upstanding citizens."[32]

In the adult entertainment zones of large cities are "rap booths."[33] Here, the prostitute and her customer occupy booths that are separated by a glass wall, and they talk via telephone for as long as the customer is willing to pay. The more money he spends, the more she engages in sexual banter and disrobing. There is no actual touching, and sex is through masturbation.

Some prostitutes have substance abuse problems, and prostitution supports their drug habits. Not all drug-addicted prostitutes barter sex for drugs, but those who do report more frequent drug abuse and physical violence than do other prostitutes.[34]

Some sex trade work is based in **massage parlours,** where prostitutes provide oral sex and manual stimulation. Photography studios and escort services are other possible covers for commercial sex. Stag party girls will service all-male parties and groups by putting on shows and having sex with participants. In years past, many hotels had live-in prostitutes, while today's hotel prostitute makes a deal with the bell captain or manager to refer customers to her for a fee.

Becoming a Prostitute. Why does someone turn to prostitution? Both male and female prostitutes often come from troubled homes marked by extreme conflict, where divorce or death has split the family.[35] Many prostitutes have long histories of sexual exploitation and abuse.[36]

For example, a study done for the Department of Justice in 2002 found that 82 percent of females and 100 percent of males in a youth prostitution survey had a background of sexual abuse before living on the street.[37] This finding was significant in terms of getting police and policymakers to rethink juvenile prostitution as sexual exploitation.

Conflict with school authorities, poor grades, and drug abuse are often factors.[38] Other personal characteristics include growing up in a slum neighbourhood, living in a single-parent home, being a member of a gang, and being unemployed. There is no evidence that people become prostitutes because of psychological problems. Money, drugs, and survival seem to be greater motivations.

Pimps may convince girls to become prostitutes through flattery and promises, but relatively few kidnap or coerce kids into prostitution. It is more likely that friends or relatives introduce kids to prostitution.[39]

Child Prostitution. Child prostitution is a worldwide problem. Girls from Latin America are sold for sex in Europe and the Middle East. Southeast Asian girls wind up in Northern Europe and the Middle East, and Russian and Ukrainian girls are sold in Hungary, Poland, and the Baltic States. In Asia an estimated one million children are part of the sex trade. Thailand is the leader, but child prostitution is a problem in India, Bangladesh, and the Philippines. Sex tours are a common practice in these nations, and the UN wants sanctions to punish operators. Canada now has laws to prosecute sex tourism with minors. In some poor Asian nations, such as Thailand, most young girls are forced into prostitution because they are poor.

Pimps. A pimp derives his livelihood from the earnings of a prostitute. The pimp helps steer customers to the prostitute, stays on the alert for police, posts bail, and protects his prostitutes from unruly customers. Pimps can pick up established "working girls" or they can "turn out" young girls who have never been in "the life." Occasionally they pick up young runaways, buy them clothes and jewellery, and turn them into street prostitutes.

The role of the pimp is changing. The decline of the brothel, the development of independent prostitutes, and the control of prostitution by organized crime have decreased the number of full-time pimps. Many prostitutes are drug-dependent, and in some areas drug dealers have replaced pimps as the controlling force in prostitution.[40] Pimps are often reluctant to work with younger prostitutes because they face more severe penalties if caught running juveniles.[41]

Johns. It is primarily men who buy the sexual services of both male and female prostitutes, although there is very little research on the topic. The men are virtually invisible as attention is focused on the female prostitute. Johns are usually between 20 and 40 years old, married, and consider themselves heterosexual even if they pick up young men. Their reasons for seeking out prostitutes are as varied as the desire for discreet sex to wanting sexual services they are unable to obtain elsewhere.[42]

Legalize Prostitution? Prostitution is a minor offence, punishable by a fine or a short jail sentence. In some jurisdictions johns must attend "john school," where they listen to stories of women forced to work in prostitution. John schools originated in San Francisco in 1995, and today more than a dozen john school programs operate successfully in Canada. They focus on educating offenders on the legal ramifications of prostitution, the health risks, and the effects of prostitution on women. In 1999 a john school was started in Vancouver, operated by the John Howard Society. The school is a precharge diversion program. Offenders arrested in the course of police undercover sting operations for communication are screened by police and offered the option of attending a Prostitution Offender Program class. The cost of attending is $400, and during the day the john will hear various speakers, including community members, legal experts, former sex trade workers, police officers, and health professionals.

To some feminists, women are victims of male dominance, and in patriarchal societies prostitution is a clear example of gender exploitation.[43] For other feminists, prostitution should be a matter of free choice.[44] Advocates of both sides argue that the penalties for prostitution should be reduced. Decriminalization would relieve already desperate women of the additional burden of severe legal punishment.

Pornography

The term **pornography** derives from the Greek *porne*, meaning "prostitute," and *graphein*, meaning "to write." Pornographic books, magazines, films, and websites that depict explicit sex acts are widely available.

One problem of controlling pornography is its relation to **obscenity**, defined as deeply offensive to morality or decency.[45] Police and law enforcement officials can legally seize only material that is judged obscene. But who is to judge what is obscene? For example, the novel *Tropic of Cancer* by Henry Miller was once banned in the United States because it was considered obscene, but today it is considered a work of great literary value.

Opponents of pornography argue that pornographers exploit their models, who may include underage children or victims of physical and psychological coercion.

Child Pornography Rings. Many of the hard-core pictures that find their way into hands of collectors are the work of pornographic rings that exploit children and adolescents for sex. A typical ring contains three to eleven children, predominantly males, some of nursery-school age. Adults who control the ring use a position of trust to recruit the children and then exploit them through material and psychological rewards.

Solo sex rings involve several children and a single adult who uses a position of trust (counsellor, teacher, Boy Scout leader) to recruit children into sexual activity. Transition rings are impromptu groups set up to sell and trade photos and sex, whereas syndicated rings are well-structured and create extensive networks of customers who desire sexual services.[46] The sexual exploitation involved causes physical and psychological problems of a variety of forms.

Given the frequency with which child pornography is now traded over the Internet, Parliament debated passing a law prohibiting the intentional viewing of any child pornography. Previously, a person had to possess it to be charged.[47]

Does Pornography Cause Violence? Serial killer Ted Bundy claimed that his murderous rampage was fuelled by reading pornography.

However, what evidence exists that viewing sexually explicit material has an effect on behaviour? An American national commission on pornography could find no relationship between pornography and violence.[48] Another commission called for legal attacks on hard-core pornography and condemnation of all sexually related material but also found little evidence that obscenity is a cause of antisocial behaviour.

How can we account for this surprisingly insignificant association? In Denmark, research showed that sex offences actually declined shortly after pornography was decriminalized in 1967.[49] Other research found that sex offenders report less exposure to pornography than nonoffenders.[50]

Viewing pornography may have the side effect of satisfying erotic impulses that otherwise might result in more sexually aggressive behaviour. Although some criminologists believe that there is a relationship between pornography and rape, others say that people exposed to violent material are likely to be sexually aggressive.[51] Laboratory experiments have found that men exposed to violence in pornography are more likely to act aggressively toward women.[52] Adult-only books and films often have sexually violent themes, such as rape, bondage, and mutilation.[53]

It is also felt that violent pornography leads to a greater acceptance of rape myths and violence against women, and to more tolerance of sexual aggression.

 InfoTrac®

In a thoughtful analysis, conservative columnist William F. Buckley argues that pornography has insinuated itself everywhere in American culture: William F. Buckley, "Porn, Pervasive Presence: The Creepy Wallpaper of Our Daily Lives," *National Review* 53, no. 22 (2001): 38–43.

Pornography and the Law. In Canada it is an offence to publish or circulate any obscene "thing" (section 163 CCC), where "obscenity" is defined as the undue exploitation of sex and crime, horror, cruelty, and violence. The key question is whether the material violates community standards. There is a high level of tolerance for adult nudity in magazines but not for pictures of adult–child sex.

The Supreme Court of Canada, in the 1992 *Butler* decision, identified the objective of this section of the *Criminal Code* as the protection of society from harm caused by exposure to obscene materials. Under section 163(8) of the *Criminal Code* and the federal *Customs Act*, officers had been in the habit of detaining materials bound for gay bookstores, so in 1998 the Little Sisters Bookstore in Vancouver challenged the law. The court found the law constitutional, but that it had been enforced in a discriminating way.

In the case where *NOW* magazine was charged for running sex ads in its business personals section, there was community support for the magazine and little for the police. Similarly, in Halifax in 1998, some police officers took it on themselves to contact businesses that advertised in *The Coast* about the "Savage Love" advice column. The column had been investigated by the morality section in 1996 and found not to be obscene, but this didn't prevent the police from trying to enforce what they thought were community standards, in this case, their standards.

The punishment of pornographers often creates moral and legal dilemmas, as in the posthumous 1990 exhibition of photographer Robert Mapplethorpe in Cincinnati. The exhibition was heavily criticized by conservative politicians because it contained images of nude children and of men in homoerotic poses. Obscenity

charges were brought against its director, but he was acquitted. The actions taken against the Mapplethorpe exhibit brought protests from artists and performers, and from civil libertarians, who fear government control over art, music, and theatre.

Obviously, a plebiscite cannot be held to determine the community's attitude for every trial concerning the sale of pornography. Works that are considered obscene in Orillia might be considered acceptable in Toronto.

Controlling Sex for Profit

Sex for profit predates Western civilization, and law enforcement crusades can make sex-related goods and services a relatively scarce commodity, driving up prices. The threat of government regulation may also convince some participants in the sex-for-profit industry to police themselves. Fear of government control probably influences mainstream sex magazines to alter their content rather than risk provoking public officials. Fewer controls exist for Internet-based material.

Technological change will challenge the sex-for-profit industry as people buy or rent tapes in local video stores to play in their homes. Adult CD-ROMs are now a staple of the computer industry. Internet sex services (cybersex) include live, interactive stripping and sexual activities. The government has moved to control the broadcast of obscene films via satellite and other technological innovations.[54] Police have also moved to control Internet-based pornography.[55]

Substance Abuse

The problem of substance abuse is widespread in modern societies. Large urban areas are beset by drug-dealing gangs, drug users who engage in crime to support their habits, and alcohol-related violence. Rural and coastal areas are important staging centres for the shipment of drugs across the country, and the production of synthetic drugs and marijuana farming are important parts of the underground economy.[56]

Another indication of the concern about drugs is simply the volume of cases, although as with prostitution, this is partly a product of police enforcement. In 2003 there were 85 953 drug crimes known to the police, a decrease of 2 percent since 1999. Cannabis accounted for 71 percent of the total (68 percent for possession). Most of those charged are adults.

The drug problem, for the most part, is a victimless crime. The Canadian Centre on Substance Abuse (CCSA) says that penalties for marijuana possession have done nothing to enhance public safety and health, and it recommends that possession be decriminalized. This is one side of the debate, that drug use is a private matter and that drug control is simply the government's intrusion into people's private lives. These people support **decriminalization**. Furthermore, legalization could reduce the profit of selling illegal substances and drive suppliers out of the market.[57] Others see these substances as dangerous, believing that the criminal activity of users makes the term "victimless" nonsensical. Still another position favours limited regulation: that the possession and use of all drugs and alcohol should be legalized but that the sale and distribution of drugs should be heavily penalized. This would punish those profiting from drugs and would enable users to be helped without fear of criminal punishment.

When Did Drug Use Begin?

The use of chemical substances to change reality and provide stimulation or relaxation has gone on for thousands of years. In Mesopotamia, opium was known four thousand years ago as the "plant of joy."[58] The ancient Greeks knew of drug use, and during the Crusades Arabs used marijuana. In the West, natives of Mexico and South America chewed coca leaves for endurance and used "magic mushrooms" in their religious ceremonies.[59] In fact, coca leaf aids in the uptake of oxygen in the thin air of the Peruvian Andes. Drug use was also accepted in Europe well into the twentieth century. Recently uncovered pharmacy records circa 1900 to 1920 showed sales of cocaine and heroin solutions to members of the British royal family. Winston Churchill, then a member of Parliament, bought a cocaine solution while staying in Scotland in 1912.[60]

In the early years of Canada and the United States, opium-based drugs were used in various patent medicine cure-alls. Morphine was used extensively to relieve the pain experienced by wounded soldiers. By the turn of the twentieth century, many citizens were opiate users.

Several factors precipitated the stringent drug laws that are in force today. The rural religious creeds of the nineteenth century—for example, those of the Methodists, Presbyterians, and Baptists—emphasized individual human toil and self-sufficiency while designating the use of intoxicating substances as an unwholesome surrender to the evils of urban morality. The medical literature of the late nineteenth century began to designate the use of morphine and opium as a vice and a disease. Late nineteenth- and early twentieth-century police literature described drug users as habitual criminals. Moral crusaders defined drug use as evil and urged lawmakers to outlaw the sale and possession of drugs. Some well-publicized research efforts categorized drug use as highly dangerous.[61] Foreign immigrants who were recruited to work in factories and mines were the focus of early antidrug legislation.[62]

In Canada, large numbers of Asian immigrants, brought in as cheap labour by industrialists in the nineteenth century, were used as a pool of cheap labour.

Asian workers, paid one-half to two-thirds what European workers received, were single men who planned to return to their home country, and they kept to themselves. Their habits of gambling and opium smuggling, although legal in Canada, were thought immoral. By 1907 many of these workers were no longer needed for large construction projects and they began to compete more directly for other jobs. This created political and labour unrest. In 1907 the Asiatic Exclusion League and its supporters rioted in downtown Vancouver. An estimated 20 000 people caused extensive damage to the shops of Chinese and Japanese people.

Deputy Minister of Labour Mackenzie King was appointed to investigate and settle Chinese property damage claims. He discovered the use of opium among the Chinese population and decided that the only means of eliminating the civil unrest was to eliminate the Chinese. He based his report, "The Need for the Suppression of Opium Traffic in Canada," on sensational newspaper stories depicting the ruin of White women caused by opium use. The *Opium Narcotic Act* of 1908 criminalized opium, and in 1911, the *Opium and Drug Act* expanded the list of prohibited drugs, made simple use and possession of the prohibited drugs an offence, and widened police powers of search and seizure.[63]

In 1920, one year before Mackenzie King became prime minister of Canada, the Opium and Drug Branch was established by the Department of Health and was put in charge of enforcing narcotics legislation. *Maclean's* magazine ran a series of articles about the illicit drug trade written by Emily Murphy, a police magistrate and judge of the Juvenile Court in Edmonton, under the pen name "Janey Canuck." They were later compiled into a larger book entitled *The Black Candle*. The articles that Murphy wrote were biased and sensational. In one oft-quoted section, a Los Angeles County Chief of Police is quoted as saying that

> persons using this narcotic smoke the dry leaves of the plant, which has the effect of driving them completely insane. The addict loses all sense of moral responsibility. Addicts to this drug, while under its influence, are immune to pain. While in this condition they become raving maniacs and are liable to kill or indulge in any forms of violence to other persons, using the most savage methods of cruelty without, as said before, any sense of moral responsibility.

When *The Black Candle* was released in 1922, it aroused public opinion and resulted in pressure on the government to create stricter drug laws. Cannabis hemp was made illegal under the *Opium and Narcotic Drug Act* of 1923 with seemingly little discussion. The film *Reefer Madness* in 1936 further reinforced this opinion. It was not until the LeDain Commission of 1969–1971 that marijuana was recommended for decriminalization.

The film *Reefer Madness* (1936) came to symbolize the danger of marijuana: the life of a promising young man brought to ruin, madness, and murder.

Alcohol and Its Prohibition

The history of alcohol and the law has also been controversial and dramatic. At the turn of the century, a drive was mustered to prohibit the sale of alcohol. The **temperance movement** was fuelled by the belief that the purity of agrarian culture was being destroyed. The growth of the city was viewed as a threat to the lifestyle of people living on farms and in villages. The Anti-Saloon League led by Carrie Nation, the Woman's Christian Temperance Union, and the Protestant clergy of the Baptist, Methodist, and Congregationalist faiths viewed the growing city, filled with newly arriving Irish, Italian, and Eastern European immigrants, as centres of degradation and wickedness. The propensity of these ethnic people to drink heavily was viewed as the main force behind their degenerate lifestyle.[64]

Prohibition turned out to be a failure. Organized crime was only too happy to supply illicit liquor. Law enforcement agencies were inadequate, and officials were more than likely to be corrupted by wealthy bootleggers. The smuggling of alcohol from Canada into the United States was especially lucrative. However, one unanticipated consequence of Prohibition in Canada between 1921 and 1929 was the growth of provincial and territorial police forces.[65]

Commonly Used and Abused Drugs

A wide variety of drugs are available to drug abusers, only some of which are addicting. Various effects include hallucinations, depression, relaxation, and exhilaration. These drugs are controlled by the *Food and Drugs Act* and the *Narcotic Control Act*. The following are some of the most widely used illegal drugs.[66]

Crime in the News

The Sinking of the *I'm Alone*

For more than a day the US Coast Cutter Dexter, with others, pursued the British schooner *I'm Alone*, admitted to be a rum-runner that had long laughed at the vigilance of the marine enforcers of prohibition. The captain of the felonious craft had refused to heave to. On Friday night she was shelled copiously. The sea was rough. The Coast Guard is righteously rough in the discharge of its function. Only one man on the refractory schooner was lost, and he fell overboard. The sinking occurred over 200 miles from the Louisiana coast. The prime question is where it began. The pursuers assert that she was within ten or eleven miles of the coast and therefore legally subject to seizure. The captain of the *I'm Alone* that he was anchored fourteen or fifteen miles offshore when first hailed by the cutter.

Here we draw near the "twelve mile limit," a modern expression of the older formula in leagues and embalmed for revenue and prohibition purposes. In the treaty of 1924 between Great Britain and the US the rights of boarding, search and seizure outside of our territorial waters shall not be exercised at a greater distance from the coast of the US than can be traversed in one hour by the vessel suspected of endeavoring to commit the offense. . . .

Source: *New York Times,* March 29, 1929.

Anesthetics. Anesthetic drugs are nervous system depressants. They act on the brain to produce a generalized loss of sensation or unconsciousness. The most widely abused anesthetic drug is phencyclidine (PCP) or "angel dust." PCP can be sprayed on marijuana and smoked, or it can be drunk or injected. PCP is an animal tranquillizer and causes hallucinations.

Volatile Liquids. Volatile liquids that are easily vaporized and inhaled include lighter fluid, paint thinner, cleaning fluid, and model airplane glue. The psychological effect is a short-term sense of excitement and euphoria followed by disorientation, slurred speech, and drowsiness. Amyl nitrate ("poppers") is sold in capsules that are broken and inhaled, used during sexual activity to prolong and intensify the experience.

Barbiturates. These hypnotic-sedative drugs depress the central nervous system into a sleeplike condition. Prescribed by doctors as sleeping pills, on the illegal market they are called "downers" and are known by the colour of the capsules—"reds" (Seconal), "blue dragons" (Amytal), and "rainbows" (Tuinal). They create relaxed, sociable, and good-humoured feelings but are probably the major cause of drug overdose deaths.

Tranquillizers. Tranquillizers have the ability to reduce anxiety, easing tension. Ampazine, Thorazine, Pacatal, and Sparine are used by people with mental illness who experience psychoses, aggressiveness, and agitation. Valium, Librium, Miltown, and Equanil are used by the average citizen to combat anxiety, tension, fast heart rate, and headaches. These mild tranquillizers are obtained by prescription; however, they can lead to addiction and painful withdrawal.

Amphetamines. "Uppers" are synthetic drugs that stimulate the central nervous system to produce elevated blood pressure, increased breathing rate, and elevated mood. Psychological effects include increased confidence, euphoria, fearlessness, impulsivity, and appetite loss. Uppers include Benzedrine ("bennies"), Dexedrine ("dex"), Dexamyl, Bephetamine ("whites"), and Methedrine ("meth," "speed," "crystal meth," "ice"). Speed is the most widely used and the most dangerous. Swallowed in pill form or injected, long-term heavy use can result in exhaustion, anxiety, prolonged depression, and hallucinations.

Cannabis (Marijuana). "Pot," "grass," "ganja," "maryjane," or "dope" is produced from the leaves of *Cannabis sativa*, a hemp plant grown throughout the world. Hashish is made from resin from the female plant. Various effects include changes in auditory and visual perception of time and space, excitement, drowsiness, and increased appetite. Marijuana is not addicting, and it has been decriminalized in Canada for medical use.

In 1972, the LeDain Commission into the Non-Medical Use of Drugs concluded that the Canadian marijuana market was free of professional criminal involvement. However, now the RCMP says that almost every large-scale grow operation is linked to organized crime. In the past this was largely outlaw motorcycle gangs, but now Asian-based criminal gangs predominate.

Technological developments and the use of cloning methods have led to a rise in the potency of the drug. Marijuana with a THC content of 2 percent was considered high quality in 1965, whereas now THC can exceed more than 10 percent. Grown hydroponically, potency can go as high as the mid-teens.[67]

Cannabis is often referred to as the gateway drug, whose use leads to progressively more serious drug abuse. However, this idea has been disproven.[68]

Hallucinogens. Hallucinogens, either natural or synthetic, produce vivid sensory distortions without greatly disturbing consciousness. Some produce hallucinations, while others cause psychotic behaviour. One common hallucinogen is mescaline, which occurs naturally in the peyote cactus. Mescaline produces vivid hallucinations, a feeling of depersonalization, and out-of-body sensations. Alkaloid compounds, either natural or made in the laboratory, include DMT, morning glory seeds, and psilocybin. Transformed into D-lysergic acid diethylamide-25 (LSD), this substance (eight hundred times more potent than mescaline) stimulates cerebral sensory centres to produce visual hallucinations, intensifies hearing, increases sensitivity, and induces euphoria.

Cocaine. Cocaine is a derivative of the coca leaf first isolated in 1860 by Albert Niemann of Göttingen, Germany. Originally considered a medicinal breakthrough that could relieve fatigue and depression, it was endorsed by psychologists such as Sigmund Freud and used in popular patent medicines. When pharmacist John Styth Pemberton first brewed his new soft drink in 1886, he added cocaine to act as a "brain tonic" and called the drink Coca-Cola; this secret ingredient was taken out in 1906.

When its addictive qualities and dangerous side effects became apparent, cocaine's use was controlled by such legislative bills as Ontario's Anti-Cocaine Bill, an Act to amend the *Pharmacy Act* of 1908. Awareness was growing of the dangerous effects of cocaine, and physicians and pharmacists were trying to control "medications" in a wider climate of moral reform. For example, in a flyer issued by the Children's Aid Society of Montreal, there appeared the following claim:

> The cocaine habit must be stamped out of Canada. It is undermining our boyhood and cutting away the moral fibre of our girls. It is turning our young people into criminals and imbeciles. . . . Will YOU help the Children's Aid

Society fight cocaine? You can do so by asking your clergyman to preach about it, [and] by writing to your member of parliament.[69]

Until the 1970s, cocaine remained underground, used by artists, jazz musicians, beatniks, and jetsetters. Cocaine produces euphoria and excitement. Overdoses cause delirium, increased reflexes, violent manic behaviour, and respiratory failure. Cocaine can be sniffed, or snorted, into the nostrils or injected. Mixing cocaine and heroin is called "speedballing"; this practice is highly dangerous and is alleged to have killed comedian John Belushi. When cocaine is treated with a liquid to remove the hydrochloric acid, the resultant "freebase" is dissolved in a solvent such as ether and crystallized, producing a high more powerful than cocaine but dangerous to make. The creation of **crack cocaine** also involves using ammonia or baking soda to remove the hydrochlorides and create a crystalline form of cocaine base that can then be smoked.[70]

The use of crack and other cocaine derivatives is not widespread. In 1993, for example, the RCMP seized less than three kilograms of crack in Ontario, while almost three thousand kilograms of cocaine were seized by police in Canada overall.[71] However, because crack cocaine is relatively cheap, it is concentrated among the poor and lower classes, who are susceptible to this powerful and inexpensive drug. Between 1993 and 1995, the percentage of students reporting the use of crack cocaine increased from 0.5 percent to 1.9 percent; it had increased to 2.7 percent by 2003, hardly an epidemic.[72] So although crack may not be the national epidemic among the middle class as some thought it would turn into, its use has had a powerful effect in the inner city.[73]

Narcotics. These drugs produce insensibility to pain, relieve anxiety, and create sedation. Users experience euphoria, reduced fear, apprehension, and tension. Narcotics can be injected under the skin or into a muscle or directly into the bloodstream (mainlining). Some come in pill form.

The most common narcotics are derivatives of opium, produced from the opium poppy. The Chinese popularized the habit of smoking or chewing opium extract to produce euphoric feelings. Morphine (from Morpheus, the Greek god of dreams), a derivative of opium, is about 10 times as strong and is used legally by physicians to relieve pain. Heroin was first produced as a painkilling alternative to morphine in 1875 because, although 25 times more powerful, it was considered non-addictive by its creator, Heinrich Dreser. The drug's name derives from the fact that it was originally considered heroic because of its painkilling ability.

Heroin is today a commonly used narcotic, although less than 2 percent of all drug offences are for heroin. Dealers cut it with neutral substances such as sugar, and it is often only 1 percent to 4 percent pure. Users can build up a tolerance, so larger doses or a changed method of ingestion are needed. Withdrawal symptoms include irritability, depression, extreme nervousness, abdominal pain, and nausea. Heroin abuse is generally considered a lower-class phenomenon, although a fair number of middle- and upper-class users exist, such as physicians.[74] The popularity of heroin in the 1990s has been linked to its relatively low cost, ready supply, and the effect of government efforts to control other substances such as crack cocaine. The drug of choice seems to be shifting from crack to heroin. Although the popularity of heroin is increasing among the middle class, it is still common to associate heroin addiction with minority youths in lower-class, inner-city neighbourhoods.

In 2003, a class-action suit was announced against Purdue Pharma, the makers of OxyContin, a powerful, highly addictive medication. It is nicknamed "hillbilly heroin" because of its popularity in poor regions.

Other opium derivatives include codeine, Dilaudid, Percodan, and Prinadol. Synthetics include Demerol, Methadone, Nalline, and Darvon.

Steroids. Anabolic steroids are used to gain muscle bulk and strength for athletics and bodybuilding. Although not physically addicting, steroids are dangerous because of the significant health problems associated with long-term use: liver ailments, tumours, hepatitis, kidney problems, sexual dysfunction, hypertension, and depression. Steroid users often share needles, which puts them at high risk for contracting human immunodeficiency virus (HIV).

After Canadian sprinter Ben Johnson tested positive for steroid use at the 1988 Olympic Games, the Dubin Inquiry found widespread use of steroids among professional athletes, who use the performance-enhancing drugs to stay competitive.[75] In 1998, a scandal rocked the Tour de France bicycle race after athletes were tested for banned substances, including synthetic hormones.

Designer Drugs. **Designer drugs** are chemical substances made in small batches that induce mood-altering effects. They include MDMA ("ecstasy"), which combines an amphetamine-like rush with hallucinogenic experiences; the hallucinogens DMT and 2c-B or "Nexus"; and the steroid substitute GHB, which causes drowsiness.

Alcohol. Although the sale and purchase of alcohol is legal today, excessive alcohol consumption is considered a major substance abuse problem.

The cost of alcohol abuse is quite high. In 1992 almost seven thousand deaths were attributed to alcohol in Ontario alone, accounting for almost 10 percent of all deaths in the province. The bulk of these deaths were indirectly related: for example, 110 homicides, 295 suicides, and 490 deaths resulting from motor vehicle accidents.[76]

Alcohol reduces tension, diverts worries, enhances pleasure, improves social skills, and transforms experiences for the better.[77] However, higher doses act as a sedative and depressant. Long-term use has been linked with depression, heart disease, cirrhosis of the liver, and a diminished sexual response.[78] Moderate drinking has been linked to a reduced probability of heart attack.[79]

The Extent of Substance Abuse

Surveys. In surveying drug use, self-report evidence is subject to error. This is true for any crime, but especially for those with high social disapproval levels. Drug users may boastfully overinflate the extent of their substance abuse, underreport out of fear, or simply be unaware or forgetful.

Another problem is that surveys can overlook important segments of the drug-using population: for example, people who are homeless, in prison, in drug rehabilitation clinics, or in AIDS clinics. A survey can miss kids who are institutionalized and those who have dropped out of school.[80] A number of studies indicate that serious abusers underreport drug use in surveys.[81]

Despite these weaknesses, surveys can get at information that would be difficult to collect otherwise, for example, on student drug use, with most provinces and territories administering self-report surveys.

Patterns. Despite a continuing effort to control it, the use of mood-altering substances persists. Despite the media attention given to the incidence of drug abuse, there is controversy over the extent of drug use. National surveys show that drug use is not substantially greater than it was two decades ago. Drug possession offences declined during the 1980s, except for cocaine, which tripled from 1985 to 1991. By 1996 drug offences were up, but almost 70 percent of that increase was for marijuana, which is very sensitive to police enforcement.[82]

Health Canada reports that cannabis use was 6.5 percent in 1989, 7.4 percent in 1994, and more than 12 percent in 2002.[83] Overall, 2.4 percent of Canadians had used one of cocaine/crack, ecstasy, LSD, amphetamines, or heroin.

The continued trend in drug abuse among adolescents indicates that the drug problem has not gone away and may be on the increase. When drug use declined in the 1980s, one reason may have been changing perceptions about the harmfulness of drugs, such as cocaine and marijuana; as people come to view these drugs as harmful, they tend to use them less. Considering the widespread publicity linking drug use, needle sharing, and the acquired immune deficiency syndrome (AIDS) virus, it comes as no surprise that people began to see drug taking as dangerous and risky. In the 1990s, however, the perceived risk of drugs was on the decline.

A survey of almost five thousand Manitoba high school students found that about 40 percent smoked tobacco, 81 percent had drunk alcohol in the past year,

and 33 percent drank once a week or more. Of those who drink, 30 percent do so in cars and 15 percent at school. About 38 percent of students used cannabis, the most commonly used drug. In Ontario, a 1999 survey on student drug use conducted by the Centre for Addiction and Mental Health showed that alcohol use had increased to 67 percent since 1993, cannabis use had more than doubled to 29 percent, and 28 percent of students smoked tobacco.[84]

The 2002 New Brunswick Student Drug Use Survey found an increase in cannabis, Ritalin, and psilocybin use, a decrease in tobacco and LSD use, and stable patterns in alcohol use.

The longest ongoing survey, the Ontario Student Drug Use Survey, found a significant amount of alcohol and drug use, as shown in Table 14.1.

Overall, research shows that when drug use declines, youths report greater disapproval of drug use among their friends, and peer pressure may contribute to lower use rates. In the 1990s the number of youths disapproving of drugs declined (although a majority still disapproved); with lower disapproval has come increased usage. It should come as no surprise that a cohort of young people who perceive little peer rejection for drug use, who consider drugs risk-free and easily available, and whose parents either ignore or condone drug use will increase the frequency of their substance abuse.

Drug-Involved Youths Who Continue to Commit Crimes as Adults. Although about two-thirds of substance-abusing youths continue to use drugs after they reach adulthood, about half desist from other criminal activities. Those who persist in both substance abuse and crime as adults tend to come from poor families, have other criminals in the family, do poorly in school, start using drugs and committing delinquent acts at a young age, and have few opportunities in late adolescence to participate in legitimate and rewarding adult activities.

Some evidence also exists that these drug-using persisters have low nonverbal IQs and poor physical coordination. Nonetheless, there is still little scientific evidence to indicate why some drug-abusing kids drop out of crime while others remain active into their adulthood.

InfoTrac®

Use InfoTrac® to find this article relevant to youths and drugs: "CASA Study Links Stress, Boredom, Money to Teen Substance Abuse," *Alcohol and Drug Abuse Weekly* 15, no. 32 (2003): 1–4.

Smugglers. Smugglers import drugs into the country. They are generally middle-aged men who have strong organizational skills, established connections, capital to invest, and a willingness to take large business risks. There

TABLE 14.1 Past Year Drug Use (%) by Total, Sex, and Grade, 2003

	Total	Males	Females		G7	G8	G9	G10	G11	G12	
Alcohol	**66.2**	68.3	64.3	*	39.1	48.9	65.1	75.1	79.9	82.5	*
Cannabis	**29.6**	30.9	28.3		6.2	10.7	27.9	35.9	45.0	44.8	*
Binge Drinking	**26.5**	29.4	23.8	*	5.8	7.7	23.5	29.8	40.9	45.2	*
Cigarettes	**19.2**	18.0	20.3		4.4	10.2	17.0	21.8	28.3	30.2	*
Hallucinogens	**10.0**	12.1	8.0	*	1.8	2.6	7.8	12.5	17.4	15.3	*
Solvents	**6.1**	5.9	6.3		10.2	9.5	6.5	4.2	3.6	3.9	*
Stimulants (NM)	**5.8**	4.7	6.7	*	1.6	3.7	5.6	6.6	8.2	7.8	*
Cocaine	**4.8**	5.4	4.3		3.1	1.9	4.9	4.6	6.8	6.7	*
Ecstasy (MDMA)	**4.1**	4.2	3.9		0.5	0.8	3.7	4.6	6.6	7.2	*
Methamphetamine	**3.3**	3.8	2.9		1.0	0.9	3.8	4.2	5.4	3.6	*
LSD	**2.9**	3.5	2.3	*	0.7	1.1	3.7	4.2	4.0	2.7	*
Ritalin (NM)	**2.9**	3.4	2.5		1.2	1.2	3.0	3.3	5.0	3.1	*
Glue	**2.8**	3.0	2.6		5.2	3.2	2.4	2.4	2.3	1.8	*
Crack	**2.7**	2.8	2.6		1.7	1.7	3.1	3.0	3.6	2.5	
Barbiturates (NM)	**2.5**	2.6	2.5		1.8	2.2	3.0	2.8	3.1	1.8	
PCP	**2.2**	2.9	1.6	*	1.3	0.8	2.1	3.6	2.6	2.7	*
Tranquillizers (NM)	**2.2**	2.7	1.8	*	0.6	1.2	1.8	2.4	4.1	2.7	*
Ketamine	**2.2**	3.0	1.6	*	1.0	s	1.7	1.6	4.7	3.7	*
Rohypnol	**1.6**	1.7	1.5		1.2	1.2	1.4	2.0	2.3	1.3	
Heroin	**1.4**	1.9	0.9	*	1.4	0.8	1.5	2.0	1.3	1.1	
Ice	**1.2**	1.3	1.0		1.2	0.8	1.3	1.0	1.1	1.5	
GHB	**0.7**	0.8	0.6		s	s	s	0.9	1.7	s	
Any Illicit, including cannabis	**32.2**	33.1	31.3		10.1	13.9	29.6	38.6	47.5	47.1	*
Any Illicit, excluding cannabis	**15.3**	16.6	14.2	*	6.6	8.0	13.0	18.0	21.7	22.3	*
Steroids (lifetime)	**3.0**	4.4	1.7	*	0.7	1.8	1.6	3.8	4.6	5.3	*

Source: Edward M. Adlaf and Angela Paglia, *Drug Use Among Ontario Students, Detailed Ontario Student Drug Use Survey Findings, 1977–2003* (Toronto: Centre for Addiction and Mental Health, 2003).

Notes: binge drinking (5+ drinks on one occasion) refers to the past 4 weeks time period; NM = non-medical use; s = estimate suppressed; * indicates a significant sex difference or grade difference ($p < .05$) *not* controlling for other factors.

is a constant flow in and out of the business as some sources become the target of law enforcement activities, new drug sources become available, older smugglers become dealers, and former dealers become smugglers.

Adult Predatory Drug Users. Many users who abuse substances early in adolescence will continue in drugs and crime in adulthood. Getting arrested, doing time, using multiple drugs, and committing predatory crimes is

a way of life for them. They have few skills, did poorly in school, and have a long criminal record specializing in robberies, burglaries, thefts, and drug sales. They filter in and out of the justice system and begin committing crimes as soon as they are released.[85]

However, some drug users commit hundreds of crimes each year but are rarely arrested. Known for calculated violence, they plan their crimes carefully. They often work with partners and are more likely to use recreational drugs, such as coke and pot, than the more addicting heroin or opiates. Some may become high-frequency users and risk apprehension and punishment. But for the lucky few, their criminal careers can stretch for up to 15 years without interruption by the justice system.

AIDS and Drug Use

There is a link between drug use and the risk of contracting HIV.[86] Since monitoring of the spread of AIDS began in 1981, about one-fourth of all adult AIDS cases reported to the Centers for Disease Control in Atlanta have occurred among intravenous (IV) drug users.[87]

In Canada the percentage of HIV positive cases among injection drug users reached its peak in 1997 at 34 percent. In comparison, cases attributable to heterosexual contact were 17 percent, and 40 percent can be traced to homosexual contact. Women are more likely to be exposed through injection drug use (IDU) than are men. In 2000, 40 percent of 226 HIV-positive females and 17 percent of 1085 HIV-positive males were due to IDU.[88]

One reason for the AIDS–drug use relationship is the widespread habit of needle sharing among IV users without disinfecting.[89] Because HIV is spread through blood transfer, sharing HIV-contaminated needles is the primary mechanism for transmitting AIDS among the drug-using population. Any attempt to control drugs by outlawing the sale of hypodermic needles has the unfortunate consequence of promoting needle reuse and sharing. Consequently, legal jurisdictions have developed outreach programs to help these drug users; others have made an effort to teach users how to clean their needles and syringes; some have gone so far as to provide addicts with sterile needles.[90]

In 2002, the most common forms of exposure to HIV for youths aged 15 to 19 were heterosexual contact (55 percent) and injection drug use (36 percent). Half of all new infections occurring worldwide are occurring among young people, with youths aged 15 to 29 accounting for 28 percent of all positive HIV test reports in Canada.[91]

Statistics Canada reports that since 1981, the exposure to HIV through homosexual contact has decreased from 80 percent to 40 percent; exposure through IDU has increased to 30 percent; and exposure through heterosexual contact has increased to almost 25 percent.[92]

Drug users also have a significant exposure to AIDS because they tend to have multiple sex partners, some of whom may be engaging in prostitution to support a drug habit.[93] What further complicates the link among prostitution, drug use, and AIDS is that women are more likely to contract HIV from men than the reverse. This was especially true in the early 1990s, when the main risk for women was heterosexual sex; however, by 2000, the main risk was injection drug use.[94]

In Vancouver's downtown eastside, a public health emergency was declared among the estimated six thousand to 10 000 heroin addicts, who live in poor housing, share needles, and engage in prostitution. In 1993, 356 people died of drug overdoses at the peak of the epidemic. More alarming is that the area's HIV transmission rate of 19 percent is the highest rate in the developed world, with 40 percent of HIV-positive addicts lending needles despite needle exchange programs. British Columbia's chief coroner proposed the federal government decriminalize heroin so that the issue can be dealt with in a medical rather than a criminal manner.[95]

In 2003, North America's first supervised safe injection site opened in Vancouver. As many as eight hundred addicts a day were expected to use the site, out of the five thousand injection drug users estimated to live in the neighbourhood.[96] Health Canada provided some money for research, and an exemption was granted under the *Controlled Drugs and Substances Act*.

Although the threat of AIDS may be having an impact on the drug-taking behaviour of recreational and middle-class users, drug use may be increasing among the poor, high-school dropouts, and other disadvantaged groups.

The Cause of Substance Abuse

What causes people to abuse drugs? Although there are many views on the causes of drug use, most can be characterized by whether they view the onset of an addictive career as either an environmental or a personal matter.

Subcultural View. Those who view drug abuse as having an environmental basis concentrate on lower-class addiction. Because many drug abusers are poor, the onset of drug use can be tied to devalued identities, low self-esteem, and poor socioeconomic status.

Alienated youths living in depressed areas will come in contact with established drug users, who teach them that narcotics relieve feelings of personal inadequacy and stress.[97] Youths will join with peers to learn techniques of drug use and receive social support for their habit, involving them in the drug use subculture.[98] However, upward mobility is available to only a few.[99]

Psychodynamic View. Yet not all drug abusers reside in lower-class slum areas; the problem of middle-class substance abuse is very real. Some have linked substance abuse to emotional problems that can strike people in any class. This explanation of substance abuse suggests that drugs help youths control or express unconscious needs and impulses. Drinking alcohol may also be associated with dependence and depression. A young teen may resort to drug abuse to reduce the emotional turmoil of adolescence. Addicts might have personality disorders characterized by a weak ego, low frustration tolerance, anxiety, and fantasies of omnipotence.

Some research also shows an association between mental illness and drug abuse.[100]

Genetic Factors. It is also possible that substance abuse has a genetic basis. The biological children of alcoholics reared by nonalcoholic adoptive parents more often develop alcohol problems than do the biological children of the adoptive parents.[101] Studies comparing alcoholism between identical twins and fraternal twins have found that the likelihood of both siblings behaving identically is twice as high among the identical twin groups. However, identical twins are more likely to be treated similarly than fraternal twins are and therefore are more likely to be influenced by environmental conditions.

Taken as a group, people whose parents were alcoholic or drug dependent have a greater chance of developing a problem than children of nonabusers do. Nonetheless, most children of abusing parents do not become drug dependent, suggesting that even if drug abuse is heritable, environment and socialization play a role in the onset of abuse.[102]

Social Learning. Social psychologists suggest drug abuse patterns may result from the observation of parental drug use. Parental drug abuse begins to have a damaging effect on children as young as two years old, especially when parents manifest drug-related personality problems such as depression or poor impulse control.[103]

People who learn that drugs provide pleasurable sensations may be the most likely to experiment with illegal substances; a habit may develop if the user experiences lower anxiety, fear, and tension levels.[104] Having a history of family drug and alcohol abuse has been found to be a characteristic of violent teenage sexual abusers.[105] Heroin abusers report an unhappy childhood, which included harsh physical punishment and parental neglect and rejection.[106]

Drinking with an adult present, presumably a parent, was also a significant precursor of future substance abuse and delinquency.[107]

Problem Behaviour Syndrome (PBS). For many people, substance abuse is just one of many problem behaviours. Longitudinal studies show that drug abusers are maladjusted, alienated, and emotionally distressed.[108] A deviant lifestyle begins early and is punctuated with criminal relationships, a family history of substance abuse, educational failure, alienation, and low commitment to religious values. Research on problem behaviour syndrome (PBS) has found support for the connection among problem drinking, drug abuse, delinquency, precocious sexual behaviour, school failure, family conflict, and other similar social problems.[109]

Connection

Chapter 10 looks at PBS as part of an overall integrated theory of criminality.

Rational Choice. Some people choose to use drugs and alcohol because they want to enjoy the effects: get high, relax, improve creativity, escape reality, increase sexual responsiveness. Adolescent alcohol abusers believe that getting high will make them powerful, increase their sexual performance, and facilitate their social behaviour; they care little about negative future consequences.[110] Research on middle-class, drug-abusing women shows that most were introduced by friends or lovers in the context of just having some fun.[111]

Substance use/abuse, then, may be a function of the rational belief that drugs can be of benefit to the user. The decision to use drugs involves evaluating personal consequences (addiction, disease, legal punishment) and the expected benefits of drug use (peer approval, positive affective states, heightened awareness, relaxation).[112]

Constructionist. Not all theories of drugs and crime start from the presupposition that drug use is automatically bad or that it leads to crime. The social constructionist position looks at who is in a position to influence the ideological characterization of drugs. In the example discussed above with regard to the criminalization of opium, labour leaders and politicians were able to trade on the prejudice against Asians prevalent in British Columbia to successfully outlaw opium at the turn of the twentieth century. The criminalization of cocaine around the same time turned on a fear promoted by police officers and religious leaders that Black men addicted to cocaine were corrupting White women. People who are able to influence public opinion in such a manner are called **claimsmakers**.[113]

In sum, there are many views of the reasons that people take drugs, and no one theory has proved to be an adequate explanation of all forms of substance abuse. However, research does show that drug users tend to suffer a variety of family and socialization difficulties, have addiction-prone personalities, and are generally at risk for many other social problems.[114]

Drugs and Crime

One reason for the criminalization of particular substances is the association believed to exist between drug abuse and crime. Many criminal offenders have extensive experience with drug use, and drug users do in fact commit an enormous amount of crime. Alcohol abuse has also been linked to criminality and appears to be an important precipitating factor in domestic assault and homicide cases.[115] Arrestees who test positive for drugs are also more likely to recidivate than are nonusers.[116]

However, it is uncertain whether the relationship between drug abuse and crime is causal, as many users had a history of criminal activity before the onset of their substance abuse.[117] As well, many people use drugs recreationally without ever committing other crimes. If drug use is not a cause of crime, perhaps it can amplify the frequency and seriousness of criminality.[118]

InfoTrac®

Use InfoTrac® to find relevant articles linking drugs and crime: David Boyum and Mark A.R. Kleiman, "Breaking the Drug–Crime Link," *Public Interest* (Summer 2003): 19–40.

Research Methods

Two approaches have been used to study the relationship between drugs and crime. One has been to survey known addicts to assess the extent of their law violations; the other has been to survey known criminals to see whether they were or are drug users.

User Surveys. Research on the criminal activity of drug users shows that people who take drugs have extensive involvement in crime. Alcohol abuse has been linked to serious, violent offending patterns. Although research indicates that drug use is not an initiator of crime (since many users had committed crime before turning to drugs), there was strong evidence that the amount and value of crime increased proportionately with the frequency of the subjects' drug involvement.[119]

A survey of 144 untreated illicit opiate users in Toronto found a high rate of property and drug-related offences for income-generating purposes.[120] This is a significant finding, given that there are an estimated 60 000 to 90 000 illicit opiates users in Canada.

Surveys of Known Criminals. The second method used to link drugs and crime is testing known criminals to determine the extent of their substance abuse. A survey of prison inmates disclosed that most (80 percent) had engaged in a lifetime of drug and alcohol abuse, more than one-third claimed to have been under the influence of drugs when they committed their last offence, and 62 percent claimed to have used drugs such as heroin, cocaine, PCP, or LSD, on a regular basis before their arrest.[121] This supports the association between substance abuse and serious crime.

The drug–crime relationship may thus be explained in three ways: Some may commit crime to support a drug habit; others may become violent while under the influence of drugs or alcohol, which lowers inhibitions and increases aggression levels; or the drug–crime connection may be a function of the violent world of drug distributors, who regularly use violence to do business.[122]

In sum, research testing both the criminality of known narcotics users and the narcotics use of known criminals produces a strong association between drug use and crime. Even if the crime rate of drug users were actually half that reported in the research literature, users would be responsible for a significant portion of total criminal activity.

The Cycle of Addiction

The drug–crime connection may also be mediated by the amount of drugs that users require and their ability to support their habit through conventional means. Occasional users are people just beginning their addiction, who use small amounts and whose habit can be

---

Exhibit 14.2	The Drug–Crime Relationship

Dependence on illicit drugs and alcohol

- 38% male federal inmates dependent on alcohol or drugs
- 43% of provincial inmates rated as drug dependent
- 54% of all arrestees judged abusers of alcohol or drugs by arresting officer

Relationship of dependency to type of offence

- alcohol-dependent federal inmates more likely to have committed a violent crime
- drug-dependent inmates more likely to have committed a gainful crime

Use and dependency as they relate to volumes of crimes committed

- inmates who used neither drugs or alcohol committed 1.7 crimes per week
- inmates who used one or more substances committed 3.3 crimes per week
- inmates dependent on drugs/alcohol committed 7.1 crimes per week

Intoxication at the time of committing a crime

- police officers reported 51% arrestees under influence of psychoactive substance
- 39% assault offenders under influence of alcohol
- 32% thefts committed under influence of drugs

Proportion of crimes attributable to drugs and alcohol

- 49% violent crimes, 50% gainful crimes, and 24% drug crimes attributed to alcohol and/or illicit drugs

Source: Kai Pernanen, Marie-Marthe Cousineau, Serge Brochu, and Fu Sun, *Proportions of Crimes Associated with Alcohol and Other Drugs in Canada* (Ottawa: Canadian Centre on Substance Abuse, 2002).

Famous Canadian Criminals

The High Life of Brian O'Dea

In 1975, Brian O'Dea, a marijuana smuggler, and a pilot flew a decrepit DC-6 to a town in Colombia, where they were to pick up eight tonnes of high-grade pot. Shortly before touchdown, the plane's nose gear failed, and the four-engine aircraft plunged through a fence and into a field of cacti. When the plane took off again, it was with one less engine.

When they were about a mile out over the water, a second engine died, and they crash-landed in the water.

After he was picked up by US authorities, he received a ten-year sentence for importing marijuana into the US. This was only one dramatic incident in a life lived outside the law.

By February 2001, out of jail and wanting to put his criminal past behind him, O'Dea decided to try his hand at a different career. He placed an ad in the National Post featuring the fact that he had been a marijuana smuggler and showing how this had given him business experience. The response was phenomenal. His ad circulated on the Internet, drawing mail from Egypt, China, and Australia. Talent agents, script brokers, and movie producers called from New York, Los Angeles, and Vancouver. His face turned up in the *Financial Times* and the *National Enquirer*. He appeared on *Good Morning America* and *Court TV*. *Playboy* wanted an interview. So did the *Wall Street Journal*.

There were a few job offers, too, though mostly from cold-call sales outfits and people operating on the fringes of the law. One man asked O'Dea to join what he described as an "offshore organ transplant" business.

Employment Wanted

Former Marijuana Smuggler

Having successfully completed a ten-year sentence, incident-free, for importing 75 tons of marijuana into the US, I am now seeking a legal and legitimate means to support myself and my family.

Business Experience: Owned and operated a successful fishing business— multi-vessel, one airplane, one island and processing facility. Simultaneously owned and operated a fleet of tractor-trailer trucks conducting business in the Western US. During this time I also co-owned and participated in the executive level manage-ment of 120 people worldwide in a successful pot smuggling venture with revenues in excess of US$100 million annually. I took responsibility for my own actions, and received a ten-year sentence in the US while others walked free for their cooperation.

Attributes: I am an expert in all levels of security; I have extensive computer skills, am personable, outgoing, well-educated, reliable, clean and sober. I have spoken in schools to thousands of kids and parent groups over the past ten years on "the consequences of choice," and received public recognition from the RCMP for community service. I am well-traveled and speak English, French and Spanish. References available from friends, family, the US District Attorney, etc.

Please direct replies to

Box 375, National Post Classified, 1450 Don Mills, ON, M3B 3R5

He has survived a troubled childhood, a cocaine addiction and numerous encounters with the world's most dangerous drug lords. He has served time in federal penitentiaries in Canada and the US and lived to tell his story. Now he needs a job, and telling that story is turning out to be it.

Part of O'Dea's new life is as a motivational speaker for the Congress of Canadian Student Associations to talk about his journey into the drug world.

At a Conference Centre in downtown Calgary, this is what he might say: "Good morning, I'm Brian O'Dea. For much of my life, if you'd asked me my name I would have told you something different. I'm going to teach you how to smuggle drugs. I ended up with way too much money and way too few brains, and way too big a coke habit . . . that's what cocaine is. It wants everything from you, and it takes it."

O'Dea was born in St. John's, Newfoundland, in 1948. When he was 11, his parents enrolled him in St. Bonaventure's school, a Roman Catholic institution run by the Christian Brothers. O'Dea says he endured two years of sexual abuse at the hands of a senior staff member there, a fact he kept to himself until he was 40. He downplays the impact, but admits it affected his sense of self-worth. He became a people-pleaser, often stealing from his parents to impress his friends.

By the time he reached his second year of university, in 1968, at St. Mary's in Halifax, O'Dea was using the tuition money his parents gave him to buy marijuana and hashish. Soon, he started dealing for most of his income. Within a couple of years, he was circumventing his expensive Toronto suppliers by taking buying trips to Britain. In 1972, when he mailed himself a half-kilogram of hash from England through the mail, Canada Customs intercepted the package and notified the RCMP. He received 18 months.

Eighteen hours after his release from prison, O'Dea booked a ticket to Bogotá, Colombia, and bought 55 grams of coke. That was the first of many trips to Colombia. But by the end of the 1970s, a string of failures had driven him to the brink of bankruptcy.

Then an old acquaintance came to him with news of an abandoned shipyard on Anacortes Island, near Seattle, that was an ideal landing spot for marijuana shipments. With William and Christopher Schaffer, two brothers from Los Angeles with legendary marijuana-growing connections, O'Dea undertook

what turned out to be a lucrative marijuana smuggling business.

O'Dea started by creating SeaCal Fisheries, an Alaska-based salmon-packing company, to land, vacuum-pack, and conceal the marijuana among its boxes of fresh fish. He hired five tractor-trailer units under the auspices of a friend's company to pick up the pot in Washington State and transport it to California. And to ensure that every state trooper and weigh-scale operator on US Interstate 5 should believe his company was legitimate, he set up a phantom roofing company to provide his trucks with cargo and waybills. For 12 months, one of his semis drove up and down the highway with the same load of cedar shingles, just to create cover.

The first load of dope arrived on Forrester Island, a speck of rock off southern Alaska, on Aug. 25, 1986, and made its way south without a hitch. According to prosecutors, the organization made more than $26-million from the deal. The second shipment ran into trouble. A disgruntled former group member had alerted the US Drug Enforcement Agency (DEA) to the group's plans. US authorities and RCMP were watching as the shipment arrived off Alaska with 42 tonnes of marijuana.

Although the DEA and RCMP continued to have O'Dea and his outfit under observation, they were not able to get concrete evidence. In 1989, however, the US Attorney's office in Seattle started squeezing confessions out of deckhands from O'Dea's boats, gradually working its way up the chain of command. "There was no way," says O'Dea, "they were going to walk away from $100-million worth of drugs."

By the time DEA officers arrived, in April 1990, to search his house, O'Dea was living in a spartan apartment, surviving on fruit juice and natural foods. He had sworn off drugs and alcohol and dedicated his life to good works. The turning point had come on the eve of his 40th birthday, he says, when he suffered a near-fatal drug overdose.

When he reflects on the changes in his life, he believes nothing he did was morally wrong. "I think the laws against marijuana are bad laws. So how do you change bad laws? Through Parliament? No way. Bad laws only get changed if somebody breaks them."

Source: Charlie Gillis, "You're Gonna Love This," *National Post,* December 8, 2001. Material reprinted with the express permission of "National Post Company," a CanWest partnership.

supported by income from conventional jobs. In contrast, stabilized users have learned the skills needed to purchase and process larger amounts of drugs. Their addiction enables them to maintain their normal lifestyles, although they may turn to drug dealing to create contacts with drug suppliers. Full-time working people involved in drugs actually commit more crime than those not in the labour force. Employment, then, does little to reduce their criminal activity.[123]

If stable users make a score through a successful drug deal, they may increase their drug use, destabilizing their lifestyle, destroying family and career ties. Addiction is not a unidimensional process. There are various stages in the career of a hard-drug user, and

criminal activity may vary according to the user's drug lifestyle. Perhaps crime is a "drug facilitator," enabling addicts to increase their drug consumption according to the success of their criminal careers.

Drugs and the Law

Both Canada and the United States initiated legal action to curtail the use of some drugs early in the twentieth century. Canada criminalized opium before 1910; in the United States, the 1914 *Harrison Narcotics Act* restricted the importation, manufacture, sale, and dispensing of narcotics. Marijuana was criminalized in Canada in 1923, and in the United States the *Marijuana Tax Act* of 1937 required registration and payment of a tax by all persons who imported, sold, or manufactured marijuana.

In later years, other federal laws were passed to clarify existing drug statutes and revise penalties. For example, psilocybin, a chemical component of some mushrooms, was criminalized before 1982 in Canada. This is a good example of the social constructionist position, in which the reaction defines the crime. Although no research has demonstrated a link between the consumption of psilocybin and the commission of crime, it is classified as a restricted drug under the *Food and Drug Act* (FDA). The FDA and the *Narcotic Control Act* (NCA) give the state wide-sweeping power to control the recreational use of drugs. For example, section 10 of the NCA gives the police the power to enter any place other than a house without a warrant if they believe narcotics are on the premises.

Sometimes police are accused of enforcing drug laws too zealously. In 1971 a Royal Commission was established in Vancouver under the *Public Inquiries Act* to inquire into the circumstances surrounding a police intervention at a marijuana "smoke-in." The inquiry established that the police officers had acted with unwarranted and excessive force when they charged a peaceful crowd by using horses and riot gear.[124]

Alcohol Abuse

Although drug control laws have been enacted on both the federal and the provincial or territorial levels, provincial and territorial legislatures have also acted to control alcohol-related crimes. One of the more serious problems is the alarming number of highway fatalities linked to drunk driving. Governments are beginning to create more

InfoTrac®

Treating alcohol abusers is a major social goal. To research current treatment programs, read these articles:

- Deborah Pappas, Chudley E. Werch, and Joan M. Carlson, "Recruitment and Retention in an Alcohol Prevention Program of Two Inner-City Middle Schools," *Journal of School Health* 68, no. 6 (1998): 231–237.
- John P. Allen, "Project MATCH: A Clarification," *Behavioral Health Management* 18, no. 4 (1998): 42–44.

This article looks at the relationship between illegal drug use and violent crime: Andrew J. Resignato, "Violent Crime: A Function of Drug Use or Drug Enforcement?" *Applied Economics* 32, no. 6 (2000): 681.

stringent penalties for drunk driving, for example, prohibiting the driving of cars after a criminal offence.

Mothers Against Drunk Driving, for example, wants to have the legal limit for blood alcohol reduced from .08 percent to .05 percent, and it is true that more people die as a result of impaired driving than are killed in homicides.

One caution in interpreting the success of drug control programs, such as those designed to control drunk driving, is that they are sensitive to levels of enforcement; if the number of roadside checks is reduced, the number of offences will appear to drop, although it might simply reflect the level of policing.

Connections

In Chapter 3 we talked about how crime rates can reflect changes in actual crimes, in levels of reporting by the public, and in reaction to policing activity.

Drug Control Strategies

Substance abuse remains a major social problem, and politicians looking for a campaign issue can call for a "war on drugs."[125] Yet can illegal drug use be eliminated or controlled?

Drug control strategies have varying degrees of success. Some aim at deterring drug use by stopping the flow of drugs into the country, apprehending and punishing dealers, and cracking down on street-level drug deals. Others focus on preventing drug use by educating potential users to the dangers of substance abuse ("just say no") and by organizing community groups to work with the at-risk population in their area. Still another approach is to treat known users so they can control their addictions.

Source Control

One approach to drug control is to apprehend large-volume drug dealers. Destroying overseas crops and arresting members of drug cartels in Central and South America, Asia, and the Middle East, where drugs are grown and manufactured, is known as source control. However, drug lords are able to fight back and will use violence and assassination to protect their interests. The United States invaded Panama with 20 000 troops in 1989 to stop its leader, General Manuel Noriega, from dealing cocaine and then tried to suppress evidence that the CIA had been involved in the cocaine smuggling.

However, *The Economist* says that "there is no sign that government intervention has cut supply, although it may sometimes divert it . . . instead the drug's purity seems to have increased."[126]

The amount of narcotics produced each year is so vast that even if three-quarters of the opium crop were destroyed, the Canadian market would still require only a small portion of the remainder to sustain its drug trade.[127] Drug users in North America and Europe are willing to pay more for drugs than are any other users in the world, so if the supply were reduced, whatever drugs existed would find their way to the country. One study of the impact of supply-side control of illicit drugs found that even after a massive heroin seizure, there was no effect on availability, use, or price. This is a significant finding, given that 93 percent of the $500 million spent on Canada's drug strategy is devoted to efforts to reduce that supply.[128]

Adding to control problems is the fact the drug trade is an important source of revenue for many countries, and destroying the drug trade would undermine the economies of some developing nations. People in Peru, Bolivia, Colombia, Burma, Thailand, and Laos are engaged in cultivating and processing drugs. Even if one nation cooperates in drug suppression, suppliers in other nations, eager to cash in on the seller's market, would be encouraged to turn more acreage over to coca or poppy production.

The difficulty of source control is illustrated by the pursuit, capture, and slaying in 1993, of billionaire drug lord Pablo Escobar. His Medellin drug cartel controlled more than 80 percent of the cocaine imported into North America. While he was in hiding, his drug empire had been replaced by that of his competitors, the Cali cartel. When the Colombian government put pressure on the drug cartels, even more powerful Mexican organizations emerged to take over the drug trade. In 1997 Mexico's government announced that it had arrested General Jesus Guttierrez Rebello, its top antinarcotics enforcer, for his suspected links to drug traffickers.[129]

Eradication efforts in one country may encourage crop development in another. For example, the Bolivian government's voluntary coca eradication program surpassed its annual target in 1996, kept cultivation levels from significantly expanding, and reduced potential coca leaf production by 12 percent. Unfortunately, this decline was more than offset by a 32 percent increase in both coca cultivation and production in Colombia, despite an aggressive aerial eradication program by authorities. Colombian coca cultivation has nearly tripled since 1987, and source control efforts have convinced the Colombian drug cartels of the importance of controlling all facets of cocaine production at home.[130]

The drug trade remains a dynamic force, with its wealth, power, and organization exceeding the resources of many governments. Hundreds of tonnes of cocaine flow to North America, Western Europe, Latin America, Asia, Africa, and the countries of the former Soviet Union. The lines between cocaine-consuming and heroin-consuming countries are blurring. Colombian cocaine syndicates have established distribution centres on virtually every continent, and recently, large Mexican drug organizations have gained control of much of the cocaine traffic formerly dominated by the Colombians.

Synthetic drugs have been gaining in popularity over the last decade. Methamphetamines (MDMA or "ecstasy") may be displacing cocaine as the stimulant of choice on the world drug market. Mexico is one of the principal suppliers, but there are centres of methamphetamine production in Poland, Japan, Burma, and the Philippines.

Law Enforcement Strategies

Law enforcement efforts to intercept drug supplies entering the country involve border patrols and military personnel using sophisticated hardware. However, homegrown marijuana and laboratory-made drugs, such as "ice," LSD, and PCP, could become the drugs of choice. Their easy availability and relatively low cost are increasing their popularity among the at-risk population.

Law enforcement agencies have tried to direct efforts at large-scale drug rings. However, the long-term consequence has been to decentralize drug dealing and encourage younger independent dealers to become major suppliers. Since it is difficult to infiltrate and prosecute drug-dealing gangs, some nontraditional groups have broken into the drug trade. For example, the Hells Angels motorcycle club has become one of the primary distributors of cocaine and amphetamines.[131] Police can also target, intimidate, and arrest street-level dealers and users in an effort to make drug use so much of a hassle that consumption is cut back and the crime rate reduced. Approaches that have been tried include "reverse stings" in which undercover agents pose as dealers to arrest users who approach them for a buy. Police have attacked fortified crack houses by using heavy equipment to breach their defences. Special police task forces have used undercover operations and drug sweeps to discourage both dealers and users.[132]

Police have also used "asset forfeiture" laws to seize the assets of known dealers. Under section 462.37 of the *Criminal Code*, property can be seized if it is believed to have been derived from the proceeds of crime. Because the wealth generated from drug sales can be so immense, it is necessary to make it seem legitimate. Buying real estate, investing in legitimate businesses, and transferring money internationally are all preferred methods of hiding illegally gained wealth. Such methods of concealing the proceeds of crime, called "money laundering," require sophisticated expertise.

Although street-level enforcement efforts have had success, drug cases have clogged courts and correctional facilities with petty offenders while proving a costly drain on police resources. There are also suspicions that a displacement effect occurs: Stepped-up efforts to curb drug dealing in one area or city simply encourage dealers to seek out friendlier "business" territory.[133] However, occasionally, law enforcement strategies do succeed: In the summer of 1998 the RCMP busted the Cuntrera-Caruana crime empire in Montreal. Described by some as the largest, most powerful drug-smuggling and money-laundering organization in the world, the Cuntrera-Caruanas acted as intermediaries between the Colombians and the Mafia.[134]

Community Strategies

Citizen-sponsored programs attempt to restore a sense of community in drug-infested areas, to reduce fear, and to promote conventional norms and values.[135] These efforts can be classified into one of four distinct categories.[136] The first involves law enforcement efforts, which may include block watches, cooperative police–community efforts, and citizen patrols. Some of these citizen groups are nonconfrontational, willing to simply observe or photograph dealers, take down their licence plate number, then notify police. On occasion, telephone hotlines have been set up to take anonymous tips on drug activity. Some of these community-based efforts are homegrown, while others attract outside organizations, such as the Guardian Angels. Area residents have gone as far as contracting with private security firms to conduct neighbourhood patrols.

Another tactic is to use the civil justice system to harass offenders. Landlords have been sued for owning properties that house drug dealers; neighbourhood groups have formed and have scrutinized drug houses for building code violations. Information acquired from these sources is turned over to police and housing agencies for more formal action.

In community-based treatment efforts, citizen volunteers participate in self-help support programs, such as Narcotics Anonymous or Cocaine Anonymous. Other programs provide youths with martial arts training, dances, and social events as an alternative to the drug life. Healing centres and treatment facilities, often organized around a theme, such as Native healing, also operate to counter the effects of drug abuse.

Community drug prevention efforts are designed to enhance the quality of life, improve interpersonal relationships, and upgrade the neighbourhood's physical environment. Activities might include the creation of drug-free school zones, demonstrations and marches to publicize the drug problem, and better police protection or tougher laws. Residents have cleaned up streets, fixed broken streetlights, and planted gardens in empty lots to broadcast the message that they have local pride and do not want drug dealers in their neighbourhood.

Community crime-prevention efforts seem appealing, but there is little conclusive evidence that they are an effective drug control strategy. Most residents do not participate in programs, and they tend to work best in stable, middle-income areas. Although these findings are discouraging, some studies have also found the opposite: that deteriorated areas can sustain successful antidrug programs.[137]

InfoTrac®

Drug Abuse Resistance Education (DARE) is an elementary-school course designed to give students the skills for resisting peer pressure to experiment with tobacco, drugs, and alcohol. To learn more about the research, read this article: "DARE: Doubtful after 10 Years," *Harvard Mental Health Letter* 17, no. 2 (2000). You can also read some of the criticisms: Terry O'Neill, "Redesigning DARE: But Promised Changes to the Popular Anti-Drug Abuse Program Will Not Silence Its Critics," *The Report Newsmagazine*, March 19, 2001.

Drug Testing Programs

Drug testing of private employees, government workers, and criminal offenders is believed to prevent people from involvement in substance abuse. Employees are tested to enhance on-the-job safety and productivity. In some industries, such as mining and transportation, drug testing is considered essential because abuse can pose a threat to the public. Mandatory drug testing programs in government and industry are common.

Drug testing is not without legal controversy, however. In 1991 the Canadian Civil Liberties Association filed a complaint with the Canadian Human Rights Commission over the Toronto-Dominion Bank's drug-testing policy. New bank employees were required to submit to a drug test within 48 hours of being offered a job; refusal to do so would be grounds for dismissal. A federal human rights tribunal ruled the bank's policy was intrusive and an invasion of privacy, and in 1998, the Canadian Federal Court of Appeal ruled that the bank's policy of testing new employees for drugs constituted a violation under the *Human Rights Act*. Key to the decision was that there was no demonstrable evidence that finding traces of drugs in a person's system meant that their performance on the job would be affected.[138]

In 1995 it was reported that doctors and nurses working in neonatal units of Toronto hospitals were surreptitiously testing infants' hair for traces of cocaine.

Acting on suspicion of mothers' drug use, staff sent samples to the Hospital for Sick Children for analysis, and positive results were sent to the Children's Aid Society. The director of the clinical pharmacology and toxicology program at the Hospital for Sick Children was quoted as saying that physicians had a right to know such information. The co-chairperson of the reproductive technology committee of the National Action Committee on the Status of Women criticized the practice as an invasion of the mother's privacy.[139]

InfoTrac®

Did you know that the state of New York is implementing sweeping new drug court reforms that will increase the number of nonviolent drug-addicted offenders who go into court-mandated substance abuse treatment? To learn more, go to InfoTrac® College Edition and read this article: "New York Drug Reforms Call for Drug Treatment, Not Incarceration," *Alcoholism & Drug Abuse Weekly* 12, no. 27 (2000): 1. Also see: Constance Weisner, Helen Matzger, Tammy Tam, and Laura Schmidt, "Who Goes to Drug and Alcohol Treatment? Understanding Drug Utilization within the Context of Insurance," *Journal of Studies on Alcohol* 63, no. 6 (2002): 673–683.

Legalization

Despite the massive effort to control drugs through prevention, deterrence, education, and treatment strategies, the fight against substance abuse has not proved successful. It is difficult to get people out of the drug culture because of the enormous profits involved in the drug trade: five hundred kilograms of coca leaves, worth $4000 to a grower, yield about eight kilograms of street cocaine, valued at about $300 000.

Considering these problems, some commentators have called for the legalization or decriminalization of restricted drugs. Legalization is warranted, according to Ethan Nadelmann, because the use of mood-altering substances is customary in almost all human societies.[140] Banning drugs serves to create networks of manufacturers and distributors, many of whom use violence as part of their standard operating procedures. Although some may charge that drug use is immoral, Nadelmann questions whether it is really any worse than the unrestricted use of alcohol and cigarettes, both

of which are addicting and unhealthful. Far more people die each year because they abuse these legal substances than are killed in drug wars or from abusing illegal substances.

Prohibition failed to stop the flow of alcohol in the 1920s while at the same time increasing the power of organized crime. When drugs were legal and freely available earlier in this century, the proportion of people using drugs was not much greater than today; most users managed to lead normal lives, probably because of the legal status of their drug use.[141]

If drugs were legalized, price and distribution could be controlled by government, reducing addicts' cash requirements, and bringing down crime rates as users would no longer need the same cash flow to support their habit. Drug-related deaths would decline because government control would reduce needle sharing and the spread of AIDS, and drugs would not be cut with other toxic substances. Legalization would also destroy the drug-importing cartels and gangs. Since drugs would be bought and sold openly, the government would get taxes on the sale of drugs and the income taxes paid by drug dealers on profits that have been part of the hidden economy. Of course, drug distribution would be regulated, like alcohol, keeping it out of the hands of adolescents, public servants, such as police and airline pilots, and known felons. Those who favour legalization point to the Netherlands as a country that has legalized drugs and remains relatively crime-free.[142]

However, if drugs were legalized and freely available, drug users might significantly increase their daily intake. In countries such as Iran and Thailand, where drugs are cheap and readily available, the rate of narcotics use is quite high. Historically, the availability of cheap narcotics has preceded drug use epidemics, as was the case when British and American merchants sold opium in nineteenth-century China.[143]

Efforts to control legal use would backfire. If juveniles, criminals, and members of other at-risk groups were forbidden to buy drugs, would not that create an underground market almost as vast as the current one? If the government tried to raise money by taxing legal drugs, as it now does for liquor and cigarettes, might that not encourage drug smuggling to avoid tax payments?

What effect would a policy of partial decriminalization (for example, legalizing small amounts of marijuana) have on drug use rates? Would a get-tough policy help "widen the net" of the justice system and actually deepen some youths' involvement in substance abuse? Can society provide alternatives to drugs that will reduce teenage drug dependency?[144]

The various efforts at drug control are summarized in Figure 14.2.

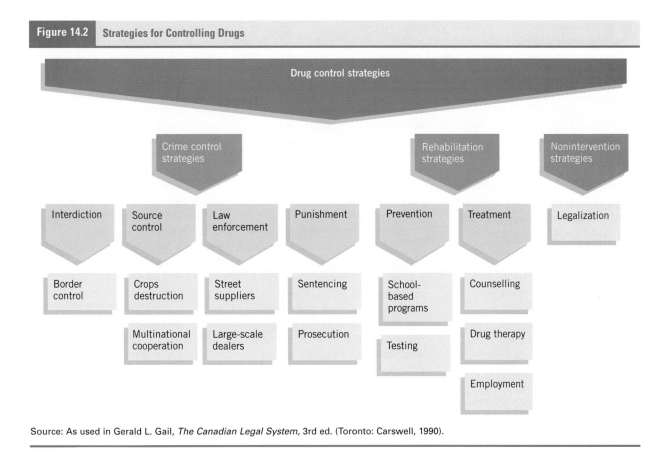

Figure 14.2   Strategies for Controlling Drugs

Source: As used in Gerald L. Gail, *The Canadian Legal System,* 3rd ed. (Toronto: Carswell, 1990).

Emerging Issues

A chapter on the legislation of morality would not be complete without looking at issues that have become the focus of debate in contemporary society. Euthanasia and gambling are two examples of such issues.

Euthanasia

Euthanasia tests the moral resolve of a society interested in protecting human rights while also respecting human dignity. There are two different types of euthanasia: passive and active; the difference is whether a patient is capable of making a decision to end his or her life. In Quebec in 1991, Nancy B petitioned the court to allow her doctor and the hospital to disconnect her life-support equipment. The judge said he had to respect the patient's right to choose to discontinue treatment and ruled that doing so would not make the physician guilty of euthanasia.[145] However, when Sue Rodriguez petitioned the Supreme Court of Canada in 1993 for the right to assisted suicide, her request was denied (see the Famous Canadian Court Case feature). In 1997 a Halifax doctor was charged with first-degree murder when she gave a patient suffering from terminal cancer an injection to ease his pain. Because this charge requires proof of premeditation, it was subsequently thrown out of court for lack of evidence.

Gambling

Gambling is a good example of decriminalization, in which the law gradually changes to allow a behaviour previously prohibited. A hundred years ago, gambling was illegal in Canada. In 1900 an exemption was granted for religious and charity bazaars to hold small raffles under $50. This charitable exemption opened the door for gambling in Canada. In 1910 an amendment was passed allowing pari-mutuel betting at fairs in order to encourage horse breeding, and in 1952 games of chance were allowed at agricultural fairs to promote the rural economy.

Lotteries were legalized in 1969, and a national lottery helped finance the 1976 Olympic games in Montreal. By 1985 exclusive control over lotteries had passed to the provinces and territories, regulated by provincial and territorial Crown monopolies, such as the Atlantic Lottery Commission, and revenues are used for the benefit of all citizens.

Famous Canadian Court Case

Sue Rodriguez

Until recently in Canadian society, suicide was more than taboo; it was a crime punishable by law. The state could charge, prosecute, and incarcerate individuals for trying to take their own life. Although attempted suicide was stricken from the *Criminal Code* in 1972, aiding and abetting suicide remains illegal. Assisted suicide is illegal under section 214(b) of the *Code* with punishment of up to 14 years in prison. Major debate exists on whether this legislation is unconstitutional. Sue Rodriguez's Supreme Court case challenged this prohibition, and although she may not have won her case, it helped fuel the debate.

Sue Rodriguez was diagnosed in 1992 with the debilitating terminal illness amyotrophic lateral sclerosis (ALS), also known as Lou Gehrig's disease. As her condition worsened and her life expectancy shortened to mere months, Rodriguez decided that she would prefer to take her own life, which is legally permitted in Canada. However, due to her disease she was unable to commit suicide without assistance. Rodriguez took her plight to the Supreme Court of Canada to challenge the law prohibiting assisted suicide on the grounds that it violated her constitutional rights.

Under section seven of the *Canadian Charter of Rights and Freedoms,* every person has the right to life, liberty, and security of the person. This right can only be deprived in accordance with fundamental justice. Rodriguez used this section of the *Charter* to frame her case, believing that she was being denied autonomy and personal liberty. She took her case to the Supreme Court, and twice it ruled that the deprivation of her rights was not violating fundamental justice. However, in her 1993 appearance, the ruling was split 5 to 4, perceived to be a major break in the battle for the decriminalization of assisted suicide. With their ruling, the Supreme Court justices urged Parliament to deal with this issue. Despite losing her case, Sue Rodriguez committed suicide in 1994 with the assistance of a doctor and parliamentarian Svend Robinson.

There has been a growing movement to change assisted suicide legislation since the 1970s. What has made the right-to-die debate so controversial is that it is charged with religious beliefs. Although religion has no place in the formation of legislation, pro-life groups have used the suggestion that suicide is morally wrong to sway Parliament. There is also the fear that assisted suicide will be abused by those taking care of the terminally ill. Conversely, pro-choice groups believe that individuals should be able to control the time and circumstances of their own deaths. Whatever the debate, assisted suicide remains illegal in Canada today. Sue Rodriguez's case, and her death, helped frame the debate.

Prepared by Sarah Gilliss.

Casinos came on the scene in the late 1980s and early 1990s. By 1995, Quebec, Ontario, and Manitoba had large casinos, while Alberta, British Columbia, Nova Scotia, and Saskatchewan allowed video lottery terminals. Provincial and territorial governments can realize huge profits from legalized gambling: The Windsor Casino in Ontario, for example, generated more than $200 million in profits in its first year, while Montreal's casino made more than $70 million in its first six months.[146]

Canadians spend hundreds of dollars per year per capita on gambling. People also tend to underreport the amount they spend on gambling because of the perceived stigma attached to it. In all provinces and territories, people spend the most on lotteries, followed by bingo, horseracing, and other forms of gaming.

In 1994, Statistics Canada estimated that gambling accounted for about 4 percent of total provincial and territorial revenue, millions more than gathered through corporate taxes.[147]

In 2002, revenues to government reached $11 billion, with a profit level more than three times the profit realized in 1992. Although the likelihood of gambling increases with income, the proportion spent decreases. On average Canadians spent $447 on gambling in 2001.[148]

Lotteries are regulated under section 207 of the *Criminal Code,* which gives provinces and territories the lawful right to "manage a lottery scheme," as shown in Exhibit 14.3. The *Criminal Code* also prohibits keeping a common gaming or betting house (section 201), betting or bookmaking (section 202), placing bets on behalf of others (section 203), promoting lotteries (section 206), and cheating at play (section 209), among others. A new concern is whether the law can adapt to handle the increasing interest in gambling on the Internet, where overhead costs are low and the potential for profits is high.

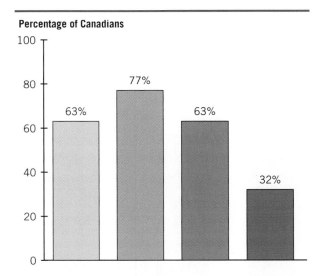

Percentage of Canadians

Attitudes on Gambling

- 63 percent of Canadians say it is their right to gamble regardless of the consequences.

- 77 percent say that government should do more to limit the negative effects of problem gambling.

- 63 percent of Canadians say that gambling is an acceptable activity.

- 32 percent say they know someone who is a problem gambler.

Source: J. Azmier, *Canadian Gambling Behaviour and Attitudes: Main Report* (Calgary: Canada West Foundation, 2001), Ontario Problem Gambling Research Centre, http://www.gamblingresearch.org/contentdetail.sz?cid=2388 (accessed May 2, 2005).

There is a lot of controversy over the link between gambling and crime. When the Nova Scotia government announced that it was going to open a casino in Halifax, there was widespread opposition on the part of the police, citizens' groups, and church groups. Three government commissions advised against it, and 40 000 people signed petitions in opposition. Police predicted an increase in prostitution, drug abuse, organized crime, and other spinoff crimes from gambling.[149] Such opposition is not unusual: for example, in Alberta, a series of plebiscites were held in 1998 on whether communities could prohibit VLTs; in British Columbia, citizens rejected a casino in 1994.

Research has shown that the social costs of gambling are high. Problem gamblers tend to have a high involvement in other drug and alcohol abuse and to have higher rates of suicide, more absenteeism from work, lower productivity, and higher rates of job loss due to gambling. Problem and pathological gamblers tend to turn to crime to support their habits, such as stealing from work and from friends and family. Although men are more likely to be problem gamblers than are women,

| Exhibit 14.3 | Quick Code: Permitted Lotteries |

207. (1) Notwithstanding any of the provisions of this Part relating to gaming and betting, it is lawful

(a) for the government of a province, either alone or in conjunction with the government of another province, to conduct and manage a lottery scheme in that province, or in that and the other province, in accordance with any law enacted by the legislature of that province;

(b) for a charitable or religious organization, pursuant to a licence issued by the Lieutenant Governor in Council of a province or by such other person or authority in the province as may be specified by the Lieutenant Governor in Council thereof, to conduct and manage a lottery scheme in that province if the proceeds from the lottery scheme are used for a charitable or religious object or purpose;

(c) for the board of a fair or of an exhibition, or an operator of a concession leased by that board, to conduct and manage a lottery scheme in a province where the Lieutenant Governor in Council of the province or such other person or authority in the province as may be specified by the Lieutenant Governor in Council thereof has

(i) designated that fair or exhibition as a fair or exhibition where a lottery scheme may be conducted and managed, and

(ii) issued a licence for the conduct and management of a lottery scheme to that board or operator;

(d) for any person, pursuant to a licence issued by the Lieutenant Governor in Council of a province or by such other person or authority in the province as may be specified by the Lieutenant Governor in Council thereof, to conduct and manage a lottery scheme at a public place of amusement in that province if

(i) the amount or value of each prize awarded does not exceed five hundred dollars, and

(ii) the money or other valuable consideration paid to secure a chance to win a prize does not exceed two dollars. . . .

women gamblers are more likely to be young, single, and unemployed and to have less than a high-school education. Women are "escape" gamblers, and men are "excitement" gamblers.

The amount spent on lottery tickets per household varies by social class (see Figure 14.3). In 1996, 52 percent of households with incomes under $20 000 bought lottery tickets compared with 77 percent of those with

Figure 14.3	Lottery Play Is Tied to Household Income

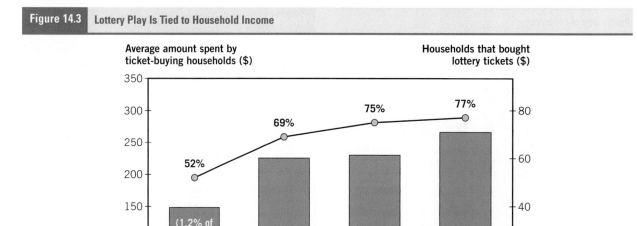

incomes over $60 000. However, low-income households spent 1.2 percent of their income on lotteries, compared with 0.3 percent for the highest income category. A survey of the Montreal casino found that the typical visitor was from Montreal (85 percent), had a high-school education (47 percent), and had a household income of less than $40 000 (48 percent).

Internet gambling is developing quickly and is now becoming a concern. By 2001, police had announced that one of Canada's largest organized crime families was operating an illegal online bookmaking ring that took in $200 million a year.

The Kahnawake Gaming Commission, established in 1996 in violation of provincial law, announced it was starting its 20th online casino five years later.

Cryptologic, the creator of encryption technology used in online gambling, announced in 2000 that registered users of its electronic payment system had reached 680 000. The company had processed more than U.S.$5 billion in transactions.[150]

Industry profiles suggest that the online gambler tends to be in the lowest income demographic, similar to other forms of gambling.

Summary

Public order crimes are acts considered illegal because they conflict with social policy, accepted moral rules, and public opinion. There is usually great debate over public order crimes. Some charge that they are not really crimes at all and that it is foolish to legislate morality. Others view such morally tinged acts as prostitution, gambling, and drug abuse as harmful and therefore subject to public control.

Prostitution is a sex-related public order crime that has been practised for thousands of years. There are several kinds of prostitutes, including streetwalkers, B-girls, and call girls. Prostitutes often come from poor, troubled families and have abusive parents. However, there is little evidence that prostitutes are emotionally disturbed, addicted to drugs, or sexually abnormal. Although the exchange of money for sex, and sex for money is legal, society and its law enforcement agents make it virtually impossible to practise.

Pornography involves the sale of sexually explicit material intended to sexually excite paying customers. The depiction of sex and nudity is not illegal, but it does violate the law when it is judged obscene. Obscenity is a legal term defined as material offensive to community standards. Thus, each local jurisdiction must decide what pornographic material is obscene. A growing problem is the exploitation of children in obscene materials. There is no hard evidence that pornography is related to crime or aggression, but data suggest that sexual material with a violent theme is related to sexual violence by those who view it.

Substance abuse is another type of public order crime. Debate continues over the legalization of drugs, usually centring on such nonaddicting drugs as marijuana. However, the federal government outlaws a wide variety of drugs, including narcotics, amphetamines, barbiturates, cocaine, hallucinogens, and marijuana. One of the main reasons for the continued ban on drugs is their relationship to crime. Numerous studies have found that drug addicts commit enormous amounts of property crime.

Alcohol is another commonly abused substance. Although it is legal to possess, it too has been linked to crime. Drunk driving and deaths caused by drunk drivers are growing national problems. Many strategies are used to control substance abuse, ranging from source control to treatment. So far, no single method seems effective. Although legalization is debated, the facts that so many people already take drugs and that drug abuse is associated with crime make legalization unlikely in the near future.

Gambling is one of the more interesting "victimless crimes" discussed in this chapter because it illustrates the process of decriminalization. As governments increasingly come to depend on income from gaming revenues, it will become an expanding province- or territory-run business.

Thinking Like a Criminologist

According to data from a 1997 national school survey, high school boys who have been physically or sexually abused are at least twice as likely as nonabused boys are to drink, smoke, or use drugs. The survey was an in-class questionnaire completed by 3162 boys in grades 5 to 12 at a nationally representative sample of 265 public, private, and parochial schools from December 1996 to June 1997. The survey included roughly equal samples of adolescent boys in grades 5 to 8 and 9 to 12. All responses were weighted to reflect grade, region, race and ethnicity, and gender.

Thirteen percent of boys in grades 9 to 12 said that they had been physically or sexually abused. Thirty percent of abused boys reported that they drank frequently, and 34 percent reported that they had used drugs in the past month, compared with 16 percent and 15 percent, respectively, of nonabused boys. Abused boys were also nearly three times more likely to smoke frequently (27 percent versus 10 percent).

As a criminologist, what would be your interpretation of these data? What is the association between child abuse and substance abuse?

Key Terms

brothels	madams	pornography
call girls	massage parlours	prostitution
claimsmakers	moral crusades	public order crimes
crack cocaine	moral entrepreneurs	temperance movement
decriminalization	obscenity	victimless crimes
designer drugs	paraphilia	vigilante

Critical Thinking Questions

1. Alcohol is highly related to violence, while marijuana is not. Under what circumstances, if any, might the legalization or decriminalization of drugs be beneficial to society?

2. Do TV shows and films glorify drug usage and encourage youths to enter the drug trade? Should all images on TV of drugs and alcohol be banned?

3. Is prostitution really a crime? Should a man or woman have the right to sell and buy sexual favours if they so choose?

4. Do you believe there should be greater controls placed on the

distribution of sexually explicit material on the Internet? Would you approve of the online sale of sexually explicit photos of children if they were artificial images created by computer animation?

5. Are there objective standards of morality? Does the existing *Criminal Code* reflect contemporary national moral standards? Or are laws banning sexual behaviours and substance abuse the product of a relatively few "moral entrepreneurs" who seek to control other people's behaviours?

6. Some researchers conclude that if pornography consumption per se is not a cause of aggression toward women, it may still be a contributing factor. Is it possible that sexually aggressive men are drawn to the images in pornography because it reinforces their preexisting hostile orientation to sexuality?

7. The findings suggest the need for increased research attention on the use and impact of pornography in men at elevated risk for sexual aggression. Given the potential for problems, should Internet pornography be strictly controlled or banned until conclusive research is conducted?

 See the book-specific website at http://www.siegelcriminology3e.nelson.com for additional chapter links, discussions, and quizzes.

Glossary

acquaintance-related crime Similar to intimate violence, in some crimes there is a prior relationship between the offender and the victim; date rape is such a crime.

active precipitation The view that the source of many criminal incidents is the aggressive or provocative behaviour of victims.

actus reus An illegal act. The *actus reus* can be an affirmative act, such as taking money or shooting someone, or a failure to act, such as failing to take proper precautions while driving a car.

adolescent-limited In the life-course view of crime, this refers to the fact that the prevalence and frequency of antisocial behaviour for most offenders peak in adolescence and then diminish.

aggravating factor Some circumstances make the crime seem more serious in the eyes of others; in hate crime, for example, racism makes an assault a more serious offence and can result in a harsher sentence.

aging out The process by which individuals reduce the frequency of their offending behaviour as they age. It is also known as spontaneous remission, because people are believed to spontaneously reduce the rate of their criminal behaviour as they mature. Aging out is thought to occur among all groups of offenders.

alien conspiracy theory The view that organized crime was imported from Europe and that crime cartels have a policy of restricting their membership to people of their own ethnic background.

androgens Male sex hormones, linked to criminality.

anomie A condition produced by normlessness. Because of rapidly shifting moral values, the individual has few guides to what is socially acceptable. According to Merton, anomie is a condition that occurs when personal goals cannot be achieved by available means.

antisocial personality Synonymous with psychopath, the antisocial personality is characterized by a lack of normal responses to life situations, the inability to learn from punishment, and violent reactions to nonthreatening events.

arbitrage The practice of buying large blocks of stock in companies that are believed to be the target of corporate buyouts or takeovers.

arousal theory A view of crime suggesting that people who have a high arousal level seek powerful stimuli in their environment to maintain an optimal level of arousal. These stimuli are often associated with violence and aggression. Sociopaths may need greater than average stimulation to bring them up to comfortable levels of living; this need explains their criminal tendencies.

arson The intentional or negligent burning of a home, structure, or vehicle for criminal purposes such as profit, revenge, insurance fraud, or crime concealment; different from the traditional stereotype of the pyromaniac.

assisted suicide The practice of seeking help in committing suicide; not legal in Canada.

atavistic traits or anomalies According to Lombroso, the physical characteristics of born criminals that indicate they are throwbacks to animals or primitive people.

at-risk In Oscar Lewis's work, Lewis argued that the lifestyle of slum areas produces a "culture of poverty" passed from one generation to the next, marked by apathy, cynicism, helplessness, and mistrust of social institutions, making each generation more prone to criminality.

attention deficit/hyperactivity disorder (AD/HD) A condition in which a child shows a developmentally inappropriate lack of attention, impulsivity, and hyperactivity.

attrition This refers to the "wearing away" of or decrease in cases as they make their way through the criminal justice system; the number of cases investigated by the police that ever result in convictions is a small percentage of the total. Also called crime funnel.

authority conflict pathway The path to a criminal career that begins with early stubborn behaviour and defiance of parents.

behaviour modelling The belief that in modern society, aggressive acts are usually modelled after three principal sources: family members, environmental experiences, and the mass media.

behaviour theory The approach that holds the view that human actions are developed through a variety of learning experiences over the course of a lifetime.

blameworthy The amount of culpability or guilt a person maintains for participating in a particular criminal offence.

booster A professional shoplifter; see *heel*.

bourgeoisie In Marxist theory, the owners of the means of production; the capitalist ruling class.

break and enter Breaking into a house to commit theft.

brothel A house of prostitution, typically run by a madam who sets prices and handles "business" arrangements.

brutalization effect The belief that capital punishment creates an atmosphere of brutality that enhances rather than deters the level of violence in society. The death penalty reinforces the view that violence is an appropriate response to provocation.

brutalization process According to Athens, the first stage in a violent career during which parents victimize children, causing them to develop a belligerent, angry demeanour.

burglary Breaking into and entering a home or structure for the purposes of committing a felony.

call girls Prostitutes who make dates via the phone and then service customers in hotel rooms or apartments. Call girls typically have a steady clientele that is made up of repeat customers.

capable guardians In routine activities theory, the presence of police, homeowners, neighbours, friends, and relatives can have a deterrent effect on crime; these are the "capable guardians."

career criminal A person whose criminality is like a career and who repeatedly violates the law. They devote many aspects of their life to criminality and commit a large portion of the total amount of crime in a community.

carjacking A new form of crime, where a car is stolen while the person is driving it; it has a low likelihood of occurring but a high news value.

Chicago School A type of sociological research begun in the early twentieth century by Robert Ezra Park, Ernest W. Burgess, Louis Wirth, and their colleagues in the Sociology Department at the University of Chicago. These sociologists pioneered research on the social ecology of the city and the study of urban crime. The Canadian counterpart was called the McGill School, under the direction of Charles Dawson, a former Baptist minister.

child abuse Any physical, emotional, or sexual trauma to a child for which no reasonable explanation, such as an accident, can be found. Child abuse can also be a function of neglecting to give proper care and attention to a young child.

chivalry hypothesis The idea that low female crime and delinquency rates are a reflection of the leniency with which police treat female offenders.

choice theory The school of thought holding that people will engage in delinquent and criminal behaviour after weighing the consequences and benefits of their actions. Delinquent behaviour is a rational choice made by a motivated offender who perceives that the chances of gain outweigh any perceived punishment or loss.

chronic offender According to Wolfgang, the small percentage of delinquent offenders who are arrested five or more times before they are 18, and who stand a good chance of becoming adult criminals; such offenders are responsible for more than half of all serious crimes.

churning A white-collar crime in which a stockbroker makes repeated trades to fraudulently increase his or her commissions.

claimsmakers An important concept in media analysis, where it is assumed that there are people located to significantly influence the social construction of crime images.

classical criminology The theoretical perspective suggesting that (1) people have free will to choose criminal or conventional behaviours; (2) people choose to commit crime for reasons of greed or personal need; and (3) crime can be controlled only by the fear of criminal sanctions.

cleared Crimes that are determined to be founded, which are then solved or cleared away by the police.

Code of Hammurabi The first written criminal code developed in Babylonia about 2000 B.C.E.

cognitive school (perspective) A theory that studies the perception of reality and of the mental processes required to understand the world we live in.

cohort A sample of subjects whose behaviour is followed over a period.

commitment to conformity In control theory, this is a logical reason to obey the rules of society.

common law Early English law, developed by judges, that incorporated Anglo-Saxon tribal custom, feudal rules and practices, and the everyday rules of behaviour of local villages. Common law became the standardized law of the land in England and eventually formed the basis of the criminal law in Canada and the United States.

community notification Recent legislative efforts that require convicted sex offenders to register with local police when they move into an area or neighbourhood.

compliance A white-collar enforcement strategy that encourages law-abiding behaviour through both the threat of economic sanctions and the promise of rewards for conformity.

concentration effect This occurs when working- and middle-class families flee inner-city poverty areas, taking with them their financial and institutional resources and support elements, leaving the most disadvantaged population consolidated in urban ghettos.

conduct norms Behaviours expected of social group members. If group norms conflict with those of the general culture, members of the group may find themselves described as outcasts or criminals.

confidence games A form of fraud.

conflict related An approach that holds the view that human behaviour is shaped by socioeconomic inequality and that those who maintain social power will use it to further their own needs.

conflict-related crime or violence An example of this type of crime would be murder, which is often an expressive crime of passion involving people who know each other and who may be under the influence of drugs or suffering from the burdens of poverty. These factors may either prevent or inhibit rational evaluation of the long-term consequences of an immediate violent act.

consent The lack of which is a legal element in the charge of sexual assault; cannot be extinguished by drunkenness.

constructive intent The finding of criminal liability for an unintentional act that is the result of negligence or recklessness.

constructive possession In the crime of larceny, willingly giving up temporary physical possession of property but retaining legal ownership.

containments According to Reckless, internal and external factors and conditions that help insulate youths from delinquency-promoting situations. Most important of the internal containments is a strong self-concept, while external containments include positive support from parents and teachers.

continuity of crime The view that crime begins early in life and continues throughout the life course. Thus, the best predictor of future criminality is past criminality.

control theory An approach that looks at the ability of society and its institutions to control, manage, restrain, or direct human behaviour, sometimes called social control theory.

corporate crime White-collar crime involving a legal violation by a corporate entity, such as price fixing, restraint of trade, or hazardous waste dumping. It can also include large corporations and their efforts to control the marketplace and earn huge profits through unlawful bidding, unfair advertising, monopolistic practices, or other illegal means.

corroboration Before 1983 it was required that someone alleging sexual assault have someone corroborate, or back up, their claim; no longer required.

covert pathway A path to a criminal career that begins with minor underhanded behaviour and progresses to firestarting and theft.

crack cocaine A smokeable form of purified cocaine that provides an immediate and powerful high.

crackdown The concentration of police resources on a particular problem area, such as street-level drug dealing, to eradicate or displace criminal activity.

crime displacement An effect of crime prevention efforts in which efforts to control crime in one area shift illegal activities to another.

crime funnel As cases move further into the justice system, the number of cases being dealt with gradually drops. Also called attrition.

crime rate This number is derived by calculating the ratio of crimes in the whole population; usually expressed as per 100 000 people, it gives the criminologist a sense of the relative likelihood of crime occurring.

crime-related violence When the violence is committed during the course of another crime, usually between strangers; see *conflict-linked crime or violence.*

criminal anthropology Early efforts to discover a biological basis of crime through measurement of physical and mental processes; associated with Cesare Lombroso and the biological positivists.

criminal justice system The complete institutional process of decision-making from the initial investigation or arrest by police to the eventual release of the offender and his or her reentry into society; the various sequential criminal justice stages through which the offender passes: police, courts, corrections.

criminological enterprise This refers to the totality of criminology, even though there are many fields or subareas of study.

criminologist One who brings objectivity and method to the study of crime and its consequences; also see *criminology.*

criminology The scientific study of the nature, extent, cause, and control of criminal behaviour.

crisis intervention A form of program provided to victims of crime, many of whom are feeling isolated, vulnerable, and in need of immediate services; might involve counselling.

cross-sectional research Surveys that use data that derive from all age, race, gender, and income segments of the population being measured simultaneously. Since people from every age group are represented, age-specific crime rates can be determined. Proponents believe that this is a sufficient substitute for the more expensive longitudinal approach that follows a group of subjects over time to measure crime rate changes.

cult killings When members of religious cults, some of which are devoted to devil worship, are ordered to kill as part of the cult's rituals; examples might include Jonestown, Guyana, or the Solar Temple cult.

cultural deviance theory This is a variation of structural theory that combines elements of both strain and social disorganization. According to this view, because of strain and social isolation, unique lower-class subcultures develop in disorganized neighbourhoods that maintain a set of values and beliefs that are in conflict with conventional social norms. Criminal behaviour is an expression of conformity to lower-class subcultural values.

cultural transmission The concept that conduct norms are passed down from one generation to the next so that they become stable within the boundaries of a culture. Cultural transmission guarantees that group lifestyle and behaviour are stable and predictable.

culture conflict According to Sellin, a condition brought about when the rules and norms of an individual's subcultural affiliation conflict with the role demands of conventional society.

culture of poverty The view that people in the lower class of society form a separate culture with its own values and norms that are in conflict with conventional society; the culture is self-maintaining and ongoing.

cybercrime Using computer technology for illicit gain, such as fraud, and for moral crimes, such as child pornography and stalking.

cycle of violence Research in this area describes a phenomenon of child victims becoming adult criminals later in life due to their early experiences.

dangerous classes An idea in conflict theory that personal characteristics (single, young, urban, male) linked to the so-called dangerous classes can result in harsher treatment in the criminal justice system.

date rape A form of sexual assault that occurs between acquaintances; it has the lowest level of reporting.

deconstructionism A modern approach that focuses on the critical analysis of communication and language in legal codes. Rules and regulations are analyzed to determine whether they contain language and content that forces racism or sexism to become institutionalized.

decriminalization Reducing the penalty for a criminal act but not actually legalizing it.

defensible space The principle that crime prevention can be achieved through modifying the physical environment to reduce the opportunity individuals have to commit crime.

definition-sensitive crimes This is a category of crimes that are sensitive to legislative activity; gambling, for example, has steadily been decriminalized in the twentieth century by a loosening of criminal sanctions around gaming.

degradation This form of shaming is an ongoing process in which the offender is branded as an evil person and cast out of society. This is a practice of exclusion that is very ritualistic and can occur at a school disciplinary hearing or a criminal court trial.

designer drugs Chemical substances made and distributed in relatively small batches that induce mood-altering effects.

desistance phenomenon The process in which crime rate declines with the perpetrator's age; synonymous with the aging-out process.

deterrence The act of preventing crime before it occurs by means of the threat of criminal sanctions. Deterrence involves the perception that the pain of apprehension and punishment outweighs any chances of criminal gain or profit.

developmental criminology A branch of criminology that examines change in a criminal career over the life course. Developmental factors include biological, social, and psychological change. Among the topics of developmental criminology are desistance, resistance, escalation, and specialization.

deviant behaviour Behaviour that departs from the social norm.

deviant place hypothesis Otherwise known as the proximity hypothesis, a theory that suggests there are natural areas for crime, which are poor, densely populated, highly transient neighbourhoods in which commercial and residential property exist side by side.

differential association (DA) theory According to Sutherland, the principle that criminal acts are related to a person's exposure to an excess amount of antisocial attitudes and values.

differential opportunity The idea that those who see themselves as failures within conventional society and who feel that there is little hope for advancement by legitimate means may join with like-minded peers to form a gang. This association provides the opportunity and socialization requisite to committing crime.

differential reinforcement (DR) theory In social learning theory, the attempt to explain crime as a type of learned behaviour, combining a focus on differential association with elements of psychological learning.

diffusion of benefits An effect that occurs when an effort to control one type of crime has the unexpected benefit of reducing the incidence of another.

disclosure A principle established in *R. v. Stinchcombe* (1991), which ruled that the prosecution must give all the evidence gathered by the police to the defendant in order to make a complete defence to the charges.

discouragement An effect that occurs when an effort made to eliminate one type of crime also controls others because it reduces the value of criminal activity by limiting access to desirable targets.

displacement Heavy law enforcement in one area, for example, might only serve to drive crime to another, less well-enforced area, thus making it ineffective overall as a policing strategy; however, politically, sometimes people just don't want crime in their neighbourhood.

dramatization of evil In Tannenbaum's pioneering study of labelling, this refers to the process where the reaction to deviance sets up a feedback effect that the individual internalizes.

drift According to Matza, the view that youths move in and out of delinquency and that their lifestyles can embrace both conventional and deviant values.

duress This is one of the grounds that excuse an accused from responsibility from an act, if it can be shown that they were forced or compelled by someone else to commit a criminal act.

early onset A term that refers to the assumption that a criminal career begins early in life and that people who are deviant at a very young age are the ones most likely to persist in crime.

economic crime An act in violation of the criminal law that is designed to bring financial gain to the offender.

egalitarian Where there is an equal sharing of authority and power, for example, between the two partners in a family.

electroencephalograph (EEG) A device that can record the electronic impulses given off by the brain, commonly called brain waves.

embezzlement A type of larceny that involves taking the possessions of another (fraudulent conversion) that have been placed in the thief's lawful possession for safekeeping, such as a bank teller misappropriating deposits or a stockbroker making off with a customer's account.

enterprise crimes Crimes of opportunity for financial gain that involve breaking regulatory rules but not personal victimization.

entrapment A criminal defence maintaining that the police originated the criminal idea or initiated the criminal action.

equipotentiality View that all individuals are equal at birth and are thereafter influenced by their environment.

equivalent group hypothesis The lifestyle view that victims and criminals share similar characteristics because they are not actually separate groups and that in fact a criminal lifestyle exposes people to increased levels of victimization risk.

eros Freud maintained that humans have two opposing instinctual drives that interact to control behaviour: *eros*, the life instinct, which drives people to self-fulfillment and enjoyment, and *thanatos*, the death instinct, which produces self-destruction.

expressive crimes Crimes that have no purpose except to accomplish the behaviour at hand, such as shooting someone.

expressive violence Violence that is designed not for profit but to vent anger or frustration.

extinction The phenomenon in which a crime prevention effort has an immediate impact that dissipates as criminals adjust to new conditions.

false pretences Illegally obtaining money, goods, or merchandise from another by fraud or misrepresentation.

fence A buyer and seller of stolen merchandise.

flash houses In the eighteenth century, skilled thieves and pickpockets congregated in public meeting places, often taverns, that served as headquarters for gangs.

focal concerns According to Miller, the value orientations of lower-class cultures; features include the needs for excitement, trouble, smartness, fate, and personal autonomy.

folkways Generally followed customs that do not have moral values attached to them, such as not interrupting people when they are speaking.

founded This is the percentage of crimes reported to the police that they believe to be real; otherwise known as actual.

fraud Taking the possessions of another through deception or cheating, such as selling a person a desk that is represented as an antique but is known to be a copy.

gang killings For example, when teenage gangs make violence part of their group activity, engaging in warfare over territory or control of the drug trade.

gendered violence The concept that some forms of violence tend to be committed against women, by men, e.g., sexual assault.

general deterrence A crime control policy that depends on the fear of criminal penalties. General deterrence measures, such as long prison sentences for violent crimes, are aimed at convincing the potential law violator that the pains associated with crime outweigh its benefits.

general strain theory (GST) A micro-level, or individual, analysis of the effects of strain and how individuals who feel stress and strain are more likely to commit crimes.

general theory of crime (GTC) In Gottfredson and Hirschi's GTC model, the earlier elements of social control theory are integrated with the concepts of biosocial, psychological, routine activities, and rational choice theories.

genocide An extreme form of state-sponsored terrorism when a government seeks to wipe out a minority group within the jurisdiction it controls.

heel A professional shoplifter; see *booster*.

hypoglycemia Some trait theorists believe that biochemical conditions, including both those that are genetically predetermined and those acquired through diet and environment, control and influence antisocial behaviour; in this case, criminality is influenced by a deficiency of sugar.

identity crisis A psychological state, identified by Erikson, in which youths face inner turmoil and uncertainty about life roles.

inchoate crimes Incomplete or contemplated crimes such as solicitation or criminal attempts.

incidence The number of crimes reported to the police in a given time period.

incident-based data Compared to the aggregate (UCR) crime information, since 1988 incident-based data give the criminologist a more complete picture of such factors as the relationship between the offender and the victim, location, and the level of violence used.

income inequality The basic principle that differences in personal income create structural inequalities in society that might be at the root of crime.

indictable offence A serious offence that carries a serious penalty, as compared to a summary offence.

inferiority complex A term used to describe people who compensate for feelings of inferiority with a drive for superiority; controlling others may help reduce personal inadequacies.

informal sanctions These may have a greater crime-reducing impact than the fear of formal legal punishments and occur when significant others, such as parents, peers, neighbours, and teachers, direct their disapproval, anger, and indignation toward an offender. This is a form of public humiliation.

insider trading Illegal buying of stock in a company based on information provided by someone who has a fiduciary interest in the company, such as an employee or an attorney or accountant retained by the firm.

instincts The view held by biosocial theorists is that learning is influenced by instinctual drives.

instrumental crimes Those unable to obtain desired goods and services through conventional means may resort to theft and other illegal activities, such as the sale of narcotics, to obtain them.

instrumental violence Violence designed to improve the financial or social position of the criminal.

integrated structural Marxist theory In this approach, it is felt that a crime control policy cannot be formulated without regard for its root causes. Coercive punishments or misguided treatments cannot be effective unless the core relationships of material production are changed.

interactional theory The idea that interaction with institutions and events during the life course determines criminal behaviour patterns; criminogenic influences evolve over time.

intimate violence A form of violent behaviour that occurs in a context of familiarity, such as wife abuse or child abuse.

just desert The philosophy of justice that asserts that those who violate the rights of others deserve to be punished. The severity of punishment should be commensurate with the seriousness of the crime.

labelling theory Theory that views society as creating deviance through a system of social control agencies that designate certain individuals as deviants. The stigmatized individual is made to feel unwanted in the normal social order. Eventually, the individual begins to believe that the label is accurate, assumes it as a personal identity, and enters into a deviant or criminal career.

larceny Usually known as theft, the taking of property unlawfully is one of the oldest common law crimes.

latent delinquency The idea that there must be a mental predisposition that prepares youths psychologically for antisocial acts.

latent trait A stable feature, characteristic, property, or condition, present at birth or soon after, that makes some people crime-prone over the life course.

left realism A branch of conflict theory that holds that crime is a real social problem experienced by the lower classes and that lower-class concerns about crime must be addressed by criminologists.

lex talionis Punishment based on physical retaliation ("an eye for an eye").

liberal feminist theory This is an approach that focuses attention on the social and economic role of women in society and its relationship to female crime rates.

life-course theory An approach that looks at the study of changes in criminal offending patterns over a person's entire life. Are there conditions or events that occur later in life that influence the way people behave or is behaviour predetermined by social or personal conditions at birth?

lifestyle In some theories, the lifestyle of the victim is seen as an important factor in the likelihood of a crime being committed against them. An example might be the number of times they go out per month or the people they hang around with.

longitudinal (cohort) research Research that tracks the development of a group of subjects over time.

M'Naghten rule In 1843 an English court established that Daniel M'Naghten could not be held responsible in a case of murder because his delusions had caused him to act. This underlies the principle of criminal responsibility, that an accused cannot be held legally liable for his or her act if he or she does not know what he or she is doing or cannot distinguish right from wrong.

macro perspective A large-scale view of a situation or event takes into account contextual, social, and economic reasons, for example, to explain the phenomenon. This is relevant to such theories as Marxism and functionalism.

madam The traditional name for a woman who ran a brothel; more common today is the male pimp.

mala in se Crimes that are rooted in the core values inherent in our culture.

mala prohibitum Crimes that involve violations of laws that reflect current public opinion and social values.

marginalization When people are forced outside the economic mainstream, a larger portion of the population is forced to live in areas more conducive to crime. Once this happens, commitment to the system declines, producing another criminogenic force: a weakened bond to society.

marital exemption The practice in some places of prohibiting the prosecution of husbands for the rape of their wives.

Marxist feminists In this approach, gender inequality stems from the unequal power of men and women in a capitalist society, and gender inequality is a function of the exploitation of females by fathers and husbands. The origin of gender differences can be traced to the development of private property and male domination over the laws of inheritance. Marxist feminists link criminal behaviour patterns to the gender conflict created by the economic and social struggles common in postindustrial societies.

masculinity hypothesis The view that women who commit crimes have biological and psychological traits similar to those of men.

mass murderer One who kills a large number of people in a single incident.

massage parlours The more hidden side of prostitution includes seemingly legitimate businesses where men can buy sex under the guise of massage therapy.

media-sensitive crimes This is a category of crimes that is sensitive to manipulation by the media; serial homicide, for example, is relatively rare, but gets incredible exposure in the media and thus increases public fear.

mens rea The intent to commit the criminal act.

mental disorder A "disease of the mind" as determined by a trial judge. It includes an illness, disorder, or abnormal condition that impairs the functioning of the mind, excluding self-induced states caused by alcohol or drugs and transitory mental states, such as hysteria and concussion.

micro perspective A small-scale view of events, looking at interaction to explain how and why things happen.

minimal brain dysfunction (MBD) MBD is related to an abnormality in cerebral structure, an abruptly appearing maladaptive behaviour that interrupts the lifestyle and life flow of an individual linked to serious antisocial acts, an imbalance in the urge-control mechanisms of the brain, and chemical abnormality.

mitigating factor Unlike an aggravating factor, this serves to make the crime appear less serious to other people; for example, it is now widely accepted that abused people might react more extremely than other people when threatened, based on the perception that their lives are at risk. These classes of circumstances might serve to make the sentence lighter, or might serve as an entire defence.

moral crusades Efforts by interest-group members to stamp out behaviour they find objectionable. Typically, moral crusades are directed at public order crimes, such as drug use or pornography.

moral entrepreneurs Interest groups that attempt to control social life and the legal order in order to promote their own personal set of moral values.

mores Customs or conventions regarded as essential to a community, which are often at the basis of criminal law.

Mosaic Code By tradition, the covenant between God and the tribes of Israel in which they agreed to obey his law, as presented to them by Moses, in return for God's special care and protection.

motivated criminals or offenders The potential offenders in a population. According to rational choice theory, crime rates will vary according to the number of motivated offenders.

multifactor theories The attempt to integrate individual factors and independent concepts into complex, coherent explanations of criminality.

murder Colloquially refers to the killing of one person by another; homicide is separated into the categories of first- and second-degree murder, manslaughter, and infanticide.

natural areas Pioneering research in sociology conducted at the Chicago School and the McGill School looked at the social ecology of the city and how social forces operating in urban areas create criminal interactions resulting in some neighbourhoods becoming natural areas for crime.

negative affective states According to Agnew, the anger, depression, disappointment, fear, and other adverse emotions that derive from strain.

neurophysiology The study of brain activity that looks at neurological and physical abnormalities acquired during the fetal or perinatal stage, which is thought to control behaviour.

neurosis A syndrome in psychodynamic theory that posits that people suffer when they experience feelings of mental anguish and are afraid they are losing control of their personalities.

neuroticism A personality trait marked by unfounded anxiety, tension, and emotional instability.

neutralization theory Neutralization theory looks at the ability to overcome social norms and controls. This approach holds that offenders adhere to conventional values while drifting into periods of illegal behaviour by neutralizing legal and moral values.

norm resistance In a branch of conflict theory, this refers to how interaction between authorities and subjects eventually produces open conflict between the two groups.

oath-helpers During the Middle Ages, groups of 12 to 25 people who would support the accused's innocence.

obscenity According to current legal theory, sexually explicit material that lacks a serious purpose and appeals solely to the prurient interest of the viewer. While nudity per se is not usually considered obscene, open sexual behaviour, masturbation, and exhibition of the genitals is banned in most communities.

occasional criminal Unlike the professional criminal, does not derive a significant income from crime.

occupational crime Crime committed by employees for personal gain using the structural advantage provided by their employment.

offence-specific crime Offenders will react selectively to the characteristics of particular offences. This is particularly relevant to routine activities theory, where there is an assessment of opportunity, guardianship, and so on.

offender-specific crime Refers to the fact that offenders do not usually engage in random acts of antisocial behaviour.

organized crime Crime committed by a gang, e.g., drug trafficking.

overt pathway In the study of the course of criminal careers, this refers to the escalation of aggressive acts beginning with aggression (annoying others, bullying) leading to physical (and gang) fighting and on to violence (attacking someone, strong-arming, forced theft).

paraphilias Bizarre or abnormal sexual practices that may involve recurrent sexual urges focused on objects, humiliation, or children.

passive precipitation The view that some people become victims because of personal and social characteristics that make them "attractive" targets for predatory criminals.

paternalistic The way in which leaders in government or organizations are seen as father figures and others are treated as "children."

peacemaking A branch of conflict theory that stresses humanism, mediation, and conflict resolution as a means to end crime.

percentage change Calculating the increase or decrease in crime rates over a period of years, for example, can tell the criminologist whether society is becoming more dangerous.

perceptual deterrence The perceived risk of being caught or the threat of severe punishments can deter active criminal offenders.

personality An idea used to explain how psychological conflict or underdevelopment might result in neurotic or psychotic behaviour patterns.

pilferage Theft by employees through stealth or deception.

policing-sensitive crimes This is a category of crimes that are particularly sensitive to law enforcement; if drug crime, for example, was not proactively investigated by the police, it is unlikely that many drug transactions would come to the attention of the police.

pornography In feminism, this is distinguished from erotica, and involves the exploitation of women and children for male pleasure; it exists in a variety of forms and is usually defined in relation to community standards of obscenity.

positivism The branch of social science that uses the scientific method of the natural sciences and suggests that human behaviour is a product of social, biological, psychological, or economic forces.

predatory crime A violent, opportunistic crime, not usually familiar-related, such as stealing brand-name clothing from strangers.

preemptive deterrence An approach advocated by left realists in which community organization efforts can eliminate or reduce crime before it becomes necessary to use police forces.

premeditation In a case of first-degree homicide, the prosecution must prove that the offence was thought out and planned.

premenstrual syndrome (PMS) The biogenetic theory (unfortunately caricaturized as a stereotype) that several days prior to and during menstruation females are beset by irritability and poor judgment as a result of hormonal changes, and that this puts them at a greater risk for criminality.

price-fixing A form of corporate crime, where companies conspire together to artificially inflate the price of goods.

primary deviance According to Lemert, deviant acts that do not help redefine the self and public image of the offender.

privilege In conflict theory, this concept refers to the wealth and prestige enjoyed by some, which puts them in conflict with those less well off in society.

problem behaviour syndrome (PBS) In the life-course view of crime, antisocial behaviours cluster together and typically include family dysfunction, substance abuse, smoking, precocious sexuality and early pregnancy, educational under-achievement, suicide attempts, sensation seeking, and unemployment.

professional criminals Make a significant portion of their income from crime.

proletariat In Marxist theory, the bourgeoisie controls the means of production, and the proletariat provides the labour; sometimes referred to as the working class.

pro-social bonds In the social development model, the way in which to control the risk of antisocial behaviour is to maintain pro-social bonds developed within the context of a family life; providing pro-social opportunities and consistent positive feedback.

prostitution The buying and selling of sex is technically not illegal in Canada, although there are various prostitution-related offences, such as pimping, brothel-keeping, and communication.

proximity hypothesis The view that people become crime victims because they live or work in areas with large criminal populations.

pseudomaturity Kids who mature faster have a greater chance of becoming life-course persisters; see *adolescent-limited*.

psychodynamic (psychoanalytic) approach Branch of psychology holding that the human personality is controlled by unconscious mental processes developed early in childhood.

psychopathy A mental disorder, especially when manifested as antisocial behaviour. The term is used interchangeably with sociopathy and antisocial personality disorder.

psychopharmacological A mood-altering substance has this effect when it produces a change in behaviour, including violence and aggression, e.g., alcohol, PCP, amphetamines.

psychosis This is what people who have lost total control and are dominated by their primitive id are said to be suffering from. They are referred to as psychotics, and their behaviour may be marked by bizarre episodes, hallucinations, and inappropriate responses to situations.

public order crimes Sometimes called victimless crimes, these acts interfere with public order, such as loitering for the purposes of prostitution.

r/k theory An evolutionary theory of crime that holds that k-oriented people are more cooperative and sensitive to others, while r-oriented people are more cunning and deceptive; corresponding to a female/male split in criminality.

radical feminists In this view, female crime is caused by male supremacy (patriarchy), the subsequent subordination of women, male aggression, and the efforts of men to control females sexually.

rational choice theory The view that crime is a function of a decision-making process in which the potential offender weighs the potential costs and benefits of an illegal act.

reaction formation According to Cohen, rejecting goals and standards that seem impossible to achieve. Because a boy cannot hope to get into college, for example, he considers higher education a waste of time.

reflected appraisal According to Matsueda and Heimer, a youth's self-evaluation based on his or her perceptions of how others evaluate him or her.

reflective role-taking According to Matsueda and Heimer, the phenomenon that occurs when youths who view themselves as delinquents are giving an inner-voice to their perceptions how significant others feel about them.

reintegrative shaming A method of correction that encourages offenders to confront their misdeeds, experience shame because of the harm they caused, and then be reincluded in society.

relative deprivation The condition that exists when people of wealth and poverty live in close proximity to one another. Some criminologists attribute crime rate differentials to relative deprivation.

report-sensitive crimes This is a category of crimes that are particularly sensitive to the willingness of victims to report them; if a victim of sexual assault, for example, does not report the crime, then it is unlikely that the police will ever know about it.

repression A process identified in psychodynamic theory that the unconscious mind contains feelings about sex and hostility, which people keep below the surface of consciousness.

restorative justice A restorative system of justice views crime as an injury to personal and community relations rather than as an abstract legal violation against society; it focuses on mediation and conflict resolution as an alternative to the more formalistic workings of the court system.

robbery A crime of violence involving the use of force to obtain money or goods.

routine activities theory An approach that holds the view that crime is a "normal" function of the routine activities of modern living. Offences can be expected if there is a suitable target that is not protected by capable guardians.

schizophrenia A type of psychosis often marked by bizarre behaviour, hallucinations, loss of thought control, and inappropriate emotional responses. Schizophrenic types include catatonic, which characteristically involves impairment of motor activity; paranoid, which is characterized by delusions of persecution; and hebephrenic, which is characterized by immature behaviour and giddiness.

secondary deviance According to Lemert, accepting deviant labels as a personal identity. Acts become secondary when they form a basis for self-concept.

seductions of crime According to Katz, the visceral and emotional appeal that the situation of crime has for those who engage in illegal acts.

selective incapacitation The policy of creating enhanced prison sentences for the relatively small group of dangerous chronic offenders.

self-rejection The consequence of successfully being labelled, where the negative stigma is internalized.

self-report survey A research approach that requires subjects to reveal their own participation in delinquent or criminal acts.

semiotics In this approach, language is studied as a set of signs that indicate more than the mere meaning of words; words are not mere descriptors, but convey a meaning understood by their audience.

sex offender registration A police registry of known sex offenders. Released offenders are required to register with the police, report to them, and keep the police informed of their whereabouts, including any change of address.

sexual abuse A form of violence, usually familiar-related, that can occur in wife abuse, child abuse, and elder abuse.

shield laws Laws designed to protect rape victims by prohibiting the defence attorney from inquiring about their previous sexual relationships.

siege mentality A consequence and symptom of community disorganization, where community fear causes the development of belief that the outside world is an enemy out to destroy the neighbourhood.

situational crime prevention A method of crime prevention that stresses tactics and strategies to eliminate or reduce particular crimes in narrow settings, such as reducing burglaries in a housing project by increasing lighting and installing security alarms.

situational inducement Crimes such as occasional property crime occur when there is an opportunity to commit crime; these are usually short-run influences on a person's behaviour that increase risk taking.

snitches Most shoplifters are amateur pilferers who think of themselves as respectable people.

social capital Positive relations with individuals and institutions that are life sustaining.

social control theory An approach that looks at the ability of society and its institutions to control, manage, restrain, or direct human behaviour, sometimes called control theory.

social development model (SDM) The attempt to integrate social control, social learning, and structural models of crime.

social deviant In labelling theory, the degree to which a person is perceived as a social deviant may affect his or her treatment at home, at work, at school, and in other social situations.

social disorganization theory An approach that looks at how neighbourhoods or areas are marked by culture conflict, lack of cohesiveness, transient population, insufficient social organizations, and anomie.

social distance In labelling theory, a person is labelled deviant primarily as a consequence of the differences in power between the labeller and the person labelled, differences located in race, class, and ethnicity.

social ecologists A modern variant of disorganization theory that looks at community-level indicators of social disorganization, including disorder, poverty, alienation, disassociation, and fear of crime.

social injustice In communities where the poor and wealthy live in close proximity, and people can see how poorly off they are, the consequent perception of injustice leads to a state of disorganization and anger; see *income inequality*.

social learning theory The view that human behaviour is modelled through observation of human social interactions, either directly from observing those who are close and from intimate contact, or indirectly through the media. Interactions that are rewarded are copied, while those that are punished are avoided.

social process theories Approaches that look at the operations of formal and informal social institutions. Elements of social processes include socialization within family and peer groups, the educational process, and the justice system.

social reality of crime Quinney's conflict theory about how power, society, and criminality are interrelated.

social structure theory An approach that looks at the various stratifications that characterize the fabric of postindustrial society.

socialization Process of human development and enculturation. Socialization is influenced by key social processes and institutions.

sociobiology Branch of science that views human behaviour as being motivated by inborn biological urges and desires. The urge to survive and preserve the species motivates human behaviour.

sociopathy A mental disorder characterized by lack of warmth and affection, inappropriate responses, and an inability to learn from experience. The term is used interchangeably with psychopathy and antisocial personality disorder.

somatype An idea used in a system developed for categorizing people on the basis of their body build, associated with the work of William Sheldon.

specific deterrence A crime control policy suggesting that punishment be severe enough to convince convicted offenders never to repeat their criminal activity. It is based on the principle that an individual can be prevented from committing a crime if the cost outweighs the benefit; see *utilitarianism*.

stalking Laws that make it a criminal offence to stalk or harass a victim even though no actual assault or battery has occurred.

stare decisis The principle that the courts are bound to follow the law established in previously decided cases (precedent) unless the law was overruled by a higher authority.

status frustration In subcultural theory, it is the view that because social conditions make lower-class youths incapable of achieving success legitimately, they experience a form of culture conflict that results in many of them joining in gangs and engaging in behaviour that is nonutilitarian, malicious, and negativistic.

stigmatize To create an enduring label that taints a person's identity and changes him or her in the eyes of others.

strain theory An approach that looks at the emotional turmoil and conflict caused when people believe they cannot achieve their desires and goals through legitimate means. Members of the lower class might feel strain because they are denied access to adequate educational opportunities and social support.

stranger-related crime Unlike acquaintance-related crime, some crimes do not require or arise from a prior relationship between the offender and the victim; an example would be carjacking.

street crime Illegal acts designed to prey on the public through theft, damage, and violence.

strict-liability crimes Illegal acts whose elements do not contain the need for intent, or *mens rea*; they are usually acts that endanger the public welfare, such as illegal dumping of toxic wastes.

structural Marxists Researchers who support the view that the law and the justice system are designed to maintain the capitalist system and that members of both the owner and the worker classes whose behaviour threatens the stability of the system will be sanctioned.

structural violence A form of state-sponsored terrorism that involves physical harm caused by the unequal distribution of wealth; a set of social conditions from which flows poverty, disease, hunger, malnutrition, poor sanitation, premature death, and high infant mortality.

subculture A group that is loosely a part of the dominant culture but maintains a unique set of values, beliefs, and traditions; a subculture of violence focuses on violent criminality.

subterranean values Important to neutralization theory, these are the morally tinged influences that have become entrenched in the culture but are publicly condemned by "right thinking" members of society.

suitable target According to routine activities theory, a target for crime that is relatively valuable, easily transportable, and not capably guarded.

summary offence Minor offences for which the penalty is restricted to a maximum of six months in jail, or a fine, or both.

surplus value The Marxist view that the labouring classes produce wealth that far exceeds their wages and goes to the capitalist class as profits.

swindling Stealing through deception by individuals who have no legitimate job and whose entire purpose is to bilk people out of their money, e.g., door-to-door sale of faulty merchandise.

symbolic interaction theory The sociological view that people communicate through symbols. People interpret symbolic communication and incorporate it within their personality. A person's view of reality, then, depends on his or her interpretation of symbolic gestures.

systematic forgers Fraud artists who make a substantial living by passing bad cheques.

target hardening Making one's home and business crime-proof through locks, bars, alarms, and other devices; this approach is based in routine activities theory, and is based on an analysis of potential risk factors.

target reduction strategies See *target hardening*.

technique of neutralization According to neutralization theory, the ability of delinquent youth to neutralize moral constraints so they may drift into criminal acts.

temperance movement An effort to prohibit the sale of liquor, largely seen as unsuccessful.

terrorism Includes a wide variety of violent acts that have a political motivation, committed against a state, and also by a state.

testosterone An androgen, or male hormone, which controls secondary sex characteristics and can alter behaviour.

thanatos According to Freud, the instinctual drive toward aggression and violence.

thrill killings Impulsive violence motivated by the killer's decision to kill a stranger as an act of daring or recklessness.

tort law The law of personal wrongs and damage. Tort actions include negligence, libel, slander, assault, and trespass.

trait theories This approach looks at the combination of biological or psychological attributes that might explain criminality. Each offender is considered unique, physically and mentally; consequently, there must be a unique explanation for each person's behaviour.

transferred intent The principle that if an illegal yet unintended act results from the intent to commit a crime, that act is also considered illegal.

transitional neighbourhood An area undergoing a shift in population and structure, usually from middle-class residential to lower-class mixed use.

turning points According to Laub and Sampson, the life events that alter the development of a criminal career.

underclass In Gunnar Myrdal's work, he described a world cut off from society, its members lacking the education and skills needed to survive in the modern world; this became a breeding ground for criminality.

Uniform Crime Report (UCR) This is an aggregate census based on reports from about 420 different police forces across Canada; it is the official basis for criminological research in Canada.

utilitarianism A view that believes that the punishment of crime should be balanced and fair, which underlies the belief in classical criminology that even criminal behaviour must be seen as purposeful and reasonable.

vagrancy Today vagrancy is a summary offence crime, but because it has been a capital offence in the past, it is a good example of historical changes in the law.

value conflict What occurs when the deviant values of teenage law-violating groups, an essential element of youthful misbehaviour in slum areas, come into conflict with existing middle-class norms, which demand strict obedience to the legal code.

victim compensation Financial restitution to the victim of crime, usually provided by the state and funded by a surcharge levied in criminal cases.

victim precipitation Refers to crime in which the victim's behaviour was the spark that ignited the subsequent offence, as when the victim abused the offender verbally or physically.

victimless crime Acts such as prostitution and drug transactions where there are two willing parties to the crime; enforcement has to be proactive.

victimologist Researchers who study the important role victims play in the crime process.

victimology The study of the victim's role in criminal transactions.

vigilante Someone who takes the law into their own hands, who acts outside the law in the interest of justice.

wergild Under medieval law, the money paid by the offender to compensate the victim and the state for a criminal offence.

white-collar crime Illegal acts that capitalize on a person's status in the marketplace. White-collar crimes can involve theft, embezzlement, fraud, market manipulation, restraint of trade, and false advertising.

Notes

Chapter 1

1. See, generally, Joel Milner, ed., "Special Issue: Physical Child Abuse," *Criminal Justice and Behavior* 18 (1991); Russell Dobash, R. Emerson Dobash, Margo Wilson, and Martin Daly, "The Myth of Sexual Symmetry in Marital Violence," *Social Problems* 39 (1992): 71–86; Martin Schwartz and Walter DeKeseredy, "The Return of the 'Battered Husband Syndrome': Typification of Women as Violent," *Crime, Law and Social Change* 4 (1993): 37–43.

2. For a thorough review, see Robin Malinosky-Rummell and David Hansen, "Long-Term Consequences of Childhood Physical Abuse," *Psychological Bulletin* 114 (1993): 68–79.

3. Sandra Besserer and Catherine Trainor, "Criminal Victimization in Canada, 1999," *Juristat* 20, no. 10 (2000); Canadian Centre for Justice Statistics, *A Profile of Criminal Victimization: Results of the 1999 General Social Survey* (Ottawa: CCJS, 2000); Sandra Besserer, "Criminal Victimization: An International Perspective: Results of the 2000 International Crime Victimization Survey," *Juristat* 22, no. 4 (2002).

4. Council for Canadian Unity, "Canada Needs to Get Back to Basics," http://www.cric.ca/en_html/opinion/ (accessed May 25, 2000).

5. Edwin Sutherland and Donald Cressey, *Principles of Criminology*, 6th ed. (Philadelphia: J.B. Lippincott, 1960), 3.

6. For a review of the development of criminal justice as a field of study, see Frank Remington, "Development of Criminal Justice as an Academic Field," *Journal of Criminal Justice Education* 1 (1990): 9–20.

7. Marvin Zalman, *A Heuristic Model of Criminology and Criminal Justice* (Chicago: Joint Commission on Criminology Education and Standards, University of Illinois, Chicago Circle, 1981), 9–11; John Ekstedt, "Canadian Justice Policy," in *Canadian Criminology: Perspectives on Crime and Criminality*, 2nd ed., ed. Margaret A. Jackson and Curt T. Griffiths (Toronto: Harcourt Brace and Co., 1995).

8. Charles McCaghy, *Deviant Behavior* (New York: Macmillan, 1976), 2–3; Vincent F. Sacco, *Deviance: Conformity and Control in Canadian Society*, 2nd ed. (Scarborough: Prentice-Hall, 1992), 4–7.

9. Cyberpages International Inc., "The 1999 Canada Drug Poll," http://www.cyberpages.com/polls/R40.HTM (accessed May 22, 2005).

10. "Vancouver Residents Soften Views on Drugs," *Vancouver Sun*, January 31, 2001.

11. John Hagan, *The Disreputable Pleasures: Crime and Deviance in Canada*, 3rd ed. (Toronto: McGraw-Hill, 1991), 13.

12. Patricia Erickson, *Cannabis Criminals: The Social Effects of Punishment on Drug Users* (Toronto: ARF, 1980); Edward Brecher, *Licit and Illicit Drugs* (Boston: Little, Brown, 1972), 413–416; Hagan, *The Disreputable Pleasures*, 27–30.

13. Sacco, *Deviance: Conformity and Control in Canadian Society*.

14. Cesare Beccaria, *On Crimes and Punishments* (originally published in 1764; Bobbs-Merrill, 1963).

15. Described in David Lykken, "Psychopathy, Sociopathy, and Crime," *Society* 34 (1996): 29–38.

16. See Peter Scott, "Henry Maudsley," in *Pioneers in Criminology*, ed. Hermann Mannheim (Montclair, N.J.: Prentice-Hall, 1981).

17. Nicole Hahn Rafter, "Criminal Anthropology in the United States," *Criminology* 30 (1992): 525–547.

18. L.A.J. Quetelet, *A Treatise on Man and the Development of His Faculties* (Gainesville, Fla.: Scholars' Facsimiles and Reprints, 1969), 82–96.

19. Piers Beirne, "The Invention of Positivist Criminology: An Introduction to Quetelet's Social Mechanics of Crime," in *Crime and Society: Readings in Critical Criminology*, ed. Brian C. MacLean (Toronto: Copp Clark, 1996).

20. See, generally, Robert Nisbet, *The Sociology of Emile Durkheim* (New York: Oxford University Press, 1974), 209; Emile Durkheim, *Rules of the Sociological Method*, trans. S.A. Solvay and J.H. Mueller, ed. G. Catlin (New York: Free Press, 1966), 65–73; Emile Durkheim, *De la division de travail social: Étude sur l'organisation des sociétés supérieures* (Paris: Félix Alcan, 1893); Emile Durkheim, *The Division of Labor in Society* (New York: Free Press, 1964); Emile Durkheim, *Suicide: A Study in Sociology* (Glencoe, Ill.: Free Press, 1951).

21. Robert Park and Ernest Burgess, *The City* (Chicago: University of Chicago Press, 1925).

22. Marlene Shore, *The Science of Social Redemption: McGill, the Chicago School, and the Origins of Social Research in Canada* (Toronto: University of Toronto Press, 1987).

23. Karl Marx and Friedrich Engels, *Capital: A Critique of Political Economy*, trans. E. Aveling (Chicago: Charles Kern, 1906); Karl Marx, *Selected Writings in Sociology and Social Philosophy*, trans. P.B. Bottomore (New York: McGraw-Hill, 1956). For a general discussion of Marxist thought, see Michael Lynch and W. Byron Groves, *A Primer in Radical Criminology* (New York: Harrow and Heston, 1986), 6–26.

24. Willem Bonger, *Criminality and Economic Conditions* (1916, abridged ed., Bloomington: Indiana University Press, 1969); Ralf Dahrendorf, *Class and Class Conflict in Industrial Society* (Palo Alto, Calif.: Stanford University Press, 1959).

25. Marvin Wolfgang and Franco Ferracuti, *The Subculture of Violence* (London: Social Science Paperbacks, 1967), 20.

26. "Lawyer to Probe Rodriguez Suicide," *Globe and Mail*, January 11, 1995, A1.

27. Associated Press, "Michigan Senate Acts to Outlaw Aiding Suicides," *Boston Globe*, March 20, 1994, 22.

28. Marvin Wolfgang, *Patterns in Criminal Homicide* (Philadelphia: University of Pennsylvania Press, 1958).

29. Edwin H. Sutherland, "White-Collar Criminality," *American Sociological Review* 5, no. 1 (1940): 2–10.

30. Hans von Hentig, *The Criminal and His Victim* (New Haven, Conn.: Yale University Press, 1948); Stephen Schafer, *The Victim and His Criminal* (New York: Random House, 1968).

31. Sutherland and Cressey, *Principles of Criminology*, 8.

32. Eugene Doleschal and Nora Klapmuts, "Toward a New Criminology," *Crime and Delinquency* 5 (1973): 607.

33. Michael Lynch and W. Byron Groves, *A Primer in Radical Criminology* (Albany, N.Y.: Harrow and Heston, 1989), 32.

34. See Herbert Blumer, *Symbolic Interactionism* (Englewood Cliffs, N.J.: Prentice-Hall, 1969).

35. Howard Becker, *Outsiders* (New York: The Free Press, 1963), 9.

36. Michael Gottfredson and Travis Hirschi, "The Methodological Adequacy of Longitudinal Research on Crime," *Criminology* 25 (1987): 581–614.

37. See, generally, David Farrington, Lloyd Ohlin, and James Q. Wilson, *Understanding and Controlling Crime* (New York: Springer-Verlag, 1986), 11–18.

38. Cathy Spaatz Widom, "Child Abuse, Neglect, and Adult Behavior," *American Journal of Orthopsychiatry* 15 (1989): 355–367.

39. "Statscan Says More Drivers Staying Sober," *Globe and Mail*, November 18, 1997, A8.

40. Claire Sterck-Elifson, "Just for Fun? Cocaine Use among Middle-Class Women," *Journal of Drug Issues* 26 (1996): 63–76.

41. William F. Whyte, *Street Corner Society* (Chicago: University of Chicago Press, 1955).

42. Herman Schwendinger and Julia Schwendinger, *Adolescent Subcultures and Delinquency* (New York: Praeger, 1985).

43. For a review of these studies, see L. Rowell Huesmann and Neil Malamuth, eds., "Media Violence and Antisocial Behavior," *Journal of Social Issues* 42 (1986): 31–53.

44. Luis T. Garcia, "Exposure to Pornography and Attitudes About Women and Rape: A Correlational Study," *Journal of Sex Research* 23 (1986): 378–385; N.M. Malamuth and E. Donnerstein, "The Effects of Aggressive-Pornographic Mass Media Stimuli," in *Advances in Experimental Social Psychology*, ed. L. Berkowitz (New York: Academic Press, 1982), 104–136.

45. Don Clairmont, "In Defence of Liberal Models of Research and Policy," *Canadian Journal of Criminology* 41 (1999): 151–160.

46. See, for example, Michael Hindelang and Travis Hirschi, "Intelligence and Delinquency: A Revisionist Review," *American Sociological Review* 42 (1977): 471–486.

47. Richard Herrnstein and Charles Murray, *The Bell Curve* (New York: Free Press, 1994).

48. Alan Ryan, "Apocalypse Now?" in *The Bell Curve Debate: History, Documents, Opinions*, ed. Russell Jacoby and Naomi Glauberman (New York: Random, 1995), 21.

Chapter 2

1. The historical material in the following sections was derived from a number of sources. The most important include Rene Wormser, *The Story of Law*, rev. ed. (New York: Simon & Schuster, 1962); Jackson Spielvogel, *Western Civilization* (St. Paul: West Publishing, 1991); Eugen Weber, *A Modern History of Europe* (New York: W.W. Norton, 1971); James Heath, *Eighteenth-Century Penal Theory* (New York: Oxford University Press, 1963); David Jones, *History of Criminology* (Westport, Conn.: Greenwood Press, 1986); Fred Inbau, James Thompson, and James Zagel, *Criminal Law and Its Administration* (Mineola, N.Y.: Foundation Press, 1974); Wayne LaFave and Austin Scott, *Criminal Law*, 2nd ed. (St. Paul: West Publishing, 1986); and Sanford Kadish and Monrad Paulsen, *Criminal Law and Its Processes* (Boston: Little, Brown, 1975).

2. Chris McCormick, "Matters of Record: Documenting Discipline in Nova Scotia Baptist Churches, circa 1800," paper presented to the 12th Church History Workshop, 2001.

3. Wayne LaFave and Austin Scott, *Handbook on Criminal Law* (St. Paul, Minn.: West Publishing, 1982), 528–529.

4. Caldwell 397 (1784), cited in LaFave and Scott, *Handbook on Criminal Law*, 422.

5. 9 George I, C. 22, 1723, cited in Douglas Hay, "Crime and Justice in Eighteenth and Nineteenth Century England," in *Crime and Justice*, vol. 2, ed. Norval Norris and Michael Tonrey (Chicago: University of Chicago Press, 1980), 51.

6. See, generally, Alfred Lindesmith, *The Addict and the Law* (New York: Vintage Books, 1965), Chapter 1.

7. A. Elizabeth Comack, "The Origins of Canadian Drug Legislation: Labelling versus Class Analysis," in *The New Criminologies in Canada*, ed. Tom Fleming (Toronto: Oxford, 1985).

8. This section owes much to Alison J. Hatch, for her excellent review: "Historical Legacies of Crime and Criminal Justice in Canada," in *Canadian Criminology: Perspectives on Crime and Criminality*, ed. Margaret A. Jackson and Curt T. Griffiths (Toronto: Harcourt Brace, 1995).

9. Pierre Berton, *Klondike: The Last Great Gold Rush, 1896–1899* (Toronto: McClelland and Stewart, 1981).

10. L. Brown and C. Brown, *An Unauthorized History of the R.C.M.P.* (Toronto: James Lorimer, 1973).

11. G.H. Crouse, "A Critique of Canadian Criminal Legislation," *Canadian Bar Review*, 12 (1934): 545–578.

12. William Henry, "Did the Music Say 'Do It'?" *Time*, July 30, 1990, 65; Doug Ireland, "Press Sins," *Village Voice*, March 20, 1990; Linda B. Deutschmann, *Deviance and Social Control* (Scarborough, Ont.: Nelson, 1994), 91.

13. For example, see *Brinegar v. United States*, 388 U.S. 160 (1949); *Speiser v. Randall*, 357 U.S. 513 (1958); *In re Winship*, 397 U.S. 358 (1970).

14. Richard Barnhorst, Sherrie Barnhorst, and Kenneth L. Clarke, *Criminal Law and the Canadian Criminal Code*, 2nd ed. (Toronto: McGraw-Hill Ryerson, 1992).

15. Curt T. Griffiths and Simon N. Verdun-Jones, *Canadian Criminal Justice*, 2nd ed. (Toronto: Harcourt Brace, 1994); for a good example of the conflict model, see, generally, R.S. Ratner and John L. McMullan, *State Control: Criminal Justice Politics in Canada* (Vancouver: UBC Press, 1987).

16. Oliver Wendell Holmes, *The Common Law*, ed. Mark De Wolf (Boston: Little, Brown, 1881), 36.

17. William Chambliss, "A Sociological Analysis of the Law of Vagrancy," *Social Problems* 12 (1964): 67–77; William Chambliss, "On Trashing Marxist Criminology," *Criminology* 27 (1989): 231–239.

18. Jeffrey Adler, "A Historical Analysis of the Law of Vagrancy," *Criminology* 27 (1989): 209–230; "Vagging the Demons and Scoundrels: Vagrancy and the Growth of St. Louis, 1830–1861," *Journal of Urban History* 13 (1986): 3–30.

19. *Carrier's case*, Y.B. 13 Edw. 4, f. 9, pl. 5 (Star Chamber and Exchequer Chamber, 1473), discussed at length in Jerome Hall, *Theft, Law and Society* (Indianapolis: Bobbs-Merrill, 1952), Chapter 1.

20. University of Montreal, *R. v. Parks* [1992] 2 S.C.R. 871 (S.C.C.), http://www.lexum.umontreal.ca/csc-scc/en/pub/1992/vol2/html/1992scr2_0871.html (accessed May 22, 2005).

21. 8 Eng. Rep. 718 (1843).

22. *Regina v. Dudley and Stephens*, 14 Q.B. 273 (1884).

23. "Canadian Rescue Pilot of Plane Lost a Month in Arctic," *New York Times*, December 10, 1972, 1; "Pilot Rescued after 32-Day Ordeal in Arctic," *The Globe and Mail*, December 11, 1972, A1; "Pilot Resorted to Cannibalism to Keep Alive, Statement Says," *Globe and Mail*, March 1, 1973, A1; "Bush Pilot Tells of Cannibalism," *New York Times*, March 2, 1973, 5.

24. Zalman et al., "Michigan Assisted Suicide Three Ring Circus"; 1992 P.A. 270 as amended by 1993 P.A. 3, M.C.L. ss. 752.1021 to 752.1027.

25. Brian Bergman, "The Final Hours," *Maclean's*, March 9, 1998, 46–49.

26. National Institute of Justice, *Project to Develop a Model Anti-stalking Statute* (Washington, D.C.: National Institute of Justice, 1994).

27. "Clinton Signs Tougher Megan's Law," CNN News Service, May 17, 1996.

28. Roger Fillion, "Cracking Down on Internet Crime," *Boston Globe*, December 28, 1995, 65.

Chapter 3

1. Timothy F. Hartnagel, "Crime among the Provinces: The Effect of Geographic Mobility," *Canadian Journal of Criminology*, October 1997: 387–402.

2. Statistics Canada, "Family Violence 1999," *The Daily*, July 25, 2000.

3. Craig Perkins and Patsy Klaus, *Criminal Victimization, 1994* (Washington, D.C.: Bureau of Justice Statistics, 1996) (hereinafter cited as NCVS, 1994); Rosemary Gartner and Anthony N. Doob, "Trends in Criminal Victimization: 1988–1993," *Juristat* 14 (1994).

4. *The 2000 British Crime Survey, England and Wales* (London: British Home Office, 2000).

5. Paul Tappan, *Crime, Justice and Corrections* (New York: McGraw-Hill, 1960); Daniel Bell, *The End of Ideology* (New York: Free Press, 1967), 152.

6. Jim Hackler and Wasanti Paranjape, "Juvenile Justice Statistics: Mythmaking or Measure of System Response," *Canadian Journal of Criminology* 25 (1983): 209–226.

7. Lawrence Sherman and Barry Glick, "The Quality of Arrest Statistics," *Police Foundation Reports* 2 (1984): 1–8; David Seidman and Michael Couzens, "Getting the Crime Rate Down: Political Pressure and Crime Reporting," *Law and Society Review* 8 (1974): 457; Robert O'Brien, "Police Productivity and Crime Rates: 1973–1992," *Criminology* 34 (1996): 183–207.

8. Duncan Chappell, Gilbert Geis, Stephen Schafer, and Larry Siegel, "Forcible Rape: A Comparative Study of Offenses Known to the Police in Boston and Los Angeles," in *Studies in the Sociology of Sex*, ed. James Henslin (New York: Appleton-Century-Crofts, 1971), 169–193.

9. Patrick Jackson, "Assessing the Validity of Official Data on Arson," *Criminology* 26 (1988): 181–195.

10. Peter Carrington, *Factors Affecting Police Diversion of Young Offenders: A Statistical Analysis* (Ottawa: Solicitor General of Canada, 1998).

11. "Arson in Canada," *Juristat* 12 (1992).

12. "Youth Courts Hear Fewer Cases," *Daily News*, May 1, 1998; Paul Robinson, "Youth Court Statistics, 2002/03," *Juristat* 24, no. 2 (2004).

13. R.P. Ericson, M. Baranek, and J. Chan, *Visualizing Deviance: A Study of News Sources* (Toronto: University of Toronto Press, 1989); R.P. Ericson, M. Baranek, and J. Chan, *Negotiating Control: A Study of News Sources* (Toronto: University of Toronto Press, 1989); R.P. Ericson, M. Baranek, and J. Chan, *Representing Order* (Toronto: University of Toronto Press, 1991).

14. M. Maltz, "Crime Statistics: A Historical Perspective," *Crime and Delinquency* 23 (1977): 32–40.

15. A. Doyle and R. Ericson, "Breaking into Prison: News Sources and Correctional Institutions," *Canadian Journal of Criminology* 38: 155–190.

16. Leonard Savitz, "Official Statistics," in *Contemporary Criminology*, ed. Leonard Savitz and Norman Johnston (New York: Wiley, 1982), 3–15.

17. A pioneering effort in self-report research is A.L. Porterfield, *Youth in Trouble* (Fort Worth, Tex.: Leo Potishman Foundation, 1946); for a review, see Robert Hardt and George Bodine, *Development of Self-Report Instruments in Delinquency Research: A Conference Report* (Syracuse, N.Y.: Syracuse University Youth Development Center, 1965). See also Fred Murphy, Mary Shirley, and Helen Witner, "The Incidence of Hidden Delinquency," *American Journal of Orthopsychology* 16 (1946): 686–696.

18. Franklyn Dunford and Delbert Elliott, "Identifying Career Criminals Using Self-Reported Data," *Journal of Research in Crime and Delinquency* 21 (1983): 57–86.

19. For example, see E. Vaz, "Middle Class Delinquency: Self Reported Delinquency and Youth Culture," *Canadian Review of Sociology and Anthropology* 2 (1965): 52–70; M. LeBlanc, "Middle Class Delinquency," in *Crime in Canadian Society*, ed. Robert A. Silverman and James J. Teevan (Toronto: Butterworths, 1975); I.M. Gomme, Mary E. Morton, and W. Gordon West, "Rates, Types, and Patterns of Male and Female Delinquency in an Ontario County," *Canadian Journal of Criminology* 26 (1984): 313–324.

20. Thomas Gabor, "Methodological Orthodoxy or Eclecticism? The Case of Youth Violence," *Canadian Journal of Criminology* 42 (2000): 77–83.

21. See, for example, Spencer Rathus and Larry Siegel, "Crime and Personality Revisited: Effects of MMPI Sets on Self-Report Studies," *Criminology* 18 (1980): 245–251; John Clark and Larry Tifft, "Polygraph and Interview Validation of Self-Reported Deviant Behavior," *American Sociological Review* 31 (1966): 516–523.

22. See, for example, Harwin Voss, "Ethnic Differences in Delinquency in Honolulu," *Journal of Criminal Law, Criminology and Police Science* 54 (1963): 322–327; Maynard Erickson and LaMar Empey, "Court Records, Undetected Delinquency and Decision Making," *Journal of Criminal Law, Criminology and Police Science* 54 (1963): 456–459; H.B. Gibson, Sylvia Morrison, and D.J. West, "The Confession of Known Offenses in Response to a Self-Reported Delinquency Schedule," *British Journal of Criminology* 10 (1970): 277–280; John Blackmore, "The Relationship between Self-Reported Delinquency and Official Convictions amongst Adolescent Boys," *British Journal of Criminology* 14 (1974): 172–176; Clark and Tifft, "Polygraph and Interview Validation of Self-Reported Deviant Behavior"; Michael Hindelang, Travis Hirschi, and Joseph Weis, *Measuring Delinquency* (Beverly Hills, Calif.: Sage, 1981).

23. Terence Thornberry, Beth Bjerregaard, and William Miles, "The Consequences of Respondent Attrition in Panel Studies: A Simulation Based on the Rochester Youth Development Study," *Journal of Quantitative Criminology* 9 (1993): 127–158.

24. Minu Mathur, Richard Dodder, and Harjit Sandhu, "Inmate Self-Report Data: A Study of Reliability," *Criminal Justice Review* 17 (1992): 258–267.

25. Thomas Gray and Eric Wish, *Maryland Youth at Risk: A Study of Drug Use in Juvenile Detainees* (College Park, Md.: Center for Substance Abuse Research, 1993); Eric Wish and Christina Polsenberg, "Arrestee Urine Tests and Self-Reports of Drug Use: Which Is More Related to Rearrest?" paper presented at the annual meeting of the American Society of Criminology, Phoenix, Ariz., November 1993.

26. L. Edward Wells and Joseph Rankin, "Juvenile Victimization: Convergent Validation of Alternative Measurements," *Journal of Research in Crime and Delinquency* 32 (1995): 287–307.

27. Alfred Blumstein, Jacqueline Cohen, and Richard Rosenfeld, "Trend and Deviation in Crime Rates: A Comparison of UCR and NCVS Data for Burglary and Robbery," *Criminology* 29 (1991): 237–248. See also Hindelang, Hirschi, and Weis, *Measuring Delinquency*.

28. For a critique, see Scott Menard, "Residual Gains, Reliability, and the UCR–NCVS Relationship: A Comment on Blumstein, Cohen and Rosenfeld (1991)," *Criminology* 30 (1992): 105–115; David McDowall and Colin Loftin, "Comparing the UCR and NCVS over Time," *Criminology* 30 (1992): 125–133.

29. D. Cole and M. Gittens, *Report of the Commission on Systemic Racism in the Ontario Criminal Justice System* (Toronto: Queen's Printer for Ontario, 1995).

30. Nova Scotia, *Royal Commission into the Wrongful Incarceration of Donald Marshall, Jr.* (Halifax: Queen's Printer, 1989).

31. Alberta, *Justice on Trial: Report of the Task Force on the Criminal Justice System and Its Impact on the Indian and Métis People of Alberta* (Edmonton: The Task Force, 1991).

32. Manitoba, *Report of the Aboriginal Justice Inquiry* (Winnipeg: Queen's Printer, 1991).

33. Saskatchewan, *Report of the Saskatchewan Indian Justice Review Committee* (Regina: The Indian Justice Review Committee, 1992); Saskatchewan, *Report of Commission of Inquiry into the Shooting Death of Leo Lachance* (Regina: Saskatchewan Justice, 1993).

34. Michael Harris, *The Royal Commission of Inquiry into the Response of the Newfoundland Criminal Justice System to Complaints* (St. John's: Queen's Printer, 1991).

35. The Honourable Stuart G. Stratton, Q.C., *Report of an Independent Investigation in Respect of Incidents and Allegations of Sexual and Other Physical Abuse at Five Nova Scotia Residential Institutions*, June 30, 1995.

36. Mennonite Central Committee, "Justice in Crisis: A Report on Canada's Criminal Justice System," http://www.mennonitecc.ca/mcc/misc/justice-in-crisis.html (accessed May 22, 2001).

37. Vincent F. Sacco and Leslie W. Kennedy, *The Criminal Event*, 2nd ed. (Toronto: ITP Nelson, 1998); M. Martin and L. Ogrodnik, "Canadian Crime Trends," in *Crime Counts*, ed. L.W. Kennedy and V.F. Sacco (Toronto: ITP Nelson, 1996).

38. L.W. Kennedy and D. Veitch, "Why Are the Crime Rates Going Down? A Case Study in Edmonton," *Canadian Journal of Criminology* 39 (1997): 51–69.

39. Glenn Pierce and James Alan Fox, *Recent Trends in Violent Crime: A Closer Look* (Boston: National Crime Analysis Program, Northeastern University, 1992).

40. Ron Logan, "Crime Statistics in Canada, 2000," *Juristat* 21 (2001).

41. Anthony N. Doob and Jane B. Sprott, "Is the 'Quality' of Youth Violence Becoming More Serious," *Canadian Journal of Criminology* 4 (1998): 185–194; Thomas Gabor, "Trends in Youth Crime: Some Evidence Pointing to Increases in the Severity and Volume of Violence on the Part of Young People," *Canadian Journal of Criminology* 7 (1999): 385–392.

42. Donald J. Auger, Anthony N. Doob, Raymond P. Auger, and Paul Driben, "Crime and Control in Three Nishnawbe-Aski Nation Communities: An Exploratory Investigation," *Canadian Journal of Criminology* 10 (1992): 317–338; Carol LaPrairie, "The Role of Sentencing in the Over-Representation of Aboriginal People in Correctional Institutions," *Canadian Journal of Criminology* 32 (1990): 429–440.

43. Canadian Centre for Justice Statistics, *Aboriginal Peoples in Canada* (Ottawa: Statistics Canada, 2001).

44. National Crime Prevention Centre, *Aboriginal Canadians: Violence, Victimization and Prevention* (Ottawa: Department of Justice, 2001).

45. M. Ouimet, "Explaining the American and Canadian Crime Drop in the 1990s," *Canadian Journal of Criminology* 44, no. 1 (2002): 33–50.

46. John McMullan, "A Social Economy of Arson," *Canadian Journal of Criminology* 31 (1989).

47. Rosemary Gartner, "Family Structure, Welfare Spending, and Child Homicide in Developed Democracies," *Journal of Marriage and the Family* 53 (1991): 231–240.

48. John Donohue and Steven Levitt, "The Impact of Legalized Abortion on Crime," National Bureau of Economic Research Working Paper, November 2000.

49. Rosemary Gartner and Robert Nash Parker, "Cross-National Evidence on Homicide and the Age Structure of the Population," *Social Forces* 69 (1990): 351–371.

50. John Braithwaite, *Crime, Shame and Reintegration* (Cambridge: Cambridge University Press, 1989).

51. Koichiro Ito, "Research on the Fear of Crime: Perceptions and Realities of Crime in Japan," *Crime and Delinquency* 39 (1993): 392–395; Joachim Kersten, "Street Youths, Bosozoku, and Yakuza: Subculture Formation and Social Reactions in Japan," *Crime and Delinquency* 39 (1993): 277–295; Michael Vaughn and Nobuho Tomita, "A Longitudinal Analysis of Japanese Crime from 1926–1987: The Pre-War, War and Post-War Eras," *International Journal of Comparative and Applied Criminal Justice* 14 (1990): 145–160; Ted Westermann and James Burfeind, *Crime and Justice in Two Societies: Japan and the United States* (Pacific Grove, Calif.: Brooks/Cole, 1991).

52. Joseph Sheley and James Wright, *In the Line of Fire: Youth, Guns, and Violence in Urban America* (New York: Aldine de Gruyter, 1995).

53. Canadian Centre for Justice Statistics, *Juristat* (2002).

54. Thomas Gabor, "Canadians Rarely Use Firearms for Self-protection," *Canadian Journal of Criminology* 38 (1996): 217–220; Gary Mauser, "Do Canadians Use Firearms in Self-protection," *Canadian Journal of Criminology* 37 (1995): 556–562.

55. Alfred Blumstein, "Violence by Young People: Why the Deadly Nexus," *National Institute of Justice Journal* 229 (1995): 2–9.

56. Steven Dillingham, *Violent Crime in the United States* (Washington, D.C.: Bureau of Justice Statistics, 1991), 17; Bruce Johnson, Andrew Golub, and Jeffrey Fagan, "Careers in Crack, Drug Use, Drug Distribution, and Nondrug Criminality," *Crime and Delinquency* 41 (1995): 275–295.

57. J.Q. Wilson and G. Kelling, "Broken Windows: The Police and Neighborhood Safety," *Atlantic Monthly* (March 19, 1996), 29–38; and George L. Kelling and Catherine M. Coles, *Fixing Broken Windows: Reducing Order and Reducing Crime in Our Communities* (New York: Martin Kessler Books/Free Press, 1997).

58. Darrell Steffensmeier and Miles Harer, "Did Crime Rise or Fall during the Reagan Presidency? The Effects of an 'Aging' U.S. Population on the Nation's Crime Rate," *Journal of Research in Crime and Delinquency* 28 (1991): 330–339.

59. James A. Fox, *Trends in Juvenile Violence: A Report to the United States Attorney General on Current and Future Rates of Juvenile Offending* (Boston, Mass.: Northeastern University, 1996).

60. Ellen Cohn, "The Effect of Weather and Temporal Variations on Calls for Police Service," *American Journal of Police* 15 (1996): 23–43.

61. R.A. Baron, "Aggression as a Function of Ambient Temperature and Prior Anger Arousal," *Journal of Personality and Social Psychology* 21 (1972): 183–189; Ellen Cohn, "The Prediction of Police Calls for Service: The Influence of Weather and Temporal Variables on Rape and Domestic Violence," *Journal of Environmental Psychology* 13 (1993): 71–83; Derral Cheatwood, "The Effects of Weather on Homicide," *Journal of Quantitative Criminology* 11 (1995): 51–70; Ellen Cohn and James Rotton, "Assault as a Function of Time and Temperature: A Moderator-Variable Times-Series Analysis," paper presented at the annual meeting of the American Society of Criminology, Chicago, November 1996, 23.

62. Robert Nash Parker, "Bringing 'Booze' Back In: The Relationship between Alcohol and Homicide," *Journal of Research in Crime and Delinquency* 32 (1995): 3–38.

63. Victoria Brewer and M. Dwayne Smith, "Gender Inequality and Rates of Female Homicide Victimization Across U.S. Cities," *Journal of Research in Crime and Delinquency* 32 (1995): 175–190.

64. F. Ivan Nye, James Short, and Virgil Olsen, "Socio-economic Status and Delinquent Behavior," *American Journal of Sociology* 63 (1958): 381–389; Robert Dentler and Lawrence Monroe, "Social Correlates of Early Adolescent Theft," *American Sociological Review* 63 (1961): 733–743. See also Terence Thornberry and Margaret Farnworth, "Social Correlates of Criminal Involvement: Further Evidence of the Relationship between Social Status and Criminal Behavior," *American Sociological Review* 47 (1982): 505–518.

65. Charles Tittle, Wayne Villemez, and Douglas Smith, "The Myth of Social Class and Criminality: An Empirical Assessment of the Empirical Evidence," *American Sociological Review* 43 (1978): 643–656.

66. Charles Tittle and Robert Meier, "Specifying the SES/Delinquency Relationship," *Criminology* 28 (1990): 271–301.

67. Delbert Elliott and Suzanne Ageton, "Reconciling Race and Class Differences in Self-Reported and Official Estimates of Delinquency," *American Sociological Review* 45 (1980): 95–110.

68. See also Delbert Elliott and David Huizinga, "Social Class and Delinquent Behavior in a National Youth Panel: 1976–1980," *Criminology* 21 (1983): 149–177. For a similar view, see John Braithwaite, "The Myth of Social Class and Criminality Reconsidered," *American Sociological Review* 46 (1981): 35–58, and Hindelang, Hirschi, and Weis, *Measuring Delinquency*, 196.

69. Jane B. Sprott, Anthony N. Doob, and Jennifer M. Jenkins, "Problem Behaviour and Delinquency in Children and Youth," *Juristat* 21, no. 4 (2001).

70. David Brownfield, "Social Class and Violent Behavior," *Criminology* 24 (1986): 421–439.

71. Douglas Smith and Laura Davidson, "Interfacing Indicators and Constructs in Criminological Research: A Note on the Comparability of Self-Report Violence Data for Race and Sex Groups," *Criminology* 24 (1986): 473–488.

72. Sally Simpson and Lori Elis, "Doing Gender: Sorting out the Case and Crime Conundrum," *Criminology* 33 (1995): 47–81.

73. Judith Blau and Peter Blau, "The Cost of Inequality: Metropolitan Structure and Violent Crime," *American Sociological Review* 147 (1982): 114–129; Richard Block, "Community Environment and Violent Crime," *Criminology* 17 (1979): 46–57; Robert Sampson, "Structural Sources of Variation in Race-Age-Specific Rates of Offending across Major U.S. Cities," *Criminology* 23 (1985): 647–673.

74. Chin-Chi Hsieh and M.D. Pugh, "Poverty, Income Inequality, and Violent Crime: A Meta-Analysis of Recent Aggregate Data Studies," *Criminal Justice Review* 18 (1993): 182–199.

75. Alan Lizotte, Terence Thornberry, Marvin Krohn, Deborah Chard-Wierschem, and David McDowall, "Neighborhood Context and Delinquency: A Longitudinal Analysis," in *Cross National Longitudinal Research on Human Development and Criminal Behavior*, ed. E.M. Weitekamp and H.J. Kerner (Stavernstr, Netherlands: Kluwer, 1994), 217–227.

76. Travis Hirschi and Michael Gottfredson, "Age and the Explanation of Crime," *American Journal of Sociology* 89 (1983): 552–584.

77. Darrell Steffensmeier and Cathy Streifel, "Age, Gender, and Crime Across Three Historical Periods: 1935, 1960 and 1985," *Social Forces* 69 (1991): 869–894; John Laub, David Clark, Leslie Siegel, and James Garofolo, *Trends in Juvenile Crime in the United States: 1973–1983* (Albany, N.Y.: Hindelang Research Center, 1987). On another note, for a comprehensive review of crime and the elderly, see Kyle Kercher, "Causes and Correlates of Crime Committed by the Elderly," in *Critical Issues in Aging Policy*, ed. E. Borgatta and R. Montgomery (Beverly Hills: Sage, 1987), 254–306, and Darrell Steffensmeier, "The Invention of the 'New' Senior Citizen Criminal," *Research on Aging* 9 (1987): 281–311.

78. Hirschi and Gottfredson, "Age and the Explanation of Crime"; Michael Gottfredson and Travis Hirschi, "The True Value of Lambda Would Appear to Be Zero: An Essay on Career Criminals, Criminal Careers, Selective Incapacitation, Cohort Studies and Related Topics," *Criminology* 24 (1986): 213–234; further support for their position can be found in Lawrence Cohen and Kenneth Land, "Age Structure and Crime," *American Sociological Review* 52 (1987): 170–183.

79. John H. Laub and Robert J. Sampson, *Shared Beginnings, Divergent Lives: Delinquent Boys to Age 70* (Cambridge: Harvard, 2003).

80. Kyle Kercher, "Explaining the Relationship between Age and Crime: The Biological Versus Sociological Model," paper presented at the American Society of Criminology meeting, Montreal, November 1987; Alfred Blumstein, Jacqueline Cohen, and David Farrington, "Criminal Career Research: Its Value for Criminology," *Criminology* 26 (1988): 1–37; Sung Joon Jang and Marvin Krohn, "Developmental Patterns of Sex Differences in Delinquency among African American Adolescents: A Test of the Sex-Invariance Hypothesis," *Journal of Quantitative Criminology* 11 (1995): 195–220; Candace Kruttschnitt, "Violence by and against Women: A Comparative and Cross-National Analysis," *Violence and Victims* 8 (1994): 1–28; Josee Savoie, "Homicide in Canada, 2002," *Juristat* 23, no. 8 (2003).

81. David Greenberg, "Age, Crime, and Social Explanation," *American Journal of Sociology* 91 (1985): 1–21; Marvin Wolfgang, Robert Figlio, and Thorsten Sellin, *Delinquency in a Birth Cohort* (Chicago: University of Chicago Press, 1972); Lyle Shannon, *Assessing the Relationship of Adult Criminal Careers to Juvenile Careers: A Summary* (Washington, D.C.: U.S. Department of Justice, 1982); D.J. West and David P. Farrington, *The Delinquent Way of Life* (London: Hienemann, 1977); Donna Hamparian, Richard Schuster, Simon Dinitz, and John Conrad, *The Violent Few* (Lexington, Mass.: Lexington Books, 1978); Rolf Loeber, Magda Stouthamer-Loeber, and Stephanie Green, "Age at Onset of Problem Behaviour in Boys and Later Disruptive and Delinquent Behaviours," *Criminal Behaviour and Mental Health* 1 (1991): 229–246.

82. Darrell Steffensmeier, Emilie Andersen Allan, Miles Harer, and Cathy Streifel, "Age and the Distribution of Crime: Variant or Invariant?" paper presented at the American Society of Criminology meeting, Montreal, November 1987; Hilary Saner, Robert MacCoun, and Peter Reuter, "On the Ubiquity of Drug Selling among Youthful Offenders in Washington, DC, 1985–1991: Age, Period, or Cohort Effect?" *Journal of Quantitative Criminology* 11 (1995): 362–373.

83. Arnold Barnett, Alfred Blumstein, and David Farrington, "Probabilistic Models of Youthful Criminal Careers," *Criminology* 25 (1987): 83–107.

84. Peter Greenwood, "Differences in Criminal Behavior and Court Responses among Juvenile and Young Adult Defendants," in *Crime and Justice, An Annual Review of Research*, ed. Michael Tonry and Norval Morris (Chicago: University of Chicago Press, 1986), 151–189.

85. John Hagan and Alberto Palloni, "Crimes as Social Events in the Life Course: Reconceiving a Criminological Controversy," *Criminology* 26 (1988): 87–101.

86. Alison Cunningham, *One Step Forward: Lessons Learned from a Randomized Study of Multisystemic Therapy in Canada* (London, Ont.: Centre for Children and Families in the Justice System, 2002).

87. Travis Hirschi and Michael Gottfredson, "Age and Crime, Logic and Scholarship: Comment on Greenberg," *American Journal of Sociology* 91 (1985): 22–27; "All Wise after the Fact Learning Theory, Again: Reply to Baldwin," *American Journal of Sociology* 90 (1985): 1330–1333; John Baldwin, "Thrill and Adventure Seeking and the Age Distribution of Crime: Comment on Hirschi and Gottfredson," *American Journal of Sociology* 90 (1985): 1326–1329; Per-Olof Wikstrom, "Age and Crime in a Stockholm Cohort," *Journal of Quantitative Criminology* 6 (1990): 61–82.

88. Edward Mulvey and John LaRosa, "Delinquency Cessation and Adolescent Development: Preliminary Data," *American Journal of Orthopsychiatry* 56 (1986): 212–224.

89. Gordon Trasler, "Cautions for a Biological Approach to Crime," in *The Causes of Crime, New Biological Approaches*, ed. Sarnoff Mednick, Terrie Moffitt, and Susan Stack, 7–25 (Cambridge: Cambridge University Press, 1987).

90. James Q. Wilson and Richard Herrnstein, *Crime and Human Nature* (New York: Simon & Schuster, 1985), 126–147.

91. Charles Tittle, "Two Empirical Regularities (Maybe) in Search of an Explanation: Commentary on the Age/Crime Debate," *Criminology* 26 (1988): 75–85.

92. Neal Shover and Carol Thompson, "Age, Differential Expectations and Crime Desistance," *Criminology* 30 (1992): 89–105.

93. Erich Labouvie, "Maturing Out of Substance Use: Selection and Self-Correction," *Journal of Drug Issues* 26 (1996): 457–474.

94. Walter Gove, "The Effect of Age and Gender on Deviant Behavior: A Biopsychosocial Perspective," in *Gender and the Life Course*, ed. A. Ross, 131 (Chicago: Aldine, 1985).

95. Steven D. Levitt, "The Limited Role of Changing Age Structure in Explaining Aggregate Crime Rates," *Criminology* 37 (1999): 581–597.

96. Cesare Lombroso, *The Female Offender* (New York: Appleton Publishers, 1895/1920).

97. Otto Pollack, *The Criminality of Women* (Philadelphia: University of Pennsylvania, 1950).

98. For a review of this issue, see Darrell Steffensmeier, "Assessing the Impact of the Women's Movement on Sex-Based Differences in the Handling of Adult Criminal Defendants," *Crime and Delinquency* 26 (1980): 344–357.

99. Alan Booth and D. Wayne Osgood, "The Influence of Testosterone on Deviance in Adulthood: Assessing and Explaining the Relationship," *Criminology* 31 (1993): 93–118.

100. Darrell Steffensmeier and Robert Clark, "Sociocultural Versus Biological/Sexist Explanations of Sex Differences in Crime: A Survey of American Criminology Textbooks, 1918–1965," *American Sociologist* 15 (1980): 246–255.

101. Gisela Konopka, *The Adolescent Girl in Conflict* (Englewood Cliffs, N.J.: Prentice-Hall, 1966); Clyde Vedder and Dora Somerville, *The Delinquent Girl* (Springfield, Ill.: Charles C Thomas, 1970).

102. John Mirowsky and Catherine Ross, "Sex Differences in Distress: Real or Artifact?" *American Sociological Review* 60 (1995): 449–468; for a review of this issue, see Anne Campbell, *Men, Women and Aggression* (New York: Basic Books, 1993).

103. Robert Hoge, D.A. Andrews, and Alan Leschied, "Tests of Three Hypotheses Regarding the Predictors of Delinquency," *Journal of Abnormal Child Psychology* 22 (1994): 547–559.

104. Freda Adler, *Sisters in Crime* (New York: McGraw-Hill, 1975); Rita James Simon, *The Contemporary Woman and Crime* (Washington, D.C.: U.S. Government Printing Office, 1975).

105. Timothy F. Hartnagel and Muhammad Mizanuddin, "Modernization, Gender Role Convergence, and Female Crime," *International Journal of Comparative Sociology* 27 (1986): 1–14.

106. David Rowe, Alexander Vazsonyi, and Daniel Flannery, "Sex Differences in Crime: Do Mean and Within-Sex Variation Have Similar Causes?" *Journal of Research in Crime and Delinquency* 32 (1995): 84–100; Michael Hindelang, "Age, Sex, and the Versatility of Delinquency Involvements," *Social Forces* 14 (1971): 525–534; Martin Gold, *Delinquent Behavior in an American City* (Belmont, Calif.: Brooks/Cole, 1970); Gary Jensen and Raymond Eve, "Sex Differences in Delinquency: An Examination of Popular Sociological Explanations," *Criminology* 13 (1976): 427–448.

107. Darrel Steffensmeier and Renee Hoffman Steffensmeier, "Trends in Female Delinquency," *Criminology* 18 (1980): 62–85; see also Darrel Steffensmeier and Renee Hoffman Steffensmeier, "Crime and the Contemporary Woman: An Analysis of Changing Levels of Female Property Crime, 1960–1975," *Social Forces* 57 (1978): 566–584; Joseph Weis, "Liberation and Crime: The Invention of the New Female Criminal," *Crime and Social Justice* 1 (1976): 17–27; Carol Smart, "The New Female Offender: Reality or Myth," *British Journal of Criminology* 19 (1979): 50–59; Steven Box and Chris Hale, "Liberation/ Emancipation, Economic Marginalization or Less Chivalry," *Criminology* 22 (1984): 473–478.

108. Meda Chesney-Lind, "Female Offenders: Paternalism Reexamined," in *Women, the Courts and Equality*, ed. Laura Crites and Winifred Hepperle, 114–139 (Newberry Park, Calif.: Sage, 1987).

109. Darrell Steffensmeier, Emilie Allan, and Cathy Streifel, "Development and Female Crime: A Cross-National Test of Alternative Explanations," *Social Forces* 68 (1989): 262–283.

110. Roy Austin, "Recent Trends in the Male and Female Crime Rate: The Convergence Controversy," *Journal of Criminal Justice* 21 (1993): 447–466.

111. Mikhail Thomas, Howard Hurley, and Craig Rimes, "Pilot Analysis of Recidivism among Convicted Youth and Young Adults: 1999/00," *Juristat* 22, no. 9 (2002).

112. Marvin Wolfgang, Robert Figlio, and Thorsten Sellin, *Delinquency in a Birth Cohort* (Chicago: University of Chicago Press, 1972).

113. See Thorsten Sellin and Marvin Wolfgang, *The Measurement of Delinquency* (New York: Wiley, 1964), p. 120.

114. Paul Tracy and Robert Figlio, "Chronic Recidivism in the 1950 Birth Cohort," paper presented at the American Society of Criminology meeting, Toronto, October 1982; Marvin Wolfgang, "Delinquency in Two Birth Cohorts," in *Perspective Studies of Crime and Delinquency*, ed. Katherine Teilmann Van Dusen and Sarnoff Mednick, 7–17 (Boston: Kluwer-Nijhoff, 1983). The sections that follow rely heavily on these sources.

115. Lyle Shannon, *Criminal Career Opportunity* (New York: Human Sciences Press, 1988); Lyle Shannon, *Assessing the Relationship of Adult Criminal Careers to Juvenile Careers*.

116. D.J. West and David P. Farrington, *The Delinquent Way of Life* (London: Heinemann, 1977); David Farrington and D.J. West, "Criminal, Penal and Life Histories of Chronic Offenders: Risk and Protective Factors and Early Identification," in *Integrating Individual and Ecological Aspects of Crime* (Stockholm: National Council for Crime Prevention, 1993).

117. See, generally, M. Wolfgang, T. Thornberry, and R. Figlio, eds., *From Boy to Man, from Delinquency to Crime* (Chicago: University of Chicago Press, 1987); Paul Tracy and Kimberly Kempf-Leonard, *Continuity and Discontinuity in Criminal Careers* (New York: Plenum Press, 1996).

118. R. Tremblay, R. Loeber, C. Gagnon, P. Charlebois, S. Larivee, and M. LeBlanc, "Disruptive Boys with Stable and Unstable High Fighting Behavior Patterns During Junior Elementary School," *Journal of Abnormal Child Psychology* 19 (1991): 285–300; Jennifer White, Terrie Moffitt, Felton Earls, Lee Robins, and Phil Silva, "How Early Can We Tell? Predictors of Childhood Conduct Disorder and Adolescent Delinquency," *Criminology* 28 (1990): 507–535; John Laub and Robert Sampson, "Unemployment, Marital Discord, and Deviant Behavior: The Long-Term Correlates of Childhood Misbehavior," paper presented at the annual meeting of the American Society of Criminology, Baltimore, November 1990, rev. version.

119. Jane B. Sprott and Anthony N. Doob, "Bad, Sad, and Rejected: The Lives of Aggressive Children," *Canadian Journal of Criminology* 42 (2000): 123–134.

120. David Farrington and J. David Hawkins, "Predicting Participation, Early Onset, and Later Persistence in Officially Recorded Offending," *Criminal Behavior and Mental Health* 1 (1991): 1–33; Daniel Nagin, David Farrington, and Terrie Moffitt, "Life-Course Trajectories of Different Types of Offenders," *Criminology* 33 (1995): 111–139.

121. Susan Martin, "Policing Career Criminals: An Examination of an Innovative Crime Control Program," *Journal of Criminal Law and Criminology* 77 (1986): 1159–1182.

122. "A One-Day Snapshot of Inmates in Canada's Adult Correctional Facilities," *Juristat* 18 (1998).

Chapter 4

1. Arthur Lurigio, "Are All Victims Alike? The Adverse, Generalized, and Differential Impact of Crime," *Crime and Delinquency* 33 (1987): 452–467.

2. Ted Miller, Mark Cohen, and Brian Wiersema, *The Extent and Costs of Crime Victimization: A New Look* (Washington, D.C.: National Institute of Justice, 1996).

3. Peter Finn, *Victims* (Washington, D.C.: Bureau of Justice Statistics, 1988); Alison Hatch Cunningham and Curt T. Griffiths, *Canadian Criminal Justice: A Primer* (Toronto: Harcourt Brace, 1997).

4. Susan Leslie Bryant and Lillian Range, "Suicidality in College Women Who Were Sexually and Physically Abused and Physically Punished by Parents," *Violence and Victims* 10 (1995): 195–215.

5. Sally Davies-Netley, Michael Hurlburt, and Richard Hough, "Childhood Abuse as a Precursor to Homelessness for Homeless Women with Severe Mental Illness," *Violence and Victims* 11 (1996): 129–142.

6. See, generally, M.D. Pagelow, *Woman Battering: Victims and Their Experiences* (Beverly Hills, Calif.: Sage, 1981); Walter Gleason, "Mental Disorders in Battered Women," *Violence and Victims* 8 (1993): 53–66; Daniel Saunders, "Posttraumatic Stress Symptom Profiles of Battered Women: A Comparison of Survivors in Two Settings," *Violence and Victims* 9 (1994): 31–43.

7. Trevor Markesteyn, *The Psychological Impact of Nonsexual Criminal Offenses on Victims*, prepared for the Corrections Branch, Ministry of the Solicitor General of Canada. Report No. 1992-21.

8. Elizabeth Stanko and Kathy Hobdell, "Assault on Men, Masculinity and Male Victimization," *British Journal of Criminology* 33 (1993): 400–415.

9. John McKendy, "Dialogue and the Risk of Responsibility," *Humanity & Society* 23 (1999): 238–253; see also, "Ideological Practices and the Management of Emotions: The Case of Wife Abusers," *Critical Sociology* 19 (1992): 61–80.

10. Alex C. Michalos and Bruno D. Zumbo, "Criminal Victimization and the Quality of Life," *Social Indicators Research* 50 (2000): 245–295.

11. Robert Davis, Bruce Taylor, and Arthur Lurigio, "Adjusting to Criminal Victimization: The Correlates of Postcrime Distress," *Violence and Victimization* 11 (1996): 21–34.

12. James Anderson, Terry Grandison, and Laronistine Dyson, "Victims of Random Violence and the Public Health Implication: A Health Care of Criminal Justice Issue," *Journal of Criminal Justice* 24 (1996): 379–393.

13. Derek Janhevich, *Hate Crime in Canada: An Overview of Issues and Data Sources* (Ottawa: Statistics Canada, 2001).

14. Rosemary Gartner and Anthony Doob, "Trends in Criminal Victimization in 1988–1993," *Juristat* 14 (1994).

15. "Toronto: Crime and Safety in the City," Ipsos-Reid poll, September 9, 2003.

16. Paul Brantingham and Stephen Easton, "The Costs of Crime: Who Pays and How Much?" *Fraser Institute Critical Issues Bulletin* (1998).

17. "Murder Rate Down for Fourth Year in a Row—TV Coverage Up," *The Fraser Institute's National Media Archive*, 1996.

18. Sandra Besserer and Catherine Trainor, "Criminal Victimization in Canada, 1999," *Juristat* 20 (2000).

19. For some interesting studies in this area, see Vincent F. Sacco, "The Effects of Mass Media on Perceptions of Crime," *Pacific Sociological Review* 25 (1982): 475–493; Julian V. Roberts and Michelle G. Grossman, "Crime Prevention and Public Opinion," *Canadian Journal of Criminology*, January (1990): 75–90; and "The Effect of Pretrial Publicity: The Bernardo

20. Timothy Ireland and Cathy Spatz Widom, *Childhood Victimization and Risk for Alcohol and Drug Arrests* (Washington, D.C.: National Institute of Justice, 1995).

21. Cathy Spatz Widom, *The Cycle of Violence* (Washington, D.C.: National Institute of Justice, 1992), 1; Cathy Spatz Widom, "The Cycle of Violence," *Science* 244 (1989): 160–166.

22. Steve Spaccarelli, J. Douglas Coatsworth, and Blake Sperry Bowden, "Exposure to Serious Family Violence among Incarcerated Boys: Its Association with Violent Offending and Potential Mediating Variables," *Violence and Victims* 10 (1995): 163–180.

23. Jerome Kolbo, "Risk and Resilience among Children Exposed to Family Violence," *Violence and Victims* 11 (1996): 113–127.

24. Jane B. Sprott, Anthony N. Doob, and Jennifer M. Jenkins, "Problem Behaviour and Delinquency in Children and Youth," *Juristat* 21, no. 4 (2001).

25. *Annual Report of the Correctional Investigator, 2002–2003* (Ottawa: Minister of Public Works and Government Services, 2003).

26. Canadian Centre for Justice Statistics, *Family Violence in Canada: A Statistical Profile 2004* (Ottawa: Statistics Canada, 2004).

27. P. Rock, *A View from the Shadows: The Ministry of the Solicitor General Canada and the Justice for Victims of Crime Initiative* (Oxford: Clarendon Press, 1986); Brian D. Maclean, "A Program of Local Crime-Survey Research for Canada," in *Crime in Society: Readings in Critical Criminology*, ed. Brian D. Maclean (Toronto: Copp Clark, 1996).

28. Solicitor General Canada, *Reported and Unreported Crimes: Canadian Urban Victimization Survey*, Bulletin 2 (Ottawa: Ministry Secretariat, 1984).

29. V.F. Sacco and H. Johnson, *Patterns of Criminal Victimization in Canada*, General Social Survey Analysis Services, Statistics Canada, Catalogue 11-612E, No. 2. (Ottawa: Ministry of Supply and Services, 1990).

30. Ronet Bachman, *Violence against Women* (Washington, D.C.: Bureau of Justice Statistics, 1994).

31. Statistics Canada, "Criminal Harassment," *The Daily*, November 29, 2000.

32. Wendy Chan and George Rigakos, "Risk, Crime and Gender," *British Journal of Criminology* 42 (2002): 743–761.

33. Holly Johnson and Gary Lazarus, "The Impact of Age on Crime Victimization Rates," *Canadian Journal of Criminology* 31 (1989): 309–317.

34. William Meloff and Robert A. Silverman, "Canadian Kids Who Kill," *Canadian Journal of Criminology* (1992): 15–34.

35. Murray Straus, Richard Gelles, and Suzanne Steinmetz, *Behind Closed Doors: Violence in the American Family* (Garden City, N.Y.: Anchor Books, 1980); Richard Gelles and Murray Straus, "Violence in the American Family," *Journal of Social Issues* 35 (1979): 15–39; Richard Gelles and Murray Straus, *Is Violence toward Children Increasing? A Comparison of 1975 and 1985 National Survey Rates* (Durham, N.H.: Family Violence Research Program, 1985).

36. Ching-Tung Lung and Deborah Daro, *Current Trends in Child Abuse Reporting and Fatalities: The Results of the 1995 Annual Fifty-State Survey* (Chicago: National Committee to Prevent Child Abuse, 1996).

37. Nico Trocme and David Wolfe, *The Canadian Incidence Study of Reported Child Abuse and Neglect* (Ottawa: Health Canada, Spring 2001).

38. Walter S. DeKeseredy and Ronald Hinch, *Woman Abuse: Sociological Perspectives* (Toronto: Thompson, 1991); Karen Rodgers, "Wife Assault: The Findings of a National Survey," *Juristat* 14 (1990).

Case," *Canadian Journal of Criminology*, July (1996): 253–270.

39. Josee Savoie, "Homicide in Canada, 2002," *Juristat* 23, no. 8 (2003); Ruth Code, "Canada's Shelters for Abused Women," *Juristat* 23, no. 4 (2003); Tina Hotton, "Spousal Violence after Marital Separation," *Juristat* 21, no. 7 (2001); Valerie Pottie Bunge, "National Trends in Intimate-Partner Homicides, 1974–2000," *Juristat* 22, no. 5 (2002).

40. Yasmin Jiwani, "The 1999 General Social Survey on Spousal Violence: An Analysis," The FREDA Centre for Research on Violence against Women and Children, August 2000; also, Daisy Locke, "Family Homicide," in *Family Violence in Canada: A Statistical Profile* (Ottawa: Statistics Canada, 2000), 39–44; Holly Johnson, *Dangerous Domains: Violence Against Women in Canada* (Scarborough, Ont.: Nelson Canada, 1996); and Robin Fitzgerald, *Family Violence in Canada: A Statistical Profile* (Ottawa: Statistics Canada, 1999).

41. *R. v. Whynot* (1983), 9 C.C.C. 449 (N.S.C.A.).

42. Holly Johnson, "Children and Youths as Victims of Violent Crimes," *Juristat* 15 (1995).

43. N. Trocme, D. McPhee, and K. Kwon Tam, "Child Abuse and Neglect in Ontario: Incidence and Characteristics," *Child Welfare* 74 (1995): 563–586.

44. Janet Lauritsen and Kenna Davis Quinet, "Repeat Victimizations among Adolescents and Young Adults," *Journal of Quantitative Criminology* 11 (1995): 143–163.

45. Denise Osborn, Dan Ellingworth, Tim Hope, and Alan Trickett, "Are Repeatedly Victimized Households Different?" *Journal of Quantitative Criminology* 12 (1996): 223–245.

46. Jon Simmons and Tricia Dodd, *Home Office Statistical Bulletin: Crime in England and Wales, 2002/03*; Ron Melchers, "Do Toronto Police Engage in Racial Profiling?" *Canadian Journal of Criminology and Criminal Justice* 7 (2003): 347–366.

47. David Finkelhor and Nancy Asdigian, "Risk Factors for Youth Victimization: Beyond a Lifestyles/Routine Activities Theory Approach," *Violence and Victimization* 11 (1996): 3–19.

48. Graham Farrell, "Predicting and Preventing Revictimization," in *Crime and Justice: An Annual Review of Research*, vol. 20, ed. Michael Tonry and David Farrington (Chicago: University of Chicago Press, 1995), 61–126.

49. Lauritsen and Quinet, "Repeat Victimizations," p. 161.

50. Graham Farrell, Coretta Phillips, and Ken Pease, "Like Taking Candy, Why Does Repeat Victimization Occur?" *British Journal of Criminology* 35 (1995): 384–399.

51. Alex C. Michalos and Bruno D. Zumbo, "Criminal Victimization and the Qualiy of Life," *Social Indicators Research* 50 (2000): 245–295.

52. A. Karmen, *Crime Victims: An Introduction to Victimology* (Pacific Grove, Calif.: Brooks/Cole, 1990).

53. Hans Von Hentig, *The Criminal and His Victim: Studies in the Sociobiology of Crime* (New Haven, Conn.: Yale University Press, 1948), 384.

54. Stephen Schafer, *The Victim and His Criminal* (New York: Random House, 1968), 152.

55. Marvin Wolfgang, *Patterns of Criminal Homicide* (Philadelphia: University of Pennsylvania Press, 1958).

56. Menachim Amir, *Patterns in Forcible Rape* (Chicago: University of Chicago Press, 1971).

57. Susan Estrich, *Real Rape* (Cambridge, Mass.: Harvard University Press, 1987), 69; L. Clark and D. Lewis, *Rape: The Price of Coercive Sexuality* (Toronto: Women's Press, 1977), 150.

58. "McClung Letter Throws Canadian Legal Circles into Turmoil," *The Globe and Mail*, March 1, 1999, A3.

59. Martin Yaqzan, "'Rape'—Yesterday and Today!" *The Brunswickan*, November 5, 1993; "Dispatch Case," *The Chronicle of Higher Education* (November 24, 1993), A34; "Date Rape Comments Cause Campus Furor: It's a Natural Outlet, Says Professor," *The Globe and Mail*, November 9, 1993, A4.

60. E.A. Fattah, "Some Recent Theoretical Developments in Victimology," *Victimology: An International Journal* 4 (1979): 198–213; see also, E.A. Fattah, "Canada's Successful Experience with the Abolition of the Death Penalty," *Canadian Journal of Criminology* 25 (1983): 421–431; E.A. Fattah, "Victimology: Past, Present and Future," *Criminologie* 33 (2000): 17–46.

61. Martin Daly and Margo Wilson, *Homicide* (New York: Aldine de Gruyter, 1988).

62. "Bill Won't Foster Gay Lifestyle, Rock Says," *The Globe and Mail*, November 18, 1994, A3; "Bill C-41 (Sentencing Reform) Passes Third Reading in House of Commons," Parliamentary press release, June 15, 1995.

63. Rosemary Gartner and Bill McCarthy, "The Social Distribution of Femicide in Urban Canada, 1921–1988," *Law and Society Review* 25 (1991): 287–311.

64. Julian V. Roberts, "Disproportionate Harm: Hate Crime in Canada," Department of Justice Canada, Working Document 1995-11e, 1995.

65. "ADL Survey Analyzes Neo-Nazi Skinhead Menace and International Connections," *CJ International* 12 (1996): 7; FBI, news release, November 4, 1996.

66. Derek E. Janhevich, *Hate Crime in Canada: An Overview of Issues and Data Sources*, Canadian Centre for Justice Statistics Catalogue no. 85-551-XIE, January 2001.

67. James Garofalo, "Bias and Non-Bias Crimes in New York City: Preliminary Findings," paper presented at the annual meeting of the American Society of Criminology, Baltimore, November 1990.

68. Ronald Powers, "Bensonhurst Man Guilty," *Boston Globe*, May 18, 1990, 3.

69. "Boy Gets 18 Years in Fatal Park Beating of Transient," *Los Angeles Times*, December 24, 1987, 9B.

70. Mike McPhee, "In Denver, Attacks Stir Fears of Racism," *Boston Globe*, December 10, 1990, 3.

71. Jack McDevitt, "The Study of the Character of Civil Rights Crimes in Massachusetts (1983–1987)," paper presented at the annual meeting of the American Society of Criminology, Reno, NV, November 1989; see also, Jack Levin and Jack McDevitt, *Hate Crimes: The Rising Tide of Bigotry and Bloodshed* (New York: Plenum, 1993); Jack Levin and Jack McDevitt, *Hate Crimes: A Study of Offenders' Motivations* (Boston, Mass.: Northeastern University, 1993).

72. Derek Janhevich, *Hate Crime in Canada: An Overview of Issues and Data Sources* (Ottawa: Canadian Centre for Justice Statistics, 2001).

73. Lawrence Cohen and Marcus Felson, "Social Change and Crime Rate Trends: A Routine Activities Approach," *American Sociological Review* 44 (1979): 588–608; L. Cohen, James Kleugel, and Kenneth Land, "Social Inequality and Predatory Criminal Victimization: An Exposition and Test of a Formal Theory," *American Sociological Review* 46 (1981): 505–524; Steven Messner and Kenneth Tardiff, "The Social Ecology of Urban Homicide: An Application of the Routine Activities Approach," *Criminology* 23 (1985): 241–267.

74. See, generally, Gary Gottfredson and Denise Gottfredson, *Victimization in Schools* (New York: Plenum Press, 1985), and "Children as Victims of Violent Crime," *Juristat* 11 (1991).

75. Gary Jensen and David Brownfield, "Gender, Lifestyles, and Victimization: Beyond Routine Activity Theory," *Violence and Victims* 1 (1986): 85–99.

76. Less Whitbeck and Ronald Simons, "A Comparison of Adaptive Strategies and Patterns of Victimization among Homeless Adolescents and Adults," *Violence and Victims* 8 (1993): 135–151; Kevin Fitzpatrick, Mark La Gory, and Ferris Ritchey, "Criminal Victimization among the Homeless," *Justice Quarterly* 10 (1993): 353–368.

77. John Lowman, "Violence and the Outlaw Status of (Street) Prostitution in Canada," *Violence Against Women* 6, no. 9 (2000): 987–1011.

78. Josee Savoie, "Homicide in Canada, 2002," *Juristat* 23, no. 8 (2003): 10.

79. Joan McDermott, "Crime in the School and in the Community: Offenders, Victims and Fearful Youth," *Crime and Delinquency* 29 (1983): 270–283.

80. Simon Singer, "Homogeneous Victim–Offender Populations: A Review and Some Research Implications," *Journal of Criminal Law and Criminology* 72 (1981): 779–799.

81. Janet Lauritsen, John Laub, and Robert Sampson, "Conventional and Delinquent Activities: Implications for the Prevention of Violent Victimization Among Adolescents," *Violence and Victims* 7 (1992): 91–102.

82. Gary Jensen and David Brownfield, "Gender, Lifestyles and Victimization: Beyond Routine Activities," *Violence and Victims* 1 (1986): 85–101.

83. Ross Vasta, "Physical Child Abuse: A Dual Component Analysis," *Developmental Review* 2 (1982): 128–135.

84. Elise Lake, "An Exploration of the Violent Victim Experiences of Female Offenders," *Violence and Victims* 8 (1993): 41–50.

85. Jeffrey Fagan, Elizabeth Piper, and Yu-Teh Cheng, "Contributions of Victimization to Delinquency in Inner Cities," *Journal of Criminal Law and Criminology* 78 (1987): 586–613.

86. M. Hindelang, M. Gottfredson, and J. Garofalo, *Victims of Personal Crime: An Empirical Foundation for a Theory of Personal Victimization* (Cambridge, Mass.: Ballinger, 1978).

87. James Garofalo, "Reassessing the Lifestyle Model of Criminal Victimization," in *Positive Criminology*, ed. Michael Gottfredson and Travis Hirschi (Newbury Park, Calif.: Sage Publications, 1987), 23–42.

88. Terance Miethe and David McDowall, "Contextual Effects in Models of Criminal Victimization," *Social Forces* 71 (1993): 741–759.

89. Terance Miethe and Robert Meier, "Opportunity, Choice, and Criminal Victimization: A Test of a Theoretical Model," *Journal of Research in Crime and Delinquency* 27 (1990): 243–266.

90. Robert Sampson and Janet Lauritsen, "Deviant Lifestyles, Proximity to Crime and the Offender–Deviant Link in Personal Violence," *Journal of Research in Crime and Delinquency* 27 (1990): 110–139.

91. Rodney Stark, "Deviant Places: A Theory of the Ecology of Crime," *Criminology* 25 (1987): 893–911.

92. William Julius Wilson, *The Truly Disadvantaged* (Chicago: University of Chicago Press, 1987); Allen Liska and Paul Bellair, "Violent-Crime Rates and Racial Composition: Convergence over Time," *American Journal of Sociology* 101 (1995): 578–610.

93. Lawrence Cohen and Marcus Felson, "Social Change and Crime Rate Trends: A Routine Activities Approach," *American Sociological Review* 44 (1979): 588–608.

94. Lawrence Cohen, Marcus Felson, and Kenneth Land, "Property Crime Rates in the United States: A Macrodynamic Analysis, 1947–1977, with Ex-ante Forecasts for the Mid-1980s," *American Journal of Sociology* 86 (1980): 90–118.

95. Terance Miethe and Robert Meier, *Crime and Its Social Context: Toward an Integrated Theory of Offenders, Victims, and Situations* (Albany: State University of New York Press, 1994).

96. Jon Gunnar Bernburg and Thorolfur Thorlindsson, "Routine Activities in Social Context: A Closer Look at the Role of Opportunity in Deviant Behavior," *Justice Quarterly* 18 (2001): 543–568.

97. Martin Schwartz, Walter DeKeseredy, David Tait, and Shahid Alvi, "Male Peer Support and a Feminist Routine Activities Theory: Understanding Sexual Assault on the College Campus," *Justice Quarterly* 18 (2001): 623–650.

98. See Messner and Tardiff, "The Social Ecology of Urban Homicide"; Philip Cook, "The Demand and Supply of Criminal Opportunities," in *Crime and Justice*, vol. 7, ed. Michael Tonry and Norval Morris, 1–28 (Chicago: University of Chicago Press, 1986); Ronald Clarke and Derek Cornish, "Modeling Offender's Decisions: A Framework for Research and Policy," in *Crime and Justice*, vol. 6, ed. Michael Tonry and Norval Morris, 147–187 (Chicago: University of Chicago Press, 1985).

99. Michael Maxfield, "Household Composition, Routine Activity, and Victimization: A Comparative Analysis," *Journal of Quantitative Criminology* 3 (1987): 301–320.

100. James Lynch and David Cantor, "Ecological and Behavioral Influences on Property Victimization at Home: Implications for Opportunity Theory," *Journal of Research in Crime and Delinquency* 29 (1992): 335–362.

101. David Maume, "Inequality and Metropolitan Rape Rates: A Routine Activities Approach," *Justice Quarterly* 6 (1989): 513–527.

102. James Massey, Marvin Krohn, and Lisa Bonati, "Property Crime and the Routine Activities of Individuals," *Journal of Research in Crime and Delinquency* 26 (1989): 378–400.

103. Terance Miethe, Mark Stafford, and Douglas Stone, "Lifestyle Changes and Risks of Criminal Victimization," *Journal of Quantitative Criminology* 6 (1990): 357–375.

104. R.R. Corado, R. Roesch, W. Glackman, J.L. Evans, and G.J. Leger, "Lifestyles and Personal Victimization: A Test of the Model with Canadian Survey Data," *Journal of Crime and Justice* 3 (1980): 129–139.

105. Messner and Tardiff, "The Social Ecology of Urban Homicide."

106. James Lasley, "Drinking Routines, Lifestyles and Predatory Victimization: A Causal Analysis," *Justice Quarterly* 6 (1989): 529–542.

107. Richard R. Benett, "Development and Crime," *The Sociological Quarterly* 32 (1991): 343–363.

108. Christopher Birkbeck and Gary LaFree, "The Situational Analysis of Crime and Deviance," *Annual Review of Sociology* 19 (1993): 113–137.

109. T.D. Miethe, M.C. Stafford, and J.S. Long, "Routine Activities/Lifestyle and Victimization," *American Sociological Review* 52 (1987): 184–194.

110. Leslie Kennedy and Stephen Baron, "Routine Activities and a Subculture of Violence: A Study of Violence on the Street," *Journal of Research in Crime and Delinquency* 30 (1993): 88–112.

111. Marcus Felson, *Crime and Everday Life* (Thousand Oaks, Calif.: Pine Forge Press, 1994).

112. M. Hough and P. Matthew, *The British Crime Survey's First Report* (London: Her Majesty's Stationery Office, 1983).

113. Patricia Resnick, "Psychological Effects of Victimization: Implications for the Criminal Justice System," *Crime and Delinquency* 33 (1987): 468–478.

114. Dean Kilpatrick, Benjamin Saunders, Lois Veronen, Connie Best, and Judith Von, "Criminal Victimization: Lifetime Prevalence, Reporting to Police, and Psychological Impact," *Crime and Delinquency* 33 (1987): 479–489.

115. Mark Santello and Harold Leitenberg, "Sexual Aggression by an Acquaintance: Methods of Coping and Later Psychological Adjustment," *Violence and Victims* 8 (1993): 91–103.

116. U.S. Department of Justice, *Report of the President's Task Force on Victims of Crime* (Washington, D.C.: U.S. Government Printing Office, 1983).

117. U.S. Department of Justice, *Report of the President's Task Force on Victims of Crime* (Washington, D.C.: U.S. Government Printing Office, 1983), 2–10; and "Review on Victims—Witnesses of Crime," *Massachusetts Lawyers Weekly*, April 25, 1983, 26; Robert Davis, *Crime Victims: Learning How to Help Them* (Washington, D.C.: National Institute of Justice, 1987).

118. Alan Young, *Victims of Crime Research Series. The Role of the Victim in the Criminal Process: A Literature Review—1989 to 1999* (Ottawa: Department of Justice, 2001).

119. John Howard Society of Alberta, "Victim Impact Statements, 1997," http://www.johnhoward.ab.ca/PUB/C53.htm (accessed May 22, 2005).

120. Randall Schmidt, "Crime Victim Compensation Legislation: A Comparative Study," *Victimology* 5 (1980): 428–437.

121. A.C. Bowland, "Sexual Assault Trials and the Protection of 'Bad Girls': The Battle between the Courts and Parliament," in *Confronting Sexual Assault: A Decade of Legal and Social Change*, ed. Julian Roberts and R.M. Mohr (Toronto: University of Toronto Press, 1994).

122. Peter Jaffe, Marlies Sudermann, Deborah Reitzel, and Steve Killip, "An Evaluation of a Secondary School Primary Prevention Program on Violence in Intimate Relationships," *Violence and Victims* 7 (1992): 129–145; *Healthy Relationships: A Violence-Prevention Curriculum* (Halifax: Men for Change, 1994).

123. Vicki McNickel Rose, "Rape as a Social Problem: A By-Product of the Feminist Movement," *Social Problems* 25 (1977): 75–89.

124. Janet Gornick, Martha Burt, and Karen Pittman, "Structure and Activities of Rape Crisis Centers in the Early 1980s," *Crime and Delinquency* 31 (1985): 247–268.

125. Andrew Karmen, "Victim–Offender Reconciliation Programs: Pro and Con," *Perspectives of the American Probation and Parole Association* 20 (1996): 11–14.

126. See Frank Carrington, "Victim's Rights Litigation: A Wave of the Future," in *Perspectives on Crime Victims*, ed. Burt Galaway and Joe Hudson (St. Louis: Mosby, 1981).

127. Alison Hatch Cunningham and Curt T. Griffiths, *Canadian Criminal Justice: A Primer* (Toronto: Harcourt Brace, 1997).

128. Ontario Ministry of the Attorney General, *Victim's Bill of Rights* (Toronto: Queen's Printer, 1996).

129. Pamela Wilcox Rountree and Kenneth Land, "Burglary Victimization, Perceptions of Crime Risk, and Routine Activities: A Multilevel Analysis across Seattle Neighborhoods and Census Tracts," *Journal of Research in Crime and Delinquency* 33 (1996): 1147–1180.

130. Leslie Kennedy, "Going It Alone: Unreported Crime and Individual Self-Help," *Journal of Criminal Justice* 16 (1988): 403–413.

131. Rosemary Gartner and Anthony Doob, "Trends in Criminal Victimization: 1988–1993," *Juristat* 14 (1994).

132. Ronald Clarke, "Situational Crime Prevention: Its Theoretical Basis and Practical Scope," in *Annual Review of Criminal Justice Research*, ed. Michael Tonry and Norval Morris (Chicago: University of Chicago Press, 1983).

133. D.P. Rosenbaum, "Community Crime Protection, A Review and Synthesis of the Literature," *Justice Quarterly* 5 (1988): 323–395.

134. Andrew Buck, Simon Hakim, and George Rengert, "Burglar Alarms and the Choice Behavior of Burglars," *Journal of Criminal Justice* 21 (1993): 497–507; for an opposing view, see Lynch and Cantor, "Ecological and Behavioral Influences on Property Victimization at Home."

135. R. McNamara, *Crime Displacement: The Other Side of Prevention* (East Rockaway, N.Y.: Cummings and Hathaway, 1994).

136. Alan Lizotte, "Determinants of Completing Rape and Assault," *Journal of Quantitative Criminology* 2 (1986): 213–217; Polly Marchbanks, Kung-Jong Lui, and James Mercy, "Risk of Injury from Resisting Rape," *American Journal of Epidemiology* 132 (1990): 540–549.

137. Caroline Wolf Harlow, *Robbery Victims* (Washington, D.C.: Bureau of Justice Statistics, 1987).

138. Gary Kleck, "Guns and Violence: An Interpretive Review of the Field," *Social Pathology* 1 (1995): 12–45.

139. James Fyfe, "Police Use of Deadly Force: Research and Reform," *Justice Quarterly* 5 (1988): 157–176.

140. Gary Kleck, "Rape and Resistance," *Social Problems* 37 (1990): 149–162.

141. Gary Mauser, "Armed Self Defense: The Canadian Case," *Journal of Criminal Justice* 24 (1996): 393–406; see also, Gary Mauser, "Canadians Do Use Firearms in Self-Protection," *Canadian Journal of Criminology*, October (1996): 485–488; Gary Mauser, "Armed Self Defense: The Canadian Case," *Journal of Criminal Justice* 24 (1996): 393–406; Gary Mauser and Richard Holmes, "An Evaluation of the 1977 Canadian Firearms Legislation," *Evaluation Review* 16 (1992): 603–617; Gary Mauser and Michael Margolis, "The Politics of Gun Control: Comparing Canadian and American Patterns," *Government and Policy* 10 (1992): 189–209.

142. Gary Green, "Citizen Gun Ownership and Criminal Deterrence: Theory, Research and Policy," *Criminology* 25 (1987): 63–81.

143. James Garofalo and Maureen McLeod, *Improving the Use and Effectiveness of Neighborhood Watch Programs* (Washington, D.C.: National Institute of Justice, 1988); Kevin D. Carriere and Richard V. Ericson, *CrimeStoppers: A Study in the Organization of Community Policing* (University of Toronto: Centre of Criminology, 1989); Dennis P. Forcese, *Policing Canadian Society* (Scarborough: Prentice Hall, 1992).

144. Peter Finn, *Block Watches Help Crime Victims in Philadelphia* (Washington, D.C.: National Institute of Justice, 1986).

Chapter 5

1. Cesare Beccaria, *On Crimes and Punishments*, excerpted in Joseph E. Jacoby, *Classics of Criminology*, 2nd ed. (Prospect Heights, Ill.: Waveland, 1994): 277–286; Francis Edward Devine, "Cesare Beccaria and the Theoretical Foundations of Modern Penal Jurisprudence," *New England Journal on Prison Law* 7 (1982): 8–21; Marcello Maestro, *Cesare Beccaria and the Origins of Penal Reform* (Philadelphia: Temple University, 1973).

2. Graeme Newman and Pietro Marongiu, "Penological Reform and the Myth of Beccaria," *Criminology* 28 (1990): 325–346.

3. Bob Roshier, *Controlling Crime* (Chicago: Lyceum Books, 1989), 10.

4. Jeremy Bentham, *A Fragment on Government and an Introduction to the Principle of Morals and Legislation*, ed. Wilfred Harrison (Oxford: Basil Blackwell, 1967).

5. Robert Martinson, "What Works?—Questions and Answers about Prison Reform," *Public Interest* 35 (1974): 22–54.

6. Charles Murray and Louis Cox, *Beyond Probation* (Beverly Hills, Calif.: Sage, 1979).

7. Ronald Bayer, "Crime, Punishment and the Decline of Liberal Optimism," *Crime and Delinquency* 27 (1981): 190.

8. James Q. Wilson, *Thinking About Crime*, rev. ed. (New York: Vintage Books, 1983), 128, 260.

9. Pierre Tremblay and Carlo Morselli, "Patterns in Criminal Achievement: Wilson and Abrhamse Revisited," *Criminology* 38 (2000): 633–660.

10. Frederick J. Desroches, *Force and Fear: Robbery in Canada* (Toronto: Nelson, 1995).

11. Phonse Jessome, *Murder at McDonald's: The Killers Next Door* (Halifax: Nimbus, 1994).

12. See, generally, Derek Cornish and Ronald Clarke, eds., *The Reasoning Criminal: Rational Choice Perspectives on Offending* (New York: Springer Verlag, 1986); Philip Cook, "The Demand and Supply of Criminal Opportunities," in *Crime and Justice*, vol. 7, ed. Michael Tonry and Norval Morris (Chicago: University of Chicago Press, 1986), 1–28; Ronald Clarke and Derek Cornish, "Modeling Offender's

Decisions: A Framework for Research and Policy," in *Crime and Justice*, vol. 6, ed. Michael Tonry and Norval Morris (Chicago: University of Chicago Press, 1985), 147–187; Morgan Reynolds, *Crime by Choice: An Economic Analysis* (Dallas: Fisher Institute, 1985).

13. George Rengert and John Wasilchick, *Suburban Burglary: A Time and Place for Everything* (Springfield, Ill.: Charles C Thomas, 1985).

14. John McIver, "Criminal Mobility: A Review of Empirical Studies," in *Crime Spillover*, eds. Simon Hakim and George Rengert (Beverly Hills, Calif.: Sage, 1981), 110–121; Carol Kohfeld and John Sprague, "Demography, Police Behavior, and Deterrence," *Criminology* 28 (1990): 111–136.

15. Derek Cornish and Ronald Clarke, "Understanding Crime Displacement: An Application of Rational Choice Theory," *Criminology* 25 (1987): 933–947.

16. Lloyd Phillips and Harold Votey, "The Influence of Police Interventions and Alternative Income Sources on the Dynamic Process of Choosing Crime as a Career," *Journal of Quantitative Criminology* 3 (1987): 251–274.

17. Michael Gottfredson and Travis Hirschi, *A General Theory of Crime* (Stanford, Calif.: Stanford University Press, 1990).

18. Liliana Pezzin, "Earnings Prospects, Matching Effects, and the Decision to Terminate a Criminal Career," *Journal of Quantitative Criminology* 11 (1995): 29–50.

19. Neal Shover, *Aging Criminals* (Beverly Hills, Calif.: Sage, 1985).

20. Ronald Akers, "Rational Choice, Deterrence and Social Learning Theory in Criminology: The Path Not Taken," *Journal of Criminal Law and Criminology* 81 (1990): 653–676.

21. Robert Agnew, "Determinism, Indeterminism, and Crime: An Empirical Exploration," *Criminology* 33 (1995): 83–109.

22. Bruce Jacobs, "Crack Dealers' Apprehension Avoidance Techniques: A Case of Restrictive Deterrence," *Justice Quarterly* 13 (1996): 359–381.

23. Paul Cromwell, James Olson, and D'Aunn Wester Avery, *Breaking and Entering: An Ethnographic Analysis of Burglary* (Newbury Park, Calif.: Sage, 1989).

24. John Gibbs and Peggy Shelly, "Life in the Fast Lane: A Retrospective View by Commercial Thieves," *Journal of Research in Crime and Delinquency* 19 (1982): 229–230.

25. George Rengert and John Wasilchick, *Space, Time and Crime: Ethnographic Insights into Residential Burglary* (Washington, D.C.: National Institute of Justice, 1989); see also George Rengert and John Wasilchick, *Suburban Burglary*.

26. Leanne Fiftal Alarid, James Marquart, Velmer Burton, Francis Cullen, and Steven Cuvelier, "Women's Roles in Serious Offenses: A Study of Adult Felons," *Justice Quarterly* 13 (1996): 431–454.

27. Ronald Clarke and Marcus Felson, "Introduction: Criminology, Routine Activity and Rational Choice," in *Routine Activity and Rational Choice* (New Brunswick, N.J.: Transaction Publishers, 1993), 1–14.

28. Andrew Buck, Simon Hakim, and George Rengert, "Burglar Alarms and the Choice Behavior of Burglars: A Suburban Phenomenon," *Journal of Criminal Justice* 21 (1993): 497–507.

29. Ralph Taylor and Stephen Gottfredson, "Environmental Design, Crime, and Prevention: An Examination of Community Dynamics," in *Communities and Crime*, ed. Albert Reiss and Michael Tonry (Chicago: University of Chicago Press, 1986), 387–416.

30. Michael Costanzo, William Halperin, and Nathan Gale, "Criminal Mobility and the Directional Component in Journeys to Crime," in *Metropolitan Crime Patterns*, ed. Robert Figlio, Simon Hakim, and George Rengert (Monsey, N.Y.: Criminal Justice Press, 1986), 73–95.

31. Garland White, "Neighborhood Permeability and Burglary Rates," *Justice Quarterly* 7 (1990): 57–67.

32. William Smith, Sharon Glave Frazee, and Elizabeth Davison, "Furthering the Integration of Routine Activity and Social Disorganization Theories: Small Units of Analysis and the Study of Street Robbery as a Diffusion Process," *Criminology* 38 (2000): 489–521.

33. Paul Bellair, "Informal Surveillance and Street Crime: A Complex Relationship," *Criminology* 38 (2000): 137–167.

34. James Massey, Marvin Krohn, and Lisa Bonati, "Property Crime and the Routine Activities of Individuals," *Journal of Research in Crime and Delinquency* 26 (1989): 378–400; note, however, that the findings here generally disagree with routine activities theory.

35. Gary Kleck and Don Kates, *Armed: New Perspectives on Guns* (Amherst, N.Y.: Prometheus Books, 2001).

36. Kenneth Tunnell, *Choosing Crime* (Chicago: Nelson-Hall, 1992), 105.

37. Robert Sampson and Jacqueline Cohen, "Deterrent Effects of the Police on Crime: A Replication and Theoretical Extension," *Law and Society Review* 22 (1988): 163–188.

38. Marcus Felson et al., "Preventing Crime at Newark Subway Stations," *Security Journal* 1 (1990): 137–140.

39. Sandra Besserer, "Criminal Victimization: An International Perspective: Results of the 2000 International Crime Victimization Survey," *Juristat* 22, no. 4 (2002).

40. Simha Landau and Daniel Fridman, "The Seasonality of Violent Crime: The Case of Robbery and Homicide in Israel," *Journal of Research in Crime and Delinquency* 30 (1993): 163–191.

41. Tunnell, *Choosing Crime*, 67.

42. Angela Browne and Kirk Williams, "Exploring the Effect of Resource Availability and the Likelihood of Female-Perpetrated Homicides," *Law and Society Review* 23 (1989): 89–93.

43. John Z. Wang, "Bank Robberies by an Asian Gang: An Assessment of the Routine Activities Theory," *International Journal of Offender Therapy and Comparative Criminology* 46, no. 5 (2002): 555–568.

44. Ronald Clarke, "Situational Crime Prevention," in *Building a Safer Society: Strategic Approaches to Crime Prevention*, vol. 19 of *Crime and Justice: A Review of Research*, ed. Michael Tonry and David Farrington, 91–151 (Chicago: University of Chicago Press, 1995).

45. Mark Warr, "Parents, Peers, and Delinquency," *Social Forces* 72 (1993): 247–264.

46. John Hagan, "Destiny and Drift: Subcultural Preferences, Status Attainments, and the Risks and Rewards of Youth," *American Sociological Review* 56 (1991): 567–582.

47. D. Wayne Osgood, Janet Wilson, Patrick O'Malley, Jerald Bachman, and Lloyd Johnston, "Routine Activities and Individual Deviant Behavior," *American Sociological Review* 61 (1996): 635–655.

48. Brent Snook, David Canter, and Craig Bennell, "Predicting the Home Location of Serial Offenders: A Preliminary Comparison of the Accuracy of Human Judges with a Geographic Profiling System," *Behavioral Sciences and the Law* 20 (2002): 109–118.

49. Associated Press, "Thrift Hearings Resume Today in Senate," *Boston Globe*, January 2, 1991, 10.

50. Ronald Clarke and Patricia Harris, "Auto Theft and Its Prevention," in *Crime and Justice: An Annual Edition*, ed. Michael Tonry and Norval Morris, 1–54, at 20–21 (Chicago: University of Chicago Press, 1992).

51. Lisa Maher, "Hidden in the Light: Occupational Norms Among Crack-Using Street-Level Sex Workers," *Journal of Drug Issues* 26 (1996): 143–173.

52. John Petraitis, Brian Flay, and Todd Miller, "Reviewing Theories of Adolescent Substance Use: Organizing Pieces in the Puzzle," *Psychological Bulletin* 117 (1995): 67–86.

53. Bruce Jacobs, "Crack Dealers' Apprehension Avoidance Techniques: A Case of Restrictive Deterrence," *Justice Quarterly* 13 (1996): 359–381.

54. Patricia Morgan and Karen Ann Joe, "Citizens and Outlaws: The Private Lives and Public Lifestyles of Women in the Illicit Drug Economy," *Journal of Drug Issues* 26 (1996): 125–142.

55. Robert MacCoun and Peter Reuter, "Are the Wages of Sin $30 an Hour? Economic Aspects of Street-Level Drug Dealing," *Crime and Delinquency* 38, no. 4 (1992): 477–491.

56. Alan Lizotte, James Tesoriero, Terence Thornberry, and Marvin Krohn, "Patterns of Adolescent Firearms Ownership and Use," *Justice Quarterly* 11 (1994): 54–74.

57. Alan Lizotte, Marvin Krohn, James Howell, Kimberly Tobin, and Gregory Howard, "Factors Influencing Gun Carrying among Young Urban Males over the Adolescent-Young Adult Life Course," *Criminology* 38 (2000): 811–834.

58. Richard Felson and Steven Messner, "To Kill or Not to Kill? Lethal Outcomes in Injurious Attacks," *Criminology* 34 (1996): 519–545.

59. James Wright and Peter Rossi, *Armed and Considered Dangerous: A Survey of Felons and Their Firearms* (Hawthorne, N.Y.: Aldine, 1983), 141–159.

60. Eric Hickey, *Serial Murderers and Their Victims* (Pacific Grove, Calif.: Brooks/Cole, 1991), 84.

61. Scott Decker, "Deviant Homicide: A New Look at the Role of Motives and Victim-Offender Relationships," *Journal of Research in Crime and Delinquency* 33 (1996): 427–449.

62. Felson and Messner, "To Kill or Not to Kill?"

63. Christopher Birkbeck and Gary LaFree, "The Situational Analysis of Crime and Deviance," *American Review of Sociology* 19 (1993): 113–137; Karen Heimer and Ross Matsueda, "Role-Taking, Role Commitment, and Delinquency: A Theory of Differential Social Control," *American Sociological Review* 59 (1994): 111–131.

64. Jack Katz, *Seductions of Crime* (New York: Basic Books, 1988).

65. Bill McCarthy and John Hagan, "Mean Streets: The Theoretical Significance of Situational Delinquency Among Homeless Youths," *American Journal of Sociology* 3 (1992): 597–627.

66. Bill McCarthy, "Not Just 'For the Thrill of It': An Instrumentalist Elaboration of Katz's Explanation of Sneaky Thrill Property Crime," *Criminology* 33 (1995): 519–539.

67. William O'Grady and Mark Ashbridge, "Illegal Tobacco Sales to Youth: A View from Rational Choice Theory," *Canadian Journal of Criminology* 42 (2000): 1–21.

68. George Rengert, "Spatial Justice and Criminal Victimization," *Justice Quarterly* 6 (1989): 543–564.

69. Oscar Newman, *Defensible Space: Crime Prevention through Urban Design* (New York: Macmillan, 1973).

70. C. Ray Jeffery, *Crime Prevention through Environmental Design* (Beverly Hills, Calif.: Sage, 1971).

71. See also Pochara Theerathorn, "Architectural Style, Aesthetic Landscaping, Home Value, and Crime Prevention," *International Journal of Comparative and Applied Criminal Justice* 12 (1988): 269–277.

72. Ronald Clarke, *Situational Crime Prevention: Successful Case Studies* (Albany, N.Y.: Harrow and Heston, 1992).

73. Patricia Brantingham and Paul Brantingham, "The Relative Spatial Concentration on Criminality and Its Analysis: Toward a Revival of Environmental Criminology" (in French), *Criminologie* 27 (1994): 81–97; Paul Brantingham and Patricia Brantingham, "The Spatial Patterning of Burglary," *Howard Journal of Penology and Crime Prevention* 14 (1975): 11–23; Paul Brantingham and Patricia Brantingham, "How Public Transit Feeds Private Crime: Notes on the Vancouver 'Sky Train' Experience," *Security Journal* 2 (1991): 91–95; Patricia L. Brantingham and Paul J. Brantingham, "Situational Crime Prevention in British Columbia," *Journal of Security Administration* 11 (1988): 18–27; Paul Brantingham and Patricia Brantingham, "Situational Crime Prevention in Practice," *Canadian Journal of Criminology* 32 (1990): 17–40.

74. Marcus Felson, "Routine Activities and Crime Prevention," in *Studies on Crime and Crime Prevention, Annual Review*, vol. 1, 30–34, National Council for Crime Prevention (Stockholm: Scandinavian University Press, 1992).

75. Anthony A. Braga, David M. Kennedy, Elin J. Waring, and Anne Morrison Piehl, "Problem-Oriented Policing, Deterrence, and Youth Violence: An Evaluation of Boston's Operation Ceasefire," *Journal of Research in Crime and Delinquency* 38 (2001).

76. Barry Webb, "Steering Column Locks and Motor Vehicle Theft: Evaluations for Three Countries," in *Crime Prevention Studies*, ed. Ronald Clarke, 71–89 (Monsey, N.Y.: Criminal Justice Press, 1994).

77. Barbara Morse and Delbert Elliott, "Effects of Ignition Interlock Devices on DUI Recidivism: Findings from a Longitudinal Study in Hamilton County, Ohio," *Crime and Delinquency* 38 (1992): 131–157.

78. Brian R. Abraham and Peter J. Baldassaro Jr., "Leaving Robbers Barren," *Security Management* 45, no. 2 (2001): 42.

79. L. Blake and R.T. Coupe, "The Impact of Single and Two-officer Patrols on Catching Burglars in the Act," *British Journal of Criminology* 41 (2001): 381–396.

80. Nancy LaVigne, "Gasoline Drive-Offs: Designing a Less Convenient Environment," in *Crime Prevention Studies*, vol. 2, ed. Ronald Clarke, 91–114 (Monsey, N.Y.: Criminal Justice Press, 1994).

81. Ronald Clark, "Deterring Obscene Phone Callers: The New Jersey Experience," *Situational Crime Prevention*, ed. Ronald Clark, 124–132 (Albany, N.Y.: Harrow and Heston, 1992).

82. Alice Morse Earle, "The Scarlett Letter," *Curious Punishments of Bygone Days* (Chicago: HS Stone & Company, 1896), text available online at http://www.getchwood.com/punishments/curious/chapter-7.html (accessed May 10, 2005).

83. Michael Levi, "Suite Justice or Sweet Charity? Some Explorations of Shaming and Incapacitating Business Fraudsters," *Punishment and Society* 2, no. 4 (2002): 147–163.

84. Marcus Felson, "Those Who Discourage Crime," in *Crime and Place*, Crime Prevention Studies, vol. 4, ed. John Eck and David Weisburd, 53–66 (Monsey, N.Y.: Criminal Justice Press, 1995); John Eck, *Drug Markets and Drug Places: A Case-Control Study of the Spatial Structure of Illicit Drug Dealing*, Doctoral dissertation, University of Maryland, College Park, 1994.

85. Robert Barr and Ken Pease, "Crime Placement, Displacement, and Deflection," in *Crime and Justice: A Review of Research*, vol. 12, ed. Michael Tonry and Norval Morris, 277–319 (Chicago: University of Chicago Press, 1990).

86. Evan Wood et al., "Displacement of Canada's Largest Public Illicit Drug Market in Response to a Police Crackdown," *Canadian Medical Association Journal* 170, no. 10 (2004): 1551–1556; "Crackdown Hasn't Cut Drug Sales in Downtown Eastside," *Vancouver Sun*, May 11, 2004.

87. Keith Harries, *Mapping Crime: Principle and Practice* (Washington, D.C.: U.S. Department of Justice, Office of Justice Programs, National Institute of Justice, 1999).

88. Thomas Gabor, "Crime Displacement and Situational Prevention: Toward the Development of Some Principles," *Canadian Journal of Criminology* 32 (1990): 41–71.

89. Ronald Clarke and David Weisburd, "Diffusion of Crime Control Benefits: Observations of the Reverse of Displacement," in *Crime Prevention Studies*, vol. 2, ed. Ronald Clarke (New York: Criminal Justice Press, 1994).

90. David Weisburd and Lorraine Green, "Policing Drug Hot Spots: The Jersey City Drug Market Analysis Experiment," *Justice Quarterly* 12 (1995): 711–734.

91. Lorraine Green, "Cleaning Up Drug Hot Spots in Oakland, California: The Displacement and Diffusion Effects," *Justice Quarterly* 12 (1995): 737–754.

92. Anthony N. Doob and Carla Cesaroni, "The Political Attractiveness of Mandatory Minimum Sentences," *Osgoode Hall Law Journal* 39 (2001): 287–304; Carla Cesaroni and Anthony N. Doob, "The Decline in Support for Penal Welfarism," *British Journal of Criminology* 43, no. 2 (2003): 434–441.

93. R. Yeaman, *The Deterrent Effectiveness of Criminal Justice Sanction Strategies: Summary Report* (Washington, D.C.: U.S. Government Printing Office, 1972); see, generally, Jack Gibbs, "Crime Punishment and Deterrence," *Social Science Quarterly* 48 (1968): 515–530.

94. Daniel Nagin and Greg Pogarsky, "Integrating Celerity, Impulsivity, and Extralegal Sanction Threats into a Model of General Deterrence: Theory and Evidence," *Criminology* 39 (2001): 865–892.

95. Charles Tittle and Alan Rowe, "Certainty of Arrest and Crime Rates: A Further Test of the Deterrence Hypothesis," *Social Forces* 52 (1974): 455–462.

96. Robert Bursik, Harold Grasmick, and Mitchell Chamlin, "The Effect of Longitudinal Arrest Patterns on the Development of Robbery Trends at the Neighborhood Level," *Criminology* 28 (1990): 431–450; Theodore Chiricos and Gordon Waldo, "Punishment and Crime: An Examination of Some Empirical Evidence," *Social Problems* 18 (1970): 200–217.

97. Jiang Wu and Allen Liska, "The Certainty of Punishment: A Reference Group Effect and Its Functional Form," *Criminology* 31 (1993): 447–464.

98. Edwin Zedlewski, "Deterrence Findings and Data Sources: A Comparison of the Uniform Crime Rates and the National Crime Surveys," *Journal of Research in Crime and Delinquency* 20 (1983): 262–276.

99. Kimberly N. Varma, and Anthony N. Doob, "Deterring Economic Crimes: The Case of Tax Evasion," *Canadian Journal of Criminology* 40 (1998): 165–184.

100. "First Marathon Fined $4-million," *Report on Business, Globe and Mail*, July 21, 1998, B1; "OSC to Hire More Investigators," *Report on Business, Globe and Mail*, July 18, 1998, B1.

101. "Mine Disaster Sparks Call for Corporate Liability in Criminal Code," *Edmonton Journal*, August 4, 1998; *The Westray Story: A Predictable Path to Disaster. Report of the Westray Mine Public Inquiry* (Halifax: Province of Nova Scotia, 1997).

102. David Bayley, *Policing for the Future* (New York: Oxford, 1994).

103. Tomislav V. Kovandzic and John J. Sloan, "Police Levels and Crime Rates Revisited, A Country-Level Analysis from Florida (1980–1998)," *Journal of Criminal Justice* 30 (2002): 65–76; Steven Levitt, "Using Electoral Cycles in Police Hiring to Estimate the Effect of Police on Crime," *American Economic Review* 87 (1997): 70–91; Thomas Marvell and Carlisle Moody, "Specification Problems, Police Levels, and Crime Rates," *Criminology* 34 (1996): 609–646.

104. For a review, see Marvell and Moody, "Specification Problems, Police Levels, and Crime Rates."

105. Joseph P. Hornick, Barry N. Leighton, and Barbara A. Burrows, "Evaluating Community Policing: The Edmonton Project," in *Evaluating Justice: Canadian Policies and Programs*, ed. Joe Hudson and Julian Roberts (Toronto: Thompson Educational Publishing, 1993).

106. S.G. Walker, C. Walker, C. Johnson, J. Sauvageau, and S. Williams, *You Can Do It: A Practical Guide to Evaluating Police and Community Crime Prevention Programs* (Ottawa: National Crime Prevention Centre, 2001).

107. George Kelling, Tony Pate, Duane Dieckman, and Charles Brown, *The Kansas City Preventive Patrol Experiment: A Summary Report* (Washington, D.C.: Police Foundation, 1974).

108. Michael Smith, "Police-Led Crackdowns and Cleanups: An Evaluation of a Crime Control Initiative in Richmond, Virginia," *Crime and Delinquency* 47 (2001): 60–68.

109. Lawrence Sherman, "Police Crackdowns," *NIJ Reports*, March/April 1990, 2–6; George L. Kelling and Catherine M. Coles, *Fixing Broken Windows: Restoring Order and Reducing Crime in Our Communities* (New York: Martin Kessler, 1997).

110. Lawrence Sherman, "Police Crackdowns," *NIJ Reports*, March/April 1990: 3; "Local Radar," *Canadian Living*, August 1997, 15; "Ontario May Try Tough 'Big Apple' Approach to Crime," *Halifax Daily News*, December 10, 1997.

111. Gary Green, "General Deterrence and Television Cable Crime: A Field Experiment in Social Crime," *Criminology* 23 (1986): 629–645.

112. H. Laurence Ross, "Implications of Drinking-and-Driving Law Studies for Deterrence Research," in *Critique and Explanation: Essays in Honor of Gwynne Nettler*, ed. Timothy Hartnagel and Robert Silverman (New Brunswick, N.J.: Transaction Books, 1986), 159–171.

113. H. Laurence Ross, Richard McCleary, and Gary LaFree, "Can Mandatory Jail Laws Deter Drunk Driving? The Arizona Case," *Journal of Criminal Law and Criminology* 81 (1990): 156–167.

114. For a review, see Jeffrey Roth, *Firearms and Violence* (Washington, D.C.: National Institute of Justice, 1994).

115. Thomas Marvell and Carlisle Moody, "The Impact of Enhanced Prison Terms for Felonies Committed with Guns," *Criminology* 33 (1995): 247–281.

116. Robert Dann, "The Deterrent Effect of Capital Punishment," *Friends Social Service Series* 29 (1935).

117. William Bowers and Glenn Pierce, "Deterrence or Brutalization: What Is the Effect of Executions?" *Crime and Delinquency* 26 (1980): 453–484; John Cochran, Mitchell Chamlin, and Mark Seth, "Deterrence or Brutalization? An Impact Assessment of Oklahoma's Return to Capital Punishment," *Criminology* 32 (1994): 107–134.

118. David Phillips, "The Deterrent Effect of Capital Punishment," *American Journal of Sociology* 86 (1980): 139–148; Hans Zeisel, "A Comment on 'The Deterrent Effect of Capital Punishment' by Phillips," *American Journal of Sociology* 88 (1982): 167–169; see also Sam McFarland, "Is Capital Punishment a Short-Term Deterrent to Homicide? A Study of the Effects of Four Recent American Executions," *Journal of Criminal Law and Criminology* 74 (1984): 1014–1032.

119. Steven Stack, "Publicized Executions and Homicide, 1950–1980," *American Sociological Review* 52 (1987): 532–540; for a study challenging Stack's methods, see William Bailey and Ruth Peterson, "Murder and Capital Punishment: A Monthly Time-Series Analysis of Execution Publicity," *American Sociological Review* 54 (1989): 722–743.

120. Karl Schuessler, "The Deterrent Influence of the Death Penalty," *Annals of the Academy of Political and Social Sciences* 284 (1952): 54–62; Thorsten Sellin, *The Death Penalty* (Philadelphia: American Law Institute, 1959); Walter Reckless, "Use of the Death Penalty," *Crime and Delinquency* 15 (1969): 43–51; Richard Lempert, "The Effect of Executions on Homicides: A New Look in an Old Light," *Crime and Delinquency* 29 (1983): 88–115; Derral Cheatwood, "Capital Punishment and the Deterrence of Violent Crime in Comparable Counties," *Criminal Justice Review* 18 (1993): 165–181.

121. James Yunker, "A New Statistical Analysis of Capital Punishment Incorporating U.S. Postmoratorium Data," *Social Science Quarterly* 82 (2001): 297–312.

122. Dane Archer, Rosemary Gartner, and Marc Beittel, "Homicide and the Death Penalty: A Cross-National Test of a Deterrence Hypothesis," *Journal of Criminal Law and Criminology* 74 (1983): 991–1014.

123. Isaac Ehrlich, "The Deterrent Effect on Capital Punishment: A Question of Life and Death," *American Economic Review* 65 (1975): 397–417.

124. James Fox and Michael Radelet, "Persistent Flaws in Econometric Studies of the Deterrent Effect of the Death Penalty," *Loyola of Los Angeles Law Review* 23 (1987): 29–44; William B. Bowers and Glenn Pierce, "The Illusion of Deterrence in Isaac Ehrlich's Research on Capital Punishment," *Yale Law Journal* 85 (1975): 187–208.

125. Angela D. West, "Death as Deterrent or Prosecutorial Tool? Examining the Impact of Louisiana's Child Rape Law," *Criminal Justice Policy Review* 13, no. 2 (2002): 156–191.

126. William Bailey, "Disaggregation in Deterrence and Death Penalty Research: The Case of Murder in Chicago," *Journal of Criminal Law and Criminology* 74 (1986): 827–859.

127. Steven Messner and Kenneth Tardiff, "Economic Inequality and Level of Homicide: An Analysis of Urban Neighborhoods," *Criminology* 24 (1986): 297–317.

128. Donald Green, "Past Behavior as a Measure of Actual Future Behavior: An Unresolved Issue in Perceptual Deterrence Research," *Journal of Criminal Law and Criminology* 80 (1989): 781–804.

129. Donna Bishop, "Deterrence: A Panel Analysis," *Justice Quarterly* 1 (1984): 311–328; Julie Horney and Ineke Haen Marshall, "Risk Perceptions Among Serious Offenders: The Role of Crime and Punishment," *Criminology* 30 (1992): 575–594.

130. Raymond Paternoster, "Decisions to Participate in and Desist from Four Types of Common Delinquency: Deterrence and the Rational Choice Perspective," *Law and Society Review* 23 (1989): 7–29; idem, "Examining Three-Wave Deterrence Models: A Question of Temporal Order and Specification," *Journal of Criminal Law and Criminology* 79 (1988): 135–163; Raymond Paternoster, Linda Saltzman, Gordon Waldo, and Theodore Chiricos, "Estimating Perceptual Stability and Deterrent Effects: The Role of Perceived Legal Punishment in the Inhibition of Criminal Involvement," *Journal of Criminal Law and Criminology* 74 (1983): 270–297; M. William Minor and Joseph Harry, "Deterrent and Experiential Effects in Perceptual Deterrence Research: A Replication and Extension," *Journal of Research in Crime and Delinquency* 19 (1982): 190–203; Lonn Lanza-Kaduce, "Perceptual Deterrence and Drinking and Driving Among College Students," *Criminology* 26 (1988): 321–341.

131. Harold Grasmick and Robert Bursik, "Conscience, Significant Others, and Rational Choice: Extending the Deterrence Model," *Law and Society Review* 24 (1990): 837–861.

132. Steven Klepper and Daniel Nagin, "The Deterrent Effect of Perceived Certainty and Severity of Punishment Revisited," *Criminology* 27 (1989): 721–746.

133. Scott Decker, Richard Wright, and Robert Logie, "Perceptual Deterrence Among Active Residential Burglars: A Research Note," *Criminology* 31 (1993): 135–147.

134. Irving Piliavin, Rosemary Gartner, Craig Thornton, and Ross Matsueda, "Crime, Deterrence, and Rational Choice," *American Sociological Review* 51 (1986): 101–119.

135. Eleni Apospori, Geoffrey Alpert, and Raymond Paternoster, "The Effect of Involvement with the Criminal Justice System: A Neglected Dimension of the Relationship Between Experience and Perceptions," *Justice Quarterly* 9 (1992): 379–392.

136. Eleni Apospori and Geoffrey Alpert, "Research Note: The Role of Differential Experience with the Criminal Justice System in Changes in Perceptions of Severity of Legal Sanctions over Time," *Crime and Delinquency* 39 (1993): 184–194.

137. Bradley R.E. Wright, Avshalom Caspi, Terrie E. Moffitt, and Ray Peternoster, "Does the Perceived Risk of Punishment Deter Criminally Prone Individuals? Rational Choice, Self-Control, and Crime," *Journal of Research in Crime and Delinquency* 41, no. 2 (2004): 180–213.

138. Harold Grasmick and George Bryjak, "The Deterrent Effect of Perceived Severity of Punishment," *Social Forces* 59 (1980): 471–491.

139. Harold Grasmick, Robert Bursik, and Karyl Kinsey, "Shame and Embarrassment as Deterrents to Noncompliance with the Law: The Case of an Anti-Littering Campaign," paper presented at the annual meeting of the American Society of Criminology, Baltimore, November 1990, 3.

140. Charles Tittle, *Sanctions and Social Deviance* (New York: Praeger, 1980).

141. For an opposite view, see Steven Burkett and David Ward, "A Note on Perceptual Deterrence, Religiously Based Moral Condemnation, and Social Control," *Criminology* 31 (1993): 119–134.

142. John Snortum, "Drinking-Driving Compliance in Great Britain: The Role of Law as a 'Threat' and as a 'Moral Eye-Opener,'" *Journal of Criminal Justice* 18 (1990): 479–499.

143. Green, "Past Behavior as a Measure of Actual Future Behavior," p. 803; Matthew Silberman, "Toward a Theory of Criminal Deterrence," *American Sociological Review* 41 (1976): 442–461; Linda Anderson, Theodore Chiricos, and Gordon Waldo, "Formal and Informal Sanctions: A Comparison of Deterrent Effects," *Social Problems* 25 (1977): 103–114; see also Maynard Erickson and Jack Gibbs, "Objective and Perceptual Properties of Legal Punishment and Deterrence Doctrine," *Social Problems* 25 (1978): 253–264.

144. Grasmick and Bursik, "Conscience, Significant Others, and Rational Choices," p. 854.

145. Grasmick, Bursik, and Kinsey, "Shame and Embarrassment as Deterrents to Noncompliance with the Law"; Harold Grasmick, Robert Bursik, and Bruce Arneklev, "Reduction in Drunk Driving as a Response to Increased Threats of Shame, Embarrassment, and Legal Sanctions," *Criminology* 31 (1993): 41–69.

146. Harold Grasmick, Brenda Sims Blackwell, and Robert Bursik, "Changes in the Sex Patterning of Perceived Threats of Sanctions," *Law and Society Review* 27 (1993): 679–699.

147. Daniel Nagin and Raymond Paternoster, "Enduring Individual Differences and Rational Choice Theories of Crime," *Law and Society Review* 27 (1993): 467–485.

148. Kirk Williams and Richard Hawkins, "The Meaning of Arrest for Wife Assault," *Criminology* 27 (1989): 163–181.

149. Thomas Peete, Trudie Milner, and Michael Welch, "Levels of Social Integration in Group Contexts and the Effects of Informal Sanction Threat on Deviance," *Criminology* 32 (1994): 85–105.

150. Ronet Bachman, Raymond Paternoster, and Sally Ward, "The Rationality of Sexual Offending: Testing a Deterrence/Rational Choice Conception of Sexual Assault," *Law and Society Review* 26 (1992): 343–358.

151. "Does Closed Circuit Television Prevent Crime? An Evaluation of the Use of CCTV Surveillance Cameras in Airdrie Town Centre," *Crime and Criminal Justice Research Findings No. 8* (Edinburgh: The Scottish Office, Central Research Office, 1995).

152. Marcus Nieto, *Public Video Surveillance: Is It an Effective Crime Prevention Tool?* (Sacramento, Calif.: California Research Bureau, 1997).

153. International Center for the Prevention of Crime, "Crime Prevention Digest, 1997," http://www.crime-prevention-intl.org (accessed May 22, 2001).

154. Robert D. Bickel, "Legal Issues Related to Silent Video Surveillance," paper presented to the Security Industry Association and the Private Sector Liaison Committee, 1999.

155. Nieto, "Public Video Surveillance: Is It an Effective Crime Prevention Tool?"

156. David H. Flaherty, "Investigation Report: Video Surveillance by Public Bodies," Investigation P98-012, March 31, 1998,

Office of the Information and Privacy Commissioner for British Columbia, http://www.oipcbc.org/investigations/reports/invrpt12.html (accessed May 22, 2005).

157. Roy Coleman and Joe Sim, "'You'll Never Walk Alone': CCTV Surveillance, Order and Neo-liberal Rule in Liverpool City Centre," *British Journal of Sociology* 51 (2000): 623–639.

158. Ernest Van Den Haag, "The Criminal Law as a Threat System," *Journal of Criminal Law and Criminology* 73 (1982): 709–785.

159. Thomas Feucht, *Drug Use Forecasting* (Washington, D.C.: National Institute of Justice, 1996).

160. David Lykken, "Psychopathy, Sociopathy, and Crime," *Society* 34 (1996): 30–38.

161. Ken Auletta, *The Under Class* (New York: Random House, 1982).

162. David Klinger, "Policing Spousal Assault," *Journal of Research in Crime and Delinquency* 32 (1995): 308–324.

163. Paternoster, "Decisions to Participate in and Desist from Four Types of Common Delinquency."

164. James Williams and Daniel Rodeheaver, "Processing of Criminal Homicide Cases in a Large Southern City," *Sociology and Social Research* 75 (1991): 80–88.

165. Wilson, *Thinking About Crime.*

166. James Q. Wilson and Richard Herrnstein, *Crime and Human Nature* (New York: Simon & Schuster, 1985), 494.

167. Paul Tracy and Kimberly Kempf-Leonard, *Continuity and Discontinuity in Criminal Careers* (New York: Plenum Press, 1996).

168. Solicitor General of Canada (Correctional Services of Canada), *Basic Facts about Corrections in Canada* (Ottawa: Public Works and Government Services, 1997), 26.

169. Lawrence Greenfeld, *Examining Recidivism* (Washington, D.C.: U.S. Government Printing Office, 1985); Allen Beck and Bernard Shipley, *Recidivism of Prisoners Released in 1983* (Washington, D.C.: Bureau of Justice Statistics, 1989).

170. Mikhail Thomas, Howard Hurley, and Craig Grimes, "Pilot Analysis of Recidivism among Convicted Youth and Young Adults, 1999/00," *Juristat* 22, no. 9 (2002).

171. David Weisburd, Elin Waring, and Ellen Chayet, "Specific Deterrence in a Sample of Offenders Convicted of White-Collar Crimes," *Criminology* 33 (1995): 587–607.

172. Raymond Paternoster and Alex Piquero, "Reconceptualizing Deterrence: An Empirical Test of Personal and Vicarious Experiences," *Journal of Research in Crime and Delinquency* 32 (1995): 201–228.

173. Michael Weinrath and John Gartrell, "Specific Deterrence and Sentence Length: The Case of Drunk Drivers," *Journal of Contemporary Criminal Justice* 17, no. 2 (2001): 105–122; Canadian Press, "Drunk Driver Says It's No Wonder Suspended Drivers Hit the Road Illegally," May 31, 2004.

174. Charles Murray and Louis Cox, *Beyond Probation* (Beverly Hills, Calif.: Sage, 1979); Perry Shapiro and Harold Votey, "Deterrence and Subjective Probabilities of Arrest: Modeling Individual Decisions to Drink and Drive in Sweden," *Law and Society Review* 18 (1984): 111–149; Douglas Smith and Patrick Gartin, "Specifying Specific Deterrence: The Influence of Arrest on Future Criminal Activity," *American Sociological Review* 54 (1989): 94–105.

175. Graeme Newman, *Just and Painful* (New York: Macmillan, 1983), 139–143.

176. John Braithwaite, *Crime, Shame and Reintegration* (Melbourne, Australia: Cambridge University Press, 1989).

177. John Braithwaite, "Shame and Criminal Justice," *Canadian Journal of Criminology* 42, no. 3 (2000): 281.

178. Harold Garfinkel, "Conditions of Successful Degradation Ceremonies," *American Journal of Sociology* 61 (1956): 420–424.

179. For more on this approach, see Jane Mugford and Stephen Mugford, "Shame and Reintegration in the Punishment and Deterrence of Spouse Assault," paper presented at the annual meeting of the American Society of Criminology, San Francisco, 1991.

180. John Braithwaite, "Shame and Criminal Justice," *Canadian Journal of Criminology* 42, no. 3 (2000): 281.

181. Carter Hay, "An Exploratory Test of Braithwaite's Reintegrative Shaming Theory," *Journal of Research in Crime and Delinquency* 38 (2001): 132–153.

182. John Braithwaite and Stephen Mugford, "Conditions of Successful Reintegration Ceremonies: Dealing with Juvenile Offenders," *British Journal of Criminology* 34, no. 2 (1994): 129–171.

183. Mark Stafford and Mark Warr, "A Reconceptualization of General and Specific Deterrence," *Journal of Research on Crime and Delinquency* 30 (1993): 123–135.

184. Paternoster and Piquero, "Reconceptualizing Deterrence: An Empirical Test of Personal and Vicarious Experiences."

185. Michele Peterson-Badali, Martin D. Ruck, and Christopher J. Koegl, "Youth Court Dispositions: Perceptions of Canadian Juvenile Offenders," *International Journal of Offender Therapy and Comparative Criminology* 45, no. 5 (2001): 593–605.

186. Andrew Karmen, "Why Is New York City's Murder Rate Dropping So Sharply?" John Jay College, New York City, preliminary draft, 1996.

187. See, generally, Raymond Paternoster, "Absolute and Restrictive Deterrence in a Panel of Youth: Explaining the Onset, Persistence/Desistance, and Frequency of Delinquent Offending," *Social Problems* 36 (1989): 289–307; Raymond Paternoster, "The Deterrent Effect of Perceived Severity of Punishment: A Review of the Evidence and Issues," *Justice Quarterly* 42 (1987): 173–217.

188. David Greenberg, "The Incapacitative Effects of Imprisonment: Some Estimates," *Law and Society Review* 9 (1975): 541–580.

189. Isaac Ehrlich, "Participation in Illegitimate Activities: An Economic Analysis," *Journal of Political Economy* 81 (1973): 521–567; Lee Bowker, "Crime and the Use of Prisons in the United States: A Time Series Analysis," *Crime and Delinquency* 27 (1981): 206–212.

190. Reuel Shinnar and Shlomo Shinnar, "The Effects of the Criminal Justice System on the Control of Crime: A Quantitative Approach," *Law and Society Review* 9 (1975): 581–611.

191. Stephan Van Dine, Simon Dinitz, and John Conrad, *Restraining the Wicked: The Dangerous Offender Project* (Lexington, Mass.: Lexington Books, 1979).

192. For a review of this issue, see James Austin and John Irwin, *Does Imprisonment Reduce Crime? A Critique of "Voodoo" Criminology* (San Francisco: National Council of Crime and Delinquency, 1993).

193. John Wallerstedt, *Returning to Prison*, Bureau of Justice Statistics Special Report (Washington, D.C.: U.S. Department of Justice, 1984).

194. *Justice Spending in Canada* (Ottawa: Canadian Centre for Justice Statistics, 1997), 3, 17.

195. Peter Greenwood, *Selective Incapacitation* (Santa Monica, Calif.: Rand Corporation, 1982).

196. Paul Gendreau and Claire Coggin, *The Effect of Prison Sentences on Recidivism* (Ottawa: Solicitor General of Canada, 1999).

197. Stephen Markman and Paul Cassell, "Protecting the Innocent: A Response to the Bedeau-Radelet Study," *Stanford Law Review* 41 (1988): 121–170 at 153.

198. James Stephan and Tracy Snell, *Capital Punishment, 1994* (Washington, D.C.: Bureau of Justice Statistics, 1996), 8.

199. Andrew Von Hirsch, *Doing Justice* (New York: Hill and Wang, 1976).

Chapter 6

1. "Guilty Plea From Man Who Allegedly Planned Shooting Spree Rejected," Canadian Press, August 20, 2004; "Dog Ends Gunman's Plan for Shooting Rampage," *The Globe and Mail*, June 24, 2004; "Man Who Wanted to Kill Torontonians Ordered to Undergo Psychiatric Testing," Canadian Press, June 25, 2004; "Poor Health and a Messy Life Produced Mass-Murder Ploy," *The Globe and Mail*, June 25, 2004.

2. Dalton Conley and Neil Bennett, "Is Biology Destiny? Birth Weight and Life Chances," *American Sociological Review* 654 (2000): 458–467.

3. Israel Nachshon, "Neurological Bases of Crime, Psychopathy and Aggression," in *Crime in Biological, Social and Moral Contexts*, ed. Lee Ellis and Harry Hoffman (New York: Praeger, 1990).

4. Raffaele Garofalo, *Criminology*, trans. Robert Miller (Boston: Little, Brown, 1914), 92.

5. Enrico Ferri, *Criminal Sociology* (New York: D. Appleton, 1909).

6. Richard Dugdale, *The Jukes: A Study in Crime, Pauperism, Disease, and Heredity* (New York: Putnam, 1910); Arthur Estabrook, *The Jukes in 1915* (Washington, D.C.: Carnegie Institute of Washington, 1916).

7. William Sheldon, *Varieties of Delinquent Youth* (New York: Harper Bros., 1949); William Sheldon, *Atlas of Men: A Guide for Somatyping the Adult Male at All Ages* (New York: Harper and Row, 1954).

8. Lee Ellis, "A Discipline in Peril: Sociology's Future Hinges on Curing Biophobia," *American Sociologist* 27 (1996): 21–41.

9. Pierre van den Bergle, "Bringing the Beast Back In: Toward a Biosocial Theory of Aggression," *American Sociological Review* 39 (1974): 779.

10. Edmund O. Wilson, *Sociobiology* (Cambridge: Harvard University Press, 1975).

11. Anthony Walsh, "Behavior Genetics and Anomie/Strain Theory," *Criminology* 38 (2000): 1075–1108.

12. See, generally, Lee Ellis, "Introduction: The Nature of the Biosocial Perspective," *Crime in Biological, Social and Moral Contexts*, 3–18 (New York: Praeger, 1990).

13. See, for example, Tracy Bennett Herbert and Sheldon Cohen, "Depression and Immunity: A Meta-Analytic Review," *Psychological Bulletin* 113 (1993): 472–486.

14. See, generally, Lee Ellis, *Theories of Rape* (New York: Hemisphere Publications, 1989).

15. Leonard Hippchen, "Some Possible Biochemical Aspects of Criminal Behavior," *Journal of Behavioral Ecology* 2 (1981): 1–6; Sarnoff Mednick and Jan Volavka, "Biology and Crime," in *Crime and Justice*, ed. Norval Morris and Michael Tonry, 85–159 (Chicago: University of Chicago Press, 1980); Saleem Shah and Loren Roth, "Biological and Psychophysiological Factors in Criminality," in *Handbook of Criminology*, ed. Daniel Glazer, 125–140 (Chicago: Rand McNally, 1974).

16. *Time*, May 28, 1979, 57.

17. Ulric Neisser et al., "Intelligence: Knowns and Unknowns," *American Psychologist* 51 (1996): 77–101.

18. Leonard Hippchen, ed., *Ecologic-Biochemical Approaches to Treatment of Delinquents and Criminals* (New York: Von Nostrand Reinhold, 1978), 14.

19. Stephen Schoenthaler, *Intelligence, Academic Performance, and Brain Function* (California State University, Stanislaus, 2000); see also, S. Schoenthaler and I. Bier, "The Effect of Vitamin-Mineral Supplementation on Juvenile Delinquency among American Schoolchildren: A Randomized Double-Blind Placebo-Controlled Trial," *Journal of Alternative and Complementary Medicine: Research on Paradigm, Practice, and Policy* 6 (2000): 7–18.

20. Michael Krassner, "Diet and Brain Function," *Nutrition Reviews* 44 (1986): 12–15.

21. J. Kershner and W. Hawke, "Megavitamins and Learning Disorders: A Controlled Double-Blind Experiment," *Journal of Nutrition* 109 (1979): 819–826.

22. Richard Knox, "Test Shows Smart People's Brains Use Nutrients Better," *Boston Globe*, February 16, 1988, 9; Ronald Prinz and David Riddle, "Associations between Nutrition and Behavior in 5-Year-Old Children," *Nutrition Reviews Supplement* 44 (1986): 151–158.

23. Stephen Schoenthaler and Walter Doraz, "Types of Offenses Which Can Be Reduced in an Institutional Setting Using Nutritional Intervention," *International Journal of Biosocial Research* 4 (1983): 74–84; Stephen Schoenthaler and Walter Doraz, "Diet and Crime," *International Journal of Biosocial Research* 4 (1983): 85–94. See also A.G. Schauss, "Differential Outcomes among Probationers Comparing Orthomolecular Approaches to Conventional Casework Counseling," paper presented at the annual meeting of the American Society of Criminology, Dallas, November 9, 1978; A. Schauss and C. Simonsen, "A Critical Analysis of the Diets of Chronic Juvenile Offenders, Part I," *Journal of Orthomolecular Psychiatry* 8 (1979): 222–226; A. Hoffer, "Children with Learning and Behavioral Disorders," *Journal of Orthomolecular Psychiatry* 5 (1976): 229.

24. H. Bruce Ferguson, Clare Stoddart, and Jovan Simeon, "Double-Blind Challenge Studies of Behavioral and Cognitive Effects of Sucrose-Aspartame Ingestion in Normal Children," *Nutrition Reviews Supplement* 44 (1986): 144–158; Gregory Gray, "Diet, Crime and Delinquency: A Critique," *Nutrition Reviews Supplement* 44 (1986): 89–94.

25. Mark Wolraich, Scott Lindgren, Phyllis Stumbo, Lewis Steginck, Mark Appelbaum, and Mary Kiritsy, "Effects of Diets High in Sucrose or Aspartame on the Behavior and Cognitive Performance of Children," *The New England Journal of Medicine* 330 (1994): 303–306.

26. Dian Gans, "Sucrose and Unusual Childhood Behavior," *Nutrition Today* 26 (1991): 8–14.

27. Diana Fishbein, "Neuropsychological Function, Drug Abuse, and Violence, a Conceptual Framework," *Criminal Justice and Behavior* 27 (2000): 139–159.

28. D. Hill and W. Sargent, "A Case of Matricide," *Lancet* 244 (1943): 526–527; E. Podolsky, "The Chemistry of Murder," *Pakistan Medical Journal* 15 (1964): 9–14.

29. J.A. Yaryura-Tobias and F. Neziroglu, "Violent Behavior, Brain Dysrhythmia and Glucose Dysfunction: A New Syndrome," *Journal of Orthopsychiatry* 4 (1975): 182–188; Matti Virkkunen, "Reactive Hypoglycemic Tendency Among Habitually Violent Offenders," *Nutrition Reviews Supplement* 44 (1986): 94–103.

30. James Q. Wilson, *The Moral Sense* (New York: Free Press, 1993).

31. Walter Gove, "The Effect of Age and Gender on Deviant Behavior: A Biopsychosocial Perspective," in *Gender and the Life Course*, ed. A.S. Rossi, 115–144 (New York: Aldine, 1985).

32. Alan Booth and D. Wayne Osgood, "The Influence of Testosterone on Deviance in Adulthood: Assessing and Explaining the Relationship," *Criminology* 31 (1993): 93–118.

33. Christy Miller Buchanan, Jacquelynne Eccles, and Jill Becker, "Are Adolescents the Victims of Raging Hormones? Evidence for Activational Effects of Hormones on Moods and Behavior at Adolescence," *Psychological Bulletin* 111 (1992): 62–107.

34. Alex Piquero and Timothy Brezina, "Testing Moffitt's Account of Adolescent-Limited Delinquency," *Criminology* 39 (2001): 353–370.

35. Loren E. McMaster, Jennifer Connolly, Debra Pepler, and Wendy M. Craig, "Peer to Peer Sexual Harassment in Early Adolescence: A Developmental Perspective," *Development and Psychopathology* 14 (2002): 91–105.

36. Albert Reiss and Jeffrey Roth, eds., *Understanding and Preventing Violence* (Washington, D.C.: National Academy Press, 1993), 118. This report by the National Research Council Panel on the Understanding and Control of Violent Behavior is hereafter cited as *Understanding Violence*.

37. L.E. Kreuz and R.M. Rose, "Assessment of Aggressive Behavior and Plasma Testosterone in a Young Criminal Population," *Psychosomatic Medicine* 34 (1972): 321–332.

38. Anne McIlroy, "Must Men Fight? Probably," *The Globe and Mail*, January 27, 2001.

39. Angela S. Book, Katherine B. Starzyk, and Vernon L. Quinsey, "The Relationship between Testosterone and Aggression: A Meta-Analysis," *Aggression and Violent Behaviour* 6 (2001): 579–599.

40. Lee Ellis, "Evolutionary and Neurochemical Causes of Sex Differences in Victimizing Behavior: Toward a Unified Theory of Criminal Behavior and Social Stratification," *Social Science Information* 28 (1989): 605–636.

41. For a general review, see Lee Ellis and Phyllis Coontz, "Androgens, Brain Functioning, and Criminality: The Neurohormonal Foundations of Antisociality," in *Crime in Biological, Social and Moral Contexts*, ed. Lee Ellis and Harry Hoffman, 162–193 (New York: Praeger, 1990). Also see Robert Rubin, "The Neuroendocrinology and Neurochemistry of Antisocial Behavior," in *The Causes of Crime, New Biological Appoaches*, ed. Sarnoff Mednick, Terrie Moffitt, and Susan Stack, 239–262 (Cambridge: Cambridge University Press, 1987).

42. J. Money, "Influence of Hormones on Psychosexual Differentiation," *Medical Aspects of Nutrition* 30 (1976): 165.

43. For a review of this concept see Anne E. Figert, "The Three Faces of PMS: The Professional, Gendered, and Scientific Structuring of a Psychiatric Disorder," *Social Problems* 42 (1995): 56–72.

44. Katharina Dalton, *The Premenstrual Syndrome* (Springfield, Ill.: Charles C. Thomas, 1971).

45. Julie Horney, "Menstrual Cycles and Criminal Responsibility," *Law and Human Nature* 2 (1978): 25–36.

46. Diana Fishbein, "Selected Studies on the Biology of Antisocial Behavior," in *New Perspectives in Criminology*, ed. John Conklin (Needham Heights, Mass.: Allyn & Bacon, 1985), 26–38.

47. Daniel J. Curran and Claire M. Renzetti, *Theories of Crime* (Boston: Allyn and Bacon, 1994); "Woman's Syndrome Brings Leniency," *Vancouver Sun*, February 10, 1987; "Should PMT Be a Woman's All-Purpose Excuse?" *London Times*, November 12, 1981, 12. See also J.C. Chisler and K.B. Levy, "The Media Construct a Menstrual Monster: A Content Analysis of PMS Articles in the Popular Press," *Women and Health* (1990): 89–104.

48. Fishbein, "Selected Studies on the Biology of Antisocial Behavior"; Karen Paige, "Effects of Oral Contraceptives on Affective Fluctuations Associated with the Menstrual Cycle," *Psychosomatic Medicine* 33 (1971): 515–537.

49. H.E. Amos and J.J.P. Drake, "Problems Posed by Food Additives," *Journal of Human Nutrition* 30 (1976): 165.

50. Ray Wunderlich, "Neuroallergy as a Contributing Factor to Social Misfits: Diagnosis and Treatment," in *Ecologic-Biochemical Approaches to Treatment of Delinquents and Criminals* (New York: Van Nostrand Reinhold, 1978), 229–253; Paul Marshall, "Allergy and Depression: A Neurochemical Threshold Model of the Relation Between the Illnesses," *Psychological Bulletin* 113 (1993): 23–39.

51. A.R. Mawson and K.J. Jacobs, "Corn Consumption, Tryptophan, and Cross-National Homicide Rates," *Journal of Orthomolecular Psychiatry* 7 (1978): 227–230.

52. Alexander Schauss, *Diet, Crime and Delinquency* (Berkeley, Calif.: Parker House, 1980).

53. C. Hawley and R.E. Buckley, "Food Dyes and Hyperkinetic Children," *Academy Therapy* 10 (1974): 27–32.

54. John Ott, "The Effects of Light and Radiation on Human Health and Behavior," in *Ecologic-Biochemical Approaches to Treatment of Delinquents and Criminals* (New York: Van Nostrand Reinhold, 1978), 105–183. See also A. Kreuger and S. Sigel, "Ions in the Air," *Human Nature* (July 1978): 46–47; Harry Wohlfarth, "The Effect of Color Psychodynamic Environmental Modification on Discipline Incidents in Elementary Schools over One School Year: A Controlled Study," *International Journal of Biosocial Research* 6 (1984): 44–53.

55. Paul Stretesky and Michael Lynch, "The Relationship between Lead Exposure and Homicide," *Archives of Pediatric Adolescent Medicine* 155 (2001): 579–582.

56. Oliver David, Stanley Hoffman, Jeffrey Sverd, Julian Clark, and Kytja Voeller, "Lead and Hyperactivity, Behavior Response to Chelation: A Pilot Study," *American Journal of Psychiatry* 133 (1976): 1155–1158.

57. Deborah Denno, "Considering Lead Poisoning as a Criminal Defense," *Fordham Urban Law Journal* 20 (1993): 377–400; Herbert Needleman, Julie Riess, Michael Tobin, Gretchen Biesecker, and Joel Greenohouse, "Bone Lead Levels and Delinquent Behavior," *Journal of the American Medical Association* 275 (1996): 363–369.

58. Ulric Neisser et al., "Intelligence: Knowns and Unknowns," *American Psychologist* 51 (1996): 77–101.

59. Terrie Moffitt, "The Neuropsychology of Juvenile Delinquency: A Critical Review," in *Crime and Justice: An Annual Review*, vol. 12, ed. Norval Morris and Michael Tonry, 99–169 (Chicago: University of Chicago Press, 1990); Terrie Moffitt, Donald Lyman, and Phil Silva, "Neuropsychological Tests Predicting Persistent Male Delinquency," *Criminology* 32 (1994): 277–300; Elizabeth Kandel and Sarnoff Mednick, "Perinatal Complications Predict Violent Offending," *Criminology* 29 (1991): 519–529; Sarnoff Mednick, Ricardo Machon, Matti Virkkunen, and Douglas Bonett, "Adult Schizophrenia Following Prenatal Exposure to an Influenza Epidemic," *Archives of General Psychiatry* 44 (1987): 35–46; C.A. Fogel, S.A. Mednick, and N. Michelson, "Hyperactive Behavior and Minor Physical Anomalies," *Acta Psychiatrica Scandinavia* 72 (1985): 551–556.

60. R. Johnson, *Aggression in Man and Animals* (Philadelphia: Saunders, 1972), 79.

61. Jean Seguin, Robert Pihl, Philip Harden, Richard Tremblay, and Bernard Boulerice, "Cognitive and Neuropsychological Characteristics of Physically Aggressive Boys," *Journal of Abnormal Psychology* 104 (1995): 614–624; Deborah Denno, "Gender, Crime and the Criminal Law Defenses," *Journal of Criminal Law and Criminology* 85 (1994): 80–180.

62. Deborah Denno, *Biology, Crime and Violence: New Evidence* (Cambridge: Cambridge University Press, 1989).

63. Diana Fishbein and Robert Thatcher, "New Diagnostic Methods in Criminology: Assessing Organic Sources of Behavioral Disorders," *Journal of Research in Crime and Delinquency* 23 (1986): 240–267.

64. See, generally, David Rowe, *Biology and Crime* (Los Angeles: Roxbury Press, 2001).

65. Lorne Yeudall, "A Neuropsychosocial Perspective of Persistent Juvenile Delinquency and Criminal Behavior," paper presented at the New York Academy of Sciences, September 26, 1979.

66. R.W. Aind and T. Yamamoto, "Behavior Disorders of Childhood," *Electroencephalography and Clinical Neurophysiology* 21 (1966): 148–156.

67. See, generally, Jan Volavka, "Electroencephalogram among Criminals," in *The Causes of Crime, New Biological Approaches*, ed. Sarnoff Mednick, Terrie Moffitt, and Susan Stack, 137–145 (Cambridge: Cambridge University Press, 1987).

68. Z.A. Zayed, S.A. Lewis, and R.P. Britain, "An Encephalographic and Psychiatric Study of 32 Insane Murderers," *British Journal of Psychiatry* 115 (1969): 1115–1124.

69. Gideon Koren, Irena Nulman, Albert E. Chudley, and Christine Loocke, "Fetal Alcohol Spectrum Disorder," *Canadian Medical Association Journal* 11 (2003): 169–180; "The Curse of Alcohol and Pregnancy," *Toronto Star*, November 27, 2002, A23; David Milne, "MDs Urged to Pursue Alcohol Screening of Pregnant Patients," *Journal of the American Medical Association* 3 (2003): 168–174; "Fetal Alcohol Syndrome Linked to Crime," *Saskatoon Star Phoenix*, March 10, 1998, A1.

70. D.R. Robin, R.M. Starles, T.J. Kenney, B.J. Reynolds, and F.P. Heald, "Adolescents Who Attempt Suicide," *Journal of Pediatrics* 90 (1977): 636–638.

71. R.R. Monroe, *Brain Dysfunction in Aggressive Criminals* (Lexington, Mass.: D.C. Heath, 1978).

72. L.T. Yeudall, *Childhood Experiences as Causes of Criminal Behavior* (Ottawa: Senate of Canada, 1977).

73. Stephen Faraone et al., "Intellectual Performance and School Failure in Children with Attention Deficit Hyperactivity Disorder and in Their Siblings," *Journal of Abnormal Psychology* 102 (1993): 616–623.

74. Terrie Moffitt and Phil Silva, "Self-Reported Delinquency, Neuropsychological Deficit, and History of Attention Deficit Disorder," *Journal of Abnormal Child Psychology* 16 (1988): 553–569.

75. Eugene Maguin, Rolf Loeber, and Paul LeMahieu, "Does the Relationship between Poor Reading and Delinquency Hold for Males of Different Ages and Ethnic Groups?" *Journal of Emotional and Behavioral Disorders* 1 (1993): 88–100.

76. Elizabeth Hart et al., "Developmental Change in Attention-Deficit Hyperactivity Disorder in Boys: A Four-Year Longitudinal Study," *Journal of Consulting and Clinical Psychology* 62 (1994): 472–491.

77. Margaret Weiss and Candice Murray, "Assessment and Management of Attention-Deficit Hyperactivity Disorder," *Canadian Medical Association Journal* 3 (2003): 168–174.

78. Lorne Yeudall, "A Neuropsychosocial Perspective of Persistent Juvenile Delinquency and Criminal Behavior," paper presented at the New York Academy of Sciences, September 26, 1979, p. 4; F.A. Elliott, "Neurological Aspects of Antisocial Behavior," in *The Psychopath: A Comprehensive Study of Antisocial Disorders and Behaviors*, ed. W.H. Reid, 146–189 (New York: Brunner/Mazel, 1978).

79. Lorne Yeudall, Orestes Fedora, and Delee Fromm, "A Neuropsychosocial Theory of Persistent Criminality: Implications for Assessment and Treatment," in *Advances in Forensic Psychology and Psychiatry*, ed. Robert Rieber, 119–191 (Norwood, N.J.: Ablex Publishing, 1987).

80. Donald D. Dutton, "The Neurobiology of Abandonment Homicide," *Aggression and Violent Behavior* 2 (2002): 407–421.

81. H.K. Kletschka, "Violent Behavior Associated with Brain Tumor," *Minnesota Medicine* 49 (1966): 1853–1855.

82. V.E. Krynicki, "Cerebral Dysfunction in Repetitively Assaultive Adolescents," *Journal of Nervous and Mental Disease* 166 (1978): 59–67.

83. C.E. Lyght, ed., *The Merck Manual of Diagnosis and Therapy* (West Point, Fla.: Merck, 1966).

84. "Obstetrical Complications and Violent Delinquency: Testing Two Developmental Pathways," *Child Development* 73, no. 2 (2002): 496–509.

85. M. Virkkunen, M.J. DeJong, J. Bartko, and M. Linnoila, "Psychobiological Concomitants of History of Suicide Attempts among Violent Offenders and Impulsive Fire Starters," *Archives of General Psychiatry* 46 (1989): 604–606; Matti Virkkunen, David Goldman, and Markku Linnoila, "Serotonin in Alcoholic Violent Offenders," *The Ciba Foundation Symposium*, *Genetics of Criminal and Antisocial Behavior* (Chichester, England: Wiley, 1995).

86. E. Jane Garland, "Facing the Evidence: Antidepressant Treatment in Children and Adolescents," *Canadian Medical Association Journal* 2 (2004): 170–174.

87. Lee Ellis, "Left- and Mixed-Handedness and Criminality: Explanations for a Probable Relationship," in *Left-Handedness: Behavioral Implications and Anomalies*, ed. S. Coren, 485–507 (Amsterdam: Elsevier, 1990).

88. Lee Ellis, "Monoamine Oxidase and Criminality: Identifying an Apparent Biological Marker for Antisocial Behavior," *Journal of Research in Crime and Delinquency* 28 (1991): 227–251.

89. "Gene Linked to Abused Children Who Become Violent," Associated Press, August 2, 2002; Erik Stokstad, "Violent Effects of Abuse Tied to Gene," *Science* 297, no. 5582 (2002); "Role of Genotype in the Cycle of Violence in Maltreated Children," *Science* 297, no. 5582 (2002): 851–854.

90. Walter Gove and Charles Wilmoth, "Risk, Crime and Neurophysiologic Highs: A Consideration of Brain Processes That May Reinforce Delinquent and Criminal Behavior," in *Crime in Biological, Social and Moral Contexts*, ed. Lee Ellis and Harry Hoffman, 261–293 (New York: Praeger, 1990).

91. Jack Katz, *Seduction of Crime: Moral and Sensual Attractions of Doing Evil* (New York: Basic Books, 1988), 12–15.

92. Lee Ellis, "Arousal Theory and the Religiosity–Criminality Relationship," in *Contemporary Criminological Theory*, ed. Peter Cordella and Larry Siegel, 65–84 (Boston, Mass.: Northeastern University, 1996).

93. For a general view, see Richard Lerner and Terryl Foch, *Biological-Psychosocial Interactions in Early Adolescence* (Hilldale, N.J.: Lawrence Erlbaum Associates, 1987); Kerry Jang, W. John Livesley, and Philip Vernon, "Heritability of the Big Five Personality Dimensions and Their Facets: A Twin Study," *Journal of Personality* 64 (1996): 577–589.

94. David Rowe, "As the Twig Is Bent: The Myth of Child-Rearing Influences on Personality Development," *Journal of Counseling and Development* 68 (1990): 606–611; David Rowe, Joseph Rogers, and Sylvia Meseck-Bushey, "Sibling Delinquency and the Family Environment: Shared and Unshared Influences," *Child Development* 63 (1992): 59–67; Patricia Brennan, Sarnoff Mednick, and Bjorn Jacobsen, "Assessing the Role of Genetics in Crime Using Adoption Cohorts," *Genetics of Criminal and Antisocial Behavior*, 115–128; Gregory Carey and David DiLalla, "Personality and Psychopathology: Genetic Perspectives," *Journal of Abnormal Psychology* 103 (1994): 32–43.

95. T.R. Sarbin and L.E. Miller, "Demonism Revisited: The XYY Chromosome Anomaly," *Issues in Criminology* 5 (1970): 195–207.

96. See Sarnoff A. Mednick and Karl O. Christiansen, eds., *Biosocial Bases in Criminal Behavior* (New York: Gardner Press, 1977); David Rowe, "Genetic and Environmental Components of Antisocial Behavior: A Study of 265 Twin Pairs," *Criminology* 24 (1986): 513–532; David Rowe and D. Wayne Osgood, "Heredity and Sociological Theories of Delinquency: A Reconsideration," *American Sociological Review* 49 (1984): 526–540.

97. Edwin J.C.G. van den Oord, Frank Verhulst, and Dorret Boomsma, "A Genetic Study of Maternal and Paternal Ratings of Problem Behaviors in 3-Year-Old Twins," *Journal of Abnormal Psychology* 105 (1996): 349–357.

98. Michael Lyons, "A Twin Study of Self-Reported Criminal Behavior"; Judy Silberg, Joanne Meyer, Andrew Pickles, Emily Simonoff, Lindon Eaves, John Hewitt, Hermine Maes, and Michael Rutter, "Heterogeneity among Juvenile Antisocial Behaviors: Findings from the Virginia Twin Study of Adolescent

Behavioral Development," in *The Ciba Foundation Symposium, Genetics of Criminal and Antisocial Behavior* (Chichester, England: Wiley, 1995).

99. Gregory Carey, "Twin Imitation for Antisocial Behavior: Implications for Genetic and Family Environment Research," *Journal of Abnormal Psychology* 101 (1992): 18–25; David Rowe and Joseph Rodgers, "The Ohio Twin Project and ADSEX Studies: Behavior Genetic Approaches to Understanding Antisocial Behavior," paper presented at the American Society of Criminology Meeting, Montreal, November 1987.

100. David Rowe, *The Limits of Family Influence: Genes, Experiences and Behavior* (New York: Guilford Press, 1995), 64.

101. R.J. Cadoret, C. Cain, and R.R. Crowe, "Evidence for a Gene-Environment Interaction in the Development of Adolescent Antisocial Behavior," *Behavior Genetics* 13 (1983): 301–310.

102. Barry Hutchings and Sarnoff A. Mednick, "Criminality in Adoptees and Their Adoptive and Biological Parents: A Pilot Study," in *Biological Bases in Criminal Behavior*, ed. S.A. Mednick and K.O. Christiansen (New York: Gardner Press, 1977).

103. For similar results, see Sarnoff Mednick, Terrie Moffitt, William Gabrielli, and Barry Hutchings, "Genetic Factors in Criminal Behavior: A Review," *Development of Antisocial and Prosocial Behavior* (New York: Academic Press, 1986), 3–50; Sarnoff Mednick, William Gabrielli, and Barry Hutchings, "Genetic Influences in Criminal Behavior: Evidence from an Adoption Cohort," in *Perspective Studies of Crime and Delinquency*, ed. Katherine Teilmann Van Dusen and Sarnoff Mednick (Boston: Kluver-Nijhoff, 1983), 39–57.

104. Michael Bohman, "Predisposition to Criminality: Swedish Adoption Studies in Retrospect," in *Genetics of Criminal and Antisocial Behavior*, 99–114.

105. Glenn Walters, "A Meta-Analysis of the Gene-Crime Relationship," *Criminology* 30 (1992): 595–613.

106. Marshall Jones and Donald Jones, "The Contagious Nature of Antisocial Behavior," *Criminology* 38 (2000): 25–46.

107. David Rowe and Bill Gulley, "Sibling Effects on Substance Use and Delinquency," *Criminology* 30 (1992): 217–232; see also, David Rowe, Joseph Rogers, and Sylvia Meseck-Bushey, "Sibling Delinquency and the Family Environment: Shared and Unshared Influences," *Child Development* 63 (1992): 59–67.

108. Lawrence Cohen and Richard Machalek, "A General Theory of Expropriative Crime: An Evolutionary Ecological Approach," *American Journal of Sociology* 94 (1988): 465–501.

109. "Sex, Lies, and Jealousy," *Toronto Star*, October 11, 2002, F05; Margie Wyle, "Are Humans Hard-Wired to Behave Aggressively?" *Toronto Star*, March 21, 2003, D04.

110. Lee Ellis, "The Evolution of Violent Criminal Behavior and Its Nonlegal Equivalent," in *Crime in Biological, Social and Moral Contexts*, ed. Lee Ellis and Harry Hoffman, 63–65 (New York: Praeger, 1990).

111. Lee Ellis and Anthony Walsh, "Gene-Based Evolutionary Theories of Criminology," *Criminology* 35 (1997): 229–276; Lee Ellis, "Sex Differences in Criminality: An Explanation Based on the Concept of r/k Selection," *Mankind Quarterly* 30 (1990): 17–37; Byron Roth, "Crime and Child Rearing," *Society* 34 (1996): 39–45.

112. Deborah Denno, "Sociological and Human Developmental Explanations of Crime: Conflict or Consensus," *Criminology* 23 (1985): 711–741.

113. Israel Nachshon and Deborah Denno, "Violence and Cerebral Function," in *The Causes of Crime, New Biological Approaches*, ed. Sarnoff Mednick, Terrie Moffitt, and Susan Stack, 185–217 (Cambridge: Cambridge University Press, 1987).

114. Avshalom Caspi, Donald Lyman, Terrie Moffitt, and Phil Silva, "Unraveling Girls' Delinquency: Biological, Dispositional, and Contextual Contributions to Adolescent Misbehavior," *Developmental Psychology* 29 (1993): 283–289.

115. Glenn Walters and Thomas White, "Heredity and Crime: Bad Genes or Bad Research," *Criminology* 27 (1989): 455–486.

116. Charles Goring, *The English Convict: A Statistical Study, 1913* (Montclair, N.J.: Patterson Smith, 1972); Edwin Driver, "Charles Buckman Goring," in *Pioneers in Criminology*, ed. Hermann Mannheim (Montclair, N.J.: Patterson Smith, 1970), 440.

117. Gabriel Tarde, *Penal Philosophy*, trans. R. Howell (Boston: Little, Brown, 1912).

118. See, generally, Donn Byrne and Kathryn Kelly, *An Introduction to Personality* (Englewood Cliffs, N.J.: Prentice-Hall, 1981).

119. Frank R. Farnham, David V. James, and Paul Cantrell, "Association Between Violence, Psychosis, and Relationship to Victim in Stalkers," *The Lancet*, January 15, 2000, 199.

120. "Schizophrenia Linked to Urban Living," *Canadian Medical Association Journal* 2 (2004): 170–174.

121. Sigmund Freud, "The Ego and the Id," in *Complete Psychological Works of Sigmund Freud*, vol. 19, 52 (London: Hogarth, 1948).

122. August Aichorn, *Wayward Youth* (New York: Viking Press, 1935).

123. David Abrahamsen, *Crime and the Human Mind* (New York: Columbia University Press, 1944), 137; see, generally, Fritz Redl and Hans Toch, "The Psychoanalytic Perspective," in *Psychology of Crime and Criminal Justice*, ed. Hans Toch, 193–195 (New York: Holt, Rinehart and Winston, 1979).

124. See, generally, D.A. Andrews and James Bonta, *The Psychology of Criminal Conduct* (Cincinnati: Anderson, 1994), 72–75.

125. Robert Krueger, Avshalom Caspi, Phil Silva, and Rob McGee, "Personality Traits Are Differentially Linked to Mental Disorders: A Multitrait-Multidiagnosis Study of an Adolescent Birth Cohort," *Journal of Abnormal Psychology* 105 (1996): 299–312; Seymour Halleck, *Psychiatry and the Dilemmas of Crime* (Berkeley: University of California Press, 1971).

126. This discussion is based on three works by Albert Bandura: *Aggression: A Social Learning Analysis* (Englewood Cliffs, N.J.: Prentice-Hall, 1973), *Social Learning Theory* (Englewood Cliffs, N.J.: Prentice-Hall, 1977), and "The Social Learning Perspective: Mechanisms of Aggression," in *Psychology of Crime and Criminal Justice*, 198–236.

127. David Phillips, "The Impact of Mass Media Violence on U.S. Homicides," *American Sociological Review* 48 (1983): 560–568.

128. See, generally, Jean Piaget, *The Moral Judgment of the Child* (London: Kegan Paul, 1932).

129. Lawrence Kohlberg, *Stages in the Development of Moral Thought and Action* (New York: Holt, Rinehart and Winston, 1969).

130. Lawrence Kohlberg, K. Kauffman, P. Scharf, and J. Hickey, *The Just Community Approach in Corrections: A Manual* (Niantic: Connecticut Department of Corrections, 1973); Scott Henggeler, *Delinquency in Adolescence* (Newbury Park, Calif.: Sage, 1989), 26.

131. Carol Veneziano and Louis Veneziano, "The Relationship between Deterrence and Moral Reasoning," *Criminal Justice Review* 17 (1992): 209–216.

132. K.A. Dodge, "A Social Information Processing Model of Social Competence in Children," in *Minnesota Symposium in Child Psychology*, vol. 18, ed. M. Perlmutter, 77–125 (Hillsdale, N.J.: Lawrence Erlbaum, 1986).

133. L. Huesman and L. Eron, "Individual Differences and the Trait of Aggression," *European Journal of Personality* 3 (1989): 95–106.

134. J.E. Lochman, "Self and Peer Perceptions and Attributional Biases of Aggressive and Nonaggressive Boys in Dyadic Interactions," *Journal of Consulting and Clinical Psychology* 55 (1987): 404–410.

135. Calvin M. Langton, and W.L. Marshall, "Cognition in Rapists. Theoretical Patterns by Typological Breakdown," *Aggression and Violent Behavior* 6 (2001): 499–518.

136. D. Lipton, E.C. McDonel, and R. McFall, "Heterosocial Perception in Rapists," *Journal of Consulting and Clinical Psychology* 55 (1987): 17–21.

137. "Stressed Parents at 'Loggerheads' with Children, Report Says," *Canadian Medical Association Journal* 164, no. 1 (2001): 84; "The Wild, Sick, Lost Children of Ontario," *National Post*, April 13, 2004; "Justice System the Wrong Route to Help for Mentally Ill," *Canadian Medical Association Journal* 170, no. 9 (2004): 1381; "Mental Illness Widespread, Untreated," Associated Press, June 1, 2004.

138. James Sorrells, "Kids Who Kill," *Crime and Delinquency* 23 (1977): 312–320.

139. Richard Rosner, "Adolescents Accused of Murder and Manslaughter: A Five-Year Descriptive Study," *Bulletin of the American Academy of Psychiatry and the Law* 7 (1979): 342–351.

140. Richard Famularo, Robert Kinscherff, and Terence Fenton, "Psychiatric Diagnoses of Abusive Mothers: A Preliminary Report," *Journal of Nervous and Mental Disease* 180 (1992): 658–660.

141. Richard Wagner, Dawn Taylor, Joy Wright, Alison Sloat, Gwynneth Springett, Sandy Arnold, and Heather Weinberg, "Substance Abuse Among the Mentally Ill," *American Journal of Orthopsychiatry* 64 (1994): 30–38.

142. Bruce Link, Howard Andrews, and Francis Cullen, "The Violent and Illegal Behavior of Mental Patients Reconsidered," *American Sociological Review* 57 (1992): 275–292; Ellen Hochstedler Steury, "Criminal Defendants with Psychiatric Impairment: Prevalence, Probabilities and Rates," *Journal of Criminal Law and Criminology* 84 (1993): 354–374.

143. Marc Hillbrand, John Krystal, Kimberly Sharpe, and Hilliard Foster, "Clinical Predictors of Self-Mutilation in Hospitalized Patients," *Journal of Nervous and Mental Disease* 182 (1994): 9–13.

144. Carmen Cirincione, Henry Steadman, Pamela Clark Robbins, and John Monahan, *Mental Illness as a Factor in Criminality: A Study of Prisoners and Mental Patients* (Delmar, N.Y.: Policy Research Associates, 1991). See also Carmen Cirincione, Henry Steadman, Pamela Clark Robbins, and John Monahan, *Schizophrenia as a Contingent Risk Factor for Criminal Violence* (Delmar, N.Y.: Policy Research Associates, 1991).

145. John Monahan, *Mental Illness and Violent Crime* (Washington, D.C.: National Institute of Justice, 1996).

146. Howard Berenbaum and Frank Fujita, "Schizophrenia and Personality: Exploring the Boundaries and Connections between Vulnerability and Outcome," *Journal of Abnormal Psychology* 103 (1994): 148–158.

147. Eric Silver, "Extending Social Disorganization Theory: A Multilevel Approach to the Study of Violence among Persons with Mental Illness," *Criminology* 38 (2000): 1043–1074.

148. Stacy DeCoster and Karen Heimer, "The Relationship between Law Violation and Depression: An Interactionist Analysis," *Criminology* 39 (2001): 799–837.

149. Jeffrey Wanson, Randy Borum, Marvin Swartz, Virginia Hidaym, H. Ryan Wagner, and Barbara Burns, "Can Involuntary Outpatient Commitment Reduce Arrests among Persons with Severe Mental Illness?" *Criminal Justice and Behavior* 28 (2001): 156–189.

150. D.A. Andrews and J. Stephen Wormith, "Personality and Crime: Knowledge and Construction in Criminology," *Justice Quarterly* 6 (1989): 289–310; Donald Gibbons, "Comment—Personality and Crime: Non-Issues, Real Issues, and a Theory and Research Agenda," *Justice Quarterly* (1989): 311–324.

151. Sheldon Glueck and Eleanor Glueck, *Unraveling Juvenile Delinquency* (Cambridge: Harvard University Press, 1950).

152. See, generally, Hans Eysenck, *Personality and Crime* (London: Routledge & Kegan Paul, 1977).

153. Edelyn Verona and Joyce Carbonell, "Female Violence and Personality," *Criminal Justice and Behavior* 27 (2000): 176–195.

154. Hans Eysenck and M.W. Eysenck, *Personality and Individual Differences* (New York: Plenum, 1985).

155. Joshua Miller and Donald Lynam, "Personality and Antisocial Behavior," *Criminology* 39 (2001): 765–799.

156. David Farrington, "Psychobiological Factors in the Explanation and Reduction of Delinquency," *Today's Delinquent* (1988): 37–51; Laurie Frost, Terrie Moffitt, and Rob McGee, "Neuropsychological Correlates of Psychopathology in an Unselected Cohort of Young Adolescents," *Journal of Abnormal Psychology* 98 (1989): 307–313.

157. David Lykken, "Psychopathy, Sociopathy, and Crime," *Society* 34 (1996): 30–38.

158. Lykken, "Psychopathy, Sociopathy, and Crime"; Lawrence Cohen and Bryan Vila, "Self-Control and Social Control: An Exposition of the Gottfredson-Hirschi/Sampson-Laub Debate," *Studies on Crime and Crime Prevention* 5 (1996): 1–21; Donald Lynam, "Early Identification of Chronic Offenders: Who Is the Fledgling Psychopath?" *Psychological Bulletin* 120 (1996): 209–234; James Ogloff and Stephen Wong, "Electrodermal and Cardiovascular Evidence of a Coping Response in Psychopaths," *Criminal Justice and Behaviour* 17 (1990): 231–245; Laurie Frost, Terrie Moffitt, and Rob McGee, "Neuropsychological Correlates of Psychopathology in an Unselected Cohort of Young Adolescents," *Journal of Abnormal Psychology* 98 (1989): 307–313; Hervey Cleckley, "Psychopathic States," in *American Handbook of Psychiatry*, ed. S. Aneti, 567–569 (New York: Basic Books, 1959); Spencer Rathus and Jeffrey Nevid, *Abnormal Psychology* (Englewood Cliffs, N.J.: Prentice-Hall, 1991), 310–316; Helene Raskin White, Erich Labouvie, and Marsha Bates, "The Relationship between Sensation Seeking and Delinquency: A Longitudinal Analysis," *Journal of Research in Crime and Delinquency* 22 (1985): 197–211.

159. Sheldon Glueck and Eleanor Glueck, *Delinquents and Nondelinquents in Perspective* (Cambridge, Mass.: Harvard University Press, 1968).

160. See, generally, R. Starke Hathaway and Elio Monachesi, *Analyzing and Predicting Juvenile Delinquency with the MMPI* (Minneapolis: University of Minnesota Press, 1953).

161. R. Starke Hathaway, Elio Monachesi, and Lawrence Young, "Delinquency Rates and Personality," *Journal of Criminal Law, Criminology, and Police Science* 51 (1960): 443–460; Michael Hindelang and Joseph Weis, "Personality and Self-Reported Delinquency: An Application of Cluster Analysis," *Criminology* 10 (1972): 268; Spencer Rathus and Larry Siegel, "Crime and Personality Revisited," *Criminology* 18 (1980): 245–251; see, generally, Edward Megargee, *The California Psychological Inventory Handbook* (San Francisco: Jossey-Bass, 1972).

162. Karl Schuessler and Donald Cressey, "Personality Characteristics of Criminals," *American Journal of Sociology* 55 (1950): 476–484; Gordon Waldo and Simon Dinitz, "Personality Attributes of the Criminal: An Analysis of Research Studies 1950–1965," *Journal of Research in Crime and Delinquency* 4 (1967): 185–201; David Tennenbaum, "Research Studies of Personality and Criminality," *Journal of Criminal Justice* 5 (1977): 1–19.

163. Edward Helmes and John Reddon, "A Perspective on Developments in Assessing Psychopathology: A Critical Review of the MMPI and MMPI-2," *Psychological Bulletin* 113 (1993): 453–471.

164. Avshalom Caspi, Terrie Moffitt, Phil Silva, Magda Stouthamer-Loeber, Robert Krueger, and Pamela Schmutte, "Are Some People Crime-Prone? Replications of the Personality-Crime Relationship Across Countries, Genders, Races and Methods," *Criminology* 32 (1994): 163–195.

165. "Interrelated Harms: Examining the Associations between Victimization, Accidents, and Criminal Behavior," *Injury Control and Safety Production* 8, no. 1 (2001): 13–28; Kevin S. Douglas and Donald G. Dutton, "Assessing the Link between Stalking and Domestic Violence," *Aggression and Violent Behaviour* 6 (2001): 519–546.

166. Henry Goddard, *Efficiency and Levels of Intelligence* (Princeton, N.J.: Princeton University Press, 1920); Edwin Sutherland, "Mental Deficiency and Crime," in *Social Attitudes*, ed. Kimball Young (New York: Henry Holt, 1931), Chapter 15.

167. William Healy and Augusta Bronner, *Delinquency and Criminals: Their Making and Unmaking* (New York: Macmillan, 1926).

168. Joseph Lee Rogers, H. Harrington Cleveland, Edwin van den Oord, and David Rowe, "Resolving the Debate Over Birth Order, Family Size and Intelligence," *American Psychologist* 55 (2000): 599–612.

169. John Slawson, *The Delinquent Boys* (Boston: Budget Press, 1926).

170. Sutherland, "Mental Deficiency and Crime."

171. Travis Hirschi and Michael Hindelang, "Intelligence and Delinquency: A Revisionist Review," *American Sociological Review* 42 (1977): 471–586.

172. Deborah Denno, "Sociological and Human Developmental Explanations of Crime: Conflict or Consensus," *Criminology* 23 (1985): 711–741; Christine Ward and Richard McFall, "Further Validation of the Problem Inventory for Adolescent Girls: Comparing Caucasian and Black Delinquents and Nondelinquents," *Journal of Consulting and Clinical Psychology* 54 (1986): 732–733; L. Hubble and M. Groff, "Magnitude and Direction of WISC-R Verbal Performance IQ Discrepancies among Adjudicated Male Delinquents," *Journal of Youth and Adolescence* 10 (1981): 179–183; Robert Gordon, "IQ Commensurability of Black–White Differences in Crime and Delinquency," paper presented at the annual meeting of the American Psychological Association, Washington, D.C., August 1986; Robert Gordon, "Two Illustrations of the IQ-Surrogate Hypothesis: IQ versus Parental Education and Occupational Status in the Race-IQ-Delinquency Model," paper presented at the annual meeting of the American Society of Criminology, Montreal, Canada, November 1987.

173. Donald Lynam, Terrie Moffitt, and Magda Stouthamer-Loeber, "Explaining the Relation between IQ and Delinquency: Class, Race, Test Motivation, School Failure or Self-Control," *Journal of Abnormal Psychology* 102 (1993): 187–196.

174. Alex Piquero, "Frequency, Specialization, and Violence in Offending Careers," *Journal of Research in Crime and Delinquency* 37 (2000): 392–418.

175. Deborah Denno, "Sociological and Human Developmental Explanations of Crime: Conflict or Consensus," *Criminology* 23 (1985): 711–741; Christine Ward and Richard McFall, "Further Validation of the Problem Inventory for Adolescent Girls: Comparing Caucasian and Black Delinquents and Nondelinquents," *Journal of Consulting and Clinical Psychology* 54 (1986): 732–733; L. Hubble and M. Groff, "Magnitude and Direction of WISC-R Verbal Performance IQ Discrepancies among Adjudicated Male Delinquents," *Journal of Youth and Adolescence* 10 (1981): 179–183; Robert Gordon, "IQ Commensurability of Black-White Differences in Crime and Delinquency," paper presented at the annual meeting of the American Psychological Association, Washington, DC, August 1986; Robert Gordon, "Two Illustrations of the IQ-Surrogate Hypothesis: IQ Versus Parental Education and Occupational

Status in the Race-IQ-Delinquency Model," paper presented at the annual meeting of the American Society of Criminology, Montreal, November 1987; Donald Lynam, Terrie Moffitt, and Magda Stouthamer-Loeber, "Explaining the Relation Between IQ and Delinquency: Class, Race, Test Motivation, School Failure or Self-Control," *Journal of Abnormal Psychology* 102 (1993): 187–196.

176. James Q. Wilson and Richard Herrnstein, *Crime and Human Nature* (New York: Simon & Schuster, 1985), 148.

177. Terrie Moffitt, William Gabrielli, Sarnoff Mednick, and Fini Schulsinger, "Socioeconomic Status, IQ, and Delinquency," *Journal of Abnormal Psychology* 90 (1981): 152–156; for a similar finding, see Hubble and Groff, "Magnitude and Direction of WISC-R Verbal Performance IQ Discrepancies." See also Lorne Yeudall, Delee Fromm-Auch, and Priscilla Davies, "Neuropsychological Impairment of Persistent Delinquency," *Journal of Nervous and Mental Diseases* 170 (1982): 257–265. And, Hakan Stattin and Ingrid Klackenberg-Larsson, "Early Language and Intelligence Development and Their Relationship to Future Criminal Behavior," *Journal of Abnormal Psychology* 102 (1993): 369–378.

178. Scott Menard and Barbara Morse, "A Structuralist Critique of the IQ–Delinquency Hypothesis: Theory and Evidence," *American Journal of Sociology* 89 (1984): 1347–1378; Denno, "Sociological and Human Developmental Explanations of Crime."

179. Ulric Neisser et al., "Intelligence: Knowns and Unknowns," *American Psychologist* 51 (1996): 77–101.

180. Richard Herrnstein and Charles Murray, *The Bell Curve: Intelligence and Class Structure in American Life* (New York: Free Press, 1994).

181. Julian V. Roberts and Simon Verdun-Jones, "Directing Traffic at the Crossroads of Criminal Justice and Mental Health: Conditional Sentencing after the Judgment in Knoblauch," *Alberta Law Review* 39, no. 4 (2002): 788–809; "Comparative Examination of the Prevalence of Mental Disorders among Jailed Inmates in Canada and the United States," *International Journal of Law and Psychiatry* 23, no. 5–6 (2002): 633–647; Shirley Steller, *Special Study on Mentally Disordered Accused and the Criminal Justice System* (Ottawa: Canadian Centre for Justice Statistics, 2003).

182. Susan Pease and Craig T. Love, "Optimal Methods and Issues in Nutrition Research in the Correctional Setting," *Nutrition Reviews Supplement* 44 (1986): 122–131.

183. Mark O'Callaghan and Douglas Carroll, "The Role of Psychosurgical Studies in the Control of Antisocial Behavior," in *The Causes of Crime, New Biological Approaches*, ed. Sarnoff Mednick, Terrie Moffitt, and Susan Stack, 312–328 (Cambridge: Cambridge University Press, 1987).

184. Mednick, Moffitt, Gabrielli, and Hutchings, "Genetic Factors in Criminal Behavior: A Review," 47–48.

Chapter 7

1. Steven Messner and Richard Rosenfeld, *Crime and the American Dream* (Belmont, Calif.: Wadsworth, 1994), 11.

2. Robert Park, "The City: Suggestions for the Investigation of Behavior in the City Environment," *American Journal of Sociology* 20 (1915): 579–583.

3. Robert Park, Ernest Burgess, and Roderic McKenzie, *The City* (Chicago: University of Chicago Press, 1925).

4. Harvey Zorbaugh, *The Gold Coast and the Slum* (Chicago: University of Chicago Press, 1929); Frederic Thrasher, *The Gang* (Chicago: University of Chicago Press, 1927); Louis Wirth, *The Ghetto* (Chicago: University of Chicago Press, 1928).

5. Daniel Bell, *The Coming of Post-Industrial Society* (New York: Basic Books, 1973).

6. See, generally, Stephen Cernkovich and Peggy Giordano, "Family Relationships and Delinquency," *Criminology* 25 (1987): 295–321; Paul Howes and Howard Markman, "Marital Quality and Child Functioning: A Longitudinal Investigation," *Child Development* 60 (1989): 1044–1051.

7. Emilie Andersen Allan and Darrell Steffensmeier, "Youth, Underemployment, and Property Crime: Differential Effects of Job Availability and Job Quality on Juvenile and Young Adult Arrest Rates," *American Sociological Review* 54 (1989): 107–123.

8. Edwin Lemert, *Human Deviance, Social Problems and Social Control* (Englewood Cliffs, N.J.: Prentice-Hall, 1967).

9. Stephen W. Baron and Timothy F. Hartnagel, "Street Youth and Labour Market Strain," *Journal of Criminal Justice* 30 (2002): 519–533; "Double Spending on Child Poverty, Campaign Asks," *Canadian Medical Association Journal* 3 (2003): 168–174; John M. Bolland, "Hopelessness and Risk Behaviour among Adolescents Living in High-Poverty Inner-City Neighbourhoods," *Journal of Adolescence* 26 (2003): 145–158.

10. Jonathan Crane, "The Epidemic Theory of Ghettos and Neighborhood Effects on Dropping Out and Teenage Childbearing," *American Journal of Sociology* 96 (1991): 1226–1259; see also Rodrick Wallace, "Expanding Coupled Shock Fronts of Urban Decay and Criminal Behavior: How U.S. Cities Are Becoming 'Hollowed Out,'" *Journal of Quantitative Criminology* 7 (1991): 333–355.

11. Kevin J.P. Craib et al., "Risk Factors for Elevated HIV Incidence among Aboriginal Injection Drug Users in Vancouver," *Canadian Medical Association Journal* 1, no. 168 (2001): 19–24.

12. Carol LaPrairie, "Aboriginal Over-Representation in the Criminal Justice: A Tale of Nine Cities," *Canadian Journal of Criminology* 4 (2002): 181–208.

13. Douglas Massey and Mitchell Eggers, "The Ecology of Inequality: Minorities and the Concentration of Poverty, 1970–1980," *American Journal of Sociology* 95 (1990): 1153–1188; Melvin Thomas, "Race, Class and Personal Income: An Empirical Test of the Declining Significance of Race Thesis, 1968–1988," *Social Problems* 40 (1993): 328–339.

14. "Domestic Violence. Low-Income Native American Women Suffer High Rates of Domestic Abuse," *Women's Health Weekly*, June 10, 2004, 51–52; "Raise Welfare Rates to Help Women Leave Abusive Relationships: Study," Canadian Press, April 5, 2004.

15. Oscar Lewis, "The Culture of Poverty," *Scientific American* 215 (1966): 19–25.

16. Gunnar Myrdal, *The Challenge of World Poverty* (New York: Vintage Books, 1970); Ken Auletta, *The Under Class* (New York: Random House, 1982).

17. Herbert Gans, "Deconstructing the Underclass: The Term's Danger as a Planning Concept," *Journal of the American Planning Association* 56 (1990): 271–277.

18. Laurence Lynn and Michael G.H. McGeary, eds., *Inner-City Poverty in the United States* (Washington, D.C.: National Academy Press, 1990), 3; Cynthia Rexroat, *Declining Economic Status of Black Children: Examining the Change* (Washington, D.C.: Joint Center for Political and Economic Studies, 1990), 1.

19. David Brownfield, "Social Class and Violent Behavior," *Criminology* 24 (1986): 421–438; Charles Tittle and Robert Meier, "Specifying the SES/Delinquency Relationship," *Criminology* 28 (1990): 271–295.

20. Ruth Kornhauser, *Social Sources of Delinquency* (Chicago: University of Chicago Press, 1978), 75.

21. Clifford R. Shaw and Henry D. McKay, *Juvenile Delinquency and Urban Areas*, rev. ed. (Chicago: University of Chicago Press, 1972).

22. Anthony Platt, *The Child Savers: The Invention of Delinquency* (Chicago: University of Chicago Press, 1968).

23. Shaw and McKay, *Juvenile Delinquency and Urban Areas*, 52.

24. For a discussion of these issues, see Robert Bursik, "Social Disorganization and Theories of Crime and Delinquency: Problems and Prospects," *Criminology* 26 (1988): 521–539.

25. Robert Sampson, "Effects of Socioeconomic Context of Official Reaction to Juvenile Delinquency," *American Sociological Review* 51 (1986): 876–885; Jeffrey Fagan, Ellen Slaughter, and Eliot Hartstone, "Blind Justice? The Impact of Race on the Juvenile Justice Process," *Crime and Delinquency* 33 (1987): 224–258; Merry Morash, "Establishment of a Juvenile Police Record," *Criminology* 22 (1984): 97–113.

26. Bernard Lander, *Towards an Understanding of Juvenile Delinquency* (New York: Columbia University Press, 1954); David Bordua, "Juvenile Delinquency and 'Anomie': An Attempt at Replication," *Social Problems* 6 (1958): 230–238; Roland Chilton, "Continuities in Delinquency Area Research: A Comparison of Studies in Baltimore, Detroit, and Indianapolis," *American Sociological Review* 29 (1964): 71–73.

27. For a general review, see James Byrne and Robert Sampson, eds., *The Social Ecology of Crime* (New York: Springer Verlag, 1985).

28. Christopher T. Lowenkamp, Francis T. Cullen, and Travis C. Pratt, "Replicating Sampson and Groves' Test of Social Disorganization Theory: Revisiting a Criminological Classic," *Journal of Research in Crime and Delinquency* 40, no. 4 (2003): 351–373.

29. See, generally, Bursik, "Social Disorganization and Theories of Crime and Delinquency," 519–551.

30. William Spelman, "Abandoned Buildings: Magnets for Crime?" *Journal of Criminal Justice* 21 (1993): 481–493.

31. Keith Harries and Andrea Powell, "Juvenile Gun Crime and Social Stress: Baltimore, 1980–1990," *Urban Geography* 15 (1994): 45–63.

32. Steven Messner and Kenneth Tardiff, "Economic Inequality and Levels of Homicide: An Analysis of Urban Neighborhoods," *Criminology* 24 (1986): 297–317.

33. G. David Curry and Irving Spergel, "Gang Homicide, Delinquency, and Community," *Criminology* 26 (1988): 381–407.

34. Jennifer L. Schulenberg, "The Social Context of Police Discretion and Young Offenders: An Ecological Analysis," *Canadian Journal of Criminology and Criminal Justice* 4 (2003): 127–157.

35. Per-Olof Wikstrom and Lars Dolmen, "Crime and Crime Trends in Different Urban Environments," *Journal of Quantitative Criminology* 6 (1990): 7–28.

36. Robert Sampson and W. Byron Groves, "Community Structure and Crime: Testing Social Disorganization Theory," *American Journal of Sociology* 94 (1989): 774–802.

37. Steven Messner, Lawrence Raffalovich, and Richard McMillan, "Economic Deprivation and Changes in Homicide Arrest Rates for White and Black Youths, 1967–1998: A National Time Series Analysis," *Criminology* 39 (2001): 591–614.

38. Bursik, "Social Disorganization and Theories of Crime and Delinquency," p. 520.

39. Darrell Steffensmeier and Dana Haynie, "Gender, Structural Disadvantage, and Urban Crime: Do Macrosocial Variables Also Explain Female Offending Rates?" *Criminology* 38 (2000): 403–438; Richard McGahey, "Economic Conditions, Organization, and Urban Crime," in *Communities and Crime*, ed. Albert Reiss and Michael Tonry, 231–270 (Chicago: University of Chicago Press, 1986).

40. Richard McGahey, "Economic Conditions, Organization, and Urban Crime," in *Communities and Crime*, ed. Albert Reiss and Michael Tonry, 231–270 (Chicago: University of Chicago Press, 1986); Scott Menard and Delbert Elliott, "Self-Reported Offending, Maturational Reform, and the Easterlin Hypothesis," *Journal of Quantitative Criminology* 6 (1990): 237–268.

41. Elijah Anderson, *Streetwise: Race, Class and Change in an Urban Community* (Chicago: University of Chicago Press, 1990), 243–244.

42. Pamela Wilcox Rountree and Kenneth Land, "Burglary Victimization, Perceptions of Crime Risk, and Routine Activities: A Multilevel Analysis Across Seattle Neighborhoods and Census Tracts," *Journal of Research in Crime and Delinquency* 33 (1996): 147–180.

43. Randy LaGrange, Kenneth Ferraro, and Michael Supancic, "Perceived Risk and Fear of Crime: Role of Social and Physical Incivilities," *Journal of Research in Crime and Delinquency* 29 (1992): 311–334.

44. Catherine E. Ross, John Mirowsky, and Shana Pribesh, "Powerlessness and the Amplification of Threat: Neighborhood Disadvantage, Disorder, and Mistrust," *American Sociological Review* 66 (2001): 568–580.

45. Ralph Taylor and Jeanette Covington, "Community Structural Change and Fear of Crime," *Social Problems* 40 (1993): 374–392.

46. Wesley Skogan, "Fear of Crime and Neighborhood Change," in *Communities and Crime*, ed. Albert Reiss and Michael Tonry, 191–232 (Chicago: University of Chicago Press, 1986).

47. Stephanie Greenberg, "Fear and Its Relationship to Crime, Neighborhood Deterioration and Informal Social Control," in *The Social Ecology of Crime*, ed. James Byrne and Robert Sampson, 47–62 (New York: Springer Verlag, 1985).

48. Anderson, *Streetwise: Race, Class and Change in an Urban Community*, 245.

49. Finn Aage-Esbensen and David Huizinga, "Community Structure and Drug Use: From a Social Disorganization Perspective," *Justice Quarterly* 7 (1990): 691–709; Allen Liska and Paul Bellair, "Violent-Crime Rates and Racial Composition: Convergence over Time," *American Journal of Sociology* 101 (1995): 578–610; Wesley Skogan, *Disorder and Decline: Crime and the Spiral of Decay in American Neighborhoods* (New York: Free Press, 1990), 15–35.

50. Ralph Taylor and Jeanette Covington, "Neighborhood Changes in Ecology and Violence," *Criminology* 26 (1988): 553–589.

51. Leo Scheurman and Solomon Kobrin, "Community Careers in Crime," in *Communities and Crime*, ed. Albert Reiss and Michael Tonry, 67–100 (Chicago: University of Chicago Press, 1986).

52. See, generally, Robert Bursik, "Delinquency Rates as Sources of Ecological Change," in *The Social Ecology of Crime*, ed. Byrne and Sampson, 63–77; Janet Heitgerd and Robert Bursik, "Extracommunity Dynamics and the Ecology of Delinquency," *American Journal of Sociology* 92 (1987): 775–787.

53. Jeffrey Morenoff, Robert Sampson, and Stephen Raudenbush, "Neighborhood Inequality, Collective Efficacy, and the Spatial Dynamics of Urban Violence," *Criminology* 39 (2001): 517–560.

54. Karen Parker and Matthew Pruitt, "Poverty, Poverty Concentration, and Homicide," *Social Science Quarterly* 81 (2000): 555–582.

55. Carolyn Rebecca Block and Richard Block, *Street Gang Crime in Chicago* (Washington, D.C.: National Institute of Justice, 1993), 7.

56. Barbara Warner and Glenn Pierce, "Reexamining Social Disorganization Theory Using Calls to the Police as a Measure of Crime," *Criminology* 31 (1993): 493–519.

57. Donald Black, "Social Control as a Dependent Variable," in *Toward a General Theory of Social Control*, ed. D. Black (Orlando, Fla.: Academic Press, 1990).

58. Rodney Stark, "Deviant Places: A Theory of the Ecology of Crime," *Criminology* 25 (1987): 893–911.

59. Delbert Elliott, William Julius Wilson, David Huizinga, Robert Sampson, Amanda Elliott, and Bruce Rankin, "The Effects of Neighborhood Disadvantage on Adolescent Development," *Journal of Research in Crime and Delinquency* 33 (1996): 389–426.

60. Robert Bursik and Harold Grasmick, "Economic Deprivation and Neighborhood Crime Rates, 1960–1980," *Law and Society Review* 27 (1993): 263–278.

61. Skogan, *Disorder and Decline*.

62. Robert Sampson and W. Byron Groves, "Community Structure and Crime: Testing Social Disorganization Theory," *American Journal of Sociology* 94 (1989): 774–802; Denise Gottfredson, Richard McNeill, and Gary Gottfredson, "Social Area Influences on Delinquency: A Multilevel Analysis," *Journal of Research in Crime and Delinquency* 28 (1991): 197–206.

63. Felton Earls, *Linking Community Factors and Individual Development* (Washington, D.C.: National Institute of Justice, 1998).

64. Robert J. Sampson and Stephen W. Raudenbush, *Disorder in Urban Neighborhoods: Does It Lead to Crime?* (Washington, D.C.: National Institute of Justice, 2001).

65. Robert J. Sampson, Jeffrey Morenoff, and Felton Earls, "Beyond Social Capital: Spatial Dynamics of Collective Efficacy for Children," *American Sociological Review* 64 (1999): 633–660.

66. Donald Black, "Social Control as a Dependent Variable," in *Toward a General Theory of Social Control*, ed. D. Black (Orlando: Academic Press, 1990).

67. Paul Bellair, "Informal Surveillance and Street Crime: A Complex Relationship," *Criminology* 38 (2000): 137–170.

68. Robert Sampson and W. Byron Groves, "Community Structure and Crime: Testing Social Disorganization Theory," *American Journal of Sociology* 94 (1989): 774–802; Denise Gottfredson, Richard McNeill, and Gary Gottfredson, "Social Area Influences on Delinquency: A Multilevel Analysis," *Journal of Research in Crime and Delinquency* 28 (1991): 197–206.

69. Fred Markowitz, Paul Bellair, Allen Liska, and Jianhong Liu, "Extending Social Disorganization Theory: Modeling the Relationships between Cohesion, Disorder, and Fear," *Criminology* 39 (2001): 293–320.

70. Robert Bursik and Harold Grasmick, "The Multiple Layers of Social Disorganization," paper presented at the annual meeting of the American Society of Criminology, New Orleans, November 1992.

71. Ruth Peterson, Lauren Krivo, and Mark Harris, "Disadvantage and Neighborhood Violent Crime: Do Local Institutions Matter?" *Journal of Research in Crime and Delinquency* 37 (2000): 31–63.

72. Maria Velez, "The Role of Public Social Control in Urban Neighborhoods: A Multi-Level Analysis of Victimization Risk," *Criminology* 39 (2001): 837–864.

73. David Klinger, "Negotiating Order in Patrol Work: An Ecological Theory of Police Response to Deviance," *Criminology* 35 (1997): 277–306.

74. Rodney Stark, "Deviant Places: A Theory of the Ecology of Crime," *Criminology* 25 (1987): 893–911.

75. Robert Bursik and Harold Grasmick, "Economic Deprivation and Neighborhood Crime Rates, 1960–1980," *Law and Society Review* 27 (1993): 263–278.

76. Delbert Elliott, William Julius Wilson, David Huizinga, Robert Sampson, Amanda Elliott, and Bruce Rankin, "The Effects of Neighborhood Disadvantage on Adolescent Development," *Journal of Research in Crime and Delinquency* 33 (1996): 389–426.

77. Robert Sampson, Jeffrey Morenoff, and Felton Earls, "Beyond Social Capital: Spatial Dynamics of Collective Efficacy for Children," *American Sociological Review* 64 (1999): 633–660.

78. Thomas McNulty, "Assessing the Race–Violence Relationship at the Macro Level: The Assumption of Racial Invariance and the Problem of Restricted Distribution," *Criminology* 39 (2001): 467–490.

79. Mitchell Chamlin and John Cochran, "Social Altruism and Crime," *Criminology* 35 (1997): 203–228.

80. Robert Merton, *Social Theory and Social Structure*, enlarged ed. (New York: Free Press, 1968); for an analysis, see Richard Hilbert, "Durkheim and Merton on Anomie: An Unexplored Contrast in Its Derivatives," *Social Problems* 36 (1989): 242–256.

81. Richard Hilbert, "Durkheim and Merton on Anomie: An Unexplored Contrast in Its Derivatives," *Social Problems* 36 (1989): 243.

82. Albert Cohen, "The Sociology of the Deviant Act: Anomie Theory and Beyond," *American Sociological Review* 30 (1965): 5–14.

83. See Robert Agnew, "The Contribution of Social Psychological Strain Theory to the Explanation of Crime and Delinquency," in *Advances in Criminological Theory* 6 (1995): 113–122.

84. Steven Messner and Richard Rosenfeld, *Crime and the American Dream*, 60.

85. Stephen A. Cernkovich, Peggy C. Giordano, and Jennifer L. Rudolph, "Race, Crime, and the American Dream," *Journal of Research in Crime and Delinquency* 37, no. 2 (2000): 131–170.

86. Martin Sanchez-Jankowski, "Gangs and Social Change," *Theoretical Criminology* 7, no. 2 (2003): 191–216.

87. Scott Menard, "A Developmental Test of Mertonian Anomie Theory," *Journal of Research in Crime and Delinquency* 32 (1995): 136–174.

88. John Hagan, Hans Merkens, and Klaus Boehnke, "Delinquency and Disdain: Social Capital and Control of Right-Wing Extremism among East and West Berlin Youth," *American Journal of Sociology* 100 (1995): 1028–1052.

89. Steven Messner and Richard Rosenfeld, "An Institutional-Anomie Theory of the Social Distribution of Crime," paper presented at the annual meeting of the American Society of Criminology, Phoenix, Arizona, November 1993.

90. Mitchell Chamlin and John Cochran, "Assessing Messner and Rosenfeld's Institutional Anomie Theory: A Partial Test," *Criminology* 33 (1995): 411–429.

91. Stephen Cernkovich, Peggy Giordano, and Jennifer Rudolph, "Race, Crime, and the American Dream," *Journal of Research in Crime and Delinquency* 37 (2000): 131–170.

92. Jukka Savolainen, "Inequality, Welfare State and Homicide: Further Support for the Institutional Anomie Theory," *Criminology* 38 (2000): 1021–1042.

93. Jeffrey Morenoff, Robert Sampson, and Stephen Raudenbush, "Neighborhood Inequality, Collective Efficacy, and the Spatial Dynamics of Urban Violence," *Criminology* 39 (2001): 517–560.

94. John Braithwaite, "Poverty Power, White-Collar Crime and the Paradoxes of Criminological Theory," *Australian and New Zealand Journal of Criminology* 24 (1991): 40–58.

95. Judith Blau and Peter Blau, "The Cost of Inequality: Metropolitan Structure and Violent Crime," *American Sociological Review* 147 (1982): 114–129.

96. Peter Blau and Joseph Schwartz, *Crosscutting Social Circles* (New York: Academic Press, 1984).

97. Scott South and Steven Messner, "Structural Determinants of Intergroup Association," *American Journal of Sociology* 91 (1986): 1409–1430; Steven Messner and Scott South, "Economic Deprivation, Opportunity Structure and Robbery Victimization," *Social Forces* 64 (1986): 975–991.

98. Richard Fowles and Mary Merva, "Wage Inequality and Criminal Activity: An Extreme Bounds Analysis for the United States, 1975–1990," *Criminology* 34 (1996): 163–182.

99. Taylor and Covington, "Neighborhood Changes in Ecology and Violence," p. 582; Richard Block, "Community Environment and Violent Crime," *Criminology* 17 (1979): 46–57; Robert Sampson, "Structural Sources of Variation in Race-Age-Specific Rates of Offending Across Major U.S. Cities," *Criminology* 23 (1985): 647–673; Richard Rosenfeld, "Urban Crime Rates: Effects of Inequality, Welfare Dependency, Region and Race," in *The Social Ecology of Crime*, ed. James Byrne and Robert Sampson, 116–130 (New York: Springer Verlag, 1985).

100. Fowles and Merva, "Wage Inequality and Criminal Activity"; Ruth Peterson and William Bailey, "Rape and Dimensions of Gender Socioeconomic Inequality in U.S. Metropolitan Areas," *Journal of Research in Crime and Delinquency* 29 (1992): 162–177; Gary LaFree, Kriss Drass, and Patrick O'Day, "Race and Crime in Postwar America: Determinants of African-American and White Rates, 1957–1988," *Criminology* 30 (1992): 157–188.

101. Martin Daly, Margo Wilson, and Shawn Vasdev, "Income Inequality and Homicide Rates in Canada and the United States," *Canadian Journal of Criminology* 4 (2001): 219–236.

102. Kenneth Land, Patricia McCall, and Lawrence Cohen, "Structural Covariates of Homicide Rates: Are There Any Invariances Across Time and Social Space?" *American Journal of Sociology* 95 (1990): 922–963; Robert Bursik and James Webb, "Community Change and Patterns of Delinquency," *American Journal of Sociology* 88 (1982): 24–42.

103. Robert Agnew, "A Durkheimian Strain Theory of Delinquency," paper presented at the annual meeting of the American Society of Criminology, Baltimore, November 1990.

104. Jeanne Brooks-Gunn, Greg Duncan, Pamela Klato Klebanov, and Naomi Sealand, "Do Neighborhoods Influence Child and Adolescent Development?" *American Journal of Sociology* 99 (1993): 353–395.

105. Nikos Passas, "Anomie and Relative Deprivation," paper presented at the annual meeting of the Eastern Sociological Society, Boston, 1987.

106. Robert Agnew, "Foundation for a General Strain Theory of Crime and Delinquency," *Criminology* 30 (1992): 47–87.

107. Paul Mazerolle and Alex Piquero, "Linking General Strain with Anger: Investigating the Instrumental, Escapist, and Violent Adaptations to Strain," paper presented at the American Society of Criminology meeting, Boston, November 1995.

108. Robert Agnew, Timothy Brezina, John Paul Wright, and Frances Cullen, "Strain, Personality Traits, and Delinquency: Extending General Strain Theory," *Criminology* 40 (2002): 43–72; Robert Agnew, "Stability and Change in Crime over the Life Course: A Strain Theory Explanation," in *Advances in Criminological Theory*, vol. 7: *Developmental Theories of Crime and Delinquency*, ed. Terence Thornberry (New Brunswick, N.J.: Transaction Books, 1995), 113–137.

109. Robert Agnew, "Stability and Change in Crime over the Life Course: A Strain Theory Explanation," in *Advances in Criminological Theory*, vol. 7: *Developmental Theories of Crime and Delinquency*, ed. Terence Thornberry (New Brunswick, N.J.: Transaction Books, 1995), 113–137.

110. Lawrence Wu, "Effects of Family Instability, Income and Income Instability on the Risk of Premarital Birth," *American Sociological Review* 61 (1996): 386–406.

111. Anthony Walsh, "Behavior Genetics and Anomie/Strain Theory," *Criminology* 38 (2000): 1075–1108.

112. George E. Capowich, Paul Mazerolle, and Alex Piquero, "General Strain Theory, Situational Anger, and Social Networks: An Assessment of Conditioning Influences," *Journal of Criminal Justice* 29 (2001): 445–461.

113. Robert Agnew and Helene Raskin White, "An Empirical Test of General Strain Theory," *Criminology* 30 (1992): 475–499.

114. John Hoffman and Alan Miller, "A Latent Variable Analysis of General Strain Theory," *Journal of Quantitative Criminology* 14 (1998): 83–110; Raymond Paternoster and Paul Mazerolle, "General Strain Theory and Delinquency: A Replication and Extension," *Journal of Research in Crime and Delinquency* 31 (1994): 235–263.

115. G. Roger Jarjoura, "The Conditional Effect of Social Class on the Dropout-Delinquency Relationship," *Journal of Research in Crime and Delinquency* 33 (1996): 232–255.

116. Teresa Lagrange and Robert Silverman, "Perceived Strain and Delinquency Motivation: An Empirical Evaluation of General Strain Theory," paper presented at the American Society of Criminology meeting, Boston, November 1995.

117. Thomas Ashby Wills, Donato Vaccaro, Grace McNamara, and A. Elizabeth Hirky, "Escalated Substance Use: A Longitudinal Grouping Analysis from Early to Middle Adolescence," *Journal of Abnormal Psychology* 105 (1996): 166–180.

118. Timothy Brezina, "Adapting to Strain: An Examination of Delinquent Coping Responses," *Criminology* 34 (1996): 39–61.

119. Stephen W. Baron, "Street Youth Labour Market Experience and Crime," *Canadian Review of Sociology and Anthropology* 38, no. 2 (2001): 189–216.

120. Lisa Broidy, "A Test of General Strain Theory," *Criminology* 39 (2001): 9–36; Robert Agnew and Timothy Brezina, "Relational Problems with Peers, Gender and Delinquency," *Youth and Society* 29 (1997): 84–111.

121. John Hoffman and S. Susan Su, "The Conditional Effects of Stress on Delinquency and Drug Use: A Strain Theory in Assessment of Sex Differences," *Journal of Research in Crime and Delinquency* 34 (1997): 46–78.

122. Lisa Broidy, "The Role of Gender in General Strain Theory," paper presented at the American Society of Criminology meeting, Boston, November 1995.

123. Robbin Ogle, Daniel Maier-Katkin, and Thomas Bernard, "A Theory of Homicidal Behavior Among Women," *Criminology* 33 (1995): 173–193.

124. Thorsten Sellin, *Culture Conflict and Crime*, bulletin no. 41 (New York: Social Science Research Council, 1938).

125. Walter Miller, "Lower-Class Culture as a Generating Milieu of Gang Delinquency," *Journal of Social Issues* 14 (1958): 5–19.

126. Elijah Anderson, *Code of the Street: Decency, Violence, and the Moral Life of the Inner City* (New York: Norton, 2000).

127. Albert Cohen, *Delinquent Boys* (New York: Free Press, 1955).

128. Carlo Morselli, "The Relational Dynamics of Illegal Firearm Transactions," *Canadian Journal of Criminology* 44, no. 3 (2002): 255–277.

129. Stephen W. Baron, David R. Forde, and Leslie W. Kennedy, "Rough Justice: Street Youth and Violence," *Journal of Interpersonal Violence* 16, no. 7 (2001): 662–678.

130. Clarence Schrag, *Crime and Justice American Style* (Washington, D.C.: U.S. Government Printing Office, 1971), 74.

131. J. Johnstone, "Social Class, Social Areas, and Delinquency," *Sociology and Social Research* 63 (1978): 49–72; Joseph Harry, "Social Class and Delinquency: One More Time," *Sociological Quarterly* 15 (1974): 294–301.

132. Stephen Baron and Leslie Kennedy, "Deterrence and Homeless Male Street Youths," *Canadian Journal of Criminology* 40 (1998): 27–52.

133. Richard Cloward and Lloyd Ohlin, *Delinquency and Opportunity* (New York: Free Press, 1960).

134. Christopher Uggen, "Work as a Turning Point in the Life Course of Criminals: A Duration Model of Age, Employment and Recidivism," *American Sociological Review* 65 (2000): 529–546.

135. G. David Curry, Robert Fox, Richard Ball, and Daryl Stone, *National Assessment and Law Enforcement Anti-Gang Information Resources, Final Report* (Morgantown, W.Va.: National Assessment Survey, 1992); G. David Curry, *Gang Crime and Law Enforcement Record Keeping* (Washington, D.C.: National Institute of Justice, 1994); G. David Curry, Richard Ball, and Scott Decker, "Estimating the National Scope of Gang Crime from Law Enforcement Data," in *Gangs in America*, 2nd ed., ed. C. Ronald Huff (Newbury Park, Calif.: Sage, 1996).

136. Malcolm Klein, *The American Street Gang, Its Nature, Prevalence and Control* (New York: Oxford University Press, 1995), 31–35.

137. Finn-Aage Esbensen and David Huizinga, "Gangs, Drugs, and Delinquency in a Survey of Urban Youth," *Criminology* 31 (1993): 565–591; Malcom Klein, Cheryl Maxson, and Lea Cunningham, "Crack, Street Gangs, and Violence," *Criminology* 29 (1991): 623–650; see also Irving Spergel, "Youth Gangs: Continuity and Change," in *Crime and Justice*, vol. 12, ed. Michael Tonry and Norval Morris, 171–277 (Chicago: University of Chicago Press, 1990).

138. Melanie Nimmo, *The "Invisible" Gang Members: A Report on Female Gang Association in Winnipeg* (Ottawa: Canadian Centre for Policy Alternatives, 2001).

139. Felix Padilla, *The Gang as an American Enterprise* (New Brunswick, N.J.: Rutgers University Press, 1992); see also Jeffery Fagan, "The Political Economy of Drug Dealing Among Urban Gangs," in *Drugs and the Community*, ed. Robert Davis, Arthur Lurigio, and Dennis Rosenbaum, 19–54 (Springfield, Ill.: Charles C Thomas, 1993).

140. Pamela Irving Jackson, "Crime, Youth Gangs, and Urban Transition: The Social Dislocations of Postindustrial Economic Development," *Justice Quarterly* 8 (1991): 379–397.

141. Robert Sampson and William Julius Wilson, "Toward a Theory of Race, Crime and Urban Inequality," in *Crime and Inequality*, ed. John Hagan and Ruth Peterson, 37–54 (Stanford, Calif.: Stanford University Press, 1995).

142. For a general criticism, see Kornhauser, *Social Sources of Delinquency*.

143. Charles Tittle, "Social Class and Criminal Behavior: A Critique of the Theoretical Foundations," *Social Forces* 62 (1983): 334–358.

144. James Q. Wilson and Richard Herrnstein, *Crime and Human Nature* (New York: Simon & Schuster, 1985).

145. Kenneth Polk and F. Lynn Richmond, "Those Who Fail," in *Schools and Delinquency*, ed. Kenneth Polk and Walter Schafer, 67 (Englewood Cliffs, N.J.: Prentice-Hall, 1974).

146. James DeFronzo, "Welfare and Burglary," *Crime and Delinquency* 42 (1996): 223–230.

147. Solomon Kobrin, "The Chicago Area Project—25-Year Assessment," *Annals of the American Academy of Political and Social Science* 322 (1959): 20–29.

Chapter 8

1. See, for example, James Q. Wilson and Allan Abrahamse, "Does Crime Pay?" *Justice Quarterly* 9 (1992): 359–378.

2. Callie Marie Rennison, *Criminal Victimization 2000 Bureau of Justice Statistics Changes 1999–2000 with Trends 1993–2000* (Washington, D.C.: Bureau of Justice Statistics, 2001).

3. Alan Lizotte, Terence Thornberry, Marvin Krohn, Deborah Chard-Wierschem, and David McDowall, "Neighborhood Context and Delinquency: A Longitudinal Analysis," in *Cross-National Longitudinal Research on Human Development and Criminal Behavior*, ed. E.M. Weitekamp and H.J. Kerner (Netherlands: Kluwer, 1994), 217–227.

4. Charles Tittle and Robert Meier, "Specifying the SES/Delinquency Relationship," *Criminology* 28 (1990): 271–299.

5. Alan Lizotte, Terence Thornberry, Marvin Krohn, Deborah Chard-Wierschem, and David McDowall, "Neighborhood Context and Delinquency: A Longitudinal Analysis," in *Cross National Longitudinal Research on Human Development and Criminal Behavior*, ed. E.M. Weitekamp and H.J. Kerner (Stavernstr, Netherlands: Kluwer, 1994), 217–227.

6. Denise Kandel, "The Parental and Peer Contexts of Adolescent Deviance: An Algebra of Interpersonal Influences," *Journal of Drug Issues* 26 (1996): 289–315; Ann Goetting, "The Parenting Crime Connection," *Journal of Primary Prevention* 14 (1994): 167–184; Sheldon Glueck and Eleanor Glueck, *Unraveling Juvenile Delinquency* (Cambridge, Mass.: Harvard University Press, 1950); Ashley Weeks, "Predicting Juvenile Delinquency," *American Sociological Review* 8 (1943): 40–46.

7. For general reviews of the relationship between families and delinquency, see Alan Jay Lincoln and Murray Straus, *Crime and the Family* (Springfield, Ill.: Charles C. Thomas, 1985); Rolf Loeber and Magda Stouthamer-Loeber, "Family Factors as Correlates and Predictors of Juvenile Conduct Problems and Delinquency," in *Crime and Justice, An Annual Review of Research*, vol. 7, ed. Michael Tonry and Norval Morris, 29–151 (Chicago: University of Chicago Press, 1986); Goetting, "The Parenting Crime Connection."

8. David J. Pevalin, Terrance J. Wade, and Augustine Brannigan, "Precursors, Consequences and Implications for Stability and Change in Pre-adolescent Antisocial Behaviours," *Prevention Science* 4, no. 2 (2003): 123–136.

9. Joseph Weis, Katherine Worsley, and Carol Zeiss, *The Family and Delinquency: Organizing the Conceptual Chaos* (Center for Law and Justice, University of Washington, 1982, Monograph).

10. Susan Stern and Carolyn Smith, "Family Processes and Delinquency in an Ecological Context," *Social Service Review* 37 (1995): 707–731.

11. *Families with Children Under 18 by Type: 1995 to 2010, Series 1, 2, and 3* (Washington, D.C.: U.S. Bureau of the Census, 1996); "Household Type, in Private Households, Percentage Change (1996–2001), for Canada, Provinces and Territories," Census 2001, Statistics Canada.

12. Jukka Savolainen, "Relative Cohort Size and Age-Specific Arrest Rates: A Conditional Interpretation of the Easterlin Effect," *Criminology* 38 (2000): 117–136.

13. Lawrence Rosen and Kathleen Neilson, "Broken Homes," in *Contemporary Criminology*, ed. Leonard Savitz and Norman Johnston, 126–135 (New York: Wiley, 1982).

14. James Q. Wilson and Richard Herrnstein, *Crime and Human Nature* (New York: Simon & Schuster, 1985), 249.

15. L. Edward Wells and Joseph Rankin, "Families and Delinquency: A Meta-Analysis of the Impact of Broken Homes," *Social Problems* 38 (1991): 71–90.

16. Nan Marie Astone and Sara McLanahan, "Family Structure, Parental Practices and High School Completion," *American Sociological Review* 56 (1991): 309–320.

17. Mary Pat Traxler, "The Influence of the Father and Alternative Male Role Models on African-American Boys' Involvement in Antisocial Behavior," paper presented at the annual meeting of the American Society of Criminology, New Orleans, November 1992.

18. Robert E. Emery, Mary C. Waldron, Jeffrey Aaron, and Katherine M. Kitzmann, "Delinquent Behavior, Future Divorce or Nonmarital Childbearing, and Externalizing Behavior among Offspring: A 14-Year Prospective Study," *Journal of Family Psychology* 13, no. 4 (1999).

19. Paul Amato and Bruce Keith, "Parental Divorce and the Well-Being of Children: A Meta-Analysis," *Psychological Bulletin* 110 (1991): 26–46.

20. Cathy Keen, "UF Study: Delinquency Risk no Greater in Families with Stepparents," *University of Florida News*, November 4, 1998.

21. Joseph Rankin and L. Edward Wells, "The Effect of Parental Attachments and Direct Controls on Delinquency," *Journal of Research in Crime and Delinquency* 27 (1990): 140–165.

22. John Paul Wright and Francis Cullen, "Parental Efficacy and Delinquent Behavior: Do Control and Support Matter?" *Criminology* 39 (2001): 677–706.

23. Carter Hay, "Parenting, Self-Control, and Delinquency: A Test of Self-Control Theory," *Criminology* 39 (2001): 707–736.

24. Robert Roberts and Vern Bengston, "Affective Ties to Parents in Early Adulthood and Self-Esteem Across 20 Years," *Social Psychology Quarterly* 59 (1996): 96–106.

25. Robert Johnson, S. Susan Su, Dean Gerstein, Hee-Choon Shin, and John Hoffman, "Parental Influences on Deviant Behavior in Early Adolescence: A Logistic Response Analysis of Age- and Gender-Differentiated Effects," *Journal of Quantitative Criminology* 11 (1995): 167–192.

26. Judith Brook and Li-Jng Tseng, "Influences of Parental Drug Use, Personality, and Child Rearing on the Toddler's Anger and Negativity," *Genetic, Social and General Psychology Monographs* 122 (1996): 107–128.

27. Thomas Ashby Wills, Donato Vaccaro, Grace McNamara, and A. Elizabeth Hirky, "Escalated Substance Use: A Longitudinal Grouping Analysis from Early to Middle Adolescence," *Journal of Abnormal Psychology* 105 (1996): 166–180.

28. John Laub and Robert Sampson, "Unraveling Families and Delinquency: A Reanalysis of the Gluecks' Data," *Criminology* 26 (1988): 355–380.

29. Richard Famularo, Karen Stone, Richard Barnum, and Robert Wharton, "Alcoholism and Severe Child Maltreatment," *American Journal of Orthopsychiatry* 56 (1987): 481–485; Richard Gelles, "Child Abuse and Violence in Single-Parent Families: Parent Absence and Economic Deprivation," *American Journal of Orthopsychiatry* 59 (1989): 492–501; Cecil Willis and Richard Wells, "The Police and Child Abuse: An Analysis of Police Decisions to Report Illegal Behavior," *Criminology* 26 (1988): 695–716; Carolyn Webster-Stratton, "Comparison of Abusive and Nonabusive Families with Conduct-Disordered Children," *American Journal of Orthopsychiatry* 55 (1985): 59–69.

30. Carolyn Smith and Terence Thornberry, "The Relationship between Childhood Maltreatment and Adolescent Involvement in Delinquency," *Criminology* 33 (1995): 451–479.

31. Herman Daldin, "The Fate of the Sexually Abused Child," *Clinical Social Work Journal* 16 (1988): 20–26; Gerald Ellenson, "Horror, Rage and Defenses in the Symptoms of Female Sexual Abuse Survivors," *Social Casework: The Journal of Contemporary Social Work* 70 (1989): 589–596.

32. Richard E. Heyman and Amy M. Smith Slep, "Do Child Abuse and Interpersonal Violence Lead to Adulthood Family Violence?" *Journal of Marriage and Family* 64 (2002): 864–870.

33. Jennie G. Noll, Lisa A. Horowitz, George A. Bonanno, Penelope K. Trickett, and Frank W. Putnam, "Revictimization and Self-Harm in Females Who Experienced Childhood Sexual Abuse: Results from a Prospective Study," *Journal of Interpersonal Violence* 18, no. 12 (2003): 1452–1471.

34. Susan Zuravin, "The Ecology of Child Abuse and Neglect: Review of the Literature and Presentation of Data," *Violence and Victims* 4 (1989): 101–120.

35. Jodi-Anne Brzozowski, *Family Violence in Canada: A Statistical Profile 2004* (Ottawa: Statistics Canada, 2004).

36. Lening Zhang and Steven Messner, "Family Deviance and Delinquency in China," *Criminology* 33 (1995): 359–387.

37. *The Forgotten Half: Pathways to Success for America's Youth and Young Families* (Washington, D.C.: William T. Grant Foundation, 1988); Lee Jussim, "Teacher Expectations: Self-Fulfilling Prophecies, Perceptual Biases, and Accuracy," *Journal of Personality and Social Psychology* 57 (1989): 469–480.

38. Eugene Maguin and Rolf Loeber, "Academic Performance and Delinquency," in *Crime and Justice: A Review of Research*, vol. 20, ed. Michael Tonry, 145–264 (Chicago: University of Chicago Press, 1996).

39. Jane B. Sprott, Anthony N. Doob, and Jennifer M. Jenkins, "Problem Behaviour and Delinquency in Children and Youth," *Juristat* 21, no. 4 (2001).

40. Jeannie Oakes, *Keeping Track: How Schools Structure Inequality* (New Haven, Conn.: Yale University Press, 1985); Marc LeBlanc, Evelyne Valliere, and Pierre McDuff, "Adolescents' School Experience and Self-Reported Offending: A Longitudinal Test of Social Control Theory," paper presented at the annual meeting of the American Society of Criminology, Baltimore, November 1990.

41. G. Roger Jarjoura, "Does Dropping Out of School Enhance Delinquent Involvement? Results from a Large-Scale National Probability Sample," *Criminology* 31 (1993): 149–712; Terence Thornberry, Melanie Moore, and R.L. Christenson, "The Effect of Dropping Out of High School on Subsequent Criminal Behavior," *Criminology* 23 (1985): 3–18.

42. Carolyn Smith, Alan Lizotte, Terence Thornberry, and Marvin Krohn, *Resilient Youth: Identifying Factors That Prevent High Risk Youth from Engaging in Delinquency and Drug Use* (Albany, N.Y.: Rochester Youth Development Study, 1994), 19–21.

43. Irving Janis, *Groupthink: Psychological Studies of Policy Decisions and Fiascoes* (Boston: Houghton Mifflin, 1982); Lening Zhang and Steven Messner, "Family Deviance and Delinquency in China," *Criminology* 33 (1995): 359–387.

44. Thomas Berndt, "The Features and Effects of Friendships in Early Adolescence," *Child Development* 53 (1982): 1447–1469; Thomas Berndt and T.B. Perry, "Children's Perceptions of Friendships as Supportive Relationships," *Developmental Psychology* 22 (1986): 640–648; Spencer Rathus, *Understanding Child Development* (New York: Holt, Rinehart and Winston, 1988), 462.

45. Peggy Giordano, "The Wider Circle of Friends in Adolescence," *American Journal of Sociology* 101 (1995): 661–697.

46. Andre Picard, "Obese Girls and Boys Bullied More Often, Research Finds," *The Globe and Mail*, May 3, 2004.

47. Delbert Elliott, David Huizinga, and Suzanne Ageton, *Explaining Delinquency and Drug Use* (Beverly Hills, Calif.: Sage, 1985); Helene Raskin White, Robert Padina, and Randy LaGrange, "Longitudinal Predictors of Serious Substance Use and Delinquency," *Criminology* 6 (1987): 715–740.

48. Ximena B. Arriaga and Vangie A. Foshee, "Adolescent Dating Violence: Do Adolescents Follow in their Friends', or Their Parents', Footsteps?" *Journal of Interpersonal Violence* 19, no. 2 (2004): 162–184.

49. See, generally, John Hagedorn, *People and Folks: Gangs, Crime and the Underclass in a Rustbelt City* (Chicago: Lakeview Press, 1988).

50. Scott Menard, "Demographic and Theoretical Variables in the Age-Period Cohort Analysis of Illegal Behavior," *Journal of Research in Crime and Delinquency* 29 (1992): 178–199.

51. Patrick Jackson, "Theories and Findings About Youth Gangs," *Criminal Justice Abstracts* 6 (1989), 313–327.

52. Marvin Krohn and Terence Thornberry, "Network Theory: A Model for Understanding Drug Abuse among African-American and Hispanic Youth," in *Drug Abuse among Minority Youth: Advances in Research and Methodology*, ed. Mario De La Rosa and Juan-Luis Recio Adrados (Washington, D.C.: U.S. Department of Health and Human Services, 1993).

53. D. Wayne Osgood, Janet Wilson, Patrick O'Malley, Jerald Bachman, and Lloyd Johnston, "Routine Activities and Individual Deviant Behavior," *American Sociological Review* 61 (1996): 635–655.

54. Mark Warr, "Age, Peers, and Delinquency," *Criminology* 31 (1993): 17–40.

55. Mark Warr, "Organization and Instigation in Delinquent Groups," *Criminology* 34 (1996): 11–35.

56. Marc Bertucco, "Bad Behaviour: Aggressive Children Are Also Unhappy," *Psychology Today* 34, no. 3 (2001): 28.

57. Travis Hirschi and Rodney Stark, "Hellfire and Delinquency," *Social Problems* 17 (1969): 202–213.

58. Colin Baier and Bradley Wright, "If You Love Me, Keep My Commandments: A Meta-Analysis of the Effect of Religion on Crime," *Journal of Research in Crime and Delinquency* 38 (2001): 3–21; Byron Johnson, Sung Joon Jang, David Larson, and Spencer De Li, "Does Adolescent Religious Commitment Matter? A Reexamination of the Effects of Religiosity on Delinquency," *Journal of Research in Crime and Delinquency* 38 (2001): 22–44.

59. Sung Joon Jang and Byron Johnson, "Neighborhood Disorder, Individual Religiosity, and Adolescent Use of Illicit Drugs: A Test of a Multilevel Hypothesis," *Criminology* 39 (2001): 109–144.

60. T. David Evans, Francis Cullen, R. Gregory Dunaway, and Velmer Burton, Jr., "Religion and Crime Reexamined: The Impact of Religion, Secular Controls, and Social Ecology on Adult Criminality," *Criminology* 33 (1995): 195–224.

61. Lee Ellis and James Patterson, "Crime and Religion: An International Comparison Among Thirteen Industrial Nations," *Personal Individual Differences* 20 (1996): 761–768.

62. Walter Miller, *Violence by Youth Gangs and Youth Groups as a Crime Problem in Major American Cities* (Washington, D.C.: U.S. Government Printing Office, 1975).

63. Edwin Sutherland, *Principles of Criminology* (Philadelphia: Lippincott, 1939).

64. See, for example, Edwin Sutherland, "White-Collar Criminality," *American Sociological Review* 5 (1940): 2–10.

65. This section is adapted from Clarence Schrag, *Crime and Justice: American Style* (Washington, D.C.: U.S. Government Printing Office, 1971), 46.

66. See Edwin Sutherland and Donald Cressey, *Criminology*, 8th ed. (Philadelphia: Lippincott, 1970), 77–79.

67. Sandra Brown, Vicki Creamer, and Barbara Stetson, "Adolescent Alcohol Expectancies in Relation to Personal and Parental Drinking Patterns," *Journal of Abnormal Psychology* 96 (1987): 117–121.

68. Ross Matsueda and Karen Heimer, "Race, Family Structure and Delinquency: A Test of Differential Association and Social Control Theories," *American Sociological Review* 52 (1987): 826–840.

69. James Short, "Differential Association as a Hypothesis: Problems of Empirical Testing," *Social Problems* 8 (1960): 14–25.

70. Albert Reiss and A. Lewis Rhodes, "The Distribution of Delinquency in the Social Class Structure," *American Sociological Review* 26 (1961): 732.

71. Douglas Smith, Christy Visher, and G. Roger Jarjoura, "Dimensions of Delinquency: Exploring the Correlates of Participation, Frequency, and Persistence of Delinquent Behavior," *Journal of Research in Crime and Delinquency* 28 (1991): 6–32.

72. Denise Kandel and Mark Davies, "Friendship Networks, Intimacy, and Illicit Drug Use in Young Adulthood: A Comparison of Two Competing Theories," *Criminology* 29 (1991): 441–467.

73. Kenneth Tunnell, "Inside the Drug Trade: Trafficking from the Dealer's Perspective," *Qualitative Sociology* 16 (1993): 361–381.

74. Krohn and Thornberry, "Network Theory," 123–124.

75. Charles Tittle, *Sanctions and Social Deviance* (New York: Praeger, 1980).

76. Yuet-Wah Cheung and Agnes M.C. Ng, "Social Factors in Adolescent Deviant Behavior in Hong Kong: An Integrated Theoretical Approach," *International Journal of Comparative and Applied Criminal Justice* 12 (1988): 27–44.

77. Robert Burgess and Ronald Akers, "A Differential Association–Reinforcement Theory of Criminal Behavior," *Social Problems* 14 (1966): 128–147.

78. Ross Matsueda, "The Current State of Differential Association Theory," *Crime and Delinquency* 34 (1988): 277–306.

79. Graham Ousey and David Aday, Jr., "The Interaction Hypothesis: A Test Using Social Control Theory and Social Learning Theory," paper presented at the American Society of Criminology meeting, Boston, November 1995.

80. The most influential critique of differential association is contained in Ruth Kornhauser, *Social Sources of Delinquency* (Chicago: University of Chicago Press, 1978).

81. These misconceptions are derived from Donald Cressey, "Epidemiologies and Individual Conduct: A Case from Criminology," *Pacific Sociological Review* 3 (1960): 47–58.

82. Kornhauser, *Social Sources of Delinquency*; in contrast, see Matsueda, "The Current State of Differential Association Theory."

83. Ronald Akers, "Is Differential Association/Social Learning Cultural Deviance Theory?" *Criminology* 34 (1996): 229–247; for an opposing view, see Travis Hirschi, "Theory Without Ideas: Reply to Akers," *Criminology* 34 (1996): 249–256.

84. Craig Reinerman and Jeffrey Fagan, "Social Organization and Differential Association: A Research Note from a Longitudinal Study of Violent Juvenile Offenders," *Crime and Delinquency* 34 (1988): 307–327.

85. Sue Titus Reed, *Crime and Criminology*, 2nd ed. (New York: Holt, Rinehart and Winston, 1979), 234.

86. See, for example, Albert Bandura, *Social Learning and Personality Development* (New York: Holt, Rinehart and Winston, 1963).

87. Ronald Akers, *Deviant Behavior: A Social Learning Approach*, 2nd ed. (Belmont, Calif.: Wadsworth, 1977).

88. Michele Peterson-Badali and Christopher J. Koegl, "Juveniles' Experiences of Incarceration: The Role of Correctional Staff in Peer Violence," *Journal of Criminal Justice* 30 (2002): 41–49.

89. Ronald Akers, Marvin Krohn, Lonn Lonza-Kaduce, and Marcia Radosevich, "Social Learning and Deviant Behavior: A Specific Test of a General Theory," *American Sociological Review* 44 (1979): 638.

90. Marvin Krohn, William Skinner, James Massey, and Ronald Akers, "Social Learning Theory and Adolescent Cigarette Smoking: A Longitudinal Study," *Social Problems* 32 (1985): 455–471.

91. Ronald Akers and Gang Lee, "A Longitudinal Test of Social Learning Theory: Adolescent Smoking," *Journal of Drug Issues* 26 (1996): 317–343.

92. Gary Jensen and David Brownfield, "Parents and Drugs," *Criminology* 21 (1983): 543–554.

93. Ronald Akers, "Rational Choice, Deterrence and Social Learning Theory in Criminology: The Path Not Taken," *Journal of Criminal Law and Criminology* 81 (1990): 653–676.

94. Gresham Sykes and David Matza, "Techniques of Neutralization: A Theory of Delinquency," *American Sociological Review* 22 (1957): 664–670; David Matza, *Delinquency and Drift* (New York: Wiley, 1964).

95. Sykes and Matza, "Techniques of Neutralization," 664–670; see also David Matza, "Subterranean Traditions of Youths," *Annals of the American Academy of Political and Social Science* 378 (1961): 116.

96. Michael Hindelang, "The Commitment of Delinquents to Their Misdeeds: Do Delinquents Drift?" *Social Problems* 17 (1970): 509.

97. Robert Regoli and Eric Poole, "The Commitment of Delinquents to Their Misdeeds: A Reexamination," *Journal of Criminal Justice* 6 (1978): 261–269.

98. Robert Agnew, "The Techniques of Neutralization and Violence," *Criminology* 32 (1994): 555–579.

99. Robert Ball, "An Empirical Exploration of Neutralization Theory," *Criminologica* 4 (1966): 22–32. For a similar view, see M. William Minor, "The Neutralization of Criminal Offense," *Criminology* 18 (1980): 103–120.

100. Mark Pogrebin, Eric Poole, and Amos Martinez, "Accounts of Professional Misdeeds: The Sexual Exploitation of Clients by Psychotherapists," *Deviant Behavior* 13 (1992): 229–252.

101. Eric Wish, *Drug Use Forecasting 1990* (Washington, D.C.: National Institute of Justice, 1991).

102. Scott Briar and Irvin Piliavin, "Delinquency: Situational Inducements and Commitment to Conformity," *Social Problems* 13 (1965–1966): 35–45.

103. Lawrence Sherman and Douglas Smith, with Janell Schmidt and Dennis Rogan, "Crime, Punishment, and Stake in Conformity: Legal and Informal Control of Domestic Violence," *American Sociological Review* 57 (1992): 680–690.

104. Albert Reiss, "Delinquency as the Failure of Personal and Social Controls," *American Sociological Review* 16 (1951): 196–207.

105. John McCarthy and Dean Hoge, "The Dynamics of Self-Esteem and Delinquency," *American Journal of Sociology* 90 (1984): 396–410; Edward Wells and Joseph Rankin, "Self-Concept as a Mediating Concept in Delinquency," *Social Psychology Quarterly* 46 (1983): 11–22.

106. Howard Kaplan, *Deviant Behavior in Defense of Self* (New York: Academic Press, 1980); Howard Kaplan, "Self-Attitudes and Deviant Response," *Social Forces* 54 (1978): 788–801.

107. Howard Kaplan, Robert Johnson, and Carol Bailey, "Self-Rejection and the Explanation of Deviance: Refinement and Elaboration of a Latent Structure," *Social Psychology Quarterly* 49 (1986): 110–128.

108. L. Edward Wells, "Self-Enhancement through Delinquency: A Conditional Test of Self-Derogation Theory," *Journal of Research in Crime and Delinquency* 26 (1989): 226–252.

109. See, generally, Walter Reckless, *The Crime Problem* (New York: Appleton-Century-Crofts, 1967). Among the many research reports by Walter Reckless and his colleagues are Walter Reckless, Simon Dinitz, and Ellen Murray, "Self-Concept as an Insulator Against Delinquency," *American Sociological Review* 21 (1956): 744–746; Reckless, Dinitz, and Murray, "The Good Boy in a High Delinquency Area," *Journal of Criminal Law, Criminology, and Police Science* 48 (1957): 1826; Walter Reckless, Simon Dinitz, and Barbara Kay, "The Self-Component in Potential Delinquency and Potential Nondelinquency," *American Sociological Review* 22 (1957): 566–570; Reckless and Dinitz, "Pioneering with Self-Concept as a Vulnerability Factor in Delinquency," *Journal of Criminal Law, Criminology, and Police Science* 58 (1967): 515–523.

110. Travis Hirschi, *Causes of Delinquency* (Berkeley: University of California Press, 1969).

111. Marc LeBlanc, "Family Dynamics, Adolescent Delinquency, and Adult Criminality," paper presented at the Society for Life History Research Conference, Keystone, CO, October 1990, 6.

112. Patricia Van Voorhis, Francis Cullen, Richard Mathers, and Connie Chenoweth Garner, "The Impact of Family Structure and Quality on Delinquency: A Comparative Assessment of Structural and Functional Factors," *Criminology* 26 (1988): 235–261.

113. Marc LeBlanc, Evelyne Valliere, and Pierre McDuff, "Adolescents' School Experience and Self-Reported Offending: A Longitudinal Test of Social Control Theory," paper presented at the annual meeting of the American Society of Criminology, Baltimore, November 1990.

114. Marianne Junger and Wim Polder, "Some Explanations of Crime Among Four Ethnic Groups in the Netherlands," *Journal of Quantitative Criminology* 8 (1992): 51–78.

115. Margit Wiesner and Rainer K. Silbereisen, "Trajectories of Delinquent Behaviour in Adolescence and Their Covariates: Relations with Initial and Time-Averaged Factors," *Journal of Adolescence* 26 (2003): 753–771.

116. Ji-Min Lee, and Nancy J. Bell, "Individual Differences in Attachment-Autonomy Configurations: Linkages with Substance Use and Youth Competencies" *Journal of Asdolescence* 26 (2003): 347–361.

117. Christopher A. Kierkus, and Douglas Baer, "A Social Control Explanation of the Relationship between Family Structure and Delinquent Behaviour," *Canadian Journal of Criminology* 44, no. 4 (2002): 425–459.

118. John Cochran and Ronald Akers, "An Exploration of the Variable Effects of Religiosity on Adolescent Marijuana and Alcohol Use," *Journal of Research in Crime and Delinquency* 26 (1989): 198–225.

119. Robert Agnew and David Peterson, "Leisure and Delinquency," *Social Problems* 36 (1989): 332–348.

120. Josine Junger-Tas, "An Empirical Test of Social Control Theory," *Journal of Quantitative Criminology* 8 (1992): 18–29.

121. Teresa Lagrange and Robert Silverman, "Perceived Strain and Delinquency Motivation: An Empirical Evaluation of General Strain Theory," paper presented at the American Society of Criminology meeting, Boston, November 1995.

122. For a review of exciting research, see Kimberly Kempf, "The Empirical Status of Hirschi's Control Theory," in *Advances in Criminological Theory*, ed. Bill Laufer and Freda Adler (New Brunswick, N.J.: Transaction Publishers, 1992).

123. Richard Lawrence, "Parents, Peers, School—and Delinquency," paper presented at the American Society of Criminology meeting, Boston, November 1995.

124. Peggy Giordano, Stephen Cernkovich, and M.D. Pugh, "Friendships and Delinquency," *American Journal of Sociology* 91 (1986): 1170–1202.

125. Denise Kandel and Mark Davies, "Friendship Networks, Intimacy, and Illicit Drug Use in Young Adulthood: A Comparison of Two Competing Theories," *Criminology* 29 (1991): 441–467.

126. Velmer Burton, Francis Cullen, T. David Evans, R. Gregory Dunaway, Sesha Kethineni, and Gary Payne, "The Impact of Parental Controls on Delinquency," *Journal of Criminal Justice* 23 (1995): 111–126.

127. Kimberly Kempf Leonard and Scott Decker, "The Theory of Social Control: Does It Apply to the Very Young?" *Journal of Criminal Justice* 22 (1994): 89–105.

128. Michael Hindelang, "Causes of Delinquency: A Partial Replication and Extension," *Social Problems* 21 (1973): 471–487.

129. Gary Jensen and David Brownfield, "Parents and Drugs," *Criminology* 21 (1983): 543–554. See also M. Wiatrowski, D. Griswold, and M. Roberts, "Social Control Theory and Delinquency," *American Sociological Review* 46 (1981): 525–541.

130. Leslie Samuelson, Timothy Hartnagel, and Harvey Krahn, "Crime and Social Control Among High School Dropouts," *Journal of Crime and Justice* 18 (1990): 129–161.

131. Mark Warr, "Parents, Peers, and Delinquency," *Social Forces* 72 (1993): 247–264.

132. Marvin Krohn and James Massey, "Social Control and Delinquent Behavior: An Examination of the Elements of the Social Bond," *Sociological Quarterly* 21 (1980): 529–543.

133. Jill Leslie Rosenbaum and James Lasley, "School, Community Context, and Delinquency: Rethinking the Gender Gap," *Justice Quarterly* 7 (1990): 493–513.

134. Randy LaGrange and Helene Raskin White, "Age Differences in Delinquency: A Test of Theory," *Criminology* 23 (1985): 19–45.

135. Robert Agnew, "Social Control Theory and Delinquency: A Longitudinal Test," *Criminology* 23 (1985): 47–61.

136. Alan E. Liska and M.D. Reed, "Ties to Conventional Institutions and Delinquency: Estimating Reciprocal Effects," *American Sociological Review* 50 (1985): 547–560.

137. Michael Wiatrowski, David Griswold, and Mary K. Roberts, "Social Control Theory and Delinquency," *American Sociological Review* 46 (1981): 525–541.

138. George Herbert Mead, *Mind, Self and Society* (Chicago: University of Chicago Press, 1934); George Herbert Mead, *The Philosophy of the Act* (Chicago: University of Chicago Press, 1938); Charles Horton Cooley, *Human Nature and the Social Order* (New York: Schocken, 1964, originally published 1902); Herbert Blumer, *Symbolic Interactionism: Perspective and Method* (Englewood Cliffs, N.J.: Prentice Hall, 1969).

139. Bruce Link, Elmer Streuning, Francis Cullen, Patrick Shrout, and Bruce Dohrenwend, "A Modified Labeling Theory Approach to Mental Disorders: An Empirical Assessment," *American Sociological Review* 54 (1989): 400–423.

140. Linda Jackson, John Hunter, and Carole Hodge, "Physical Attractiveness and Intellectual Competence: A Meta-Analytic Review," *Social Psychology Quarterly* 58 (1995): 108–122.

141. Anthony Matarazzo, Peter J. Carrington, and Robert D. Hiscott, "The Effect of Prior Youth Court Dispositions on Current Disposition: An Application of Societal-Reaction Theory," *Journal of Quantitative Criminology* 17, no. 2 (2001): 169–200.

142. Kai Erickson, "Notes on the Sociology of Deviance," *Social Problems* 9 (1962): 397–414.

143. Edwin Schur, *Labeling Deviant Behavior* (New York: Harper & Row, 1972), 21.

144. Howard Becker, *Outsiders: Studies in the Sociology of Deviance* (New York: Macmillan, 1963), 9.

145. Christy Visher, "Gender, Police Arrest Decision, and Notions of Chivalry," *Criminology* 21 (1983): 5–28.

146. Marjorie Zatz, "Race, Ethnicity and Determinate Sentencing," *Criminology* 22 (1984): 147–171.

147. Roland Chilton and Jim Galvin, "Race, Crime and Criminal Justice," *Crime and Delinquency* 31 (1985): 3–14.

148. Joan Petersilia, "Racial Disparities in the Criminal Justice System: A Summary," *Crime and Delinquency* 31 (1985): 15–34.

149. Walter Gove, *The Labeling of Deviance: Evaluating a Perspective* (New York: Wiley, 1975), 5.

150. Harold Garfinkle, "Conditions of Successful Degradation Ceremonies," *American Journal of Sociology* 61 (1956): 420–424.

151. John Lofland, *Deviance and Identity* (Englewood Cliffs, N.J.: Prentice-Hall, 1969).

152. Frank Tannenbaum, *Crime and the Community* (New York: Columbia University Press, 1938), 19–20.

153. Edwin Lemert, *Social Pathology* (New York: McGraw-Hill, 1951).

154. See, for example, Howard Kaplan and Hiroshi Fukurai, "Negative Social Sanctions, Self-Rejection, and Drug Use," *Youth and Society* 23 (1992): 275–298.

155. Howard Kaplan, *Toward a General Theory of Deviance: Contributions from Perspectives on Deviance and Criminality* (College Station: Texas A&M University, n.d.).

156. Howard Kaplan and Robert Johnson, "Negative Social Sanctions and Juvenile Delinquency: Effects of Labeling in a Model of Deviant Behavior," *Social Science Quarterly* 72 (1991): 98–122; Howard Kaplan, Robert Johnson, and Carol Bailey, "Deviant Peers and Deviant Behavior: Further Elaboration of a Model," *Social Psychology Quarterly* 30 (1987): 277–284.

157. Karen Heimer and Ross Matsueda, "Role-Taking, Role-Commitment and Delinquency: A Theory of Differential Social Control," *American Sociological Review* 59 (1994): 400–437.

158. Stacy DeCoster and Karen Heimer, "The Relationship between Law Violation and Depression: An Interactionist Analysis," *Criminology* 39 (2001): 799–837.

159. Karen Heimer, "Gender, Race, and the Pathways to Delinquency: An Interactionist Explanation," in *Crime and Inequality*, ed. John Hagan and Ruth Peterson (Stanford, Calif.: Stanford University Press, 1995).

160. National Minority Council on Criminal Justice, *The Inequality of Justice* (Washington, D.C.: National Minority Advisory Council on Criminal Justice, 1981), 200.

161. Carl Pope and William Feyerherm, "Minority Status and Juvenile Justice Processing," *Criminal Justice Abstracts* 22 (1990): 327–336; see also Carl Pope, "Race and Crime Revisited," *Crime and Delinquency* 25 (1979): 347–357.

162. Leslie Margolin, "Deviance on Record: Techniques for Labeling Child Abusers in Official Documents," *Social Problems* 39 (1992): 58–68.

163. Charles Corley, Stephen Cernkovich, and Peggy Giordano, "Sex and the Likelihood of Sanction," *Journal of Criminal Law and Criminology* 80 (1989): 540–553.

164. Kaplan and Johnson, "Negative Social Sanctions and Juvenile Delinquency: Effects of Labeling in a Model of Deviant Behavior."

165. Ruth Triplett, "The Conflict Perspective, Symbolic Interactionism, and the Status Characteristics Hypothesis," *Justice Quarterly* 10 (1993): 540–558.

166. Ross Matsueda, "Reflected Appraisals, Parental Labeling, and Delinquency: Specifying a Symbolic Interactionist Theory," *American Journal of Sociology* 97 (1992): 1577–1611.

167. Suzanne Ageton and Delbert Elliott, *The Effect of Legal Processing on Self-Concept* (Boulder, Colo.: Institute of Behavioral Science, 1973).

168. Christine Bowditch, "Getting Rid of Troublemakers: High School Disciplinary Procedures and the Production of Dropouts," *Social Problems* 40 (1993): 493–507.

169. Melvin Ray and William Downs, "An Empirical Test of Labeling Theory Using Longitudinal Data," *Journal of Research in Crime and Delinquency* 23 (1986): 169–194.

170. Sherman and Smith, with Schmidt and Rogan, "Crime, Punishment, and Stake in Conformity."

171. Charles Tittle, "Two Empirical Regularities (Maybe) in Search of an Explanation: Commentary on the Age/Crime Debate," *Criminology* 26 (1988): 75–85.

172. Douglas Smith and Robert Brame, "On the Initiation and Continuation of Delinquency," *Criminology* 4 (1994): 607–630.

173. Jack Gibbs, "Conceptions of Deviant Behavior: The Old and the New," *Pacific Sociological Review* 9 (1966): 11–13.

174. Ronald Akers, "Problems in the Sociology of Deviance," *Social Problems* 46 (1968): 463.

175. Charles Wellford, "Labeling Theory and Criminology: An Assessment," *Social Problems* 22 (1975): 335–347.

176. Alexander Liazos, "The Poverty of the Sociology of Deviance: Nuts, Sluts, and Perverts," *Social Problems* 20 (1971): 103–120.

177. Paul Lipsett, "The Juvenile Offender's Perception," *Crime and Delinquency* 14 (1968): 49; Jack Foster, Simon Dinitz, and Walter Reckless, "Perception of Stigma Following Public Intervention for Delinquent Behavior," *Social Problems* 20 (1972): 202.

178. Charles Tittle, "Labeling and Crime: An Empirical Evaluation," in *The Labeling of Deviance: Evaluating a Perspective*, ed. Walter Gove, 157–179 (New York: Wiley, 1975).

179. David Farrington, "Early Predictors of Adolescent Aggression and Adult Violence," *Violence and Victims* 4 (1989): 79–100.

180. Raymond Paternoster and Leeann Iovanni, "The Labeling Perspective and Delinquency: An Elaboration of the Theory and an Assessment of the Evidence," *Justice Quarterly* 6 (1989): 358–394.

181. Gillian Livingston, "Justice Program for Youths to Expand," Canadian Press, June 14, 2004; Neena Chowdhury, "Youth Justice Program Moves to Malvern," Canadian Press, June 15, 2004; James McCarten, "Ont. Spends $39M to Lower Dropout Rate," Canadian Press, June 8, 2004; Sarah Schmidt, "Campus Camps Reach out to Native Students," CanWest, August 3, 2004; Craig Dowden, and D.A. Andrews, "Does Family Intervention Work for Delinquents? Results of a Meta-Analysis," *Canadian Journal of Criminology and Criminal Justice*, July 2003, 327–342.

182. Doug Hillian and Marge Reitsma-Street, "Parents and Youth Justice," *Canadian Journal of Criminology* 45, no. 1 (2003): 19–42.

183. *Multisystemic Therapy: Treating Violent and Chronic Juvenile Offenders* (Canberra: Australian Institute of Criminology, 2000); "Multisystemic Therapy," *American Youth Policy Forum*, n.d.; *Effective Interventions for Young Offenders: Interim Results of a Four-Year Randomized Study of Multisystemic Therapy in Ontario, Canada* (London, Ont.: London Family Court Clinic, 2002); Allan Cunningham, *Lessons Learned from a Randomized Study of Multisystemic Therapy in Canada* (London, Ont.: Centre for Children and Families in the Justice System, London Family Court Clinic, 2002).

Chapter 9

1. Michael Lynch, "Rediscovering Criminology: Lessons from the Marxist Tradition," in *Marxist Sociology: Surveys of Contemporary Theory and Research*, ed. Donald McQuarie and Patrick McGuire (New York: General Hall Press, 1994).

2. Michael Lynch and W. Byron Groves, *A Primer in Radical Criminology*, 2nd ed. (Albany, N.Y.: Harrow and Heston, 1989), 32–33.

3. See, generally, Karl Marx and Friedrich Engels, *Capital: A Critique of Political Economy*, trans. E. Aveling (Chicago: Charles Kern, 1906); Karl Marx, *Selected Writings in Sociology and Social Philosophy*, trans. P.B. Bottomore (New York: McGraw-Hill, 1956). For a general discussion of Marxist thought, see Lynch and Groves, *A Primer in Radical Criminology*, 6–26.

4. Karl Marx, *Grundrisse: Introduction to the Critique of Political Economy*, trans. Martin Nicolaus (New York: Vintage, 1973), 106–107.

5. Karl Marx, "Population, Crime and Pauperism," in Karl Marx and Friedrich Engels, *Ireland and the Irish Question* (Moscow: Progress, 1859, reprinted 1971), 92.

6. Friedrich Engels, *The Condition of the Working Class in England in 1844* (London: Allen & Unwin, 1950).

7. Willem Bonger, *Criminality and Economic Conditions* (1916, abridged ed., Bloomington: Indiana University Press, 1969).

8. Ralf Dahrendorf, *Class and Class Conflict in Industrial Society* (Palo Alto, Calif.: Stanford University Press, 1959).

9. George Vold, *Theoretical Criminology* (New York: Oxford University Press, 1958).

10. James Short and F. Ivan Nye, "Extent of Undetected Delinquency: Tentative Conclusions," *Journal of Criminal Law, Criminology, and Police Science* 49 (1958): 296–302.

11. For a general view, see David Friedrichs, "Crime, Deviance and Criminal Justice: In Search of a Radical Humanistic Perspective," *Humanity and Society* 6 (1982): 200–226.

12. Edwin Lemert, *Social Pathology* (New York: McGraw-Hill, 1951); Howard Becker, *Outsiders: Studies in the Sociology of Deviance* (New York: Macmillan, 1963).

13. Alexander Liazos, "The Poverty of the Sociology of Deviance: Nuts, Sluts and Perverts," *Social Problems* 20 (1972): 103–120.

14. See, generally, Robert Meier, "The New Criminology: Continuity in Criminological Theory," *Journal of Criminal Law and Criminology* 67 (1977): 461–469.

15. David Greenberg, ed., *Crime and Capitalism* (Palo Alto, Calif.: Mayfield Publishing, 1981), 3.

16. William Chambliss and Robert Seidman, *Law, Order and Power* (Reading, Mass.: Addison-Wesley, 1971), 503.

17. John Braithwaite, "Retributivism, Punishment and Privilege," in *Punishment and Privilege*, ed. W. Byron Groves and Graeme Newman, 55–66 (Albany, N.Y.: Harrow and Heston, 1986).

18. Austin Turk, "Class, Conflict and Criminology," *Sociological Focus* 10 (1977): 209–220.

19. Karen Swol, "Private Security and Public Policing in Canada," *Juristat* 18, no. 13 (1998).

20. Daniel Georges-Abeyie, "Race, Ethnicity, and the Spatial Dynamic: Toward a Realistic Study of Black Crime, Crime Victimization, and Criminal Justice Processing of Blacks," *Social Justice* 16 (1989): 35–54.

21. John Hagan and Celesta Albonetti, "Race, Class and the Perception of Criminal Injustice in America," *American Journal of Sociology* 88 (1982): 329–355.

22. Richard Quinney, *The Social Reality of Crime* (Boston: Little, Brown, 1970), 15–23.

23. Austin Turk, *Criminality and Legal Order* (Chicago: Rand McNally, 1969), 58.

24. Lynch and Groves, *A Primer in Radical Criminology*, 2nd ed., 38.

25. Andrea McCalla and Vic Satzewich, "Settler Capitalism and the Construction of Immigrants and 'Indians' as Racialized Others," in *Crimes of Colour: Racialization and the Criminal Justice System in Canada*, ed. Wendy Chan and Kiran Mirchandani (Peterborough, Ont.: Broadview Press, 2002); "Mediation Offered in Kanesatake Standoff," *The Globe and Mail*, June 15, 2004; "Fire Damages Kanesatake Police Station," Canadian Press, June 11, 2004.

26. Austin Turk, *Criminality and Legal Order* (Chicago: Rand McNally, 1969).

27. David McDowall, "Poverty and Homicide in Detroit, 1926–1978," *Victims and Violence* 1 (1986): 23–34; David McDowall and Sandra Norris, "Poverty and Homicide in Baltimore, Cleveland, and Memphis, 1937–1980," paper presented at the annual meeting of the American Society of Criminology, Montreal, November 1987.

28. Judith Blau and Peter Blau, "The Cost of Inequality: Metropolitan Structure and Violent Crime," *American Sociological Review* 147 (1982): 114–129; Richard Block, "Community Environment and Violent Crime," *Criminology* 17 (1979): 46–57; Robert Sampson, "Structural Sources of Variation in Race-Age-Specific Rates of Offending across Major U.S. Cities," *Criminology* 23 (1985): 647–673.

29. David Jacobs and David Britt, "Inequality and Police Use of Deadly Force: An Empirical Assessment of a Conflict Hypothesis," *Social Problems* 26 (1979): 403–412.

30. Alan Lizotte, "Extra-Legal Factors in Chicago's Criminal Courts: Testing the Conflict Model of Criminal Justice," *Social Problems* 25 (1978): 564–580.

31. Terance Miethe and Charles Moore, "Racial Differences in Criminal Processing: The Consequences of Model Selection on Conclusions About Differential Treatment," *Sociological Quarterly* 27 (1987): 217–237.

32. Gail Kellough and Scot Wortley, "Remand for Plea: Bail Decisions and Plea Bargaining as Commensurate Decisions," *British Journal of Criminology* 42 (2002): 186–210; Yasmin Jiwani, "The Criminalization of 'Race,' the Racialization of Crime," in *Crimes of Colour: Racialization and the Criminal Justice System in Canada*, ed. Wendy Chan and Kiran Mirchandani (Peterborough, Ont.: Broadview Press, 2002).

33. Ron Melchers, "Do Toronto Police Engage in Racial Profiling?" *Canadian Review of Criminology and Criminal Justice* 7 (2003): 347–366; Scot Wortley and Julian Tanner, "Data, Denials, and Confusion: The Racial Profiling Debate in Toronto," *Canadian Review of Criminology and Criminal Justice* (2003): 367–389; Alan D. Gold, "Media Hype, Racial Profiling, and Good Science," *Canadian Review of Criminology and Criminal Justice* (2003): 391–399.

34. Douglas Smith, Christy Visher, and Laura Davidson, "Equity and Discretionary Justice: The Influence of Race on Police Arrest Decisions," *Journal of Criminal Law and Criminology* 75 (1984): 234–249.

35. Thomas Arvanites, "Increasing Imprisonment: A Function of Crime or Socioeconomic Factors?" *American Journal of Criminal Justice* 17 (1992): 19–38.

36. Nancy Wonders, "Determinate Sentencing: A Feminist and Postmodern Story," *Justice Quarterly* 13 (1996): 610–648.

37. Michael Leiber, Anne Woodrick, and E. Michele Roudebush, "Religion, Discriminatory Attitudes and the Orientations of Juvenile Justice Personnel: A Research Note," *Criminology* 33 (1995): 431–447.

38. Michael Leiber and Katherine Jamieson, "Race and Decision Making Within Juvenile Justice: The Importance of Context," *Journal of Quantitative Criminology* 11 (1995): 363–388.

39. Dragan Milovanovic, "Postmodern Criminology: Mapping the Terrain," *Justice Quarterly* 13 (1996): 567–610.

40. Richard Greenleaf and Lonn Lanza-Kaduce, "Sophistication, Organization and Authority-Subject Conflict: Rediscovering and Unraveling Turk's Theory of Norm Resistance," *Criminology* 33 (1995): 565–585.

41. Ab Currie, *Research Report: The New Brunswick Aboriginal Duty Counsel Project* (Ottawa: Department of Justice, 2000).

42. Jackson Toby, "The New Criminology Is the Old Sentimentality," *Criminology* 16 (1979): 513–526.

43. Kenneth Land and Marcus Felson, "A General Framework for Building Dynamic Macro Social Indicator Models: An Analysis of Changes in Crime Rates and Police Expenditures," *American Journal of Sociology* 82 (1976): 565–604.

44. See, generally, William Wilbanks, *The Myth of a Racist Criminal Justice System* (Monterey, Calif.: Brooks/Cole, 1987).

45. Theodore Chiricos and Gordon Waldo, "Socioeconomic Status and Criminal Sentencing: An Empirical Assessment of a Conflict Proposition," *American Sociological Review* 40 (1975): 753–772.

46. Stephen Klein, Joan Petersilia, and Susan Turner, "Race and Imprisonment Decisions in California," *Science* 247 (1990): 812–816.

47. Basil Owomero, "Crime in Tanzania: Contradictions of a Socialist Experiment," *International Journal of Comparative and Applied Criminal Justice* 12 (1988): 177–189.

48. This section borrows heavily from Richard Sparks, "A Critique of Marxist Criminology," in *Crime and Justice*, vol. 2, ed. Norval Morris and Michael Tonry (Chicago: University of Chicago Press, 1980), 159–208.

49. Jeffery Reiman, *The Rich Get Richer and the Poor Get Prison* (New York: Wiley, 1984), 43–44.

50. For a general review of Marxist criminology, see Lynch and Groves, *A Primer in Radical Criminology*, 2nd ed.

51. Ian Taylor, Paul Walton, and Jock Young, *The New Criminology: For a Social Theory of Deviance* (London: Routledge & Kegan Paul, 1973).

52. Barry Krisberg, *Crime and Privilege: Toward a New Criminology* (Englewood Cliffs, N.J.: Prentice-Hall, 1975), 167.

53. David Friedrichs, "Critical Criminology and Critical Legal Studies," *Critical Criminologist* 1 (1989): 7.

54. See, for example, Larry Tifft and Dennis Sullivan, *The Struggle to Be Human: Crime, Criminology and Anarchism* (Orkney

Islands, Over-the-Water-Sanday: Cienfuegos Press, 1979); Dennis Sullivan, *The Mask of Love* (Port Washington, N.Y.: Kennikat Press, 1980).

55. R.M. Bohm, "Radical Criminology: An Explication," *Criminology* 19 (1982): 565–589.

56. Robert Bohm, "Radical Criminology: Back to the Basics," paper presented at the annual meeting of the American Society of Criminology, Phoenix, Ariz., November 1993, 2.

57. W. Byron Groves and Robert Sampson, "Critical Theory and Criminology," *Social Problems* 33 (1986): 58–80.

58. Gregg Barak, "'Crimes of the Homeless' or the 'Crime of Homelessness': A Self-Reflexive, New-Marxist Analysis of Crime and Social Control," paper presented at the annual meeting of the American Society of Criminology, Montreal, November 1987.

59. Michael Lynch, "Assessing the State of Radical Criminology: Toward the Year 2000," paper presented at the annual meeting of the American Society of Criminology, Phoenix, Ariz., November 1993.

60. Gresham Sykes, "The Rise of Critical Criminology," *Journal of Criminal Law and Criminology* 65 (1974): 211; David Jacobs, "Corporate Economic Power and the State: A Longitudinal Assessment of Two Explanations," *American Journal of Sociology* 93 (1988): 852–881.

61. Deanna Alexander, "Victims of the L.A. Riots: A Theoretical Consideration," paper presented at the annual meeting of the American Society of Criminology, Phoenix, Ariz., November 1993.

62. Richard Quinney, "Crime Control in Capitalist Society," in *Critical Criminology*, ed. Ian Taylor, Paul Walton, and Jock Young, 199 (London: Routledge and Kegan Paul, 1975).

63. Herman Schwendinger and Julia Schwendinger, "Delinquency and Social Reform: A Radical Perspective," in *Juvenile Justice*, ed. Lamar Empey, 246–290 (Charlottesville: University of Virginia Press, 1979).

64. Michael Lynch, Raymond Michalowski, and W. Byron Groves, *The New Primer in Radical Criminology: Critical Perspectives on Crime, Power, and Identity*, 3rd ed. (Monsey, N.Y.: Criminal Justice Press, 2000), 45; herein cited as *The New Primer*; Malcolm Homes, "Minority Threat and Police Brutality: Determinants of Civil Rights Criminal Complaints in U.S. Municipalities," *Criminology* 38 (2000): 343–368.

65. Laureen Snider, "The Sociology of Corporate Crime: An Obituary," *Theoretical Criminology* 4, no. 2 (2000): 169–206.

66. Elliott Currie, "A Dialogue with Anthony M. Platt," *Issues in Criminology* 8 (1973): 28.

67. John Hagan, *Structural Criminology* (New Brunswick, N.J.: Rutgers University Press, 1989), 110–119.

68. Stephen Spitzer, "Toward a Marxian Theory of Deviance," *Social Problems* 22 (1975): 638–651.

69. Roy Bhaskar, "Empiricism," in *A Dictionary of Marxist Thought*, ed. T. Bottomore, 149–150 (Cambridge: Harvard University Press, 1983).

70. Byron Groves, "Marxism and Positivism," *Crime and Social Justice* 23 (1985): 129–150; Michael Lynch, "Quantitative Analysis and Marxist Criminology: Some Old Answers to a Dilemma in Marxist Criminology," *Crime and Social Justice* 29 (1987): 110–117.

71. Alan Lizotte, James Mercy, and Eric Monkkonen, "Crime and Police Strength in an Urban Setting: Chicago, 1947–1970," in *Quantitative Criminology*, ed. John Hagan, 129–148 (Beverly Hills, Calif.: Sage, 1982).

72. William Chambliss, "The State, the Law and the Definition of Behavior as Criminal or Delinquent," in *Handbook of Criminology*, ed. D. Glazer, 7–44 (Chicago: Rand McNally, 1974).

73. Timothy Carter and Donald Clelland, "A Neo-Marxian Critique, Formulation and Test of Juvenile Dispositions as a Function of Social Class," *Social Problems* 27 (1979): 96–108.

74. David Greenberg, "Socio-Economic Status and Criminal Sentences: Is There an Association?" *American Sociological Review* 42 (1977): 174–175; David Greenberg and Drew Humphries, "The Co-optation of Fixed Sentencing Reform," *Crime and Delinquency* 26 (1980): 206–225.

75. Steven Box, *Power, Crime and Mystification* (London: Tavistock, 1984); Gregg Barak, *In Defense of Whom? A Critique of Criminal Justice Reform* (Cincinnati: Anderson Publishing, 1980); for an opposing view, see Franklin Williams, "Conflict Theory and Differential Processing: An Analysis of the Research Literature," in *Radical Criminology: The Coming Crisis*, ed. J. Inciardi, 213–231 (Beverly Hills, Calif.: Sage, 1980).

76. Herman Schwendinger and Julia Schwendinger, "Rape Victims and the False Sense of Guilt," *Crime and Social Justice* 13 (1980): 4–17.

77. For more of their work, see Herman Schwendinger and Julia Schwendinger, *Adolescent Subcultures and Delinquency* (New York: Praeger, 1985); Herman Schwendinger and Julia Schwendinger, "The Paradigmatic Crisis in Delinquency Theory," *Crime and Social Justice* 18 (1982): 70–78; Herman Schwendinger and Julia Schwendinger, "The Collective Varieties of Youth," *Crime and Social Justice* 5 (1976): 7–25; Herman Schwendinger and Julia Schwendinger, "Marginal Youth and Social Policy," *Social Problems* 24 (1976): 184–191.

78. David Greenberg and Valerie West, "State Prison Populations and Their Growth, 1971–1991," *Criminology* 39 (2001): 615–654.

79. Robert Weiss, "Repatriating Low-Wage Work: The Political Economy of Prison Labor Reprivatization in the Postindustrial United States," *Criminology* 39 (2001): 253–292.

80. W. Gordon West and Ruth Morris, *The Case for Penal Abolition* (Toronto: Canadian Scholar's Press, 2000).

81. Michael Rustigan, "A Reinterpretation of Criminal Law Reform in Nineteenth-Century England," in *Crime and Capitalism*, ed. D. Greenberg (Palo Alto, Calif.: Mayfield Publishing, 1981), 255–278; Rosalind Petchesky, "At Hard Labor: Penal Confinement and Production in Nineteenth-Century America," in *Crime and Capitalism*, ed. D. Greenberg, 341–357; Paul Takagi, "The Walnut Street Jail: A Penal Reform to Centralize the Powers of the State," *Federal Probation* 49 (1975): 18–26.

82. Steven Spitzer and Andrew Scull, "Privatization and Capitalist Development: The Case of the Private Police," *Social Problems* 25 (1977): 18–29; Dennis Hoffman, "Cops and Wobblies," Ph.D. dissertation, Portland State University, 1977.

83. Sidney Harring, "Policing a Class Society: The Expansion of the Urban Police in the Late Nineteenth and Early Twentieth Centuries," in *Crime and Capitalism*, ed. D. Greenberg, 292–313.

84. Jack Gibbs, "An Incorrigible Positivist," *Criminologist* 12 (1987): 2–3.

85. Carl Klockars, "The Contemporary Crises of Marxist Criminology," in *Radical Criminology: The Coming Crisis*, ed. J. Inciardi, 92–123 (Beverly Hills, Calif.: Sage, 1980).

86. Michael Lynch, W. Byron Groves, and Alan Lizotte, "The Rate of Surplus Value and Crime: A Theoretical and Empirical Examination of Marxian Economic Theory and Criminology," *Crime, Law and Social Change* 1 (1994): 1–11.

87. Anthony Platt, "Criminology in the 1980s: Progressive Alternatives to 'Law and Order,'" *Crime and Social Justice* 21–22 (1985): 191–199.

88. See, generally, Roger Matthews and Jock Young, eds., *Confronting Crime* (London: Sage, 1986); for a thorough review of left realism, see Martin Schwartz and Walter DeKeseredy, "Left Realist Criminology: Strengths, Weaknesses and the Feminist Critique," *Crime, Law and Social Change* 15 (1991): 51–72.

89. John Lea and Jock Young, *What Is to Be Done About Law and Order?* (Harmondsworth, England: Penguin, 1984).

90. Richard Kinsey, John Lea, and Jock Young, *Losing the Fight against Crime* (London: Blackwell, 1986).

91. Martin Schwartz and Walter DeKeseredy, *Contemporary Criminology* (Belmont, Calif.: Wadsworth, 1996), 249.

92. For a general review of this issue, see Kathleen Daly and Meda Chesney-Lind, "Feminism and Criminology," *Justice Quarterly* 5 (1988): 497–538; Douglas Smith and Raymond Paternoster, "The Gender Gap in Theories of Deviance: Issues and Evidence," *Journal of Research in Crime and Delinquency* 24 (1987): 140–172; Pat Carlen, "Women, Crime, Feminism, and Realism," *Social Justice* 17 (1990): 106–123.

93. Julia Schwendinger and Herman Schwendinger, *Rape and Inequality* (Beverly Hills, Calif.: Sage, 1983).

94. Bernard Schissel, "Boys against Girls. The Structural and Interpersonal Dimensions or Violent Patriarchal Culture in the Lives of Young Men," *Violence Against Women* 6, no. 9 (2000): 960–986.

95. James Messerschmidt, *Capitalism, Patriarchy and Crime* (Totowa, N.J.: Rowman and Littlefield, 1986); for a critique of this work, see Herman Schwendinger and Julia Schwendinger, "The World According to James Messerschmidt," *Social Justice* 15 (1988): 123–145.

96. Kathleen Daly, "Gender and Varieties of White-Collar Crime," *Criminology* 27 (1989): 769–793.

97. Jane Roberts Chapman, "Violence against Women as a Violation of Human Rights," *Social Justice* 17 (1990): 54–71.

98. James Messerschmidt, *Masculinities and Crime: Critique and Reconceptualization of Theory* (Lanham, Md.: Rowman and Littlefield, 1993).

99. For a review of feminist theory, see Sally Simpson, "Feminist Theory, Crime and Justice," *Criminology* 27 (1989): 605–632.

100. Suzie Dod Thomas and Nancy Stein, "Criminality, Imprisonment, and Women's Rights in the 1990s," *Social Justice* 17 (1990): 1–5.

101. Walter DeKeseredy and Martin Schwartz, "Male Peer Support and Woman Abuse: An Expansion of DeKeseredy's Model," *Sociological Spectrum* 13 (1993): 393–413.

102. Daly and Chesney-Lind, "Feminism and Criminology." See also Drew Humphries and Susan Caringella-MacDonald, "Murdered Mothers, Missing Wives: Reconsidering Female Victimization," *Social Justice* 17 (1990): 71–78.

103. Center for Research on Women, *Secrets in Public: Sexual Harassment in Our Schools* (Wellesley, Mass.: Wellesley College, 1993).

104. Sandy Cook and Susanne Davies, eds., *Harsh Punishment. International Experiences of Women's Imprisonment* (Boston: Northeastern University Press, 1999).

105. Jane Siegel and Linda Meyer Williams, "Aggressive Behavior among Women Sexually Abused as Children," paper presented at the American Society of Criminology meeting, Phoenix, Ariz., 1993, rev. version.

106. Susan Ehrlich Martin and Nancy Jurik, *Doing Justice, Doing Gender* (Thousand Oaks, Calif.: Sage, 1996), 27.

107. Ruth Alexander, *The "Girl Problem": Female Sexual Delinquency in New York, 1900–1930* (Ithaca, N.Y.: Cornell University Press, 1995).

108. Steven Bittle, "When Protection is Punishment: Neo-liberalism and Secure Care Approaches to Youth Prostitution," *Canadian Journal of Criminology* 44, no. 3 (2002): 317–351.

109. Raymond R. Corrado, Candice Odgers, and Irwin M. Cohen, "The Incarceration of Female Young Offenders: Protection for Whom?" *Canadian Journal of Criminology* 42, no. 2 (2000): 189–208.

110. Mary Odem and Steven Schlossman, "Guardians of Virtue: The Juvenile Court and Female Delinquency in Early 20th-Century Los Angeles," *Crime and Delinquency* 37 (1991): 186–203.

111. Meda Chesney-Lind, "Judicial Enforcement of the Female Sex Role: The Family Court and the Female Delinquent," *Issues in Criminology* 8 (1973): 51–69; see also Meda Chesney-Lind, "Women and Crime: The Female Offender," *Signs: Journal of Women in Culture and Society* 12 (1986): 78–96; Meda Chesney-Lind, "Female Offenders: Paternalism Reexamined," in *Women, the Courts, and Equality*, ed. Laura L. Crites and Winifred L. Hepperle, 114–139 (Newbury Park, Calif.: Sage, 1987); Meda Chesney-Lind, "Girls' Crime and a Woman's Place: Toward a Feminist Model of Female Delinquency," paper presented at a meeting of the American Society of Criminology, Montreal, 1987.

112. John Hagan, A.R. Gillis, and John Simpson, "The Class Structure and Delinquency: Toward a Power-Control Theory of Common Delinquent Behavior," *American Journal of Sociology* 90 (1985): 1151–1178; John Hagan, John Simpson, and A.R. Gillis, "Class in the Household: A Power-Control Theory of Gender and Delinquency," *American Journal of Sociology* 92 (1987): 788–816.

113. John Hagan, Bill McCarthy, and Holly Foster, "A Gendered Theory of Delinquency and Despair in the Life Course," *Acta Sociologica* 45 (2002): 37–47.

114. Brenda Sims Blackwell, "Perceived Sanction Threats, Gender, and Crime: A Test and Elaboration of Power-Control Theory," *Criminology* 38 (2000): 439–488.

115. Christopher Uggen, "Class, Gender, and Arrest: An Intergenerational Analysis of Workplace Power and Control," *Criminology* 38 (2000): 835–862.

116. Gary Jensen, "Power-Control versus Social-Control Theory: Identifying Crucial Differences for Future Research," paper presented at the annual meeting of the American Society of Criminology, Baltimore, November 1990.

117. Gary Jensen and Kevin Thompson, "What's Class Got to Do with It? A Further Examination of Power-Control Theory," *American Journal of Sociology* 95 (1990): 1009–1023. For some critical research, see Simon Singer and Murray Levine, "Power Control Theory, Gender and Delinquency: A Partial Replication with Additional Evidence on the Effects of Peers," *Criminology* 26 (1988): 627–648.

118. Kevin Thompson, "Gender and Adolescent Drinking Problems: The Effects of Occupational Structure," *Social Problems* 36 (1989): 30–38.

119. Dragan Milovanovic, *A Primer in the Sociology of Law* (New York: Harrow and Heston, 1988) 127–128.

120. Gladys L. Symons, "Police Constructions of Race and Gender in Street Gangs," in *Crimes of Colour: Racialization and the Criminal Justice System in Canada*, ed. Wendy Chan and Kiran Mirchandani (Peterborough, Ont.: Broadview Press, 2002).

121. Kathryn Campbell, Martin Dufresne, and Richard MacLure, "Amending Youth Justice Policy in Canada: Discourse, Mediation and Ambiguity," *The Howard Journal* 40, no. 3 (2001): 272–284.

122. Howard Zehr, *Changing Lenses* (Scottdale, Pa.: Herald Press, 1990), 181.

123. The Anabaptist Brethren and Mennonite Churches as well as the Quaker religious denomination have long since been recognized as peacemaking churches. Individuals who identify themselves as Brethren, Mennonite, or Quaker have committed themselves to living simple and pacifist lifestyles. Brethren, Mennonites, and Quakers are typically very actively involved with many community-based restorative justice programs. Some of these restorative justice programs are sponsored either by the Mennonite Central Committee or by the Canadian Friends (Quakers) Service Committee. Agape comes from the Greek

word meaning "to love one's brother in the same way that one loves oneself." Agape is distinct from eros (romantic love) and philia (friendship or platonic love). *The Bible*, New International Version, 2 Peter 1:7

124. Dennis Sullivan and Larry Tifft, *Restorative Justice: Healing the Foundations of Our Everyday Lives* (Monsey, N.Y.: Willow Tree Press, 2001), 49.

125. John L. McKnight, "Redefining Community," *Social Policy* Fall–Winter (1992): 56–62.

126. Robin J. Wilson, Bria Huculak, and Andrew McWhinnie, "Restorative Justice Innovations in Canada," *Behavioural Science and the Law* 20 (2002): 363–380.

127. Bas Van Stokkom, "Moral Emotions in Restorative Justice Conferences: Managing Shame, Designing Empathy," *Theoretical Criminology* 6 (2002): 339–360.

128. Alan N. Young, *Victims of Crime: The Role of the Victim in the Criminal Process: A Literature Review—1989 to 1999* (Ottawa, Ont.: Department of Justice Canada, 2001), 60.

129. Robert C. Depew, "Popular Justice and Aboriginal Communities," *Journal of Legal Pluralism* 36 (1996): 21–67.

130. Ruth Morris, *Stories of Transformative Justice* (Toronto, Ont.: Canadian Scholar's Press, 2000).

131. Peter Cordella, *Restorative Justice* (unpublished paper, Manchester, N.H.: St. Anselm College, 1997); see also Herbert Bianchi, *Justice as Sanctuary* (Bloomington: Indiana University Press, 1994); Nils Christie, "Conflicts as Property," *The British Journal of Criminology* 17 (1977): 1–15; L. Hulsman, "Critical Criminology and the Concept of Crime," *Contemporary Crises* 10 (1986): 63–80.

132. This section adapted with the assistance of Stephen Pidwysocky.

133. Richard Quinney, "The Way of Peace: On Crime, Suffering and Service," in *Criminology as Peacemaking*, ed. Harold Pepinsky and Richard Quinney (Bloomington: Indiana University Press, 1991), 8–9.

134. John Paul Lederach, Building Peace: Sustainable Reconciliation in Divided Societies (Washington, D.C.: United States Institute of Peace Press, 1997); Denise Breton and Stephen Lehman, *The Mystic Heart of Justice* (West Chester, Pa.: Chrysalis Books, 2001); Harold Pepinsky and Richard Quinney, eds., *Criminology as Peace-Making* (Indianapolis, Ind.: Indiana University Press, 1991), p. 10.

135. Gregg Barak, *Violence and Nonviolence: Pathways to Understanding* (Thousand Oaks, Calif.: Sage Publications, 2003), 120.

136. See, for example, Tifft and Sullivan, *The Struggle to Be Human*; and Sullivan, *The Mask of Love*.

137. Dennis Sullivan and Larry Tifft, *Restorative Justice* (Monsey, N.Y.: Willow Tree Press, 2001).

138. Richard Quinney, "The Way of Peace: On Crime, Suffering and Service," in *Criminology as Peacemaking*, ed. Harold Pepinsky and Richard Quinney, 8–9 (Bloomington: Indiana University Press, 1991). To read about the evolution of Quinney's work, see Kevin Anderson, "Richard Quinney's Journey: The Marxist Dimension," *Crime and Delinquency* 48 (2002): 232–243.

139. Denise Breton and Stephen Lehman, *The Mystic Heart of Justice* (West Chester, Pa.: Chrysalis Books, 2001), 181–182.

140. John Paul Lederach, *Building Peace: Sustainable Reconciliation in Divided Societies* (Washington, D.C.: United States Institute of Peace Press, 2002), 24.

141. For more resources on restorative justice and peacemaking, see Gene Stephens, "The Future of Policing: From a War Model to a Peace Model," in *The Past, Present, and Future of American Criminal Justice*, ed. Brendan Maguire and Polly Radosh, 77–93 (Dix Hills, N.Y.: General Hall, 1996); Kay Pranis, "Peacemaking Circles: Restorative Justice in Practice Allows Victims and Offenders to Begin Repairing the Harm," *Corrections Today* 59 (1997): 74; Carol LaPrairie, "The 'New'

Justice: Some Implications for Aboriginal Communities," *Canadian Journal of Criminology* 40 (1998): 61–79; David R. Karp and Beau Breslin, "Restorative Justice in School Communities," *Youth and Society* 33 (2001): 249–272; Paul Jesilow and Deborah Parsons, "Community Policing as Peacemaking," *Policing and Society* 10 (2000): 163–183; Gordon Bazemore and Curt Taylor Griffiths, "Conferences, Circles, Boards, and Mediations: The 'New Wave' of Community Justice Decision Making," *Federal Probation* 61 (1997): 25–37; John Braithwaite, "Setting Standards for Restorative Justice," *British Journal of Criminology* 42 (2002): 563–577; David Altschuler, "Community Justice Initiatives: Issues and Challenges in the U.S. Context," *Federal Probation* 65 (2001): 28–33; Lois Presser and Patricia Van Voorhis, "Values and Evaluation: Assessing Processes and Outcomes of Restorative Justice Programs," *Crime and Delinquency* 48 (2002): 162–189; Sharon Levrant, Francis Cullen, Betsy Fulton, and John Wozniak, "Reconsidering Restorative Justice: The Corruption of Benevolence Revisited?" *Crime and Delinquency* 45 (1999): 3–28.

Chapter 10

1. Emilie Andersen Allan, "Theory Is Not a Zero-Sum Game: The Quest for an Integrated Theory," paper presented at the annual meeting of the American Society of Criminology, Phoenix, Ariz., November 1993.

2. Gerald Patterson and Karen Yoerger, "Developmental Models for Delinquent Behavior," in *Mental Disorder and Crime*, ed. Sheilagh Higdins (Newbury Park, Calif.: Sage, 1993), 150–159.

3. David Rowe, D. Wayne Osgood, and W. Alan Nicewander, "A Latent Trait Approach to Unifying Criminal Careers," *Criminology* 28 (1990): 237–270.

4. David Rowe, Alexander Vazsonyi, and Daniel Flannery, "Sex Differences in Crime: Do Means and Within-Sex Variation Have Similar Causes?" *Journal of Research in Crime and Delinquency* 32 (1995): 84–100.

5. G.R. Patterson, Barbara DeBaryshe, and Elizabeth Ramsey, "A Developmental Perspective on Antisocial Behavior," *American Psychologist* 44 (1989): 329–335.

6. Kenneth Land and Daniel Nagin, "Micro-Models of Criminal Careers: A Synthesis of the Criminal Careers and Life-Course Approaches via Semiparametric Mixed Poisson Regression Models with Empirical Applications," *Journal of Quantitative Criminology* 12 (1996): 163–190.

7. Daniel Glazer, *Crime in Our Changing Society* (New York: Holt, Rinehart and Winston, 1978).

8. Joseph Weis and J. David Hawkins, Reports of the National Juvenile Justice Assessment Centers, *Preventing Delinquency* (Washington, D.C.: U.S. Department of Justice, 1981); Joseph Weis and John Sederstrom, Reports of the National Juvenile Justice Assessment Centers, *The Prevention of Serious Delinquency: What to Do* (Washington, D.C.: U.S. Department of Justice, 1981).

9. Julie O'Donnell, J. David Hawkins, and Robert Abbott, "Predicting Serious Delinquency and Substance Use among Aggressive Boys," *Journal of Consulting and Clinical Psychology* 63 (1995): 529–537.

10. Julie O'Donnell, J. David Hawkins, and Robert Abbott, "Predicting Serious Delinquency and Substance Use among Aggressive Boys," *Journal of Consulting and Clinical Psychology* 63 (1995): 534–536; Richard Catalano, Rick Kosterman, J. David Hawkins, Michael Newcomb, and Robert Abbott, "Modeling the Etiology of Adolescent Substance Use: A Test of the Social Development Model," *Journal of Drug Issues* 26 (1996): 429–455.

11. Todd Herrenkohl, Bu Huang, Rick Kosterman, J. David Hawkins, Richard Catalano, and Brian Smith, "A Comparison of Social Development Processes Leading to Violent Behavior in Late Adolescence for Childhood Initiators and Adolescent Initiators of Violence," *Journal of Research in Crime and Delinquency* 38 (2001): 45–63.

12. David Brownfield, Kevin Thompson, and Ann Marie Sorenson, "Correlates of Gang Membership: A Test of Strain, Social Learning, and Control-Bonding Theories," paper presented at the annual meeting of the American Society of Criminology, Chicago, November 1996.

13. Bu Huang, Rick Kosterman, Richard Catalano, J. David Hawkins, and Robert Abbott, "Modeling Mediation in the Etiology of Violent Behavior in Adolescence: A Test of the Social Development Model," *Criminology* 39 (2001): 75–107.

14. J. David Hawkins, Richard Catalano, Diane Morrison, Julie O'Donnell, Robert Abbott, and L. Edward Day, "The Seattle Social Development Project," in *The Prevention of Antisocial Behavior in Children*, ed. Joan McCord and Richard Tremblay, 139–160 (New York: Guilford, 1992).

15. Delbert Elliott, David Huizinga, and Suzanne Ageton, *Explaining Delinquency and Drug Use* (Beverly Hills, Calif.: Sage, 1985).

16. Scott Menard and Delbert Elliott, "Delinquent Bonding, Moral Beliefs, and Illegal Behavior: A Three Wave–Panel Model," *Justice Quarterly* 11 (1994): 173–188.

17. Mark Colvin and John Pauly, "A Critique of Criminology: Toward an Integrated Structural-Marxist Theory of Delinquency Production," *American Journal of Sociology* 89 (1983): 513–551.

18. Steven Messner and Marvin Krohn, "Class, Compliance Structures, and Delinquency: Assessing Integrated Structural-Marxist Theory," *American Journal of Sociology* 96 (1990): 300–328.

19. Lee Ellis, "Neurohormonal Bases of Varying Tendencies to Learn Delinquent and Criminal Behavior," in *Behavioral Approaches to Crime and Delinquency*, ed. E. Morris and C. Braukmann, 499–518 (New York: Plenum, 1988).

20. James Q. Wilson and Richard Herrnstein, *Crime and Human Nature* (New York: Simon & Schuster, 1985).

21. Michael Gottfredson and Travis Hirschi, *A General Theory of Crime* (Stanford, Calif.: Stanford University Press, 1990).

22. Alex Piquero and Stephen Tibbetts, "Specifying the Direct and Indirect Effects of Low Self-Control and Situational Factors in Offenders' Decision Making: Toward a More Complete Model of Rational Offending," *Justice Quarterly* 13 (1996): 481–508.

23. Dennis Giever, "An Empirical Assessment of the Core Elements of Gottfredson and Hirschi's General Theory of Crime," paper presented at the American Society of Criminology meeting, Boston, November 1995.

24. Robert Agnew, "The Contribution of Social-Psychological Strain Theory to the Explanation of Crime and Delinquency," *Advances in Criminological Theory* 6 (1994).

25. Travis Hirschi and Michael Gottfredson, "Rethinking the Juvenile Justice System," *Crime and Delinquency* 39 (1993): 262–271.

26. David Brownfield and Ann Marie Sorenson, "Self-Control and Juvenile Delinquency: Theoretical Issues and an Empirical Assessment of Selected Elements of a General Theory of Crime," *Deviant Behavior* 14 (1993): 243–264; Harold Grasmick, Charles Tittle, Robert Bursik, and Bruce Arneklev, "Testing the Core Empirical Implications of Gottfredson and Hirschi's General Theory of Crime," *Journal of Research in Crime and Delinquency* 30 (1993): 5–29; John Cochran, Peter Wood, and Bruce Arneklev, "Is the Religiosity-Delinquency Relationship Spurious? A Test of Arousal and Social Control Theories," *Journal of Research in Crime and Delinquency* 31 (1994): 92–123.

27. Carl Keane, Paul Maxim, and James Teevan, "Drinking and Driving, Self-Control, and Gender: Testing a General Theory of Crime," *Journal of Research in Crime and Delinquency* 30 (1993): 30–46.

28. Judith DeJong, Matti Virkkunen, and Marku Linnoila, "Factors Associated with Recidivism in a Criminal Population," *The Journal of Nervous and Mental Disease* 180 (1992): 543–550.

29. David Cantor, "Drug Involvement and Offending Among Incarcerated Juveniles," paper presented at the American Society of Criminology meeting, Boston, November 1995.

30. Brownfield and Sorenson, "Self-Control and Juvenile Delinquency."

31. Jon Gibbs and Dennis Giever, "Self-Control and Its Manifestations among University Students: An Empirical Test of Gottfredson and Hirschi's General Theory," *Justice Quarterly* 12 (1995): 231–255.

32. Dennis Giever, "An Empirical Assessment of the Core Elements of Gottfredson and Hirschi's General Theory of Crime," paper presented at the American Society of Criminology meeting, Boston, November 1995.

33. Marc LeBlanc, Marc Ouimet, and Richard Tremblay, "An Integrative Control Theory of Delinquent Behavior: A Validation, 1976–1985," *Psychiatry* 51 (1988): 164–176.

34. Alexander Vazsonyi, Lloyd Pickering, Marianne Junger, and Dick Hessing, "An Empirical Test of a General Theory of Crime: A Four-Nation Comparative Study of Self-Control and the Prediction of Deviance," *Journal of Research in Crime and Delinquency* 38 (2001): 91–131.

35. See, for example, Douglas Longshore, Susan Turner, and Judith Stein, "Self-Control in a Criminal Sample: An Examination of Construct Validity," *Criminology* 34 (1996): 209–228; Grasmick et al., "Testing the Core Empirical Implications of Gottfredson and Hirschi's General Theory of Crime"; Daniel Nagin and Raymond Paternoster, "Enduring Individual Differences and Rational Choice Theories of Crime," *Law and Society Review* 27 (1993): 467–489.

36. Bruce Link, Elmer Streuning, Francis Cullen, Patrick Shrout, and Bruce Dohrenwend, "A Modified Labeling Theory Approach to Mental Disorders: An Empirical Assessment," *American Sociological Review* 54 (1989): 400–423.

37. Michael Benson and Elizabeth Moore, "Are White-Collar and Common Offenders the Same? An Empirical and Theoretical Critique of a Recently Proposed General Theory of Crime," *Journal of Research in Crime and Delinquency* 29 (1992): 251–272.

38. For a general review and critique, see Kenneth Polk's book review in *Crime and Delinquency* 37 (1991): 575–581.

39. Ronald Akers, "Self-Control as a General Theory of Crime," *Journal of Quantitative Criminology* 7 (1991): 201–211.

40. Samuel Yochelson and Clifford Samenow, *The Criminal Personality* (New York: Jason Aronson, 1977).

41. Ann Marie Sorenson and David Brownfield, "Normative Concepts in Social Control," paper presented at the annual meeting of the American Society of Criminology, Phoenix, Ariz., November 1993.

42. Scott Menard, Delbert Elliott, and Sharon Wofford, "Social Control Theories in Developmental Perspective," *Studies on Crime and Crime Prevention* 2 (1993): 69–87.

43. Delbert Elliott and Scott Menard, "Delinquent Friends and Delinquent Behavior: Temporal and Developmental Patterns," in *Current Theories of Crime and Deviance*, ed. J. David Hawkins (Newbury, Calif.: Sage Publications, 1996).

44. Graham Ousey and David Aday, Jr., "The Interaction Hypothesis: A Test Using Social Control Theory and Social Learning Theory," paper presented at the American Society of Criminology meeting, Boston, November 1995.

45. Julie Horney, D. Wayne Osgood, and Ineke Haen Marshall, "Criminal Careers in the Short-Term: Intra-Individual Variability in Crime and Its Relations to Local Life Circumstances," *American Sociological Review* 60 (1995): 655–673.

46. Otwin Marenin and Michael Resig, "A General Theory of Crime and Patterns of Crime in Nigeria: An Exploration of Methodological Assumptions," *Journal of Criminal Justice* 23 (1995): 501–518.

47. Bruce Arneklev, Harold Grasmick, Charles Tittle, and Robert Bursik, "Low Self-Control and Imprudent Behavior," *Journal of Quantitative Criminology* 9 (1993): 225–246.

48. Terrie Moffitt, "Adolescence-Limited and Life-Course Persistent Antisocial Behaviors: A Developmental Taxonomy," *Psychological Review* 100 (1993): 674–701.

49. Alex R. Piquero and He Len Chung, "On the Relationships between Gender, Early Onset, and the Seriousness of Offending," *Journal of Criminal Justice* 29 (2001): 189–206.

50. Delbert Elliott and Scott Menard, "Delinquent Friends and Delinquent Behavior: Temporal and Developmental Patterns," in *Crime and Delinquency: Current Theories*, ed. J. David Hawkins (Cambridge: Cambridge University Press, 1996).

51. Graham Ousey and David Aday, "The Interaction Hypothesis: A Test Using Social Control Theory and Social Learning Theory," paper presented at the American Society of Criminology Meeting, Boston, 1995.

52. Bradley Entner Wright, Avashalom Caspi, Terrie Moffitt, and Phil Silva, "The Effects of Social Ties on Crime Vary by Criminal Propensity: A Life-Course Model of Interdependence," *Criminology* 39 (2001): 321–352.

53. Carter Hay, "Parenting, Self-Control, and Delinquency: A Test of Self-Control Theory," *Criminology* 39 (2001): 707–736; Douglas Longshore, "Self-Control and Criminal Opportunity: A Prospective Test of the General Theory of Crime," *Social Problems* 45 (1998): 102–114; Finn-Aage Esbensen and Elizabeth Piper Deschenes, "A Multisite Examination of Youth Gang Membership: Does Gender Matter?" *Criminology* 36 (1998): 799–828.

54. Raymond Paternoster and Robert Brame, "The Structural Similarity of Processes Generating Criminal and Analogous Behaviors," *Criminology* 36 (1998): 633–670.

55. Kevin Thompson, "Sexual Harassment and Low Self-Control: An Application of Gottfredson and Hirschi's General Theory of Crime," paper presented at the annual meeting of the American Society of Criminology, Phoenix, Ariz., November 1993.

56. R.E. Tremblay and L.C. Masse, "Cognitive Deficits, School Achievement, Disruptive Behavior and Juvenile Delinquency: A Longitudinal Look at Their Developmental Sequence," paper presented at the annual meeting of the American Society of Criminology, Phoenix, Ariz., November 1993.

57. David Nurco, Timothy Kinlock, and Mitchell Balter, "The Severity of Preaddiction Criminal Behavior among Urban, Male Narcotic Addicts and Two Nonaddicted Control Groups," *Journal of Research in Crime and Delinquency* 30 (1993): 293–316.

58. G.R. Patterson and Karen Yoerger, "Differentiating Outcomes and Histories for Early and Late Onset Arrests," paper presented at the annual meeting of the American Society of Criminology, Phoenix, Ariz., November 1993.

59. David Farrington, Darrick Jolliffe, Rolf Loeber, Madga Stouthamer-Loeber, and Larry Kalb, "The Concentration of Offenders in Families, and Family Criminality in the Prediction of Boys' Delinquency," *Journal of Adolescence* 24 (2001): 579–596.

60. Joan McCord, "Family Relationships, Juvenile Delinquency, and Adult Criminality," *Criminology* 29 (1991): 397–417.

61. Robert Sampson and John Laub, "Crime and Deviance in the Life Course," *American Review of Sociology* 18 (1992): 63–84.

62. Gerald Patterson, J.B. Reid, and Thomas Dishion, *A Social Interactional Approach: Antisocial Boys* (Eugene, Ore.: Castalia Press, 1992).

63. Francois Poulin, Thomas Dishion, Mike Stoolmiller, and Gerald Patterson, "Modeling Growth in Adolescent Delinquency: The Combined Effect and Developmental Specificity of Parent Bonding and Deviant Peers," paper presented at the annual meeting of the American Society of Criminology, Chicago, November 1996.

64. See, generally, Sheldon Glueck and Eleanor Glueck, *500 Criminal Careers* (New York: Knopf, 1930); Sheldon Glueck and Eleanor Glueck, *One Thousand Juvenile Delinquents* (Cambridge, Mass.: Harvard University Press, 1934); Sheldon Glueck and Eleanor Glueck, *Predicting Delinquency and Crime* (Cambridge, Mass.: Harvard University Press, 1967), 82–83.

65. Sheldon Glueck and Eleanor Glueck, *Unraveling Juvenile Delinquency* (Cambridge, Mass.: Harvard University Press, 1950).

66. See, generally, John Laub and Robert Sampson, "The Sutherland-Glueck Debate: On the Sociology of Criminological Knowledge," *American Journal of Sociology* 96 (1991): 1402–1440; John Laub and Robert Sampson, "Unraveling Families and Delinquency: A Reanalysis of the Gluecks' Data," *Criminology* 26 (1988): 355–380.

67. Rolf Loeber and Marc LeBlanc, "Toward a Developmental Criminology," in *Crime and Justice*, vol. 12, ed. Norval Morris and Michael Tonry, 375–473 (Chicago: University of Chicago Press, 1990).

68. G.R. Patterson, L. Crosby, and S. Vuchinich, "Predicting Risk for Early Police Arrest," *Journal of Quantitative Criminology* 8 (1992): 335–355.

69. Patterson, DeBaryshe, and Ramsey, "A Developmental Perspective on Antisocial Behavior," 331–333.

70. Rolf Loeber, Magda Southamer-Loeber, Welmoet Van Kammen, and David Farrington, "Initiation, Escalation and Desistance in Juvenile Offending and Their Correlates," *Journal of Criminal Law and Criminology* 82 (1991): 36–82.

71. Richard Jessor, John Donovan, and Francis Costa, *Beyond Adolescence: Problem Behavior and Young Adult Development* (New York: Cambridge University Press, 1991).

72. Richard Jessor, "Risk Behavior in Adolescence: A Psychosocial Framework for Understanding and Action," in *Adolescents at Risk: Medical and Social Perspectives*, ed. D.E. Rogers and E. Ginzburg (Boulder, Colo.: Westview, 1992).

73. Magda Stouthamer-Loeber and Evelyn Wei, "The Precursors of Young Fatherhood and Its Effect on Delinquency of Teenage Males," *Journal of Adolescent Health* 22 (1998): 56–65; Richard Jessor, John Donovan, and Francis Costa, *Beyond Adolescence: Problem Behavior and Young Adult Development* (New York: Cambridge University Press, 1991); Xavier Coll, Fergus Law, Aurelio Tobias, Keith Hawton, and Josep Tomas, "Abuse and Deliberate Self-Poisoning in Women: A Matched Case-Control Study," *Child Abuse and Neglect* 25 (2001): 1291–1293.

74. Deborah Capaldi and Gerald Patterson, "Can Violent Offenders Be Distinguished from Frequent Offenders: Prediction from Childhood to Adolescence," *Journal of Research in Crime and Delinquency* 33 (1996): 206–231; D. Wayne Osgood, "The Covariation among Adolescent Problem Behaviors," paper presented at the annual meeting of the American Society of Criminology, Baltimore, November 1990.

75. Todd Miller, Timothy Smith, Charles Turner, Margarita Guijarro, and Amanda Hallet, "A Meta-Analytic Review of Research on Hostility and Physical Health," *Psychological Bulletin* 119 (1996): 322–348; Marianne Junger, "Accidents and Crime," in *The Generality of Deviance*, ed. T. Hirschi and M. Gottfredson (New Brunswick, N.J.: Transaction Press, 1993).

76. Robert Johnson, S. Susan Su, Dean Gerstein, Hee-Choon Shin, and John Hoffman, "Parental Influences on Deviant Behavior in Early Adolescence: A Logistic Response Analysis of Age- and Gender-Differentiated Effects," *Journal of Quantitative Criminology* 11 (1995): 167–192; Judith Brooks, Martin Whiteman, and Patricia Cohen, "Stage of Drug Use, Aggression, and Theft/Vandalism," in *Drugs, Crime and Other Deviant Adaptations: Longitudinal Studies*, ed. Howard Kaplan (New York: Plenum Press, 1995), 83–96; Robert Hoge, D.A. Andrews, and Alan Leschied, "Tests of Three Hypotheses Regarding the Predictors of Delinquency," *Journal of Abnormal Child Psychology* 22 (1994): 547–559.

77. Rolf Loeber and David Farrington, "Young Children Who Commit Crime: Epidemiology, Developmental Origins, Risk Factors, Early Interventions, and Policy Implications," *Development and Psychopathology* 12 (2000): 737–762.

78. David Huizinga, Rolf Loeber, and Terence Thornberry, "Longitudinal Study of Delinquency, Drug Use, Sexual Activity, and Pregnancy among Children and Youth in Three Cities," *Public Health Reports* 108 (1993): 90–96.

79. Helene Raskin White, Peter Tice, Rolf Loeber, and Magda Stouthamer-Loeber, "Illegal Acts Committed by Adolescents under the Influence of Alcohol and Drugs," *Journal of Research in Crime and Delinquency* 39 (2002): 131–153.

80. Jeanne Hernandez, "The Concurrence of Eating Disorders with Histories of Child Abuse among Adolescents," paper presented at the annual meeting of the American Society of Criminology, Phoenix, Ariz., November 1993.

81. Candace Kruttschnitt, Jane McLeod, and Maude Dornfeld, "The Economic Environment of Child Abuse," *Social Problems* 41 (1994): 299–312.

82. James Marquart, Victoria Brewer, Patricia Simon, and Edward Morse, "Lifestyle Factors among Female Prisoners with Histories of Psychiatric Treatment," *Journal of Criminal Justice* 29 (2001): 319–328.

83. Helene Raskin White, "Early Problem Behavior and Later Drug Problems," *Journal of Research in Crime and Delinquency* 29 (1992): 412–429.

84. Helene Raskin White and Erich Labouvie, "Generality Versus Specificity of Problem Behavior: Psychological and Functional Differences," *Journal of Drug Issues* 24 (1994): 55–74.

85. See, generally, Richard Dembo, Linda Williams, Werner Wothke, James Schmeidier, Alan Getreu, Estrellita Berry, and Eric Wish, "The Generality of Deviance: Replication of a Structural Model Among High-Risk Youths," *Journal of Research in Crime and Delinquency* 29 (1992): 200–216.

86. Rolf Loeber, Phen Wung, Kate Keenan, Bruce Giroux, Magda Stouthamer-Loeber, Wemoet Van Kammen, and Barbara Maughan, "Developmental Pathways in Disruptive Behavior," *Development and Psychopathology* (1993): 12–48.

87. Sheila Royo Maxwell and Christopher Maxwell, "Examining the 'Criminal Careers' of Prostitutes within the Nexus of Drug Use, Drug Selling, and Other Illicit Activities," *Criminology* 38 (2000): 787–809.

88. Alex Piquero and Timothy Brezina, "Testing Moffitt's Account of Adolescent-Limited Delinquency," *Criminology* 39 (2001): 353–370.

89. Amy D'Unger, Kenneth Land, Patricia McCall, and Daniel Nagin, "How Many Latent Classes of Delinquent/Criminal Careers? Results from Mixed Poisson Regression Analyses of the London, Philadelphia, and Racine Cohort Studies," paper presented at the annual meeting of the American Society of Criminology, Chicago, November 1996.

90. Terrie Moffitt, "Natural Histories of Delinquency," in *Cross-National Longitudinal Research on Human Development and Criminal Behavior*, ed. Elmar Weitekamp and Hans-Jurgen Kerner, 3–65 (Dordrecht, Netherlands: Kluwer, 1994).

91. Terrie Moffitt, "Adolescence-Limited and Life-Course Persistent Antisocial Behavior: A Developmental Taxonomy," *Psychological Review* 100 (1993): 674–701.

92. Michael Newcomb, "Pseudomaturity among Adolescents: Construct Validation, Sex Differences, and Associations in Adulthood," *Journal of Drug Issues* 26 (1996): 477–504.

93. Paul Tracy and Kimberly Kempf-Leonard, *Continuity and Discontinuity in Criminal Careers* (New York: Plenum Press, 1996), 208.

94. Paul Mazerolle, Robert Brame, Ray Paternoster, Alex Piquero, and Charles Dean, "Onset Age, Persistence, and Offending Versatility: Comparisons across Sex," *Criminology* 38 (2000): 1143–1172.

95. Alex Piquero, Robert Brame, Paul Mazerolle, and Rudy Haapanen, "Crime in Emerging Adulthood," *Criminology* 40 (2002): 137–170.

96. David Nurco, Timothy Kinlock, and Mitchell Balter, "The Severity of Preaddiction Criminal Behavior among Urban, Male Narcotic Addicts and Two Nonaddicted Control Groups," *Journal of Research in Crime and Delinquency* 30 (1993): 293–316.

97. Ronald Simons, Chyi-In Wu, Rand Conger, and Frederick Lorenz, "Two Routes to Delinquency: Differences Between Early and Later Starters in the Impact of Parenting and Deviant Careers," *Criminology* 32 (1994): 247–275.

98. Paul Mazerolle, "Understanding the Theoretical and Empirical Dimensions of Late Onset to Delinquent Behavior," paper presented at the annual meeting of the American Society of Criminology, Boston, November 1995.

99. Charles Dean, Robert Brame, and Alex Piquero, "Criminal Propensities, Discrete Groups of Offenders, and Persistence of Crime," *Criminology* 34 (1966): 547–573.

100. Ick-Joong Chung, Karl G Hill, J. David Hawkins, Lewayne Gilchrist, and Daniel Nagin, "Childhood Predictors of Offense Trajectories," *Journal of Research in Crime and Delinquency* 39 (2002): 60–91.

101. Amy D'Unger, Kenneth Land, Patricia McCall, and Daniel Nagin, "How Many Latent Classes of Delinquent/Criminal Careers? Results from Mixed Poisson Regression Analyses," *American Journal of Sociology* 103 (1998): 1593–1630.

102. See, for example, the *Rochester Youth Development Study* (Hindelang Criminal Justice Research Center, 135 Western Avenue, Albany, New York 12222).

103. David Farrington, "The Development of Offending and Antisocial Behavior from Childhood to Adulthood," paper presented at the Congress on Rethinking Delinquency, University of Minho, Braga, Portugal, July 1992.

104. See, generally, D.J. West and David P. Farrington, *The Delinquent Way of Life* (London: Heinemann, 1977).

105. The material in the following sections is summarized from Farrington, "The Development of Offending and Antisocial Behavior from Childhood to Adulthood"; David Farrington, "Psychobiological Factors in the Explanation and Reduction of Delinquency," *Today's Delinquent* 7 (1988): 44–46; David Farrington, "Childhood Origins of Teenage Antisocial Behaviour and Adult Social Dysfunction," *Journal of the Royal Society of Medicine* 86 (1993): 13–17; David Farrington, "Psychosocial Influences on the Development of Antisocial Personality," paper presented at the annual meeting of the American Society of Criminology, Phoenix, Ariz., November 1993.

106. Terence Thornberry, "Toward an Interactional Theory of Delinquency," *Criminology* 25 (1987): 863–891.

107. See, for example, Jean Piaget, *The Grasp of Consciousness* (Cambridge, Mass.: Harvard University Press, 1976).

108. This research is known as the *Rochester Youth Development Study*. Thornberry's colleagues on the project include Alan Lizotte, Margaret Farnworth, Marvin Krohn, and Susan Stern.

109. Terence Thornberry, Alan Lizotte, Marvin Krohn, and Margaret Farnworth, "The Role of Delinquent Peers in the Initiation of Delinquent Behavior," working paper no. 6, rev., Rochester Youth Development Study (Albany, N.Y.: Hindelang Criminal Justice Research Center, 1993).

110. Terence Thornberry, Alan Lizotte, Marvin Krohn, Margaret Farnworth, and Sung Joon Jang, "Delinquent Peers, Beliefs, and Delinquent Behavior: A Longitudinal Test of Interactional Theory," *Criminology* 32 (1994): 601–637.

111. Terence Thornberry, Alan Lizotte, Marvin Krohn, Margaret Farnworth, and Sung Joon Jang, "Delinquent Peers, Beliefs, and Delinquent Behavior: A Longitudinal Test of Interactional Theory," working paper no. 6, rev., Rochester Youth Development Study (Albany, N.Y.: Hindelang Criminal Justice Research Center, 1992).

112. Terence Thornberry, Alan Lizotte, Marvin Krohn, Margaret Farnworth, and Sung Joon Jang, "Testing Interactional Theory: An Examination of Reciprocal Causal Relationships Among Family, School and Delinquency," *Journal of Criminal Law and Criminology* 82 (1991): 3–35.

113. Scott Menard and Delbert Elliott, "Delinquent Bonding, Moral Beliefs, and Illegal Behavior: A Three Wave–Panel Model," *Justice Quarterly* 11 (1994): 173–188.

114. Carolyn Smith, Alan Lizotte, Terence Thornberry, and Marvin Krohn, *Resilient Youth: Identifying Factors That Prevent High-Risk Youth from Engaging in Delinquency and Drug Use* (Albany, N.Y.: Rochester Youth Development Study, 1994).

115. Robert Sampson and John Laub, *Crime in the Making: Pathways and Turning Points through Life* (Cambridge, Mass.: Harvard University Press, 1993); John Laub and Robert Sampson, "Turning Points in the Life Course: Why Change Matters to the Study of Crime," paper presented at the annual meeting of the American Society of Criminology, New Orleans, November 1992.

116. Terri Orbuch, James House, Richard Mero, and Pamela Webster, "Marital Quality over the Life Course," *Social Psychology Quarterly* 59 (1996): 162–171; Lee Lillard and Linda Waite, "'Til Death Do Us Part: Marital Disruption and Mortality," *American Journal of Sociology* 100 (1995): 1131–1156.

117. Pamela Webster, Terri Orbuch, and James House, "Effects of Childhood Family Background on Adult Marital Quality and Perceived Stability," *American Journal of Sociology* 101 (1995): 404–432.

118. John Hagan, Ross MacMillan, and Blair Wheaton, "New Kid in Town: Social Capital and the Life Course Effects of Family Migration on Children," *American Sociological Review* 61 (1996): 368–385.

119. Robert Hoge, D.A. Andrews, and Alan Leschied, "An Investigation of Risk and Protective Factors in a Sample of Youthful Offenders," *Journal of Child Psychology and Psychiatry* 37 (1996): 419–424.

120. For a discussion see Mark Collins and Don Weatherburn, "Unemployment and the Dynamics of Offender Populations," *Journal of Quantitative Criminology* 11 (1995): 231–245.

121. Erich Labouvie, "Maturing Out of Substance Use: Selection and Self-Correction," *Journal of Drug Issues* 26 (1996): 457–474.

122. Robert Sampson and John Laub, "Socioeconomic Achievement in the Life Course of Disadvantaged Men: Military Service as a Turning Point, circa 1940–1965," *American Sociological Review* 61 (1996): 347–367.

123. Daniel Nagin and Raymond Paternoster, "Personal Capital and Social Control: The Deterrence Implications of a Theory of Criminal Offending," *Criminology* 32 (1994): 581–606.

124. Eloise Dunlop and Bruce Johnson, "Family and Human Resources in the Development of a Female Crack-Seller Career: Case Study of a Hidden Population," *Journal of Drug Issues* 26 (1996): 175–198.

125. Mark Warr, "Life-Course Transitions and Desistance from Crime," *Criminology* 36 (1998): 502–535.

126. Doris Layton MacKenzie and Spencer De Li, "The Impact of Formal and Informal Social Controls on the Criminal Activities of Probationers," *Journal of Research in Crime and Delinquency* 39 (2002): 243–278.

127. Alex Piquero, John MacDonald, and Karen Parker, "Race, Local Life Circumstances, and Criminal Activity over the Life-Course," *Social Science Quarterly* 83 (2002): 654–671.

128. Ronald Simons, Eric Stewart, Leslie Gordon, Rand Conger, and Glen Elder, Jr., "Test of Life-Course Explanations for Stability and Change in Antisocial Behavior from Adolescence to Young Adulthood," *Criminology* 40 (2002): 401–435.

Chapter 11

1. Albert Reiss and Jeffrey Roth, *Understanding and Preventing Violence* (Washington, D.C.: National Academy Press, 1993); Jeffrey Ian Ross, ed., *Violence in Canada: Sociopolitical Perspectives* (Don Mills, Ont.: Oxford, 1995).

2. *Stanford v. Kentucky*, 109 Supreme Court, 2969 (1989).

3. Josee Savoie, "Homicide in Canada, 2002," *Juristat* 23, no. 8 (2003).

4. Robert Nash Parker and Catherine Colony, "Relationships, Homicides, and Weapons: A Detailed Analysis," paper presented at the annual meeting of the American Society of Criminology, Montreal, November 1987.

5. Stryker McGuire, "The Dunblane Effect," *Newsweek*, October 28, 1996, 46; "Gunman Kills 14, Self. Letter Blames Feminists," *Mail Star* (Halifax), December 7, 1989, A1.

6. Laura Bender, "Children and Adolescents Who Have Killed," *American Journal of Psychiatry* 116 (1959): 510–516.

7. Dorothy Otnow Lewis, Ernest Moy, Lori Jackson, Robert Aaronson, Nicholas Restifo, Susan Serra, and Alexander Simos, "Biopsychosocial Characteristics of Children Who Later Murder," *American Journal of Psychiatry* 142 (1985): 1161–1167.

8. Amy Holtzworth-Munroe and Gregory Stuart, "Typologies of Male Batterers: Three Subtypes and the Differences Among Them," *Psychological Bulletin* 116 (1994): 476–497.

9. "Jury Recommends Death for Florida Killer of Five," *New York Times*, March 25, 1994, A14.

10. Deborah Capaldi and Gerald Patterson, "Can Violent Offenders Be Distinguished from Frequent Offenders? Prediction from Childhood to Adolescence," *Journal of Research in Crime and Delinquency* 33 (1996): 206–231; see also, Pamela Lattimore, Christy Visher, and Richard Linster, "Predicting Rearrest for Violence Among Serious Youthful Offenders," *Journal of Research in Crime and Delinquency* 32 (1995): 54–83.

11. Robert Scudder, William Blount, Kathleen Heide, and Ira Silverman, "Important Links between Child Abuse, Neglect, and Delinquency," *International Journal of Offender Therapy* 37 (1993): 315–323.

12. Dorothy Lewis et al., "Neuropsychiatric, Psychoeducational, and Family Characteristics of 14 Juveniles Condemned to Death in the United States," *American Journal of Psychiatry* 145 (1988): 584–588.

13. Charles Patrick Ewing, *When Children Kill* (Lexington, Mass.: Lexington Books, 1990), 22.

14. Murray Straus, "Discipline and Deviance: Physical Punishment of Children and Violence and Other Crime in Adulthood," *Social Problems* 38 (1991): 133–154.

15. Lonnie Athens, *The Creation of Dangerous Violent Criminals* (Urbana: University of Illinois Press, 1992), 27–80.

16. Cathy Spatz Widom, "Child Abuse, Neglect, and Violent Criminal Behavior," *Criminology* 27 (1989): 251–271; Beverly Rivera and Cathy Spatz Widom, "Childhood Victimization and Violent Offending," *Violence and Victims* 5 (1990): 19–34.

17. Sigmund Freud, *Beyond the Pleasure Principle* (London: Inter-Psychoanalytic Press, 1922).

18. Konrad Lorenz, *On Aggression* (New York: Harcourt Brace Jovanovich, 1966).

19. See, generally, Lee Ellis and Anthony Walsh, "Gene-Based Evolutionary Theories in Criminology," *Criminology* 35 (1997): 229–276.

20. Paul Joubert and Craig Forsyth, "A Macro View of Two Decades of Violence in America," *American Journal of Criminal Justice* 13 (1988): 10–25; M. Dwayne Smith and Victoria Brewer, "A Sex-Specific Analysis of Correlates of Homicide Victimization in United States Cities," *Violence and Victims* 7 (1992): 279–285.

21. Marvin Wolfgang and Franco Ferracuti, *The Subculture of Violence* (London: Tavistock, 1967).

22. David Luckenbill and Daniel Doyle, "Structural Position and Violence: Developing a Cultural Explanation," *Criminology* 27 (1989): 419–436.

23. Steven Messner, "Regional and Racial Effects on the Urban Homicide Rate: The Subculture of Violence Revisited," *American Journal of Sociology* 88 (1983): 997–1007; Steven Messner and Kenneth Tardiff, "Economic Inequality and Levels of Homicide: An Analysis of Urban Neighborhoods," *Criminology* 24 (1986): 297–317.

24. Beth Bjerregaard and Alan Lizotte, "Gun Ownership and Gang Membership," *Journal of Criminal Law and Criminology* 86 (1995): 37–58.

25. Scott Decker, "Gangs and Violence: The Expressive Character of Collective Involvement," unpublished manuscript, University of Missouri–St. Louis, 1994.

26. Carolyn Rebecca Block, "Chicago Homicide from the Sixties to the Nineties: Have Patterns of Lethal Violence Changed?" paper presented at the annual meeting of the American Society of Criminology, Baltimore, November 1990.

27. Vincent F. Sacco and Leslie W. Kennedy, *The Criminal Event*, 2nd ed. (Toronto, Ont.: ITP Nelson, 1998).

28. See, generally, Kirk Williams and Robert Flewelling, "The Social Production of Criminal Homicide: A Comparative Study of Disaggregated Rates in American Cities," *American Sociological Review* 53 (1988): 421–431.

29. Raymond Gastil, "Homicide and the Regional Culture of Violence," *American Sociological Review* 36 (1971): 12–27; Keith Harries, *Serious Violence: Patterns of Homicide and Assault in America* (Springfield, Ill.: Charles C. Thomas, 1990).

30. Howard Erlanger, "Is There a Subculture of Violence in the South?" *Journal of Criminal Law and Criminology* 66 (1976): 483–490; Colin Loftin and Robert Hill, "Regional Subculture of Violence: An Examination of the Gastil-Hackney Thesis," *American Sociological Review* 39 (1974): 714–724; Raymond Gastil, "Comments," *Criminology* 16 (1975): 60–64; F. Frederick Hawley and Steven Messner, "The Southern Violence Construct: A Review of Arguments, Evidence, and the Normative Context," *Justice Quarterly* 6 (1989): 481–511.

31. T.F. Hartnagel, "The Effect of Age and Sex Compositions of Provincial Populations on Provincial Crime Rates," *Canadian Journal of Criminology* 20 (1978): 28–33; C. Lindsay, "Trends in the Crime Rate in Canada, 1970–1985," *Canadian Social Trends* (Autumn 1986): 33–38; L.W. Kennedy, R.A. Silverman,

and D.R. Forde, "Homicide in Urban Canada," *Canadian Journal of Sociology* 16 (1991): 397–410; for the United States, see Gregory Kowalski and Thomas Petee, "Sunbelt Effects on Homicide Rates," *Sociology and Social Research* 76 (1991): 73–79.

32. Leslie Kennedy, Robert Silverman, and David Forde, "Homicide in Urban Canada: Testing the Impact of Economic Inequality and Social Disorganization," *Canadian Journal of Sociology* 16 (1991): 397.

33. Paul Goldstein, Henry Brownstein, and Patrick Ryan, "Drug-Related Homicide in New York: 1984–1988," *Crime and Delinquency* 38 (1992): 459–476.

34. James Collins and Pamela Messerschmidt, "Epidemiology of Alcohol-Related Violence," *Alcohol Health and Research World* 17 (1993): 93–100.

35. Thomas Feucht, *Drug Use Forecasting 1995* (Washington, D.C.: National Institute of Justice, 1996).

36. Christopher Innes, *Profile of State Prison Inmates 1986* (Washington, D.C.: Bureau of Justice Statistics, 1988).

37. Paul Goldstein, Patricia Bellucci, Barry Spunt, and Thomas Miller, "Volume of Cocaine Use and Violence: A Comparison between Men and Women," *Journal of Drug Issues* 21 (1991): 345–367; Paul Goldstein, Henry Brownstein, Patrick Ryan, and Patricia Bellucci, "Crack and Homicide in New York City, 1988: A Conceptually Based Event Analysis," unpublished paper, Narcotic and Drug Research, New York, 1989; Goldstein, Brownstein, and Ryan, "Drug-Related Homicide in New York: 1984–1988," p. 473.

38. Tracey Leesti, "Weapons and Violent Crime," *Juristat* 17 (1997); Orest Fedowycz, "Homicide in Canada–1999," *Juristat* 20 (2000); Josee Savoie, "Homicide in Canada, 2002," *Juristat* 23, no. 8 (2003).

39. David Brent, Joshua Perper, Christopher Allman, Grace Moritz, Mary Wartella, and Janice Zelenak, "The Presence and Accessibility of Firearms in the Home and Adolescent Suicides," *Journal of the American Medical Association* 266 (1991): 2989–2995.

40. Linda Saltzman, James Mercy, Patrick O'Carroll, Mark Rosenberg, and Philip Rhodes, "Weapon Involvement and Injury Outcomes in Family and Intimate Assaults," *Journal of the American Medical Association* 267 (1992): 3043–3047.

41. David Lester, "Gun Availability and the Use of Guns for Suicide and Homicide in Canada," *Canadian Journal of Public Health* 91, no. 3 (2000): 186; "Unintentional Firearm Deaths: Can They Be Reduced by Lowering Gun Ownership Levels," *Canadian Journal of Public Health* 92, no. 5 (2001): 396–398.

42. Philip C. Stenning, "Long Gun Registration: A Poorly Aimed Longshot," *Canadian Journal of Crime and Criminal Justice* 10 (2003): 479–488; Neil Boyd, "Gun Control: Placing Costs in Context," *Canadian Journal of Crime and Criminal Justice* 10 (2003): 473–478.

43. "Gunshot Wounds: The New Public Health Issue," *Journal of the American Medical Association* 3 (2004): 170–175; "Shooting Ourselves in the Foot: Why Mandatory Reporting of Gunshot Wounds Is a Bad Idea," *Canadian Medical Association Journal* 4 (2004): 170–178; "Why Mandatory Reporting of Gunshot Wounds Is Necessary," *Canadian Medical Association Journal* 4 (2004): 170–178.

44. "More Canadians Oppose Gun Ownership by General Public, but Majority Still Favours Stricter Gun Laws," Gallup Canada, November 28, 2001; "Majority of Canadians Say Gun Registry Should Be Scrapped," Ipsos Reid poll, December 13, 2002.

45. Timothy Hartnagel, "Gun Control in Alberta: Explaining Public Attitudes Concerning Legislative Change," *Canadian Journal of Criminology* 44, no. 4 (2002): 403–424; see also Thomas Gabor, "Universal Firearm Registration in Canada: Three Perspectives," *Canadian Journal of Crime and Criminal Justice*

10 (2003): 465–471; Thomas Gabor, "The Federal Gun Registry: An Urgent Need for Independent, Non-Partisan Research," *Canadian Journal of Crime and Criminal Justice* 10 (2003): 489–498.

46. William Green, *Rape* (Lexington, Mass.: Lexington Books, 1988), 5.

47. Susan Randall and Vicki McNickle Rose, "Forcible Rape," in *Major Forms of Crime*, ed. Robert Meyer (Beverly Hills, Calif.: Sage, 1984), 47.

48. As cited in Chris McCormick, "Contemporary Sociological Thought," in *Canadian Criminology: Perspectives in Crime and Criminality*, 2nd ed., ed. Margaret A. Jackson and Curt T. Griffiths (Toronto, Ont.: Harcourt Brace, 1995), 129.

49. Associated Press, "Judge Who Told Rape Suspect to Get a Girlfriend Orders Him into Custody," *Manchester Union Leader*, February 19, 1994, 2.

50. Susan Brownmiller, *Against Our Will: Men, Women and Rape* (New York: Simon & Schuster, 1975).

51. Diego Ribadeneira, "In Haiti's Poorest Areas, Women Tell of Rape by Armed Men," *Boston Globe*, August 29, 1993, 6.

52. Canadian Centre for Justice Statistics, *Canadian Crime Statistics 2002* (Ottawa: Statistics Canada, 2003), catalogue no. 85-205 XPE.

53. Julian V. Roberts, "Criminal Justice Processing of Sexual Assault Cases," *Juristat* 14 (1994).

54. Robin Warshaw, *I Never Called It Rape: The Ms. Report on Recognizing, Fighting, and Surviving Date and Acquaintance Rape* (New York: Harper and Row, 1988), 26.

55. Elisa Romano and Rayleen V. De Luca, "Male Sexual Abuse: A Review of Effects, Abuse Characteristics, and Links with Later Psychological Functioning," *Aggression and Violent Behaviour* 6 (2001): 55–78.

56. Myriam S. Denov, "A Culture of Denial: Exploring Professional Perspectives on Female Sex Offending," *Canadian Journal of Criminology* 43, no. 3 (2001): 303–330.

57. Angela Browne, "Violence against Women: Relevance for Medical Practitioners," *Journal of the American Medical Association* 267 (1992): 3184–3189.

58. Roberts, "Criminal Justice Processing of Sexual Assault Cases."

59. *The Final Report of the Task Force on Sexual Abuse of Patients* (Toronto: Ontario College of Physicians and Surgeons, 1991).

60. Mark Warr, "Rape, Burglary and Opportunity," *Journal of Quantitative Criminology* 4 (1988): 275–288.

61. James LeBeau, "Patterns of Stranger and Serial Rape Offending Factors Distinguishing Apprehended and At-Large Offenders," *Journal of Criminal Law and Delinquency* 78 (1987): 309–326.

62. A. Nicholas Groth and Jean Birnbaum, *Men Who Rape* (New York: Plenum Press, 1979).

63. Raymond Knight, "Validation of a Typology of Rapists," in *Sex Offender Research and Treatment: State-of-the-Art in North America and Europe*, ed. W.L. Marshall and J. Frenken (Beverly Hills, Calif.: Sage, 1997).

64. Rebecca Kong, Holly Johnson, Sara Beattie, and Andrea Cardillo, "Sexual Offences in Canada," *Juristat* 23, no. 6 (2003).

65. Canadian Centre for Justice Statistics, *Canadian Crime Statistics, 1995* (Ottawa: Statistics Canada, 1996); Canadian Centre for Justice Statistics, *Canadian Crime Statistics 1999* (Ottawa: Statistics Canada, 2000), catalogue 85-205-XPE.

66. R. Lance Shotland, "A Model of the Causes of Date Rape in Developing and Close Relationships," in *Close Relationships*, ed. C. Hendrick, 247–270 (Newbury Park, Calif.: Sage, 1989).

67. Walter DeKeseredy, Martin Schwartz, and Karen Tait, "Sexual Assault and Stranger Aggression on a Canadian Campus," *Sex Roles* 28 (1993): 263–277; Thomas Meyer, "Date Rape: A Serious Campus Problem That Few Talk About," *Chronicle of Higher Education* 29 (December 1984): 15.

68. Martin Schwartz, "Humanist Sociology and Date Rape on the College Campus," *Humanity and Society* 15 (1991): 304–316.

69. Mark Starr, "The Writing on the Wall," *Newsweek*, November 26, 1990, 64.

70. Peggy Reeves Sanday, *Fraternity Gang Rape: Sex, Brotherhood, and Privilege on Campus* (New York: New York University, 1990); Sarah Elton, "McMaster: Rohypol [sic] and Sexual Assault," *The Brunswickan*, March 13, 1998, 4.

71. David Finkelhor and K. Yllo, *License to Rape: Sexual Abuse of Wives* (New York: Holt, Rinehart and Winston, 1985).

72. Cited in Diana Russell, "Wife Rape," in *Acquaintance Rape: The Hidden Crime*, ed. A. Parrot and L. Bechhofer (New York: Wiley, 1991).

73. Associated Press, "British Court Rejects Precedent, Finds a Man Guilty of Raping Wife," *Boston Globe*, March 15, 1991, 68.

74. Donald Symons, *The Evolution of Human Sexuality* (Oxford: Oxford University Press, 1979).

75. Lee Ellis, "A Synthesized (Biosocial) Theory of Rape," *Journal of Consulting and Clinical Psychology* 39 (1991): 631–642.

76. Diana Russell, *The Politics of Rape* (New York: Stein & Day, 1975).

77. Paul Gebhard, John Gagnon, Wardell Pomeroy, and Cornelia Christenson, *Sex Offenders: An Analysis of Types* (New York: Harper & Row, 1965), 198–205; Richard Rada, ed., *Clinical Aspects of the Rapist* (New York: Grune & Stratton, 1978), 122–130.

78. See, generally, Edward Donnerstein, Daniel Linz, and Steven Penrod, *The Question of Pornography* (New York: Free Press, 1987); Diana Russell, *Sexual Exploitation* (Beverly Hills, Calif.: Sage, 1985), 115–116; Neil Malamuth and John Briere, "Sexual Violence in the Media: Indirect Effects on Aggression Against Women," *Journal of Social Issues* 42 (1986): 75–92.

79. Associated Press, "Trial on TV May Have Influenced Boy Facing Sexual-Assault Count," *Omaha World Herald*, April 18, 1984, 50.

80. Richard Felson and Marvin Krohn, "Motives for Rape," *Journal of Research in Crime and Delinquency* 27 (1990): 222–242.

81. Larry Baron and Murray Straus, "Four Theories of Rape: A Macrosociological Analysis," *Social Problems* 34 (1987): 467–489.

82. Julie Horney and Cassia Spohn, "The Influence of Blame and Believability Factors on the Processing of Simple versus Aggravated Rape Cases," *Criminology* 34 (1996): 135–163.

83. "Woman Urges Dotson's Release," *Omaha World Herald*, April 25, 1985, 3; Associated Press, "Apology Is Aired for Lie about Rape," *Boston Globe*, September 6, 1990, 12; Associated Press, "Protection Urged for Rape Suspects," *Boston Globe*, January 13, 1997, A5.

84. Gerald Robin, "Forcible Rape: Institutionalized Sexism in the Criminal Justice System," *Crime and Delinquency* 23 (1977): 136–153.

85. Associated Press, "Jury Stirs Furor by Citing Dress in Rape Acquittal," *Boston Globe*, October 6, 1989, 12.

86. *Michigan v. Lucas* 90–149 (1991); Comment, "The Rape Shield Paradox: Complainant Protection Amidst Oscillating Trends of State Judicial Interpretation," *Journal of Criminal Law and Criminology* 78 (1987): 644–698.

87. Andrew Karmen, *Crime Victims* (Pacific Grove, Calif.: Brooks/Cole, 1990), 252.

88. See, for example, Michigan Comprehensive Laws Annotated, 750.5200-(1); Florida Statutes Annotated, Sec. 794.011. See, generally, Gary LaFree, "Official Reactions to Rape," *American Sociological Review* 45 (1980): 842–854; Martin Schwartz and Todd Clear, "Toward a New Law on Rape," *Crime and Delinquency* 26 (1980): 129–151; Susan Caringella-MacDonald,

"The Comparability in Sexual and Nonsexual Assault Case Treatment: Did Statute Change Meet the Objective?" *Crime and Delinquency* 31 (1985): 206–223.

89. Linda Coates, "Causal Attributions in Sexual Assault Trial Judgments," *Journal of Language and Social Psychology* 16 (1997): 287–296; Linda Coates, Janet Bavelas, and James Gibson, "Anomalous Language in Sexual Assault Trial Judgments," *Discourse and Society* 5 (1994): 189–206.

90. The legal principles here come from Wayne LaFave and Austin Scott, *Criminal Law* (St. Paul: West Publishing, 1986; updated, 1993).

91. Josee Savoie, "Homicide in Canada, 2002," *Juristat* 23, no. 8 (2003).

92. Angela Browne and Kirk Williams, "Gender, Intimacy, and Lethal Violence: Trends from 1976 through 1987," *Gender and Society* 7 (1993): 78–98. See also, Linda Saltzman and James Mercy, "Assaults between Intimates: The Range of Relationships Involved," in *Homicide, The Victim/Offender Connection*, ed. Anna Victoria Wilson (Cincinnati: Anderson Publishing, 1993), 65–74; Angela Browne and Kirk Williams, "Exploring the Effect of Resource Availability and the Likelihood of Female-Perpetrated Homicides," *Law and Society Review* 23 (1989): 75–94; Joseph A. Kuypers, *Man's Will to Hurt: Investigating the Causes, Supports and Varieties of His Violence* (Halifax: Fernwood, 1992).

93. Valerie Pottie Bunge, "National Trends in Intimate Partner Homicides, 1974–2000," *Juristat* 22, no. 5 (2002); Tina Hotton, "Spousal Violence After Marital Separation," *Juristat* 21, no. 7 (2001); Myrna Dawson, *Examination of Declining Intimate Partner Homicide Rates* (Ottawa: Department of Justice, 2001).

94. Robert Silverman and Leslie Kennedy, "Women Who Kill Their Children," *Violence and Victims* 3 (1988): 113.

95. Robert Silverman and William Meloff, "Canadian Kids Who Kill," *Canadian Journal of Criminology*, January (1992): 15.

96. Margaret Zahn and Philip Sagi, "Stranger Homicides in Nine American Cities," *Journal of Criminal Law and Criminology* 78 (1987): 377–397.

97. David Luckenbill, "Criminal Homicide as a Situational Transaction," *Social Problems* 25 (1977): 176–186.

98. Leslie Kennedy and Robert Silverman, "The Elderly Victim of Homicide: An Application of the Routine Activities Approach," *Sociological Quarterly* 31 (1990): 308.

99. Stephen Baron and Leslie Kennedy, "Routine Activities and a Subculture of Violence: A Study of Violence on the Street," *Journal of Research in Crime and Delinquency* 30 (1993): 88.

100. Michael Hazlett and Thomas Tomlinson, "Females Involved in Homicides: Victims and Offenders in Two Southern States," paper presented at the annual meeting of the American Society of Criminology, Montreal, November 1987; rev. 1988.

101. Scott Decker, "Deviant Homicide: A New Look at the Role of Motives and Victim-Offender Relationships," *Journal of Research in Crime and Delinquency* 33 (1996): 427–449.

102. Scott Decker, "Exploring Victim–Offender Relationships in Homicide: The Role of Individual and Event Characteristics," *Justice Quarterly* 10 (1993): 585–613.

103. James A. Fox and Jack Levin, *Mass Murder*, 2nd ed. (New York: Plenum Press, 1991).

104. Cindy Horswell, "Teen Held in Mom's Shooting Death: 'The Devil Made Me Do It,'" *Houston Chronicle*, May 19, 1993, 1.

105. Thomas Palmer, "A Doctor Smelled Arsenic, Leading to Arrest of Serial Killer," *Boston Globe*, August 20, 1987, 3.

106. "Police Suspect 'Something Snapped' to Ignite Wilder's Crime Spree," *Omaha World Herald*, April 15, 1984, 21A; Mark Starr, "The Random Killers," *Newsweek*, November 26, 1984, 100–106; Thomas Palmer, "Ex-Hospital Aide Admits Killing 24 in Cincinnati," *Boston Globe*, August 19, 1987, 3.

107. Ronald Holmes and Stephen Homes, *Murder in America* (Thousand Oaks, Calif.: Sage, 1994), 6.

108. Jenkins, "Serial Murder in England, 1940–1985," p. 9.

109. Ronald Holmes and James DeBurger, *Serial Murder* (Newbury Park, Calif.: Sage, 1988), 58–59.

110. Belea Keeney and Kathleen Heide, "Gender Differences in Serial Murderers: A Preliminary Analysis," *Journal of Interpersonal Violence* 9 (1994): 37–56.

111. Royal Canadian Mounted Police, "Violent Crime Linkage Analysis System (ViCLAS)," http://www.rcmp-grc.gc.ca/viclas/viclas_e.htm (accessed May 24, 2005); Jennifer Browdy, "VI-CAP System to Be Operational This Summer," *Law Enforcement News*, May 21, 1984, 1.

112. Philip Jenkins, "A Murder 'Wave'? Trends in American Serial Homicide 1940–1990," *Criminal Justice Review* 17 (1992): 1–18.

113. See, generally, Joel Milner, ed., "Special Issue: Physical Child Abuse," *Criminal Justice and Behavior* 18 (1991); see, generally, Ruth S. Kempe and C. Henry Kempe, *Child Abuse* (Cambridge, Mass.: Harvard University Press, 1978).

114. Catherine Trainor, *Family Violence in Canada: A Statistical Profile 2002* (Ottawa: Canadian Centre for Justice Statistics, 2002).

115. Holly Johnson, "Children and Youths as Victims of Violent Crimes," *Juristat* 15 (1995); for the United States, see David Wiese and Deborah Daro, *Current Trends in Child Abuse Reporting and Fatalities: The Results of the 1994 Annual Fifty-State Survey* (Chicago: National Committee to Prevent Child Abuse, 1995).

116. Richard Gelles and Murray Straus, "Violence in the American Family," *Journal of Social Issues* 35 (1979): 15–39.

117. Steve Geissinger, "Boy Scouts Dismissed 1,800 Suspected Molesters from 1971–91," *Boston Globe*, October 15, 1993, 3.

118. Diana Russell, "The Incidence and Prevalence of Intrafamilial and Extrafamilial Sexual Abuse of Female Children," *Child Abuse and Neglect* 7 (1983): 133–146; see also David Finkelhor, *Sexually Victimized Children* (New York: Free Press, 1979), 88.

119. Jeanne Hernandez, "Eating Disorders and Sexual Abuse in Adolescents," paper presented at the annual meeting of the American Psychosomatic Society, Charleston, S.C., March 1993; Glenn Wolfner and Richard Gelles, "A Profile of Violence Toward Children: A National Study," *Child Abuse and Neglect* 17 (1993): 197–212.

120. Louanne Lawson and Mark Chaffin, "False Negatives in Sexual Abuse Disclosure Interviews," *Journal of Interpersonal Violence* 7 (1992): 532–542.

121. For a thorough review, see Kathleen Kendall-Tackett, Linda Meyer Williams, and David Finkelhor, "Impact of Sexual Abuse on Children: A Review and Synthesis of Recent Empirical Studies," *Psychological Bulletin* 133 (1993): 164–180.

122. Brandt Steele, "Violence within the Family," in *Child Abuse and Neglect: The Family and the Community*, ed. R. Helfer and C.H. Kempe, 12 (Cambridge, Mass.: Ballinger Publishing, 1976).

123. M. O'Keefe, "Predictors of Child Abuse in Maritally Violent Families," *Journal of Interpersonal Violence* 10 (1995): 3–25; as cited in Johnson, "Children and Youths as Victims of Violent Crimes."

124. Ruth Inglis, *Sins of the Fathers: A Study of the Physical and Emotional Abuse of Children* (New York: St. Martin's Press, 1978), 68.

125. Associated Press, "Lorena Freed," *Manchester Union Leader*, March 1, 1994, 44.

126. Russell Dobash, R. Emerson Dobash, Margo Wilson, and Martin Daly, "The Myth of Sexual Symmetry in Marital Violence," *Social Problems* 39 (1992): 71–86; Martin Schwartz and Walter DeKeseredy, "The Return of the 'Battered Husband Syndrome': Typification of Women as Violent," *Crime, Law and Social Change* 8 (1993): 11–27.

127. Schwartz and DeKeseredy, "The Return of the 'Battered Husband Syndrome.'"

128. R. Emerson Dobash and Russell Dobash, *Violence against Wives* (New York: Free Press, 1979); Julia O'Faolain and Laura Martines, eds., *Not in God's Image: Women in History* (Glasgow: Fontana/Collins, 1974); Laurence Stone, "The Rise of the Nuclear Family in Modern England: The Patriarchal Stage," in *The Family in History*, ed. Charles Rosenberg, 53 (Philadelphia: University of Pennsylvania Press, 1975). See also John Braithwaite, "Inequality and Republican Criminology," paper presented at the annual meeting of the American Society of Criminology, San Francisco, November 1991, 20.

129. Merlin Brinkenhoff and Eugene Lupri, "Interspousal Violence," *Canadian Journal of Sociology* 13 (1988): 407.

130. Karen Rodgers, "Wife Assault: The Findings of a National Survey," *Juristat* 14 (1994).

131. James Makepeace, "Social Factor and Victim-Offender Differences in Courtship Violence," *Family Relations* 33 (1987): 87–91.

132. Graeme Newman, *Understanding Violence* (New York: Lippincott, 1979), 145–146.

133. Gerald Hotaling and David Sugarman, "An Analysis of Risk Markers in Husband to Wife Violence," *Violence and Victims* 1 (1986): 101–124; Ronald Simons, Chyi-In Wu, Christine Johnson, and Rand Conger, "A Test of Various Perspectives on the Intergenerational Transmission of Domestic Violence," *Criminology* 33 (1995): 141–171.

134. Canadian Centre for Justice Statistics, *Canadian Crime Statistics 2003* (Ottawa: Statistics Canada, 2004), catalogue 85-205-XPE.

135. F.H. McClintock and Evelyn Gibson, *Robbery in London* (London: Macmillan, 1961), 15.

136. John Conklin, *Robbery and the Criminal Justice System* (New York: Lippincott, 1972), 1–80.

137. James Calder and John Bauer, "Convenience Store Robberies: Security Measures and Store Robbery Incidents," *Journal of Criminal Justice* 20 (1992): 553–566.

138. John Scott Cameron, *Lessons from the Fabrikant File: A Report to the Board of Governors of Concordia University*, May 1994.

139. "Health and Safety Canada 2005—Violence in the Workplace Spotlighted at Canada's Largest Health and Safety Conference," Canada Newswire Group, http://www.newswire.ca/en/releases/archive/April2005/01/c0983.html (accessed May 12, 2005).

140. James Alan Fox and Jack Levin, "Firing Back: The Growing Threat of Workplace Homicide," *Annals* 536 (1994): 16–30.

141. Associated Press, "Gunman Wounds 3 Doctors in L.A. Hospital," *Cleveland Plain Dealer*, February 9, 1993, 1B.

142. Neil Boyd, "Violence in the Workplace in British Columbia: A Preliminary Investigation," *Canadian Journal of Criminology*, October (1995): 491.

143. Stephen Schafer, *The Political Criminal* (New York: Free Press, 1974), 1.

144. Robert Friedlander, *Terrorism* (Dobbs Ferry, N.Y.: Oceana Publishers, 1979); Walter Laquer, *The Age of Terrorism* (Boston: Little, Brown, 1987), 72; National Advisory Commission on Criminal Justice Standards and Goals, *Report of the Task Force on Disorders and Terrorism* (Washington, D.C.: U.S. Government Printing Office, 1976), 3.

145. Paul Wilkinson, *Terrorism and the Liberal State* (New York: Wiley, 1977), 49.

146. Jack Gibbs, "Conceptualization of Terrorism," *American Sociological Review* 54 (1989): 329–340.

147. Daniel Georges-Abeyie, "Political Crime and Terrorism," in *Crime and Deviance: A Comparative Perspective*, ed. Graeme Newman, 313–333 (Beverly Hills, Calif.: Sage, 1980).

148. This section relies heavily on Friedlander, *Terrorism*, 8–20.

149. For a general view, see Jonathan White, *Terrorism* (Pacific Grove, Calif.: Brooks/Cole, 1991).

150. Jonathan Kaufman, "Trauma of a German Slaying," *Boston Globe*, April 3, 1991, 2.

151. Claire Sterling, "Gen. Dozier and the International Terror Network," *Wall Street Journal*, December 29, 1981, 12.

152. Associated Press—Reuters, "Saudi Exile Is America's Most Wanted," *Toronto Star*, August 21, 1998.

153. Peter Annin and Mark Hosenball, "A Showdown in Montana," *Newsweek*, April 8, 1996, 39.

154. Reuters, "Five White Separatists Indicted in Robberies," *Boston Globe*, January 31, 1997, A8.

155. William Smith, "Libya's Ministry of Fear," *Time*, April 30, 1984, 36–38.

156. Reuters, "Nile Tour Boat Is Attacked; Blast Hits Egyptian Resort," *Boston Globe*, April 10, 1993, 5.

157. Associated Press, "31 Decapitated South of Algiers," *Boston Globe*, February 3, 1997, A5.

158. "Ottawa Is Prepared to Go Any Distance to Stop FLQ, Trudeau Says," *Globe and Mail*, October 14, 1970.

159. Charles Hillsinger and Mark Stein, "Militant Vegetarians Tied to Attacks on Livestock Industry," *Boston Globe*, November 23, 1989, A34.

160. Ted Robert Gurr, "Political Terrorism in the United States: Historical Antecedents and Contemporary Trends," in *The Politics of Terrorism*, ed. Michael Stohl (New York: Dekker, 1988); Martha Crenshaw, ed., *Terrorism, Legitimacy, and Power* (Middletown, Conn.: Wesleyan University Press, 1983), 1–10.

161. Reuters, "New Haiti Police Have Executed 15, Rights Group Asserts," *Boston Globe*, January 24, 1997, A10.

162. Amnesty International, *Annual Report, 1992* (Washington, D.C.), released July 1993.

163. This report on state action in Peru can be obtained on the Amnesty International Web site at http://www.amnesty.org/ailib/aipub/1996/AMR/2460396.html.

164. "Human Rights Watch/Americas Faults Ombudsman's First Year As President of Guatemala," Human Rights Watch news release, June 14, 1994.

165. Ronald Kramer, "Structural Violence and State Terrorism: Neglected Forms of Criminal Violence," paper presented at the annual meeting of the American Society of Criminology, Phoenix, Ariz., November 1993.

166. Dick Ward, "The Nuclear Terror Threat," *CJ International* 12 (1996): 1–4.

167. Jeffrey Kluger, "The Nuke Pipeline: The Trade in Nuclear Contraband Is Approaching Critical Mass. Can We Turn Off the Spigot?" *Time*, December 17, 2001, 40.

168. Chris Dishman, "Terrorism, Crime, and Transformation," *Studies in Conflict and Terrorism* 24 (2001): 43–56.

169. Peter L. Bergen, *Holy War, Inc.: Inside the Secret World of Osama bin Laden* (New York, Free Press, 2001), 41–50; Yonah Alexander and Michael S. Swetnam, *Usama bin Laden's al-Qaida: Profile of a Terrorist Network* (New York: Transnational Publishers, 2001); Michael Kranish and Anthony Shadid, "Bin Laden Zeal for Stature Used Psychology, Religion," *Boston Globe*, November 19, 2001, 3.

170. Mark Jurgensmeyer, *Terror in the Mind of God* (Berkeley and Los Angeles: University of California Press, 2000).

171. Jerrold M. Post, "Terrorist Psycho-Logic: Terrorist Behavior as a Product of Psychological Forces," in *Origins of Terrorism: Psychologies, Ideologies, Theologies, States of Mind*, ed. Walter Reich (Cambridge: Cambridge University Press, 1990), 12.

172. Haruki Murakami, *Underground* (New York: Vintage Books, 2001).

173. Theodore Gurr, *Why Men Rebel* (Princeton, N.J.: Princeton University Press, 1970).

174. M. Cherif Bassiouni, "Terrorism, Law Enforcement, and Mass Media: Perspectives, Problems and Proposals," *Journal of Criminal Law and Criminology* 72 (1981): 1–51.

175. Austin Turk, "Political Crime," in *Major Forms of Crime*, ed. R. Meier, 119–135 (Beverly Hills, Calif.: Sage, 1984).
176. Reuters, "18 Beheaded in Sri Lanka; Revenge for Slaying Seen," *Boston Globe*, October 6, 1989, 13.
177. "Chapter 3: National Security in Canada—The 2001 Anti-Terrorism Initiative," *Report of the Auditor General of Canada to the House of Commons* (Ottawa: Office of the Auditor General, 2004); Ronald J. Daniels, Patrick Macklem, and Kent Roach, eds., *The Security of Freedom: Essays on Canada's Anti-Terrorism Bill* (Toronto: University of Toronto Press, 2001).
178. The Special Senate Committee on the Subject-Matter of Bill C-36, 2001; "Justice Minister Preparing for Possible Changes to Anti-terrorism Bill," *National Post*, November 15, 2001.
179. "Hunting Terrorists Using Confidential Informant Reward Programs," *The FBI Law Enforcement Bulletin* 71 (2002): 26–28; Sara Sun Beale and James Felman, "The Consequences of Enlisting Federal Grand Juries in the War on Terrorism: Assessing the USA Patriot Act's Changes to Grand Jury Secrecy," *Harvard Journal of Law and Public Policy* 25 (2002): 699–721.
180. Morton Halperin, "Less Secure, Less Free: Striking Terror at Civil Liberty," *The American Prospect* 12 (2001): 10–13.
181. "Ottawa Compiles 'No-Fly' List of Banned Passengers," *The Globe and Mail*, September 3, 2004; "Terror Czar Demands More Power," *Ottawa Citizen*, June 24, 2004; "Top Court Backs Sun Challenge of Secret Air India Hearings," CanWest News Services, June 24, 2004; "Slow Border 'Dire' for Canada," *Financial Post*, June 7, 2004; "Crime Link Probe on at Airports," *National Post*, May 10, 2004.

Chapter 12

1. Andrew McCall, *The Medieval Underworld* (London: Hamish Hamilton, 1979), 86.
2. J.J. Tobias, *Crime and Police in England, 1700–1900* (London: Gill and Macmillan, 1979).
3. Marilyn Walsh, *The Fence* (Westport, Conn.: Greenwood Press, 1977), 18–25.
4. Sandra Besserer and Catherine Trainor, "Criminal Victimization in Canada, 1999," *Juristat* 20 (2000): Figure 3; Rosemary Garter and Anthony N. Doob, "Trends in Criminal Victimization: 1988–1993," *Juristat* 14 (1994): Table 7.
5. John Hepburn, "Occasional Criminals," in *Major Forms of Crime*, ed. Robert Meier, 73–94 (Beverly Hills, Calif.: Sage, 1984).
6. P.F. Cromwell, J.N. Olson, and D.W. Avary, *Breaking and Entering: An Ethnographic Analysis of Burglary* (Newbury Park, Calif.: Sage, 1991).
7. Dianne Hendrick, "Theft," in *Crime Counts: A Criminal Event Analysis*, ed. Leslie W. Kennedy and Vincent F. Sacco (Toronto: ITP Nelson, 1996).
8. Harry King and William Chambliss, *Box Man: A Professional Thief's Journal* (New York: Harper & Row, 1972), 24.
9. Edwin Sutherland, "White-Collar Criminality," *American Sociological Review* 5 (1940): 2–10.
10. Gilbert Geis, "Avocational Crime," in *Handbook of Criminology*, ed. D. Glazer (Chicago: Rand McNally, 1974), 284.
11. Edwin Sutherland and Chic Conwell, *The Professional Thief* (Chicago: University of Chicago Press, 1937).
12. See, for example, Edwin Lemert, "The Behavior of the Systematic Check Forger," *Social Problems* 6 (1958): 141–148.
13. Carl Klockars, *The Professional Fence* (New York: Free Press, 1976); Darrell Steffensmeier, *The Fence: In the Shadow of Two Worlds* (Totowa, N.J.: Rowman and Littlefield, 1986); Walsh, *The Fence*, 25–28.
14. Paul Cromwell, James Olson, and D'Aunn Avary, "Who Buys Stolen Property? A New Look at Criminal Receiving," *Journal of Crime and Justice* 16 (1993): 75–95.
15. This section depends heavily on a classic book: Wayne LaFave and Austin Scott, *Handbook on Criminal Law* (St. Paul: West Publishing, 1972).
16. L.E. Cohen and M. Felson, "Social Change and Crime Rate Trends: A Routine Activity Approach," *American Sociological Review* 44 (1979): 588–608.
17. Paul McPhie, "Fraud," in *Crime Counts: A Criminal Event Analysis*, ed. Leslie W. Kennedy and Vincent F. Sacco (Toronto: Nelson, 1996).
18. D. Hartmann, D. Gelfand, B. Page, and P. Walder, "Rates of Bystander Observation and Reporting of Contrived Shoplifting Incidents," *Criminology* 10 (1972): 248.
19. Mary Owen Cameron, *The Booster and the Snitch* (New York: Free Press, 1964).
20. Lawrence Cohen and Rodney Stark, "Discriminatory Labeling and the Five-Finger Discount: An Empirical Analysis of Differential Shoplifting Dispositions," *Journal of Research on Crime and Delinquency* 11 (1974): 25–35.
21. Lloyd Klemke, "Does Apprehension for Shoplifting Amplify or Terminate Shoplifting Activity?" *Law and Society Review* 12 (1978): 390–403.
22. Erhard Blankenburg, "The Selectivity of Legal Sanctions: An Empirical Investigation of Shoplifting," *Law and Society Review* 11 (1976): 109–129.
23. Michael Hindelang, "Decisions of Shoplifting Victims to Invoke the Criminal Justice Process," *Social Problems* 21 (1974): 580–595.
24. George Keckeisen, *Retail Security versus the Shoplifter* (Springfield, Ill.: Charles C. Thomas, 1993), 31–32.
25. Melissa Davis, Richard Lundman, and Ramiro Martinez, Jr., "Private Corporate Justice: Store Police, Shoplifters, and Civil Recovery," *Social Problems* 38 (1991): 395–408.
26. Peter Morrison, "Motor-Vehicle Crimes," in *Crime Counts: A Criminal Event Analysis*, ed. Leslie W. Kennedy and Vincent F. Sacco (Toronto: Nelson, 1996).
27. "Challenges and Champions," Canadian Coalition Against Insurance Fraud, April 2001.
28. Charles McCaghy, Peggy Giordano, and Trudy Knicely Henson, "Auto Theft," *Criminology* 15 (1977): 367–381.
29. Donald Gibbons, *Society, Crime and Criminal Careers* (Englewood Cliffs, N.J.: Prentice-Hall, 1977), 310.
30. Kim Hazelbaker, "Insurance Industry Analyses and the Prevention of Motor Vehicle Theft," in *Business and Crime Prevention*, ed. Marcus Felson and Ronald Clarke, 283–293 (Monsey, N.Y.: Criminal Justice Press, 1997).
31. "Vehicle Crime Profits Can Be Used to Support Terrorist Organizations, Interpol's Chief Says," Interpol press release, November 19, 2000, http://www.interpol.int (accessed May 24, 2001).
32. Michael Rand, *Carjacking* (Washington, D.C.: Bureau of Justice Statistics, 1994), 1.
33. Frederick J. Desroches, *Force and Fear: Robbery in Canada* (Toronto: ITP Nelson, 1995).
34. "Home Invasions," Melanie Kowalski, Canadian Centre for Justice Statistics, Bulletin, June 2002.
35. Ronald Clarke and Patricia Harris, "Auto Theft and Its Prevention," in *Crime and Justice, An Annual Review*, ed. N. Morris and M. Tonry (Chicago: University of Chicago Press, 1992).
36. R. Light, C. Nee, and H. Ingham, *Car Theft: The Offender's Perspective*, Home Office Research Study No. 130 (London: Home Office, 1993); R.V. Clarke and P.M. Harris, "Auto Theft and Its Prevention," in *Crime and Justice: A Review of Research*, ed. M. Tonry (Chicago: University of Chicago Press, 1992).

37. P.J. Brantingham and P.L. Brantingham, *Patterns in Crime* (New York: Macmillan, 1984).

38. La Fave and Scott, *Handbook on Criminal Law*, 655.

39. 30 Geo. III, C.24 (1975).

40. Michael Friscolanti, "Canada Fails to Combat Counterfeits," *National Post*, May 4, 2004; James Mccaryten, "Ontario Driver's Licenses Sell for $90US on Internet," Canadian Press, June 8, 2004; "Stronger ID-Theft Laws Needed, CBA Says," Canadian Press, August 23, 2004.

41. As described in Charles McCaghy, *Deviant Behavior* (New York: Macmillan, 1976), 230–231.

42. Susan Gembrowski and Tim Dahlberg, "Over 100 Here Indicted after Telemarketing Fraud Probe around the U.S.," *San Diego Daily Transcript Online*, December 8, 1995.

43. Edwin Lemert, "An Isolation and Closure Theory of Naive Check Forgery," *Journal of Criminal Law, Criminology and Police Science* 44 (1953): 297–298.

44. Canadian Bankers' Association, http://www.cba.ca (accessed February 2, 2005).

45. Jerome Hall, *Theft, Law and Society* (Indianapolis: Bobbs-Merrill, 1952), 36.

46. La Fave and Scott, *Handbook on Criminal Law*, 644.

47. E. Blackstone, *Commentaries on the Laws of England* (London: 1769), 224.

48. Frank Hoheimer, *The Home Invaders: Confessions of a Cat Burglar* (Chicago: Chicago Review, 1975).

49. Richard Wright, Robert Logie, and Scott Decker, "Criminal Expertise and Offender Decision Making: An Experimental Study of the Target Selection Process in Residential Burglary," *Journal of Research in Crime and Delinquency* 32 (1995): 39–53.

50. Richard Wright and Scott Decker, *Burglars on the Job: Streetlife and Residential Break-Ins* (Boston: Northeastern University Press, 1994).

51. See, generally, Neal Shover, "Structures and Careers in Burglary," *Journal of Criminal Law, Criminology and Police Science* 63 (1972): 540–549.

52. Paul Cromwell, James Olson, and D'Aunn Wester Avary, *Breaking and Entering: An Ethnographic Analysis of Burglary* (Newbury Park, Calif.: Sage, 1991), 48–51.

53. See M. Taylor and C. Nee, "The Role of Cues in Simulated Residential Burglary: A Preliminary Investigation," *British Journal of Criminology* 28 (1988): 398–401; Julia MacDonald and Robert Gifford, "Territorial Cues and Defensible Space Theory: The Burglar's Point of View," *Journal of Environmental Psychology* 9 (1989): 193–205.

54. Roger Litton, "Crime Prevention and the Insurance Industry," in *Business and Crime Prevention*, ed. Marcus Felson and Ronald Clarke, 162 (Monsey, N.Y.: Criminal Justice Press, 1997).

55. Graham Farrell, Coretta Phillips, and Ken Pease, "Like Taking Candy, Why Does Repeat Victimization Occur?" *British Journal of Criminology* 35 (1995): 384–399.

56. Scott Decker, Richard Wright, Allison Redfern, and Dietrich Smith, "A Woman's Place Is in the Home: Females and Residential Burglary," *Justice Quarterly* 10 (1993): 143–163.

57. Eileen M. Garry, *Juvenile Firesetting and Arson* (Washington, D.C.: Office of Juvenile Justice and Delinquency Prevention, 1997).

58. Wayne Wooden, "Juvenile Firesetters in Cross-Cultural Perspective: How Should Society Respond," in *Official Responses to Problem Juveniles: Some International Reflections*, ed. James Hackler, 339–348 (Onati, Spain: Onati Publications, 1991).

59. Nancy Webb, George Sakheim, Luz Towns-Miranda, and Charles Wagner, "Collaborative Treatment of Juvenile Firestarters: Assessment and Outreach," *American Journal of Orthopsychiatry* 60 (1990): 305–310.

60. Vernon Quinsey, Terry Chaplin, and Douglas Unfold, "Arsonists and Sexual Arousal to Fire Setting: Correlations Unsupported," *Journal of Behavior Therapy and Experimental Psychiatry* 20 (1989): 203–209.

61. Leigh Edward Somers, *Economic Crimes* (New York: Clark Boardman, 1984), 158–168.

62. Michael Rogers, "The Fire Next Time," *Newsweek*, November 26, 1990, 63.

63. National Fraud Information Center, "2001 Internet Fraud Statistics," http://www.fraud.org (accessed May 15, 2005).

Chapter 13

1. Constance Hays, "ImClone Founder Pleads Guilty to 6 Charges," *New York Times*, October 16, 2002, A1.

2. Dwight Smith, Jr., "White-Collar Crime, Organized Crime and the Business Establishment: Resolving a Crisis in Criminological Theory," in *White Collar and Economic Crime: A Multidisciplinary and Crossnational Perspective*, ed. P. Wickman and T. Dailey, 53 (Lexington, Mass.: Lexington Books, 1982).

3. See, generally, Dwight Smith, Jr., "Organized Crime and Entrepreneurship," *International Journal of Criminology and Penology* 6 (1978): 161–177; Dwight Smith, Jr., "Paragons, Pariahs, and Pirates: A Spectrum-Based Theory of Enterprise," *Crime and Delinquency* 26 (1980): 358–386; Dwight Smith, Jr. and Richard S. Alba, "Organized Crime and American Life," *Society* 16 (1979): 32–38.

4. Mark Haller, "Illegal Enterprise: A Theoretical and Historical Interpretation," *Criminology* 28 (1990): 207–235.

5. Nancy Frank and Michael Lynch, *Corporate Crime, Corporate Violence* (Albany, N.Y.: Harrow and Heston, 1992), 7.

6. Nikos Passas and David Nelken, "The Thin Line between Legitimate and Criminal Enterprises: Subsidy Frauds in the European Community," *Crime, Law and Social Change* 19 (1993): 223–243.

7. For a thorough review, see David Friedrichs, *Trusted Criminals* (Belmont, Calif.: Wadsworth, 1996).

8. Kitty Calavita and Henry Pontell, "Savings and Loan Fraud as Organized Crime: Toward a Conceptual Typology of Corporate Illegality," *Criminology* 31 (1993): 519–548.

9. Edwin Sutherland, *White-Collar Crime: The Uncut Version* (New Haven, Conn.: Yale University Press, 1983).

10. Edwin Sutherland, "White-Collar Criminality," *American Sociological Review* 5 (1940): 2–10.

11. See, generally, Herbert Edelhertz, The Nature, Impact and Prosecution of White-Collar Crime (Washington, D.C.: U.S. Government Printing Office, 1970), 73–75.

12. James Coleman, "What Is White Collar Crime? New Battles in the War of Definitions," in James Helmkamp, Richard Ball, and Kitty Townsend, Proceedings of the Academic Workshop, "Definitional Dilemma: Can and Should There Be a Universal Definition of White Collar Crime?" (Morgantown, WV: National White Collar Crime Center, 1996), 77–86.

13. James Helmkamp and Richard Ball, "Progress in the Definition and Exploration of White-Collar Crime," paper presented at the annual meeting of the American Society of Criminology, Chicago, November 1996, 9.

14. David Weisburd and Kip Schlegel, "Returning to the Mainstream," in *White-Collar Crime Reconsidered*, ed. Kip Schlegel and David Weisburd, 352–365 (Boston: Northeastern University Press, 1992).

15. Gilbert Geis, "Avocational Crime," in *Handbook of Criminology*, ed. Daniel Glazer, 284 (Chicago: Rand McNally, 1974); Ronald Kramer and Raymond Michalowski, "State-Corporate Crime," paper presented at the annual meeting of the American Society of Criminology, Baltimore, November 1990.

16. Elizabeth Moore and Michael Mills, "The Neglected Victims and Unexamined Costs of White-Collar Crime," *Crime and Delinquency* 36 (1990): 408–418.

17. Stuart Traub, "Battling Employee Crime: A Review of Corporate Strategies and Programs," *Crime and Delinquency* 42 (1996): 244–256.

18. Laura Schrager and James Short, "Toward a Sociology of Organizational Crime," *Social Problems* 25 (1978): 415–425.

19. Gilbert Geis, "White-Collar and Corporate Crime," in *Major Forms of Crime*, ed. Robert Meier, 145 (Beverly Hills, Calif.: Sage, 1984).

20. Bureau of Justice Statistics, *The Severity of Crime* (Washington, D.C.: U.S. Government Printing Office, 1984).

21. Xie Baogue, "The Function of the Chinese Procuratorial Organ in Combat Against Corruption," *Police Studies* 11 (1988): 38–43; Dai Yisheng, "Expanding Economy and Growing Crime," *CJ International* 11 (1995): 916.

22. Jim Moran, "Thailand, Crime and Corruption Become Increasing Threat," *CJ International* 12 (1996): 5.

23. Sam Perry, "Economic Espionage and Corporate Responsibility," *CJ International* 11 (1995): 3–4.

24. Nikos Passas and David Nelkin, "The Fight against Fraud in the European Community: Cacophony Rather Than Harmony," *Corruption and Reform* 6 (1991): 237–266.

25. Nikos Passas, "European Integration, Protectionism, and Criminogenesis: A Case Study on Farm Subsidy Frauds," *Mediterranean Quarterly* 5 (1994): 66–84.

26. Marshall Clinard and Richard Quinney, *Criminal Behavior Systems: A Typology* (New York: Holt, Rinehart and Winston, 1973), 117.

27. Mark Moore, "Notes Toward a National Strategy to Deal with White-Collar Crime," in *A National Strategy for Containing White-Collar Crime*, ed. Herbert Edelhertz and Charles Rogovin, 32–44 (Lexington, Mass.: Lexington Books, 1980); For a general review, see John Braithwaite, "White-Collar Crime," *Annual Review of Sociology* 11 (1985): 1–25.

28. Scott Paltrow, "Goldblum Now in Consulting and on Parole," *Wall Street Journal*, March 22, 1982, 25.

29. Nikos Passas, "Structural Sources of International Crime: Policy Lessons from the BCCI Affair," *Crime, Law and Social Change* 19 (1994): 223–231.

30. Nikos Passas, "Accounting for Fraud: Auditors' Ethical Dilemmas in the BCCI Affair," in *The Ethics of Accounting and Finance*, ed. W. Michael Hoffman, Judith Brown Kamm, Robert Frederick, and Edward Petry, 85–99 (Westport, Conn.: Quorum Books, 1996).

31. Paul Nowell, "Bakker Convicted of Fraud," *Boston Globe*, October 6, 1989, 1.

32. Earl Gottschalk, "Churchgoers Are the Prey as Scams Rise," *Wall Street Journal*, August 7, 1989, C1.

33. Diana Henriques, "10 Percent of Fruit Juice Sold in U.S. Is Not All Juice, Regulators Say," *New York Times*, October 31, 1993, 1.

34. Richard Quinney, "Occupational Structure and Criminal Behavior: Prescription Violation of Retail Pharmacists," *Social Problems* 11 (1963): 179–185; see also John Braithwaite, *Corporate Crime in the Pharmaceutical Industry* (London: Routledge and Kegan Paul, 1984).

35. Amy Dockser Marcus, "Thievery by Lawyers Is on the Increase, with Duped Clients Losing Bigger Sums," *Wall Street Journal*, November 26, 1990, B1.

36. James Armstrong et al., "Securities Fraud," *American Criminal Law Review* 33 (1995): 973–1016.

37. Robert Rose and Jeff Bailey, "Traders in CBOT Soybean Pit Indicted," *Wall Street Journal*, August 3, 1989, A4.

38. Scott McMurray, "Futures Pit Trader Goes to Trial," *Wall Street Journal*, May 8, 1990, C1; Scott McMurray, "Chicago Pits' Dazzling Growth Permitted a Free-for-All Mecca," *Wall Street Journal*, August 3, 1989, A4.

39. *Carpenter v. United States*, 484 U.S. 19 (1987); also see John Boland, "The SEC Trims the First Amendment," *Wall Street Journal*, December 4, 1986, 28.

40. Tim Metz and Michael Miller, "Boesky's Rise and Fall Illustrate a Compulsion to Profit by Getting Inside Track on Market," *Wall Street Journal*, November 17, 1986, 28; Wade Lambert, "FDIC Receives Cooperation of Milken Aide," *Wall Street Journal*, April 25, 1991, A3.

41. This section depends heavily on Frank Browning and John Gerassi, *The American Way of Crime* (New York: Putnam, 1980), 151.

42. Edward Ranzal, "City Report Finds Building Industry Infested by Graft," *New York Times*, November 8, 1974, 1.

43. Rod Macdonell, "Tory Senator Must Pay Fine," *Halifax Daily News*, July 8, 1998; Toni Locy, "Former Lawmaker Gets Plea Deal," *Washington Post*, April 17, 1996.

44. Marshall Clinard and Peter Yeager, *Corporate Crime* (New York: Free Press, 1980), 166–167.

45. *Fraud Update, The White Paper* (1991): 3–4.

46. United Press International, "Minority Leader in N.Y. Senate Is Charged," *Boston Globe*, September 17, 1987, 20.

47. "Rail Deal Debate Heats Up: Provincial Government Reveals Billion-Dollar Operational Lease for BC Rail Could Last a Lot Longer Than 90 Years," *Penticton Herald*, April 20, 2004; "Furor in British Columbia Grows over Bribery Probe," Mark Hume, *The Globe and Mail*, March 4, 2004.

48. "More Charges Laid in Police Scandal," Canada.com, October 15, 2004; Oliver Moore, "Toronto Police Officers Charged," *The Globe and Mail*, May 3, 2004; Jonathan Fowlie, "Toronto Officers Charged in 'Shakedown' Case," *The Globe and Mail*, May 4, 2004; Steve Fairbairn, "Outside Force Won't Probe Toronto Cops," Canadian Press, April 27, 2004.

49. Daniel Leblanc, Campbell Clark, and Ingrid Peritz, "Pair Held in Sponsorship Scandal," *The Globe and Mail*, May 11, 2004; Jack Aubry, "Ex-Adman Alleges Liberal Kickback Scheme," *Ottawa Citizen*, April 8, 2004; "Judicial Inquiry into Scandal Officially Begins," Canadian Press, May 7, 2004.

50. "Now Williams—Last, Not Least of ABSCAM Trials," *New York Times*, April 5, 1982, E7.

51. Edward Pound, "Honored Employee Is a Key in Huge Fraud in Defense Purchasing," *Wall Street Journal*, March 2, 1988, 1.

52. Larry Tye, "A Tide of State Corruption Sweeps from Coast to Coast," *Boston Globe*, March 25, 1991, 1.

53. *The Knapp Commission Report on Police Corruption* (New York: George Braziller, 1973), 1–3, 170–182.

54. Michael Rezendes, "N.Y. Hears of Police Corrupted," *Boston Globe*, October 10, 1993, 1.

55. Cited in Hugh Barlow, *Introduction to Criminology*, 2nd ed. (Boston: Little, Brown, 1984).

56. Thomas Burton, "The More Baxter Hides Its Israeli Boycott Role, the More Flak It Gets," *Wall Street Journal*, April 25, 1991, 1.

57. "Newsbreaks," *Aviation Week and Space Technology*, July 10, 1995, 19.

58. Charles McCaghy, *Deviant Behavior* (New York: Macmillan, 1976), 178.

59. John Clark and Richard Hollinger, *Theft by Employees in Work Organizations* (Washington, D.C.: U.S. Government Printing Office, 1983), 2–3.

60. "Business Fraud Prevails, May Worsen, Study Says," *Wall Street Journal*, August 17, 1993, A4.

61. J. Sorenson, H. Grove, and T. Sorenson, "Detecting Management Fraud: The Role of the Independent Auditor," in *White-Collar Crime, Theory and Research*, ed. G. Geis and E. Stotland, 221–251 (Beverly Hills, Calif.: Sage, 1980).

62. Teri Agins, "Report Is Said to Show Pervasive Fraud at Leslie Fay," *Wall Street Journal*, October 27, 1993, B4.

63. KPMG, "KPMG Fraud Survey, 2003," http://www.kpmg.com/aci/docs/Fraud%20Survey_040855_R5.pdf (accessed May 24, 2005).

64. Henry Pontell, Kitty Calavita, and Robert Tillman, *Fraud in the Savings and Loan Industry: White-Collar Crime and*

Government Response (Report to the National Institute of Justice, Washington, D.C., 1994); Robert Tillman and Henry Pontell, "Organizations and Fraud in the Savings and Loan Industry," *Social Forces* 73 (1995): 1439–1463; Kitty Calavita and Henry Pontell, "Savings and Loan Fraud as Organized Crime: Toward a Conceptual Typology of Corporate Illegality," *Criminology* 31 (1993): 519–548; Kitty Calavita and Henry Pontell, "'Heads I Win, Tails You Lose': Deregulation, Crime, and Crisis in the Savings and Loan Industry," *Crime and Delinquency* 36 (1990): 309–341; Rich Thomas, "Sit Down Taxpayers," *Newsweek*, June 4, 1990, 60; John Gallagher, "Good Old Bad Boy," *Time*, June 25, 1990, 42–43; L. Gordon Crovitz, "Milken's Tragedy: Oh, How the Mighty Fall before RICO," *Wall Street Journal*, May 2, 1990, A17.

65. See Kristine DeBry, Bonny Harbinger, and Susan Rotkis, "Health Care Fraud," *American Criminal Law Review* 33 (1995): 818–838.

66. Henry Thomas Stelfox and Donald A. Redelmeier, "An Analysis of One Potential Form of Health Care Fraud in Canada," *Canadian Medical Association Journal* 7 (2003): 169–171; Moe Litman, "Self-Referral and Kickbacks: Fiduciary Law and the Regulation of 'Trafficking in Patients,'" *Canadian Medical Association Journal* 3 (2004): 170–177.

67. Bruce Lambert, "12 Chiropractors among 20 Arrested in Insurance Fraud Sting," *New York Times*, May 22, 1997, A30.

68. Laura Johannes and Wendy Bounds, "Corning Agrees to Pay $6.8 Million to Settle Medicare Billing Charges," *Wall Street Journal*, February 22, 1996, B2.

69. Carl Hartman, "Study Says Underground Economy May Represent 33 Percent of Production," *Boston Globe*, February 16, 1988, 38.

70. Alan Murray, "IRS in Losing Battle against Tax Evaders Despite Its New Gear," *Wall Street Journal*, April 10, 1984, 1; "The Police Perspective on Organized Crime," *RCMP Gazette*, n.d.; Canadian Taxpayers Federation, "The Oldest Profession, the Underground Economy and Swiss Cheese," February 28, 2002, http://www.taxpayer.com/main/news.php?news_id=110 (accessed May 24, 2005).

71. Paul Duke, "IRS Excels at Tracking the Average Earner but Not the Wealthy," *Wall Street Journal*, April 15, 1991, 1.

72. Nancy Frank and Michael Lynch, *Corporate Crime, Corporate Violence* (Albany, N.Y.: Harrow and Heston), 12–13.

73. Sutherland, "White-Collar Criminality," 2–10.

74. Michael Maltz and Stephen Pollack, "Suspected Collusion Among Bidders," in *White-Collar Crime, Theory and Research*, ed. G. Geis and E. Stotland, 174–198 (Beverly Hills, Calif.: Sage, 1980).

75. Bruce Ingersoll and Alecia Swasy, "FDA Puts Squeeze on P&G over Citrus Hill Labeling," *Wall Street Journal*, April 25, 1991, B1.

76. John Conklin, *Illegal but Not Criminal* (Englewood Cliffs, N.J.: Prentice-Hall, 1972), 45–46.

77. For an analysis of false claims, see Jonathan Kaye and John Patrick Sullivan, "False Claims," in *Eighth Survey of White-Collar Crime, American Criminal Law Review* 30 (1993): 643–657.

78. "Union Carbide Says Bhopal Plant Should Have Been Closed," *Wall Street Journal*, March 21, 1985, 18.

79. "Judge Rejects Exxon Alaska Spill Pact," *Wall Street Journal*, April 25, 1991, A3.

80. Christopher Marquis, "U.S. Says It Broke Pornography Ring Featuring Youths," *New York Times*, August 9, 2001, 6.

81. Computer Security Institute, "Cyber Crime Bleeds U.S. Corporations, Survey Shows; Financial Losses from Attacks Climb for Third Year in a Row," Press Release, April 7, 2002.

82. Jeanne Capachin and Dave Potterton, "Online Card Payments, Fraud Solutions Bid to Win," *Meridien Research Report*, 18 January 2001.

83. Bruce Swartz, Deputy Assistant General, Criminal Division, Justice Department, *Internet Fraud Testimony Before the House Energy and Commerce Committee*, 23 May 2001.

84. Shirley Won and Simon Avery, "Hackers Step up E-Commerce Attacks," *The Globe and Mail*, September 20, 2004; Jack Kapica, "Cyber Threats on Rise: Report," *The Globe and Mail*, July 28, 2004.

85. M. Swanson and J. Terriot, "Computer Crime: Dimensions, Types, Causes and Investigations," *Journal of Political Science and Administration* 8 (1980): 305–306; Donn Parker, "Computer-Related White-Collar Crime," in *White-Collar Crime, Theory and Research*, ed. G. Geis and E. Stotland, 199–220 (Beverly Hills, Calif.: Sage, 1980).

86. Anne Branscomb, "Rogue Computer Programs and Computer Rogues: Tailoring Punishment to Fit the Crime," *Rutgers Computer and Technology Law Journal* 16 (1990): 24–26.

87. David Stipp, "Computer Virus Maker Is Given Probation, Fine," *Wall Street Journal*, May 7, 1990, B3.

88. Erik Larson, "Computers Turn Out to Be Valuable Aid in Employee Crime," *Wall Street Journal*, January 14, 1985, 1.

89. Computer Security Institute, "Cyber Crime Bleeds U.S. Corporations, Survey Shows; Financial Losses from Attacks Climb for Third Year in a Row," Press Release, April 7, 2002.

90. Business Software Alliance, *BSA Seventh Annual Global Software Piracy Study*, http://www.bsa.org/resources/2001-05-21.55.pdf (accessed October 21, 2002).

91. Kathleen Daly, "Gender and Varieties of White-Collar Crime," *Criminology* 27 (1989): 769–793.

92. Quoted in Metz and Miller, "Boesky's Rise and Fall Illustrate a Compulsion to Profit by Getting Inside Track on Market," p. 28.

93. Donald Cressey, *Other People's Money: A Study of the Social Psychology of Embezzlement* (Glencoe, Ill.: Free Press, 1973).

94. Ronald Kramer, "Corporate Crime: An Organizational Perspective," in *White-Collar and Economic Crime: A Multidisciplinary and Crossnational Perspective*, ed. P. Wickman and T. Dailey, 75–94 (Lexington, Mass.: Lexington Books, 1982).

95. John Braithwaite, "Toward a Theory of Organizational Crime," paper presented at the annual meeting of the American Society of Criminology, Montreal, November 1987.

96. Travis Hirschi and Michael Gottfredson, "Causes of White-Collar Crime," *Criminology* 25 (1987): 949–974.

97. Michael Gottfredson and Travis Hirschi, *A General Theory of Crime* (Stanford, Calif.: Stanford University Press, 1990), 191.

98. David Weisburd, Ellen Chayet, and Elin Waring, "White-Collar and Criminal Careers: Some Preliminary Findings," *Crime and Delinquency* 36 (1990): 342–355.

99. Michael Benson and Elizabeth Moore, "Are White-Collar and Common Offenders the Same? An Empirical and Theoretical Critique of a Recently Proposed General Theory of Crime," *Journal of Research in Crime and Delinquency* 29 (1992): 251–272.

100. David Simon and D. Stanley Eitzen, *Elite Deviance* (Boston: Allyn & Bacon, 1982), 28.

101. Jesilow, Pontell, and Geis, "Physician Immunity from Prosecution and Punishment for Medical Program Fraud," p. 19.

102. Peter Yeager, "Structural Bias in Regulatory Law Enforcement: The Case of the U.S. Environmental Protection Agency," *Social Problems* 34 (1987): 330–344.

103. See, generally, Stanton Wheeler, David Weisburd, Elin Waring, and Nancy Bode, "White-Collar Crimes and Criminals," *American Criminal Law Review* 25 (1988): 331–357.

104. Susanne Schafer, "One General Fired, Two Punished for Mismanaging C-17 Plane," *Boston Globe*, May 1, 1993, 3.

105. Paul Blustein, "Disputes Arise over Value of Laws on Insider Trading," *Wall Street Journal*, November 17, 1986, 28.

106. Paul Barrett, "For Many Dalkon Shield Claimants Settlement Won't End the Trauma," *Wall Street Journal*, March 9, 1988, 29.

107. This section relies on Daniel Skoler, "White-Collar Crime and the Criminal Justice System: Problems and Challenges," in *A National Strategy for Containing White-Collar Crime*, ed. Herbert Edelhertz and Charles Rogovin, 57–76 (Lexington, Mass.: Lexington Books, 1980).

108. Michael Benson, Francis Cullen, and William Maakestad, "Local Prosecutors and Corporate Crime," *Crime and Delinquency* 36 (1990): 356–372.

109. Traub, "Battling Employee Crime: A Review of Corporate Strategies and Programs," 248–252.

110. Alan Otten, "States Begin to Protect Employees Who Blow Whistle on Their Firms," *Wall Street Journal*, December 31, 1984, 11.

111. This section relies heavily on Albert Reiss, Jr., "Selecting Strategies of Social Control over Organizational Life," in *Enforcing Regulation*, ed. Keith Hawkins and John M. Thomas, 25–37 (Boston: Klowver Publications, 1984).

112. John Braithwaite, "The Limits of Economism in Controlling Harmful Corporate Conduct," *Law and Society Review* 16 (1981–1982): 481–504.

113. "EPA Sues Sherwin-Williams: Pattern of Pollution at Paint Factory Is Alleged," *Wall Street Journal*, July 19, 1993, 1; "Making Firms Liable for Cleaning Toxic Sites," *Wall Street Journal*, March 9, 1988, 29.

114. Rhonda Rundle, "Computer Sciences Will Pay $2.1 Million to Settle Charges by U.S. Government," *Wall Street Journal*, July 19, 1993, B8.

115. Wayne Gray and John Scholz, "Does Regulatory Enforcement Work? A Panel Analysis of OSHA Enforcement," *Law and Society Review* 27 (1993): 177–191.

116. Michael Benson, "Emotions and Adjudication: Status Degradation Among White-Collar Criminals," *Justice Quarterly* 7 (1990): 515–528; John Braithwaite, *Crime, Shame and Reintegration* (Sydney: Cambridge University Press, 1989).

117. John Braithwaite and Gilbert Geis, "On Theory and Action for Corporate Crime Control," *Crime and Delinquency* 28 (1982): 292–314.

118. James Miller, "U.S. Ban on Baxter International Bids Hurt Reputation More Than Business," *Wall Street Journal*, August 16, 1993, A3.

119. Kip Schlegel, "Desert, Retribution and Corporate Criminality," *Justice Quarterly* 5 (1988): 615–634.

120. Raymond Michalowski and Ronald Kramer, "The Space Between Laws: The Problem of Corporate Crime in a Transnational Context," *Social Problems* 34 (1987): 34–53.

121. Steven Klepper and Daniel Nagin, "The Deterrent Effect of Perceived Certainty and Severity of Punishment Revisited," *Criminology* 27 (1989): 721–746.

122. "The Follies Go On," *Time*, April 15, 1991, 45.

123. Bill Richards and Alex Kotlowitz, "Judge Finds Three Corporate Officials Guilty of Murder in Cyanide Death of Worker," *Wall Street Journal*, June 17, 1985, 2.

124. Donald Manson, *Tracking Offenders: White-Collar Crime* (Washington, D.C.: Bureau of Justice Statistics, 1986); Kenneth Carlson and Jan Chaiken, *White-Collar Crime* (Washington, D.C.: Bureau of Justice Statistics, 1987); Robert Bennett, "Foreword: Eighth Survey of White-Collar Crime," *American Criminal Law Review* 30 (1993).

125. David Weisburd, Elin Waring, and Stanton Wheeler, "Class, Status, and the Punishment of White-Collar Criminals," *Law and Social Inquiry* 15 (1990): 223–243.

126. Mark Cohen, "Environmental Crime and Punishment: Legal/Economic Theory and Empirical Evidence on Enforcement of Federal Environmental Statutes," *Journal of Criminal Law and Criminology* 82 (1992): 1054–1109.

127. See, generally, President's Commission on Organized Crime, Report to the President and the Attorney General, *The Impact: Organized Crime Today* (Washington, D.C.: U.S. Government Printing Office, 1986). Herein cited as *Organized Crime Today*.

128. Frederick Martens and Michele Cunningham-Niederer, "Media Magic, Mafia Mania," *Federal Probation* 49 (1985): 60–68.

129. Alan Block and William Chambliss, *Organizing Crime* (New York: Elsevier, 1981).

130. Attorney General's Commission on Pornography, *Final Report* (Washington, D.C.: U.S. Government Printing Office, 1986), 1053.

131. Alan Block, *East Side/West Side* (New Brunswick, N.J.: Transaction Books, 1983), vii, 10–11; G.R. Blakey and M. Goldsmith, "Criminal Redistribution of Stolen Property: The Need for Law Reform," *Michigan Law Review* 81 (August 1976): 45–46.

132. Merry Morash, "Organized Crime," in *Major Forms of Crime*, ed. Robert Meier, 198 (Beverly Hills, Calif.: Sage, 1984).

133. Stephen Koepp, "Dirty Cash and Tarnished Vaults," *Time*, February 25, 1985, 65; Roy Rowan, "The 50 Biggest Mafia Bosses," *Fortune*, November 10, 1986, 24.

134. Donald Cressey, *Theft of the Nation* (New York: Harper and Row, 1969).

135. Dwight Smith, Jr., *The Mafia Mystique* (New York: Basic Books, 1975).

136. *Organized Crime Today*, 489; Robert Rhodes, *Organized Crime: Crime Control versus Civil Liberties* (New York: Random House, 1984).

137. This section borrows heavily from Browning and Gerassi, *The American Way of Crime*, 288–472; and August Bequai, *Organized Crime* (Lexington, Mass.: Lexington Books, 1979).

138. Jay Albanese, "God and the Mafia Revisited: From Valachi to Frantianno," paper presented at the annual meeting of the American Society of Criminology, Toronto, 1982.

139. Philip Jenkins and Gary Potter, "The Politics and Mythology of Organized Crime: A Philadelphia Case Study," *Journal of Criminal Justice* 15 (1987): 473–484.

140. Based on the 2001 Report on Organized Crime in Canada prepared by the Criminal Intelligence Service of Canada, available at http://www.cisc.gc.ca/AnnualReport2001/Cisc2001/frontpage2001.html (accessed May 24, 2005).

141. Criminal Intelligence Service Canada, *2004 Annual Report on Organized Crime in Canada* (Ottawa: Criminal Intelligence Service Canada, 2004).

142. Robert Kelly and Rufus Schatzberg, "Types of Minority Organized Crime: Some Considerations," paper presented at the annual meeting of the American Society of Criminology, Montreal, November 1987.

143. Chad Skelton, "Losing the War on Bikers," *Vancouver Sun*, October 9, 2004; Adrian Humphreys, "Forces Fear Bikergang Infiltration," *National Post*, August 30, 2004.

144. Omar Bartos, "Growth of Russian Organized Crime Poses Serious Threat," *CJ International* 11 (1995): 8–9; Francis Ianni, *Black Mafia: Ethnic Succession in Organized Crime* (New York: Pocket Books, 1975).

145. Peter Kerr, "Chinese Now Dominate New York Heroin Trade," *New York Times*, August 9, 1987, 1; Ian McDermid Gomme, *The Shadow Line: Deviance and Crime in Canada*, 2nd ed. (Toronto: Harcourt Brace, 1998).

146. Jenkins and Potter, "The Politics and Mythology of Organized Crime."

147. William Chambliss, *On the Take* (Bloomington: Indiana University Press, 1978).

148. Russell Watson, "Death on the Spot," *Newsweek*, December 13, 1993, 18–20.

149. Yumiko Ono, "Top Kirin Brewery Executives Resign Amid Reports of Paying off Racketeers," *Wall Street Journal*, July 19, 1993, A6.

150. Michael Elliott, "Global Mafia," *Newsweek*, December 13, 1993, 22–29.

151. Associated Press, "Gangland Violence Rises and Startles in Moscow," *Boston Globe*, July 22, 1993, 44.

152. George Vold, *Theoretical Criminology*, 2nd ed., rev. Thomas Bernard (New York: Oxford University Press, 1979).

153. Selwyn Raab, "A Battered and Ailing Mafia Is Losing Its Grip on America," *New York Times*, October 22, 1990, 1.

154. Jay Albanese, *Organized Crime in America*, 2nd ed. (Cincinnati: Anderson, 1989), 68.

Chapter 14

1. "Guess Found Guilty," *The Globe and Mail*, June 20, 1998; "Prosecutor Says Juror Knew Affair Was Wrong," *Telegraph Journal*, June 18, 1998, D1; "Crown's Summation Brings Guess to Tears," *Halifax Herald*, June 18, 1998.

2. Edwin Schur, *Crimes without Victims* (Englewood Cliffs, N.J.: Prentice-Hall, 1965).

3. Andrea Dworkin, quoted in "Where Do We Stand on Pornography," *Ms*, January–February 1994, 34.

4. Jennifer Williard, *Juvenile Prostitution* (Washington, D.C.: National Victim Resource Center, 1991).

5. The Committee on Sexual Offences against Children and Youth (the Badgley Committee), 1984; and the *Report of the Special Committee on Pornography and Prostitution* (the Fraser Committee), 1985.

6. The Royal Commission on the Criminal Law Relating to Criminal Sexual Psychopaths, 1956.

7. Morris Cohen, "Moral Aspects of the Criminal Law," *Yale Law Journal* 49 (1940): 1017.

8. Sir Patrick Devlin, *The Enforcement of Morals* (New York: Oxford University Press, 1959), 20.

9. See Joel Feinberg, *Social Philosophy* (Englewood Cliffs, N.J.: Prentice-Hall, 1973), Chapters 2, 3.

10. *United States v. 12 200-ft Reels of Super 8mm Film*, 413 U.S. 123 (1973) at 137.

11. David Kaplan, "Is It Torture or Tradition?" *Newsweek*, December 20, 1993, 124.

12. H.L.A. Hart, "Immorality and Treason," *Listener* 62 (1959): 163.

13. Joseph Gusfield, "On Legislating Morals: The Symbolic Process of Designating Deviancy," *California Law Review* 56 (1968): 58–59.

14. E. Hatfield, S. Sprecher, and J. Traupman, "Men and Women's Reactions to Sexually Explicit Films: A Serendipitous Finding," *Archives of Sexual Behavior* 6 (1978): 583–592; Henry Lesieur and Joseph Sheley, "Illegal Appended Enterprises: Selling the Lines," *Social Problems* 34 (1987): 249–260.

15. Wayne LaFave and Austin Scott, Jr., *Criminal Law* (St. Paul, Minn.: West Publishing, 1986), 12.

16. Bill Curry, "Canadians Back Legalized Euthanasia: Numbers down from Past Polls, Yet Half Still Support MD-Assisted Suicide," *Ottawa Citizen*, September 7, 2003.

17. Tina Loo and Lorna McLean, *Historical Perspectives on Law and Society in Canada* (Toronto: Copp Clark, 1994); Bryan D. Palmer, "Discordant Music: Charivaris and White-Capping in Nineteenth-Century North America," *Labour/Le Travail* 3 (1978): 5–62.

18. Howard Becker, *Outsiders* (New York: Macmillan, 1963), 13–14.

19. Daniel Claster, *Bad Guys and Good Guys, Moral Polarization and Crime* (Westport, Conn.: Greenwood Press, 1992), 28–29.

20. "Amsterdam Cafe Raided," *Cannabis Culture Magazine Online*, May 15, 1998, http://www.hempbc.com/library/bust/amsterdam.html (accessed May 24, 2005).

21. Reuters, "Belgians Promise to Clean up Courts," *Boston Globe*, October 22, 1996, A17.

22. See, generally, Spencer Rathus and Jeffery Nevid, *Abnormal Psychology* (Englewood Cliffs, N.J.: Prentice-Hall, 1991), 373–411.

23. *Canadian Crime Statistics 2000* (Ottawa: Canadian Centre for Crime Statistics, 2001).

24. G. Kinsman, "'Character Weaknesses' and 'Fruit Machines': Towards an Analysis of the Anti-homosexual Security Campaign in the Canadian Civil Service," *Labour/Le Travail* 35 (1995): 133–161; Gary Kinsman and Patrizia Gentile, "'In the Interests of the State': The Anti-gay, Anti-lesbian National Security Campaign in Canada," unpublished report.

25. See, generally, V. Bullogh, *Sexual Variance in Society and History* (Chicago: University of Chicago Press, 1958), 143–144; Spencer Rathus, *Human Sexuality* (New York: Holt, Rinehart and Winston), 463; Annette Jolin, "On the Backs of Working Prostitutes: Feminist Theory and Prostitution Policy," *Crime and Delinquency* 40 (1994): 60–83.

26. "The Court and the Soliciting Law," *The Globe and Mail*, June 6, 1990; Richard Barnhorst, Sherrie Barnhorst, and Kenneth Clarke, *Criminal Law and the Canadian Criminal Code* (Toronto: McGraw-Hill Ryerson, 1992).

27. "NOW Charges Dropped. Alright!" *NOW*, September 27, 1990; "Crown Finds No Legal Basis, Drops NOW Charges," *NOW*, September 27, 1990, 15.

28. Charles McCaghy, *Deviant Behavior* (New York: Macmillan, 1976), 348–349.

29. Information for the following section draws on various sources, including Charles Winick and Paul Kinsie, *The Lively Commerce* (Chicago: Quadrangle Books, 1971); Jennifer James, "Prostitutes and Prostitution," in *Deviants: Voluntary Action in a Hostile World*, ed. E. Sagarin and F. Montanino (New York: Scott, Foresman, 1977).

30. Mark-David Janus, Barbara Scanlon, and Virginia Price, "Youth Prostitution," in *Child Pornography and Sex Rings*, ed. Ann Wolbert Burgess, 127–146 (Lexington, Mass.: Lexington Books, 1989).

31. Paul Goldstein, "Occupational Mobility in the World of Prostitution: Becoming a Madam," *Deviant Behavior* 4 (1983): 267–279.

32. Goldstein, "Occupational Mobility in the World of Prostitution," 267–270.

33. Described in Rathus, *Human Sexuality*, 468.

34. Paul Goldstein, Lawrence Ouellet, and Michael Fendrich, "From Bag Brides to Skeezers: A Historical Perspective on Sex-for-Drugs Behavior," *Journal of Psychoactive Drugs* 24 (1992): 349–361; Lisa Maher and Kathleen Daly, "Women in the Street-Level Drug Economy: Continuity or Change?" *Criminology* 34 (1996): 465–491.

35. D. Kelly Weisberg, *Children of the Night: A Study of Adolescent Prostitution* (Lexington, Mass.: Lexington Books, 1985), 44–55.

36. Gerald Hotaling and David Finkelhor, *The Sexual Exploitation of Missing Children* (Washington, D.C.: U.S. Department of Justice, 1988).

37. Carolyn McIntyre, *Strolling Away* (Ottawa: Department of Justice, 2002). See also, Steven Bittle, *Youth Involvement in Prostitution: A Focus on Intrafamilial Violence. A Literature Review* (Ottawa: Department of Justice, n.d.); and Steven Bittle, *Youth Involvement in Prostitution: A Literature Review and Annotated Bibliography* (Ottawa: Department of Justice, Research and Statistics, 2002).

38. N. Jackman, Richard O'Toole, and Gilbert Geis, "The Self-Image of the Prostitute," in *Sexual Deviance*, ed. J. Gagnon and W. Simon, 152–153 (New York: Harper & Row, 1967).

39. Paul Gebhard, "Misconceptions about Female Prostitutes," *Medical Aspects of Human Sexuality* 3 (July 1969): 28–30.

40. Reuters, "UN Cites Sharp Rise in Child Labor, Prostitution," *Boston Globe*, November 12, 1996, A6.

41. Dorothy Bracey, *"Baby Pros": Preliminary Profiles of Juvenile Prostitutes* (New York: JohnJay Press, 1979).

42. A. Brannigan, L. Knafla, and C. Levy, *Street Prostitution. Assessing the Impact of the Law: Calgary* (Ottawa: Department

of Justice, 1989); N. Crook, *A Report on Prostitution in the Atlantic Provinces*, Working Papers on Pornography and Prostitution, Report No. 12 (Ottawa: Department of Justice, 1984); J. Lowman, *Vancouver Field Study of Prostitution*, Working Papers on Pornography and Prostitution, Report No. 8 (Ottawa: Department of Justice, 1984).

43. Andrea Dworkin, *Pornography* (New York: Dutton, 1989).

44. Jolin, "On the Backs of Working Prostitutes," 76–77.

45. *Merriam-Webster Dictionary* (New York: Pocket Books, 1974), 484.

46. Albert Belanger et al., "Typology of Sex Rings Exploiting Children," in *Child Pornography and Sex Rings*, ed. Ann Wolbert Burgess, 51–81 (Lexington, Mass.: Lexington Books, 1984).

47. "Battling Child Porn," *Maclean's*, April 8, 2002, 55.

48. *The Report of the Commission on Obscenity and Pornography* (Washington, D.C.: U.S. Government Printing Office, 1970).

49. Berl Kutchinsky, "The Effect of Easy Availability of Pornography on the Incidence of Sex Crimes," *Journal of Social Issues* 29 (1973): 95–112.

50. Michael Goldstein, "Exposure to Erotic Stimuli and Sexual Deviance," *Journal of Social Issues* 29 (1973): 197–219.

51. John Court, "Sex and Violence: A Ripple Effect," *Pornography and Aggression*, ed. Neal Malamuth and Edward Donnerstein (Orlando, Fla.: Academic Press, 1984); also see Edward Donnerstein, Daniel Linz, and Steven Penrod, *The Question of Pornography* (New York: Free Press, 1987).

52. Edward Donnerstein, "Pornography and Violence against Women," *Annals of the New York Academy of Science* 347 (1980): 277–288; E. Donnerstein and J. Hallam, "Facilitating Effects of Erotica on Aggression against Women," *Journal of Personality and Social Psychology* 36 (1977): 1270–1277; Seymour Fishbach and Neil Malamuth, "Sex and Aggression: Proving the Link," *Psychology Today* 12 (1978): 111–122.

53. Don Smith, "Sexual Aggression in American Pornography: The Stereotype of Rape," paper presented at the annual meeting of the American Sociological Association, 1976.

54. Associated Press, "N.Y. Firm Fined for Broadcasting Pornographic Films by Satellite," *Boston Globe*, February 16, 1991, 12.

55. Jared Sandberg, "U.S. Cracks Down on On-Line Child Pornography," *Wall Street Journal*, September 14, 1995, A3.

56. Ralph Weisheit, "Studying Drugs in Rural Areas: Notes from the Field," *Journal of Research in Crime and Delinquency* 30 (1993): 213–232.

57. Arnold Trebach, *The Heroin Solution* (New Haven, Conn.: Yale University Press, 1982).

58. James Inciardi, *The War on Drugs* (Palo Alto, Calif.: Mayfield, 1986), 2.

59. See, generally, David Pittman, "Drug Addiction and Crime," in *Handbook of Criminology*, ed. D. Glazer, 209–232 (Chicago: Rand McNally, 1974); Board of Directors, National Council on Crime and Delinquency, "Drug Addiction: A Medical, Not a Law Enforcement, Problem," *Crime and Delinquency* 20 (1974): 4–9.

60. Associated Press, "Records Detail Royals' Turn-of-Century Drug Use," *Boston Globe*, August 29, 1993, 13.

61. James Inciardi, *Reflections on Crime* (New York: Holt, Rinehart and Winston, 1978), 15.

62. William Bates and Betty Crowther, "Drug Abuse," in *Deviants: Voluntary Actors in a Hostile World*, ed. E. Sagarin and F. Montanino, 269 (New York: Foresman and Co., 1977).

63. A. Elizabeth Comack, "The Origins of Canadian Drug Legislation: Labelling versus Class Analysis," in *The New Criminologies in Canada*, ed. Brian Fleming (Toronto: Oxford, 1985).

64. Inciardi, *Reflections on Crime*, 8–10; see also A. Greeley, William McCready, and Gary Theisen, *Ethnic Drinking Subcultures*

(New York: Praeger, 1980); Joseph Gusfield, *Symbolic Crusade* (Urbana: University of Illinois Press, 1963), Chapter 3.

65. John Phyne, "Prohibition's Legacy: The Emergence of Provincial Policing in Nova Scotia, 1921–1932," *Canadian Journal of Law and Society* 7 (1992): 157–184.

66. This section relies heavily on the descriptions in Kenneth Jones, Louis Shainberg, and Curtin Byer, *Drugs and Alcohol* (New York: Harper & Row, 1979), 57–114.

67. "Drug Situation in Canada—2002," Organized Crime Analysis Section, Royal Canadian Mounted Police, Ottawa, July 2003.

68. *Cannabis: Our Position for a Canadian Public Policy. Report of the Special Senate Committee on Illegal Drugs* (Ottawa: Senate Committee, 2002).

69. Glenn F. Murray, "Cocaine Use in the Era of Social Reform: The Natural History of a Social Problem in Canada, 1880–1911," *Canadian Journal of Law and Society* 2 (1987): 29–43; Jeffrey Fagan and Ko-Lin Chin, "Initiation into Crack and Powdered Cocaine: A Tale of Two Epidemics," *Contemporary Drug Problems* 16 (1989): 579–617.

70. Thomas Mieczkowski, "The Damage Done: Cocaine Methods in Detroit," *International Journal of Comparative and Applied Criminal Justice* 12 (1988): 261–267.

71. *RCMP National Drug Intelligence Estimate 1994* (Ottawa: Minister of Supply and Services, 1994).

72. The Metro Toronto Research Group on Drug Use, "Drug Use in Toronto, 2001," http://www.city.toronto.on.ca/health/rgdu/rgdu_2001.htm (accessed May 24, 2005).

73. John Hagedorn, "Homeboys, Dope Fiends, Legits, and New Jacks," *Criminology* 32 (1994): 197–220.

74. Charles Winick, "Physician Narcotics Addicts," *Social Problems* 9 (1961): 174–186.

75. *Commission of Inquiry into the Use of Drugs and Banned Practices Intended to Increase Athletic Performance* (Ottawa: Supply and Services Canada, 1990).

76. Addiction Research Foundation, "Deaths Due to Alcohol," Statistical Information Service.

77. D.J. Rohsenow, "Drinking Habits and Expectancies about Alcohol's Effects for Self Versus Others," *Journal of Consulting and Clinical Psychology* 51 (1983): 752–756.

78. Spencer Rathus, *Psychology*, 4th ed. (New York: Holt, Rinehart and Winston, 1990), 161.

79. G. Kolata, "Study Backs Heart Benefits in Light Drinking," *New York Times*, August 3, 1988, A24.

80. Eric Wish, *Drug Use Forecasting Program*, Annual Report 1990 (Washington, D.C.: National Institute of Justice, 1990).

81. Thomas Gray and Eric Wish, *Maryland Youth at Risk: A Study of Drug Use in Juvenile Detainees* (College Park, Md.: Center for Substance Abuse Research, 1993); Eric Wish and Christina Polsenberg, "Arrestee Urine Tests and Self-Reports of Drug Use: Which Is More Related to Rearrest?" paper presented at the annual meeting of the American Society of Criminology, Phoenix, Ariz., November 1993.

82. "Canadian Crime Statistics, 1996," *Juristat* 17 (1997); "Drug Offences in Canada," *Juristat* 10 (1990).

83. Michael Tjepkema, "Use of Cannabis and Other Illicit Drugs," *Statistics Canada Health Reports* 15, no. 4 (2004).

84. David Patton, David Brown, Brian Broszeit, and Jastej Dhaliwal, "Substance Abuse among Manitoba High School Students, 2001," Addiction Foundation of Manitoba, http://www.afm.mb.ca/pdfs/HSSU.pdf (accessed May 24, 2005); E.M. Adlaf, A. Pagli, and F.J. Ivis, *Drug Use Among Ontario Students 1977 to 1999: Findings from the Ontario Student Drug Use Survey* (Toronto: Centre for Addiction and Mental Health, 1999).

85. Hilary Saner, Robert MacCoun, and Peter Reuter, "On the Ubiquity of Drug Selling among Youthful Offenders in

Washington, D.C., 1985–1991: Age, Period, or Cohort Effect?" *Journal of Quantitative Criminology* 11 (1995): 362–373.

86. See, generally, Mark Blumberg, ed., *AIDS: The Impact on the Criminal Justice System* (Columbus, Ohio: Merrill Publishing, 1990).

87. Scott Decker and Richard Rosenfeld, "Intravenous Drug Use and the AIDS Epidemic: Findings for a Twenty-City Sample of Arrestees," paper presented at the annual meeting of the American Society of Criminology, Baltimore, November 1990.

88. *HIV and AIDS in Canada. Surveillance Report to June 30, 2000* (Ottawa: Health Canada, 2000), http://www.phac-aspc.gc.ca/publicat/aids-sida/hiv-aic11-00/index.html (accessed May 24, 2005).

89. Douglas Longshore, "Prevalence and Circumstances of Drug Injection at Los Angeles Shooting Galleries," *Crime and Delinquency* 42 (1996): 21–35.

90. Mark Blumberg, "AIDS and the Criminal Justice System: An Overview," in *AIDS: The Impact on the Criminal Justice System*, 11.

91. Aids Committee of Toronto, "HIV/AIDS Statistics—Youth," July 23, 2004.

92. *Estimates of HIV Prevalence and Incidence in Canada, 2002* (Ottawa: Health Canada, 2003).

93. Bruce Johnson, Andrew Golub, and Jeffrey Fagan, "Careers in Crack, Drug Use, Drug Distribution, and Nondrug Criminality," *Crime and Delinquency* 41 (1995): 275–295.

94. "Women's AIDS Blamed on Men," *Toronto Star*, September 30, 1994, A1.

95. "Where Death Gets a Double Shot. The Call to Clean Up a Hotbed of Heroin and HIV in Canada's Poorest Ghetto," *The Globe and Mail*, October 8, 1997.

96. "Safe Injection Site Opens," Vancouver CBC, September 15, 2003. See also "Potential Use of Safer Injecting Facilities among Injection Drug Users in Vancouver's Downtown Eastside," *Canadian Medical Association Journal* 10 (2003): 169–177.

97. C. Bowden, "Determinants of Initial Use of Opioids," *Comprehensive Psychiatry* 12 (1971): 136–140.

98. Marvin Krohn, Alan Lizotte, Terence Thornberry, Carolyn Smith, and David McDowall, "Reciprocal Causal Relationships among Drug Use, Peers, and Beliefs: A Five-Wave Panel Model," *Journal of Drug Issues* 26 (1996): 205–428; R. Cloward and L. Ohlin, *Delinquency and Opportunity: A Theory of Delinquent Gangs* (Glencoe, Ill.: Free Press, 1960).

99. Kellie Barr, Michael Farrell, Grace Barnes, and John Welte, "Race, Class, and Gender Differences in Substance Abuse: Evidence of Middle-Class/Underclass Polarization among Black Males," *Social Problems* 40 (1993): 314–326.

100. Alison Bass, "Mental Ills, Drug Abuse Linked," *Boston Globe*, November 21, 1990, 3.

101. D.W. Goodwin, "Alcoholism and Genetics," *Archives of General Psychiatry* 42 (1985): 171–174.

102. For a thorough review of this issue, see John Petraitis, Brian Flay, and Todd Miller, "Reviewing Theories of Adolescent Substance Use: Organizing Pieces in the Puzzle," *Psychological Bulletin* 117 (1995): 67–86.

103. Judith Brooks and Li-Jung Tseng, "Influences of Parental Drug Use, Personality, and Child Rearing on the Toddler's Anger and Negativity," *Genetic, Social and General Psychology Monographs* 122 (1996): 107–128; Thomas Ashby Wills, Donato Vaccaro, Grace McNamara, and A. Elizabeth Hirky, "Escalated Substance Use: A Longitudinal Grouping Analysis from Early to Middle Adolescence," *Journal of Abnormal Psychology* 105 (1996): 166–180.

104. Denise Kandel and Mark Davies, "Friendship Networks, Intimacy and Illicit Drug Use in Young Adulthood: A Comparison of Two Competing Theories," *Criminology* 29 (1991): 441–471.

105. J.S. Mio, G. Nanjundappa, D.E. Verlur, and M.D. DeRios, "Drug Abuse and the Adolescent Sex Offender: A Preliminary Analysis," *Journal of Psychoactive Drugs* 18 (1986): 65–72.

106. D. Baer and J. Corrado, "Heroin Addict Relationships with Parents during Childhood and Early Adolescent Years," *Journal of Genetic Psychology* 124 (1974): 99–103.

107. James Inciardi, Ruth Horowitz, and Anne Pottieger, *Street Kids, Street Drugs, Street Crime: An Examination of Drug Use and Serious Delinquency in Miami* (Belmont, Calif.: Wadsworth, 1993), 43.

108. John Wallace and Jerald Bachman, "Explaining Racial/Ethnic Differences in Adolescent Drug Use: The Impact of Background and Lifestyle," *Social Problems* 38 (1991): 333–357.

109. John Donovan, "Problem-Behavior Theory and the Explanation of Adolescent Marijuana Use," *Journal of Drug Issues* 26 (1996): 379–404.

110. A. Christiansen, G.T. Smith, V. Roehling, and M.S. Goldman, "Using Alcohol Expectancies to Predict Adolescent Drinking Behavior after One Year," *Journal of Counseling and Clinical Psychology* 57 (1989): 93–99.

111. Claire Sterck-Elifson, "Just for Fun? Cocaine Use among Middle-Class Women," *Journal of Drug Issues* 26 (1996): 63–76.

112. Icek Ajzen, *Attitudes, Personality and Behavior* (Homewood, Ill.: Dorsey Press, 1988).

113. Lester Grinspoon and James B. Bakalar, *Cocaine: A Drug and Its Social Evolution*, rev. ed. (New York: Basic Books, 1985).

114. Judith Brook, Martin Whiteman, Elinor Balka, and Beatrix Hamburg, "African-American and Puerto Rican Drug Use: Personality, Familial, and Other Environmental Risk Factors," *Genetic, Social, and General Psychology Monographs* 118 (1992): 419–438.

115. Carolyn Rebecca Block and Antigone Christakos, "Intimate Partner Homicide in Chicago over 29 Years," *Crime and Delinquency* 41 (1995): 496–526.

116. Douglas Smith and Christina Polsenberg, "Specifying the Relationship between Arrestee Drug Test Results and Recidivism," *Journal of Criminal Law and Criminology* 83 (1992): 364–377.

117. George Speckart and M. Douglas Anglin, "Narcotics Use and Crime: An Overview of Recent Research Advances," *Contemporary Drug Problems* 13 (1986): 741–769; Charles Faupel and Carl Klockars, "Drugs-Crime Connections: Elaborations from the Life Histories of Hard-Core Heroin Addicts," *Social Problems* 34 (1987): 54–68.

118. Speckart and Anglin, "Narcotics Use and Crime: An Overview of Recent Research Advances," p. 752.

119. Helene Raskin White and Stephen Hansell, "The Moderating Effects of Gender and Hostility on the Alcohol-Aggression Relationship," *Journal of Research in Crime and Delinquency* 33 (1996): 450–470; James Inciardi, "Heroin Use and Street Crime," *Crime and Delinquency* 25 (1979): 335–346; see also W. McGlothlin, M. Anglin, and B. Wilson, "Narcotic Addiction and Crime," *Criminology* 16 (1978): 293–311; M. Douglas Anglin and George Speckart, "Narcotics Use and Crime: A Multisample, Multimethod Analysis," *Criminology* 26 (1988): 197–235; David Nurco, Ira Cisin, and John Ball, "Crime as a Source of Income for Narcotics Addicts," *Journal of Substance Abuse Treatment* 2 (1985): 113–115.

120. Benedikt Fischer, Wendy Medved, Maritt Kirst, Jurgen Rehm, and Louis Glicksman, "Illicit Opiates and Crime: Results of an Untreated User Cohort Study in Toronto," *Canadian Journal of Criminology* 43, no. 2 (2001): 197.

121. Allen Beck, Darrell Gilliard, Lawrence Greenfeld, Caroline Harlow, Thomas Hester, Lewis Jankowski, Tracy Snell, James Stephen, and Danielle Morton, *Survey of State Prison Inmates, 1991* (Washington, D.C.: Bureau of Justice Statistics, 1993).

The survey of prison inmates is conducted by the Bureau of Justice Statistics every five to seven years.

122. Paul Goldstein, "The Drugs-Violence Nexus: A Tripartite Conceptual Framework," *Journal of Drug Issues* 15 (1985): 493–506.

123. Charles Faupel, "Heroin Use, Crime and Unemployment Status," *Journal of Drug Issues* 18 (1988): 467–479.

124. Royal Commission on Disturbances in a Portion of the City of Vancouver known as "Gastown," as cited in *Royal Commissions and Commissions of Inquiry in British Columbia, 1943–1980* (B.C. Legislative Library, 1982).

125. Eric Jensen, Jurg Gerber, and Ginna Babcock, "The New War on Drugs: Grass Roots Movement or Political Construction?" *Journal of Drug Issues* 21 (1991): 651–667.

126. "Just Say Maybe," *The Economist* 366, no. 8318 (2003).

127. *RCMP National Drug Intelligence Estimate, 1994* (Ottawa: Minister of Supply and Services, 1994).

128. "Impact of Supply-Side Policies for Control of Illicit Drugs in the Face of the Aids and Overdose Epidemics: Investigation of a Massive Heroin Seizure," *Canadian Medical Association Journal* 1 (2003): 168–170.

129. Christopher Wren, "U.S. Is Certifying Mexico as an Ally in Fighting Drugs," *New York Times*, March 1, 1997, 1; Diego Ribadneira, "In Escobar Death, No Curb in Drugs Seen," *Boston Globe*, December 4, 1993, 2.

130. Bureau for International Narcotics and Law Enforcement Affairs, *International Narcotics Control Strategy Report, 1996* (Washington, D.C.: U.S. Department of State, 1997).

131. Walter Shapiro, "Going After the Hell's Angels," *Newsweek*, May 13, 1985, 41.

132. David Hayeslip, "Local-Level Drug Enforcement: New Strategies," *NIJ Reports*, March/April 1989.

133. Mark Moore, *Drug Trafficking* (Washington, D.C.: National Institute of Justice, 1988).

134. "Why It Took 30 Years to Bust a Crime Family," *Globe and Mail*, July 17, 1998, A1.

135. Robert Davis, Arthur Lurigio, and Dennis Rosenbaum, eds., *Drugs and the Community* (Springfield, Ill.: Charles C. Thomas, 1993), xii–xv.

136. Saul Weingart, "A Typology of Community Responses to Drugs," in *Drugs and the Community*, ed. Davis, Lurigio, and Rosenbaum, 85–105.

137. Bureau of Justice Statistics, *Drugs, Crime and the Justice System* (Washington, D.C.: Bureau of Justice Statistics, 1992), 109–112.

138. "TD's Drug-Testing Policy Wrong, Court Rules," *Globe and Mail*, July 25, 1998, A3; "Drug Testing in the Workplace," *Daily News*, August 21, 1994, 19; "Just Say No to Testing," *Toronto Star*, August 23, 1994, A12; "Submission on Mandatory Drug Testing in the Workplace," Canadian Civil Liberties Association, http://www.ccla.org/pos/briefs/drugtest. html (accessed May 24, 2005)

139. "Infants' Hair Tested without Moms Knowing," *Toronto Star*, April 15, 1995, A1.

140. Ethan Nadelmann, "America's Drug Problem," *Bulletin of the American Academy of Arts and Sciences* 65 (1991): 24–40.

141. Ethan Nadelmann, "Should We Legalize Drugs? History Answers Yes," *American Heritage* (February/March 1993): 41–56.

142. See, generally, Ralph Weisheit, *Drugs, Crime and the Criminal Justice System* (Cincinnati: Anderson, 1990).

143. David Courtwright, "Should We Legalize Drugs? History Answers No," *American Heritage* (February/March 1993): 43–56; James Inciardi and Duane McBride, "Legalizing Drugs: A Gormless, Naive Idea," *Criminologist* 15 (1990): 1–4.

144. Kathryn Ann Farr, "Revitalizing the Drug Decriminalization Debate," *Crime and Delinquency* 36 (1990): 223–237.

145. "Nancy B's Gift," *Mail Star*, January 8, 1992, C1; "Nancy B.'s Right to Die," *Montreal Gazette*, January 7, 1992, B2; "Exercising the Right to Die," *The Globe and Mail*, November 29, 1991, A18.

146. "The Government as Bookie," *The Globe and Mail*, May 23, 1995, A18.

147. "Bernie Bets Big on Gambling Gains," *Halifax Herald*, April 12, 1995, A1; "A Sure Bet Industry," *Perspectives* 8 (1996): 3–6.

148. "Gambling: An update, 2002," *The Daily*, April 22, 2003.

149. "RCMP Fears Fuel N.S. Casino Debate," *The Globe and Mail*, April 27, 1994, A3; "Casino Will Boost Crime, Windsor Police Report Says," *The Globe and Mail*, August 4, 1993, A4; "Mobsters Bet on Niagara Falls to Win Casino," *Toronto Star*, May 16, 1994, A1.

150. Robin Kelley, Peter Todosichuk, and Jason Azmier, *Gambling@Home: Internet Gambling in Canada* (Calgary: Canada West Foundation, 2001). See also "Gambling@Home: Internet Gambling in Canada Background," Ontario Problem Gambling Research Centre Home Page, http://www.gamblingresearch.org/contentdetail.sz?cid=2379&pageid=1200 &r=s (accessed May 24, 2005).

Photo Credits

Chapter 1

p. 3: The Toronto Star/P. Power; **p. 4**: CP Archive/Remi Lemee; **p. 9**: © T.H. Matteson/The Peabody Essex Museum

Chapter 2

p. 28: © Pool/Reuters/CORBIS; **p. 33**: Internet Medieval Handbook; **p. 37**: CP Picture Archive/Kevin Frayer; **p. 43**: CP Photo/Jacques Boissinot; **p. 51**: CP Photo/Maclean's Photo/Gerard Kwiatkowski

Chapter 3

p. 54: CP Picture Archive; **p. 65**: CP Picture Archive/Fredericton Daily Gleaner/Bob Wilson; **p. 67**: Mike Graston/Windsor Star; **p. 76**: CP Picture Archive/Joe Bryska AP; **p. 84**: © Reuters/Reinhard Krause/CORBIS

Chapter 4

p. 87: CP Photo/Aaron Harris; **p. 88**: © The Toronto Star/Ron Bull; **p. 100**: © Provincial Archives of Alberta, Photo Collection OB2562; **p. 117**: © Pete Wagner

Chapter 5

p. 123: The Toronto Sun/Stan Behal

Chapter 6

p. 157: © Bettman/CORBIS/MAGMA; **p. 179**: © Dick Hemingway; **p. 185**: © Chris Carroll/CORBIS

Chapter 7

p. 189: © Ken Faught/The Toronto Star; **p. 192**: © Dick Hemingway; **p. 206**: © CP Picture Archive/Fred Thornhill; **p. 216**: The Toronto Star/K. Faught

Chapter 8

p. 222: CP Picture Archive/Cheryl Hnatiuk; **p. 239**: © Stockphoto.com/Black Star/Todd Yates; **p. 240**: CP Picture Archive; **p. 244**: © Sygma/Brooks Kraft/Magma/CORBIS; **p. 246**: CP Picture Archive/Kevin Frayer

Chapter 9

p. 253: CP Photo/Ryan Remiorz; **p. 258**: CP Picture Archive/Paul Chiasson; **p. 265**: CP Picture Archive/Kevin Frayer

Chapter 10

p. 277: © Robert Brenner/PhotoEdit; **p. 296**: The Gazette (Montreal)/John Kennedy; **p. 299**: © Christina Kennedy/PhotoEdit

Chapter 11

p. 305: AP Photo/APTV; **p. 319**: © Press Association; **p. 330**: CP Picture Archive/Moshe Bursurker/AP; **p. 331**: CP Picture Archive/Chuck Mitchell

Chapter 12

p. 339: © Photographer's Choice/Getty; **p. 340**: Roy 20 CVii f.41v British Library/Bridgeman Art Library International; **p. 346**: © Courtesy of the Toronto and Regional Crimestoppers; **p. 355**: CP Picture Archive/Hamilton Spectator; **p. 363**: © The Toronto Star/J. Mahler

Chapter 13

p. 367: © Mike Segar/Reuters/Landov; **p. 371**: CP Picture Archive/Daniel Beltra/EFE; **p. 374**: © Sygma/CORBIS; **p. 388**: © Reuters/CORBIS

Chapter 14

p. 403: © Dick Hemingway; **p. 406**: © The Toronto Sun/Cassese; **p. 415**: © Bettman/Corbis/Magma

Index